Nineteenth-Century Literature Criticism

Guide to Gale Literary Criticism Series

For criticism on	Consult these Gale series
Authors now living or who died after December 31, 1999	*CONTEMPORARY LITERARY CRITICISM (CLC)*
Authors who died between 1900 and 1999	*TWENTIETH-CENTURY LITERARY CRITICISM (TCLC)*
Authors who died between 1800 and 1899	*NINETEENTH-CENTURY LITERATURE CRITICISM (NCLC)*
Authors who died between 1400 and 1799	*LITERATURE CRITICISM FROM 1400 TO 1800 (LC)* *SHAKESPEAREAN CRITICISM (SC)*
Authors who died before 1400	*CLASSICAL AND MEDIEVAL LITERATURE CRITICISM (CMLC)*
Authors of books for children and young adults	*CHILDREN'S LITERATURE REVIEW (CLR)*
Dramatists	*DRAMA CRITICISM (DC)*
Poets	*POETRY CRITICISM (PC)*
Short story writers	*SHORT STORY CRITICISM (SSC)*
Literary topics and movements	*HARLEM RENAISSANCE: A GALE CRITICAL COMPANION (HR)* *THE BEAT GENERATION: A GALE CRITICAL COMPANION (BG)* *FEMINISM IN LITERATURE: A GALE CRITICAL COMPANION (FL)* *GOTHIC LITERATURE: A GALE CRITICAL COMPANION (GL)*
Asian American writers of the last two hundred years	*ASIAN AMERICAN LITERATURE (AAL)*
Black writers of the past two hundred years	*BLACK LITERATURE CRITICISM (BLC)* *BLACK LITERATURE CRITICISM SUPPLEMENT (BLCS)* *BLACK LITERATURE CRITICISM: CLASSIC AND EMERGING AUTHORS SINCE 1950 (BLC-2)*
Hispanic writers of the late nineteenth and twentieth centuries	*HISPANIC LITERATURE CRITICISM (HLC)* *HISPANIC LITERATURE CRITICISM SUPPLEMENT (HLCS)*
Native North American writers and orators of the eighteenth, nineteenth, and twentieth centuries	*NATIVE NORTH AMERICAN LITERATURE (NNAL)*
Major authors from the Renaissance to the present	*WORLD LITERATURE CRITICISM, 1500 TO THE PRESENT (WLC)* *WORLD LITERATURE CRITICISM SUPPLEMENT (WLCS)*

ISSN 0732-1864

Volume 213

Nineteenth-Century Literature Criticism

Criticism of the
Works of Novelists, Philosophers, and Other
Creative Writers Who Died between 1800
and 1899, from the First Published Critical
Appraisals to Current Evaluations

Kathy D. Darrow
Project Editor

GALE
CENGAGE Learning

Detroit • New York • San Francisco • New Haven, Conn • Waterville, Maine • London

Nineteenth-Century Literature Criticism, Vol. 213

Project Editor: Kathy D. Darrow

Editorial: Dana Barnes, Elizabeth Cranston, Kristen Dorsch, Jeffrey W. Hunter, Jelena O. Krstović, Michelle Lee, Thomas J. Schoenberg, Lawrence J. Trudeau

Data Capture: Katrina D. Coach, Gwen Tucker

Rights and Acquisitions: Jennifer Altschul, Kelly Quin, Timothy Sisler

Composition and Electronic Capture: Gary Oudersluys

Manufacturing: Cynde Bishop

Associate Product Manager: Marc Cormier

For product information and technology assistance, contact us at **Gale Customer Support, 1-800-877-4253.** For permission to use material from this text or product, submit all requests online at **www.cengage.com/permissions.** Further permissions questions can be emailed to **permissionrequest@cengage.com**

Gale
27500 Drake Rd.
Farmington Hills, MI, 48331-3535

LIBRARY OF CONGRESS CATALOG CARD NUMBER 84-643008

ISBN-13: 978-1-4144-3411-7
ISBN-10: 1-4144-3411-1

ISSN 0732-1864

Printed in the United States of America
1 2 3 4 5 6 7 13 12 11 10 09

Contents

Preface vii

Acknowledgments xi

Literary Criticism Series Advisory Board xiii

Preface

S ince its inception in 1981, *Nineteenth-Century Literature Criticism* (*NCLC*) has been a valuable resource for students and librarians seeking critical commentary on writers of this transitional period in world history. Designated an "Outstanding Reference Source" by the American Library Association with the publication of is first volume, *NCLC* has since been purchased by over 6,000 school, public, and university libraries. The series has covered more than 500 authors representing 38 nationalities and over 28,000 titles. No other reference source has surveyed the critical reaction to nineteenth-century authors and literature as thoroughly as *NCLC*.

Scope of the Series

NCLC is designed to introduce students and advanced readers to the authors of the nineteenth century and to the most significant interpretations of these authors' works. The great poets, novelists, short story writers, playwrights, and philosophers of this period are frequently studied in high school and college literature courses. By organizing and reprinting commentary written on these authors, *NCLC* helps students develop valuable insight into literary history, promotes a better understanding of the texts, and sparks ideas for papers and assignments. Each entry in *NCLC* presents a comprehensive survey of an author's career or an individual work of literature and provides the user with a multiplicity of interpretations and assessments. Such variety allows students to pursue their own interests; furthermore, it fosters an awareness that literature is dynamic and responsive to many different opinions.

Every fourth volume of *NCLC* is devoted to literary topics that cannot be covered under the author approach used in the rest of the series. Such topics include literary movements, prominent themes in nineteenth-century literature, literary reaction to political and historical events, significant eras in literary history, prominent literary anniversaries, and the literatures of cultures that are often overlooked by English-speaking readers.

NCLC continues the survey of criticism of world literature begun by Gale's *Contemporary Literary Criticism* (*CLC*) and *Twentieth-Century Literary Criticism* (*TCLC*).

Organization of the Book

An *NCLC* entry consists of the following elements:

- The **Author Heading** cites the name under which the author most commonly wrote, followed by birth and death dates. Also located here are any name variations under which an author wrote, including transliterated forms for authors whose native languages use nonroman alphabets. If the author wrote consistently under a pseudonym, the pseudonym will be listed in the author heading and the author's actual name given in parenthesis on the first line of the biographical and critical information. Uncertain birth or death dates are indicated by question marks. Single-work entries are preceded by a heading that consists of the most common form of the title in English translation (if applicable) and the original date of composition.

- The **Introduction** contains background information that introduces the reader to the author, work, or topic that is the subject of the entry.

- The list of **Principal Works** is ordered chronologically by date of first publication and lists the most important works by the author. The genre and publication date of each work is given. In the case of foreign authors whose works have been translated into English, the list will focus primarily on twentieth-century translations, selecting those works most commonly considered the best by critics. Unless otherwise indicated, dramas are dated by first performance, not first publication. Lists of **Representative Works** by different authors appear with topic entries.

- Reprinted **Criticism** is arranged chronologically in each entry to provide a useful perspective on changes in critical evaluation over time. The critic's name and the date of composition or publication of the critical work are given at the beginning of each piece of criticism. Unsigned criticism is preceded by the title of the source in which it appeared. All titles by the author featured in the text are printed in boldface type. Footnotes are reprinted at the end of each essay or excerpt. In the case of excerpted criticism, only those footnotes that pertain to the excerpted texts are included. Criticism in topic entries is arranged chronologically under a variety of subheadings to facilitate the study of different aspects of the topic.

- A complete **Bibliographical Citation** of the original essay or book precedes each piece of criticism.

- Critical essays are prefaced by brief **Annotations** explicating each piece.

- An annotated bibliography of **Further Reading** appears at the end of each entry and suggests resources for additional study. In some cases, significant essays for which the editors could not obtain reprint rights are included here. Boxed material following the further reading list provides references to other biographical and critical sources on the author in series published by Gale.

Indexes

Each volume of *NCLC* contains a **Cumulative Author Index** listing all authors who have appeared in a wide variety of reference sources published by Gale, including *NCLC*. A complete list of these sources is found facing the first page of the Author Index. The index also includes birth and death dates and cross references between pseudonyms and actual names.

A **Cumulative Nationality Index** lists all authors featured in *NCLC* by nationality, followed by the number of the *NCLC* volume in which their entry appears.

A **Cumulative Topic Index** lists the literary themes and topics treated in the series as well as in *Classical and Medieval Literature Criticism, Literature Criticism from 1400 to 1800, Twentieth-Century Literary Criticism,* and the *Contemporary Literary Criticism* Yearbook, which was discontinued in 1998.

An alphabetical **Title Index** accompanies each volume of *NCLC*, with the exception of the Topics volumes. Listings of titles by authors covered in the given volume are followed by the author's name and the corresponding page numbers where the titles are discussed. English translations of foreign titles and variations of titles are cross-referenced to the title under which a work was originally published. Titles of novels, dramas, nonfiction books, and poetry, short story, or essay collections are printed in italics, while individual poems, short stories, and essays are printed in roman type within quotation marks.

In response to numerous suggestions from librarians, Gale also produces an annual paperbound edition of the *NCLC* cumulative title index. This annual cumulation, which alphabetically lists all titles reviewed in the series, is available to all customers. Additional copies of this index are available upon request. Librarians and patrons will welcome this separate index; it saves shelf space, is easy to use, and is recyclable upon receipt of the next edition.

Citing *Nineteenth-Century Literature Criticism*

When citing criticism reprinted in the Literary Criticism Series, students should provide complete bibliographic information so that the cited essay can be located in the original print or electronic source. Students who quote directly from reprinted criticism may use any accepted bibliographic format, such as University of Chicago Press style or Modern Language Association style.

The examples below follow recommendations for preparing a bibliography set forth in *The Chicago Manual of Style,* 14th ed. (Chicago: The University of Chicago Press, 1993); the first example pertains to material drawn from periodicals, the second to material reprinted from books:

Franklin, J. Jeffrey. "The Victorian Discourse of Gambling: Speculations on *Middlemarch* and *The Duke's Children*." *ELH* 61, no. 4 (winter 1994): 899-921. Reprinted in *Nineteenth-Century Literature Criticism*. Vol. 168, edited by Jessica Bomarito and Russel Whitaker, 39-51. Detroit: Thomson Gale, 2006.

Frank, Joseph. "*The Gambler*: A Study in Ethnopsychology." In *Freedom and Responsibility in Russian Literature: Essays in Honor of Robert Louis Jackson,* edited by Elizabeth Cheresh Allen and Gary Saul Morson, 69-85. Evanston, Ill.: Northwestern University Press, 1995. Reprinted in *Nineteenth-Century Literature Criticism*. Vol. 168, edited by Jessica Bomarito and Russel Whitaker, 75-84. Detroit: Thomson Gale, 2006.

The examples below follow recommendations for preparing a works cited list set forth in the *MLA Handbook for Writers of Research Papers,* 6th ed. (New York: The Modern Language Association of America, 2003); the first example pertains to material drawn from periodicals, the second to material reprinted from books:

Franklin, J. Jeffrey. "The Victorian Discourse of Gambling: Speculations on *Middlemarch* and *The Duke's Children*." *ELH* 61.4 (winter 1994): 899-921. Reprinted in *Nineteenth-Century Literature Criticism*. Eds. Jessica Bomarito and Russel Whitaker. Vol. 168. Detroit: Thomson Gale, 2006. 39-51.

Frank, Joseph. "*The Gambler*: A Study in Ethnopsychology." *Freedom and Responsibility in Russian Literature: Essays in Honor of Robert Louis Jackson*. Eds. Elizabeth Cheresh Allen and Gary Saul Morson. Evanston, Ill.: Northwestern University Press, 1995. 69-85. Reprinted in *Nineteenth-Century Literature Criticism*. Eds. Jessica Bomarito and Russel Whitaker. Vol. 168. Detroit: Thomson Gale, 2006. 75-84.

Suggestions are Welcome

Readers who wish to suggest new features, topics, or authors to appear in future volumes, or who have other suggestions or comments are cordially invited to call, write, or fax the Associate Product Manager:

Associate Product Manager, Literary Criticism Series
Gale
27500 Drake Road
Farmington Hills, MI 48331-3535
1-800-347-4253 (GALE)
Fax: 248-699-8054

Acknowledgments

The editors wish to thank the copyright holders of the criticism included in this volume and the permissions managers of many book and magazine publishing companies for assisting us in securing reproduction rights. Following is a list of the copyright holders who have granted us permission to reproduce material in this volume of *NCLC*. Every effort has been made to trace copyright, but if omissions have been made, please let us know.

COPYRIGHTED MATERIAL IN *NCLC*, VOLUME 213, WAS REPRODUCED FROM THE FOLLOWING PERIODICALS:

CLIO: A Journal of Literature, History, and the Philosophy of History, v. 31, fall, 2001. Copyright © 2001 by Purdue Research Foundation. Reproduced by permission.—*The Edinburgh Review,* v. 205, April, 1907. Reproduced by permission.—*ELH,* v. 58, spring, 1991. Copyright © 1991 The Johns Hopkins University Press. Reproduced by permission.—*French Literature Series,* v. 11, 1984. Copyright © 1984 Editions Rodopi B. V. Reproduced by permission.—*The French Review,* v. 73, October, 1999. Copyright © 1999 by the American Association of Teachers of French. Reproduced by permission.—*French Studies,* v. 61, April, 2007 for "The Myth of the Female Dandy," by Miranda Gill. Copyright © 2007 Oxford University Press. Reproduced by permission of the publisher and the author.—*Genre: Forms of Discourse and Culture,* v. 29, fall, 1996 for "Empires at Stake: Gambling and the Economic Unconscious in Thackeray" by Elizabeth Rosdeitcher. Copyright © 1996 by the University of Oklahoma. Reproduced by permission of *Genre,* the University of Oklahoma and the author.—*Journal of Anthropological Research,* v. 39, spring, 1983. Copyright © 1983 The University of New Mexico. Reproduced by permission.—*Journal of Victorian Culture,* v. 11, spring, 2006. Reproduced by permission of Edinburgh University Press, www.euppublishing.com.—*MLN,* v. 98, May, 1983. Copyright © 1983 The Johns Hopkins University Press. Reproduced by permission.—*Modern Language Studies,* v. 15, fall, 1985 for "The Priest or the Mob: Religious Violence in Three Novels of Barbey d'Aurevilly" by Thomas Buckley; v. 29, spring, 1999 for "Dandyism in the Literary Works of Barbey d'Aurevilly: Ideology, Gender, and Narration" by Susanne Rossbach. Copyright © 1985, 1999 Northeast Modern Language Association. Both reproduced by permission of the publisher and the respective authors.—*Nineteenth-Century French Studies,* v. 24, fall-winter, 1995-96; v. 31, spring-summer, 2003. Copyright © 1995-96, 2003 by *Nineteenth-Century French Studies.* Both reproduced by permission.—*Nineteenth-Century Literature,* v. 56, June, 2001 for "Brushes with Fame: Thackeray and the Work of Celebrity" by Nicholas Dames; v. 61, September, 2006 for "The Aristocrat in the Mirror: Male Vanity and Bourgeois Desire in William Makepeace Thackeray's *Vanity Fair*" by Sarah Rose Cole. Copyright © 2001, 2006 by The Regents of the University of California. Both reproduced by permission of the publisher and the respective authors.—*Nineteenth Century Prose,* v. 17, winter, 1989/90. Reproduced by permission.—*Novel: A Forum on Fiction,* v. 32, summer, 1999. Copyright © 1999 NOVEL Corp. Reproduced with permission.—*Philological Quarterly,* v. 50, April, 1971. Copyright © 1971 by The University of Iowa. Reproduced by permission.—*Romance Quarterly,* v. 35, November, 1988. Copyright © 1988 by Helen Dwight Reid Educational Foundation. Reproduced with permission of the Helen Dwight Reid Educational Foundation, published by Heldref Publications, 1319 18th Street, NW, Washington, DC 20036-1802.—*The Romanic Review,* v. 74, May, 1983; v. 90, May, 1999. Copyright © 1983, 1999 by the Trustees of Columbia University in the City of New York. Both reproduced by permission.—*The Scottish Historical Review,* v. 86, April, 2007. Reproduced by permission.—*Studies in the Novel,* v. 13, spring-summer, 1981; v. 17, summer, 1985. Copyright © 1981, 1985 by the University of North Texas. Both reproduced by permission.—*Symposium,* v. 41, fall, 1987. Copyright © 1987 by Helen Dwight Reid Educational Foundation. Reproduced with permission of the Helen Dwight Reid Educational Foundation, published by Heldref Publications, 1319 18th Street, NW, Washington, DC 20036-1802.—*Victorian Periodicals Review,* v. 39, summer, 2006. Copyright © 2006 University of Toronto Press. Reproduced by permission of University of Toronto Press Incorporated.—*Victorian Poetry,* v. 39, fall, 2001. Copyright © 2001 West Virginia University. Reproduced by permission.—*Victorian Studies,* v. 10, June, 1967; v. 22, winter, 1979; v. 26, autumn, 1982; v. 48, winter, 2006. Copyright © 1967, 1979, 1982, 2006 Indiana University Press. All reproduced by permission.

COPYRIGHTED MATERIAL IN *NCLC*, VOLUME 213, WAS REPRODUCED FROM THE FOLLOWING BOOKS:

Greene, John. From "The Grotesque Characters in Barbey d'Aurevilly's *Le Chevalier des Touches*," in *L'Hénaurme Siècle: A Miscellany of Essays on Nineteenth-Century French Literature.* Edited by Will L. McLendon. Carl Winter Uni-

Gale Literature Product Advisory Board

The members of the Gale Literature Product Advisory Board—reference librarians from public and academic library systems—represent a cross-section of our customer base and offer a variety of informed perspectives on both the presentation and content of our literature products. Advisory board members assess and define such quality issues as the relevance, currency, and usefulness of the author coverage, critical content, and literary topics included in our series; evaluate the layout, presentation, and general quality of our printed volumes; provide feedback on the criteria used for selecting authors and topics covered in our series; provide suggestions for potential enhancements to our series; identify any gaps in our coverage of authors or literary topics, recommending authors or topics for inclusion; analyze the appropriateness of our content and presentation for various user audiences, such as high school students, undergraduates, graduate students, librarians, and educators; and offer feedback on any proposed changes/enhancements to our series. We wish to thank the following advisors for their advice throughout the year.

Jules-Amédée Barbey d'Aurevilly
1808-1889

French novelist, short story writer, critic, journalist, letter writer, essayist, and poet.

The following entry presents an overview of Barbey d'Aurevilly's life and works. For additional information on Barbey d'Aurevilly's career, see *NCLC,* Volume 1.

INTRODUCTION

Many scholars consider Jules-Amédée Barbey d'Aurevilly to be among the most eccentric and original writers of nineteenth-century France. His name is typically associated with literary dandyism, a school of nineteenth-century writing defined by stylistic elegance, an obsession with decadent subject matter and themes, and an iconoclastic refusal to adhere to religious, cultural, and sexual norms. Barbey d'Aurevilly's life and career were marked by numerous contradictions, among them that he was both a staunch Catholic and a scandalous author whose erotic writings shocked Parisian literary circles and that he adamantly eschewed the liberal principles of political and social progress while continually defying the conventional moral values of his aristocratic upbringing.

Barbey d'Aurevilly was renowned throughout his career for his extravagance, both in his personal life and in his writing. In such fictional works as *Une vieille Maîtresse* (1851) and *Les diaboliques* (1874), he explored extreme states of sexual perversion, frequently transgressing the limits of mainstream social and moral proprieties. In his long career as a critic, Barbey d'Aurevilly stunned readers with his vitriolic and contemptuous assessments of some of France's leading literary icons, notably Victor Hugo and Émile Zola; not unexpectedly, his negative critiques earned him many enemies over the years, and he spent the majority of his career at odds with the Paris literary establishment. While Barbey d'Aurevilly alienated a number of his contemporaries, he was also among the earliest champions of works now considered canonical by modern literary critics, and his glowing assessments of such writers as Honoré de Balzac, Charles Baudelaire, and Stendhal contributed a great deal to solidifying the lasting reputations of those authors.

BIOGRAPHICAL INFORMATION

Barbey d'Aurevilly was born Jules-Amédée Barbey on November 2, 1808, in Saint-Sauveur-le-Vicomte, a small town in the Normandy region of France. His father, Théophile Barbey, was a member of the landed nobility and was deeply embittered by the decline of aristocratic society after the French Revolution. According to biographer and critic Armand B. Chartier, Barbey's resentment tyrannized his son in his early childhood and helped shape many of Barbey d'Aurevilly's own grim attitudes toward modern society. Barbey d'Aurevilly's mother, Ernestine Ango Barbey, did little to mitigate the negative impact of her husband's animosity; although sociable and creative, she was generally inattentive to her son's emotional needs, and Barbey d'Aurevilly's youth was marked by intense isolation and solitude. In spite of his gloomy circumstances, he found solace in the storytelling talents of his maid, who introduced the boy to a wealth of local folk tales and legends. Barbey d'Aurevilly was also captivated by the history surrounding the Chouannerie, a royalist uprising against the French Revolution in which a number of his family members had participated. As biographers have noted, these stories of Normandy sparked the young boy's literary imagination, and the geography and history of his native region played a central role in his mature writings.

At the age of ten, Barbey d'Aurevilly went to live with his wealthy uncle, Jean-Louis Pontas-Duméril, in the nearby town of Valognes. As mayor of Valognes, Pontas-Duméril enjoyed considerable prestige and influence in the community, and during this period Barbey d'Aurevilly discovered a life of privilege and culture that he had not experienced during his formative years in Saint-Sauveur-le-Vicomte. Pontas-Duméril entrusted his nephew's education to a prominent Catholic abbot, who supervised his instruction in Latin. During these years Barbey d'Aurevilly also read widely in contemporary French and English literature, devouring the works of Sir Walter Scott, François-René de Chateaubriand, and Lord Byron. In 1827 Barbey d'Aurevilly moved to Paris, where for the next two years he studied at the Collège Stanislas, completing his baccalaureate in 1829. He then returned to Saint-Sauveur-le-Vicomte, intent on asking his father's permission to join the military. Théophile Barbey, still deeply hostile toward the Republican government, adamantly denied his son's petition. Despondent, Barbey d'Aurevilly reluctantly agreed to attend law school in Caen.

Shortly after arriving in Caen, Barbey d'Aurevilly entered into an illicit affair with Louise Cantru de Costils, the wife of a cousin. Although their relationship ultimately floundered, Barbey d'Aurevilly idolized Louise for the remainder of his life, using her as a model for several of his female protagonists. In Caen, Barbey d'Aurevilly also became close friends with Guillaume Stanislas Trébutien, a local publisher and librarian, who encouraged the young law student to try his hand at writing stories. Their voluminous correspondence, spanning twenty-five years of friendship, was published in two major editions (1899 and 1927) in the decades after Barbey d'Aurevilly's death as *Lettres à Trébutien.*

Although Barbey d'Aurevilly showed little desire to pursue a legal vocation, his law school years exerted a powerful influence on his later life. Upon completing his studies in 1833, he received a small inheritance that allowed him to pursue a literary career in Paris. He was confident of his future success and fame, and he lived well beyond his means during his early years in the city, adopting the social habits of a dandy and abusing alcohol and drugs. At this stage, Barbey d'Aurevilly allied himself with the liberal philosophy of the Romantic movement, primarily as a reaction to his father's autocratic, domineering personality. One of the major turning points of his career came when he befriended a young poet, Maurice de Guérin, whose advice on writing played a key role in shaping Barbey d'Aurevilly's emerging literary aesthetic. On his friend's recommendation, he began keeping a journal, a habit he maintained for much of his career; these writings were published as *Memoranda* in 1883.

While Barbey d'Aurevilly made a few connections with journal and magazine editors and became a notable presence at some of the city's elite literary salons, he failed to produce much publishable work, and he eventually found himself deep in debt. Forced to earn a living, Barbey d'Aurevilly began working as a journalist. He contributed articles to various periodicals and later joined the staff of *Nouvelliste,* a prominent left-wing newspaper. Barbey d'Aurevilly quickly emerged as one of the city's most combative critics, earning widespread notoriety for his unapologetically scathing theater reviews.

While he was busy establishing himself in Parisian literary circles, Barbey d'Aurevilly suffered two severe personal losses, both of which would have a profound effect on his aesthetic and moral sensibility. The first trauma came in 1837, when he ended his friendship with Guillaume Trébutien. Although the two men reconciled four years later, the period of their estrangement was, as Armand Chartier describes it, an "emotional desert" for Barbey d'Aurevilly, during which he exerted "considerable will power to conceal his sorrows" from others. The second, more tragic event came in 1839, when Maurice de Guérin died of consumption at the age of twenty-eight. Embittered by these losses,

Barbey d'Aurevilly began to cultivate a contemptuous bearing toward the world, one characterized by, in Chartier's words, a "need to astound and to shock through irony and scorn." These attitudes became the trademarks of Barbey d'Aurevilly's distinctive prose style.

In the first half of the 1840s, Barbey d'Aurevilly published two minor works of fiction, the novel *L'amour impossible* (1841) and the story "La bague d'Annibal" (1843), as well as an influential essay on the phenomenon of dandyism, *Du dandysme et de George Brummell* (1845; *The Anatomy of Dandyism, with Some Observations on Beau Brummell,* 1928). During these years, Barbey d'Aurevilly became increasingly conservative in his views, largely as a revolt against the political liberalism that had come to dominate the Paris salons. In 1846, inspired by the monarchism and religious conservatism of novelist Honoré de Balzac, he underwent what several commentators have described as an "intellectual conversion" to the Catholic Church. Scholar Will McLendon has argued that Barbey d'Aurevilly's adoption of a rigid Catholicism reveals a deep-seated nostalgia for aristocratic social values as much as it reflected the author's moral and spiritual beliefs. After the Paris Revolution of 1848, he became even more entrenched in his reactionary philosophy; disenchanted with the cultural milieu of the French capital, he began exploring the history and traditions of Normandy, discovering in his native province a rich source of themes and subject matter for his writings.

Barbey d'Aurevilly's first major novel, *Une vieille maîtresse,* came out in 1851. The same year, he published *Les prophètes du passé* (1851), a collection of elegiac biographical pieces on such writers as François-René de Chateaubriand, Joseph de Maistre, and others. Around this time Barbey d'Aurevilly began a love affair with Adelaide-Emilie de Sommervogel, a widowed baroness whose piety had a strong impact on the author's religious views over the next several years. In 1854 he published his first collection of poetry, *Poésies,* as well as his second major novel, *L'ensorcelée.* In the midst of this productive phase, Barbey d'Aurevilly developed an intimate friendship with the poet Charles Baudelaire, with whom he shared a deep contempt for contemporary culture and morality. The two authors inspired each other to pursue even greater extremes of artistic decadence and perversion; Chartier has noted that Barbey d'Aurevilly regarded Baudelaire as "the dear horror" of his life, while Baudelaire nicknamed his friend the "perfect monster."

Barbey d'Aurevilly began actively practicing Catholicism in 1855 with the encouragement of de Sommervogel. During the late 1850s he began writing literary criticism for *Le Pays,* a conservative newspaper that supported the repressive government of Napoléon III.

He was recognized for his favorable assessments of Balzac's novels, which he compared to the works of Molière and Shakespeare; at the same time, his harsh criticism of works by Flaubert and Hugo caused a stir within the city's salons. When the publication of Baudelaire's *Fleurs du Mal* (1857) resulted in an obscenity trial, Barbey d'Aurevilly published a landmark review of the work, defending both its artistic and ethical integrity and comparing his friend's verse to the work of Dante. A year later, Barbey d'Aurevilly's long friendship with Guillaume Trébutien abruptly ended for the second time after Trébutien decided that he could no longer tolerate what he considered the immorality of his friend's aesthetic views.

In 1860, Barbey d'Aurevilly published the first volume of his epic collection of criticism, *Les œuvres et les hommes* (1860-1895); the work eventually encompassed fourteen volumes, the last of which were published in the years following the author's death. Most biographical accounts describe the 1860s as a desperate period for Barbey d'Aurevilly. He became bitter about his failure to achieve widespread fame as an author and drank heavily; his criticism of contemporary literature, notably the work of Stephane Mallarmé and other Parnassian poets, became exceptionally brutal. Barbey d'Aurevilly still managed to publish two important novels during the decade, *Le Chevalier des Touches* (1864) and *Un prêtre marié* (1865). He also composed the novellas that would make up what many critics consider his masterpiece, *Les diaboliques* (*The Diaboliques*, 1925). The collection caused substantial controversy upon its publication in 1874; outraged by its explicit treatment of sexual themes, authorities banned sales of the book, and Barbey d'Aurevilly evaded prosecution only after agreeing to destroy all remaining copies of the work.

Following the sensation surrounding the publication of *Les diaboliques*, Barbey d'Aurevilly began to attract the admiration of a younger generation of French authors, a group that included Joris-Karl Huysmans, Edmond de Goncourt, Jean Lorrain, and José-Maria de Hérédia. His next novel, *Une histoire sans nom* (*The Story Without a Name*, 1891), appeared in 1882; that year he also published a second edition of *Les diaboliques*. In 1883 Barbey d'Aurevilly released his final major works: his *Memoranda* and the novel *Ce qui ne meurt pas* (*What Never Dies*, 1902). In his remaining years he continued to write criticism while also arranging for the republication of many of his earlier works. Barbey d'Aurevilly died in Paris on April 23, 1889.

MAJOR WORKS

A versatile and prolific author, Barbey d'Aurevilly produced noteworthy work in a variety of genres. To most modern scholars and readers, he remains best known for his fiction. Themes of transgression, sexual role reversals, and mortality dominate his novels and stories. Barbey d'Aurevilly's first major novel, *Une vieille maîtresse,* revolves around a dark love affair between a womanizing young man, Ryno de Marigny, and an androgynous Spanish woman, la Vellini. Domineering and cruel, la Vellini eventually imposes a form of psychological bondage on her younger lover that continues even after he enters into a conventional marriage with a beautiful young noblewoman.

The author's 1874 masterpiece, *Les diaboliques,* a collection of thematically related novellas, contains some of his most shocking portraits of sexual and psychological deviance. In the novella *Le rideau cramoisi,* an army officer is haunted by the aggressive sexual overtures of a young *femme fatale. Le dessous de cartes d'une partie de whist*concerns a scandalous love affair between two members of a Paris literary salon. In *Le bonheur dans le crime,* Hauteclaire Stassin, a beautiful young fencing instructor of modest birth, murders the wife of her employer, the Comte de Savigny, in order to become his lover. Hauteclaire embodies many of the unorthodox qualities typical of Barbey d'Aurevilly's heroines, including sexual confidence and an aggressiveness and physical strength usually associated with male protagonists. The novellas in *Les diaboliques* are also notable for containing detailed depictions of the traditions and social customs of Normandy.

Barbey d'Aurevilly's *Memoranda,* a collection of journal writings that chronicle his early years in Paris, offers a vivid portrait of the young writer's development, both creative and psychological. In the estimation of most scholars, the journal entries hauntingly depict Barbey d'Aurevilly's dark imaginative perspective; describing *Memoranda* in his 1977 study *Barbey d'Aurevilly,* Chartier characterizes the work as a record of "a man in quest of himself" that captures "the sufferings of a flayed heart and a boredom verging on the metaphysical." Barbey d'Aurevilly's voluminous critical writings, collected in the monumental *Les œuvres et les hommes,* also provide an in-depth look into the author's idiosyncratic views on literature and art; the volumes are known for including Barbey d'Aurevilly's legendary reviews of such authors as Hugo, Flaubert, Balzac, and Baudelaire.

CRITICAL RECEPTION

Although he was admired by a number of his contemporaries, Barbey d'Aurevilly struggled for critical recognition throughout his career. One of the first significant treatments of Barbey d'Aurevilly's work came not in a conventional review but through a work of fiction. In his 1884 novel *A rebours* (*Against the Grain,* 1922),

Joris-Karl Huysmans described his nonconformist protagonist, Des Esseintes, as enthralled by Barbey d'Aurevilly's novels, particularly by their dark explorations of sadism and blasphemy, as well as the by vigor and energy of their prose. In the early twentieth century a few prominent critics, among them Edgar Saltus, recognized the importance of Barbey d'Aurevilly's work; in his introduction to the 1919 English edition of *The Story Without a Name,* Saltus praised the artistry of Barbey d'Aurevilly's writings, comparing their enduring power to "the gargoyles of Notre Dame."

During the 1960s French scholar Jacques Petit played a key role in reawakening critical interest in the author's life and career; Petit's edition of *Œuvres romanesques complètes* (1964-66) introduced Barbey d'Aurevilly's work to modern readers, while his study of the author's critical writings, *Barbey d'Aurevilly critique* (1963), offered the first significant in-depth exploration of Barbey d'Aurevilly's unique aesthetic sensibility. In the 1980s scholars began to explore some of the major narrative strategies and themes of Barbey d'Aurevilly's fiction; Charles Bernheimer examines psychosexual elements in the author's depictions of his female protagonists, while Emanuel J. Mickel analyzes the role of religion and the supernatural in his later novels. In 1999, Susan Rossbach evaluates the relationship between Barbey d'Aurevilly's dandyism and his attitudes toward sexual and artistic power. Later, Miranda Gill analyzes Barbey d'Aurevilly's dandyism as it relates to gender roles in nineteenth-century France.

PRINCIPAL WORKS

L'amour impossible (novel) 1841

"La bague d'Annibal" (short story) 1843

Du dandysme et de George Brummell [*The Anatomy of Dandyism, with Some Observations on Beau Brummell*] (essay) 1845

Les prophètes du passé (prose) 1851

Une vieille maîtresse. 3 vols. (novel) 1851

L'ensorcelée. 2 vols. (novel) 1854

Poésies (poetry) 1854

Les œuvres et les hommes. 14 vols. (criticism) 1860-95

Le Chevalier des Touches (novel) 1864

Un prêtre marié. 2 vols. (novel) 1865

Poésies (poetry) 1870

*Les diaboliques [*The Diaboliques*; also published as *The She-Devils*] (novellas) 1874

Une histoire sans nom [*The Story Without a Name*] (novel) 1882

"Une page d'histoire" (short story) 1882

Ce qui ne meurt pas [*What Never Dies*] (novel) 1883

Memoranda (journals) 1883

Lettres à Trébutien, extraits, 1843-1851 (letters) 1899

Œuvres complètes. 17 vols. (novels, novellas, short stories, letters, essays, poetry, and prose) 1926-27

Lettres à Trébutien. 4 vols. (letters) 1927

Lettres et fragments (letters and prose) 1958

Œuvres romanesques complètes. 2 vols. (novels, short stories, essays, and journals) 1964-66

*This work contains the novellas *Le rideau cramoisi, Le plus bel amour de Don Juan, Le bonheur dans le crime, Le dessous de cartes d'une partie de whist, A un dîner d'athées,* and *La vengeance d'une femme.*

CRITICISM

George Saintsbury (essay date 1904)

SOURCE: Saintsbury, George. "The Successors of Sainte-Beuve." In *A History of Criticism and Literary Taste in Europe,* pp. 431-70. New York: Dodd, Mead, and Co., 1904.

[*In the following excerpt, Saintsbury offers a brief assessment of Barbey d'Aurevilly's critical writings.*]

A dandy and an apostle of Dandyism, a practitioner of the most "precious" style, a transgressor as to forbidden subjects, and at the same time one of the most formidable of those free lances of Catholicism of whom Ourliac, Pontmartin, and Veuillot are the chief others in his time and country, Barbey d'Aurévilly did a good deal to invite the title of charlatan, which was freely bestowed on him by his numerous and recklessly provoked enemies. But I do not think he quite deserved it at any time: and in a very large part of his extensive work[1] he did not deserve it at all. Nor are many people likely to follow me in reading this without acknowledging him as a chief example of that steady improvement in critical power with age, which has been so often noted. He never, indeed, became a good critic *sans phrase*—that is to say, a trustworthy one. In his country the danger-flag is constantly flying; or, rather, there are all sorts of danger-flags some of which even the tolerably wary may not always recognise as such.

Note

1. It fills perhaps the major part of the great collection of articles called *Les Œuvres et les Hommes* (15 vols., Paris, 1860-95).

Edinburgh Review (review date April 1907)

SOURCE: "Peasant Studies in French Fiction." *Edinburgh Review* 205, no. 420 (April 1907): 299-325.

[*In the following excerpt, the reviewer considers qualities of excess and decadence in Barbey d'Aurevilly's novel L'ensorcelée.*]

Barbey d'Aurevilly, the strange harlequin of ultraromanticism, nine years after the publication of *Les Paysans,* expended the graphic energy of his uncertain talent in the composition of his decadent extravaganza *L'Ensorcelée.* Here the counter-spirit of revolt, a fanatical feudal devotion, is embodied in the person of the palsied village Herodias of his Chouan *légende.* Idealist d'Aurevilly was not, and frequently his ultraromanticism evinces incongruous impulses of realistic insight. Nevertheless, dwelling, according to the wont of the school he survived so long,[1] upon the abnormal and the fantastic, carrying to æsthetic excess the juxtaposition of moral contrasts, he occasionally vindicates in his own productions his belief 'que 'l'imagination continuera d'être d'ici longtemps la plus puissante 'réalité qu'il y ait dans la vie des hommes.'

Note

1. Barbey d'Aurevilly died at the age of eighty in 1889.

C. H. Conrad Wright (essay date 1912)

SOURCE: Wright, C. H. Conrad. "Fiction." In *A History of French Literature,* pp. 757-78. New York: Oxford University Press, 1912.

[*In the following excerpt, Wright examines the diversity and range of Barbey d'Aurevilly's body of work. Wright identifies a contradictory quality in the author's career, arguing that his writings contain "almost diametrically opposed views" on religion, politics, and art.*]

Jules Barbey d'Aurevilly (1808-1889) was an impecunious bohemian, novelist, journalist, and critic, and the permanent embodiment of the actor on parade as well as the connecting link, across a generation, between the old Romantic egotists and the neo-Romantic individualists who, especially in poetry, followed after the Parnassians. He posed as an intellectual aristocrat (legend had it that he was descended from Louis XV) and as a fashionable dandy, though his costume grew more grotesque and his manner more extraordinary. He expressed, at different periods, almost diametrically opposed views as he ranged from incredulity to mystical Catholicism, from liberalism through Bonapartism to monarchism. His voluminous criticisms have no value of interpretation, but are examples of brilliant irony and vituperation, showing by stinging epigrammatic phrases the failings of his victims. He prided himself on having his hand against every man, on being an iconoclast, an *éreinteur,* or as he called it, a "sagittaire." He was the mediæval paladin, the "constable of France of letters" fighting modern Philistinism.

In early life Barbey d'Aurevilly had known and sympathised with troubled spirits like his intimate friend Maurice de Guérin and the latter's sister Eugénie, and was held in check somewhat by his friend, the publisher Trébutien, of Caen. Later, under the influence of drugs and the growing megalomania of the Byronic rebel, he developed an attitude of "artistic" Romanticism, which we should call eccentric or decadent. His rigid mediæval Catholicism, after the order of Joseph de Maistre and Bonald, became a neurotic perversion of faith and a belief in Satanism, in the Devil as an active force set up against God, an attitude finding expression in symbolism, psychological and sentimental. All this may seem to verge on lunacy, yet Barbey d'Aurevilly found admirers and followers, not only in persons like Huysmans, but also among the coteries of the Symbolist poets and the adepts of the "advanced" reviews, such as the *Revue blanche, la Plume,* and *le Mercure de France.*

Barbey d'Aurevilly's writings spread over a wide field and include his miscellaneous literary, dramatic, and artistic criticisms, some poetry, confessions or memoranda of the Rousseau order ("vomitoria" of the soul), a study of dandyism and Beau Brummell. But his chief significance as an influence lies rather in his not very numerous works of fiction. They are steeped in the atmosphere of his native Normandy, but particularly they exemplify the spirit of the perverse and an amoralism which at least once brought him in danger of prosecution. The chief ones are *l'Amour impossible, Une vieille maîtresse, l'Ensorcelée, le Chevalier des Touches, Un prêtre marié,* and *les Diaboliques.*

Edgar Saltus (essay date 1919)

SOURCE: Saltus, Edgar. "Barbey D'Aurevilly." In *The Story Without a Name,* by Barbey d'Aurevilly, pp. 5-23. New York: Brentano's, 1919.

[*In the following introduction, Saltus meditates on the style and central themes of Barbey d'Aurevilly's novel. Saltus describes Barbey d'Aurevilly's prose style as "canonical" while characterizing the novel as "unexceeded in fiendishness."*]

We usually get what we want, if we know how to want it, but we get too the consequences. Balzac wanted fame. The strumpet came and killed him. Barbey d'Aurevilly wanted obscurity and acquired it so amply that when I presented an earlier translation of *The Story Without a Name,* a local critic, who contrived to be both complimentary and amusing, said I had invented Barbey and that the vile story was my own vile work. Inique mais folichon.

The Story Without a Name is a masterpiece in duodecimo. Very soberly told, it is unexceeded in fiendishness, except by the Huns and the *Conte cruel* that ¨Vllieṛṣ told of the fervent Inquisition. Another man overboard. Outside the cénacle—where he is much overrated—Villiers de l'Isle Adam is remarkably unknown. But that story of his will live when French is a dead language. It may be that *Salammbô* will survive it. Personally, I would rather have written *Salammbô* than own New York. For second choice I would take Villiers' little horror and, for third, Barbey's.

Barbey's other novels are more colored and less poignant. It is not given to every writer to surprise an unsuspecting reader in bed and make him shriek with fright. Barbey did it once and once is enormous. Twice would be excessive. Sacrilege and sorcery, shapes of sin, les vieux castels, these, together with cognate accessories, he manipulated in an atmosphere charged with shivers and occasionally with chic. Here and there the chic is circumambient. In the odor of that opopanax you might fancy that if he ever stopped writing, it was because of imperative intrigues with incandescent duchesses who, save for him, would be ice. As a matter of fact, his main diversion consisted in exchanging the time of day with his concierge. I would give a red pippin to have seen him at it.

Otherwise his life was very enviable. He wrote for himself—which is the only way to write—and for thirty-six unknown friends. That is the ideal. Too fair though. Bourget, always pertinacious, ferreted him out, turned him into copy.

> At the hour when, the curtains drawn, the candles lighted, this alchemist elaborates his work, little he cares whether or not it will interest you. You, the future reader, are absent from his mind. Is there without a world of vulgar sensations and commonplace destinies? He knows nothing of it. He is absorbed in his characters. Yes, in the literal meaning of the word, *his* characters, for he has projected them from his brain, as Jupiter projected Minerva, engendered and nourished by the purest substance of his being.

If I did not know that Bourget wrote the foregoing, I would suspect him of it. Barring only Georges Ohnet, I know of no French writer who has succeeded so perfectly in being both emphatic and banal. Besides, as my friend Willy somewhere remarked: "Quand Ohnet mord c'est pour longtemps." Ohnet is very satisfying. In reading him you realise that nowhere, at any time, has there been anything worse. Bourget lacks that distinction. He gives the impression that there may be something worse and yet manages to leave you wondering.

Paul de Saint-Victor strums a different guitar. Hugo said it was a joy to write a book which Saint-Victor would write about. Barbey said nothing. He preferred to be ignored.

Here is the guitar.

> In Barbey d'Aurevilly's work there is something brutal and exquisite, violent and tender. It is like the philters that sorcerers brewed in which were asphodels and vipers, tiger's blood and honey. Never has language been raised to a prouder paroxysm.

One may wonder what a proud paroxysm is, but otherwise the image leaps. Barbey wrote on a piano. You might guess it, precisely as you might guess that Hugo wrote in a pulpit. Hugo lifted the pulpit to where all of this world and portions of the next could see it. Barbey turned the piano into a palette. After Balzac it was assumed that no one could startle a printer. Balzac wrote on proof-sheets, rewrote the proofs, made abracadabras of them and ran in debt for the costs. He owed as much as Dumas made. Dumas was prince of the pen—without at all being lord of language—and Balzac the galley-slave. Fame has her forms.

Barbey's method was more ornate. On his piano were inks—gold, blue, red, green, black. Every emotion has its color, every note in music has. Rimbaud, a poet—one of the poètes maudits—sang a sonnet about the colors of the vowels. Unphilosophic persons who get in a temper may not see red but psychically they radiate it. The aura of the jealous shows not green but yellow. The auræ of sweethearts and swains are blue. What recent occultism has discovered, Barbey divined. According to the emotion that he depicted he used the corresponding ink. It was certainly ornate. Yet, as no one except his printer saw the rainbows, it was perhaps also insane. The rainbows had another charm. I have examined a few of them. Not a correction in the lot. They were painted with a pen that ran.

An ability to write in that fashion may indicate the genius, but hardly the purist. Geniuses often write badly and as much the better for them. Balzac is atrocious. It is only in inferior artists that you get what young ladies call style. Style consists in sandpaper, the choice of words and in so manipulating both that occasionally the words seem to leap, laugh and explode.

Grammar is an adjunct, not an obligation. No grammarian ever wrote a thing that is fit to read.

Barbey's sentences are none the less canonical. How, without revision, he managed it, is conjectural only on the supposition that he rehearsed them, at the top of his lungs, as Flaubert did, before putting them down. In a minor matter, he had another similarity with Flaubert. A minor matter may be momentous. Any conversation with a stranger gave him a pain in the stomach. He was shy and yet, through an agreeable contradiction, superb or so regarded himself. The leveled eyeglass, the curl of the lip, the easy insolence, the attitude which it pleased him to affect, all that was modeled after Brummell whose cigarette stumps he had pocketed.

Zola called him a clown. Well, why not? A clown is often brilliant, which Zola never was. Moreover, Barbey's sentences in addition to being canonical are often profound, and any profundities of Zola could play tag on the head of a pin. But Zola had his hour. During it he was Jupiter Feuilletonant. As such, homage was indicated. All he got from Barbey was an ignoring stare. In return, Zola ridiculed him, laughed at his clothes, at his garret. Perhaps afterward he wished he had held his pen. In a café that Barbey frequented, Vallès, the mad anarchist, shouted: "We want the heads of a hundred thousand imbeciles." Negligently Barbey yawned: "Zola's ought to suffice." At that, some one cut in: "He will be astonished when he hears it." Now for the superb. Barbey raised his eyeglass: "Since civilization began, men such as I, have been created to astonish men such as he." A trifle too superb perhaps, but finer than Zola's brickbats.

Barbey came by it naturally. Villiers was more or less authentically comte and claimed a more or less authentic descent from a problematic crusader. But if I have the facts correctly, Barbey descended from one of the numbered Louis' of France. Nowadays, the blood of kings—unless you can take it away from them—is not much to boast of. Yet, at the time, it produced the superb which Barbey and Villiers paraded. Apart from that, Barbey was Gautier in black.

Gautier was a poet, and if I bring that coal to Newcastle it is only that with it I may note that a poet is not a human being. I lived with one once—but not twice. There are towers of jade to which the muse may come but from which sanity departs. Gautier's enthusiasms were very violent. They were splendid, lavish and noisy. He too had a palette. On Barbey's piano there was ink of every color. Gautier used but one. It was gold. But was it with ink that he wrote? The first Francis of France wrote with a diamond, which is the proper pen for a sovereign. In the *Emaux et Camées* Gautier commends a humming-bird's feather. I doubt that he ever tried one but I suspect that, drunk every morning, as a poet should be, with the nectar he had sipped in dream, he kept a cup of it before him. What Barbey's brew was, Saint-Victor has told.

There is a deeper antithesis. Gautier was pagan. Before him was the joy of life. Barbey was a Catholic. Behind him was the fear of hell. Gautier went to Spain and afterward wrote about Russia. Whether he went there is uncertain. He said he had and he believed it. Huysmans passed an evening at Henry's bar—around the corner from the rue de la Paix—and believed he had been in London. But if Gautier omitted to go to Russia, he made himself at home in the Pays des songes. Barbey followed him to that realm, strange and unique, which all of us interpret temperamentally and which each must visit alone. Back of the doors that close behind our birth crouch shapes beautiful or diabolic, shapes fashioned perhaps in our anterior lives. In the land of dreams they greet us. Occultists say that these shapes are not figments of fancy but actual entities that move and have their being as, in the gulfs of sleep, many of us do move and have our being, on another plane. It is hazardous to argue with an occultist. The only safe way is to agree. But real or unreal, the shapes that Gautier met had mouths of many tunes. Apart from inflammatory duchesses, those that Barbey saw were silent. They came clad in grey or else blood-red, with faces cicatrised and ashen. They fed him sorrow with a long spoon. They fed him horror also.

I think he enjoyed it. Madmen have a point of view that interests them and which, I am sure, is very enviable. Barbey's enjoyment induced anthropophobia which, in his case, was not an aversion to humanity but a desire to be undisturbed at his piano, alone with the hypnogogic hallucinations that it evoked.

At the time, he too had had his hour. In age he resembled Dante, not physically merely, but figuratively. He also had been in hell. But in his youth he stood for Balzac's portrait of Lucien de Rubempré. Fame ogled Lucien and the hussy made eyes at Barbey. On the boulevards he was Somebody. As he passed before the terraced cafés, you knew it. "Regarde un peu! C'est Barbey d'Aurevilly!"

He was worth it. If you had not known better you would have said: "Mais non, c'est d'Orsay!" The same air, if you please: the same costume; the blue coat, high-collared, gold-buttoned, short-waisted, long-tailed: the skin-tight trousers; the curled-brim beaver; the jeweled cane, the jeweled snuff-box, the fob, the neckcloth, that air!—and the insolence on the tip of the tongue. Not so long ago, either. I saw him at a moment when, just across the Channel, there were Gaiety Girls, a gardenia in your buttonhole and the inflated proprieties of the Victorian régime.

In that fashion he promenaded, always alone. Meanwhile something had happened. It is said that in the temple of Zeus Lycæos, men lost their shadow, their future as well. Villiers may have ventured there. He disappeared. He was gone for years, though where no one knew. Barbey also executed a fugue, perhaps to the Cévennes, where this horrible story, the Story without a Smile, occurred. But meanwhile something had happened, some incident that contrived to be catastrophic. It drove him away, not omitting to put a mark on him and more profoundly than Brummell—whom he had known—put another. It made him seek what the solitary ever do seek, obscurity. He courted it, as imbeciles court fame. Thereafter it was only at his garret in the rue Rousselet—a garret furnished, I was told, in buhl and ormolu, the rickety remnants of early ease—it was only there that fame presumed to knock.

At Caen, when Brummell entertained, his servant bawled: "The Duchess of Devonshire! His royal highness, the Regent! My lord Avanly!" To the phantom guests Brummell bowed, aired his wit. Barbey had no servant. It was he who opened the door and to guests nobler than those that appeared at Caen. Fame came and with her Love, sister visions, indistinguishably fair, indistinguishably false. On the threshold, with lips that said, Drink me! with arms that cried, Take us! before him they stood. The door closed on them. Barbey was back at his piano, disdainful of either, indifferent to both, a host still, but the host of wraiths brain-created and not desire-born.

Gautier had a ballet in his mind, Barbey a morgue. Of the two, I like Barbey best, not because he is superior—he is not—but because affection does not always go with the river. Besides, it is easy enough to like an author whom you have read, though, by the same token, it is easier still to loathe him. Georges Ohnet makes me vomit.

Gautier had two daughters. One married Catulle Mendès; the other, Emile Bergerat. Mendès wrote a hundred novels and not a single book. Bergerat wrote one book, and if you can obtain a copy, you will get glimmers of the charm made man which Gautier was.

Barbey had daughters also, daughters of dream, born on a piano which was a palette. Nowadays, like Bergerat's book, they are mainly *o. p.* [out of print]. Books have their destinies. Æschylus dedicated his tragedies to Time. Time, always the gentleman, acknowledged the compliment by storing in camphor as many of them as the fates and the fathers allowed. Barbey, more subtly, I think, dedicated his wares to Art. Time passes, nations crumble, only art survives. There are sunetoi who still swear by Æschylus. His sublimity is too antique for me. But I can and do admire Barbey, whose art, which endures, has in it the malignity of the gargoyles of Notre Dame—monsters leaning from the turrets that they may mark across the ages the sameness of the joys and griefs of man. What but monsters could be compelled to do that? Barbey created a brood that differs from the griffons and chimeras of Our Lady, yet only in this, the litter is alive and therefore more horrible.

The effect, very comforting in itself, achieved its purpose. Popularity never annoyed him, fame he let pass by. Gautier's karma was fairer—or more vulgar, according to the point of view. He was the torch of an epoch of which Barbey is now the ghost.

Donald Aynesworth (essay date May 1983)

SOURCE: Aynesworth, Donald. "The Telling of Time in *L'ensorcelée*." *MLN* 98, no. 4 (May 1983): 639-56.

[*In the following essay, Aynesworth investigates the relationship between temporality and the supernatural in Barbey d'Aurevilly's novel.*]

Barbey d'Aurevilly locates *L'Ensorcelée* in a historical lacuna. The text to which he refers in the preface to this work occupies a gap in the written record, a blank formed by the loss of the one published account of his subject, "la Chouannerie du Cotentin."[1] The disappearance of the document in question has left a vacant space which Barbey identifies as the locus of poetry and the novel. In the absence of recorded time, mnemonic evocation is the only access to the period which the writer seeks to recall. He treats of time and of history as a function of the voice, an act of speech: "Ce mot de Chouans . . . évoqua . . . ces fantômes du temps passé devant lesquels toute réalité présente pâlit et s'efface" (pp. 47-48). In the spell of the word which brings the dead to life, history assumes a form suggestive of the supernatural and acquires the power of fiction to violate chronological order.

Of the various forms of violence active in *L'Ensorcelée*, none has greater narrative significance than the subversion of temporal succession. The work is filled with forms of reversal, revision, and regression, all of which begin with the interruption of a certain sequence in time. The novel recounts a series of homecomings, each of which is marked by the unforeseen, a deviation from the "droit chemin" which occasions its own recitation and thus the process of repetition which prolongs the journey, lends it the form of a digression, and equates the time of travel with the origins of narrative. The most enduring of these journeys, the one most chronically effective in the text of the novel, is the narrator's crossing of the "lande de Lessay," a nocturnal venture whose spatiotemporal significance is inscribed in the narrative community which it establishes between the narrator and his guide, Louis Tainnebouy, a local "herbager." The verbal bond which develops between the two originates in the silence of a spatial void, the Norman moors, empty, barren expanses which suspend the production of life, arrest progress, and leave the traveler at a loss for words: "on ne saurait dire l'effet qu'elles produisent sur l'imagination de ceux qui les traversent, de quel charme bizarre et profond elles saisissent les yeux et le coeur" (p. 18).

The "lande de Lessay" is the scene of events whose inhumanity literally identifies the place with death in life: "On parlait vaguement d'assassinats qui s'y étaient commis à d'autres époques" (pp. 19-20). Fabled for its association with crime, the "lande" also lends itself to forms of horror which reduce nature to an aspect of the supernatural: "Dans le langage du pays, *il y revenait*" (p. 20). Still more telling in this context is the narrator's second use of the "langage du pays." Describing the ease with which the traveler may lose his way on the moor, he cites the peasants' "picturesque and superstitious" description of such wanderings: "Ils disent du voyageur ainsi dévoyé qu'il a *marché sur mal herbe*, et par là ils entendent quelque 'charme' méchant et caché dont l'idée les contente par le vague même de son mystère" (p. 32).

The charm of the "lande" is most active in the form of these deviations, events whose causes cannot be factually determined and whose primary locus of occurrence is language itself or, more precisely, the pleasure which the peasants take in conniving, verbally and proverbially, with mystery. The apparent absence of fact is occupied by fictional constructs in whose guise one attempts to spell out the operation of the deviant and the indeterminate. Especially significant in this regard is the incident which interrupts the narrator's journey. Tainnebouy's mare sustains an injury whose "explanation" is critical to the novelist's history of superstition. In the absence of any visible sign of harm, Tainnebouy imagines the animal's limp to be the work of a sorcerer. He is realist enough to appreciate the improbability of such a notion: "vous allez p't-être vous moquer de moi" (p. 43), and he qualifies his statement in the form of a confession, a mode of expression generically suited to the authorization and aggravation of "secrets": "certaines choses avérées parmi nous autres herbagers et fermiers . . ., comme, par exemple, des secrets qu'ont d'aucunes personnes et qu'on appelle des *sorts* parmi nous" (p. 43).

The commentary occasioned by this confession reveals a danger whose threat to realism is still more ominous than the imagined "ensorcellement" of the horse: "Il y a dans la presqu'île du Cotentin (depuis combien de temps? on l'ignore) de ces bergers errants qui se taisent sur leurs origines. . . . Espèces de pâtres bohémiens auxquels la voix du peuple des campagnes attribue des pouvoirs occultes et la connaissance des secrets et des sortilèges. D'où viennent-ils? Où vont-ils? ils passent" (p. 44). A people whose origins are kept secret enters local life and originates in the "récit" itself in the form of various gaps in the historical record: Who? Whence? When? Where? questions which threaten narrative completion and which the Norman peasants identify as the locus of the supernatural. The significance which the shepherds assume in the novel derives from their power to generate such fictions: interpretations of fact which deviate from the laws of cause and effect, change the course of communication, and modify the speaker's sense of his audience.

Tainnebouy's confession prefigures a second form of violence, a fiction whose deviation from the natural order of things is still more extreme than was his explanation of the injury to the horse. Close on the stroke of midnight, the two travelers are stopped dead in their tracks by a second sound, a bell tolling in the distance, so strange and sinister in its effects that the narrator is tempted to believe that he is hearing things: "C'est bien étrange." And his companion echoes: "étrange, en effet, mais réel?" (p. 53) What they have heard is the bell

sounding "la messe de l'Abbé de la Croix-Jugan . . . une messe des morts . . ." (p. 54), a mass whose meaning is summed up in the questions it generates: "mais réel?" *L'Ensorcelée* is punctuated by such self-readings, moments of uncertainty which typify the impression made by things seen and heard in the time and space of the "lande." Reality is stigmatized by the implausibility of its appearance, the visual and acoustical secretion of occult forces, a phenomenon which the narrator accredits in terms of Catholic dogma: "l'Eglise romaine . . . a condamné . . . la magie, la sorcellerie, les charmes, non comme choses vaines et pernicieusement fausses, mais comme choses REELLES, et que ses dogmes expliquaient très bien" (p. 56). This is an ethical epitome of the novel and is one answer to Tainnebouy's "mais réel?" A second answer, one esthetically true to the spirit of the question, appears in the story which is about to be told and in its effect on the listener.

* * *

When Marie Hecquet discovers the body of the dying Chouan priest, Jéhoël de la Croix-Jugan, she initiates the tortuous return to life of a man fated to survive various forms of violence—suicide, torture, murder— and to figure thus as the protagonist of a horror story, a "revenant" whose supernatural subversion of the natural order signifies the fictional potential of crime. This story is originally the work of a blacksmith, Pierre Cloud. Returning home from a night of revelry, he is halted by the sound of a bell, nine strokes tolling the mass in the dead of night. He sees a strange light in the nearby church and there, through a hole in the church door, witnesses a scene whose horror he cannot resist: the spectacle of a man disfigured in body and mind, the murdered priest attempting to reconstruct and complete the ceremony of his consecration, the event interrupted by the murderer's bullet. Tainnebouy's retelling of this story prolongs the life of the dead and identifies the narrative process as the locus of death in life, a form of violence which alters the voice of the speaker and, still more, the identity of the listener, the narrator; he is compelled to a form of belief which is not of his times: "je cessai d'être un instant du XIXe siècle . . . je crus à tout ce que m'avait dit Tainnebouy comme il y croyait" (p. 268).

The narrator's momentary departure from the 19th century attests to the anachronistic force of language and, as an instance of enchantment, forms a commentary on the event in whose "récit" it originates: the "ensorcellement" of the woman referred to in the title of the novel. When Jeanne-Madeleine Le Hardouey first sees the Abbé de la Croix-Jugan, she feels a loss for words which will alter the course of her life. The political passions which ruined the face of the priest have produced a visual monstrosity which provokes in the witness a sense of the indeterminate: "elle eut un frisson . . . une espèce de vertige . . . une sensation sans nom, produite par ce visage qui était aussi une chose sans nom" (p. 82). The disfiguration of the priest distracts Jeanne from the religious service and causes her to break the silence appropriate to vespers. In an effort to identify the unnameable, she turns to question her friend, Nonon Cocouan, a "commère" whose ambulatory habits and talent for gossip give her an unrivalled narrative command of local comings and goings. Nonon satisfies Jeanne's curiosity in terms which prompt the narrator to characterize "les commères": "poétesses au petit pied qui aiment les récits, les secrets dévoilés, les exagérations mensongères, aliment éternel de toute poésie . . . matrones de l'invention humaine qui pétrissent, à leur manière, les réalités de l'Histoire" (p. 84).

The crisis in Jeanne's life coincides thus with a singular departure from fact: the origins of a language whose poetry will detail the pathology of her enchantment and literally prefigure the course of her passion. The question she asks her friend initiates a form of narrative discourse, "commérage," which is essential to the circulation of the unspeakable and whose various modes—"chuchottements," "diries," "mauvaises paroles"—symptomize secrecy and scandal: the love of a married woman for a priest.

The time Jeanne spends with the "commère" delays her return home long enough to prepare the second crisis of her life, the "mise-en-scène" of a local superstition. I am referring to her encounter with the shepherd at the "vieux Presbytère," a place as ill-famed as the "lande" itself: "On disait que c'était un lieu hanté par les mauvais esprits . . ." (p. 87). This saying identifies the collective origins of the diabolical and prefigures the initial oral intervention in the novel of the sorcerer, "le Pâtre." What is said in the person of the indefinite "on," the pronominal form of the people, authorizes what the shepherd says to Jeanne-Madeleine. He captures the significance of a "haunted place" in the form of an omen and thus turns on Jeanne the malevolence he feels toward her husband: "vous n'êtes pas ici sous les poutres de votre cuisine. Vous êtes . . . dans un mauvais carrefour où âme qui vive ne passera plus maintenant que demain matin" (p. 104). The shepherd is the linguistic medium of the place. He evokes the "evil spirits" of popular legend and mediates their entry into the life of an aristocrat, a woman long distinguished for her refusal to believe the superstitions of the people. This act of mediation is the first magical gesture of the novel.

The shepherd then issues a second, equally ominous warning: "Vous vous souviendrez longtemps des vêpres d'où vous sortez, maîtresse Le Hardouey" (p. 105). In these premonitory terms, the speaker introduces a language complementary to "commérage." Arresting and memorable by virtue of its sibylline form, this warning

intimates the inaugural potential of place, the power of a crossroads, "un mauvais carrefour," to generate the language of omen and augury. It is at such ill-omened intersections that the stranger enters and occupies the city, and it is in terms of this event that literature most tellingly identifies the curse of language, the form of bondage we call "fate," *fatum,* "that which has been spoken."[2] The Latin etymon clearly substantiates the ominous quality of the act of speech.[3]

With the casting of a spell, the sorcerer subjects Jeanne-Madeleine to his sense of time and space and thereby initiates an oral tradition which vivifies and transfigures one of the oldest themes of western literature. Jeanne's predicament is analogous to the dilemma described long ago by Helen of Troy. Speaking her mind to Hector, she wishes herself dead, unborn, and refers thus to the fatal couple:

> us two, on whom Zeus set a vile destiny, so that here-
> after
> we shall be made into things of song for the men of
> the future.[4]

(*Iliad* vi. 357-58)

Helen was a prophet and, in her moment of insight, something like the poet himself. Her words have the value of an archetype and may stand for the experience of many another adulteress. And, as Barbey's novel will show, it matters little that the act of adultery be a thing of the flesh or of the mind alone. In the act of infidelity, mental or physical, a woman tends to lose her domestic life and to become, verbally, the property of others, aliens, "men of the future." The loss of life to language entails a collapse of social order which is one of the principle themes of **L'Ensorcelée.**

Between her meeting with Nonon Cocouan and her encounter with the shepherd, Jeanne becomes the locus of a paradox whose terms will spell her ruin; the loss of language occasioned by the disfiguration of the priest makes her a source and a subject of verbal invention. In the form of her enchantment, she becomes the person in whose life gossip and prophecy intersect. Her presence is chronically subverted by those versions of the past and the future established in the several narratives of which she forms the audience. This constant temporal displacement determines her mental and social alienation.

The relevance of gossip to the form of Jeanne's fate ultimately appears in the violence which loose talk does to language. In the guise of "commérage," language is distinguished by its decomposition. Grammar and syntax are subverted by the oral evidence of secrecy: "des bruits vagues, un mot dit par-ci et par-là, des souffles plutôt que des mots . . ." (p. 158). In this context, the act of speech is a choral production, a process of anonymization in which the voice becomes a vestige of the collective. Rumor thus reduces society to a volatile, unstable form and literally masses the subversive forces essential to personal crisis and popular indiscretion.

Ironically, the linguistic subversion of Jeanne's life is partly the work of her friend, Clothilde Mauduit, a person who proves to be the sorcerer's second. Isolated by poverty and paralysis, by her royalist sympathies and the contempt she feels for her contemporaries, this woman leads a life which is as marginal as that of "les pâtres bohémiens." Generally reputed to be herself a "sorcière," la Clotte is, in fact, a gifted storyteller and, as such, Jeanne's only access to the aristocratic life into which she was born. Though she is married to a rich farmer, Thomas Le Hardouey, Jeanne is still, to Clothilde, Mlle de Feuardent. La Clotte's refusal to acknowledge Jeanne's legal identity expresses her nostalgia for the world epitomized in the noble name. In her narrative reconstruction of Jeanne's maiden name, she contrives a genealogy in whose terms she seeks to refute the facts of modern life, to reverse and revise history. Her companion willingly complies in this effort: "Jeanne-Madeleine . . . ne sentait vivement, ne vivait réellement qu'avec la Clotte . . . ses récits étaient la poésie" (p. 122).

The life which Jeanne lives in the language of these stories is, unfortunately, fatal. As she listens to Clothilde recall the past, she fulfills the shepherd's prophecy: "Vous vous souviendrez longtemps . . ." In la Clotte's account of Dlaïde Malgy, Jeanne-Madeleine discovers a person whose fate foreshadows her own. Adélaïde's unrequited love for la Croix-Jugan led her to consult "les faiseuses de breuvages" and to dabble in black magic. But her venture into sorcery merely accelerated the loss of her life and formed a history of madness whose "récit" may be construed as the art of damnation, a narrative which prefigures and precipitates the demise of the woman who forms its audience.

Doomed for her original transgression of the sacred, love for a priest, Jeanne is doubly damned because she believes herself to be "ensorcelée." Her interpretation of her passion is ominous and ultimately fatal, for it entails a recourse to the occult which compels her to a second form of sacrilege, the profanation of prayer, a practice which violates her religion, alters her identity, and portends her self-destruction. She confesses her secret life to la Clotte, her visits to the shepherds: "Je m'en étais longtemps moquée, d'eux et de leurs sortilèges, mais j'y suis allée. . . . J'ai reconnu celui . . . qui m'avait fait cette menace et que je n'ai jamais pu oublier. Je l'ai prié . . . ce vagabond . . . comme on ne doit prier que Dieu, d'avoir pitié de moi et de m'ôter le sort qu'il m'avait jeté . . ." (p. 170).

Enchantment equals sacrilege, an abuse of language whose potential for violence is realized in Jeanne's suicide and its spectacular sequel; her loss of religion reproduces itself in the public at large in terms of an alienation whose linguistic form is exactly analogous to the profane use of prayer. The event in question occurs on the day of her funeral: "On vint . . . aux obsèques de Jeanne encore plus pour parler de sa mort extraordinaire et inexpliquée que pour s'acquitter envers elle d'un dernier devoir. La *jaserie,* ce mouvement éternel de la langue humaine, ne s'arrête ni sur une tombe fermée ni en suivant un cercueil . . ." (p. 213). One of the definitions which Robert gives of "jaser" is: "parler avec indiscretion de ce qu'on devrait taire."[5] In the context in which the novelist uses this word, the indiscretion is especially excessive. A funeral is a time for meditation or "recueillement" when the mere act of speech may be more than indiscreet, may be, in fact, scandalous, sacrilegious, subversive. On this occasion, the disruption of silence originates in the absence of the persons primarily responsible for its preservation. Neither Jeanne's own relations nor those of her husband deign to attend the ceremony. The mismatch of the farmer and the aristocrat has attacked society at its center, the family itself. Left empty in the funeral cortege is the space reserved for mourning, the very life of the dead. Thus is Jeanne murdered by her "mésalliance." But this is also the suicide of a society, a void in whose visual presence the common townsfolk of Blanchelande, those most peripheral to the event, begin to lose their own religion and to produce an idiom appropriate to the scandal of such a loss.

The violence which language does to death can be still more virulent than this. In his introduction to the novel, Barbey refers to the form assumed by the crisis of this contagion. To explain the scandal and the mystery of Jeanne's degradation, the ruin of "une âme . . . ineffaçablement chrétienne," the townspeople are obliged to "remonter jusqu'à des idées surnaturelles" (pp. 12-13). Regressive as it is, such an interpretation momentarily undoes the town. Recourse to the idea of the supernatural occasions the commission of a crime, an act of profanation which is fatal to la Clotte. The appearance of the old woman at her friend's funeral inspires a popular version of their relationship, an instant "précis" whose distortion of the facts is literally lethal. Notorious as she is for her long neglect of Catholic practice, Clothilde's mere presence magnifies her years of absence and confirms the monstrous suspicions produced by her marginal existence. Her attendance at church is unheard-of and, in this context, her very name is horrible to hear: "Ce nom de la Clotte, sa présence inattendue . . . firent passer dans la foule cette vibration attentive qui précède . . . les grandes scènes et les grands malheurs" (p. 219).

Like the sacred itself, la Clotte is at once central and peripheral to the community. An essential outsider, her sudden emergence in public suffices to resolve a massive uncertainty and to generate an equally massive fiction, "une exagération mensongère" in whose form she perishes.⁶ Clothilde is murdered because she is orally and collectively identified as a "sorcière" and Jeanne herself as "ensorcelée" (p. 220). This accusation is initiated by the son of a man at whose hands Clothilde became, years earlier, "la Tousée," a woman shorn of her hair and publicly humiliated for her Chouan sympathies. Her accuser knows and names her as such, "vieille Tousée" (p. 219), but when she asks to be allowed to bless her dead friend, her adversary uses a word expressive of horror, a noun which disfigures those who use it and whose force far exceeds that of "la Tousée." Whatever form it may assume—"sort," "sorcière," "ensorcelée"—every such utterance prefigures and ultimately produces an act of violence: sacrilege, suicide, madness, murder, all of which demonstrate the socially subversive effect of superstition.

Throughout *L'Ensorcelée,* the belief in sorcery is atavistic in its effects. It revives passions which were originally political in nature and thus exposes the pathology of local history. Social excesses which originated in the form of civil war return to life anachronistically with the mere utterance of the word "sorcière," a sound whose sense is catastrophically inscribed in the body of la Clotte. The system of subversion inaugurated by the revolution surfaces in an attack of communal madness, a collective "ensorcellement" produced by the use of the word most appropriate to such a phenomenon, a noun whose repetition alone is enough to create a mob and therein a force sufficient to a fatal, fictional deviation from fact. The generation of violence is divided thus between politics and the belief in magic. Calling la Clotte a sorceress is analogous to the production of a fiction, a process which may be likened to the interpretation of a disease, a pathological condition which linguistically contaminates the community in which and by which it is formulated.

This contamination originates in Jeanne-Madeleine's unspeakable, unspoken passion for the priest: "elle s'était *imposé le devoir* de cacher la passion qui la minait et de ne révéler à personne l'énigme cruelle de sa vie" (p. 158). This silence forms a second enigma, a lacuna, an unknown whose effect on society is equivalent to that of the face of the abbé, "une chose sans nom," on the woman herself. Jeanne's silence is the locus of a language which demonstrates the murderous potential of secrecy. When the narrator refers to the "commères" as "mothers of invention," poets who love "les récits, les secrets dévoilés, les exagérations mensongères," he identifies the idiom essential to the accreditation of the supernatural, an idiom which will literally fill the gap formed by Jeanne's refusal to speak.

The various linguistic modes at work in the text of *L'Ensorcelée*—prophecy, horror stories, "commérage," "jaserie," "dirie,"—are meant, in part, to spell out the unity of gossip and the supernatural. More importantly, they fashion the polemic of an author whose work is styled to voice the collective, a community of wisdom and superstition whose several voices modulate and ultimately stage a *creatio ex nihilo,* a magical performance which marks the textual "prise de pouvoir" of the popular imagination. The verbal and proverbial power of the people articulates the form in which the impersonal and the ahistorical penetrate and appropriate the narrative. This is most tellingly worked out in the strange peregrination of Thomas Le Hardouey. Of all the characters in the novel, this "acquéreur des biens d'Eglise" is initially the least likely to credit popular beliefs or the reality of the occult (p. 110). Materialist though he may be, however, he is haunted by the "état sans nom" of Jeanne-Madeleine and by the growing secrecy of her life, a mystery made all the more maddening by the language which it generates: "ses visites à la Clotte, ses rencontres . . . avec ce Chouan dont on glosait tant dans la contrée, et enfin les propos de chacun, ramassés en miettes, à droite et à gauche . . ." (pp. 174-75).

Still more troubling to Le Hardouey are the conditions in which he is told the secret in question. Crossing the moor on his return from a business trip, he is arrested by the sound of a voice whose source he cannot identify: "Tout esprit fort que fut maître Le Hardouey, ces sons humains sans personne, dans ces landages ouverts aux chimères et aux monstres de l'imagination populaire produisirent sur ses sens un effet singulier et nouveau et le disposèrent sans doute à la scène inouïe qui allait suivre" (p. 176). The "un-heard-of scene" in which he is about to participate originates in the recitation of a poem, "une complainte de vagabond":

> Je rode par tout chemin
> Et de village en village,
> L'un m'donne un morcet de pain,
> L'autre un morcet de fromage . . .
> Et quelquefois, par hasard,
> Un petit morcet de lard . . .
>
> (p. 177)

The shepherds survive by virtue of a faculty comparable to that of a poet, the power to subvert skepticism, to suspend disbelief, and so create an audience essential to the working of their spells. The "complainte" which they intone on the moor is a brief history of their talent for survival, a gift whose most effective form is its narrative "précis"; as such, it forms an esthetic intervention in the life of a man for whom such language marks a radically subversive departure from the "droit chemin," a loss of direction in the course of which he will become one of those "voyageurs dévoyés" of peasant lore. The power which the nomads assume over the farmer is, in part, a function of the context in which he hears the poem. During his homecoming, his life becomes a locus of verbal invention originating in a loss of language. The nameless state of Jeanne-Madeleine and the dead silence of the "lande" provoke a sense of "malaise" which can be specified only in interrogative terms: "était-ce l'heure? était-ce la réputation du lieu où il se trouvait? étaient-ce les superstitions qui enveloppaient ces pâtres contemplatifs . . . ?" (p. 179).

These questions form the text of a crisis which the traveler shares with the teller of the tale. Interrogation suspends the "récit" and transforms the narrator into a reader. In the form of this reading, he identifies the element of the indeterminate which occasions Le Hardouey's change of mind: was it the hour? the reputation of the place? the superstitions? These uncertainties articulate the form in which fact becomes fiction and compel a form of belief analogous to the action of poetry. In his crossing of the moor, Le Hardouey wanders into an area of silence where communal storytelling, "the chimeras and the monsters of the popular imagination," prove more potent than his own skepticism. His conversion to the occult reflects the power of narrative to suspend disbelief. This change of mind confirms the connection which Marcel Mauss made between narrative recitation, stories and legends, and magical performance: "ces contes et ces légendes ne sont pas seulement . . . un aliment traditionnel de la fantaisie collective; leur constante répétition . . . entretient un état d'attente, de crainte, qui peut, au moindre choc, produire des illusions et conduire à des actes . . . l'image du magicien . . . se constitue par une infinité de 'on dit'. . . ."[7] Such is the sense of a crisis, a "péripétie," in the life of a traveler; his thoughts and gestures suddenly originate in the mind of the collective, the anonymous, indefinite "on."

It is appropriate that the enchantment of a wealthy farmer be set in a "terrain vague." A no-man's land, the "lande de Lessay" belongs to everyone and to no one. Here, where distinctions based on law and property signify nothing, one person's life becomes, literally and materially, the territory of another. As such, the moor may be reckoned a theatre or, more precisely, a utopia, a "no-place" which functions precisely as does a blank page in the genesis of a fiction. It provides a spatial context for a utopian attack on the idea of property. Witness the shepherd's response when Le Hardouey orders him to move from the path of his horse: "—'La terre appartient à tout le monde'" (p. 179)! Thus is the language of revolution appropriated by those who have no history, no social status—no place—at all; thus does the shepherd voice the violence which history does to property. To cite the narrator, it was as if he had proclaimed "d'avance l'axiome menaçant du communisme moderne . . . l'expropriation du genre humain . . ." (p. 179). Ominous as it is, the shepherd's statement is merely a polemical revision of his personal threat to Jeanne-Madeleine. The "lande de Lessay" is itself "un mauvais carrefour ou âme qui vive ne passera plus maintenant que demain matin," and it was once so described by Louis Tainnebouy, "sans âme qui vive" (p. 41).

The enchantment of maître Le Hardouey culminates in his expropriation: the mental and material losses he suffers in the person of his wife. From the shepherd himself, the farmer learns the extremes of Jeanne's madness, the gifts which she made to this man in her attempt to gain the love of the priest, gifts which the nomad now uses to expose her as a menace to her society, a woman whose adulterous passion engenders a form of circulation and exchange which supercedes money and subverts private property. Thus does he tell Le Hardouey a secret long since the subject of local gossip: "Les propos qui lui étaient revenus sur sa femme, vagues . . . sans consistance, sans netteté, comme tous les propos qui reviennent, étaient donc bien positifs et bien hardis puisque ces misérables bergers les répétaient. . . . Jeanne-Madeleine, cette femme d'un si grand sens autrefois, avait des rapports avec ces bergers" (p. 182)!

The nomad's contention that the earth belongs to everyone was prophetic in more ways than one. It prefigured his provocation of a purely linguistic community which effectively dissolves legally constituted society. Gossip produces relationships in which social status and personal distinction come to nothing; society is subverted by a language which exists to promote the idea of adultery and which mimics the act itself by the promiscuous ease of its own circulation. Significantly, it is from this same subversive idiom that the sorcerer contrives the vernacular of the supernatural. Witness the farmer's response to the shepherd's version of Jeanne's fall: "il faut que tu me prouves tout à l'heure ce que tu me dis." And the shepherd: "Mais qué que vous me payerez, maître Le Hardouey, si je vous montre que ce que je dis, c'est la pure et vraie vérité?—Ce que tu voudras!— dit le paysan dévoré du désir qui perdent ceux qui l'éprouvent, le désir de voir son destin" (p. 182).

The desire to "see his destiny" creates a "sortilège" which transforms Le Hardouey into the peasant that he is, "tel qu'en lui-même enfin la sorcellerie le change." Drawing a small mirror from his bag, the sorcerer tells Le Hardouey to look into it, utters "des mots étranges, inconnus à maître Le Hardouey," then commands him to recount what he sees in the glass. Thus prompted, the farmer recites a passage from his life: "je commence . . . je vois . . . je vois comme une salle . . . je vois du monde dans la salle . . . V'là que je revois . . ." (pp. 183-84). In this instance, narration is initiated by incantation, a form of vocalization which reduces language to a mode of the unknown and whose effect on maître Thomas is equivalent to that of the face of the abbé on his wife; it promotes a state of alienation which is identical to enchantment. What Le Hardouey finally sees in the surface of the magical "mirette," two people turning his heart on a spit, reflects only what he suspects, the complicity of his wife with the priest, and verifies "les propos qui reviennent."

The mirror is the moor itself "mise en abîme," a diminutive version of a spatial void in which time and life appear only as an effect of language and only in the image of death. Lest one be tempted to dismiss this as mere magic, consider its relevance to the making—the reading and the writing—of a novel. Conjured, created, *ex nihilo,* the image which the shepherd offers in proof to the peasant illuminates Proust's remarks on the affective power of the esthetic elimination of life. Given the reality of joy and sorrow, "la joie ou l'infortune d'un personnage réel," such reality touches us only indirectly, imagistically, in the act of reading: "l'ingéniosité du premier romancier consista à comprendre que dans l'appareil de nos émotions, l'image étant le seul élément essentiel, la simplification qui consisterait à supprimer purement et simplement les personnages réels, serait un perfectionnement décisif."[8] In his own image, Le Hardouey suffers the most radical form of suppression a real person can sustain and yet survive. Shall we say, then, that a nomadic shepherd is a model of the first novelist? And is his collaborator, his narrator—the man who says what he sees—an avatar of the first reader? "Il faut dire ce que vous véyez . . . autrement le sort va s'évanir" (p. 186). Such is the principle of this fiction: a vocal production of a visual horror, a tale told by an idiot who sees and speaks by virtue of the art of another, a sorcerer whose sources are the same as those of the "commère" and the "romancier."

A community born of its verbal excesses—the linguistic secretion of the unspeakable—attains perfection in the art of the magician. He coaxes Le Hardouey to see and speak in a manner consonant with suspicion and thereby demonstrates the charm, the poetic force, of public opinion. And, like the crowd assembled at the grave of his wife, maître Thomas is literally maddened by his belief in sorcery. His crime, like that of the mob, is provoked by a magical revival of political passion. He murders la Croix-Jugan less for love of Jeanne-Madeleine than he does for the sake of partisan prejudice: "c'était le Bleu, plus encore que le mari, qui aspirait à la vengeance" (p. 187). Thus, in the person of his fool, his "guignol," the sorcerer authors an act of violence which subverts the social order created by the revolution, an order designed, in part, to discredit occult practices and to sap the authority of the Catholic church, the institution most closely associated with the survival of superstition.

* * *

The criminal effects of enchantment might be treated as a moment from the "grand Guignol," a form of melodrama episodically endemic in a work which treats of the absurdity and extravagance of horror. Various losses of mind and of life are told and foretold in ways which systematically undermine nature, attack reason, and subvert realism. This process of subversion identifies Barbey's text with a paradox generically rooted in the "romanesque." The novel violates the conventions of its own operation; it secretes in its subject matter forms of violence sufficient to sabotage the novel itself and to voice the author's polemical attack on post-revolutionary civilization, "époque, grossièrement matérialiste et utilitaire . . ." (p. 18). This polemic is the work of a man who identifies himself as a "conteur" and his narrative as a "histoire," a text whose truth he equates with its lack of "vraisemblance" and its exclusion of psychological analysis (pp. 156-57).

Critical disaffection with the canon of his medium is an irony typical of the process of authorization which defines the work of the novelist. In this case, it identifies that radical disenchantment with his times characteristic of the intellectual aristocrat, the dandy. An anachronism, by definition, the dandy survives by virtue of his ethical and esthetic departure from contemporary life. Hence, in the narrator's construction of history, the priority which he gives to the oral over the written. Historical truth, "la véritable histoire," is not "celle des cartons et des chancelleries" (p. 48). It is something known "de vive voix," "l'histoire orale, le discours, la tradition vivante" (p. 48). Access to this truth is a matter of verbal initiation. It passes from one generation to another by word of mouth, and, like the secrets of the shepherds, is the genetic principle of a temporal community. Time originates in these acts of speech and survives by virtue of the voice alone.

As one who cultivates this sort of discourse, the narrator might be styled a collector of archaic modes, an archaeologist of verbal gestures whose collective formation threatens the notion of individual authority. Time and place become significant in terms of their ability to generate the passions of superstition and therein a form of community whose most enduring form is the priority it assumes in the narrative act. In this context, the narrator himself is simply an analogue of Jeanne-Madeleine, la Clotte, la Croix-Jugan, and others. Together, these persons form a "récit" whose several voices spell out the fictional potential of a lost cause in the person of its most militant survivor, the "monstrueux défiguré de la Fosse" (p. 157), a hero completely absent from "l'histoire écrite" but eminently present, legend itself, "dans l'histoire qui ne s'écrit pas . . . dans l'esprit des foules" (p. 260)!

Jéhoël de la Croix-Jugan is a catalyst of the mass mind. But the subversion of the individual author and of the historical originality implicit in this idea is ultimately the work of the shepherd, the sorcerer. In this regard, one need only consider the education of the narrator, or, more precisely, the generic distinction of those stories whose telling has so long spelled the coming of night in his life. The love of a beautiful, noble woman for a man monstrously disfigured is the stuff of a fairy tale. Reading *L'Ensorcelée,* one might easily subscribe to it as a version, or a subversion, of *La Belle et la bête,* a story whose antiquity and whose many revivals constitute the history of a spell, "un charme bizarre et profond." But this fairy tale, set in *L'Ensorcelée,* exists only to frame and to elaborate a second such bedtime story. In response to Tainnebouy's account of the tales told of the wandering shepherds, the narrator says: "j'ai été bercé avec ces histoires . . ." (p. 44). The passive construction and the sense of the verb signify the quality of the narrator's subjection to the oral tradition into which he was born. The passage from waking to sleeping is, and was, a critical moment in the genesis of narrative forms and in the generation of time itself. It is the locus of those nocturnal enchantments in whose form the collective bears most tellingly on the diurnal ego of the narrator. The anonymity of this person is a novelist's tribute to the authority of local, Norman folklore, a body of learning which long antedates the birth of the speaker and which educates one not to seek to tell the truth in one's own name.

* * *

Writing some seventy-five years after Barbey d'Aurevilly, Walter Benjamin was to describe a form of exchange identical to that which occurs between Louis Tainnebouy, his anonymous companion, and the reader: "people imagine the storyteller as someone who has come from afar. But they enjoy no less listening to the man who has stayed at home, making an honest living, and who knows the local tales and traditions."[9] The novelist's narrator, the reader's guide, is a man returning from afar. The pleasure he takes in "listening to the man who has stayed at home" attests to the esthetic force of nostalgia, or to what the German critic terms, "the beauty in what is vanishing," the recession of storytelling itself "into the archaic" (pp. 87-88). Benjamin attributes the decline of the art of the storyteller to the devaluation of experience, and his focus on this phenomenon is essentially the same as that of Barbey's nameless traveler: the acceleration and mechanization of life, the appetite for information and explanation, the passion for the printed page, the desire for the novel itself. Barbey's narrator seeks out the recesses of rural life because he finds there, in Tainnebouy's own speech, something essential to the narrative preservation of experience, that is, "sagacité fine et . . . bon sens," qualities of mind neglected in "ce pauvre siècle de mouvement perpétuel et de gesticulation cérébrale" (p. 39). To Benjamin, the giving of "counsel" was ethically central to the art of the storyteller, counsel which he called "the epic side of truth, wisdom" (p. 87), an esthetically enduring form of intelligence which commends itself to memory and to repetition precisely because the explanation, the pure prose of the thing, has been left out.

In *L'Ensorcelée,* counsel is crucial, but it comes in a form critical of the text and the context in which it originates. As set in Barbey's novel, among women, storytelling is a risk which runs to scandal and worse. The tales women tell one another generate energies which revive the dead and disfigure the living, and it falls to the lot of another storyteller to draw the moral. Thus Tainnebouy: "Les femmes se perdent avec les histoires . . ." (p. 135)! Tainnebouy's critique of storytelling qualifies the narrator's attack on the novel. The counsel which Barbey's storyteller affords is a word of caution against the art of damnation, a warning which recalls the ominous utterances of the sorcerer. But we can apply what he says of women to society at large, to the town of Blanchelande. The oral tradition in whose terms the narrator tells his tale originates on the moor itself, in the anonymous, collective generation of the diabolical. The "ensorcellement" of Jeanne-Madeleine shows the devil to abide in certain abuses of language, an evil as distinct in the mass as it is in the individual. To present the multiformity of this evil, the author is obliged to multiply the forms of speech collected by the narrator and to construe demonic possession in diachronic terms, as a history of linguistic degeneration and profanation occasioned by a sacrilegious breach of silence. From the first whisperings of "commérage" to the "jaserie" of the crowd to the unknown tongue of the sorcerer's incantation, the oral modes assembled in the narrative are meant to pace the progress of a superstition and to plot the textual appropriation of the unspeakable. For the devil, in *L'Ensorcelée,* is precisely that, "une chose sans nom," a face whose disfiguration sets the standard of sacrilege and its linguistic reproduction, the novel, itself a nameless thing, a generic monstrosity whose creation equals an act of self-destruction. The violence of this paradox is surely a fitting form for the death in life of Jéhoël de la Croix-Jugan.

Notes

1. Jules Amédée Barbey d'Aurevilly, *L'Ensorcelée,* in *Œuvres complètes,* 17 vols. (Paris: François Bernouard, 1926-27), II, 8. Subsequent page references to the novel will be given in parentheses in the text.

2. *Oxford English Dictionary,* Compact Edition, 2 vols. (Oxford: Oxford University Press, 1971), I, 968.

3. In his reading of *L'Ensorcelée,* Michel Serres traces "sort," "sortilége," and "sorcellerie" to their Latin and Greek roots and localizes a form of activity analogous to that at work in the shaping of a

fiction, that is, "entrelacer, tisser, joindre." "Analyse spectrale de Barbey d'Aurevilly," in *Critique*, 349-50 (June-July, 1976), p. 592. The terms cited by Serres illuminate the sense of "text" itself, a web of words which might be reckoned the fate of a reader.

4. Homer, *Iliad,* trans. and intr. Richard Lattimore, Phoenix Books (Chicago: University of Chicago Press, 1961), p. 162.

5. Paul Robert, *Petit Robert,* Nouvelle édition (Paris: Société du Nouveau Littré, 1977), p. 1043.

6. In writing this passage, I was inevitably influenced by *La Violence et le sacré.* As a scapegoat, Clothilde Mauduit comes very close to enacting René Girard's idea of the sacred. Much of the violence latent in the community does center, momentarily, on her person. But the catharsis proves to be abortive. As Naomi Schor has pointed out, the death of la Clotte is not truly conciliatory in its effects. "*L'Ensorcelée* ou la scandalisée," in *MLN* [*Modern Language Notes*], 94:4 (1979) pp. 731-41. The murder awakens la Croix-Jugan to a sense of his Christian charge, but his moral assumption of the priesthood culminates in his own murder, a second act of violence which undoes whatever unanimity was attained in the first.

7. Marcel Mauss, *Esquisse d'une théorie générale de la magie,* in *Sociologie et anthropologie,* intr. Claude Levi-Strauss (Paris: PUF, 1950), p. 25.

8. Marcel Proust, *A la recherche du temps perdu,* ed. Pierre Clarac and André Ferré, Pléiade, 3 vols. (Paris: Gallimard, 1954), I, 85.

9. Walter Benjamin, *Illuminations,* ed. and intr. Hannah Arendt, trans. Harry Zohn (New York: Harcourt, Brace, and World, 1968), p. 84. Future page references to this essay will be given in parentheses in the text.

Charles Bernheimer (essay date May 1983)

SOURCE: Bernheimer, Charles. "Female Sexuality and Narrative Closure: Barbey's *La vengeance d'une femme* and *Á un dîner d'athées.*" *Romanic Review* 74, no. 3 (May 1983): 330-41.

[*In the following essay, Bernheimer presents a psychoanalytic reading of the two novellas. Bernheimer highlights undercurrents of sexual repression in Barbey d'Aurevilly's storytelling strategies.*]

Etymologically, prostitution is a placing or setting forth in public, a public exposition. The word is made up of the Latin preposition *pro,* here with the sense of "for-

ward," "towards the front," "into a public position," plus *statuere* "to cause to stand," "set up," "place." The psychoanalytic significance of prostitution in the male imagination suggests another meaning of the Latin prefix *pro*: "instead of," "in place of," "serving as a substitute for." In the male erotic imagination, according to Freud, the prostitute stands unconsciously in place of the mother as the degraded object of those sensual feelings that the incest barrier prevents from being directed toward maternally derived object choices.[1] In this sense the prostitute functions as a veil, a cover-up, a disguise to obscure the primary object of male desire. The prostitute's indiscriminate availability to public scrutiny and sexual purchase is related in a dramatically ambiguous way to her private role as a substitute in a secret incestuous fantasy.

The dynamics of exposure and concealment are, of course, essential to the novelistic imagination, and it is consequently no accident that the prostitute figures so prominently in nineteenth century fiction. Her fascination, however, seems to derive as much from the way she serves to focus male ambivalence about female sexual desire as it does from her role in splitting the object of male desire. Indeed, in the case of Barbey d'Aurevilly ambivalence seems too balanced a term. Like a strikingly large number of novelists in nineteenth century France, he portrays the prostitute's open and aggressive eroticism less as an invitation to desire than as a justification to fear it and to repress active female sexuality. As I propose to demonstrate here, in the two stories about prostitution included in *Les Diaboliques, La Vengeance d'une femme* and *À un dîner d'athées,* Barbey reflexively links the very possibility of narrative control and closure to the successful repression, even obliteration, of the female sexual body.

Tressignies in *La Vengeance* [*La Vengeance d'une femme*], "un libertin fortement intellectualisé" (283),[2] follows an attractive prostitute not as much out of desire as out of curiosity. He wonders what story might explain how such a strikingly beautiful woman "n'était qu'une fille du plus bas étage" (283). Moreover, "cette femme était pour lui une ressemblance" (284). It does indeed turn out that he has encountered her previously, as a great Spanish duchess, but the memory, the semblance, also involves an unconscious maternal image. So the quest for story by this intellectual, "qui avait assez réfléchi sur ses sensations pour ne plus pouvoir en être dupe" (283), is motivated unconsciously by a quest for the primary love object to which all erotic resemblances refer. Intercourse with this woman, however, is so terrifyingly intense, her sensuality is "quelque chose de si fauve et de si acharné" (291), that the experience cancels Tressignies' reflexive defensiveness and causes him to forget everything "—et ce qu'elle était, et ce pour quoi il était venu" (291). Her body is an abyss that sucks his soul into it ("Positivement, elle lui soutira son âme, à lui, dans son corps, à elle"—292), thereby destroying, symbolically castrating, his intellectual identity and his narrative curiosity.

But then Tressignies discovers that this violently voluptuous body has actually been merely an instrument in a highly intellectualized representational scenario. He suddenly realizes that his partner, in the midst of sexual intimacy, has been absorbed in the contemplation of a man's portrait on her bracelet. His first interpretation is typically oedipal and casts him in a substitutive role similar to the one she has played in his own fantasy: He angrily imagines "qu'il *posait pour un autre*—qu'il était là pour le compte d'un autre" (292). The mother seems to have acknowledged the father's unique privilege just when the son thought he had her all to himself. This gesture violates a crucial principle of the prostitute's appeal, her ability to camouflage oedipal dynamics by making herself equally available to all.

At this point this passionate whore reveals that she is actually the Duchess of Sierra Leone and that she hates rather than loves her husband, the Duke, whose portrait is on her bracelet. This revelation reverses the oedipal model affectively but maintains, in a negative mode, the bond of the mother to the father. For Tressignies, it is as if the incest taboo had suddenly taken effect: He now recognizes the source of the mysterious resemblance that had initially intrigued him. Immediately he loses all sexual desire for this maternal figure, whose identity as a prostitute has been totally erased ("La duchesse, en émergeant à travers la fille, l'avait anéanti"—296). She is now appealing to him only in terms of her story. Indeed he looks at her with such intense curiosity that he seems to want her dead so that she can be revived entirely as a function of narrative: "Il la regardait comme s'il avait désiré assister à l'autopsie de son cadavre. Allait-elle le faire revivre pour lui?" (297). A measure of her success is that, in the course of telling her story, she regains in Tressignies' eyes the perfect chastity and fantasized virginity of the ideal mother (see p. 300).

The Duchess is happy to tell Tressignies the story of her life, for narration is the vehicle of her vengeance against her husband, or more precisely against his name, the symbol of the family honor, which is all the Duke really cares about. She has degraded herself to the level of "fille publique" so as to drag his nominal heritage "en honte, en immondice, en excrément" (305). She hopes that the story of her dishonor will reach the Duke through one of her clients, but, if not, she is counting on her dead body, putrified with venereal disease, to tell the story of her prostitution. By using her body as a common place of male desire, the Duchess is turning the possessive privilege inherent in the father's name against the patriarchal order that name sustains.

Her strategy shows her to be more than Tressignies' match in the intellectual mastery of sensual experience.

Indeed he has been entirely her dupe, to the point that the intensity of her voluptuous sensuality led him to believe that she "ne pouvait être ainsi avec tous les autres" (292). Her narrative reveals not only that he is no different from the others, no better than one in a series, but also that her motive for substitution is not economic gain but imaginary stimulation. Whereas he had followed her in order to become master of her story, as a corollary of his sexual mastery, she instead makes use of his phallus within her own representational scenario. His phallus is valuable to her only insofar as she can imagine it as seen by the Duke's painted eyes in the portrait on her bracelet. Tressignies has been for nothing in her sexual pleasure: "Son image excite mes transports" (307), she tells him. The Duke's image serves as a sadistic phallus in a masochistic scenario that puts sexuality entirely in the service of the imaginary: "Je m'enfonçais cette exécrable image dans les yeux et dans le coeur, pour mieux bondir sous vous quand vous me teniez" (307). Thus Tressignies is castrated twice over by the Duchess, first by the violence of her sexual desire, then by the violence of her denial of that desire.

The crime the Duchess intends to revenge by staging her own debasement repeats this theme of castration. The context is once again sexuality and its denial, but that denial is now sublimated as purity and innocence. This was the ideal mode of the Duchess's chaste love for Don Esteban, the Duke's cousin, whom she met after some years of her unhappy marriage. Their love is a positive version of the imaginary, visual relationship that later binds the Duchess in hatred to her husband. The Duke's crime is precipitated by his coming upon the lovers "comme nous étions toujours, comme nous passions notre vie depuis que nous nous aimions, tête à tête, *unis par le regard seul*; lui, à mes pieds, devant moi, comme devant la Vierge Marie, dans une contemplation si profonde que nous n'avions besoin d'aucune caresse" (303; my emphasis). This scene, conventional though it may be, clearly fulfills a central fantasy in this text, the fantasy of an asexual union modeled on the infant's relation to the nurturant mother. The potentially incestuous encounter is sublimated ("jamais les lèvres d'Esteban n'ont touché les miennes"—302) and a fusion is imagined that dissolves sexual difference ("Nous étions . . . fondus l'un dans l'autre"—302). The mother here has nothing of the whore about her. To contemplate her is to desire only death ("Nous désirions mourir"—302).

The Duchess's description of this love as "chevalresque, romanesque" (301) suggests the same association between the sublimation of sexuality and the entry into narrative that provided the impetus for her storytelling to begin with. Her husband, however, can only read this sublimated love in entirely physical terms according to a scenario of oedipal rivalry. His revenge is to murder Esteban, symbolically castrate him by cutting out his heart, and profane this love organ by feeding it as meat to his dogs. For the Duchess the heart is a symbol of her soul-mating with Esteban and she demands in vain that she be allowed to eat it herself: "J'aurais communié avec ce coeur, comme avec une hostie" (304). The Duke's vengeful action, which connects oedipal sexuality and castrating violence, can be seen as the model for the Duchess's own strategy of revenge. By becoming a prostitute, she is actually fulfilling the role her husband was the first to cast her in. Her plan is to castrate him by attacking the only symbolic value he cherishes, his name, the source of the patriarchal narrative of generational continuity with which he completely identifies. He has violated her soul by interpreting its "transparent" (302) love story literally, that is, sexually; now she will turn this literalization of the body against his soul-equivalent, his name.

Since the diffusion of her story is an important aspect of the Duchess's strategy, the fact that Tressignies deliberately holds onto it for himself, instead of repeating it as she had requested, suggests that he is trying to extricate himself from the oedipal structure in which she has implicated him. Indeed, his attitude toward the narrative, cloistering himself with his memories of the evening in a "tête à tête" (312), burying the story in "le coin le plus mystérieux de son être" (313), suggests that he is trying to recreate with the story a relationship not unlike Esteban's with the Duchess. Instead of the Duchess's physical body, her story is now the source of sublimating contemplation. It is as if this story had come to replace the nurturing maternal body, thereby enabling Tressignies to luxuriate in a narcissistic fantasy of union: "Aussi passa-t-il bien des heures, accoudé aux bras de son fauteuil, à feuilleter rêveusement en lui les pages toujours ouvertes de ce poème d'une hideuse énergie" (313). The Duchess's disturbing sexual availability to many has been translated into her narrative availability to him alone.

One fear still troubles Tressignies, however: The same female body that was his narrative source remains open to others. Thus "il n'aborda jamais un de ses amis sans avoir peur de lui entendre raconter, comme lui étant arrivé, l'aventure qui était la sienne" (313). The mother's physical prostitution threatens to dispossess Tressignies of her story: The female sexual body as the source of narrative remains irrepressibly outside it. This perception, it would appear, is what causes Tressignies' own physical degeneration, as if by refusing the life of the body—he shows no interest in women, loses his usual animation in society, and finally appears quite sickly—he could come closer to the suspended life of narrative. His sudden disappearance from Paris "comme par un trou" (314) radicalizes this movement to cancel his physical presence.

But Barbey's story does not end there. The female body must be conclusively destroyed before the narrative itself can conclude. Tressignies returns to Paris after a year's absence and, at a swank dinner party, witnesses the first public revelation of the Duchess's prostitution: A newspaper notice announcing her burial as a common whore is read to the scandalized assembly. Her story of revenge, however, is not yet known, and Tressignies does not tell it. Instead he visits the religious establishment where the Duchess was buried and requests information from a priest about her final illness. He learns that she had indeed contracted the venereal disease she had wished for and that her body had rotted with decay. The text pays special attention to the gruesome fate of her eyes: One eye had popped out of its socket and fallen at her feet while the other had liquefied and melted. The imagery of castration is evident here and relates specifically to the metaphorical sense in which the Duchess's soul was in her eyes. Her love for Esteban had been a communion of souls through the spiritual path of visual contemplation. She had expressed her hatred of the Duke by contemplating his portrait imagined as the voyeuristic witness to her prostitution. So the Duchess's fate is twice over a revenge for Tressignies' double castration: She is mutilated in both body and soul.

"Contre quoi échanger le récit? Que 'vaut' le récit?"[3] This, says Roland Barthes, is probably the key question posed, *en abyme,* in any narration. In *La Vengeance* the answer is clear: Tressignies obtains full possession of the Duchess's story at the expense of her death and mutilation. *La Vengeance d'une femme,* which is really that of a man, ends with Tressignies exulting in his privileged knowledge of the Duchess's plot. He considers himself the only reader qualified to establish the truth of her posthumous text. Whereas the deluded priest believes that humility prompted her to want the word "repentie" removed from the phrase "fille repentie" in her epitaph, Tressignies' command of her narrative enables him to read this gesture as a final refinement in her masochistic scenario of revenge. The Duchess's masochism, which makes her sexuality a pleasure-denying instrument of her death drive, now appears to correspond perfectly to Tressignies' sadism. Her story is indeed his story ("l'aventure qui était la sienne"), the story of female sexuality repressed and degraded to the point where its fantasized castrating power is made to turn against itself. Female sexuality then becomes a purely narrative impulse subject to male control and closure. Or rather that closure is not so much male as it is desexualized. We saw earlier that Tressignies' desire for narrative entailed a wish for the storyteller's death and that her revival in narrative involved the rebirth on his part of a maternal fantasy. Now that Tressignies has himself symbolically died (his departure from Paris) and been revived as a function of his identification with the dead Duchess's narrative, by implication his rebirth also identifies him with the chaste and virginal mother. Thus the power of narrative closure depends not only on the closure of the "literal" female body but also on the inception of a fantasy that dissolves sexual difference in a dream of maternal union.

A similar narrative and psychological structure is discernible in *À un dîner d'athées.* The main story is introduced by its narrator, Mesnilgrand, after a lengthy description of the society of erstwhile soldiers and officers of Napoleon's army, now living in a provincial town, of which the proud, aristocratic Mesnilgrand is the acknowledged leader. The active life of these men is essentially over ("ils avaient . . . leur vie finie avant la mort"—238). The present exists for them as a vehicle to narrate the past, to tell its romantic and heroic story, and thereby to forget the banality of contemporary existence. Mesnilgrand stands out as forcefully in this narrative enterprise as he had once on the fields of battle. His eloquence is so extraordinarily intense that it strikes his listeners with a physical impact. Mesnilgrand has transformed his life entirely in the service of representation. After a few initial forays into the local salons, this once passionate lover of women has retired from the social scene, although he continues to dress with the most tasteful elegance as if his dandyism "survivait à cette vie finie, enterrée" (231). He spends his days at an occupation as removed from war as possible—landscape painting, and his somewhat dated patrician appearance actually makes him resemble "un portrait qui marche" (231).

When Mesnilgrand finally tells his story, it becomes apparent that his "transfiguration" (241) from soldier to artistic creator and creation was not so much a response to the loss of his military identity as to the loss of his sexual identity. As in *La Vengeance d'une femme,* the crucial confrontation here is with a prostitute figure. Unlike the Duchess of Sierra Leone, however, la Rosalba is not a whore who, subsequent to intercourse, reveals herself to be a mother, but a woman who, even in the midst of the sexual act, is simultaneously mother and whore. Mesnilgrand dwells on this paradox. La Rosalba, mistress of a certain captain Ydow, provokes the entire regiment through "la composition diabolique de son être . . . qui faisait d'elle la plus enragée des courtisanes, avec la figure d'une des plus célestes madones de Raphaël" (263). Happily she satisfies the desire she invites and sleeps with the whole officer corps, maintaining all the while the blushing virginal modesty that earned her the nickname "la Pudica."

Mesnilgrand has his turn with la Rosalba, thereby becoming one in a series of others for whom she remains the same (the regimental view of her position stresses the logic of substitution: "Puisqu'elle s'était donnée à [Ydow], elle pouvait bien se donner à un autre, et, ma foi, tout le monde pouvait être cet autre-là!"—258). But he experiences his otherness to her, the principle of her sexual openness, as a castrating refusal of his desire.

Like Tressignies, who momentarily imagines himself exceptional, Mesnilgrand wants la Rosalba to admit to loving him, even though he has no love for her "dans le sens élevé et romanesque qu'on donne à ce mot, moi tout le premier" (265). She, however, refuses to romanticize their affair, to give him any kind of linguistic privilege over her sexuality, to narrativize her body. Physically penetrated, she remains "impénétrable comme le sphinx" (266). Although stories are circulated about her among her lovers, "elle ne donnait pas prise sur elle ouvertement par sa conduite" (264). Her body, which Mesnilgrand calls "sa seule âme" (265), remains outside any narrative plot.

The depth of her sensuality ("Ce fut la plus profonde des sensualités"—265) serves much the same function for her as does the Duchess's similarly limitless capacity for sensual pleasure. It ensures her self-possession, keeping all men alien to her and denying their temporal as well as their sexual experience: "On était toujours au début avec elle, même après le dénouement" (261).

Just as Tressignies felt castrated by his immersion in the abyss of the Duchess's sensuality, so Mesnilgrand responds to Rosalba's impenetrability as a castration which leaves him "fort tranquille et fort indifférent avec toutes les femmes" (266). He sees this state, however, as a distinct advantage, relating it to Achilles' (near) invulnerability after being dipped in the river Styx. Out of "dégoût moral" (266) he has dissociated himself from his sexual body and thereby preserved his spiritual soul: "J'avais ôté mon âme de cette liaison" (269). Like the Duchess, Mesnilgrand associates morality and the soul with "le sens élevé et romanesque" commonly given to the word "love." He saves himself from the terribly unreadability of female sexuality ("le langage périrait à exprimer cela!"—261) by resorting to shared, narratable formulations.

The climax of his story, however, dramatizes the dependence of narrative on precisely the erotic female body that it cannot express. Perhaps because of his Achilles heel, Mesnilgrand returns to see, that is, to make love to, Rosalba. But in the unconscious structure of the story, it seems as if the violent act of sexual revenge that interrupts his erotic encounter actually fulfills his deepest wish. Surprised by the unexpected appearance of Ydow, Rosalba hides Mesnilgrand in a closet, from the dark, protected space of which he overhears Ydow verbally abusing her. Ydow is in a jealous rage over a letter of assignation he has found unaddressed on her table and wants to know who the intended recipient is. She refuses to name her lover and goes on to further provoke the captain by declaring that she has never loved him.

Thus far the scene repeats Mesnilgrand's emasculating experience with Rosalba, her insistence on the substitutability of her sex partners, and her denial of romantic feeling. But now she goes a step further to mock the entire symbolic order of male authority associated with the name of the father. She denies that Ydow was the father of her son, who died a few months after birth, lists all the men who could potentially have claimed paternity, and then suddenly names as the actual father the other man in the room, Mesnilgrand, "le seul homme que j'aie jamais aimé, que j'aie jamais idolâtré" (275). Mesnilgrand knows this declaration of love to be a fiction and hence cannot help but doubt his alleged paternity, although his name pronounced in this context "[l]'atteignit comme une balle à travers [son] placard" (275). Thus Rosalba repudiates that most cherished of male stories, the history of generations, and, on the basis of the impenetrable interiority of her body, unmans both Ydow, who wanted to believe himself the father, and Mesnilgrand, who did not.

Earlier in the story Mesnilgrand had already reflected that "ce qu'il y a de plus affreux dans les amours partagés, . . . c'est cette anxiété terrible qui vous empêche d'écouter la voix de la nature, et qui l'étouffe dans un doute dont il est impossible de sortir" (267).[4] The voice Mesnilgrand considers natural speaks to a man of his right to possess a woman, control her sexuality, and inscribe her in his genealogical story. By placing her body outside this patriarchal scheme, Rosalba throws the scheme into confusion: Paternity becomes a mere fiction, a matter of her arbitrary naming. Thus, as in *La Vengeance,* woman generates narrative precisely by asserting her independence of it. The father's nomination is her prerogative, "dont il est impossible de sortir."

But Barbey cannot allow the subversive power of female fictionalizing to determine the outcome of his narrative. Rosalba's open sexuality must be sealed up so that Mesnilgrand's anxiety can be calmed and he can take possession of her story. By pouring hot wax into his mistress's sexual organs, Ydow is fulfilling both his own and Mesnilgrand's vengeful impulses. Thus it is no accident that Mesnilgrand bursts out of his closet only *after* the mutilated Rosalba has let out a cry "comme d'une vulve de louve" (277). Indeed this startling phrase suggests that Rosalba's sexuality is bestial and predatory and thus warrants extermination. Mesnilgrand, however, cannot accept his implication in Ydow's act and runs him through the back with a sword.[5] Just at this point, thankfully, a call to arms sounds and the heroic violence of the battlefield displaces and veils the far more troubling arena of sexual violation.

Mesnilgrand never hears of Rosalba again—she is as good as dead, having been rejected from the narrative—but he has taken with him the heart of the child she called his. This heart, lovingly embalmed by Ydow when he thought he was the child's father, served, hideously, as a projectile in his fight with Rosalba. Its fate relates the end of the story to its beginning. After years of carrying the heart around with him like a relic, Mesnilgrand decides to give it to a priest. This accounts for his having been in the church where a scandalized fellow soldier-atheist, Rançonnet, glimpsed him in the text's opening scene. Mesnilgrand's story is a response to Rançonnet's demand to know what he was doing in this religious haunt.

One psychoanalytic interpretation of this ending, offered by Jacques Petit, is that Mesnilgrand is returning the phallus (the child's heart) to a maternal refuge (the church).[6] This analysis, however, needs to be nuanced, especially in regard to Petit's conclusion that Mesnilgrand is hereby accepting his own castration. The heart, for Mesnilgrand, is associated above all with anxiety about the potentially fictional status of paternity. He refers to it as "ce coeur d'enfant dont je doutais" (278). Earlier he had reflected that uncertainty about the patriarchal status of the phallus in determining the order of nature could drive a man mad: "Si on pensait longtemps à cela [l'indigne partage auquel on s'est honteusement soumis], quand on a du coeur, on deviendrait fou" (267). "Quand on a du coeur". . . . Clearly it is to this metaphorical meaning of "having the heart" that the child's actual organ must be assimilated if the madness generated by the impenetrable abyss of female sexuality is to be controlled. "Heart" in this sense corresponds to "le sens élevé et romanesque" Mesnilgrand attributes to "love." Religion for him has this same romanticizing function of metaphorical elevation. To depose the child's heart with the church thus is to elevate the whole question of the uncertain origin of paternal authority into the sphere of imaginary representation. Only in this sphere can the priest to whom Mesnilgrand hands over the "objet indiscernable" be called "mon père" (223). The father's nomination becomes a male prerogative once the sexual basis of paternity has been eliminated.

In this scene of symbolic restitution, the phallus, veiled, indiscernible, is returned to the father, in name only, whose place is inside the darkened body of the maternal church, itself associated with death ("À cette heure là, on sent vraiment très bien que la religion chrétienne est la fille des catacombes"—219). Physical presence is dissolved in a proliferation of symbolic substitutes. The maternal space, which provides the story's narrative frame, is protective precisely insofar as it sublimates the body and fictionalizes the whole issue of sexual differentiation.[7] The worshippers in the church are described as "âmes" rather than as men and women. In the "lueur fantômale" of this edifice, "il était possible de se voir douteusement et confusément, mais il était impossible de se reconnaître" (220). This is not the doubt generated by sexual anxiety, but a reassuring confusion that allows sexual difference to be hidden by a veil of uncertainty.[8]

In the unfolding of the *récit,* the description of the church precedes the description of Mesnilgrand's post-Napoleonic life style. In effect, the one appears to derive from the other. Mesnilgrand, who was struck by "l'aspect presque tombal de cette église" (221) at present "ne demande plus rien de la vie" (232). In his roles as painter, storyteller, and dandy, he has made life over as representation, image, artifice. His having apparently renounced all sexual activity does indeed suggest an acceptance of castration. But his dandyism is more accurately understood as a way of putting the fixity of sexual identity in doubt. The narrator tells us that Mesnilgrand "n'était pas de la même espèce" (241) as his fellow soldiers. In his essay on Beau Brummell, Barbey explicitly associates dandyism with a kind of androgynous interchangeability of sexual characteristics. Dandys, he declares, are "natures doubles et multiples, d'un sexe intellectuel indécis, où la grâce est plus grâce encore dans la force, et où la force se retrouve encore dans la grâce."[9] This sexually undecidable mixture of strength and grace is what gives Mesnilgrand such remarkable control over his story, for it constitutes an essential Aurevillian principle of narrative closure. Mesnilgrand is as intimately identified with "l'aventure qui était la sienne" as Tressignies is with his. In both cases this identification, based on the elimination of female sexuality within the story's plot, gives access to a sublimating fiction that cancels the threat of sexual difference.[10] True, that access in both stories is a male privilege. Indeed, Mesnilgrand as narrator tells his story as if he were directing a battle: "Reste dans le rang," he tells Rançonnet. "Laisse moi manoeuvrer, comme je l'entends, mon histoire" (257-58). But the goal of this specifically narrative manoeuvre is a victory over the sexual determinants of the story's violence.[11] Masculinity achieves its (hollow) triumph by emptying sexuality of its physical reference and closing with the resultant fictional world in a fantasy of maternal union.

A traditional psychoanalytic interpretation would have no trouble finding the "source" in Barbey's biography of the narrative patterns I have traced here. His need for maternal protection can be seen as a response to the coldness his actual mother displayed in his childhood and his masochistic fascination with the dominating, masculinized female can be shown to have the same origin, via a reversal typical of the psyche ("L'amour maternel est le *châtreur* de l'autre amour," he once wrote[12]). His hostility toward the father, representative of the sexually active male, can be traced back to an unresolved Oedipus complex (which, inversely, also leads him to desire a powerful authority worthy of his rebellion).[13] But a reading along these lines, however fruitful, would focus attention on the eccentricities of individual neurotic symptomatology, whereas a broader analysis might, indeed *would* in my opinion, demonstrate that Barbey's narrative strategies were shared by many male fiction writers in nineteenth century France. The prostitute is the key figure in this fictional production. At the crossroads of the energies of desire and the modes of substitution, she subverts genealogy and patronymic lineage. In her inviting openness, she appears to be easily readable; in her refusal to be possessed, in the depth of her sensuality, she remains alien, impenetrable. In this sense, as Eileen Sivert has argued, her body is like a text, promising more than it reveals, at once accessible and opaque, teasing the reader with the illusion of mastery but ultimately escaping his design.[14] In this escape the textual becomes literal, the body asserts its presence as that which cannot be marked, penetrated, deciphered, named (think of Alberte's provocative refusal to articulate her desire in *Le Rideau cramoisi*). It is the potentially spreading scandal of this immunity that male discursive strategies attempt to control. One of the most powerful of these strategies, I have argued here, is the sublimation and fictionalization of sexual difference. Domination is thus acquired not by the assertion of power within a binary structure but by the destabilization of that structure and its assimilation into the sphere of artistic play, where the body is "d'un sexe intellectuel indécis." Once sexual difference has been intellectualized to this extent, the undecidability of fatherhood, generative of intense male anxiety, can be interpreted as a necessary fiction, indeed *the* necessary fiction. And on the basis of this eviscerating sublimation, fiction regains its threatened authority.

Notes

1. See Freud, "A Special Type of Object Choice Made by Men" (1910) and "The Most Prevalent Form of Degradation in Erotic Life" (1912) in *Sexuality and the Psychology of Love,* ed. Rieff (New York: Collier, 1963).

2. All page numbers in the text refer to the Garnier-Flammarion edition of *Les Diaboliques* (Paris, 1967).

3. Roland Barthes, *S/Z* (Paris: Seuil, 1970), p. 95.

4. In an illuminating article, "La Question du père dans les romans de Barbey d'Aurevilly" (*La Revue des lettres modernes,* 600-604, 1981), Philippe Berthier notes that the problem of paternity haunts all of Barbey's works: "*Qui est le Père?* Sous des formes diverses, plus ou moins ruineuses, la question retentit partout dans l'oeuvre aurevillienne, où l'on est à la recherche d'un Père qui ne peut être dit" (p. 13).

5. At least two critics interpret this act as symbolic sodomy, Claudine Herrmann (*Les Voleuses de langue,* Paris: Editions des femmes, 1967, pp. 118-19) and Pierre Tranouez ("Un Récit révocatoire: *À un dîner d'athées," Littérature,* no. 38, May 1980, pp. 31-33). They see Rosalba as a mediating fig-

ure between Mesnilgrand and the ambivalent object of his homosexual desire, Ydow. Once Rosalba's function is terminated, Mesnilgrand's powerful ambivalence expresses itself in a murder that is simultaneously a rape. Philippe Berthier discusses the evidence of repressed homosexual tendencies in Barbey on pp. 174-75 of his fine book *Barbey d'Aurevilly et l'imagination* (Geneva: Droz, 1978).

6. Jacques Petit, *Essais de lectures des "Diaboliques" de Barbey d'Aurevilly* (Paris: Minard, 1974), p. 159.

7. Marielle Marini observes a marked instability of sexual identity in all the principal characters of *Les Diaboliques*. "Il n'y a point de véritable classification des personnages selon le sexe, ni même selon l'alternance phallique/châtré," she notes. "Les indices de castration ou de puissance phallique, les signes que le texte donne pour marque de féminité ou de virilité, circulent de personnage en personnage" ("Ricochets de lecture: Le fantasmatique des *Diaboliques,*" *Litterature,* no. 10, May 1973, p. 16). I hope to have shown that the circulation of sexual signs is not as arbitrary as this comment suggests but is a function of an overriding fear of female sexuality, which motivates a regressive desire to erase all signs of sexual difference.

8. The imagery of veiling is made explicit in a description of the night falling within the church. The narrator refers here to "un voile" where the metaphorical context would lead one to expect "une voile": "La nuit, épaisse déjà dans l'église, y étalait sa grande draperie d'ombre qui semblait, comme un voile tombant d'un mat, déferler des cintres" (220).

9. Barbey d'Aurevilly, "Du Dandysme et de George Brummell" in *Œuvres romanesques complètes,* vol. 2, ed. Petit (Paris: Bibliothèque de la Pleiade, 1966), p. 718.

10. In the article referred to in note 5 above, Pierre Tranouez reads Mesnilgrand's narration as the vehicle of his homoerotic seduction of his most excitedly attentive listener, Rançonnet. Thus, for Tranouez, the scene of narration is homologous to the crucial scene of desire and horror in which Mesnilgrand symbolically sodomizes Ydow by killing him. Although to my mind this ingenious argument does not give enough weight to the sublimating function of narration, it does provide a provocative alternative way of understanding Barbey's powerful impulse to deny sexual difference. Tranouez has addressed the question of narrative closure in another stimulating article, "La narration neutralisante: Étude de quatre *Diaboliques,*" *Poétique* 17 (1974).

11. This may explain the strange metaphor in which Mesnilgrand's being seized by an opportunity to display his eloquence is compared to Perseus cutting off the Gorgon's head (see 241).

12. Barbey d'Aurevilly, *Disjecta Membra,* vol. 2 (Paris: La Connaissance, 1925), p. 177. Quoted by Philippe Berthier, op. cit., note 5 above, p. 167.

13. Philippe Berthier (op. cit., note 4 above) puts it very well: "Telle est l'aporie aurevillienne: pour défendre et illustrer la cause sacrée du Père, cette oeuvre ne doit, et d'ailleurs ne peut, que dire l'excès, la transgression et le révolte qui menacent le Père" (p. 41).

14. Eileen Sivert, "Text, Body, and Reader in Barbey d'Aurevilly's *Les Diaboliques,*" Symposium, Summer 1977. Sivert's excellent article, which focusses on the same two stories I analyse here, elaborates an erotics of reading on the basis of Barthesian notions. See also her article "Narration and Exhibitionism in *Le Rideau cramoisi,*" *Romanic Review,* vol. LXX, no. 2 (March 1979).

Robert Willard Artinian (essay date 1984)

SOURCE: Artinian, Robert Willard. "Barbey's Decadence: The Test of Time." *French Literature Series* 11 (1984): 89-96.

[*In the following essay, Artinian discusses elements of modernity in Barbey d'Aurevilly's depictions of immorality and corruption.*]

There are many associations which tie Barbey d'Aurevilly to the manifestation of decadence in France.[1] For the public at large Barbey has remained primarily a fantastic figure who believed in the Devil—perhaps worshipped him—and who not only wrote a book about Beau Brummell, but exemplified the philosophy of the "dandy" in his own person, to the delight of the Boulevards. He was also a vehement critic who conceived his calling as a kind of crusade against all that was tawdry and vulgar in contemporary life. Wanting in dignity, detachment, and coherence, his figure as a quixotic crusader and champion of Christianity in an atheistic age, fits in well with the fantastic legend which has stood in the way of his serious acceptance. Few have cared to dive below the troubled surface of a man whose vices and vanities appear sufficiently demonstrated by the title of his works.[2] Huysmans set the final seal of Barbey's diabolism when he penned the highly colored analysis of *Un Prêtre marié* in *A rebours*.[3] In fact, Huysmans was simply acknowledging a kindred spirit, as had Baudelaire already: both put passion into their pursuit of the exotic, the macabre and the sinister, and into their portrayal of delicate shades of corruption. Baudelaire finally concluded that the essence of decadence, the "demoniac tendency," was an essential characteristic of modern art.[4] In Baudelaire this remains in its metaphysical state. In Barbey d'Aurevilly it takes a theological turn and produces the devil.

But decadence is so much more than diabolism. It seems too easy, and a result unconvincing in the final analysis, to simply point to the theme of the devil in an author and label him decadent.[5] For Barbey as for Byron, the criminal was fascinating because of his force and strange distinction and, because he was at war with society and considered the conventional moral code irrelevant. In him, something of the passion and self-reliance of primitive man is displayed, and he may readily be made to seem heroic, a superhuman. It was just such a sentiment that made Stendhal in Italy welcome manifestations of atrocious crime because they proved that that country could still produce "characters!" Barbey d'Aurevilly's books abound in Byronic figures, male and female. With this difference, however: while Byron's criminals derive much of their romantic suggestion from the exotic coloring of their exploits, which are generally little more than ordinary acts of assault and murder, Barbey's derive theirs rather from the secrecy, or from the peculiar violence and perversity, of their acts. This is characteristic of the decadent attitude, and it is here that he possesses a distinct advantage as a Catholic writer. For not only does the spiritual significance of crime become immeasurably deepened and intensified when it is regarded as sin, but the casuistry of the Catholic conscience, developed through the secular experience of the confessional, suggests varieties and subtleties of wrong-doing with which a less completely evolved legal and social conscience cannot compete.

Another distinction must be made: Barbey depicts a criminal altogether different from any to be found in Byron. The Byronic criminal commits an act of crime or violence in a dimension tinged with moral stress: remorse, mingled with no little sense of pride—this is the very hallmark of the Byronic criminal. But Barbey, with consummate skill, eliminates all sense of guilt from the heart of his criminal protagonists: he gives us the *absolute* criminal. Such characters—we have the Marquise in *Les Liaisons dangereuses* as an example— are likely to appear somewhat unreal, unless, indeed, as in Feuillet's *La Morte,* they are presented as frankly pathological. These people, one feels, live in a region "beyond good and evil." They are part of the decadent notion of superiority, anticipating the theory of the Superman. Being of the elect who win the right to a special moral standard by living up to the full level of their passions, they are, from Barbey's point of view, the elect of the devil rather than of nature. This in fact constitutes the only divergence from Nietzsche's idea. And this is merely a superficial difference, after all. If the

German is a Greek at heart, Barbey d'Aurevilly is a child of the early Renaissance. He is, as it were, a Pollaiuolo of the pen. He is absorbed and fascinated by manifestations of power and forms of personal distinction. The devil still terrifies him. This shows itself in contortion and grimace. But he is already beginning to feel the fiend dissolving into the complexity of natural forces and to interpret these physically and psychologically. Meanwhile the pagan finds, or believes to find, a certain support in the primitive Christian—a justification for the broad and liberal representation of life to which he is drawn.

If Barbey actually believed that his profession of an edifying purpose would set him right with Christian orthodoxy he was sorely mistaken, and he might as well have made full profession of paganism. It is one thing to accept the devil and another to accord him a seat in the sanctuary. Hence like another but unrepentant Tannhäuser, Barbey was dismissed from the conclave and left free to return to the Horselberg of his imagination. And for him no staff has ever broken into miraculous blossom. *Les Diaboliques,* in fact, where the flimsy pretext of a moral intention is more or less abandoned, was prosecuted on its appearance, being the third of the famous trilogy of works thus treated in France during the nineteenth century. The other two, of course, were *Madame Bovary* and the *Fleurs du Mal.* The author was found innocent but public sentiment has never quite acquitted him of crime in the execution of that daring but profoundly beautiful and artistic work.

The general cast of Barbey's imagination, then, undoubtedly qualifies him as decadent, as do his themes. The critical next step concerns his use of language. Might this be considered decadent? His vocabulary is scarcely *recherché.* Nowhere does one find the hermeticism that characterizes Mallarmé or Huysmans. To put Barbey to the stylistic test we will examine one of his novels, *Le Chevalier des Touches* (1864), where to all intents and purposes the reader was presented with a traditional work of prose: a narrative dealing with the revolt of some Bretons against the French revolution. The principal agent of the *émigrés,* the Chevalier is one of those mysterious Byronic characters referred to earlier and who stalk across Barbey d'Aurevilly's pages. He appears for a time to lead a charmed life, miraculously eluding his pursuers. He is eventually captured and condemned, though, and his followers plan a desperate rescue. Twelve aristocrats disguised as wheat-dealers go to the town where the Chevalier is confined, on the market day, and while one of the group attempts to gain access to the prisoner, the others, by way of creating a diversion, start a disturbance in the market. From disturbance to ugly riot is the work of a moment. Surrounded by throngs of peasants who have discovered their true identity, the nobles fight back to back, ferociously. A stampede of cattle in the market-place is all that saves the little band which, having failed in its attempt to rescue the leader, slowly makes its retreat along lanes opened by horns and hoofs. A second expedition is more successful and the Chevalier eventually escapes to England. This is all there is to the story, or nearly all, for there is a slender thread of romantic love interwoven in the main action.

The *Chevalier des Touches* is thus not precisely a novel, but a tale. And as there is no complication of plot, its effectiveness proceeds almost entirely from the manner in which it is told, and from the personality of the supposed narrator, a *vieille fille* of good family, a veritable Amazon, who had herself participated in the second expedition. The scene of the recital is a quiet provincial drawing-room, where a group of old nobles congregate years after the events recorded, and the savage violence of the tale is thus thrown into vivid contrast with the peaceful repose of an interior as *quotidien* as one of Maeterlinck's. All the portraits—the delicate spinsters with their needlework, the old baron intent on the delights of the tea-table, and the aristocratic abbé with his witty sallies—are sketched with an exquisite delicacy that does not preclude broad, bold strokes of characterization. These are particularly telling in the case of the Amazon, whose grotesque ugliness, brusque masculine speech and peremptory gestures make her the perfect type of the old soldier in petticoats. Barbey d'Aurevilly as a master of portraiture suggests the very threads of personality. A similar atmosphere is created from inanimate objects, so that in this story the spirit of the past exudes from the gray, wainscoted walls and time-darkened portraits of the salon with a subtlety that makes Barbey d'Aurevilly the predecessor of Henry James in this manner of mute evocation. In the events themselves, one will note the bent of the author to interpret high action heroically, to see life in a sublime light of daring and sacrifice, and to extract from even the most trivial incident an epic significance.

Thus for the contemporary reader, who may not be attuned to the idiosyncrasies of the nineteenth-century novel, *Le Chevalier des Touches* may not appear as an unqualified success. Certain *procédés* may be considered offensive, e.g. the melodramatic opening pages, the authorial interventions, the conventional structure of a story within a story; in fact, the true intrigue does not begin until some fifty pages into the narrative.

What redeems the novel is it decadent attitude presented in a highly artistic, unified structure. A model text will illustrate this: the portrait of the *demoiselles* de Touffedelys:

> Toutes deux avaient été belles, mais l'antiquaire le plus habile à deviner le sens des médailles effacées n'aurait pu retrouver les lignes de ces deux camées, rongés par le temps et par le plus épouvantable des acides, une

virginité aigrie. La Révolution leur avait tout pris: famille, fortune, bonheur du foyer, et ce poème du cœur, l'amour dans le mariage, plus beau que la gloire! disait Mme de Staël, et enfin la maternité. Elle ne leur avait laissé que leurs têtes, mais blanchies et affaiblies par tous les genres de douleur. Orphelines quand elle éclata, les Touffedelys n'avaient point émigré. Elles étaient restées, comme beaucoup de nobles, dans le Cotentin. Imprudence qu'elles auraient payée de leur vie, si Thermidor ne les avait sauvées, en ouvrant les maisons d'arrêt. Vêtues toujours des mêmes couleurs, se ressemblant beaucoup, de la même taille et de la même voix, c'était comme une répétion dans la nature que ces demoiselles de Touffedelys.[6]

First impressions suggest the numerous ties which associate this text with Balzac. In fact, the entire novel exudes a Balzacian air. The stereotyping of characters, the method of preparing the reader for the appearance of major characters and their ultimate presentation, character analysis, the frequent digressions and generalizations, all bear the imprint of Balzac. And it is no secret that Barbey had before him a copy of *La Vieille Fille* as he composed this novel.[7]

But *au degré zéro de l'écriture,* what is most impressive about this text is the image which predominates, the metaphor of the *demoiselles* as *médailles, camées.* Again, an echo of Balzac, drawn from both *La Vielle Fille* and *Le Cabinet des Antiques,* but more important is the fact that the image, obviously of some importance to Barbey, is carefully orchestrated throughout the novel. To cite but a few examples, the abbé himself is described in terms of a *camée*: ". . . il avait un de ces teints dont la couleur semble avoir l'épaisseur de l'émail et que l'émotion ne traverse pas" (I:747). The heroine, Barbe, is presented with the qualities of a *médaille*: "Solide de laideur, elle avait reçu le soufflet . . . du Temps, comme elle disait, sur un bronze que rien ne pouvait entamer;" (I:751). The Baron is described on several occasions in terms of a miniature portrait (I:753, 754); and finally, the entire gathering in the salon is portrayed as having "des yeux faïencés" (I:754). The importance of this metaphor is that it sets in relief the total impact of the novel. For the larger significance of the work goes far beyond the adventure of the Chevalier des Touches. Had the adventure been the major interest of Barbey, the exploits would have been more rigidly structured, with an appropriate reduction of the introductory and concluding pages. Nor could the major concern have been the exploits of the Twelve. We are forced to conclude that, given the amount of time and energy expended on recreation of atmosphere and in-depth characterization, the focus of the novel is upon the participants of the salon who are reminiscing about the Chevalier. They are attempting to recapture their *temps perdu.* This is not a conventional novel, in terms of a character in action. On the contrary, there is precious little physical action *now.* Instead, the past is viewed as something sacred, which explains the abundant religious imagery and the constant emphasis on the passage of time, including numerous references to a symbolic clock. Within this context, then, the presentation of the demoiselles as médailles acquires a special significance. For their persons, like religious medallions, are external symbols of a sacred past, sacred to them and to the cause they serve, and particularly for Barbey and the established families of the mid-nineteenth century for whom the coming of the Revolution was a very real event. Even the name of the demoiselles reinforces this impression: Touffedelys, or cluster of lilies, symbolic of the royalty they served.

It is this constant use of a religious metaphorical structure that permits Barbey d'Aurevilly to freeze the dramatic action of the past into an ever-present *instantané,* to use the term of Jacques Dubois.[8] By thus fragmenting the concept of human time Barbey announces a decadent quality of despair which can be distinguished from Romanticism. From its Gothic heritage, Barbey d'Aurevilly helps take the novel into the twentieth century. Expanding the themes of sterility and impotence, he anticipates the need for *engagement,* even on the part of an elderly noblewoman! And especially in his representation of the very modern confrontation of self and world, he gives precise shape to the self-conscious concern with the nature of the object in an "atmosphere of the mind." This comes at a time when artists throughout Europe created a climate which forced realism in literature into a radical crisis. For the novel, based on sequential time, has its last great representatives in Flaubert and Zola; later Gide, Proust, Joyce, and Mann concerned themselves not with telling stories conveying through characters a criticism of the society to which these characters belonged, but rather aimed at conveying the moment of present experience and intensity which, whether it embraces twenty-four hours or twenty-four years, brings together the simultaneity of events which form the duration of a human consciousness. Whitehead describes that moment as the "creativity of the world which is the throbbing emotion of the past hurling itself into a new transcendent fact." It is the search for time lost and time regained of Proust, it is the abolition of time and matter of Dostoevski and the moment of dénouement of Gide. *L'Après-midi d'un Faune, La Jeune Parque, Ulysses,* and, later on *Four Quartets,* are above all records of journeys of discovery across various *états d'âme*; centered around a story as is the case with *Ulysses* and *L'Après-midi d'un Faune,* around a myth, in the case of Valéry, and concrete experiences in the case of Eliot, with whom the structure of the poem approximates most to the structure of a musical composition.

Baudelaire, Barbey, Huysmans, Mallarmé and Valéry found in the German idealists support for their views; their views were not derived from them, but confirmed by them much as G. M. Hopkins' views were confirmed by his reading of Duns Scotus. Artists have long felt with Kant that the "thing-in-itself" could never be apprehended but only hinted at. The famous theory of the oneness of the universe apprehended in moments of mystical union is as old as Plotinus, and again, is only a derivation of Plato's beliefs. It is also Schelling's theory, it fits with the Kantian theory of the "noumenon," and it was quite widespread in England and in France, too, through the writings of Carlyle, Victor Cousin, Taine and others. Carlyle had said: "The universe is but a vast symbol of God; nay, if thou wilt have it, what is man himself but a symbol of God?"[9] Barbey's nobles are in fact gods: their contact with ordinary humanity is brief, and they remain uncontaminated. They are immortal, and the stylistic image used to portray them is also of a timeless quality. This is decadence in its best sense without the fanfare, without the outrage, but satisfying and enduring.

Notes

1. A selected bibliography on Barbey d'Aurevilly would include the following: Philippe Berthier, *Barbey d'Aurevilly et l'imagination* (Geneve: Droz, 1977); Jean-Pierre Boucher, Les Diaboliques *de Barbey d'Aurevilly: une esthétique de la dissimulation et de la provocation* (Québec: Presses Universitaires de Québec, 1976); Jean Canu, *Barbey d'Aurevilly* (Paris: Laffont, 1965); Armand B. Chartier, *Barbey d'Aurevilly* (Boston: Twayne, 1977); Karen N. Fuglie, "Narrative Techniques in the Works of Barbey d'Aurevilly," Ph.D. dissertation, University of Wisconsin, 1973; John Greene, "Barbey d'Aurevilly et *A rebours,*" *Revue des Lettres Modernes* 260-263 (1971):121-124; E. Grelé, *Barbey d'Aurevilly, sa vie et son oeuvre* (Caen: L. Jouan, 1902), 2 vols.; Jacques Petit, *Essais de lectures des "Diaboliques" de Barbey d'Aurevilly* (Paris: Minard, 1974); and *Revue des Lettres Modernes* 491-497 (1977): a special issue devoted to Barbey d'Aurevilly.

2. *Les Diaboliques* (1874), including these stories: *A un dîner d'athées, Le Bonheur dans le crime, La Vengeance d'une femme; L'Ensorcelée* (1854); *Un Prêtre marié* (1881); *Une Vieille maîtresse* (1851).

3. J. K. Huysmans, *A rebours* (Paris: Fasquelle, 1955): pp. 200-201.

4. Quoted by Maximilian Rudwin, *The Devil in Legend and Literature* (Chicago: Open Court Publishing Company, 1931), p. 252. An essential bibliography of French literary decadence should include the following: Robert Willard Artinian, "Literary Decadence and the *Frisson Nouveau,*" *The Naussau Review* 2:5 (1974), 19-24; Anna Balakian, *The Symbolist Movement: A Critical Appraisal* (New York: Random House, 1967); André Barre, *Le Symbolisme* (Paris: Jouve, 1911); A. E. Carter,

The Idea of Decadence in French Literature (Toronto: University of Toronto Press, 1958); Kenneth Cornell, *The Symbolist Movement* (New Haven: Yale University Press, 1951); Jacques Gengoux, "Le Symbolisme et les symboles," *Lettres Romanes* 5 (1951), 3-37; Alice R. Kaminsky, "The Literary Concept of Decadence," *Nineteenth-Century French Studies* 4 (1976), 71-84; A. G. Lehmann, *The Symbolist Aesthetic in France, 1885-1895* (Oxford: Blackwell, 1950); Jacques Lethève, "Le Thème de la décadence dans les lettres françaises à la fin du XIX(e) siècle," *Revue d'Histoire Littéraire de la France,* 63 (1963), 46-61; Jean Pierrot, *L'Imaginaire décadent* (Paris: Presses Universitaires de France, 1977); Jean-Pierre Richard, *Microlectures* (Paris: Seuil, 1979); and James M. Smith, "Concepts of Decadence in Nineteenth-Century French Literature," *Studies in Philology,* 50 (1953), 640-651.

5. Full, fascinating development of the theme of the devil may be found in the work of Maximilian Rudwin, cited above.

6. Barbey d'Aurevilly, *Le Chevalier des Touches,* in *Œuvres romanesques complètes* (Paris: Gallimard, 1964), I, 750. Subsequent citations will refer to this edition by volume and page number.

7. Jacques Petit develops this notion in his notes to the Pléiade edition [*Œuvres romanes ques complètes*] (Pans: Gallimard, 1964)], I, 1391 ff.

8. Jacques Dubois, *Romanciers français de l'instantané au XIX(e) siècle* (Bruxelles: Palais des Académies, 1963).

9. Thomas Carlyle, *Sartor Resartus* (London: Walter Scott, 1888), p. 198.

John Greene (essay date 1984)

SOURCE: Greene, John. "The Grotesque Characters in Barbey d'Aurevilly's *Le Chevalier des Touches.*" In *L'Hénaurme Siècle: A Miscellany of Essays on Nineteenth-Century French Literature,* edited by Will L. McLendon, pp. 103-10. Heidelberg: Carl Winter Universitätverlag, 1984.

[*In the following essay, Greene analyzes Barbey d'Aurevilly's use of realist storytelling techniques to depict unrealistic characters in* Le Chevalier des Touches. *In Greene's view, the novel represents a "deliberate provocation of the reader of realist novels."*]

Philip Thomson in his book on *The Grotesque* describes the grotesque as "the unresolved clash of incompatibles in both work and effect".[1] Barbey d'Aurevilly confronts his reader with such a clash in the opening chapter of *Le Chevalier des Touches,* a novel purporting to present a real episode of the *chouannerie,* in a style that bears all the hallmarks of the realists—detailed descriptions, local color, frequent circumstantial allusions to well-known places, people and events, realistic dialogue, and so on. The traditions of Scott and Balzac are in evidence. However, flying in the face of contemporary realist practice, later to be summed up in Maupassant's suggestion that the school be called "illusionniste" for its art in lending verisimilitude to fiction,[2] Barbey uses the style of the realists to present truth in the most outrageously improbable manner.

He goes far beyond the misnamed "grotesque characters" usually found in realist novels, those who are simply individualized by means of an eccentricity, usually a loveable one, and confronts the public with characters it is not possible to accept as real. In short, the novel is an assault upon the naïve reader by what Boucher calls Barbey's "esthetics of provocation"[3]—by asking the audience of the Second Empire to believe the unbelievable, Barbey deliberately provokes a scandalized reaction.

Developing a technique used by Balzac in such stories as *l'Auberge rouge,* Barbey concentrates our attention as much on the characters telling the story as on the tale itself. Not that a clear-cut distinction can be made, for the narrator and several of her companions are actors in the story of des Touches, and the crucial point of the novel is the thirty-odd year gap between the events and their recounting, followed by another thirty-year delay between the telling and the writing. People change, as do our perceptions of them, over such periods of time, and Barbey is interested much less in the rescue of a royalist messenger than in his characters and his perceptions of them.

And they are definitely arresting characters. Barbe de Percy, an ancient Amazon whose Christian name has unfortunately become appropriate, and who will be the narrator, is presented thus:

> Coiffée habituellement d'une espèce de baril de soie orange et violette, qui aurait défié par sa forme la plus audacieuse fantaisie et qu'elle fabriquait de ses propres mains . . . elle ressemblait, avec son nez recourbé comme un sabre oriental dans son fourreau grenu de maroquin rouge, à la reine de Saba, interprétée par un Callot chinois, surexcité par l'opium. . . . Cette femme avait un grotesque si supérieur qu'on l'eût remarquée même en Angleterre, ce pays de grotesques, où le spleen, l'excentricité, la richesse et le gin travaillent perpétuellement à faire un carnaval de figures auprès desquelles les masques du carnaval de Venise ne seraient que du carton vulgairement badigeonné.[4]

The description continues in this vein, and the others present are given the same sort of treatment, although somewhat more subtly at times. The improbably named

Touffedelys sisters are two identical dry old sticks, eternally fussing and misinterpreting what others say. Barbe's brother is a fat, jolly and horribly ugly old *abbé,* whose nose is the only purple he is ever likely to wear.

But it is the Baron de Fierdrap who has undergone the most incredible accretion of characteristics. I have shown elsewhere[5] that his addiction to tea, among other symptoms of Anglomania, and his astounding habit of wearing *seven* jackets—«nombre sacrementel et mystérieux» (*Chevalier* [*Le Chevalier des Touches*], p. 754)—one on top of the other, can be traced to real sources in Normandy. It has long been known that his all-pervasive obsession with fish has been borrowed from an uncle of Barbey's, after whom the character was named, le chevalier de Beaudrap. Barbey has simply superimposed the peculiar traits of different people, the end result being, as he says, «que, comme le chat du bonhomme Misère, autre diction normand, il ne ressemblait plus à personne» (*Chevalier,* p. 753). Or at least, he no longer resembles what my high-school literature teacher used to call a "well-rounded character."

Although less evidence is available, what there is suggests that the other characters of this opening scene are equally rooted in reality, as the notes to the Pléiade edition make clear. It is odd to reflect that in marked contrast, as Andrée Hirschi has pointed out,[6] Barbey is quite willing to play fast and loose with history in recounting the actual episode of des Touches' rescue. However, the changes Barbey makes in the real events all contribute to the basic theme of the novel: Madame Hirschi demonstrates that his concentration of the action in April 1799, a date at which the *chouannerie* was petering out, strengthens our sense of the degradation that time inflicts on all things. She also speculates that the change of the title, from *l'Enlèvement* to the present one, reflects a shift of emphasis in Barbey's mind during composition, from the story to the human types embodied in it.

These confrontations of the text with its putative historical referents make clear that whatever Barbey is doing, he is quite far from fulfilling the expectations of a public hoping to be edified by a "novelization" of a historical event. What he is doing should become apparent as we move beyond the gallery of grotesques which opens the novel.

Two other characters, who are only marginally grotesque, are introduced before Barbe's narration gets under way: des Touches himself, who makes a brief Lear-like appearance as a madman in a storm at night, and Aimée de Spens, a still-beautiful spinster who is cut off from human reality through her deafness. Insofar as des Touches is grotesque, he is so in the terrible rather than the comic vein; there is nothing intrinsically grotesque

about Aimée, but by a certain exaggeration in description she is made to seem not out of place in the collection of caricatures who gather to hear the story. What is happening with these two characters in that already at the outset, the comic grotesque is being tempered by the tragic and the pathetic; these latter two elements will grow throughout the novel until they come to dominate it. And yet the comic never loses its importance: in the thick of the action we have an old woman emptying her bedpan almost on top of the rescue squad, or the timid and stupid watchmaker with the grossly improbable name of Couyart blundering into them later. A grossly improbable name, perhaps, but again, a real one. The man lived at Saint-Sauveur-le-Vicomte, Barbey's birthplace.[7]

I have maintained elsewhere[8] that part of Barbey's purpose in creating this gallery of cartoon characters was to rival the English eighteenth-century masters of the grotesque, notably Fielding, but also Hogarth and Goldsmith, and not, curiously enough, his logical competitors in his own century, Dickens and Balzac. My confidence in this last assertion has, however, been shaken by my subsequent discovery that le cousin Pons wears three vests, one over the other, under his ancient coat.[9] But I would like to deal here with a more important function of the grotesque, which is fulfilled by a transformation of the severely flawed characters of the nineteenth century, when the tale is told, into their heroic ideal selves, at the time of the Revolution, when the action takes place.

In order to demonstrate this transformation, I will compare some other descriptions of Barbe de Percy with the one already quoted. Space does not permit me to show the similar changes in descriptions of other characters who have a role in both parts of the novel—that is, the other female characters and des Touches (Fierdrap and the abbé de Percy are confined to the role of audience).

As she begins to tell the story, the modulation of Barbe from comic figure to heroic starts with the transformation of her needlework into weaponry:

> Mlle de Percy, dont l'impatience ressemblait à une menace d'apoplexie et qui débâtissait convulsivement les points qu'elle avait faits à son travail de tapisserie, repoussa son canevas dans sa corbeille; et tenant ses ciseaux, les seules armes dont sa main d'héroïne fût maintenant armée et dont elle tambourinait de temps en temps sur le guéridon contre lequel elle était accoudée, elle commença son récit . . . Histoire militaire, digne d'un bien autre tambour!
>
> (775)

The fact the she actually has borne arms makes the phrase «sa main d'héroïne» only partly ironic. Shortly thereafter, her brother's opinion of her turns out to be more respectful than we had previously suspected, which is important, as the reactions of Fierdrap and the *abbé* are the reader's chief touchstones in this novel:

> J'étais la chirurgienne en chef. On m'appelait: «le Major,» parce que je savais mieux débrider une blessure que toutes ces trembleuses . . .
>
> —Tu la débridais comme tu l'aurais faite! dit l'abbé.
>
> Pour Mlle de Percy, cette héroïne inconnue, l'opinion de l'abbé représentait la Gloire. Elle devint plus pivoine que jamais à l'observation de son frère.

(788)

From this point on, the military allusions are constant, until Barbe becomes a character in her own tale, taking an active part in the second expedition. At the outset of this part of the story, she is established as a person of feeling, as she plays the violin for the dance at Aimée's engagement ceremony; in telling of it, she alludes to the imminent death of Aimée's fiancé in the second expedition:

> Je ne touche plus à cet alto qui allait si bien à ma figure de polichinelle . . . et je me suis punie, en l'accrochant à mon lambris, d'avoir, à cette noce d'Aimée, si follement accompagné les derniers moments de son bonheur et sonné si joyeusement une agonie.
>
> —Tu es une bonne fille, après tout, Percy, que le bon Dieu a mise dans le fond d'un vaillant homme!—dit l'abbé, que sa soeur touchait, malgré lui.

(831)

Her hitherto little-suspected capacity for sentiment allows us in the end to conclude this savagely grisly story on a reasonably humane note, as Barbe interrupts the torture of the double agent who had betrayed des Touches to the revolutionaries:

> —Pour Dieu! chevalier, abrégez un pareil supplice. Et je lui tendis ma carabine, à lui qui était désarmé.
>
> —Pour Dieu et pour vous, Mademoiselle!—répondit-il.—Vous avez fait assez cette nuit même, pour que je ne puisse vous rien refuser.

(857)

We are never allowed to forget the caricatural aspects of this woman, but the underlying heroism and humanity of the character are brought out gradually. Thus we arrive at the full meaning of the "unresolved clash of incompatibles": not only is the unbelievable true, but the cartoon is a real person. The same thing happens with other characters, as we learn of the beauty and devotion of the Touffedelys sisters, of the love, imagination and capacity for action of Aimée, or of the seriousness of purpose of the pretty-boy sadist des Touches.

The final comment is given by the child who has overheard the story, and thirty years later is writing it:

> L'abbé, sa soeur et le baron étaient plus ou moins impressionnés par cette histoire d'un des héros de leur jeunesse, mais ils l'étaient moins à coup sûr qu'*une autre personne* qui était là . . . Cette autre personne n'était qu'un enfant, auquel ils n'avaient pas pris garde, tant ils étaient à leur histoire! . . . il était resté dans ce salon antique, regardant et gravant dans sa jeune mémoire ces figures comme on n'en voyait que rarement dans ce temps-là, et comme maintenant on n'en voit plus, s'intéressant déjà à ces types dans lesquels la bonhomie, la comédie et le burlesque se mêlaient, avec tant de caractère, à des sentiments hauts et grands!

(865)

This passage reminds us, in its very different vocabulary, of Michael Steig's comment on the function of the grotesque:

> In what is usually called the comic-grotesque, the comic in its various forms lessens the threat of identification with infantile drives by means of ridicule; at the same time, it lulls the inhibitions and makes possible on a pre-conscious level the same identification that it appears to the conscience or super-ego to prevent.[10]

The identification being made here is primarily the narrator's identification with the past, and his implicit rejection of the present, with its lack of heroism and feeling.

It is very tempting to relate the narrator to the circumstances of Barbey's personal experience at this point in his life, when he was undergoing a difficult reconciliation with his father. However that may be, the point of greatest importance is the concept of the accessibility of the past through the narrator's capacity to see the deep reality underlying the superficial grotesquerie. The child-narrator is first introduced in the following passage:

> Mais eux, l'oubli doit les dévorer . . . si Dieu . . . ne jetait parfois un enfant entre leurs genoux, une tête aux cheveux bouclés sur laquelle ils posent un instant la main, et qui, devenu plus tard Goldsmith ou Fielding, se souviendra d'eux dans quelque roman de génie et paraîtra créer ce qu'elle aura simplement copié, en se ressouvenant!

(775)

The legitimization of the narrator and his version of the past are underlined both by the equation with Goldsmith and Fielding, and by the gesture of benediction the old people bestow upon the cild.

The effectiveness of the identification Barbey feels and imposes on the reader is in great part due to the grotesque characters—«ces individualités exceptionnelles qui entrent violemment dans la mémoire lorsqu'on les a rencontrées, et dont l'image y reste soudée, comme une patte-fiche dans un mur.» (751)

Balzac had shown the way to convert a figure of fun into a profound lesson in humanity, within the realist style, in such novels as *le Cousin Pons.* Dickens also had turned caricatures into human beings in the *Pickwick Papers*—but there is no question of Barbey having imitated him, for he read Dickens for the first time at a late stage of composition of **Le Chevalier des Touches,** and declared himself unimpressed.[11] One may suspect a certain element of sour grapes in that opinion without taking away from the originality of **Le Chevalier des Touches** and other books of the same period.

Barbey's generation was to adapt the technique of Balzac and Dickens to create a window into the past, as Flaubert, for example, followed Barbey with his remarkable exercise in pathos, *Un Cœur simple,* bringing the reader to the brink of adopting Félicité's ridiculous identification of a stuffed parrot with the Holy Ghost. Flaubert also was reaching imaginatively into the world of those who were adults when he was a child. In another example, of slighter literary importance and less central to the novel in which it appears, Jules Verne lightly evoked the grandeur and terror of the American Civil War with a brief glimpse into the minds of the incredible human debris that constitute the Baltimore Gun Club, in *Autour de la lune.*

Barbey, however, not only brings alive an admired past, he rejects the present. His persistence in wearing 1835 fashions, his intransigently reactionary opinions, his vicious literary criticism, the sadistic violence and overt sexuality of his novels: all are an outrageous defiance of the present in the name of an irrevocably lost but infinitely desirable past. Similarly, the pathetic contrast of the revolutionary period with the degraded nineteenth century is brought out by Barbey's deliberate provocation of the reader of realist novels with his grotesque characters.

Notes

1. Philip Thomson, *The Grotesque* (London: Methuen, 1972).

2. Preface to *Pierre et Jean* in Gershman and Whitworth, *Anthologie des préfaces de romans frances du dix-neuvième siècle* (Paris: Julliard, 1964), p. 312.

3. J.-P. Boucher, Les Diaboliques *de Barbey d'Aurevilly: Une Esthétique de la dissimulation et de la provocation* (Montréal: Presses de l'Université de Québec, 1976).

4. Barbey d'Aurevilly, *Le Chevalier des Touches,* in *Œuvres romanesques complètes,* ed. de la Pléiade (Paris: Gallimard, 1964), I, p. 751. Further quotations from this edition will be indicated parenthetically in my text.

5. «Quelques éclaircissements sur *Le Chevalier des Touches,*» *Revue des lettres modernes,* Nos. 491-497 («Barbey d'Aurevilly 10»), Paris, 1977, pp. 146-49.

6. «Les Sources historiques», *Revue des lettres modernes,* issue cited, pp. 63-82.

7. «Quelques éclaircissements . . . », p. 160.

8. *Ibid.,* pp. 147-48.

9. Balzac, *Le Cousin Pons* (Paris: Nelson, 1937), pp. 8-9.

10. Quoted by Thomson, *The Grotesque,* p. 60.

11. *Nicholas Nickleby* Cf. *Quatrième Memorandum* in *Œuvres romanesques complètes,* II, p. 1086.

Thomas Buckley (essay date fall 1985)

SOURCE: Buckley, Thomas. "The Priest or the Mob: Religious Violence in Three Novels of Barbey d'Aurevilly." *Modern Language Studies* 15, no. 4 (fall 1985): 245-60.

[*In the following essay, Buckley examines ritualized violence in Barbey d'Aurevilly's fiction.*]

In **L'Ensorcelée,** there is a striking alternation between group religious ritual and punitive mob violence. The pattern is also noticeable in **Un Prêtre Marié** and **Une Histoire sans Nom,** where it suggests not only a narrative arrangement of tension—release, but also a thematic relation between religion and violence. The phenomenon has its origin in Barbey's earliest prose work, **"Le Cachet d'Onyx,"** where social authority is portrayed as a cruel, violent force that punishes adulterers. Before tracing it back to that narrative, however, I would like to propose some ideological background for such an odd configuration in the works of a Catholic novelist.

According to Georges Bataille, early man's respect and fear of bloodshed led him to equate it with the sacred world.[1] Cadavers, criminal violence, incest, and sorcery were seen as belonging to the domain of impure sacredness, while carefully chosen transgressions such as bloody sacrifice and orgiastic harvest festivals belonged to that of pure sacredness, the domain of religion in general.

René Girard points out that sacrifice was made necessary not only by a belief in the sacred character of blood, which defined the sacrificial act as a purification of the community; it also served the mechanism of the emissary victim or scapegoat, channelling potentially disruptive violence onto a safely removed, unanimous target.[2] The De Maistrean principle of expiation, to which some critics have attributed Barbey's enthusiasm for violence,[3] also fits into this perspective. Joseph De Maistre contended that the blood of innocent victims vicariously redeems evil in the world.[4] Girard goes further, however, affirming that the distinction between pure and impure sacredness was crucial, for it prevented sacrificial bloodshed from degenerating into the chain of self-righteous vengeance which he calls "the sacrificial crisis:"

> *La crise sacrificielle,* c'est-à-dire la perte du sacrifice, est perte de la différence entre violence impure et violence purificatrice. Quand cette différence est perdue, il n'y a plus de purification possible et la violence impure, contagieuse, c'est-à-dire réciproque, se répand dans la communauté.[5]

Pagans of antiquity practiced ritual transgressions of bloody sacrifice and sacred orgies, and they believed that the power of sorcery was derived from bold, illicit transgressions of the blood taboo. Christianity suppressed these sacred violations, making moral prohibitions absolute. The crucifixion need not be literally repeated, for it was believed that the transubstantiation made possible the miraculous renewal of this ritual, without bloodshed. The pagan category of impure sacredness was transformed into the notion of sin.[6]

Barbey recalls paganism by depicting a religion which either depends on bloodshed for ritual renewal and purification of the community, or is horrified by blood in a way which suggests that blood is impure sacred.

* * *

According to the narrator of Barbey's early story **"Le Cachet d'Onyx,"** it is society's condemnation of adulterous love which makes that love impure. He also hints that social opinion causes Auguste Dorsay to punish cruelly his lover Hortense for her infidelity. The injustice of Dorsay's punishment of Hortense is partially explained by the arbitrary, unjust character of a society which pins non-conformists under a bright light of surveillance. The story implies that the society of the Parisian salon world during the Restoration imposes its authority illegitimately. The same point of view characterizes most of Barbey's early stories, despite their tendency to make fun of love and courtship. In **"La Bague d'Annibal"** the metaphor of human sacrifice expresses the author's criticism of social authority:

> Le médisance, inconstante personne qui veut chaque jour des sacrifices nouveaux, comme ces divinités du Mexique auxquelles il fallait chaque matin une nouvelle victime humaine.

(I, p. 152)

L'Amour Impossible expresses the same idea in a different way when it shows that social pressure makes love impossible. Love represents a sacred ideal that is profaned by a cruel, unjust society.

The meaning of social opinion is different in **L'Ensorcelée,** primarily because a different society is concerned: the setting is the Norman countryside during the revolutionary years. Barbey feels that the ancien régime is legitimate and time-tested, and he admires it as a monument of civilization and tradition. The Revolution complicates the question of society's moral authority, however, and the townsmen described in **L'Ensorcelée** are divided into pro- and counter-revolutionary factions. The legitimist author chooses a royalist sympathizer as victim of a republican mob, thereby making the Revolution seem unjust. Political considerations decide that the murder is a sacrilege rather than a sacrifice.

The other factor which colors the group-victim relationship in **L'Ensorcelée** and in all of Barbey's works, is sexuality. The fact that a woman has been "tarnished" always figures as part of the group's reason for punishing her. Female sexual promiscuity thus functions in the Aurevillian universe as do the "victimary signs" (sexual crimes, rape, incest, bestiality) which, according to Girard,[7] trigger the crowd's unanimous punishment response.

One finds in the novel the suggestion that mob judgment is instinctively just: "les âmes religieuses et tranquilles . . . devraient faire l'opinion dans tous les pays . . ." (I, p. 665). But at this point the narrator condemns the mob's violent actions in the name of Catholicism. The blood of crime is a sacrilegious threat to the Church. The sacrificial crisis describes one aspect of the situation: the impure blood of crime comes dangerously close to merging with the purity or the "pure blood" of religious ritual. The Catholic Mass involves no real blood, but only wine "miraculously transformed" into the blood of Christ. The Christian fear that the purity of the host and the wine will be desecrated nonetheless resembles the pagan fear that the pure blood of sacrifice will be contaminated by contact with impure blood.

L'Ensorcelée deals with the mystical power of Jéhoël de la Croix-Jugan over Jeanne Le Hardouey. La Croix-Jugan is a priest who temporarily quits the priesthood in order to fight in the counter-revolutionary Chouannerie. He represents the royalists at a time when French society was divided between supporters and opponents of the Revolution. When he returns to the Church to do penance, Jeanne falls in love with him, and eventually drowns herself in a pond out of despair that her love will never be returned. Because of the priest's ill-defined involvement in Jeanne's fate, and because of his guerrilla warfare, the novel is centered on the forces which oppose and favor La Croix-Jugan.

In the opening pages of **L'Ensorcelée,** Jéhoël de la Croix-Jugan is being tortured by five revolutionary soldiers. The author emphasizes the soldiers' intentional cruelty against the heroic Chouan leader, but the characteristics of religious violence emerge from this cruelty. In proportion as the narrator suggests sacrilege, the scene appears sacrificial. It appears that inhuman violence resembles religious violence. The Blue soldiers are meant to appear diabolic, since they feel no fear or disgust at their actions. But the surpassing of this human boundary comes to be identified with "divine-commanded" violence as well.

The five soldiers find the wounded La Croix-Jugan lying in an old woman's hut, and they amuse themselves by burning his face with a red-hot poker. Their wanton cruelty prompts them all to participate in the act, and their disrespect causes them to refer to the victim as a piece of meat being grilled:

> Et tous les cinq prirent de la braise rouge dans l'âtre embrasé. . . .
>
> Nous avons pris le feu pour cuire la grillade de ce Chouan. . . .
>
> (I, p. 597)

Unanimity is one of the key attributes of pagan sacrifice, as is the eating of the victim.[8] But at this point Barbey is far from suggesting that cruel, unjust violence possesses spiritual value. The only hint in that direction is the fact that La Croix-Jugan's facial scars become associated with satanism, a kind of negative spirituality. The scars are vaguely involved in the bewitching of Jeanne Le Hardouey.

La Clotte, victim in the novel's main punishment scene, is also caught up in the revolutionary conflict. Her fidelity to the aristocracy makes her remain aloof from post-revolutionary society. On the other hand, she is rejected by that society for having once compromised herself with members of the decadent noble class. The narrator toys with the idea that she is in fact "unclean" and deserves punishment for her sin, but his condemnation of the revolutionary mob finally surpasses his condemnation of an "immoral woman." A close analysis of the scene in which La Clotte is stoned reveals, however, that Barbey's attitude toward the group's punishment motive is still full of contradictions.

The author does not attribute any religious or judicial authority to this mob, in spite of his previous reference to the moral authority of the "religious, peaceful souls." A funeral crowd is emerging from church, when several of its members notice that the banned La Clotte has also attended the service for her old friend Jeanne Le Hardouey. There is a natural transfer of mood from the ritual of sprinkling holy water upon the casket, to the emotional contagion which leads to La Clotte's death. The emotion stirred by the ritual is contagious, as is the hatred for La Clotte:

> Instant pathétique et redoubtable! Le coeur de l'homme le plus fort n'y résiste pas, lorsque, rangés en cercle, leurs cierges éteints, au bord de la tombe entr'ouverte, les prêtres versent l'eau bénite, dans un requiescat suprême. . . .
>
> (I, p. 704)

(The butcher Augé provokes the crowd's sentiment against La Clotte):

> "Est-ce pour maléficier aussi son cadavre que tu t'en viens. . . ." L'idée qu'il exprimait saisit tout à coup cette foule. . . . Un long et confus murmure circula parmi ces têtes pressées dans le cimetière. . . .
>
> (I, pp. 705-706)

Ritual and violence are both emotional, instinctive events to which the people cannot help ceding, even though the first is supposed to be divine, and the second criminal. This illustrates the sacrificial crisis, insofar as a passionate ritual overflows into and becomes indistinguishable from vengeance.[9] Barbey, however, explains the events differently. Although he believes that ritual must be emotional or "passionate," and that God communicates religion to men through emotional rituals, he indicates that any blood is capable of tarnishing the purity of Catholic ritual. The crowd ends up committing a crime in the name of religious purification, and the leader of the stoning chases a horrified priest back into the church. But why is the priest horrified? Is it because a sacrilege is being committed or because the town has reverted to mob rule? The horror stems from both religious transgression, i.e. sacrilege, and from judicial transgression, i.e. crime. Pagan terms, according to which the distinction between pure and impure sacredness has broken down, express both kinds of transgression. Barbey's perspective similarly suggests that civil and religious authority are combined, a hint that his viewpoint is regressing.

Other factors nonetheless make the stoning a successful scapegoat mechanism. One is the unanimity with which the group finally turns against La Clotte, deciding that she caused the death of Jeanne Le Hardouey which has disturbed and divided the community. There is little chance that anyone will avenge La Clotte, since she is removed from the rest of society. Through an apparent coincidence, Jéhoël de la Croix-Jugan later finds her lying out on the heath, and though it is too late to defend her, he administers the last sacraments. Her only sympathizer is unable to divide the community's united hatred of her, and he too will become a victim of the revolutionary forces.

The second factor which recalls pagan sacrifice is the old woman's partially superior, partially inferior position:

> Son sang d'autrefois, son vieux sang de concubine des seigneurs du pays monta à sa joue sillonnée comme une lueur dernière. . . .
>
> (I, p. 706)

From the sacrificers' perspective only certain blood is capable of purifying the community, and during the sacrifice they alternately see this blood as being purer and less pure than that of a member of the community; the murderers see their victim now as a scorned scapegoat, now as a noble savior.[10] If the victim were a "normal" member of the community, his death would be avenged, provoking a socially disruptive chain of vengeance.

The group murder of La Clotte stops short of both sacrifice and satanism, unlike the Blues' torture of La Croix-Jugan. The former is not entirely "sacralized." After dragging the old woman out of town on a metal grill, the murderers shrink in fear upon arriving in the haunted Lessay heath. They leave the body here and flee, lest their act incur supernatural wrath.

The priestly power of Aurevillian soldiers depends on their ability to confront the supernatural (sin or crime) without fear. Passionate lovers and sorcerers are similarly credited with supernatural power for infringing upon that realm without fear of punishment. If the sacrificial phenomenon remains incomplete in the murder of La Clotte, it is partially because of this failure to go beyond the limits of the natural world. Her murderers have a religious fear of having sinned. This is why the Blues' fearless cruelty against La Croix-Jugan has as much in common with pagan sacrifice as does the self-righteous punishment of a sinner. The Blues' boldly handle blood, which here represents the sacred world.

The sacrificers' attitude poses a problem in the death of La Clotte, as in primitive sacrifice. Since the author ultimately attributes no spiritual value to this atrocity, he depicts its perpetrators as sinners or madmen. Pagans pray that their murder be excused as a sacrifice dictated by the divinity.[11] They may also treat their victim as a king prior to his execution, as if in recognition of the beneficial effect of his sacrifice upon the community. These prayers correspond to the sacrificial priest's purification of himself before and after the sacrifice as a sign of respect for the sacred world, or in order to keep the sacred (i.e. the blood of the victim) separate from the profane. This symbolizes his change of attitude upon confronting ritual transgressions. Because of this change, his act is not seen as a crime, as is the Blues' torturing of La Croix-Jugan. The "pious" symbolism of the former oddly resembles the impious, playful cruelty of the latter. Both seem unnatural or inhuman.

The Christian attitude toward the crucifixion of Christ is even more ambiguous than the pagan's, for Christianity condemns all violence without exception, leaving no place for ritual transgression. The murderers of Christ are seen as sinners or criminals, resembling the Blue torturers of Jéhoël rather than pagan sacrificers. The crucifixion is nonetheless believed to redeem the sins of mankind. But the spiritual value of Christ's death is contingent upon its voluntary nature.[12] His murderers appear to be mere tools and are given no credit for man's redemption. Christians see themselves as the sacrificers of Christ and, like pagans, pray God to excuse the crime of the crucifixion. In contrast, Jéhoël's "sacrifice" is involuntary—hence his torturers are entirely responsible and, since the fact is accorded no spiritual value, they are seen in a negative light.

La Clotte's murder provokes fear of sacrilege. The purity of the church risks being contaminated by a violent act. The final incident in *L'Ensorcelée,* the assassination of La Croix-Jugan, also involves the risk of sacrilege. The scene does not appear to be one of group violence, but rather of a religious ritual, an Easter Sunday Mass. The event recalls the sacrificial crisis, not in the sense of a chain reaction of violence, but in the sense that the arbitrary distinction between sacrifice and crime becomes blurred. La Croix-Jugan is shot while consecrating the host, which is spattered with his blood. An assisting priest quickly consumes the bloody host in order to put an end to the sacrilege.

It is interesting to note that, at the beginning of this passage, the author discredits the mob's authority, explaining that the Church resists "the fury and confusion of the tongues." In fact, however, the goals of Church and mob are not at odds: both are concerned with punishing the sinner. The Church has merely decided, and convinced the crowd, that La Croix-Jugan's penance was sufficient to pay for his errors.

The difference in the foregoing scene between the apparent meaning of the events, and the narrator's explanation of them, reflects a similar gap between apparent and assigned meaning in the novel as a whole. The apparent subject of *L'Ensorcelée* is La Croix-Jugan's bewitching of Jeanne Le Hardouey, but the novel is equally concerned with the sacrificial killing of La Croix-Jugan by a member of the revolutionary forces which kill La Clotte. This suggests an explanation for the enigmatic fact, noted by Naomi Schor, that the lapidation (unanimous violence) fails to engender a socially unifying ritual, whereas the vengeance (reciprocal violence) which kills La Croix-Jugan at the end of the novel accompanies a ritual which does unite the community.[13] The murder of Jéhoël can be seen as the logical completion of the sacrificial configuration which develops at Jeanne's funeral. Jeanne and Jéhoël, the only two characters who come into contact with La Clotte, both fall prey to the "victimary" contagion which emanates from this social outcast. Previewed in the opening pages of the work, the assassination of La Croix-Jugan takes place at the end, where the rumor circulates that the re-instated priest was killed by Thomas Le Hardouey, Jeanne's husband and an acquirer of Church goods after the Revolution. Barbey chooses, however, to stress sorcery and sacrilege rather than sacrifice. The author of *L'Ensorcelée* constantly juxtaposes Catholic ritual and sacrificial violence, but goes no further than the suggestion that blood on the alter is logical in revolutionary times.

* * *

Un Prêtre Marié focuses on the concept of expiation. The idea is stressed repeatedly in reference to Calixte's mysterious wounds and suffering on account of his father, the married priest. The question of social opinion is nonetheless of central importance, because of the relationship between Sombreval, his daughter, and society. The sins of the married priest are said to hurt God, but society attempts to punish him, since the narrator accords society responsibility for the enforcement of divine justice.

The novel contains passages similar to those seen in *L'Ensorcelée,* but here they are viewed in a different light. The narrator still strives to show the horror and violence of sacrilege, but instead of society being tainted with the impure blood of the Revolution as in *L'Ensorcelée,* sacrilegious impurity is identified with the pariah, Jean Sombreval, a defrocked, married priest. The community's anger against Sombreval and his daughter Calixte is mystified and portrayed as just, sacrificial anger. The storyteller is more concerned with mystical justice than with human justice, for he portrays impiety as being more violent than expiatory violence. This constitutes a further step in his increasing mystification of violence.

The Revolution is relegated to the background of the novel. Its violence does not constitute a socially divisive force in the main plot, as in *L'Ensorcelée.* The bloodshed of the Revolution is briefly depicted as a disgusting, horrible sacrilege in Paris where, as a young man, Sombreval flees from the priesthood and marries. Like the Blues' torturing of La Croix-Jugan in *L'Ensorcelée,* descriptions of revolutionaries carrying torn-out human hearts in bouquets of carnations suggest deliberate cruelty, cannabalism, or primitive religious violence. They appear unnatural and inhuman:

> L'abbé Sombreval continua d'habiter Paris—le Paris de Marat, de Fouquier-Tinville, des têtes fichées au bout des piques, des coeurs chauds et tressaillant encore portés dans des bouquets d'oeillets blancs. . . .
>
> (I, p. 892)

These crimes hover in the distance, as if to imply that the retribution to come is inevitable, amply deserved and perhaps less cruel than the transgressions which it will punish. By contrast, all of the violence in *L'Ensorcelée,* including sacrificial violence, was depicted with equal horror, since all of it was associated with the sacrilegious Blues or with sorcerers. Here religious violence seems natural, in contrast with the unnatural violence of sacrilege. The narrator comes to accept the De Maistrean imperative of expiation as if it

were a Christian principle. In *L'Ensorcelée* he showed self-righteous mob justice as being at odds with the Church. There the narrator did not adopt the persecutors' point of view, but showed their violence to be criminal even though it claimed religious motives. In *Un Prêtre Marié* the situation is different, first because group violence is skirted there, and secondly because Calixte's suffering is believed to pay for other impure, threatening violence.

Sombreval's marriage is depicted as a violent blow that kills his father and causes his daughter to be born with a wound on her forehead. But God is not held responsible for these deaths. The priest's taboo marriage is portrayed as a catalyst which unchains a mysterious force; sacrilege is associated with this uncontrollable, dangerous flowing of blood. His subsequent devotion to the chemical study of blood is likewise suggested to be unnatural and dangerous, further implying that blood is a formidable, sacred substance. Medicine and scientific research are opposed to religion and to God's will, and related to sorcery.

Still other aspects of Sombreval link sacrilege with blood. His antisocial character leads him to buy the Du Quesnay castle, previously owned by a ruined noble family, since respect for the fallen family prevents anyone else from buying the dwelling. The narrator compares the incident to an injured animal's being devoured by another, once more directly associating blood with sacrilege:

> Une meute de créanciers s'était levée. Ayant déjà goûté par l'usure à ce patrimoine déshonoré, ces ignobles chiens, qui avaient au museau du sang de cette belle fortune, dont ils voulaient boire, hurlèrent pour qu'on leur en donnât la dernière gorge-chaude. . . .
>
> (I, p. 885)

The community's hatred of Sombreval coincides with its respect for religious principles and its hatred of sinners. Hence, when Sombreval attends church at the request of his pious daughter Calixte, the narrator is able to justify the angry crowd that threatens both of them. They are righteously indignant at the priest's sacrilege, and want to punish him for sullying the church. The crowd's anger is associated with divine anger, and the narrator rationalizes their seemingly indiscriminate desire to punish the innocent Calixte as well, explaining that Calixte remains tarnished by her father's crime:

> Ils avaient raison contre Calixte elle-même, et elle le reconnaissait bien, tant l'esprit de cette enfant avait de clarté et de profondeur!
>
> L'élève de l'abbé Hugon était trop chrétienne pour admettre l'irresponsabilité des enfants dans le crime ou la faute des pères . . .—le lien inextricable qui unit le père aux enfants.
>
> (I, p. 937)

This expresses the De Maistrean principle of hereditary sin.[14] What is interesting here is that the narrator now adopts and defends the point of view of the persecutors. Instead of demystifying religious violence, as Girard does, he mystifies a mob's anger, assigning it theological motives. If these are not precisely pagan motives, they nonetheless constitute a regressive religious perspective, i.e. a perspective that moves toward paganism. They go in the opposite direction from the modern position which, as Girard points out in *Le Bouc Emissaire,* renders self-righteous violence increasingly transparent.[15]

In accordance with the idea that the law of the crowd is a higher, fairer one than official law in post-revolutionary France, the narrator refers to the illegitimacy of the "atheist" government:

> Le peuple est naturellement exécuteur des hautes oeuvres d'une justice dont il a l'instinct et à laquelle, sans ses tribuns, je me fierais. Ici, il n'avait que sa huée pour tout supplice, et ce supplice, il voulait l'appliquer à un grand coupable impuni qu'une législation athée protégeait. Il avait raison.

> (I, p. 936)

This mob violence is portrayed as being pure and righteous, unlike that seen in *L'Ensorcelée,* which was associated with sacrilege and animality:

> Dans un coin de terre chrétienne encore, cette poignée de paysans allait châtier, du seul châtiment que la loi n'eût pas enlevé aux moeurs, un homme . . . décide autant qu'un homme peut l'être.

> (I, p. 936)

Instead, it is Sombreval's defensive reaction against the crowd which is depicted as being bloodthirsty and sacrilegious:

> La colère léchait de sa langue de tigre, qui veut du sang, l'intérieur de la poitrine de Sombreval, de cette poitrine qui avait l'énergie ardente et le développement d'un poitrail.

> (I, p. 938)

Narrative rhetoric contributes importantly to the thematic opposition between "sacrificial" violence and other violence, suggesting the arbitrary distinction between sacrifice and sacrilege.[16]

The crowd's unanimous desire to cleanse the church by expelling these "impure" individuals brings to mind the murder of La Clotte. But in *Un Prêtre Marié* violence is prevented by a friend of the victims who is also a member of the community. Néel de Néhou impedes the crowd's "righteous, pure" intentions from being blemished by an act as brutal as the one described in *L'Ensorcelée.* Then, as the crowd's mood changes, the narrator dwells on its different reactions to Sombreval and Néel. He describes the crowd as something more than or less than a human being, its humor changing from anger and scorn to religious respect for Néel. This transformation suggests that its "instinct for justice" is temporarily forgotten. On the other hand, it illustrates strikingly well the change of attitude which reflects sacrificers' mystification or "sacralization" of their violence:

> l'étonnement—un étonnement sans bornes—leur coupa la parole; ils se turent. . . . Il avait les dons irrésistibles qui plaisent à l'imagination des foules.

> (I, p. 939)

It seems illogical that Néel's personal charm would be able to sway so easily the same crowd whose punishing instinct wisely corresponded to God's will, but the nebulous terms "instinct" and "imagination" join the two incidents with no apparent contradiction.

The narrator subsequently describes public opinion as a force which continues to grow, threatening Sombreval and Calixte. He now emphasizes its violence, which he calls "le coup de lanière" or "l'ennemi invisible, cette chose sans visage qu'on appelle le bruit public." But instead of concluding from this violence that social opinion is unjust, the narrator suggests that it is inevitable, and that it can be put to good use. Faced with the realization that Calixte's name is being slandered on account of his "crime," Sombreval decides to repent by going to live in a monastery.

As in previous works, the crowd cites the impurity of its victim. When rumor contends that Calixte has an incestuous relationship with Sombreval, the narrator insists on the idea of incest, as if intending to horrify the reader. He implies that it is cruel and antithetical that the immaculate, ascetic Calixte should be tarnished by such a rumor. In sacrificial terms, however, Calixte possesses the purity of the perfect victim; moreover, the accusation of incest here serves to justify punishment of her. Girard mentions incest as a "victimary" sign which typically designates individuals as objects of sacrificial violence. Here the narrator implies, as the author of a primitive myth or a Medieval text might state unequivocally, that the victim deserves punishment and has provoked a crisis in the community. De Maistrean theology allows him to emphasize both the cruelty and the necessity of the crowd's action, thereby heightening the effect of the passage on the modern reader's sensibility. What is shocking and unusual is that these events, situated in a modern context, are described from a regressive point of view.

Another explanation for the contradiction between the "piety" of the crowd and that of Calixte can be found in the writings of William Robertson Smith, scholar of early Semitic religion. He observes that, in ancient religion, precedence is given to ritual, while in modern religion, precedence is given to beliefs.[17] In these terms, the church crowd and its "justice" represent primitive, ritual-based religion, while the inward, expiatory suffering of Calixte derives from modern, belief-oriented religion, in this case Christianity. The novel shows the two to be in conflict. Father Méautis, the local priest, announces to his congregation that Sombreval has retired to the Coutances monastery as an act of repentance. The purpose of the announcement is to absolve Calixte in the minds of the community members who have thus far slandered her. The narrator describes the appeasement of the crowd with as much fascination as he described its arousal:

> (the message) . . . frappa d'étonnement les paysans comme si la main de Dieu fût sortie visiblement du Tabernacle et eût projeté son ombre gigantesque sur la voûte de leur église.
>
> (I, p. 1123)

Here the priest's voice represents divine authority and apparently supersedes the authority of the crowd. The event seems to contradict the previously expressed notion of crowd justice. But the priest is later proven wrong, when science confirms a clairvoyant woman's revelation that Sombreval has only feigned repentance. The conclusion supports Barbey's theory that instinct and imagination are synonymous with religious sensitivity.

Un Prêtre Marié ostensibly explores the theme of individual expiation, but inadvertently reveals much about society as a moral judge. Alongside the elaborate descriptions of Calixte's penance, appears and disappears the notion of a society in which moral and judicial authority have merged. Calixte dies of a mysterious catalepsy, presumably because she knows that her father has not truly repented. But it is logical to assume that she finally succumbs to the social force which has all along designated her as a victim. At the end of the novel the narrator no longer expresses this idea, even though he enunciated it earlier as a religious principle. He reconciles the Christian piety of the community with that of Calixte, by portraying Sombreval's apostasy as a violent force which destroys his daughter. Townspeople now express devoted respect for Calixte. This apparently contradictory change of heart strains the limits of Catholic theology, but it makes sense from the sacrificial perspective, recalling sacrificers who alternately scorn and adore their victims.

The De Maistrean concept of expiation fits into pre-Christian religious thought inasmuch as both assign to bloodshed the role of redeeming previous faults. But *Un Prêtre Marié* strays from the sacrificial perspective and becomes enmeshed in the complexities of Christian thought as the drama becomes Sombreval's false repentance, or his failure to believe in God. Belief finally takes precedence over ritual. Sombreval sheds his blood in an attempt to assuage Calixte's fears that he will be damned, but his lack of belief continues to haunt the girl. This suggests why the crowd motif fades away at the end of the novel: the concern of the crowd always centers on the observance of emotional, outwardly expressed social habits, rather than on internal, intellectually formed beliefs. Barbey attempts to return to a modern, Christian perspective. He compromises his theory of instinctive religion by explaining that Sombreval's apostasy is a crime against God. But the God which he has portrayed in *Un Prêtre Marié* is no New Testament God. The die has already been cast in favor of pre-Christian theology.

* * *

Une Histoire sans Nom straddles the same two themes of expiation and crowd justice. It concerns a daughter's expiation of her mother's sin, but indirectly reveals much about the power of social opinion, and its tendency to claim victims. In the work, geographical descriptions suggest a religion which punishes for no reason at all. That seems even crueller than De Maistre's principle of expiatory bloodshed.

In the novel's opening scene, the narrator describes the small town in the Cévennes where the first part of the story takes place. He dwells on the fact that the town is smothered beneath the mountains which surround it, hinting with little subtlety that the tale's psychological climate will also be heavy and crushing. When it is mentioned that the church's architecture is "écrasante," and that the Barbarian had to prostrate himself before the Christian faith, the reader can expect this stifling atmosphere to claim a victim. There is something strange about this "fervent Catholic town." But the story soon centers on two devout churchgoers, Mme de Ferjol and her daughter Lasthénie, and, at this point, it appears that the church crowd will not assume the explicit role which it did in previous novels.

The narrator is nonetheless fascinated by Mme de Ferjol's relationship with the community, a social position which recalls that of La Clotte in *L'Ensorcelée.* Ferjol had previously eloped and married a man from this small town but, since his death, has maintained a "sovereign coldness" toward her neighbors. The portrait suggests that she is half aloof and half outcast, as was La Clotte. A difference between the two women is that the community respects Mme de Ferjol because of her noble blood and her strict piety, whereas La Clotte was scorned on account of her promiscuous youth. The narrator compares Ferjol's role to that of a king in pagan antiquity:

> Si ce n'était pas comme les Rois de Perse, invisibles, et dont elle ne pouvait avoir l'invisibilité absolue, c'était du moins un peu comme eux, par l'éloignement dans lequel elle se tint toujours au sein étroit de ce petit monde, avec qui elle ne se familiarisa jamais.
>
> (II, p. 285)

It soon becomes evident that, if the woman is respected for her virtue, it is only because she carefully monitors her public image. The novel focuses on the peculiar psychological factors which enable Ferjol to remain a saint in the eyes of society.

The mother and daughter live in near isolation, spending their time only at church, in their gigantic, awesome house, or on occasional walks up the sides of their mountainous prison. Mme de Ferjol is thus mystified when she discovers that Lasthénie is pregnant, and the next eighty pages describe how the mother cruelly punishes her daughter for her "sin," attempting to find out who her partner was. The narrator documents the religious education which causes Mme de Ferjol to punish in the name of virtue. Her Jansenism compels her to squelch her own love for her daughter and to become inhumanly virtuous.

The concept of expiation enters with the narrator's suggestion that, in punishing Lasthénie, Mme de Ferjol punishes herself. The mother's elopement was a fault which went unpunished and, as she finally reveals, Lasthénie was conceived out of wedlock. The daughter's pregnancy constitutes a "shameful sin" like that which Mme de Ferjol has kept hidden all her life, and the narrator suggests that the mother unknowingly makes her daughter pay for her hidden mistake, as Calixte paid for Sombreval's "evil" acts. But Lasthénie's torture is much crueller than that of Calixte; Lasthénie does not know why she is being tortured, while Calixte willingly and knowingly accepted her expiatory suffering. The narrator of *Une Histoire sans Nom* reiterates the religious and psychological factors which contribute to Mme de Ferjol's "well-intentioned" punishment of her daughter, and the end of the novel describes the woman's dramatic remorse.

The narrator explains logically Mme de Ferjol's cruelty toward her daughter without successfully hiding his admiration for Mme de Ferjol's "staunch virtue," as Jacques Petit points out in the notes to the novel (II, p. 1255). She is enforcing the kind of justice which fascinated the narrator of *Un Prêtre Marié.* He continually mentions the small town's respect for Mme de Ferjol, and the woman's fear that the townspeople should discover Lasthénie's pregnancy. But never does he suggest that, in punishing her daughter, Mme de Ferjol is the instrument of a religious community which, like those seen in the two previous novels, demands a victim. Instead, the narrator proposes a total lack of continuity between events inside the Ferjol family, and events of the outside world. He sees the severe, suffocating atmosphere of the Cévennes village as a cruel coincidence, and Lasthénie, destroyed for a crime of which she was innocent, as the purest, most perfect victim. According to the logic suggested in *L'Ensorcelée* and established in *Un Prêtre Marié,* mysterious, inhuman cruelty signals supernatural motives. But here the narrator does not assign a spiritual purpose to the violence. He implies instead that peculiar circumstances have caused Mme de Ferjol's strict virtue to serve evil intentions unwillingly.

While punishing herself and her daughter for the mysterious pregnancy, Mme de Ferjol is unaware that the girl was unknowingly violated in her sleep by a visiting priest. The narrator never suggests that this "virtuous punishment" is an expression of the woman's submission to the expectations of a watchful small town which incarnates the pagan god mentioned in Barbey's early tales. He similarly avoids the suggestion that Mme de Ferjol's pride has been nurtured by religious concerns, and asserts that it has only remained *despite* the humbling influence of Catholicism:

> L'orgueil que la religion n'avait pas domptén en Mme de Ferjol se soulevait dans le coeur de cette femme de race. . . .
>
> (II, p. 310)

She badgers Lasthénie for the name of her child's father, in order that a marriage might resolve the embarrassing problem, just as it resolved hers years ago. Only the surface really counts in this religion, despite descriptions of Mme de Ferjol's private mortification and self-questioning.

The community has always respected the piety of the otherwise non-conformist Mme de Ferjol. It is the only aspect of her life which she shares with other townspeople. It is thus no coincidence if she remains "sovereign" in the town, and if her cruel virtue punishes a pregnancy which would cause the town to scorn her and her daughter.

Social opinion is an invisible force within the novel, since the townspeople are faceless. The narrator merely alludes to the danger of gossiping tongues when, after her husband's death, Mme de Ferjol dismisses her servants, and when the washing women enter her lonely kingdom. He implies on those occasions that the tongues are a force that always lies waiting for a new victim. Mme de Ferjol defuses this force, first by leaving the small town in the Cévennes in order to hide Lasthénie's pregnancy, and secondly by hiding their arrival in her native Norman village until after the dead infant has been buried. In both instances, Mme de Ferjol has her servant Agathe announce the news to the local peasants, as if Agathe were the spokesperson for a public figure who wanted to control his reputation:

> Mme de Ferjol, qui ne voyait personne, fit répandre, un matin, par Agathe, au marché du bourg, qu'elle retournait en son pays. . . .
>
> (II, p. 324)

> Elle avait pensé que *maintenant* elle et sa fille devaient sortir de ce strict et formidable incognito qu'elle avait voulu et gardé jusque là.—"Vous pouvez—dit-elle à Agathe—annoncer au fermier de la terre que nous sommes arrivées. . . ."
>
> (II, p. 343)

The narrator never elucidates Mme de Ferjol's reasons for being so cautious with society, but this caution contradicts his previous suggestion that she was independent of others, and beyond their criticism. Mme de Ferjol personifies virtue only by forcing herself to conform to an unwritten moral law. The horror which she expresses upon discovering that her daughter is pregnant is no different from the horror expressed by angry, scornful crowds in *L'Ensorcelée* and *Un Prêtre Marié*. They cited La Clotte's impurity and Calixte's illegitimate birth as if these were shocking, punishable sins, and Mme de Ferjol acts in the same way with Lasthénie's "fault." She is only independent from social opinion insofar as her own moral judgment represents that of society.

While Mme de Ferjol's punishing attitude requires explanation, Lasthénie's attitude becomes a total mystery. Unable to believe that she is pregnant, she first wonders why her mother insists on punishing her. Later, confused and only half conscious after the constant pestering, Lasthénie becomes a willing victim. After she dies, it becomes clear that she has killed herself by poking eighteen needles into her heart. But there is no explanation for this self-imposed torture. On the contrary, the narrator leaves it mysterious as if to imply that it might have a religious motive.

The outside world apparently remains unaware of Lasthénie's pregnancy and wounds. But there is an indirect indication late in the novel that society is cognizant of the girl's approaching death:

> Quand elle et sa mère paraissaient le dimanche à l'église, on comprenait, en les voyant, que Mme de Ferjol ne voulût recevoir personne, pour se consacrer tout entière à la santé de sa fille. L'opinion fut que cette enfant qu'elle y traînait avec elle, elle ne l'y traînerait pas longtemps.
>
> (II, p. 345)

The community appears to have a passive, innocent role in this sacrifice, unlike the community's active role in the persecution described in the two previous novels. And although society has not literally ordered Lasthénie's death, the repression of the girl's pregnancy and the mother's guilt would not have been necessary in the absence of a watchful, moralizing society. The priest's violation of Lasthénie does not mysteriously generate violence, as the narrator suggests, and as he suggested with Sombreval's marriage in *Un Prêtre Marié*. It is society's reaction to sexuality which turns it into a violent, destructive force in all three novels. Having demystified the phenomenon in his early stories, albeit paradoxically by means of a reference to society as a pagan god, Barbey goes on to mystify and eventually "sacralize" society's violence in his novels. Ironically, however, the Aurevillian narrator no longer refers to pagan gods and sacrifices, now that events in

his narrative suggest them more strongly than ever. Barbey's perspective is the exact opposite of the contemporary attitude which Girard assails in *Le Bouc Emissaire*:[18] he portrays primitive religious violence as surpassing in horror the ire of a modern day self-righteous mob. Barbey remains "under the spell" of the "Christian" mob.

Barbey appears unable to resolve the question of a group's role in punishing sexual promiscuity. He ultimately abandons the De Maistrean principle enunciated in *Un Prêtre Marié* (innocent victims must pay for other people's sins), and re-explains punitive violence (in *Une Histoire sans Nom*) in terms of Jansenism and abnormal psychology.

Mme de Ferjol discovers twenty-five years after Lasthénie's death that the girl had been violated while sleepwalking. The woman feels great remorse at the thought that she punished her daughter unjustly and pushed her to the point of suicide. She now realizes that she has committed a crime in the name of religion, which once again recalls the sacrificial crisis. But what has become of the pagan perspective which, up to this point, has explained so much of Barbey's religious thought?

In the Aurevillian universe, the moral law is based on passion, which represents transgression or blood, as in paganism. This is repeatedly proposed as an explanation for self-righteous violence in the novels. Since, however, there is no social, cultural or theological basis for such a law in the society described in the three novels, their conclusions seem inexplicably brutal or sinful.[19] The scapegoat principle operates successfully in the works, but the author hovers back and forth between the sacrificial and the Christian perspective, and the principle is obscured. The crowds in *L'Ensorcelée* and *Un Prêtre Marié*, and Mme de Ferjol in *Une Histoire sans Nom* behave instinctively as pagan sacrificers, but later they return to a Christian point of view, seeing their acts as sacrilege.

Notes

N.B. "I" refers to: Jules Barbey d'Aurevilly, *Œuvres romanesques complètes* (Paris: Editions Gallimard "de la Pléiade," 1973). "II" refers to Volume II of that edition.

1. Georges Bataille, *L'Erotisme* (Paris: Les Editions de Munuit, 1957), p. 54.

2. René Girard, *La Violence et le Sacré* (Paris: Editions Bernard Grasset, 1972), p. 146.

3. Joyce B. Lowrie, *The Violent Mystique: thematics of retribution and expiation in Balzac, Barbey d'Aurevilly, Bloy and Huysmans* (Genève: Droz, 1974), pp. 74-76.

4. Joseph De Maistre, "Eclaircissements sur les sacrifices," in *Les Soirées de Saint-Pétersbourg*, II (Lyon: Vitte et Pérussel, 1892), p. 300.

5. René Girard, *La Violence et le Sacré,* p. 76.

6. Bataille, pp. 134-137.

7. René Girard, *Le Bouc Emissaire* (Paris: Editions Bernard Grasset, 1982), p. 26. In *La Violence et le Sacré,* Girard explains and demystifies the scapegoat mechanism involved in sacrifice which, in primitive society, derives its efficacity from the fact that it remains mysterious. In *Le Bouc Emissaire,* he goes on to contend that the absence of this system in the modern world is responsible for the proliferation of socially disruptive, "reciprocal" violence. In no way suggesting a return to the artificial and cruel stability of the sacrificial order, however, Girard argues that the only chance for the survival of human society lies in non-violence, the lesson of the New Testament. De Maistre, on the other hand, proclaims the theological necessity and social utility of all violence, although he expresses horror at human sacrifice per se. The De Maistrean theory, which claims that the bloodshed of innocent victims helps redeem the faults of mankind, nonetheless comes very close to an argument in favor of human sacrifice for the benefit of society. His philosophy mystifies violence; it is regressive. Girard's progressive viewpoint demystifies violence.

8. René Girard, *La Violence et le Sacré,* p. 22.

9. René Girard, *La Violence et le Sacré,* p. 64.

10. René Girard, *La Violence et le Sacré,* p. 417.

11. René Girard, *La Violence et le Sacré,* p. 29.

12. This interpretation is confirmed in the New Testament, Matthew 20, 28: ". . . the Son of man came not to be served but to serve, and to give his life as a ransom for many." *The New Oxford Annotated Bible with the Apocrypha* (New York: Oxford University Press, 1973), p. 1198. It remains true, moreover, both in the perspective of René Girard, (("Dans les Evangiles, la passion nous est bien présentée comme un acte qui apporte le salut à l'humanité, mais nullement comme un sacrifice." René Girard, *Des choses cachées depuis la fondation du monde* (Paris: Editions Grasset et Fasquelle, 1978), p. 204.)) and in the official Catholic version: "Consequently, the sacrifice of the Cross, at which Christ functions as sole priest, must likewise be referred to the free offering of His blood for us men, inasmuch as the Redeemer, while outwardly submitting to the forcible shedding of His blood by His executioners, simultaneously offered it to God in the spirit of sacrifice." *The Catholic Encyclopedia* (New York: The Encyclopedia Press, 1913), vol. 13, p. 317. It implies no "sacralization of the crucifixion."

13. Naomi Schor, *"L'Ensorcelée* ou la Scandalisée," *Modern Language Notes,* 94 (1979), p. 731.

14. De Maistre, p. 161.

15. René Girard, *Le Bouc Emissaire,* p. 16-17.

16. René Girard, *La Violence et le Sacré,* pp. 13-26.

17. William Robertson Smith, *Lectures on the Religion of the Semites* (1889; rpt. n.p.: New Matter, 1969), p. 16.

18. René Girard, *Le Bouc Emissaire,* pp. 79-80.

19. The notion that the moral law is based on passion returns in *Le Bonheur dans le Crime,* where the author finds a cultural setting in which to illustrate it: 16th century France. The marriage law derives its meaning from the offenses (duels, adultery) which, representing its "other side," place it in relief. The narrator of the story reproaches modern French society for having replaced the sacred, passion-based law with a profanely legalistic law: "Dans nos plates moeurs, où la loi a remplacé la passion . . ." (II, p. 105). Even though this story concerns adultery rather than mob violence, it illuminates in retrospect the moral problem raised in the three novels.

Nichola Anne Haxell (essay date fall 1987)

SOURCE: Haxell, Nichola Anne. "Barbey d'Aurevilly, 'Creative Critic' of Baudelaire." *Symposium* 41, no. 3 (fall 1987): 174-87.

[*In the following essay, Haxell evaluates Barbey d'Aurevilly's development as a literary critic, focusing on his unpublished review of Charles Baudelaire's* Les fleurs du mal.]

1857 SAW a neatly executed *quid pro quo* between Barbey D'Aurevilly and Baudelaire that reflected their dual vocations as campaigning literary critics and creative artists. Barbey's assessment of *Les Fleurs du Mal* is well known. Written in July 1857 (but never in fact published), it was, nonetheless, cited at Baudelaire's trial later in the year by lawyers for the defense, as an "article justificatif." This was presumably because of its sensitive appreciation of Baudelaire's moral and aesthetic concerns, but also because of Barbey's own reputation (in Baudelaire's words) as "un écrivain absolument catholique, autoritaire et non-suspect" ("Notes pour mon avocat," *OC* [*Œuvres Complètes*], i, 195).[1] A few months later Baudelaire replied with a brief but vivid analysis of the Aurevillian novel. This appeared in an article on *Madame Bovary,* which had itself fought prosecution in February of that same year.

Rosemary Lloyd has recently investigated Baudelaire's "creative criticism"[2] as an arena where exegesis and evaluation can "cross-fertilize with the literary imagination" (p. 40), and "exploration of another's style" interact with "[the] refinement of one's own" (p. 38). To illustrate Baudelaire's mastery of the single-sentence, throw-away "pastiche d'admiration" she quotes from this 1857 assessment of Barbey d'Aurevilly the novelist, or rather, of one of Barbey's narrative styles—that of myth-making and passionate ferment: "D'Aurevilly, vrai catholique, évoquant la passion pour la vaincre, chantant, pleurant et criant au milieu de l'orage, planté comme Ajax sur un rocher de désolation et ayant toujours l'air de dire à son rival—homme, foudre, dieu ou matière—enlève-moi, ou je t'enlève" (*OC*, ii, 78). What Lloyd identifies as the interaction of interpretative assessment and autonomous creativity is also present, as this article will seek to demonstrate, in Barbey d'Aurevilly's own critical writings. The *Fleurs du Mal* review is a case in point. Quite apart from the role it played in reinforcing Baudelaire's poetic credentials at this critical time, the review is important for Barbey's own development as a literary critic. It was one of his first full-length studies of a contemporary poet (following articles in 1856 on Hugo and Banville), and as such was crucial in establishing the paradigm for his subsequent appraisals of other poetic works. At the formal level, it served as an initial presentation of certain images and metaphors that would recur in, and indeed come to dominate, later critical writings on poets and poetry.

The primary mechanism that permits the exercise of creative criticism in Baudelaire's work, isolated by R. Lloyd, is that of pastiche. In the illustration quoted above, this involves a reconstruction of Barbey's thematic and metaphoric repertoire of untamed land- and soul-scapes, frenetic passions, and spiritual defiance or construction (familiar to readers of *Une Vieille maîtresse* and *L'Ensorcelée*). Also featured is what Proust identified in his own pastiches as "[le] jeu de reproduire, avec l'allure générale de la pensée, la même gesticulation de style".[3] The constituent elements of Baudelairian pastiche, on the basis of the "Barbey" example and others, can be said to include the following: admiration for one's model and an explicit intention to convey the essence of that model; the desire to emulate principally stylistic features; the exercise of one's own technical skills, and—that mark of a true critic—the capacity to enter into and absorb the work of one's subject.

R. Lloyd tends to equate the exercise of creative criticism with the particular medium of pastiche. My analysis, however, will employ "creative criticism" as the generic term. In part this avoids the persistent suggestion of ludism present in any reference to "pastiche": it also helps to clarify the distinctions between Baudelarian and Aurevillian approaches and achievements in this domain. Not all the elements constituting R. Lloyd's definition of Baudelarian pastiche are present in Barbey's critical work. The major distinction is this: despite his reputation as a responsible and well-seasoned critic, Barbey turns inwards, more frequently than does Baudelaire, away from a critical communion with his "host" subject and towards an autoreflexive identification with, and reiteration of, his own creative concerns. Self-generative and self-nourishing, Barbey's creative criticism could be viewed by the unsympathetic as more properly anti-creative, since it is forever restating familiar concerns and permits little expansion of stylistic or thematic horizons through emulation of his Subject. In this respect his output diverges from the generative capacity of Baudelaire's criticism and from pastiche itself. As used in this article, the term "creative criticism" refers to the percolation of features from an author's novelistic or poetic repertoire into the more analytical format of his criticism. In general, it can be applied to any attempt to turn critical *reaction* into literary *action*.[4]

The Aurevillian process of creative criticism can be illustrated by three passages taken from the *Fleurs du Mal* review. These cover an intuitive analysis of the work's structure, a discussion of Baudelaire's style and language, and a thumb-nail sketch of two particularly accomplished poems. In each instance the critical response is linked to Barbey's own creative works and is conveyed through an image from sculpture and statuary, frequently that of marble. It is interesting that Rosemary Lloyd herself employs a similar image of substance and materiality to describe the practice of creative criticism in Baudelaire's portrait of Barbey: "all these elements of Barbey d'Aurevilly's style are caught like wasps in the amber of a single sentence" (p. 39).

The first passage places Baudelaire's imagery, diction and prosody in the service of his "architecture secrète": not that rigorous and austere construction of theme and tone through which Barbey himself had uncovered the collection's pitiless didacticism, but, on the contrary, an ornate and decadent model here applied to formal concerns of syntax and language-structure:

> Figurez-vous cette langue, plus plastique encore que poétique, maniée et taillée comme le bronze et la pierre, et où la phrase a des enroulements et des canelures; figurez-vous quelque chose du gothique fleuri ou de l'architecture moresque appliqué à cetter simple construction qui a un sujet, un régime et un verbe. . . .
>
> (*OH* [*Les œuvres et les hommes*], xxiii, 105)

Images of metal and mineral and their artistic confection are conveyed in the two parallel clauses ("Figurez-vous . . . figurez-vous . . .")—language as substance, and language as structure, both decadently complex and ornate. In the first, its formative properties are presented: resilient to the artist's creative will, it requires the same crafting and polish as would a stone block or bronze casting. Contrasts of texture and density (as between stone and bronze) are echoed in the second sequence where language is viewed in the service of design and structure. Here also, two images are presented as being equally valid—the florid architecture of high medieval Catholicism and/or the elaborate tracery of Moorish styling; Christianity and/or Islam; stone carving, shadow, burnished metal and/or filigree arabesques of light and space. Neither image-sequence is especially germane to Baudelaire's poetic universe (hence neither are pastiches), but both are employed by Barbey in his own. For example, the gothic virtuosity of his description of nightfall in the nave which opens the account of **"A un diner d'athées"** (*ORC* [*Œuvres Romanesques Complètes*], ii, 173-75), and the claustrophobic bedroom of insomnia and delirium in the prose-poem **"Les Yeux caméléons"**: "La goutte d'or filtra le long des lambris sombres et, tombant comme une larme dans ma glace frissonnante au fond de son cadre d'ébène, attacha sa faible étincelle jusque sur la pointe des genoux crispés du noir crucifix de bronze" (1209-10); alternatively, the ornamental stylization of **"Les Arabesques d'un tapis"**: "La ligne mystérieuse et fantasque courait, se tordait, s'allongeait, se carrait, et prenait toutes les formes d'une géométrie impossible . . ." (1213).

In the second extract, Barbey conveys his appreciation of two of Baudelaire's poems, again through images of sculpture and stone: "la pièce *La Géante,* ou [dans] *Don Juan aux Enfers,*—un groupe de marbre blanc et noir, une poésie de pierre (*di sasso*) comme le Commandeur" (*OH,* xxiii, 106). Evoking the legend of Don Juan in terms of a stone statue ("grand homme de pierre": "Don Juan aux Enfers," *OC,* i, 20) is perhaps predictable; "La Géante" is a "magnifique[s] forme[s]" and hence undisputedly statuesque, but the image of black and white marble is unexpected.

On one level it does schematize the *chiaroscuro* oppositions present in "Don Juan aux Enfers": "sombre, noir firmament, front blanc, brillât, deuil, flot noir." It also translates in terms of color symbolism, the "double postulation simultanée" present throughout the *Fleurs du mal*: the confrontation or alternation of absolute oppositions (Spleen/Idéal, bien/mal, beau/laid) leading to the reconciliation of such irrefutably contradictory elements through poetic creation. Georges Poulet explores Baudelaire's interplay of light and shadow in *Les Fleurs du Mal* as evidence of the poet's transcendent vision. His conclusions on "Chanson de l'après midi" are equally valid for "Don Juan aux Enfers"—as for Barbey's marble image itself: "la dichotomie [noirceur/clarté] est extrêmement nette. Elle ressemble à une de ces oppositions entre blanc et noir, si fréquente dans la poésie pétrarquiste ou baroque. Néanmoins la poésie baudelairienne tend plus souvent à suggérer une complicité équivoque entre la lumière et la nuit."[5]

It is of interest for this study that Barbey's image of baroque marble formations predates by almost a decade Baudelaire's own appreciation of the ecclesiastical architecture of Brussels and Antwerp in *Pauvre Belgique.*

In several of his notes, attention is drawn to the frequent use of black and white marble for funerary monuments: "Deuil en marbre (noir et blanc)" (*OC,* ii, 943, 949) and a particularly fine example of the genre, the tomb of Charles d'Hovye in the Béguine church of Brussels: "Un squelette blanc se penchant hors d'une tombe de marbre noir suspendue au mur" (p. 945). *Les Fleurs du Mal* of 1857 has a single reference to this sepulchral property of marble: "Lorsque tu dormiras, ma belle ténébreuse / Au fond d'un monument construit en marbre noir" ("Remords posthume," 34), but the motif is amply developed in *Pauvre Belgique* where it serves as a vital ingredient in Baudelaire's analysis of the "style jésuite" (or "jésuitique"). The definition-by-enumeration that he proposes is one of Baroque rhetoric and dramatic oppositions: "Je suis belle, ô mortels! comme un rêve de pierre, / Et mon sein, où chacun s'est meurtri tour á tour, / Est fait pour inspirer au poète un amour / Eternel et muet ainsi que la matière" (21). The theme recurs in the dispassionate charms of his corrupt and corrupting Muse: "Ranimeras-tu donc tes épaules marbrées / Aux nocturnes rayons qui percent les volets?" ("La Muse Vénale", 15é), and in the warmer image of the caressed body of his mistress-idol ("Sur ton beau corps poli comme le cuivre") in the condemned poem "Le Léthé" (156).

The most famous of Baudelaire's *femmes-statues,* however, date from 1859: Andromaque, in "Le Cygne," and the woman of "Le Masque". The frigid but triumphal beauty of mistress and Muse has here been replaced by statuesque symbols of grief and mourning, figures that R. D. E. Burton interprets as "incarnation[s] of a universal, unending and irredeemable grief":[6]

> Pauvre grande beauté! le magnifique fleuve
> De tes pleurs aboutit dans mon coeur soucieux;
> Ton mensonge m'enivre, et mon âme s'abreuve
> Aux flots que la Douleur fait jaillir de tes yeux!
>
> ["Le Masque," 24]
>
> L'immense majesté de vos douleurs de veuve
>
> ["Le Cygne," 85]

The statuary frame of reference in "Le Masque" is uncontrovertible, since it was inspired by Baudelaire's admiration for Ernest Christophe's 1858 statuette, *La Comédie humaine,* and this is made explicit in the poem's subtitle and dedication: "Statue allégorique dans le goût de la Renaissance. A Ernest Christophe, statuaire." As for Andromaque, it is the marmoreal quality of her evocation that establishes the theme. Victor Brombert has isolated, as evidence, the nominal mode of stanza ten: "Andromaque, des bras d'un grand époux tombée, / Vil bétail, sous la main du superbe Pyrrhus, / Auprès d'un tombeau vide en extase courbée; / Veuve d'Hector, hélas! et femme d'Hélénus," which fixes the image outside time and tense in a static conformation.[7] Both these figures, immovable in their desolation and mourning, are representative of a familiar classical model and frequent artistic allegory for female grief, that of Niobe. The legend tells of a fertile mother, whose fourteen children were destroyed by the gods because of her maternal arrogance and *hubris,* and who, distraught with grief, was eventually transformed into a marble statue. Barbey's analysis of the moral and artistic aims of *Les Fleurs du Mal* (in the third passage from his 1857 article) is intrinsically bound up with his own creative exploitation of the Niobe myth and iconography.

At first sight, Barbey's summation of the "moralité, inattendue, involontaire peut-être, mais certaine, qui sortira de ce livre cruel et osé" [*OH,* xxiii, 99] has little relationship with the image of Niobe: "Le poète, terrible et terrifié, a voulu nous faire respirer l'abomination de cette épouvantable corbeille qu'il porte, pâle canéphore, sur sa tête, hérissée d'horreur [*OH,* xxiii, 100]." The single sentence would certainly be a pastiche as defined by Rosemary Lloyd, since it incorporates (and in the appropriate lexicon) many of the *leitmotifs* of Baudelaire's collection: the tension of contrast and contradiction present in the *Fleurs du Mal* title and the work's bifrontal dynamic structure ("Spleen et idéal": "terrible et terrifiée"); the flower-image itself ("respirer," "corbeille," "canéphore,") and the metaphor, used earlier in the analysis, of "fleurs horribles de fauve éclat et de senteur" (p. 98), as well as that of "mal" ("terrible," "abomination," "épouvantable," "hérissée d'horreur"). Present also is the poet's moral responsibility in exposing the horrors of such vice and corruption: "porte, pâle . . . sur sa tête," an image of guilt, solemnity and burden conveyed in similar terms in the admission, "on n'a rien vu de plus tragique que la tristesse de cette poésie coupable, qui porte le faix de ses vices sur son front livide" (p. 100); and a craftsman's concern for mood and expression through language: the fearful gasps of "hérissée d'horreur," the relentlessly repeated plosives: "poète, respirer, abomination, épouvantable, corbeille, porté, pâle."

Close parallels of theme and diction link this critical assessment with a short passage from a prose-poem written by Barbey in 1844 (but probably revised in the 1850s in preparation for a privately published edition of several of his poems) entitled **"Niobé."** In a sequence of ten prose stanzas, Barbey develops and intertwines three representatives of Niobé, three time scales, and references to two "real" women. The poem's opening is set in Barbey's present reality as he admires a cameo of Niobé which his companion is wearing in her hair: "Pâle camée de ton diadème, [. . .] cette inerte figure de Niobé, mise comme parure sur un front jeune," (*ORC,* ii, 1203). Memories are evoked of a fondly familiar bust of Niobé from his childhood home: "Il y avait, dans un angle obscur de salmigandis, jeu d'échecs, chandeliers, boudoir mystique et terrible, deuil en marbre, confessionaux théâtraux, théâtre et boudoir, gloires

et transparents, anges at amours, apothéoses et béatifications . . . (949)." When a sober rigorism is coupled with the luxurious abandon of the Baroque, the result is an intensely dramatic atmosphere of confrontation between the forces of evil and the glory of the Church triumphant. These characteristics of the Jesuit aesthetic ideal are, *in petto,* and in spiritual rather than explicitly religious terms, the ideals of Baudelaire's poetic-cum-redemptive quest in *Les Fleurs du Mal.*[8] Barbey recognized this spiritual dimension in the work of the poet "[qui] ne se croit pas chrétien et qui, dans son livre, positivement ne veut pas l'être" (*OH,* xxiii, 103), and sought to encapsulate it in the lapidary critical/creative image of "un groupe de marbre blanc et noir, une poésie de pierre."

In spite of his proclamation of the inadequacies of sculpture and statuary in general (in the *Salon de 1846*: "Pourquoi la sculpture est ennuyeuse . . . ," [*OC,* ii, 487-49]),[9] the theme of woman-as-statue is developed in several poems from the Jeanne Duval cycle of *Les Fleurs du Mal,* composed in the late 1840s. It is present in the impassive and statuesque dedicatee of "Je te donne ces vers": "O toi, qui, comme une ombre à la trace éphémère, / Foules d'un pied léger et d'un regard serein / Les stupides mortels qui t'ont jugée amère, / Statue aux yeux de jais, grand ange au front d'airain" [411], as in the inscrutable model of "La Beauté": "la maison paternelle, un buste blanc, noyé dans l'ombre . . ." (p. 1204). This bust is dually associated with motherhood: Niobé, the prolific mother ("seins au vent . . . calices d'albâtre auxquels j'ignorais que quatorze enfants avaient bu"), and the poet's own ("les cheveux relevés et tordus négligemment derrière la tête, comme j'avais vu souvent ma mère, le matin"). Simultaneously there is rejection of the mother-figure ("Je préférais l'intrépide contour de cette lèvre entr'ouverte et muette, mate et pâle, sans souffle et glacée . . . à celle qui, rouge de vie et chaude de tendresse me tiédissait le front chaque soir," 1205). Memories of pubescent sexual awakening are evident in correspondence with Trebutien as in a later verse treatment of the Niobé theme: "Car ce buste, ce fut . . . oui! mon premier amour, / Le premier amour fou de mon coeur solitaire" ("Le buste jaune," 1188), and "ce buste que j'avais tant regardé dans mon enfance en suçant mon pouce jusqu'au sang" (*CG* [*Correspondance Générale*], ii, 196). In this way the psychological stage is set for the succession of *fantasmes marmoréens/femmes statufiées*[10] idealized in his private life and present throughout his narratives.[11]

After Niobé as cameo and as bust, the third representation of Niobé as icon from Greek mythology is introduced. She serves as that symbol for maternity, grief and impassive beauty that had become an integral part of Barbey's psychological and literary trousseau. According to the sentiments expressed in the poem, Niobé represents an aesthetic model and moral code based on an idealized past more valid and "real" than the life and society which surround him:

C'est bien Elle; c'est bien cette physionomie unique dans les temps anciens, où l'étincelante beauté était seule adorée . . . C'est bien Elle, la seule triste, la seule pâle que j'aie vue parmi tous ces visages riants et gracieux, ceints de guirlandes ou courbés sous le poids des corbeilles . . . Image de la force morale, qui se détourne amèrement de la Providence pour ne s'appuyer que sur soi, ô Femme Antique, qui pense à ce que ton nom rappelle, dans nos jours légers et oublieux? Excepté moi, peut-être, qui te détache du front que j'aime, où la fantaisie, devenue sévère, te plaça, de préférence à une fleur . . .

(1204, 1206)[12]

The recurrence of the flower-motif takes the analysis back to Barbey's critique of the *Fleurs du Mal* and the striking similarity of treatment between mythological representation and living poet. For ease of comparison, the two passages are presented in parallel sequence, and to emphasize the repeated elements, certain key words are schematized:

Barbey: "Charles Baudelaire" (1857) [OH, xxiii, 97-123]	Barbey: "Niobé" (1844 and reviewed 1853) [ORC, ii, 1203-06]
"l'abomination de cette épouvantable corbeille qu'il porte, pâle canéphore* sur sa tête hérissée d'horreur" (p 100)	"étrange choéphore* qui portait sur sa tête maudite—mais toujours droite—ces grandes fleurs empoisonnées de la terre: la Douleur, l'Orgueil et l'Impiété" (p. 1204)

*canéphore: terme d'antiquité greque. Jeune fille portant des corbeilles en certaines fêtes. En architecture: statue de décoration avec une corbeille sur la tête (*Littré*)

*choéphore: terme d'antiquité grecque. Femme qui porte les offrandes destinées aux morts (*Littré*)

ETRANGETE: épouvantable	étrange
FEMME: canéphore	choéphore, Niobé [Vellini, mère]
FLEUR: corbeille [*Fleurs* . . .]	grandes fleurs empoisonnées
MAL: abomination, horreur, [. . . *du Mal*]	maudite, empoisonnées, Douleur, Orgueil (tête . . . toujours droite), Impiété
MORT: [fleurs funestes, p. 100; poésie sinistre et violente, déchirante et meurtrère, p. 106]	choéphore, empoisonnées
PALEUR: pâle [livide, p. 100]	[pâle camée, p. 1203; la seule pâle . . . La figure, sinistre et blanche, p. 1204; blanche figure, plâtre morne et blême, p. 1205]
PORTER: porte, (cané)-phore	portait, (choé)-phore
STATUE: canéphore [architecture]	Niobé, [buste]
TETE: tête hérissée d'horreur	tête maudite

At one and the same time a creative exploitation of various Baudelarian themes, and a reprise of memories and motifs present in his own poetic repertoire, Barbey's critique of *Les Fleurs du Mal* satisfies the criteria of "creative criticism." This interreaction of criticism

and creativity was doubtless stimulated by the particular association of blasphemy and the marmoreal beauty of despair uncovered in *Les Fleurs du Mal,* together with the centrality of the Niobé image to Barbey's mythology. That the confrontation of Impiété/Statue-Douleur is the principal generative force behind the creative critique is corroborated by two further reviews written by Barbey, one on Alfred de Vigny's *Les Destinées, Poèmes philosophiques* (1864), another on Louise Ackermann's *Poésies philosophiques* of 1873, both of which feature the figure of Niobé.

As Barbey develops and refines his Niobé over the productive years from 1844 (**"Niobé"**) to 1873 (**"Madame Ackermann"**), so the substance of the representation is transformed and progressively petrified. The plaster-cast bust from his Saint-Sauveur home ("cette blanche figure . . . du plâtre grossier et fragile," **"Niobé,"** *ORC,* ii, 1205) becomes "le beau buste blond,—d'un blond pâle,—en argile" of "le Buste jaune," recalled many years later, whose resilience and durability, both physical and psychological, compare favourably with subsequent human loves: "Tous les bustes vivants que j'ai pris sur mon coeur / S'y sont brisés, usés, déformés par la vie . . . / Leur argile de chair s'est plus vite amollie / Que ton argile, ô buste! immobile effigie / Et du temps inerte vainqueur!" (1189). In the later critical reviews, it is the strength and density of marble that predominates: "Niobé devenue marbre" (**"Alfred de Vigny,"** *OH,* xi, 355) and "Cette vieille Niobé . . . elle n'en a pas moins gardé *l'irréprochabilité* . . . de son marbre" (referring to Mme. Ackermann, *OH,* xxiii, 219).

The article on Louise Ackermann herself recasts the elements of the Greek legend into a modern formula. A fiercely independent thinker and poets remains defiant in her atheism but suffering through her awareness of the absurdity of an existence without the possibility of redemption: "cette femme mûre, calme et grave . . . est, au fond, quelque chose comme un démon . . . par la certitude de son impiété et la douleur de sa pensée . . . Elle y souffre comme toutes les âmes fortes, qui périssent d'orgueil, déchirées dans leur force vaine . . . Ces cruelles et sacrilèges *Poésies* . . . rappellent involontairement les plus grandes douleurs de l'orgueil humain, et on y retrouve comme un grandiose souvenir des yeux convulsés de la Niobé antique" [*OH,* 166-67]. The image of marble is used to convey the irredeemability of Louise Ackermann's damnation and despair (what Barbey acknowledges as the sublime dignity her metaphysical suffering bestows on her), as well as the purity ("irréprochabilité," xxiii, 219) of her apostatical vision, and its expression through language: "Ses blasphèmes . . . sont taillés dans un marbre radieux de blancheur idéale, avec une vigueur et une sûreté de main . . . le mode terrible de cette impiété, carré et solide comme un cube . . . sous le marbre de son expression" [*OH,* xi, 159-60]. The same criteria apply to the posthumous expression of Alfred de Vigny's poetic vision, *Les Destinées,* in 1864. Barbey identifies the "double caractère fatal et stoïque" (*OH,* xi, 357) of his last compositions where, as with Louise Ackermann, "philosophique" seems to be equated with "détourné des choses de l'âme" (*OH,* xxiii, 17). Their immaculate crafting of word, theme and tone is once again compared to a marble Niobé; but as opposed to the frenetic agonizing of Ackermann's defiant *alter ego,* the figure is here dignified and resigned to her suffering, as was Vigny (implicitly) to the approach of his own death, and Christ, to his imminent betrayal and Crucifixion: "dans une pièce intitulée: *Jésus au mont des Oliviers,* où l'âme du chrétien rouverte un moment, se referme tout à coup, redevenue rigide, je trouve ces vers d'une stoïcité presque impie: 'Le juste opposera le dédain à l'absence / Et ne répondra plus que par un froid silence / Au silence éternel de la Divinité.' Telle donc est l'inspiration dernière d'Alfred de Vigny; tel de sentiment amer, mais dompté, qui donne une beauté de douleur calme, de beauté de Niobé devenue marbre, aux compositions de sa vieillesse" (pp. 355-56).[13]

Barbey's tendency to depict a literary work's moral import or formal expression through an image of a marble artistic representation can be found in studies of other poets, including Pierre Dupont, Gérard de Nerval, Heinrich Heine and Maurice Rollinat. In his review of the latter's *Névroses,* this tendency simply takes the form of a reference to the visually descriptive nature of one poem, "La vache au taureau": "un groupe qui vaut le marbre dans sa plasticité et digne de la main de Michel-Ange ou de Puget" (*OH,* xi, 343). A certain delicacy and sensitivity of tone found in Nerval's *Œuvres Complètes* is the basis of a comparison between "le talent de Nerval" and (quoting Gautier) "un marbre grec, légèrement teinté de pastel aux joues et aux lèvres par un caprice de sculpteur" (*OH,* xxiii, 206). With Pierre Dupont, it is the facile quantity and vociferously proletarian nature of his poetry that offends Barbey's refined sensibilities and gives rise to the felicitous image of a marble gargoyle spewing forth torrents of loud and popularist balladry: "Je ne connaissais pas M. Pierre Dupont, et j'avoue que cette formidable gueule de marbre (pardon!) ne donnait pas une très-vive envie d'entendre les sons qui devaient en sortir, les chansons ou plutôt les clameurs que devait vomir cet effrayable trou de fontaine publique, creusé en plein visage humain . . . cette gargouille à vociférations de cabaret" (*OH,* iii, 240).

The final example in this series of Aurevillian "transpositions d'art" is from the critical essay on Heine [*OH,* xi, 111-23], which recapitulates a vast array of associations from the Niobé cycle of poems and creative critiques. Barbey wishes to evoke Heine's philosophical skylarking, a fish/fowl mixed metaphor, since Barbey himself uses a marine reference: "il se joue dans la philosophie comme le dauphin dans la mer," (p. 113) and his deftness and intellectual lightness of touch:

> Il allège la philosophie. Elle ne lui pése plus, ni à vous non plus qui le lisez, et véritablement il rappelle ces femmes qui ressemblent presque à des magies de ces maladies nerveuses et mystérieuses comme l'utérus dont elles sont sorties, lèvent une table de marbre de l'extrémité de leurs doigts tournés en fuseau et la portent comme une corbeille de fleurs!

> (*OH,* xi, 119)

It is curious how so many key "Niobé elements" can be densely packed into such a short passage: "marbre," "femme-mère" ["magiciennes, femmes, utérus"], "fleurs" ["corbeille de fleurs"], "mal" ["magies, malades, maladies nerveuses"], "étrangeté" ["mystérieuses"], "porter" ["lèvent, portent"], "transformation" ["tournés en fuseau"], but reassembled in such a way as to create an image far removed from that of dignified grief—one of hysterical table-turning!

This study has attempted to draw attention to an underestimated facet of Barbey's prolific (and well-documented) critical portfolio,[14] that of "creative criticism," where reflective or polemical judgment interreacts with the exercise of the poetic, imaginative faculties. My starting point is Barbey's famous appreciation of *Les Fleurs du Mal,* and the method chosen has been to trace the use and evolution of one recurrent metaphor, that of marble as artistic configuration (particularly the Niobé image), through his analyses of Baudelaire, Vigny, and Ackermann. Through my focus on critical studies of Baudelaire and other poets, and on the thematic links with Barbey's poetic output in prose and verse, I have attempted to complement the broader-based studies of Petit and Corbière-Gille on Aurevillian literary criticism. It also seemed a worthwhile exercise to test Rosemary Lloyd's analysis of creative criticism in Baudelaire by applying her definition and methods of approach to similar manifestations in the critical oeuvre of a close contemporary. There is certainly scope for pursuing the critical and circumstantial evidence which links Barbey and Baudelaire during the crucial year of 1857, the year that witnessed the publication of *Les Fleurs du Mal,* Barbey's sensitive review, the work's legal condemnation in spite of Barbey's approbation, and the inception of a quasi-regular correspondence between the two writers.[15] Eighteen-fifty-seven is also significant as the year in which both writers published inaugural formulations of the prose-poetic enterprise each was undertaking independently.[16] The foregoing analysis has traced the Niobé and marble themes through Barbey's prose-poetry, across the dividing line of his (creative) criticisms of Baudelaire's verse poetry in the direction of the latter's prose-poetic activity. In the process, I have hoped to reveal something of Barbey's attitude toward contemporaneous poets and his view of the theory of poetry and the practice of poetic composition, applied to his own works as to those of others. The question of his personal interpretation of the role of a literary critic is open to discussion, as are his views on the essence and function of criticism itself.

One of Barbey's most developed statements on the latter issue is to be found in his early review of Charles Monselet's *Œuvres diverses* (1854). To convey the skeptical attitude of Monselet and his clique of fellow artists who despise what they consider the sterile exercise of criticism and whose pride in their own achievements is overweening and "uncritical," Barbey first uses the image which is so regularly exploited in his later critiques of poetry and poets, that of Niobé: "Selon ces fiers esprits [qui ont la sainte horreur de la Critique, p. 47] qui, comme Niobé, ont l'orgueil de leur progéniture, même avant de l'avoir mise au monde" [*OH*, xxiii, 45]. Working with motifs of fertility and impotence taken from the Niobé legend, Barbey goes on to argue a strong case for criticism being accepted as primarily a *creative* activity: "Selon ces fiers esprits . . . la Critique est toujours une oeuvre stérile pour le moins, lorsque c'est pis encore: une envieuse occupation d'impuissant . . . [ils] n'ont pas vu ou n'ont pas voulu précisément l'emploi des facultés à l'aide desquelles l'esprit invente: l'observation qui cherche et l'intuition qui devine . . ." [*OH,* xxiii, 45-46]. Baudelaire's "imagination" is unrelated to the above definition of poetic "invention"; as such, Rosemary Lloyd's contribution on Baudelaire's creative criticism is also a valid one for Barbey's: "an arena in which he flexes his muscles, trains his reactions, sharpens his awareness of language and stimulates that queen of faculties, his imagination" (p. 44).

Notes

1. Abbreviations used: *OC*: Charles Baudelaire, *Œuvres Complètes* (Claude Pichois, ed.), 2 vols. [i, ii], (Pléïade, 1975); *ORC*: J. Barbey d'Aurevilly, *Œuvres Romanesques Complètes* (J. Petit, ed.), 2 vols. [i, ii] (Pléïade, 1996); *OH*: J. Barbey d'Aurevilly, *Les œuvres et les hommes,* 26 vol. [i, ii etc.] (Geneva: Slatkine, 1968); *CG*: J. Barbey d'Aurevilly, *Correspondance Générale,* Centre de recherches Jacques-Petit, 5 vols. to date (Belles Lettres, 1980-85). The place of publication is Paris unless otherwise stated.

2. R. Lloyd, "Baudelaire's creative criticism," *French Studies,* 36 (1982), 37-44.

3. Marcel Proust, *Correspondance,* P. Kalb ed., 12 vols. to date (Librarie Plon, 1970-) ix, 135 ("A Robert Dreyfus," 7 juillet 1909).

4. See M. Proust, note 3: "Quant aux pastiches . . . C'était par paresse de faire de la critique littérature, amusement de faire de la critique littéraire 'en action'" (iv, 61: "A Robert Dreyfus," 17 mars 1908).

5. Georges Poulet, *La Poésie éclatée* (PUF, 1980), p. 60. I am grateful to G. Chesters for drawing my attention to this analysis and to the Yves Bonnefoy article (note 6, below).

6. R. D. E. Burton, *The Context of Baudelaire's "Le Cygne"* (Durham UP, 1980), p. 58.

7. Victor Brombert, "Le Cygne de Baudelaire: Douleur, Souvenir, Travail," *Etudes Baudelairiennes,* 3 (1973), p. 257: "Rituel de la douleur et de la beauté: la strophe fige le personnage en une pose qui se prolonge dans un présent éternel."

8. Y. Bonnefoy introduces this notion in his discussion of Baudelaire's response to Belgian architecture: "intuition d'un couple de forces à la fois unies de façon intime et divergentes qui sans cesse se réaffirment. Et ce qui les signifie c'est l'opposition du blanc et noir marque de deuil, emblème de ce catholicisme que Baudelaire a réputé 'triste' . . . sa double postulation vers Dieu et la terre, ce qui scellait l'artiste dans son déchirement semble devenu le lieu même ou l'instrument d'une réconciliation à soi-même—d'un salut" ("Baudelaire contre Rubens," in *Le Nuage rouge* (Mercure de France, 1977), pp. 34-35).

9. "Pourquoi la sculpture est ennuyeuse" in "Salon de 1846" (*OC,* ii, 487-49). The issue is discussed by Marcel Raymond in "Baudelaire et la sculpture," *Journées Baudelaire, Actes du Colloque de Namur-Bruxelles, 1967* (Bruxelles: Académie Royale, 1968), pp. 66-74.

10. Philippe Berthier, *Barbey d'Aurevilly et l'Imagination* (Geneva: Droz, 1978), p. 158. For further discussion of this theme see: D. Mounier-Daumas, "La maternité, blessure et désir de mort," *Barbey d'Aurevilly,* XI (1981), pp. 49-65, and "Un univers de la stérilité," *Barbey d'Aurevilly,* X (1977), pp. 9-34; P. Tranouez, "L'Asthénique, l'Amazone, l'Androgyne," *Barbey d'Aurevilly,* X (1977), pp. 85-113.

11. Note the following allusions to Niobé from his *Journal*: "[Louise] c'est Ninon jusqu'à la ceinture. La ressemblance ne descend pas plus bas que ses hanches superbes, dignes de la Niobé antique" ("Premier memorandum," 8 novembre 1837, *ORC,* ii, 855); "La marquise *frappée de* pâleur . . . les yeux sombres, l'air vague, le sourire distrait, les poses appesanties, idéale enfin comme la Niobé" ("Premier memorandum," 12 juillet 1838, 926); "Allé flâner chez Ap[olline] qui a pris enfin une assez belle créature pour aide de camp. Trente ans, un teint blanc mat . . . cheveux noirs tordus à la Niobé" (22 novembre 1838, 933). Also those from his narrative works: *Le Cachet d'onyx* (1831), Hortense: "Cette femme que l'on avait vue fière d'elle-même comme Niobé l'était de ses enfants" (*ORC,* i, 8); *L'Amour Impossible* (1841),

Bérangère de Gesvres: "La femme et toutes ses ondoyances, ses morbidezzes, ses gaietés moqueuses, se remontraient dans cette grande statue désespérée parfois et silencieuse comme la Niobé" (*ORC*, i, 103); *L'Ensorcelée* (1852), Bernadine de Lieusaint: "ce corsage à la Niobé, auquel des grappes d'enfants devaient se suspendre" (*ORC*, i, 1002); *Ce qui ne meurt pas* (1853), Germaine de Scudémor: "cheveux bruns, tordus à la Nobé" (*ORC*, ii, 455); "devenue si bien la Niobé avec son éternelle impassibilité de marbre" (491); "grande Niobé qui n'avait qu'à l'âme le marbre éternel" (601). Silent heroines with flesh as white as marble, whose evocation resembles that of Niobé, abound in the narratives: Madame d'Angline (*L'Amour Impossible*), Madame de *** (*Un Prêtre marié*), Joséphine d'Alcy ("La Bague d'Annibal"), Hermangarde (*Une Vieille maîtresse*); see Berthier [note 12] for further details, pp. 157-64.

12. Note the phonetic pun: "courbé/corbeille," an infrequent but salient feature of his prose poetry, involving the ludic manipulation (or exploration of the poetic possibilities) of his prose.

13. Compare Barbey's use of the marble metaphor with Vigny's own, when he evokes the creation and construction of a poetic work: "Un livre, tel que je le conçois, doit être composé, sculpté, posé, taillé, fini et limé, et poli comme une statue de marbre de Paros. Sur son piédestal, tous ses membres doivent être dessinés purement, mesurés dans de justes proportions; il faut qu'on les trouve aussi pures de forme en profil qu'en face. Une fois, *exposés* en cet état sur le piédestal, le groupe ou la statue doit conserver pour toujours chaque pli de son manteau invariablement sculpté" (*Journal d'un poète*, L. Ratisbonne ed. [Delagrave, 1903], p. 260).

14. For a comprehensive survey of Barbey's critical output, see J. Petit, *Barbey d'Aurevilly, critique* (Belles Lettres, 1963), and G. Corbière-Gille, *Barbey d'Aurevilly, critique littéraire* (Geneva: Droz, 1962).

15. For details, see Baudelaire's *Correspondance*, J. Petit ed., 2 vols. (Pléiade, 1973), i. 280, 297, 305, 342, 494, 545; ii, 61, 475; Barbey's *CG*: ii: 283; iv: 62, 64, 102, 145, 156; v: 51, 85, 138, 152, 242, 243; see also *Lettres à Baudelaire*, Cl. Pichois ed., *Etudes Baudelairiennes* IV-V (Neuchâtel: A la Baconnière, 1973).

16. "Le Crépuscule du soir" and "La Solitude" had previously appeared in *Fontainebleau* in 1855, but it was only in *Le Présent* that Baudelaire gave a selection of such prose pieces a generic title.

Emanuel J. Mickel Jr. (essay date November 1988)

SOURCE: Mickel, Emanuel J., Jr. "Barbey's 'Poetic' Technique in *L'ensorcelée*." *Romance Quarterly* 35, no. 4 (November 1988): 415-34.

[*In the following essay, Mickel assesses the impact of Barbey d'Aurevilly's religious conversion on his later novels. Mickel attributes the predominance of supernatural themes in* L'ensorcelée *to Barbey d'Aurevilly's Catholic faith.*]

In his discussion of Jules Barbey d'Aurevilly's novels, Jacques Petit astutely remarked that *La Vieille maîtresse* represented a turning point in the novelist's career, for it was in this novel that he really discovered the manner and technique which were to characterize his subsequent work.[1] Professor Petit sees that alteration in the novelist's manner as a reflection of a basic change which had taken place in the author's life: his conversion to Catholicism. For Barbey conversion represented more than active membership in the Church as an organization. Catholicism became the living symbol of an order of society, a political system, and a philosophical perspective to which he was deeply committed. It represented an acceptance of himself and his past, a return to the memories and beliefs of his childhood. In becoming a defender of the faith, Barbey sought to retain, one might even say resurrect, and establish in his fiction a reality which was disappearing as a result of the advent of modern industrial society.

As Professor Petit notes, one sees the change in Barbey's manner in the second half of *La Vieille maîtresse.* In his letters to Trebutien, Barbey's longtime friend and correspondent, there is considerable evidence to support this thesis. In what sense does the second part of *La Vieille maîtresse* represent a new mode of composition for the author? Essentially it is not in the adoption of new themes or ideas. In his early work one already finds some of his favorite themes, such as incest and the impossibility of love. Rather Barbey finds the personal novelistic technique particularly suited to the development of his novels. Prior to the second half of *La Vieille maîtresse,* Barbey's novels were realistic in nature and did not manifest his later preoccupation with the "fantastique." In the second half of *La Vieille maîtresse,* he places greater emphasis on the supernatural influence of the vow sealed by an exchange of blood. The attachment between Marigny and Vellini transcends the realm of the psychological. There is a strong implication that the "blood-tie" exercises a power over Marigny which he is incapable of overcoming. Moreover, Vellini's magnetic hold on Marigny goes beyond her mysterious charm; the introduction of the magic mirror[2] suggests a link with the supernatural and lends credence to the suggestion that her hold over Marigny transcends the bonds of any human relationship.

It is also in the second half of *La Vieille maîtresse* that Barbey's abiding interest in Normandy becomes manifest, as he sets this portion of the novel at Carteret. For the first time the setting of the novel becomes as important as the action itself. But it is not a graphic, realistic description of Normandy which one finds. Rather, it is a transformed Norman countryside, an attempt to recapture a Normandy which Barbey sees through the eyes of his childhood. The author recreates a social and intellectual atmosphere which he considers the essence of the Normandy of his youth. More than that, he resurrects the old order, society prior to the ravages of the revolution. It is a Normandy transformed by his imagination, a resurrection of his past, a search for an essential reality buried under the avalanche of change.

If Barbey's early works were realistic in nature, such is not the case in the novels which follow *La Vieille maîtresse.* In *L'Ensorcelée* it is the "fantastique" which dominates. Following the second half of *La Vieille maîtresse,* Barbey again uses the Norman setting. Only his hesitant use of the supernatural in *La Vieille maîtresse* is replaced by a plot boldly set in an atmosphere filled with the suggestion of the supernatural. As Barbey wrote to Trebutien in a letter dated 22 November 1851, "il y a là-dedans encore l'audacieuse tentative d'un *fantastique* nouveau, sinistre et crânement surnaturel. . . ."[3]

In spite of Barbey's increased use of the supernatural, however, he continued to insist that he was interested in "le réel" and that his work was basically realistic. Professor Petit sees in the novelist's stance a realistic pose in whose reality the author himself comes to believe: "Son désir d'être 'réel' est une prétention, un masque, ou mieux une justification, dont il est lui-même dupe. La réalité ne l'intéresse pas; elle n'est qu'incitation."[4]

In my judgment this assessment emphasizes too strongly Barbey's departure from "le réel" and implies that Barbey's interest was only a pretense which he came to believe. In his earliest writings Barbey expressed a strong interest in reality and historicity. He consistently maintained that the novelist was a kind of historian. Gradually he seems to have formulated a clearer idea of what he meant by reality and of the relationship between reality, history, and poetry. It is my contention that the change in his novels is a direct result of his new understanding of the relationship between these concepts. However, only in *L'Ensorcelée* does he find a narrative technique which succeeds in accomplishing his ideal. But before discussing the novel, it is important that one understand Barbey's idea of history and poetry and their relationship to reality.

That Barbey was interested in gathering factual information on subjects about which he wrote is manifest in his letters to Trebutien. Basically his attitude in this respect remains rather constant, though he seems to recognize with time that he is seeking a special kind of information which he will use in his own way. In June of 1843 he requests details on Brummell and frequently asks about the countryside or seeks information concerning figures who were involved with the Chouans, such as M. d'Aché, whose physical description he requests. There was, of course, historical documentation which he could have consulted, but he was more interested in information gleaned from the inhabitants of the area. On 24 April 1850 he writes to Trebutien: "Consultez pour moi, dans votre pays, tout le monde. Walter Scott causait avec les postillons et les cabaretières. Des renseignements, pour être bons, doivent être pris à toutes les hauteurs de la société" (*Trebutien* [*Lettres de Jules Barbey d'Aurevilly a Trebutien*], Vol I, 171-72). True, his historical interest shows none of the care for scientific control of his sources; he seems unconcerned about the reliability of the information obtained. The reason for this, however, lies more in his concept of the truth in history than his willingness to set forth what may be untrue. It is true that Barbey replied to Trebutien concerning M. de Lasalle's review of his *Amour impossible*: "J'ai pensé que le romancier était un historien à sa manière et qu'il n'avait qu'à rapporter ce qu'il a vu ou ce qui est" (29 September 1843, *Trebutien,* Vol I, 56). But in the ordinary use of the word realistic, Barbey was never a realistic novelist, just as the realities which he sought to portray could not be considered historically reliable. Yet, he seriously considered his novels to include a truth in the historical sense, a truth more significant and accurate than the external details of a historical narrative.

What did Barbey consider historical? He was never patient enough to study a subject in the manner of a historian, carefully analyzing the extant documents and laying a sound foundation for reconstructing the events within the proper sequence in order to establish the correct relationships among things. In reconstructing the historical reality, the historian hopes to uncover the real motives and causes which led to the situation which he is studying and which determined the configuration of events. In this desire Barbey would have considered himself to have been the historian's counterpart or to have had the same goals. He too sought to discover the hidden motives of his "historical" personages, he wished to seize the essence of their natures, to recapture, for example, the collective soul or spirit of the people involved in the "chouannerie" movement. However, if Barbey's interest in disclosing the true essence of things accorded with the historian's goal, his method was clearly different, even unhistorical by scientific historical standards. To a certain extent he recognized his failing in this respect: "J'aspire tous les jours à devenir impersonnel et je ne puis" (16 September 1846, *Trebutien,* Vol I, 121). Not unlike Balzac, whose influence was great in this period, Barbey saw an intimate relationship between a character's personality and his mode of dress, physical characteristics, and speech. In seeking information on Brummell for his planned essay, he especially requested to be furnished with some of his aphorisms: "Les aphorismes d'un homme valent mieux que ses os pour le reconstituer ce qu'il était de son vivant. Avec un aphorisme de Brummell, je me fais fort d'être son Cuvier" (6 June 1843, *Trebutien,* Vol I, 48). In a man's aphorisms one perceives the distilled essence of his thoughts, the concise, vivid, and vibrant sayings which so aptly reveal the inner marrow of his being.

In perceiving the true significance of the aphorism lies the personal element which Barbey knew to be such an important factor in his method. That he was aware of this personal element and defended its validity in a historical sense is evident in comments to Trebutien concerning the proposed biography of Brummell by Captain Jesse. He notes that his essay will not in any way infringe on Jesse's work: ". . . je me suis mis à penser *sur Brummell* et sur le Dandysme bien plutôt que je n'ai écrit une histoire, fondée sur les commérages les plus incertains" (29 February [1844], *Trebutien,* Vol I, 71). His remarks disclose a scorn for the facts gleaned by a more historical method, which he calls "commérages incertains." His will be observations drawn from meditation on Brummell and dandyism. His material will be the items he considers significant and they will yield the inner truth to his own perceptive genius.

For Barbey the principal instrument of one's perceptive genius is the imagination. In fact, the imagination is far more significant than the information which he gathers about the place or event in question. In requesting topographical details from Trebutien concerning the "lande de Lessay," which Barbey confesses never to have seen, he stresses a confidence in the image of the area which he has formed from his childhood memories:

> Je suis bien sûr que je l'imagine telle qu'elle est, mais pourtant, pour me rassurer à cet égard, je voudrais bien quelques détails *topographiques.* Je suis persuadé qu'avec des impressions comme celle des récits de mon enfance et de l'imagination, on arrive à une espèce de somnambulisme très *lucide,* mais je voudrais que la lucidité du mien me fût attestée par une expérience.

> (1 May 1850, *Trebutien,* Vol I, 177)

In addition to pointing up his consistent concern that his personal assessment be in accord with an impersonal judgment, the passage highlights the nature of the reality he wishes to seize. The "impressions" which he has formed from the "récits" of his "enfance" coupled with the work of his "imagination" have given him "une espèce de somnambulisme très *lucide*" concerning the spirit, atmosphere, or true nature of the "lande de Lessay." Clearly the association with "somnambulisme" indicates that the image he has comprises a sense of the

inner reality of the "lande" which transcends any mere physical description of it. The underlined "lucide" refers particularly to the traditional veracity of visions seen in the somnambulistic state and thus indicates that there is an inner historical reality inherent in his vision. It is a reality which goes behind appearances, one which is synonymous with the essence of the "lande de Lessay."

Although he does not believe his novel on the Chevalier des Touches to be historical in the ordinary sense of the word, he does consider it historical (see the letter to Trebutien of 23 September 1850, Vol I, 208). Barbey conceives of the novel as a kind of historical vehicle which joins the ideal with the real. Some nine months later he reaffirms his belief in the historical nature of the novel in his response to Trebutien's lack of enthusiasm for *La Vieille maîtresse* (6 June 1851, Vol I, 232). He agrees that *La Vieille maîtresse* is not a historical novel in the sense of a *roman à clef,* but this does not negate the verity of its portraits or its essential truth. The novelist always draws his "idéal" from real life, from the blood and tears he has seen. In his artistic harvest lie the hidden realities which all great books conceal beneath their narrative surfaces.

It is not difficult to see that Barbey is drawing near to an equation of the poetic essence of things with their true historical nature. Just as the aphorisms of a Brummell translate his inner being, so does the "patois" of an area bear the historical essence of the people who use it: "La poésie, pour moi, n'existe qu'au fin fond de la réalité, et la réalité parle patois. Les langues sont le clavier des artistes: ils les animent, ils les idéalisent; ils en doublent, triplent, multiplient le jeu, les fonctions, la portée, et qui le croirait? le sens et même le son" (31 October 1851, *Trebutien,* Vol I, 273). Barbey's comment here on *L'Ensorcelée* recalls his earlier comment on the future *Chevalier Des Touches,* where he asserts that he will portray history but only "dans les fonds." However, in this quotation he equates this "fond de la réalité" with "la poésie." By means of the realistic detail (patois), the imagination perceives and creates the "fond de la réalité," the inner historical truth. For Barbey "la poésie" lies at the heart of this reality. In a letter to Trebutien on 1 January 1852 he exuberantly praises the poetic quality of *L'Ensorcelée,* while at the same time affirming that it is as much history as the work of the antiquarian (Vol I, 297).[5]

So much were the poetic essence of a place and its true reality synonymous in the mind of Barbey that the destruction of one necessarily entailed the elimination of the other. This is why he so desperately needed to create the reality of Normandy as he saw it in his imagination. By capturing the poetic essence of his beloved country as it was in his childhood (or as it was in his memory), he preserved it from destruction by the execrable enemies, materialism and progress. In September 1856 he revisited the Normandy of his youth only to find that it had indeed lost its poetry (see the letter to Trebutien of 12 September 1856, Vol II, 281). To Barbey it was not a question of facing the fact that the reality of Normandy had merely changed. Rather, Normandy no longer existed. The poetic essence of the true Normandy, its inner reality, was destroyed. The beliefs, the superstitions, the patois, the personality of a people and area whose roots extended into the Norman/Viking racial heritage were being obliterated by the levelling, homogenizing effect of the modern, industrial society. For Barbey the poetic, spiritual death of Normandy was in reality its historical demise.

* * *

In the second half of *La Vieille maîtresse* and in his subsequent novels, Barbey attempted to capture the poetic essence of a historical moment as it appeared in his imagination. As Hubert Juin has noted, "son instrument, c'est la poésie . . . son ambition: c'est l,épopée."[6] Barbey never completed all the novels which were to form a part of his "epic." Of those which he did write, *L'Ensorcelée* is the most successful and is unique among them, because he discovered a technique which was perfectly suited to the notion of poetry which he had conceived.

In the novels of this period one finds many of the author's favorite techniques.[7] In *La Vieille maîtresse, L'Ensorcelée,* the *Chevalier Des Touches* and *Un Prêtre marié,* Barbey introduces characters shrouded in mystery. The description of the countryside, the events which form the intrigue of the text, and the motives of the characters are all veiled in mystery. Beneath the surface of this mysterious atmosphere, one sees human passions seething, struggling against an adverse destiny which they at one time create and seek to overcome. He is fond of the shocking scenes in which the violence of these emotions is displayed. The mist which has covered both characters and events is no longer able to hide the gruesome explosion of frustrated passion. One need only recall the scene in which Vellini burns her own dead child on the shores of the Adriatic, the moment when Jeanne Le Hardouey's body is found, or the dreadful conclusion of *Un Prêtre marié,* when Sombreval digs up the corpse of his beloved Calixte and, like a raving madman, carries her off to the quagmire. Within the mystery Barbey suggests the influence of the supernatural, an element which lies beyond the power of the characters involved, one which makes them face an adversary of indefinable and superhuman proportions. As a result the text takes on an epic tone: one senses that he is witnessing a struggle between man and his destiny.

Each novel retains the framework so often used by the short-story writer. *L'Ensorcelée, Chevalier Des Touches,* and *Un Prêtre marié* are all tales told within a frame story. If *La Vieille maîtresse* does not use this mechanism as such, there is the long narrative of Marigny to Mme de Flers, which dominates the first half of the novel.

All of these novels include themes and techniques for which the author is well known. However, *L'Ensorcelée* differs significantly from the others in its narrative technique. While the narrative voice of the other texts is that of a "raconteur" who relates the events of a tale to his listeners, the narrative voice of *L'Ensorcelée* is much more complex. Strictly speaking, *L'Ensorcelée* does not have a single narrative voice.[8] It is a composite narrative assembled from the observations of many characters who participated in the events. But what is more important, not one of the persons whose observations are used by the narrator provides factual evidence which can elucidate the events or the motives of the main characters. In *L'Ensorcelée* Barbey created a text whose fabric is woven entirely out of "commérages." No longer does he look upon the "commérages" with scorn as he did in the letter of 29 February 1844 concerning the historical work of Captain Jesse. Rather, he had come to see the "commère" as a poetic figure whose imagination penetrated to the heart of reality. In the "commérage" Barbey found the poetic essence, that "fin fond de la réalité" which was the goal of his work. His comment on Nônon Cocouan who had "cet air ineffable et particulier aux commères" is significant. As Barbey notes, he does not mean this to be an insulting remark, "car les commères, après tout, sont des poétesses au petit pied qui aiment les récits, les secrets dévoilés, les exagérations mensongères, aliment éternel de toute poésie; ce sont les matrones de l'invention humaine qui pétrissent, à leur manière, les réalités de l'Histoire."[9] By use of her imagination the "commère" molds the events and ultimately distills the essential reality from them. Barbey's technique in *L'Ensorcelée* includes many kinds of what one might call "commérages." At the heart of his technique is the imagination, for the conclusion which is drawn is based ultimately on innuendo and not fact. Frequently someone in the text draws conclusions which come to represent beliefs. And, at times, it is the reader who must use his imagination to form his own conclusions. In the end, one believes that he understands the events and motives which comprise the tale, so certain is he that his conclusions are essentially true. Yet an impartial review of the factual evidence discloses that nothing has been established with certainty. Basically the motives and events of the other novels of the period are eventually elucidated by the narrator. If one never learns the secret of Jacques in the *Chevalier Des Touches,* he does discover the mystery concerning Aimée de Spens and her relationship with the Chevalier Des Touches. Throughout *Un Prêtre marié* one is never in doubt concerning the Abbé Sombreval's alleged conversion. Characters in the novel are duped, but the reader understands what he has done and why. Only *L'Ensorcelée* remains as a tale in which nothing is revealed through fact. The "truth" is revealed through the poetic device, the "commérage."

* * *

Essentially the introductory chapters of *L'Ensorcelée* remind one of the typical short-story writer's use of the conventional frame narrative to introduce the "true narrator" of the tale. It is a device which Barbey used for other novels and of which he was very fond, prompting critics to see him as a writer more at home with the short narrative than with the novel. But the first two chapters of *L'Ensorcelée* serve a more important purpose than the simple introduction to the tale itself. In them we meet the first character of the novel, the "lande de Lessay." The "lande" is more than an atmospheric setting in which the action takes place; it is a brooding, sinister, mysterious entity which has a personality all its own. That personality is the life and spirit of the Norman people buried in the depths of the barren marshes, hidden by the mists which enshroud the paths leading through the endless wasteland. Within the bosom of this timeless, spaceless "lande" lies the primitive, poetic essence of Normandy. To perceive this essence, the author cannot use the data of modern society. Only the intuitive insights of the imagination can capture the essence which is its true reality. To create the "lande de Lessay" for the reader Barbey uses the kind of "commérage" which dominates the entire novel. Nothing is fact. The character of the "lande" is created from the impression made on the imaginations of those whose testimony is used. Barbey himself has never seen the "lande" yet feels that he has its essence from what he has heard about it. In the tales of the "charretiers" one perceives the reality: "Si l'on en croyait les récits des charretiers qui s'y attardaient, la lande de Lessay était le théâtre des plus singulières apparitions . . . c'était là le côté véritablement sinistre et menaçant de la lande, car l'imagination continuera d'être, d'ici longtemps, la plus puissante réalité qu'il y ait dans la vie des hommes" (p. 557). In stark contrast with the down-to-earth peasant, rooted in reality, are the "apparitions," the hidden essence, the "fin fond de la réalité." Even the etymology of the name, Blanchelande, though shrouded in doubt and offering various possibilities, adds to one's "knowledge" only by analogy, through the intuition of the folk etymology and not through its actual derivation.

Barbey's own imaginative reminiscences from the "récits" of his youth and those "récits" transformed by the imaginations of the "charretiers" form one vision of the "lande." But even the events of the present chapter, while adding to one's impression, do not add any real element of fact. The *Taureau Rouge,* a real inn which the narrator encounters on his way, is known only by its ominous reputation as a meeting place for highwaymen.

The old lady who owns the *Taureau Rouge* adds to the lack of certainty which characterizes the "lande." In addition to the uncertainty of the roads through the area, the author's lack of knowledge concerning his route, and the growing darkness of the night, one is faced with the doubt concerning the old lady herself. Is she in league with the highwaymen and are her directions deliberately unclear?

Thus, in the opening chapter, Barbey evokes the nature of the "lande de Lessay" without stepping into reality in the ordinary sense of the word. Moreover, the essential characteristics of the "lande" coincide perfectly with the story we are about to hear: it is a remote place, apart from modern society, both mysterious and sinister, a poetic, timeless reality which has not lost its primitive nature, a reality of the imagination in which the supernatural becomes the spiritual extension of the natural.

If Barbey's introduction to "la lande de Lessay" is based on hearsay, such is not the case with Maître Tainnebouy, the peasant who will accompany the narrator throughout the night and who will relate the story of the Abbé de la Croix-Jugan. It is important to note that very little in the book is couched in factual reality. When such is the case Barbey inevitably has a purpose in mind. When introduced, Maître Tainnebouy is an unknown quantity. Clearly one might suspect him of being connected with highwaymen or in league with the owner of the *Tareau Rouge.* However, Barbey quickly dispels such an idea. Maître Tainnebouy's honesty, open nature, courage, and common sense quickly establish one's confidence in him. This is important not so much for allaying any fears concerning his companionship on the night ride, but to root the future tale in reality, despite its unrealistic qualities. Barbey has created an atmosphere in which the supernatural nature of the tale is acceptable; now he wishes to persuade the reader that the supernatural element is credible. One finds that the world of the supernatural is accepted as a part of reality by a level-headed, brave peasant who does not fear to ride through the "lande" alone at night. Throughout the novel the author departs from the narrative technique of using hearsay only to establish a realistic element important precisely because of its factual nature.

In the second chapter, two other elements of the story are introduced. Both are significant to the text, yet each escapes the clarifying light of day. It is interesting that when Maître Tainnebouy mentions the "bergers" who live in the area, he is able to tell us nothing factual about them, except to state that they live in that part of the country yet remain apart from the Norman inhabitants. Very little is known about their activities and way of life. Their reputation is formed from the deductions and intuitive assumptions of the Norman peasants. Not only are they of a different racial background (in the French sense of the term), but their origins are obscure.

The reality of the "bergers" is perceived only through the hostile, fearful impression of them in the minds of the people.

In speaking of the Chouans Barbey uses the same technique. One is left with an impression concerning their nature and purpose. Their very name implies the secrecy which surrounds the text. They were guerilla soldiers fighting an underground war and using assumed nicknames to hide their identities. It was a hidden army which rode by night. Thus were the soldiers called Chouans.

In the introductory chapters, then, Barbey establishes a background for his tale by means of the narrative technique which he will use throughout the novel. In Chapter 3 Maître Tainnebouy begins to recount the events which are designed to explain the meaning of the ghostly midnight mass performed by the Abbé de La Croix-Jugan. At this point Barbey multiplies the narrative voice of the text. One could expect to hear Maître Tainnebouy's version of the story gleaned from all the people who had contributed to his knowledge of the events. It is a tale composed of rumor, deductions, and innuendo complemented by the imaginative conclusions drawn by Maître Tainnebouy and his sources. Yet it is further complicated. Barbey's own imagination was so stirred by what he heard that he resolved to penetrate the true reality by further investigation (p. 584). What the reader ultimately hears is Maître Tainnebouy's version transformed by the original narrator himself.

The unique narrative technique which Barbey employs in the text can be seen clearly by following the development of the principal male character. By the end of the novel one is certain that he understands the true nature of the Abbé, his relationship to Jeanne, and the motives which caused him to act in the way that he did. This, of course, is exactly the impression which Barbey hoped to create. The reader should be convinced that he perceives the poetic truth or essence of the Abbé and of the drama. Only if the reader goes back over the narrative and reconstructs the reality from the reliable factual information provided does he perceive that his knowledge is based entirely on imaginative speculation, the intuitive judgment which is at the heart of the "commérage."

Seemingly Chapter 3 provides a factual background leading to the appearance of the disfigured Abbé at Blanchelande. Except for those rare scenes in which the Abbé himself appears and speaks, this background narrative is as close as one gets to an omniscient point of view. Even here, however, the facts are qualified by an element of doubt. Barbey's choice of vocabulary and use of verb tenses indicate the uncertainty in the narrative. The narrator describes the events not as one who knows, but as an observer drawing conclusions from what he sees.[10]

Ostensibly the Abbé has just left the scene of a great battle which has spelled the doom of his cause. In his despair he tries to commit suicide. Actually this is the assumption which the narrator and reader make. The text only shows a man hurrying along the edge of the woods. The narrator notes that he "paraissait brisé de fatigue. Il avait peut-être marché depuis le matin" (p. 585). Both the verb "paraissait" and the qualifying word, "peut-être," indicate the deductive nature of the conclusion. Similarly the narrator concludes, "ce devait être un Chouan" (p. 585), a conclusion drawn from his costume, his proximity to the woods, and an indefinable aura about him. Before the fact, the narrator surmises that the man is about to commit suicide: "Pour qui connaît la physionomie, il était évident que cet homme allait se tuer" (p. 588). His motive for committing suicide is related to his being a Chouan ("Selon toute probabilité, il était de ceux qui avaient pris part à un engagement de troupes républicaines et de Chouans . . ." [p. 588]), and this leads to the deduction that he is one of the leaders, for only a leader would be so committed to the cause. A final detail of importance is his attitude toward the "cachet de cire" of the parchment which he chews and swallows. The royal seal is the symbol of the Ancien Régime, the embodiment of his cause, emblematic of an entire way of life which is now lost. At least this is the conclusion which one draws from the narrator's own interpretation of what he saw:

> . . . on le vit contempler rêveusement, et avec l'adoration mouillée de pleurs d'un amour sans bornes, ce cachet à la profonde empreinte, comme s'il eût voulu graver un peu plus avant dans son âme le portrait d'une maîtresse dont il eût été idolâtre.
>
> (p. 589)

The key phrases in the passage are all subjective evaluations of the scene. The words "adoration" and "idolâtre" and the phrase "amour sans bornes" contribute to a conclusion which is especially important in view of later events. In fact, the deductions throughout this scene are influenced by the religious overtones of the vocabulary, and they temper our judgment of the Abbé's actions and motives in the rest of the story. Despite the paucity of real information, the reader believes (with some reservations) that the man is a dedicated Chouan, a devoted aristocrat who worships the old order and is capable of giving it a place ahead of God in his life.

Our next encounter with the Abbé occurs several years later after his attempted suicide, disfigurement by republican soldiers, and physical recovery. Because of his horrible disfigurement,[11] he keeps his face covered by the cowl as much as possible. In this chapter, one sees the Abbé through the eyes of his future "victim," Jeanne Le Hardouey. The narrator relates that she saw the strange Abbé "monter à l'une des stalles du choeur placées en face d'elle et s'y tenir dans une attitude d'orgueil sombre que la religion dont il était le ministre n'avait pu plier" (p. 600). The specific interpretation that his attitude was marked by an "orgueil sombre" is the narrator's account of Jeanne's reaction. The phrase is one of many such descriptions linking the Abbé to Satan.

> . . . il tenait un cierge, presque à bras tendus, comme s'il eût essayé d'écarter la lumière de son visage. Dieu du ciel! avait-il la conscience de son horreur? Seulement, s'il l'avait, cette conscience, ce n'était pas pour lui, c'était pour les autres. Lui, sous ce masque de cicatrices, il gardait une âme dans laquelle, comme dans cette face labourée, on ne pouvait marquer une blessure de plus.
>
> (p. 603)

The pluperfect subjunctive, "eût essayé," significantly adds the speculative reason for the Abbé's gesture. His marred face is the mirror of his disfigured soul. It cannot stand the light. His activities as Chouan are related to the darkness which enshrouds the actions of his soul. The rebelliousness which has caused his facial disfigurement is symbolic of a deeper rebellion against God. The overtones of these deductions are summed up in the comments of Nônon Cocouan, one of Barbey's "commères." She recounts the Abbé's arrival as it was described to her by Barbe Causseron, another "commère" who is employed by the "curé." Even when the Abbé arrived at Blanchelande, he had on the garb of the Chouans. One also learns that he had refused a bishopric from the new government (p. 605), wishing only to serve the king. Nônon's own assessment of the Abbé is reflected in her conclusion that she could not confess to this priest: "M'est avis que j'aurais toujours peur, en recevant l'absolution, de penser plus au diable qu'au bon Dieu!" (p. 107).

An excellent example of the "commérage" technique occurs in Chapter 9 (pp. 652-53) when Barbe Causseron's comments are used to reflect to what extent this Abbé had caught the imagination of the people. Their conclusions are dominated by the disfigurement of face and soul; one represents the wounds from his activities as a Chouan, the other his satanic association and rebellion against God.

In Chapter 6 one sees the Abbé through the eyes of the Abbé Caillemer ("commère comme il était," p. 625), a source which one might expect to be more factually enlightening. The Abbé Caillemer confirms the Abbé's activities as a Chouan and is scarcely concerned over them: "on n'aurait encore rien à dire s'il n'avait que chouanné, mais . . ." (p. 627). In these suspension points lie the real commentary of the Abbé Caillemer. He is, of course, thinking of the attempted suicide, the act of Judas Iscariot. The hushed tones in which he discloses the Abbé's act insinuate the diabolical association of the attempt. Because the Abbé is seen in satanic terms, his attempted suicide is viewed less in terms of an individual who allows his despair to shut him off from God's mercy than as a gesture of the supreme rebel who refuses to yield to God. The act of suicide here represents the refusal to live on other than one's own terms. Interpreted in this way, it is the Abbé's refusal to repent.

The next two chapters form a very important stage in the development of the text. Ostensibly one moves away from hearsay and innuendo and toward factual material. In these two chapters the reader sees the Abbé through the eyes of Clotilde Mauduit, known as la Clotte, an old woman who knows the Abbé personally from previous association and, more importantly, an individual favorably disposed to him. Moreover, the Abbé actually appears and speaks for himself in Chapter 8. Nonetheless, the facts themselves add little to one's knowledge of the Abbé's character. Rather, it is from the tone of voice, the deductions drawn from his attitude, and the metaphorical language that one derives an impression.

In Chapter 7 la Clotte speaks of the early days of the Abbé, using his given name, Jéhoël,[12] a detail which emphasizes his aristocratic background. Through la Clotte the reader learns that the young Abbé frequented without participating in the debauched society of Remy de Sang-d'Aiglon, seigneur de Haut-Mesnil. She also relates that one of the women, Dlaide Malgy, conceived a fatal passion for the Abbé, tried desperately to arouse his interest, and failed. Essentially the factual details which la Clotte recounts add little to one's knowledge of the Abbé's character and motives. One sees only the surface of a silent, enigmatic individual. However, la Clotte's own imaginative interpretation of the Abbé's personality plays a key role in the reader's assessment of the Abbé's true nature. In answering the question why he should associate with companions whose debauchery and bent for blasphemy made them so unlike him, she replies that it was his aristocratic nature which drew him there. He loved the hunt and felt at home among his own kind. But in the feeling of blood kinship, la Clotte perceives a key to his character. His aristocratic pride becomes symbolic of the rebelliousness which causes him to remain intransigent, a figure apart from his fellow man and even from the religion he has vowed to serve. La Clotte's description of the Abbé's reactions hints at his satanic nature. In those days he was young, yet even then "sombre comme un vieux. Jamais son visage ne s'éclaircissait" (p. 638). The adjective "sombre" and the timeless quality rendered by the noun "vieux" indicate that the Abbé's morose attitude goes beyond the melancholy of an ordinary young man. That his "visage ne s'éclaircissait," with the play on light and darkness, contributes to the impression of an individual whose disposition is unnaturally bleak. This might, of course, be the result of his unhappiness over the debauchery which he sees about him. La Clotte's further description of his silence dispels this notion. When his friends blasphemed, "il continuait de boire en silence, sombre comme le bois de Limore et froid comme un rocher de la mer devant les excès dont il était témoin" (pp. 638-39). Here the silence and somber demeanor are associated with images of coldness and hardness. In the adjective "froid" and in the two nouns, "bois" and "rocher," one sees the key to the Abbé's spirit. He is not outraged by what he sees but indifferent and impervious to those about him. When the Revolution broke out, this "man of the cloth" was among the first to disappear from his convent. This fact is less important than the rumors which la Clotte reports: it was said that he killed as many republicans as he had formerly killed wolves when hunting.[13]

Far from considering his failure to respond to the advances of Dlaide Malgy as a mark in his favor, la Clotte sees in it an extension of his pride and unnatural indifference toward his fellow man: "Jéhoël avait des pensées qu'on ne savait pas. L'acier de son fusil de chasse était moins dur que son coeur orgueilleux, et le sang des bêtes massacrées qu'il rapportait sur ses mains du fond des fôrets, il ne l'essuya jamais à nos tabliers! Nous ne lui étions rien!" (p. 641). In the first line one sees the fact, "Jéhoël avait des pensées qu'on ne savait pas." But by her imagery la Clotte interprets the enigma. The Abbé's heart or soul is as cold and hard as the steel of his murderous weapon. Even after the slaughter there is no pity, no wiping of the hands, no human fraternization. La Clotte gives her own interpretation to his lack of interest in Dlaide: "Nous ne lui étions rien!" The Abbé's indifference to women is not a result of his religious vows; rather, it is a mark of his satanic nature. Satan fell through pride, never through the seduction of a woman.[14] Such is the implication of la Clotte's comment on the principal quality of the Abbé's character: "Il était haut comme le ciel, et je crois que l'orgueil était son plus grand vice" (p. 638).

To further the portrait which has been drawn, Barbey causes the Abbé to appear mysteriously out of the shadows, as if called forth by the mention of his name. One cannot help but think of the famous proverb, "Speak of the devil. . . ." La Clotte herself is troubled by the supernatural aura of his appearance. This is one of only two times in the novel when the reader has the opportunity to hear the Abbé speak. Even so, it is not so much his words which add to our understanding of his character as the narrator's comments and his elaboration of what the Abbé's comments mean.

When la Clotte refers to him by his former religious name, frère Ranulphe, the Abbé replies: "Il n'y a plus de frère Ranulphe, Clotilde!" (p. 644). What this statement means is implied by the narrator's description of the Abbé's tone of voice: "dit le prêtre d'une voix âpre en jetant ces paroles comme la dernière pelletée de terre

sur un cercueil" (p. 644). The adjective, "âpre," accompanied by the simile, provides the key to the Abbé's attitude, one of bitterness rather than acceptance. Without the narrator's comments, the Abbé's following speech might be interpreted as evidence of his recognition of the errors of his past. Instead one feels that the priest in him has been buried (pp. 644-45). Even with the obvious tone of bitterness inherent in his denunciation of the revolutionary forces, there is room for believing that he has perhaps accepted the defeat which he and his cause have suffered. However, the narrator's description of the removal of his cowl leaves no doubt in the reader's mind. Ostensibly it is the final act to show the disaster wrought by the "vanités folles du vouloir humain"; nevertheless, the act and the disfigured face, symbol of the defeat, have the reverse effect. The majesty, strength, and beauty of the Abbé, inspite of his disfigurement, turn one's thoughts from his words to the rebellious figure still very much alive:

> Ses yeux, deux réchauds de pensées allumés et asphyxiants de lumière, éclairaient tout cela, comme la foudre éclaire un piton qu'elle a fracassé. Le sang faufilait, comme un ruban de flamme, ses paupières brûlées, semblables aux paupières à vif d'un lion qui a traversé l'incendie. C'était magnifique et c'était affreux!
>
> (p. 645)

In sharp contrast with the images of darkness which dominated the previous chapter and the Abbé's initial appearance, the current description of the hideous face unveiled is resplendent. The reader concludes that the Abbé has suffered an external defeat symbolized by his black habit and the cowl which covers his disfigured face, but the inner man remains undaunted.[15] The brilliance shines in his eyes, the power in his lightning glances; the heat of his passion is luminous in the flaming, heated blood, his thirst for vengeance in the image of the lion.[16]

Another device related to the "commérage," or which might broadly be classified under the same heading, is the author's use of the "pâtre's" magic mirror, his curse, and the prediction of the "tireuse de cartes." In each instance what is involved surpasses the world of realism and fact. The characters in question are sinister and are linked with an infernal, supernatural element. From a factual standpoint their comments would seem to count for little in establishing the reality of the supernatural and in the conclusions which the reader ultimately forms.

Barbey cleverly establishes the credibility of the "berger's" foreknowledge early in the text. Jeanne is returning from the mass where she first saw the Abbé and meets the shepherd on her way home. After a hostile exchange of words, the shepherd concludes with a prediction which clearly relates to the encounter she has

just had at mass (p. 620). There is no logical explanation for the prediction, except to conclude that the shepherd is aware of a destiny which awaits Jeanne. That
the shepherds are linked with the supernatural and can
see into the destiny of people is important in our assessment of the Abbé's suggested satanic association.
When Thomas Le Hardouey, the would-be rationalist
and son of the revolution, returns to seek vengeance on
the Abbé, he encounters the shepherds and comes to believe in their powers. In his hate he tries to persuade
them to cast a lot against the Abbé. They merely laugh
at him derisively, "car les sorts ne peuvent rien sur
l'abbé de La Croix-Jugan" (p. 719). When Thomas derides them for their lack of power, the shepherd answers, "Du pouvai! j'n'en avons pas contre li,—dit le
pâtre,—il a sur li un signe plus fort que nous!" (p. 720).
Le Hardouey tries to discover what they mean, but they
refuse to say more and remain ominously quiet. By his
handling of the shepherds and the scene, Barbey creates
in the reader, as in Le Hardouey, an implicit faith that
the shepherds have supernatural powers and that their
statements are true, even though unsupported by fact.
Even so, the shepherds do not actually divulge what is
meant by their lack of power against him and by the
sign on him. Nonetheless, the intuitive conclusion which
the reader draws is that the Abbé is closer to the source
of infernal power than they.[17]

Another significant element which should be included
in a study of Barbey's technique in this novel is the use
of the magic mirror.[18] It plays a dominant role as a catalyst in precipitating the events which lead to the fatal
mass, and its revelations remind one of the "commérages" themselves.

As the story develops it becomes clear that Jeanne loves
the Abbé de La Croix-Jugan. Initially one has only the
deductions of Barbe Causseron and the general opinion
of the townsmen;[19] eventually, however, the narrator
confirms their intuition (again adopting a tone of
omniscience) by informing the reader that she does indeed love the Abbé and later by having Jeanne confess
her love to la Clotte. But the more mysterious question
relates to the Abbé. Has Jeanne been bewitched by him
and does he have any love for her?[20]

Doubt concerning the exact nature of Jeanne's relationship with the Abbé preys on the mind of Thomas Le
Hardouey, Jeanne's husband. In his desire to know the
truth, he looks into the mirror provided by the shepherd. Ostensibly the mirror allows one to see things
happening at a distance. Yet nothing could be more dubious than what the mirror reveals. Essentially it seems
to reveal only the fears of the person who peers into it.
It represents a reflection of the assumptions and conclusions which the feverish, jealous mind has conceived
from the fragments of information and rumor which it
has heard. Thomas must wish to see his destiny for the

mirror to work. Furthermore, he must continue to tell
the shepherd what he sees for the mirror to continue to
produce an image. Although the actions of Thomas's
horse suggest a supernatural presence, the events in the
mirror are really the construction of Thomas's imagination. In fact, what he sees—the Abbé and Jeanne standing before a fireplace roasting a human heart on a
spit—is no suggestion that the Abbé and Jeanne are in
love, only that their association is literally roasting Thomas's jealous heart. What he believes about them has
the effect of the action depicted. There is nothing supernatural in the fact that the shepherd is able to comment
that the heart being roasted belongs to Thomas. What
the mirror shows is true; what Thomas's imagination
deduces from the "mirror's insinuations" is even more
important.

After Jeanne's death (was it suicide or murder?), Thomas disappears. He reappears just at the moment when
the Abbé de La Croix-Jugan, his penance completed, is
to perform his first mass. Thomas again encounters the
shepherds, who manage to suggest indirectly to Thomas
that only a bullet can stop the Abbé. When the Abbé is
shot during the mass, the reader deduces that the killer
must have been Thomas. Many things indicate as much
without so proving directly.

However, the greater question which remains unanswered stems from the account of the drunk "forgeron"
who witnessed one of the attempted ghostly masses
supposedly performed by the Abbé. According to the
blacksmith, who witnessed the scene through some bullet holes in the portal, the Abbé's ghost appeared to celebrate the mass again and again. Just at the moment
when he lifted the Host, the very moment when he was
shot in real life, he was prevented from continuing. To
this point one has only the facts of the event as they
were witnessed by those in the church. However, the
importance of the blacksmith's story lies in the interpretation which is made of the ghostly scene. Each time
the Abbé is unable to consecrate the Host, he undergoes
unspeakable agony and frustration. The scene thus becomes emblematic of the Abbé's life. Is not his failure
to gain absolution symbolic of his inability to repent of
his sins and to cleanse his soul? His frustration in being
unable to complete the mass represents his failure to
become a bona fide priest. Moreover, once one has become convinced of the significance of the ghostly mass,
a further deduction is reached quickly. Is there not significance in the fact that the assassin was not seen by
an eyewitness? The seemingly accidental details begin
to form a pattern. Thomas arrives by chance just when
the Abbé is to serve his first mass. His chance encounter with the shepherds provokes him and stimulates him
to action. Is it chance which has the Abbé shot just at
the moment when he was to consecrate the Host and
not at the mass's conclusion? The factual details of the
assassination, the alleged account of the mass, and the

drunken blacksmith's interpretation of the ghost's attitude conspire to persuade one that Divine Providence intervened. One is persuaded that the Abbé was struck down by God. The blacksmith's story and the important truth which is deduced from it recall one of Barbey's most significant comments on the nature of reality and truth:

> Ce qui sort de ces drames cachés, étouffés, que j'appellerai presque à *transpiration rentrée,* est plus sinistre, et d'un effet plus poignant sur l'imagination et sur le souvenir, que si le drame tout entier s'était déroulé sous vos yeux. Ce qu'on ne sait pas centuple l'impression de ce qu'on sait. Me trompé-je? Mais je me figure que l'enfer, vu par un soupirail, devrait être plus effrayant que si, d'un seul et planant regard, on pouvait l'embrasser tout entier.[21]

What is significant in this quotation is not merely the importance it places on the imagination in creating a literary effect which is striking and esthetically successful, but in accenting the imagination's role in perceiving reality as it actually is. To see hell laid out before one as if it were merely another setting might cause one to overlook the horror which it should inspire. To see it only "par un soupirail," however, focuses the mind on a few salient and awe-inspiring details. The stimulated imagination then completes the nightmarish reality. It is true that the reality of the imagination might well be different from that which an overview of the real hell might reveal. Barbey's point is that the external details of hell are less important than its essential reality. If the imagination makes the essential horror of hell vivid in the mind of the beholder, then this image has more truth in it than the object seen without horror in all its plenitude.

The factual element in **L'Ensorcelée** is indeed slight. One encounters an Abbé who has left his religious order to become a Chouan. In the opening chapter of the book he attempts suicide. Some time after his suicide attempt, he appears at Blanchelande as a penitent priest. Jeanne Le Hardouey falls in love with the Abbé and subsequently commits suicide or is murdered. Thomas Le Hardouey disappears at the time of her death and returns to the area on the day when the Abbé is to perform his first mass. The Abbé is shot while attempting to perform the mass which would mark his reinstatement.

The truth of the story is not found in the known facts, nor does the author play the role of an omniscient storyteller. The truth which lies beneath the surface of the text is derived from the hearsay accounts of various individuals whose intuitive remarks, imaginative embellishment, and silent innuendo constitute the essential substance of the tale.

In his other novels Barbey used various narrative devices to create the esthetic effect which he was seeking.

Only in **L'Ensorcelée** did he succeed completely in capturing that poetic reality which lies in the imagination beyond the realm of known fact.

Basically the novel is a text of "commérages" recounted by many "commères." The narrative of Maître Tainnebouy, the author's asides and analogies, the comments and facial gestures of Barbe Causseron and Nônon Cocouan, the innocent accounts of mère Ingou's child, the illuminating hypotheses of la Clotte, the hushed and fearful remarks of the Abbé Caillemer, the affirmative but strangely unenlightening assertions of the Comtesse de Montsurvent, the drunken vision of the blacksmith, the uncanny predictions and foreknowledge of the shepherd, and even the reflections of his mirror of destiny—together they comprise the substance of the text and provide the key to its meaning.

Notes

1. Jules Barbey d'Aurevilly, *Œuvres romanesques complètes*. Textes présentés, établis at annotés par Jacques Petit. Vol. I (Paris: La Nouvelle Revue Française, 1964). Citations from *L'Ensorcelée* have been taken from this edition. See also Jacques Petit, *Barbey d'Aurevilly Critique* (Paris: Les Belles Letters, 1963).

2. The magic mirror plays an important role in *L'Ensorcelée*.

3. *Lettres de Jules Barbey d'Aurevilly à Trebutien,* I (Paris: Blaizot, 1908), 278. Subsequent citations from the letters of Barbey are drawn from this edition.

4. *Œuvres romanesques* [*Œuvres romanesques Complètes*], p. xxv.

5. Barbey's concept of poetry has more to do with the effect and quality of the work than with any fixed notion of form. See his comments to Trebutien on the poetry of Maurice Guérin (II, 67). For further discussion of Barbey's conception of poetry, see Jacques Petit's work cited above and Gisèle Corbière-Gille, *Barbey d'Aurevilly* (Geneva: Droz, 1967).

6. Jules Barbey d'Aurevilly, *L'Ensorcelée,* texte présenté, établi et annoté par Jacques Petit. Préface de Hubert Juin (Paris: Gallimard, 1964), p. 17.

7. For a discussion of narrative technique in Barbey's novels see B. G. Rogers, *The Novels and Stories of Barbey d'Aurevilly* (Geneva: Droz, 1967).

8. In *Chevalier Des Touches* both the Abbé and his sister play the role of narrator. The narrations are sequential, however. The Abbé's only sets the stage for the actual tale related by the sister.

9. *Œuvres romanesques*, pp. 604-05.

10. The narrative stance of the author virtually places the reader in the same position as the narrator. He, too, is observing a series of surface actions whose connection and meaning must be supplied by his own imagination. In so involving the reader's imagination, Barbey accomplishes his esthetic objective. The reader himself perceives the essence of the story through his own imaginative reconstruction of it.

11. After shooting himself in the face, the Abbé is further marked by republican soldiers who spread burning embers in the open facial wounds made by the shot.

12. It is specifically noted that the Abbé's aristocratic friends deliberately used the name Jéhoël to remind him of his noble background. Barbey uses this name when he is stressing the conflict between the Abbé's aristocratic pride and his adopted profession as the humble servant of God.

13. The image of the wolf is intended to reflect the Abbé's own thoughts about the republicans and their desire to prey on the nobility.

14. This is precisely the response which la Clotte makes to Jeanne when she suggests that even a priest might be seduced: "'Les anges sont bien tombés!' dit Jeanne. 'Par orgueil,' répondit la vieille; 'aucun n'est tombé par amour'" (p. 670). Note la Clotte's further interpretation of Dlaide's attempted use of potions and Jeanne's reactions to la Clotte's interpretation.

15. The Abbé himself notes with acrimony that the white habit of former years is gone forever.

16. See p. 648. That the Abbé is not the confirmed rebel that one finds in *Un Prêtre marié*, despite the satanic associations, is shown in Chapter 13 when he comes upon the dying la Clotte. Although one sees the scene through the eyes of the narrator, it has none of the uncertainty of hearsay. The narrator here takes the role of the omniscient novelist, relating what the Abbé thinks and what he says, even though there was no one present to witness the scene. the Abbé blames the republicans for the old woman's death. Filled with hate, he mounts his horse, caresses and unholsters his gun as if to take vengeance. At this point one sees the sincerity of his desire to repent: "'Ah!' dit-il, replongeant l'arme aux fontes de la selle,—tu seras donc toujours le même pécheur, insensé Jéhoël" (p. 711). He reproaches himself, gets down from his horse, prays, and gives the old woman last rites. This account confirms one in his ideas that Jéhoël is still a Chouan at heart—his own use of his given name emphasizes the point. More im-portantly, it shows that Jéhoël sincerely wishes to repent. His later comment that both la Clotte and he have been led astray by "orgueil" indicates his recognition of their sin and his sorrow for it. He is a sinner stubbornly drawn to his sin while wishing repentance.

17. Similar confirmation of the Abbé's power comes from the fortune-tellers whom the desperate Jeanne consulted at the fair (p. 669).

18. Vellini's magic mirror plays a minor role in *La Vieille maîtresse*. It represents Barbey's first overt use of the supernatural.

19. The reader is referred to the scene in Chapter 9 where Barbe speculates on the reasons why the Abbé and Jeanne went into the "sacristie" together.

20. In Chapter 9 Barbey introduces the idea by telling the story of a seventeenth-century woman reputedly bewitched by the magnetic will of a certain abbé. It is no coincidence that the woman's name is Madeleine, also Jeanne's second name. Barbey treats the seventeenth-century account as if it were an accepted fact in an effort to establish the plausibility of such an occurrence. More important to the novelist, though, is the suggestive truth which he intends to impart by means of an analogy. The Comtesse de Montsurvent, a long-time associate and close friend of the Abbé, whom the narrator later consulted to obtain more factual information, rejects the idea that the Abbé deliberately bewitched Jeanne and categorically denies that the Abbé had any romantic attachment to her. It is interesting how little the Comtesse adds to the factual presentation. Although the Abbé made regular visits to her chateau, where he remained throughout the night, the Comtesse knows little more about him than the reader has already learned. In fact, her account only adds to the deep mystery which surrounds his true nature. In despair over the failure of his continued attempts at conspiracy, the Abbé sat in the same chair for hours on end in silence. One assumes that he was brooding over the lost cause; yet his somber silence, because it is so unnatural in both length and intensity, adds to one's impression that there is something not entirely human connected with the Abbé.

21. *Œuvres romanesques complètes*, II, "Les Dessous de cartes d'une partie de whist," 132-33.

Herta Rodina (essay date fall-winter 1995-96)

SOURCE: Rodina, Herta. "Textual Harassment: Barbey d'Aurevilly's *Les Diaboliques*." *Nineteenth-Century French Studies* 24, nos. 1-2 (fall-winter 1995-96): 144-53.

[*In the following essay, Rodina probes Barbey d'Aurevilly's use of repression as a storytelling tech-*

nique in the novellas Le bonheur dans le crime *and* La vengeance d'une femme.]

The publication and censorship of Barbey d'Aurevilly's *Les Diaboliques* reveal a dialectic of expression/ repression in the reactions of both the literary community and the author, a real-life dialectic that reflects, retroactively, themes and structures central to the collection itself. Using *Le Bonheur dans le crime* and *La Vengeance d'une femme,* I hope to show that the text develops by abuses of communication that harass the characters, the narrator, and by extension, the author and his readers. *Le Bonheur dans le crime* is distinct because it is the only story in the collection where repression of information allows a crime to be committed and apparently to remain unpunished. *La Vengeance d'une femme,* as the last story written, was closest in time to the author's state of mind at publication. In this text, eventual expression leads to the destruction of self and others. Examining the differences between the stories may help illuminate changes in the author as he faces a coincidence of fact and fiction during the censorship of his work.

To prepare for the textual analysis, we must first review biographically the stance Barbey adopted towards his readers. That his text becomes a target of social harassment will seem inevitable—but complicated by Barbey's own response to the legal proceedings begun against him. This response—retreat from and fear of scandal—is strangely inconsistent with lifelong attitudes and previous behavior.

From the outset of his career, scandal and provocation were an integral part of Barbey's artistic, intellectual, and critical stance. Although a fervent Catholic, as early as 1850 Barbey recognized that religion could repress art and that braving scandal was in a sense the antidote for this danger: "'Que notre catholicisme n'éclope pas l'Art de peur du scandale!'" (Boschian-Campaner [*Barbey d'Aurevilly*] 165). When the first *Diabolique, Le Dessous de cartes,* appeared in the same year, Barbey was already envisioning a collection featuring thinly disguised members of Parisian society:

> Mon intention est de donner deux ou trois nouvelles intitulées comme cette première, *Ricochets de conversation,* avec des sous-titres différents. Tous les personnages de ces nouvelles sont réels et à Paris, on les nomme quand je lis dans quelque salon.
>
> (Letter to Trébutien, 4 May 1850 in *Correspondance générale* 2: 156)

Scandal, exposition, the revelation of secrets, then, could also serve as a vehicle for artistic recognition. When this recognition was denied, when the *Revue des Deux Mondes* refused *Le Dessous de cartes,* Barbey's response was to increase the provocation. "Ainsi, mon

cher Trébutien," he wrote to his friend, "sous prétexte d'être un *incendiaire,* voilà que les portes se ferment devant moi (j'entends les portes de la Publicité!). C'est égal, je les forcerai. J'ai la patience de la colère rentrée, de la colère Eternelle!" (12 Jan. 1850, *Correspondance Générale* 2: 146). From 1850 to 1865, when he began the other five *Diaboliques,* Barbey acquired some of this much-sought-after publicity—not through scandalous fiction, but through the relentless acidity of his reviews of contemporary literature and drama (Bornecque [*Les Diaboliques*] v-vi).

Alongside Barbey's desire to provoke was an equally strong conviction that he was an outsider by virtue of his superiority, persecuted by the stupidity of his century. Writing to long-time correspondent Elisabeth Bouillet, Barbey comments: "Partout où je parais, . . . je trouve toute la bêtise humaine,—une forte armée! debout et en bataille contre moi" (2 Jan. 1880, *Correspondance générale* 8: 222). There is some indication that others besides the author himself felt that Barbey was the victim of a unique persecution that took the form of an undeserved conspiracy of silence surrounding his fiction. Alcide Dusolier, critic, writes in 1862:

> Comment, doué de toutes ces qualités fortes ou délicates, propres à trapper les esprits naïfs autant qu'à séduire les esprits raffinés, n'a-t-il pas emporté la réputation? Encore une fois, demandez à la Critique contemporaine qui a, pour *empêcher* un livre, quelque chose de plus sûr que l'Index romain: le silence.
>
> (qtd. in Bornecque iv)

Barbey, then, had been a long-silent journalist and an almost forgotten novelist when the publisher Dentu accepted the collected *Diaboliques* in the spring of 1873. Given the political and moral climate in France so soon after the defeat of the Commune, it is difficult to imagine that Barbey, even though a staunch Catholic and supporter of the new government, did not foresee problems of censure. After all, shortly before the appearance of *Les Diaboliques* in the fall of 1874, he had dealt with similar accusations concerning *Le Prêtre marié* (Bornecque x). The only substantive difference between the first preface, written in 1870 for the manuscript, and the final, published one dated May 1874, is the addition of the third and fourth paragraphs, both of which carefully defend the morality of the collection. *La Vengeance d'une femme,* completed well after the other five stories and shortly before publication, expands the arguments presented in the preface, opening with a lengthy (and somewhat gratuitous) discussion of the need for increased boldness in contemporary literature. This self-described "moraliste chrétien" (23), then, clearly knew the potential for scandal and censure contained within his *Diaboliques.*

On sale from 10 November to 11 December 1874, when the remaining copies were seized, *Les Diaboliques* was an immediate success. In one short month 1,500 copies were sold, which was substantial for the time (Boschian-Campaner 163). Without detailing the events that led up to the seizure and subsequent charges of outrage to public morals (see Hirschi for a discussion of these events), we can say that opinions were divided. In the end, the motivation behind the charges brought against the author was as much political as moral, if not more so. Intriguing for our purposes is Barbey's reaction to being, for once, the center of attention, for **Les Diaboliques** had clearly broken the conspiracy of silence.

Previous to the threat of a trial, Barbey's sense of artistic superiority provided refuge from negative criticism. To Léon Bloy, his secretary at the time, Barbey wrote:

> . . . je profite de l'occasion [writing a flattering review of Houssaye's *La Messaline blonde,* which might, in return, earn him one for **Les Diaboliques**] pour aplatir le bec des bégueules en littérature, qui, selon l'évangéliste Dentu, doivent, contre mes pauvres diablesses, pousser les hauts cris! . . . *Les Diaboliques* ne peuvent avoir contre elles que les imbéciles, mais c'est un gros bataillon, et la victoire est aux gros bataillons.

> (26 Nov. 1874, *Correspondance générale* 7: 234)

Another letter, written a few days before the seizure, reiterated this position and, incidentally, used similar images of cacophony to characterize his opponents:

> *Les Diaboliques* font, à ce qu'il paraît, un bruit diabolique. Il y a des imbéciles qui ne savent pas lire dans les entre-deux des lignes d'un livre,—qui n'ont pas d'écho dans leurs âmes idiotes pour la Moralité Souterrraine, mais perceptible, d'un livre hardi,—et tout cela pour l'heure braille contre moi!!!

> (Letter to Alexandre Piédagnel, 7 Dec. 1874, *Correspondance générale* 7: 238)

After all this, Barbey completely reversed himself when scandal and publicity culminated in charges of outrage to public morals. Suddenly he took all available measures to avoid public scrutiny and to silence condemnation—this despite the recognition a scandal would clearly bring to an under-recognized author and despite having consciously provoked such a reaction. At his home in Valognes when he learned of the events in Paris, Barbey immediately wrote to his publisher: "Si nous n'avons pas évité la saisie, tâchons du moins d'éviter le procès. Combinons tous nos efforts pour cela . . ." (Letter to Dentu, 9 Dec. 1874, *Correspondance générale* 7: 238). These efforts included successful lobbying for support from various political parties, as well as personal intervention from local deputies (Bornecque xxxi). In addition, Barbey prepared a careful defense of the offending passages when the interrogation first opened on 15 December 1874. (For a complete list of these passages, see Hirschi.) His initial statement responded to the charges in general terms, but its tone was characteristic of the rest of his defence:

> Je m'indigne à cette pensée qu'on peut me soupçonner d'avoir jamais manqué à la morale publique. Le but de ma vie est d'apporter à la société le contingent de bonnes choses dont tout honnête homme doit être pourvu en ce monde. Le but de mon œuvre a été de moraliser mes semblables en leur donnant l'horreur du vice.

> (Hirschi ["Le 'Procès' des *Diaboliques*"] 17-18)

On 22 January 1875, during the second interrogation that led to the dismissal of his case, the indignation expressed five weeks earlier turned to complete surrender:

> Je prends devant vous l'engagement de m'opposer à ce qu'à l'avenir des exemplaires de mon ouvrage, intitulé: **Les Diaboliques** soient mis en vente, et je m'engage également à ce que défense soit faite à tous éditeurs et libraires d'imprimer jamais nouvelle édition dudit ouvrage.

> (Hirschi 23)

Barbey gave some indication of his state of mind in a request for assistance from Arsène Houssaye:

> Ce n'est pas la condamnation qui m'inquiète, c'est l'exhibition de ma personne (devant un tribunal) qui me fait vomir. . . . Vous avez des relations immenses et vous êtes puissant parce que vous êtes séduisant. Par vous ou par vos amis pouvez-vous agir sur le procureur de la République et sur le procureur général?

> (Dec. 1874, *Correspondance générale* 7: 243)

Paradoxically, a desire to provoke has led to its diametrical opposite, a need to repress scandal and a fear of the public eye with the sexual implications contained in the phrase *l'exhibition de ma personne*. This apparent contradiction resolves itself if we examine the texts closely. In the stories, scandal, provocation, and expression are balanced—and eventually overcome—by an opposing need for privacy, secrecy, and repression. When critics viewed **Les Diaboliques** as morally decadent, the level of extratextual repression had not only been foreseen but, in an inversion of mimesis, Barbey's refusal to express himself in his own defence became to some extent a reflection of his art.

In **Les Diaboliques,** a dialectic of expression/repression affects even the act of reading. Most notable are the strategies that routinely delay, or harass, the progress of the narrative and the promise of information. The series of portraits that occupy the first few pages of **Le Bonheur dans le crime,** for instance—Torty's, then the panther's, followed by Serlon's, and finally Hauteclaire's—retards the first significant revelation, namely that Torty was the strange couple's doctor. Likewise, in **La Vengeance d'une femme,** the lengthy preamble about contemporary literature, the portrait of Tressignies and then of the prostitute, and the detailed account of him following her to her apartment withhold the duchess's revelation of her identity and, consequently, the telling of the real story. In *Le Bonheur dans le crime* the function of these delays is fairly transparent. From time to time, the first narrator intervenes with remarks such as the following: "Le docteur fit ce qu'on appelle un temps, voulant faire un effet, car en tout il était rusé, le compère!" (119). In *La Vengeance d'une femme,* however, the strategy is concealed as long as possible. Aside from the preamble, the descriptions that follow— comprising approximately one quarter of the text—do appear, during a first reading, to be part of the main story. In *La Vengeance d'une femme,* then, the narrative technique has been refined, for not only is the central story repressed by these passages, their very function is repressed during the initial—and often only— reading.

Similar delays continue even once the telling of the real story has begun. The interventions of the first narrator, "je," during Torty's narration appear to serve no other purpose than to interrupt the flow of the narrative, both visually and conceptually. Although this first narrator— Barbey himself?—effaces himself from the text in favor of Torty, he regularly reminds us of his presence with short exclamations, questions, and interjections, usually devoid of narrational value. A few examples will illustrate: "—Quoi, c'est vous, docteur!—m'écriai-je" (119), "—La comtesse de Savigny!—m'écriai-je" (124), or "—Empoisonnée! m'écriai-je" (155). Tressignies's comments during the duchess's narration, although not without content and hence not as superfluous as "je's" in *Le Bonheur dans le crime,* also postpone the progression of the story.

Postponement is a modus operandi for these texts and would be nothing more than structural suspense, if not for its persistence to the very end. Tressignies's sudden disappearance after hearing the duchess's story, like the series of questions without answers that punctuates Torty's narration, not only delays, but delays forever the possibility of a final revelation. After the end of *La Vengeance d'une femme,* we, as well as the characters, still do not know Tressignies's reasons for his silence or the duke's reaction to the circumstances of his wife's death. Torty never does provide answers to his own questions, nor does his self-described proficiency at observation express anything but his inability to reveal the reasons underlying Hauteclaire's and Serlon's longlasting happiness. These texts, like the others in the collection, end with an enigma for which we have insufficient clues, with repression of information instead of an expected resolution.

Combatting this narrative reticence is a pathological desire among all the main characters for scandal, for exciting public commentary. In *Le Bonheur dans le crime,* Torty, with his "plaisanterie légèrement sacrilège," is "un de ces esprits hardis et vigoureux qui ne chaussent point de mitaines" (112); Stassin arouses curiosity by

having a child late in life; Hauteclaire first invites gossip by excelling in an exclusively male activity, then censure by marrying the husband of the poisoned countess; and Serlon, even without his involvement with Hauteclaire, displays "assez de dédain pour les goûts et les idées du jour" (116). In *La Vengeance d'une femme,* the duchess' evolution as a woman is described in terms of a violent release of energy: "La solitude dans laquelle je vivais ne pesait point sur mon âme, tranquille comme les montagnes de marbre rouge qui entourent Sierra-Leone. Je ne soupçonnais pas que sous ces marbres dormait un volcan" (316). After recognizing her love for Esteban, she dares her lover to reveal his affection in her husband's presence. As for Tressignies, he is presented from the outset as a confirmed libertine (298).

However, despite their penchant for public display, these characters conceal best, whether by diegetic intention or by authorial irony, at those times when their observers are convinced that they have revealed most. The more that events and characters appear to be revealed to other characters, to the narrator, and to the reader, the more they are hidden; paradoxically, they are concealed under the guise of revelation. Two key scenes illustrate in microcosm the mechanism of the entire collection.

In *Le Bonheur dans le crime,* when Torty glimpses Hauteclaire and Serlon embracing on the balcony after a night-time fencing match, he is convinced that he has finally been granted the eye-witness proof of their affair that he has been seeking for so long: "En voyant ces caresses et cette intimité qui me révélaient tout, j'en tirais, en médecin, les conséquences" (151). Up to this point, Torty's fondness for observation has been continually frustrated; the suspected lovers are skilled at concealment, especially Hauteclaire, who never abandons her mask and who never confides in anyone and, consequently, whose defences not even Torty can penetrate. The balcony scene, then, provides a unique opportunity. But what has the doctor actually observed? Contrary to his own claims, he does not witness their love-making, which for this couple is synonymous with the fencing match held behind closed doors (itself a euphemism, a concealment behind a publicly acceptable metaphor). Although the window is open, the blinds, "à moitié fermées et zébrées de lumière sur le balcon," (150) allow only sound to pass. Torty can only listen to this "assaut d'armes entre amants qui s'étaient aimés les armes à la main et qui continuaient de s'aimer ainsi" (150). They continue to succeed, then, in hiding their affair. In fact, well before Torty hears strange sounds in the neighborhood of the château, the description of the moon touching, "de la pointe inférieure de son croissant, la pointe des hauts sapins de Savigny" (149) provides a metaphoric account of the couple's love-making that has been denied to Torty. Their subsequent appearance on the balcony, then, only gives the semblance of expression—although fully clothed, their "vêtements serrés . . . ressemblaient à une nudité" (151)—and only leads to false conclusions, namely Torty's conviction that this apparent intercourse will one day result in a child. Indeed, the entire text can be read as a story of incorrect diagnosis, failed observation, and frustrated voyeurism resulting in part from a simultaneous combination of repression and expression. When miscues are repeated so strenuously, the narrative strategy is not simply contrary and obscurantist, but aggressive and polemical. It is the repeated nature of the attacks on truth and knowledge, the harrying, which converts the text into harassment.

In the second key scene, a similar combination in *La Vengeance d'une femme* takes the form of literal and figurative veiling and unveiling. When Tressignies first enters the prostitute's apartment, an initial clue to the narrative process that follows is provided by the name plate on the door. Considerable narrative energy is expended in simultaneously focusing on and concealing the woman's name. Although we are told that the bronze candelabra are positioned to illuminate the name, Tressignies "fit plus attention à ces torchères . . . qu'à la carte et au nom de la femme" (302). Information is withheld because Tressignies is distracted by the very means of expression.

This phenomenon continues. To Tressignies, aristocracy is a visible and polar opposite to degradation. When he enters the apartment and looks carefully at the prostitute, he notices her resemblance to a duchess he once glimpsed (303). This information, however, is contained narratively between descriptions of the room and of her body, both of which confirm her as a prostitute. Further on, the details of her face, which most resembles the duchess's, are framed by references to her body. Interestingly, Tressignies never sees her naked, but draped in a transparent veil that irrefutably proclaims her as a prostitute:

> Mais cette fille . . . avait combiné la transparence insidieuse des voiles et l'*osé* de la chair, avec le génie et le mauvais goût d'un libertinage atroce.
>
> (306)

This veil, revealing her body while at the same time covering it, like the partially-open blinds in *Le Bonheur dans le crime,* serves as a metaphor for the entire text. Veils reveal, and the removal of veils conceals.

This dialectic of veiling/revealing is reinforced by the duchess's choice of profession. In itself, successful prostitution may depend on repressing one's true emotions, habits of dress, and physical attitudes in order to express artificial ones. Her proficiency at concealment is such that even cynical Tressignies is duped into thinking that her ardor might be for him:

> Oui, Robert de Tressignies, qui avait presque dans la trempe la froideur d'acier de son patron Robert Love-

lace, crut avoir inspiré au moins un caprice à cette prostituée, qui ne pouvait être ainsi avec tous les autres . . .

> (308)

It is not until she speaks her name that the prostitute and consequently the disguise disappear: "En se révélant, la duchesse avait emporté la courtisane!" (312). In the case of the duchess, however, this faking has revealed her true identity while at the same time hiding it, since the passion she brings to her profession, although not for her client, is for her estranged husband.

Triggered by this play of revealing and re-veiling, voyeurism plays a key role in *Le Bonheur dans le crime* and *La Vengeance d'une femme* alike and has implications for a study of the dialectic of repression/ expression. Both stories involve allowing and sometimes forcing an outsider to witness a sexually-related crime, while at the same time compelling him to keep what is witnessed repressed. Torty sees "le concubinage dans la maison conjugale" (147) and keeps silent hoping to see more. Hauteclaire encourages Torty's observations—which soon degenerate into "espionnage" with its contingent of "petites bassesses" (147)—not only by challenging him with her gaze as the count's lover (137) and as his wife's assassin (164), but also by continuing to call on his services after marrying. Similarly, the duchess wants the duke to see, knowing that he must remain silent about what he sees in order to maintain his honor. By wearing the bracelet with the duke's picture on it, she forces him to witness her debasement, while at the same time allowing herself to watch him as his image watches her and as the mirrors in her room reflect ad infinitum this mise en abime of voyeurism. More importantly, the duchess forces Tressignies—the only client willing to listen to her story (314)—to visualize the original event by describing in detail Esteban's murder and by showing him her blood-stained dress. The fact that Tressignies is silenced by this sight is not accidental, for he occupies symbolically the same place as the murdered lover, with the enraged husband witnessing this scandal from the bracelet. Ironically, it is Tressignies himself who brings about this metaphoric assassination. Upon seeing the duchess's preoccupation with the portrait in the bracelet, he demands an explanation and thus triggers the telling of the story as well as his subsequent inability to retell it.

Giving and receiving confession—the verbal equivalents of exhibitionism and voyeurism—are essential to storytelling in both *Diaboliques*. Claiming that literature doesn't begin to tell society's darkest crimes, the narrator at the beginning of *La Vengeance d'une femme* adds: "Demandez à tous les confesseurs,—qui seraient les plus grands romanciers que le monde aurait eus, s'ils pouvaient raconter les histoires qu'on leur coule dans l'oreille au confessionnal" (293). Throughout *Le Bonheur dans le crime,* Torty sees himself as a surrogate priest: "Le médecin est le confesseur des temps modernes . . . Il a remplacé le prêtre . . ." (120-21). In both texts, confession/voyeurism is put in place of participation (priests by definition do not participate in the confessed sins). These repeated attacks on the ability to act—harassment—culminate in the death, whether metaphoric or literal, of the storyteller/voyeur. When carried to the death, "harassment" seems to be an even more accurate descriptor; the word derives from an older verb in which dogs are set upon game. In *La Vengeance d'une femme,* the duchess self-destructs by reviewing her story every time she acquires a client. Significantly, the only details we are given about her death concern her loss of sight: "Un de ses yeux avait sauté . . . de son orbite et était tombé à ses pieds comme un gros sou . . . L'autre s'était liquifié et fondu . . ."(336). In the case of Tressignies, destruction comes in the form of symbolic castration. Learning her true identity constitutes the first blow:

> Ah! cette découverte abominable le frappait à la poitrine et au front d'un coup de massue de glace. L'homme, en lui, qui flambait il n'y avait qu'une minute, . . . restait désenivré, transi, écrasé.
>
> (312)

After this "Gorgone" (322) has finished speaking, Tressignies realizes that "[e]n jetant son histoire entre elle et lui, elle avait coupé, comme avec une hache, ces liens d'une minute qu'ils venaient de nouer" (326-327). The story, as well as the woman, silences Tressignies's words and desires. Not only is he incapable of repeating her story, despite her fervent wishes that he do so, he also removes himself from society—and women (333).

As storyteller/voyeur, Torty too is cut off. The one character Torty's powers of observation cannot penetrate or dominate is Hauteclaire, the fencing champion. Why Hauteclaire and Serlon remain happy despite their heinous crime, why they choose to stay at Savigny and face ostracization when they could have moved elsewhere, are among the questions he cannot answer. Consequently, as a narrator, Torty is far less credible at the end than at the beginning—he ends his story, we are told, on an item "qu'il *croyait* profond" (169; emphasis added).

Unlike Tressignies, however, Torty does not self-destruct, but saves himself in a unique way. While Torty may have healing abilities as a character and a narrator, as a narrator the doctor also menaces his listener with his metaphoric scalpel/sword. By alternately delaying and revealing information, Torty forces frustration and surprise on his interlocutor in the same way that Hauteclaire triggered these same reactions in him by alter-

nately concealing and displaying her "story." Torty provokes because he has been provoked; in short, he engages his interlocutor in a verbal fencing match in which he is clearly superior. This superiority reverses the position he was in when the events took place, for at that time Torty lost to Hauteclaire literal (131) as well as figurative fencing matches. As narrator, Torty menaces in a way that he could not, or dared not, menace Hauteclaire when he was a character. The physician, then, heals only himself and does so by taking the wound he himself received as a participant and inflicting it onto his interlocutor—"je," Barbey—who in turn, as if by contagion, passes it on to his listener/reader. By this process, the contagion lifts from the story to the narrator and from the narrator to the listener, from the fictional page to the flesh-and-blood readers, who then, historically, took the published work to the public courts.

It is in this public arena of censorship and suppression where fact and fiction begin to coincide. According to a view expressed by an acquaintance, Charles Buet, Barbey's collection was threatened because of a conspiracy that was female:

> *Les Diaboliques* avaient excité la colère de quelques femmes du monde, plus ou moins compromises par d'anciennes aventures, qu'elles voulurent y reconnaître. Il y eut toute une conspiration féminine. On fit jouer des influences. On menaça quelques libraires des environs de sainte Clotilde de mettre à l'index s'ils exposaient encore dans leurs vitrines les œuvres du Ravila, du **"Plus bel amour de Don Juan."**
>
> (Buet [*J. Barbey d'Aurevilly*] 411-412)

As time elapsed, Barbey became convinced that women were indeed responsible for the seizure of *Les Diaboliques.* A letter from his secretary, Léon Bloy, to Joséphin Péladan supports this notion:

> M. d'Aurevilly me charge de vous dire, qu'il ne lui déplaît pas qu'on le nomme l'auteur des *Diaboliques,* mais qu'il pourrait être *dangereux* pour lui d'être désigné à l'attention ignoble des magistrats embusqués sous les jupons de quatre ou cinq salopes des lettres. *Il ne faut donc pas* annoncer la nouvelle édition.
>
> (qtd. in Bornecque xliv)

We know that Barbey disliked and feared virile women, and for him, virile women were most often writers. He describes them in detail in *Les Bas-Bleus:*

> La femme qui se croit cerveau d'homme et demande sa part dans la publicité et dans la gloire. Or, cette espèce est très moderne en France et il a fallu les transformations successives par lesquelles nous sommes passés depuis la Révolution française, pour que des femmes qui n'étaient ni bossues, ni laides, ni bréhaignes eussent l'idée de se mettre en équation avec l'homme, et que les hommes devenus aussi femmes qu'elles, eussent la bassesse de le souffrir.
>
> (qtd. in Buet 366)

Armed not with a sword or a foil, but a pen, in general they disputed man his God-given superiority by engaging in what Barbey thought should be an exclusively male activity, and in particular "killed" his *Diaboliques* by using their feminine charms to pressure officials for censure.

On the one hand, repressing a story, harassing it by making it incomplete or unavailable, is no ordinary wound for Barbey, but a castrating one. After the countess' death, Torty remarks: "j'avais la fatuité de croire qu'elle redoutait la pénétration de mon regard; mais, à présent, elle n'avait plus à la craindre" (163). Later on, he describes in terms of unsuccessful penetration his failure to detect signs of the couple's unhappiness: "Je puis dire que je continuai de m'acharner à regarder et à percer dans l'intimité de ces deux êtres, si complètement heureux par l'amour" (166).

On the other hand, by telling the story, Torty retrieves the "sword" that Barbey felt the men of his time had surrendered to women. In this context, the fact that the first narrator's listener is a woman—"Madame" (113)—is significant, especially since this detail appears to be unnecessary. By telling Torty's story to a woman, this narrator is re-enacting the initial "castration" of the female as proposed by Freud: he is creating an ideal woman by removing her phallus, an operation performed by being actively engaged in creating a story.

We are participating, then, in an intra- and extra-textual castration that "ricochets" from one witness/voyeur/listener/reader/critic to another. Similarly, the act of storytelling passes from one narrator to another throughout *Les Diaboliques*—the initial title of the collection being, after all, *Ricochets de conversation.*

In a text that equates lovemaking, fencing, storytelling, and death, the implications for an artistic career seem inescapable. Storytelling and fencing (the ability to kill elegantly) are equally deadly and both are art. However, since fencing/storytelling is also lovemaking, the view of art expressed in *Le Bonheur dans le crime* remains primarily optimistic. Although a death results from repression, since the countess would rather die of poison than expose herself to scandal, expression exists as a possible antidote, available but declined.

La Vengeance d'une femme, however, presents a resoundingly pessimistic view. By defiling herself to the point of death by venereal disease, the duchess expresses her anger and ruins her husband. In this case, the terms have reversed and expression has become the poison, though ironically, her means of revenge exist only because of the strength of the social repression surrounding her actions. Like Torty who transmits his wound by means of his narrative, the duchess passes on her disease as she repeats her story. In her case, though, textual transmission does not heal her, but instead ensures her ruin. Moreover, the last text that she authors, her own epitaph, is grounded in falsehood and repression, since she dies anything but "une fille repentie" (335). This transition from narration as salvation in *Le Bonheur dans le crime* to narration as self-destruction in *La Vengeance d'une femme,* the last story in the collection and the last to be written, coincides with the suppression and self-suppression of Barbey's artistic career. While Barbey inflicted his share of wounds through scathing criticism of his literary peers, the ones his own career sustained were never addressed.

In the aftermath of the seizure of *Les Diaboliques,* why decline the public means of passing on his wounds? Could his fictional simulation have convinced him of the futility of the public hearing that a trial provides, of its inability to cleanse and save? Or did it provide an opportunity to provoke yet again, with a non-response, a non-ending? In this reaction to censure that contradicts his past, I suggest we should see the author's life imitating and re-viewing what his art has previewed. The text has harassed and repressed the author well before the authorities.

Works Consulted

Annales Littéraires de l'Université de Besançon. *Barbey d'Aurevilly: Correspondance générale.* 11 vols. Paris: Les Belles Lettres, 1987-89.

Barbey d'Aurevilly, Jules. *Les Diaboliques.* Ed. Jacques Petit. Paris: Gallimard, 1973. All textual references are to this edition.

Bornecque, Jacques-Henry, ed. *Les Diaboliques.* By Jules Barbey d'Aurevilly. Paris: Garnier, 1963.

Boschian-Campaner, Catherine. *Barbey d'Aurevilly: Biographie.* Paris: Séguier, 1989.

Boucher, Jean-Pierre. Les Diaboliques *de Barbey d'Aurevilly: Une esthétique de la dissimulation et de la provocation.* Montréal: PU du Québec, 1976.

Buet, Charles. *J. Barbey d'Aurevilly: Impressions et souvenirs.* Paris: Albert Savine, 1891.

Chartier, Armand B. *Barbey d'Aurevilly.* Boston: Twayne, 1977.

Debray-Genette, Raymonde. "Un récit autologique: *Le Bonheur dans le crime." Romanic Review* 1 (1973): 38-53.

Fréchet, Georges, and Geneviève Dormann, eds. *Barbey d'Aurevilly 1808-1889.* Paris: Bibliothèque historique de la ville de Paris, 1989.

Hirschi, Andrée. "Le 'Procès' des *Diaboliques." Barbey d'Aurevilly 9: l'histoire des Diaboliques.* Spec. issue of *La Revue des lettres modernes* (1974): 6-64.

L'Ensorcelée et les Diaboliques. Actes du Colloque du 16 janvier 1988. Paris: Sedes, 1988.

Marini, Marcelle. "Ricochets de lecture: la fantasmatique des *Diaboliques.*" *Littérature* 10 (1973): 3-19.

Petit, Jacques. *Essais de lectures des "Diaboliques."* Paris: Minard, 1974.

Tranouez, Pierre. *Fascination et narration dans l'œuvre romanesque de Barbey d'Aurevilly: la scène capitale.* Paris: Minard, 1987.

Yarrow, Philip John. *La Pensée politique et religieuse de Barbey d'Aurevilly.* Paris: Minard, 1961.

Susanne Rossbach (essay date spring 1999)

SOURCE: Rossbach, Susanne. "Dandyism in the Literary Works of Barbey d'Aurevilly: Ideology, Gender, and Narration." *Modern Language Studies* 29, no. 1 (spring 1999): 81-102.

[*In the following essay, Rossbach studies the intellectual and psychological underpinnings of Barbey d'Aurevilly's depictions of dandyism. According to Rossbach, Barbey d'Aurevilly's approach to narrative represents an assertion of "sexual and textual control" over his subject matter.*]

Jules Amédée Barbey d'Aurevilly was a dandy of some notoriety in the Parisian circles of his time, and with Balzac and Baudelaire an important theorist of French dandyism.[1] With his essay **Du Dandysme et de George Brummell,** first published in 1845, he helped transform the superficial "beau" of the British Isles into an intellectual being of psychological depth and thus rid dandyism of its negative connotations.[2] Barbey was moreover a writer who made dandyism the thematic focus and the narrative principle of his literary production and whose literary output is rife with dandy heros as well as dandy narratives.

Barbey d'Aurevilly was also a convert to Catholicism and a staunch monarchist who deeply resented the nineteenth-century bourgeois society in which he lived. Like many of his contemporaries, he yearned for an idealized society in France's prerevolutionary past, believing his own time to be an era of decline and decay, "un siècle malade," "grossièrement matérialiste et utilitaire."[3] Dandyism and the aristocratic, stoic, and aesthetic lifestyle it stood for represented a means of revolt for the Catholic and reactionary Barbey who called the French revolution "[la] fille de Satan" and "une révolution contre Dieu."[4] It enabled him to react against the increasingly utilitarian and democratic society that his declared enemy, the bourgeoisie, epitomized. As a philosophy of life for the superior man, dandyism also rep-

resented for Barbey an avenue to power and authority. On the literary level it provided the author, deprived of any real influence in an increasingly modern and rapidly changing world, with powerful means of sexual and textual control. Dandyism was for Barbey not simply a superficial statement of fashion or an interesting but negligible element of his writing but, on the contrary, the key to understanding his text.

In the following, I plan to show that the dandy's ideologically motivated revolt as well as his striving for power and control affect every level of Barbey's text. I will first discuss the role of Barbey's numerous dandy heroes who—as we will see—struggle to dominate the bourgeois society they abhor and the erotic woman they fear. Second, I will focus on Barbey's dandy narrators. I plan to reveal the aggressive and authoritative nature of their narration and show how deeply their narrative strategies are shaped by dandyism. We will see that the art of conversation in which the dandy excels, the aesthetic of dissimulation that he cultivates as well as the art of the unexpected that he perfects characterize and determine the narrative structures of Barbey's text.

* * *

A large number of Barbey's male protagonists are either explicitly described as dandies or clearly manifest dandy characteristics.[5] These dandy heroes of Barbey's text live without exception in postrevolutionary and postnapoleonic France, "ce temps d'égoïsme sans grandeur" (*Œuvres* [*Œuvres romanesques complètes*] 1: 205), yet seem to be remnants of an earlier and—as the text implies—more noble and more virile age. Better than their surroundings and superior to their contemporaries, they suffer from the "mediocrity" and "vulgarity" of their time. Destined to be heroes yet caught in an "unheroic" age, these "âmes fortes dépaysées par les circonstances" (*Œuvres* 1: 254) deeply resent the materialistic and utilitarian society of nineteenth-century France. But unlike the typical romantic hero who flees bourgeois society to seek refuge in nature or love, Barbey's dandy protagonists instead hide their frustration behind an impenetrable mask or an air of scornful aloofness and set out to provoke, fascinate, and dominate the society they despise.

Ryno de Marigny, dandy hero of Barbey's novel **Une Vieille maîtresse,** is for example "un homme d'une distinction presque grandiose" (*Œuvres* 1: 244) whose captivating personality, striking wit, and stunning elegance seem to be unparalleled in the Parisian salons he frequents. For the increasingly bourgeois society that surrounds him, this dandy harbors nothing but contempt and makes no effort to conceal it: "Le voile diaphane et brun délicatement lamé d'or de [sa] moustache orientale . . . cachait mal le dédain de ses lèvres" (*Œuvres* 1: 253). Marigny's distinguished appearance and arrogant demeanor are meant to irritate, shock, and provoke and so they do: they pit the aristocratic dandy against his bourgeois contemporaries in an ideologically charged confrontation. By means of an aggressive and military language, a vocabulary of dominance and conquest, Barbey's narrator turns the nineteenth-century salon society into a metaphorical battleground.[6] The dandy Marigny comes to represent the French monarchy and—as if transported back to the revolutionary wars—has to fend off attacks by what Barbey's narrator disparagingly calls "la plèbe":

> [Marigny] n'avait d'ennemis que les gens vulgaires. Même physiquement, il les choquait. . . . On le critiquait dans sa mise, dans sa physionomie, dans sa personne extérieure,—la pire critique pour les gens du monde. Quoi d'étonnant? Avec les mœurs égalitaires et jalouses de notre temps, il y a des physionomies qu'on voudrait briser comme une couronne. C'est de la royauté de droit si divin pour cette plèbe qui n'y croit plus!
>
> (*Œuvres* 1: 253)

Marigny, "[ce] conquérant," "né pour le commandement" (*Œuvres* 1: 254, 210), is able to keep the upper hand in this salon warfare: He is safe behind the dandy's mask as if behind a strong shield, retaliates with biting scorn, and manages to captivate the Parisian society he loathes.[7]

The dandy hero Marmor de Karkoël (*Le Dessous de cartes d'une partie de whist, Les Diaboliques*) is even more successful in dominating a small provincial town than Marigny in fascinating the Faubourg Saint Germain. The impassive Marmor is able to elevate whist, the popular passtime activity of a bored and powerless aristocracy, "jusqu'à la hauteur de la plus difficile et de la plus magnifique escrime" (*Œuvres* 2: 152). In the presence of Marmor, the card game becomes a substitute for glorious battle and Marmor, this king of whist, the most influential and sought-after man in town:

> Comment ce Karkoël n'eût-il pas été puissant? Il avait ce qui fait la force des gouvernements . . . Aussi arriva-t-il à cette domination qui ressemble à un ensorcellement. On se l'arrachait. Tout le temps qu'il resta dans cette ville, il fut toujours reçu avec le même accueil, et cet acceuil était une fiévreuse recherche.
>
> (*Œuvres* 2: 152)

Barbey's dandy protagonists are "chevaliers errants" (*Œuvres* 2: 183), former soldiers or would-be warriors bereft of a theater of war. Unlike the heroic Sir des Touches (*Le Chevalier des Touches*), who singlehandedly takes on Republican forces during France's revolutionary years, Barbey's dandy protagonists are no longer able to wage open war against the society they abhor. Instead they make life over as representation and artifice and stage their revolt in a more subtle manner.

Barbey's hero Mesnilgrand (*A un Dîner d'athées, Les Diaboliques*) was for example a brilliant army officer before becoming a full-blown dandy. Forced to retire from the military, "ce monstre de fureur" (*Œuvres* 2: 182) proves at first unable to cope with the inglorious life as a civilian that he has to lead in postrevolutionary and bourgeois society. Threatened by madness, Mesnilgrand considers suicide but eventually is able to give vent to his frustration and rage through art. He exchanges the stiff elegance of his officer's uniform for the dandy's much more artistic and tasteful dress. Mesnilgrand becomes a dandy and a painter, an orator and a storyteller whose weapons are no longer swords and explosives but paintbrushes and words: "l'artiste avait passé par le soldat et l'avait transfiguré . . ." (*Œuvres* 2: 193). It is with his necktie, his sabering brush strokes, and especially with his extraordinary eloquence that he now marks his superiority and voices his discontent.[8] The following excerpt from *A un Dîner d'athées* describes Mesnilgrand as an orator in action:

> Il fallait le voir, . . . sa poitrine de volcan soulevée, . . . le front labouré de houles de rides,—comme la mer dans l'ouragan de sa colère,—les pupilles jaillissant de leur cornée, comme pour frapper ceux à qui il parlait,—deux balles flamboyantes! Il fallait le voir haletant, palpitant, l'haleine courte, la voix plus pathétique à mesure qu'elle se brisait davantage, l'ironie faisant trembler l'écume sur ses lèvres, longtemps vibrantes après qu'il avait parlé. . . .
>
> (*Œuvres* 2: 183)

Mesnilgrand has transferred the aggressions he harbors against postrevolutionary and bourgeois society from the realm of deeds to that of words and replaced the "virility" of military action with that of narration and representation. Like Mesnilgrand, Barbey's dandy protagonists redress no longer "les torts avec la lance, mais les ridicules avec la raillerie" (*Œuvres* 2: 183). It is in the salon that—by way of substitution—these warriors-turned-dandies seek to satisfy their longing for superiority, heroism, and power. And, as we will see, this is especially valid in their dealings with women.

Barbey's dandy protagonist excels not only in the art of (salon) warfare but also in that of love and seduction. Yet, unlike the classical Don Juan, he does not savor the transports of passion or the rapture of lust but rather his own seductive power and erotic appeal. In matters of love, Barbey's dandy hero is "un conquérant plus pour l'exercise du pouvoir que pour les jouissances de l'amour" (*Œuvres* 1: 254). In his essay *Du Dandysme et de George Brummell* Barbey claims that love, even in its purely sensual form, is incompatible with dandyism because it makes the dandy dependent on women as well as on his own desire, thus threatening his stoic aloofness and superiority. George Brummell, the prototype of English dandyism and the model for Barbey's seducer-heroes, successfully avoided this danger because he knew how to seduce und thus exercise power without being seduced himself:

> Aimer, . . . désirer, c'est toujours dépendre, c'est être esclave de son désir. Les bras le plus tendrement fermés sur vous sont encore une chaîne. . . . Voilà l'esclavage auquel Brummell échappa. Ses triomphes eurent l'insolence du désintéressement. Il n'avait jamais le vertige des têtes qu'il tournait.
>
> (*Œuvres* 2: 686)

According to Barbey, Brummell was an indifferent and dispassionate seducer who sought protection from woman, love, and lust behind "cette élégante froideur qu'il portait sur lui comme une armure et qui le rendait invulnérable" (*Œuvres* 2: 703). His insensitivity guaranteed not only his independence but also his power.

By no means all of Barbey's dandy heroes are as successful as Brummell in avoiding the threat that love, passion, and the often demonized woman pose to their superiority and independence. Yet the emotional and sensual coldness of some of them easily compares with that of Brummell. Marmor de Karkoël displays for example "une impassibilité superbe" that surpasses the callousness and mysteriousness of stone sphinxes: "A côté de lui, les sphinx accroupis dans la lave de leur basalte auraient semblé les statues des génies de la confiance et de l'expansion" (*Œuvres* 2: 143). Not even the sweet-scented hair of thirty beautiful young women can awaken the senses or soften the countenance of this dandy:

> Les dernières brises de cette soirée d'août déferlaient en vagues de souffles et de parfums sur ces trente chevelures de jeunes filles, nu-tête, pour arriver chargées de nouveaux parfums et d'effluves virginales, prises à ce champ de têtes radieuses, et se briser contre ce front cuivré, large et bas, écueil de marbre humain qui ne faisait pas un seul pli. Il ne s'en apercevait même pas. Ses nerfs étaient muets. En cet instant, il faut bien l'avouer, il portait bien son nom de Marmor!
>
> (*Œuvres* 2: 143)

Despite his indifference, Marmor is able to please and seduce. The aura of mysterious opacity with which he surrounds himself has great erotic appeal. Even the strongwilled Comtesse de Stasseville whose stoic aloofness equals that of Marmor is inflamed by him yet has to pay for the ardent attack on Marmor's freedom with her death.

Nowhere in Barbey's literary works are the dispassionate dandy's erotic appeal and seductive power more obvious and more celebrated than in the short story *Le plus bel amour de Don Juan*. In this story the elderly count Ravila de Ravilès (*celui qui la/les ravit*) is invited for dinner by twelve of his former mistresses. He presides at the dinner table "comme un roi—comme le maître" (*Œuvres* 2: 63) and clearly relishes the el-

egance, sensuality, and charm that the twelve ladies display exclusively for him. The dandy Ravila then proceeds to impress, astonish, and thus "seduce" his female admirers with a skilfully told story, the story of the most beautiful romance of his life. Instead of the romantic and sensual adventure his listeners anticipate with suspense, Ravila tells them about an unattractive and devout thirteen year old girl whom he was able to "seduce" without his knowledge and against her will. When the innocent and naive girl sat in an armchair from which Ravila had just gotten up, she thought she had fallen into a fire and conceived a child through this indirect contact. The greatest love of Don Juan is not the count's most sensual and most intoxicating adventure but on the contrary one in which he remained emotionally and physically uninvolved; one in which he was able to triumph over the will of a deeply religious girl by inspiring a purely mental passion and causing an imaginary pregnancy. Ravila is an impassive Don Juan and an intellectualized seducer who prefers the triumphs of the will to those of the flesh. Afraid of losing his superiority and independence, he seeks not the transport of passion but domination and control, savoring above all his own virile power and erotic appeal.[9]

Since his appearance in early nineteenth-century England and his subsequent importation into France, the dandy has time and again been hailed as a mythical being, the androgyne. Thus associated with androgyny, dandyism is generally seen to represent a challenge to the dichotomy of gender and an attempt to merge the two opposite sexes into an ideal and superior being. Yet although the dandy appropriates certain female characteristics, his attitude toward women—be it on the historical or the literary level—is generally one of dislike, of fear, or of outright hostility. In nineteenth-century French literature misogynous statements by dandy writers abound[10]; among these the following one by Baudelaire is probably the most ferocious and the most disturbing:

> La femme est le contraire du dandy.
> Donc elle doit faire horreur.
> La femme a faim et elle veut manger. Soif, et elle veut boire.
> Elle est en rut et elle veut être foutue.
> Le beau mérite!
> La femme est naturelle, c'est à dire abominable.
> Aussi est-elle toujours vulgaire, c'est-à-dire le contraire du dandy.
>
> (1272)

Unlike Baudelaire, Barbey does not systematically oppose the dandy to woman. In his essay *Du Dandysme et de George Brummell*, he describes the two instead as having certain traits in common: "un Dandy est femme par certains côtés" (*Œuvres* 2: 710). Like a woman, the famous Brummell was graceful, attached great importance to elegance, and always sought to seduce:

"*Paraître,* c'est *être* pour les Dandys, comme pour les femmes" (*Œuvres* 2: 703). In the conclusion to his essay, Barbey even explicitly takes up the theme of androgyny: he calls dandies such as Brummell "Androgynes de l'Histoire" and describes them as "natures doubles et multiples, d'un sexe intellectuel indécis, où la grâce est plus grâce encore dans la force, et où la force se retrouve encore dans la grâce" (*Œuvres* 2: 718). Not merely Brummell but also numerous protagonists of Barbey's novels and short stories possess attributes of both sexes: male heroes are regularly feminized and female ones masculinized.[11] Whereas Marcelle Marini in her article "Ricochets de lecture" comes to the conclusion that Barbey negates und thus eliminates sexual difference,[12] I am arguing here, on the contrary, that this difference is not abolished but merely redefined. Although Barbey's male protagonists take on female characteristics, the mutually exclusive categories of the masculine and the feminine remain intact. Barbey redefines masculinity and femininity yet leaves the polarity of gender untouched. Virility is not perceived in opposition to traditional conceptions of femininity but describes instead a new, perfect, and integral being that possesses both grace and power, that is both male and female: a pseudoandrogynous "supermale" who, in Barbey's literary text, is represented by either the warrior or the dandy.[13] In contrast to this improved male, woman remains imperfect and incomplete. The hero Des Touches, royalist fighter in France's revolutionary wars, is a good example of Barbey's perfect and well-rounded man. He has "[une] taille fine et cambrée, comme celle d'une femme en corset" and "[une] délicate figure d'ange de missel," yet is at the same time "un des Chouans les plus redoutables." His feminine and angelic beauty is complemented by "l'âme d'un homme," "une vaillance acharnée et féroce," and "la force terrassante du taureau" (*Œuvres* 1: 782, 778). The Chevalier Des Touches combines in his male person the most beautiful as well as the strongest and bravest being one can imagine. The women that surround him are less perfect: the delicate Aimée possesses solely beauty and charm, whereas Mademoiselle de Percy, described as "[un] homme manqué" and "un assez brave laideron," is forceful and courageous yet unattractive (*Œuvres* 1: 802, 783). If a woman comes to resemble the virile ideal, if like the dandy or warrior she combines charm and power, if like him she can both seduce and dominate[14], she is perceived as a threat, demonized, and physically punished. Two short stories, **"Le Cachet d'onyx"** and *A un Dîner d'athées,* tell of the ultimate punishment for such a woman: in each story the dandy hero, sexually attracted yet rejected by a strong, beautiful, and independent minded heroine, seals her vagina with hot, melted sealing-wax.

As we have seen, Barbey's dandy protagonists strive to provoke, fascinate, and dominate the society they abhor and the women they fear. Yet these heroes seek control not solely on the social and sexual level but also and especially on the narrative level. The dandy Ravila, although surrounded by twelve beautiful and sensual women, does not have romantic or erotic escapades in mind but instead sets out to fascinate and "seduce" the ladies by telling them a story. He replaces the sexual with the narrative act and rules supreme not with caresses but with words. Numerous other dandies of Barbey's text are, like Ravila, not only heroes but also narrators who manage to spellbind their audience with their much-celebrated eloquence, stories, and narrative techniques. The narrative act is of particular importance in Barbey's literary works and, as a theme, omnipresent: indirectly because of the highly complex and multi-layered structure of these works, directly by frequent remarks on the quality, strategies, or problems of narration. In fact, the narrative act gains at times such prominence that it tends to overshadow the story that is told. This is especially valid for *Les Diaboliques,* Barbey's collection of short stories. Each of the six tales from this collection is embedded in an unusually detailed and elaborate frame that does more than just authenticate the story that is told. By reducing the traditional opposition between cadre and récit, by linking the diegetic and extradiegetic levels[15] of his text with a complex net of symbols, reflections, and mises en abyme, Barbey revalorizes this frame as well as the narrative act it harbors and pushes the story—often ambiguous and incomplete—into the background. Since the 1960s scholars have shown great interest in Barbey's unusual and often highly complex narrative techniques.[16] Although proposing quite different readings of Barbey's literary works, they all wrestle with the following questions: What is the relationship between cadre and récit in *Les Diaboliques*? Are Barbey and his narrators primarily interested in telling a story or in undermining and destroying it?[17] I would like to contribute to this ongoing discussion by showing that the true originality of Barbey's literary text lies in the close linking of the narrative act with dandyism. The dandy's ideologically motivated revolt as well as his striving for power and control shape the narrative and aesthetic structures of this text and account for the unusual relationship between frame and story in *Les Diaboliques.*

The salon constitutes the dandy's sphere of action: it is here that this king of fashion and eloquence fascinates and provokes, it is here that he rules supreme thanks to his stunning elegance and striking wit. However, according to Barbey, nineteenth-century salon culture does not measure up to the past. Barbey and his narrators criticize time and again the tedium and prudery of modern society life and deplore the decadence of the great French art of conversation.[18] This art—so they claim—had reached its climax in the aristocratic salon of the seventeenth and eighteenth centuries yet has largely disappeared in the bourgeois salon of the nineteenth century. In each of his novels and short stories Barbey evokes the great salon culture of an idealized era of the past. The storytelling circles of his framing stories—regardless whether they take place in a living room, in a carriage, or on a park bench—constitute the last strongholds of artful conversation and aristocratic salon culture in a "utilitarian" nineteenth-century society. The salon of the Baronne de Mascranny (*Le Dessous de cartes d'une partie de whist*) is an example of such a stronghold in which a talented "causeur" reveals the gruesome background of a game of whist. The narrator describes this salon as follows:

> Avec l'esprit et les manières de son nom, la baronne de Mascranny a fait de son salon une espèce de Coblentz délicieux où s'est réfugiée la conversation d'autrefois, la dernière gloire de l'esprit françis, forcé d'émigrer devant les mœurs utilitaires et occupées de notre temps. C'est là que chaque soir, jusqu'à ce qu'il se taise tout à fait, il chante divinement son chant de cygne. Là, comme dans les rares maisons de Paris où l'on a conservé les grandes traditions de la causerie, on ne carre guères de phrases, et le monologue est à peu près inconnu. Rien n'y rappelle l'article du journal et le discours politique, ces deux moules si vulgaires de la pensée, au dix-neuvième siècle. L'esprit se contente d'y briller en mots charmants ou profonds, mais bientôt dits; quelquefois même en de simples intonations, et moins que cela encore, en quelque petit geste de génie.
>
> (*Œuvres* 2: 130)

The narrator clearly distinguishes here between a written and monological form of communication on the one hand and an oral and dialogical one on the other ("l'article du journal" and "le discours politique" versus "la causerie" and "la conversation d'autrefois"). Whereas the former, described as being vulgar, is identified with the nineteenth century, the latter, of a subtle and artistic quality, is said to represent the ideal vehicle for "l'esprit français." I would argue that "la conversation d'autrefois" is not only highly praised in Barbey's literary works but characterizes also the dandy's storytelling skills and defines the narrative and aesthetic structures of Barbey's literary text. The above quotation describes not only the salon of the Baronne de Mascranny but also the author's principle of literary production. In his novels and especially in his short stories Barbey seeks to reproduce stylistically as well as structurally the specific character of the aristocratic salon conversation of an idealized and bygone age. He tries to achieve this on the one hand with a literary style rich in images, comparisons, and metaphors that testifies to Barbey's wish for artistic subtlety and aesthetic originality.[19] On the other hand he hopes to imitate "la conversation d'autrefois" by giving the framing stories in *Les Diaboliques* the same dialogical structure and oral character that characterizes the narrative situation in the salon. Seen in this light, the extradiegetic level of Barbey's literary text takes on an important ideological function.

For Barbey, the spoken word clearly takes precedence over the written word. His first person narrators, who record the stories told in the salon for the reader, look upon their own written texts unfavorably. The narrator of the novel *Un Prêtre marié,* comparing a skilfully told story with his own written version, warns the reader as follows: "Les pages qui vont suivre ressembleront au plâtre avec lequel on essaie de lever une empreinte de la vie, et qui n'en est qu'une ironie!" (*Œuvres* 1: 882) And the narrator in the short story *Le Dessous de cartes* [*Le Dessous de cartes dune partie de whist*] asks himself:

> Mais pourrai-je rappeler, sans l'affaiblir, ce récit, nuancé par la voix et le geste, et surtout faire ressortir le contrecoup de l'impression qu'il produisit sur toutes les personnes rassemblées dans l'atmosphère sympathique de ce salon?
>
> (*Œuvres* 2: 113-34)

Both fear that the spontaneous interaction between storyteller and listener as well as the richness of the spoken word, nuanced by intonation and gestures, are lost in their written versions. The challenge of Barbey's narrators therefore consists in avoiding this loss. They hope to achieve this primarily by giving their written text the same dialogical structure that characterizes the conversational situation in the salon.

As the first title of *Les Diaboliques, Ricochets de conversation,*[20] suggests, the stories of this collection simulate conversational situations in which the reactions and objections of the audience influence the narrative strategies of the storyteller. The listeners in Barbey's framing stories are by no means passive, docile, and silent but are on the contrary active interlocutors. They interrupt the narrator time and again with impatient remarks, commentaries, and rivalling stories so that a fierce struggle for mastery of the narrative situation ensues.[21] For example, the dandy narrator Mesnilgrand (*A un Dîner d'athées*), his narrative authority in jeopardy, resorts to an authoritative language and military metaphors to defend himself. This is how he reprimands an especially fierce contender, the captain Rançonnet:

> —Reste donc dans le rang, Rançonnet!—fit Mesnil, comme s'il eût commandé un mouvement à son escadron,—et tiens-toi tranquille! . . . Laisse-moi manœuvrer, comme je l'entends, mon histoire.
>
> (*Œuvres* 2: 208)

The dandy Mesnilgrand, in every respect superior to his rebellious listeners, emerges victoriously from this battle. He is able to conquer the word and reduce his opponents to silence thanks to his unequalled storytelling skills:

> Le capitaine Rançonnet . . . ne prononça pas une syllabe, les autres non plus. Nulle réflexion ne fut risquée. Un silence plus expressif que toutes les réflexions leur pesait sur la bouche à tous.
>
> (*Œuvres* 2: 228)

The narrative endeavors of Barbey's heroes are not always as openly militaristic as Mesnilgrand's. But each of Barbey's dandy narrators wrestles with and eventually overcomes the initial reluctance or impatience of his audience. And each is in the end able to fascinate, irritate or shock his listeners, causing them to shiver or perspire, to cry out with surprise or indignation, leaving them—once the story is completed—pensive, dumbfounded or plain speechless. Barbey's dandy narrator firmly holds his audience "sous la griffe de son récit" (*Œuvres* 2: 164).

It is not solely with the dialogical structure of his text that Barbey's narrator seeks to overcome the "deficiency" and "poverty" of the written word. He also tries to render the oral qualities of the speech act by describing in detail the gestures and especially the voice of the storyteller, "[les] moindres nuances de sa voix" (*Œuvres* 2: 25). In *Le Rideau cramoisi,* for example, the storyteller's voice plays an important role. Since Brassard tells his unsettling tale at night in a dark carriage, his travelling companion can make out neither his gestures nor his facial expressions and therefore pays heightened attention to his voice and intonation. The listener and first person narrator of the short story describes not only Brassard's "forte voix un peu brisée" (*Œuvres* 2: 56), but records every important change in tone and accent.[22] Barbey attributes the success of his dandy narrators—as he does that of Beau Brummell—to the immediacy and complexity of their modes of communication. In his essay **Du Dandysme et de George Brummell** he writes the following about the famous English dandy:

> Son action sur les autres était plus immédiate que celle qui s'exerce uniquement par le language. [Brummell] la produisait par l'intonation, le regard, le geste, l'intention transparente, le silence même. . . .
>
> (*Œuvres* 2: 696)

It is the directness of communication that enables Brummell to captivate British salon society and it is this same directness that Barbey seeks to imitate in his framing stories.

By seeking to reproduce the oral and dialogical character of the conversational (and often confrontational) situation in the salon, Barbey lends considerable weight to the narrative process in his literary works. The story that is told thus necessarily loses importance and tends to get pushed into the background. Whereas the narrative aspects of this extradiegetic upgrading have interested scholars since the sixties, the ideologically motivated revolt that lies behind it has been next to ignored. By making the art of conversation the narrative and aesthetic principle of his literary production, Barbey celebrates not only the salon culture of prerevolutionary times but aims also at reviving a discourse formerly characteristic of the absolutist court and the aristocratic

salon. Joan B. Landes has shown that, in the eighteenth century, language and style played an important role in the development of an oppositional bourgeois ideology.[23] It was on a linguistic level that absolutist France and a new bourgeois public sphere clashed and staged important ideological struggles. During the Enlightenment the discourse characteristic of the *ancien régime* was increasingly differentiated by a set of binary oppositions from a new bourgeois style that eventually replaced it. The oppositional public sphere that emerged predicated simplicity, naturalness, transparency, and universality and rejected the high-flown, artificial, opaque, and particular discourse associated with aristocratic and courtly circles. Whereas the new bourgeois discourse was associated with greatness and virility, the oral, ornate, and playful conversations of the aristocratic salon were labeled effeminate: the "salonnière," that educated and influential woman of the world, came to symbolize a detested, absolutist (life)style. To a large extent, the oppositional public sphere owed its emergence to the liberalization of the press laws and caused an unprecedented boom in the printing industry. It attributed a heightened symbolic significance to the printed word and rejected the art of conversation that had flourished in the aristocratic salon, associating it with orality, femininity, and artificiality.[24]

By making salon conversation the narrative and aesthetic principle of his literary production, Barbey places himself within the discursive battles mentioned above, siding clearly with an absolutist and against a bourgeois aesthetic, language, and ideology. He reverses the bourgeois premises and celebrates in his novels and short stories not the printed but the spoken word, not naturalness but preciosity, not transparency but ambiguity and opacity. Only the "salonnière" remains excluded from this transvaluation of all bourgeois values: Barbey hails not her but the dandy as the representative of an ideal (life)style, as the symbol of a "regenerated" language, literature, and culture.

The dandy narrator is celebrated in Barbey's literary works as an exceptionally talented storyteller who is destined to renew nineteenth-century French literature. His narrative skills are not only highly and abundantly praised but also measured by his audience's reactions. Rollon Langrune, the narrator of the novel **Un Prêtre marié,** is for example able to captivate his listeners to such an extent that they feel neither the cold evening wind nor their great fatigue when he tells them his long story. He is "[un] conteur sans égal," "un robuste génie," and "un des grands talents *genuine* qui renouvellent, d'une source inespérée, les littératures défaillantes" (*Œuvres* 1: 882, 878). The narrator of the short story **Le Dessous de cartes** is introduced to the reader as "le plus étincelant causeur" (*Œuvres* 2: 132) in the salon of the Baronne de Mascranny. Whereas the frightening story that he tells causes his listeners to shiver and to cry out, Ryno de Marigny (*Une Vieille maîtresse*) can move the Marquise de Flers to tears because "les plus simples paroles [prennent] en passant dans sa bouche des vibrations extraordinaires" (*Œuvres* 1: 264).[25] What characterizes the dandy's narration that would merit such praise and yield such power?

In the introduction to the short story *La Vengeance d'une femme* Barbey's first person narrator defines the subject matter of a regenerated literature by first discrediting and rejecting the narrative traditions of his time. He disputes the claim of realist and naturalist writers to truthfully reflect nineteenth-century society by asserting that they depict only what is conspicuous and ordinary yet fail to explore the hidden horrors of the modern "enfer social" (*Œuvres* 2: 229). If Barbey's narrator accuses the literature of his time of recording only a superficial reality characteristic of a materialistic and positivistic age, he himself on the contrary promises to portray the extraordinary, to sound the darkest and most fascinating aspects of this reality. Whereas the dandy seeks to strike his contemporaries with the originality of his appearance and his attitude, the dandy narrator wishes to stand out for the originality of his subject matter. He portrays not the Homais and Lantiers of his time but the unusual Calixte who painfully yet happily atones for her father's sins (*Un Prêtre marié*); the vindictive Duchesse d'Archos, who seeks to discredit her husband's name by becoming a prostitute and intentionally contracting syphilis (*La Vengeance d'une femme*); or the mysterious Marmor who hides unbridled passion and murderous cruelty behind the whist player's impassive mask (*Le Dessous de cartes*).

While Barbey's dandy narrator sets out to depict the uncommon and hidden aspects of modern existence, he is not interested in illuminating society's darker side in a positivistic manner. On the contrary, Barbey's storyteller confronts the "enlightened" nineteenth century reader with a world of opacity and ambiguity that is supposed to shock and surprise. A basic narrative principle of Barbey's dandy text thus consists in generating darkness and mystery. This principle is of particular importance in Barbey's literary works and, as a theme, omnipresent. The introduction to the short story *A un Dîner d'athées* should, for example, be read as a figurative representation of the narrative principle at work in this story as well as in Barbey's literary text in general.[26] In this introduction the narrator paints the mysterious darkness in a church that allows the faithful to better communicate with God. This darkness, referred to eighteen times in the first paragraph alone,[27] is described as a deep human need and as a prerequisite for true and intensive communication:

> . . . ces nuits mystérieuses des nefs vides, qui répondent certainement au plus profond besoin de l'âme humaine, car si, pour nous autres, mondains et passion-

nés, le tête-à-tête en cachette avec la femme aimée nous paraît plus intime et plus troublant dans les ténèbres, pourquoi n'en serait-il pas de même pour les âmes religieuses avec Dieu, quand il fait noir devant les tabernacles, et qu'elles lui parlent, de bouche à oreille, dans l'obscurité?

> (*Œuvres* 2: 173-74)

Compared to a curtain, a falling sail or cloth, and a filter[28], the obscurity of the church corresponds on the narrative level to the lacuna. Barbey weaves narrative gaps into his text so that the stories that are told remain to a certain degree incomplete, opaque, and impenetrable. If "[la] grande draperie d'ombre" and "[la] filtration de clarté incertaine" permit a more intensive communication with God, the lacuna is, according to Barbey, essential for an effective storytelling and a literary renewal. "Ce qu'on ne sait pas centuple l'impression de ce qu'on sait," claims the narrator of *Le Dessous de cartes* and adds: "Je me figure que l'enfer, vu par un soupirail, devrait etre plus effrayant que si, d'un seul et planant regard, on pouvait l'embrasser tout entier" (*Œuvres* 2: 132-33). While the dandy hides behind a cold and indifferent mask in order to astonish, irritate, and thus dominate, the dandy narrator makes use of a "filtered," "masked," or even "blocked" narration[29] in order to maximize the interest of his listeners and the control over his audience.

Barbey's narrators, often imperfectly or indirectly informed, cannot always entirely reconstruct their stories' plots, thus leaving them incomplete or unfinished. "Et après?" asks for example the still curious listener at the end of the short story *Le Rideau cramoisi.* "Eh bien! voilà! . . . il n'y a pas d'après!" replies the narrator Brassard (*Œuvres* 2: 56). The events after Alberte's sudden death and Brassard's desperate flight are not told and the listener's curiosity is not satisfied. Barbey's dandy narrators withhold information, relating merely "les surfaces" and "les extrémités" of their stories.[30] Remarks such as "ici l'histoire est fort obscure" and "voilà ce qu'il est impossible de savoir" (*Œuvres* 2: 167, 169) abound and mark together with vague speculations and unanswered questions the narrative gaps in Barbey's text.

Opacity is also generated by omissions of a psychological nature. A great number of Barbey's protagonists are mysterious beings whose behavior astounds and eludes explanation. Their actions often lack a motive and the intensity of their feelings remains incomprehensible. Barbey's dandy hero and narrator Brassard (*Le Rideau cramoisi*) is for example deeply bewildered by Alberte's contradictory conduct. The bold schoolgirl who passionately seized his hand under the dinner table and enflamed the young man with this "monstrueuse avance" (*Œuvres* 2: 35) treats him the next day with cold and cruel indifference. Throughout the short story the alternation between unbridled passion and complete emotional control that Alberte seems to master with such ease remains incomprehensible; the psychological profile of this "Mademoiselle Impassible"—as well as that of numerous other protagonists in Barbey's literary works—remains enigmatic.

Mystery is generated not solely by omissions of a narrative and psychological nature. Darkness exists also on the linguistic level of Barbey's text, since grammatical, lexical, as well as rhetorical details also contribute to the arcane atmosphere of the dandy narrative. As Anne Giard has shown, Barbey's narrators have recourse to "une grammaire de l'incertitude" and "un vocabulaire du mystère" (47, 46) in order to communicate the mysterious nature of their protagonists and to express their own insecurity, incomprehension, and perplexity. Narrators such as Brassard and Torty accumulate unanswered questions as well as vague suppositions and conjectures. They also pair factual statements with conditional clauses as, for example, in the following sentence from *Le Bonheur dans le crime*: "Ce qui se passa entre [Serlon] et Hauteclaire, *s'il se passa quelque chose,* aucun, à cette époque, ne l'a su ou ne s'en douta" (*Œuvres* 2: 96, my italics). By adding the conditional clause the narrator challenges the assertion put forth in the same sentence. Barbey's "grammaire de l'incertitude" reaches a climax in the short story *Le Dessous de cartes* in which the net of suppositions, searching questions, and conditional objections is so tightly knit that little room for unequivocal facts and clarity remains:

> Si ce fut là un mensonge de plus, jamais mensonge ne fut mieux osé. Tenait-elle [la comtesse de Stasseville] cette effrayante faculté de dissimuler de son organisation sèche et contractile? Mais pourquoi s'en servait-elle, elle, l'indépendance en personne par sa position et la fierté moqueuse du caractère? Pourquoi, si elle aimait Kerkoël et si elle en était aimée, le cachait-elle sous les ridicules qu'elle lui jetait de temps à autre, sous ces plaisanteries apostates, renégates, impies, qui dégradent l'idole adorée . . . les plus grands sacrilèges en amour? Mon Dieu! qui sait? il y avait peut-être en tout cela du bonheur pour elle . . .
>
> (*Œuvres* 2: 153)

On the lexical level mysteriousness and opacity are created by the choice of vocabulary as well as by the impossibility of that choice. The dandy narrator Brassard describes for example the attractive yet at the same time uncanny and "demonic" Alberte by using "un lexique du mystère" (Giard 46) that includes the following nine adjectives: "énigmatique," "étrange," "singulier," "incomparable," "incroyable," "inexplicable," "incompréhensible," "impénétrable," "impassible."[31] These adjectives that all belong to the same word field and in most cases are repeated at least once give Alberte something indecipherable and indefinable. If the young woman is inscrutable—as the prefixes *im-* and *in-*sug-

gest—, she is also indescribable. Brassard hesitates in his choice of words when he seeks to describe Alberte's striking behavior and amazing bearing because the appropriate adjective for which he is looking does not seem to exist:

> . . . l'air qu'elle avait, et qui était singulier dans une jeune fille aussi jeune qu'elle, car c'était une espèce d'air impassible, très difficile à caractériser. . . . *L'Infante à l'épagneul,* de Velasquez, pourrait, si vous la connaissez, vous donner une idée de cet air-là, qui n'était ni fier, ni méprisant, ni dédaigneux, non! mais tout simplement impassible. . . .
>
> (*Œuvres* 2: 31)

The narrator tries to compensate for the inadequacy of language with a reference to the pictorial arts. He also seeks to approach the missing word by listing and then eliminating inapplicable adjectives. Yet the adequate word remains absent and the linguistic gap cannot be closed.

Omissions of a narrative kind are thus joined by those of a linguistic kind, that which is untold by that which is "untellable," nameless, and unspeakable. In the short stories of *Les Diaboliques* linguistic lacunas are primarily produced by oxymoron, a figure of speech so common in Barbey's dandy text that it constitutes not only a stylistic device but also a *Weltanschauung.*[32] When Barbey's narrator describes Alberte as "infernalement calme," Ravila's eye color as "bleu d'enfer," and the attitude of the Comtesse de Stasseville as "amoureusement cruelle,"[33] he links two contradictory terms that cannot be united and thus disturbs the "order" of language: the two mutually exclusive words joined in the oxymoron lose their original meaning and serve as a substitute for a third word that is absent and inexistent. The close connection between the *signifiant* and the *signifié* is undermined so that "cruelle," coupled with "amoureusement," loses its transparency as a linguistic sign. The paradoxical word combination in the oxymoron refers to something beyond language that has no linguistic sign of its own and thus remains unreachable, dark, and mysterious.

* * *

The dandy's ideologically motivated revolt as well as his striving for power and control affect every level of Barbey's text and account for the unusual relationship between frame and story in *Les Diaboliques*. The art of conversation in which the dandy excels constitutes the principle of Barbey's literary production. Hailed as a talented storyteller and a renewing force in literature, Barbey's dandy narrators set out to revive a discourse characteristic of the aristocratic salon and the absolutist court. The aesthetic of dissimulation that the dandy cultivates determines the narrative and linguistic structures of Barbey's dandy text. Omissions and lacunas characterize especially the short stories of *Les Diaboliques* and create on the narrative as well as on the grammatical, lexical, and rhetorical level darkness, mysteriousness, and ambiguity. By masking his story as the dandy masks himself, Barbey's narrator also perfects the art of the unexpected. He seeks to surprise and thus dominate his salon audience, to disappoint the traditional reader's expectations and shake his positivistic world view. While the reader might feel mocked or fooled, might be irritated or shocked by the dandy's story, he is also fascinated and captivated by it. The dandy's narrative act surely constituted for the reactionary Barbey a means of revolt, a weapon of sorts with which to subtly attack and artfully deride a society he abhorred and rejected. The narrative act, coupled with dandyism, was for Barbey thus of great importance. As for his hero-narrators, it represented for the author an ideologically charged and aggressive act that provided him with powerful means of sexual and textual control. It allowed Barbey to create a male world of the word in which postrevolutionary France, deemed decadent and effeminate, is reviled and in which the erotic woman, desired and feared, falls victim to his narrative violence.

Notes

1. See Barbey, "Du Dandysme et de George Brummell," *Œuvres* [*Œuvres romanesques complètes*] 2: 667-733. Charles Baudelaire discusses dandyism in his essay "Le Dandy" as well as sporadically in his diaries "Fusées" and "Mon coeur mis à nu" (Baudelaire [*Œuvres complètes*] 1177-80, 1247-65, 1271-1301). Honoré de Balzac discusses dandyism under the name of "elegance" in his "Traité de la vie élégante" (Balzac [*La Comédie humaine*] 12:238-86).

2. Ellen Moers' study *The Dandy: Brummell to Beerbohm* provides a very good historical account of dandyism. Other most useful studies on historical and literary dandyism are: Prevost, *Le Dandysme en France (1817-39)*; Lemaire, *Le Dandysme de Baudelaire à Mallarmé*; Carassus, *Le Mythe du dandy*; Gnüg, *Kult der Kälte. Der klassische Dandy im Spiegel der Weltliteratur*; Stanton, *The Aristocrat as Art. A Study of the Honnête Homme and the Dandy in Seventeenth and Nineteenth Century French Literature*; Kempf, *Dandies: Baudelaire et Cie.*

3. Barbey, *Les Prophètes du passé* 48; Barbey, *Œuvres* 1: 555. Yarrow's *La Pensée politique et religieuse de Barbey d'Aurevilly* is an informative study on Barbey's political and religious thought. See also: Schwartz, *Idéologie et art romanesque chez Jules Barbey d'Aurevilly*.

4. Barbey, *Œuvres* 1: 627; Barbey, *Revue du monde catholique*, 4 July 1847, 53, quoted in Yarrow 76.

5. Among these dandy heroes of Barbey's text are the Vicomte de Brassard (*Le Rideau cramoisi*), Ryno de Marigny (*Une Vieille maîtresse*), Marmor de Kerkoël (*Le Dessous de cartes d'une partie de whist*), and Mesnilgrand (*A un Dîner d'athées*).

6. For a more extensive discussion of metaphors of war and dandyism, see Stanton 62-105 (chapter 2).

7. See also Barbey, *Œuvres* 1: 253, 221.

8. See also Barbey, *Œuvres* 2: 184 ("il était toujours divinement mis"), 181 ("sabrant la toile de son pinceau"), 183 ("il avait . . . une extraordinaire éloquence").

9. See Barbey, *Œuvres* 2: 64: "C'est qu'au fond, et malgré tout ce qui pourrait empêcher de le croire, c'est un rude spiritualiste que Don Juan! Il l'est comme le démon lui-même, qui aime les âmes encore plus que les corps, et qui fait même cette traite-là de préférence à l'autre, ce négrier infernal!" See also Gnüg 207-24.

10. See Feldman, *Gender on the Divide. The Dandy in Modernist Literature* 6.

11. See for example Alberte and Brassard in *Le Rideau cramoisi* as well as Hauteclaire and Serlon in *Le Bonheur dans le crime*.

12. See Marini 12.

13. Jessica Feldman, on the contrary, claims that the dandy is not a pseudoandrogynous but a genuinely androgynous being. See Feldman 6-7.

14. As for example Alberte in *Le Rideau cramoisi*, Hauteclaire in *Le Bonheur dans le crime*, Rosalba in *A un Dîner d'athées*, and Vellini in *Une Vieille maîtresse*.

15. I am using the terminology of Gérard Genette. See Genette, *Figures III* 238.

16. See for example: Petit, "Note sur la structure des *Diaboliques*"; Debray-Genette, "Un récit autologique? *Le Bonheur dans le crime*"; Ropars-Wuilleumier, "*Le plus bel amour de Don Juan*: Narration et signification"; Petit, *Essais de lectures des* Diaboliques; Tranouez, "La Narration neutralisante"; Boucher, Les Diaboliques *de Barbey d'Aurevilly: Une esthétique de la dissimulation et de la provocation*; Sivert, "Text, Body, and Reader in Barbey d'Aurevilly's *Les Diaboliques*"; Sivert, "Narration and Exhibitionism in *Le Rideau cramoisi*"; Giard, "Le récit lacunaire dans *Les Diaboliques*"; Bernheimer, "Female Sexuality and Narrative Closure: Barbey d'Aurevilly's *La Vengeance d'une femme* and *A un Dîner d'athées*"; Cardonne-Arlyck, "Nom, corps, métaphore dans

Les Diaboliques de Barbey d'Aurevilly"; Tranouez, *Fascination et narration dans l'œuvre romanesque de Barbey d'Aurevilly: La scène capitale*; Unwin, "Barbey d'Aurevilly conteur: Discours et narration dans *Les Diaboliques*"; Stivale "'Like the Sculptor's Chisel': Voices 'On' and 'Off' in Barbey d'Aurevilly's *Les Diaboliques*"; Holder, "Séduction narrative et donjuanisme chez Barbey d'Aurevilly"; Eisenberg, *The Figure of the Dandy in Barbey d'Aurevilly's* Le bonheur dans le crime.

17. See also Unwin 354.

18. See for example Barbey, *Œuvres* 1: 214, 1313; 2: 130.

19. For an analysis of Barbey's literary style see: Lemaire 109; Gnüg 217-21.

20. See Barbey, *Œuvres* 2: 1274-75.

21. See also Stivale 323.

22. See Barbey, *Œuvres* 2: 24 ("avec mélancholie"), 38 ("assez froidement"), 49 ("d'un ton plus grave"), 57 ("avec amertume").

23. See Landes, *Women and the Public Sphere in the Age of the French Revolution*.

24. See Landes 39-65.

25. See also Barbey, *Œuvres* 2: 155, 169.

26. See Sivert, "Text, Body, and Reader" ["Text, Body, and Reader in Barbey d'Aurevilly's *Les Diaboliques*"] 152.

27. In the first paragraph of the short story *A un Dîner d'athées* the following terms or expressions belong to the word field "darkness": "nuit," "sombres," "ombres," "la mort . . . du jour," "vespérale," "agonise," "catacombes," "cachette," "ténèbres," "obscurité." See Barbey, *Œuvres* 2: 173-74.

28. See Barbey, *Œuvres* 2: 174: "sa grande draperie d'ombre," "comme une voile tombant d'un mât," "cette filtration de clarté incertaine."

29. "'Blocked' narration" is an expression used by Eileen Sivert. See Sivert, "Text, Body, and Reader" 151.

30. See Barbey, *Œuvres* 1: 584 (*L'Ensorcelée*): "Cette histoire, mon compagnon de route me la raconta comme il la savait, et il n'en savait que les surfaces." See also Barbey, *Œuvres* 2: 170 (*Le Dessous de cartes*): "Le conteur avait fini son histoire, ce roman qu'il avait promis et dont il n'avait montré que ce qu'il en savait, c'est-à-dire les extrémités."

31. See Barbey, *Œuvres*: "cette énigmatique Alberte" (2: 43); "étrange personne" (2: 47); "l'air [. . .]

singulier" (2: 31); "cette singulière fille" (2: 47); "une aisance et une gracieuse langueur de mouvement incomparables," "un incroyable sang-froid" (2: 34); "incroyable ton" (2: 39); "cette froideur inexplicable" (2: 46); "incompréhensible physionomie" (2: 39); "cette incompréhensible Alberte" (2: 43); "ses grands yeux impénétrables" (2: 39); "aussi impénétrable qu'elle" (2: 48); "air impassible," "tout simplement impassible" (2: 31); "Mademoiselle Impassible" (2: 41). See Giard 46.

32. See Crouzet, "Barbey d'Aurevilly et l'oxymore: ou la rhétorique du diable".

33. Barbey, *Œuvres* 2: 41, 63, 168. Other examples are: "délicieusement étouffée" (2: 33); "lâcheté si hardie" (2: 46); "marbre humain" (2: 143); "larve élégante" (2: 148); "sombre gaîté" (2: 161); "silencieux et sonore" (2: 174); "la furie joyeuse" (2: 223); "splendide de mauvais goût" (2: 234); "innocente meutrière" (1: 614); "la grandiose laideur" (1: 622).

Works Cited

Balzac, Honoré de. *La Comédie humaine*. vol. 12. Paris: Gallimard, 1981.

Barbey d'Aurevilly, Jules. *Œuvres romanesques complètes*. 2 vols. Paris: Gallimard, 1964-66.

———. *Les Prophètes du passé*. Paris: Lévy, 1889.

Baudelaire, Charles. *Œuvres complètes*. Paris: Gallimard, 1961.

Bernheimer, Charles. "Female Sexuality and Narrative Closure: Barbey d'Aurevilly's *La Vengeance d'une femme* and *A un Dîner d'athées*." *The Romanic Review* LXXIV.3 (May 1983): 330-41.

Boucher, Jean-Pierre. Les Diaboliques *de Barbey d'Aurevilly: Une esthétique de la dissimulation et de la provocation*. Montréal: Les Presses de l'université de Québec, 1976.

Carassus, Emilien. *Le Mythe du dandy*. Paris: Colin, 1971.

Cardonne-Arlyck, Elisabeth. "Nom, corps, métaphore dans *Les Diaboliques* de Barbey d'Aurevilly." *Littérature* 54 (May 1984): 3-19.

Crouzet, Michel. "Barbey d'Aurevilly et l'oxymore: ou la rhétorique du diable." *Barbey d'Aurevilly—* L'Ensorcelée *et* Les Diaboliques: *La chose sans nom*. Paris: Sedes, 1988. 83-98.

Debray-Genette, Raymonde. "Un récit autologique? *Le Bonheur dans le crime*." *The Romanic Review* LXIV.1 (January 1973): 38-53.

Eisenberg, Davina L. *The Figure of the Dandy in Barbey d'Aurevilly's* Le bonheur dans le crime. New York: Peter Lang, 1996.

Feldman, Jessica. *Gender on the Divide. The Dandy in Modernist Literature.* Ithaca and London: Cornell UP, 1993.

Genette, Gérard. *Figures III.* Paris: Seuil, 1972.

Giard, Anne. "Le récit lacunaire dans *Les Diaboliques.*" *Poétique* 41 (February 1980): 39-50.

Gnüg, Hiltrud. *Kult der Kälte. Der klassische Dandy im Spiegel der Weltliteratur.* Stuttgart: Metzler, 1988.

Holder, Guillemette I. "Séduction narrative et donjuanisme chez Barbey d'Aurevilly." *Nineteenth Century French Studies* 23.1-2 (Fall 1994-Winter 1995): 166-74.

Kempf, Roger. *Dandies: Baudelaire et Cie.* Paris: Seuil, 1989.

Landes, Joan B. *Women and the Public Sphere in the Age of the French Revolution.* Ithaca and London: Cornell UP, 1988.

Lemaire, Michel. *Le Dandysme de Baudelaire à Mallarmé.* Montreal and Paris: Klincksieck, 1978.

Marini, Marcelle. "Ricochets de lecture. La Fantasmatique des *Diaboliques.*" *Littérature* 10 (May 1973): 3-19.

Moers, Ellen. *The Dandy: Brummell to Beerbohm.* Lincoln: U of Nebraska P, 1960.

Petit, Jacques. *Essais de lectures des* Diaboliques. Paris: Minard, 1974.

———. "Note sur la structure des *Diaboliques.*" *Revue des lettres modernes* 199-202 (1969): 85-89.

Prevost, John C. *Le Dandysme en France (1817-39).* Genève: Droz, 1957.

Ropars-Wuilleumier, Marie-Claire. "*Le plus bel amour de Don Juan*: Narration et signification." *Littérature* 9 (February 1973): 118-25.

Schwartz, Helmut. *Idéologie et art romanesque chez Jules Barbey d'Aurevilly.* München: Fink, 1971.

Sivert, Eileen. "Text, Body, and Reader in Barbey d'Aurevilly's *Les Diaboliques.*" *Symposium* XXXI.2 (Summer 1977): 151-64.

———. "Narration and Exhibitionism in *Le Rideau cramoisi.*" *The Romanic Review* LXX (March 1979): 146-58.

Stanton, Domna C. *The Aristocrat as Art. A Study of the Honnête Homme and the Dandy in Seventeenth and Nineteenth Century French Literature.* New York: Columbia UP, 1980.

Stivale, Charles. "'Like the Sculptor's Chisel': Voices 'On' and 'Off' in Barbey d'Aurevilly's *Les Diaboliques.*" *The Romanic Review* LXXXII.2 (March 1991): 317-30.

Tranouez, Pierre. "La Narration neutralisante." *Poétique* 17 (1974): 39-49.

———. *Fascination et narration dans l'oeuvre romanesque de Barbey d'Aurevilly: La scène capitale.* Paris: Lettres Modernes, 1987.

Unwin, Timothy. "Barbey d'Aurevilly conteur: Discours et narration dans *Les Diaboliques.*" *Neophilologus* 72.3 (1988): 353-65.

Yarrow, Philip J. *La Pensée politique et religieuse de Barbey d'Aurevilly.* Genève: Droz, 1961.

Joyce O. Lowrie (essay date May 1999)

SOURCE: Lowrie, Joyce O. "Barbey d'Aurevilly's 'Une Page d'histoire': A Poetics of Incest." *Romantic Review* 90, no. 3 (May 1999): 379-95.

[*In the following essay, Lowrie follows themes of transgression and narcissism in Barbey d'Aurevilly's short story.*]

> In every way, repetition is transgression. It questions law, denouncing its nominal or general characteristics, to the benefit of a more profound and artistic reality.
>
> Gilles Deleuze[1]

The ourobouros, the serpent biting its tail that remains iconographically intact so as to signify unity, the end in the beginning, the Omega in the Alpha, will not do as a symbol for Barbey d'Aurevilly's short story, **"Une Page d'histoire"** (1882). But the witticism about the two snakes seen devouring each other that concludes with the punch line, "and when I looked again, they were *both* gone," will do. One might even say that it is an appropriate emblem for one of Barbey's most intriguing short stories, a narrative about transgression in which the real author elaborates what might be termed a "poetics of incest."

The narrator of **"Une Page d'histoire"** asserts that very few facts about Julien and Marguerite de Ravalet can be uncovered in the chronicle of their fate. What is known, the reader is told, is that at the end of the 16th century, during the reign of Henri IV, the beautiful Marguerite and Julien were brother and sister in a family made infamous for its crimes ever since it had come from Brittany to the chateau of Tourlaville in Normandy around 1400. After the brother and sister fell in love, their imperious father exiled his son and married off his daughter to an old man, Jean Le Fauconnier. Julien returned from exile, abducted Marguerite, and their traces were lost for more than a year. They were found in Paris, on a sad day in December, on their way to the scaffold. The most vivid historical detail available is that of Marguerite's being so beautiful that as she climbed the steps of the platform where she was going to die, she caused the executioner to become distraught. She slapped him smartly to bring him to his senses.[2]

Barbey's short story is symbolically "undone" in the tale of the Ravalets. As a decadent writer, Barbey was extremely fond of ambiguity and duplicity. This penchant was translated, semiologically, into a fondness for double entendres. The seme *Ravalet* recalls the verb *ravaler,* "to swallow again," and, as such, it emphasizes the termination of the family's race:

> La famille qui vivait là [in the chateau of Tourlaville] portait sans le savoir un nom faridique. C'était la famille de Ravalet . . . Et de fait, elle devait un jour le *ravaler,* ce nom sinistre! Après le crime de ses deux derniers descendants, elle s'excommunia elle-même de son nom.

> * * *

> [The family who lived there bore, without knowing it, a fateful name. They were called the Ravalets . . . And in fact, one day the family would *swallow down again* that sinister name! Following the crime of its last two descendants, it excommunicated itself from its own name.] Underlining in text.

(369)[3]

The incestuous crime of Julien and Marguerite led to their deaths, to the end of the Ravalet family, and to the conclusion of the narrator's story. It also happens that **"Une Page d'histoire"** was the last narrative written by Barbey d'Aurevilly (1882).[4]

Ravalet—Ravaler: Barbey clearly plays with the polysemy of the words. *Ravaler* means not only "to swallow again," but also "to lower, throw down, cause to fall." Its first meaning relates to masonry, the "completion of a house's exterior walls," a work that goes from top to bottom, signifying "descent." Its figurative meanings are "to lower, depreciate, vilify, deprave, denigrate, disparage." In the 16th century the word acquired the meaning of *avaler de nouveau,* "to swallow again," or simply "to swallow," as in *ravaler sa salive,* "to swallow one's saliva," or metaphorically, *je lui ferai ravaler ses paroles,* "I will make him swallow his words." (In English people are made to *eat* their words—in French, to swallow them). Barbey has the last descendants of the *Ravalets* "swallowing their own name,"—gone, gone—as well as depreciating, denigrating, depraving it. This was a perfect word for a decadent writer, since, as we know, "decadence" comes from the medieval Latin word *cadere,* to fall.[5]

The narrator of **"Une Page d'histoire"** not only plays with double meanings, but he is also ambivalent about the crime. He finds himself identifying with the protagonists of his story. Though the narrator states that incest is "a shame, the termination of a race," he will also

say that the protagonists *"se sont enfoncés en moi comme si je les avais connus"* "they *had burrowed down into me* as if I had known them" (368). And he uses the word "charme" twice, a troubling charm that renders the happiness of the brother and sister "enviously shared" by him, and he prays, "may God forgive us for that" (368). He and his characters swallow each other up, as it were. The surrealist notion that was introduced later in the history of poetics by Breton's *Vases communicants,* of "the one in the other," is clearly at work in the metaphorically incestuous relationship that exists between the narrator and his heroes.

PROLOGUE AND PARTS: HISTORY AND STORY

The tale of Tourlaville is divided into five parts. In what I entitle the "Prologue" (Part I), the narrator talks about himself, about his "Norman birthplace," about the specters that haunt the land. He talks about his town, which he calls "the town of *my* specters," and about the two specific specters whose story he will tell and who will, he says, join "the company of the others."

After the "Prologue" (Part I), the family's place in history is told in Parts II and III.[6] The Ravalet saga took place at the end of the 16th century, the century that brought to the fore Catherine de Médicis and the race of the Valois, "the Borgias of France" (369), as the narrator calls them. This was the age of "la reine Margot," whose adventures were made famous by Dumas, and more recently, by Patrice Chéreau's film *La Reine Margot.* It is no accident that the narrator alludes not only to Marguerite de Valois's incestuous past, but poetically foregrounds the names "Marguerite de Valois" and "Marguerite de Ravalet." Both share first names, and their last names share similar syllables, namely, "*Val*ois" and "Ra*val*et." One thinks of the connotations of the word "*val*" or "valley," or of the expression *à val,* which means "down dale," or "to go downhill." Does not one also think of *Val*mont as well, that scandalous oxymoron?

Marguerite de Valois, the narrator says, "had attributed to her, to her soul, so many incests as to punish herself in Marguerite de Ravalet's incest" (372). The narrator is referring to the beheading of the Ravalet brother and sister, which had occurred during the reign of Henri IV. While Henri IV hesitated to execute them, his wife Marguerite de Valois had no pity. To expiate her own incestuous past, she encouraged her husband to effectuate justice upon the guilty pair. One incest precedes the other, making of incest a repetitive or doubled act in the historical structure of the tale.[7] Historical incests were sources of interest to Romantic and Decadent writers.

The family's history had more than its share of murders, rapes, debauchery and sacrilege, all of which could not but whet the appetite of the real author of *Les Di-*

aboliques. Many of these crimes are named and described briefly by the narrator in Parts II and III. But, he says, while the public awaited some new monster to come forth from the bloodied and sullied Ravalets, two beautiful roses appeared instead, Julien and Marguerite, who were "as beautiful as innocence" (371). The family crest, in fact, carried "une rose en pointe."[8] When the two roses joined together to become one, in "reality," as well as symbolically, the family's history came to an end.

FIRST CHIASTIC SIGHTING

While Parts II and III emphasize the place in *history* of the Ravalet family, the narrator uses his imagination to tell their *story* in Parts IV and V. Because the meanings of both *history* and *story* are contained in the word *histoire,* ambiguity is present in the short story's title, **"Une Page d'histoire."** The story will consist of a *"page* d'histoire," but it will be a fiction based upon a historical event, a "page d'*histoire.*" Both meanings are made distinct by the narrator. When he writes *History* with a capital "H" he talks about his *spectres* coming to him after "trois siècles d'*Histoire*;" and when he writes *story* with a lower-case "h" he speaks of "l'*histoire* de ces deux *spectres*" (368).

"Spectres—Histoire—histoire—spectres": this first chiasmus, used in the Prologue of the narrative, accentuates, through its disposition of words, both the duality of *histoire,* on the one hand, and the unity of both, on the other. The story is, after all, based upon the history of an incestual relationship, sparse though the historical details may be. In frustration, the narrator says in Part IV:

> Et voilà tout ce que l'on sait de cette triste et cruelle histoire. Mais ce qui passionnerait bien davantage serait ce que l'on n'en sait pas! . . . Or, où les historiens s'arrêtent, ne sachant plus rien, les poètes apparaissent et devinent. Ils voient encore, quand les historiens ne voient plus.
>
> * * *
>
> [And that is all we know about this sad and cruel story. But what could be even more passionate is what we do not know! . . . So, where historians stop, knowing nothing more, poets appear and guess. They go on seeing, when historians fail.]
>
> (373)

It is up to the poet to use imagination to turn the tapestry of history inside out, "to find out what is behind that tapestry, fascinating precisely because of what it hides from us . . ." (373). A mirror is appropriate for this imagery, since the narrator's task is that of coating the glass on the underside so that it will reveal what has been hidden so far.

Even then, the narrator indicates uncertainty by asking one question after another, and each question mark is followed by suspension points: "Who ever knew the origin of this disastrous love, which had probably already come to fruition by the time anyone noticed it? . . . At what moment in their infancy or their youth did they find the cantharis of incest in the bottom of their hearts, subterraneously dormant, and which of the two taught the other one it was there?" (371-372). Six questions ending with ellipses appear in one paragraph.

ARTIFACT BEFORE FACT

In one of Murray Krieger's essays on *ekphrasis,*[9] he shows how a number of factually based questions in Keats's "Ode on a Grecian Urn" end in suspension periods: "What men or gods are these? What maidens loth? . . . Who are these coming to the sacrifice? To what green altar . . . ?" Krieger concludes that "these ellipses have guaranteed the poet's exasperation at the inadequacy of empirical data before beauty's archetypal perfection, the inadequacy of fact before artifact" (284).

Barbey's narrator expresses impatience at the lack of historical data available to him, so much so that in Part IV, he will opt for artifact before fact. He begins by using poetic custom to evoke those writers and poets who had gone before him for whom the question of incest was unquestionably a provocative one. He mentions, intratextually, Chateaubriand's *René,* and Byron's *Parisina* and *Manfred,* all texts dealing with incest.[10] Barbey's text is grounded primarily in literary textuality, even as it narrates historical incest intratextually. The writer himself was fascinated by incest, and elaborates a poetics of incest not only in **"Une Page d'histoire"** but also in *Ce qui ne meurt pas* (written in the 1830's but published in 1883), in the novella *Léa* (1832), and in the poem **"Treize ans"** (dated approximately around 1869-1870).

TRACES

The narrator/poet will use the well-known topos, *captatio henevolentiae* (which might be interpreted as a friendly seduction), in Part IV, to disavow rhetoric, only to use it to pull in his readers, thereby rendering them sensitive to rhetorical strategies: "Il faut, pour suivre les spectres, avoir plus foi en eux qu'en des figures de rhétorique" "In order to follow specters, one must have more faith in them than in rhetorical figures" (374). As Lévi-Strauss might say, Barbey testifies that he found "traces" of "les beaux Incestueux," and he uses anaphora, in which there is repetition of the same word at the beginning of successive clauses or verses, to show what those traces are. The usage of antimetabole ("inverting the order of repeated words [ABBA] to sharpen their sense or to contrast the ideas they convey, or both. . . . Chiasmus and commutatio sometimes imply a more precise balance and reversal, antimetabole a looser, but they are virtual synonyms," (Lanham, 14) and repetition is a basic element of Barbey's poetics of incest: "same into same" as well as "different into same" express the structural basis of such a poetics.

The phrase the narrator first uses in the *middle* of his first sentence, and then at the beginning of four successive phrases, is *je les ai retrouvés,* "I rediscovered them." He begins: "Les spectres qui m'avaient fait venir, *je les ai retrouvés* partout dans ce château, entrelacés après leur mort comme ils l'étaient pendant leur vie" "I rediscovered, everywhere in the chateau, the specters who had called me forth, intertwined after their death as they had been during their lifetime" (374).

In the first usage of the refrain *je les ai retrouvés* at the beginning of a sentence, the narrator mentions the scattered poetic inscriptions found on the walls throughout the chateau: "I rediscovered them as they strolled about, below the panellings that were filled with tragically amorous inscriptions" (374). He cites those inscriptions in a footnote. It is as if, placed together, they formed a prose poem:

> Un seul me suffit.—Ce qui donne la vie me cause la mort.—Sa froideur me glace les veines et son ardeur brûle mon coeur.—Les deux n'en font qu'un.—Ainsi puissé-je mourir!
>
> [One only suffices.—That which gives life causes my death.—His [or her] coldness makes my blood run cold, and his [or her] ardour burns my heart.—Two are but one.—Thus may I die!]

The inscriptions are poetically rendered: "un *seul* me suffit" is echoed in "les *deux* n'en font qu'*un*." The long sentence in the middle uses repetition and contrast: "froideur"/"glance"/"veines" contrasts with "ardeur"/ "brûle"/"cœur." The second and fifth sentences echo each other in their references to death.

The second anaphora, *je les ai retrouvés* "I rediscovered them", "finds" traces of the lovers in the octagonal tower of the chateau, where the narrator opposes "absent warmth" to the "frozen satin" of the blue boudoir in the tower. Like Keats's Grecian urn, the tower of Tourlaville stands archetypically cold in its reminder of warm life and loves past.

WITHIN THE MIRROR

In the third *je les ai retrouvés,* the narrator "finds" the incestuous lovers in a mirror of the chateau, "dans la glace oblongue de la cheminée, avec leurs grands yeux pâles et mornes de fantômes, me regardant du fond de ce cristal qui, moi parti, ne gardera pas leur image!" "in the oblong mirror above the fireplace, with their large, pale, and lukewarm fantom's eyes, looking at me from the bottom of the crystal, which, once I was gone, would not keep their image" (374).[11]

The "literal," or referential mirror in the text, "la glace oblongue de la cheminée," raises the question of focalization, of "who sees?," of point of view. The narrator reflects the reader in and of the text, the doubled "eyes"

of the "I." The lovers "exist" insofar as the reader-spectator is in dialogue with their *imago.* Reader criticism, and Iser in particular, has taught us that the Book exists *in relationship* to its reader. There is no clearer example of this than in Barbey's having his narrator/ poet's specters "come to life" so long as the spectator sees them in the mirror. Once the spectator has stopped "reading" them, they are gone. They can be "re-found," so to speak, once we readers "read" the spectator's "reading" them in the oblong mirror he describes in the text. The mirror is in the text as the text is in the mirror.

WITHIN THE PORTRAIT

The spectator/poet's fourth and final *je les ai retrouvés* is an admirable exercise in *ekphrasis*:

> Je les ai retrouvés enfin devant le portrait de Marguerite, et le frère disait passionément et mélancoliquement à la sœur: "Pourquoi ne t'ont-ils pas fait ressemblante?"
>
> * * *
>
> ["I rediscovered them, finally, in front of Marguerite's portrait, and the brother was saying, passionately and mournfully to his sister: 'Why could they not have painted a true likeness of you?'"]
>
> (374)

Again, the questions of point of view and mimesis are raised. To the brother/lover the portrait of his sister/ lover cannot possibly "resemble" her. To him, the lover, the mimetic qualities of painting are a failure. But this will not keep the narrator from painting, ekphrastically, a portrait of Marguerite for his readers. *His* "painting" will supposedly "resemble" her, since it is semiologically engraved.

And so, to the portrait. Just as the "reader" gazed at the lovers in the oblong mirror and they returned his gaze ("me regardant du fond de ce cristal"), so does Marguerite de Ravalet look at the spectator, in the narrator's version, rather than at the Cupids surrounding her: "She is standing in this portrait,—a full-faced picture,— and she is not looking at the Cupids that surround her (one more proof that they were added to the portrait), but at the spectator. . . . She seems . . . to be doing the honors, her right hand graciously opened, to the person who is looking at her portrait" (375).[12]

There is a difference between the gaze in the mirror and the gaze described in the painting. While it is the narrator who rediscovers the lovers in the oblong mirror, and they gaze back at him, the initiative comes from *within* in the ekphrastic depiction. Were one to juxtapose them, the point of view of the eyes in the mirror and those in the painting would be chiastically related, since a mirror reverses images. In the painting, Marguerite looks at the generic spectator, or at "the person looking at the portrait." She thus encodes that person within the portrait. Semiologically that person is as much a part of the portrait as are King Felipe IV and Queen María Ana, in Velásquez's painting of *Las Meninas*.[13] In Velásquez, most of the persons represented gaze at the King and Queen, who are "spectators" being "spectated," to use a neologism. They are looking at each other, in one way or another, even as we "spectate" both sides. Although in Velázquez the King and Queen are supposedly "outside" of the painting, their painted reflection in the mirror places them "inside" of the painting as well. Colie, Foucault, Kahr, Vaizey, Searle, Synder, Cohen, *et al.* agree on this point, even as they disagree on other interpretations of that famous painting.[14]

While there is no "literal" mirror represented within the *portrait* of Marguerite, the ekphrastic "painter" of **"Une Page d'histoire,"** its narrator also becomes "the spectator" who is being observed. He becomes the object of Marguerite's gaze as well as the equivalent of the real and implied readers of **"Une Page d'histoire."** The spectator becomes a mirror of the reflexive activity that takes place in the act of reading, in the act of reading about a portrait in which the subject gazes at her "reader" to the point that her "reader/spectator" is pulled into the text. On February 4th, 1995, in *Le Figaro Magazine* (17), Anne Sinclair, a popular television personality in France, made the following statement about herself: "One is consumed . . . because one is seen." Marguerite "consumes" *her* spectators, inversing the relationship just described between television viewer and viewed.

SECOND CHIASTIC SIGHTING

It should not be surprising that one of the two most deliberate and evident uses of chiasmus in **"Une Page d'histoire"** should be located at the conclusion of Part IV. While it is not found exactly at the "hinge," or at the center of the text's structure, it concludes the most self-consciously tropological section of the text, the most rhetorically charged in that it opposes "la Chronique" to "l'imagination des poètes" (373).

Part IV began with opposition between history and poetry, and so does it end. This appears in the intentionally striking chiasmus:

> La Chronique, qui dit si peu de choses, a dit seulement qu'elle prononça que c'était elle [Marguerite de Ravalet] qui avait entraîné son frère. Elle accueillit, sans se plaindre et sans protester, *l'échafaud,* comme elle avait accueilli *l'inceste,* et simplement, parce que la conséquence de *l'inceste* érait, dans ce temps-là, *l'échafaud.*

* * *

> [The Chronicle, that says so little, reveals only that it was she who told that she had seduced her brother. She

accepted, without complaining or protesting, *the scaffold,* just as she accepted *incest,* and she did this simply because the *consequence of incest* was, at that time, the *scaffold.*]

(376)

In the chiasmus "échafaud-inceste—inceste-échafaud," the historical consequence of incest is placed before the cause in the first part ("échafaud-inceste"), and cause precedes effect in the second part ("inceste-échafaud"). It is as if the narrator (1) reverses, rhetorically, in the chiastic disposition, the natural order of things, since incest at least calls into question "the natural order of things," and (2) mirrors his own ambiguity in his condemnation of, but fascination with, incest. By being repeated in the center of the chiasmus, "inceste" is valorized. It is also framed by death because it leads to *l'échafaud.*

Ravaler: to swallow twice, *avaler de nouveau.* The chiasmus does that. As Richard Lahnam says, "chiasmus seems to set up a natural internal dynamic that draws the parts closer together, as if the second element wanted to flip over and back over the first . . ." (33). The poetics of incest does that too: it is the interpenetration of two similar entities.

Murray Krieger, and many other commentators upon *ekphrasis,* including Wendy Steiner, emphasize the relationship that exists between the imitation of a spatial work and the question of temporality. One of the principal objects Krieger studies is the urn in literature (Keats's, Thomas Browne's, Shakespeare's, Donne's, etc.). Because the urn is a container of ashes for the dead, it represents both life and death, both movement and stillness. Its circular shape emblematizes the beginning and the end. Krieger states that the circularity of the urn adds complex dimensions to the temporal aspects of *ekphrasis.* It is an "always-in-motion but never-to-be-completed action." "As with Keats's urn," Krieger says, "it accompanies the introduction, in accordance with the ekphrastic principle of spatial forms within literature's temporality" (270-271). It brings to the literary work a doubleness that reveals "continual, deliberate advance, a 'succession,' yet a forever movement, 'without progress'" (271).

Time is integral to the ekphrastic portrait painted by the narrator of **"Une Page d'histoire."** When Marguerite "seems to be doing the honors, with her beautiful right hand hospitably open to the person who looks at the portrait" (375), she is represented as making a living, loving, inviting gesture to the percipient.[15] The bloody-winged Cupid painted next to her, however, was painted "après coup," *after* her death. The linear movement of her life and death are inscribed in the painting in several ways: both love and death are portrayed, the passage of time is represented because it was painted both before and after her death, and the static description of a static object is "brought to life" by focalization. Even though *ekphrasis* is related to a descriptive pause, it forms part of a narrative that moves through time, that has a beginning and an ending.[16] The passage of time and the lasting elements of art are not only in tension—they are deliberately "woven" and "unwoven," deconstructively, like Penelope's tapestry.

The inviting gesture Marguerite de Ravalet makes with her right hand contrasts with that depicted by her left. Both gestures seem to be inviting the reader to a hermeneutical task, as do the arm and hand painted by Parmigianino in his *Self-Portrait in a Convex Mirror*. Some critics interpret Parmigianino's arm as a barrier to interpretation. In Marguerite's portrait, she crumples up a handkerchief with her left hand "similar to the contraction of a secret one is hiding" (375). The right hand knows but does not reveal what the left hand is doing. While the right hand invites, the left one hides, in what one is led to assume is either a guilty, or obsessive, but in any case, highly symbolic contraction.

Mary Ann Caws is thought-provoking when she juxtaposes John Ashbery's poem on Parmigianino's painting to the painting itself. While Ashbery sees the arm as a barrier, as if it were painted there "to protest what it advertises," Caws suggests another interpretation. The hand, she says, can be viewed as a pointer, pointing inwards, back *into* the convex "mirror" of the self-portrait (51). Both Marguerite de Ravalet's hands manifest a visible disparity in the manner in which they are depicted. One invites the outsider in, while the other manifests the tension of privatization. The portrait as mirror shows the tension existing in the 19th century between private and public domains—with the private coming to dominate in Romanticism, in Symbolism, and in Decadence.

In the ekphrastic description of Marguerite's dress, the narrator says she is wearing "a *formal* white and rose-colored dress, whose cloth seems to have been braided together, and whose colors are *one in the other*, as one says in heraldic language" (375, emphases in text). We return to the surrealist injunction to join "one in the other." But "l'une en l'autre," as Jacques Petit reminds us, is also heraldic language, meaning "alternation of enamel between joints and partitions" (1362). While *alternance* appears in heraldic vocabulary, the word *tressée* the narrator uses seems equally appropriate to the meaning he is giving to his ekphrastic description: two colors, pink and white, are woven together so as to form one iridescent color. One imagines the material looking pinker at times and whiter at others, depending upon the nap of the material as well as the point of view of the spectator.

The "mingling" of colors or the braiding of two entities into one in **"Une Page d'histoire,"** the colors of which

go "from one to the other," not only describes, ekphrastically, the color of Marguerite's dress, but also reminds the reader of Ovid's paradigmatic myth of Narcissus, where his flesh is both white and pink. Ovid's narrator intertwines the colors pink and white in the description of Narcissus's admiring "the glorious beauty of his face, the blush mingled with snowy white" (155). After he comes to know himself and to despair, Narcissus beats his breast until it becomes pink, "just as apples sometimes, though white in part, flush red in other part, or as grapes hanging in clusters take on a purple hue when not yet ripe" (159). In the end, before he dies, the "ruddy colour" no longer mingles with the white. The "mingling," the joining of two in one is a metaphor for life, love, and death. It is also a metaphor for chiastic rhetoric. It achieves further import by being a metaphor for the poetics of incest itself, since Narcissism and incest have many rhetorical elements in common.

OF TIME AND CONTESTATION

The notion of difference in similarity brings us to Barbey's having his narrator call into question various aspects of narrative, mainly, verbal inscriptions and ekphrastic description: "These inscriptions and this portrait have been contested" (374). Both "callings into question" have to do with the idea of time. The inscriptions were most likely added to the wall panellings *after* the lovers' deaths. It would be most implausible, in the narrator's mind, for them to have been placed there at a time in which the lovers were trying to hide their passion:

> As for the inscriptions, I myself could never admit that they were imprinted by them, the poor creatures! and [it is not likely] that two lovers who knew themselves to be guilty, and whose life was spent in hiding their love from the eyes of a father who had the right to be terrible, would have imprinted upon the walls, with such lack of prudence, the secrets of their heart and the fury of their incest.
>
> (374)

The narrator surmises that the inscriptions were added "après coup" "after the fact." The same is true of the Cupids depicted in the painting. They are called a "détail suspect" (374). This is especially true of the Cupid with the bloodied wings: "That blood on its wings indicates, surely, that it was placed there after Marguerite's death" (374-75).

Poetic inscriptions and the use of *ekphrasis* affirm literary creation, on the one hand, and call it into question, on the other. The narrator both "constructs" and "deconstructs" his tale. Marguerite and Julien both live their love and die because of it. The narrator both creates and undermines, both condemns incest and envies it, both decries rhetoric and uses it.

The Third Chiasmus

The relationship of the text's two principal uses of chiasmus to the contexts of Parts IV and V is compelling. The first, located in the "Prologue," is of less consequence than are the second and third. Part V begins by referring, as did Part IV, to textuality when the narrator mentions having read a few printed letters that the brother and sister had exchanged. But even here there is contradiction. Although "one cannot find in these letters one single word that indicates the type of intimacy one is looking for" (376), words of passion are found in the quotations from Marguerite's letters that are italicized by the narrator:

"Votre lettre que j'ai *brûlée*," "*vostre passion à mon bien dont les* FELICITES *me sont encore présentes au cœur . . .*;" "*Vos récits de Paris me mettent en joie sur les marques seures de vostre passion qui me sont plus chères que la vie . . .*"

* * *

['your letter that I *burned*,' 'your passion for my good whose FELICITIES *are still present in my heart*'; 'Your letters from Paris give me such joy that they are *certain proof of your passion that is more dear to me than is life*.']

(376-77, emphases in text)

After noting the existence of the epistles, and reading quotations from them, the reader learns that Marguerite's father forced her to marry the old but rich "messire Le Fauconnier," and at this point the two usages of the words *adultère* frame the two usages of the word *inceste,* making, once again, *inceste* the principal part of the third chiasmus: "Later, she was forced to marry that Sir Le Fauconnier, and that is how she introduced *adultery* into *incest*; but *incest* devoured *adultery,* and of both crimes was the strongest" (377).

Adultery is first introduced into *incest,* but then *incest* wins out, "devouring" *adultery.* The frame of the chiasmus is "consumed"—swallowed twice, as it were—since the word *adultère* appears at both beginning and ending of the "a-b—b-a" structure. As in the second usage of chiasmus, in Part IV, emphasis is placed upon the central part of the trope. The narrator's doing this in two locations of the text creates for the word an epistemological instrument that gives seeming ontological status to incest. In the first instance the trope undermines incest's consequence, *l'échafaud,* and in the second it states that of the two crimes, incest or adultery, incest is the strongest (a plus in Barbey's mind). The real author of *Les Diaboliques* believed that the worse the crime the "better" it was.

Immediately after using the chiastic phrase "adultère-inceste—inceste-adultère," the reader is told that Marguerite had children from both "crimes" (from Le Fau-

connier as well as from her brother), but that both children died. She was thus able to climb the steps to the scaffold without looking back. Her eyes were riveted upon her brother, instead, who went before her, preceding her into death (377).

Marguerite's having conceived children from both husband and brother creates echoes with another one of Barbey's tales of incest, *Ce qui ne meurt pas.* Although it was written in the 1830's, Barbey did not publish it until 1883. Its writing, then, precedes **"Une Page d'histoire,"** but its publication follows it. In this novel, Allan de Cynthry falls in love with his adoptive mother, Yseult de Scudemor, who is disillusioned with life and love, and is unable to reciprocate Allan's sensual desires. She does, however, become his mistress, out of pity for him. Her aim is to destroy the boy's passion by revealing to him her own boredom and sense of affective sterility. After having achieved her purpose, since Allan's own passion dies, Allan falls in love with Camille, Yseult's daughter (his adoptive sister). They marry, but Allan loses his passion for her as well. The climax of the story takes place when both mother and daughter give birth to one child each, fathered by Allan. At the end of the novel, Yseult de Scudemor dies soon after childbirth, and Allan and Camille are left with both children, Jeanne and Marie. Allan has no love left, but intends to be faithful to his adoptive sister/wife and to both of his children.

The antimetabolic structure of this complicated affair might be viewed in the following way:

Adoptive mother-Allan—Allan-Adoptive sister
↓   ↓
Jeanne   Marie

The novel is written in two parts, a structure that is appropriate for what is a doubled incest. As an *Epilogue,* Allan writes a letter to his friend, André d'Albany, a name that rhymes with his own, Allan de Cynthry, another semantic mirroring, to tell him that life holds no meaning for him.

Barbey frequently reminds his readers, particularly in his correspondence, that he was born on All Saints' Day, the day devoted to the celebration of the dead. He makes of his own birth a pattern that is repeated over and over again in his poetics. He lives to construct, to imprint, to make permanent the prose he creates, even as he reminds his readers that he was born on the Day of the Dead and that death is part of life. His life and work, then, ever repeat binary formulations and ideas, the attraction and repulsion of opposites, or, as we see in **"Une Page d'histoire,"** the contestation of one by the other, even as both become one.

If we consider the last paragraph of **"Une Page d'histoire"** as a coda that the narrator adds to his tale, we find that it reveals another facet of the tale of Tourlaville. Having recently visited the castle, the narrator had seen two swans glide by on the lake next to it. Their description brings to mind the Narcissus paradigm as related not by Ovid but by Pausanias, of Narcissus falling in love with the imagined reflection of his twin sister. It is as if they were the boy and his Other, close together, with nothing separating them: "They were pressed together, squeezed against one another as if they were brother and sister, quivering upon that shimmering water. They could have made one think of the souls of the last Ravalets, departed and then revived in this charming form" (378). But even the analogy to metamorphosis is immediately disavowed: "they were too white to be the souls of the guilty brother and sister. In order for one to believe that, they would have had to be black, their necks stained with blood . . ." (378). Analogy and its immediate disavowal represent both circularity and its negation, both closure and openness.

The word-play implicit in the name of *"Tour-*la-ville" is obvious, and its relationship to rhetoric is striking. The word evokes a tower, solid and stable, as well as its opposite, movement in a circumference. As Etienne Souriau says, "Chiasmus takes off in one direction; then, even as it continues in the same linear and irreversible direction, thus continuing the phrase, it turns back upon itself by making the same components march past, in another pattern, in reverse" (362-363).

Readers of this story cannot "faire le tour" of **"Une Page d'histoire"** without encountering transgression, ambiguity, hermeneutic challenges, inscriptions, ekphrastic depictions, interpretative contestations, elements of Narcissism, the ideas of "same into same" and "different into same," questions of stillness and time, and chiastic framing devices that are both reflexive and reflective, all of which constitute a poetics of incest. This text foregrounds the making of texts in its use of rhetoric and in the negation of its usage. The text reflects itself in itself, and causes the reader to reflect upon what is reflected in the text. The reader says to herself, in the end: "And when I looked again, they were both gone . . . ," and no one, not even the writer, was left to swallow his own tale.

Notes

1. All translations in this essay are my own. This is the case in short sentences, in particular, when it seems that they might otherwise interrupt the flow of the prose. The original French passages have been maintained, with translations, when deemed appropriate for the sake of clarity.

2. Unless otherwise stated, all page references are to vol. II of the Pléiade edition of Barbey d'Aurevilly, *Œuvres romanesques complètes* [1966], 372. Hereafter cited parenthetically in the text.

3. Unless otherwise noted, all emphases have been added.

4. See Jacques Petit's *Notice* of *Ce qui ne meurt pas*: "Other elements come into play. Incest, for example, a theme that will become obsessive in the last pages written by Barbey: 'Une Page d'histoire' . . ." (1366).

5. See *Le Robert* for meanings of both *ravaler* and *décadence*.

6. Jacques Petit tells us that the characters in the story belonged to Norman history, and that Barbey had doubtlessly known about them for a long time. Around 1872 Barbey noted, in *Disjecta Membra,* that he needed to read up on the subject. A while later, he took copious notes on it, from a *Notice* by M. de Pontaumont. He calls it "Ravalet de Tourlaville." He begins: "The Ravalet family, having come from Brittany to Normandy in 1480. Lords of Tourlaville. Horrible! One of them assassinated his brother, another had his vassals hung because they hadn't ground their wheat in the lordly mill. A third stole the wife of a watchman from Tourlaville . . . etc." Barbey then places the brother and sister in this context: "And finally, it was Marguerite and Julien de Tourlaville, incestuous brother and sister, who had their heads cut off in the Place de Grève, 1603. It was Marguerite de Valois who, being suspected, herself, of having committed incest, kept her husband, Henry IV, from granting them pardon (see P. de L'Etoile)."

7. Jacques Petit reminds the reader in a note that although Barbey did not invent this fact, in 1599 Henri IV and Marguerite de Valois were divorced. In 1603, it was Marie de Médicis who was on the throne. Petit also doubts the veracity of "la reine Margot's" incest: "while Marguerite de Valois's life was adventurous, it does not seem to be the case that she was accused of incest" (1361). Petit is at odds with Dumas, Barbey, and others on this question.

8. In heraldic language, "en pointe" can mean either the place where an emblem is placed on an escutcheon, or the top of an isosceles triangle. It is clear that the narrator is using the second meaning, as he has the brother and sister meet, as one, at the top of the rose "en pointe" on the family crest.

9. Krieger's essay, "*Ekphrasis* and the Still Movement of Poetry; or *Laokoön* Revisited" (1967), was reprinted as an Appendix in *Ekphrasis, The Illusion of the Natural Sign,* 263-288.

10. The reference to *René* is obvious. The one to Byron is less explicit. Philippe Berthier reminds us that *Parisina* "relates the incestuous loves of Hugo, illegitimate child of the Duke of Este in Ferrara, with his father's wife; Hugo was decapi-

tated, Parisina went crazy and died." As for *Manfred,* says Berthier, one suspects that the hero's torments come, in part, from his incestuous relationship with his sister, Astarte. But one is also reminded of *The Fiancée from Ahydos,* in which the loves of Selim and Zuleika seem to be, in the beginning, most incestuous, because Selim is supposedly Zuleika's brother; and we know, from Bourget, that it was exactly these passages that appealed to Barbey in Byron, those nuances that were "the most tenderly mysterious and culpable" (169). Byron's biography contained incest, just as did Barbey's: Barbey's early love for his cousin, Ernestine du Méril, is considered incestuous.

11. While the word "crystal" is used, here, in a referential manner by Barbey, one of the definitions of the word has import in regard to the subject of repetition: "A solidified form of a substance in which the atoms or molecules are arranged in a definite repeating pattern so that the external shape of a particle or mass of the substance is made up of plane faces in a symmetrical arrangement" (Webster's *New Twentieth Century Dictionary*).

12. In the notes Barbey takes from the *Notice de M. de Pontaumont,* it is obvious that he never saw the portrait that the narrator of "Une Page d'histoire" describes: "Renaissance chateau. When one visits it, one would prefer seeing, to the chateau itself, the portrait of Marguerite de Ravalet that was taken away. They say she was painted standing, surrounded by blindfolded Cupids whom she rejects in favor of one, in particular, who is not blindfolded, and whose wings are *spotted with blood*" (underlining in text). Coming out of her mouth, one sentence is painted in, as if she were saying it: "One only suffices". It is obvious that Barbey's *ekphrasis* betrays or changes the *ekphrasis* in the notes he took from M. de Pontaumont. While Pontaumont has Marguerite smile at the Cupid whose wings are bloodied, Barbey has Marguerite face the spectator.

13. Interpretations of *Las Meninas* are multiple and complex. Some of the most interesting include Rosalie L. Colie's chapter entitled "Problems of Self-Reference" in *Paradoxia Epidemica*; Michel Foucault's *The Order of Things* (in French *Les Mots et les choses*); Madlyn Millner Kahr's *Velásquez: The Art of Painting*; H. W. Janson's *A Basic History of Art*; Marina Vaizey's *One Hundred Masterpieces of Art*; John R. Searle's "*Las Meninas* and the Paradoxes of Pictorial Representation"; Joel Snyder and Ted Cohen's "Reflexions on *Las Meninas*: Paradox Lost."

14. The authors of the last two articles listed in note #13 (Searle's, and Snyder and Cohn's) disagree with each other in their interpretations of *Las Meninas.* All three authors have profound things to say, nevertheless, about point of view, about where the King and Queen are located, about what they are doing on "this side" of the picture, about the reflection in the mirror, and about what the painter is painting on the represented canvas. While I shall not take sides in these scholars' disagreements, I do wish to say that, in my view, one of the most interesting remarks Searle makes is that "the painter is painting the picture we are seeing: that is, he is painting *Las Meninas* by Velásque" (485). Snyder and Cohn's conclusions are also illuminating. They say the following about what Velásquez probably wished:

> He wanted the mirror to depend upon the unseeable painted canvas for its image. Why should he want that? The luminous image in the mirror appears to reflect the king and queen themselves, but it does more than just this: the mirror outdoes nature. The mirror image is only a reflection. A reflection of what? Of the real thing—of the art of Velásquez. In the presence of his divinely ordained monarchs . . . Velásquez exults in his artistry and counsels Philip and María not to look for the revelation of their image in the natural reflection of a looking glass but rather in the penetrating vision of their master painter. In the presence of Velásquez, a mirror image is a poor imitation of the real.
>
> (447)

What interests me particularly is that most people who have written about *Las Meninas* agree that the King and Queen are on "this side" of the painting, and that the image in the mirror is that of Felipe IV and Queen María Ana. Searle as well as Snyder and Cohn also come to a meeting of minds on the notion that it is the art of Velásquez that matters.

15. "Percipient" is used by J. Kittay in "Descriptive Limits" 225-43, on p. 234.

16. See D. P. Fowler's instructive article, "Narrate and Describe: The Problem of Ekphrasis," 25-35, as well as Wendy Steiner's chapters on "The Painting-Literature Analogy," and "The Temporal versus the Spatial Arts".

Works Cited

Barbey d'Aurevilly, Jules Amédée. *Œuvres romanesques,* ed. Jacques Petit. Paris: Gallimard, II, 1966.

Berthier, Philippe. *Barbey d'Aurevilly et l'Imagination.* Genève: Droz, 1978.

Caws, Mary Ann. *The Eye in the Text: Essays on Perception, Mannerist to Modern.* Princeton: Princeton University Press, 1982.

Colie, Rosalie L. "Problems of Reference." *Paradoxia Epidemica.* Princeton: Princeton University Press, 1966.

Foucault, Michel. *The Order of Things.* New York: Vintage Books, 1973.

Fowler, D. P. "Narrate and Describe: The Problem of Ekphrasis." *Journal of Roman Studies* 6, Spring 1980.

Janson, H. W. *A Basic History of Art.* New York: Harry N. Abrams, 1971 & 1977.

Kahr, Madlyn Milner. *Velásquez: The Art of Painting.* New York: Harper & Row, 1976.

Kittay, Jay. "Descriptive Limits." *Yale French Studies* 61, 1981.

Krieger, Murray. *Ekphrasis, The Illusion of the Natural Sign.* Baltimore: The Johns Hopkins University Press, 1992.

Lanham, Richard A. *A Handlist of Rhetorical Terms,* 2nd ed. Berkeley: University of California Press, 1991.

Le Robert. Paris: Société du Nouveau Littré, 1966.

Ovid. *Metamorphoses,* transl. Frank Justus Miller. Cambridge: Harvard University Press, 1984.

Searle, John R. "*Las Meninas* and the Paradoxes of Pictorial Representation." *Critical Inquiry* 6, Spring, 1980.

Snyder, Joel and Cohen, Ted. "Reflexions on *Las Meninas*: Paradox Lost." *Critical Inquiry* 6, Spring, 1980.

Steiner, Wendy. *The Colors of Rhetoric.* Chicago: University of Chicago Press, 1982.

Souriau, Etienne. *Vocabulaire d'esthétique.* Paris: PUF, 1990.

Vaizey, Marina. *One Hundred Masterpieces of Art.* New York: Putnam, 1979.

Webster's New Twentieth Century Dictionary, 1979.

Michèle M. Respaut (essay date October 1999)

SOURCE: Respaut, Michèle M. "The Doctor's Discourse: Emblems of Science, Sexual Fantasy, and Myth in Barbey d'Aurevilly's *Le bonheur dans le crime.*" *French Review* 73, no. 1 (October 1999): 71-80.

[*In the following essay, Respaut explores the relationship between sexuality, power, and the uncanny in Barbey d'Aurevilly's novella.*]

Caduceus: Emblem of the medical corps, consisting of a cluster of rods or wands, around which is entwined the serpent of Epidaurus, famous for its cult of Asclepius, Greek god of medicine, and which is crowned by a mirror, symbolic of self-reflection, insight, prudence. Related to other ancient emblems, including the caduceus of Hermes, which variously featured two serpents, cups, wings. The dual nature of the serpent, feared for its venom, symbolic of resurrection in its ability to slough its skin, is related to the physician's ability to confront death and restore health, to the use of poisonous substances as curatives, to the interaction of body and spirit, and ultimately to the struggle between chaos and equilibrium not only in the individual but in the cosmos. The phallic nature of the wands and the entwined serpent emphasize the centrality of sexuality, with its ambiguous potential for fecundity or barrenness, for conflict or the androgynous union of the sexes.[1]

Nineteenth-century French literature is famous for its fascination with doctors and medicine, as many a reader has discovered in works by Balzac, Flaubert, and Zola. Less widely known, Barbey d'Aurevilly draws on and intensifies that fascination in *Le Bonheur dans le crime,* one of the *Diaboliques,* a collection of stories about diabolical women. In the preface to the work, Barbey says that the stories are true, and he relates them to the contradictory moral nature of his historical period, which in an explicitly Manichean way he calls both divine and diabolical. *Le Bonheur dans le crime* is a case in point, an exploration of how the most intense happiness can be achieved through crime—and one of the worst crimes at that, the murder of a spouse.[2] The exploration is conducted by a doctor, *le docteur* Torty, who is presented as the ideal observer, diagnosing moral as well as physical illness, and as the ideal narrator, provoking in his interlocutor—and perhaps in his readers—an intense investment of interest and passion.[3]

In a much analyzed framing arrangement, Barbey has an unnamed male speaker recount to an unnamed woman an event involving a beautiful couple and dangerous behavior. This is followed by Torty's narration, to the original speaker, and by extension to the woman as well as the reader, of the couple's past. The doctor's diagnostic skills are essential to the narrative, but—in keeping with the description of the caduceus—his observations go far beyond objective and scientific treatment of physical illness, involving psychosexual and historicomythic themes of the most profound sort, resonating with extreme violence and love, utter revulsion and absolute desire.

In the opening scene, set in the Jardin des Plantes in Paris, the first speaker and Torty come upon a couple, in their forties but still strikingly (and androgynously) beautiful, and seemingly belonging to the highest rank in Parisian society. After a kind of staring match with a rare female Javanese panther, whose coat is compared to black velvet, and who blinks first, the woman takes the risk of slapping it with the long glove that she has removed from her "avant-bras magnifique" (86). This results in the loss of the glove if not of her limb. Oblivious to the resulting uproar, and without recognizing Torty, who is their family doctor, the couple, caught up in the embrace of their passionate love, depart. The woman, who resembles the panther in being dressed in black, drags her train in the dust of the garden like a disdainful peacock (84-87).

These opening actions and motifs—danger and violence, the visual confrontation, the female animal and the emblem of male sexuality, the vigorous forearm—will recurrently represent the magnetism, for Torty, his listener, and his reader, of the androgynous main figure in the doctor's story. His ensuing narrative is sexually tinted, not only because of the first speaker's subsequent address to the unnamed woman, but also in his appreciation of the doctor's bodily attributes. Though he is past seventy, Torty's penetrating eye requires no glasses (it is, literally, "vierge de lunettes" [82]). His hand and thigh are still powerfully muscular (92); later, in a moment of excitement during his story, the doctor grabs his listener by the knee with his knotty fingers, strong as a pair of tongs—or forceps ("pince" [117]). And Torty's narration is marked by the delays, interruptions, apparent refusals that critics from Barthes to Brooks have shown to stimulate what Freud claimed is our libidinal investment in reading. Indeed, at the outset Torty himself identifies the doctor as the quintessential modern narrator: "Le médecin est le confesseur des temps modernes . . . Il a remplacé le prêtre . . . et il est obligé au secret de la confession comme le prêtre" (89). But of course he tells the story, at the end admitting that it is the first time he has done so, under the stimulation of the scene witnessed in the Jardin des Plantes (120).[4]

The story, which begins long ago, in the years following the defeat in 1815 of Napoleon and the restoration of the monarchy (89), concerns the dismaying Hauteclaire Stassin. She is the daughter of a *grisette* (a word designating lower-class female store employees of easy morals) and a retired soldier. Her father has established a fencing establishment in the provincial town of V . . . , whose population remains devoted to France's ancient class system, the Catholic religion, and to swordsmanship. Under his tutelage she becomes uncannily adept at swordplay, superior to all men, hence fearful and fascinating. After the death of her widowed father in the wake of the July Revolution (1830), she reopens his business, giving proof of considerable independence. Then she vanishes, apparently without a trace. Some years later she is found living under the assumed name Eulalie as the servant of Count Serlon de Savigny, whose wife has died under mysterious circumstances, and whom she now marries, to the consternation and disapproval of polite society. Only Torty, through his activity as a doctor, learns the details of the story, including the fact that Eulalie murdered the countess, supposedly by "mistakenly" giving her poison instead of medicine.

Everything in the opening scene in fact situates Torty in a medical tradition familiar to readers of novels by Balzac, Flaubert, and Zola, specifically *Le Médecin de*

campagne (1833), *Le Père Goriot* (1835), *Madame Bovary* (1857), and *Le Docteur Pascal* (1893). Having practiced in the country, now virtually retired in Paris but still dressing like a country doctor, Torty lives on the rue Cuvier, near the Jardin des Plantes and the Parisian hospitals that recall Balzac's character, Bianchon, medical student then doctor, and the dialectic of province and capital at work in these texts by him as well as by Flaubert and Zola. When we learn that the famous black panther has since died of consumption like a young girl ("comme une jeune fille, de la poitrine" [84]), we cannot miss the allusion to another Balzac novel, *La Fille aux yeux d'or,* which is not about doctors but *is* about murderously androgynous forms of sexuality.[5] All of this fits with the first speaker's claim that Torty is a representative of modern medicine, anticlerical and resolutely materialist (82), yet nonetheless "grand observateur, en plus, de bien d'autres cas que de cas simplement physiologiques et pathologiques" (81). What are cases that go beyond the physiological and pathological, which here mean "physical" and "psychological"? Torty will tell us—about Hauteclaire and Eulalie and Serlon and the Countess de Savigny.

He can do so because of his activities as a doctor—his visits on horseback throughout the countryside, his examinations by auscultation and pulse-taking, his diagnoses and prescriptions, his presence at childbirths. Frequently too he explains his observations, his pursuit of the truth, through reference to medical instruments, *sonde* (probe) and *serres,*[6] and in fact he begins his story with a medical analogy: "c'est là une histoire qu'il faut aller chercher déjà loin, comme une balle perdue sous des chairs revenues" (89). The murderous implications are not lost on the reader. Of course therefore he knows about Hauteclaire's mother, since he delivered all of her kind; surely too he notices the "enflamed" interest provoked by Hauteclaire among the young noblewomen of the vicinity, encountered during his medical visits (91, 94). Since his diagnostic skill is sound, he predicts her father's death (95). During her unexplained absence, however, he has no clue about her whereabouts. But he is the Savigny family doctor, and when called to care for the countess, it is he and he alone who recognizes her maidservant "Eulalie" as Hauteclaire, and who therefore understands the clandestine adulterous relationship between her and Savigny.

As I have already implied, Torty's treatment of the countess is only a prelude to his passionate interest in this adulterous relationship. The countess is feverish, but beyond that her symptoms are vague and therefore dangerous, according to Torty, who disdainfully notes that the "médecins de ce temps énervé" would diagnose her as anemic (110). On the contrary, when taking her pulse, which in its normal state is languid, he sees her white, soft flesh, pale arm with its pearl-blue veins, her aristocratically fine wrist, "fin et de race," as those of a woman created to be a victim (106). This, like everything else about the town of V . . . , suggests a reactionary sociohistorical undertone to the psychosexual thematics of the work. Naturally the powerful forearms and "belles mains" of Eulalie, bringing the potion he has ordered for the countess, are in constant contrast (101).

Attempting to get to the bottom of the mystery of this curious family romance, Torty tries not so much to cure the countess as to find out if she suspects the relationship between her husband and her servant. Asserting "Qui confesse le corps tient vite le cœur," he begins to "ausculter doublement" the countess, by implication examining her physically but also in terms of her awareness of the situation. Referring again to a medical instrument, he admits that he is unsuccessful in thus manipulating her with his "serre de médecin." Realizing that she has no suspicion, he risks a final probe ("coup de sonde"), warning her that Eulalie is too beautiful. The countess refuses to take the hint, absorbed instead in her mirror, which is framed in green velvet and peacock feathers (106-08). In these last details we may recall partial echoes of the description of Hauteclaire in the scene in the Jardin des Plantes. Closer by, Torty perceives her approach to the countess as that of a snake moving threateningly toward the bed of a sleeping woman (107).

It is, of course, Hauteclaire that most fascinates Torty, who from this point on in no way maintains the scientific stance which is supposed to typify the physician. After the initial surprise of discovering Hauteclaire as Eulalie, he strives to regain his scientific objectivity, his "attitude passive de médecin et d'observateur." However, since she is wearing her hair in the style of *grisettes,* with long serpentine curls, he cannot avoid his emotion at the contrast between her modest bearing and the fact that "elles font bien tout ce qu'elles veulent de leurs satanés corps, ces couleuvres de femelles" (102). Woman as diabolical snake: the pathological, and the more than simply pathological, as suggested at the outset, is expressed, but by and in Torty himself.[7]

When Torty realizes that not only Eulalie but also Servan know that *he* knows, it opens the way to a depiction of the doctor-narrator as ultimate *voyeur.* Relying on his physician's discretion, they will be safe. As for Torty, based on his duty as doctor to observe, he can have his fill of "ces plaisirs impersonnels et solitaires de l'observateur," pursued at will in this isolated provincial chateau. "Solitary" is hardly ambiguous here, despite the accompanying "impersonal." And all under the guise of scientific inquiry: "Je pourrais donc étudier, avec autant d'intérêt et de suite qu'une maladie, le mystère d'une situation qui, racontée à n'importe qui, aurait semblé impossible." He adds that the mystery he pursues stimulates "la faculté ratiocinante, qui est le bâ-

ton d'aveugle du savant et surtout du médecin, dans la curiosité acharnée de leurs recherches . . ." (103).

Here it is plain, and it has in fact been visible from the outset of the work, that the doctor/narrator is the vehicle for a fantasmatic sexual discourse that is scarcely disguised by its pseudo-scientific form. Given its flagrant expression in **Le Bonheur dans le crime,** this discourse is aptly characterized as a representation of the phallic woman and the androgynous woman or couple.

Hence in the opening scene, in the "maître-couple," these "créatures supérieures," it is Serlon who appears the effeminate dandy, his wife who is muscular. Upon seeing her, the opening narrator even wonders if she is a woman—"si c'en était un." However, not only do they seem to exchange sexual roles; they also seem to fuse androgynously. For when they leave it seems to him that they form "un seul corps à eux deux" (86-87). We have already seen that Hauteclaire is linked to female panther and male peacock (as well as to snakes, associated with women but phallic in form). Moreover, the panther is described in what seems a classic example of nineteenth-century French exoticism, since nature in Java is said to be the most intense in the world, "tout à la fois enchantante et empoisonnante, tout ensemble Armide et Locuste" (84). Here the allusions to entrancing feminine magician and female poisoner,[8] while reminding us of the symbolism of the caduceus, about poison and cure, about the ancient origins of medicine, also foreshadow the overpowering and murderous nature of Hauteclaire.

After that opening scene, when Torty begins his story, the androgynous nature of Hauteclaire is emphasized. Her name itself (after the sword of Olivier, Roland's companion in *La Chanson de Roland*), together with numerous other dangerously bisexual allusions and transformations,[9] corresponds to Torty's statement that she was two children in one (92). (Her "other" name, Eulalie, that of a third-century virgin martyr, emphasizes her capacity for duplicity.) Her skill in horsemanship is surpassed only by her prowess with the sword, "ce talent phénoménal si peu fait pour une femme" (97). It is, however, the view of her body, dressed for male swordplay, yet so abundantly and vigorously female, that is most striking: thighs, bust, waist, like those of the Louvre's statue Pallas de Velletri, depicting Athena as virgin warrior (95). All of this contributes to a fundamental strangeness ("étrangeté"), an advantage in a woman, according to Torty (96). Here the Freud of the "uncanny" becomes inescapably relevant.

Indeed, Freud's essay on the *unheimlich* has been translated into French as *L'Inquiétante Etrangeté,* roughly "the uncanny strangeness." Freud notes that the German term has no direct equivalent in other languages, listing "uncanny" and "étrange" among other words. In his argument, "unheimlich" designates experiences that should be familiar but that provoke extreme fear and that therefore involve repression. It refers among much else to forbidden sexual activities and the sexual organs. Fundamental, according to him, is the fear of castration, involving the death of the father and the substitution of eye for penis, and, in some neurotic men, repressed fear of the female sexual organs. The relevance of all of this to many features in Barbey's tale (the fascination with eyes, the threat of the phallic and potentially fatal sword, disturbingly ambiguous sexuality) is clear. So too is another uncanny experience, that of the double (two women, two names, poisoning by what is described as "encre double," and particularly the uncanny pair formed by Hauteclaire and Torty himself). Freud concludes that the uncanny involves a resurgence of "primitive" magic thinking (as when one believes one can kill someone simply by wishing), and that literary works that mix a claim to truthfulness with uncanny elements are the most unsettling. *Le Bonheur dans le crime,* preceded by a preface that claims truthfulness, presents the enigma of a murder that is desired and carried out without difficulty or guilt.[10] Like the caduceus, too, Barbey's story roots medical science in repressed layers of the psyche and in ancient myth.

Torty's narrative of the adulterous love between Serlon and Eulalie intensifies many of these motifs. After witnessing a suggestively sensuous contact between the two, he imagines the intensity of their pleasure, their "fameuses jouissances." He reminds us that he was still young at the time, subject to "le tapage des molécules dans l'organisation" (110)! He begins to observe the lovers' symptoms, rather than those of the countess (110-11, 114-15). Supposedly by chance, but really again because of his medical duties, in this case a prolonged delivery, he discovers after midnight "leur manière de faire l'amour," as they duel, then appear on a balcony in an embrace that seems like "une nudité." As earlier, Hauteclaire's abbreviated costume seems to expose her utter femaleness, yet her superb muscularity; again they seem fused as one. His position is again voyeuristic: "Je les discernais à merveille." Once more he measures his strong physical response in medically accurate fashion: their kiss lasted "bien soixante pulsations comptées à ce pouls qui allait plus vite qu'à présent, et que ce spectacle fit aller plus vite encore" (112-13).

However, the most strikingly phallic/androgynous evocation of Hauteclaire appears in the passage in which she brings pen and ink so that Torty may engage in the doctorly activity of writing a prescription for the countess. As usual in her diurnal role of servant, she has been sewing, and arrives with her steel thimble on her finger. The needle she had been using is threaded on her tempting breasts ("provocante poitrine"), where

there are in fact masses of other steel needles. This inevitably recalls her fencing outfit, her cuirasse, and provokes in the doctor the thought that she would have worn steel in the Middle Ages. Thus provocatively female and male, she uses the "noble et moelleux mouvement dans les avant-bras que l'habitude de faire des armes lui avait donné plus qu'à personne" to provide the surface for Torty's writing (115).

The physical closeness of the two, the stress on breast and phallic form—thimble, finger, needle, forearm, sword—with no specific mention of the writing implement, the pen, and the fact that later the countess will be poisoned by Hauteclaire with a form of ink (116)[11]—all of this embodies the closest form of cooperation between Hauteclaire and Torty. In a theme heavy with significance in the history of literature in the nineteenth century, she *almost* writes; she provides the bodily support for writing.[12] But she also poisons with the substance of writing.

The conclusion of the story exacerbates the ambivalent role of the doctor and the troubling nature of the love between Serlon and Hauteclaire. The dying countess swears him to silence about the crime—*as her doctor*; so that in some sense he is the author (he wrote the prescription?), concealer, and finally revealer of the crime (118-19). Ever since the murder he has been attempting to comprehend the protagonists' criminal and simultaneously exalting love—he who wants to write a book on monstrous congenital deformations, "un traité de tératologie," who has been studying their love "microscopiquement," taking the pulse for so long of this "bonheur incompréhensible" (125-26).

However, his attempt to comprehend, to explain what seems so morally contradictory—absolute love, produced by and undiminished by murder—ultimately yields no insight. Except that such a love, so intense, so incomprehensible, is barren. Hauteclaire wants no children, wishing no intrusion on her union with Serlon, which leads to Torty's judgment: "Le feu,—qui dévore,—consume et ne produit pas" (127). Nonetheless, the last exchange, significantly between the two male speakers in this masculine narratological system, emphasizes the persistent fascination of Hauteclaire. Despite her crime, even with her crime, they agree that Serlon's love is understandable. But so is the attraction she exercises on Torty, who has the last word: "Et moi aussi!" (128).

Le Bonheur dans le crime is upon first reflection open to the feminist critique of male-authored works that project bizarre, fascinating, and destructive representations of women.[13] Certainly the figure of the doctor, as I have shown throughout, illustrates not scientific observation and veracity, but an immensely voyeuristic obsession with a fantastic conception of women.

It is not to diminish the appropriateness of the feminist critique that, reverting to the symbolism of the caduceus, I suggest further, related, meanings. The elements of the caduceus and their significance are strewn throughout the text—the doctor himself, the flagrantly phallic motifs, snakes and the mirror, androgynous sexuality, the effort (unsuccessful) to understand and balance the most extreme of contraries—murderous crime and ecstatic love. There is also the theme of fecundity or rather, and strikingly, its opposite: despite all the births at which Torty assists, the countess and Hauteclaire are childless.

In light of these features and their ancient meanings, Barbey's tale may be seen as a tortured reenactment, in a relatively recent period, of archaic themes. The claim in the preface to recount true stories reflective of the ambivalent moral nature of his period may in this perspective seem more profoundly true than merely self-protective. The sociohistorical dimension of the text has been mentioned. However, the devotion to swordplay among the provincial nobility of V . . . may ultimately have less to do with the trappings of class than with a recrudescence of ancient modes of experience. I have indicated Hauteclaire's association with the primal nature of the Javanese panther and the unsettling strangeness of her skill with the sword. It was right to think of Freud's argument on the uncanny at that point. For Freud the experience of the uncanny, which from the point of view of the reality principle he criticizes, is a reemergence of primitive magical thinking, the belief in something that, according to him, cannot exist or occur.

To the extent that Freud contributed to distorted representations of women, it is reasonable to assume that he was subject to another form of primitive thinking.[14] Something of the same may be said of Torty, for all his cynical materialism. Does he not dismiss the diagnosis of anemia made by the "médecins de ce temps énervé" (110)? And is he not a fascinated observer "d'autres cas que de cas simplement physiologiques et pathologiques" (81)? In pursuing the fascinating Hauteclaire, he is going beyond the limits of medical science, just as in the representation of the phallic or androgynous woman Barbey is resurrecting an ancient myth.

The myth, and Barbey's version of it, may be irremediably sexist. However, two features in his story make it more complex, in their divergence from the traditional symbolism of the caduceus. Although androgynous, Hauteclaire is barren. Moreover, the mirror, which ought to figure the doctor's self-reflection and intellectual power, is displaced, in the scene in which Torty attempts to warn the countess. She is uninterested, utterly absorbed in examining her face in her mirror. Here we have feminine narcissism, but also an indication of Torty's powerlessness. He does not succeed in warning the countess or preventing her death; nor can he finally fathom the mystery of "le bonheur dans le crime." Barbey's tale appears to celebrate both the doctor's mastery and the ideal of an androgynous being. True to his preface, however, in his world both are fatally flawed.

Notes

1. See Chevalier and Gheerbrant 153-55. Given the complexity of the symbolism, it is not surprising that representations of the medical caduceus vary. American television spots on medical issues often are accompanied by an emblem that includes Hermes's wings, whereas *Webster's Third New International Dictionary* 2219 shows only a staff and a single snake. French dictionaries and encyclopedias, including current and older publications by Larousse, e.g., *Petit Larousse illustré 1990* 165, include the mirror and specify that it represents prudence.

2. For a comprehensive treatment, see Tranouez, *Fascination et narration dans l'œuvre romanesque de Barbey d'Aurevilly* 485-530. On the preface see Kanbar.

3. I have found no fully detailed discussion of the doctor in this story. For a brief and accurate paragraph see Stivale 326.

4. See Barthes and Brooks. For complexities of narrative form in Barbey see Rodina, Giard, Holder, Sivert, and Unwin.

5. In *La Fille aux yeux d'or* (1835) in the trilogy *Histoire des Treize,* Paquita is the object of the violent love of a man and a woman, who until the end are unaware that they are half-siblings. Both wish to murder Paquita, but the sister succeeds. At the end the brother dismisses the murder by explaining that Paquita died "de la poitrine" (425).

6. Or "serres fines," a small spring-equipped instrument for holding the edges of a wound together (*Nouveau Larousse illustré* 663).

7. When Torty tries to dominate Eulalie in this scene by staring at her, she does not blink—her eyes and will are stronger than those of the panther.

8. The first ensnares the hero of Tasso's *Jerusalem Delivered,* the second was a famous Roman poisoner.

9. In addition to several Old Testament references, she is likened to Lady Macbeth, to a female Saint George, and to an Amazon. See 88, 93, 94, 102, 109, 114.

10. See Freud, *L'Inquiétante Etrangeté* 209-63.

11. *Encre double.* Nineteenth-century industrially produced inks were "double" in combining a solid pigment with a fluid element. Although to my

knowledge Barbey criticism is silent on this explicit reference in the text, we recall Torty's *double* auscultation of the countess, as well as the figure of the double throughout. Not only the subject but also the form of the written work are fundamentally ambivalent—the crime committed, the story written with an *encre double.*

12. See Respaut.

13. See Dodille, Milner, Petit, Peylet, and Tranouez, "L'Asthénique, l'amazone et l'androgyne."

14. Amid the vast critical literature on this theme one may single out Bernheimer and Kahane.

Works Cited

Balzac, Honoré de. *Histoire des Treize: Ferragus, La Duchesse de Langeais, La Fille aux yeux d'or.* Paris: Presses Pocket, 1992.

Barbey d'Aurevilly, Jules. "Le Bonheur dans le crime." *Œuvres romanesques complètes.* Vol. 2. Paris: Gallimard, Bibl. de la Pléiade, 1966. 2 vols.

Barthes, Roland. *S/Z.* Paris: Seuil, 1970.

Bernheimer, Charles, and Claire Kahane, eds. *In Dora's Case: Freud—Hysteria—Feminism.* New York: Columbia UP, 1985.

Brooks, Peter. *Reading for the Plot: Design and Intention in Narrative.* New York: Vintage, 1985.

Chevalier, Jean, and Alain Gheerbrant. *Dictionnaire des symboles: mythes, rêves, coutumes, gestes, formes, figures, couleurs, nombres.* Rev. ed. Paris: Robert Laffont/ Jupiter, 1982.

Dodille, Norbert. "Les Femmes de l'écrivain." *Romantisme* 16 (1986): 45-56.

Freud, Sigmund. *L'Inquiétante Etrangeté et autres essais.* Trans. Bertrand Féron. Paris: Gallimard, 1985. 209-63.

Giard, Ann. "Le Récit lacunaire dans *Les Diaboliques.*" *Poétique* 11 (1980): 39-50.

Holder, Guillemette I. "Séduction narrative et donjuanisme chez Barbey d'Aurevilly." *Nineteenth-Century French Studies* 23 (1994-95): 166-74.

Kanbar, Nabih. "Analyse pragmatique de la préface des *Diaboliques.*" *La Revue des Lettres Modernes* 1183-92 (1994): 145-86.

Milner, Max. "Identification psychanalytique de la perversion dans *Les Diaboliques.*" *Barbey d'Aurevilly cent ans après (1889-1989).* Ed. Philippe Berthier. Geneva: Droz, 1990. 313-25.

Nouveau Larousse Illustré. 7 vols. Paris: Larousse, 1897-1904.

Petit, Jacques. "La Femme dominatrice." *La Revue des Lettres Modernes* 351-54 (1973): 124-30.

Petit Larousse illustré 1990. Paris: Larousse, 1989.

Peylet, Gérard. "Entre 1832 et 1882, l'image de la femme dans quelques œuvres majeures de Barbey d'Aurevilly." *Littérature* 18 (1988): 67-80.

Respaut, Michèle. "Regards d'hommes/corps de femmes: *Germinie Lacerteux* des Frères Goncourt." *French Review* 65 (1991): 46-54.

Rodina, Herta. "Textual Harassment: Barbey d'Aurevilly's *Les Diaboliques.*" *Nineteenth-Century French Studies* 24 (1995-96): 144-53.

Sivert, Eileen. "Text, Body, and Reader in Barbey d'Aurevilly's *Les Diaboliques.*" *Symposium* 31 (1977): 151-64.

Stivale, Charles J. "'Like the Sculptor's Chisel': Voices 'On' and 'Off' in Barbey d'Aurevilly's *Les Diaboliques.*" *Romanic Review* 82 (1991): 317-30.

Tranouez, Pierre. "L'Asthénique, l'amazone et l'androgyne." *La Revue des Lettres Modernes* 491-97 (1977): 85-113.

———. *Fascination et narration dans l'œuvre romanesque de Barbey d'Aurevilly: la scène capitale.* Paris: Minard, 1987.

Unwin, Timothy. "Barbey d'Aurevilly conteur: discours et narration dans *Les Diaboliques.*" *Neophilologus* 72 (1988): 353-65.

Webster's Third New International Dictionary of the English Language Unabridged. Springfield, MA: Merriam-Webster, 1986.

Karen Humphreys (essay date spring-summer 2003)

SOURCE: Humphreys, Karen. "Dandyism, Gems, and Epigrams: Lapidary Style and Genre Transformation in Barbey's *Les diaboliques.*" *Nineteenth-Century French Studies* 31, nos. 3-4 (spring-summer 2003): 259-77.

[*In the following essay, Humphreys examines elements of ornamentation and apocalyptic prophecy in* Les diaboliques. *Humphreys asserts that Barbey d'Aurevilly's aesthetic vision owes a profound debt to medieval theology.*]

In a letter dated May 1887, Jean Lorrain writes to Barbey d'Aurevilly, "Je me permets de vous envoyer un article où je vous ai fort pillé, mais on ne pille que des trésors . . ."[1] Lorrain had previously paid homage to Barbey in his 1897 *Monsieur de Bougrelon,* a parody of an eccentric based largely on the persona of Barbey. Lorrain's peculiar story of two French expatriates in

Amsterdam is, in part, a tribute to Barbey and his literary influence. It is not only by dint of compliment that Lorrain refers to Barbey's writings as "trésors"; in the form of a collection of gems and precious stones, treasure is a fundamental trope in Barbey's œuvre and it is likely that Lorrain understood the relevance of lapidary metaphors in Barbey's text.

The following portrait reveals Barbey as a prototype for the protagonist of Lorrain's novel and suggests that the association between Barbey and precious stones is symbolic of both literary inspiration and creative transformation. In Lorrain's text, Bougrelon, "la silhouette épique," (Lorrain, *Monsieur de Bougrelon* 17) has left France for the Netherlands; he had acquired his "prestigieuse élégance" (35) from his native "Normandie royaliste," (35) which is a clue to his alias.[2] As a sign of his maverick nobility, he sports "Des gants extraordinaires, monsieur, dont chaque doigt était onglé d'agate, une patte de tigre ou la main du diable: une invention à lui d'une bizarrerie tout à fait délicieuse, et qui lui ressemblait" (36). The elegant and outlandish aspects of his appearance are basic tenets of dandyism as outlined by Barbey in **Du Dandysme et de George Brummell** (1844). Although there is no prescribed dress code for the dandy, the text of whatever garb he chooses signifies an attitude, a renegade *parti pris* by which he differentiates himself from society. Barbey claims in **Du Dandysme** [**Du Dandysme et de George Brummell**], "Ce n'est pas un habit qui marche tout seul! au contraire! C'est une certaine manière de le porter qui crée le Dandysme . . ." ([*Œuvres romanes ques complètes*] 2:673). Barbey's *silhouette épique* is testimony to his reputation as a master storyteller and his literary influence on a younger generation of artists. Lorrain's interest in Barbey was perhaps enhanced by his own desire to challenge literary convention and contemporary gender stereotypes; consequently he saw in Barbey a model or mentor, a *maître*[3] as the afflatus for his own work.

In this essay, I show that Barbey's apparent status as a unique "styliste" (1295) is the result of a complex process of innovation and genre transformation—specifically the genres of the epigram and the lapidary. I argue that Barbey's lapidary imagery is fundamental to his narrative dandyism and that epigrams and precious stones are stylistic features that generate the transformative process of his creative endeavor in **Les Diaboliques**. My allusions to Lorrain are not the basis of an intertextual analysis in this essay, but rather serve to support my claim that in Barbey's text, gems and semiprecious stones are privileged media of artistic expression and emphasize the abstraction and the multi-faceted aspect of the creative process.

Although the traditional epigrammatic genre and the formal lapidary differ significantly from each other, both genres have in common the production of meaning through the use of lapidary imagery. Epigrams and precious stones correspond to the appropriation and representation of artistic identity in the Aurevillian text. Barbey cultivated certain qualities that he desired for his own persona such as strength or power ("raconter chez Barbey signifie savoir dominer," Boucher [Les Diaboliques *de Barbey d'Aurevilly*] 135), or the singularity and uniqueness he associated with genius, and cast these attributes into a permanent aesthetic form. "Barbey created others that he might form himself, all the while insisting upon his own integrity, his own sovereignty over the world of shadowy figures he commanded" (Feldman [*Gender on the Divide*] 57). He elucidates the complexity of this selective process through the short story form and suggests that these motifs recur, both as individual elements, and as parts in the larger scheme of the collection. For example, in **Le Dessous de cartes d'une partie de whist,** the pearls of perspiration on the countess Damnaglia's back initially seem like a simple narrative detail (2:170). However, they are part of a greater configuration of precious stones and human jewels, and more importantly their presence signifies the story telling *process*. (The figure of speech *où perlait une sueur légère* evokes a gem that is the consequence or result of a grain of sand that is transformed by friction over time). The narrator's story produces an impassioned physical response in the countess. At the same time, Barbey's story is the result of labor, nervous anticipation, erotic desire; ultimately it is the material jewel of his imagination.

Despite the seemingly ephemeral and fragile nature of many of Barbey's glyptic images, they are set firmly in the structure of the work itself, evoking a more durable fate. Characters like Hauteclaire and Savigny are elusive, but share an undying passion of mythic proportion (the narrator refers to them as "Philémon et Baucis," 2:87) which endows them with a sense of permanence. Hauteclaire, like many of Barbey's protagonists, resembles a gem and embodies paradoxically both fragile and solid qualities. Such paradox is also the *modus operandi* for the dandy who is the very incarnation of opposites and ambiguity—as Barbey says of the dandy par excellence, George Brummell, "il versait à doses parfaitement égales la terreur et la sympathie, et il en composait le philtre magique de son influence" (2:694).

In **Les Diaboliques,** characters are cut and chiseled out of stone and become ornaments themselves. Ravila is a "dandy taillé," (62) as calm as the "Guest of Stone," and the duchess de Sierra Leone is a "statuette" (239). Marmor de Karkoël has "des mains blanches et bien sculptées" (142). His name, derived from "marmoréen" alludes to the texture and properties of marble. Although lapidary images often suggest the notion of inherent worth or value, in Barbey's text, they specifically connote craftsmanship, talent, and originality. Swords, scissors, arrows, and other tools refer to the narrator's craft, of writer as lapidary who pares down language to emphasize the valor of the individual word. In addition to experimenting with language and the "alphabet des romanciers" (1291) Barbey has selected pieces from the massive ruins of his predecessors to cut and refine for his own creative lapidary.

A lapidary style suggests the elegance and precision of works engraved in stone. Barbey strove to capture that elegance as though to avoid oncoming oblivion. His style consists of reinstating the old, the forgotten, or the worthy, while at the same time it reveals a conscious effort to forge a unique style tinged with artifice, perversity, and irreverence. Style, says Barbey "c'est ce qui donne aux œuvres littéraires leur durée et leur virilité. Otez le style, ôtez la forme, que reste-t-il dans l'esprit humain qui n'appartienne plus ou moins à tous?"[4] Barbey emphasizes the importance of duration or longevity throughout his work; an original technique might ensure endurance or possibly an inimitable mark of distinction. Barbey composed many epigrams for his journal *Disjecta Membra* and for *Pensées detachées*; consequently this pointed style was something he had worked on extensively, over time, and which he integrated in his story telling.

Even though the epigrammatic genre usually refers to ancient sources such as Martial or to sixteenth century Latinist writers, it is incorporated in the nineteenth century as part of the dandy aesthetic.[5] The nineteenth-century meaning of epigram is much broader than that of either Renaissance or ancient Greek and Latin poems; and its form is not clearly defined. Pierre Laurens, in an extensive study of the epigram, briefly sketches the history of the genre, and shows how many of the earlier characteristics are retained in the modern sense of the word.[6] Literally, epigram means inscription, and since the words were etched in stone, whether statues, monuments or temples, the message had to be succinct. Consequently, the message appeared telegraphic and left out clues in favor of brevity. Its purpose was often to pique curiosity as well as to ornament. Like the early writers of epigrams, the dandy's goal is to create a lasting impression.

Laurens shows the various transformations in Latin epigrams, particularly those of Catullus and Martial and concludes with the general modern understanding developed by Lessing and Voltaire. "L'épigramme néolatine est, en comparaison, beaucoup plus riche: elle aussi a retenu la leçon rhétorique; mais, armée de la pointe, qu'elle affine encore (John Owen), elle part à la reconquête de la diversité originelle" (Laurens [*L'Abeille dans l'ambre*] 27). In the nineteenth century, the epigram was still noteworthy for its satire, simplicity, rhetoric, and strategy, even though it no longer required the poetic form of the ancients. For the purposes of studying Barbey's style in relation to the epigram, it is helpful to approach it from a more modern understanding of the term with the primary traits that were retained from the earlier versions, rather than from a study of the whole tradition. Since the cultural context of a literary genre both shapes and is shaped by that genre, Laurens claims, "Naturellement il ne suffisait pas, pour comprendre un moment de l'épigramme, de la mettre en rapport avec la châine épigrammatique tout entière: il s'éclaire tout autant par sa relation avec les structures intellectuelles et spirituelles de son époque" (21).

Lessing's essay on the epigram informs current perceptions of the genre, although it does not appear to have had a profound impact on nineteenth-century French avatars of the epigram. First the epigram incites curiosity and then gratifies that curiosity. For Lessing, the epigram consists of two parts, the expectation and the explanation. "The epigram is a poem, in which, in the manner of an inscription, our attention and curiosity are excited by some individual object, in respect to which we are more or less kept in suspense, in order to be the more piquantly gratified at the close" (Lessing [*Fables and Epigrams*] 169-70). The phrase "more piquantly gratified" seems ambiguous, as though the more curious or the more unconventional, the more satisfying the ending (from the perspective of the epigrammatist). At the close of his essay he refers to "those epigrams in which our expectation is rather amused, and agreeably deceived, than satisfied" (203). The desired effect of deceit, or ambiguity on behalf of the epigrammatist, is also typical of the dandy, only he does not grant his reader or spectator any final satisfaction. Through deceit and ambiguity, he produces the unexpected, for as Lessing states, a necessary condition for ambiguity is that it is unexpected. Barbey echoes this idea in his treatise on Brummell; "Ainsi, une des conséquences du Dandysme, un de ses principaux caractères . . . est-il de produire toujours l'imprévu" . . . (2:675).

Nineteenth-century knowledge of epigrams was derived in part from readings of the Ancients. Although certain critics assert that very few nineteenth-century artists were actually familiar with the poets and styles they praised and sought to imitate, some of them were.[7] For example, Remy de Gourmont analyzes numerous Latin poets, explaining the attraction of nineteenth-century artists to these works. Many of the detailed crystalline images of ancient Latin poems are reset in the prose and poetry of the fin de siècle. In the 1913 preface to *Le Latin Mystique*, Gourmont quotes Arnaud de Villeneuve and suggests that literary style is the result of ongoing transformation of earlier sources: "Les éléments ne peuvent être engendrés que par leur propre semence" (Gourmont [*Le Latin Mystique*] x). Des Esseintes's library pays homage to Latin works by Archelaus, Albertus Magnus, Raymond Llully and Arnaud de Villeneuve, but the narrator does not elaborate on why he is partial to them. The only other comparison he draws is in relation to Barbey—"les œuvres de Barbey d'Aurevilly étaient encore les seules dont les idées et le style présentassent ces faisandages, ces taches morbides, ces épidermes talés et ce goût blet, qu'il aimait tant à savourer parmi les écrivains décadents, latins et monastiques des vieux âges" (Huysmans [*A Rebours*] 193). Huysmans most likely compared Barbey to these writers to emphasize Barbey's role as a herald of fin de siècle *décadentisme*; however he too, could have perceived a deeper correspondence based on Barbey's interest in the stylistic transformation of earlier genres.

The nineteenth-century interest in Latin works was based not only on an attraction to detail, mysticism and bygone cultures, but also on the challenge of reviving language. How was the artist to revitalize and renovate tradition in light of previous literary history and the cultural malaise at the end of the nineteenth century?[8]

The epigram provides a response to this question for it illustrates the process of derivation and renovation. The use of epigrams also contributed to the refined style that was in vogue at the fin de siècle. Lorrain, for example, includes many epigrams in his *La Nostalgie de la Beauté* (1900) which, like Barbey's **Pensées détachées** is a collection of various observations and selected musings. Oscar Wilde (who translated Barbey's novel **Ce qui ne meurt pas,** originally published in 1883) was also a master of the epigram; his countless pithy phrases and witticisms appear throughout his work and in separate publications of epigrams. Verlaine also compiled numerous epigrams, dedicated to friends and contemporaries.[9]

Certain characteristics of the earlier epigrammatic genre clearly appealed to its nineteenth-century practitioners: the delicate combination of artifice, wit, and ornament represented an expression of genius that not only differentiated the artist from others, but that linked him with the past. The dandy's tailored speech and witty commentary are also associated with aristocratic mannerisms that distinguish him from the democratic society he scorns.[10] Epigrams consequently provide a means of rebellion against bourgeois conventions of propriety and good conduct. For example Barbey writes in an *album* to a friend, Mademoiselle S[arah] L[afaye]:

> Je me nomme le Sagittaire!
> Je suis né sous ce signe et je le mets partout!
> Et dans ce monde, inerte, ennuyeux et vulgaire,
> J'aime à lancer ma flèche à tout.
>
> Ma flèche . . . Ce n'est plus ce trait au vol de flamme
> Qui partait de mon arc, en vibrant, - autrefois,
> Quand, amoureux archer, c'est au cœur d'une femme
> Que j'envoyais tout mon carquois!
>
> La flèche de mon arc, à présent est cruelle,
> Je n'ai plus de l'amour les traits brûlants et doux . . .

> Mais si j'en avais un encor, Mademoiselle,
> Je voudrais que ce fût pour vous!

(2:1597)

The dandy's barbed verse lashes out against his own ennui and at bourgeois culture (*ce monde, inerte, ennuyeux et vulgaire*). In Barbey's case, "Le Sagittaire" his pen name, is an alter ego whose mask he dons to attack social convention. The poem recalls the erotic epigrams of Antiquity, in a form that has been radically transfigured, but that still carries vestiges of the ancient epigram in the modern version.[11]

The epigram is a textual detail or *skandalon,* a textual protrusion that trips the reader as s/he progresses through the narrative.[12] In addition it functions as a creative metaphor, a tool for whittling down language to the most pointed expression, the smallest detail. Epigrams condense maximum meaning and impact through the most succinct phrase. For example in **Le Dessous de cartes d'une partie de whist** the narrator adds to his anecdote, "Permettez moi-encore une parenthèse: Les Normands me font toujours l'effet de ce renard si fort en sorite dans Montaigne. Où ils mettent la patte, on est sûr que la rivière est bien prise, et qu'ils peuvent, de cette puissante patte, appuyer" (2:139). Not only do the parentheses briefly convey the Norman sense of cleverness but they represent a gesture of narrative authority. The very emphasis on the last word, *appuyer,* refers directly to the epigram itself—that which carries weight, or impresses upon. After this aside, the dandy narrator's use of epigram is implicitly compared to that of the other expert conversationalists at the gathering:

> C'était un joueur de la grande espèce, un homme dont la vie (véritable fantasmagorie d'ailleurs) n'avait de signification et de réalité que quand il tenait des cartes, un homme, enfin, qui répétait sans cesse que le premier bonheur était de gagner au jeu, et que le second était d'y perdre: magnifique axiome qu'il avait pris à Sheridan, mais qu'il appliquait de manière à se faire absoudre de l'avoir pris.

(139)

This passage illustrates a subtle jousting for excellence among dandies over whom the narrator presides. Moreover, the utterance recalls the prophetic omniscience typically associated with axioms or aphorisms which are avatars of epigrams. The narrator, too, reinscribes Sheridan's phrase in a manner similar to that of Marmor—by transforming it in such a way so that it is not obvious that it was borrowed.[13] Barbey does the same with various stylistic features of the epigram and the lapidary throughout **Les Diaboliques.**

In **A un dîner d'athées,** the narrator says of M. Mesnilgrand, "en conversation, il gravait le mot. Il avait le style lapidaire—et même lapidant, car il était né caustique, et les pierres qu'il jetait dans le jardin des autres atteignaient toujours quelqu'un" (187). The epigram is the preferred mode of expression for the dandy; through it, he emphasizes an economization of language and by means of irony and proper delivery, he creates the "philtre magique de son influence."

In the example of Mesnilgrand, his style is also "lapidant," and evokes the stinging delivery of a projectile. Such is the goal of the epigram—or a sharp but passing dandy quip. "Quelle *pierre infernale* que le mépris! . . ." (2:808). For Barbey, the word is a stone not only to be cut, but that cuts another substance or surface or that wounds someone, once again evoking the dandy paradox only this time to the tune of Baudelaire's verse, "je suis la plaie et le couteau" (1:79). Most of Barbey's heroes hone their edges on the characters around them, exercising their mental acumen as if to refine and distinguish themselves from the company they frequent or the places and crowds they haunt.

The initial title of **Les Diaboliques** was **Ricochets de conversation** which suggests the reverberations of a projectile. Barbey includes words and expressions which recall such a pattern of repetition within his own texts, as well as in those of his predecessors. *Ricochet* also carries the meaning of an old expression whose meaning has become obscured. Barbey, forever in search of the rare and outmoded revalorizes such words and phrases. Like an article of clothing for the dandy, the *mot recherché* is a means to reinstate a former elegance and at the same time, an attempt to attract attention: for example, "On se coiffait en *ferronnière,* ce qui faisait dans son visage, avec ses deux yeux incendiaires dont la flamme emphêchait de voir la couleur, comme un triangle de trois rubis" (2:70).

The word *ferronnière* tacitly declares the narrator's social alliances with the aristocracy through esoteric language and the company of women who hang jewels on their forehead. Like the *mot recherché,* the dandy puzzles and provokes, with the intent to stand out like a shining star—a task which the *ferronnière* carries out literally. The word becomes an antique lexical jewel reset in Barbey's narrative.

Not only do words and themes resonate throughout **Les Diaboliques,** but they inevitably derive from earlier influences. The writer's challenge then, is to carve his own place in literary tradition. The arrows, scissors, chisels and swords that abound in Barbey's text are even drawn into some of the manuscripts. These references not only illustrate the pivotal position he holds in the dandy tradition, by evoking the figure of the epigram, but they insist on the importance of mastery and artifice in the creative project.

Many of Barbey's dandies—characters and narrators alike, are expert conversationalists and skilled practitioners of the oral epigram. La comtesse de Stasseville in

Le Dessous de cartes d'une partie de whist is "une espèce de *femme-dandy*" whose noble society "ne voyait, elle, dans la rigidité de cette lèvre étroite et meurtrière que le fil d'acier sur lequel dansait incessament la flèche barbeléé de l'épigramme" (145). Ironically though, she never utters a word in the story and the reader must take the narrator's word. Since she is a near match for Marmor in card-sharking, the reader is perhaps likely to believe in her verbal finesse as well. Voice is a "ciseau d'or avec lequel nous sculptons nos pensées dans l'âme de ceux qui nous écoutent et y gravons la séduction" (141); Barbey inscribes the dandy's voice with his steel quill and immortalizes it by preserving its effect in writing.

Although there are relatively few epigrams articulated by the characters throughout **Les Diaboliques,** the narrators integrate numerous epigrams into the text. Most obvious are the quotations and epigraphs that precede the stories and that serve as cryptic preludes to his tales of terror. For example, "Dans ce temps délicieux, quand on raconte une histoire vraie, c'est à croire que le Diable a dicté" (81). This tantalizing prelude leaves the reader in anticipation of the story. What creates the effect is the ambiguity produced by the allusion to the devil as speaker of the truth. The epigraph also refers to the narrator himself (since he is telling the story) who reinforces the self-conscious and ironic pose the dandy must maintain. In addition, the phrase establishes an alliance between the narrator and Satan, thereby making the reader an accomplice to his *pécheresses* as he calls his stories in the preface.

The epigrams of le docteur Torty are stylized to reflect his personality. Also a dandy, Torty is skeptical of women: "Il ne faut pas regarder aux origines, pas plus pour les femmes que pour les nations; il ne faut regarder au berceau de personne" (91). Or "Une femme qui fait ce que fait un homme, le ferait-elle beaucoup moins bien, aura toujours sur l'homme, en France, un avantage marqué" (97). He explains to the narrator why Hauteclaire and Savigny never had children, "Le feu,—qui dévore,—consume et ne produit pas" (127).

The twist often added at the end of the epigram, for example, "c'est à croire que le Diable a dicté," or "a un avantage marqué" is also a dandy gesture. He takes a single truth or topic of common knowledge and adds a provocative turn of phrase. One critic claims that "the authors of collections of epigrams have usually stated specifically why they wrote these short, salty poems. In each case the poet intends to reveal the incongruity, the injustice, insincerity, and falsehood in the life around us" (Holum ["The Epigram"] 21). According to Barbey, the falsehood around us is not the artifice he valorizes, but rather the mundane hypocrisy of bourgeois culture. For example, in an exchange between Ravila and an astonished guest in **Le Plus Bel Amour de Don Juan**:

"Comment? . . . C'est donc dans le boudoir qu'on aura soupé?" / —Oui Madame, c'est dans le boudoir. Et pourquoi pas? On dîne bien sur un champ de bataille . . ." (2: 60), the analogy between bedroom and battlefield is a provocation aimed at the bourgeois reader. He shows that what is in fact out of place, or "false" is not only the imposed social taboo of dining in the boudoir but also narrating a bedroom scene. At the same time he integrates an age-old topos—the comparison between love and war. The epigram becomes a rhetorical device that the dandy narrator manipulates according to the situation and desired effect.

The epigram, both as pointed saying and metaphor for the creative process itself, accomplishes the effects of ambiguity sought by the dandy artist: it piques curiosity by addressing subjects of general interest in a unique style, particular to the author. Whether its solution or explanation as Lessing maintains, is ambiguous, gratifying or both, depends on the author's intent to surprise or perplex his reader. Barbey withholds gratification and shows that the more ironic the ending, the sharper the point, the more impressive the effect, and perhaps the more lasting.

Barbey's use of epigram transforms an ancient genre (sifting through the remains of history is, after all, a dandy pastime) and renews it within the context of modern French society. Just as the dandy seeks to imitate certain aspects of his forefathers,[14] the nineteenth-century artist revives and recreates literature of previous eras. The creative work, derived from earlier models is altered through a new style characterized by personal genius and cultural influence.

Barbey's inclusion of epigrams figures into a larger context of lapidary images in **Les Diaboliques.** One can argue that the collection could be read as a metatext for the very process of transforming literary genres—not only the genres of the epigram and the lapidary, as argued in this essay. Barbey also experiments with the short story genre, with oral tradition (**Ricochets de conversation**), autobiography and even *tombeau*.[15] As a figural lapidary, the stories refer to the process of creative transformation. Although ancient and medieval lapidaries listed properties of gems in the form of a mystical catalogue, Barbey's allusions to individual jewels are subtle and scattered, like reflections through light. They develop a complex rendering of character, tradition and style throughout the stories, with each stone illuminating a unique personality trait or a dandy flair. In the traditional lapidary a gem forms a distinctive entity in its own right and is also a part of a whole, like Barbey's collection of stories. Rather than list the corresponding meanings of precious stones in the text, Barbey leaves their secrets intact and thereby endows them with a mystical significance.[16] By refusing a code according to which the stones can be neatly catego-

rized, Barbey avoids judgements such as that of Gaston Paris who refers to the emptiness and repetition of canonical lapidary tradition and claims that the lapidary genre is "dénué de toute valeur et de toute originalité" (Baisier [*The Lapidaire Chrétien*] 21). Barbey did not list or categorize the actual properties of stones in **Les Diaboliques**—the words of a nineteenth-century scholar describing a fourteenth-century lapidary apply equally as well to Barbey's collection: "Ce n'est certainement pas un receuil de recettes que l'auteur a voulu écrire, mais une collection de talismans. Il se soucie peu de guérir le corps, il veut surtout frapper l'imagination" (Pannier [*Les Lapidaires français du moyen-âge*] 11). In Barbey's work and specifically in **Les Diaboliques,** gems ultimately symbolize the power of the imagination to transform the banal realities of the world outside.

It is helpful to adumbrate aspects of previous lapidary tradition to illustrate the metamorphosis of the genre in relation to Barbey's text. The ancient lapidaries included precious and semi-precious stones; Pliny's *Historia Naturalis* (27-79 AD) is one of the earliest of the Classical lapidaries and was preceded by the *Libellus de Lapidibus* of Theophrastus. Pliny attributes both curative as well as magical properties to stones and includes myths and folklore associated with certain gems. Saint Isidore, who read Pliny, was a possible medieval source for Barbey as well as Albertus Magnus, who in the thirteenth century focused on the more scientific approach to gems in his *De mineralibus*. The *Liber de Gemmis* of Marbode was the most popular medieval lapidary translated into French in about the mid-twelfth century. This work blends scientific and mythical aspects of stones in the tradition of Pliny, but also combines them with the notion that the stones form the foundation of the celestial Jerusalem. Several versions and translations of the Marbode lapidary were available in the nineteenth century (Studer [*Anglo-Norman Lapidaries*] 2). The *Apocalyptic Lapidary* by Phillippe de Thaon (c. 1140) focuses mainly on the jewels in the books of Exodus and Revelation in which the stones on Aaron's breastplate and of the New Jerusalem hold religious symbolic significance.[17] Rémy Belleau in his 1576 *Les Amours et les eschanges des pierres precieueses* reverts to ancient tradition and composes a mythical lapidary drawing on the curative properties of stone and an Ovidian-like cast of characters.

Barbey cultivated a personal interest in gems and gemology. The conspicuously large piece of lapus lazuli on his cane, the glass "jewels" in the special edition of **Le Prêtre marié,** as well as their presence in his fiction bear testimony to this fascination.[18] Gems were regularly mentioned in his journal **Memoranda**: "Reçu Ar[istide] B[oissière] qui m'a rapporté une bague en aigue-marine que je lui avais donnée à rétrécir" (2:857). When he recounts his visits to various women friends, their choice of jewels never escapes him: of the marquise du Vallon he observes "Elle était d'une beauté splendide, grave, pâle, idéale, et que je ne lui connaissais pas; les cheveux en bandeaux et une émeraude sur le front . . ." (887). Another entry compares sunlight to the sparkle of jewels: "M'a reçu en robe de chambre et les cheveux relevés, digne du soleil qui lui pleuvait son or et son opale sur la tête" (891) and reinforces the tension between nature and artifice, between natural genius and cultivated beauty. Since jewels are both natural and crafted, Barbey tests the boundaries between the natural and the artificial exploring aspects of his own dual nature. His affection for a "coupante plume de cristal, taillée à facettes" (896) suggests the desire to capture images in writing. Jewels catch the eye by casting refracted images that can distort and trick. Barbey appropriates their properties for the purposes of his own project; after all, most of the stories in *Les Diaboliques* are generated by a play of distorted and reflected images—a series of episodic and textual *skandalons*.[19] The epigram as well in its desired effect of ambiguity distorts convention by playing upon the expectations of the reader/listener.

The metaphor for the creative work as unblemished and unchanging in a changing world corresponds to a quest of the self through art. The figure of lapidary images evokes this personal quest as well as the dynamics between stasis and movement. The allusions to stone as both crystal clear jewel and hard opaque substance are juxtaposed throughout the text, and emphasize the complex nature of Barbey's text and his own persona.

Crystallization evokes both petrification and permanence, as well as movement through light. An entry in Barbey's journal recounts a typical day and illustrates this tension between stasis and vibrancy.

> Allé chez la Geslin; pris des gants. Convoité un magnifique flacon de cristal ciselé à bouchon d'or pur dont ma fatuité s'arrangerait et peut-être s'arrangera. Les caprices de mon âme sont aussi nombreux que les plis sur la mer, *un jour d'ouragon.*—Fait un *véritable cours* d'éventails. Peut-être en donnerai-je un à ma belle-sœur, symbole de la fraîcheur de mes sentiments pour elle.—Tué le temps avec ces graves *élucubrations.*
>
> (2:760)

For Barbey, the apparent frivolity of fans and crystal bottles breaks the monotony of quotidian experience. Like a stone making ripples on a lake, or a prism refracting light, these crystals and bibelots create movement through their very petrification. According to Barbey, "S'il y a plus beau que le contour, c'est le mouvement" (1634); yet these solid and staid objects move him to desire and aesthetic inspiration. By "killing time," by preoccupying himself with fetish objects and sentimentalism, he mitigates the effects of ennui and projects himself into the crystal or gem to capture beauty, to survive the passage of time.

The metaphors and curious facts made available to him from previous lapidary tradition along with his own experience stimulate the power of his imagination to lend an epic or at least mythic dimension to his stories. For example, in a note to one of his prose poems in *Rythmes oubliés,* he observes, "Le saphir, comme le rubis, n'est qu'un peu de terre glaise que le fer colore (Voir tous les Minéralogistes)" (1219). In the same collection he refers to the cherished "Pierre Noire" in Arab tradition. Barbey's interest in the folkloric properties of stones is linked to a general interest in natural history and more specifically it figures into the alchemy of his narrative imagery.

Precious stones signify numerous themes in *Les Diaboliques* such as intelligence, creative legacy, poetic inspiration, even hypnotic power. Ultimately they comprise the treasure Barbey leaves behind. Prisms and crystals are signifiers of ultimate perfection and unmatched genius. In *Pensées Détachées,* he remarks "Le Diamant, le graphite, et le charbon ordinaire sont chimiquement le même corps."[20] The observation corresponds to a similar comparison of genius in artists. He claims "Je ne crois qu'à ce qui est rare: Les grands esprits, les grands caractères, les grands hommes. . . . Le plus grand éloge qu'on puisse faire d'un diamant c'est de l'appeler un solitaire" (1236-37). Barbey evokes the fervent, almost frantic desire to be unique. In *Le Plus Bel Amour de Don Juan* he insists that one lover always stands out among the others: "c'est la vérité, qu'il y en a *un,* entre tous les sentiments de la vie, qui rayonne toujours dans le souvenir plus fort que les autres, à mesure que la vie s'avance, et pour lequel on les donnerait tous!—Le diamant de l'écrin,—dit la comtesse de Chiffrevas songeuse, qui regardait peut-être dans les facettes du sien" (66-67).

The comparison between exceptional stone and exceptional human being corresponds to the brilliance of personality and intellect. While humans are fundamentally similar, only certain ones, according to Barbey, are endowed with the gift of brilliance or genius (clearly he saw himself as one of the happy few). By recuperating properties of precious stones, he calls attention to the paradox of ready-made or self-made man, a constant theme throughout his work. "As a dandy writing about dandyism, Barbey parsed the central paradox of identity: its need to take in the identities of others—whatever their nationality, personality, native tongue, gender—even as it contracts to a formidably private crystalline core" (Feldman [*Gender on the Divide*] 96).

Artistic transmission and creative metamorphosis are represented through specific lapidary tropes in Barbey's text. For example, Cleopatra drinking pearls dissolved in vinegar is a striking metaphor in Barbey's work. In *Ce qui ne meurt pas* the narrator uses the myth in reference to the effects of decomposed love: "vase de vinaigre où se dissolvent les perles de Cléopâtre, toutes les richesses du cœur dépensées, plus lentement et plus misérablement perdues que dans la somptuosité d'un seul soir" (590).[21] Barbey also evokes the image in a critique of Gautier's *Emaux et Camées*: "Le livre de M. Gautier devrait s'appeler plutôt: *Perles fondues,* car presque toutes ces perles de poésies, que l'esprit boit avec des voluptés de Cléopâtre, se fondent en larmes aux dernières strophes de chacune d'elles, et c'est là un charme,—un charme encore meilleur que leur beauté" (*Les Œuvres et les hommes,* "Les Poètes," 71). Through this image, Barbey duplicates the queen's cold countenance and figuratively imbibes the nacrous liquid of tradition. It is the transmission of a pure and precious substance by which he produces his own gem.

Barbey makes himself a monument to his time in another example that emphasizes creative transformation. In the **"Dessous de cartes d'une partie de whist,"** the narrator affirms, "Il semblait qu'en se retirant de toute la surface du pays, envahi chaque jour par une bourgeoisie insolente, l'aristocratie se fût concentrée là, comme dans le fond d'un creuset, et y jetât, comme un rubis brûlé, le tenace éclat qui tient à la substance même de la pierre, et qui ne disparaîtra qu'avec elle" (2:134). The words *creuset, rubis, éclat,* and *pierre* create an isolated structure within the passage. The metaphor is a funereal monument: this crucible of aristocracy becomes a jeweled coffin or tombstone in memory of a world past. At the same time, it suggests the distillation of the creative process, an alchemical procedure in search of the philosopher's stone—that evasive substance, an elixir of life.

By immortalizing himself and his work in stone, Barbey ensures that his stories, his crafted gems, will remain. After his own demise and the end of this "triste siècle" his stones would rise from the ruins, like a *phénix,* a dandy, a treasure within a pyramid to be opened to posterity:

> Comme à l'angle tournant d'un pâle mausolée
> Un nom qui fait penser quelquefois vient s'offrir . . .
> Ton œil rêveur, un jour, sur la page isolée
> Où je t'écris mon nom verra mon souvenir.
>
> Et tu le reliras, comme on lit, sur la pierre,
> Le nom que l'on aimait préservé de l'oubli . . .
> Et tu diras: "Ce livre est comme un cimetière
> Où pour moi dort son cœur,—son cœur enseveli!"[22]

Barbey was petrified of death; painfully aware of imminent obscurity, his response was a careful exquisite travail that contrasted with the dark undignified effects of death. It was Barbey's fervent hope that future readers would see his tomb through the pages of his work.

The refracted images projected by crystal or cut gems are an apt metaphor for creative crisis. Crisis entails splinter and fragmentation (from the Greek *krinein,* to

separate). A staunch Catholic who envisioned apocalyptic ruin, Barbey clearly evokes the world's fate as well as his own in *Les Diaboliques* (see Hofer's "Apocalypse et Fin de siècle: Le cas de Barbey d'Aurevilly"). His project was to include twelve short stories and in the preface to the 1874 edition he states: "Voici les six premières! Si le public y mord, et les trouve à son goût, on publiera prochainement les six autres, car elles sont douze—comme une douzaine de pêches—ces pécheresses!" (2:1290). (Barbey lists the titles of the stories he hoped to add to the six *Diaboliques* in his *Disjecta Membra.* Among the stories never-to-be-written were "L'honneur des femmes," "Madame Henri III," "Entre adultères," "L'Avorteur," "Valognes," and "Les Deux vieux hommes d'état de l'amour.") At the end of the preface he concludes, "Après *les Diaboliques, les Célestes. . . .* si on trouve du bleu assez pur . . . Mais y en a-t-il?" (1292). Similarly the last line of the 1870 *projet de préface* reads "En ce cas-là, après *les Diaboliques* viendraient *les Célestes*" (1293). The epithet, *les Célestes* evokes the contrasting elements of Barbey's manichean universe; it also recalls the *murailles célestes* of the New City in the book of *Revelation* and invites Biblical exegesis of the proposed installments. In addition, it recalls the early lapidaries of Saint Isidore and the Bishop of Marbode. In particular, Barbey's projected twelve stories, his gems, as the twelve stones of the Apocalypse, correspond to a twelfth-century lapidary attributed to Philippe de Thaon. According to one source, Thaon's Alphabetical Lapidary has an addendum that appears to introduce another lapidary. The final lines read:

> E Deus m'aït al comencer
> E al finer et al traiter!
> Ci fine li livre terrestre
> E [si] comence li celestre.

(Studer [*Anglo-Norman Lapidaries*] 262)[23]

This second lapidary was perhaps announced as *céleste* because it alludes to the twelve stones of the Heavenly City which would be detailed in a sequel, the Apocalyptic Lapidary (262).

The comparison between Barbey's preface and this medieval text supports the notion that *Les Diaboliques* reconfigures earlier genres and traditional literary forms. The reference to the Heavenly City links Barbey's vision to earlier manifestations of apocalyptic prophecy and suggests the lapidary as yet another source of inspiration for Barbey's collection of stories. The emphasis on *les Célestes* evokes not only the gemmed foundation of the New City but ultimately it reveals Barbey's hope that his work would also rise from the ashes.

Notes

1. Jean Lorrain, *Correspondance* 25.

2. Barbey allied himself with the Norman *chouans* who were among the last militant supporters to combat the republic.

3. Lorrain's letter greetings to Barbey often contain the conventional use of "Cher maître"; at the same time he playfully intended to emphasize the connotation of mastery or connaisseurship in "maître." In another letter dated 1886 he remarks "vous êtes le grand maître" (Lorrain, *Correspondance* 23).

4. Philippe Berthier, *Barbey d'Aurevilly et l'imagination* [Geneva: Droz, 1978] 238, from "Premiers articles" 26 avril 1846, 120.

5. Barbey writes in a footnote in *Du Dandysme* [*Du Dandysme et de George Brummell*], "Le Dandysme introduit le calme antique au sein des agitations modernes; mais le calme des Anciens venait de l'harmonie de leurs facultés et de la plénitude d'une vie librement développée, tandis que le calme du Dandysme est la pose d'un esprit qui doit avoir fait le tour de beaucoup d'idées et qui est trop dégoûté pour s'animer" ([*Œuvres romanesquos complètes*] 2: 681).

6. "Cette identité de la forme épigrammatique à travers le temps ne doit pas nous cacher les profondes mutations. En l'espace de quatre siècles, de l'époque alexandrine à l'époque romaine, l'épigramme grecque amorce—et en un sens achève—son évolution interne: toujours liée à l'inscription originelle, mais ouverte à des formes et à des contenus nouveaux, elle réussit à être et à dire le contraire de ce qu'elle était et disait:

   —Elle était la lettre figée dans la pierre, et elle réussit à capter la parole la plus éphémère.

   —Elle disait l'éloge (du guerrier, de l'athlète), et voici que l'éloge se retourne, d'abord dans la parodie, puis dans le trait comique et satirique, et que d'épigramme *sur,* elle devient épigramme *contre.*

   —Elle était simple, consistant en un énoncé nu: elle se dédouble et, non contente d'accentuer l'élément final, finit par détacher le trait"

   (Laurens [*L'Abeille dans l'ambre*] 26)

7. For example see Richard Gilman's *Decadence* [1979] and A. E. Carter's *The Idea of Decadence in French Literature* [1958].

8. By cultural malaise I refer both to the general sense of uncertainty and pessimism that was sparked by the French defeat in the Franco-Prussian war and that reached a crescendo at the fin de siècle and specifically to those fears and anxieties produced by the industrialization and commercialization of the publishing industry. Barbey in particular was deeply critical of the growing number of writers, particularly women writers who, in his opinion, made "métiers et marchandise de littérature."

9. See Paul Verlaine, "Epigrammes," *Œuvres complètes* 211-74.

10. Barbey's kindred soul Baudelaire maintains in *Le Dandy* (1863) "Le dandysme apparaît surtout aux époques transitoires où la démocratie n'est pas encore toute-puissante, où l'aristocratie n'est que partiellement chancelante et avilie. Dans le trouble de ces époques quelques hommes déclassés, dégoûtés, désœuvrés, mais tous riches de force native, peuvent concevoir le projet de fonder une espèce nouvelle d'aristocratie, d'autant plus difficile à rompre qu'elle sera basée sur les facultés les plus précieuses, les plus indestructibles, et sur les dons célestes que le travail et l'argent ne peuvent conférer" ([*Œuvres complètes*] 2: 711).

11. Barbey's verse emphasizes the symbol of the *flèche* and conflates pen, power, passion and penis. It also recalls the crafty licentiousness of the Priapic poems of ancient Rome: in particular Richard Hooper's translation of the following inscription bears a striking resemblance because of its insistence on phallic imagery and mythological references.

   Jove wields the lightening, Neptune's trident-lord.
   Minerva, yours the spear. Mars bears the sword.
   The thyrsus serves to rally Liber's band;
   the shaft speeds onward from Apollo's hand;
   for Hercules a club is standard gear;
   but it's my hard-on that inspires fear.

   (Hooper [*The Priapus Poems*] 60)

   Barbey was extremely well read and very familiar with ancient Latin and Greek texts; it is very likely that he read epigrams similar to this one. Both Meyer and Franz Buecheler published editions of the *Corpus Priapeorum* which were contemporaneous with Barbey's work.

12. René Girard's conceptualization of the *skandalon* in *Des Choses cachées depuis la fondation du monde* is particularly applicable to *Les Diaboliques* in light of Barbey's subtle incorporation of psychology, desire, and scandal. The "diabolical" aspects of Barbey's dandies are linked to the dandy's practice of subverting convention—Girard also points out that hell and Satan are associated with scandal or *skandalon*: "Satan n'est pas seulement le prince de ce monde, le principe de tout ordre mondain; il est également le principe de tout désordre, c'est à dire le scandale lui-même . . ." (441). Barbey's textualization of the *skandalon* ("généralement traduit par scandale, obstacle, pierre d'achoppement, piège placé sur le chemin," 439), is manifested in his use of the epigram.

13. Barbey also cites Sheridan in *Du Dandysme* as an inspiration for the nineteenth-century dandy: "Plus spirituel ou plus passionné, c'était Sheridan . . . Yarmouth, Byron, Sheridan, et tant d'autres de cette époque, fameux dans tous les genres de gloire, qui furent Dandys, mais quelque chose de plus" (2: 673).

14. Baudelaire also looked to the Ancients for inspiration: "Le dandysme est une institution vague, aussi bizarre que le duel; très ancienne, puisque César, Catilina, Alcibiade nous en fournissent des types éclatants . . ." (2: 709).

15. For a study of the oral "residue" in Barbey's narratives see Peter Brooks, "The Story Teller" *The Yale Journal of Criticism* 1 (1987-88): 21-38.

16. G. Peylet claims in *Les Evasions manquées ou les illusions de l'artifice* "Le minéral exerce une véritable fascination chez les artistes de la seconde moitié du siècle. Les saphirs, la topaze, l'émeraude, le diamant, le rubis sont les pierres qui reviennent le plus souvent chez Barbey d'Aurevilly . . . [Mais] l'auteur ne les exploite pas psychologiquement. Il se contente de leur pouvoir de suggestion" (Peylet 142).

17. See also Baisier's *The Lapidaire Chrétien,* Joan Evans's *English Medieval Lapidaries* (London: Humphrey Milford Press, 1933), Paul Studer and Joan Evans, *Anglo-Norman Lapidaries,* and Pannier's *Les Lapidaires Français du moyen âge.*

18. Barbey's cane was an essential accouterment to his dandy persona. Elizabeth Creed points out in *Le Dandysme de Barbey d'Aurevilly,* "la canne du dandy se dresse contre le parapluie du bourgeois."

19. See Jean-Pierre Boucher's Les Diaboliques *de Barbey d'Aurevilly: Une esthétique de la dissimulation et de la provocation.*

20. Barbey, *Disjecta Membra,* vol 2 (Paris: La Connaissance, 1925) 134.

21. Barbey refers to the image on two other occasions. In *Le Cachet d'Onyx* the metaphor evokes the fiery passion of Dorsay for Hortense: "Quand la reine d'Egypte jetait dans la coupe de vinaigre les perles qui pendaient à ses oreilles, avait-elle de l'amour comme cet amour?" (1: 8). In his *Rythmes oubliés,* he describes Cleopatra as a "Buveuse de perles" (2: 1219).

22. Barbey, "Sur un livre donné à Lily," *Dédicaces,* 1598-99.

23. Whether or not Barbey actually read a version of this lapidary still remains uncertain. Although the poem was transcribed in its entirety by Paul Meyer in *Romania* xxxviii, versions of Marbode's lapi-

dary detailing the stones of the Heavenly City were published as early as 1708, 1799 and later in 1854 (Studer 2).

Works Cited

Baisier, Léon. *The Lapidaire Chrétien, Its Composition, Its Influence, Its Sources.* Washington D.C.: Catholic University of America, 1936.

Barbey d'Aurevilly, Jules Amédée. *Œuvres romanesques complètes I-II.* ed. Jacques Petit. Paris: Gallimard, Bibliothèque de la Pléiade, 1966.

———. *Les Œuvres et les hommes* vols. 1-26. Geneva: Slatkine, 1968.

Baudelaire, Charles. *Œuvres complètes I-II.* Ed. Claude Pichois. Paris: Gallimard, Bibliothèque de la Pléiade, 1976.

Bernheimer, Charles. "Barbey's Dandy Narratives." *Figures of Ill Repute.* Cambridge: Harvard UP, 1989. 69-88.

Berthier, Philippe. "Huysmans et Barbey d'Aurevilly: l'étalon catholique," *Huysmans* Ed. Pierre Brunel et André Guyaux. Paris: Editions de l'Herne, 1985. 333-44.

Boucher, Jean-Pierre. Les Diaboliques *de Barbey d'Aurevilly: Une esthétique de la dissimulation et de la provocation.* Montréal: Les Presses Universitaires du Québec, 1976.

Brooks, Peter. "The Storyteller." *The Yale Journal of Criticism* 1 (1987-88): 21-38.

Creed, Elizabeth. *Le Dandysme de Barbey d'Aurevilly.* Paris: Droz, 1938.

Feldman, Jessica. *Gender on the Divide.* Ithaca: Cornell UP, 1993.

Girard, René. *Des Choses cachées depuis la fondation du monde.* Paris: Grasset, 1978.

Gourmont, Remy de. *Le Latin mystique.* Paris: Georges Crès, 1913.

Hofer, Hermann. "Apocalypse et Fin de Siècle: Le Cas de Barbey d'Aurevilly," *Fin de Siècle: Terme Evolution, Revolution. Actes du Congrès de la Société Française de Littérature Générale et Comparée.* Ed. Gwenhaël Ponnau. France: Presses Universitaires du Mirail, 1989. 425-32.

Holum, Karen. "The Epigram: Semantic Basis for the Pointed Ending." *Linguistics* 94 (1972): 21.

Hooper, Richard. *The Priapus Poems: Erotic epigrams from Ancient Rome.* Urbana: U of Illinois P, 1999.

Huysmans, J. K. *A Rebours.* Paris: Fasquelle Editeurs, 1974.

Laurens, Pierre. *L'Abeille dans l'ambre: Célébration de l'épigramme de l'époque alexandrine à la fin de la Renaissance.* Pairs: Les Belles Lettres, 1989.

Lessing. *Fables and Epigrams.* London: John and H. L. Hunt, 1825.

Lorrain, Jean. *Correspondance.* Paris: Editions Baudinière, 1929.

———. *Monsieur de Bougrelon.* Paris: Guillaume, 1897.

———. *La Nostalgie de la Beauté.* Paris: E. Sansot, 1900.

Pannier, L. *Les Lapidaires français du moyen-âge, des* XIIe, XIIIe, *et* XIVe *siècles.* Paris: F. Vieweg, 1882.

Petit, Jacques. *Barbey d'Aurevilly Critique. Annales Littéraires de l'Université de Besançon* vol. 53. Paris: Les Belles Lettres, 1963.

Peylet, Gérard. *Les Evasions manquées ou les illusions de l'artifice dans la littérature "fin de siècle."* Genève: Slatkine, 1986.

Redman, Alvin. ed. *The Epigrams of Oscar Wilde.* United Kingdom: Senate Press, 1996.

Studer, Paul and Joan Evans. *Anglo-Norman Lapidaries.* Paris: Librarie Ancienne Edouard Champion, 1924.

Verlaine, Paul. "Epigrammes." *Œuvres complètes.* Paris: Gallimard. Bibliothèque de la Pléiade, 1954. 639-70.

Miranda Gill (essay date April 2007)

SOURCE: Gill, Miranda. "The Myth of the Female Dandy." *French Studies* 61, no. 2 (April 2007): 167-81.

[*In the following essay, Gill analyzes the relationship between dandyism and gender in the writings of Barbey d'Aurevilly.*]

THE INVISIBLE FEMALE DANDY

According to critical commonplace, female dandyism did not exist in nineteenth-century French culture. In the words of Roger Kempf, 'La femme ne pèse guère dans l'histoire universelle du dandysme'. Even feminist critics have suggested that female dandyism only emerged in the twentieth-century interwar period with the arrival of wealthy American women artists in Paris.[1] Nineteenth-century women could not be dandies, it has typically been argued, because sexual double standards severely restricted women's freedom in social life; because concern for appearances was transgressive in men but not in women; because contemporaneous gender ideologies denied women the status of individual; and because women were associated with the natural body,

rather than with stylized self-presentation.[2] As reflections of general beliefs about sexual difference during this period, such arguments are largely accurate. However, since the dandy represented departure from convention, they cannot account for women who departed from the conventions of femininity (for fashionable women, for instance, who were associated with 'unnatural' styles of dress or with distinctly unfeminine traits such as self-assertion and emotional coldness). Critics have therefore neglected a wide body of nineteenth-century commentary on such atypical women, many of whom, I will argue, were explicitly linked to dandyism.

More generally, critics who deny the existence of female dandyism have relied upon a normative rather than an historical approach to the phenomenon of dandyism. The former consists in the view that only one model of the male dandy, namely that exemplified by the austere English Regency dandy Beau Brummell and subsequently theorized by Barbey d'Aurevilly and Baudelaire, is valid; it implies that all other figures termed 'dandies' by nineteenth-century writers are somehow inauthentic. Yet the term 'dandy' arose within unstable networks of English and French terms relating to fashionable life, a field in which there was often little consensus.[3] The dandy also appeared in an array of literary masks, from the English gentleman to the prankster, the would-be eighteenth-century libertine, the cursed Byronic 'fatal man', the Bohemian Jeune-France, the poet-hero of modernism, the Second Empire *parvenu,* and the feminized and potentially homosexual *fin-de-siècle* aesthete.[4] To cite merely two examples of nineteenth-century distinctions that have since largely been forgotten, Regency commentators differentiated between two types of English dandy, the feminized 'exquisite' and the uncouth 'ruffian', whilst French writers distinguished the understated dandy who emulated Brummell from the ostentatious *lion,* a 'dandy féroce'.[5] Once the monolithic figure of the dandy is perceived as representing a series of shifting performances rather than a timeless essence, the multiple areas of overlap with female dandyism become apparent. The following analysis focuses on the emergence of female dandyism in France during the 1840s, with particular reference to key early texts by Jules Barbey d'Aurevilly and the cultural contexts from which they emerged.

THE LEGACY OF THE PARISIAN 'PHYSIOLOGIE'

In 1845, Barbey published his influential essay ***Du dandysme et de George Brummell.*** Two of his fictional texts written around the same period portray characters explicitly framed as female dandies: Mme de Gesvres in ***L'Amour impossible*** (1841), and Mme de Stasseville in ***Ricochets de conversation: I, Le Dessous de cartes d'une partie de whist*** (1850).[6] If little attention has been devoted to Barbey's representations of female dandies, this is due to a more general lack of critical engagement with the main cultural codes through which the writer articulated this new type: the Parisian literary *physiologie* and medicine. The reworking of these discourses in Barbey's writing will be considered in turn.

Fashionable and singular women who departed from the codes of femininity were represented to a wide readership in the literary 'physiology', a moderately priced small book immensely popular with middle and lower middle class readers during the period 1830-1845. The genre attained its zenith in 1841 and 1842; in these two years alone, it has been estimated, some 500,000 copies were in circulation.[7] Each physiology treated a different social type or aspect of Parisian life. Their narrative voice was humorous and worldly, that of the male expert who, like the *flâneur,* revelled in his intimate knowledge of city life. Physiologies created a comforting sense of complicity between narrator and readers, and critics have focused on the role of the genre in ensuring the smooth reproduction of bourgeois ideology. Yet recent feminist criticism suggests that the physiology may indirectly have contributed to the liberalization of female identity.[8] The 1804 Napoleonic civil code sought to enshrine in law a monolithic model of femininity, defining women as dependent upon their fathers and husbands and devoted to domestic pursuits, but this model was inadvertently called into question by the emergence of a body of writing aimed at cataloguing the different strata of Parisian life. 'Panoramic literature' such as the physiology highlighted the variable nature of female roles, characteristics, and class affiliations, from the flower seller and seamstress to the blue stocking and *femme politique*: 'les identités féminines semblent se multiplier'.[9] The physiology also provides a crucial point of reference for understanding contemporaneous literary production, for when nineteenth-century readers made sense of fiction by writers such as Sand, Balzac, Barbey d'Aurevilly and Stendhal, they implicitly drew on a range of cultural references linked to the physiology that have since faded from sight. Two female types strongly influenced discourse on female dandyism: the *femme à la mode* and the *lionne.*

During the July Monarchy, symbolic dominance of Parisian society was linked to the *femme à la mode,* portrayed in physiological sketches as a figure obsessed by monopolizing the public gaze at social gatherings. None 'reigned' for very long: the public's attention span appeared to be decreasing at a time when commodity culture was encouraging objects to be perceived as expendable. A description of a *femme à la mode* in *Les Français peints par eux-mêmes* (1840-42) depicts her anguish in front of the mirror as she fears her celebrity is waning; she is wholly indifferent to her husband and family. Another, from Delphine de Girardin's *Lettres parisiennes,* attempts to defuse the transgressive implications of such 'unfeminine' characteristics by showing the figure weeping, desperate for the love and friendship enjoyed by less fashionable women.[10] The *femme à la mode* took the vanity widely considered to be characteristic of Parisian women to a pathological extreme. Structurally close to the model of narcissistic coldness associated with Beau Brummell, her creation of a fashionable persona was managed with the same pragmatic calculation: 'Sa toilette ne fut plus le chaste vêtement de la femme modeste', one commentator writes: 'Ce fut d'abord et à tout prix le luxe, la variété, la magnificence et l'éclat; puis des idées bizarres, des recherches piquantes pour ranimer constamment l'attention fugitive'.[11]

If this figure represented anxious self-scrutiny, the *lionne,* a subcategory of the *femme à la mode,* was associated with independence and bodily vitality. For many commentators, the 'dandy' was the fashionable type of the Restoration and the 'lion' that of the July Monarchy, hence the dandy's direct successor.[12] Sketches typically depicted *lionnes* as aspirant members of the anglophile male elite of the July Monarchy:

> infatigables amazones, dédaignant les paisibles recréations de leur sexe, et abdiquant le doux empire des grâces discrètes pour suivre nos dandys à la course, et se mêler aux grandes et aux petites manœuvres du Jockey's-Club; reines du monde cavalier, que l'on a surnommées *les Lionnes,* pour rendre hommage à la force, à l'intrépidité et à l'inépuisable ardeur dont elles donnent chaque jour tant de preuves.[13]

Their surrogate masculinity is expressed in strenuous physical exercise such as horse riding, pigeon shooting and swimming, in eating with a hearty appetite (unlike the fasting romantic heroine of the late 1820s), and in adopting manly habits such as drinking and smoking.

Yet reference to the *lionne*'s 'inépuisable ardeur' hints at her femininity, and ambiguity is created by the term *merveilleuse.* Though the equivalent of *merveilleux,* one of the types cited by nineteenth-century commentators as a precursor to the dandy, the term had been used around the start of the century to refer to courtesans. Indeed, the semantic field of the term 'lionne', with its connotations of erotic pursuit, underwent a significant shift after 1848. Associated with fashionable aristocrats during the July Monarchy, it became synonymous with clandestine prostitution during the Second Empire, largely as a consequence of Émile Augier and Édouard Foussier's popular play *Les Lionnes pauvres* (1858). The worldly 'philosopher' of the play, Bourgnon, describes the *lionne* in the following terms:

> Qu'est-ce qu'une *lionne* dans cet argot qu'on nomme le langage du monde? Une femme à la mode, n'est ce pas, c'est-à-dire un de ces dandys femelles qu'on rencontre invariablement où il est bon ton de se montrer, aux courses, au bois de Boulogne, aux premières représentations . . . Ajoute une pointe d'excentricité, tu as la lionne: supprime la fortune, tu as la lionne pauvre.[14]

Both memoirs and histories of fashion subsequently cited the *lionne* as a key symbol of a new mood of gender experimentation dating back to the July Monarchy. Some commentators suggested that the *lionne*'s masculine traits were merely feigned; others retrospectively (and inaccurately) associated her with radicalism, linking her to George Sand's daring heroines, even to the revolutionary *Vésuviennes* of 1848.[15]

Thus when, in 1841, the young Barbey d'Aurevilly published a novel entitled **L'Amour impossible,** the vocabulary of the *physiologie* was the interpretive framework within which both he and his readers made sense of its unusual heroine. The narrative recounts a psychological battle between a young man, Maulévrier, and an emotionally cold older woman, Mme de Gesvres, each of whom seeks to seduce the other whilst preserving his or her autonomy. Having sacrificed to Mme de Gesvres his hyperbolically feminine lover Mme d'Anglure, who dies of grief, Maulévrier is contaminated by Mme de Gesvre's inability to love, and the narrative closes with a depiction of their joint emotional sterility. In an anonymous review published in *La Revue des deux mondes* in 1841, the novel is described as quintessentially fashionable:

> Il s'agit d'une *femme à la mode,* d'une lionne qui vole son amant à une autre femme de ses amies, et qui, pourtant n'en profite guère; car elle et lui sont blasés . . . Le style, le langage, le costume et les mœurs de cette nouvelle sont du dernier moderne; la mode y joue un grand rôle, le jargon n'y est pas étranger[16]

The review also compares Mme de Gesvres to a *panthère* (a wealthy kept woman), interpreting the novel within the framework of the Parisian physiology. Barbey knew this discourse well, for much of his writing on dandyism first appeared in the related genre of the fashion magazine. He himself describes Mme de Gesvres as a *femme à la mode* and a *fat,* a close synonym of 'dandy'. Reinserted into the cultural context of the July Monarchy physiology, such descriptions of **L'Amour impossible** suggest that Gesvres embodies the narcissistic coldness of the *femme à la mode,* the masculine self-assurance of the *lionne,* and the sexual immorality of the *panthère.* Elaborated by Barbey into a model of female dandyism during the 1840s, this combination of traits proved considerably more threatening than any one alone.[17]

The Dandy's Temperament

Just as they reworked well-known themes from the literary physiology, Barbey's texts presupposed that their readers would grasp the cultural meanings sedimented around medical concepts. Four of these underpinned Barbey's codification of both male *and* female dandies, though with different cultural implications in each case: temperament, hermaphrodism, melancholia and sadism.

First, and in line with the models of national temperament that retained their prestige well into the century, Barbey associated dandies with the phlegmatic and cold north, as opposed to the sanguine and passionate Latin south. Since masculinity was culturally associated with self-control and femininity with 'nerves', these concepts were strongly gendered. When, in his essay on dandyism, Barbey opposes the 'race nervo-sanguine de France' to 'ces hommes du Nord, lymphatiques et pâles', the latter the home of dandies such as Brummell, he implicitly feminizes the entire French race. He refers elsewhere to the 'système physiologique anglais' (*O.r.c.* [*Œuvres romanesques complètes*], II, 671, 705n). Such comments echo the nineteenth-century doxa of national temperament, in which Frenchmen were construed as too emotionally unpredictable to trade on the stock market and too sociable and enthusiastic to become true dandies, compared with their phlegmatic English counterparts.[18] Female coldness was frequently interpreted according to such geographical models of temperament: Frenchwomen were held to be coquettish and vain, forming an intermediary stage between passionate Italian women and cold and spiritual German women.[19] Since female coldness *per se* was considered pathological within the medical codes of the period, 'normal' French women were doubly identified with emotional warmth, by virtue of their race as well as their sex.[20] The French female dandy thus appeared an alarming exception to both geographical and medical norms.

The pathologization of female coldness centred at first on the enigmatic figure of the *femme froide*. Doctors believed that civilization cooled down women's innately hysterical tendencies and made them wiser.[21] However, excessively cold women were associated with frigidity and 'manliness' within a burgeoning medical discourse of sexual difference, disseminated to a wide audience by figures such as the medical publicist J.-J. Virey. Upon meeting the Marquise de Vallon, the woman on whom Mme de Gesvres was closely modelled, Barbey placed her in the category of female exception: 'Malgré quelques vouloirs insensés et le besoin de tendresse, ancré au cœur des femmes, elle est sous la sauvegarde d'un esprit mâle et d'une incorruptible froideur. Son esprit désire plus que son cœur' (*O.r.c.,* II, 853). He evokes Vallon's austere coldness with imagery of snow. In turn, Gesvres's name hints at her frostiness ('givre'), and she is compared to Niobe, a woman turned to stone (*O.r.c.,* I, 103).[22] Female coldness was also suggestive of sexual immorality: during the July Monarchy, writers produced numerous fictional portraits of courtesans as *femmes froides,* associating them with dehumanized imagery of sculpture, marble and machinery.

Second, Barbey stressed the dandy's androgyny, a concept which often overlapped with hermaphrodism in nineteenth-century writing. His essay on dandyism closes with a lyrical invocation of the dandy's transcendence of sexual difference: 'Natures doubles et multiples, d'un sexe intellectuel indécis, où la grâce est plus grâce encore dans la force, et où la force se retrouve encore dans la grâce'. He terms them 'androgynes de l'histoire' (*O.r.c.,* II, 718). Critical discussion has focused overwhelmingly upon the psychological androgyny of the male dandy, arising from his partial feminization, but Barbey's comment simultaneously refers to the androgyny of the *female* dandy, linked to her partial 'virilization'. In his vision of dandyism, masculinity (associated with hardness, cruelty and violence), is tempered by femininity (associated with softness, sensuality and delicacy).[23] Mme de Gesvres represents precisely such psychological hybridity: 'c'était un hermaphrodisme si bien fondu entre ce qui charme et ce qui impose, entre ce qui subjugue et ce qui enivre, que jamais l'art et ses incomparables fantaisies n'avaient rien produit de pareil' (*O.r.c.,* I, 46-7).

Barbey's image of the monster evokes both an aesthetic trope of Romanticism, the monstrously original work emerging from the male artistic imagination, and a highly topical medical concept. Isidore Geoffroy Saint-Hilaire's *Traité de tératologie* (1830-38), the most important nineteenth-century analysis of congenital malformations, cites as an example of the female pole of the hermaphroditic spectrum the cold and frigid woman.[24] French doctors were intrigued by the problem of the hermaphrodite's desire, since dominant medical theories of sexual difference proposed that men and women were complementary, drawn together by a mutual sense of lack. J.-J. Virey's medical description of the hermaphrodite was typical: '[il] n'aurait plus de désirs; il serait neutre et comme rassasié, il n'aimerait donc pas, et ne serait pas capable d'être aimé. Ce serait un individu équivoque, ambigu, indifférent, froid en tous sens'.[25] For Virey, hermaphrodites are condemned to emotional indifference since they cannot be propelled towards a member of the opposite sex with complementary characteristics; they already contain inner equilibrium. In an illustration of the close imaginative links between medical and literary discourse in the period, his vision is startlingly close to Barbey's psychology of dandyism, and specifically to the inability of the androgynous Gesvres and Maulévrier to experience love.

Third, a historically specific set of categories lies behind many nineteenth-century representations of problematic desire: melancholia, discussed during the first half of the century in terms of *mal du siècle,* ennui and spleen (terms often used loosely). Gesves and Maulévrier are portrayed as suffering from pervasive ennui, and linked to a social type associated with the absence of desire: the *fat*. This figure, characterized by his arrogant indifference to others, was known to a wide audience from the Parisian physiology. In a sketch published one year after *L'Amour impossible,* for instance,

the *fat* is depicted in terms of calculated world-weariness and the task of seducing him described as 'une chose impossible', a phrase which resonates with the title of Barbey's narrative.[26] The *fat* was forbidden from manifesting desire, for this would weaken his ability to mystify and seduce his audience.[27] Barbey claims that he was tempted to place as the epigraph to his essay on dandyism 'D'un fat, par un fat, à des fats' (*O.r.c.,* II, 1438), and evinces strong identification with the type in his autobiographical writing.[28]

Barbey's depiction of Mme de Gesvres as a female *fat* departs strikingly from the cultural convention that the *fat* was a male subject, symbolized by the absence of a female form of the term; indeed, the writer subsequently experimented in his 1845 essay on dandyism with approximate equivalents such as 'femmes fates' (*O.r.c.,* II, 700n.). In the preface to the second edition of *L'Amour impossible* in 1859, however, he portrays himself as being embarrassed by his earlier depiction of female fatuity. He emphasizes the text's historical referentiality, in notably Stendhalian terms, to defend it against charges of implausibility (and implicitly of immorality):[29]

> *L'Amour impossible* est à peine un roman, c'est une chronique, et la dédicace qu'on y a laissée atteste sa réalité. C'est l'histoire d'une de ces femmes comme les classes élégantes et oisives—le *high life* d'un pays où le mot d'aristocratie ne devrait même plus se prononcer—nous en ont tant offert le modèle depuis 1839 jusqu'à 1848. A cette époque, si on se le rappelle, les femmes les plus jeunes, les plus belles, et, j'oserais ajouter, physiologiquement les plus parfaits, se vantaient de leur froideur, comme de vieux fats se vantent d'être blasés, même avant d'être vieux. Singulières hypocrites, elles jouaient, les unes à l'ange, les autres au démon, mais toutes, anges ou démons, prétendaient avoir horreur de l'émotion
>
> (*O.r.c.,* I. 1254)

By creating a female *fat,* Barbey was transforming a literary model with strongly masculine associations. This bold move accounts for his subsequent embarrassment, as well as his attempt (like many of the writers who portrayed the *lionne*) to argue that such women were merely feigning their unfeminine absence of emotion. Similarly appropriating a traditionally male theme, George Sand had provided a powerful elaboration of female *mal du siècle* in her partially autobiographical novel *Lélia* (1833); it forms an important intertextual reference at the end of Barbey's novel when a momentarily guilty Mme de Gesvres claims to identify with Sand's impotent heroine. An unpublished section of the novel explores this theme at length.[30] Yet Barbey subsequently dismissed Sand's heroine as 'une impossibilité', echoing the cultural doxa which posited a necessary link between femininity and sensibility.[31]

Finally, the text suggests that only one force can rouse the dandy from the absence of desire: the drive for domination, and in particular the murderous desire to subjugate the consciousness of the other. Male and female dandies ward off pervasive ennui and generate narrative energy by attempting an 'impossible' erotic conquest in which cruelty rather than affection predominates. The love of cruelty is defined by Barbey as a key characteristic of the dandy. A master of the paradoxical 'art de plaire en déplaisant', the dandy attracts a submissive audience through his sadistic contempt. Beau Brummell's insolent disdain for his audience was stressed in both English and French commentary,[32] and Barbey tellingly compares all those entranced by the dandy to female masochists: 'Ne reconnaît-on pas là le besoin d'être battues qui prend quelquefois les femmes puissantes et débauchées?' (*O.r.c.,* II, 715). His representations of female dandyism transform the passive female viewer seduced by the male dandy into a sadistic agent who seeks to dominate others.

The parity of male and female sadism is repeatedly emphasized by Barbey. The crime at the centre of *L'Amour impossible* is the destruction of the saintly Mme d'Anglure by Gesvres and Maulévrier. In the preface to the second edition, Barbey describes the pair as 'deux monstres moraux, et deux monstres par impuissance— les plus laids de tous, car qui est puissant n'est monstre qu'à moitié' (*O.r.c.,* II, 1255). He immediately reminds his readers that he wrote the novel around the same time as his essay *Du dandysme et de George Brummell,* implicitly evoking his description of the dandy in the latter as 'un de ces monstres chez qui la tête est au-dessus du cœur' (*O.r.c.,* II, 710 n). Though evidently intended to create closure, his reference to 'impuissance' in fact destabilizes the meaning of the passage. It suggests at once a congenital abnormality (lack of conscience) against which Maulévrier and Gesvres are helpless; morally culpable weakness of will; and sexual sterility, a characteristic of both effeminate men and virile women in contemporaneous medicine, the latter exemplified by Sand's Lélia. The multiple meanings accrued by concepts such as coldness, ennui, and monstrosity in *L'Amour impossible* exemplify the ability of Barbey's narratives of dandyism to generate irreconcilable interpretive paradigms.

THE DOCTOR'S GAZE

This problematization of interpretation was typical of the uncertainty surrounding the mysterious figure of the dandy. Barbey draws repeatedly on imagery of sphinxes and hieroglyphs to describe both his male and female characters. Substituting for actual analysis, the images raise the possibility that dandies are merely riddles without answers, breaking the tacit contract on the basis of which the realist narrative functions and thwarting the operation of the hermeneutic code.[33] The reader finds a structural double in the figure of the doctor, keen to prevent such interpretive instability by 'diagnosing' the aberrant psychology of the dandy. Bar-

bey continued to experiment with narratives that paired together androgynous male and female dandies, particularly *Le Dessous de cartes d'une partie de whist* (1850) and *Le Bonheur dans le crime* (1874). As though to underline the centrality of medical rhetoric in the codification of the dandy, both place doctors in key positions in the narrative. The former foregrounds the reflections of two doctors upon Mme de Stasseville's 'character'; in the latter Dr Torty, the source of the narrator's information, wishes to write a treatise on teratology, announcing that the androgynous dandies Hauteclaire and Savigny interest him 'comme des monstres' (*O.r.c.,* II, 125).

Despite the critical interest generated by *Le Dessous de cartes,* one key aspect of the text has been little remarked upon: the description of Mme de Stasseville as a 'femme-dandy', and the close relationship between this comment and Barbey's earlier characterization of Mme de Gesvres as a 'lionne', 'femme à la mode' and female 'fat'. The narrative famously recounts the psychological impenetrability of Marmor de Karkoël and the aristocratic Mme de Stasseville, culminating in the revelation of their secret affair and the latter's double infanticide. Stasseville is, like Mme de Gesvres, expert in concealing her thoughts and emotionally indifferent, but is hers a spiritual or a medical condition, aristocratic superiority or illness?

> C'était une nature stagnante, une espèce de *femme-dandy,* auraient dit les Anglais. . . . "Elle est de la race des animaux à sang blanc", répétait son médecin dans le tuyau de l'oreille, croyant l'expliquer par une image, comme on expliquerait une maladie par un symptôme. Quoiqu'elle eût l'air malade, le médecin dépaysé niait la maladie. Etait-ce haute discrétion? ou bien réellement ne la voyait-il pas? jamais elle ne se plaignait ni de son corps ni de son âme. Elle n'avait pas même cette ombre presque physique de mélancolie, étendue d'ordinaire sur le front meurtri des femmes qui ont quarante ans. Ses jours se détachaient d'elle et ne s'en arrachaient pas. Elle les voyait tomber de ce regard d'Ondine, glauque et moqueur, dont elle regardait toutes choses. Elle semblait mentir à sa réputation de femme spirituelle, en ne nuançant sa conduite d'aucune de ces manières d'être personnelles, appelées des excentricités. Elle faisait naturellement, simplement, tout ce que faisaient les autres femmes dans sa société, et ni plus ni moins.
>
> (*O.r.c.,* II, 148)

The narrator's interrogatives, together with his qualification of the phrase 'femme-dandy', mirror the disorientation of both the text's narratees and its readers. Through his suggestion that the doctor might be incompetent, he appears to posit illness as the explanation for the enigma of Stasseville's persona, but this is immediately qualified by his recognition that the main symptom consists precisely in the absence of symptoms, indeed of libidinal investment itself. The narrator's explicit denial of melancholia and eccentricity further complicates the meaning of the passage. Stasseville's absence of desire, within the cultural codes of the period, clearly suggests a form of ennui similar to that afflicting Mme de Gesvres and Sand's Lélia, whilst her lack of sensibility is thoroughly eccentric according to dominant medical theories of female nature. Her abnormality is so far-reaching that it can be evoked only by negation (the absence of colour, desire and movement), and the anaphoric 'elle' suggests a series of futile attempts to unravel an enigma.

Together with melancholia, many of the other medicalized elements of dandyism are implicitly present in this description: the narrator's reference to race and white-bloodedness echoes Barbey's linking of dandyism to national temperament and phlegm, and Stasseville's apparent indifference appears typical of the hermaphrodite described by Virey ('un individu équivoque, ambigu, indifférent, froid en tous sens'). Most importantly, the subsequent dénouement, with its revelation of Stasseville's unnatural crimes, implies that rather than an easily readable malady she suffers from a more alarming condition that increasingly preoccupied psychiatrists in the latter part of the century, namely moral insanity (*la folie morale* or *la folie lucide*).[34] It leaves uncertain the question of responsibility, in line with Barbey's description of Gesvres and Maulévrier as 'moral monsters', a phrase with simultaneously medical and religious connotations. Does Stasseville's insensibility signify a 'teratological' lack of conscience or a depravity suggestive of original sin? Are her symptoms genuine, feigned or non-existent? The narratees within the text are unable to reach a conclusion about her character, just as the doctor's attempt at diagnosis is here undermined.[35]

Indeed, the spectre of the dissimulating woman was, as Barbey was writing, coming to occupy a key role in the medical imaginary. Doctors drew unconsciously on cultural models of female depravity in their depictions of manipulative female patients. To cite one example, the narrator's description of Mme de Stasseville alternates conviction with expressions of doubt and a need for confirmation from the doctor:

> A la voir, on ne pouvait douter qu'elle ne fût, en femme, une de ces organisations comme il y en a dans tous les règnes de la nature, qui, de préférence ou d'instinct, recherchent le fond au lieu de la surface des choses; un de ces êtres destinés à des cohabitations occultes . . . Peut-être ces sortes d'organisations aiment-elles le mensonge pour le mensonge, comme on aime l'art pour l'art, comme les Polonais aiment les batailles.—(Le docteur inclina gravement la tête en signe d'adhésion.)—Vous le pensez, n'est-ce pas? et moi aussi! je suis convaincu que, pour certaines âmes il y a le bonheur de l'imposture. Il y a une effroyable, mais enivrante félicité dans l'idée qu'on ment et qu'on trompe; dans la pensée qu'on se sait seul soi-même, et qu'on joue à la société une comédie dont elle est la

> dupe, et dont on se rembourse les frais de mise en scène par toutes les voluptés du mépris.

(*O.r.c.*, , 154-55)

The following description of the perverse female hysteric was published in 1880 for a general readership by Charles Richet, a physiologist and disciple of Jean-Martin Charcot. It reformulates Barbey's description of female depravity almost word for word:

> elles sont toutes plus ou moins menteuses, moins peut-être pour faire un mensonge intéressé que pour en forger d'inutiles. Elles ont l'amour du mensonge ou plutôt de la tromperie. Rien ne leur plaît plus que d'induire en erreur ceux qui les interrogent, de raconter des histoires absolument fausses, qui n'ont même pas l'excuse de la vraisemblance . . . avec un luxe incroyable de faux détails. Ces gros mensonges sont dits audacieusement, crûment, avec un sang-froid qui déconcerte.[36]

The scene of dissimulation is that of the clinical encounter: doctors are led astray in their quest for knowledge. Richet's characterization is echoed by the psychiatrist Jules Falret fils's description of hysterics ten years later as 'de véritables comédiennes', mixing up truth and falsity 'de manière à tromper les plus clairvoyants', again testifying to doctors' fears of being duped by perverse female patients.[37]

Barbey's text, however, ultimately refuses to assent to the medicalization of the female dandy or to identify with the doctor's gaze. Immediately before the passage in which he describes Stasseville as a dissimulator, Barbey's narrator explains that he wishes to examine her with 'un de ces bons regards *physiologistes*', seemingly qualifying his attitude as medical rather than moral (*O.r.c.*, II, 154). However, the term simultaneously denotes the medical *and* the literary physiology. The passage, more generally, provides the reader with conflicting interpretative models. References to 'organisations' and 'nature' medicalize Stasseville yet terms such as 'âme' and 'occultes' hint at a spiritual realm inaccessible to medical science. The comparison between her love of deception for its own sake and the theory of art for art's sake evokes at once the dandy's persona as an autotelic work of art, the aristocratic rejection of bourgeois materialism, and the novelist's love of fictitious literary masks.[38] Just as it appears to pathologize Mme de Stasseville, the passage endows her dissimulation with ethical complexity absent from medical descriptions.

Dr Jean-Louis Brachet asserted in 1847 that women were naturally undifferentiated: 'les femmes semblent jetées dans un moule commun . . . les exceptions sont une méprise de la nature'.[39] Barbey drew consistently on medical discourse, a key element of nineteenth-century efforts to understand the enigmas of human behaviour. However, he did not strive, like Brachet and his peers, to reduce the meaning of such apparently monstrous 'impossibilities' to a single, stable diagnosis, and his writing testifies far more openly than theirs to the erotic appeal of the exceptional woman. Both these tendencies were echoed in contemporaneous and subsequent literary representations of female dandyism, which will briefly be considered in conclusion.

'ANDROGYNES BIZARRES'

Barbey's codification of female dandyism in the 1840s was inseparable from a number of wider cultural developments, particularly the emergence of unconventional female icons in the Parisian *physiologie* and the growing popularity of medical theories of sexual difference. All three developments coincided with a surge of literary interest in female singularity, forming a crucial link between Ancien Régime portraits of female libertines and *fin-de-siècle* representations of female sadism.

Barbey himself retrospectively highlighted the similarities of Hauteclaire to Stendhal's heroine Mathilde de la Mole, referring to the latter in an essay on dandyism (*O.r.c.*, II, 724, 1281). Stendhal's literary 'amazons', a category typically held to include Mathilde, Mme Grandet and Lamiel, subvert ideologies of female temperament in similar ways to Barbey's female dandies. Independent and self-possessed, they are described with the language of monstrosity and exception, and have well-established affinities with the medical model of the *femme froide*.[40] In her memoirs, Daniel Stern proposed that the *lionne* typified young women's thirst for dangerous experiences in reaction to the monotonous 'comme il faut' of the Restoration salon; Mathilde suffers from precisely such ennui and requires 'anxiety' to stimulate her jaded nerves.[41] Balzac's portrait of the aristocratic Lady Arabelle Dudley in *Le Lys dans la vallée* (1836) explored similar tropes, with particular emphasis on the rhetoric of national temperament. Lady Dudley is prone to boredom and spleen, and is described as having a typically English need for shocking and extraordinary sensations; she is also compared to a lioness.[42]

Baudelaire subsequently addressed the theme of female dandyism. In *Mon cœur mis à nu* he notoriously dismisses 'la femme' as the antithesis of the dandy,[43] but in his essay on Flaubert of 1857 he describes Emma Bovary as 'ce bizarre androgyne', explicitly referring to her dandyism: 'Goût immodéré de la séduction, de la domination et même de tous les moyens vulgaires de séduction . . .—le tout se résumant en deux mots: dandysme, amour exclusif de la domination'.[44] Though Baudelaire's comments have elicited many theories about Emma's relationship to gender stereotypes, none has situated them in relation to preceding discourses of female dandyism in Parisian culture. Yet their relevance

is immediately evident: the *lionne* was notorious for her virile persona and quasi-masculine attire, whilst the spectre of the *femme froide* and the perverse hysteric haunts Flaubert's description of Emma during her affair with Léon in Rouen ('Où donc avait-elle appris cette corruption, presque immatérielle à force d'être profonde et dissimulée?').[45] The narrator also portrays Emma in terms of male fantasies of masochism and role-reversal, like a number of other representations of female dandies.[46] Indeed, the eroticism of the female dandy appeared increasingly threatening as the century progressed, and she began to foreshadow the 'idols of perversity' of *fin-de-siècle* art and literature.[47]

What were the concrete historical effects of literary representations of female dandies? These are difficult to determine, despite the fact that the phenomenon certainly had some basis in social experience (the 'lionne', for example, was described in a range of non-fictional texts). As cultural historians have recognized, it proves impossible to disentangle the actual identity and behaviour of nineteenth-century women from the myths of femininity which proliferated across art, advertising and religion.[48] The figure of the female dandy emerged into cultural consciousness in the context of the social and literary experimentation of the July Monarchy, and evolved in response to both the obsessions of individual writers and the shifting contours of the wider social order. In their resistance to dominant gender stereotypes, these diverse and often contradictory representations widened the imaginary parameters of female identity, and it is therein that their real significance lies.

Notes

1. *Dandies: Baudelaire et Cie* (Paris, Seuil, 1977), p. 157; see also, for instance, Michelle Perrot, 'En marge: célibataires et solitaires', in *Histoire de la vie privée*, IV, *De la Révolution à la Grande Guerre,* ed. by Michelle Perrot (Paris, Seuil, 1987), pp. 287-303 (p. 302).

2. Thus the 'artificial' prostitute and actress have been described as the real equivalents of the male dandy by Marie-Christine Natta, *La Grandeur sans convictions: essai sur le dandysme* (Paris, Félin, 1991), pp. 160-61, and Rhonda Garelick, *Rising Star: Dandyism, Gender, and Performance in the fin de siècle* (Princeton University Press, 1998), p. 3; both too hastily dismiss direct equivalents.

3. For terminological vagueness and disagreement, see, for instance, Charles Baudelaire, *Œuvres complètes,* ed. by Claude Pichois, 2 vols (Paris, Gallimard, 1975-76), II, 711, and Eugène Chapus, *Théorie de l'élégance* (Paris, Comptoir des imprimeurs-unis, 1844), p. 134.

4. See in particular Domna C. Stanton's *The Aristocrat as Art: A Study of the Honnête Homme and*

Dandy in Seventeenth- and Nineteenth-Century French Literature (New York, Columbia University Press, 1980), pp. 30-62.

5. See John C. Prevost, *Le Dandysme en France: 1817-1839* (Paris, Minard, 1957), pp. 22-23 and Félix Deriège, *Physiologie du lion* (Paris, J. Delahaye, 1842), p. 17.

6. The latter formed the kernel of *Les Diaboliques* (1874). Marie-Christine Natta, the only critic to consider Stasseville's description as a 'femme-dandy' in detail (*Grandeur sans convictions*, pp. 158-60), does not situate the text within either Barbey's writing of the 1840s or wider cultural developments.

7. See Claude Pichois, 'Le Succès des physiologies', in *Les Physiologies*, ed. by Andrée Lhéritier (Paris, Université de Paris, 1958), pp. 59-66 (p. 63).

8. On the former, see Richard Sieburth, 'Same Difference: The French Physiologies, 1840-1842', *Notebooks in Cultural Analysis*, I (1984), 163-200.

9. *Histoire des femmes en Occident*, IV, *Le XIXe siècle*, ed. by Geneviève Fraisse and Michelle Perrot (Paris, Plon, 1992), p. 16. Victoria Thompson argues that representations of sexuality and gender were fairly fluid during the July Monarchy, in contrast with rigid Second Empire attitudes: see 'Creating Boundaries: Homosexuality and the Changing Social Order in France, 1830-1870', in *Homosexuality in Modern France*, ed. by Jeffrey Merrick and Bryant T. Ragan (Oxford University Press, 1996), pp. 102-27 (p. 121).

10. *Lettres parisiennes*, 3 vols (Paris, Librairie nouvelle, 1856), II, 282-84.

11. Mme Ancelot, 'Une femme à la mode', in *Les Français peints par eux-mêmes*, 8 vols (Paris, Curmer, 1840-42), I, 57-64 (p. 59).

12. On the *lionne*, see Louis Maigron, *Le Romantisme et la mode* (Paris, Champion, 1911), p. 48 and Honoré de Balzac, *La Comédie humaine*, ed. by Pierre-Georges Castex, 12 vols (Paris, Gallimard, 1976-81), I, 916-17 and XII, 167.

13. Eugène Guinot, 'La Lionne', in *Les Français peints par eux-mêmes*, II, 9-16 (p. 10).

14. *Les Lionnes pauvres* (Paris, A. Lemerre, 1884), p. 45.

15. See, for instance, Octave Uzanne, *La Française du siècle: la femme et la mode* (Paris, May, 1894), p. 194.

16. Quoted in Barbey d'Aurevilly, *Œuvres romanesques complètes*, ed. by Jacques Petit, 2 vols (Paris, Gallimard, 1964-66), I, 1252 (future references abbreviated to *O.r.c.*).

17. Charles Bernheimer opposes women/prostitution/passion to men/dandyism/coldness in Barbey's writing, ignoring the *female* dandies who undermine such polarities; see *Figures of Ill Repute: Representing Prostitution in Nineteenth-Century France* (Cambridge, MA, Harvard University Press, 1989), pp. 75-88.

18. See J.-J. Virey, 'La Femme', *Dictionnaire des sciences médicales*, 15 vols (Paris, Panckoucke, 1812-22), XIV, 503-72 (pp. 517-18).

19. See J.-J. Virey, *De la femme sous ses rapports physiologique, moral et littéraire* (Paris, Crochard, 1823), pp. 78, 96.

20. For an overview of nineteenth-century gender norms, see Robert A. Nye, *Masculinity and Male Codes of Honor in Modern France* (Berkeley, CA, University of California Press, 1998), pp. 47-71. Female sadism was doubly perverse for the sexologist Krafft-Ebing, who argued that women had a 'natural instinct for servitude'; see Vernon A. Rosario, *The Erotic Imagination: French Histories of Perversity* (Oxford University Press, 1997), pp. 148-50.

21. See Nicole Edelman, *Métamorphoses de l'hystérique: du début du XIXe siècle à la Grande Guerre* (Paris, La Découverte, 2003), p. 522.

22. See Philippe Berthier, *Barbey d'Aurevilly et l'imagination* (Geneva, Droz, 1978), pp. 160-64.

23. See Stanton, *Aristocrat as Art*, pp. 146-47.

24. See Nye, *Masculinity and Male Codes of Honor*, pp. 59-65.

25. Virey, 'La Femme', p. 551.

26. Eugénie Foa, 'Le Fat', in *Les Français peints par eux-mêmes*, III, 297-304 (p. 61).

27. See Prince Korasoff's advice to Julien Sorel on 'la haute fatuité' in *Le Rouge et le noir*: Stendhal, *Romans*, ed. by Henri Martineau, 2 vols (Paris, Gallimard, 1948-52), I, 590.

28. On Maulévrier as a *fat*, see *O.r.c.*, I, 62.

29. See Christopher Prendergast's discussion of Stendhal's 'impossible' Mathilde in *The Order of Mimesis: Balzac, Stendhal, Nerval, Flaubert* (Cambridge University Press, 1986), pp. 120-25.

30. Compare Barbey's portrayal of Vallon, *O.r.c.*, II, 133-35 and 1247-48.

31. *Lettres à Trébutien*, 4 vols (Geneva, Slatkine, 1979), II, 21.

32. See Stanton, *Aristocrat as Art*, pp. 146-47.

33. See Françoise Coblence, *Le Dandysme: obligation d'incertitude* (Paris, PUF, 1988), pp. 293-94.

34. See, for instance, Ulysse Trélat, *La Folie lucide* (Paris, A. Delahaye, 1861).

35. See, for instance, *O.r.c.,* II, 149.

36. 'Les Démoniaques d'aujourd'hui', *Revue des deux mondes,* 15 January 1880, 340-72 (p. 344).

37. *Études cliniques* (Paris, Baillière, 1890), pp. 501-02.

38. See Stanton, *Aristocrat as Art,* pp. 178-84.

39. *Traité de l'hystérie* (Paris, Baillière, 1847), p. 64.

40. See especially C. W. Thompson, *Lamiel, fille du feu: essai sur Stendhal et l'énergie* (Paris, L'Harmattan, 1997), pp. 31-37.

41. See Stern, *Mes souvenirs* (Paris, Calmann Lévy, 1880), p. 335 and Stendhal, *Romans,* I, 513.

42. See *La Comédie humaine,* IX, 1142-43.

43. *Œuvres complètes,* I, 677.

44. *Œuvres complètes,* II, 81-82. For a bibliographical overview see Mary Orr, *Flaubert: Writing the Masculine* (Oxford University Press, 2000), p. 41, n.3.

45. *Œuvres,* ed. by Bernard Masson, 2 vols (Paris, Seuil, 1964), I, 668; see also 675.

46. Compare Flaubert's comment, regarding Léon and Emma, 'il devenait sa maîtresse plutôt qu'elle n'était la sienne' (*Œuvres,* I, 668) to Barbey's description of Hauteclaire and Savigny: 'c'était la femme qui avait les muscles, et l'homme qui avait les nerfs' (*O.r.c.,* II, 85).

47. More generally, representations of sexuality and gender were relatively fluid during the July Monarchy but subsequently became more intolerant. See Victoria Thompson's 'Creating Boundaries: Homosexuality and the Changing Social Order in France, 1830-1870', in *Homosexuality in Modern France,* pp. 102-27 (p. 121).

48. See Anne Higonnet, 'Femmes et images: apparences, loisirs, subsistance', in *Histoire des femmes en Occident,* IV, 303-33 (p. 304).

FURTHER READING

Biography

Chartier, Armand B. *Barbey d'Aurevilly.* Boston: Twayne Publishers, 1977, 182 p.

Investigates the impact of Barbey d'Aurevilly's personal life on his career as an author and on the formation of his literary persona.

Criticism

Cogman, P. W. M. "Criminal Conversation: Telling and Knowing in Barbey's *La vengeance d'une femme.*" *French Studies* 51, no. 1 (January 1997): 30-42.
Discusses the psychological underpinnings of vengeance in the novella.

Doucette, Clarice M. "Power in Perspective: Barbey d'Aurevilly's *Le bonheur dans le crime.*" *Dalhousie French Studies* 44 (fall 1998): 55-64.
Considers the thematic significance of observation in Barbey d'Aurevilly's approach to narrative.

Eisenberg, Davina L. *The Figure of the Dandy in Barbey d'Aurevilly's* Le bonheur dans le crime. New York: Peter Lang, 1996. 144 p.
Examines the connections among dandyism, fashion, and sexuality in Barbey d'Aurevilly's novella.

Esteban, Manuel A. "Arch-Enemies: Zola and Barbey d'Aurevilly." *Michigan Academician: Papers of the Michigan Academy of Science, Arts, and Letters* 12 (1979): 193-200.
Addresses the combative and at times vicious literary relationship between the two authors, reviewing their criticisms of each other's work within the context of their opposing aesthetic sensibilities.

Haxell, N. A. "Hermaphrodites and Winged Monsters: Images of Prose-Poetic Creation in the Writings of Barbey-d'Aurevilly." *Forum for Modern Language Studies* 22, no. 4 (October 1986): 354-64.
Underscores Barbey d'Aurevilly's ambivalence toward questions of gender, sexuality, and beauty in his writings.

Humphreys, Karen. "Barbey, Baudelaire, and the 'Imprévu': Strategies in Literary Dandyism." *Modern Language Studies* 29, no. 1 (April 1999): 63-80.
Concentrates on elements of irony in the two authors' representations of dandyism.

Moers, Ellen. "Barbey D'Aurevilly." In *The Dandy: Brummell to Beerbohm,* pp. 253-70. New York: The Viking Press, 1960.
Analyzes Barbey d'Aurevilly's landmark essay *Du dandysme et de Georges Brummell* (1845), assessing the work's subsequent influence on dandy literature and culture in France and England.

Moger, Angela S. "Gödel's 'Incompleteness Theorem' and Barbey: Raising Story to a Higher Power." *SubStance: A Review of Theory and Literary Criticism* 12, no. 4 (1983): 17-30.

Assesses Barbey d'Aurevilly's use of a frame narrative in the novella *Le dessous de cartes d'une partie de whist.*

Place, E. B. "Spanish Sources of the 'Diabolism' of Barbey d'Aurevilly." *Romanic Review* 19, no. 3 (October-December 1928): 332-38.
  Identifies plot and character elements from María de Zayas's *Novelas amorosas* (1637) in Barbey d'Aurevilly's *Une vielle maîtresse.*

Sivert, Eileen Boyd. "Text, Body and Reader in Barbey d'Aurevilly's *Les diaboliques.*" *Symposium* 31, no. 2 (summer 1977): 151-64.

Describes the relationship between masculine narration and female action in the novellas.

———. "Narration and Exhibitionism in *Le rideau cramoisi.*" *Romanic Review* 70, no. 2 (March 1979): 146-58.
  Studies the tension between voyeuristic and exhibitionistic narrative techniques in the novella.

Stivale, Charles J. "'Like the Sculptor's Chisel': Voices 'On' and 'Off' in Barbey d'Aurevilly's *Les diaboliques.*" *Romanic Review* 82, no. 3 (May 1991): 317-30.
  Explores layers of narration in Barbey d'Aurevilly's novellas.

Additional coverage of Barbey d'Aurevilly's life and career is contained in the following sources published by Gale: *Dictionary of Literary Biography,* **Vol. 119;** *Guide to French Literature, 1789 to the Present;* *Literature Resource Center;* *Nineteenth-Century Literature Criticism,* **Vol. 1; and** *Short Story Criticism,* **Vol. 17.**

William Ewart Gladstone
1809-1898

English statesman, essayist, orator, critic, and letter writer.

The following entry presents an overview of Gladstone's life and works.

INTRODUCTION

In the eyes of modern scholars, William Ewart Gladstone was one of the most influential and dominant figures of Victorian political life. A four-time prime minister of England, Gladstone oversaw a period of intense social, economic, and cultural transformation during which Great Britain emerged as a global power. He was a dedicated supporter of free trade, individual liberty, and social and economic reform. Associated with the modern Liberal Party in England, he earned such widespread popularity that he became known as the Grand Old Man to his many supporters. Though primarily remembered for his achievements in the political arena, Gladstone was also an important literary figure during his lifetime. An author of varied interests and versatile talents, he wrote on topics ranging from Homer to the relationship between church and state and the issue of Irish independence. These writings, though not well known among twenty-first-century readers, reveal a figure of probing intelligence and unwavering morality, while at the same time they offer a vital glimpse into the central cultural, political, and social issues of the Victorian age. Gladstone's accomplishments as both an author and a statesman also exerted a powerful influence on later British politicians, notably Winston Churchill.

BIOGRAPHICAL INFORMATION

Gladstone was born in Liverpool, England, on December 29, 1809, the fifth of six children. His father, Sir John Gladstone, was a prosperous sugar trader who owned several plantations in the British West Indies; his mother, Anne MacKenzie Gladstone, was of Scottish descent. Raised in a strict Anglican household, Gladstone developed a strong sense of moral principles at a young age; his early religious beliefs were later the bedrock of his public career. As a child Gladstone studied at a local preparatory school; he later attended Eton College. In 1828, shortly after graduating from Eton, he

matriculated at Christ Church College, Oxford. He thrived at Oxford, excelling at mathematics, classics, and literature while establishing a reputation as a formidable debater. During his years at Oxford, Gladstone also became more outspoken in his conservative political beliefs. According to biographers, he delivered one of his first memorable speeches at the Oxford Student Union, in 1831; in the address he argued against passage of the Reform Act—a bill that proposed a more equitable restructuring of parliamentary representation—on the grounds that it would lead to civil unrest.

After completing his university examinations in 1831, Gladstone briefly considered entering the Church of England; his father strenuously objected to this career path, however, steering him instead toward commerce and politics. Gladstone first ran for public office in 1832, winning a seat as the Tory representative of Newark-on-Trent in the House of Commons. A year later he began studying law, joining the Honourable Society of Lincoln's Inn, one of London's prestigious legal associations. Gladstone was invited to join the Conservative administration of Prime Minister Robert Peel in 1834, first as a junior lord of the treasury and later as undersecretary of state for the War and Colonial Office. Although Peel resigned as prime minister a year later, Gladstone had already established himself as a leading young figure in the burgeoning Conservative Party. During this time, Gladstone also met Benjamin Disraeli, a popular author and aspiring politician who later served two terms as prime minister of England. The two men quickly became fierce political rivals, initiating a personal enmity that would endure throughout their long careers in public office.

Gladstone published his first book, *The State in Its Relations with the Church,* in 1838. A year later he married Catherine Glynne, the daughter of a prominent baronet, with whom he would have eight children. The couple moved to London in 1840, and Gladstone published his second book, *Church Principles Considered in Their Results* (1840). In 1841 Gladstone was drawn back into politics when Robert Peel, newly reelected as prime minister, named him vice president of the government's Board of Trade; two years later he rose to the rank of president of the board, and he later served as Britain's colonial secretary. Gladstone's political views began to shift from conservative to liberal in the 1840s. Scholar Robert O'Kell has noted that Gladstone's years in the second Peel administration helped shape his views on economic policy, in particular his conviction that fiscal responsibility was an inherently moral issue. During this time Gladstone authored his first significant policy paper, "The Course of Commercial Policy at Home and Abroad," which appeared in the *Foreign and Colonial Quarterly Review* in January 1843. He also became active in various social causes, devoting himself in particular to alleviating the economic and moral problems associated with prostitution.

In 1852 Prime Minister George Hamilton Gordon appointed Gladstone chancellor of the exchequer, a position he held until 1855. Throughout these years Gladstone developed the political and economic philosophy that would become the foundation of the Liberal Party, a movement that called for decreased government involvement in economic affairs, greater protection of civil liberties and individual freedoms, and the promotion of a range of social reforms, notably the expansion of suffrage rights. His part in the creation of the liberal platform was so significant that the doctrine eventually became known as Gladstonian Liberalism. Gladstone was also increasingly vocal in his opposition to the Vatican's expanding role in British social and political life, views he elucidated in two influential essays published in the *Quarterly Review* after he left the exchequer: "The Declining Efficiency of Parliament" (1856) and "The New Parliament and Its Work" (1857). In 1858 Gladstone published his first significant work of classical scholarship, *Studies on Homer and the Homeric Age.* Rejoining the government in 1859, he served as chancellor of the exchequer under Whig Prime Minister Lord Palmerston until 1865. In November 1865 Gladstone gave his famous *Address on the Place of Ancient Greece in the Providential Order of the World; Delivered Before the University of Edinburgh, on the Third of November, 1865,* a speech emphasizing the value of a classical education.

As Gladstonian ideals gained popularity, the Liberal Party became stronger, and in December 1868 Gladstone was elected prime minister of England. During the following six years he spearheaded a host of significant reforms, promoting the causes of improving education, reorganizing the military, and establishing free trade with other European nations. He also supervised the passage of several laws designed to promote peace in colonial Ireland, among them the Irish Land Act. After the Liberals lost the general elections of 1874, Gladstone temporarily retired from public office, although he remained involved in the important political debates of the period. In 1876 he published *Bulgarian Horrors and the Question of the East,* a critique of Prime Minister Disraeli's foreign policy, and a new work of classical scholarship, *Homeric Synchronism: An Enquiry into the Time and Place of Homer.* His seven-volume *Gleanings of Past Years, 1843-78,* a collection of essays, was published in 1879.

Gladstone returned to public life in 1880, when he was elected to a second term as prime minister. He remained in office until June 1885 and later served a third term from February to July 1886. That year he delivered two milestone speeches on the question of English rule over Ireland, *The Home Rule Manifesto. Address . . . to the Electors of Midlothian, May 1st, 1886* and *The Irish Question. I: History of an Idea. II: Lessons of the Election.* In 1890, returning to the classics, he published *Landmarks of Homeric Study.* He won a fourth term as prime minister in 1892 and served until March 1894, when he retired from politics permanently. William Gladstone died on May 19, 1898, and was buried in Westminster Abbey.

MAJOR WORKS

Scholars generally divide Gladstone's body of work into three categories: religious writings, political speeches and essays, and scholarly studies. Gladstone launched his literary career in 1838 with the publication of *The State in Its Relations with the Church.* In this work Gladstone examined the connection between religious belief and practical action, particularly as it related to the conscience of the individual politician. In the course of his investigation, he concluded that the British government had a moral obligation to promote the agenda of the Anglican Church. He explored these ideas further in *Church Principles Considered in Their Results,* a study of the evolution of the Church of England throughout history.

Gladstone's political writings generally reflect his liberal attitudes toward such issues as trade, individual liberty, and social reform. In the early essay "The Course of Commercial Policy at Home and Abroad," he argued on behalf of British economic supremacy in an increasingly industrialized world while also outlining the central tenets of Prime Minister Robert Peel's free-trade policies. His major political works also include a number of influential speeches, among them two important addresses on the political climate in Ireland: *Home Rule Manifesto. Address . . . to the Electors of Midlothian, May 1st, 1886,* in which he insisted on achieving a balance between Irish autonomy and the "Imperial prerogative" of England; and *The Irish Question. I: History of an Idea. II: Lessons of the Election,* which stresses the need for "safety and prudence" in the pursuit of reform. Both speeches were delivered in 1886 and were published the same year.

Gladstone's writings on Homer and ancient Greek literature made important contributions to the field of classical scholarship; important works in this area include *Studies on Homer and the Homeric Age* and *Landmarks of Homeric Study.* In his benchmark *Address on the Place of Ancient Greece in the Providential Order of the World,* Gladstone offered his most in-depth analysis of the role of classical studies in Britain's educational system.

CRITICAL RECEPTION

For nineteenth-century observers, Gladstone's career as a politician largely eclipsed his accomplishments as a writer. Notable early studies of his career include George Barnett Smith's *The Life of the Right Honourable William Ewart Gladstone* (1880), which does include a discussion of Gladstone's varied literary accomplishments. James Bryce, in his essay "William Ewart Gladstone," examined the relationship between Gladstone's speeches and his writings, arguing that his literary style was deeply informed by his oratory talents. Later in the twentieth century a handful of critical works devoted to Gladstone's career—particularly to his work on the classics—gradually emerged. Sir John L. Myres included a valuable study of Gladstone's writings on Greek poetry, "Gladstone's View of Homer," in his 1958 work *Homer and His Critics* [See Further Reading]. In her essay "Gladstone's Ethnolinguistics: The Language of Experience in the Nineteenth Century," Nancy Parrott Hickerson discussed Gladstone's classical scholarship within the framework of anthropological and linguistic concerns.

In the first decade of the twenty-first century, scholars began to reexamine Gladstone's career against the backdrop of Victorian politics and culture. Matthew Bevis analyzes the influence of Gladstone's Ireland policies on Tennyson's later poetry in "Tennyson, Ireland, and 'The Powers of Speech'." Tobias Döring explores the political significance of Gladstone's Homeric writings, particularly their relationship to the issue of British colonial power.

PRINCIPAL WORKS

The State in Its Relations with the Church (nonfiction) 1838

Church Principles Considered in Their Results (nonfiction) 1840

"The Course of Commercial Policy at Home and Abroad" (essay) 1843; published in journal *Foreign and Colonial Quarterly Review*

"The Declining Efficiency of Parliament" (essay) 1856

"The New Parliament and Its Work" (essay) 1857; published in journal *Quarterly Review*

*Studies on Homer and the Homeric Age. 3 vols. (criticism) 1858

Address on the Place of Ancient Greece in the Providential Order of the World; Delivered before the University of Edinburgh, on the Third of November, 1865 (speech) 1865

Juventus Mundi: The Gods and Men of the Heroic Age (criticism) 1869

Bulgarian Horrors and the Question of the East (essay) 1876

Homeric Synchronism: An Enquiry into the Time and Place of Homer (criticism) 1876

Gleanings of Past Years, 1843-78. 7 vols. (essays) 1879

The Home Rule Manifesto. Address . . . to the Electors of Midlothian, May 1st, 1886 (speech) 1886

The Irish Question. I: History of an Idea. II: Lessons of the Election (speech) 1886

Speeches on the Irish Question in 1886; With an Appendix Containing the Full Text of the Government of Ireland and the Sale and Purchase of Land Bills of 1886 (speeches) 1886

Landmarks of Homeric Study (criticism) 1890

Female Suffrage. A Letter to Samuel Smith, M.P. (letter) 1892

The Speeches and Public Addresses of the Right Hon. W. E. Gladstone, M.P., with Notes and Introductions. 2 vols. (speeches) 1892

Later Gleanings: A New Series of Gleanings of Past Years, Theological and Ecclesiastical (essays) 1897

Gladstone's Speeches (speeches) 1916

Gladstone and Palmerston: Being the Correspondence of Lord Palmerston with Mr. Gladstone, 1851-1865 (letters) 1928

The Gladstone Diaries. 14 vols. (diaries) 1968-94

*This work includes the essays "Homer and His Successors in Epic Poetry" and "Homeric Characters In and Out of Homer," which were originally published in the *Quarterly Review* in January 1857 and July 1857, respectively.

CRITICISM

George Barnett Smith (essay date 1880)

SOURCE: Smith, George Barnett. "Mr. Gladstone's Miscellaneous Writings, Etc." In *The Life of the Right Honourable William Ewart Gladstone,* pp. 555-70. New York: G. P. Putnam's Sons, 1880.

[In the following essay, Smith assesses the versatility and scope of Gladstone's literary interests. Smith contends that Gladstone's writings often reveal more about Gladstone himself than about their subject matter.]

The plenitude and variety of Mr. Gladstone's intellectual powers have been the subject of such frequent comment that it would be superfluous to insist upon them here. On the political side of his career his life has been as unresting and active as that of any other great party leader; and, if we regard him in the literary aspect, we are equally astonished at his energy and versatility. Putting out of view his various works upon Homer, his miscellaneous writings of themselves, with the reading they involve, would entitle their author to take high rank on the score of industry with the majority of the literary craft. As a writer, indeed, fluency may be said to be his besetting sin. Great ideas do not come either to the world or to individuals in battalions; they are the product of thought, action, comparison. So, while we stand amazed at the infinity of topics which have received Mr. Gladstone's attention, we do not always acquire from his essays that high dry light which it is the privilege of the greatest critics to shed upon the subjects and the men they undertake to interpret.

A recent reviewer, while scarcely doing Mr. Gladstone justice in certain respects, furnishes some apposite observations—or partially apposite, at least—upon the general character of his essays as well as their style. 'It is,' he says, 'the light they throw on Mr. Gladstone and upon his habits and modes of thought, far more than any light they throw upon the special subjects they deal with, that gives these essays their strongest claim. And this internal unity of thought and temperament is made the more prominent by the comparative absence of any corresponding unity of style. Indeed, of a style, in the strict sense of the term, Mr. Gladstone has almost little or none, and the reader is almost startled to find how well he gets along without it. Sometimes we have a sentence so long and involved that nothing but a passionate intensity of meaning and a profuse vocabulary could have averted a disastrous collapse. Elsewhere, as for instance in his controversy with Mr. Lowe, the "Tempter," as Mr. Gladstone might say, leads him to imitate, with very partial success, the nimble dialectics of his skilful opponent. His writing, it is true, is often vigorous and trenchant, his phrases not unfrequently happy and well turned; but a distinctive style, such for instance as Lord Macaulay's, he most certainly has not.'[1] The essays remind the reader more of the flowing eloquence and the declamation of a Burke than of the massiveness, the dignity, and the majesty of a Bacon.

The whole of Mr. Gladstone's miscellaneous writings—with the exception of essays of a strictly controversial and classical kind—have recently been collected in a uniform edition.[2] The first volume has no fewer than four articles upon the life and character of the Prince Consort, two of them being based upon Mr. Martin's life. The critic writes sympathetically upon the virtues of the Prince, who was deserving of the eulogy passed upon him, and who undoubtedly raised the life of the Court, and the influence and usefulness of our highest institution, to their highest point. He also laments the loss which society has sustained from the slackening of that beneficial action to which the Prince so powerfully contributed. These essays are followed by three papers on the County Franchise, being a response to the deliverances of Mr. Lowe upon this subject. Mr. Gladstone claims to regard this question with strict impartiality, for he looks upon it as one which calls upon him for adhesion as an individual, but not for the guidance of others in any larger capacity. He warns Englishmen, however, against one of the greatest moral dangers that can beset the politics of a self-governed country—the danger of having a great question insincerely dealt with. The Conservatives are ready to step in between the Liberal leaders and their work, and to do the exact opposite of that which was done by Sir Robert Peel in 1829 and 1846:—'They will handle the subject, to the best of their judgment, as one which may legitimately be used, either by adoption or by a faint and procrastinating repulse, as shall best suit the interests of their party.' The speech of the present majority will say one thing, while its heart conceals another. In legislating upon this subject, Mr. Gladstone is not afraid that we shall fall down the precipice into national ruin, inasmuch as we fell down a much greater precipice in 1832, and another one in 1867, and are none the worse for it. His arguments upon the whole question are well worthy of study.

The last essay in this volume, **'Kin Beyond Sea,'** is one for which Mr. Gladstone was taken severely to task by many English journals, on its appearance originally in the *North American Review* for September, 1878. Reading through this essay now after the excitement it created has calmed down, it seems to us to contain much food for reflection for Englishmen. Mr. Gladstone is not alone in taking the following view of the future of America, and we should do well to heed the advice with which he closes:—'She will probably become what we are now, the head servant in the great household of the world, the employer of all employed; because her services will be the most and ablest. We have no more title against her than Venice, or Genoa, or Holland has had against us. One great duty is entailed upon us, which we, unfortunately, neglect; the duty of preparing, by a resolute and sturdy effort, to reduce our public burdens, in preparation for a day when we shall probably have less capacity than we have now to bear them.' Again, 'the England and the America of the present are probably the two strongest nations in the world. But there can hardly be a doubt, as between the America and the England of the future, that the daughter, at some no very distant time, will, whether fairer or less fair, be unquestionably yet stronger than the mother.' Mr. Gladstone argues in support of this position from the concentrated continuous empire which America possesses, and the enormous progress she has made within a century. The writer's brief review of the British Constitution, and his summary of possible dangers which may beset the mother-country, are deserving of careful consideration, especially when we reflect that these things have driven one who is perhaps better acquainted with them than most students of the Constitution to this general conclusion:—'We of this island are not great political philosophers; and we contend with an earnest but disproportioned vehemence about changes which are palpable, such as the extension of the suffrage, or the re-distribution of Parliamentary seats, neglecting wholly other processes of change which work beneath the surface, and in the dark, but which are even more fertile of great organic results.'

The second volume consists of essays exclusively personal and literary. The author discourses both pleasantly and profitably upon such differently constituted beings as Blanco White, Giacomo Leopardi, Bishop Patteson, Dr. Norman Macleod, Macaulay, Tennyson, and Wedgwood. While we could willingly linger over each of these names, it is only the last three to which we can give some attention. In treating of Macaulay, Mr. Gladstone is not so incisive as some other English critics— Mr. John Morley, for example; but the essay is written with admirable temper and a certain largeness of spirit. 'Prosperous and brilliant, a prodigy, a meteor, almost a portent, in literary history,' the great Whig historian is described, and yet withal there was much of the commonplace about him; while his fierceness as an advocate prevented him from attaining to that atmosphere of calm impartiality which surrounds the greatest historians. An accurate man, in the long run, is of more service to the world than a fascinating man, though the latter may in the outset absorb all the honours; and this rule will, we think, be found to hold good in all kinds of intellectual effort. Mr. Gladstone observes that 'as the serious flaw in Macaulay's mind was want of depth, so the central defect with which his productions appear to be chargeable, is a pervading strain of more or less exaggeration.' The truth is that 'Macaulay was not only accustomed, like many more of us, to go out hobby-riding, but, from the portentous vigour of the animal he mounted, was liable, more than most of us, to be run away with.' Once more—in drawing a comparison between Macaulay and Thucydides, the latter of whom was greatly admired by the modern historian—'Ease, brilliancy, pellucid clearness, commanding fascination, the effective marshalling of all facts belonging to the external world as if on parade; all these gifts Macaulay has, and Thucydides has not. But weight, breadth, proportion, deep discernment, habitual contemplation of the springs of character and conduct, and the power to hold the scales of human action with firm and even hand, these must be sought in Thucydides, and are rarely observable in Macaulay.' Yet with all his defects—and they are nearly as pronounced and conspicuous as his excellences—Macaulay remains one of the most considerable figures in English literature in the nineteenth century.

The merits of Mr. Tennyson, as a poet, excite less controversy. As the essayist remarks, 'from his very first appearance he has had the form and fashion of a true poet; the delicate insight into beauty, the refined perception of harmony, the faculty of suggestion, the eye both in the physical and moral world for motion, light, and colour, the sympathetic and close observation of nature, the dominance of the constructive faculty, and that rare gift, the thorough mastery and loving use of his native tongue. His turn for metaphysical analysis is closely associated with a deep ethical insight; and many of his verses form sayings of so high a class that we trust they are destined to contribute a permanent part of the household words of England.' It is twenty years since these words were written, and each of those years has witnessed something towards their fulfilment. Like Wordsworth, Mr. Tennyson has won his way with the public against the vaticinations of the reviewers, and this way has been a laborious one. Few poets have aimed at perfection so persistently, so devotedly, as Mr. Tennyson. Unquestionably fine as his genius is, it is not inspiration alone, but a spirit of unrelaxing effort which has assisted in raising him to the high position he occupies amongst English singers.

Most valuable, perhaps, of all these gleanings of a personal character is the address on Wedgwood, originally spoken at Burslem, Staffordshire, on the occasion of laying the foundation-stone of the Wedgwood Institute. We not only meet here with many true and beautiful things about art, but with much sound advice calculated to be of profit to all classes of British workmen. Considering the products of industry with reference to their utility, their cheapness, their influence upon the condition of those who produce them, and their beauty, Mr. Gladstone conceives it to be in the last-named department that we are to look for the peculiar pre-eminence, he does not scruple to say the peculiar greatness, of Wedgwood. The association of beauty with convenience is not a matter light and fanciful; beauty is not an accident of things, it pertains to their essence; it pervades the wide range of creation; and wherever it is impaired or banished we perceive proofs of the moral disorder which disturbs the world. God hath made everything 'beautiful in his time.' 'Among all the devices of creation, there is not one more wonderful, whether it be the movement of the heavenly bodies, or the succession of the seasons and the years, or the adaptation of the world and its phenomena to the conditions of human life, or the structure of the eye, or hand, or any other part of the frame of man—not one of all these is more wonderful than the profuseness with which the Mighty Maker has been pleased to shed over the works of his hands an endless and boundless beauty.' England has long taken a lead among the nations of Europe for the cheapness of her manufactures; and Mr. Gladstone believes that if the day is ever to come when she shall be as eminent in true taste and beauty as she is now in economy of production, that result will probably be due to no other single man in so great a degree as to Wedgwood. In the words of his epitaph, he 'converted a rude and inconsiderable manufacture into an elegant art and an important branch of national commerce.' Unaided by the national or the royal gifts which were found necessary to uphold the glories of Svres, of Chelsea, and of Dresden, he produced works truer, perhaps, to the inexorable laws of art, than the fine fabrics that proceeded from those establishments. The lessons to be deduced from a career of toil, and one devoted to the highest ends, like Wedgwood's, are admirably pointed out and enforced. Mr. Gladstone's address especially deserves praise for its insistence upon the great truth that the mean and the lowly are not divorced from the beautiful. 'Down to the humblest condition of life, down to the lowest and most backward grade of civilisation, the nature of man craves, and seems even as it were to cry aloud, for something, some sign or token at the least, of what is beautiful, in some of the many spheres of mind or sense.'

In an address delivered at Chester,[3] Mr. Gladstone once more spoke concerning art in its relations to English manufactures. He denied that the promotion of excellence for its own sake was a visionary idea; for every excellence that was real, whether it related in the first instance to utility or beauty, had got its price, its value in the market. It was an element of strength. In France, the standard of taste, taken as a whole, was very much higher than in England. This was a great national want—a want that had been felt at all times, and a national want that was now specially felt because of the depression of British commerce, and the increased difficulties in finding a way into the markets of many foreign countries. Yet it was a very significant thing that this want should exist, because it was admitted that England is a country which, in the production of beauty in its highest form, showed no deficiency at all. The very highest form in which the beautiful could be produced was that of poetry, and the English poetry of the nineteenth century has been at the head of the poetry of the world. With the English people there was some deficiency in that quality or habit which connects the sense of beauty with the production of works of utility. 'With the English those two things are quite distinct; but in the oldest times of human industry—that is to say, amongst the Greeks—there was no separation whatever, no gap at all, between the idea of beauty and the idea of utility. Whatever the ancient Greek produced he made as useful as he could; and at the same time a cardinal law with him was to make it as beautiful as he could.' In the industrial productions of America there was very little idea of beauty: an American's axe, for example, was not intended to cut away a tree neatly, but quickly. The object was to clear the ground, and that is the history of American industry up to the present time. In England, schools of art were producing an excellent effect upon almost every branch of industry. 'We want a workman to understand that if he can learn to appreciate beauty in industrial productions, he is thereby doing good to himself, first of all in the improvement of his mind, and in the pleasure he derives from his work, and likewise that literally he is increasing his own capital, which is his labour.' He looked to the union of beauty and utility in industrial production as the true way to ensure success in our national enterprise and commerce.

Mr. Gladstone's third series of essays, which are of an historical and speculative character, opens with **'The Theses of Erastus and the Scottish Church Establishment, 1844.'** The writer strongly condemns Erastianism, and though his subject is one which does not profoundly concern the great body of the people, it has a special interest for those who have followed the deep ecclesiastical upheaval in Scotland. The articles on *Ecce Homo* take a wider range, and are written with considerable eloquence and power. That remarkable work is closely examined, with the object of showing that the method and order of religious teaching may vary, as between the period of first introduction, on the one hand, and of established possession and hereditary transmission on the other; that there were seasons in the state of the world, at the period of the Advent, for a careful and delicate regulation of the approaches for the new religion to the mind of man: and that in the matter and succession of the Gospels we may find a succinct testimony to this system of providential adjustment. He next discusses what was the order or economy observed by the Saviour in making known to the world the religion he had come on earth to found. On the great question whether the world has gained on the whole in Christian ages as compared with those of heathenism, Mr. Gladstone cites social changes of a vast and wide range, which decisively settle the problem in favour of Christianity. He concludes his survey by expressing a hope 'that the present tendency to treat the old belief of man with a precipitate, shallow, and unexamining disparagement, is simply a distemper that infects for a time the moral atmosphere; that is due, like plagues and fevers, to our own previous folly and neglect; and that, when it has served its work of admonition and reform, will be allowed to pass away. Towards this result the author of *Ecce Homo,* if I read him right, will have the consolation and the praise of having furnished an earnest, powerful, and original contribution.' Seldom has the work to be effected in man by the Christian religion been so felicitously expressed as in the following passage:—

> No more in the inner than the outer sphere did Christ come among us as a conqueror, making His appeal to force. We were neither to be consumed by the heat of the Divine presence, nor were we to be dazzled by its brightness; God was not in the storm, nor in the fire, nor in the flood, but He was in the still small voice. This vast treasure was not only to be conveyed to us,

and to be set down as it were at our doors; it was to enter into us, to become part of us, and to become that part which should rule the rest; it was to assimilate alike the mind and heart of every class and description of men. While, as a moral system, it aimed at an entire dominion in the heart, this dominion was to be founded upon an essential conformity to the whole of our original and true essence. It, therefore, recognised the freedom of man, and respected his understanding, even while it absolutely required him both to learn and to unlearn so largely; the whole of the new lessons were founded upon principles that were based in the deepest and best regions of his nature, and that had the sanction of his highest faculties in their moments of calm, and in circumstances of impartiality. The work was one of restoration, of return, and of enlargement, not of innovation. A space was to be bridged over, and it was vast: but a space where all the piers, and every foundation-stone of the connecting structure, were to be laid in the reason and common sense, in the history and experience of man. This movement was to be a revolutionary movement, but only in the sense of a return from anarchy to order.

The remaining essays of an historical and ecclesiastical type are 'The Courses of Religious Thought,' 'The Sixteenth Century and the Nineteenth,' and 'The Influence of Authority in Matters of Opinion'—the main argument of the last-named paper being suggested by Sir G. C. Lewis's well-known essay upon the same subject.

In the Foreign essays are to be found the letters to Lord Aberdeen on the Neapolitan prisons, which have been already referred to at length in another part of this work. In an article upon 'Germany, France, and England,' contributed to the *Edinburgh Review*, in 1870, Mr. Gladstone pleads for the time when nations shall do to each other as they would wish to be done by. 'The greatest triumph of our time, a triumph in a region loftier than that of electricity and steam, will be the enthronement of the idea of Public Right, as the governing idea of European policy; as the common and precious inheritance of all lands, but superior to the passing opinion of any. The foremost among the nations will be that one which by its conduct shall gradually engender in the mind of the others a fixed belief that it is just. In the competition for this prize, the bounty of Providence has given us a place of vantage; and nothing save our own fault or folly can wrest it from our grasp.' Dealing with 'The Hellenic Factor in the Eastern Problem,' Mr. Gladstone traces the course of British policy with respect to Greece, and redeems the memory of Lord Palmerston from the wrong done it by those who believe or argue that, if now alive, he would have been found to plead the obligation of maintaining the integrity of the Ottoman Power as paramount to the duty of granting to her afflicted subjects simple, broad, and effective guarantees for their personal and civil liberties. In no spirit of unfriendliness to the Porte, Earl Russell and Lord Palmerston wished for the assignment of Thessaly and Epirus to Greece, subject to the conditions of suzerain and tribute. Mr. Gladstone shows that there is an opportunity for England to acquire the lasting gratitude of Greece. 'Of that people who still fondle in their memories the names of Canning and Byron, there are in the Levant, we may safely say, four millions, on whose affections we may take a standing hold, by giving a little friendly care at this juncture to the case of the Hellenic provinces. They want not Russian institutions, but such a freedom as we enjoy. They want for their cause an advocate who is not likely to turn into an adversary, one whose temptations lie in other quarters; who cannot (as they fondly trust) ask anything from them; or, in any possible contingency, through durable opposition of sympathies or interests, inflict anything upon them.' Such a thorough and steadfast friend England has not yet proved herself. Mr. Gladstone relates, in another article, the long struggle of the noble and heroic people of Montenegro against their hereditary oppressors; and he has further something to say anent '**Aggression in Egypt, and Freedom in the East.**'[4] He does not hide the difficulties besetting British encroachments in the East. Enlargements of the empire are for us an evil fraught with serious if not with immediate danger. We have left many old tasks undone; 'our currency, our local government, our liquor laws, portions even of our taxation, remain in a state either positively discreditable or at the least inviting and demanding great improvements; but, for want of time and strength, we cannot handle them. For the romance of political travel we are ready to scour the world, and yet of capital defect in duties lying at our door we are not ashamed.' By way of reply to the fears and arguments of those who advocate the strengthening of our position in the East, Mr. Gladstone does not believe that Russian power on the Bosphorus is a practical possibility. But if the worst came to the worst, and Russia accomplished the designs attributed to her, and stopped also the Suez Canal, she would have done nothing more than introduce an average delay of about three weeks into our military communications with Bombay, and less with Calcutta. In time of war, this would not make the difference to us between life and death in the maintenance of our Indian Empire.

Mr. Gladstone's position on Ritualism, and his answer to the question whether the Church of England is worth preserving, have already been defined in a previous chapter. He has reprinted the essays in which he expounded his views on these questions in two volumes, which also contain papers entitled '**Remarks on the Royal Supremacy,**' '**Present Aspect of the Church, 1843,**' '**Ward's Ideal of a Christian Church,**' '**On the Functions of Laymen in the Church,**' '**The Bill for Divorce,**' and '**Italy and Her Church.**' These essays are undoubtedly valuable as affording materials to add to the general stock 'from which the religious history of a critical period will have finally to be written.'

They do not, however, possess the same general interest as the volume of miscellaneous essays which succeeds them. This volume includes the admirable **'Inaugural Address'** delivered to the students of Edinburgh University in 1860; the address on the **'Place of Ancient Greece in the Providential Order'**; a **'Chapter of Autobiography'**; **'Probability as a Guide of Conduct,'** and the very entertaining narrative of the parentage, progress, and issue of the Evangelical movement in England [**'The Evangelical Movement'**].[5] Mr. Gladstone's strength does not lie in discovering and exposing the deep roots of those great principles which have governed the growth of nations in the various ages of the world; he rather, by graphic and picturesque antithesis, illustrates the outer effects and manifestations of those principles in national life. Take, for example, this comparison between Greece and Palestine, extracted from the essay on the **'Place of Ancient Greece'**:—

> For the exercises of strength and skill, for the achievements and for the enchantments of wit, of eloquence, of art, of genius, for the imperial games of politics and war—let us seek them on the shores of Greece. But if the first among the problems of life be how to establish the peace and restore the balance of our inward being; if the highest of all conditions in the existence of the creature be his aspect towards the God to whom he owes his being, and in whose great hand he stands; then let us make our search elsewhere. All the wonders of the Greek civilisation heaped together are less wonderful than is the single Book of Psalms. Palestine was weak and despised, always obscure, oftentimes and long trodden down beneath the feet of imperious masters. On the other hand, Greece for a thousand years,
>
> 'Confident from foreign purposes,'
>
> repelled every invader from her shores. Fostering her strength in the keen air of freedom, she defied, and at length overthrew, the mightiest of existing empires; and when finally she felt the resistless grasp of the masters of all the world, them, too, at the very moment of their subjugation, she herself subdued to her literature, language, arts, and manners. Palestine, in a word, had no share of the glories of our race; while they blaze on every page of the history of Greece with an overpowering splendour. Greece had valour, policy, reason, genius, wisdom, wit; she had all, in a word, that this world could give her; but the flowers of Paradise, which blossom at the best but thinly, blossomed in Palestine alone.

One article by Mr. Gladstone—which does not appear in the collected edition of his essays, on account of its political and controversial character—still claims attention. It does so on the ground of its exposition of the writer's views as to the dangers attendant upon an Imperial policy. This article is entitled **'England's Mission.'**[6] The writer is alarmed by recent developments of English statesmanship. He maintains that 'not peace, not humanity, not reverence for the traditions established by the thought and care of the mighty dead, not anxiety to secure the equal rights of nations, not the golden rule to do to others as we would fain have them

do to us, not far-seeing provision for the future, have been the sources from which the present Ministers have drawn their strength.' On the contrary, 'they are the men, and the political heirs of the men, who passed the Six Acts and the Corn Laws; who impoverished the population, who fettered enterprise by legislative restraint, who withheld those franchises that have given voice and vent to the public wishes, whose policy, in a word, kept the Throne insecure and the empire weak; and would, unless happily arrested in 1832, and again in 1846, have plunged the country into revolution.' They have abandoned all idea, such as inspired Sir Robert Peel, that Government should live by great measures of legislation framed for the national benefit, and have substituted a careful regard to interest and class, from bishops down to beer-houses. This inglorious existence being unable to bear the concentrated force of criticism, however, they sought out a vigorous foreign policy. The first care of the Liberal party has been held to be the care of her own children within her own shores, the redress of wrongs, the supply of needs, the improvements of laws and institutions; but against this doctrine, the present Government appears to set up territorial aggrandisement, large establishments, and the accumulation of a multitude of fictitious interests abroad, as if our real interests were not enough. Mr. Gladstone deprecates the multiplication of British possessions beyond the sea, and especially condemns such acquisitions as that of Cyprus, which can never become truly British in character. As every possible road to India threatens to become a British interest, he observes that there is no saying what preposterous guarantees may be proposed for Khiva, or Bokhara, or Badakshan. Nay, as China is a possible road to India, why should it not also have a guarantee? All the old doctrines of statesmanship which should have been jealously guarded by Ministers have been left to the advocacy of unofficial persons. The writer maintains that the Government have, on the whole, opened up and relied on an illegitimate source of power; and that one of the damning signs of the politics of the school is their total blindness to the fact that the central strength of England lies in England. He further complains that 'we have undertaken in the matter of Governments far more than ever in the history of the world has been previously attempted by the children of men. None of the great continuous empires of ancient or modern times ever grappled with such a task.' Meanwhile, during the prevalence of this lust of empire, what has become of domestic legislation? Mr. Gladstone supplies the following list of questions not (so far) grappled with, and 'the neglect of which amounts, in not a few instances, to positive scandal:' London Municipal Reform; County Government; County Franchise; Liquor Laws; Irish Borough Franchise; Irish University Question; Opium Revenue; Criminal Law Procedure; Responsibility of Masters for Injuries to Workmen; Reduction of Public Expenditure; Probate Duty; Indian

Finance; Working of the Home Government of India; City Companies; Burial Laws; Valuation of Property; Law of the Medical Profession; Law of Entail and Settlement; Corrupt Practices at Elections; Expenses of Election; Reorganisation of the Revenue Departments; and the Currency. In a later article, entitled **'The Country and the Government,'** Mr. Gladstone added to these subjects waiting to be dealt with, the Laws of Bankruptcy, of Banking, of Distress, of Charities, and Mortmain, Loans for Local Purposes, Game, Distribution as well as Redistribution of Seats, Savings Bank Finance, and the Bright Clauses of the Irish Land Act. Instead of dealing with these matters, the Government of Lord Beaconsfield had raised up as from a virgin soil a whole forest of new questions, in themselves enough to occupy a Parliament and a State which had nothing else to do. Of these new and thorny subjects, he gave the following enumeration, which, while probably incomplete, might suffice for present purposes:—1. Eastern Roumelia; 2. The Greek Frontier; 3. Crete and the other European Provinces of Turkey; 4. The Armenians; 5. Turkey in Asia; 6. Cyprus; 7. Suez Canal Shares and Management; 8. Egyptian Debt; 9. Egyptian Succession; 10. North-west Frontier of India; 11. Supervision of Afghanistan; 12. East Indian Finance; 13. Arms Act, Press Act, and Taxing Legislation of India; 14. Cape—Annexation of the Transvaal: the act of the present Administration; and 15. Cape—Zulu War: the result of the mission of Sir Bartle Frere. Of these, the first three come under the Treaty of Berlin; the fourth, fifth, and sixth under the Anglo-Turkish Convention; the seventh, eighth, and ninth are assumed to result from the purchase of shares in the Suez Canal; while the tenth, eleventh, twelfth, and thirteenth result from the mission of Lord Lytton. After reviewing the home and foreign policy of the Government, the right hon. gentleman compared its claims with those of its predecessor, and said that though there had been times when men of ardent minds had complained that they could scarcely distinguish between one party and another, assuredly no such complaint could now be made, and the nation must choose between them in the light afforded by the experience of the last six years.

Mr. Gladstone has supplemented this indictment by other charges in a speech at Chester.[7] He maintained, as he had assured the electors of Midlothian, that at no period of his public life had the issues inviting the judgment of the nation been of such profound importance—including the management of finance, the scale of expenditure, and the constantly growing arrears of legislation—as now. 'I hold,' he continued, 'that the faith and honour of the country have been gravely compromised by the foreign policy of the Ministry; that by the disturbance of confidence, and lately even of peace, which they have brought about, they have prolonged and aggravated public distress; that they have augmented the power and interest of the Russian Empire,

even while estranging the feelings of its population; that they have embarked the Crown and people in an unjust war; that their Afghan war is full of mischief, if not of positive danger, to India; and that by their use of the treaty-making and war-making powers of the Crown they have abridged the just rights of Parliament, and have presented its prerogatives to the nation under an unconstitutional aspect, which tends to make it insecure.' Mr. Gladstone added that these were the characters he had inscribed on his colours, and he had nailed them to the mast. He again reiterated his charge that the Ministry had played the game of Russia, and had enabled her to take the part which belonged to our forefathers—and which ought to have belonged to us—that of promoting the interests of liberty and justice. Further, although it was perfectly well known that we had invaded the country of the Zulus, Lord Salisbury, the Foreign Secretary—who ought to be among the best informed men—had lately announced that we had engaged in a war in South Africa which was brought upon us in order to repel an attack made by savages upon our colonial dominions. It was coolly asserted by a responsible Minister of the Crown that the people of the country which we invaded invaded us. The Zulus, denounced as savages by Lord Salisbury, showed us an evidence of the right feeling which was rather to have been expected from a Christian people, and refused to cross the little thread of a stream that separated their land from ours, being simply contented to await within their own territories a renewal of our wanton, unprovoked, mischievous, and deplorable attacks. Describing our latest acquisition, Mr. Gladstone said, 'You know what Cyprus is. It is a small island, but it is a great imposture.' In that great and wonderful arsenal which was to contain an army that would frighten Russia out of its wits, there were now three hundred English soldiers, and so inadequate were they even to the duty of keeping the people in order that, notwithstanding the promise given that Cyprus should not cost a shilling for civil government, one of the last acts of the Administration had been to carry a vote through Parliament for the support of the civil police of the island. With regard to financial matters, Mr. Gladstone said that at the beginning of the year the deficiency stood at six millions sterling, and there would be a deficiency of three and a half millions more at the end of the financial year. It would be a great stroke for the Government if they could postpone the presentation of the bill for expenses until after the dissolution. From the Liberal party had proceeded all the measures which had made the country so great and so strong, that had led to the prosperity which lasted in an unbroken term for such a number of years until this crisis had arrived—a crisis so unhappily prolonged and aggravated as the present crisis had been unhappily prolonged and aggravated by the financial extravagance of the Government, and by that want of confidence which they had introduced into their relations with the different countries of the globe. When the dissolution came, if they did their duty, there was no fear for the Liberals.

This address by the ex-Premier, delivered in his seventieth year, exhibited all the energy and vigour usually associated with a political chief of fifty. It demonstrated that, though he had retired from the leadership of his party, he answered the call to the political battle as the war-horse scents the conflict from afar.

A final word remains to be said upon the Anglo-Turkish Convention and the Ministerial policy generally. The acquisition of Cyprus was Lord Beaconsfield's set-off against the territorial cessions to Russia under the Treaty of Berlin. It was deemed necessary for England to do something at this juncture, and, to obtain Cyprus, the Premier even pledged England to that immense responsibility (whose results no man can possibly foresee), the Protectorate over the Turkish dominions in Asia. Lord Beaconsfield had fixed his attention upon Cyprus some time before its cession to Great Britain, for Lord Derby, in explaining the reasons for his secession from the Cabinet, said, 'When I quitted the Cabinet I did so mainly because it was said that it was necessary to secure a naval station in the Eastern part of the Mediterranean; and that, for that purpose, it was necessary to seize and occupy the island of Cyprus, together with a point upon the Syrian coast. That was to be done by means of a Syrian expedition sent out from India, with or without the consent of the Sultan.' The Premier has not only pursued a policy now widely recognised under the term 'Imperial,' but he has pursued this policy in secret, and has shown so great a contempt for Parliamentary and constitutional usage as to take little thought for the nation, or its representatives in the House of Commons. For some time back, however, the sinister effects of this policy have been in process of demonstration, and the country is beginning to ask whether the vast concerns of this great empire should continue practically to remain at the will and disposal of one man. We have—as all must have—a genuine admiration for Lord Beaconsfield's talents and genius; but we have arrived at so grave a crisis in our national history that it becomes the duty of every man to speak out, and with no uncertain voice. What would Pym, Hampden, and their compatriots have said to the system of government which now prevails in England. Yet the Premier is not wholly, though chiefly, responsible for this. The country should remember that he would have been powerless but for the support of a majority of the House of Commons; and in order to destroy personal government, the nation must change its representatives. The results of recent policy have been thus described by Mr. Gladstone:—'There is not a nation upon earth with which we have drawn the bonds of friendship closer by the transactions of these last years, but we have played perilous tricks with the loyalty of India, have estranged the

ninety millions who inhabit Russia, and have severed ourselves from the Christians of Turkey, Greek and Slav alike, without gaining the respect of the Moslem. And all this we have done, not to increase our power, but only our engagements.' A statesman who neglects every home interest to boast of our power before other nations; who enters upon engagements lightly, and without thinking of the enormous responsibilities they must devolve upon us in the future; who enacts the swashbuckler in foreign politics, and endeavours to flatter us by a sense of our own grandeur—such a statesman, whatever may be his claims in other respects, is to be dreaded as the most dangerous foe that England could possess.

We have now reached the close of our survey of Mr. Gladstone's literary and political career. In both aspects the average reader seems to toil after him in vain, so great is his fertility in resource, so extraordinary his power of seizing upon and comprehending the facts and bearings of our foreign and domestic policy, so copious and inexhaustible the eloquence with which he illustrates and enforces his views—whether those views relate to the immortal works of Homer, the scandals of the Neapolitan prisons, the questions raised by *Ecce Homo,* the details of the last budget, the principles which should pervade industrial art, the dogmas of the Romish Church, the duty of man in relation to education and religion, or the policy of the Beaconsfield Administration. The strength and vehemence of his denunciations of the Government—as we have already had occasion to remark—have been sometimes severely commented upon; but, without defending his addresses in every particular, it may be observed that strong language is sometimes called for in English politics, provided it be just. Moreover, in addition to the force which Mr. Gladstone's addresses have always derived from the natural ardour of his temperament, they owe much of their polemical character to the firm and settled conviction of the ex-Premier—that the policy of Lord Beaconsfield's Ministry has been derogatory to the honour and interests of England, at home and abroad.

Notes

1. The *Athenæum,* Feb. 1879.

2. *Gleanings of Past Years.* In seven volumes. London: 1879.

3. Opening of an Art Loan Exhibition, August 11, 1879.

4. Egypt may yet prove a source of serious difficulty to England. It was stated in a communication to the *Times* from Alexandria, dated August 24, 1879, that when Ismail Pasha was still Viceroy of Egypt, and was being pressed to sign his abdication, he used these words:—'You English have made a mistake; whatever I have been or done, I made

English interests in Egypt paramount. You have the railways, the customs, the post-office, the telegraphs, and the ports entirely under English Administration. To gain more you have called in the French. You then hesitated, and Bismarck, who looks far ahead, pushed you on till you have come to direct intervention. Mark my words, Bismarck sees what I see, that Egypt will become the Schleswig-Holstein of England and France.'

5. This article on the Evangelical movement in England originally appeared in the *British Quarterly Review* [70 (July 1879): 15].

6. See the *Nineteenth Century* for September, 1878.

7. Delivered August 19, 1879.

J. L. M. Curry (essay date 1891)

SOURCE: Curry, J. L. M. "Authorship—Homeric Writings—The Vatican Decree." In *William Ewart Gladstone*, pp. 183-90. Richmond, Va.: B. F. Johnson & Co., 1891.

[*In the following essay, Curry evaluates Gladstone's writings on politics and religion, focusing on his attitudes toward the question of Papal doctrine.*]

Like his celebrated rival, Mr. Gladstone has been a writer of books and a frequent contributor to magazines and reviews. So wide are his reading and sympathies, such the variety and plenitude of his intellectual powers and acquisitions, that his writings are numerous and inclusive of a great range of topics. Subjects—historical, political, ecclesiastical, religious, artistic, economic, literary and practical, have engaged his prolific pen. Some books have owed their reputation or circulation to his commendation of them. When he was serving as Lord High Commissioner to arrange the cession of the Ionian Islands, at a banquet in Athens he addressed the assembly in the ancient Greek language, and because of his fluency, pronunciation and accent was declared a great Greek orator. The ability to accomplish this intellectual feat was the result, in some degree, of his Homeric studies. For many years he has applied himself to the study of Homer. It is his recreation, his passion, and his mind is saturated with the spirit, and his memory is filled with the images and the language, of the Homeric poems. He may not be a Greek scholar of the verbal nicety and critical accuracy of some professors who have given their lives to the grammar of the language, but his *Studies on Homer, Juventus Mundi, Homeric Synchronism,* and various contributions to the reviews, show a profound acquaintance with the history, the thought, the atmosphere of the period.

In the course of this study frequent reference has been made to, and several quotations taken from, *Church and State* and *Gleanings of Past Years.* No writings

have been more read, or have provoked more bitter comment, than those in which he discussed Vaticanism. His high churchism, and his strenuous and successful efforts for the disestablishment of the Anglican Church in Ireland, and his courageous purpose to mete out fullest justice to Roman Catholics, have caused Mr. Gladstone to be charged with drifting toward the Church of Rome, and even with being a pervert to that faith. In some respects that ecclesiastical organization has had no more persistent nor able opponent. Pius IX, resolving to crown his long pontificate by the formal assumption, under the sanction of the collective episcopate of his church, of semi-divine attributes, summoned, in 1870, a council to Rome, which assented to his wishes, and decreed papal infallibility.

In 1874 the public mind in England was much aroused by ritualistic practices in some of the churches of the establishment, by the aggressive activity of the Roman Church, and by the apprehension of an organized and powerful influence for Romanizing Great Britain. This awakened much controversy on church power and papal power. Mr. Gladstone, in an article in *Contemporary Review* on ritualism, used this language: "At no time since the sanguinary reign of Mary has such a scheme been possible [Romanizing the church and people of England]. But if it had been possible in the seventeenth or eighteenth centuries, it would still have become impossible in the nineteenth, when Rome has substituted for the proud boast of *semper eadem* a policy of violence and change in faith; when she has refurbished and paraded anew every rusty tool she was fondly thought to have disused; when no one can become her convert without renouncing his moral and mental freedom, and placing his civil loyalty and duty at the mercy of another; and when she has equally repudiated modern thought and ancient history." This courageous attack created much excitement and discussion. During the ecclesiastical warfare which prevailed, he defended his position by a pamphlet on *The Vatican Decrees in their Bearing on Civil Allegiance: a Political Expostulation.* In restating the four distinct propositions included in the foregoing extract, he proceeded to their demonstration with thorough familiarity with ecclesiastical history, with great boldness, with most careful polemical fairness, but with inexpugnable logic. His contention was that the design of Vaticanism was to disturb civil society and to proceed, when requisite and practicable, to the issue of blood for the accomplishment of its aims; that the hierarchical power aimed, internally, at the total destruction of right, not of right as opposed to wrong, but of right as opposed to arbitrary will, and, externally, it maintained the right and duty of the organized spirituality to override at will, in respect of right and wrong, the entire action of the civil power, and likewise to employ force, as and when it may think fit, for the fulfillment of its purposes, and thus to establish "absolutism of the church and absolutism in the church." The Pope claimed to determine, by spiritual prerogative, questions of the civil sphere, and thus those who acknowledge his authority forfeit mental and moral freedom and place loyalty and civil duty in his hands. "Absolute obedience, it is declared, is due to the Pope at the peril of salvation, not alone in faith, in morals, but in all things which concern the discipline and government of the church." "Duty is a power which rises with us in the morning, goes to rest with us at night. It is co-extensive with the action of our intelligence." Mr. Gladstone thus summed up his conclusions:

1. That the Pope, authorized by his council, claims for himself the domain (*a*) of faith, (*b*) of morals, and (*c*) of all that concerns the discipline and government of the church.

2. That he, in like manner, claims the power of determining the limits of those domains.

3. That he does not sever them, by any acknowledged or intelligible line, from the domains of civil duty and allegiance.

4. That he therefore claims, and claims from the month of July, 1870, onwards, with plenary authority, from every convert and member of his church that he shall place his loyalty and civil duty at the mercy of himself.

The angry discussion provoked by the essay on Ritualism was quietude compared with the storm of wrath which the pamphlet evoked. The writer was fiercely and bitterly assailed in many tongues. Replies innumerable poured forth from the press in Europe and the United States. Besides anonymous and editorial strictures, such antagonists as Cardinals Newman and Manning, Monsignor Capel, Bishops Ullathorne, Clifford, Vaughn, etc., and hosts of others made replies. The little book was placed on the *Index Librorum Prohibitorum.* The Duc de Decages, on behalf of the government of France, refused to allow the free sale of the translation at the railway book-stalls, on the public highways and in the kiosks. The efforts to restrain the circulation only increased the desire of the public to read. In the course of a few weeks 120,000 copies were sold in England. The circulation in this country was immense, and translations were made into all the European languages. *An Answer to Reproofs and Replies* shows marvelous dialectical skill and self-control. *A Review of the Speeches of Pope Pius IX* is one of the most trenchant and indignant exposures of papal assumptions to be found in our language. The three papers make Vol. 1524 of the Tauchnitz Collection of British Authors.

James Bryce (essay date 1903)

SOURCE: Bryce, James. "William Ewart Gladstone." In *Studies in Contemporary Biography,* pp. 400-80. New York: The Macmillan Company, 1903.

[*In the following excerpt, Bryce examines the relationship between Gladstone's oratory style and his writings. Bryce suggests that Gladstone's renown as a public speaker played a key role in bolstering his literary reputation.*]

The best proof of his [Gladstone's] swiftness, industry, and skill in economising time is supplied by the quantity of his literary work, which, considering the abstruse nature of the subjects to which much of it is related, would have been creditable to the diligence of a German professor sitting alone in his study. The merits of the work have been disputed. Mankind are slow to credit the same person with eminence in various fields. When they read the prose of a great poet, they try it by severer tests than would be applied to other writers. When a painter has won credit by his landscapes or his cattle pieces, he is seldom encouraged to venture into other lines. So Mr. Gladstone's reputation as an orator stood in his own light when he appeared as an author. He was read by thousands who would not have looked at the article or book had it borne some other name; but he was judged by the standard, not of his finest printed speeches, for his speeches were seldom models of composition, but rather by the impression which his finest speeches made on those who heard them. Since his warmest admirers could not claim for him as a writer of prose any such pre-eminence as belonged to him as a speaker, it followed that his written work was not duly appreciated. Had he been a writer and nothing else, he would have been eminent and powerful by his pen.

He might, however, have failed to secure a place in the front rank. His style was forcible, copious, rich with various knowledge, warm with the ardour of his temperament. But it suffered from an inborn tendency to exuberance which the long practice of oratory had confirmed. It was diffuse, apt to pursue a topic into details, when these might have been left to the reader's own reflection. It was redundant, employing more words than were needed to convey the substance. It was unchastened, indulging too freely in tropes and metaphors, in quotations and adapted phrases even when the quotation added nothing to the sense but was suggested merely by some association in his own mind. Thus it seldom reached a high level of purity and grace, and though one might excuse the faults as natural to the work of a swift and busy man, they were sufficient to reduce the pleasure to be derived from the form and dress of his thoughts. Nevertheless there are not a few passages of rare merit, both in the books and in the articles, among which may be cited (not as exceptionally good, but as typical of his strong points) the striking picture of his own youthful feeling toward the Church of England contained in the *Chapter of Autobiography,* and the refined criticism of *Robert Elsmere,* published in 1888. Almost the last thing he wrote, a pamphlet on the Greek and Cretan question, published in the spring of 1897, has the force and cogency of his best days. Two things were never wanting to him: vigour of expression and an admirable command of appropriate words.

His writings fall into three classes: political, theological, and literary—the last chiefly consisting of his books and articles upon Homer and the Homeric question. All the political writings, except the books on *The State in its Relations to the Church* and *Church Principles Considered in their Results,* belong to the class of occasional literature, being pamphlets or articles produced with a view to some current crisis or controversy. They are valuable chiefly as proceeding from one who bore a leading part in the affairs they relate to, and as embodying vividly the opinions and aspirations of the moment, less frequently in respect of permanent lessons of political wisdom, such as one finds in Machiavelli or Tocqueville or Edmund Burke. Like Pitt and Peel, Mr. Gladstone had a mind which, whatever its original tendencies, had come to be rather practical than meditative. He was fond of generalisations and principles, but they were always directly related to the questions that came before him in actual politics; and the number of weighty maxims or illuminative suggestions to be found in his writings and speeches is small in proportion to the sustained vigour they display. Even Disraeli, though his views were often fanciful and his epigrams often forced, gives us more frequently a brilliant (if only half true) historical *aperçu,* or throws a flash of light into some corner of human character. Of the theological essays, which are mainly apologetic and concerned with the authenticity and authority of Scripture, it is enough to say that they were the work of an accomplished amateur, who had been too busy to follow the progress of critical inquiry. His Homeric treatises, the most elaborate piece of work that proceeded from Mr. Gladstone's pen, are in one sense worthless, in another sense admirable. Those parts of them which deal with early Greek mythology, genealogy, and religion, and, in a less degree, the theories about Homeric geography and the use of Homeric epithets, have been condemned by the unanimous voice of scholars as fantastic. The premises are assumed without sufficient investigation, while the reasonings are fine-drawn and flimsy. Extraordinary ingenuity is shown in piling up a lofty fabric, but the foundation is of sand, and the edifice has hardly a solid wall or beam in it. A conjecture is treated as a fact; then an inference, possible but not certain, is drawn from this conjecture; a second possible inference is based upon the first; and we are made to forget that the probability of this second is at most only half the probability of the first. So the process goes on; and when the superstructure is complete, the reader is provoked to perceive how much dialectical skill has been wasted upon a series of hypotheses which a breath of common-sense criticism dissipates. If one is asked to explain the weakness in this particular department of a mind otherwise so strong, the answer would seem to be that the element of fancifulness in Mr. Gladstone's intellect, and his tendency to mistake mere argumentation for verification, were checked in practical politics by constant intercourse with friends and colleagues as well as by the need of convincing visible audiences, while in theological or historical inquiries his ingenuity roamed with fatal freedom over wide plains where no obstacles checked its course. Something may also be due to the fact that his philosophical and historical education was received at a time when the modern critical spirit and the canons it recognises had scarcely begun to assert themselves at Oxford. Similar defects may be discerned in other eminent writers of his own and the preceding generation of Oxford men, defects from which persons of inferior power in later days might be free. In some of these writers, and particularly in Cardinal Newman, the contrast between dialectical acumen, coupled with surpassing rhetorical skill, and the vitiation of the argument by a want of the critical faculty, is scarcely less striking; and the example of that illustrious man suggests that the dominance of the theological view of literary and historical problems, a dominance evident in Mr. Gladstone, counts for something in producing the phenomenon.

With these defects, Mr. Gladstone's Homeric work had the merit of being based on a full and thorough knowledge of the Homeric text. He had seen, at a time when few people in England had seen it, that the Homeric poems are an historical source of the highest value, a treasure-house of data for the study of early Greek life and thought, an authority all the more trustworthy because an unconscious authority, addressing not posterity but contemporaries. This mastery of the matter contained in the poems enabled him to present valuable pictures of the political and social life of Homeric Greece, while the interspersed literary criticisms are often subtle and suggestive, erring, when they do err, chiefly through the over-earnestness of his mind. He often takes the poet too seriously; reading an ethical purpose into descriptive or dramatic touches which are merely descriptive or dramatic. Passages whose moral tendency offends him are reprobated as later insertions with a naïveté which forgets the character of a primitive age. But he has for his author not only that sympathy which is the best basis for criticism, but a justness of poetic taste which the learned and painstaking German commentator frequently wants. That Mr. Gladstone was a sound scholar in that narrower sense of the word which denotes a grammatical and literary command of Greek and Latin, goes without saying. Men of his generation kept a closer hold upon the ancient classics than we do to-day; and his habit of reading Greek for the sake of his Homeric studies, and Latin for the sake of his theological, made this familiarity more than usually thorough. Like most Etonians, he loved and knew the poets by preference. Dante was his favourite poet, perhaps because Dante is the most theological and ethical of the great poets, and because the tongue and the memories of Italy had a peculiar attraction for him. He used to say that he found Dante's thought incomparably inspiring, but hard to follow, it was so high and so abstract. Theology claimed a place beside poetry; history came next, though he did not study it systematically. It seemed odd that he was sometimes at fault in the constitutional antiquities of England; but this subject was, until the day of Dr. Stubbs, pre-eminently a Whig subject, and Mr. Gladstone never was a Whig, never learned to think upon the lines of the great Whigs of former days. His historical knowledge was not exceptionally wide, but it was generally accurate in matters of fact, however fanciful he might be in reasoning from the facts, however wild his conjectures in the prehistoric region. In metaphysics strictly so called his reading did not go far beyond those companions of his youth, Aristotle and Bishop Butler; and philosophical speculation interested him only so far as it bore on Christian doctrine. Keen as was his interest in theology and in history, it is not certain that he would have produced work of permanent value in either sphere even had his life been wholly devoted to study. His mind seemed to need to be steadied, his ingenuity restrained, by having to deal with concrete matter for a practical end. Neither, in spite of his eminence as a financier and an advocate of free trade, did he show much taste for economic studies. On practical topics, such as the working of protective tariffs, the abuse of charitable endowments, the development of fruit-culture in England, the duty of liberal giving by the rich, the utility of thrift among the poor, his remarks were full of point, clearness, and good sense, but he seldom launched out into the wider sea of economic theory. He took a first-class in mathematics at Oxford, at the same time as his first in classics, but did not pursue the subject in later life. Regarding the sciences of experiment and observation, he seemed to feel as little curiosity as any educated man who notes the enormous part they play in the modern world can feel. Sayings of his have been quoted which show that he imperfectly comprehended the character of the evidence they rely upon and of the methods they employ. On one occasion he horrified a dinner-table of younger friends by refusing to accept some of the most certain conclusions of modern geology. No doubt he belonged, as Lord Derby (the Prime Minister) once said of himself, to a pre-scientific age. Perhaps he was unconsciously biassed by the notion that such sciences as geology and biology, for instance, were being used by some students to sap the foundations of revealed religion. But I can recall no sign of disposition to dissuade free inquiry either into those among the sciences of nature which have been supposed to touch theology, or into the date, authorship, and authority of the books of the Bible. He had faith not only in his creed, but in God as a God of truth, and in the power of research to elicit truth.

General propositions are dangerous, yet it seems safe to observe that great men have seldom been obscurantists or persecutors. Either the sympathy with intellectual effort which is natural to a powerful intellect, or the sense that free inquiry, though it may be checked by repression for a certain time or within a certain area, will ultimately have its course, dissuades them from that attempt to dam up the stream of thought which smaller minds regard as the obvious expedient for saving souls or institutions.

It ought to be added, for this was a remarkable feature of his character, that he had the deepest reverence for the great poets and philosophers, placing the career of the statesman on a far lower plane than that of those who rule the world by their thoughts enshrined in literature. He expressed in a striking letter to Tennyson's eldest son his sense of the immense superiority of the poet's life and work. Once, in the lobby of the House of Commons, seeing his countenance saddened by the troubles of Ireland, I told him, in order to divert his thoughts, how some one had recently discovered that Dante had in his last years been appointed at Ravenna to a lectureship which raised him above the pinch of want. Mr. Gladstone's face lit up at once, and he said, "How strange it is to think that these great souls whose words are a beacon-light to all the generations that have come after them, should have had cares and anxieties to vex them in their daily life, just like the rest of us common mortals." The phrase reminded me that a few days before I had heard Mr. Darwin, in dwelling upon the pleasure a visit paid by Mr. Gladstone had given him, say, "And he talked just as if he had been an ordinary person like one of ourselves." The two great men were alike unconscious of their greatness.

It was an unspeakable benefit to Mr. Gladstone that his love of letters and learning enabled him to find in the pursuit of knowledge a relief from anxieties and a solace under disappointments. Without some such relief his fiery and restless spirit would have worn itself out.

Agatha Ramm (lecture date 28 May 1981)

SOURCE: Ramm, Agatha. "Gladstone as Man of Letters." *Nineteenth Century Prose* 17, no. 1 (winter 1989/90): 1-29.

[*In the following essay, which was originally presented on May 28, 1981, as a James Bryce memorial lecture at Somerville College (Oxford), Ramm explores the diversity of Gladstone's intellectual interests. Ramm asserts that Gladstone's writings, in particular his essays and reviews, are characterized primarily by his deep passion for literature and books.*]

It is a supreme honor to have been asked to deliver a lecture in memory of Lord Bryce. He was a considerable historian and jurist, a notable ambassador and a great humanitarian. It is fitting that the subject should be Mr. Gladstone, who was Prime Minister when James Bryce was parliamentary under-secretary for foreign affairs (1886) and the Prime Minister who, in 1892, brought him into the cabinet. Gladstone was also something of an historian—his Romanes lecture, the first of the series, was an historical sketch of the University—and as Bulgarians and Armenians to this day know, a great humanitarian.

Sir Adolphus Ward, the historian, wrote of Gladstone's scholarship and of his love of classical and Italian literature, "But," continues he, "he could not be called . . . a man of letters."[1] I am encouraged to demur because James Bryce himself was "forcibly struck" by "the source of strength as well as enjoyment" which Gladstone "found in cherishing the love of letters . . . among the occupations of practical life."[2] I am emboldened in my demurrer because the published *Diaries* [*The Gladstone Diaries*] and unpublished letters and papers, none of them accessible to Ward, have told us now what books he read—the number is beyond that of reading men, let alone of men with full public lives—how thoroughly he read and remembered them, and how and why he wrote his many review articles and established himself as an authority on Homer; have brought us, in short, closer than Ward was, to the imagination, to the musical ear and to the intellect of a good and constant writer in the quarterlies and monthlies, of a man with a universal curiosity and a life-long book-lover.

Certainly the beginning of review-writing was not typical of the romantic novelist's idea of a man of letters; for the spur was neither money nor fame. The beginning was in 1842. By then he has already published two books [*The State in Its Relations with the Church* and *Church Principles Considered in Their Results*];[3] he has married and his two eldest children have been born; he will soon have been ten years a Tory M.P.; he has a reputation for intellect and oratory. He is a junior minister and because of his indispensability with the customs tariff changes in the previous spring, Sir Robert Peel is about to appoint him to the cabinet. The year is drawing to its close and parliament is in recess. Although he is putting in some six hours a day at the Board of Trade, he has time free. The urge to systematise and record takes possession of him and he resolves "to try my hand at an article about tariff."[4] He is in touch with Hatchard, bookseller and publisher, and with John Murray, his own publisher. There is ground to surmise that one or the other gave him the name of the Rev. Dr. James Worthington who, with Murray's advice, was collecting material to start a new review, to be called the *Foreign and Colonial Quarterly Review*. Gladstone wrote to Worthington on 6 December, received prospectuses of the new review by return and sent him the article on the 8th.[5] It duly appeared in the

first number in January 1843. The article reviewed a number of parliamentary papers and the official publication of the Prussian (Zollverein) tariff.

Worthington, eager to promote his review, offered "to assist the Government," obtained an interview with Gladstone and gained a promise of more articles. Gladstone's original article had been anonymous, but the newspapers[6] soon gossiped of his writing for the new review—he was already news—and he had laid himself open to editorial importunity when he sent nothing more.[7] Worthington was pacified with—Gladstone's second—**"The Present Aspect of the Church"** for October 1843 and—his third article—**"The Theses of Erastus"** for October 1844.[8] Both articles reviewed publications of Gladstone's choice. The third article was the end of the connection and in 1846 the review ceased publication. Of payment there is never any mention. Worthington's effusive thanks "for noble support" and his pointed remarks on the proprietors' expectation of heavy losses during the first two years suggest no payment or very little. Gladstone's circumstances enabled him to dispense with it. He had just agreed with his wife to live on the income of their inherited wealth, to pass the inheritance on to their children and "to give what we earn or save."[9]

Meanwhile, and for quite different reasons, Gladstone was supporting another new quarterly review. William Palmer of Worcester College, Oxford and B. W. Savile of Emmanuel College, Cambridge had joined together to try to change the partisan character of the Tractarian *British Critic*. By the summer of 1843 Manning and Hope, both still Anglican, were concerned about it. The editor was known to be "romanising" and had indeed "gone over" by September. The October number was the last of the *British Critic*.[10] Rivington, its publisher was approached by two sets of men to negotiate a replacement, one led by Palmer and Savile. The other was led by Gladstone and Manning. Their aim was a review which, while maintaining Church principles, should show no Tractarian bias and provoke no one. The difficulty of succeeding in that object in 1844 will be appreciated. In the end the conciliatory mind and the self-sacrifice of William Palmer prevailed. The *English Review* lasted, under his unpaid editorship, from 1844 to 1853. Gladstone wrote for it two short, anonymous articles. For the first number he sent "a paltry criticism" as he called it, but it was far from that, of Lord John Russell's translation of the Paolo and Francesca story in Dante's *Inferno* "to show," as he said, "goodwill." For the second number he sent a review of *Ellen Middleton*, a Tractarian novel, by Lady Georgiana Fullerton, of which the central idea was the need to confess one's misdeeds.[11] From the beginning Gladstone thought the new review reminded him of "petrifaction." It was never better than "feeble and dull" as such a neutral product might well appear in 1844.[12] Gladstone must find another outlet for his articles.

Except, then, in so far as a literary instinct may have been present in his support of new periodicals, Gladstone's *motive* for this group of five articles was not literary: the *character* of the five articles, in part, was literary. The three contributions to the *Foreign and Colonial* [*Foreign and Colonial Quarterly Review*] were rooted rather in public controversy than in his private, bookish life. Yet they *were* literary in their systematising, generalising, even moralising, character. The two contributions to the *English Review,* in motive partly literary, were wholly literary in character. The first with its comparisons with translations of the same episode by Cary, Dayman and Byron, could not have been written except by a man of letters. The second was certainly the work of a literary critic. This beginning of Gladstone's literary reviewing was confirmed when he made contact with John Lockhart and the *Quarterly* to which he began to send articles at the end of 1844.

One notices, however, that as he began, so he continued. The literary articles were always to be interspersed between articles which belonged only partly to his private, bookish life. To read in chronological order all the articles Gladstone wrote, is to survey the speculative controversies of the century. He took part in all of them: in the thirties and forties, in the argument about the Church establishment; in the fifties and later, in the argument over the relationship between the Hebraic tradition and the Old Testament on one side and the Homeric and ancient Greek tradition on the other, all writers, including Gladstone, calling in the new archaeological evidence to support their views; in the sixties in the argument provoked by those three strange works, D. F. Strauss, *Das Leben Jesu* (1837), Ernst Renan, *Vie de Jésus* (1863) and John Seeley, *Ecce Homo* (1865).[13] All these Gladstone read—the foreigners in the original language—and he reviewed *Ecce Homo* in a reconciling sense.[14] In the sixties and onwards all the dogmas of the Church were attacked under the watchword "free enquiry" and Gladstone entered the lists against the rationalists. In 1885 he contributed **"Dawn of Creation"** and **"Proem to Genesis"** to the arguments about the origin of life and revealed religion.[15] For good measure he took part in the sabbatarian controversy, arguing with characteristic exactitude in choice of word for a day not of rest, but of renewal.[16] Though in the learning they displayed and in their quotations, allusions and comparisons, they suggest the bookish man, these articles are in their essence what any public man who was also a Churchman might have thought it incumbent on himself to write. They are only the context in which Gladstone, man of letters, wrote.

If I may continue to digress a little longer: Gladstone's manner of working meant that the stream of writing would narrow to a trickle and even run underground in some years when he was in office. His habit was to keep a group—sometimes as many as five—of books in reading at the same time, turning to another when he tired of one. Then suddenly he would become engrossed and excited by one of them, would read it on consecutive days, always omitting Sunday which had its own kind of reading, until he finished it, and then, perhaps after a short interval, write upon what he had read. He wrote to disburden an excited mind—or imagination. After some days with short spells of writing came the crisis, when he worked on—the *Diary* replaces "wrote on" by "worked on" for the task of abridging, checking references and revising—when he worked on his essay from 7 a.m. to 3 p.m. or "all my working day" or "from early morning to late afternoon." A twelve-hour, or more, working day in his office, in parliament, in the cabinet, did not accommodate such spells of literary labour and it had to be abandoned or nearly so.

To return to my theme: the five articles which made the beginning led on to the connection with John Lockhart and the *Quarterly*. On 15 September 1844, Gladstone began to read W. G. Ward's *Ideal of a Christian Church.* The **Diary** records the day on which each of the stages I have described then followed. It tells us the day he decided to write to calm his excitement and relates that throughout the second week of November he worked on cutting down and polishing an article.[17] Through John Murray, he tested the ground first and then on November 20th sent the article to Lockhart for the *Quarterly.* This essay was not like his contributions to the *Foreign and Colonial,* rooted in his public life; for it was less theological and speculative than critical in a literary sense. Lockhart, who had already put the *Quarterly* in an aloof position towards the Tractarians, would not have accepted it had it not been a review of the manner rather than the matter of the book. As it was he made trouble enough when the article was set up in print. He had accepted it warmly as "an intellectual luxury," but insisted on much alteration when it was in print.[18] Certainly the article had polemical and ecclesiastical importance, however much Lockhart had diminished it, when it was published in January 1845. But it also confirmed Gladstone in his career as literary critic, after his first appearance in that part in the *English Review.*

The impulse to write continued to come from the excitement of mind or imagination. One cannot otherwise account for the predominance of reviews of *Memoirs, Lives* and *Letters,* in his writing. This continued from 1845 to his last article, **"Recollections of Arthur Hallam"** of 1898,[19] published a few months before he died. But I do not refer to reviews of memoirs of friends, such as that of Döllinger, the German theologian, nor to reviews which gave him scope for political apology, such as those of the successive volumes of Theodore

Martin's *Life of the Prince Consort,* written during the period of comparative leisure after the fall of his first ministry, nor to that of Fraser Rae's *Sheridan,* "patriot, orator, statesman," which allowed him to express political reflection in 1896 towards the end of his life.[20] (I need not say that Gladstone read all political memoirs as they came out and some collections of speeches, back to Bolingbroke, Horace Walpole, Chatham, Burke and Pitt and among contemporaries, Greville's *Memoirs* the last part of which he reviewed in the first number of the *English Historical Review* in 1886.) I refer not to these but to reviews which were fully rooted in his private, bookish life. I mean those of J. H. Thom's edition of the *Autobiography and Correspondence of Joseph Blanco White,* of Charlotte Yonge's *Life of Bishop Patteson,* and of W. J. Fitzgerald's *Correspondence of Daniel O'Connell, the Liberator.*[21] These are very odd choices of subject matter. They are inexplicable unless by the explanation that Gladstone's imagination was excited by vivid, commanding personalities whose lives were lived at the limits of human strain. Sometimes it was a strain of introspection that excited him, as in the case of Blanco White, sometimes the strain of practical endeavour in an alien society, as in that of Bishop Patteson, or a hostile society, as with O'Connell. One remembers that Gladstone's own life was lived under the dual strain of self-examination, self-questioning of a kind peculiar to himself as the **Diaries** record, and of endeavour quite exceptional, even by Victorian standards of self-exertion—a seventeen-hour working day occurred more than once.

Lockhart accepted the essay on Blanco White for the June 1845 number of the *Quarterly* "as the best article that could have been done on that painful subject" and sent Gladstone £46, his maximum payment for a long article.[22] Blanco White's "spirit," wrote Gladstone, "was a battlefield, upon which with fluctuating fortune and a singular intensity, the powers of belief and skepticism waged, from first to last, their unceasing war." He recounts the varying religious fancies of this Spaniard of Irish extraction, from his Roman Catholicism in Seville to Unitarianism in Liverpool in a manner that is far from lifeless, though he thought it was,[23] with respect for Blanco White's honesty, but full recognition of his instability. In 1889 Gladstone reviewed an autobiography of another "harrowed soul," an extraordinary piece of introspection by a dying woman painter, *Journal de Marie Bashkirtseff* (Paris, 1888).[24] The repetition of the choice in an exaggerated form seems to vindicate one in explaining the Blanco White review by the power of this sort of strain to hold Gladstone's imagination.

Gladstone's review of Charlotte Yonge's, "long" but not "bulky" *Life of Bishop Patteson* appeared in the *Quarterly* for October 1874. Lockhart had died and (after two other successors) W. Smith had succeeded to the editorship and Gladstone had been Liberal prime minister, but his private literary life was so far separate, that he would not abruptly break with the Tory *Quarterly.* He had found it unreceptive to his Italian political enthusiasm in 1851 and had sent his articles on that subject elsewhere[25] and he begins in 1874 to send his articles on Homer to the Liberal monthly *Contemporary,* but there was no dramatic break and the Patteson article went to the *Quarterly.* In the Patteson review Gladstone is clearly excited by the drama of the Bishop's life. He makes the most of the contrast between the happiness of childhood and youth and the hardship of the later life of this missionary in the South Sea Islands. He dwells upon Patteson's reading and practical contriving as farmer, builder, doctor as well as teacher and pastor and leads us to the catastrophe. The Bishop was tragically killed by the gentle people whom he had served and taught. Gladstone relies all the time upon quoting the letters which Charlotte Yonge prints. Patteson was one of the tribe of Coleridges and wrote vivid letters home from Eton, Oxford and, of course, the Islands. It is these last, one suspects, which so fired Gladstone's imagination.

The article on Daniel O'Connell was accepted by James Knowles for the Liberal monthly *Nineteenth Century* for the number of January 1889. Knowles had been on the staff of the *Contemporary* and when he left it to found his own review Gladstone, supporting yet another new review, went with him, and remained loyal to him for the rest of his life. The article was a eulogy to purge old prejudices—understandable during the Home Rule campaign. But it was also a piece of literature and a human document; for it revived from memory the man with whom a young Gladstone had ridden out into the Essex countryside one summer morning more than half a century before. They were in search of a witness too old and ill to appear in person before the parliamentary committee of enquiry on which he and O'Connell sat. The vividness with which O'Connell is made to live on the page suggests again a personal, imaginative impulse to write.

But there was a skill at work in these reviews of *Lives* and *Letters,* beyond the imagination which inspired them. Gladstone possessed to an extraordinary degree the ability—and the urge—to generalise at large from minute particulars. Inspired by a prosaic fact or two he would flow off into a whole philosophy. It was an ability which sometimes made him laughable, when small talk was required, and it had a disastrous effect upon his relations with the Queen, whom it embarrassed. It gives character and interest to all his reviews. It throve on biographical details. This was perhaps why he used the Prince Consort's death to give a biographical cast to the generalisations he wished to make in addressing the Mechanics' Institutes in 1862 or why he inserts his generalisations about beauty in objects of daily use, into an account of the life of Josiah Wedgewood in opening the

Wedgewood Museum in 1863.[26] It enables him to moralise about the unhappy Blanco White without exaggeration and without self-righteousness. It enables him to tell us at the beginning of the Patteson review, and to catch our interest in so doing, why all biographies of religious celebrities are flat and unreal; and to end it with general propositions about heroes, martyrs and saints. It enables him to discuss what he calls "the statesmanship" of O'Connell without drifting off into politics and losing sight of the human being he has so vividly brought back to life.

Gladstone's review of G. O. Trevelyan's *Life and Letters of Lord Macaulay* in the *Quarterly* for July 1876[27] carries one a stage further in this attempt to interpret Gladstone, the man of letters. For it was a consideration not only of Macaulay's life, but of his works. As a piece of literary and historical criticism it has considerable value. It also illustrates well the interplay in Gladstone between the excited imagination which stirred him to write and the systematising, generalising, moralising intellect which controlled and gave its character to what he wrote. He had first been struck by Macaulay's essay on Milton of 1825. And he had read Macaulay's *History* as he read Carlyle's books from *On Heroes, Hero-Worship[, and the Heroic in History]* to *Frederick the Great,* when they first appeared,[28] though he did not rely on these for his own historical knowledge. Sir Walter Scott, he wrote, was "a yet greater, and much greater, man" than either Carlyle or Macaulay. Of Macaulay, he continued, "the higher energies of his life were as completely summed up in the present, as those of Walter Scott were projected upon the past . . . [Macaulay] judges the men and institutions and events of other times by the instruments and measures of the present."[29] Scott revived the past with as little regard to the present as any man can have, who wishes still to remain intelligible. This comparison with Scott suggests that Gladstone was not judging Macaulay adversely merely in the light of his own, different assessment of the past. He certainly did not think of the past as progress towards a glorious culmination in the 1870s. Indeed, he was singularly divided about his own day. In the education and standard of living of the poorer classes there had been spectacular improvement; in scientific discovery there had been many marvels; in the chances of all men to share in political life there had been progress. But in the bowing of the mind to material wealth, in the extravagant waste of taxpayers' money on large armaments and inefficient administration, and in the widespread questioning of religious belief, there had been great decline. Gladstone had one thing only in common with Macaulay. He, like Macaulay, after a glance at Magna Carta, saw the true beginning of English history in the Tudor period. Then, for Gladstone, but not for Macaulay, there were three peaks of greatness: during the reign of the "sagacious" Elizabeth, during the reign of Charles I, patron of literature and the arts, and during the reign of Charles II, with its re-affirmation of Anglicanism and the glory of the Caroline divines. For Gladstone the Glorious Revolution was but the vindication of liberties inherited and already possessed. He is clearly not much enamoured of the "great dualism" which he believed entered our history with the Reformation: the dualism wherein stability faced change, authority faced freedom, Tory faced Whig.[30]

It is indicative of the good reviewer that Gladstone was, that he said nothing of this in his discussion of Macaulay as an historian. He might have said it all. Gladstone judged Macaulay adversely only in so far as he was ill-balanced. He merely suggests Macaulay had a *parti pris,* not that he was wrong, except in one thing. Macaulay's strictures on the Restoration clergy he answers sentence by sentence from an array of first-hand authorities.[31] His value as a reviewer was that he showed readers of Macaulay how to discriminate between the acceptable and the possibly prejudiced. He showed them, too, how to discriminate among Macaulay's literary merits. He put his works "among the prodigies of literature." He could not find praise too high for the liveliness and artistry of his narrative. But he deprecated his deficiency of reflection. Macaulay's mind, he wrote, "like a dredging-net at the bottom of the sea, took up all that it encountered, both bad and good, nor ever seemed to feel the burden." Gladstone, the generaliser, the systematiser, the drawer of fine distinctions, controls the whole essay and marks it with characteristic apothegms, as for example "truth depends above all on proportion and relation."[32]

To read Gladstone's writing on poetry, especially Italian poetry, is to become aware most sharply of the difference between the excited, imaginative impulse to write and the systematising, generalising, prosaic intellect which controls what Gladstone wrote. It is as if there were, indeed, two Mr. Gladstones. My "indeed" refers to the two desks in the bookroom at Hawarden. The one Mr. Gladstone was imaginative, passionate, impulsive. "He is a man of versatile mind and great impulsiveness," wrote Mr. Tennyson. The other Mr. Gladstone was balanced, methodical and controlled with an iron self-control. The one yields to the enchantment of the poetry. The *Diary* records his excitement: "Read Tennyson, Tennyson, Tennyson."[33] The other systematises, generalises, judges, lowers the temperature of the review—spoiling it sometimes. The one might have written novels like his rival Disraeli. The other ensured that he did not do so. Speaking as the common reader, I judge the rhythm of his own verse to be better than its poetry. He is best in his verse translations—I am thinking of his translation of Grossi's *Nelda*—where his imagination penetrates and reflects the poetry of the author and does not need to make poetry itself.[34] I think the more sympathetic Mr. Gladstone chanced to receive the specimens of his verse, neatly copied out in purple ink, which a young undergraduate of Magdalen sent him—his name was Oscar Wilde—for he replied seriously and kept them.

To return to my theme: "There is but one qualification I have for writing about Italian literature and language—an intense love of it."[35] One guesses that it was Gladstone's musical ear that found it so agreeable; for he did not love it until he heard it. He also wrote that scarce a word can be found in the Italian language which is not musical.[36] He learned it rapidly during an extended tour of Italy, made in 1831 on first going down from Oxford. After his return he kept up the colloquial language with a gossipy book and, more seriously, plunged into Ariosto, Tasso and Dante. He acquainted himself with Italian history from Sismondi and was next steeped in Risorgimento literature: Silvio Pellico, Ugo Foscolo, Alfieri, D'Azeglio, above all, Manzoni. Machiavelli he could not get on with, though he understood him better at a second attempt and with the *Discorsi* instead of the *Prince*.[37] But it was Dante on whom his imagination fed. He was to call him in the critique of Lord John Russell's translation, "the great Christian philosopher . . . who was like the ancient Egyptians of whom it was said they wrought upon the scale of giants with the nicety of jewellers."[38] He read first the *Inferno* and after a year's interval, while he was in Peel's administration of 1835, the *Purgatorio,* and after another two months, the *Paradiso.* He read steadily at the rate of two cantos a day and later returned to it all "with the greatest anticipations of delight."[39]

It is a pity that his one piece of writing on Dante was a half serious *jeu d'esprit* towards the end of his life.[40] It is a wonderfully clever argument to prove that Dante visited Oxford. Part at least of its cleverness lay in leaving anything like a shred of evidence to the end when it appeared to clinch a series of tendentious deductions from poetry. As it is, Dante is much present in his reviews by allusion and quotation.

Then, one day, in Italy, in 1849 Gladstone discovered Giacomo Leopardi. Everything about the poet touched his imagination from the very first reading of his name. This was in the brief, vivid account of the young poet's last days in the early summer of 1837, read in Vicenzo Gioberti's *Il Gesuita moderno* in May 1848.[41] In July a year later, Gladstone in Rome bought the four-volume edition of the *Opere* and began to read the *canti*.[42] He was bewitched. But he set the music aside to probe further into the life. One notices again how Gladstone was stirred by a life under great strain. The relationship between son and father moved him, himself all too familiar with the experience of an exacting and dominating father. He wrote to Leopardi senior, read his account of the supposed house of the Virgin Mary at Loreto, and wrote to Panizzi, Principal Librarian of the British Museum and a friend, for further information.[43]

Gladstone already deep in Homeric studies was interested in the poet's philological learning and critical powers and skill as translator of Homer. He was sympathetic, too, to the tension in Leopardi between a rationalist belief in material progress and a deep feeling about the unhappiness of men.[44] He believed he had found in G. Casati's *Il poema tartaro* the source of Leopardi's satirical poem.[45] But, set it aside as he would, it was the music of his lyrical verse, "forcible, noble, graceful" which sounded so pleasant in his ear; the matter of it "wonderfully imaginative" and the puzzle of it: so much nobility and beauty and so little sensitivity to the religious experience.

An earlier reviewer of the *Opere* in *Fraser's Magazine* had made no impression. Gladstone wrote such a review in the number of the *Quarterly* for March 1850 that Leopardi found a permanent place in England. One passage may help to explain why Gladstone succeeded. "In the Dorian metre of the *terza rima* the image of Dante comes before us; in his blank verse we think of Milton; in his lighter letters, and in the extreme elegance of touch with which he describes mental gloom and oppression, we are reminded of the grace of Cowper." English scholars of the seventeenth and eighteenth century and Shelley and Coleridge take their places in further comparisons. The earlier reviewer had enlarged to his English readers only upon Leopardi's alien quality.[46]

Tennyson was the poet of Gladstone's middle life as Leopardi was of his youth. Tennyson and Gladstone were coevals and were both friends of Arthur Hallam, Gladstone at Eton and Tennyson at Trinity College, Cambridge. Hallam wrote or talked of the one to the other and after Hallam's death, Tennyson called on Gladstone in London. In June 1855 they had a long talk in Oxford, where Tennyson had come to receive his doctorate.[47] They met [for] dinner at "The Club," that venerable [survivor] from Dr. Johnson's day to which Tennyson was elected in 1865, Gladstone being already a member.[48] In 1871 Gladstone made his first visit to Farringford. In 1876 Tennyson stayed at Hawarden. In the 1880s there were several meetings and in 1883 they were for two weeks together on a sea voyage. Hallam Tennyson records their conversation on the poets Homer, Dante, Chaucer and Shakespeare.[49]

The essay on Tennyson to which the excitement of August 1859, already referred to, led, appeared in the *Quarterly* for October 1859.[50] Hallam Tennyson in the *Memoir* of his father treats it as three reviews and records his father's high opinion of each of two and the "noble" recantation over *Maud*.[51] Gladstone's main concern was with the four *Idylls of the King* just published which "had laid hold" of him "with a power" he had not felt, even "suffered" for many years.[52] But he recalls Tennyson's *Poems, Chiefly Lyrical* of 1830, *Poems* of December 1832, draws attention to "Oenone" and "Ulysses" published in 1842. He then passes to *The Princess* of 1847 and *In Memoriam* of 1850. In all this he reflects his excitement straightforwardly; for by quoting, he lets Tennyson speak for himself. When he turns to *Maud* the other Mr. Gladstone holds the pen, and lowers the poem to the prosaic level of political economy. He thought its beginning was written in praise of war—it was published in the second year of the Crimean War—and war he argues with force and in detail, far from being a cure for materialism, the "mammon Worship" of the age, stimulated production, economic growth and the desire for wealth. This Mr. Gladstone fortunately withdraws. Mr. Gladstone of the fiery imagination writes on the *Idylls. Guinevere* has especially moved him: "No one can read the poem without feeling when it ends . . . that void in heart and mind for the want of the continuance, of which we are conscious when some noble strain of music ceases." He learnt it by heart.[53]

As literary criticism, the essay was not without value. He places Tennyson as he had placed Leopardi. "The music and the just and pure modulation of his verse carry us back not only to the fine ear of Shelley, but to Milton and to Shakespeare." He notices that Tennyson's "extraordinary felicity and force in the use of metaphor and simile" had "grown with his years, alike in abundance, truth and grace." One's assessment of Gladstone's literary *scholarship* depends upon one's view of Gladstone the system-builder, the generaliser. He has read Malory—in Southey's edition of 1817—and is well aware that Malory expresses ideas older than the reign of Edward IV in language also older than those times. But then Gladstone the systematiser writes: "Lofty example in comprehensive form is, without doubt, one of the great standing needs of our race." This the ancient world found in the heroes of Homer. "At length, after many generations, and great revolutions of mind and of events, another age arrived, like, if not equal in creative power, to that of Homer." The Christian era had begun and it, too, had its need of models. Two great epic cycles sprang into begin: that of Arthur in England, of Charlemagne on the continent. Lancelot in the one: Orlando or Roland in the other; Guinevere in one: Angelica in the other.[54] Not perhaps Arthurian scholarship as today understood! Yet the instinct which led him to read Lady Charlotte Guest's *Mabinogion*, A. F. Cruese de Lesser, *Les Chevaliers de la table ronde* (1812), Geoffrey of Monmouth and the *Niebelungenlied*, as well as to re-read *Orlando Furioso* before he wrote the sentences I have quoted, would not be miscalled, if one named it scholarly.[55]

He wrote once more on Tennyson, in 1887. Remembering Scott's second title for *Waverley*, "Tis Sixty Years Since," he compared Tennyson's *Locksley Hall Sixty Years After* with the "Locksley Hall" of 1842 and commended Tennyson's objectivity in commenting on his own age.[56]

Remembering that "letters" in the phrase "man of letters" are "literae humaniores," classical studies, I turn to Gladstone on Homer. Gladstone wrote three full versions of his ideas: ***Studies on Homer and the Homeric Age*** in three volumes, Oxford, 1858; ***Juventus Mundi. The Gods and Men of the Homeric Age,*** revising this and reducing it to one volume, London, Macmillan, 1869; and ***Landmarks in Homeric Study,*** revising the Juventus and reducing it to 160 pages, London, Macmillan, 1890. These successive revisions show the intellectual development and the constant reshaping of thought to accommodate new material, characteristic of the pragmatic Gladstone. In addition in ***Homeric Synchronism*** (London: Macmillan, 1876), he discussed specifically *The Time and Place of Homer,* (the book's subtitle) which he had already touched on in the introduction to the ***Juventus*** [***Juventus Mundi***] and alluded to in the ***Studies*** [***Studies on Homer and the Homeric Age***].

There was an element of chance in the beginning of Gladstone's work on Homer. In 1840 T. S. Brandreth, a fellow Etonian and like Gladstone a mathematician as well as a classicist, sent him the proofs of his edition of the *Iliad* and the punctilious Gladstone read them through.[57] When six years later Gladstone read Brandreth's verse translation he was stimulated to re-read *Iliad* and *Odyssey*.[58] He recovered his fluency in Greek and his "intense delight" in that world of spare beauty and began to write short essays as he read. Yet work on Homer satisfied a need in Gladstone "to fill up my time"[59] after an abrupt relaxation of parliamentary or ministerial tension. The circumstances were always the same. When he returned to Homer in 1846-7 he was temporarily without a seat in the Commons after the Maynooth crisis and the outcome was his first article on a Homeric subject.[60] When he returned again in 1855 it was after his first spell as Chancellor of the Exchequer and the ***Studies*** resulted. In July 1867 when a great struggle with Disraeli over parliamentary reform had ended, he returned yet again to Homer and wrote the ***Juventus.*** In 1890 he stood between the two peaks of Home Rule effort.

Work on Homer may have filled a need for Gladstone but publication in 1858 was still premature. It was so for three reasons. His ideas were immature and were almost at once rendered out-of-date by new discoveries and new theories, and publication was justified to himself by a perhaps passing personal motive. "The remote idea of publication of the fruits of study as intended to reach others" was a remedy for the temptation to selfishness which his great enjoyment had engendered.[61] Yet there was consistency between the three books as well as development. Their topics were always the same: the movement and settlement of peoples, religion, politics, certain literary themes and, a subject rather by itself, the geography of *Odyssey* and *Iliad*. One subject is consistently absent: the so-called Homeric question. Gladstone was familiar with books in German (e.g. by F. W. Wolf) and French (e.g. by J. B. Le Chevalier) which at the end of the eighteenth century had opened the question of the single or multiple identity of Homer and the unity or disunity of *Iliad* and *Odyssey*. From the *Studies* onwards to the end he preferred to treat Homer as one poet and the texts as fixed data. Though in the introduction to the *Juventus* he indicated Wolf's argument, he insisted that "internal evidence" supported "both the soundness of the texts as well as . . . the unity of the Poems,"[62] i.e. that they were written by one poet. He preferred the attitude of J. B. Friedrich who taught scholars to think about the *Realien of Homer.*[63] In the *Landmarks* [*Landmarks in Homeric Study*] he most eloquently pleaded for "close, minute, and comprehensive study of the matters contained in the Poems" and urged students "steadily to mine deeper and deeper into the text by observation and comparison."[64]

Of these matters the ethnographical took pride of place. He began the *Studies* by trying to solve the puzzle of Homer's apparent use of three different "appellations" to describe one people. He was a most observant reader, tabulating the different ways the words Danaan, Achaian and Argive were used in different passages, adding a fourth word, Hellas, and going through the catalogues of ships in the *Iliad* and the genealogies to find other racial terms and counting the number of times the four main words were used. He concluded with a scheme of settlement. The Pelasgians were "the bulk of the Greeks . . . under the sway of ruling tribes or families belonging to another race," the Achaian, more warlike, of later arrival and rulers wherever they were. Danaan was used to refer to the soldiery; Argos, a geographical term, to refer to the lowlands of the Peloponnese and Hellas to describe northern or middle Greece. What had begun as tentative speculations became premises for fresh arguments and the discussion ended with the surprising remark that Homer's purpose "was to unite more closely the elements of the Achaian nation, not to record that they had once been separate."[65]

In the *Juventus* the emphasis on nationality was even stronger, because he began by describing the pastoral and cultivating Pelasgians as the indigenous inhabitants of both the Greek and Italian peninsulas and the Achaians as a greater people coming in from outside, eventually, he suggested, to absorb them. He then gave his proofs. He dealt with the other racial and geographic terms, but now had more to say about the Phoenicians whose influence he rightly showed came in through Crete. His etymological evidence, confined in the *Studies* to the names of heroes and legendary characters, was now more extensive. He listed words similar in Greek and Latin to show that these related to pastoral life and tillage, but rarely to religion, the use of metals or to war. A modern reader is more impressed by his

force and learning than convinced by his argument, for it is not clear whether he used this discovery to prove that the Pelasgians were the original people in both peninsulas or whether this is the premise which has led him to seek out the similar words. The rhetorical conclusion was still the same; Homer was "intensely national in feeling,"[66] and he repeated the sentence already quoted from the *Studies.*

The *Landmarks* is an even more marked indication that for Gladstone nationality was the supreme force of his own age. He stated at the beginning that Homer's purpose was "before all things" national. The book with very little exaggeration might be called "in praise of the Achaian nation." He ascribed great importance to the Phoenician element in Greece and claimed that Ulysses and Ithaca showed "distinct Phoenician characters." But "the two ideas in Homer that are really cardinal, central, generative, are the nation, and its reflection in the Thearchy, or Olympic society." Homer "had to launch into the world the Greek idea," a nation and its religion.[67]

The idea of Thearchy had not been present in Gladstone's first discussion of Homeric religion. He had begun in the *Studies* with a theory never widely acceptable and rendered quite old-fashioned by the sociological approach to religion founded by Johann Bachofen within three years of its publication.[68] Gladstone rightly appreciated the religious sense of the Homeric heroes, their piety, their respect for the supernatural world,[69] but for him religion could never be the mere product of social conditions though he came to understand how much it was influenced by them. For the young Gladstone the truths of divine revelation and of Christianity, which embodied it, were absolutes and the only way to validate Homeric religion was to give it some share in these truths. This he did by postulating an original revelation of one God to all people for all time and drawing a distinction between Homer's "tradi-tive" Gods (who preserved the tradition of it), as Zeus, Hera, Apollo and Athene, and his "invented" gods and goddesses. Aphrodite and Ares, for example, were mere "personalized attributes" and without the special powers which Gladstone had observed in Apollo and Athene, in relation, for example, to death. Indeed, Apollo, the son of Latona, might have been a kind of pre-figuring of Christ, born of the seed of Woman, the Deliverer. But the reflective reader is not sure quite where Gladstone is leading him, for the argument up to now has demanded survival not foreshadowing. So far he had argued that by the time of Homer the original revelation had been corrupted, or rather, disintegrated, so that the idea of one God had been broken up into many gods and a tradition of it only preserved in those whom he had called "tradi-tive." He had shown that Genesis recorded the original revelation and (without answering obvious objections) all the elements of Christianity. He had strengthened his argument of corruption by analogy with the parallel Hebrew corruption which had made the original revelation the monopoly of a single people.[70] The modern reader is impressed by his exact and detailed knowledge of Old Testament and Hebrew sources rather than convinced by his eccentric argument.

In the *Juventus* he made no attempt to sustain the idea of an original universal revelation and its disintegration. He now wrote that "Homer from living in the midst of an intermixture and fusion of bloods constantly proceeding in Greece, acquired a vast amount of materials, and by his skillful use of them exercised an immense influence on the construction of the Greek religion."[71] Gladstone included Egyptian and Assyrian elements among those materials, but is especially well-informed on the Phoenician.[72] He devoted twenty-one sections to individual gods and goddesses and the ideas connected with them. He showed how together they composed a single Olympian society "or Polity formed on the human model with a king, an aristocracy and even a people or multitude."[73] After calling these sections a discussion of the Olympian system, he ended by calling this the Olympian religion.[74] In the *Landmarks* which he concluded with an essay on the Assyrian tablets and their points of contrast with the Homeric texts, Gladstone put his whole emphasis on Homer, the maker of "a formula of concord, a *modus vivendi*" among the multitude of religious traditions among which he felt himself to live. "Divine revelation is not here supposed," he wrote, while insisting that religious unity was the necessary condition of national unity. He had made Homer "the maker of a religion" as well as "the maker of a nation."[75]

Like the discussions of nationality and religion the discussion on politics was governed by a personal conviction. He believed in free government and he believed in its Greek, even Homeric origin. The idealization of Greek institutions was so characteristically English that it has been said that all German histories of Greece after the mid-century were an answer to George Grote who typified it. His twelve volumes were read by Gladstone as they came out between 1845 and 1856. Gladstone plainly stated in the *Studies* that all the best ideas on government were to be seen in their ancient form in the *Iliad* and *Odyssey*. There "the strength and simplicity" of social relations was remarkable and the characters in the poems were pervaded by "an intense political spirit."[76] He developed his meaning by showing that alongside the characteristic features of a patriarchical society—he had discussed Homeric kingship at length—"we find the full, constant and effective use, of two great instruments of popular government . . . namely, publicity and persuasion."[77] He illustrated this from the eight assemblies of the Greek army and from Telemachus's assembly in the *Odyssey*. He noticed how much of the *Iliad* was composed of speeches and how each

speech answered another one. In the liveliest part of the discussion he characterized each speaker in turn. Gladstone on the art of persuasion became Gladstone on his own oratory. "And if we regard it," he wrote of Thersites' speech, "as every speech should be regarded, with reference to some paramount purpose, it is really senseless and incompetent."[78] The reader senses a note of personal experience. He began in the *Juventus* too by showing that all ideas of free government were derived from the Greeks and listed them as: responsibility in rulers, their use of persuasion rather than force, of open rather than secret methods, their reconciliation of freedom with order and their rule by law. After again discussing kingship, he noticed the absence of ideas such as the submission of the minority to the vote of the majority and of law-making as later understood, but "in the Homeric ideas upon Polity perhaps the most remarkable of all is the distinction accorded to the power of speech." "The voice and the sword are the twin powers by which the Greek world is governed."[79] Corporate or political life was intense and the organ of consensus or "the common soul" was *Tis*, often translated as public opinion.[80] He characterized individual speakers more tersely and without the personal note of the *Studies*. In the *Landmarks* he began the political discussion with slavery, left to the last in the *Juventus*. He soon dismissed it since it had so little importance in the Homeric world, and moved on to kingship. He summed up his first conclusion: "the Poet sets a high value on the personal freedom of the human being as such." He made a second point: "another characteristic and singularly striking idea of the Poems is the power of the spoken word."[81] The Greek epithet, "glory-giving", was applied only to success in speech or battle. There was no higher gift. It could change public opinion or *Tis*.[82] He remarked that styles of speaking were varied and "singularly diversified," but he did not consider individual speakers.

To turn to literary themes: he treated them in volume three of the *Studies,* more briefly in the *Juventus* and largely omitted them from the Landmarks. He commented on Homer's similes, his epithets especially of movement, his special feeling for the horse and for some other animals, his use of number, not as an instrument of calculation but as an inexact yet vivid tool of description, and his attitude to color, where he described intensity rather than named a pigment. On the geography of *Odyssey* and *Iliad* he had to change his ideas between 1858 and 1890 but in all three works he was ingenious, mathematically fascinated and immensely knowledgeable.

From 1858 onwards Gladstone treated Homer as a real person, living either at or soon after the time when he composed the poems for oral recitation. Nevertheless he faced the question, When did Homer live?—and sought an answer. His method was to consider what could be learnt of the use of metals from the texts and from archaeological evidence and to weigh up what could be learnt by comparisons between ancient Greece and ancient Egypt and Assyria. Gladstone here had lasting importance since he contributed to making widely known the results of excavations and the deciphering of Egyptian papyri and Assyrian tablets.[83] I illustrate this from his relations with H. Schliemann who was associated with the excavations at Troy and Mycene. Gladstone met Schliemann in London in the summer of 1875. In company with the historian of eighteenth-century England, Lord Stanhope, Gladstone attended him to the Society of Antiquaries, heard his lecture on Troy and intervened in the discussion to question his dating.[84] They subsequently corresponded. He read some of the German edition of Schliemann's book on Troy when it first came out in 1874, but after the lecture, relied for working purposes on the English edition, *Troy and its Remains,* which by then had appeared. He also read German commentaries. Then he wrote a lengthy preface for Schliemann's *Mycene: a narrative of excavations and discoveries at Mycene and Tyrene* [*Mycenae: A Narrative of Researches and Discoveries at Mycenae and Tiryns*] (London, 1878). Meanwhile in **Homeric Synchronism** he described Schliemann's excavations at Hissarlik: the burnt-out town in the fourth layer down and the remains of successive later towns in the three layers above. He gave his reasons for accepting Hissarlik as the site of Troy. He passed on to the general layout of Priam's Palace, the wall and the Scanian Gate, the remains of objects in daily use, the two headdresses and the six blades of silver. He gave his reasons for accepting Schliemann's interpretation of it all, adding conjectures of his own. He concluded that Homer supplied reliable evidence on Greek society, and its customs, of a period just before the time at which he himself lived. He next dismissed claims that Homer was the author of the *Hymn to Apollo,* which also survived from prehistoric Greece, or was the blind poet of Chios. These dismissals helped to give the reader confidence in Gladstone's argument on what mattered most: the date when Homer lived. Here he used the recently established Egyptian chronology and especially that of the years 1316 to 1226 B.C. because he found "correspondences" between the Egyptian nineteenth dynasty and the material for dating which Homer supplied in the genealogies of his heroes and in the legends he recounted about happenings before the siege of Troy. His conclusion was that 1316 and 1226 were respectively the earliest and the latest dates at which the siege of Troy could have taken place. According to the modern view that Homer (whatever is meant by that name) may have lived in the late bronze age, perhaps the eighth century B.C. Gladstone put him too early, but some of his method is acceptable. The interest of it all is in what it shows us of Gladstone's mind. He argued like a barrister in a court of law, determined to convince. He was deeply and imaginatively stirred by the worlds archaeology, Egyptology and Assyriology were opening up.

Gladstone had always been interested in the plot of the *Iliad.* In the *Studies* he noticed the problem in composition Homer faced: the double mechanism of the plot.[85] Homer had to maintain a clear superiority in the Greeks because they were going to win and yet make the Trojans an enemy worth beating. In the **Studies** he noticed the other duality: two stories, one of heroes, one of gods. In the **Juventus** he made less of this last, only showing how the balance was redressed for the Trojans by "the Theotechny, or divine movement of the Poem."[86] In both the **Studies** and the **Juventus** he showed how Homer succeeded in making Achilles head and shoulders above the other heroes yet never allowing Ulysses to be diminished by him and in keeping Achilles supreme while making Agamemnon and Hector great men in relation to him. In the **Landmarks** he wrote only that there was not a single episode which did not contribute to the structure of the whole and that Homer had surmounted both the difficulty of the twofold movement and that of proportion as between Greeks and Trojans and between Achilles and the other heroes.[87] He omitted here what he had made the primary interest of the plot in the **Juventus**: the theme of justice. There, after writing that the *Iliad* was not about the fate of Troy but about Achilles, "in whose marvelous character the Greek nationality is to find its supreme satisfaction," he went on to name the successive steps in its development. Achilles had withdrawn from the battlefield in wrath. The Greeks will show that they can get on without him. They failed, so the Wrath had its first triumph. The next step was the second triumph of the Wrath, or the second defeat of the Greeks. Then came the slaying of Patroclus, the dear companion of Achilles. "That which was to be the last triumph of his wounded pride . . . now becomes the cause of an agony so intense, as by far to surpass . . . the emotions he has suffered from anger." So Achilles was punished for allowing "indignation to degenerate into revenge"[88] as the Greeks had been punished for the wrong they had done or allowed to be done to Achilles. Next, Homer turned, wrote Gladstone, upon the Trojans and Hector was slain. The Trojan king then repented and offered reparation which was justly refused. Next the dishonoring of Hector's body became another crime for which Achilles must pay the price. Gladstone's imagination had clearly been fired, but Gladstone the systemiser had invented a theory of retributive justice which simply did not exist in prehistoric Greece.

To complete this vindication of Gladstone, man of letters, I should like to revert to his literary reviewing and to notice that his habit in reviewing novels was to recount the story first, to comment in doing so on the character-drawing and then to discuss the novel's central idea. This was his method with the review of *Ellen Middleton,* already mentioned, of *From Oxford to Rome* by Elizabeth Harris in the *Quarterly* for January 1847 and of *Robert Elsmere* by Mrs. Humphrey Ward in the *Nineteenth Century* for May 1888.[89] All had the human stuff and religious interest which always caught his imagination. He had plenty of material on which to draw for comparisons and to exercise his generalising habit; for he was well read in Scott, Jane Austen and the new publications. He read as they appeared the novels of George Eliot, the Brontës, William Thackeray—*Vanity Fair* he thought in 1849, "a work of genius, to be admired in some respects" and read a second time in 1864[90]—Mrs. Gaskell, Dumas, Trollope, Disraeli, Victor Hugo, but not Dickens, except for *Pickwick.*

His review of one more novel deserves comment, *For the Right* by Karl Emil Franços. This was contributed to a new series which Gladstone opened in the *Nineteenth Century,* of occasional articles called "Noticeable Books."[91] The novel was translated from the German. It is not surprising that it should fall into Gladstone's hands, for his reputation among continental liberals was such that it might well have been sent to him. One is more surprised that he should have thought it so important—until one grasps its central idea. The hero is a quite humble man, a village magistrate. The plot is summed up in his nature. "He is impelled by an enthusiasm for justice, alike passionate, persistent and profound." All Gladstone's generalising, system-building, balancing was governed by the search for justice as he understood it. Aristotle's *Politics* was a strong influence on all Gladstone's thought. Gladstone's obsession with justice—justice in the sense of balance of interests, what he called right relationship—runs through all his thought. His appeal to justice made him popular with the people, men like the dour hard-working men from which his Scottish forebears came; his pretension to a monopoly of it alienated from him in the end the class to which by education, marriage and occupation he belonged. When he thought he had found justice he proclaimed it alike in politics, domestic, foreign or Irish, and in his literary work, though "proclaimed" is too loud a word to use here. Yet it may perhaps be the bridge between the two sides of his personal nature, both nourishing the fiery imagination of the one and directing the intellect of the other.

I should like in conclusion to speak of Gladstone's love of books. He wrote: "In a room well filled with them no one has felt or can feel solitary." They are "the allies of the thought of man," his means of talking with "the vast human procession" of the dead. He understood the desirable harmony between subject-matter, paper, type, ink and binding "the dress in which a book went forth into the world."[92] He knew better than most others how to shelve and arrange books and something of his knowledge, so I am told, survives in Bodley's stacks.

The present London Library, as well as St. Deiniol's, is a memorial to him. He with Carlyle and ten others were founders of the London Library and composed the committee that met on 18 July 1840 to found the Library which opened in the following May.[93]

Nothing better bespeaks the love of books of a bookish man than a characteristic manner of quoting—in Gladstone's case of quoting poetry. I refer to quotation external to the argument, used not to convey his meaning, nor to provide evidence or authority, but to grace his text. I have not counted the quotations from Tennyson in the article on Tennyson; I have considered some 133 quotations taken from some 60 articles and addresses, political, speculative and literary. Leaving aside quotations from Scripture which outnumber all the rest, I can say that Homer he alludes to most often, but Virgil, Dante, Shakespeare are the poets he most often quotes. Next in frequency is Tennyson, then Wordsworth, Milton and Horace; in the next group are Juvenal, Gray, Goethe, Manzoni and Shelley. He quotes a single time from Chaucer, Dryden, Voltaire, Schiller, Thomas Campbell and others. One notices the range and the element of standard Great Authors. Of course he quotes as all quoters do, to distance something that is difficult to say directly as when he apologises for vehemence with "Let Kent be unmannerly when Lear is mad"; he quotes like others to notice an especially happy way of saying something one has already oneself said as when he quotes Gray "And blended form, with artful strife/ the strength and harmony of life"; he quotes to compliment his readers by assuming they share his own enjoyment, as when he disposes of Annie Besant's inflated self-satisfaction as capable of bearing her through tracts of air, buoyant and copious enough to carry the Dircaean swan, in allusion to Horace's ode to Pindar.

But the interesting quotations bear a personal stamp. This is caused by their being called up by some association of ideas personal to himself. One can show that they *are* called from memory because the ***Diaries*** notice when he read the works from which they come. They do not come from what he is reading when he is writing, but from something read long before or some time before. The quotations are lines that *he* has remembered, because they chime with some thought of *his own,* not because they are especially poetic, not because they are especially important in conveying the meaning of the poet who has written them. Dante's "in la sua voluntade e nostra pace," "in God's will is our peace," he quotes several times either alone or with neighbouring lines and he seldom uses a quotation more than once. It tells us more about Gladstone than about Dante. Tom Moore's *Lallah Rookh* (1817) was not a likely place to go deliberately for an encouraging passage for undergraduates. Yet he finds there, "And when he dies he leaves a lofty name / A light, a landmark on the cliffs of fame" and uses it both in his **"Inaugural"**

(1860) and in his **"Valedictory Address"** (1865) as Rector of Edinburgh University. To go where Gladstone's quotations lead one is to follow the path of his thought and his personal literary enjoyment.

Gladstone, man of letters, was a quieter character than the man in politics. Among his books he is open-minded, excitable yet balancing arguments on both sides of what he has read, and then releasing his mind in writing. He is a private, enclosed man, who yet must needs come forth from his privacy. He wrote:

> The authority of literary inquiries depends on care, comprehensiveness, and precision, in collecting facts, and on great caution in concluding from them. There is no democracy so levelling as the Republic of Letters. Liberty and equality here are absolute, though fraternity may be sometimes absent on a holiday. And a literary labour, be it critical, be it technical, be it archaeological, when it has done its immediate duty of disposing of a cause . . . must come into the light, and be turned round and round . . .[94]

He may not much have relished the coming forth from his books into print, but the need seems to have been stronger than the man.

Notes

1. *Cambridge History of English Literature,* xiv (1916) p. 135.

2. Bryce to Mrs. Gladstone, 18 Jan. 1884, Bodleian Library, MS Bryce 11, fol. 79.

3. *The State in its relations with the Church* (1838); *Church Principles considered in their Results* (1840).

4. M. R. D. Foot and H. C. G. Matthew (editors) *The Gladstone Diaries* (1968-) vol. iii. 26 Nov. 1842.

5. Worthington in fact published with Smith Elder, not Murray, but told Gladstone of Murray's advice; see Gladstone to Worthington, copies, 8, 9, Dec. 1842, British Library, Gladstone Papers, Add. Ms. 44527, fol. 106; Worthington to Gladstone, 9, 13, Dec. 1842, Add. Ms. 44359, fols. 238, 291; see also *Diaries,* iii.28, 30 Nov., 3, 6, 8, 12, 16, 20 Dec. 1842.

6. The *Globe* and *Chronicle,* according to Worthington.

7. Worthington to Gladstone, 18 Apr., 4/5 May, 2 Sept., undated, 13, 20 Sept. 1843, Add. Ms. 44360, fols. 118, 133, 239, 243, 245, 249.

8. Reprinted in W. E. Gladstone, *Gleanings of Past Years 1843-78* (1879) vol. v. p. 1, vol. iii. p. 1, reviewing respectively an anonymous *Letter to the Bishops of the Church of England on the necessity of Liturgical Adjustment* (1843), Rev. J. Sutcliffe,

A Letter to . . . Bishop of London (1843), Rev. Dr. Holloway, *Reply to the Charge of . . . Bishop of London* (1842), Rev. C. J. Yorke, *A Respectful Address to . . . Bishop of London* (1842); *Theses of Erastus,* translated with an introduction by Dr. R. Lee (1844); *Diaries,* iii. 31 Aug., 3 Sept. 1844.

9. *Diaries,* iii. 4 Feb. 1844.

10. T. Mozley, *Reminiscences* (1882) ii. pp. 310ff; *Diaries,* iii. 236, footnote 11.

11. *Inferno,* v. 73-142; Lord John Russell's translation is in *Literary Souvenir* (1844); Gladstone's review in *English Review,* i. p. 164 (Apr. 1844); *Ellen Middleton: A Tale* by Lady Georgiana Fullerton, 3 vols. (1844) *English Review,* i. (Jul. 1844)336; quotation from Gladstone to Manning, 8 Apr. 1844, Add. Ms. 44247, fol. 211.

12. *Diaries,* iii, 1 Apr. 1844.

13. *Diaries,* iv, 15 Feb.-8 Apr., 22 Aug.-8 Sept., 26 Oct.-3 Nov. 1848 for reading of Strauss but op. 24 Mar. 1847; on 3 Nov. he commented on Strauss "a painful book but has its uses as well as dangers"; 21-25 Dec. 1865 for Seeley when he also "recommended Renan," continuing with the *Vie de Jésus* until 2 Jan. 1866; his first reading unrecorded but v. 30 Jan.-14 Feb. 1858 he was reading Renan, *Études d'histoire religieuse* (1858) and vi. 24 Jan. 1864 W. Lee, *Recent forms of unbelief: some account of Renan's "Vie de Jésus"* (1864).

14. "J. R. Seeley, *Ecce Homo: A Survey of the Life and Works of Jesus Christ* (1865)," *Good Words,* ix (Jan., Feb., Mar. 1868)33, 80, 177; reprinted in *Gleanings [Gleanings of Past Years],* iii. 41.

15. "Dawn of Creation and of Worship," *Nineteenth Century,* xviii (Nov. 1885) 685; "Proem to Genesis. A Plea for a Fair Trial," *Nineteenth Century* xix (Jan. 1886) 1; both reprinted in *Gleanings,* viii. 1 and 40.

16. "The Lord's Day," *Church Monthly,* viii (Mar., Apr. 1895) 51, 75.

17. *Diaries,* iii. 15 Sept., 12 Oct.-13 Dec. 1844 *passim.*

18. See J. Murray to Gladstone, 15 Nov. 1844 and encl. and further letters esp. 21 Nov. and 3 Dec. also enclosing letters from Lockhart to Murray, Add. Ms. 44259, fols. 43ff; see also Lockhart to Gladstone, direct, 18 Dec. 1844, Add. Ms. 44237, fols. 371ff; Gladstone to Manning, 14, 17, 23 Nov., 3, 6, 24 Dec. 1884, Add. Ms. 44247, fols. 226-246; the *Diaries* record a visit to Lockhart on 5 Dec. to go through his corrections and modify the article accordingly; review reprinted in *Gleanings,* v. 81.

19. *Daily Telegraph,* 25 Jan. 1898.

20. "Dr. Döllinger's Posthumous Remains," *Speaker*, 30 Aug. 1890; "Life and Speeches of the Prince Consort," *Contemporary Review*, xxvi (June 1875) 1; "Life of the Prince Consort," *Church Quarterly Review*, iii (Jan. 1877) 465; v (Jan. 1878) 469; all three reprinted, *Gleanings*, i. 23-130; "Sheridan," *Nineteenth Century*, xxxiv (June 1896) 1037.

21. *Quarterly Review*, lxxvi (June 1845) 164; cxxxvii (Oct. 1874) 458. *Nineteenth Century* xxv (Jan. 1889) 149; the first two reprinted, *Gleanings*, ii. 1 and 213.

22. Lockhart to Gladstone, 7, 19 June 1845, Add. Ms. 44237, fols. 379, 383.

23. He wrote of the review in the *Christian Remembrancer*, "it breathes, mine does not," *Diaries*, iii. 3 Jul. 1845; for quotations see *Gleanings*, ii. 2.

24. See *Nineteenth Century*, xxvi. (Oct. 1889) 602.

25. See Gladstone to Lacaita, referring especially to his *Letter to Aberdeen* (1851) on the Neapolitan prisons, 11 Oct. 1855, Add. Ms. 44233, fol. 66; for hostile review of his translation of Farini's *Stato Romano*, see *Quarterly Review*, xc (Dec. 1851) 226; for his own review of that book see *Edinburgh Review*, xcv (Apr. 1852) 357.

26. Both these addresses he reprinted, *Gleanings*, "Death of the Prince Consort," i. 1, "Wedgwood," ii. 181.

27. Reprinted *Gleanings*, ii. 265.

28. For Carlyle see *Diaries*, iii. 6 Sept. 1841 (*On Heroes, Hero Worship. . . .*) 28 Dec. 1842, 5 Jan. 1843 (*Sartor Resartus*) 22, 24, 27 Jul. 1843 (*Past and Present*) iv. 18 Feb. 1850 (*Latter-day papers*) v. 25-27 Aug. 1857 (*On German Romances*, 1827, and *Biographical Essays*) v. 19 Oct. 1858, vi. 9 Jul. 1862 (*Frederick the Great*) 22 Dec. 1862-17 Jan. 1863 (*Oliver Cromwell's Letters & Speeches*). For Macaulay see *Diaries*, iii. 3 Nov. 1842 (*Lays of Ancient Rome*) iv. 2-19 Feb. and occasionally up to 9 June 1849 (*History*, vols. i & ii) v. 18 Dec. 1855-5 Jan. 1856 (*History*, vols. iii & iv) 27 May-15 June 1858 (*Historical Essays*) 10-16 Mar. 1860. (*Biographies in Encyclopaedia Britannica*) vi. 23-27 Mar. 1861 (*History*, vol. v).

29. See *Gleanings*, ii. 286-7, 336; for comparison of Macaulay with Carlyle whose "licentious, though striking, peculiarities of style" he deplored, pp. 287-8.

30. As the *Diaries* indicate Gladstone relied for historical knowledge in addition to Burnet, Clarendon, Strype, on D. Hume, *History of England* (1754-61), Henry Hallam, *Constitutional History of England*, 3 vols. (1827). P. H. Stanhope (Mahon), *History of England from the Peace of Utrecht to the Peace of Versailles*, 7 vols. (1836-54), J. A. Froude, *History of England from the Fall of Wolsey to the Death of Elizabeth*, 12 vols. (1856-70), J. Lingard, *History of England*, 8 vols. (1819-30), T. E. May, *Constitutional History of England, 1760-1860*, 2 vols. (1861), W. N. Massey, *A History of England during the Reign of George III* (1855-60). The views about the past summarised here are gleaned from a variety of parliamentary speeches and a number of articles, see especially "Kin Beyond Sea," *Gleanings*, 1.210 for the "great dualism"; "Wedgwood", *Gleanings* ii. 201; "The Sixteenth Century arraigned before the Nineteenth," *Gleanings* iii. 227 for Elizabeth; "Examination of the Reply of the Neapolitan Government," *Gleanings* iv. 127 for Charles I.

31. *Gleanings*, ii. 320ff. quoting John Eachard, *Contempt of the Clergy* (1670), Anthony Wood, *Athenae Oxonienses* (1691-2), Gilbert Burnet, *Pastoral Care, History of his Own Time* (1723-34). Isaac Barrow, *Opuscula* [1687], Clarendon, *History of the Rebellion* [1807], White Kennet, *Collectanea Curiosa* [1781], John Walker, *Sufferings of the Clergy* [1807], Jeremy Collier, *Immorality and Profaneness of the English Stage* (1698). Barnabas Oley, preface to George Herbert's *Country Parson* (1675) and Herbert himself.

32. For quotations see respectively *Gleanings*, ii. 341, 339, 290, 311.

33. *Diaries*, v. 13 Aug. 1859.

34. *Fraser's Magazine*, lx (Dec. 1859) 668.

35. Gladstone to Panizzi, 4 Dec. 1849, quoted from the Panizzi papers in the British Library by D. E. Rhodes, "The Composition of Mr. Gladstone's Essay on Leopardi," *Italian Studies*, viii (1953) p. 70.

36. *Gleanings*, vi. 112-13.

37. *Diaries* i. 5 Mar., 2 Apr. 1832; ii. 9, 15 Aug. 1833, 28 Mar.-16 Apr. 1836 for Ariosto and Tasso; 9-28 Feb., 27 Mar., 15, 22 May-1 June 1833 for G. Pecchio, *Osservazioni semiserie di un Esule sull' Inghilterra* (1831); 6, 8-16 Apr. 1833 for Sismondi, taking full notes and recording his delight; 3-19 June 1833, 18-29 Mar., 12-16 Jul. 1834 for Silvio Pellico; 23-28 Aug. 1833; 12 Aug. 1833 for *I Promessi Sposi*; 2 Mar.-23 May 1833 for d'Azeglio, *Ettore Fieramosca*; 9 Mar., 30 Oct. 1834, 28 Apr.-24 May 1836 (i.e. after Dante) for Machiavelli; references continue at intervals throughout later vols.

38. *English Review*, vol. i, no. 1 (Apr. 1844) 164, 180.

39. *Diaries,* ii. 16 Sept.-14 Oct. 1834, 10 Nov.-4 Dec. 1835, 23 Feb.-23 Mar. 1836. He translated some of the *Paradiso* into blank verse, found cantos iii and iv "veramente deliziosi" and xviii "delightful"; 11-23 Nov. 1836 for his return to Dante.

40. "Did Dante study in Oxford?" *Nineteenth Century,* xxxi (June 1892) 1032.

41. In vol. i. p. cxcviii in the edition of 1846-7 in 5 vols., *Diaries,* iv. 4 May-18 June, 24 Aug.-11 Sept., 16 Sept.-12 Dec. 1848, records his reading and note taking.

42. *Diaries,* iv. 28 Jul. 1849; see also D. E. Rhodes, "The Composition of Mr. Gladstone's Essay on Leopardi," *Italian Studies,* viii (1953) 59.

43. *Diaries* iv. 12 Aug. 1849 records his letter to "Count Recanati" and 7 Oct. 1849 his reading of Count Monaldo Leopardi, *La Santa casa di Loreto* (1841); for letters to Panizzi, see D. E. Rhodes, p. 59.

44. See Sebastiano Timpanaro, *Classicismo e illuminismo nell' ottocento italiano* (Pisa 1965) pp. 150-1.

45. I.e. his [Homer's] *Batrachomyomachia. Diaries,* iv. 9, 13 Aug. 1849 records his reading of G. Casati, *Il poema tartaro,* 2 vols. (1803); 6 Oct.-10 Nov. 1849 records his reading of the prose works and letters of Leopardi, the latter sent to him by Panizzi, and then the writing of his essay, his "working on" and revising it.

46. "Giacomo Leopardi," *Quarterly Review,* lxxxvi (Mar. 1850) 295 reprinted in *Gleanings,* ii. 89 and 128 for quoted passages; for first review see *Fraser's Magazine,* xxxviii (Dec. 1848) 659.

47. See Hallam Tennyson, *Tennyson. A Memoir* (1899) 138, 324.

48. *Diaries,* v. 21 Apr. 1857 records first time he dined having been just elected.

49. Tennyson, *Memoir* [*Tennyson. A Memoir*], pp. 433, 507, 651-6.

50. *Quarterly Review,* cvi (Oct. 1859) 454; reprinted *Gleanings,* ii. 131.

51. Tennyson, *Memoir,* pp. 250, 336, 373.

52. *Diaries,* v. 14 Jul. 1859.

53. *Gleanings,* ii. 169; cp. "I have always thought that the prettiest English hexametre is Longfellow's 'when she had passed it seemed like the ceasing of exquisite music,'" *Evangeline,* part i line 62, Gladstone to Granville, 5 Nov. 1876, Ramm, *Political Correspondence of Mr Gladstone and Lord Granville* (1961) i. 17. *Diaries,* v. 14 Oct. 1859 for learning of *Guinevere.*

54. *Gleanings,* ii. quotations respectively at pp. 175, 159, 148-50.

55. See *Diaries,* v. 14 Aug.-15 Sept., 21 Sept.-1 Oct., 1 Nov. 1859 as well as references in the article to these works.

56. *Nineteenth Century,* xxi (Jan. 1887) 1.

57. *Diaries,* iii. 1 Dec. 40. See *Ilias. Littera digamma restituta ad metri leges redegit, et notatione brevi illustravit T. S. Brandreth* (London, 1841). The section on Homer was not in the original lecture.

58. T. S. Brandreth, *The Iliad translated,* 2 vols. (London, 1846).

59. *Diaries,* iii. 15 Jan. 1847.

60. *Quarterly Review,* lxxxi. (Sept. 1847), article iii. pp. 381-417, reviewing Karl Lachmann, *Uber die ersten zehn Bücher des Ilias* (1839) and his *fernere Betrachtungen* (1843).

61. *Diaries,* iii. 6 Nov. 46.

62. [W. E. Gladstone] *Juventus* [*Juventus Mundi. The Gods and Men of the Homeric Age* (London, 1869)], p. 24.

63. *Juventus* pp. 14ff. See J. B. Friedrich, *Die Realien in der Iliade und Odyssen* (Erlangen, 1851). He also mentions E. A. W. Buchholz, whose *Die Homerischen Realien,* 3 vols. (Berlin, 1871-85) was not yet published. *Die Realien* are the realities of the Homeric text.

64. [W. E. Gladstone] *Landmarks* [*Landmarks in Homeric Studies* (London, 1890)], pp. 6, 12.

65. [W. E. Gladstone] *Studies* [*Studies on Homer and the Homeric Age,* 3 vols. (Oxford, 1858)], i. 370, 373, 386, 423; i. 361 for the final quotation.

66. *Juventus,* p. 38.

67. *Landmarks,* pp. 30, 55, 88.

68. J. J. Bachofen, *Versuch über der Grabersymbolik der Alten* (1859) and *Das Mutterrecht. Eine Unternehmung über der Genikrotie der Alten* (1861). Modern editions of his works belong only to 1938 (Berlin) and 1943 (Basle). An English translation, *Myth, Religion and Mother right* came from Princeton in 1973.

69. Cp. Jasper Griffin, *Homer on Life and Death* (Oxford, 1980) pp. 40-44, 148-78, 201-2.

70. *Studies,* ii. 3, 5, 47-52.

71. *Juventus,* p. 179.

72. In January 1868 he had published a review of Ernst Renan, *Mission de Phoenicie,* 3 vols. (1864-7), *Quarterly Review,* cxxiv article vii. 199-225.

73. *Juventus,* p. 193.

74. *Juventus,* p. 377.

75. *Landmarks,* pp. 56, 83, 87-8.

76. *Studies,* iii. 2-3.

77. *Studies,* iii. 7.

78. *Studies,* iii, 122-3.

79. *Juventus,* p. 431.

80. *Juventus,* p. 436.

81. *Landmarks,* pp. 98, 99.

82. *Landmarks,* p. 100.

83. He relied much on F. Lenormant, *Histoire des premieres civilizations* (1874), F. J. Lauth, *Homer und Aegypten* (1867) and in a minor way on G. Rawlinson, *The five great monarchies of the ancient eastern world,* 4 vols. (1862-67). Lauthlater (1877) published *Aegyptische chronologie.*

84. *Diaries,* ix. 24 June 75 and note 8.

85. Cp. *Juventus,* p. 490.

86. *Juventus,* p. 491.

87. *Landmarks,* pp, 106ff.

88. *Juventus,* pp. 493ff.

89. He reprinted no reviews of novels except that of *Robert Elsmere* for which see *Gleanings,* viii. 77.

90. *Diaries,* iv. 11-23 Jan. 1849, vi. 16 Aug.-17 Sept. 1864, "on this reperusal after a long interval I think it a very remarkable and on the whole a *good* book."

91. *Nineteenth Century,* xxv (Feb. 1889) 213 for first of the series to which Gladstone contributed an account of Margaret Lee, *Faithful and Unfaithful* (1889); xxv (Apr. 1889) 615 for account of *For the Right.*

92. "On books and the housing of them," *Nineteenth Century,* xxvii (Mar. 1890) 384.

93. The minute books of the committee of the London Library show that Gladstone with Carlyle and ten others attended its first meeting, 18 July 1840, Lord Lyttelton in the chair. He was again present, Carlyle absent, on 25 July. Meetings were then intermitted until Nov. 1840. Gladstone did not attend again until 3 Feb. 1841, an important meeting since it appointed the first librarian and the first committee for purchasing books, and 20 Feb., when the "laws" of the Library were drawn up. In Apr. 1841 he was appointed to the general committee for the first year of the Library's existence. My thanks are due to Mr. Higgins, the Deputy Librarian, for showing me the minute books. See also *Diaries,* iii, 18, 25 Jul. 1840, 3, 11, 20, 27, Feb., 5 Mar., 26 Apr. 1841.

94. *Gleanings,* vi. 178.

Nancy Parrott Hickerson (essay date spring 1983)

SOURCE: Hickerson, Nancy Parrott. "Gladstone's Ethnolinguistics: The Language of Experience in the Nineteenth Century." *Journal of Anthropological Research* 39, no. 1 (spring 1983): 26-41.

[*In the following essay, Hickerson considers the linguistic and anthropological foundations of Gladstone's classical scholarship.*]

The American psychologist R. W. Woodworth, in a short paper in the *Psychological Bulletin* for 15 October 1910, recalled the previous fifty years of scholarly interest in a "puzzle" toward the solution of which he himself had expended time and effort: the "puzzle of color vocabularies." As Woodworth (1910 ["The Puzzle of Color Vocabularies"]: 226) defined it the puzzle consisted of a "discrepancy between color vision and color vocabulary" seen, for example, in the absence or poverty of color terms in certain languages, and in the fact that various regions of the spectrum may in some languages be named by a few and in others by many terms. Woodworth's historical account begins in 1858, with William E. Gladstone, who was a classical scholar as well as a gentleman of state. Gladstone's studies of early Greek literature had led him to remark on the "extraordinary vagueness" of the references to color and to conclude that the sense of color of the ancient Greeks was inferior to that of modern Europeans. His lead was followed by a number of scholars who amplified and extended the focus of investigation to other ancient literary sources such as the Bible, Vedic scriptures, and Germanic sagas (e.g., Hopkins 1883; Furrel 1885; Mead 1889), and to direct observations of the color vocabulary used by various nonliterate peoples (Magnus 1880; Gatschett 1879; Kirschoff 1879). During this same period color vision, as one aspect of sensory perception, became a favorite subject for study in the new field of experimental psychology (Boring 1942). By the turn of the century a number of theories—biological, psychological, and cultural—had been coined to account for the development of the color sense and to explain how and why color terms originate (Geiger 1878; Allen 1879; Magnus 1877; Wundt 1900; Rivers 1901).[1]

By 1910 broad deterministic theories were falling out of favor in the social sciences; Woodworth (1910) traced a steady progress from a naive sort of biological determinism, which he attributed to Gladstone, to an ever-increasing awareness of and emphasis on cultural factors. After reviewing his own researches on color vision, he himself came down firmly in the culturalist camp, arriving at what an anthropologist might recognize as a truly Boasian solution to the puzzle of color vocabulary: color terms are invented "as they are needed."[2] He declared (1910:332) this solution to be "simple and devoid of psychological interest," and he must have felt that he had laid the matter to rest once and for all.

It may be that Woodworth's commonsense appraisal did have a short-term discouraging effect, since he himself did not pursue the problem any further, and there is little evidence of interest in color vocabulary in social science journals over the next two to three decades. However, if there was a lull in research, it was brief; by the middle of the twentieth century, experimental psychologists had renewed their interest in the use of colored stimulus materials for tests involving verbal responses such as identification, discrimination, matching, and recall (e.g., Lenneberg 1953; Brown and Lenneberg 1954; Burnham and Clark 1955), and a number of anthropologists were at work with similar materials and techniques in the field (e.g., Ray 1952, 1953; Beaglehole 1939; W. R. Geddes 1946; White 1943; Lenneberg and Roberts 1956).

Eric Lenneberg and John M. Roberts's innovative study of the Zuni color lexicon, *The Language of Experience* (1956), published almost fifty years after Woodworth's article, marked a near century of ethnolinguistic studies of color. Woodworth's work had heralded an end to the search for laws and evolutionary principles to explain the growth of color vocabulary and had evoked a simple relativistic appreciation of cultural differences. Lenneberg and Roberts's (1956) study reflects an established tradition of relativism, but in retrospect is recognized as an important turning point. It applied methods and concepts developed in the context of experimental psychology, relating to the internal structure and cognitive processing of the field of color, and stimulated a new kind of ethnolinguistic research. This led, indirectly, to the revival of interest in regular and universal tendencies in the growth of lexicon (Brown 1976; Tornay 1978 [Voir et nommer les couleurs]: xxiv-xxvi), culminating in *Basic Color Terms,* by B. Berlin and P. Kay (1969), another turning point.

The prevailing emphasis in color-term research since the publication of *Basic Color Terms* has been the documenting of universal (or near universal) tendencies, and a downplaying of the importance of unique historical developments in specific cultural contexts. This had led, in turn, to the positing of biological determinants (the anatomy of the eye, the neurological "wiring," genetic programming, etc.) as underlying factors which determine the "emergence" of similar color categories in various languages. On the other hand, cultural factors are invoked to explain, for example, variations in the total number of categories, differences in their boundaries, additions to or omissions from the inventory, or a range of variation in symbolic or metaphoric uses of color. Acceptance of such a biocultural perspective can be seen, in a very general sense, as a return to the type of theoretical posture typical of mid-nineteenth-century researchers such as Gladstone.

GLADSTONE AND ETHNOLINGUISTIC THEORY

When modern scholars review the history of research in visual perception and color vocabulary, they, like Woodworth, still invoke Gladstone's name as an early contributor (Segall, Campbell, and Herskovits 1956 [*The Influence of Culture on Visual Perception*]: 38; Berlin and Kay 1969 [*Basic Color Terms*]: 134; Tornay 1978:xi). Although it is customary to credit Gladstone with an innovative role, he usually makes a very brief appearance in print, entering and exiting in a single sentence or short paragraph. Curiously, opinions about his views and contributions seem unclear and even contradictory. As we have seen, Woodworth counted Gladstone as a biological determinist, the first of a series of misguided evolutionists whose views he saw giving way to a more judicious relativism. On the other hand, W. H. R. Rivers, a near contemporary of Woodworth, seems to have regarded Gladstone simply as a befuddled literary commentator; he credited him only with comments on ambiguities in Homer's terminology and with the suggestion that early Greek ideas about color may have been different from those of the modern world. Later investigators, according to Rivers (1901 ["Primitive Color Vision"]: 44), introduced the possibility of differences in biological endowment and of a gradual evolutionary development of the color sense, leading up to Rivers's own universalist theories.

More recent writers seem to echo these two sources, though differing in the positive or negative evaluation which they put on Gladstone's contribution. For example, Segall, Herskovits, and Campbell, in *The Influence of Culture on Visual Perception* (1966), describe Gladstone as an early culturalist, in basic agreement with their own views. Three years later, Berlin and Kay (1969), citing Woodworth, congratulate Gladstone on the beginnings of an evolutionist position anticipating, and consistent with, their own.

There are, then, at least two different traditions of interpretation of Gladstone's views: the tradition of Rivers and Segall, Herskovits, and Campbell, which aligns Gladstone with a theoretical position of cultural relativism, and the Woodworth and Berlin and Kay tradition, which claims him as an evolutionist or biological determinist. One might suspect that disagreement in the secondary sources reveals more about the biasing effects of time and differing scientific paradigms on the interpretation of prior scholarship than about the intrinsic value of that scholarship itself. The examination of Gladstone's work which is the basis for the present paper was undertaken, first, because of the innovative role which he played in a still ongoing tradition of research; he had an enduring influence on the work of others both directly, in his own lifetime, and indirectly, in ours. Further, I was intrigued by the chronic disagreement about his theoretical views, and anticipated both that they might be complex, and that they might not fit either the culturalist or the evolutionist position—the two interpretive paradigms which twentieth-century social scientists are accustomed to oppose to one another. Finally, I hoped that, in some perhaps intangible or indirect fashion, an insight into the issues toward which Gladstone's researches were directed would provide a perspective relevant to the interpretation of modern research of a similar sort.

THE HISTORIC GLADSTONE

William E. Gladstone was born in Liverpool in December 1809, the fifth of six children in a well-to-do family with extensive commercial interests. He was educated at Eton and Oxford, where he graduated in 1831 with high honors in classics and mathematics. He entered politics almost immediately, elected to his first term in Parliament in 1832. Gladstone's political career lasted more than sixty years, virtually spanning the long reign of Queen Victoria. He resigned from his fourth term as prime minister in 1894, four years before his death. Though first elected from a Tory pocket borough, he soon became a member of the Liberal party; through most of the years before he became head of the government, in 1868, he was the M.P. representing Oxford University. Gladstone's connections with Oxford remained strong throughout his life, and so did his interest in the classics; he frequently returned to Oxford to speak on classical topics, as well as on theological, pedagogical, and political issues.

Gladstone's magnum opus as a classicist, *Studies in Homer and the Homeric Age* (1858), was written during a hiatus of almost five years between his resignation from government precipitated by opposition to the Crimean War, and his appointment as chancellor of the exchequer, in 1859. Following this appointment he was seldom out of high public office; however, it would seem that he was always as much at home in Homer's Greece as in his own Victorian England, and parliamentary recesses were often marked by speeches and publications on classical topics. When stricken by his final illness, in 1897, he was at work on an unfinished manuscript, a comprehensive study of "The Olympian Religion" (Morley 1903[3] [*Life of William Ewart Gladstone*]: 356).

Serious work on *Studies in Homer* [*Studies in Homer and the Homeric Age*] began, according to Gladstone's diary, in August 1855; the manuscript was sent to the publisher in February 1858. Some of the most immediate motivations for undertaking the project can be inferred from his introductory paragraphs and from comments made in his diary. For one thing, there were contemporary educational issues about which he felt strongly. The writing of *Studies in Homer* followed closely on a lecture given at Oxford, **"On the Place of Homer in Classical Education and in Historical Inquiry,"** the gist of which is incorporated in the introduction to the longer work. Classics had an important place in the traditional British curriculum; but by the 1820s, during Gladstone's own schooldays at Eton, this curriculum was under attack by a variety of educational reformers. The movement toward a national system of schools did not achieve success in Britain until the 1880s, but by the early decades of the century a number of groups—prominent among them the phrenological societies—were advocates of secular education and of a balanced curriculum emphasizing civic affairs, with a corresponding deemphasis on the classics (DeGiustino 1975 [*The Conquest of Mind*]: 166-71). Gladstone's position (**1858**[1] [*Studies in Homer and the Homeric Age*]: 5) was, on the one hand, that the ethical values embodied in the ancient literature were of continuing importance in the education of British youth; and, on the other, that the roots of English civilization lay in that very source. Based on these premises he decried the decline of interest in the Greek poets, which he detected even at Oxford.

Related to the educational issue was a religious one. While he was a student Gladstone had become a Tractarian, a member of the so-called Oxford Movement, which was dedicated to the restoration of Catholic dogma and rituals to the Church of England. The leader of that movement, John Newman, and several of the other members eventually became Roman Catholics; Gladstone remained in the Church of England during a period of doctrinal tension and religious reaction which rendered suspect, among other things, a taste for pagan literature. Part of his motivation for the Homeric studies, apparently, was his felt need to justify this taste and his devotion to the study of the mythology and culture of a non-Christian people.

STUDIES IN HOMER AND THE HOMERIC AGE

Studies in Homer is a work in three volumes, a total of 1,696 pages. The first major section, "Achais," which takes up most of the first volume, is a long historical essay which deals with the identification and interrelationships of the various "tribes" and "races" (Arcadians, Graians, Ionians, etc.) named in the Homeric sources, arguing partly on the basis of their distribution in time and space, partly from etymologies, comparisons, and collations of names; in the process, it purports to locate the sources of English culture in the more "progressive" of these groups.

The second major section, "Olympus," also a full volume in length, focuses on religion and on the social and political order traditionally associated with the deities of the Greek pantheon. It includes, for example, separate treatment of the attributes of each deity, followed by an analysis of their hierarchical relations; further on there are studies of family life, the divisions of society, the office of kingship, and the rules of political succession, as reflected in the epics. There is an inventory of occupations, including the priesthood, trades, and the military; ethical concepts are discussed in reference to homicide, feuds, and warfare; and there is, among many others, a chapter which treats the status of women and the institution of marriage. Throughout, Gladstone is at pains to demonstrate the existence of underlying parallels to the revealed religion of the Old Testament. His position was, essentially, that while the Old Testament stood as the ultimate source for religious inspiration, the origins of civilized society and culture lay in Greece; therefore, he proposed that the *Iliad* and the *Odyssey* should have equal status with the Bible, and that Homer should rank with Moses as a vehicle of divine inspiration. In effect he argued that the two bodies of literature properly complement one another and should not be held to be in conflict; that each had a divine purpose.

The third volume of *Studies in Homer* is taken up with a number of disparate topics: politics, geography, a comparison of Greek and Trojan religions, and a discussion of the plot of the *Iliad,* relating to the issue of Homer's identity and the question of the authorship of the Homeric corpus. Although Gladstone considered the Homeric texts a valid source for general statements about the mental processes of Greeks of the Heroic Age, he was a staunch defender of the unique identity of Homer and the single authorship of the texts. And while he does not commit himself outright to Bishop Ussher's famous calculation of 4004 B.C. as the date of Creation, it is clear that he was operating within just such a time frame and that he regarded the period depicted in the Homeric texts as chronologically close to the creation of the world.

Finally, at the end of the third volume, there is the section called "Aoidos," a discussion of subjective aspects of the culture depicted by Homer, based on an analysis of lexicon. It is this section which can be called a pioneering study in ethnolinguistics, since it is an attempt to draw conclusions about the mentality and world view of a people on the basis of a treatment of vocabulary and usage; and it is largely on the basis of this section that Gladstone's work is still cited by modern scholars.

Despite various caveats which might be issued because of Gladstone's academic limitations, the times in which he lived, and other considerations, *Studies in Homer* remains, in its own way, an impressive work. As a topical catalogue and collation of the sources, it can serve quite adequately as a guide to the Homeric corpus. Beyond this, to quote the assessment (Morley 1903[3]:545) of Gladstone's official biographer (who tends to minimize Gladstone's scholarly talents): "anyone who wished to have his feeling about the Iliad and Odyssey as delightful poetry refreshed and quickened, will find inspiring elements in the profusion, the eager array of Homer's own lines, the diligent exploration of aspects and bearing hitherto unthought of."

However, time and critics in general have not been kind to Gladstone's classical studies. For one thing, both in *Studies in Homer* and in later publications, there is Gladstone's almost obsessive loyalty to the unique identity of the historic Homer. The question of whether the Homeric corpus was the product of one, two, or several authors has been debated since classical times. A. F. Wolf, in 1795, outlined a view which is still widely accepted: that the epics are the product of an oral tradition, to which many individuals may have contributed.[3] Most Homeric scholars of Gladstone's period defended either the long-accepted chorizontic theory (of separate authorship of the *Odyssey* and *Iliad*) or the Wolfian position (of plural authorship) (W. D. Geddes 1878: [*The Problem of the Homeric Poems*]: 2-19). Gladstone's arguments for single authorship, in *Studies in Homer* and in later publications, such as *Juventus Mundi* (1868), rest in part on textual analysis, but also on a purely subjective appeal to overall aesthetic impression (see Morley 1903[3]:544).

Furthermore, as we have seen, Gladstone's time perspective was severely foreshortened, since he considered the Homeric period to be a very early stage in human history, and since he attempted to interpret sequences of historical events in a creationist framework; his estimates of time intervals are generally in tens and hundreds of years, rarely in thousands. He may not have been abreast of, or have taken seriously, current developments in the natural sciences; his own education in that area was slight, and his reading, though always voluminous, emphasized history and the classics. Darwin's *Origin of Species* appeared in 1859, a year later than *Studies in Homer*; Gladstone did meet Darwin, and corresponded with him on the subject of color, but only some twenty years later. Within a decade of Gladstone's 1858 publication, stratigraphic researches, in England as well as on the continent, had begun to reveal evidence of the futility of his view of prehistory. It is to his credit that he sought to relate his own research to the new discoveries in archaeology; in 1878, at the urgings of that great archaeologist, he contributed a preface to Schliemann's (1878) volume on Mycenae.

It was the "theo-mythology" propounded in the "Olympus" which attracted the most severe criticism from Gladstone's contemporaries, focusing on his efforts to separate ancient and innovative aspects of Greek religion: this amounted to a kind of internal reconstruction, which aimed at discovering a putatively earlier stratum with strong resemblances to Old Testament monotheism. Gladstone was not unique in undertaking this type of approach; the relationship of paganism to the historic religions of Europe was much discussed throughout the nineteenth century. The conservative British theological establishment held, essentially, a degenerationist view of pagan beliefs, wherever and whenever they might be found; according to this view, the Greeks of Homer's time were on a downhill path leading from the perfection of original revelation to the total corruption of pagan superstition.[4] Although Gladstone in effect paid lip service to the degenerationist position, he extended the limits of tolerance in two ways: he clearly went to extremes in his efforts to find points of agreement between the two systems of belief; and he appears to have interpreted discrepancies in too favorable a light to please even the most credulous of his readers.[5]

"Aoidos": The Homeric World View

As already noted, "Aoidos," the last major section of *Studies in Homer* (**1858**[3]:397-499), is a discussion of mentality, based on the analysis of vocabulary. For the reader who peruses these pages more than a century after they were written, the "Aoidos" holds a certain fascination simply as a depiction of some aspects of inferred world view, aesthetic and cognitive. The tenor of Gladstone's discussion constantly reminds us, however, that his research objectives included an estimate of the state of development of the mind and various mental faculties. This, undoubtedly, was the main reason for his undertaking the lexical analysis upon which the section is based.

There are three areas of expression which Gladstone chose as the bases for characterizing the mentality which he saw reflected in the epics: the senses of *beauty, number,* and *color.* The last of these is developed at the greatest length (over forty pages), and is the one which Gladstone seems to have found the most productive, since he returned to the topic for a separate publication twenty years later (1877). This is also the part of his discussion which later writers have found the most provocative of both comment and emulation.

His treatment of the sense of beauty is brief; Gladstone's premise (**1858**[3]:401) that the Homeric texts represent "a very early and chaste condition of human thought" in regard to linked ideals of beauty and divinity seems, essentially, a matter of subjective interpretation. Concepts of number, on the other hand, are discussed in a straightforward way, linking a general paucity of broad, abstract numerical concepts to the limitations of the cultural environment and other practical considerations. One is inclined to accept Gladstone's

conclusions (**1858**[3]:431) that the level of development of numerical skills and concepts was "below that of most contemporary schoolchildren," without seeing the necessity to conclude—as he does—that this entailed an underdeveloped condition of the mind itself.

"Next to the idea of number, there is none perhaps more definite to the modern mind than that of colour" (Gladstone **1858**[3]:457). I will treat the subject of color in greater detail than the other two, both because Gladstone's analysis is carried further and is more complete, and because of the greater interest which it must hold, both for myself and for others who have inherited Gladstone's preoccupation with color terminology. Let us consider, first, Gladstone's analysis of the color vocabulary and then proceed to review his interpretation of this data as a contribution to the dynamics of Lamarckian inheritance.

The analysis of the data begins with an examination, item by item, of the contexts of occurrence of those terms which are judged to have definite status as color terms, and continues with a similar treatment of those which have more problematical status in designating colors. In this analysis an attempt is made to arrive at a basic, or core, meaning for each of the terms. Eight terms are included in the first list, the first six given with a provisional English gloss: (1) *leukos,* "white"; (2) *melas,* "black"; (3) *xanthos,* "yellow"; (4) *eruthros,* "red"; (5) *porphureos,* "violet"; (6) *kuaneos,* "indigo"; (7) *phoinix*; (8) *polios.*

Gladstone matches the Greek terms as best he can with Newton's list of seven primary colors (red, orange, yellow, green, blue, indigo, and violet), plus black and white. He does not cite Newton's works, but apparently accepts the correctness and irreducibility of this set of colors which, as he states (**1858**[3]:459) "has been determined for us by Nature." Thus for Gladstone as for more recent authors (e.g., Rivers 1901; Berlin and Kay 1969) a set of English color terms serves as a standard against which to evaluate another color system.

At first glance the list of eight Greek terms might seem almost as rich as the English set of nine. However, Gladstone immediately puts aside the last two, phoinix and polios, as being either indefinite or redundant of other terms (neither occurs very frequently). Thus there is a discrepancy of three—the English categories named by orange, green, and either blue or indigo have no equivalents.[6]

However, this is just the starting point of Gladstone's demonstration of the "vagueness," or "indefiniteness," of the Homeric lexicon. He examines the Greek terms one by one and finds virtually all of them to be used with some degree of inconsistency. He postpones discussion of leukos and melas; he also has little to say about the apparent translatability of xanthos and eruthros as "yellow" and "red." Porphureos is the first term for which he discusses a "startling discrepancy" in the list of referents to which it is applied—these include blood, dark clouds, waves, and disturbed river and ocean waters; garments and carpets; the rainbow; in compounded forms, wool and woolen textiles; and, metaphorically, death, and the brooding mind. Attempting to match the term with English equivalents, he suggests (**1858**[3]:461-62), "red" (as in blood), "purple" (the sea and, perhaps, the rainbow), "grey" or "leaden" (dark clouds, etc.), and perhaps also "tawny" or "brown" shades—all aside from the metaphoric applications. Through this sort of procedure both this term and the next, kuaneos, are found to approximate a wide range of referents, with "dark" as perhaps the best general English equivalent for both. The last two terms, phoinix and polios, are similarly found to apply to "dark" and "light" fields of reference.

The second list, of "words which have not even the pretensions of those which have preceded to be treated as adjectives of definite colour," (**1858**[3]:467) includes thirteen: (1) *khloros,* (2) *aithalois,* (3) *rhodois,* (4) *ioeis,* (5) *oinops,* (6) *miltopareos,* (7) *aithops,* (8) *argos,* (9) *aiolos,* (10) *glaukos,* (11) *kharopos,* (12) *sigloeis,* (13) *marmareos.*

Several of these terms, such as rhodois, ioeis, and oinops, occur in a very restricted set of contexts; for example, ioeis is found in this form only three times, always in reference to the sea. However, since compounded or derived terms are applied to iron, wool, and sheep, Gladstone takes it as an approximate synonym for porphureos, with a similar range of referents and the general meaning of "dark." Thus, as the name of a flower, the violet, the word would have nothing in common with its applications to other objects aside from "a rather vague idea of darkness" (**1858**[3]:471).

Probably the most frequently used term in this list is the first, khloros, which is considered, and dismissed, as a candidate for "green." The term signifies "freshness" (of twigs) and "paleness" (of face, and the color of honey), besides its applications to foliage; metaphorically it is often applied to fear. Gladstone decides (**1858**[3]:467-68) that the notion of "green" is only marginally associated with the term; since verdure is so prominent a feature of the environment, he finds his analysis to be a telling argument against the Homeric sensitivity to color.

One further example can illustrate the extremes of pedantry to which Gladstone's methods could sometimes lead: rhodois, the name of the rose, is used rarely and in ways which Gladstone describes as "altogether indeterminate." He criticizes and finds wanting (**1858**[3]:470) the compounded epithet *rhododaktulos,*

translated as "rosy-fingered," applied to the dawn or morning, because the redness denoted by the term would seem to apply to the fingers in their entirety, whereas "that colour is only even admissible in the interior of the hand, which is the part not seen and therefore the part not intended." In this case it is difficult to see how Gladstone's over-literal comments can either add to or detract from an appreciation of Homer's imagery.

The last six terms are dismissed as having primary reference to motion (argos and aiolos) or to quality or intensity of light (glaukos, etc.). Thus Gladstone finds that glaukoopis, Minerva's epithet, a compound based on glaukos, should properly describe the goddess as having luminous, or flashing, eyes, rather than as "blue-eyed."

Gladstone briefly reinforces his thesis of "vagueness" in the naming of colors with another type of analysis, comparing the range of color terms applied to a few selected referents. For example, iron is alternatively described by terms originally translated as "violet," "gray," and "tawny." Taken as names of colors they "cannot be reconciled," but when the factor of light is brought in, Gladstone (**1858**[3]:476) suggests that they can be interpreted more adequately: "iron is dark or tawny if in the shade; while in the light it may appear grey."

Having completed his discussion of most of the terms which may or may not have chromatic reference, Gladstone returns to the beginning of his first list and to what he sees (**1858**[3]:476-77) as the "vast predominance in Homer of the two simple opposites, white and black." Melas ("black," "dark") occurs, by his count, 170 times, and is also represented in numerous derived verbs and adjectives, in compounds, and as a frequent element in personal names. Leukos ("white," "light") occurs 60 times, and is found in several compounded epithets and other derived terms. Besides these, which are by far the terms of most frequent occurrence, there are several others which, as we have seen, he determined to be basically descriptive of darkness or lightness rather than of chromatic hue.

Finally there are the two additional items, xanthos and eruthros, which are conceded to have status as terms with chromatic reference; but both occur only rarely and in restricted contexts. Xanthos is "yellow" or "blond," and is found only 10 times, aside from its repeated use as an epithet for Menelaus; eruthros is used only 6 times, and other terms which may designate "red" raise the total to only 13 (**1858**[3]:477).

An additional line of argument on which Gladstone relies is, essentially, an appeal to human nature as he understood it: he comments on Homer's failure to use color descriptions at times when they might properly be expected. Homer's similes are more often based on motion, force, form, or sound than on color; epithets for countries almost never involve reference to color; and despite an apparent love of horses and the occurrence of numerous passages in which horses are described, Homer almost never describes them in terms of color. Gladstone dwells on this last point; apparently it seemed natural, indeed almost inevitable to him that bays, chestnuts, roans, etc., should be properly differentiated.[7] In discussing this matter he contrasts Homer's "lax" phraseology with a series of passages quoted from the later Greek author Euripides and from the English author Macaulay. After brief comments on the paucity of descriptive passages dealing with animals other than horses, and with human pigmentation, he also notes (**1858**[3]:477-83) the "surprising" absence in Homer's works of precise color vocabulary applied to the rainbow and to the sky.

In attempting to define the basis for Homer's concepts of color, Gladstone takes up the question of blindness or, perhaps, other defects in vision. He rejects them, noting Homer's vivid images of light, his feeling for form, and other prevailingly visual types of description; the very emphasis on the interplay of light and dark calls for a denial of the possibility of blindness. However, after a comparison of Homer's descriptive imagery with that of Shakespeare, who is by comparison fairly rich in color imagery, he concludes (**1858**[3]:487) that "we must . . . seek for the basis of Homer's system . . . in something outside our own."

Understanding Gladstone's proposed explanation, at this point, requires us to suspend the belief—well inculcated in ourselves as twentieth-century social scientists—in the independence of inherited and acquired characteristics. On the one hand, Gladstone marshalls evidence to suggest environmental and technological influences on the Homeric world view: an assumed general uniformity of pigmentation in the population (olive skin, dark hair); a monotony of climate; and technological simplicity (glass did not exist, painting and dyeing were little known, and artificial or manufactured colors were few or absent, with the exception of metals). He suggests (**1858**[3]:488) that "the eye may require a familiarity with an ordered system of colors, as the condition of its being able closely to appreciate any one of them."

On the other hand, his commitment to "traducianism," the inheritance of acquired characteristics, precludes his building these insights into a theory based on the dynamics of culture. His conclusion (**1858**[3]:488), in a passage which has been often quoted but perhaps inadequately understood, is that "the organ of colour and its impressions were but partially developed among the Greeks of the heroic age." This partial development, as Gladstone saw it, amounted to a system "in lieu of colour," which was based on light and darkness, along with "some crude conceptions of colour derived from the elements." He attempts to support this, analogically, by reference (**1858**[3]:491) to naturalists' descriptions of "creatures (fishes, bats, etc.) respecting which it is known that their organs are sensitive to light and darkness, but with no perception either of colour or of form."

Thus Homer, as a representative of what Gladstone saw as a very early stage in history—the "childhood of the race"—had mental faculties which were "underdeveloped" in certain respects. This lack of development, however, attested not to overall inferiority of endowment—indeed, as has been noted, Gladstone saw Homer as little short of divine in nature—but to lack of experience. Experience, in turn, is cumulative and, over the generations, results in changes in the "organs" of the mind, which would therefore be most fully developed in the modern population. As for Homer (Gladstone **1858**[3]:495-96),

> though his organ was little trained in the discrimination of colours . . . yet he made very bold and effective use of these limited materials . . . Nor are we able to suppose that we see in this department an exception to that comparative profusion of power which marked his endowments in general and that he bore, in this respect, a crippled nature; but rather we are to learn that the perceptions so easy and familiar to us are the results of a slow, traditionary growth in knowledge and in the training of the human organ, which commenced long before we took our place in the succession of mankind.

GLADSTONE AND LITERARY STUDIES

The most productive and most lasting aspect of Gladstone's study has to do with the color lexicon itself; it resulted in inferential definitions of the intrinsic, or basic, meaning of individual terms, and in a delineation of the underlying dichotomy of dark versus light. His empirical approach to this part of his task has been emulated by some, criticized by others, and was the first of a long series of publications devoted to the color lexicons of Homer and later Greek authors. One of the latest of these studies is Evelyn Irwin's *Colour Terms in Greek Poetry* (1974), which includes a summary of previous scholarship in the field, beginning with Gladstone. Throughout a century of debate since Gladstone's time, it would appear that interpretation has varied between those scholars (including Gladstone and Geiger and extending to Irwin herself) who look for one or more common threads among the contexts in which terms are used, and from these try to arrive at an underlying system, or rationale; and others, who attempt to match each term with a specific hue, an approach which leads them generally to distinguish between "color" and "noncolor" uses of the individual terms. This division in interpretation is complicated by a second: that between those who, like Geiger, Magnus, and W. Schultz (1904), closely equated vocabulary with perception and argued for a biological basis for the lexical categories; and those who (perhaps beginning with F. Marty 1879) have insisted on a distinction between perceptual ability and vocabulary, and have treated the latter as psychological, cultural, or simply linguistic in origin.

It is worth noting that Gladstone's definition of the Homeric color system, despite his pedantry and occasional tendency to over-literal interpretation, is really very close to that of Irwin; she goes much farther than Gladstone, however, in drawing on a number of other Greek authors and in including a treatment of historical changes in color vocabulary. Although she makes few direct references to Gladstone's study, and although she chooses to base her discussion on a few exemplary words (khloros, kuaneos, and several others), rather than the exhaustive list treated by Gladstone, Irwin's analysis coincides with Gladstone's in revealing a system which does not base itself on hue but which builds, instead, on a basic, pervasive opposition of black and white. She strengthens her case by bringing in symbolic associations (which Gladstone touched on but did not develop) aligned with the black/white polarity; these include gender, organs of the body, the elements, life and death, sorrow and joy, and many other associations.[8] From Irwin's perspective Gladstone can be regarded as a pioneer in his objective of discovering pervasive, systematic features and an underlying logic revealed in the lexicon—an objective which coincides closely with the goals of both modern literary criticism and of cognitively oriented anthropology and linguistics.

GLADSTONE AND CONSTITUTIONAL PSYCHOLOGY

Finally, Gladstone's synchronic analysis of lexicon was only a means to his real theoretical ends as pursued in the "Aoidos": the pervasive theoretical issue throughout is the question of the relative importance and the interrelations of function, learning, and heredity in the development of the mind. Like most of his twentieth-century counterparts (including, for example, Lenneberg and Roberts) Gladstone intended his treatment of color to have broad implications. His concern is mentality; the sense of color, like number and beauty, was chosen simply as representative of the higher mental functions or faculties. His use of the term "organs" in relation to these functions, as well as his views on development and inheritance, strongly indicate that he assumed a constitution of the mind best represented by the charts of the phrenologists.[9]

Phrenology, which had its greatest vogue in England between 1828 and 1840, was still a respectable popular science in the 1850s. Phrenology is a type of constitutional psychology which maps the brain as approximately thirty separate, localized organs with specific functions. These are classified into two main groups. (1) Broad behavioral tendencies, including *feelings* (such as combativeness and acquisitiveness), which humans have in common with lower animals, and *sentiments* (such as self-esteem and cautiousness); the higher sentiments (such as conscientiousness and ideality) are located higher toward the crown of the head and are unique to humans. (2) The second group includes more specific conscious processes, including *intellectual faculties* (such as [the ability to perceive] form, color, time, and number), clustered in the forehead area, and the *reflective faculties* (including comparison and causality), which are higher on the forehead, toward the crown (DeGiustino 1975:12-21; Wells 1872).

It might be noted that phrenology classified number and color as two members of the perceptive group of intellectual processes, which are shared with lower animals but are more highly developed in humans. The sense of beauty is a function of ideality, one of the higher sentiments, and uniquely human. Phrenologists argued for a continuity of development of the mind from lower to higher forms of life, and also pointed to variations in the shape of the head (reflecting the relative development of these various "organs" of the mind) in different races and nations, as well as in individuals. One point of constant debate, both within and outside of the phrenological societies, was the degree of fixity or potential for growth of mental endowment. On the one hand, phrenology preached self-knowledge and called for exercise of the organs of the mind, which was supposed to lead to their growth and to improvement of the corresponding faculties; on the other hand, there seemed to be limits to improvement, since the mentality of the "lower races" was generally deemed inferior, both absolutely and potentially, to that of the civilized races. In the context of education, one of Gladstone's main concerns, many phrenologists were inclined to a conservative view and considered intelligence and aptitudes to be modifiable only within narrow limits; others shared the faith of various of their contemporaries, such as the Owenite socialists, in a boundless human potential for improvement (DeGiustino 1975:140-41).

In this context, then, Gladstone's "Aoidos" had the status of a test case: he attempted to assess the degree of development, in a given population, over a given period of time, of three representative "organs" of the mind. For all three he diagnosed a rudimentary condition in the early population and presented evidence for marked progress, over the generations, to a high degree of development in the modern race, which he believed to be, in some sense, the lineal descendants of the earlier. Thus, according to Gladstone (**1858**[3]:458), "the acquired aptitudes of one generation . . . become . . . the inherited and inborn aptitudes of another"; and the race advances, as it were, from its infancy to adulthood.[10] His best example of this Lamarckian process, again, was the development of the color sense, from a childlike condition characterized by a predominance of "the most crude and elemental forms of colour, black and white," a poor vocabulary, and demonstrated inconsistency in the naming of chromatic hues and tints; to a modern condition, with clear recognition of "the distinctions between the principal colours," reflected in an adequate and unambiguous vocabulary.

POSTSCRIPT: "THE COLOUR-SENSE"

It must be obvious that the long-term value of Gladstone's ethnolinguistic contribution lies in the power of his synchronic lexical analysis. In this respect the "Aoidos" has enduring interest and is the prototype of a large body of later research. His diachronic interpretive paradigm was much less secure; indeed, within Gladstone's own lifetime, most of his assumptions about time, history, and human psychology would become outdated. In 1877, almost twenty years after *Studies in Homer,* Gladstone published an article, **"The Colour-sense,"** in a popular journal, *The Nineteenth Century.* Here he undertook to synthesize his own earlier work with that of other literary scholars and with biological and psychological research on perception then underway, especially in Germany. In particular, he attempted to align his findings with the universalist theory proposed by the German ophthalmologist Hugo Magnus, who outlined a development of color discrimination beginning with the light-dark opposition (B-W) and adding chromatic discriminations in the sequence of the spectrum (R, Y, G, B). Gladstone disputed Magnus's placement of the Homeric Greeks in the third state (B-WRY); he preferred to see Homer just emerging from the initial stage. In accepting the broad outlines of Magnus's comparative typology, however, he implicitly accepted the principle of general stages in human evolution—something he had not broached earlier.

The 1877 article very likely reached a wider audience, or at least a different audience, from the earlier work and elicited comments and rejoinders from a number of prominent scientists, among them Grant Allen (1878); Robertson Smith (1877); E. Krause (1877), and perhaps most importantly, Charles Darwin (1877; see Allen 1879 [*The Colour Sense*]:82). A few months later, in 1878, Darwin and Gladstone met, a confrontation arranged by the naturalist and anthropologist Sir John Lubbock; we do not know what they discussed, but we do know that they subsequently exchanged letters specifically on the subject of color vocabulary (Morley 1903[2]:536-37).[11]

In 1879 Grant Allen, a comparative psychologist and a protégé of Darwin, published a book called *The Colour Sense,* which took color vision as the focus of a powerful exposition of the principles of natural selection. Although their views were diametrically opposed, Allen acknowledged Gladstone (who was by then in his first

term as prime minister) in the preface and in footnotes throughout, as a constant source of information and bibliographical suggestions. Allen traced the evolution and adaptive significance of color vision in separate chapters on insects, fish, birds, and mammals, and treated human color perception in the context of the evolutionary history of the primate order. In his final chapter he dealt with color vocabulary and countered Gladstone's theories, asserting a common human biological basis for the perception and discrimination of hues and arguing that unique traditional and historical factors are sufficient to explain variations in color use and color vocabulary.

Allen's work thus expressed a position that the human mind is, on the one hand, shaped by biological evolution but is, on the other, virtually free from biological determinism and open to almost infinite, arbitrary variation. This position underlies Woodworth's (1910) assessment of Gladstone's work, and was a main tenet of anthropological and linguistic theory during the early twentieth century. Since midcentury this position has been under attack, both by research directed toward the definition of human cognitive universals, in the field of color and in many other domains, and by the identification of specific biological and cultural determinants of cognitive variation. In a very general sense, then, Gladstone's biocultural orientation—if not his assumptions and methods—could be said to have come back into respectability.

Notes

1. Skard's annotated bibliography (1946) is an exhaustive treatment of literary studies up to that date and also includes sources in anthropology and linguistics. Conklin (1972) includes, especially, works in anthropology, psychology, and optics. Tornay's bibliography (1978) is selective but quite broad in coverage. Other works with selective but useful bibliographies are Segall, Campbell, and Herskovits (1966); Bornstein (1975); and Berlin and Kay (1969).

2. The mention of Boas here is not fortuitous. Woodworth (1910:327) cited a personal communication from Professor Boas as the authority for the statement that "some languages have no conventional color names at all." This information must have contributed to, or at least confirmed, Woodworth's relativistic position.

3. A contemporary compromise position (Kirk 1976) holds that Homer was an oral poet, or "singer," in an established tradition, but that he was also an active creator in synthesizing a number of separate traditional narratives into the epic works.

4. Gladstone dismisses suggestions that the "immortals" of Homer are either "impersonations of the

powers of nature" or transformations of human social life, and emphasizes what he perceives as "vestiges" of scriptural knowledge; the discovery of such survivals, in turn, confirm him in his faith in the Bible as a historical document. Superimposed over this base of original truth, he sees a system based on life and experience—the whole is (1858[2]:3, 8) "a true religion into which falsehood has entered," and his analysis is aimed at separating these two elements.

5. Gladstone sees the principal figures of the Olympian court as essentially a fragmenting of the original unity of the godhead, while the minor deities, associated with the forces of nature, are a later addition; he believes the polytheistic religion to be an extension of the idea of the Trinity; he detects in the relationship between Minerva and Ulysses the "tender and intimate relations which have from the first subsisted between the children of faith and their Father in Heaven"—a quality which "is not of heathen origin" (1858[2]:121); he identifies the tradition of the Blessed Virgin with Latona, the Tempter with Hector, and the Evil One with Neptune; etc.

6. Gladstone is inconsistent, as he lists "indigo" opposite kuaneos, but also calls indigo an unmatched term; clearly he must have intended "blue" rather than "indigo" in one of these contexts, or may have vacillated between the two as the appropriate translation equivalent of kuaneos (now identified as "lapis lazuli").

7. Considering the passion with which Gladstone pursues this point, one suspects that it was a crucial issue, perhaps the crucial issue, in first calling to his attention the discrepancy between the Greek and English color lexicons.

8. Both Gladstone and Irwin point out that classical Greek theories of color usually dealt with an opposition of black and white. Aristotle, for example, considered all colors to be differential mixtures of, and thus intermediate between, black and white (*De Sensoribus*; see also *De Coloribus*).

9. Phrenology originated with the writings of F. J. Gall, who conducted research in Vienna between 1790 and 1805. Gall's theories became widely disseminated in Europe through his publications, but in larger part through the writings and lectures of his associate J. C. Spurzheim. In 1814 Spurzheim made the first of several visits to Britain, speaking in London, but achieving his greatest success in Edinburgh. Largely through the efforts of George Combe, an Edinburgh lawyer and author of *The Constitution of Man,* and a circle of associates in Edinburgh, phrenology became enormously popular, especially in Scotland and the north of England, where many local phrenological societies had libraries, collections of model heads, and lectures on phrenological topics (De Giustino 1975:1-31).

10. As noted earlier, Gladstone believed that there was direct racial continuity between contemporary Britons (as well as other Western Europeans) and the Greek tribes of Homer's time. Such a tunnel view of history, which seems naive today, was commonplace in his time.

11. Lubbock (Lord Avesbury) had conducted ingenious experiments relating to the color sense of honey bees; Allen (1879:84-85) drew heavily on this work in his chapter dealing with insects.

References Cited

Allen, G., 1878, "Development of the Sense of Colour." *Mind* 3:129-32.

———, 1879, *The Colour Sense: Its Origin and Development.* London: Trubner and Co.

Beaglehole, E., 1939, "Tongan Colour-Vision." *Man* 39:170-72.

Berlin, B., and P. Kay, 1969, *Basic Color Terms.* Berkeley and Los Angeles: University of California Press.

Boring, E. G., 1942, *Sensation and Perception in the History of Experimental Psychology.* New York: Appleton-Century-Crofts.

Bornstein, M. H., 1975, "The Influence of Visual Perception on Culture." *American Anthropologist* 77:774-98.

Brown, R. W., 1958, *Words and Things.* Glencoe, Ill.: Free Press.

———, 1976, "Reference: In Memorial Tribute to Eric Lenneberg." *Cognition* 4(2):125-53.

Brown, R. W., and E. Lenneberg, 1954, "A Study in Language and Cognition." *Journal of Abnormal and Social Psychology* 49:454-62.

Burnham, R. W., and J. R. Clark, 1955, "A Test of Hue Memory." *Journal of Applied Psychology* 39(3):164-72.

Conklin, H. C., 1972, *Folk Classification: A Topically Arranged Bibliography.* New Haven: Department of Anthropology, Yale University.

Darwin, C., 1877, "Brief Communication on Color Terminology." *Kosmos,* 1877:423.

DeGiustino, D., 1975, *The Conquest of Mind: Phrenology and Victorian Social Thought.* London: Croom Helm.

Furrell, J. W., 1885, "Light from the East on the Colour Question." *Nineteenth Century* 17:321-30.

Gatschett, A. S., 1879, "Adjectives of Color in Indian Languages." *American Naturalist* 13:475-85.

Geddes, W. D., 1878, *The Problem of the Homeric Poems.* London: Macmillan.

Geddes, W. R., 1946, "The Colour Sense of Fijian Natives." *British Journal of Psychology* 37(1):30-36.

Geiger, L., 1878, *Der Ursprung der Sprache.* Stuttgart: Vorträge.

Gladstone, W. E., 1858, *Studies in Homer and the Homeric Age.* 3 vols. Oxford: Oxford University Press.

———, 1869, *Juventus Mundi.* Boston: Little, Brown and Co.

———, 1877, "The Colour Sense." *Nineteenth Century* 2:366-88.

Hopkins, E. W., 1883, "Words for Color in the Rig Veda." *American Journal of Philosophy* 4:166-91.

Irwin, E., 1974, *Colour Terms in Greek Poetry.* Toronto: Hakkert.

Kirk, G. S., 1976, *Homer and the Oral Tradition.* Cambridge: Cambridge University Press.

Kirschoff, A., 1879, "Über Farbensinn und Farbenbezeichnung der Nubier." *Zeitschrift für Ethnologie* 11:379-402.

Krause, E., 1877, "Brief Communication on Color Terminology." *Kosmos,* 1877:264.

Lenneberg, E. H., 1953, "Cognition in Ethnolinguistics." *Language* 19:463-71.

Lenneberg, E. H., and J. M. Roberts, 1956, "The Language of Experience: A Study in Methodology." *International Journal of American Linguistics,* Mem. 15.

Magnus, H., 1877, *Die geschichtliche Entwicklung des Farbensinnes.* Leipzig: Veit.

———, 1880, *Untersuchungen über den Farbensinn der Naturvölker.* Jena: Fischer.

Marty, F., 1879, *Die Frage nach der geschichtlichen Entwicklung des Farbensinnes.* Leipzig.

Mead, W. E., 1899, "Color in Old English Poetry." *Publications of the Modern Language Association* 14:169-206.

Morley, J. M., 1903, *Life of William Ewart Gladstone.* 3 vols. New York: Macmillan and Co.

Ray, V. F., 1952, "Techniques and Problems in the Study of Human Color Perception." *Southwestern Journal of Anthropology* 8:251-59.

———, 1953, "Human Color Perception and Behavioral Response." *Transactions of the New York Academy of Sciences,* Series 2, 16(2):98-104.

Rivers, W. H. R., 1901, "Primitive Color Vision." *Popular Science Monthly* 59(1):44-58.

Schliemann, H., 1878, *Mycenae: A Narrative of Researches and Discoveries at Mycenae and Tiryns.* New York: Scribners.

Schultz, W., 1904, *Das Farbenempfindungssystem der Hellenen.* Leipzig.

Segall, M. H., D. T. Campbell, and M. J. Herskovits, 1966, *The Influence of Culture on Visual Perception.* New York: Bobbs-Merrill.

Skard, S., 1946, "The Use of Color in Literature: A Survey of Research." *Proceedings of the American Philosophical Society* 90(3):163-249.

Smith, R., 1877, "The Colour-Sense of the Greeks." *Nature* 17:100.

Tornay, S., 1978, *Voir et nommer les couleurs.* Nanterre: Laboratoire d'Ethnologie et de Sociologie Comparative.

Wells, S. R., ed., 1872, *How to Read Character: A New Illustrated Hand-Book of Phrenology and Physiognomy.* New York: Samuel R. Wells.

White, L. A., 1943, "Keresan Color Terms." *Papers of the Michigan Academy of Science, Arts, and Letters* 28:559-63.

Woodworth, R. S., 1910, "The Puzzle of Color Vocabularies." *Psychological Bulletin* 7(10):325-34.

Wundt, W., 1900, *Völkerpsychologie, I. Die Sprache.* Leipzig: W. Engelmann.

Matthew Bevis (essay date fall 2001)

SOURCE: Bevis, Matthew. "Tennyson, Ireland, and 'The Powers of Speech.'" *Victorian Poetry* 39, no. 3 (fall 2001): 345-64.

[*In the following essay, Bevis investigates the literary and political foundations of Gladstone's friendship with Tennyson. Bevis argues that Gladstone's views on the question of Irish Home Rule exerted a powerful influence on Tennyson's later poetry.*]

When Tennyson and Gladstone met for the final time, the poet was in a bad mood. He initially refused to come down to dinner, angry at the politician's continued support of Home Rule for Ireland, but once the two men got talking the Laureate changed his tune:

> It was not long before it became obvious, from the energetic actions of Mr. Gladstone, that the two had got upon the Home Rule Bill, and some two hours went by before they rose from their seats. Shortly afterwards

Gladstone took his departure. 'He has quite converted me,' said Tennyson. 'I see it all; it is the best thing if one looks at it from all sides.' . . .

The following morning when the poet came down to breakfast his first words were, 'It is all right, he spellbound me for the time and I could not help agreeing with him, it was the extraordinary way he put it all; his logic is immense, but I have gone back to my own views. It is all wrong, this Home Rule, and I am going to write and tell him so.'[1]

Tennyson's interest in the finer points of contemporary political debate, and Gladstone's willingness to discuss them with him at some length, attest to the intimate, vexed relations between the two men.[2] The anecdote alerts us to the Laureate's simultaneously appreciative and wary sense of how a politician's eloquence can be both a powerful tool for altering affairs and also a medium which can simplify or distort the complexity of those affairs. The statesman's vocal art of persuasion is met by the poet's need, after thinking things through, to put pen to paper, and such an exchange offers an instructive starting-point for a study of Tennyson's public engagements during the late 1870s and 1880s.

This article has a dual concern. First, I want to situate Tennyson's late poetry in relation to political debate over the Irish question, and to argue that the Laureate's attentiveness to the emphases of public rhetoric helped to shape the rhetorical structures of his poems. Secondly, I want to use the Irish issue to examine how forms of political rhetoric and literary endeavor could meet and part company in this period. Tennyson's entry into Parliament in 1884, and his close relationships with two Liberal orators—Gladstone and the Duke of Argyll—were to be important points of focus for these men when they considered how the public should be addressed through speech and print.[3]

1

At the end of the nineteenth century, the reporter Michael MacDonagh devoted a chapter of his book on Ireland to the Irish politicians who had entered the House of Commons as a result of the Act of Union in 1801. In it he recalled a debate between George Campbell and the Irish MP, Major O'Gorman:

SIR GEORGE CAMPBELL said he had some experience of the Glasgow Irish.

MAJOR O'GORMAN (indignantly)—"Mr. Speaker, Mr. Speaker, I rise to order, sir! I wish to know, sir, whether the hon. member is justified in stigmatizing my beloved country-people as 'the blasted Irish'?"

. . . THE SPEAKER—"Order, order! But if the expression was used, it is certainly unparliamentary and most improper" (*hear, hear*).

SIR G. CAMPBELL—"Mr. Speaker, it is an entire misconception of my remarks on the part of my honourable and gallant friend. What I said was 'Glasgow Irish,' and not 'blasted Irish'" (*much laughter and cheering*).[4]

The laughter inspired by O'Gorman's mishearing is owed in part to his apparent readiness to perceive an insult, but it also acknowledges that such a mishearing has read between the lines of Sir George's "parliamentary" expressions and given voice to an attitude held by many MPs in the Commons. O'Gorman's interruption encapsulates two qualities that were prevalent in nineteenth-century conceptions of Irish politicians: namely, an inclination to quarrel, and an imaginative way with words. Such qualities were often perceived as a link between violence and verbosity, and—as Perry Curtis has shown—Victorian depictions of the Irishman in England frequently stressed his animosity as well as his animal spirits.[5] Following Curtis, Sheridan Gilley has examined the mixed caricatures of the Irish as both gregarious and quick to take offense, and observed that "both in his vices and his virtues, 'Paddy' was singularly unfitted for self-government."[6]

Tennyson's often intemperate pronouncements on the Irish were a strange compound of such views, for he saw the people as both wronged and unreasonable.[7] Irish "charm" is something to which the poet continually returns when trying to define his feelings: "I like the Irish—I admit the charm of their manners—but they're a fearful nuisance," or "Our ancestors *were* horrible brutes! And the Kelts are very charming and sweet and poetic. I love their Ossians and their Finns and so forth—but they are most damnably unreasonable!"[8] Such "charm," at once endearing and dangerous, is the marker of a nation whose poetic nature carries fearful political implications. Tennyson remarks:

The Teuton has no poetry in his nature like the Celt, and this makes the Celt much more dangerous in politics, for he yields more to his imagination than his common-sense. Yet his imagination does not allow of his realizing the sufferings of poor dumb beasts. The Irish are difficult for us to deal with. For one thing the English do not understand their innate love of fighting, words and blows.

([*Alfred Lord Tennyson: A Memoir*] *Memoir*, 2:338)

The Irish imagination is envisaged as a mixture of the commendable, the divisive, and the deficient. The "poetic" is apparently a "political" danger here, but the Laureate's own imaginative involvement with Irish politics led him to poems which were not always so ready to assume the "English" understanding of the situation.

Tennyson's complaints about "the sufferings of poor dumb beasts" and the Irishman's "innate love of fighting, words and blows" point to issues that were at the forefront of political debate in the late 1870s and early 80s. Henry Lucy, a political writer for *Punch* and the newspapers, wryly observed that "All Parliamentary roads lead to Ireland . . . it [the Irish question] is everywhere, varying as the atmosphere varies, yet ever present."[9] The pages of *Punch* were filled with allusions to the Irish at this time; R. F. Foster notes that "from late 1879, nearly every lead cartoon had an Irish reference," and these references continually focused on the Irish propensity to fighting in "words and blows" by depicting scenes of parliamentary obstructionism at Westminster and agrarian violence in Ireland.[10]

In 1879 Parnell came to the centre of the public stage. In November of that year the Irish Land League was formed in Dublin. Parnell was its first president, making him both the leader of the Irish in Parliament, and, more disconcertingly, the leader of the agrarian agitation in Ireland.[11] Lucy drew attention to the double life which Parnell was leading in and out of Westminster when he observed of one speech in the Commons that "there was a delightful unconsciousness about him of all that had happened in Ireland since the House last met. . . . As a dramatic feat it was a triumph of Art."[12] Parnell was well aware of the drama of such artifice. He noted to a friend that "a true revolutionary movement in Ireland should, in my opinion, partake of both a constitutional and an illegal character,"[13] and his position as both an astute parliamentarian and a revolutionary public speaker would be a constant negotiation between incompatible Irish pressure groups, an attempt to hold differing interests together.

Parnell's ambiguous position in 1879 was mirrored by the ambivalent rhetoric of the Land League itself, for while it was technically a legal and non-violent organization, it had alliances with a long tradition of rural crime. As Foster observes: "The government's attempts to prosecute for seditious speeches were riven with problems: the League's official slogans were brilliant, economical and unactionable. . . . What the League largely relied on was implicit violence."[14] In December "The Chief," as Parnell was now known, left Britain for America in order to raise funds for the new organization. As reports of agrarian violence—most frequently, the burning of buildings and the killing or maiming of livestock—started to fill the columns of the *Times,* Parnell's speaking tour in America was helping to raise his profile as an orator who, when away from the confines of Westminster, could shift the tenor of his speeches from the constitutional to the subversive.[15]

In the month that Parnell began his voyage for America Tennyson began writing "The Voyage of Maeldune," a poem which he continued to write during 1880.[16] Hallam noted: "By this story he intended to represent in his own original way the Celtic genius, and he wrote the poem with a genuine love of the peculiar exuberance of the Irish imagination" (*Memoir,* 2:255). The peculiar exuberance of Tennyson's imagining expresses something less than genuine love, for it has politics on its mind. He found the story of Maeldune in P. W. Joyce's *Old Celtic Romances,* a book he was sent in December, but he elaborated on the plot to create a crew of Irish-

men whose continual brawling was in marked contrast to the cheerful buoyancy of Joyce's translation. Joyce noted in his preface:

> I am forced to say that many of these specimens have been presented in a very unfavourable and unjust light—distorted to make them look *funny* and their characters debased to mere modern conventional stage Irishmen.[17]

The weirdly somber note of Tennyson's poem registers a distortion, but the predicament of the Irish is not made to seem "funny." While the Chief was attempting to tread the fine line between the demands of the Land League and those of the parliamentary party, Tennyson's speaker opens by announcing: "I was the chief of the race—he had stricken my father dead— / But I gathered my fellows together, I swore I would strike off his head."[18] Like Parnell, Tennyson's chief has difficulty keeping his party together, and his voyage to unknown lands leads to "fighting, words and blows" which recall the agrarian unrest and the rhetoric which had helped to incite it.

Allingham remembers a conversation with Tennyson in 1880 about "a speech followed by the maiming of many animals" (Allingham [*William Allingham, A Diary*], p. 293) The poet's contempt for a form of public speech which does not quite counsel what it incites, and his pity for the "poor dumb animals," lead to a strange elaboration on Joyce in "The Voyage of Maeldune." In the original version, Maeldune and his sailors arrive at the Isle of Speaking Birds, but Tennyson darkens Joyce's scene with a depiction of a violent outbreak. The Chief explains:

> And we came to the Isle of Shouting, we landed, a score of wild birds
> Cried from the topmost summit with human voices and words;
> Once in an hour they cried, and whenever their voices pealed
> The steer fell down at the plow and the harvest died from the field,
> And the men dropt dead in the valleys and half of the cattle went lame,
> And the roof sank in on the hearth, and the dwelling broke into flame;
> And the shouting of these wild birds ran into the hearts of my crew,
> Till they shouted along with the shouting and seized one another and slew;
> But I drew them one from the other; I saw that we could not stay,
> And we left the dead to the birds and we sailed with our wounded away.
>
> (ll. 27-36)

The tremors amid the rhythmic tug of this verse ("we landed," or, less abruptly, "wild birds") give us something less than a charming Irish lilt, and this Chief's voice seems more enervated than upset. The lame cattle and the flaming dwellings evoke the agitations of the Land League as voices again lead to violence, but in this instance the Irish are the victims of, as well as contributors, to the ruin. The violence is turned inwards as the crew are led astray by other voices, and the confused leader of the party tries to pacify rather than to enrage his followers. The eerie scene intimates Tennyson's distress at a contemporary political situation, but it does not seem to offer a clear political perspective on that distress.

Maeldune's ill-fated voyage and his aim to "strike off" his enemy's head lead him to isles which seem immediately welcoming but which turn out to be hostile, and the *Times* saw Parnell's voyage in similar terms, reporting American hostility to what had been termed "the new departure" in Irish politics by the Land League. One leader reprinted an article from the *New York Herald* which had this to say about Parnell's apparent "project of striking at British resistance by way of the United States":

> He is "at sea" in several other respects also—. . . utterly at sea in his theory that an oratorical noise made here and there in Irish towns can force the British Legislature to loosen the grip of landholders on Irish property.[19]

By linking Parnell's voyage to the oratorical and physical exertions of his followers, the paper casts doubt on the politician's strategy and implies that he would do better to give up the "agitation" in order to pursue a "true remedy" via constitutional means. Maeldune's metaphorical and physical state of being "at sea" nears its end with the company travelling to "the Isle of a Saint who had sailed with St Brendan of yore" (l. 115; Tennyson adds a note to hint at the analogy with Parnell: "St Brendan sailed on his voyage some time in the sixth century from Kerry, and some say he visited America"), and it is this man who tells the Chief to "Go back to the Isle of Finn and suffer the Past to be Past" (l. 124).[20]

Tennyson had some trouble deciding how Maeldune and his followers would take this advice, advice which had been offered to Parnell by politicians and press alike. The poem ends thus (the italics mark an unpublished conclusion from the poet's notebook):

> And we came to the Isle we were blown from, and there on the shore was he,
> The man that had slain my father. I saw him and let him be.
> O weary was I of the travel, the trouble, the strife and the sin,
> When I landed again, with a tithe of my men, on the Isle of Finn.
> *The few that were left to me frowned—they held it a deep disgrace.*

> *O the degenerate chief, was I fit to be chief of my race?*
> *And they rose against me to slay me because I had spared my foe.*
> *There were but five of us left and I fought them, I laid them low.*
>
> (ll. 127-130+ *Harvard Notebook* 64)

The published voice shares the emphasis of those who opposed Parnell and asked him to suffer the past to be past. But the shift from vengeance to forgiveness is not the full picture, for the notebook ending highlights Tennyson's awareness that the Chief is not only the leader of his followers, but also a response to them, a political consequence as well as a cause. If the Laureate's published words constitute a public admonition to the leader of the Irish agitations, then his notebook lines point to a fear that such discontent is not easily placated. Behind the stilted, resigned sadness of "I saw him and let him be" lies the beleaguered sound of "I fought them, I laid them low"; "The Voyage of Maeldune" aims to suppress the need to fight in order to forge a single-minded public rhetoric, but the progress of the 1880s would ask Tennyson to find a public form for these unpublished concerns.

2

The new decade saw Gladstone's conversion to Home Rule and a consequent split in the Liberal party.[21] On March 31, 1881, the Duke of Argyll resigned his position of Privy Seal in Gladstone's cabinet as a result of his opposition to the minister's Irish Land bill. A year earlier in the Lords the Duke had reproached the Conservative ministry for threatening "the interests of the empire," quoting from Tennyson's Dedication to *Idylls of the King* in order to further his cause.[22] According to Argyll, Gladstone's bill was threatening such interests by granting concessions to the Irish tenants as a result of the Land League agitation. These concessions were primarily conceived as the "Three F's" (fixity of tenure, fair rent, and freedom of sale), and while the bill did not fully establish this triad, Argyll felt that Gladstone's back-tracking was the beginning of the end, a dangerously expedient measure which capitulated to Parnell's demands.[23]

The Prime Minister's rhetorical tactics in parliament were an artful mix of the conciliatory and the adamant. He stood up in the Commons to equivocate:

> The controversy as to whether or not the "three F's" are in this Bill is one into which I have not entered. The "three F's" I have always seen printed have been three capital F's; but the "three F's" in this Bill, if they are in it at all, are three little f's.[24]

Gladstone wants to eschew short-term "controversy" for a wider view of things, but he actually enters into the controversy by obscuring it, for his "if they are there at all" neither asserts nor denies a policy. Moreover, the difference between "F" and "f" is a difference which the listener cannot always catch, and it allows the politician an oratorical amplitude which can cater to the pressures of the present while masquerading as a balanced service to time.

Tennyson was spurred into action by Argyll's criticisms of Gladstone's Irish policies.[25] Just as Argyll had alluded to the Laureate in the House, so the Laureate returned the compliment with a poem supporting the Duke's policy, "To the Duke of Argyll." When praising the "Patriot Statesman" (l. 1), Tennyson drew attention to Argyll's foresight by envisaging his heart as "a fortress to maintain / The day against the moment, and the year / Against the day" (ll. 5-7). While Gladstone exploited the medium of the spoken word to allow for a latitude in policy which could take its bearings from present exigency, here Tennyson's uncertain touch creates a tremor which the written medium intensifies. The need to maintain "The day against the moment, and the year" initially asks for a mode of ministerial action that can respond to the demands of "the day" rather than the extremes of the moment or the year; that is, "the day" is to mediate between short-term and long-term considerations. But the line runs on, and effaces this advice by insisting that the maintenance of the year should come at the expense of the day. What looks like a balanced consideration is actually part of a steadily widening viewpoint, as Tennyson backs up Argyll's vision of the Land bill as a short-term solution which would create long-term problems. Such printed effects are not to be wholly disassociated from Gladstone's disingenuous oratory; in these instances, both poet and politician allow the forms of their mediums to hint at a viewpoint which they refuse to countenance.

What Gladstone often saw as promptitude, Tennyson saw as precipitancy, and the differences between the two men over how to address the Irish problem were translated into more explicit negotiations at the end of 1883, when the Prime Minister offered Tennyson a seat in the Lords. As Richard Shannon observes, while the literary peerage "marked a historic moment in the recognition by the British state of the claims on it of the worlds of letters . . . a 'political' angle was rarely absent from such patronage. . . . Gladstone expected him to vote as a Liberal peer."[26] Introduced to the Lords by Argyll, Tennyson was to unsettle such expectations, and signalled his refusal to be a mere echo of Gladstonian policy when he took up a position on the cross-benches in the House.

The parliamentary debate over the new Reform bill gathered pace in 1884. Behind the issue of franchise reform there lurked the Irish question, for the proposed expansion of the voting community would give Parnell's party more power in parliament.[27] The Franchise

bill was reintroduced into the Lords on November 13, and the following day Tennyson sent a brief poem to Gladstone (entitled "Compromise") in which he advised him "be not precipitate in thine act" (l. 1), counselling him to avoid the "straight" (l. 4) route and to take "the bend" (l. 8). Again, Tennyson's focus is on the long-term course as opposed to short cuts, but Gladstone's reply to this public and personal statement took up the terms of the poem, and added a rider of its own:

> I think it a great honour to receive from you a suggestion in verse. . . . I have been quite willing to tread any path, direct or circuitous, which could lead me to the attainment of this end.
>
> Indeed I have, as you advise, toiled in the circuitous method: but unfortunately with this issue that, working round the labyrinth, I find myself at the end where I was at the beginning.
>
> However, in any and every way open to us, we shall continue to work for peace. "The resources of civilisation are not yet exhausted," and I will not despair.
>
> (*Letters* [*The Letters of Alfred Lord Tennyson*], 3:304)

Turning "the bend" into a labyrinth, Gladstone implies that the advice "be not precipitate" can easily overlook the opposite imperative, "be not dawdling." The politician also infuses the reform question with an Irish dimension, for his quotation is from one of his most renowned speeches during the 1880s, delivered at Leeds on October 7, 1881, on Parnell and the Irish issue. Here Gladstone issued a threat which was disguised as an appeal when considering the violent language of the Land League and their supporters:

> If the law, purged from defeat and from any taint of injustice, is still to be refused and the first condition of political society to remain unfulfilled, then I say, gentlemen, without hesitation, that the resources of civilization are not yet exhausted.
>
> (The *Times,* October 8, 1881, p. 7)

The resource to which Gladstone alluded was jail, and Parnell was imprisoned four days later for "speeches pointing to treasonable practice." By referring to this speech in his letter to Tennyson, the politician is stressing the need for something other than "the circuitous method" in political life.

These cagey altercations conducted between the Laureate and the Prime Minister through allusions to poetry and public speeches helped to temper Tennyson's own need to see beyond the moment; he eventually supported the Gladstone bill and explained that "I voted for the Franchise to avoid worse things" (Allingham, p. 325). What these "worse things" might be was broached by the progress of Parnell's career after 1882, a progress which had important corollaries for the attitudes of both Tennyson and Gladstone to public speaking and Irish politics. The Land League was dissolved in 1882, and as Parnell turned away from his links with agrarian unrest to an increased focus on parliamentary pressure, so another oratorical strategy had to be developed.

Before his prison sentence the Irish leader had divided his time in and out of the House between different types of speech (one constitutional and the other revolutionary), but he now attempted to shape a language which could contain both types of impetus in order to defend "Home Rule." What "Home Rule" was, exactly, is open to some doubt. In his study of the transition from agrarian agitation to nationalist politics, James Loughlin notes that "in Parnell the Home Rule movement was dominated by a leader whose true significance lay in his ability to pose simultaneously as a revolutionary and a constitutionalist."[28] "Simultaneously" now, and not by turns; this simultaneity was to be enacted in Parnell's carefully crafted oratory. He delivered his most famous speech at Cork in 1885, a speech from which excerpts were taken and engraved on the Chief's tombstone:

> It is given to none of us to forecast the future. . . . We cannot ask for less than the restitution of Grattan's Parliament (cheers), with its important privileges and wide and far reaching constitution. We cannot, under the British constitution, ask for more than the restitution of Grattan's parliament (renewed cheers). But no man has the right to fix the boundary to the march of a nation (great cheering); no man has the right to say to his country "Thus far shalt thou go and no further", and we have never attempted to fix the *ne plus ultra* to the progress of Ireland's nationhood, and we never shall (cheers).

> (The *Times,* January 22, 1885, p. 10)

Mark his absolute "shall." "We never shall" is, in fact, "a forecast of the future," but the forecast is at once full and empty of meaning, for Parnell's willingness to turn prophet is met by equivocations as to exactly what the "march of a nation" might be.[29] The cadences of "no more than x and no less than x" are met by the proviso that "anything is possible." When heard, the cheering of the audience seems to point toward nationalist aspirations, but when read, it points in too many directions at once. The mixture of fervor and equivocation here was noted by the *Times* that day: "The words . . . are pregnant with meaning and with mischief" (p. 8).

This meaningful mischief led to similar ambivalences in Conservative and Liberal responses to Parnell's project, as both Salisbury and Gladstone equivocated over the future direction of Irish policy. Such ambivalences might be seen as a careful unwillingness to rule out options or envisaged as dishonest temporizing; Argyll opted for the latter viewpoint. Many of his speeches after 1882 (speeches which Tennyson praised as "sane and true") objected to the way in which Parnell's wavering rhetorical had been mimicked by Gladstone's

edging towards an ambivalent language with regard to Home Rule.[30] These arguments were developed in a book which Argyll wrote and sent to Tennyson after the first Home Rule crisis. He focused on Gladstone's oratorical deceitfulness, claiming that the speaker's phrases had been infected by Parnell's eloquence; Gladstone's words now had "a boundless latitude of meaning . . . in some senses they might be 'perfectly acceptable and even desirable,' whilst in others they would be 'mischievous and revolutionary'":

> Our Parliamentary Government, especially as developed in recent times, puts an enormous premium on the powers of speech. Mr. Gladstone, more perhaps than any public man who has ever occupied a like position, uses, and depends upon this power. . . . His great parliamentary expositions bristle with ingenuities of statement. Subtle distinctions, and sometimes equally subtle confoundings of distinction, are continually involved when they are entirely unperceived by those who hear him. Dexterous appeals to different sentiments and to sections of opinion, equally refined and effective, are parts of his apparatus in the handling of the great popular assembly in which he has been so long predominant. Now this is, perhaps, of all training the most dangerous in the making of Constitutions. It leads men to be the victims of their own eloquence—firm believers in the power and virtue of mere words and phrases. For the purpose of swaying popular assemblies at the moment, these are indeed invaluable; and of course they may be yoked to service in a good cause as well as in a bad one. But of all the sources of danger and of fatal error that can beset a statesman who assumes to frame an organic statute for the government of mankind, perhaps this volubility in phrases, and this trust in them, is the most pestilent, because the most prolific.[31]

Gladstone's ambiguously (un)constitutional oratory is here associated with Parnell's ability to make his statements inflammatory when spoken, yet reticent in print. The underhand shift from the "ingenious" to the "dexterous" to the "subtle" to the "pestilent" insists upon the danger of Gladstone's abilities by implementing them against him, and such danger is again perceived as being too attentive to "the moment." In the Lords, it was Tennyson who came to mind when Argyll expressed his desire for another type of public speech:

> Is there no medium between total silence upon the greatest questions that will affect the political future of this country and the partisan utterances to which I have alluded? . . . We want men, my Lords,

> "Who never sold a truth to serve the hour,
> Nor paltered with Eternal God for power."

> (The *Times,* July 11, 1885, p. 8)

In contrast to Gladstone's perceived misuse of "the powers of speech," Argyll's peroration implements Tennyson's lines from the Wellington Ode (ll. 179-180) in order to defend the perennial against the present.[32] Outside the speech-marks, however, great public speaking is conceived as an ability to mediate between the partisan and the non-committal. For Tennyson, such a mediation was often alarmingly close to those "ingenuities of statement" and "confoundings of distinction" which Argyll had observed in Gladstone's "appeals to different sentiments and to sections of opinion." In the agonized eloquence of "Locksley Hall Sixty Years After" (1886) he set himself to examine not only the meaning of contemporary political events, but also to explore how a voice in print could shift between an appeal to different sentiments and an appalling loss of bearings.

3

"Locksley Hall Sixty Years After" is haunted by the powers of speech and by the sounds of public voices, raving against "the hustings liar" (l. 123) and "the tonguesters" (l. 130). The poem's contradictions on the tongue lament the passing of the "old political commonsense" (l. 250), but they also invade the common senses of words through a linguistic concentration which is as politically astute about the pretensions of the age's rhetoric as it is politically tentative about its own.

The speaker's criticisms of the age often turn into a worry about his own age, for while he is anxious not to sell the truth to serve the hour, he cannot seem to work out what time it is. Fearful of the encroaching political darkness, he addresses those who see the changing contemporary scene as evidence of progress:

> Nay, your pardon, cry your "forward", yours are hope
> and youth, but I—
> Eighty winters leave the dog too lame to follow with
> the cry,
>
> Lame and old, and past his time, and passing now into
> the night;
> Yet I would the rising race were half as eager for the
> light.
>
> Light the fading gleam of Even? light the glimmer of
> the dawn?
> Agèd eyes may take the growing glimmer for the
> gleam withdrawn.
>
>   (ll. 225-230)

That Tennyson's acoustic imagination should, in the first four lines, seize upon the same rhymes which described the infant crying in the night in *In Memoriam* (104:16-20) attests to the delicacy with which "hope" is articulated here. This elderly viewpoint "may" take things the wrong way, just as "our *old* England *may* go down in babble at last" (l. 8; my italics), but, then again, it may not. Whether these "agèd eyes" provide the wisdom of experience, or whether they show the loss of the speaker's faculties, was something which concerned the elderly Tennyson. Queen Victoria remembered a conversation with her Laureate at this time: "He spoke

of Ireland, and the wickedness of ill-using poor animals: 'I am afraid I think the world is darkened; I dare say it will brighten again'" (*Memoir*, 2:457).

The poet's fear that his speaking on Ireland may be subject to his seeing awry leads him back to bestial behavior in "Locksley Hall Sixty Years After." As so often in Tennyson's late verse, the liberalism of the age is intertwined with the Irish question; here, the speaker's fear that past calls for democracy in France were pernicious ("Celtic Demos rose a Demon" [l. 90]) leads him to those other Celts:

> Have we sunk below them? peasants maim the help-
> less horse, and drive
> Innocent cattle under thatch, and burn the kindlier
> brutes alive.
>
> Brutes, the brutes are not your wrongers—burnt at
> midnight, found at morn,
> Twisted hard in mortal agony with their offspring,
> born-unborn.
>
>   (ll. 95-98)

The topography of "Maeldune" (the flaming dwellings and lame cattle) is revisited, but now indignation is mixed with implication by a speaker who is himself "lame and old" (l. 226). At the very moment when the speaker tries to back off from complicity in agrarian and political outrage (when "we" becomes "your"), the point is conceded that the Irish have been wronged ("your wrongers"). The lines express terror at political crimes, but the voices within the lines register the feeling that there is more than one criminal. When the speaker goes on to admit that "here and there my lord is lower than his oxen or his swine" (l. 126), it seems that the political rulers have sunk below the objects of the Irish cruelty.

As Tennyson was writing "Locksley Hall Sixty Years After," heady democratic changes in late 1885 brought Irish matters to a head. The general election marked the end of an era, as the increased electorate created by the 1884 Franchise bill returned a parliament with a new atmosphere. For the first time in history, fewer than half the MPs returned were connected to landed society, while nearly half of the Members were returned for the first time (the highest percentage of the century).[33] After the election the Liberal government had a slender majority of sixty-eight, a majority which required them to work with Parnell's party (now exactly sixty-eight men strong in the Commons), and the sense of instability was compounded when Gladstone's conversion to Home Rule was announced.

On April 8, 1886 the Prime Minister delivered his key speech on Ireland. The *Times* claimed:

> It is not a figure of speech to affirm that Mr Gladstone's
> statement, in moving for leave to introduce a measure

of Home Rule for Ireland, was without a parallel in our Parliamentary annals. . . . Never within living memory has there been so much interest displayed in a debate.

(The *Times,* April 9, 1886, pp. 9-10)[34]

Tennyson's own interest was evidenced by a letter he wrote to the Queen a week after Gladstone's speech: "We feel deeply the state of public affairs" (*Letters,* 3:336). He then sent Gladstone a copy of a book he had been reading, Henry Maine's *Popular Government,* which echoed many of Argyll's complaints about how the dignity of public speaking at Westminster was being threatened as a result of the increased electorate and the Irish pressure.[35]

Gladstone's speech filters into the agitated cadences of "Locksley Hall Sixty Years After" at odd angles. The politician had begun his speech by adapting the temporal considerations of Argyll and Tennyson to his own ends:

> What I wish is . . . that we should take measures not merely intended for the wants of to-day and tomorrow, but, if possible, that we should look into a more distant future; that we should endeavour to anticipate and realise that future by the force of reflection; that we should, if possible, unroll it in anticipation before our eyes, and make provision now, while there is yet time, for all the results that may await upon a right or wrong decision to-day.[36]

Behind the extremity of a rhetoric which apparently wants us to consider "*all* the results" of present actions "if possible" there lies Gladstone's responsiveness to present exigency (hence his "while there is yet time"), for many contemporaries perceived that the Home Rule bill was designed as an expedient way of getting rid of the Irish MPs who were obstructing parliamentary business through prolonged debate. The politician obliquely alludes to obstructionism only twice in the speech, but it was this practical consideration which lay behind his ideal emphasis on the need for "political equality" and "equitable arrangements" between Ireland and England (Bassett [*Gladstone's Speeches*], pp. 603, 643, 615, 635).

Tennyson's speaker grapples with these issues in the following address to the "Orator":

> Chaos, Cosmos! Cosmos, Chaos! who can tell how all will end?
> Read the wide world's annals, you, and take their wisdom for your friend.
>
> Hope the best, but hold the Present faithful daughter of the Past,
> Shape your heart to front the hour, but dream not that the hour will last.
>
> Ay, if dynamite and revolver leave you courage to be wise:

> When was age so crammed with menace? madness? written, spoken lies?
>
> Envy wears the mask of Love, and, laughing sober fact to scorn,
> Cries to Weakest as to Strongest, "Ye are equals, equal-born."
>
> Equal-born? O yes, if yonder hill be level with the flat.
> Charm us, Orator, till the Lion look no larger than the Cat,
>
> Till the Cat through that mirage of overheated language loom
> Larger than the Lion,—Demos end in working its own doom.

(ll. 103-114)

"Charm us"; the contemptuous imperative recalls that Irish charm which so concerned Tennyson and which Gladstone was cultivating in his own speeches. Here the poet's speaker takes issue with the Prime Minister's vision of the present as infiltrated by past and future concerns by suggesting that such "wise" statements are prompted by the language of menace which had been employed by Irish agitators. The wisdom of the "annals" has been perverted by a speech which seeks only to further party ends, and Tennyson's printed voice aims to redress the balance. But the polemic which envisages the Lion (of England) as threatened by a rhetoric of "equality" is also that which finds it hard to tell "written, spoken lies" apart. By the end of this passage, it is difficult to know whether the speaker laments or welcomes the end of "Demos," or whether "age" (l. 108) refers to "the" age, to the Grand Old Man of the Liberal party, or to the speaker himself. Indeed, the speaker's criticism of "overheated language" will soon led to a confession: "Heated am I? you—you wonder—well, it scarce becomes mine age" (l. 151).

The dizzying trails of insinuation in "Locksley Hall Sixty Years After" bespeak a political perplexity, a feeling that public speech has let the public down, but also, a feeling that speakers should not always address themselves to public "Voices" (l. 131) and demands by capitulating to them. In his review of Tennyson's poems Walt Whitman quoted the lines on the Orator when praising Tennyson's "deep-sounding voice": "He shows how one can be royal laureate, quite elegant and 'aristocratic', and a little queer and affected, and at the same time perfectly manly and natural."[37] Such a mixture of elegant, affected, and natural accents finds an analogue in those speeches by Parnell and Gladstone which aimed to mediate between different sections of opinion, and, as with Gladstone's "subtle confoundings of distinction," the confounded politics of "Locksley Hall Sixty Years After" have often to be re-read in order to be heard. The analogue also points to a difference, though; whereas the oratory of the politicians finds its end in action, the speaker of Tennyson's monologue has seen through so many voices that he can no longer shape a future. The recreations of political speech on the page attempt to read between the lines of that which has passed out of earshot, but they also acknowledge that an ability to see voices leads not to persuasion, but to nostalgia. As the speaker himself puts it: "All I loved are vanished voices" (l. 252).

Gladstone was quick to take a hint, and a month after the poem came out he deemed the Laureate's veiled utterance important enough to review it. While Tennyson had plumbed the unspoken agenda behind Gladstone's rhetoric by re-imagining his voice in print, the poet's return to the dramatic monologue for a comment upon the age was coolly met by the politician:

> In the work . . . which is now before the world, Lord Tennyson neither claims the authority, nor charges himself with the responsibility, of one who solemnly delivers, under the weight of years, and with a shortened span before him, a confession of political or social faith. The poem is strictly a dramatic monologue.[38]

Gladstone's prose can not quite manage not to be adversely critical here, as Tennyson's modest unwillingness to claim authority gives rise to a more debatable unwillingness to accept responsibility for the words he has written. For Gladstone, "Locksley Hall Sixty Years After" is at once both too certain and not certain enough; on the one hand, the Laureate's "present survey of the age" asks a question of the last sixty years which brooks no reply: "The question demands an answer; . . . whether it is just to pronounce what seems to be a very decided censure on the immediate Past," but the "seems" in the sentence also articulates Gladstone's other view concerning both "Locksley Hall" poems: "The poems are purely subjective; . . . they do not deal with the outward world at all" (pp. 6, 18). The extremity of the politician's response belies the achievement of Tennyson's poem, for the monologue is, as we have seen and heard, neither "very decided" nor "purely subjective," and when Gladstone ends his article on the poem with the grand assertion that "justice does not require, nay rather she forbids, that the Jubilee of the Queen be marred by tragic tones" (p. 18), we may ask why these tones should be censored on public occasions.

Tennyson's public utterances in print insist upon the value of an eloquence which can express doubts as well as convictions. The politician's insistence in the same article upon focusing on the achievements of the age in "the sphere of legislation" (p. 9) met with a reply, this time in a Jubilee Ode in which the Laureate dropped the monologist's mask for an utterance honoring the fifty years "Since our Queen assumed the globe, the sceptre" (l. 3). Having asked that "the maimed in his heart rejoice / At this glad Ceremonial / And this year

of her Jubilee" (ll. 36-38), the lame, old man of "Locksley Hall Sixty Years After" is not quite forgotten as Tennyson adds a coda to match Gladstone's remarks:

> Are there thunders moaning in the distance?
> Are there spectres moving in the darkness?
> Trust the Hand of Light will lead her people,
> Till the thunders pass, the spectres vanish,
> And the Light is Victor, and the darkness
> Dawns into the Jubilee of the Ages.
>
> (ll. 66-71)

The vision of a future which holds both terror and hope stems from the sense of a past which holds the lowly, the destitute, the weary, and the needy (ll. 31-35) as well as the achievements of Commerce, Science, and Empire (ll. 51-63). For Tennyson, being jubilant about achievement involves an awareness of how the power of the "sceptre" can glide into the presence of "spectres," how behind the "ceremonial," if one listens carefully enough, one can hear "moaning."

In his essay on "The Poetic Principle" Edgar Allan Poe observed of Tennyson that "he has neglected to make precise investigation of the principles of metre; but, on the other hand, so perfect is his rhythmical instinct in general, that . . . he seems *to see with his ear*."[39] The last line of the Jubilee Ode, in contrast to the last sentence of Gladstone's article, insists upon a minute rhythmical lapse, adding an extra syllable ("the") to disrupt the steadily falling rhythms of the trochaics which the poet had been so careful to establish in the earlier lines.[40] The disturbance insists upon the integrity of a public speech which refuses to become too eloquent through an appeal to "Trust." The Laureate's last words speak of the difficulty of smooth perorations; when "seeing with his ear," Tennyson creates a civic voice which is both apprehensive and aspiring.

Notes

1. Recorded by A. G. Temple, in *Guildhall Memories* (London: John Murray, 1918), pp. 262-263. See also Lord Ernle, *Whippingham to Westminster* (London: John Murray, 1938), pp. 141-142.

2. Gladstone's continued willingness to find time for Tennyson even amid the press of his political duties is confirmed by a browse through his diaries; while preparing the budget speech in 1859, for example, he was reading "Tennyson, Tennyson, Tennyson," and a few weeks earlier he noted "Read divers pamphlets . . . Hansard's Debates—Tennyson" (*The Gladstone Diaries,* ed. H. C. G. Matthew and M. R. D. Foot, 14 vols [Oxford: Clarendon Press, 1968-94], 5:416, 411). Conversely, Hallam Tennyson records the two men talking over the differences between "poets and literary men . . . and orators," and over "the force of public

opinion" (*Alfred Lord Tennyson: A Memoir,* 2 vols [London, 1897], 2:278, 315), while William Allingham mentions discussions with the Laureate in which "we spoke of Gladstone's oratory." (*The Letters of Alfred Lord Tennyson,* ed. Cecil Lang and Edgar Shannon, 3 vols. [Oxford: Clarendon Press, 1982-90], 2:306).

3. No sustained analysis of how the relationship between Gladstone and Tennyson influenced the style of the latter's work has yet been undertaken. For brief studies, see Gerhard Joseph, "The Homeric Competitions of Tennyson and Gladstone," *BIS* [*Browning Institute Studies: An Annual of Victorian Literary and Culture History*] 10 (1982): 105-115; Jack Kolb, "Gladstone and Tennyson's *In Memoriam,*" *VP* [*Victorian Poetry*] 23 (1985): 196-199; and Richard Shannon, "Tennyson and Gladstone: From Courtship to Mutual Disenchantment," *TLS* [*Times Literary Supplement*], October 2, 1992, p. 4. There is also still much work to be done on Tennyson's relationship with Argyll. As Cecil Lang and Edgar Shannon point out: "More letters survive from Tennyson to the Duke and Duchess of Argyll than to anyone else except his wife. . . . As an *orator* he [Argyll] ranked with Bright, Gladstone, and Disraeli" (*Letters* [*The Letters of Alfred Lord Tennyson*], 2:562). The epigraph to Argyll's *The Reign of Law* (London, 1867) is taken from *In Memoriam,* and Argyll quotes Tennyson's poetry throughout his book in order to support his political and philosophical arguments.

4. Michael MacDonough, *Irish Life and Character* (London, 1898), pp. 280-281.

5. See L. Perry Curtis, *Apes and Angels: The Irishman in Victorian Caricature* (Washington, D.C.: Smithsonian Institute, c. 1977), who explores how the Irish were often represented as ungovernable apes and animals during the latter half of the nineteenth century.

6. Sheridan Gilley, "English Attitudes to the Irish in England, 1789-1900," *Immigrants and Minorities in British Society,* ed. Colin Holmes (London: Allen and Unwin, 1978), pp. 94-95.

7. On Tennyson's focus on "the unreasonable memories of the slighted Irish," see Matthew Campbell, "Tennyson and Ireland," *TRB* [*The Tennyson Research Bulletin*] 6 (1994): 161-173.

8. H. Allingham and D. Radford, eds., *William Allingham, A Diary* (1907; London: Folio Society, 1990), pp. 293, 298.

9. Henry Lucy, *A Diary of the Home Rule Parliament, 1892-1895* (London, 1896), p. 38.

10. R. F. Foster, *Paddy and Mr Punch: Connections in Irish and British History* (London: Penguin, 1993), p. 186. For a discussion of how Irish obstructionism shaped parliamentary debate in this period, see Edward Hughes, "The Changes in Parliamentary Procedure 1880-1882," *Essays Presented to Sir Lewis Namier,* ed. Richard Pares and A. J. P. Taylor (London: Macmillan, 1956), pp. 289-319.

11. As Conor Cruise O'Brien notes: "Parnell directed a movement of revolutionary inspiration, from within a relatively conservative and constitutional party. This is the peculiarity that made 'Parnellism' such an equivocal term and so elusive and effective a force" (*Parnell and His Party 1880-90* [Oxford: Clarendon Press, 1957], pp. 9-10).

12. Henry Lucy, *A Diary of Two Parliaments,* Vol. 2, *The Gladstone Parliament 1886-1885* (London: 1885), pp. 108-109.

13. Quoted in F. S. L. Lyons, *Charles Stewart Parnell* (London: Harper Collins, 1978), p. 106.

14. R. F. Foster, *Modern Ireland 1600-1972* (London: Penguin, 1989), pp. 405-406.

15. Foster notes that "Parnell's wildly successful tour of America in 1880 established him as the greatest political leader of nationalist Ireland since O'Connell" (p. 405).

16. It was published in the 1880 volume of Tennyson's poems, and became one of the most popular pieces in the collection; see *Daily News,* December 5, 1883, p. 5.

17. P. W. Joyce, *Old Celtic Romances* (London, 1879), p. vi.

18. *The Poems of Tennyson,* ed. Christopher Ricks, 3 vols. (Berkeley: Univ. of California Press, 1987), ll. 1-2. All subsequent citations refer to this edition.

19. The *Times,* January 2, 1880, p. 4.

20. In a conversation with Tennyson in 1880, Allingham had admitted of the Land League agitation that "this last phase of discontent is perhaps the worst—flavoured with Americanism and general irreverence" (Allingham, p. 298).

21. On Gladstone's change in policy, see John Vincent, "Gladstone and Ireland," *Proceedings of the British Academy* 63 (1977): 193-238.

22. Argyll had protested: "My lords, we all know who it is that in recent years has spoken, in words that have been very often quoted, of 'that fierce light which beats upon a throne.' I ask you, my Lords, whether there ever was in this world so fierce a light as that which beats upon this Afghan policy of Her Majesty's Government," The *Times,* February 21, 1880, p. 6.

23. Argyll recalls the dispute and a letter to Gladstone in which he stated: "My impression has always been, and still is, that any of the 'three F's' carries or will carry the other two" (*Autobiography and Memoirs* [London: John Murray, 1906], 2:361). For an account of the bill, see H. C. G. Matthew, *Gladstone* (Oxford: Clarendon Press, 1997), pp. 444-448.

24. *Hansard's Parliamentary Debates* 263, p. 1419 (July 20, 1881).

25. Tennyson's extensive reading of Argyll's speeches is noted in *Letters,* 3:364.

26. Richard Shannon, *Gladstone: Heroic Minister* (London: Penguin, 1999), p. 320.

27. For a discussion of the bill, see Andrew Jones, *The Politics of Reform 1884* (Cambridge: Cambridge Univ. Press, 1972). Tennyson's awareness of the link between Irish and domestic matters is shown by a letter he wrote to Gladstone on the eve of the reform debate; see *Letters,* 3:296.

28. James Loughlin, *Gladstone, Home Rule and the Ulster Question 1882-1893* (Dublin: Gill and Macmillan, 1986), p. 27. John Kendle points out that "in the 1880s, at the very beginning of the concentrated discussion, 'devolution,' 'federalism,' 'home rule,' 'federal home rule,' 'home rule all round,' and 'federal devolution' were used indiscriminately to describe proposed changes to the British constitution" (*Ireland and The Federal Solution: The Debate over the U.K. Constitution 1870-1971* [Montreal: McGill-Queen's Univ. Press, 1989], p. 4).

29. Lyons attests to the "calculated ambiguity" of the speech: "To some . . . he seemed to have left the road to full independence wide open. To others, although their knowledge of Grattan's parliament might be rusty, the phrases in which he described it sounded agreeably constitutional." (p. 261)

30. See, for example, the *Times,* June 17, 1884, p. 6.

31. George Douglas Campbell, *The New British Constitution and Its Master-Builders* (Edinburgh, 1888), pp. 125, 48.

32. When Argyll visited Tennyson at Farringford the poet read the Wellington Ode to him and stopped at the words above, adding: "As I am afraid Gladstone is doing now"; quoted in Robert Bernard Martin, *Tennyson: The Unquiet Heart* (Oxford: Clarendon Press, 1983), pp. 575-576.

33. As W. C. Lubenow observes: "This was a sudden event. The reforms of 1884-85 did what those of 1832 and 1867 did not do; they broke the numerical hold of the landed élite in the House of Commons" (*Parliamentary Politics and the Home Rule Crisis: The British House of Commons in 1886* [Oxford: Clarendon Press, 1988], p. 57). Contemporary opinion was also alert to the significance of the situation; the *Times* observed: "With today's dissolution passes away, for good or evil, the direct power of the middle classes in English politics" (November 18, 1885, p. 9).

34. The paper printed the speech whole, p. 5 onwards.

35. Henry Maine observed of the Commons and the country that "crowds of men can be got to assent to general statements, clothed in striking language, but unverified and perhaps incapable of verification; and thus there is formed a sort of sham and pretence of concurrent opinion" (*Popular Government: Four Essays* [London: 1885], p. 95).

36. Reprinted in Arthur Tilney Bassett, ed., *Gladstone's Speeches: A Descriptive Index and Bibliography* (London: Methuen, 1916), p. 602.

37. Walt Whitman, "A Word about Tennyson," *The Critic* (January 1, 1887): 1-2.

38. "'Locksley Hall' and the Jubilee," *Nineteenth Century* 21 (January 1887): 1.

39. Cited in *Lord Alfred Tennyson: The Critical Heritage,* ed. John Jump (London: Routledge, 1967), p. 418.

40. One might read "th'Ages" in order to elide the syllable, but the rhythmic tremor would still be audible. The last line is exemplary in more than just its syllable count; lines 66-70 never go beyond a disyllabic word, nor do any of these disyllables start with an unstressed syllable. Line 71 goes against such order in using "Jubilee" and "into."

Ruth Clayton Windscheffel (essay date spring 2006)

SOURCE: Windscheffel, Ruth Clayton. "Politics, Religion and Text: W. E. Gladstone and Spiritualism." *Journal of Victorian Culture* 11, no. 1: no. 221 (spring 2006): 1-29.

[*In the following essay, Windscheffel probes Gladstone's treatment of spiritualism and the occult in his writings. Windscheffel maintains that Gladstone's investigations into supernatural and psychic phenomena played a key role in shaping his later religious beliefs.*]

INTRODUCTION[1]

The tag line of *Cheiro's Language of the Hand,* first published in 1894 with its showcase of living celebrities' palm prints, reads 'as is the mind, so is the form'.[2]

Amongst the 'famous hands' reproduced in the 1897 edition was that of William Ewart Gladstone, four times Prime Minister of Great Britain, an obvious choice for any commercially minded author or publisher.[3] Ostensibly there seems little reason to suppose that Gladstone's interest in such phenomena was anything other than transient. Historiographical tradition indicates that Gladstone's intellectual and spiritual concerns were of the most serious kind: the tenets of Anglicanism; the connection between Olympian and Judaic religions, and the nature of sin. But Gladstone's sphere of serious interest did extend into realms such as cheiromancy, as this exploration of his earnest investigation into psychical phenomena, particularly spiritualism, seeks to demonstrate.

The press reported Gladstone's occasional *séance* attendances and he recorded observing other amateur paranormal experiments in his diary. Based on these sources, Gladstone's biographers (when they have addressed the question at all)[4] have suggested that his involvement was limited to mild, intermittent curiosity about the latest crazes preoccupying the élite circles in which he moved. However this evaluation does not sit well with the insights offered by other available evidence, particularly that presented by his library.

Gladstone's recorded reading and writings indicate a deep level of concern about occult practices. He accorded a prominent place to 'Magic and Spiritism' in his library classification scheme for St Deiniol's (the residential library which he established in the 1880s near his North Wales home).[5] He did not regard it as a minor collection; such were listed in a memorandum as 'Epitaphs &c. Books on marriage &c. Hymns. [and] Liturgies': subjects more obviously in keeping with his better-publicized preoccupations.[6] Moreover, the library preserves an impressive collection of arcane literature, the greater part of which Gladstone owned and annotated.

The following historical study aims, through a careful examination and integration of the St Deiniol's evidence, to reassess Gladstone's relationship with spiritualism, and, in the light of those findings, to review aspects of his broader thought and behaviour.

SPIRITUALISM IN CONTEXT

Modern spiritualism is traditionally dated from 1848 when a spate of table-rappings swept New York State. The movement soon took hold in Britain and peaked in the 1870s and 1880s.[7] To define who was or was not a spiritualist in Victorian Britain remains problematic. Victorian spiritualist belief centred on the possibility of contact between the living and the dead; beyond this it is impossible to cite a single creed embraced by its followers.[8]

Whether or not Gladstone was a spiritualist remains subordinate to questions of how and why he engaged with such beliefs, and what was its impact upon him. His involvement was not unusual, as Colin Matthew has shown:

> Involvement with spiritualism in the 1880s was common enough in the professional classes and the aristocracy. As traditional beliefs about heaven, hell, and sacramental religion declined among the intelligentsia and 'agnostic' became a common self-description, attempts to communicate beyond immediate consciousness were seen as a natural form of progress.[9]

Matthew is right to acknowledge that spiritualists expressed many preoccupations common to the period. However his theory of secularization and diametrical opposition of Christian belief and spiritualism are questionable. Many spiritualists shared Christian concerns over apparent threats from science and materialist philosophy; before 1914, the desire to discredit scientific materialism was a primary motivation for many British spiritualists.[10] Some certainly preferred to fight science with science rather than with the defensive intransigence that characterized much Christian apologetic. But when investigating Gladstone's involvement it must be remembered that there were fervent Christian as well as anti-Christian spiritualists.

GLADSTONE'S INVOLVEMENT WITH SPIRITUALISM

PSYCHICAL RESEARCH

Gladstone's main public association with spiritualism was through his honorary membership of the Society for Psychical Research (SPR), which he joined in June 1885 and with which he remained affiliated until his death.[11] This was unlikely to excite comment; other honorary members included Tennyson, Ruskin and G. F. Watts. Gladstone's interest in questions on the margins of Christian belief was longstanding: he was a founder member of the Metaphysical Society, which aimed 'to collect, arrange, and diffuse knowledge (whether objective or subjective) of mental and moral phenomena'.[12] The SPR was similarly organized. Run by respected academics and intellectuals, it had a largely congruent membership.

What does Gladstone's membership of the SPR tell us about his relations with spiritualism? Spiritualists and psychical researchers were not always identical. The SPR adopted a rigorous approach to the study of phenomena, publishing their results in an academic journal. Founder members like Henry Sidgwick and Frederick Myers were committed to achieving certainty through their experiments in order to secure tangible proof of immortality. Some spiritualists interpreted such activities as hostile to their own. In 1885, the *Light* observed, 'The real *mot d'ordre* of the Psychical Society may be summed up in the well-known phrase, "the spirit is the last thing I will give in to", a position which involves some of the most wanton assumptions possible.'[13] Gladstone, although happy to be associated with the SPR, remained distant from its activities. He was friendly with the Sidgwicks but his correspondence with Henry did not mention psychical research. His collection of the Society's transactions is preserved at St Deiniol's, but remains unbound and largely unannotated. The first two volumes, which predate membership, are the only ones so treated. In all likelihood these were given to Gladstone by the SPR, either as an encouragement to join or for information, explaining why they were read more carefully than subsequent editions.[14]

DATING

Central to understanding Gladstone's relationship with spiritualism is establishing its duration. Matthew dates Gladstone's experience of psychical phenomena from the 1880s, whilst Richard Shannon suggests the interest originated earlier, with a 'weakness for phrenology'.[15] Matthew's earliest reference is June 1884, when Gladstone and about fifty other MPs attended a 'Thought-reading' by a Mr Cumberland at the House of Commons, which Gladstone described as 'curious'; adding 'to call it imposture is [. . .] nonsense. I was myself operated upon'.[16] Immediately we see Gladstone both interested and open-minded. Many of his contemporaries denounced such things out of hand: Charles Dickens wrote in 1855, 'I have not the least belief in the awful unseen being available for evening parties at so much per night.'[17] Gladstone admitted, 'to mix myself in these things would baffle & perplex', but, unlike Dickens, he felt, 'good advice is to be remembered come how it may'.[18] And he had held such views for a significant period. In 1877 he wrote to J. T. Markley, who had sent a work on spiritualism, saying: 'I do not share the temper of simple contempt [. . .] I remain in what may be called contented reserve.'[19]

Matthew suggests that Gladstone was first drawn into spiritualism directly on 8 October 1884 at Laura Thistlethwayte's *salon* in Grosvenor Square.[20] Gladstone met and had been captivated by the recently retired courtesan in the 1860s.[21] By the 1880s her circle included numerous socialites involved in spiritualism, who eagerly entertained Gladstone. However there is evidence that Gladstone was associating with society spiritualists before this date. In 1879 he visited Sir Charles Isham and recorded:

> Sir C. I. touched on Spiritualism with me, and Mr Dasent on his favourite belief in Fairies. *Most curious* are the little low benches and stumps placed under his trees [. . .] said to be for their accommodation.[22]

Shannon suggests that Gladstone's association with Thistlethwayte's circle was just 'one of his periodic spiritualist phases',[23] citing (inaccurately) a 'table-turning' experiment at Penrhyn Castle in 1861 for com-parison.[24] But what Shannon does not mention is that, on his return to Hawarden, Gladstone made a point of reading H. Novra's *Spirit Rapping, Explained and Exposed* (1860).[25] This follow-up reading, about a phenomenon categorized as a popular diversion rather than a serious intellectual concern,[26] immediately attests a deeper interest. Such reading was to become a defining characteristic of Gladstone's response to spiritualism.

SÉANCE ATTENDANCE: SOCIETY SPIRITS AND THE VAGARIES OF CLASS

Gladstone attended his first *séance* on 29 October 1884.[27] It was conducted by William Eglinton mainly by slate writing. Gladstone participated by writing two questions,[28] and recorded the experience in his diary:

> Dined at Mrs Hartmanns. Mr Elkington [*sic*] came in evg. For the first time I was present at his operations of spiritism: quite inexplicable: not the smallest sign of imposture. I took down the particulars.[29]

As with Mr Cumberland, Gladstone perceived no reason to doubt the phenomena. But Eglinton was regarded by some as a charlatan. In the 1870s he had established a reputation as a sensational medium, whose *séances* included full-form spirit materializations, flying objects, levitation and slate writing. Following an SPR investigation into the latter in 1886, he was fiercely denounced as 'a clever conjuror' in their journal. This ignited a rancorous controversy that damaged Eglinton's reputation and provoked a split between some spiritualists and the SPR.[30] It is unclear what Gladstone thought of Eglinton subsequently; he certainly made no marginal comment on reading the following account by J. N. Maskelyne:

> Some few years ago a slight stir was made by one Eglinton [. . .] He was once invited by an old lady to meet Mr. Gladstone [. . .] On this occasion, upon a prepared slate, the property of the medium, some writing appeared, and, as a matter of course, the ex-Premier failed to discover the trick.[31]

Reports of the *séance* quickly appeared in the London newspapers to Gladstone's chagrin and Mrs Hartmann's embarrassment.[32] Eglinton promised that the true story would appear in the following week's *Light* (8 November 1884), a publication which Gladstone tried unsuccessfully to prevent.[33] The British Library preserves a copy of the article with Gladstone's scant annotations. The title, 'Mr. Gladstone at a *séance*', and preamble show the evident media interest. The body consists of an interview with Eglinton who declared that Gladstone 'had no scepticism in regard to the possibility of psychical phenomena'.[34]

Gladstone posed two questions: 'Which year do you remember to have been more dry than the present one?' To which the reply was: 'In the year 1857'. And on a locked slate: 'Is the Pope well or ill?' To which the response came back: 'He is ill in mind, not in body'. (The spirits declined to reply to another question—not from Gladstone—about the following year's Cesarwitch horse-race winner). Eglinton concluded that he thought Gladstone was 'satisfied' of 'the *bona fides* of the experiment'.[35]

It is easy to see why Eglinton was so forthcoming. It was potentially a terrific boost to his career and to the spiritualist cause to claim that the Prime Minister, who was popularly known as a great advocate of truth, had been convinced.

Gladstone, engulfed in crisis over the reintroduction of the Franchise Bill, greeted the further press coverage with annoyance. He wrote to Emma Hartmann:

> I am sorry to find an article in the *Morning Post* of today. The facts are I think pretty accurately stated, not so the conversation, though I have no doubt that the account is truthfully intended. But the serious matter is that the reporting it at all is a breach of trust & confidence; which Mr. Eglinton has properly respected in the case of yourself & the other ladies.[36]

Several aspects of Gladstone's reaction are noteworthy. Firstly observe Gladstone's assertion that the report was 'truthfully intended'. This not only indicates positive feeling towards Eglinton but is also indicative of Gladstone's liberal approach to evaluating others' beliefs. For example, he could say, of Comte's 'Religion of Humanity', that the 'profession is one which I may be unable to distinguish from an hallucination, but I am far from presuming to pronounce or believe it an imposture'.[37] The importance of such an attitude will become explicit in the following investigation of Gladstone's Christianity. But it is worth remarking how Gladstone's collected response to the inexplicable both supports Peter Lamont's recent contention that validation could be given to phenomena by rigorous, open-minded non-believers but also that such responses did not always result in 'crisis' for the informed observer.[38]

Gladstone's letter is also revelatory of his attitude to both press and public. Although by this stage Gladstone was adept at managing the media and the mass audience, he did not think either should know that the premier had attended a *séance*. This illuminates a dividing line between the public and the private aspects of his political life which is increasingly difficult to situate in the later decades. It also makes clear Gladstone's belief that such occasions should be governed by the same proprieties regulating other aspects of his social world. Ruth Brandon notes the importance of the social setting of the Society *séance,* where politeness and etiquette outranked the demands of scientific experiment.[39] With this in mind, one observes the class-conscious quality of Gladstone's annoyance. He firstly notes that the la-

dies remain nameless. In the *Light,* his hostess is styled 'a lady of distinction in Grosvenor Square' and thus worthy of anonymity. Gladstone's annotated *Light* article also bears heavy underlining and an 'NB' by Eglinton's insistence that 'I am not at liberty to say anything about my relations with the Duke of Albany'.[40] The belittling implications of differently treating the fourth son of Victoria and Albert and the fourth son of a Liverpool merchant were clearly not lost on the annoyed premier.

The letter sheds light both on Gladstone's treatment of people and their gifts, and also on his attitude to the material culture of books. In his interview, Eglinton had highlighted Gladstone's acceptance of some books.

> I asked him whether he would honour me by accepting a few books upon the subject, to which he very kindly replied that [. . .] he would most cheerfully undertake to read any book I might desire to send him, adding, 'And I shall keep them as a memento of this very interesting evening'.[41]

Gladstone's subsequently refused the gift, 'which under present circumstances I could not retain'.[42] The rejection of communication with people who had offended him was undoubtedly a character trait. In 1878 a parcel containing gifts from his sister Helen remained unopened because of an outstanding debt: 'I can have no other concern with it,' he informed her, 'while matters remain as they are.'[43] Secondly, Gladstone understood the exchange of books to both reflect and extend intimacy between people, something private and courtly; not to be broadcast in order to increase the giver's status.

The Eglinton *exposé* neither long occupied the headlines nor deterred Gladstone's interest in spiritualism, but it did limit his public engagement with it to the fashionable society world. When he next attended a *séance* it was with guaranteed privacy at Lady Sandhurst's (one of Laura Thistlethwayte's circle) on 18 November 1884, although the medium, Mrs Duncan, was still clearly of a lower class.[44] Gladstone, circumspect after the Eglinton *débâcle,* was determined to remain uninvolved. Nonetheless he gave a full résumé of Mrs Duncan's communications in his diary. Amongst other things she 'Spoke of great questions and great decisions immediately impending and promised help', 'Commended reception of the "Blessed Sacrament" but *rather as an act of obedience* than from any mystical virtue' and concluded by giving 'certain medical prescriptions'.[45] She sent a supplementary exhortation to Gladstone, via Lady Sandhurst, on 27 November 1884, in which she demanded that 'the Navy ought to be looked after, and that quickly',[46] as well as offering further reassuring words about Gladstone's political career.[47]

It is unclear whether Gladstone was influenced by Mrs Duncan but Shannon suggests Lady Sandhurst's political influence on Gladstone was of a high order.[48] It is certain that her correspondence had a definite political agenda, articulated through a heavily Christianized spiritualist discourse designed to appeal to him. Gladstone continued to attend her *soirées* and, although there is no explicit mention of further *séances,* he continued to associate with spiritualists there. In 1888 he recorded, 'Lady Sandhurst's party. All alive. Saw one who told me strange inventions.'[49]

GLADSTONE AND THE SPIRITUALIST TEXT

SURVEYING THE ST DEINIOL'S COLLECTION

Gladstone's spiritualist reading has neither featured in scholarly assessments of his involvement with the movement nor of his broader religious views. He began his reading in the 1840s and 1850s,[50] activity predating both Matthew's and Shannon's narratives.

A survey of the St Deiniol's collection reveals illuminating evidence of Gladstone's reading practice. Of a sample of 125 nineteenth-century texts, 36% (45/125) were either listed as read or annotated by Gladstone, sent by authors, or both.[51] 25% (31/125) were definitely annotated by him. A small percentage (11% [14/125]) was sent by authors but the books bear no signs of his reading.

The collection's modal decade of publication was the 1880s. Despite its incompleteness, information for Gladstone's reading mirrors this remarkably well. The pattern of the collection supports the view that Gladstone's interest and involvement in spiritualism heightened, but did not begin, during the 1880s.

The earliest annotated text is probably Gerald Massey's *Concerning Spiritualism* (1871), which Gladstone read the year after publication.[52] What is of great interest, with reference to how Gladstone related spiritualism to Christianity, is when he read such texts. Gladstone had a lifelong practice of dedicated Sunday reading which, whilst not exclusive of secular works, displayed a religio-spiritual character that distinguished it from his more eclectic weekly diet.[53] He would certainly not have read anything intentionally hostile to Christianity on Sundays. But he recorded reading Massey's book on the fourth Sunday of Lent that year.[54] This was not an isolated incident. He read other spiritualist texts on Sundays and holy days. For example he read *Life Beyond the Grave, described by A SPIRIT, through a writing medium* (1876) on Maundy Thursday and Good Friday 1879.[55] He also corresponded with spiritualists on Sundays. Thus on 8 April 1877 (the first Sunday after Easter) he wrote telling James Phillips of Dorking that 'I know of no rule which forbids a Christian to examine into the preternatural agency in the system called spiritualism'.[56]

What is striking about Gladstone's collection is firstly its variety and secondly the attention he gave to it. William Eglinton had at least accurately recorded Glad-

stone's high level of familiarity with the literature: 'He said that he already knew that the movement was represented by excellent journals, and that many eminent men had written on the question'.[57] Gladstone's collection contained works both hostile and friendly to spiritualism and it incorporated various genres including general surveys, commission reports, historical studies, poetry and direct spirit communications, which Gladstone read as closely as the critical works.

The variety of material he read indicates that his interest was not limited by a preoccupation with proving the authenticity of the supernatural phenomena discussed. Is there any evidence to suggest that he was personally moved by the material he read? He was certainly not averse to amateur divining. He was obviously intrigued by Louise Cotton's gift of her *Palmistry, and its Practical Uses* (London 1890); his annotations include direct references to his own star sign and palm. In Cotton's chapter on astral influences, Gladstone placed his precise tick next to the planets' influences on Capricorn. The sun apparently guaranteed 'small mean stature, thin and ill-proportioned, pale complexion, lank brown hair, long face, just and upright disposition, hasty, undaunted, benevolent, but sometimes indulgent in dissipation'. He did not acknowledge with any mark Jupiter's tendency to produce a 'mean-looking [. . .] peevish disposition, weak, irritable, indolent but harmless, not fortunate, nor respected by anyone'.[58]

GLADSTONE'S SPIRITUALIST CORRESPONDENTS

Gladstone was not only reading but also corresponding with ordinary practising spiritualists from the early 1870s; another important but previously ignored aspect of his spiritualist involvement. Gladstone's correspondence was, like that of Sherlock Holmes, 'a varied one'[59] and his spiritualist correspondents went into significant detail about their activities and beliefs, and provided evidence for various phenomena. In 1878, John Francis Hunt wrote to Gladstone asking permission to send 'two prose communications'. He elaborated, as if to whet Gladstone's appetite, 'one [is] a direct communication [. . .] [from] the spirit of the late president Lincoln [. . .] in which *your* name incidentally occurs'.[60] In 1886 a Madame du Guet sent Gladstone a collection of 'autographs' from the other world.[61] But why did they take such pains to write to him? Letters that Gladstone received in July 1874 from Albert Snow of Leatherhead offer some indications.

> Supposing you ignorant of such facts, and interested in you by your writings & speeches, I take the liberty of thus offering you evidence of the existence of methods of communication with our departed friends. The boys, the [automatic writing] instrument, & the writings, you can see privately and incognito, if you think the matter of sufficient importance.[62]

Snow suggested that a relationship had been inaugurated between Gladstone and one portion of the people by means of his 'writings and speeches'. He had formed an opinion of Gladstone on the basis of these and now sought to develop the relationship by inviting face to face communication. Snow's high estimation of Gladstone's character, based on his public statements, is further demonstrated by a second letter in which he accepted Gladstone's decision not to investigate, because he had confidence in his 'love of truth [. . .] *wherever it might lead*'.[63] Gladstone's popular political and religious profile was obviously attractive to spiritualists, even at a point when was resolutely seeking retirement.

* * *

What has been thus far ascertained of Gladstone's interest in spiritualism? It might be said that he was unremarkable for his personal experience of the fashionable phenomena of the day. However his serious and sustained exploration of the subject, bolstered by extensive reading and a lively, socially broad correspondence, was more unusual and has been somewhat belied by concentration merely on his non-committal relationship with the SPR and occasional *séance* attendance. Moreover St Deiniol's shows that Gladstone's arcane reading ranged well beyond the category of spiritualism and incorporated works on theosophy, demonology, witchcraft, magic, astrology, thought-reading, palmistry, mesmerism, ghosts and haunted houses. But what was the overall significance of this, both for Gladstone himself, and for our understanding of him as a Victorian politico-intellectual? There are three parts to the following explanation: the first deals with politics, the second with religion, and the third with bibliography.

GLADSTONE, POLITICS AND THE SPIRITS

Science and politics shared with spiritualism and psychical research a concern with questions about authority, influence and communication.[64] The spirits showed themselves to be deeply interested in politics. In *Life beyond the Grave,* a spirit announced '*we read your newspapers*', which Gladstone underlined and marked with two exclamation marks. The entity continued to denounce 'principal public men, from the Prime Minister [Disraeli] downwards' as 'shams' and claimed spirits 'attend your House of Commons [. . .] and make themselves personally acquainted with what goes on there'. At this Gladstone drew a line, or rather an 'x' (of disapprobation) indicating perhaps a parliamentarian's disbelief that any unauthorized person should be witness to the House's activities.[65] Neither did he accept the spirit's suggestion that 'Party feeling is only self-interest in another form'.[66]

Gladstone's annotation of these, often very radical, texts is a useful barometer of his own radicalism, just as the texts themselves are important evidence of the ways in which sections of the people conceptualized

Gladstone as a political agent in relationship with them. Logie Barrow suggests that 'Spiritualism [. . .] benefited from being strategically attractive to people of any reforming cast of mind'.[67] And there was enthusiastic vindication of Gladstonian Liberalism from the spirit world. In 1875 *Life Beyond the Grave*'s disincarnate author predicted that 'unless a healthy reaction takes place in public feeling, much mischief will ensue', due to the Conservative government.[68] During an 1890 trance-address, a 'veteran spiritualist lecturer and reformer' designated Gladstone as the panacea for society's 'monstrous inequality'. He was described as 'the agent of progressive ideas' who merely awaited the moment when 'the ideas of the people shall have progressed to the point of practical unanimity [. . .] to carry out the will of the people'.[69] Unsurprisingly, spiritualists' appropriation of Gladstone did not cease after his death. The Clapham Junction branch of the Amalgamated Society of Railway Servants was told on Gladstone's death of the 'most striking coincidence that Mr. Gladstone should be called in to the Great Unknown on Ascension Day [. . .] [this being] a confirmation of his strong belief that this life is but the introduction to a higher life hereafter'.[70] On 1 November 1909, the *Daily Chronicle* carried an 'AMAZING SPIRIT "INTERVIEW." [WITH] THE LATE MR GLADSTONE ON THE BUDGET' obtained by W. T. Stead and conducted in the presence of two clairvoyants and a stenographer. A variety of spirits communicated, including Cardinal Manning. Gladstone, characteristically unwilling to return to the 'limited and melancholy arena of party politics', nevertheless expressed himself at length as to whether he would disband the House of Lords if it threw out the Budget. 'In my opinion the Upper Chamber will act most ill-advisedly if they reject this financial measure,' his shade pronounced.[71]

It is unlikely Gladstone would have endorsed any of these characterizations of himself. For all his populist rhetoric he venerated an Aristotelian model of government by a knowledgeable hierarchy, and was wary of anything that might encourage anarchy. However a radical/conservative tension existed within Gladstone, which caused confusion not only to himself but to his contemporaries and later commentators. His radical instinct, intermittently restrained by cautious probity, is well illustrated by his exclamation both of alarm and interest ('!vl') beside Hudson Tuttle's pronouncement 'Oh, that the bright day, fast dawning, may shine forth, when every one will be his own master, his own sovereign, his own ruler, and govern himself with the strength of his manhood!'[72] Gladstone was also willing to use exchanges with practitioners of the paranormal as opportunities for self promotion. For example, when he entertained 'Cheiro' at Hawarden in 1897, Gladstone not only allowed the palmist to take impressions of his hands but, 'further to show his interest', gave his visitor his photograph.[73] It is small wonder that tension existed between Gladstone's complex and somewhat contradictory radicalism and that of some of his spiritualist admirers, or that confusion was generated by his inconsistent levels of (dis)interest.

Alison Winter's book on mesmerism suggests a direct link between concepts of the mind, particularly the communal experience of phenomena central to psychical experimentation, and the growth of mass politics and charismatic leadership. She examines the way in which Gladstone was presented, by Walter Bagehot and others, as a political mesmerist subduing the collective will of the masses to his power. She quotes Bagehot's prediction, made on the basis of Gladstone's 1871 Greenwich speech (the first Prime Ministerial speech addressed directly to the public), that Gladstone would ever afterwards 'exert a control over the masses [. . .] *directly* by the vitality of his own mind'.[74] With reference to Gladstone's spiritualist correspondence, a useful extension can be made to Winter's discussion. The evidence of reception and response (albeit from one group) in the audience that Bagehot imagined suggests that political influences were deemed not just to flow one way; it indicates how some of 'the people' conceived of being actively involved in the political process (both individually and in communities) and sought to exert influence themselves. Winter notes (and Lamont argues similarly) the independent licence that educated Victorians exhibited (and were accorded by society) when it came to judging experiments and evidence.[75] Such independence clearly characterized Gladstone's approach. A constant preoccupation of his, well illustrated by diary examples and annotations, was describing and judging phenomena that he had witnessed personally. For example, the items in the *JSPR* [*Journal of the Society for Psychical Research*] in which he showed most interest concerned phenomena he had experienced. He especially noted experiments where number guessing was involved, undoubtedly comparing them to his experience with Mr Cumberland.[76] Likewise, having been convinced that the thought-reading and slate-writing he had witnessed were genuine, Gladstone was reluctant to accept J. N. Maskelyne's assaults on them.[77] And it is no surprise to find that he disagreed with Maskelyne's co-author Lionel Wetherly in his rigid distinction between 'those with whom the spirit world is an objective reality' and 'the ordinary-thinking public'.[78]

Gladstone's recognition of and belief in the validity of individual judgement adds weight to the arguments of both Winter and Lamont. The latter demonstrates the increasing levels of confidence observable amongst Victorian witnesses.[79] And Winter describes the community-building effects of mesmerism amongst the well-to-do.[80] There is no reason to suppose that this process was restricted only to élite groups who already occupied secure collective positions from which to ask questions and govern events. What about the validity of judge-

ments of the 'ordinary-thinking public'? The ability and fitness of those of a lower class to judge matters of political import were frequently questioned by their social superiors; those involved in spiritualism regularly faced charges of fraudulence. But there is evidence to show that the practice of independent questioning and evaluation, by spiritualists and others, was fostered and encouraged across a much broader social range. For example, note that in *Cheiro's Language of the Hand* no definitive analysis was provided of the famous palms. They were to be interpreted by the individual reader, having learnt techniques from the book.[81] One can also see evidence of analytical and investigative practice encouraging confidence and proactive behaviour amongst Gladstone's ordinary spiritualist correspondents and book-givers. The combination of Gladstone's open-minded approach to spiritualism and his political appeal to the masses was a heady mixture and was understandably made much of by the spiritualists who wrote to and about him. Not only did they feel vindicated by his sympathetic attitude to the experiments he witnessed, quoting his opinion as 'the rational view of the subject',[82] but they also drew on their own experiences of investigation and experimentation, as well as on a positive sense of class status, to suggest political as well as spiritualist opinions to him. Thus Albert Snow concluded his first letter to Gladstone:

> I was formerly the Master of a Church Grammar school; you may rely on my discretion, especially as if I succeed in satisfying you and thereby rendering you an important service, I shall then ask you kindly to do me a small service in return.[83]

It is also questionable, *pace* Shannon, whether we should assume that Lady Sandhurst's role was automatically invested with more political importance than that of Mrs Duncan and her spiritual advisers. This tentative two-way communication is also evident in Gladstone's reading of spiritualist texts. Several volumes refer to Gladstone within the printed text. Remarkably, in the St Deiniol's copy of *An Angel's Message. Being a series of Angelic and Holy Communications received by a Lady.* (London, 1858), the sender, Francis Hobler, provided an extensive marginal commentary on the text for Gladstone's benefit, relating further testimony for the phenomena described from the spiritualist community of which he was a part. For example, he wrote, 'Capt. Beasely RN. has told me he has seen & touched these spirit hands & they were perfectly in sensation as natural hands would be', and with reference to a spiritual wreath: 'This is true—Mr Coleman saw it and has the wreath'. At the end of one chapter Hobler noted that the medium, Miss Juliana Fawcett, 'is a very amiable and sensible young lady—who does not assume airs or assume on superior knowledge or abilities'.[84] All of which narrative was designed to convince Gladstone by a mixture of empirical evidence, assertion of respectability, and trustworthiness within a frame of reference which recognized class distinction.

Such texts illustrate that the exertion of confident, communal powers of influence was being seriously attempted (leaving aside the question of such projects' success or failure), not only from the top down, but also from the bottom up in spiritualist communities. This had immense political and cultural implications in an era of burgeoning mass politics, especially for Gladstone, both as 'the People's William' and as private consumer of these texts. He was clearly confident about his own ability to judge the truth of both political and psychical phenomena. But the frequent assumption, by correspondents and mediums, of Gladstone's fellow-feeling (however deferential and resistible) had unsettling implications for the amount of control he could maintain over his own political identity. Versions of this identity were being acculturated into communal narratives, by ordinary spiritualists with often quite different political agendas. It was this uncomfortable situation which produced Gladstone's frequently uncertain comments and annotations, his sharp reluctance to see his spiritualist involvement become the business of the public as well as of the private sphere, but also his attempts to try and manipulate the way his image was seen and used.

SPIRITUALISM, CHRISTIANITY AND THE BURDEN
OF PROOF

There is little doubt that the most important factors motivating Gladstone's decision to investigate spiritualism were his personal Christian faith and his understanding of the nature and development of religion. Spiritualism's relationship with Christianity was complex. London Spiritualism tended to be middle-class dominated and largely Christian in emphasis. Provincial Spiritualism was more lower-middle and upper-working class and was strong in anti-Christian sentiment.[85] Where agreement occurred between the two, it most frequently concerned the relationship between belief in the supernatural and materialistic science. This aspect greatly interested Gladstone. In 1876, he published an article detailing his own religious classification system: **'The Courses of Religious Thought'**.[86] The bulk of spiritualist and theosophical material which Gladstone read most closely accorded with the 'Theistic' division outlined in this systematization. 'Materialism' belonged firmly in what he termed 'The Negative School': an aggregate of schemes which 'agree in denying [. . .] the reign of a moral Governor or Providence, and the existence of a state of discipline or probation'.[87] In his private reading he consistently annotated passages where spiritualism and materialism were defined in opposition. For example, he placed double lines of notice both beside S. C. Hall's assertion that spiritualism's purpose was 'To

CONFUTE AND DESTROY MATERIALISM, by supplying sure and certain and *palpable* evidence that to every human being God gives a soul which he ordains shall not perish when the body dies'.[88] Also by Dr G. Sexton's claim that spiritualism 'is destined to crush the materialism of the age, and hurl the scepticism, now so prevalent, from the throne which it has usurped'.[89] ('Scepticism' was number one on Gladstone's 'Negative School' list.)

Despite such sustained interest, it was difficult for Christians and spiritualists to agree on a basis of proof. Unlike mainstream Christian practice, spiritualism's prime object was to undertake practical communicative experiments with unseen beings, and to provide scientific evidence proving the veracity of both spiritualist and Christian claims. As Albert Snow explained, 'one of the main objects of this movement begun from on High, is to offer to materialists & men of science whom the Church cannot reach absolute proof of the existence of spirit and a future life'.[90]

The central question for Christian-spiritualist dialogue was whether or not this approach supported a Christian world-view, or whether it would erode traditional faith.[91] Official Anglican disapproval was proffered by such figures as Archbishop Benson of Canterbury and B. F. Westcott, Bishop of Durham, but one should be careful not to exaggerate (as Lamont does) the difference between levels of serious scientific and Christian engagement with spiritualism.[92] There was significant involvement amongst ordinary clergy and a working policy of coexistence developed. But how did Gladstone fit into this debate?

Gladstone had no time for outright attacks on Christianity and his readings indicate where he drew the line with regard to criticisms. He rejected the argument, employed by Gerard Massey and others, that 'it has almost become necessary not to be a Christian, to appreciate the beauty and significance of the life of Christ'.[93] His understanding of the incarnation as the keystone of humanity's redemption meant that he baulked at how even theistic believers could reject the 'aids, bounteous even if limited' of the incarnation 'and thus doom themselves to face with crippled resources the whole host of the enemy'.[94] With regard to criticism of the Church as an institution, he disagreed with one author ('x') who asserted 'the uselessness of modern religious teaching' and 'false teaching' by clergy.[95] Echoes of these judgements are to be found in his public writings. For example, his isolation of 'The Negative School' in **'The Courses of Religious Thought'** was governed by his estimation of its purely destructive character. He was steadfast in his veneration for the teaching role of the church and the historical nature of its traditions. Matthew's description of Gladstone as an 'orthodox sacramentalist' is largely true.[96] He was surprised by

Mrs Duncan's advice to receive communion as a duty rather than for its sacramental benefits and was repelled by spiritualists and theosophists who argued for divorce. For example in *Life Beyond the Grave* (1876) Gladstone placed an 'x' beside the assertion that people with opposing magnetisms should part,[97] and disagreed with much of this spirit's radical feminist discourse on women and marriage, including the suggestion that women who only occupy themselves with home and family on earth 'and cast no thought around them, are not qualified to enter the higher life'.[98]

But Gladstone's undoubted moral conservatism should not blind us to the pragmatism of his overall approach to Christian belief and his understanding that change must operate upon its representative institutions. Doctrine was, for Gladstone, 'the very heart of the great Christian tradition' but he was extremely critical of those unwilling to countenance change, and in particular of evangelical interpolations, such as 'personal assurance, particular election, final perseverance, and peculiar conceptions respecting the atonement of Christ and the doctrine of justification'.[99] In his 1894 review of Annie Besant's autobiography, Gladstone admitted 'rash things' had been said in defence of such doctrines, and recommended 'the application of a corrective and pruning process to retrench excesses unwittingly committed by believers'.[100]

Gladstone's 'pruning process' not only involved moderating language but also a concentration on 'the central truth of the Gospel', namely the trinity and the incarnation.[101] 'Everything besides,' he wrote (also in 1894), 'is only developments which have been embodied in the historic Christianity of the past, as auxiliary to the great central purpose of Redemption.'[102]

Gladstone's increasing broadness of religious outlook did not involve the complete repudiation of his previous positions, but one can see just how far he had moved by examining his reaction to extreme evangelical attacks on spiritualism. Over Christmas and New Year 1884-5 he read G. H. Pember's *Earth's Earliest Ages; and their Connection with Modern Spiritualism and Theosophy* (London, 1884). Gladstone's verdict on the work, which was hostile to both theosophy and spiritualism, was that it was '*awful*'.[103] Pember asserted that 'Knowledge in this life is a gift fraught with peril: for our great task here is to learn the lesson of absolute dependence upon God, and entire submission to His will'. Gladstone disagreed with this immoderate statement.[104] Anti-intellectualism was something for which Gladstone soundly criticized both catholic and protestant Christians.[105] Pember, a member of the extremely-protestant Plymouth Brethren,[106] was also rabidly anti-Catholic, which as a young man Gladstone was on occasion.[107] Here Gladstone reacted negatively to such outbursts.[108]

If there was one area where Gladstone was considerably influenced by his early evangelicalism it was in his attitude to the Bible. This he defended at length in *The Impregnable Rock of Holy Scripture*.[109] However his annotations of spiritualist texts and other later writings confirm that his position was not as intransigent as that title suggests. For example he consistently disagreed with William Carlisle who, in *An Essay on Evil Spirits* (1827) (which Gladstone read in 1885) asserted that the Bible was 'infallible truth', written by '*full* or *complete* inspiration' and that those who did not accept this had 'no resting place for thought'.[110] Such exclusive reliance on the Bible as 'a self-attested volume', resulting from 'verbal inspiration', left, to Gladstone's mind, the late nineteenth-century protestant evangelical in a weak position in the face of 'the recent assaults on the *corpus* of Scripture'. He clearly placed himself amongst those for whom the 'question [. . .] has never offered so serious dilemma' due to their recognition of a proliferated system of authority including, as well as scripture, 'the ancient constitution of the Church, and [. . .] its witnessing and teaching office'.[111] 'Scripture is not a stereotype projected into the world at a given time and place,' Gladstone asserted, 'but is a record of comprehensive and progressive teaching applicable to a nature set under providential discipline [. . .] which must vary with its growth'.[112]

There is an absence of dogmatic condemnation in Gladstone's annotation of spiritualist writing, even when authors questioned common Christian beliefs. For example, *An Angel's Message* (1858) instructs the reader to 'relinquish all idea that the natural body will ever rise again from the tomb'.[113] Belief in individual bodily resurrection from the dead was still a common expectation amongst devout Christians like Gladstone and yet his annotation of the instruction with a tick ['v'], whilst not positively approbatory is not condemnatory. Elsewhere he questioned one writer's literal belief in the Apostles' Creed by placing his querying 'ma' beside 'We believe that Christ descended into hell, and did not ascend into heaven until the *third day*'.[114] Gladstone concomitantly noted criticisms of Christian denigrations of the human condition, a mark of his increasingly incarnation-centred faith. Thus he ticked Gerald Massey's censure of those 'who profess to believe in human nature's total depravity' and his impassioned plea 'for God's sake as well as for the sake of human progress, that the world should be rescued from beliefs such as these, and from that ossification of the letter which kills the spirit of Christ'.[115]

Gladstone bestowed his most auspicious mark, '+', on the following passage from *Light Beyond the Grave* (1876), which advocated living a Christian life in the present, as opposed to setting one's sights on eternal glory.

Those who lead such a life feel the meaning of the expression, 'the Kingdom of Heaven is within you'. For them, no need to wait until the grave close on the body in order to appreciate the happiness in store for them in the spirit world.[116]

This passage, which quotes Luke's Gospel (17:20-1), was radical, and reminiscent of major arguments made by F. D. Maurice in *The Kingdom of Christ,* which Gladstone had read in 1837 and 1843.[117] Maurice is a prime example of a churchman whose beliefs combined sacramentalism and liberalism. We should not see the two as mutually exclusive in Gladstone's case either and his endorsement of such views suggests his broad church tendencies were not reluctantly admitted.

Many spiritualists yearned to uncover universal truths about knowledge and faith.[118] This understanding was not limited to spiritualism proper; 'Cheiro' defined 'occultism' in general as 'the one [religion] in whose temple all religions may meet, where Catholic and Protestant, Mahometan or Hebrew may find something in common'.[119] Gladstone's own search for religious knowledge could not be described in these terms; he never wavered in his faith in the fundamental character of existence being explicable in Christian language. Nonetheless, his understanding of the historical development of religious thought incorporated a belief that the original divine revelation had been universal—a conviction expressed in his unfinished work on Olympian religion—and also that the future life of the Church must have a universalist dimension—a belief that was embodied in his foundation of St Deiniol's Library. The final section of this investigation will examine the links between Gladstone's epistemology and spiritualism and go on to explain how and why 'magic and spiritism' formed part of his library scheme.

GLADSTONE, EPISTEMOLOGY AND ST DEINIOL'S LIBRARY

Gladstone's advice to James Philips stressed that any investigation into spiritualism should be serious, exhaustive and that the inquirer should remain open-minded and not form exaggerated conclusions either way on the basis of inconclusive evidence. Although he reminded his correspondent, 'universal knowledge is not possible', Gladstone stressed that such investigation should have a 'useful object'. Gladstone was here arguing according to the precepts of the eighteenth-century Broad Churchman Joseph Butler (1692-1752). Butler was a crucial resource for late-Victorian religious apologists;[120] he was also one of the four thinkers to whom Gladstone openly acknowledged a lifelong debt.[121] Butler had argued that by increasing in knowledge, humans do not advance towards absolute truth; rather they affirm the state of ignorance or partial knowledge in which they are bound to live. Consequently, both human knowledge and all actions based on it are only

ever probably true and the only way to reach morally credible decisions is to base one's judgements on as broad a range of evidence as possible. For, where no one piece of evidence can be said to carry conviction, the cumulative testimony of many can carry more probable truth and provide the individual with a basis for action. Such a methodology had obvious attractions for those seeking to counter the overreaching claims of scientific rationalism and reassert the value of religious knowledge: Christian as well as spiritualist.

There is no surviving evidence of James Philip's reaction to Gladstone's advice, but it is clear that some spiritualist writers recognized positive concurrences between Gladstone's intellectual priorities and their own. For example, the author of *Where are the Dead?* commended Gladstone's 'remarkable speech upon education and religion, delivered at the Liverpool College, in December, 1872'.[122] This programmatic address, which questioned materialism and a secular approach to education, had constituted a remarkably controversial statement for a serving Prime Minister to make (as Gladstone was aware) and provoked a public exchange with Herbert Spencer.[123] It questioned scientists' right to claim a superior level of authenticity for their work and queried assumptions that science was a pre-eminent system of knowledge. Gladstone's alternative vision defended the validity of reasoning and thinking theologically. He argued for a reconciliation between Christianity and modern life, which was to be achieved through liberal-minded ecumenical co-operation and the application of a Butlerian methodology.[124] Thus he counselled his Liverpool audience to

> Be slow to stir inquiries, which you do not mean patiently to pursue to their proper end. Be not afraid oftentimes to suspend your judgement; or to feel and admit to yourselves how narrow are the bounds of knowledge. Do not too readily assume that to us have been opened royal roads to truth.[125]

Gladstone envisaged that his Olympian religion monograph and St Deiniol's Library would together represent 'the proper end' of his own investigation into the relationship between human and divine systems of knowledge. In 1893, when Gladstone propounded the spiritual rationale on which he justified the foundation of St Deiniol's, he argued for 'a Christianity which is to cover the whole ground of our complete existence'.[126] There is no denying Gladstone's privileging of the Christian system here; he did not claim authenticity for all spirituality and there were clear limits to his ecumenical vision. Nonetheless his recognition of 'comprehensiveness' points to an understanding that both the Christian and spiritualist systems were part of a unified whole, although how exactly they existed in relationship was a matter for thought and study. At the beginning of his **'Courses of Religious Thought',** Gladstone expressed frustration at the 'multiform and confused' character of modern religious thought. 'It defies all attempts at reduction to an unity,' he wrote, 'refusing not only to be governed, but even to be classified.'[127]

Gladstone's urge to classify found its ultimate outlet in his lifelong collection and organization of his private library, and his particular desire to reduce knowledge, both religious and secular, to 'an unity' found concrete expression in his classification scheme for St Deiniol's. He at one stage intended to call the establishment the 'Monad',[128] or 'ultimate unity' and the institution brought together a remarkably broad literature of spirituality. A significant number of Gladstone's spiritualist texts survive in the present-day library and, as was stated clearly at the outset, they were accorded an important place in Gladstone's classification scheme. Gladstone divided St Deiniol's into two rooms: one named 'The Divinity Room' and one 'The Humanity Room'. His 'Divinity Room' contained not only theology but sections on non-Christian religions, philosophy of religion, man and nature as well as 'Magic and Spiritism'. This emphasis on comparative religion and spirituality within a theological library was both ahead of, but also clearly of its time. As well as designing this classification scheme, Gladstone left instructions about how the library should be used. The collection was not to be left as a memorializing testimony to one man's intellectual interests. It was to be put to practical use.

In his writings on religious thought Gladstone returned repeatedly to the subject of education and the need for a revitalization of religious intellectual life.[129] His priority in founding St Deiniol's was to foster a learned Christian clergy, but he insisted that their learning should involve engagement with other systems of religious thought, including spiritualism. He envisaged a non-sectarian institution, insisting that 'I by no means desire that the use of the institution should be confined to those who are in communion with that Church [Anglican], or be able to attend its services: provided only that they are set upon serious and solid studies of religion'.[130] Spiritualists and psychical researchers would thus not have been excluded for they also desired to function as reconcilers in nineteenth-century culture.[131] Gladstone's desire to discover, classify and utilize new knowledge for the ultimate benefit of humanity, as he understood the concept, contributed significantly to bolstering his attraction to spiritualism and sustained his solid, serious and open-minded engagement with it.

CONCLUSION

On the basis of this examination, it is certainly no longer possible to maintain that Gladstone's interest in spiritualism was mere curiosity. Gladstone shared a fundamental belief about the 'spirit of the age' with the spiritualists. He approved when they maintained their 'main object [. . .] is [. . .] to destroy materialism, to strengthen Bible-teaching, and lead to *belief* in *Christ*'.[132] And yet Gladstone was not an adherent of spiritualism. He was an open minded and liberal Christian thinker who, like the 'rational person' described by the spiritualist-writer P. P. Alexander, 'would [. . .] neither rush into belief of the thing, nor yet, from his *à priori* ground of experience, dogmatically contemn [. . .] it'.[133] He was more than a detached psychical researcher however, principally because of the connection he sought to explore between his belief in God, the redemptive reality of the incarnation, and the Christian aspects of spiritualism. For his own departure point was not one of doubt, like many of his contemporaries at the SPR, but faith. And yet this was faith in an inclusive not exclusive revelation.

The evidence examined above adds weight to the growing understanding we have of the important and suggestive liberalising tendency present in Gladstone's religious thinking in his later years. During his life Gladstone moved through several religious phases. He was brought up a strict evangelical, flirted with anglo-catholicism in his middle years and ended up a liberal catholic. This transformation, including Gladstone's willingness to challenge extreme evangelical positions, has been well covered elsewhere; what this material adds is evidence of his serious engagement with and readiness to endorse, often positively, spiritual discourse outside the bounds of mainstream Christian institutional structures. He was in private as well as in public 'not unmindful of the saying of an eminent Presbyterian, Dr Norman Macleod, that many an opponent of dogma is nearer to God than many an orthodox believer'.[134]

This investigation has also revealed more of the tensions and contradictions which characterized this polymath. Gladstone's involvement entailed, like his other cross-class association with prostitutes, a significant degree of discomfort and uncertainty. These conflicts were both personal—relating to the battle between his radical and conservative leanings—and also public—inherent in his position as a political figure. His varied and thoughtful correspondence with spiritualists, for example, bespoke the complex mixture of negotiation, promotion, consumption and selective assimilation which characterized much nineteenth-century discourse between politicians and public. Not only does it indicate a deeper awareness of and growing interest in the significance of psychic and supernatural phenomena on Gladstone's part, but also provides important information on the nature of his politicized and at times tense relationship with the lower classes, particularly the lower middle class; a relationship that was both direct and personal. As Jon Lawrence has argued, there are significant difficulties but great potential benefits in any historical project which seeks to recover 'the relationship between the construction and the reception of political discourse' and, we might add, the construction and reception of political image and personality.[135] In Gladstone's spiritualist correspondence we have an opportunity to study creatively and sensitively a point of direct engagement between Gladstone and at least one part of his popular constituency and recover something of the two-way flow of political discourse.

The factor that ultimately links the three aspects of Gladstone's 'otherworldly' engagement discussed here—politics, religion and text—is Gladstone's insatiable intellectual curiosity. Throughout his life this characteristic, again and again, drew him into an unpredictable no man's land betwixt public and private domains, the orthodox and unorthodox, the moral and immoral. But once drawn into an investigation, whether of sin or spirits, Gladstone's desire both to touch the numinous and also to impose a classificatory order on his findings could be relied upon to push him beyond the accepted bounds of his class, his church, and our expectations.

Notes

1. I would like to thank St Deiniol's Library, Hawarden; seminar audiences at Liverpool University, University of Chester and St Deiniol's; Graham Clayton, Alex Windscheffel and my *JVC* [*Journal of Victorian Culture*] readers for providing assistance and feedback during the preparation of this article.

2. 'Cheiro', *Cheiro's Language of the Hand: a Complete Practical Work on the Sciences of Cheirognomy and Cheiromancy,* 14th edn (London: Nichols & Co., 1910), title page.

3. For a description of Gladstone's meeting with 'Cheiro', cf. 'Cheiro', *Cheiro's Memoirs: the Reminiscences of a Society Palmist* (London: William Rider and Son Ltd, 1912), Chapter 24.

4. John Morley recorded Bulwer Lytton sending Gladstone a horoscope but did not mention other psychic phenomena. John Morley, *The Life of William Ewart Gladstone,* New edn, 2 vols (London: Macmillan and Co. Ltd, 1905), I, 196-7. More recently, only Colin Matthew and Richard Shannon have treated Gladstone's involvement with spiritualism at any length. H. C. G. Matthew, *Gladstone 1809-1898* (Oxford: Clarendon Press, 1997), 544-6, Richard Shannon, *Gladstone: Heroic Minister, 1865-1898* (London: Allen Lane, 1999), 118, 344-5, 345n, 423.

5. For information on the foundation cf. Ruth Clayton, 'Enlarging the Text: a Cultural History of William Ewart Gladstone's Library and Reading,' Unpublished PhD, Liverpool, 2003, Mary Drew and Stephen Liberty, *In the Cause of Divine Learning* (London: Henry Frowde, 1906), Hulda Friederichs, *In the Evening of his Days: a Study of Mr. Gladstone in Retirement, with some account of St. Deiniol's Library and Hostel,* Westminster Gazette Library (London: Westminster Gazette, 1896), Peter J. Jagger, 'Gladstone and his Library' *Gladstone,* ed. Peter J. Jagger (London: Hambledon, 1998), 235-53, T. W. Pritchard, *A History of St Deiniol's Library* (Hawarden: Monad Press, 1999), Frederick W. Ratcliffe, 'Mr Gladstone, the Librarian, and St Deiniol's Library, Hawarden' *Gladstone, Politics and Religion: a Collection of Founder's Day Lectures delivered at St Deiniol's Library, Hawarden, 1967-83,* ed. Peter J. Jagger (London: Macmillan, 1985).

6. 'Memorandum on St Deiniol's Library', n.d., St Deiniol's Library Uncatalogued MSS.

7. Janet Oppenheim, *The Other World: Spiritualism and Psychical Research in England, 1850-1914* (Cambridge: Cambridge University Press, 1985), 50.

8. Cf. Oppenheim, *Other World,* 59.

9. M. R. D. Foot and H. C. G. Matthew (eds), *The Gladstone Diaries: with Prime Ministerial Correspondence,* 14 vols (Oxford: Oxford University Press, 1968-96), X, clxxxix-cxc. Afterwards *GD* with date or volume.

10. Cf. Oppenheim, *Other World,* 2.

11. Cf. 'List of Honorary Members', *Journal of the Society for Psychical Research* 2 (1885).

12. R. H. Hutton, 'The Metaphysical Society: a Reminiscence', *Nineteenth Century* 18 (1885), 177-8. Quoted in Oppenheim, *Other World,* 127.

13. Quoted in Ruth Brandon, *The Spiritualists: the Passion for the Occult in the Nineteenth and Twentieth Centuries* (London: Weidenfeld and Nicolson, 1983), 87.

14. He recorded reading 'Psychical Transactions' whilst on a cruise in August 1885. *GD* 22/8/85.

15. Richard Shannon, *Gladstone: Peel's Inheritor 1809-1865* (London: Penguin, 1982), 98.

16. *The Times,* 20 June 1884, 8c. Quoted at *GD* 19/6/84.

17. Charles Dickens to Mrs Trollope, 19 June 1855. Quoted in Brandon, *The Spiritualists,* 56.

18. *GD* 18/11/84.

19. *The Times,* 18 October 1878, 8f. Quoted at *GD* 16/10/78.

20. *GD* 19/6/84.

21. Cf. J. Gilliland, *Gladstone's Dear Spirit: Laura Thistlethwayte* (London: The Author, 1994), 161-5.

22. *GD* 7/4/79.

23. Shannon, *Gladstone,* II, 344.

24. Shannon conflates two separate entries on table-turning on 13 and 14 September. Shannon, *Gladstone,* I, 448, *GD* 13-14/9/61. Cf. also *GD* 31/3/69 for a later example.

25. *GD* 17/9/61.

26. Peter Lamont, 'Spiritualism and a Mid-Victorian Crisis of Evidence', *Historical Journal* 47.4 (2004), 897-920, 900.

27. *GD* X, clxxxviii.

28. *Morning Post,* 7 November 1884, 3f. Quoted at *GD* X, clxxxix.

29. *GD* 29/10/84. Cf. (for correspondence with Mrs Hartmann) British Library Gladstone Papers (BL GP) Add. MS 44488, fol. 44; (for Gladstone's notes) BL GP Add. MS 44768, fol. 128.

30. Oppenheim, *Other World,* 139-40.

31. Lionel A. Weatherly and J. N. Maskelyne, *The Supernatural?* (Bristol: J. W. Arrowsmith, 1891), 196. The copy preserved in St Deiniol's [K41/15] was presented by the author.

32. Cf. Eglinton to Mrs Hartmann, n.d., and Mrs Hartmann to Gladstone, n.d. (docketed 1 November 1884), BL GP Add. MS 44488, fol. 4.

33. Cf. J. Farmer to Gladstone, 7 November 1884, BL GP Add. MS 44488, fol. 40.

34. BL GP Add. MS 44488, fol. 42.

35. BL GP Add. MS 44488, fol. 43.

36. Gladstone to Mrs Hartmann, 7 November 1884, BL GP Add. MS 44547, fol. 134. Quoted in *GD* at this date.

37. W. E. Gladstone, 'The Courses of Religious Thought' *Gleanings of Past Years 1844-78,* vol. III: Historical and Speculative (London: John Murray, 1879), 95-136, 126-7.

38. Lamont, 'Crisis of Evidence' ['Spiritualism and a Mid-Victorian Crisis of Evidence'], 899.

39. Brandon, *The Spiritualists,* 61-2.

40. BL GP Add. MS 44488, fol. 42.

41. BL GP Add. MS 44488, fol. 42.

42. Gladstone to Mrs Hartmann, 7 November 1884, BL GP Add. MS 44547, fol. 134. Quoted in *GD* at this date.

43. Gladstone to Helen Gladstone (1814-80), 5 January 1878, Glynne-Gladstone Papers, quoted in

44. Matthew, *Gladstone,* 329. I am grateful to one of my anonymous *JVC* readers for reminding me of this parallel.

44. Cf. BL GP Add. MS 44488, fol. 48 and *GD* 18/11/84.

45. *GD* 18/11/84.

46. Mrs Duncan/Lady Sandhurst to Gladstone, 27 November 1884, BL GP Add. MS 44488, fol. 154.

47. BL GP Add. MS 44488, fols 154-5.

48. Shannon, *Gladstone,* II, 423.

49. *GD* 6/3/88.

50. *GD* 23/8/48; *GD* 2/9/58.

51. The Library has a number of pre-1800 books on demonology etc., which are not included in this survey, but the nineteenth-century texts span practically the whole century from 1807-1896.

52. St Deiniol's Library, K47/39.

53. Cf. Roy Jenkins, *Gladstone* (London: Macmillan, 1995), 182. I am grateful to Christiane d'Haussy, Professor Emerita, Université de Paris XII, for showing me her unpublished paper on 'William Gladstone's Sundays', which contains reference to Gladstone's Sabbath reading.

54. *GD* 10/3/72.

55. *GD* 10-11/4/79. St Deiniol's, K47/74.

56. Gladstone to J. Phillips, 8 April 1877, BL GP Add. MS 44454, fol. 30, quoted in *GD* at this date.

57. BL GP Add. MS 44488, fol. 43.

58. Louise Cotton, *Palmistry, and its Practical Uses* (London: G. Redway, 1890), 82, 91.

59. Arthur Conan Doyle, 'The Dying Detective' *The Penguin Complete Sherlock Holmes* (London: Penguin, 1981), 941.

60. J. F. Hunt to Gladstone, 6 May 1878, BL GP Add. MS 44456, fol. 289. Hunt wrote again in 1883 enclosing songs communicated by 'Sarcheon Homerus', which Gladstone annotated with his '+' of approbation. J. F. Hunt to Gladstone, 23 April 1883, BL GP Add. MS 44480, fols 232-5.

61. *GD* 18/11/86.

62. Albert Snow to Gladstone, 6 July 1874, BL GP Add. MS 44444, fols 38-9.

63. Albert Snow to Gladstone, 9 July 1874. BL GP Add. MS 44444, fol. 40. Original emphasis.

64. Alison Winter, *Mesmerized: Powers of Mind in Victorian Britain* (Chicago and London: Univer-

sity of Chicago Press, 1998), 306, Lamont, 'Crisis of Evidence'.

65. For further explanation of Gladstone's annotation system, cf. Ruth Clayton, 'W. E. Gladstone: an Annotation Key', *Notes & Queries* 246:2 (2001), 140-3.

66. *Life Beyond the Grave, described by A SPIRIT, through a writing medium,* (London: E. W. Allen, 1876), 74, 122, 124.

67. Logie Barrow, *Independent Spirits: Spiritualism and English Plebeians, 1850-1910* (London: Routledge & Kegan Paul, 1986), 110.

68. *Life Beyond the Grave,* 122.

69. *Two Worlds,* 3 (1890), 33ff, quoted in Barrow, *Independent Spirits,* 242-3.

70. *Railway Review,* 27 May 1898, 2, quoted in Barrow, *Independent Spirits,* 239.

71. Brandon, *The Spiritualists,* 204-5.

72. Hudson Tuttle, *Scenes in the Spirit World* (New York: Partridge & Brittan, 1866), 50.

73. 'Cheiro', *Cheiro's Memoirs,* 169.

74. Walter Bagehot quoted in Winter, *Mesmerized,* 333.

75. Winter, *Mesmerized,* 292, Lamont, 'Crisis of Evidence', 919.

76. Malcolm Guthrie, 'An Account of Some Experiments in Thought-Transference', *Journal of the Society for Psychical Research* 2 (1884-5), 24-42, 24.

77. Weatherly and Maskelyne, *The Supernatural?,* 202, 209. Both pages annotated 'ma' (using the Italian for 'but' to express reservation).

78. Weatherly and Maskelyne, *The Supernatural?,* 240, 'ma'.

79. Lamont, 'Crisis of Evidence', 919.

80. Winter, *Mesmerized,* 304.

81. My thanks to Mark Nixon, University of Stirling, for this information. Readings were given in *Cheiro's Memoirs,* but not of Gladstone's palm.

82. Epes Sargent, *The Scientific Basis of Spiritualism* (Boston: Colby & Rich, 1881), 13. Gladstone marked with a single line.

83. Albert Snow to Gladstone, 6 July 1874, BL GP Add. MS 44444, fols 38-9.

84. *An Angel's Message. Being a series of Angelic and Holy Communications received by a Lady,* (London: John Wesley & Co., 1858), 32-3, 107.

85. Oppenheim, *Other World,* 67.

86. First published in the *Contemporary Review,* 28 (June 1876) and reprinted in *Gleanings [Gleanings of Past Years 1844-78]* (1879).

87. Gladstone, 'Religious Thought' ['The Courses of Religious Thought'], 101.

88. S. C. Hall, *The Use of Spiritualism* (London: E. W. Allen, 1884), 6.

89. F. G. Lee, *More Glimpses of the World Unseen* (London: Chatto & Windus, 1878), 7.

90. Albert Snow to Gladstone, 6 July 1874, BL GP Add. MS 44444, fols 38-9.

91. Cf. Oppenheim, *Other World,* 66.

92. Lamont, 'Crisis of Evidence', 918.

93. Gerald Massey, *Concerning Spiritualism* (London: J. Burns, n.d. [1871]), 63. Gladstone marked with 'x'.

94. Gladstone, 'Religious Thought', 125.

95. *Life Beyond the Grave,* 36-7.

96. *GD* X, cxc.

97. *Life Beyond the Grave,* 27.

98. *Life Beyond the Grave,* 129. Gladstone marked an 'x' by the text and in his endnotes.

99. Gladstone, 'Religious Thought', 113, 116.

100. W. E. Gladstone, 'True and False Conceptions of the Atonement', *Nineteenth Century* 36.211 (1894), 317-331, 330.

101. W. E. Gladstone, 'The Place of Heresy and Schism in the Modern Church', *Gleanings of Past Years, 1885-96,* vol. VIII: Theological and Ecclesiastical (London: John Murray, 1894), 280-311, 300.

102. Gladstone, 'Heresy and Schism' ['The Place of Heresy and Schism in the Modern Church'], 308.

103. *GD* 11/1/85.

104. G. H. Pember, *Earth's Earliest Ages: and their connection with Modern Spiritualism and Theosophy* (London: Hodder and Stoughton, 1884), 28. Gladstone marked with 'ma'.

105. Gladstone, 'Religious Thought', 105, 112-17.

106. I would like to thank one of this paper's reviewers for drawing this to my attention.

107. Cf. e.g. *GD* 1/2/32-28/7/32.

108. Cf. St Deiniol's copy of Pember, *Earth's Earliest Ages,* 292, 368.

109. W. E. Gladstone, *The Impregnable Rock of Holy Scripture,* Revised edn (London: Isbister, 1892).

110. William Carlisle, *An Essay on Evil Spirits* (London: The Author, 1827), ii, 25, 26.

111. Gladstone, 'Religious Thought', 116.

112. Gladstone, 'Heresy and Schism', 294.

113. *An Angel's Message,* 183.

114. 'Fritz', *Where are the Dead? Or, Spiritualism Explained,* 3rd edn (London: Simpkin, Marshall & Co., 1875), 5.

115. Massey, *Spiritualism* [*Concerning Spiritualism*], 62-3.

116. *Life Beyond the Grave,* 86.

117. *GD* 5/3/37; *GD* 16/4/43.

118. Cf. Oppenheim, *Other World,* 109.

119. 'Cheiro', *Cheiro's Memoirs,* 210.

120. Cf. Jane Garnett, 'Bishop Butler and the Zeitgeist: Butler and the Development of Christian Moral Philosophy in Victorian Britain' *Joseph Butler's Moral and Religious Thought: Tercentenary Essays,* ed. Christopher Cunliffe (Oxford: Clarendon Press, 1992), 63-96.

121. The others were Dante Alighieri, St Augustine and Aristotle.

122. 'Fritz', *Where are the Dead?,* 3. Gladstone marked with '+'.

123. Shannon, *Gladstone,* II, 118, Matthew, *Gladstone,* 238.

124. W. E. Gladstone, *Address delivered at the distribution of prizes in the Liverpool College, December 21, 1872,* 5th edn (London: John Murray, 1873), 11-12.

125. Gladstone, *Liverpool College* [see previous note], 29.

126. Uncatalogued Memorandum in St Deiniol's Library. This exists in Gladstone's original (1893) and in a later copy by Mary Drew (1895).

127. Gladstone, 'Religious Thought', 95-6.

128. Cf. Matthew, *Gladstone,* 553.

129. Cf. e.g. W. E. Gladstone, 'The Evangelical Movement; its parentage, progress, and issue' *Gleanings of Past Years, 1860-79,* ed. W. E. Gladstone, vol. VII: Miscellaneous (London: John Murray, 1879), 201-41, pp. 240-1.

130. Undated holograph preserved with BL GP Add. MS 44773, fol. 75. Reproduced at *GD* 12/11/88.

131. Oppenheim, *Other World,* 391, 396.

132. Hall, *Use of Spiritualism,* 14.

133. P. P. Alexander, *Spiritualism: a Narrative with a Discussion* (Edinburgh: W. P. Nimmo, 1871), 46.

134. Gladstone, 'Religious Thought', 127.

135. Jon Lawrence, *Speaking for the People: Party, Language and Popular Politics in England, 1867-1914* (Cambridge: Cambridge University Press, 1998), 67-8.

Ruth Clayton Windscheffel (essay date April 2007)

SOURCE: Windscheffel, Ruth Clayton. "Gladstone and Scott: Family, Identity, and Nation." *Scottish Historical Review* 86, no. 1 (April 2007): 69-95.

[*In the following essay, Windscheffel evaluates the importance of Sir Walter Scott's writings in shaping Gladstone's literary and political views. Windscheffel maintains that Scott exerted a powerful influence on both Gladstone's private life and on his career as a public figure.*]

> That day of wrath, that dreadful day,
> When heaven and earth shall pass away,
> What power shall be the sinner's stay?
> How shall he meet that dreadful day?
> When, shrivelling like a parched scroll,
> The flaming heavens together roll;
> When louder yet, and yet more dread,
> Swells the high trump that wakes the dead;
> Oh! on that day, that wrathful day,
> When man to judgement wakes from clay,
> Be THOU the trembling sinner's stay,
> Though heaven and earth shall pass away![1]

With these foreboding lines, Sir Walter Scott's 'Last Minstrel' concludes his final performance before the emasculated household of Buccleuch. In 1868, William Ewart Gladstone declared that he knew of 'nothing so sublime in any portion of the sacred poetry of modern times' than this (apparently straightforward) rendering of the *Dies Irae.* So convinced was Gladstone of the poem's quality that in May 1883 he wrote to the Reverend Orby Shipley to defend the verse against the latter's charge of derivation. 'My contention is', Gladstone argued, 'that the *Dies Irae* supplied Scott with a suggestion, not an original; and that, setting out from that suggestion, he composed what is not only an original but very decidedly the grandest piece of sacred poetry in the English language'.[2]

Gladstone's affirmation of Scott's appropriation of this ancient text, both to secure his reputation and to impart sacred truth to a new generation, is suggestive of the statesman's own relationships with Sir Walter Scott: the most profound and long-lasting British literary influence on his life, thought, and politics. Scott's poems and novels were amongst the earliest texts Gladstone read; except for the Bible, he read no works in English so consistently or completely over such a length of time. They offered Gladstone a plethora of inspirations, ideas, and language, which he imbibed, appropriated into his public and private personae, and which he poured back upon his various audiences 'in a flood'.[3] The novels, in particular, reappeared in his diary record with phenomenal regularity throughout his reading life, and Scott himself, although he died in 1832,[4] remained a constant point of reference, and an ever-present influence. Much of this influence was directly related to Gladstone's engagement with his Scottish heritage, his developing sense of identity and nationality. In his later years, it also affected his conceptualisation of the status and future of the Scottish political nation.

Gladstone was (and is) not unique amongst politicians for publicly avowing a love of Scott. When the *Review of Reviews* asked the 1906 intake of Labour MPs to name the writers and books most influential over them, a high proportion named Sir Walter Scott, and Ramsay MacDonald claimed that the Waverley novels 'opened out the great world of national life for me and led me on to politics'.[5] More recently Tony Blair has, on numerous occasions, named *Ivanhoe* his favourite novel. These latest declarations, tossed into a sceptical public domain in which Scott's name is known but in which his work is little read, have been interpreted as attempts to construct an appropriate image rather than as a straightforward acknowledgement of formative influence. This is not a charge that could have been levelled at Gladstone, partly because his audience was one to which the words as well as the name of Scott were familiar but also because of the amount of evidence which survives of his sustained engagement with the writer.

The aim of the following examination is threefold. First, it seeks to elucidate how Gladstone's consumption of Scott's writings was seminal in the formation of his private identity, both individual and familial. Second, it aims to explain how Gladstone's readings of Scott fitted into the specific and serious character of his other reading and knowledge-gathering, and third, how the details of Gladstone's response to Scott related to the broader intellectual and cultural context of his public life. In essence, what was Gladstone's Scottian frame of reference and how was it constructed and used?

CONSUMPTION: SCOTT, SCOTTISHNESS, AND THE FORMATION OF IDENTITY

In his diary, Gladstone listed reading almost fifty different titles by or about Scott, many several times. These included edited works, letters, journals, biography and memoirs, short stories, melodrama, history, poetry and novels. Of the Waverley Novels (including their constituent stories),[6] Gladstone recorded reading twenty-six in seventy-two different readings over his life; only *Redgauntlet* (1824) and *Count Robert of Paris* (1832) received no specific mention. Those most frequently read were *The Bride of Lammermoor* (six times), *The Antiquary,* and *Waverley* (five times each).

Gladstone often read several of Scott's novels in a concentrated period and interchanged them. He also combined reading Scott's novels with the record of the author's own life. The way in which Gladstone read Scott gives the strong impression that he conceptualised a seamless Scottian world. He practised the same interchangeable pattern of reading with the works of two of the greatest intellectual influences upon him: Aristotle and St. Augustine. By adopting the same technique with Scott, he was according the author extremely high status.

So fundamental was Scott to Gladstone's reading experience that, even in his almost blind old age, he remained determined to read him. His claim, made in September 1894, to have attempted 'little heavy reading' is belied by his following admission of having read 'A good deal of Walter Scott (7 novels in all)'.[7] When he was completely unable to read, he asked others (principally his daughter Helen) to read Scott for him.[8]

Gladstone read Scott under a variety of circumstances and it was more than a simple treat or recreation. Scott's works were comforters and stress relievers. For example, when at Trentham for the Dowager Duchess of Sutherland's funeral in 1868, Gladstone occupied himself by reading Scott's translation of Goethe's *Goetz of Berlichingen* (1799).[9] And at times when he was ill himself, Gladstone turned to Scott for comfort and amusement. For example, in 1873 when 'my upper jaw . . . sent me to bed early', he wrote with grim humour, 'I took to reading "Old Mortality"'.[10]

Gladstone's reading of Scott was particularly important in his domestic life. During the last illness of his sister Anne, Gladstone was 'solaced' during an afternoon in Oxford 'with a little copy of *Legend of Montrose*' and several days before his mother's death in 1835 occupied his mind with *Paul's Letter to his Kinsfolk* (1816).[11] In 1847, during a dark time in his relationship with his sister Helen Jane, Gladstone 'spent much of the later part of the day with H[elen]. She was in a sad state. However I read Marmion Intr[oduction]. & Canto I to her: on these she was generally rational. It is in a manner pleasing to be again discharging offices of brotherhood about her even as she is'.[12] Scott also featured in Gladstone's relationship with his wife. In the weeks prior to their wedding in 1839 Gladstone recorded, 'read . . . Kenilworth, aloud with dearest'. On their wedding night (and succeeding day) he 'read *Marmion* to her' and during their honeymoon 'read Lady of the Lake (aloud)'.[13] The following year Gladstone recorded reading both *Rokeby* and *Lord of the Isles* to Catherine.[14]

There is evidence to suggest that Gladstone confined his reading of Scott principally to the home. For example, he began *Peveril of the Peak* (1822) on 1 October, 1860 whilst at Hawarden, left it behind whilst on a short visit to London (where he read Wilkie Collins' *The Woman in White*), resuming *Peveril* on his return.[15] Similarly, he left *St. Ronan's Well* behind in Hawarden when returning to London on election business in 1857.[16] Several months later he repeated the same procedure with *The Heart of Midlothian,* reading almost every day, only breaking off when away from Hawarden.[17]

Nonetheless, Gladstone's reading of Scott did occasionally stray into a category of forbidden reading: that which he undertook with prostitutes who he was seeking to reform. He both read Scott to prostitutes,[18] and alone, after engaging in rescue work.[19] In the light of this it is perhaps not difficult to make sense of Gladstone's placement of a firm 'v'[20] by Rob Roy's observation that 'ye ken weel aneugh that women and gear are at the bottom of a' the mischief in the warld' in his copy of the novel.[21] But Scott remained principally to be enjoyed within the official domestic environment in the company of family. This is unsurprising as Gladstone's Scottian reading was one of the most fundamental ways in which he received, analysed and expressed his national and familial identity.

Considering the prominence of Scotland, both in Gladstone's personal and political life, it is remarkable that more has not been written exploring Gladstone's Scottishness. There is certainly little compared with the quantity of comment on his attitude towards Ireland (to which he only made two brief visits in 1877 and 1880) or even his possession of a 'European sense'.[22] As Christopher Harvie has pointed out, Gladstone's Scottish identity 'has, in the biographies, a curious, flickering quality'.[23] Sydney Checkland, when comparing the backgrounds of Disraeli and Gladstone, did briefly note that both had 'received the heritage of his peculiar people in such a way that though overlaid and amended it was never effaced'.[24] In fact it is questionable whether Gladstone, his family or contemporaries consistently sought to overlay, amend or efface Gladstone's Scottishness.

Gladstone was brought up within a family strongly conscious of its national identity. There were clear attempts to integrate the Gladstones' family history directly into the frames of reference employed by Walter Scott, as well as to construct Gladstonian biography according to Scottian models. Note the following description of the family by Gladstone's daughter, Mary Drew:

> Mr. Gladstone sprang from an old Scotch family, originally a race of Borderers (there is still an old Gledstanes Castle). One of his ancestors, Herbert de Gledstanes, appears in Sir Walter Scott as 'gude at need.' His mother was descended from Robert the Bruce. It was surely a sad lack of imagination that allowed his father and grandfather to anglicise the fine name of Gledstanes into Gladstone.[25]

Such characterisation reflected a long-standing Scottish passion for genealogy,[26] and interpretation of history in family terms. Mary firmly anchored the family's identity to that 'retrospective invention' of 'a distinct Highland culture and tradition', which, although not created by, was certainly, as Murray Pittock has phrased it, 'restored to prominence' by Scott.[27] But she also emphasised a persistent duality in the family's Scottish identity, as both lowlanders and highlanders, which, as we shall see, was also important.

Gladstonian identity was predominantly patriarchal. There is no doubt John Gladstone remained fiercely loyal to his Scottish heritage; Checkland describes him as 'a Highland chief' who 'regarded himself as the head of his clan (including his wife's kinsfolk)'.[28] John maintained links with Scotland whilst in Liverpool.[29] But it was his desire to re-establish himself and his family there, an aspiration which was satisfied by his purchase of Fasque House in 1829-30. This grand residence, which possessed estates second only in extent to Balmoral, occupied space on the borderlands between highland and lowland Scotland. It was the ultimate expression of the family's genteel and dual Scottish identity.

William's sense of a Scottish home, and of a Scottish identity was significantly bound up with his feelings for Fasque, which he represented as a bucolic paradise,[30] a wild romantic retreat, a sacred space, and a place for study. And he consciously accompanied the rich experience of Scottish family life he knew there with reading Scott. In a striking way this paralleled Scott's rendering of his protagonists' experiences. They are often sympathetic outsiders visiting a land with which they feel or develop an affinity, or exiles seeking knowledge of their lost national or familial history and identity.[31] Gladstone was little involved in the choice and purchase of Fasque, being at Oxford, and his first visit did not take place until August 1833, when he was an MP living in London.[32] But he was '*much* pleased' with the house and its environs when he did encounter them,[33] and set about learning as much as he could about his new home.

In August 1837 Gladstone recorded travelling '7-5 (by Defiance) to Fasque' and interrogating '"The Captain" [who] drove us from Perth' for 'he has much inf[orma]tio]n on men & things of these parts'.[34] On his wedding tour in 1839, Gladstone delighted in showing the glories of Fasque and the Scottish highlands to his new wife, as well as to Mary and George Lyttelton,[35] giving free rein to his feelings about his Scottish home and displaying the strength of his romantic characterisation of it.

> We were delighted & all my companions who are new to this country were in ecstasy . . . The spectacle from the rocks is indeed magnificent: they beetle over the black sleeping lake in everlasting horror . . . They do not reach round it: but form more than half a cradle: they are of very great height & extreme wildness. In

1836, I looked from their brow into mist which was almost more peaceful than the reality of the yawning chasm . . . The Garrawalt deserves its name: its channel is generally naked rock. The views from it are glorious.[36]

Gladstone, although not entirely successfully, was trying here to emulate Scott's treatment of the sublime. At the end of the tour, he continued to wax lyrical about the scenery and wildlife as well as noting 'the absence of the herd of tourists . . . which above all renders this a delightful trip';[37] a passage very reminiscent of Scott's description of the Highlands in *A Legend of Montrose,* which Gladstone marked with a 'v'.

He therefore plodded patiently on through a waste and savage wilderness, treading paths which were only known to the shepherds and cattle-drivers, and passing with much more of discomfort than satisfaction many of those sublime combinations of mountainous scenery which now draw visitors from every corner of England to feast their eyes upon Highland grandeur.[38]

Gladstone's feelings about Fasque, Scott's works, and the Scotland they embodied were acutely personalised. This in itself was distinctly Scottian. Scott's narratives relayed both present and past through the specific, personal experiences of individuals and families. The stones of Fasque, in Gladstone's mind, seemed almost literally to represent family members; the mortar holding them together symbolised their relationships. In particular, Gladstone's 'moving recollections' of Fasque in later years were closely associated with memories of Sir John Gladstone.[39] Visits to Fasque afforded Gladstone the valued opportunity to observe the ageing baronet at closer quarters and for longer periods than he had ever been able to do previously; and his feelings of love for Fasque intensified following his father's death in 1851 and his eldest brother Tom's succession to the estate and title. On a visit to Tom and sister-in-law Louisa in 1858, Gladstone recorded 'much is changed, some very well, all in the spirit of love to the place: yet I miss some marks of my Father, our foundations [*sic*] stone'.[40] And during a later stay, in 1885, he wrote: 'It is deeply interesting to me to be here. The house is still a home. I sleep in the room in which my mother died, sit in the room where my Father died. Dearest Jessy sleeps under the chapel. And my brother is in many ways an edifying sight'.[41] Several days after writing the above, Gladstone noted that 'stories of Sir J[ohn]. G[ladstone].' were told on a visit to The Burn in Fettercairn.[42] Gladstone regularly noted when the practice of family tale-telling was depicted in Scott's novels. For example, in his copy of *Waverley,* he placed his '+' of approbation next to the description of Edward Waverley listening to and appreciating 'the oft-repeated tale of narrative old age'.[43]

Just as Gladstone's idea of Fasque as home was given meaning by familial memories and associations, so his reading of Scott's texts was augmented by imagina-

tively peopling its pages with members of his own family. Thus, whilst reading *Rob Roy,* Gladstone wrote 'Sir J[ohn]. G[ladstone].' next to Scott's descriptions of Frank Osbaldistone's father, the aged and stern merchant.[44] This 'man of business' is given a prominent role in *Rob Roy,* but the novel's romantic preoccupation is with Frank himself. The story is dominated initially by the question of whether or not Frank will carry on his father's business; however, by the end, the wealth of commerce is employed in securing the son landed property and a gentleman's life.[45] This, of course, is what his father's money achieved for Gladstone, who, in his copy of *The Antiquary,* placed his own initials opposite a description of a merchant's son.[46] The 'dream of landed establishment', as Kerr terms it, was not only 'the political fantasy that animates the Waverley novels' but was also one which occupied the Gladstone family.[47]

Such was the power of Gladstone's feeling for Fasque that he sought to persuade first his brother, and then his father, to agree to a division of the Gladstone inheritance on the latter's death. He proposed that the baronetcy should go to Tom but that he should have Fasque. His Machiavellian plot came to nothing, however, and there are a number of sharp rejoinders surviving in the family papers, written in the wake of Sir John's death, ordering William to abandon his 'claims'.[48] It is clear that much of William's sadness over Fasque derived from the fact that it was no longer his.

Physical residence in Scotland, particularly at Fasque, as well as Scottish reading, encouraged Gladstone's lifelong practice of self examination. Considering the tendency for this to be a self-denigrating process, the reflection on Scott's life provided important affirmation for Gladstone in the face of his many self-established shortcomings. For, as Judith Wilt has noted, the importance of Lockhart's *Scott* in particular was that 'this was a tale of a crippled child in love with the great outlaw deeds of aristocratic forbears who did not grow up to be Byron';[49] and Gladstone also drew direct attention to Scott's triumph over physical infirmity.[50] Scott, as numerous scholars have pointed out, was acutely aware of his own history. Thus autobiography was both an important source of inspiration, and also an art he consistently practised. As Ferris notes, he frequently interchanged history and biography whilst writing.[51] Moreover, James Kerr writes: 'Scott wrote his own career over and over again in the careers of the Waverley heroes. In the process of transforming history, he revised the life of Scott, he altered his autobiography'.[52]

There is striking concurrence between Gladstone's own idea of the status of autobiography and his engagement with Scott's (auto)biography. In 1868, whilst reading *Anne of Geierstein* for the second time, Gladstone also resumed Lockhart's *Memoirs of the Life of Sir Walter Scott,* 7 vols (1837-8), which he had been reading a couple of months before in conjunction with *The Anti-quary*.[53] In 1868 Gladstone wrote *A Chapter of Autobiography,* in which he discussed the question of his personal responsibility for Irish church disestablishment.[54] It is striking to see how consistently this autobiographical project went along with reading of, and discoursing on Scott. In February 1868 he 'Worked on Scott—Lockhart's Life—Autobiogr[aphy]. and Q[uarterly]. R[eview]. & c.: and at 8.30 delivered in the . . . school a Lecture of 1h. 20m. on that great man', in which he mentioned 'the sketch which he [Scott] wrote of his own life'.[55] The simultaneous reading of Lockhart and *Geierstein* also accompanied more work on the *Chapter* [*A Chapter of Autobiography*]. Lockhart and Scott's *Life of Jonathan Swift* (1814) also featured in his list of reading for the succeeding month.[56] At the beginning of *A Chapter,* Gladstone wrote:

> One thing is clear: that if I am warranted in treating my own case as an exceptional case, I am bound so to treat it. It is only with a view to the promotion of some general interest, that the public can becomingly be invited to hear more, especially in personal history, about an individual, of whom they already hear too much.[57]

Scott had displayed the same admixture of deprecation and public spirit in a memoir (reproduced by Lockhart), expressing the hope that 'those who shall hereafter read this little Memoir may find in it some hints to be improved, for the regulation of their own mind, or the training of others'.[58] The way Gladstone used Scott as a point of reference whilst compiling his *Chapter* exemplifies his reliance upon existing knowledge and experience, also shown by the rigorous approach to study and methodological analysis of scholarly texts that he was wont to display.

RECEPTION: SCHOLARSHIP, SELF-EDUCATION, AND THE SCOTTIAN HERO

An important aspect of Scott's establishment of himself as a man of learning and as an antiquary was that he consistently made reference to the libraries and reading habits of his characters, and in a way which was often overtly critical.[59] Gladstone regularly noted these descriptions of scholarliness and textuality, particularly when they were related to his preoccupations with broad reading, and techniques of gaining knowledge. Thus he placed a 'v' next to this description of Cosmo Bradwardine in *Waverley*.

> He was a . . . scholar, according to the scholarship of Scotchmen, that is, his learning was more diffuse than accurate, and he was rather a reader than a grammarian. Of his zeal for the classic authors he is said to have given an uncommon instance.[60]

It can be argued that the influence of Scott's imaginary, library-haunting antiquaries was matched, if not exceeded, by that of his other creation: Abbotsford. In his library and study, Scott was both deconstructing and

constructing history whilst surrounded by the most amazing array of objects and symbols representing a romanticised vision of Scotland's past. The Abbotsford model—a baronial hall filled with highland weaponry and regalia located in the gently undulating and peaceful Scottish borders—was much copied. In such a location the authentic remains of a heroic but vanished culture could be displayed and classified, read and written about, whilst one remained safe in the knowledge that their practical use would never again be required. Hence the 'modern' laird could traverse the borders between highland romantic fantasy and lowland enlightenment reality, simultaneously feeding the imagination and cultivating the rational mind, whilst remaining safe in a domesticated environment. Whilst the decorative scheme at Fasque was not Abbotsfordian, Gladstone's behaviour when there exhibited a similar duality. Both the atmosphere of Fasque, and the time and space vacation residence there afforded, inspired him to seek new levels of self-education and classificatory rigour. For example, in 1834 he recorded: 'Arranging my books & meditating great doings, to work 2 h[ours]. (at least) before breakf[ast]—& go to bed at 11'.[61] Such high levels of work were punctuated by immensely long walks over the estate, which gave him the chance to think and reflect, meet and observe the tenantry—opportunities not offered by the shooting expeditions which he made occasionally but did not really enjoy[62]—and glory in the romantic scenery. It is important to recognise, however, that, just as the romantic could enter the domestic sphere, so the domestic could seek to tame the romantic: Gladstone sought to bring his classifying and rationalising side to such encounters. Thus, in December 1851, he expressed his romantic attachment to the physical landscape in a very rationalistic way: by pacing out and recording the distances on the estate.

> Walked up the hills: mist on the top but I had the same pleasure as in seeing an old friend though soiled with a journey. I noted these distances & put them down that if I look back upon this page I may love the old hills as I see them.
>
> | | |
> |---|---|
> | By West Garrol to last gate 1 ½ mile | 20 min |
> | Through the gorge to the stream, ¾ mile, | 10 min |
> | Shank of Cairdown to top 1½ mile | 24 min |
> | Down, to point of East Garrol road. 1 ¾ mile | 13 min (say 12 ½) |
> | To Annie Croals 1 ¼ mile | 14 ½ min |
> | Back to Fasque 1 ¼ mile | 12 ½ min |
> | Total eight miles & 1 h. 36 mins[63] | |

Such tangible and practical interaction between the romantic and the rational was most obvious in Gladstone when in a Scottish setting, but the influence of Scott on Gladstone's methods of study was more far reaching and universal in scope.

The tendency for readers to identify with characters or scenes of which they read is well attested,[64] and there is compelling evidence that Gladstone both identified with, and sought to improve on, the literary character of Scott's first hero—Edward Waverley—specifically in terms of his own self-education. Self-education (or autodidacticism) was an important Gladstonian family value, and Gladstone regularly drew attention to autodidactic references in Scott's life and work. Thus, in 1868, Gladstone emphasised Scott's opportunities (as an isolated, invalid child) of 'acquiring that unbounded lore in legendary knowledge of all kinds, particularly connected with the history of his own country, which gave him a literary character in subsequent life, with some features which probably have never been seen in any former case'.[65]

In Chapter Three of *Waverley,* entitled 'Education', Scott summarised Edward's erratic reading and unsystematic learning techniques. In his edition, Gladstone placed two lines and a 'v' next to the following description.

> Alas! While he was thus permitted to read only for the gratification of his own amusement, he foresaw not that he was losing for ever the opportunity of acquiring habits of firm and incumbent application, of gaining the art of controlling, directing, and concentrating the powers of his own mind for earnest investigation,—an art far more essential than even that learning which is the primary object of study.[66]

Gladstone went on to place two 'v's next to another passage, which continued in the same critical vein.

> With a desire of amusement . . . which better discipline might soon have converted into a thirst for knowledge, young Waverley drove through the sea of books, like a vessel without pilot or rudder. Nothing . . . increases by indulgence more than a desultory habit of reading, especially under such opportunities of gratifying it. I believe one reason why such numerous instances of erudition occur among the lower rank is, that, with the same powers of mind, the poor student is limited to a narrow circle for indulging his passion for books, and must necessarily make himself master of the few he possesses ere he can acquire more. Edward . . . read no volume a moment after it ceased to excite his curiosity or interest; and it necessarily happened, that the habit of seeking only this sort of gratification, rendered it daily more difficult of attainment, till the passion for reading, like other strong appetites, produced by indulgence a sort of satiety.[67]

Gladstone combined his reading of the novel with an attempt to sort out his own reading environment. Thus, on 15 August, 1826, he 'read *Waverley*' whilst also being 'hard at work getting the Library into some kind of order', and on the 18th recorded triumphantly: 'On these days finished Library—[and] finished Waverley'.[68] This amazing association lasted throughout his life. In 1871

he recorded: 'A day of unpacking, rummaging, and arranging', and reading *Waverley* in his own library in Hawarden, where he was watched over, appropriately enough, by a print of Raeburn's portrait of Sir Walter Scott.[69]

Remarkable as this association was, it was, on the surface at least, a private and personal one. Gladstone and his brothers had had their father's vision of the nature and purposes of education well impressed on them at school. As a pragmatic preparation for public life, it was to be strategic, self-directed, and exhibit 'habits of application, of close thinking and investigation of subject, and that of tracing every effect to its cause'; all of which was to be enriched by a 'general reading' of history.[70] If Gladstone was to live up to his father's pragmatism, and obey his own conceptualisation of the aims of study, then knowledge was to be gained and used for practical, public ends. To what public use did Gladstone put his Scottian influences?

APPROPRIATION: KNOWLEDGE, NATIONALITY, AND PUBLIC ASSOCIATION WITH SCOTT

At least two specific aspects of Gladstone's public life incorporated important Scottian influences: his attitude to public education and the prosecution of his later political career.

In 1906, Mary Drew claimed her father's enduring love for Scott was determined by the writer's commitment to achieving a 'sense of harmony' and 'fitness in literature', and his 'presentation to mankind of, not the ugly, the unnatural, the cruel, the base, but the lofty, the beautiful, [and] the ideal'.[71] Such a conceptualisation brings to our attention once again the often uneasy combination, in both Scott and Gladstone, of romanticism and rationalism, and the attempt of both, in their public works, especially in a Scottish context, to foster and mediate union and understanding between the two in the realms of politics, history, religion, and education.

Gladstone felt enormous respect for Scott's history writing. He particularly appreciated the author's ability to communicate facts. In his 1868 speech, Gladstone expressed his belief

> that in this extraordinary power of calling forth from the sepulchre the dry bones of former ages—clothing sinew and flesh—causing them to live and move before us, and us to live and move among them, as if we belonged to them and they belonged to us—I believe in . . . that very rare power, Scott has exceeded most of the literary men that the world has produced.[72]

Gladstone also endorsed Scott's aim of communicating a thirst for knowledge by teaching readers about their past, a desire articulated, for example, in the prefatory letter to *Peveril of the Peak,* which describes how readers might be led to deeper, more rigorous engagement with the past by reading popular, fictionalised history.

The love of knowledge wants but a beginning—the least spark will give fire when the train is properly prepared; and having been interested in fictitious adventures, ascribed to an historical period and characters, the reader begins next to be anxious to learn what the facts really were, and how far the novelist has justly represented them.[73]

Gladstone portrayed the example and works of Scott as potentially civilising and spiritualising influences on the next generation, if it would but heed them. His annotation of the Waverley novels exhibits a consistent interest in characters' expression of spiritual, religious or ethical sentiments (Wilibert of Waverley,[74] Jeannie Deans[75]) or lack of them (Prince John in *Ivanhoe*).[76]

In his 1868 Hawarden speech, made to Welsh schoolchildren, Gladstone noted, with some concern, Scott's apparent waning popularity amongst the young, calling it a 'public misfortune'.[77] For Scott to lie unread was, to Gladstone, a tragedy almost akin to that inaugurated by the destruction of Scott's strongest characters (like Lucy Ashton and Amy Robsart) who possessed both moral principles and the courage to act on them. The fact that Gladstone characterised this as a public misfortune underlines his understanding of Scott's work as knowledge that had direct relevance to the public as well as to the private domain. This was not a new idea; *Waverley* had long been seen as a text which dealt with the 'serious political concerns of the age'.[78] The *New Monthly Magazine* in 1820 observed, for example, that: 'He [the author of *Waverley*] has enriched history to us' by making it 'loftier' and 'more public'.[79] And, fifty-eight years later, Richard Hutton considered 'the most striking feature' of the Waverley novels was that:

They are pivoted on public rather than mere private interests and passions . . . And this it is which gives his books so large an interest for young and old, soldiers and statesmen, the world of society and the recluse, alike. You can hardly read any novel of Scott's and not become better aware what public life and political issues mean . . . no man can read Scott without being more of a public man, whereas the ordinary novel tends to make its readers rather less of one than before.[80]

So far it has been demonstrated how Gladstone's reading of Scott in particular reflected, and potentially informed, his own personal sense of nationality. The final section will explore the impact of Scott on Gladstone's public life as a politician.

Gladstone's earliest practical political experiences were accompanied by readings of Scott. In 1832, during the run up to his first election contest in Newark, Gladstone read Scott's *History of Napoleon*.[81] Despite engaging in frenetic canvassing and other election business, Gladstone kept up his reading and analysis of the text right through the election (although on the 8th December he was forced to admit that he had 'made very little of

it').[82] Reading Scott's account of Napoleon's career, and his own experience of political involvement combined to produce a powerful emotional effect on the young man, which he strove to articulate in his diary. On 31 December 1832, he reflected on

an eventful year . . . to this poor country . . . [and] to my own prospects. May the mercy of God be upon its sins and failings, and may His Wisdom provide against their recurrence in that which now lies before us . . . [and] may the stormy elements of agitation which are now aroused, be overruled by Him.[83]

And, as he was nearing the end of *Napoleon,* Gladstone gave one of the most vivid and physical descriptions of a reading experience that he ever made, imbued with a similarly apocalyptic and messianic tone to that he had employed to conjure up the dangers of reform.

At night I read the account in Scott of Napoleon's last days & death. While going through the detail, I literally felt an internal weakness and my stomach turned, with such a feeling as is excited upon hearing of some sudden & terrible catastrophe—with such a feeling as I should behold the sun removed out of the face of the heaven. What is so awful, as the transition of such a Spirit![84]

Such language is reminiscent of several of Scott's 'gothick' passages dwelling on the physical effects of encountering the terrible or horrific, such as Fergus MacIvor's spectral vision in Carlisle, which Gladstone much admired.[85]

We might ask if Gladstone's journey from toryism to liberalism affected his attitude to or public use of Scott. Lionel Tollemache asserted that Gladstone 'never quite forgave Walter Scott for the part he took about Queen Caroline's trial or for his somewhat servile loyalty to "that creature George IV." And he regarded Scott's Toryism as "silly."'[86] But overall, Walter Scott's political conservatism seemed to matter little to the liberal Gladstone. This was partly because Gladstone saw Scott's genius as transcending such mundane categories; there was also a shared episcopalianism and, within certain bounds, a shared appreciation for conservatism, rationalism, and unionism. In addition, the broad brushstrokes with which Gladstone painted liberal values meant that it was often extremely easy to marshal Scott to support them in general terms. Gladstone's ability to see things anew in Scott in the light of his own developing attitudes is perhaps seen most clearly in his annotations with respect to religion. As a young man, Gladstone's denominational chauvinism made him dubious about the status of the presbyterian establishment in Scotland, and sometimes anti-catholic.[87] He marked passages critical of Roman catholicism, for example, in *Waverley* and *The Monastery* where the Scottish Roman catholic church is described as 'at her last gasp'.[88] But equally, Gladstone's increased religious tolerance in later years is reflected in the marginalia, which emphasise (with clear approval) messages of accommodation and tolerance articulated by some of his characters: kirk ministers,[89] Roman catholics,[90] and episcopalians.[91]

Gladstone, in practice, favoured episcopalian Scotland. He encouraged his father to build an episcopalian church at Fasque and to invest in Trinity College, Glenalmond, the episcopalian school in Perthshire planned by James Hope Scott and himself.[92] The key attraction of episcopalianism for Gladstone was its claim to christian apostolic descent, but its representation of an unbroken Scottish history and nationality was also vitally important. The fractured nature of both Scottish history and identity were realities that preoccupied both Scott and Gladstone in public and private.

Scott is famous for his romantic depictions of Scottish history, but the fundamental message of his writings was not to foster a revival of the eighteenth-century highland world. Although Scott celebrated and idealised that strong nationalism and organic communitarian society, which he argued had existed in Scotland up to 1745, and dealt with the possibility for reform of the existing social and political order in novels such as *The Heart of Midlothian,* which Kerr describes as 'a romance of national regeneration',[93] his ultimate sense of reality (however regretful) was that this Scotland was dead and gone; the post '45 generation was severed from what had gone before. As he wrote in the 'Preface' to *Ivanhoe,* 'even within these thirty years, such an infinite change has taken place in the manners of Scotland, that men look back upon their fathers' habits of society, as we do on those of the reign of Queen Anne'.[94]

There was much in this anglicised, domesticated, and cautious Scottishness which appealed to Gladstone. Gladstone's own Scottish identity was problematic as a result of having been born and brought up in an émigré-Scots household in England. He was as attracted as Scott to a romanticised Scottish heritage, in which national identity and patriotism played a large part, but he was also cautious and, in general, supportive of the union which had been effected between the romantic, violent, irrational 'Jacobite', or highland, Scotland, and the rational 'Hanoverian' lowland Scotland. As we have seen, he was more than happy returning from the wildness of the mountains to work in the secure and rational study of the country house. In political terms, he also exhibited a baffling mixture of caution and radicalism. The message of his Midlothian speeches was essentially a conservative one, if more radical in its implications;[95] and his commitment to Scottish land reform was not immediate and instinctive. It was partly based, as Clive Dewey has demonstrated, on a careful absorption of new historicist modes of thought (exemplified by the work of W. F. Skene and J. S. Blackie), which de-

manded political recognition for indigenous agricultural traditions and customary laws.[96] However, it needed the evidence and moderate recommendations of the Napier Commission report to secure Gladstone's support, and reform was made a matter of urgency by the crofters' agitation.[97] Gladstone, as a pragmatic politician and one who believed that the 'freedom best known to us' was that 'allied with order and loyalty',[98] definitely shared Scott's overall concern to keep the Scottish cart on the Union's wheels.

Nonetheless, Gladstone believed in the persistence of an authentic and autonomous (if not unanimous)[99] Scottish national identity. When reading Scott, Gladstone was drawn to those characters who exhibited peculiarly Scottish characteristics, either in physiognomy, dress, language or behaviour, which, to him, represented the long history of Scotland's distinctness as a nation.[100] Furthermore, Gladstone was particularly attracted by those characters who exhibited a strongly nationalistic brand of politics. Thus Scott's descriptions of Fergus and Flora MacIvor in *Waverley,* the archetypal highland rebels, elicited special notice and comment.[101]

Despite his caution, Gladstone was more open than Scott to the possibility of a regeneration in Scottish nationality. In 1885, at the dedication of the newly restored town cross of Edinburgh (for which Gladstone had paid) he flagged his divergence from the political conservatism of his hero as well as his admiration for him: 'I am not able to subscribe to every article of the creed of that great man in relation to modern occurrences' he announced.[102]

Fundamentally, Gladstone was inspired by Scott's stories and language to consider the regeneration of 'Old Scotland' because of the coincidences he saw between Scott's concentric model of Scotland's nationality, rooted in the community of clan and family, and his own mature, religiously informed liberalism. He marked the following passage in *Rob Roy* with a single, vertical line.

> 'You do not know the genius of that man's country, sir,' answered Rashleigh; 'discretion, prudence, and foresight . . . modified by . . . ardent patriotism, which forms . . . the outmost of the concentric bulwarks with which a Scotchman fortifies himself . . . Surmount this mound, you find an inner and still dearer barrier—the love of his province, his village, or, most probably, his clan; storm this second obstacle, you have a third—his attachment to his own family . . . It is within these limits that a Scotchman's social affectation expands itself, never reaching those which are outermost, till all means of discharging itself in the interior circles have been exhausted'.[103]

In his second Midlothian address, Gladstone similarly called attention to the 'sacred constitution' of the family, that 'primary element of society',[104] and presented an understanding of society ordered in exactly the same concentric way. Clive Dewey suggests that Gladstone's model for regenerating an 'idealized aristocracy—an aristocracy redeemed by service,' in both Scotland and Ireland, 'was a historicist argument of his own'.[105] Whilst such an idea might not have derived directly from Gladstone's reading of Blackie *et al,* it was undoubtedly inspired by his reading of Scott.

When addressing specific contemporary political issues relating to Scotland, Gladstone was deeply influenced by his reading and understanding of Scott's Scotland. When Gladstone was preoccupied with Scottish land reform in 1885, as well as reading 'Blackie on Land Laws' and 'L[or]d Selkirk on the Highlands', he was also re-reading *The Heart of Midlothian.*[106] His conceptualisation of the Scottish people, their levels of nationalism and, indeed, how dangerous they were came straight from a personal (re)interpretation of Scott's world. For example, when he wrote to William Harcourt about the extension of the Irish Land Act to Scotland, and the problems of achieving a just settlement for the Scottish people, he described them as 'a people united by tradition, by neighbourhood, often by blood; by agitation, as it may now be added, and always by common interest'. The landowners might be different at present, but 'the representatives of the old flesh and blood, still largely on the ground' were to be treated with respect.[107] Instead of the disjunction stressed by Scott, Gladstone habitually stressed historical continuity by calling Scotland 'Old Scotland'.[108] Gladstone saw Scottish nationality as alive and well, and was keen to fight anyone who sought to belittle or underestimate the strength of it. In 1885 he criticised Parnell for alleging 'that Scotland had lost her nationality', remarking 'that Mr Parnell "is a very thoughtful man . . . but he never said a sillier thing than that"'.[109]

Unlike Scott, but within a conception importantly derived from his depiction of Scotland, Gladstone still regarded the Scots as a potential political threat. The volatility and unpredictability of Scottish national feeling, especially amongst highlanders, was a subject to which Gladstone frequently returned. In 1884, he wrote to Lord Carlingford, after reading the Napier Commission report, expressing his concern about Scottish resentment over their lack of representation at cabinet level.[110] 'The Scotch are a dangerous people', he observed in 1889, who needed to be 'treated with prudence and consideration' in a political context;[111] and this only a month after he had re-read *Peveril of the Peak,* in which the consequences of awakening the 'fury of a whole people' are discussed.[112] In the face of such power and potential danger, the only resort was to ensure that British governance of Scotland was completely and transparently just and unrepressive, respectful of the nation's long history and traditions, and careful not to arouse its hatred, which would be disastrous for both the stability of the Union as well as for the Liberal party.

The Midlothian campaigns themselves can be read explicitly within a Scottian frame of reference. David Brooks' analysis of the background to the first campaign characterises the constituency as a 'world of local rivalries and family influence', and the campaign itself as a contest, between the two noble Scottish houses of Rosebery and Buccleuch, in which 'the democratic and the feudal were at times strangely combined'.[113] The constituency was traditional Tory territory and was not going to be easy for Gladstone to win: 'It may be necessary to make a pilgrimage in the county', Gladstone duly observed in January 1879.[114] Not only was the resulting campaign rhetorically an attempt to save the nation from corrupting influences, but structurally, as a punishing schedule of tours and political rallies, it was in a striking way like the picaresque journeyings of so many of Scott's protagonists. As Kerr observes: 'Touring is not a politically innocent activity in *Waverley*', and it certainly was not for Gladstone in Midlothian.[115]

Gladstone's political speeches and writings are obvious places to look for the marks of Scott's influence upon the public man, and also to gauge the levels of Scottishness in Gladstone's world view. On this latter point, of course, caution is required. Politicians are adept at seeking to identify a link with their audience, and Gladstone did this when in Scotland. For example, in the first Midlothian speech he defended his status as a non-local parliamentary candidate, and in the second speech addressed 'the subjects most likely to have a special interest' to his audience as Scots.[116] The passion of Gladstone's Midlothian speeches was certainly Scottian, and so was their language. However, the stylistic influence Scott had over Gladstone's oratory was more diffused and integral than direct and ornamental, appropriate to his level of immersion in Scott's world and consistent (as Agatha Ramm has demonstrated) with his usual practice of quoting and alluding to literary material long after it had been read and internalised.[117]

David Bebbington has convincingly shown how the influence of Scott ensured that Gladstone conceptualised early Greek society as in many ways equivalent to patriarchal highland society.[118] In the same way, Gladstone's graphic description of the fate of women and children in Afghanistan, included in his second Dalkeith speech at the Foresters' Hall, was imagery drawn not just from his own experience and conceptualisation of highland society; it was importantly mediated through Scott's rendering of the latter world in both his fictional and non-fictional prose, a world with which Gladstone had been familiar since his schooldays. During the summer of 1826, Gladstone spoke several times in favour of the Jacobite cause at the Eton debating society.[119] One of his sources was Scott's long article on 'The Culloden Papers' in the *Quarterly Review* of 1816, which he read and from which took quotations.[120] Whilst he was reading it he noted: 'I [am] rather getting a new light on subject of Stuarts, 1745 & c.'[121] In his article, Scott had drawn attention to 'curious points of parallelism' between Scottish highland clan society and that of the Afghan or Persian mountain tribes, which 'show how the same state of society and civilisation produces similar manners, laws, and customs, even at the most remote periods of time, and in the most distant quarters of the world'.[122]

Gladstone urged the people (and particularly the women) of Dalkeith to: 'Remember the rights of the savage, as we call him. Remember that the happiness of his humble home, remember that the sanctity of life in the hill villages of Afghanistan among the winter snows, is as inviolable in the eye of Almighty God as can be your own.'[123] Here he was painting a picture of the horrors of war and pillage in Afghanistan reminiscent of Scott's graphic description of the devastation wreaked by the English army after Culloden in *Waverley*:

> The place had been sacked by the King's troops, who, in wanton mischief, had even attempted to burn it; and though the thickness of the walls had resisted the fire . . . the stables and out-houses were totally consumed. The towers and pinnacles of the main building were scorched and blackened; the pavement of the court broken and shattered; the doors torn down entirely, or hanging by a single hinge; the windows dashed in and demolished, and the court strewed with articles of furniture broken into fragments. The accessories of ancient distinction . . . were treated with peculiar contumely. The fountain was demolished, and the spring, which had supplied it, now flooded the courtyard. The stone basin seemed to be destined for a drinking-trough for cattle . . . and one or two of the family pictures, which seemed to have served as targets for the soldiers, lay on the ground in tatters . . .
>
> Amid these general marks of ravage, there were some which more particularly addressed the feelings of Waverley. Viewing the front of the building, thus wasted and defaced, his eyes naturally sought the little balcony which more properly belonged to Rose's apartment . . . It was easily discovered, for beneath it lay the stage-flowers and shrubs, with which it was her pride to decorate it, and which had been hurled from the bartizan: several of her books were mingled with broken flower-pots and other remnants. Among these Waverley distinguished one of his own, a small copy of Ariosto, and gathered it as a treasure, though wasted by the wind and rain.[124]

Scott had, through the eyes of the returning Waverley, brought home the human and personalised consequences of the Jacobite rebellion to a generation for whom Scottish society had been irrevocably altered. But, by view-

ing it from the vantage point of sixty years since, and concluding with Edward and Rose's nuptial union, Scott softened and somewhat sentimentalised the post-Culloden devastation. This world was truly 'dead and gane', as Davie Gellatley choruses at the scene.[125] But here was the difference, and where Gladstone had to go beyond Scott. When Gladstone delivered his second Midlothian speeches, the issue of Afghanistan was no longer a hot political topic, a fact which has puzzled other commentators on this speech.[126] By prodding the collective memories of another highland people, in rhetoric evoking the most famous literary description of their own treatment at the hands of the British army, Gladstone was doing his best to rekindle the flames:

> Go into the lofty hills of Afghanistan . . . and what do we there see? . . . our gallant troops . . . in its border lands, inhabited by hill tribes who enjoy more or less of political independence . . . You have seen . . . that from such and such a village attacks had been made upon the British forces, and that in consequence the village had been burned. Have you ever reflected on the meaning of these words? . . . The meaning . . . is, that the women and the children were driven forth to perish in the snows of winter . . . Is not that a fact . . . which does appeal to your hearts as women . . . which does rouse in you a sentiment of horror and grief, to think that the name of England, under no political necessity, but for a war as frivolous as ever was waged in the history of man, should be associated with consequences such as these?[127]

There is no framing or softening here. Gladstone confronts his audience with a contemporary atrocity and demands a moral response. The telling line: 'If they resisted, would not you have done the same?', is offered in the full knowledge that, as Scots, his listeners knew their ancestors had done exactly that and had paid dearly for it.

Gladstone's eagerness to be associated with the sort of Scottishness that the name of Scott conjured up, and his blatant flaunting of his 'Scottishness' during his political campaigns was not lost on his audiences, nor on contemporary commentators and caricaturists. For example, the Irish nationalist paper, *United Ireland*, referred to Gladstone as 'the renowned Wizard of the North', in 1886, using the title popularly associated with Walter Scott.[128] If, as David Brooks suggests, leading Liberals considered Midlothian to be the ideal siding into which to shunt their most controversial figure, then they had gravely miscalculated.[129] As we have seen, the rhetorical and representational resources offered by Scott, Scotland and Midlothian were substantial, and carried a number of potentially worrying implications. Gladstone was represented by some cartoonists as an heroic, but possibly dangerous, highlander. In August 1884, he was shown by Tenniel, 'Raising the "Fiery Cross" of "agitation"', in Midlothian, dressed in full highland regalia and backed by a crowd of surly looking Scots glaring out menacingly from the smoke and shadows [fig. 1].[130] But the Scott-inspired Gladstone of Midlothian also presented characteristics with which more conservative forces could work. As Kerr notes, of Edward Waverley's commissioning of an heroic portrait of himself and Fergus in full highland costume at the end of *Waverley,* political portraiture can fulfil a domesticating function: 'the preferred method of dealing with disruptive political desire is to frame it within the boundaries of a sentimental portrait'.[131] By representing Gladstone as a tartan-clad romantic rebel, cartoonists could also domesticate his increasingly radical politics by romanticising, sentimentalising, and even poking fun at them. In 1890, Harry Furniss pictured, 'The Grand Old Campaigner in Scotland', as a completely humorous figure in 'a Ravenswood costume', supposedly lent to him by the actor Henry Irving.[132] Such variety of response is also observable in the popular reception of Gladstone in Scotland. In a period during which 'English' and 'Scottish' were regularly synonymised, Gladstone's Scottish nationality and identity was acknowledged and positively celebrated by the Scots themselves. Rosebery described a meeting at which the convenor was shouted down by 'a furious shout of "Scotchman, Scotchman"', after he had referred to Gladstone as '"the greatest living Englishman"', and the Lord Provost of Dundee received the same treatment in 1890.[133] But it is important to note that recognition of Gladstone's Scottish nationality by Scots was not necessarily an anti-Union gesture (as neither was his acknowledgment of theirs), as the following description of Gladstone's visit to Glasgow in 1892 suggests:

> The exterior of the [Liberal] Club was gaily decorated with bunting and festoons. It was evidently the occasion of Scotchmen welcoming a Scotchman. Above the doorway was displayed the Scottish Coat of Arms, and at each side the Scottish flag. Overhead was a picture of The Grand Old Man; and crowing all floated proudly the Union Jack![134]

Here Scottish nationality is asserted, proudly but safely, within the context of the United Kingdom.

* * *

Gladstone's overwhelmingly positive public association with Scott continued after his death. John Morley drew a direct comparison between the composition of his biography of Gladstone and the story of Scott's life:

> I must here pause for material affairs of money and business, with which . . . in the case of its heroes the public is considered to have little concern. They can no more be altogether omitted here than the bills, acceptances, renewals, notes of hand, and all the other financial apparatus of his printers and publishers can be left out of the story of Sir Walter Scott.[135]

Equally, as is suggested in this article, neither can the fascinating engagement between Gladstone and the works of Scott be omitted from a consideration of his life and career.

This examination, although not exhaustive, has attempted to cast new light on an important and influential relationship in Gladstone's life, establishing that it was neither the superficial and recreational association some have described, nor simply a ploy of an astute politician. Gladstone's engagement with Scott was long-lasting, evidenced by the volume and technique of his reading, and the writer's influence upon him was truly remarkable. Scott functioned as a constructor and classifier of memory and identity for Gladstone. His concept of self, his understanding of family, and his sense of home, were all forged and conducted within a concentrically modelled Scottian frame of reference. In the context of Midlothian, Gladstone broadened this circle to incorporate and appeal to the collective memory of the Scots themselves, showing how crucially Scott influenced Gladstone's political understanding of the Scottish nation and its people, and his conception of how he could, acting and being represented as a fellow countryman, best serve their political interests. Gladstone shared with Scott an essential commitment to the Union but, with his principled commitment not to offer to Ireland what he could not to Scotland and Wales (essentially leaving the door open for devolution), Gladstone was to be a significant force in the reanimation of Scottish nationalism, apparently 'missing' for much of the nineteenth century. This outcome would have surprised and undoubtedly troubled the author by whom much of Gladstone's enthusiasm for his ancestral land had been inspired and, in its most separatist manifestations, Gladstone himself.

At the end of *A Legend of Montrose,* Scott addressed his reader as follows:

> He cannot be more sensible than I am, that sufficient varieties have now been exhibited of the Scottish character, to exhaust one individual's powers of observation, and that to persist would be useless and tedious. I have the vanity to suppose, that the popularity of these Novels has shewn my countrymen, and their peculiarities, in lights which were new to the Southern reader; and that many, hitherto indifferent upon the subject, have been induced to read Scottish history, from the allusions in these works of fiction.[136]

By placing Gladstone within his Scottish context we see again how frequently and significantly his private and public worlds intersected; how 'allusions in . . . works of fiction', read in the privacy of a library, underpinned so much of import in a public life.

Notes

1. Sir Walter Scott, *The Lay of the Last Minstrel* (1805), canto six, verse 31. J. Logie Robertson (ed.), *The Poetical Works of Sir Walter Scott* (Oxford, 1913), 47.

2. London, British Library [BL], W. E. Gladstone MSS, Add. MS 44546 fo. 114, W. E. Gladstone to Rev. O. Shipley, 14 May 1883.

3. W. E. Gladstone, *Studies on Homer and the Homeric age,* 3 vols (Oxford, 1858), iii, 107.

4. Gladstone never met Scott. The nearest he came was in Rome in 1832. He wrote, with obvious disappointment, 'Sir W. Scott arrived—but we could not find him out'. M. R. D. Foot and H. C. G. Matthew (eds), *The Gladstone Diaries: With Prime Ministerial Correspondence,* 14 vols (Oxford, 1968-96), 19 Apr. 1832. Afterwards *Diaries* with date. Morley recalled that Gladstone 'constantly regretted that he had never met or known Sir Walter Scott, as of course he might have done'. John Morley, *The Life of William Ewart Gladstone,* New edn, 2 vols (London, 1905), ii, 731.

5. Jonathan Rose, *The Intellectual Life of the British Working Classes* (New Haven and London, 2001), 40-1.

6. There are twenty-two Waverley novels but *Tales of My Landlord* (1816) comprises *The Black Dwarf* and *Old Mortality; Tales of My Landlord,* Third Series (1819) contains *The Bride of Lammermoor* and *A Legend of Montrose, Tales of the Crusaders* (1825) is made up of *The Betrothed* and *The Talisman; Chronicles of the Canongate* (1827) features *Two Drovers, The Highland Widow* and *The Surgeon's Daughter* and the fourth series of *Tales of My Landlord* (1832) consists of *Count Robert of Paris* and *Castle Dangerous*—making twenty-eight novels and stories in all.

7. *Diaries,* 1 Sept. 1894.

8. Cf. for example, *Diaries,* 5 Oct. 1892 and 18 Apr. 1894.

9. *Diaries,* 3 Nov. 1868.

10. *Diaries,* 13 Jan. 1873. Cf. also *Diaries,* 15 Nov. 1827. For Scott as insomnia cure, cf. *Diaries,* 3 Jan. 1883.

11. *Diaries,* 20 Feb. 1829, 18 Sept. 1835.

12. *Diaries,* 5 Oct. 1847.

13. *Diaries,* 18, 25, 26, and 31 Jul. 1839.

14. *Diaries,* 17 and 27 Jun. 1840 ff.

15. *Diaries,* 1-27 Oct. 1860.

16. *Diaries,* 9 Apr. 1857.

17. *Diaries,* 9-30 Oct. 1857.

18. On 8 April, 1859 he 'Saw Stapylton—Mrs Jarvis' (both rescue cases), 'Read *L[ady] of Lake* aloud'

to them and placed a chastising 'X' by the date. In 1875 he repeated the exercise, this time to 'Stewart & another'. *Diaries,* 9 Nov. 1875.

19. For example, *Diaries,* 22 Jan. 1884.

20. Gladstone's tick mark. Gladstone used a consistent, symbolic system of annotation throughout his life to which his own key survives. See Ruth Clayton, 'W. E. Gladstone: an annotation key', *Notes & Queries* 246 (June 2001), 140-3.

21. Sir Walter Scott, *Rob Roy,* 3rd edn, 2 vols, *Novels and Tales of the Author of Waverley,* 25 vols (Edinburgh and London, 1821-4), [NTAW], vi, 395.

22. Cf. K. A. P. Sandiford, 'Gladstone and Europe', in B. L. Kinzer (ed.), *The Gladstonian Turn of Mind: Essays Presented to J. B. Conacher* (Toronto, 1985), 177-196.

23. Christopher Harvie, 'Gladstonianism, the provinces and popular political culture, 1860-1906', in R. Bellamy (ed.), *Victorian Liberalism: Nineteenth-Century Political Thought and Practice* (London, 1990), 164.

24. S. G. Checkland, *The Gladstones: A Family Biography 1764-1851* (Cambridge, 1971), 3.

25. Mary Drew, *Catherine Gladstone* (London, 1919), 25.

26. Cf. David Allan, '"What's in a name?": pedigree and propaganda in seventeenth-century Scotland', in E. J. Cowan and R. J. Finlay (eds), *Scottish History: The Power of the Past* (Edinburgh, 2002), 147-167.

27. Murray G. H. Pittock, 'The Jacobite cult', in Cowan and Finlay (eds), *Scottish History,* 194.

28. Checkland, *The Gladstones,* xii.

29. C. R. Fay, *Huskisson and his Age* (London, 1951), 369.

30. For example, *Diaries,* 11 Aug. 1836: 'Found all well—hay making, cherries & gooseberries ripening'.

31. Judith Wilt, *Secret Leaves: The Novels of Walter Scott* (Chicago and London, 1985), 16-17.

32. *Diaries,* 20 Aug. 1833.

33. *Diaries,* 21 Aug. 1833.

34. *Diaries,* 14 Aug. 1837.

35. *Diaries,* 20 Aug. 1839.

36. *Diaries,* 3 Sept. 1839.

37. *Diaries,* 6 Sept. 1839.

38. Sir Walter Scott, *A Legend of Montrose*, 3rd edn, 2 vols, NTAW, xii, 294.

39. Cf. *Diaries,* 26 Dec. 1851.

40. *Diaries,* 7 Oct. 1858.

41. *Diaries,* 2 Sept. 1885. This refers to Catherine Jessy Gladstone, Gladstone's second daughter, who died, aged five, in 1850.

42. *Diaries,* 4 Sept. 1885. Cf. also *Diaries,* 10 Nov. 1836 note, 17 Oct. 1846 and 30 Oct. 1890.

43. Sir Walter Scott, *Waverley,* 3rd edn, NTAW, i, 36. He also noted tale-telling in *The Bride of Lammermoor*: Cf. *Diaries,* 31 Oct. 1836 and Sir Walter Scott, *The Bride of Lammermoor,* 3rd edn, 2 vols, NTAW, xii, 80.

44. Sir Walter Scott, *Rob Roy,* 3rd edn, 2 vols, NTAW, v, 265, 266. In his endnotes to his first volume of *Rob Roy* Gladstone noted '265, 6. Sir J. G. 271'.

45. Cf. Alexander Welsh, *The Hero of the Waverley Novels with New Essays on Scott,* (ed.) by L. Gossman, New edn (Princeton, 1992), 123-5.

46. Sir Walter Scott, *The Antiquary,* 3rd edn, NTAW, iv, 26.

47. James Kerr, *Fiction Against History: Scott as Storyteller* (Cambridge, 1989), 10.

48. Hawarden, Flintshire Record Office [FRO], Glynne-Gladstone MSS, MS 1252, Correspondence and papers (mainly of Thomas Gladstone and W. E. Gladstone) concerning the division of the estate of Sir John Gladstone, 1845-51. Cf. David Bebbington, *William Ewart Gladstone: Faith and Politics in Victorian Britain* (Grand Rapids, Michigan, 1993), 75-6, and Richard Shannon, *Gladstone: Peel's Inheritor 1809-1865* (London, 1982), 158-9.

49. Wilt, *Secret Leaves,* 1.

50. 'The Right Hon. W. E. Gladstone, M.P. at Hawarden, February 3, 1868', *The Chester Courant,* 3 Feb. 1868.

51. Ina Ferris, *The Achievement of Literary Authority: Gender, History, and the Waverley Novels* (Ithaca and London, 1991), 120.

52. Kerr, *Scott as Storyteller* [*Fiction Against History*: Scott as Storyteller], 9.

53. *Diaries,* 30 Jul. 1868 and 15 Sept. 1868 ff.

54. W. E. Gladstone, 'A Chapter of Autobiography', in W. E. Gladstone (ed.), *Gleanings of Past Years* (London, 1879).

55. *Diaries,* 3 Feb. 1868. *The Chester Courant,* 3 Feb. 1868. Gladstone's speech notes are at BL, W. E.

Gladstone MSS, Add. MS 44660, fo. 1. Note also that he read *The Bride of Lammermoor* on 5 February.

56. For example, *Diaries,* 28 Oct. 1868: 'Lockhart's Scott—finished—Scott's Life of Swift: began'.

57. Gladstone, 'A Chapter of Autobiography', 98.

58. J. Lockhart, *Memoirs of the Life of Sir Walter Scott,* 7 vols (Edinburgh and London, 1837-8), i, 3.

59. Cf. Robert Colby, *Fiction with a Purpose* (Bloomington, 1967), 30.

60. Scott, *Waverley,* 3rd edn, NTAW, i, 59.

61. *Diaries,* 14 Aug. 1834.

62. Cf. for example, *Diaries,* 11 Nov. 1834: 'Conf[ess]. had to kill a wounded partridge: & felt after it, as if I had shot the albatross.'

63. *Diaries,* 17 Dec. 1851.

64. Cf. Rose, *Intellectual Life* [*The Intellectual Life of the British Working Classes*], 98, 412.

65. *The Chester Courant,* 3 Feb. 1868.

66. Scott, *Waverley,* NTAW, i, 28-9. The mark on this page is possibly an '!'.

67. Scott, *Waverley,* NTAW, i, 31-2.

68. *Diaries,* 18 Aug. 1826.

69. *Diaries,* 7 Sept. 1871.

70. Sir John Gladstone to Tom Gladstone, 21 Apr., 5 May, 1820 and 9 Oct. 1822. Quoted in Checkland, *The Gladstones,* 410-12.

71. Mary Drew, 'Mr. Gladstone's Library at "St. Deiniol's Hawarden"', *Nineteenth Century* 59 (June 1906) 944-954, at 950.

72. *The Chester Courant,* 3 Feb. 1868.

73. Prefatory Letter to *Peveril of the Peak,* quoted in Kerr, *Scott as Storyteller,* 15-16.

74. Scott, *Waverley,* NTAW, i, 37.

75. Sir Walter Scott, *The Heart of Midlothian,* 3rd edn, 2 vols, *Tales of My Landlord* Series 2, NTAW, ix, 150, 157.

76. Sir Walter Scott, *Ivanhoe,* 3rd edn, 2 vols, NTAW, xiii, 118.

77. *The Chester Courant,* 3 Feb. 1868. Lionel Tollemache reported that Gladstone encountered this attitude at a dinner party in December 1891: 'A young lady present sprung a mine by saying that Scott was dull, and adding that she got more pleasure from Thackeray and George Eliot . . .

Mr. Gladstone said, "We shall never agree about novels."' Asa Briggs (ed.), *Gladstone's Boswell. Late Victorian Conversations by Lionel A. Tollemache and Other Documents* (Sussex and New York, 1984), 44.

78. Ferris, *Literary Authority* [*The Achievement of Literary Authority*], 84.

79. Quoted in Ferris, *Literary Authority,* 207.

80. Richard H. Hutton, *Sir Walter Scott* (New York, 1878), 101-2, quoted in Ferris, *Literary Authority,* 98-9.

81. Walter Scott, *The Life of Napoleon Buonaparte, Emperor of the French. With a Preliminary View of the French Revolution,* 9 vols (Edinburgh and London, 1827). *Diaries,* 16 Nov., 1832 ff. Gladstone's analysis of the text is at BL, W. E. Gladstone MSS, Add. MS 44722, fos. 75, 77.

82. *Diaries,* 8 Dec. 1832.

83. *Diaries,* 31 Dec. 1832.

84. *Diaries,* 19 Jan. 1833. Gladstone's final analysis took place on 22nd. For the death scene, cf. Scott, *Napoleon* [*The Life of Napoleon Buonaparte*], ix, 254 ff.

85. Sir Walter Scott, *Waverley,* NTAW, ii, 225. Gladstone marked '+' and noted in his diary how both 'sublime' and 'grand' he found the two chapters. *Diaries,* 4 Dec. 1848, 21 Dec. 1876.

86. Briggs, *Gladstone's Boswell,* 78.

87. Cf. Stewart J. Brown, 'Gladstone, Chalmers and the disruption of the church of Scotland', in D. W. Bebbington and R. Swift (eds), *Gladstone Centenary Essays* (Liverpool, 2000), 10-28.

88. Scott, *Waverley,* NTAW, i, 398.

89. Scott, *Waverley,* NTAW, i, 348. Here Gladstone notes (with a single line) an affirmation of presbyterian worship. Gladstone notes ('v') further favourable commentary of presbyterian attitudes and ethics in *Old Mortality.* Sir Walter Scott, *Old Mortality,* 3rd edn, *Tales of My Landlord* Series One, NTAW, viii, 115. Tollemache recorded Gladstone favourably acknowledging, in the 1890s, how much presbyterianism had changed over his lifetime. Briggs, *Gladstone's Boswell,* 146-7.

90. Scott, *Waverley,* NTAW, i, 232, 332; Sir Walter Scott, *The Abbot,* 3rd edn, 2 vols, NTAW, xvi, 380; Sir Walter Scott, *Peveril of the Peak,* 3rd edn, 3 vols, NTAW, xxii, 164.

91. Sir Walter Scott, *Guy Mannering; or, The Astrologer,* 3rd edn, NTAW, iii, 204; Sir Walter Scott, *Quentin Durward,* 3rd edn, 2 vols, NTAW, xxv, 58.

92. Cf. H. C. G. Matthew, *Gladstone 1809-1898* (Oxford, 1997), 61, 97, 100, 245.

93. Kerr, *Scott as Storyteller,* 62, 64.

94. Scott, *Ivanhoe,* NTAW, xiii, vi.

95. For example, his promise to 'consent to give Ireland no principle, nothing that is not upon equal terms offered to Scotland and to the different portions of the United Kingdom' was made much of in later years by the Scottish home rule association. W. E. Gladstone, *Political Speeches in Scotland, November and December 1879* (Edinburgh, 1879), 88. Cf. Richard Shannon, *Gladstone: Heroic Minister, 1865-1898* (London, 1999), 236-7.

96. Clive Dewey, 'Celtic agrarian legislation and the Celtic Revival: historicist implications of Gladstone's Irish and Scottish Land Acts 1870-1886', *Past & Present* 64 (1974), 30-70.

97. James Hunter, 'The politics of Highland land reform, 1873-1895', *Scottish Historical Review* 53 (1974) 45-68. Cf. also Ewen A. Cameron, *Land for the People?: The British Government and the Scottish Highlands, c. 1880-1925* (East Linton, 1996).

98. Gladstone, *Political Speeches in Scotland,* 163.

99. In December 1891 he told Tollemache: 'In Scotland [national] sentiment is not unanimous'. Briggs, *Gladstone's Boswell,* 199.

100. For example, Gladstone marked (with lines) Scott's description of an old man in *Waverley.* Scott, *Waverley,* NTAW, i, 270-1. In the endnotes to this volume, Gladstone draws attention to four references to national dress.

101. Scott, *Waverley,* NTAW, i, 206, 216, 219, 233.

102. 'The Cross of Edinburgh', *Daily News,* 24 Nov. 1885.

103. Scott, *Rob Roy,* NTAW, v, 435.

104. Gladstone, *Political Speeches in Scotland,* 84.

105. Dewey, 'Celtic agrarian legislation', 60.

106. *Diaries,* 12, 17, 19 Jan. 1885.

107. Oxford, Bodleian Library, MSS Harcourt dep. 9, fos. 120-31, letter two: W. E. Gladstone to W. V. Harcourt, 19 Jan. 1885 (quoted in *Diaries* at this date).

108. Cf. for example: BL, W. E. Gladstone MSS, Add. MS 44543, fo. 64: W. E. Gladstone to G. Young, 9 Feb. 1874 (quoted in *Diaries,* at this date); BL, W. E. Gladstone MSS, Add. MS 44316, fo. 117, W. E. Gladstone to Lord Richard Grosvenor, 27 Nov. 1885 (quoted in *Diaries* at this date).

109. *Scotsman,* 3 Sep. 1885, 4a, quoted in *Diaries,* 2 Sept. 1885 note. Cf. also 'The Cross of Edinburgh', *Daily News,* 24 Nov. 1885.

110. Taunton, Somerset Archive and Record Service, Carlingford MSS, CP1/227, W. E. Gladstone to Lord Carlingford, 7 Sept., 1884 (quoted in *Diaries* at this date).

111. *Hansard* [*Hansard's Parliamentary Debates*], 336, 1510 (quoted at *Diaries,* 30 May, 1889 note).

112. Scott, *Peveril of the Peak,* NTAW, xxii, 499.

113. David Brooks, 'Gladstone and Midlothian: the background to the first campaign', *Scottish Historical Review* 64 (1985) 42-67 at 46, 55-6.

114. BL, W. E. Gladstone MSS, Add. MS 56444: W. E. Gladstone to W. Adam, 11 Jan. 1879, quoted in Brooks, 'Gladstone and Midlothian', 47.

115. Kerr, *Scott as Storyteller,* 24.

116. Gladstone, *Political Speeches in Scotland,* 68. Tory papers at the time suggested Gladstone's reference to larger representation for Scotland constituted a bribe to electors. Brooks, 'Gladstone and Midlothian', 57.

117. A. Ramm, *Gladstone as Man of Letters. A James Bryce Memorial Lecture* (Oxford, 1981), 20-1.

118. In his *Studies on Homer and the Homeric Age,* 3 vols (Oxford, 1858). David Bebbington, *The Mind of Gladstone: Religion, Homer, and Politics* (Oxford, 2004), 150-1.

119. *Diaries,* 17 Jun. 1826. (Notes for this speech are at BL, W. E. Gladstone MSS, Add. MS 44649, fos. 17-20); cf. also *Diaries,* 24 Jun. 1826, 1 Jul. 1826 and 4 Jul. 1826.

120. *Diaries,* 30 Jun. 1826 and 3-12 Jul. 1826.

121. *Diaries,* 4 Jul. 1826.

122. Sir Walter Scott, 'Culloden Papers', *Quarterly Review* 14 (January 1816), 283-332, at 288, 290. For a recent, stimulating discussion of this piece cf. James Watt, 'Scott, the Scottish Enlightenment, and Romantic Orientalism', in L. Davis, I. Duncan, and J. Sorensen (eds), *Scotland and the Borders of Romanticism* (Cambridge, 2004), 94-112.

123. Gladstone, *Political Speeches in Scotland,* 92-4.

124. Scott, *Waverley,* NTAW, ii, 157-9.

125. Scott, *Waverley,* NTAW, i, 419.

126. Cf. Roland Quinault, 'Afghanistan and Gladstone's moral foreign policy', *History Today* 52 (Dec. 2002), 28-34.

127. Gladstone, *Political Speeches in Scotland,* 92-4.

128. [John D. Reigh], 'The Cabinet Trick. PROFESSOR GLADSTONE, the renowned Wizard of the North, in his new and original Cabinet Trick, by Special Command of the Queen, now about to be performed at the Theatre Royal, St. Stephen's:— "How will he get out of it?"', *United Ireland,* Saturday 6 Feb. 1886, supplement.

129. Brooks, 'Gladstone and Midlothian', 45.

130. Cf. 'Raising the "Fiery Cross." Midlothian, August, 1884', *Punch, or the London Charivari,* 30 Aug. 1884.

131. Kerr, *Scott as Storyteller,* 19-20.

132. 'The Grand Old Campaigner in Scotland', *Punch, or the London Charivari,* 25 Oct. 1890.

133. BL, W. E. Gladstone MSS, Add. MS 56444, Lord Rosebery to W. E. Gladstone, 9 Jan. 1879, quoted in Brooks, 'Gladstone and Midlothian,' 47; 'Mr. Gladstone in Scotland', *Glasgow Herald,* 30 Oct. 1890.

134. 'Mr. Gladstone's Visit to Glasgow', *Glasgow Herald,* 4 Jul. 1892.

135. Morley, *Life of Gladstone* [*The Life of William Ewart Gladstone*], i, 337.

136. Scott, *A Legend of Montrose,* NTAW, xii, 505. Gladstone marked this with a 'v'.

FURTHER READING

Bibliography

Dobson, Caroline J. *Gladstonia: A Bibliography of Material Relating to W. E. Gladstone at St. Deiniol's Library.* Hawarden, England: St. Deiniol's Library, 1981, 38 p.

Includes a survey of writings relating to Gladstone's life and career.

Biographies

Morley, John. *The Life of William Ewart Gladstone.* 3 volumes. London: Macmillan & Co., 1903.

Provides an exhaustive portrait of Gladstone's career as an author, a thinker, and a statesman.

Shannon, Richard. *Gladstone: God and Politics.* London: Hambledon and Continuum, 2007, 550 p.

Examines the role of religion in shaping Gladstone's notions of leadership and public policy.

Criticism

Aldous, Richard. *The Lion and the Unicorn: Gladstone vs. Disraeli.* New York: W. W. Norton & Company, 2007, 368 p.

    Addresses Gladstone's contentious relationship with novelist and statesman Benjamin Disraeli, analyzing the significance of their rivalry for modern British society.

Campbell, Kate. "W. E. Gladstone, W. T. Stead, Matthew Arnold and a New Journalism: Cultural Politics in the 1880s." *Victorian Periodicals Review* 36, no. 1 (April 2003): 20-40.

    Discusses the links between journalism and democracy in Gladstone's political career.

Clayton, Ruth. "Gladstone, Tennyson and History: 1886 and All That . . ." *Tennyson Research Bulletin* 8, no. 3 (November 2004): 151-65.

    Contrasts the views of Gladstone and Tennyson on questions of history, politics, and culture.

Davie, Mark. "'Not an After-Dinner Relaxation': Gladstone on Translating Dante." *Journal of European Studies* 24, no. 4 (December 1994): 385-401.

    Analyzes Gladstone's critique of Lord John Russell's Dante translation.

Döring, Tobias. "The Sea Is History: Historicizing the Homeric Sea in Victorian Passages." In *Fictions of the Sea: Critical Perspectives on the Ocean in British Literature and Culture,* edited by Bernhard Klein, pp. 121-40. Aldershot, England: Ashgate, 2002.

    Investigates the affinities among ideas of mythology, empire, and the sea in Gladstone's *Studies on Homer and the Homeric Age.*

Foot, M. R. D. Introduction to *The Gladstone Diaries,* Volume I: *1825-1832,* pp. xix-xlix. Oxford: Clarendon Press, 1968.

    Considers Gladstone's political and intellectual development through an analysis of his early journal writings.

Guedalla, Philip. "Commentary." In *Gladstone and Palmerston; Being the Correspondence of Lord Palmerston with Mr. Gladstone, 1851-1865,* pp. 23-78. New York: Harper and Brothers, 1928.

    Explores the various political, economic, and moral issues at the core of Gladstone's correspondence with Lord Palmerston.

Myres, Sir John L. "Gladstone's View of Homer." In *Homer and His Critics,* edited by Dorothea Gray, pp. 94-122. London: Routledge & Kegan Paul, 1958.

    Discusses Gladstone's development as a classicist.

Schreuder, Deryck. "Gladstone and the Conscience of the State." In *The Conscience of the Victorian State,* edited by Peter Marsh, pp. 73-134. Syracuse, N.Y.: Syracuse University Press, 1979.

    Appraises the relationship between government and morality in Gladstone's writings.

Towheed, Shafquat. "W. E. Gladstone's Reception of *Robert Elsmere*: A Critical Re-Evaluation." *English Literature in Transition (1880-1920)* 40, no. 4 (1997): 389-97.

    Assesses Gladstone's reaction to Mrs. Humphry Ward's unorthodox treatment of religious themes in her novel *Robert Elsmere.*

Additional coverage of Gladstone's life and career is contained in the following sources published by Gale: *Dictionary of Literary Biography,* Vols. 57, 184; and *Literature Resource Center.*

William Makepeace Thackeray
1811-1863

English novelist, short story writer, essayist, journalist, sketch writer, letter writer, lecturer, and poet.

The following entry presents an overview of Thackeray's life and works. For discussion of the novel *Vanity Fair* (1847-48), see *NCLC*, Volumes 14 and 169; for discussion of the novel *The History of Henry Esmond* (1852), see *NCLC*, Volume 22; for discussion of the novel *The Luck of Barry Lyndon* (1844), see *NCLC*, Volume 43; for additional information on Thackeray's career, see *NCLC*, Volume 5.

INTRODUCTION

William Makepeace Thackeray is widely regarded to be among the most influential and popular novelists of the Victorian age. Like his contemporary and rival Charles Dickens, Thackeray wrote prolifically, producing ten novels in a career spanning more than two decades. In his best-known work, *Vanity Fair*, which was serialized in *Fraser's Magazine* in 1847-48 and published in book form in 1848, Thackeray set new standards for realistic fiction through his incisive critique of Victorian hypocrisy, greed, and pretentiousness, as well as through his complex, ambivalent portraits of his major characters. In such novels as *The Luck of Barry Lyndon* (1844) and *The History of Henry Esmond* (1852), Thackeray delved into English history to explore themes of human ambition and folly. Other fictional works, notably *The History of Pendennis* (1848-50), are significant in providing a glimpse into Thackeray's own life and in drawing from his personal experience to examine the dominant social and cultural mores of his day.

Although primarily remembered as a novelist, Thackeray was also a successful journalist and magazine writer during his lifetime, publishing sketches, criticism, and essays in some of the leading periodicals of the era. His travel writings, collected in *The Paris Sketch Book* (1840) and *The Irish Sketch Book* (1843), introduced numerous innovations to the genre, especially in their emphasis on the character and personal impressions of the author himself. In all of his writings, Thackeray was primarily concerned with the notion of truth, particularly as it related to the manner in which men and women conducted themselves in society and as it pertained to his own obligation, as an author, to record his observations with uncompromising honesty.

Many modern scholars have asserted that in this respect, Thackeray was one of the most important social critics of nineteenth-century England.

BIOGRAPHICAL INFORMATION

Thackeray was born on July 18, 1811, in Calcutta, India. His father, Richmond Thackeray, worked for the British East India Company as a revenue collector, a position that brought the family considerable wealth and prestige. When Thackeray was still a young child, however, his father died of a fever, leaving him in the care of his mother, Anne Becher Thackeray. She sent him to live with relatives in England when he was five, while she remained in India; three months later she married an army officer. For the next three years Thackeray attended a series of boarding schools and generally led an isolated existence until his mother and stepfather returned to England in 1819. In 1822 he was enrolled in the prestigious Charterhouse School, where he received his earliest instruction in classical Greek and Latin. The educational rigors of the school, coupled with the floggings he received from both his teachers and his fellow students, made Thackeray's time at Charterhouse one of the unhappiest phases of his life. He found consolation in popular novels, reading the works of James Fenimore Cooper, Sir Walter Scott, and other leading authors of the period.

In 1829 Thackeray entered Trinity College of Cambridge University. He led a dissolute life for the next year and a half, devoting more time to debauchery than to his studies and accumulating considerable gambling debts. Thackeray managed to dedicate himself to literary pursuits in the midst of this dissipation, founding two magazines, the *Snob* and the *Gownsman,* while also forming close friendships with classmates Alfred Tennyson and Edward FitzGerald. In 1830 he dropped out of Cambridge without a degree. Able to live off of an inheritance from his father, Thackeray left England to travel throughout Europe. He spent several months in Weimar, Germany, where he learned German and met with some of the city's preeminent writers, notably Johann Wolfgang von Goethe. Uncertain of his future, he returned to London in 1831 to study law; he quickly became disenchanted with the legal profession, however, and spent most of his days and nights reading novels and socializing. In the summer of 1832, he traveled to France, where he remained until November of that year. In Paris he continued to drink and gamble a great deal while also reading contemporary French literature and dabbling in painting.

Soon after returning to London, Thackeray used some of his inheritance to purchase the *National Standard and Journal of Literature, Science, Music, Theatricals, and the Fine Arts,* a weekly newspaper, appointing himself the paper's Paris correspondent so that he could live in France. Around this time, Thackeray's financial fortunes suffered a drastic reversal: he lost the bulk of his estate in a bank failure. He returned to London to try to salvage his stake in the *National Standard,* but by February 1834, after pouring several hundred pounds into it, he was forced to abandon the enterprise. Later that year he moved back to Paris in order to live a bohemian life as an art student; he gradually realized that he had little talent for drawing or painting, however, and after a year he determined that he would need to pursue a different vocation. In the summer of 1835, while still living in Paris, Thackeray fell in love with Isabella Shawe, a seventeen-year-old Irish girl. He courted Shawe over the course of the next year despite her mother's reservations, while trying to establish himself in a viable career. Hired as a correspondent for the *Constitutional and Public Ledger* in the spring of 1836, he bought a partial ownership stake in the newspaper with the help of his stepfather. A short time later Thackeray published his first work, a collection of lithographs with captions titled *Flore et Zéphyr: Ballet Mythologique* (1836). In August Thackeray and Shawe were married.

The couple returned to London in March 1837; in June, Isabella gave birth to their first daughter, Anne. Thackeray aggressively pursued a career as a journalist and magazine writer in the ensuing months, contributing criticism, articles, and essays to such periodicals as *Fraser's Magazine* and *Punch.* His first published stories, a series of fictional letters written under the alias Charles J. Yellowplush, appeared in *Fraser's* between November 1837 and August 1838; these epistles were compiled and published pseudonymously as *The Yellowplush Correspondence.* During the next two years, Isabella gave birth to two more daughters: Jane, who died suddenly at the age of eight months, and Harriet. The demands of parenting took a heavy toll on Isabella's frail constitution; she suffered tremendous physical and mental strain, and in 1840, during a family trip to Ireland, she attempted suicide. By 1842, no longer able to provide Isabella the care she needed, Thackeray committed his wife to a mental hospital. Their daughters, Anne and Harriet, went to Paris to live with relatives. Thackeray wrote at a prodigious rate throughout these difficult times, largely in order to pay for his wife's medical care; he published several serialized novels in *Fraser's,* among them *A Shabby Genteel Story* (1840); *The History of Samuel Titmarsh and the Great Hog-garty Diamond* (1841), written under the pseudonym Michael Angelo Titmarsh; and *The Luck of Barry Lyndon,* published under the name Fitz-Boodle. During the early 1840s he also published two collections of travel essays, *The Paris Sketch Book* and *The Irish Sketch Book.*

Thackeray's first major commercial and critical success was *Vanity Fair: A Novel Without a Hero.* Regarded by many critics as one of the most important novels of Victorian England, it received favorable reviews in leading newspapers and literary journals; perhaps more importantly for Thackeray at the time, it provided him with the financial security he desperately needed. The same year, Thackeray published *The Book of Snobs* (1848), a collection of satirical essays. His next two novels, *The History of Pendennis: His Fortunes and Misfortunes, His Friends and His Greatest Enemy* and *The History of Henry Esmond, Esq., a Colonel in the Service of Her Majesty Q. Anne, Written by Himself,* also received high praise from critics while attracting an increasing readership. In the early 1850s Thackeray embarked on lecture tours of England and the United States; these talks were published as *The English Humourists of the Eighteenth Century: A Series of Lectures Delivered in England, Scotland, and the United States of America* (1853).

As Thackeray's fame grew, he became a fixture among London's elite literary circles, where he gained recognition for his talents as a raconteur. By then he had amassed considerable wealth, and in 1853 he purchased a house in London, where he lived with his daughters and his mother. Over the next several years, however, Thackeray's active social life, coupled with his unhealthy eating and drinking habits, began to take a toll on his health, and he suffered from frequent illnesses. Although his productivity slowed somewhat, Thackeray still managed to publish two noteworthy novels: *The Newcomes: Memoirs of a Most Respectable Family* (1853-55) and *The Virginians: A Tale of the Last Century* (1857-59).

In 1860 Thackeray finished the novel *Lovel the Widower;* that year he also accepted a lucrative offer to become the editor of the *Cornhill,* a new literary journal. His extensive connections helped attract contributions from some of England's most prestigious writers, and the *Cornhill* became one of the country's leading magazines. Thackeray's next novel, *The Adventures of Philip on His Way Through the World,* was serialized in it in 1861-62. In 1862, however, he resigned his editorship in order to devote more time to writing. A collection of his personal essays, *Roundabout Papers* (1863), was published a year later. Thackeray died suddenly on December 24, 1863, after suffering a massive stroke. An unfinished novel, *Denis Duval* (1864), came out the following year.

MAJOR WORKS

Thackeray remains best known for his epic novel *Vanity Fair.* Hailed by scholars and critics as a seminal work in the emergence of literary realism in the mid-nineteenth century, the novel is exceptional in its detailed character descriptions, the objectivity and intelligence of its omniscient narrator, and the candor of its observations on such issues as morality, class, and human weakness. The novel's central character, the scheming, socially ambitious Becky Sharpe, remains one of the most colorful and ruthless protagonists in English literature. Becky embodies many of the novel's central themes in her mercurial rise to prominence and wealth, in particular the crassness and cynicism that underlie modern existence.

Several of Thackeray's other novels also remain of interest to modern scholars; among the best known is *The Luck of Barry Lyndon,* the fictional memoir of a self-centered Irish rake in constant search of adventure and fortune. Thackeray's unsparing portrait of the callous, at times brutal protagonist rankled contemporary readers and the book failed to attract an audience at the time of its original publication. Other major works of fiction include *The History of Pendennis,* a sprawling portrait of bohemian life during the Victorian age; *The History of Henry Esmond,* a fictional autobiography set during the reigns of William III and Queen Anne; and *The Newcomes,* the story of an aspiring painter. These novels are also unique in that they contain strong autobiographical elements, particularly in their depictions of the artistic and social milieus Thackeray frequented throughout his career.

While recognized primarily for his fiction, Thackeray also produced several collections of essays during his prolific career. His best travel writings, compiled in the two early collections *The Paris Sketch Book* and *The Irish Sketch Book,* offer detailed—and at times humorous—glimpses into nineteenth-century life, accompanied by the author's wry commentary; the essays on Ireland are exceptional for their depictions of rural poverty, as well as for Thackeray's in-depth analysis of the purpose and value of the travel-writing genre. In *The Book of Snobs,* one of the most amusing and ruthless works of social satire in British literature, Thackeray exposed the fundamental duplicity and posturing underlying all levels of Victorian society.

CRITICAL RECEPTION

Thackeray's work attracted a wide readership during his lifetime; most of his early novels were serialized in the popular *Fraser's Magazine. Vanity Fair* and *The History of Henry Esmond* were highly acclaimed by contemporary critics. Charlotte Brontë was among Thackeray's earliest champions; in a letter to prominent editor W. S. Williams dated August 14, 1848, Brontë hailed the singularity of Thackeray's talent, describing him as "the first of modern masters, and the legitimate high priest of Truth." In a review dated July 22, 1848, John Forster dubbed *Vanity Fair* "one of the most original works of real genius" published in England.

In spite of his extensive popularity among reading audiences and reviewers, Thackeray had his share of detractors during his career, many of whom objected to his writings on moral grounds. Novelist Margaret Oliphant was one notable critic of Thackeray's fiction, describing *Vanity Fair* as a "clever, unbelieving, disagreeable book" in an 1855 article published in *Blackwood's Edinburgh Magazine.* French commentator H. A. Taine, evaluating the broader significance of the author's work in his *History of English Literature* (1863-64), lamented the superficial and cynical worldview suggested by Thackeray's fiction, accusing him of reducing humanity to "an aggregate of virtues and vices." In the decades after Thackeray's death, however, most commentators agreed on the lasting importance of his body of work. Anthony Trollope, in his landmark study *Thackeray* (1879), lauded the realism of the author's characterizations, as well as the intelligence and moral vigor of his artistic vision. In *Some Aspects of Thackeray* (1911), English author Lewis Melville presented a comprehensive overview of the author's career, including in-depth analyses of his critical writings, sketches, and poetry.

By the second half of the twentieth century, scholars had begun to examine the relevance of Thackeray's work within the larger framework of Victorian literature and culture. In a 1955 critique of *The Book of Snobs,* Thackeray scholar Gordon N. Ray explores the tensions between class divisions and universal morality underlying the author's satirical worldview [see Further Reading]. Chauncey C. Loomis Jr.'s essay, "Thackeray and the Plight of the Victorian Satirist," looks at Thackeray's pessimistic opinion of humanity within the context of Victorian attitudes toward the genre of satire [see Further Reading]. In the 1990s and the early twenty-first century, a number of commentators, among them Brian McCuskey and Sarah Rose Cole, focus on questions of sexuality and identity as they relate to the author's depictions of Victorian society, and scholar Elizabeth Rosdeitcher identifies dominant economic themes in Thackeray's work.

PRINCIPAL WORKS

The Yellowplush Correspondence [as Charles J. Yellowplush] (sketches) 1837-38; published in *Fraser's Magazine*

Catherine: A Story [as Ikey Solomons] (novel) 1839-40; published in *Fraser's Magazine*

The Paris Sketch Book. 2 vols. [as Mr. Titmarsh] (sketches) 1840

A Shabby Genteel Story (unfinished novel) 1840; published in *Fraser's Magazine*

The History of Samuel Titmarsh and the Great Hoggarty Diamond [as Michael Angelo Titmarsh] (novel) 1841; published in *Fraser's Magazine*; also published as *The Great Hoggarty Diamond,* 1848

The Irish Sketch Book [as Mr. M. A. Titmarsh] (sketches) 1843

The Luck of Barry Lyndon [as Fitz-Boodle] (novel) 1844; published in journal *Fraser's Magazine*; also published as *The Luck of Barry Lyndon: A Romance of the Last Century,* 1852-53; and as *Memoirs of Barry Lyndon, Esq.,*1856

Vanity Fair: A Novel without a Hero (novel) 1847-48

The Book of Snobs (sketches) 1848

The History of Pendennis: His Fortunes and Misfortunes, His Friends and His Greatest Enemy (novel) 1848-50

The History of Henry Esmond, Esq., a Colonel in the Service of Her Majesty Q. Anne, Written by Himself (novel) 1852

The English Humourists of the Eighteenth Century: A Series of Lectures Delivered in England, Scotland, and the United States of America (lectures) 1853

The Newcomes: Memoirs of a Most Respectable Family (novel) 1853-55

Miscellanies: Prose and Verse. 4 vols. (essays, sketches, short stories, and poetry) 1855-57

The Virginians: A Tale of the Last Century (novel) 1857-59

The Four Georges: Sketches of Manners, Morals, Court and Town Life (lectures) 1860

Lovel the Widower (novel) 1860

The Adventures of Philip on His Way through the World (novel) 1861-62; published in journal *Cornhill*

Roundabout Papers (essays) 1863

Denis Duval (unfinished novel) 1864

The Complete Works of William Makepeace Thackeray. 30 vols. (novels, short stories, sketches, poetry, essays, and letters) 1904

The Letters and Private Papers of William Makepeace Thackeray. 4 vols. (letters and journals) 1945-46

CRITICISM

Jean Sudrann (essay date June 1967)

SOURCE: Sudrann, Jean. "'The Philosopher's Property': Thackeray and the Use of Time." *Victorian Studies* 10, no. 4 (June 1967): 359-88.

[*In the following essay, Sudrann analyzes correlations between time, narration, and character in Thackeray's novels.*]

In *The Book of Snobs* Thackeray creates a metaphor out of the old custom, practiced by clubs in the City, of washing coins before they are handled by gentlemen. The passage, in its definition of Thackeray's subject matter and illustration of his method, suggests a fresh approach to certain vexing questions of Thackeray's artistic and political integrity.

> It used to be the custom of some very old-fashioned clubs in the City, when a gentleman asked for change for a guinea, always to bring it to him in *washed silver*: that which had passed immediately out of the hands of the vulgar being considered "as too coarse to soil a gentleman's fingers." So, when the City Snob's money has been washed during a generation or so; has been washed into estates, and woods, and castles, and town mansions, it is allowed to pass current as real aristocratic coin. Old Pump sweeps a shop, runs of messages, becomes a confidential clerk and partner. Pump the Second becomes chief of the house, spins more and more money, marries his son to an Earl's daughter. Pump Tertius goes on with the bank; but his chief business in life is to become the father of Pump Quartus, who comes out a full-blown aristocrat, and takes his seat as Baron Pumpington, and his race rules hereditarily over this nation of Snobs.[1]

This washing of city cash into aristocratic coin describes a persistent theme in each of Thackeray's novels from the early *Barry Lyndon* to the late and unfinished *Denis Duval.* Moreover, the transmutation is wholly dependent, as the passage clearly indicates, on the passing of time. However various the activities of the men involved, only as time passes can the vulgar pence become aristocratic coin: only because Pump Quartus has behind him the lives of his ancestors can he come into his inheritance of "hereditary rule." Anthony Powell once complained that society novelists tend to forget the necessary mobility of all aristocracies.[2] Thackeray's whole world is predicated on that mobility; his knowledge of its pace informs the activities of his characters and the judgments he passes on them; it controls the very shape of the novels they inhabit. The capsule genealogy of Baron Pumpington suggests, therefore, the reason for the extraordinary importance of the concept of time in Thackeray's fiction, an importance that springs from his realization, not his denial, of the Victorian social dilemma.

I

Historians of our own time disagree on the extent to which Thackeray's fiction can fairly be said to embody any formulation of the immensely complex public questions of his day. G. M. Trevelyan notes that "the critical analysis of actual society . . . helped to inspire and to popularize . . . Thackeray,"[3] while G. M. Young confesses that he has "rarely . . . had occasion to cite [Thackeray] as an authority on Victorian ways of thought and feeling."[4] Young goes on to depict Thackeray seated in that great Railway Carriage, which Young sees as a central symbol of Victorian life, excited neither by the adventure of the journey itself nor by the various possibilities of its destination, but simply wondering whether he holds a first class ticket. The image is delightful and compels our assent. We remember that Thackeray called himself "a Whig & a Quietist,"[5] sentimentalized the indignities suffered by the old men pensioners of the Charterhouse school,[6] and was largely responsible for transforming the incisive political satire of *Punch* into the kindly chuckle that never forgets "that if Fun is good, Truth is still better, and Love best of all" (**Book of Snobs,** ch. Last). His biography reveals a man uncertain of his own position in a society whose institutions he reveres even while he diagnoses their mortal illness. And to a greater or lesser degree these biographical facts do have their influence on the shaping of the fiction.

The obvious influence is seen in obvious ways in the novels: curious outbursts where the author scolds his characters; mechanical plot contrivances to bring about socially desirable dénouements that run counter to all that the reader expects from the action of the novel; sugary praise for characters, especially female characters, who have quite explicitly been revealed by the action as both stupid and selfish. Much of the sentimentality springs, as Gordon Ray has convincingly demonstrated, from Thackeray's unresolved personal relationships.[7] And much of the political hedging can be explained on similar grounds. The nature of Thackeray's essential conservatism is defined in young Arthur Pendennis' defense of the "hereditary legislator, who passes his time with jockeys and blacklegs and ballet-girls" simply because "he is a part of the old society to which we belong; and I submit to his lordship with acquiescence; and he takes his place above the best of us at all dinner-parties" (ch. lxi). In the novels, Thackeray often was unable to reconcile his knowledge of this corruption with his passionate acceptance of the traditional arrangements of British State, Church, and Dinner Table. Yet such tensions of belief are the very breeding grounds of art and a good part of Thackeray's development as a novelist can be read in his slowly acquired artistic control over these warring materials of knowledge and desire.

That development can be traced by a consideration of **Barry Lyndon** (1833-34), **Pendennis** (1849-50), and **The Newcomes** (1853-55), novels which clearly illustrate how Thackeray found his form and subject and the extent to which this discovery released his full creative powers, enabling him to engage, in the only way possible for him, in the great debate of his times. If **The Newcomes** takes its place with *In Memoriam* and *Bleak House* as a part of the Victorian attempt to express the sickness of the age—and I believe it does—it does so through Thackeray's vision of the historical processes on which his society is based: the creation, flourishing, and decay of a Baron Pumpington. That this vision, with its emphasis on the sheer accumulation of passing moments, removes the burden of responsibility for action from author and reader alike in no way negates the fact or the passion that informs its comment on the contemporary social scene. By embodying that comment through his use and handling of time, Thackeray gave new dimensions to the form of fiction. His most striking contribution to the structure of the novel, then, springs precisely from an awareness of the central social issues of his day. Thackeray's experimentation with the narrative form of the novel is, in fact, his version of the Victorian Compromise.

As Thackeray struggled over the writing of **Barry Lyndon,** he began to find his true subject and to work out a technique for its expression. This first person account of the life of an Irish gentleman-rogue, with its picaresque sequence of duels, war, gambling fortunes, marriage marts, and debtors' prisons, has a total effect quite other than that of the traditional rogue literature. Thackeray's admiration of and indebtedness to Henry Fielding's *Jonathan Wild* has long been recognized.[8] Yet, although Thackeray chooses to be guided by Fielding in working out the irony of the first person narrator's indictment of himself and although the general moral intention of Thackeray's fiction echoes that of Fielding's, the final statement of **Barry Lyndon** differs from that of *Jonathan Wild* as markedly as it does from the earlier adventure stories. It is by virtue of this difference that **Barry Lyndon** is so clearly instructive on the bent of Thackeray's experimentation with the novel.

There can be no question that our feelings differ markedly at the conclusion of each of these novels. Not the nature of the tale, but the way it is told effects that difference in final tone. And Thackeray's way is to enclose his protagonist within an envelope of time—time passing as well as historical time past: a single man's backward glance over the adventure that was his life as well as a century's perspective on monarchs and mores. Fielding's rogue appears to us in all the immediacy of time present; the novel, peopled by such figures as La Ruse and Fireblood, who act as companions to the Wild who practices his thievery and deception on the family of Heartfree, offers its indictment through an almost allegorical spareness that takes no account of centuries.

The hollow heroics of each rogue come to their appropriate end. Jonathan Wild rides from Newgate to swing from the gallows because he has stolen and cheated and lied. Barry Lyndon, too, has stolen and cheated and lied. But his fate is to become an old man scribbling away at his memoirs from the Fleet; the battle he loses is the battle with time. One closes **Barry Lyndon,** then, with the sense of a moral experience quite other than that created by *Jonathan Wild.* For the effect of Thackeray's placement of Barry Lyndon at the end of a long avenue of time is the creation of a point of view for the novel and a perspective on Barry Lyndon's deed which can only soften our censure and which, because we know we share his fate, invites us to compassion not judgment.

By a shift of perspective, Thackeray has woven a new form from the materials of picaresque romance and moral allegory. He has written a novel which, through its vision of the human condition as man's life in time, diminishes the urgency for the punishment of evil perpetrated by individual men while at no time does it ask us to excuse or condone the moral flaw. Moreover, he has found a point of view which he will use with increasing skill in his later work to convey his increasingly sophisticated sense of the relationship between society and the life of the individual man.

II

Critical neglect of the way in which Thackeray's newly-found perspective creates the subject of the novels has led to considerable critical confusion about the action of *Pendennis,* where the narrative flow, which takes the reader in time from Pen's adolescence to his marriage and moves him in space from country home to university to metropolis, follows the conventional outline of the Bildungsroman.[9] The path seems to be the familiar one of David Copperfield and Pip, of Stephen Dedalus and Eugene Gant. But if the term Bildungsroman is to have any validity, the *History of Pendennis* cannot be so described. The story of Arthur Pendennis is not the story of a boy who grows up but rather that of a boy who grows older. Thackeray himself makes this clear as he comments on Pen's deliberate drift toward an engagement with Blanche Amory:

> Yes, it was the same Pendennis, and time had brought to him, as to the rest of us, its ordinary consequences, consolations, developments. We alter very little. When we talk of this man or that woman being no longer the same person whom we remember in youth, and remark (of course to deplore) changes in our friends, we don't, perhaps, calculate that circumstance only brings out the latent defect or quality, and does not create it . . . our mental changes are like our grey hairs or our wrinkles—but the fulfilment of the plan of mortal growth and decay.
>
> (ch. lix)

An integral part of Thackeray's understanding of life, this sense of the fixity of the individual identity echoes through his letters as well as his art. Travelling abroad with his daughters in 1851, Thackeray writes to Mrs. Brookfield of the memories of an earlier tour: "Ah, I recollect 10 years back a poor devil, looking wistfully at the few Napoleons in his *gousset,* and giving himself no airs at all. He was a better fellow than the one you

know perhaps—not that our characters alter, only they develop, and our minds grow grey or bald &c." (*Letters* [*The Letters and Private Papers of William Makepeace Thackeray*], II, 795).

This attitude toward the fixed identity is difficult to reconcile with the writing of a novel designed to image the creation of character by tracing the protagonist's movement from youth to a maturity based on a coherent philosophy of life shaped by his experiences. Does *Pendennis* in fact contradict Thackeray's explicit statements and emerge as a Bildungsroman? The sequence of young Pen's adventures as he makes his way through that marriage mart by which Thackeray focusses the narrative interest of the novel provides us with an answer to the question.

As a young boy, Pen falls madly and delightfully in love with a provincial actress, Emily Costigan, known as the Fotheringay; he proposes marriage, is accepted, and is only rescued from this folly by the prompt action of Major Pendennis, who knows that all he has to do to save his nephew is to inform the lady of the true state of Pen's finances and then remove her from the neighborhood by opening the way for her entry onto the London stage. Later, as a law student, Pen dallies with the porter's daughter, Fanny Bolton. By now, he has learned enough worldly wisdom not to let this infatuation culminate in an offer of marriage. But the question of whether Pen has wandered far enough into the purlieus of Vanity Fair to seduce Fanny is huddled off by his fortuitous illness. As a successful author, Pen agrees to propose marriage to the wealthy and highly-placed Blanche Amory in order to gain a seat for himself in Parliament and enough money to maintain that position. But the deus ex machina reappears, this time with the incredibly contrived story of Blanche's father. As with Fanny Bolton, Pen does make a choice of a kind, but once again is saved the crucial decision and let off with simply an empty, if gentlemanly, gesture. The priggish pomposity with which he announces to the old Major that he will reject the seat in Parliament but keep his pledge to the daughter of the convict—"You have done it. You have brought this on me, sir. But you knew no better: and I forgive" (ch. lxx)—deprives even that gesture of any generosity of heart at the same time that it reveals how little Pen, at least, feels he has had any choice at all. Moreover, the convict's daughter is momentarily transferred to the brewer's son as the plot unwinds, and, in a swift paragraph, Pen is united to the "good woman," Laura, who has waited with incredible patience for this moment of recognition. The domestic felicities triumph. But Pen has neither effected that triumph nor has Thackeray convinced the reader that his union with Laura truly depicts any maturity into which Pen has grown. Arthur Pendennis simply drifts into domestic bliss. The narrative has followed the shape of the Bildungsroman seemingly only to remind us that we do not alter; we do not change.

Thackeray's own comment on Pen's conversion strengthens the validity of such a reading of the narrative. A fortuitous train ride with a young lady, Thackeray writes to Mrs. Brookfield, has given him the idea for the final Blanche-Pen episode in which the two will play at being in love "as two blase London People might act, and half deceive themselves that they were in earnest. That will complete the cycle of Mr. Pen's worldly experiences, *and then* we will make, or try and make, a good man of him. O! me, we are wicked worldlings most of us, may God better us and cleanse us" (*Letters,* IV, 425 [Italics mine]). Although we cannot put too much weight on what is, after all, a casual sketch of a proposed plot sequence, the "and then" does seem to echo exactly the wholly sequential nature of Pen's experience. Moreover, the final sentence quoted from the letter, with its implicit identification of Pen and his author, reiterates the inconclusiveness of the decision which the dénouement of the entire narrative attempts to force on the reader.

The history of Thackeray's cover illustrations for the serial publication and for the first volume of the first edition of the complete novel adds a valuable gloss to support the view that Thackeray's own attitude was ambivalent. For the wrapper of the serialized edition, he drew Pen with clinging female figures entwined around his neck, his arm, and his knee while behind him rise the spires of church or Oxbridge, At his other side there is a seductive, mermaid-like figure accompanied by two extremely cherubic devils with cloven hooves and tails. Pen's gaze is directed, in conjecture, at the reader and he stands with one foot firmly in each camp. For the title page of the 1850 edition, Thackeray adapted this drawing so as to make the critic wonder whether the artist does protest too much. He simplified the design so that there are only two figures on each side of Pen and the moral definition of the seductive figures is more firmly drawn into the half-clothed, loose-haired seductress and the devil who accompanies her. The second drawing minimizes any ambiguity that might linger around the first; the parasitic heaviness of the domestic figures is gone as is the charm of the mermaid and her half-cherubim, half-devil companions. Moreover, Pen now gazes back at the seductress and although he still stands between the two, the legs have started their motion toward the side of home and church and Pen's arm is clasped firmly around the waist of the representative of domestic bliss. No reader can mistake which choice is intended to bring Pen happiness. Yet seven years later, in a moment of weariness with London life, Thackeray writes: "The frontispiece of Pendennis is verily always going on my mind" (*Letters,* IV, 28). Thackeray's own commitment has never been made,

and the novel reflects the struggle. Unshaped by his experiences, Pen must remain poised between the two groups.

Of course it would be possible simply to write off such a work as a bad novel by a novelist who could not make up his mind what he wanted to say. Yet the reader is held back from this decision by the sure knowledge that in the description of its narrative sequence, the novel itself, as he has experienced it, has somehow disappeared. The immense amount of "felt life" which crowds its pages must be dependent, therefore, upon sources other, or more inclusive, than the simple narrative moment.

Thackeray himself suggests that we "take the trouble to look under the stream of the story" (*Letters,* II, 457). To do so is to heighten our awareness of that omniscient author-narrator who tells his story retrospectively and who, by the middle of the third chapter, is chatting unreservedly with his reader. Once again, as in *Barry Lyndon,* the teller of the tale creates a distance, a thickness of time past and passing, between the reader and the narrative, at the same time that the frequent and unabashed requests to the reader to look to his own life to validate Pen's experience are calculated to engage his sympathy thoroughly and to suggest the eternal recurrence of the events. When Geoffrey Tillotson notes that a portion of our experience in reading Thackeray is "experience of commentary,"[10] he points toward the shaping force of the artistic life of the novel. A more explicit description of the nature of that experience in the reading of *Pendennis* can bring us below "the stream of the story," closer to an understanding of the novel's statement. A single sentence will illustrate Thackeray's method. The Vicar of Clavering has been dining with the Dean of Chatteris on a midsummer evening. He leaves the other gentlemen with their port to join the Dean's wife: "Then the Doctor went up and offered Mrs. Dean his arm, and they sauntered over the ancient velvet lawn, which had been mowed and rolled for immemorial deans, in that easy, quiet, comfortable manner, in which people of middle age and good temper walk after a good dinner, in a calm golden summer evening, when the sun has but just sunk behind the enormous cathedral-towers, and the sickle-shaped moon is growing every instant brighter in the heavens" (ch. vi). The stylistic ease with which Thackeray broadens the import of this after-dinner stroll is memorable. A specific man performs a specific action at a specific moment in the recorded time of the narrative. But when the lady takes his arm, they stroll over an "ancient velvet lawn" that recalls a succession of presiding deans while the activity of the strolling couple includes into the scene all of the placid, well-fed, middle-aged who walk in their gardens everywhere as the sun sets and the moon rises. The single sentence binds together the ancient past assumed by the narrative ("immemorial deans"), the simple time past of Pen's youth ("the Doctor *went* up and *offered*") and the time present of the narrator ("people . . . *walk* . . . the . . . moon *is growing*"). Thus this post-prandial stroll of Doctor Portman and the Dean's wife—a narrative moment—is made expressive of a golden midsummer moment of all human existence by means of a commentary which, by repeating that walk in the past and in the future, evokes the common humanity of the simple single action.

This easy movement among various moments of time is so characteristic of the style of **Pendennis** that it is hard to justify any definition of the novel's action which fails to take it into account. Indeed, one begins to wonder if what "lies beneath the stream of the story" is not simply a series of mirrors manipulated by the author to catch the image of passing time. Certainly that image of passing time holds within it much of the novel's meaning. In order to explore fully its significance, Thackeray had first to make the reader himself experience the movement of time within the frame of the novel. The point of view of the narrator, reviewing completed action and noting its recurrence for other men in other times, is only part of the creation of that experience. Commenting on Major Pendennis' stay in the country with his sister-in-law, Thackeray notes, "and if he did not improve each shining hour . . . Major Pendennis made one hour after another pass as he could" (ch. xv). The skill with which the novelist makes, for each of his characters, "one hour after another pass" is the necessary condition for his success in manipulating the mirrors of time. He makes time drag for the Major in the country, race for Pen while he is courting Emily, and seem maddeningly slow while Pen waits for election to his uncle's club. By the very number of characters with which he peoples the novel, Thackeray indubitably affects our sense of the passage of the hours for each of them.[11] With each return that we make to any single group of characters, we are reminded that they have progressed on their journey in time: the Fotheringay becomes Lady Mirabel; Fanny Bolton becomes Fanny Huxter; old Bows shifts his jealous care from Emily Costigan to Fanny Bolton and is left, finally, alone; Pen furbishes up his old poems to Emily for his new love, Blanche Amory; the gold watch, so cherished by Pen's father, Pen leaves at home in his drawer, ashamed to take so old fashioned a timepiece off to the university with him. With every scene of the novel, Thackeray makes his readers aware that whatever else his characters are doing, they are growing older.

Because this is true, when one thinks of **Pendennis,** one thinks not of the fate of an individual character nor the exploration of a human problem; instead, an image rises of a crowded, somewhat tattered tapestry of such long views and deep perspectives that the activities depicted hold little enough interest as activities but serve rather to suggest a richness of design deeply satisfying when viewed from a sufficient distance: the design of man's life set into its proper framework of time.

Thackeray, however, could never have suggested the richness of that design by simply crowding the pages of his novel with a sense of the passing moment. The authenticity of the experience is borne in on the reader by the skill with which Thackeray conveys his knowledge that the figure of time is a Janus-faced figure: time preserves and time destroys; time is swift and time stands still; all things recur in time and all things cease in time. To depict these paradoxes, which constitute the human experience of time, is the function of the novel's structure and its language.

It is worth looking at its first paragraph in some detail to demonstrate the point at which Thackeray begins this difficult task.

> One fine morning in the full London season, Major Arthur Pendennis came over from his lodgings, according to his custom, to breakfast at a certain club in Pall Mall, of which he was a chief ornament. At a quarter-past ten the major invariably made his appearance in the best blacked boots in all London, with a checked morning cravat that never was rumpled until dinner-time, a buff waistcoat which bore the crown of his sovereign on the buttons, and linen so spotless that Mr. Brummell himself asked the name of his laundress, and would probably have employed her had not misfortunes compelled that great man to fly the country. Pendennis's coat, his white gloves, his whiskers, his very cane, were perfect of their kind as specimens of the costume of a military man *en retraite*. At a distance, or seeing his back merely, you would have taken him to be not more than thirty years old: it was only by a nearer inspection that you saw the factitious nature of his rich brown hair, and that there were a few crow's-feet round about the somewhat faded eyes of his handsome mottled face. His nose was of the Wellington pattern. His hands and wristbands were beautifully long and white. On the latter he wore handsome gold buttons given to him by his Royal Highness the Duke of York, and on the others more than one elegant ring, the chief and largest of them being emblazoned with the famous arms of Pendennis.
>
> (ch. i)

In its setting of time of day and year, the opening phrase suggests a moment of ripe fullness into which the Major, by the notation of specific time and regularly recurring event, is firmly established. The magnificence of his toilet makes him an appropriate partaker in the splendors of the day and the social scene: only the mention of Beau Brummell checks us with its suggestion of the ideals of an earlier day. This suggestion is amplified by the allusions to Wellington and "his Royal Highness the Duke of York": the Major's adornments, too, are memorials of an earlier age. However, the dyed hair, the crow's-feet, the mottled face—all these suggestions of physical decay—are kept subordinate to the total effect of the handsome and embellished figure of a man who has just stepped over the threshold of vigorous middle age to become a kind of lively reminder of an age just past. The seal ring emblazoned with those fictitious Pendennis arms works beautifully to make the Major a part of the history of that country whose sovereign's crown embellishes his waistcoat buttons and to establish him as a participator in the flow of historical time by its reminder of a family past kept alive into time-present on the Major's ring finger. These collocations of past and present, reminders of time-the-preserver and time-the-destroyer, are underscored by Thackeray's own explicit shift of perspective in the middle of the paragraph. Looked at from the rear, the Major may match the fullness of the day and the season, but turn him around and move closer and you can see the wrinkles and the broken veins. The most striking feature of this opening paragraph, however, is the audacity with which Thackeray has chosen his starting point for the characterization of Major Pendennis. To begin with the Major as an old man and then depict how time brings him, too, in the span of the novel, "its ordinary consequences" represents one of the major achievements of characterization in **Pendennis.**

Like any Homeric hero, the Major has his descriptive epithets through the novel, each suggesting one of his roles, all emphasizing his age: "old Wigsby," "old negotiator," "gay old traveler," "old bachelor," and "old heathen." Against this reiterated emphasis on age, Thackeray dramatizes the stages of time's action to reveal to his reader, with a force matched only by his sympathy for the human condition, the ineluctable reduction of man's powers. Nor is it a simple stripping of physical beauty and prowess. These pass, of course. But at first, the man being divested, himself unaware of the process, can still seem fully apparelled to the rest of the world. As the London season gets under way, Major Pendennis takes his place with "everybody" who "is in town." It is only his valet who notes the "meagre carcass" of "the worthy gentleman" who, wrapped in "a brilliant Turkish dressing-gown," soaks his feet of a morning as he sips his tea and reads his newspaper (ch. xxxvi). As the day goes on and the Major removes himself to the fashionable Pall Mall Club, where we found him at the beginning of the novel, the narrator notes: "Bays's is rather an old-fashioned place of resort now, and many of its members more than middle-aged." Pen and his young dandy friend, strolling on the Mall, can only describe the gentlemen looking down at them from the windows of Bays's as a "collection of old fogies," "a regular museum" fit only for some "chamber of old horrors" at "Madame Tussaud's." This appraisal and mockery of age by the youngsters is, however, only part of the vision Thackeray wishes us to see. The dialogue ends with Popjoy's parting from Pen at the entrance to the Club: "and the young sinner took leave of Pen, and the club of elder criminals, and sauntered into

Blacquière's, an adjacent establishment, frequented by reprobates of his own age" (ch. xxxvi). Popjoy's future, like the Major's present, will be to look down at the youngsters strolling on the Mall from his Club window. All things end in time and all things recur in time.

At the very height of the season, the Major brings to a climax his own efforts to ensure the continued luster of the Pendennis name by furthering Pen's suit of Blanche Amory; he obtains invitations for both young people and Lady Clavering, Blanche's mother, to Lord Steyne's entertainment at Gaunt House. Not until dawn does the party disperse. And as Thackeray describes the departure of the guests "down the great staircase of Gaunt House" into the early morning light, he creates a superb tableau from the juxtaposition of the fading and faded human figures with the early morning clarity of the spacious city square into which they emerge (ch. xlv). Like Virginia Woolf at the close of *The Years,* like Proust himself, Thackeray creates, in the vision of the fresh dawn rising at the close of the social gathering which celebrates the human community, another image of the Janus-faced time which passes and is to come, which destroys and creates.

Not until considerably later, at a time when the London season has passed and the Major is making his round of autumn visits, does he begin to acknowledge to himself the effects of time. To this acknowledgement is added the Major's recognition that his very way of life is disappearing. In a brilliant passage that interweaves awareness of physical decay with nostalgia for a disappearing society, Thackeray conveys the profoundest shock that age brings: we do not grow old comfortably in a familiar world; our most habitual responses and deepest sympathies endure only to be checked and violated by the new age. He records the Major's regret for the passing of "the old grand manner and courtly grace of life," along with his contrasting of the splendor of "*his* Lady Lorraine . . . magnificent in diamonds and velvets, daring in rouge" with "to-day's Lady Lorraine" in her black dress, talking of "the labouring classes," and going to early morning church, and with his finally achieved, painful understanding that he grows old: "they're getting past me: they laugh at us old boys" (ch. lxvii). Together, the Major and the historical era are disappearing; Thackeray makes each an image of the passing of the other.

All that remains for this experience of "time's consequences" to be completed is for the Major to acknowledge openly the end of his reign by announcing the succession of his heirs. This he does in the only way humanly possible—grudgingly and with provisos—in a letter to Pen which admits that "old Arthur Pendennis" is ready to "make room for the younger fellows; he has walked the Pall Mall *pavé* long enough" (ch. lxix).

In its own way, this letter strikes the note of "The King is dead; long live the King" with which the novel abounds. In an early chapter, the description of Pen's father's death ends when Doctor Portman makes his tactful allusion to "our dear departed friend" on the Sunday following the funeral, and it is clear that "Arthur Pendennis reigned in his stead" (ch. ii). When John Henry Foker, Esq., leaves behind the great brewery of Foker and Co., Pen hails the new lord with the proverbial cry itself (ch. lxxi). As the narrator reminds us: "How long do you wish or expect that your people will regret you? How much time does a man devote to grief before he begins to enjoy? A great man must keep his heir at his feast like a living *memento mori*" (ch. lxi).

The motif of "The King is dead, long live the King" underlines the sense of action occurring simply *because* time passes and thus reinforces our sense of the "and then" aspect of the narrative construction by which Pen's marriage to Laura is engineered. But the paradox of the "living *memento mori*," through its implication of the tutelary role of time's passage, points toward a theme which runs counter to the "and then" drift of the story. Dramatic statement of that tutelary role occurs some chapters later in the Major's letter to Pen resigning his place on the Mall. Yet time's lessons are not restricted to the acquisition of the knowledge of time's end for the individual. As tutor, Time again shows its double-face: creator as well as destroyer. What time creates for the individual life is, of course, memory. And it is through memory, the novel tells us, that the individual man shapes into significance the seemingly random, often painful, events of his own life. Once this is understood, the function of the sequential narrative and the necessity for the retrospective point of view in the creation of the novel's meaning becomes clear. If *Pendennis* is an Old Fogy's threnody on youth, it does not explore the meaning and value of youthful experience but rather the meaning and value of the memories stored up from that season of activity. Everywhere and always, throughout the novel, Thackeray is creating memories for his characters, calling on the narrator's memories, evoking the reader's memories.

In **"Memorials of Gormandizing,"** an essay Thackeray wrote for *Fraser's Magazine* in 1841, the man of thirty announces his discovery of a means for subduing the chaos of the immediate moment, the pain of loss and deprivation, of choice itself. "Yesterday," he wrote, "is the philosopher's property; and by thinking of it, and using it to advantage, he may gaily go through to-morrow, doubtful and dismal though it be" (*Works* [*The Oxford Thackeray*], III, 510-511). At forty, he wrote for *Punch* on the pleasures and benefits of being a Fogy in terms which again stress the delights of the remembered moment: "A proper management of his recollec-

tions thus constitutes a very great item in the happiness of a Fogy. I, for my part, would rather remember . . . than be in love over again" (*Works,* VIII, 358).

The *Punch* essays were written just as Thackeray was completing *Pendennis*; together with the earlier essay they justly reflect the concern for memory which permeates the novel. "The philosopher's property" is explained by the narrator of *Pendennis,* offered to the reader, and dramatically imaged in the life of the protagonist. In his first personal approach to the reader, the narrator suggests a way in which yesterday can be used "to advantage." "Look back, good friend, at your own youth, and ask how was that? I like to think of a well-nurtured boy, brave and gentle, warm-hearted and loving, and looking the world in the face with kind honest eyes. What bright colours it wore then, and how you enjoyed it! A man has not many years of such time. He does not know them whilst they are with him. It is only when they are passed long away that he remembers how dear and happy they were" (ch. iii). Youth is bright and joyous, full of noble impulse and generous feeling, but wholly unconscious of its own delights. It is as though the moment lived is not the moment perceived and hence has no reality in itself. The perception comes later, through memory; and that is the moment of joy, for that is the moment of a true consciousness of reality. Not until long after Pen leaves home for Oxbridge is he aware of the tenderness and love that sustained him at home (ch. xvi); not until long after the pleasures of London have become commonplaces does he know how much he enjoyed the balls, the tavern jokes, the dancing ladies of his first months in town (ch. xxxvi); not until after the visit of Pen's mother and Laura to the chambers of the young law students does George Warrington know that while the visit occurred he "had had the happiest days of his whole life" (ch. liii).

In this way, the vision back over the past created by the novel's retrospective point of view is not a sentimental sigh for "the good old days" but an attempt—groping, to be sure, and not always successful—to explore what is for Thackeray the very nature of reality. He seems to be working toward that metaphysic on which Proust's art rests: the belief that memory "in its brightness reveal[s] what the mock reality of experience never can and never will reveal—the real."[12]

The narrative itself, insofar as it depicts Pen's growth into the power of memory, further supports the claim that the novel's definition of reality rests on the remembered moment. In the first episode of the novel, about Pen's love for the actress, Thackeray succeeds beautifully in making the infatuation wholly credible at the same time that he makes it wholly comic. The brief affair over, the Fotheringay is not plucked either from Pen's world or from the world of the novel. The series of encounters between Pen and Emily after the lovers' parting in Chatteris dramatizes the creation of that memory which has enabled the narrator to recreate his own story with such wit and wisdom.

In college, Pen, as might be expected, rushes up to London in term-time to see the Fotheringay perform. Watching her on stage, he "recollected" rather than "renewed" his love. Although he waits for her at the stage-door, when she does pass by, neither one recognizes the other. On the second night, Pen returns to the theater but not to the stage-door. On the third night, he is off to watch Taglioni dance at the Opera (ch. xix). The following year, Pen returns to London and to the theater where the Fotheringay is "in the pride of her glory," but this time he cannot even "recollect" his love; for him the rich voice now reveals its vulgar "brogue," the graceful movement is "mechanical" and "false." He wonders what other man he was "who had so madly loved her." The illusion that love brings has quite gone, and Pen is left now only with feelings of humiliation and loneliness (ch. xix). He is obviously cured of his infatuation but has not yet inherited his yesterday, not yet approached the reality of the truly remembered moment. He comes into that inheritance only some years later, after he has settled in London. There he sees the now Lady Mirabel in her box at the theater, and shakes hands with her at a grand London party (ch. xxviii). Yet even those encounters have no power to move him to anything but wonderment at his own folly and gratitude to his uncle for having rescued him from the scrape. But late on the night after the party—and two chapters further on in the novel—Pen wanders into a tavern and recognizes the piano-player as old Bows, Emily's coach during her Chatteris days.

> Bows had seen and recollected Pen at once when the latter came into the room. . . . He now began to play an air, which Pen instantly remembered as one which used to be sung by the chorus of villagers in *The Stranger,* just before Mrs. Haller came in. It shook Pen as he heard it. He remembered how his heart used to beat as that air was played, and before the divine Emily made her entry. Nobody, save Arthur, took any notice of old Bows's playing: it was scarcely heard amidst the clatter of knives and forks, the calls for poached eggs and kidneys, and the tramp of guests and waiters.
>
> (ch. xxx)

In the midst of that racket, the old tune stirs Pen's memory to restore "the divine Emily" to his possession again—a possession now unaccompanied by either pain or foolishness.

If the novel can be said to depict in any way Pen's development, it is this growth into memory which it reflects. But such an acquisition of memory is in no way proffered as a practical guide to man's conduct in a world of choices. Instead, the sequence illustrates the way in which it is time alone that brings man to that "proper management of his recollections" in which happiness consists.

In a comment by the protagonist and narrator of ***Denis Duval,*** Thackeray makes explicit the source of the happiness created—not evoked—by memory. Moved to wonder at his own way of telling his story, Denis asks: "Why do I make zig-zag journeys? 'Tis the privilege of age to be garrulous, and its happiness to remember early days. As I sink back in my arm-chair, safe and sheltered . . . the past comes back to me—the stormy past, the strange unhappy yet happy past—and I look at it scared and astonished sometimes; as huntsmen look at the gaps and ditches over which they have leapt, and wonder how they are alive" (ch. iv). As it is being lived, life is dark and crowded, hurried and dangerous. But that which was "unhappy" in the living becomes "happy" through the sheer process of re-living in memory. One source, at least, of the joy springs from the sheer knowledge that the danger is over. This perspective of the armchair for the explorations of the dangers of existence is the perspective of all of Thackeray's novels; in *Pendennis* it permits him to create for our acceptance the Major's worldliness and Pen's follies with that same wonder and joy as the huntsmen who have made the successful leap. It also permits him to focus the central thematic concern of the novel: the nature of man's conduct in a world in which time passes. For the morality of the novel springs directly from the passage of time, just as its important events occur simply because time passes.

The speech in which Pen defends his respect for the hereditary aristocracy (ch. lxi) reflects not just an acceptance of the world as it is but goes on to assert the absolute insufficiency of individual human action. In the context of a chapter which records how time has muted Pen's image sufficiently for Fanny Bolton to console herself for his loss with the acquisition of Sam Huxter and has replaced Pen's mourning crape for his mother with a white hat, the speech is part of Pen's attempt to explain his decision to marry the seat in Parliament and the fortune of Blanche Amory. In doing so, Pen goes beyond the simple assertion that being of the world, he "will not be ashamed of it." Morality and historical perspective, he insists, support the decision to acquiesce. He admits to the contemporary corruption of the institutions of society. But, he queries, is the Revolutionary who would "'throw the throne into the Thames after the peers and the bench . . . more modest than I, who take these institutions as I find them, and wait for time and truth to develop, or fortify, or (if you like) destroy them?'" Thus he disposes of the revolutionary reformer with what might be called a modification of the let-George-do-it argument: leave it to time. He then goes on to use precisely the same argument against the rigid political conservatism that rejects all change. "'If anyone says (as some faithful souls do) that these schemes are for ever, and having been changed and modified constantly are to be subject to no further development or decay, I laugh, and let the man speak'" (ch. lxi).

Thackeray refuses to accept any responsibility for Pen's argument. He breaks out of the novel to tell the reader so in his own voice and to scold "Arthur": "if . . . you alone are to lie on your balcony and smoke your pipe out of the noise and the danger, you had better have died, or never have been at all, than such a sensual coward" (ch. lxi). Yet the very climate of the novel supports Pen's assertions and Thackeray's protest simply does not ring true. It is a conventional negative, a sentimental disregard of all that has gone on "beneath the stream of the story" to create *The History of Arthur Pendennis*. The final long sentence of the novel is, on the other hand, much more honest:

> We own, and see daily, how the false and worthless live and prosper, while the good are called away, and the dear and young perish untimely,—we perceive in every man's life the maimed happiness, the frequent falling, the bootless endeavour, the struggle of Right and Wrong, in which the strong often succumb and the swift fail: we see flowers of good blooming in foul places, as, in the most lofty and splendid fortunes, flaws of vice and meanness, and stains of evil; and, knowing how mean the best of us is, let us give a hand of charity to Arthur Pendennis, with all his faults and shortcomings, who does not claim to be a hero, but only a man and a brother.
>
> (ch. lxxv)

Struggle and quiescence, evil and righteousness, good fortune and ill fortune, are all levelled by the rhythms of a sentence that flows with the time of a man's history and is graced by the beneficence of man's compassion for man to make the wholly, and only appropriate final comment on the novelist's vision of man's life in time.

III

Through its evocation of the succession of passing moments, *Pendennis* speaks to us of the Janus-faced time who destroys man, yet, through the power of memory, redeems the days and nights of his existence into a pattern of significance and joy. Although its canvas is crowded and its scene various, its emphasis falls on the individual, on "a man and a brother." By the time Arthur Pendennis tells his next story, *The Newcomes,* Thackeray is able to extend this wisdom beyond the destiny of a single man to encompass the fate of society itself. The very fact that Pendennis now narrates Clive Newcome's story marks the shift in emphasis. His comment, as he watches the adventure of his young friend from the vantage point of his own middle age, establishes the armchair safety of Dennis Duval: "This narrative . . . is written maturely and at ease, long after the voyage is over . . . the storms, shoals, shipwrecks, islands" (ch. xxiv). Yet since not Clive but the world Clive inhabits is to be the focus of this novel, such personal distancing of personal events is not sufficient. And so even before

Pendennis takes over, Thackeray himself opens the novel with a marvelous kaleidoscopic whirl of animal fables. I am, he says, going to tell you a "fable," for "what stories are new? All types of all characters march through all fables" (ch. i).

The importance of this fabular outline for the novel cannot be overestimated. In "The Overture" (ch. i), Thackeray makes it plain that his convocation of fox and crow, lamb and wolf, frog and owl are intended to place his work in succession to that of Aesop and La Fontaine. The Fable with a Moral is as appropriate a tale for Victorian England as it has been for human beings ever since "the very first page of the human story" when "ages before Aesop . . . asses under lions' manes roared in Hebrew; and sly foxes flattered in Etruscan; and wolves in sheep's clothing gnashed their teeth in Sanscrit, no doubt." Thackeray's familiar theme of the recurrence of all events in time is given fresh expression as the opening paragraphs come to their climax: "There may be nothing new under and including the sun; but it looks fresh every morning, and we rise with it to toil, hope, scheme, laugh, struggle, love, suffer, until the night comes and quiet. And then will wake Morrow and the eyes that look on it; and so *da capo*." The simple, personal relationship between reader, narrator, and character which marks similar statements in *Pendennis* disappears here in the bare and abstract reworking of the proverb which covers all centuries of recorded and to-be-recorded time, all worlds of all men. In its insistence on the kinship of men through the recurrence of their actions, "The Overture" sweeps away any feeling that might have been present for the unique importance of the individual.

This sense of the individual as simply the agent of his own day in the perpetually retold story of human life is re-enforced by the illustrations for the wrapper of the monthly parts of the novel, later adapted for the title page of Volume I of the first edition, and by the initial letter designs for each chapter. Although Thackeray turned over the work of executing these illustrations to Richard Doyle, he was deeply concerned in their conception and his instructions to his artist were full and frequent.[13]

The title page consists of eight medallions, each an image of one of the familiar fables to which Thackeray refers in the opening pages of the novel. In the initial letter designs for the chapters, the animal fable is often linked to the events of the particular chapter to emphasize the Victorian human manifestation of the familiar story: the wily Snake of Madame la Duchesse d'Ivry (ch. xxxi), the social Lions who attend Mrs. Hobson Newcome's Soirée (ch. vii), the Crocodile who weeps over the grave of Lady Kew (ch. lv), the Vulture with the nose of Mr. Moss who broods on Colonel Newcome's bankruptcy (ch. lxxi). But other realms than those of the animal fable are also called on for the initial letter designs. From classical legend, Cupid sharpens his darts as Barnes Newcome becomes Lady Clara's suitor (ch. xxxii), the Sirens sing in vain as Clive rejects the blandishments of the Baines ladies (ch. l), and Strephon blows his pipe for Phyllis as Clive courts Ethel (ch. xlvii). And from ordinary folk tale and romance come knights slaying dragons (ch. lvi), rescuing fair ladies (ch. lviii) and riding off from inaccessible loves in despair (ch. xxx) to illuminate the opening of chapter after chapter along with the Giant (ch. xxvi), Father Time (ch. xxiv), the young heir trying on his father's crown (ch. xxxi), and the wicked old Witch (chs. xxxviii, lii, and liv).

Even more striking than these extraordinary illustrations for a novel subtitled *Memoirs of a Most Respectable Family* is the way in which its language persistently identifies the main actors in the narrative with the figures of fairy tale. Although more than one legend is called upon, the most ancient of patterns is preserved. Ethel Newcome is the Princess whose hand is sought by three Suitors, the Marquis of Kew, the Marquis of Farintosh, and Clive Newcome; her fate is governed by the wicked old Witch, the bad Fairy who was not asked to the christening, Lady Kew.[14] What would Thackeray have us make of what goes on "under the stream" of this story?

These *Memoirs,* like **The History of Arthur Pendennis,** deal with the society of Thackeray's own time, and the fairy tale of Ethel's courtship is at the center of a modern fable of "washed silver" in which the "most respectable family" of Newcomes is depicted at various stages of its rise to the rank and hereditary rule of a "Baron Pumpington." Indeed, **The Newcomes** stands out among his novels for the unusual bitterness with which Thackeray handles the ironies evoked by the spectacle of that rise. Yet here, as in **Pendennis,** he is able to contain his criticism of contemporary social problems within a never faltering respect for traditional social arrangements. By calling once again on his sense of man's life in time, he is able to control his rage at the events of the passing moment and through that control make of those events the material of art.

In **Pendennis** Thackeray demonstrated the power of memory to order the life of the individual man; in **The Newcomes** he works with the power of Fable, the memory of the race, to effect an acceptance of the life of society. Thackeray's description of the task of the novelist joins with the consistent emphasis on the fabular already noted to support the reader's feeling that the allusive style of **The Newcomes** is directed toward this end. Taking his image from contemporary science, Thackeray compares the novelist's work to that of an Owen or an Agassiz who "builds an enormous forgotten monster" from "a fragment of bone." The image is os-

tensibly used to explain how the narrator is able, from the visible fragments, to divine "the feelings in a young lady's mind." Yet the biological metaphor with its emphasis on the resurrection of the "megatherium" from "primaeval quagmires" echoes the fabulous and suggests that the sources of the novel lie in the deep past of mankind. Out of present fragments hinting of ancient forms, the biologist recovers the ancient beast to make fable into history. In the same way, the novelist makes the imaginative present from the fabular past: "the megatherium of his history" is created when he "puts this and that together: from the footprint finds the foot."[15]

This metaphor is immediately followed, as if Thackeray wished to illustrate his thesis, by a magnificent tableau of the fabulous lifetime of man. The narrative picks up the history of the cousins, Clive and Ethel Newcome, as they meet at the home of Mme. de Florac, that lady whose early love for Clive's father, Colonel Newcome, was disappointed when she had to consent to the marriage arranged by her family and who now "may be said to resemble the bird which the fables say feeds her young with her blood" (ch. xlvi). The unacknowledged love of Ethel and Clive is being cut off by Lady Kew, whose "natural liking for her brood" (ch. xlvi) has sent her in pursuit of that "noble Scottish stag" (ch. liii), the Marquis of Farintosh, as a marriage prize for her niece, a prize sufficiently grand to continue the washing of the vulgar Newcome stain from Ethel's pedigree.

> Suppose then, in the quaint old garden of the Hôtel de Florac, two young people are walking up and down in an avenue of lime-trees, which are still permitted to grow in that ancient place. In the centre of that avenue is a fountain, surmounted by a Triton so grey and moss-eaten, that though he holds his conch to his swelling lips, curling his tail in the arid basin, his instrument has had a sinecure for at least fifty years; and did not think fit even to play when the Bourbons, in whose time he was erected, came back from their exile. At the end of the lime-tree avenue is a broken-nosed damp Faun, with a marble panpipe, who pipes to the spirit ditties which I believe never had any tune. The *perron* of the hotel is at the other end of the avenue; a couple of Caesars on either side of the door-window, from which the inhabitants of the hotel issue into the garden—Caracalla frowning over his mouldy shoulder at Nerva, on to whose clipped hair the roofs of the grey chateau have been dribbling for ever so many long years. There are more statues gracing this noble place. There is Cupid, who has been at the point of kissing Psyche this half-century at least, though the delicious event has never come off, through all those blazing summers and dreary winters: there is Venus and her Boy under the damp little dome of a cracked old temple. Through the alley of this old garden, in which their ancestors have disported in hoops and powder, Monsieur de Florac's chair is wheeled by St. Jean, his attendant; Mme. de Préville's children trot about, and skip, and play at cache-cache. The R. P. de Florac (when at home) paces up and down and meditates his sermons; Madame de Florac sadly walks sometimes to look at her roses; and

Clive and Ethel Newcome are marching up and down; the children and their bonne of course being there, jumping to and fro; and Madame de Florac, having just been called away to Monsieur le Comte, whose physician has come to see him.

(ch. xlvii)

The mythological figures of Triton and Faun, of Venus, Cupid and Psyche speak ironically of a free joy of life and passion in the formal patterning of the quaint old garden. But the complex ironies weave backward and forward to comment on past as well as present. The memory of Venus' wrath at Psyche places that maiden's love in precisely the same light as Ethel's for Clive or Madame de Florac's childhood passion for Colonel Newcome. Yet Psyche's success fades to echo Madame de Florac's failure under the pressure of "all those blazing summers and dreary winters." At the same time, the note of Keats's "Ode on a Grecian Urn" reduces Psyche's story to a "cold Pastoral" in contrast to the living family group now "in the midst of" their "other woe" in the garden. Not until the end of the paragraph are the figures of the new lovers, young and doomed,[16] introduced into the scene. There they are described as walking "in the alley of this old garden" as they walk at the present end of the alley of time itself, prophesying the renewal of the play.

History mingles with Fable to create this garden of memory as Roman Emperors and Louis XIV stand behind the invalid chair of M. de Florac. The movement of time from Fable through History to Now reaches its climax in the action of the final sentence, with its catching up of all the present generations, from infancy to enfeebled old age, to underscore the rhythms of time passing, of past becoming present, of future prefigured by past and present, which the perspective of the whole paragraph has established. At the same time, the sentence catches the very moment of Now as an epitome of time's movement and hence, like Keats's Urn, becomes a moment of life snatched out of time. The figures of Clive and Ethel are sustained by those of Cupid and Psyche and by M. and Mme. de Florac to create for the reader a unique vision which contrasts present and past even while it is comparing them, which heightens the urgency of each while it distances both, and which emphasizes the ephemeral quality of both while it creates their eternity. And over the whole paragraph the voice of the narrator plays with the ironic phrases of his perspective—"curling his tail," "sinecure," "delicious event"—a perspective which reminds us that both past and present belong to "happy, harmless fable-land" (ch. lxxx) even as it calls up images of such mutability and withered passion as make us utterly deny any such retreat from rage and tears.

In such a passage, Thackeray is completely successful in conveying his wisdom that the fundamental evil practiced by man is the denial of love and his knowledge that man has survived to inflict that denial over and over again. Elsewhere in the novel he compromises with that wisdom. He does so either to meet the demands of his readers, as in the killing off of Rosey so that Clive and Ethel may marry, or to satisfy his own reluctance to take any *immediate* notice of disturbances in traditional social arrangements. The dinner table scene at Miss Honeyman's lodgings in Brighton provides a good example of the way in which Thackeray's political sentimentality can disrupt the tenor of the novel. The assembled characters create a vivid picture of the Newcome social range. At the bottom of the scale is Miss Honeyman, Colonel Newcome's sister-in-law, who keeps the Brighton boarding house and to whom Clive's childhood was entrusted while the Colonel was on duty in India. At the top of the scale is Lady Ann, wife of the Colonel's half-brother, Sir Brian Newcome, and daughter of the Countess of Kew. At the center, as always in the novel, are Ethel, Lady Ann's daughter, and her suitors, Clive and the Marquis of Farintosh. Dinner is being served at Miss Honeyman's where Lady Ann and her family are staying. Clive's sulkiness at finding the Marquis a member of the party expresses itself in his insistence that the Marquis understand that his "good old aunt" is the cook for the establishment: "Clive tried to think he had asserted his independence by showing that he was not ashamed of his old aunt; but the doubt may be whether there was any necessity for presenting her in this company, and whether Mr. Clive had not much better have left the tart question alone" (ch. xlii). In the assembling of characters for this particular scene, Thackeray has himself brought up "the tart question"; that he then chides Clive is wholly characteristic of his frequent reluctance to discuss those very questions which he has himself raised.

The novel, nevertheless, goes on presenting these embarrassing questions. By focussing the narrative interest on the arranged marriage, Thackeray is able to illuminate what seems to him, at least, the crux of the social problem of his era. In every institution of society that he surveys he sees cash value substituted for human value. Like Carlyle, then, Thackeray sees a world unified by "the cash nexus"; like Dickens, he sees a world that pays lip service to the morality of the Scriptures while it lives by the tablets of jungle law. The rambling richness of *The Newcomes* encompasses this vision through the many entangled lives whose threads we follow to their separate conclusions, through the quantity of seemingly incompatible allusive material which ranges from the Old Testament and Greek mythology through Eastern fable and Saints' Legends to Bourbon France, Elizabethan England, and nineteenth-century India; and with its free play of narrative technique and point of view as Thackeray makes use of lengthy letters (there are at least seventeen of them in the novel), playlets, impressionistic place descriptions, and attempts at internal dialogue. Out of this richness, it is possible here only to suggest the complexity with which Thackeray invests his theme. There are, for example, at least five courtships in the novel that trace various stages of the rise of a "Baron Pumpington." The destruction of Lady Clara Pulleyn, the rejection of Lord Kew by Ethel, the plight of Barnes Newcome's illegitimate family, the misery of Clive under his mother-in-law's rule, all provide explanatory footnotes by their image of the human waste these marriages create, the hypocrisy they nurture, and the strictly cash basis on which they are built. Colonel Newcome walks through the novel a naïf who does not understand the rules of the game he undertakes to play out of love for his son. Yet we see that even he has his judgment corrupted by his disastrous involvement with the Bundelcund Bank: "now, it seemed as if there was anger on Thomas Newcome's part, because . . . with every outward appliance of happiness, Clive was not happy. What young man on earth could look for more? a sweet young wife, a handsome home . . . And it was to bring about this end that Thomas Newcome had toiled and amassed a fortune!" (ch. lxiii). Enchanted by his own gold, the Colonel cannot understand what he has done: "In place of Art the colonel brings him [Clive] a ledger; and in lieu of first love, shows him Rosey" (ch. lxv). The silver coco-nut-tree, given to Mrs. Clive as a testimonial at the annual dinner of the Bundelcund Bank Company, becomes a visual image of the values which created the company and destroyed the relationship between Clive and his father. "There was a superb silver coco-nut-tree, whereof the leaves were dexterously arranged for holding candles and pickles; under the coco-nut was an Indian prince on a camel giving his hand to a cavalry officer on horseback—a howitzer, a plough, a loom, a bale of cotton, on which were the East India Company's arms, a brahmin, Britannia and Commerce, with a cornucopia were grouped round the principal figures" (ch. lxiii). The "queer expression" with which J. J. Ridley, Clive's artist-friend, eyes the trophy is sufficient comment on this marvelous representation of the union between Indian Prince and British Army brought about in order to fill the cornucopia of Commerce. This makes its final appearance in the novel along with the Court tiara and silver forks which Rosey and her mother attempt to smuggle off with them on their bankrupt flight to the Continent.

From this material, Thackeray has woven *The Newcomes*. And so it is fair to say that Ethel Newcome's fancy for "a pretty four-pronged coronet" (ch. xxviii) is nurtured by precisely the same world as that in which Bella Wilfer boasts of her mercenary aims in *Our Mutual Friend* and in which Gwendolen Harleth nourishes her aristocratic dreams in *Daniel Deronda*. What distinguishes Thackeray's treatment of this world from that of Dickens and George Eliot is the special shape of his novel as fable. One of the most memorable scenes of

the novel is Ethel's appearance at the family dinner table wearing a green ticket taken from one of the paintings at the Water-Colour Exhibition to demonstrate that she, too, is being "sold." The extent to which the novel's special shape is molded by Thackeray's particular use of "a farrago of old fables" (ch. i) can be seen by looking more closely at the structure of the chapter in which that scene occurs.

Entitled "In Which Clive Begins to See the World," chapter xxviii is set in the fashionable resort at Baden and includes three different episodes in the main stream of the narrative: Clive's introduction to the gambling tables through his encounter with the elder son of the house of de Florac, his reunion with Ethel, and his witnessing of the fainting of Lady Clara Pulleyn on the promenade when she encounters the young Guardsman, Jack Belsize. Each of the episodes is handled in under two pages, yet the chapter itself is almost twenty-five pages long. The bulk of the chapter prepares for and gives meaning to these events by a skillful combination of commentary with history of the characters to link the events and justify the chapter's title.

The locale itself, "the prettiest town of all places where Pleasure has set up her tents," has just been described as the place where one meets "wonderful countesses and princesses, whose husbands are almost always absent on their vast estates . . . while trains of suitors surround those wandering Penelopes their noble wives" (ch. xxvii). Into this world of ironically reversed fable, Clive comes like one of "those guileless virgins of romance and ballad, who walk smiling through dark forests charming off dragons and confronting lions" (ch. xxviii). Certainly he walks blithely enough through the dark forest of the gambling casino, pausing only to ensure the renewal of M. de Florac's fortune with the lucky money of the beginner. But before this episode occurs we have had a vivid picture of the young Frenchman's life of losses, including a full account of his marriage to the somewhat elderly Dissenter, Miss Higg of Manchester, which was arranged to recoup the family fortunes, but "her income"—alas!—"was greatly exaggerated." Then, the relationship between Clive and Ethel is sketched, with just the right pressure of intensity, through a series of letters written by Clive to the Colonel with marginal annotations by Ethel. Behind this account of an idyllic reunion, however, lies another tale of time past to parallel M. de Florac's account of his marriage: Ethel's appearance during the preceding London season wearing the bright green ticket from the Water-Colour Exhibition. The third episode, the fainting of Lady Clara, also has its background history in the account of the impoverishment of her family which with brutal simplicity precludes any possibility of the flowering of her love for Jack Belsize and demands her acquiescence in the courtship of the untitled but wealthy banker's son, Barnes Newcome. In these tents of Pleasure, Clive and the reader walk through a world whose principal business seems to be the selling of hearts and buying of marriage settlements. By a narrative technique of point and counterpoint, events of time present are surrounded by events of time past to picture the ever recurring and relentless sacrifice of fragile human feeling in the market place of wealth and rank.

One-third of the chapter, its entire central section, presents and comments on the Baden idyll of Clive and Ethel and can serve to illustrate even further the weaving of context which gives these episodes their meaning. Thackeray begins with a sentence that immediately diminishes the event to a single episode on Clive's journey to Rome and places it in the past as a moment to be remembered with pleasure. The resurrection of that moment comes with the disinterment of Clive's letters from Colonel Newcome's effects after the Colonel's death. Having hauled us thus mercilessly into the future to look back at the event, Thackeray then gives us the substance of those letters, Ethel's annotations on them, and one letter of her own. But just as we feel firmly located at Baden with Clive and Ethel while the letters are being written, the narrator interrupts to remind us that these are in "faded ink" on "yellow paper," that, in fact, we can all disinter our individual pasts in this way. He recalls the figure of a soldier scratched on a wall by "a boy of Herculaneum, eighteen hundred years ago" and then draws together that child of the buried city, Ethel and Clive, and the reader to ask: "Which of us that is thirty years old has not had his Pompeii"? Which of us, fingering the yellowed pages, does not "excavate" his own "heart"? Only then is Ethel allowed to take up her pen and write her news of the social scene at Baden to her uncle in India. The use of the letters, the movements backward and forward within the lifetime of the characters, and the allusion to Pompeii effectively surround the event of the reunion of Clive and Ethel with such a sense of passing time and other lives that their resort town idyll itself fades into a remembered happiness which the tangential approach of the novel brings to life only in terms of its place in a chronological sequence as yet unknown to its participants.

Yet this is absolutely all Thackeray gives us in this chapter about the meeting of Clive and Ethel. The narrator picks up with an extended description of the real sport to be had at the resort in those rooms of entertainment where "mamma . . . stakes her virgin daughter against Count Fettacker's forests and meadows . . . Lord Lackland plays his coronet . . . against Miss Bags's three per cents." Then, "because all stories are old," he transmutes the whole scene into a Scriptural tableau peopled by Mary Magdalen, the Prodigal Son, Hagar and Ishmael, Sarah and Abraham. This paragraph of description is followed by the account of the May evening when Ethel chose to appear with her green

ticket visible. The memorable scene, then, of Ethel's confrontation of her family with her knowledge of her own fate is safely buried in the past and surrounded by echoes of its recurrence in other lives and other times. Although it happened earlier, it is told to us after Clive and Ethel meet again. This reversal of the chronological order works both to underline the fadedness of the time present episode and to mitigate the pain of the time past episode by reviving, however momentarily, Ethel's previous happiness.

Yet Thackeray is not being evasive here in his depiction of Ethel's plight. He seeks simply to place it in what is, for him, its proper context. And so he moves from the London scene to the "fable" of "Tancred Pulleyn, Earl of Dorking, and Sigismunda, his wife," which looks back to comment on the Ethel-Clive story and ahead to introduce that of Lady Clara and Jack Belsize. Effortlessly, Thackeray shifts the characters of the story from Saxon barbarians to the young Indian widow being made ready for her husband's funeral pyre and on into the English earl's house where "the parents . . . are getting ready their daughter for sale." The two last tableaux fuse as "his grace the Arch Brahmin" speaks and the bride slips away to "put on a plain dress more suited for the occasion, and the house door will open—and there comes the SUTTEE in company of the body: yonder the pile is waiting on four wheels with four horses, the crowd hurrahs and the deed is done." But Thackeray has not yet finished, for the commentary on such a *"mariage de convenance"* introduces a different cast from yet another fable-land: "Let us not weep when everybody else is laughing: let us pity the agonized duchess when her daughter, Lady Atalanta, runs away with the doctor—of course, that's respectable; let us pity Lady Iphigenia's father when that venerable chief is obliged to offer up his darling child. . . . Her ladyship's sacrifice is performed, and the less said about it the better."

* * *

In such chapters, Thackeray demonstrates his full possession of the "philosopher's property." Through the manipulation of chronology and the use of legend, he manages to picture for the reader the pleasure tents of this Vanity Fair so that it seems buried as deeply in the past as that figure scratched on the wall at Herculaneum. Yet while the perspective certainly is that of the armchair's safety, the sense of danger safely past does not cancel the forceful presentation of evil ever present. Rather, as in the description of Mme. de Florac's garden, the sense of safety and the sense of danger play against each other to satisfy the reader's desire for knowledge. For if *Pendennis* points the way toward "proper management" of a man's memories of his own life, *The Newcomes* demonstrates how all our yesterdays can illuminate, define, and make bearable the existence of contemporary evil. The moral of the Fable resides in the story itself; the solace, in the retelling.

Notes

1. *The Book of Snobs, The Oxford Thackeray,* ed. George Saintsbury (London, 1908), IX, 299. All quotations from Thackeray's works are from this edition (henceforth *Works*).

2. Anthony Powell, ed., *Novels of High Society from the Victorian Era* (London, 1947), p. xiv.

3. *Illustrated English Social History* (Harmondsworth, 1964), IV, 107.

4. "Thackeray," *Victorian Essays* (London, 1962), p. 81.

5. *The Letters and Private Papers of William Makepeace Thackeray* (henceforth *Letters*), ed. Gordon N. Ray (Cambridge, Mass., 1945-46), III, 429.

6. Gordon N. Ray, *Thackeray: The Age of Wisdom* (London, 1958), pp. 272-273.

7. *The Buried Life: A Study of the Relation Between Thackeray's Fiction and His Personal History* (London, 1952), *passim.*

8. Gordon N. Ray, *Thackeray: The Uses of Adversity* (London, 1955), p. 345.

9. Ray, *Thackeray: The Age of Wisdom,* pp. 109-110.

10. *Thackeray the Novelist* (Cambridge, 1954), p. 91.

11. See Barbara Hardy, *The Appropriate Form* (London, 1964), pp. 185-186, for a discussion of the effect of "the population of a novel."

12. Samuel Beckett, *Proust* (London, 1931), p. 20.

13. John D. Gordan, *William Makepeace Thackeray: An Exhibition from the Berg Collection in Celebration of the 100th Anniversary of* Vanity Fair (New York, 1947), p. 29.

14. It is worth remembering that while Thackeray was writing *The Newcomes,* he broke off to write *The Rose and the Ring.* See Ray, *Thackeray: The Age of Wisdom,* pp. 229-230.

15. Ch. xlvii. Some of the material which I will use in this discussion of *The Newcomes* has been anticipated by the publication of John Loofbourow's *Thackeray and the Form of Fiction* (Princeton, N.J., 1964). But where Mr. Loofbourow brilliantly demonstrates the varieties of use to which Thackeray put his literary heritage, I am more concerned to demonstrate how these materials enabled the novelist to create his essential illusion: the movement of time. For Loofbourow's reference to this passage, see p. 89.

16. Thackeray was outspoken about his foolish yielding to public pressure in the ultimate marriage of Clive and Ethel; he knew it should be otherwise. See, for example, *Letters,* III, 465n.

Charles Mauskopf (essay date April 1971)

SOURCE: Mauskopf, Charles. "Thackeray's Concept of the Novel: A Study of Conflict." *Philological Quarterly* 50, no. 2 (April 1971): 239-52.

[*In the following essay, Mauskopf assesses the role of Thackeray's experiences working as a critic in shaping his concept of the novel form. According to Mauskopf, Thackeray was primarily concerned with achieving a "combination of realism and morality" in his fiction.*]

I

The articles and literary reviews by which Thackeray earned his living for almost fifteen years before the publication in 1848 of *Vanity Fair,* his first major novel and success, provide a fertile area in which to study the ideas on the nature of fiction which guided him in criticizing the novels of other writers and, more important, which are embodied in his own later novels. Thackeray's basic conception of the novel which emerges from this large body of criticism was that it should be an historical record of the manners of a particular time, encompassing all levels of society in an objective and consistent method of treatment, and should, at the same time, attempt to inculcate a moral upon the minds of its readers. Although Thackeray would comment upon other details to suit the individual work under consideration, this definition contains most of his ideas on what in general he considered the proper nature and purpose of the novel to be.

To an extent, this attitude towards the novel was typical of that of many critics of the time. A return to the ideals of eighteenth-century realism was being widely advocated in an attempt to raise the level of the novel by rescuing it from the excesses of the Gothic and the historical romance, as well as the more immediately popular Newgate and Silver fork fiction. Coupled with this demand for greater social realism and objectivity was the increasing clamor for greater moral responsibility on the part of the novelist to counteract the apparent disregard for moral considerations or the exploitation of immorality in the sensational fiction of the day.[1]

At least three major influences can be seen as shaping Thackeray's own literary taste to coincide with the prevailing critical opinion. His long-standing partiality for the eighteenth-century novelists, which went back to his earliest reading of them while a student at Charterhouse, inclined him towards their standards of realism and away from the attractions of more romantic fiction. Another important influence upon his ideas was the Evangelical training, with its consequent bias towards moral literature, which he had received from his mother and which, remaining with him throughout his life as part of his affection for her, had a stronger and more lasting effect upon him than he was perhaps aware. Yet a third influence appeared early in his career as a journalist when he came under the tutelage of William Maginn, the colorful editor of *Fraser's Magazine*. While it is impossible to determine the extent of Maginn's influence in shaping Thackeray's ideas, from the time that Thackeray was taken on the staff of *Fraser's*, he appeared to be in easy agreement with the critical values which Maginn prescribed in his magazine.[2]

A basic idea which Thackeray stressed frequently in his reviews and comments upon fiction was that one of the most important functions of a novelist was to be a social historian. In this role, the novelist could be more important, because more effective, than the professional historian in giving the readers of a later time an accurate picture of the time in which a novel is set. Thus, by implication, the serious novelist has a responsibility to catch the tone and manners of a given time as accurately as possible. In as early a work as **The Paris Sketch Book** of 1840, while berating the novelists of the *école romantique* for their lack of concern with describing the manners of the day, Thackeray turned to the eighteenth century to praise the realism of Fielding's *Jonathan Wild* because he found that it gives its readers a closer feeling for its period than does a more traditional contemporary historical work such as Smollett's *History of England*.[3]

> I am sure that a man who, a hundred years hence, should sit down to write the history of our time, would do wrong to put that great contemporary history of *Pickwick* aside as a frivolous work. It contains true character under false names; and, like *Roderick Random* an inferior work, and *Tom Jones* (one that is immeasurably superior), gives us a better idea of the state and ways of the people, than one could gather from any more pompous or authentic histories.
>
> (*Works* [*The Oxford Thackeray*], II, 98)

In a similar vein, he could admire so minor a work as Douglas Jerrold's *Mrs. Caudle's Curtain Lectures* in *The Morning Chronicle* (26 December 1845) because it presents its readers with "as accurate pictures of London life as we can get out of the pictures of Hogarth." It can be seen that this attitude stayed with him throughout his life when towards the end of his career the discussion of eighteenth-century fiction in **The English Humourists of the Eighteenth Century** led him to return to this same theme of historical realism.

> I take up a volume of Dr. Smollett, or a volume of the *Spectator,* and say the fiction carries a greater amount of truth in solution than the volume which purports to

be all true. Out of the fictitious book I get the expression of the life of the time; of the manners, of the movement, the dress, the pleasures, the laughter, the ridicules of society—the old times live again, and I travel in the old country of England.

> (*Works,* XIV, 543)

Again, almost the highest compliment which he could pay to Fielding's art was to declare that "as a picture of manners, the novel of *Tom Jones* is indeed exquisite" (**Works,** XIV, 649).

In order to adequately perform their appointed task as social historians, Thackeray urged the novelists to limit their subject matter as much as possible to that with which they were familiar from personal acquaintance, and to strive to describe this reality as faithfully as possible. The lack of a realistic intention behind the fiction was his major cause of discontent with two of the dominant types of fiction of his day, the Newgate and the Silver fork novels. In an assault upon the Newgate novel, **"Half a Crown's Worth of Cheap Knowledge,"** which he wrote for *Fraser's* in 1838 (17, 279-90), Thackeray argued that an interested reader could learn more about the habits of the lowest classes in society by perusing the penny newspapers than by reading the sensation fiction of Bulwer, Dickens, and Theodore Hook, none of whom wrote from firsthand experience. Shortly thereafter, he followed this first attack with another in *Fraser's*, **"Horae Catnachianae"** (19, 407-24), in which he cited the popular street ballads as better sources of information about low life than "Bulwer's ingenious inconsistencies, and Dickens's startling, pleasing, unnatural caricatures." In yet a third *Fraser's* article, a review of one of the most successful of all Newgate novels, Ainsworth's *Jack Sheppard* (21, 227-45), among the many faults for which he criticized Ainsworth was that of inventing sentimental scenes to replace the real ones from the *Newgate Calendar* which possess more power and force simply because of their historical truth.

> We back the reality against the romance,—the lady in her cups against the lady in her tears. Is not the whole history of the unfortunate lad's life told more graphically, and more truly, and therefore more poetically, by those three quarters of brandy, than by a tub-full of maudlin pathos?

At the same time that Thackeray was flaying the Newgate novel in this series of articles, his critical fervor led him to emulate Fielding in attempting something more original in the way of a critical satire. *Catherine,* which also appeared in *Fraser's* during 1839 and 1840, is less successful than its eighteenth-century prototypes because Thackeray was unable to decide how to assimilate his somewhat irreconcilable desires to parody the genre and to provide (especially in the concluding account of the murder, the details of which he followed very closely from the description in the *Newgate Calendar*) an example of a narrative so historically accurate, and thus so horrible, that it might act as a cathartic to purge the public's taste for violence once and for all.

Thackeray's protests against the Silver fork novels were made on similar grounds, but with the further objection that these novels violated reality by failing to present a comprehensive picture of the whole of society. Often this failure reflected a prejudice against, instead of in favor of high society. In one of the very first reviews which he wrote, that of Bulwer's *Godolphin* for the *National Standard* (15 and 22 June 1833), he complained against Bulwer's placing the entire blame for his hero's faults upon his experiences in high society, since, as Thackeray took care to point out, as much virtue can be found in high society as vice in Newgate. Again he defended high society from another such prejudiced view in his review of Lady Charlotte Bury's *Eros and Anteros* for *The Times* (11 January 1838), where he indignantly denied that such improbable and indecent events as this novel described were common in society, as its author would have had the gullible public believe. Another Silver fork novelist whom Thackeray occasionally took to task for the improbability of his fiction was Disraeli. For example, in *The Morning Chronicle* (13 May 1844) he criticized *Coningsby* for its "dandyism" which he found "intense, but not real." In the same newspaper, but in an opposite vein, he had little sympathy for Mrs. Gore's *Sketches of English Character,* which preached the moral that "the world is the most hollow, heartless, vulgar, brazen world, and those are luckiest who are out of it" (4 May 1846).

In keeping with these ideals of historical objectivity, Thackeray opposed the use of the novel for the display of any sort of prejudice or the advocacy of any cause, as not the proper sphere of interest of the novel nor the proper function of the novelist. Mrs. Trollope was one author who received a good deal of criticism on this score from Thackeray, who felt that the various causes which she was so fond of advocating in her novels were inappropriate in fiction. For example, he thought that the anti-Evangelical bias in her *The Vicar of Wrexhill* rendered the plot of that novel "as improbable as it is indecent" (*Fraser's,* 18, 79-83).[4]

This attitude is especially prevalent in the reviews of fiction which Thackeray wrote for *The Morning Chronicle,* in which he insisted repeatedly that the novel was not the proper place to attack existing institutions because the use of imaginary incidents and characters gives the novelist an unfair advantage in shaping the truth to fit his particular bias and allows him to exercise an undue influence upon his readers, by leading them to believe that what they are being given is objective reality. Of Lever's *St. Patrick's Eve* he exclaimed,

You cannot have a question fairly debated in this way. You can't allow an author to invent incidents, motives, and characters, in order that he may attack them subsequently. How many Puseyite novels, Evangelical novels, Roman Catholic novels, have we had, and how absurd and unsatisfactory are they.

(3 April 1845)

In reviewing *Sybil* (13 May 1845), he found that Disraeli had failed in his picture of the mine workers "not from want of sympathy, but from want of experience and familiarity with the subject," and he argued against Disraeli's inclusion of political and social philosophy in his novel:

We stand already committed as to our idea of the tendency and province of the novel. Morals and manners we believe to be the novelist's best themes; and hence prefer romances which do not treat of algebra, religion, political economy, or other abstract science. We doubt the fitness of the occasion, and often (it must be confessed) the competency of the teacher.

He reiterated this point even more strongly when he next came to review Gilbert à Beckett's *The Comic Blackstone* later that same year (31 December 1845):

For it no more follows, because a man is a clever novelist that he should be a great political philosopher, or an historian, or a controversialist, than that he should be able to dance the tight rope or play the flute. All virtuous indignation against grinding aristocrats, artful priests, &c., all sentimental political economy, ought, we think, to be marked and branded. It is not only wrong of authors thus to go meddle with subjects of which their small studies have given them but a faint notion, and to treat complicated and delicate questions with apologues, instead of argument—it is not only dishonest, but it is a bore.

In his comments on the technique of fiction, Thackeray had frequent recourse to the adjective "natural" by which he meant to convey the idea, as he stated in a letter to David Masson in 1851, that "the Art of Novels *is* to represent Nature: to convey as strongly as possible the sentiment of reality."[5] Although Thackeray nowhere talks at length about technique, it is clear from his scattered statements on the subject that he believed that the best way for this natural ideal to be achieved was through a fusion of plot and character to create an appearance of reality and through the author's maintaining throughout the novel the initial conception of plot and character to which he had introduced the reader from the beginning. The criterion which Thackeray appeared to follow in praising or damning the plots of the novels which he read was that the successful plot was one which had been worked to a logical conclusion with complete fidelity to probability, eschewing such contraptions as death-bed confessions or the sudden regeneration of seemingly unregenerate characters. Again it is Fielding and the artistic consistency of the plot of *Tom Jones* which called forth especial praise in *The Times* (2 September 1840). Here there is not an incident ever so trifling, but advances the story, grows out of former incidents, and is connected with the whole. . . . Roderick Random and heroes of that sort run through a series of adventures, at the end of which the fiddles are brought, and there is a marriage. But the history of Tom Jones connects the very first page with the very last.

Similarly, Thackeray insisted even more strongly that the characterization throughout the novel must be consistent both with the plot and with the initial presentation of the character. In complaining against the good-hearted prostitute and the chivalrous highwayman, Thackeray was really objecting to the unnaturalness inherent both in the too-sudden change of character with insufficient motive and to the stereotyping process which by its very nature robs these characters of their individuality and thus their reality. In keeping with historical objectivity, he also urged the need for authors to view their characters objectively; he noted, for example, that Charlotte Brontë's evident personal unhappiness, which came out in her novels, frequently made her unjust to her characters: "Novel writers should not be in a passion with their characters as I imagine, but describe them, good or bad, with a like calm."[6]

II

While Thackeray believed strongly in the importance of the novel as social history, he had no doubts that fiction must have a moral basis as well, and he insisted upon a clearly defined separation between the presentation of virtue and vice. Such an attitude, however, could only lead to a conflict between the ideals of realism and morality, a conflict which Thackeray was unable to avoid and which ultimately he was unable to reconcile. "We must insist upon it," he wrote in his review of *Jack Sheppard,* "that our thieves are nothing more than thieves, whom it is hopeless to attempt gilding over with the graces and glories of chivalry." *Catherine* had opened with a similar statement:

> We say, let your rogues in novels act like rogues, and your honest men like honest men; don't let us have any juggling and thimblerigging with virtue and vice, so that, at the end of three volumes, the bewildered reader shall not know which is which; don't let us find ourselves kindling at the generous qualities of thieves, and sympathizing with the rascalities of noble hearts.

> (*Works,* III, 31)

His sensitivity to the moral considerations of fiction occasionally led him to give undue consideration to criticizing a work on moral grounds, contributing to the unevenness and subjectivity of much of his critical writing, and made him suspicious of those authors who insert a superficial morality into their works in order to appeal to a certain segment of the reading public or to disguise what Thackeray often felt was a basic immorality in their fiction. Bulwer appeared to be a frequent offender

on this score, but Thackeray also had a healthy disdain for the ideas and ideals of Hugo, Balzac, George Sand, and the *école romantique* in general, whose morality he felt changed with the fashion and who hypocritically indulged in religious and philosophical speculation to cover the gross immorality which he found to exist in many of their works. Part of Thackeray's attitude is attributable to simple English chauvinism which caused him to distrust the morality of much French culture, the same attitude which led him to provide Becky with French antecedents to account for her questionable morals. There is also a strong note of class consciousness in his contempt for the *école romantique* which caused him to commend the little-known Charles de Bernard "for writing like a gentleman: there is ease, grace, and *ton,* in his style, which, if we judge aright, cannot be discovered in Balzac, or Soulié, or Dumas" (*Works,* II, 109). Commenting in *Fraser's* in 1843 on Eugène Sue's evident lack of knowledge when writing of the aristocracy, he added, "As for De Balzac, he is not fit for the *salon*. In point of gentility, Dumas is about as genteel as a courier; and Frederic Soulié as elegant as a *huissier*" (28, 349-62). The works of Sue struck Thackeray as especially dangerous since, as he explained to Macvey Napier when suggesting Sue as a possible subject for an article in *The Edinburgh Review,* Sue exploited a kind of "sham virtue" which passed for a novelty in French fiction.[7] In his review of Sue's *Les Mystères de Paris* for *The Foreign Quarterly Review* (31, 231-41), Thackeray stated his objections to that work in terms which are especially significant because of their similarity to his criticism of the Newgate fiction:

> To give such a story a *moral* tendency, is quite as absurd as to invent it. We have no right to be interested with the virtues of ruffianism, or to be called upon to sympathise with innocent prostitution. A person who chooses to describe such characters, should make us heartily hate them at once, as Fielding did, whose indignation is the moral of his satire; . . . The only good to be got out of the contemplation of crime is abhorrence; and as the world is too squeamish to hear the whole truth (and the world is right, no doubt), it is a shame only to tell the palatable half of it. Pity for these rascals is surely much more indecent than disgust; and the rendering them presentable for society, the very worst service a writer can do it.

As the above statement indicates, Thackeray was well aware of the apparent conflict between the novelist as social historian and as parson (a favorite analogy with him, especially after the success of *Vanity Fair*), but he frequently tried to reconcile the two points of view on aesthetic grounds, arguing that an inconsistent moral viewpoint leads directly to inconsistencies of plot and character, and is, therefore, "unnatural." For example, he complained that in *Godolphin* Bulwer's confused moral presentation of the hero, in which the reader is asked to sympathize with a dissipated character, rendered both the plot and the characterizations unbeliev-able: "Now we deny that such a character is at all natu-ral; we are quite sure that it is only in such a trashy book as the one before us that, with all his excess of re-finement, could be coupled all that is gross and sen-sual." He disliked Bulwer's *Eugene Aram* for the same reasons: "It is a very forced & absurd taste to elevate a murderer for money into a hero—The sentiments are very eloquent claptrap."[8] Not even the revered Fielding could escape censure on this point, for, although Thack-eray was fond of praising Fielding for a variety of rea-sons, he was unable to understand how Fielding could elevate so flawed a character into the hero of his novel:

> I can't say that I think Mr. Jones a virtuous character; I can't say but that I think Fielding's evident liking and admiration for Mr. Jones, shows that the great humour-ist's moral sense was blunted by his life, and that here in Art and Ethics, there is a great error. If it is right to have a hero whom we may admire, let us at least take care that he is admirable: if, as is the plan of some au-thors (a plan decidedly against their interests, be it said), it is propounded that there exists in life no such being, and therefore that in novels, the picture of life, there should appear no such character; then Mr. Tho-mas Jones becomes an admissible person, and we ex-amine his defects and good qualities, as we do those of Parson Thwackum or Miss Seagrim. But a hero with a flawed reputation; a hero spunging for a guinea; a hero who can't pay his landlady, and is obliged to let his ho-nour out to hire, is absurd, and his claim to heroic rank untenable.

(*Works,* XIV, 649-50)

When the conflict became unresolvable, Thackeray fre-quently excused his concern for the moral consequences of fiction by blaming the pressures of public opinion. "Ainsworth dared not paint his hero as the scoundrel he knew him to be," he remarked in his review of *Jack Sheppard*; "he must keep his brutalities in the back-ground, else public morals will be outraged." In **The English Humourists** [**The English Humourists of the Eighteenth Century**], he titillated his audience by re-fusing to discuss certain aspects of eighteenth-century life: "We can't tell—you would not bear to be told the whole truth regarding those men and manners. You could no more suffer in a British drawing-room, under the reign of Queen Victoria, a fine gentleman or fine lady of Queen Anne's time, or hear what they heard and said, than you would receive an ancient Briton" (***Works,*** XIV, 545). As editor of *The Cornhill,* he refused Trollope's "Mrs. General Talboys" and Mrs. Brown-ing's "Lord Walter's Wife" because they contained "things my squeamish public will not hear on Mondays though on Sundays they listen to them without scruple."[9] When forced to make the absolute choice between the claims of the social historian and those of the preacher, Thackeray, while recognizing and admitting the prob-lem, gave in to the moral imperative, as for example, in his review of *Jack Sheppard* in which he admitted that perhaps after all "public morals" were to be preferred:

The world no doubt is right in a great part of its squea-mishness; for it is good to pretend to the virtue of chas-tity even though we do not possess it; nay, the very re-straint which the hypocrisy lays on a man, is not unapt, in some instances, to profit him. . . . It is wise that public modesty should be as prudish as it is, that writ-ers should be forced to chasten their humour, and when it would play with points of life and character which are essentially immoral, that they should be compelled, by the general outcry of incensed public propriety, to be silent altogether.

III

"When my novel is written it will be something better I trust," Thackeray noted in his diary in 1832 after read-ing *Eugene Aram.*[10] Although it has become almost a cliché of Thackeray criticism to note how his fiction arose out of his critical writings and how even in his later novels he could not resist inserting bits of criti-cism, the extent to which in his own novels he followed those precepts which he formulated while judging the fiction of other writers has not been as fully appreci-ated. During the time when Thackeray was writing his major novels, the novel as a form of history was a popu-lar concept which fit in well with the new Victorian em-phasis upon realism in literature and which can be seen in the renewed popularity of the "personal history," whether of David Copperfield, Arthur Pendennis, or Henry Esmond, or the "life and adventures" of Nicho-las Nickleby or Philip Firmin. In the "histories," "lives," and "memoirs" which provide the elaborate titles and subtitles of much early Victorian fiction can be seen a desire to deny the fictive and to point up the realistic mode of the narrative in the manner of the eighteenth-century novel. However, Thackeray, following the criti-cal bent which he had been developing throughout most of his professional life, tried to extend the realistic basis of these biographical fictions still further and, in narrat-ing the histories of his central characters, to describe the times in which they live as well.

All of Thackeray's novels, even **Vanity Fair,** which is in some ways his least typical, are basically novels of growth and education in which the lives and experi-ences of the youthful heroes and heroines are consid-ered against carefully defined and closely detailed so-cial backgrounds. At the same time, it is significant that exactly half of Thackeray's novels beginning with **Van-ity Fair** are historical novels, as opposed to those which have a more contemporary setting and which do not in-volve major historical events and personages. The his-torical novel as an inheritance from the Romantic novel and from Scott retained a certain attraction throughout the nineteenth century, although with something of a new realistic basis; witness the fact that such essentially non-historical novelists as, for example, Dickens and George Eliot tried their hands at the genre. However, it is a phenomenon of Victorian literature that the novel which was considered contemporary in setting and subject matter generally was not, strictly speaking, contemporary at all. There was usually a time lapse of some decades between the time at which the novel was written and the time in which it was set, which allowed the novelist a certain limited historical perspective in which to consider the society he was portraying and at the same time helped to dull the immediacy of the realistic effect.

The fact that Thackeray viewed the novel as a history of manners does much to account for his singular success with both the contemporary and the historical novel. The voice of the narrator which plays so prominent a part in a Thackeray novel and which has been called the voice of an old man reminiscing or that of a gossip or of a born essayist, might equally be termed the voice of a social historian intent upon filling in the important background details of the society in which the narrative occurs and in pointing out the similarities to and differences from the reader's own time. The great truth which Thackeray discovered and which he exploited in all of his novels was that people and manners do not change very much; only the minor surface details change. Thus, in both the historical and the contemporary novels which he wrote, in **Henry Esmond** as in **The Newcomes,** his technique is basically the same: to place recognizable human beings in a realistic social context and to indicate to the reader those details of conduct which are specific to a particular time and those which form parallels with his own time. The major difference in his treatment is that in the historical novels he had to work up the details of manners and society with more care and had to pay attention to the accuracy of his handling of historical events. Nevertheless, in accordance with his own prescriptions, in all of his novels Thackeray concerned himself primarily with the upper middle class, that level of society with which he was best acquainted. He did not limit himself to this class, however, but, again in keeping with his own critical dictates, ranged throughout the society as the need arose, in order to present a realistic and unprejudiced complete picture. His regard for the details of everyday life creates that air of verisimilitude in his novels for which he has been perhaps most praised, and the bankruptcy of the Sedleys, Major Pendennis at his club, the language of **Henry Esmond,** the Virginians at the theatre, or Ethel Newcome at a ball strike the reader as the way it was—or at least as the way it should have been.

In his own novels, Thackeray similarly tried for consistency in characterization, and it is a measure of the success which he generally achieved that his critics have been able to single out those moments in **Vanity Fair** when Becky seems to them untrue to her essential nature. His idea that a character should be as fully drawn as possible from the outset and act in accordance with the reader's original conception of him led him to introduce his characters in situations which quickly define their personalities, often at the expense of greater character development later on. At the same time, his belief in the universality of certain generalized character traits caused him to repeat basic character types against differing social backgrounds, so that, on the one hand, he could bring off the transformation of Beatrix Esmond into the Baroness Bernstein, but, on the other hand, Henry Esmond has been accused of being a good example of a proper Victorian gentleman.

When Thackeray aspired to apply the novel of manners, with the realistic implications inherent in its type, to the *Bildungsroman,* the problem of morality in fiction which he had stressed in his criticism became crucial in his own art. As he became more successful he took the moral responsibilities of the novelist more seriously. "A few years ago I should have sneered at the idea of setting up as a teacher at all . . ." he admitted, "but I have got to believe in the business, and in many other things since then. And our profession seems to me to be as serious as the Parson's own."[11] Thus he could not avoid the fact that, especially in a novel like **Pendennis,** the realistic ideal demanded a narration of the youthful experience which was at variance with his equal desire to encourage the morality of his readers by providing a kind of moral exemplum. As his own comments upon *Tom Jones* have indicated, Thackeray realized that his version of reality had no place for the heroic; **Vanity Fair** is "A Novel without a Hero," not because it has heroines instead of heroes, but because its heroines and all of its characters are conceived in a realistic manner, with their faults as well as their virtues, and thus do not provide the kind of admirable model which Thackeray's uncompromising version of the heroic, and the moral requirements of fiction as he saw them, demanded. To an extent, he attempted to remedy the problem by providing a running moral commentary from the *persona* of the narrator, but this was at best an unhappy solution. As in Byron, a poet whose works Thackeray knew well and whose technique Thackeray's own technique surprisingly resembles, the voice of the narrator is in danger of drowning the narrative.

If he could not resolve this conflict successfully in his novels, at least Thackeray did not hesitate to bring it to the attention of his public. "Since the author of *Tom Jones* was buried, no writer of fiction among us has been permitted to depict to his utmost a Man," he declared in his famous Preface to **Pendennis.** "We must drape him, and give him a certain conventional simper." But if "Society will not tolerate the Natural in our Art," the fault was as much that of Thackeray and his fellow critics as Society's, since, in attempting to restore the level of fiction to something more serious than Romantic escapism, they had taught the public to expect a combination of the natural and the moral. It is ironic that Thackeray, who as a critic helped to create the problem by advocating the two conflicting demands upon the novel, should have been one of the first major novelists to be caught by the dilemma. Although in later novels he became, in Gordon Ray's apt phrase, "expert . . . in innuendo,"[12] he was never able to adequately solve the problem, whatever partial release he may have found in occasional Dickensian grotesques or in the public's easier acceptance of licentiousness within an historical, rather than a contemporary, setting.

Because this failure is so very striking in his novels, Thackeray in many ways may be considered the representative early Victorian novelist. In the works of few other novelists of the time are the twin demands which the culture and its critics made upon the writers of fiction so apparent and so obviously irreconcilable, and few novelists claimed to be so concerned to meet the challenge squarely. As its problems became increasingly complex, the conscience of the society made it need to see itself more clearly in an historical perspective, and it looked to its novelists to provide the mirror through the new realism. The pressures upon the society and the reflection of itself which it saw emphasized the necessity for an increasing morality as a possible help in solving its problems or at least as a possible escape from them. The fiction of the immediate past, the Gothic, the Newgate, and the Silver fork novels fulfilled none of these requirements, and a new or a different aesthetic was called for, which Thackeray, among others, was attempting to provide.

At the same time, the juxtaposition of the realistic and the moral in the novel may have been a necessary historical development to restore and revitalize a genre which, with a few exceptions, had lain in abeyance for some time. In reacting against the various manifestations of romantic fiction, Thackeray and his fellow critics were trying to engraft a moral tendency upon realistic values which had been widely disregarded since the great masters of the eighteenth-century novel and, in a way, to fashion a new aesthetic. Thackeray's own novels were among the first outgrowths of this initial attempt to provide a critical alternative to the romantic novel, since they spring from the ideas about the nature of fiction which he had developed during his years as a journalistic reviewer. Although Dickens is frequently cited by the critics for venturing into territories which Thackeray claimed were forbidden to him, Dickens's achievement was the more successful because he softened the line between realism and morality with sentiment and grotesquerie which Thackeray recognized as being at variance with his own realistic ideal. In his own day Thackeray enjoyed the reputation for being both an outspoken realist and a stern moralist, and even when he failed, he called attention to the difficulty if not the impossibility of achieving this combination of realism and morality, at least in its ideal form. The

problem which beset him and with which he was one of the first of a long line of novelists to grapple—the relationship between realism and the moral imperative, or whether there should be any such relationship—was one which continued to pursue novelists down through the nineteenth century into the present. To disregard the moral imperative is merely another way of handling the same problem that faced Thackeray and which faces every writer of the realistic novel, but it is a solution which Thackeray and his contemporaries, struggling to restore realism to fiction on an artistic level, could not accept.

Notes

1. See Richard Stang, *The Theory of the Novel in England, 1850-1870* (Columbia U. Press, 1959), pp. 139-51.

2. The most thorough study of the relationship between Thackeray and Maginn is by Miriam Thrall, *Rebellious* Fraser's (Columbia U. Press, 1934), pp. 55-114.

3. William Makepeace Thackeray, *The Oxford Thackeray,* ed. George Saintsbury (Oxford U. Press, 1908), II, 174. Hereafter, all references to this edition will be cited in the text as *Works*.

4. Thackeray is said to have declined meeting that estimable lady at a dinner party because, as he insisted, "she tells lies." Lewis Benjamin (pseud. of Lewis Melville), *Some Aspects of Thackeray* (Boston, 1911), p. 38.

5. William Makepeace Thackeray, *The Letters and Private Papers of William Makepeace Thackeray,* ed. Gordon N. Ray (London and Harvard U. Press, 1945-1946), II, 771.

6. *Ibid.,* III, 67.

7. *Ibid.,* II, 202.

8. *Ibid.,* I, 198.

9. *Ibid.,* IV, 226-27.

10. *Ibid.,* I, 198.

11. *Ibid.,* II, 282.

12. Gordon N. Ray, *Thackeray, The Age of Wisdom, 1847-1863* (New York, 1958), p. 125.

Joan Garrett-Goodyear (essay date winter 1979)

SOURCE: Garrett-Goodyear, Joan. "Stylized Emotions, Unrealized Selves: Expressive Characterization in Thackeray." *Victorian Studies* 22, no. 2 (winter 1979): 173-92.

[*In the following essay, Garrett-Goodyear investigates Thackeray's portrayal of emotional intensity in his char-*

acters. In Garrett-Goodyear's view, Thackeray's depictions of human vanity and self-delusion reflect his belief that human beings are fundamentally isolated from each other.]

The skill of Thackeray's characterization is a puzzling matter and has been open to debate. Acclaimed by some readers for his subtlety and profundity, Thackeray is dismissed by others for his easygoing superficiality. While some follow the careers of his characters with gusto, others feel that his fiction "is merely a matter of going on and on."[1] It has been common in the past for critics to nod approvingly at Thackeray's panoramic view of society and his sense of history but to feel that his characters lack depth, that they are not presented with much introspective insight. More recently, a number of sensitive and illuminating critical studies have argued persuasively that his characterization is both skillfully expressive and psychologically penetrating.[2] Yet responses to Thackeray have been divided along these lines from the beginning. William Roscoe, who considered Thackeray "probably the greatest painter of manners that ever lived," noted that, "man is his study; but man the social animal . . . never man the individual soul. He never penetrates into the interior, secret, *real* life that every man leads in isolation from his fellows."[3] George Henry Lewes, on the other hand, proclaimed that Thackeray "seizes *characters* where other writers seize only characteristics; he does not give you a peculiarity for the man, he places the man himself, that 'bundle of motives,' before you."[4]

Thackeray elicits such divided responses because he often composes his characters from stereotypes, and he prefers to emphasize in each individual a few prominent, essentially unchanging traits; yet he presents these characters with surprising expressive intensity and in ways which suggest the force of profound emotional compulsions in determining their actions. Thackeray sees very clearly how conceptions of character which are social and literary clichés serve as expressions of irrational psychological energy (Loofbourow [*Thackeray and the Form of Fiction*], p. 4). His characters are trapped in rigid responses, given to extravagant extremes. They ask for too much or not enough, are generous or selfish to a fault, abandon desires too readily or pursue them too desperately.[5] Although Thackeray has been particularly celebrated for his sensitivity to the infinite variety of self-delusion, to the vanity which can make even painful situations a matter of self-congratulation,[6] he sees much more than vanity in his characters. The patterns of exploitation so prevalent in his fiction are shaped to inner requirements for conquest and defeat, for self-aggrandizement and for self-denial.

My concern in this essay is not, however, to demonstrate the profundity of Thackeray's psychological conceptions, for that has been done elsewhere. Rather, I am interested in considering some of the techniques which establish the expressive power of Thackeray's characterizations and what those techniques imply about Thackeray's view of the self. They convey the sense of an intense emotional life which eludes expression. Thackeray's characters are very often in situations of deciding that they should conceal or deny their feelings or, worse, of being unable to confront their feelings at all. The frequency of such situations in his fiction suggests a pessimistic doubt that whatever vital energies are within could ever enrich or liberate the articulated shape the self presents to the world. Instead, he sees the deepest reaches of the self as a reservoir of disappointment and despair, of an emotionality which is incompatible with the demands of life as it may be lived in a social context. His characters seem to speak to each other across barriers, and the manner of their speaking dramatizes a sense that their fullest feelings are being held back or are entangled in unresolvable contradictions. Thackeray's ability to convey the pressure such uncharted emotional regions bring to bear on sensitive individuals in an indifferent or even hostile world is one of the major accomplishments of his fiction.

The way a character in a novel by Thackeray can avoid coming to terms with feelings shows very clearly in Amelia Sedley's reflections on her marriage to George Osborne when she visits her parents' home just a short time afterwards. What comes into her head are not fully formed thoughts but a succession of images which stand in their place. First, she recalls "that image of George to which she had knelt before marriage." Then "Rebecca's twinkling green eyes and baleful smile lighted upon her." Next, she looks at "the little white bed" of her girlhood and thinks that "she would like to sleep in it that night"; finally, she thinks "with terror" of her marriage bed, "the great funereal damask pavilion in the vast and dingy state bed-room."[7] Her bewilderment when the reality of marriage replaces the fantasy of romance, her longing to return to childish simplicities, her helplessness to combat Rebecca, her sexual immaturity are embodied concretely, without abstract intellectual formulation, just as Amelia would experience them. The effect is that while her understanding is clearly judged inadequate, she is also shown to be pathetically at the mercy of feelings which elude her simplifications.

The point is worth emphasizing because it represents a deliberate restriction on Thackeray's part. Instead of concentrating on a level of subjectivity where thoughts are rationally ordered and move towards clarified perception, Thackeray depicts a less rational, less deliberately conscious level on which anxieties and despairs come as images, one after the other, without the intervening control of directed intention. In this way, he suggests that Amelia is not only unwilling but also unable to come to terms with her own perceptions. The sequence of her thoughts enables the reader to supply the causal links Amelia omits: instead of understanding how far sexual disappointment and even dread have replaced her girlish daydreams, Amelia retreats into prayer; but Thackeray's analysis of the situation is clear enough. At the same time, Thackeray's use of symbolically resonant imagery enables him to convey the emotional intensity of the subjective experience he criticizes: the image of Amelia's funereal bed is movingly suggestive in a way that the enumeration of her timorous misgivings would not be.

Limited characters who are presented with psychological acumen and expressive intensity abound in Thackeray's fiction, but the novels most dominated by the pathos of characters whose passionate feelings must be forever frustrated are *Henry Esmond* and *The Newcomes.* In the fiction before these two novels, many characters are caught in the grip of such wild and extravagant compulsions that the absurdity deflects—without wholly destroying—the pathos, as with the characters in *The Yellowplush Papers* [*The Yellowplush Correspondence*], for example, or the minor characters in *Pendennis*; in the fiction which follows, there is a slackening of Thackeray's artistic grasp, so that the characters are neither as interesting nor as emotionally compelling. That Thackeray should have written his most consistently moving fiction in *Henry Esmond* and *The Newcomes* is not surprising, as these are the two works written most directly after his cherished intimacy with Jane Brookfield was broken off. The stunning impact of this rupture forced Thackeray into a more searching analysis of his own feelings, and of Mrs. Brookfield's, than he had been willing to make in the past. His heightened awareness figures particularly in his brilliant characterizations of the Esmond family, and a sense of terrible deprivation permeates both novels. However much the central characters merit criticism, their feelings are taken with great seriousness, and their suffering is clearly to be mourned.[8]

I

Because *Henry Esmond* and *The Newcomes* are so prominently concerned with characters who cannot or will not acknowledge their feelings, the use of concrete objects which call attention to those feelings, the sort of objective correlative already discussed in relation to Amelia, plays an important role. John Loofbourow has described the way recurrent metaphorical motifs and epical allusions articulate and intensify the emotional experience of the characters in *Henry Esmond* (Loofbourow, chaps. 6, 7, 8); but indeed, in this novel even the simplest repetitions of a phrase or an image can become laden with expressive implications. For example, Esmond's impressions of Lady Castlewood are studded throughout with apparently casual references to her hands. While hands traditionally figure in gestures of trust and generosity, they also have erotic connotations and symbolic connections with marriage—and all of these associations are important to what Esmond is feeling. In the long course of his devotion to Lady Castlewood, Esmond frequently misunderstands the nature of his love for her, but his recurring attention to her hands defines the increasingly erotic aspect of his feelings even when he imagines himself wholly infatuated with Beatrix.[9]

Throughout his childhood memories, Esmond's impressions of Lady Castlewood's graciousness and beauty focus on the loveliness of her hands. At their first meeting, "she stretched out her hand—indeed when was it that that hand would not stretch out to do an act of kindness, or to protect grief and ill-fortune?" (*Henry Esmond,* I, chap. 1). When she upbraids him for "polluting" the Castlewood household with smallpox and moral dissolution, he is "bewildered with grief and rage at the injustice of such a stab from such a hand" (I, chap. 8). When she blames him for her husband's death, Esmond is too stunned to protest, "stricken only with the more pain at thinking it was that soft and beloved hand which should stab him so cruelly" (II, chap 1). By the time of their reconciliation, Lady Castlewood's hand is laden with emotional significance for Esmond, so that when "she gave him her hand, her little fair hand; there was only her marriage ring on it," his sudden awareness of the wedding band he has never previously mentioned indicates a specifically erotic direction in his feelings. This erotic emphasis continues as he muses, "Where lies it? the secret which makes one little hand the dearest of all? Whoever can unriddle that mystery?" (II, chap. 6). Even after Esmond has seen Beatrix in her newly dazzling maturity, his attention fastens obsessively on Rachel's wedding band: "He . . . took one of her fair little hands—it was that which had her marriage ring on—and kissed it" (II, chap. 8). The note of sensual attraction sounds still more clearly somewhat later in Esmond's comment that Rachel's hand is "the prettiest dimpled little hand in the world" (II, chap. 15). This recurrent pattern of attention suggests that Esmond is passionately, if ambiguously, drawn to Lady Castlewood throughout his courtship of Beatrix; but Rachel, because she lacks the reader's privilege of following Henry's thoughts and can see only his courtly performances, concludes wrongly that his devotion to her is purely filial. That Thackeray dramatizes Esmond's continuing love by emphasizing its subtle influence on the way he perceives reflects his sensitivity to the importance of unconscious desire in shaping subjective experience, and his wish to convey this influence is central to his best fiction.

In *Henry Esmond* both Beatrix and Rachel are torn by powerful feelings which pull in opposite directions and are unresolvable. Thackeray is at his expressive best when he is depicting such situations; he creates for his characters a stylized manner of speaking which impels the reader to look between the lines and recognize the pressure of unacknowledged emotion. The techniques Thackeray adopts may be found throughout his fiction, but they are especially prominent in *Esmond,* which is so decisively flavored with divided longings and frustrated impulse.

When Lady Castlewood attempts to explain to Henry why they were not reconciled earlier, the manner of her speech suggests turbulent passion reined in by decorous convention:

> I know how wicked my heart has been; and I have suffered too, my dear. I confessed to Mr. Atterbury—I must not tell any more. He—I said I would not write to you or go to you—and it was better even that, having parted, we should part. But I knew you would come back—I own that. That is no one's fault. And to-day, Henry, in the anthem, when they sang it, "When the Lord turned the captivity of Zion, we were like them that dream," I thought, yes, like them that dream—them that dream. . . . Do you know what day it is? . . . It is the 29th of December—it is your birthday! But last year we did not drink it—no, no. My lord was cold, and my Harry was likely to die; and my brain was in a fever; and we had no wine. But now—now you are come again, bringing your sheaves with you, my dear.
>
> (*Henry Esmond,* II, chap. 6)

Rachel constructs her speech around a series of oppositions. She has been wicked, but she has suffered for it; she has confessed, but must say no more. It was better that she and Esmond part, but she knew he would come back. As she half confesses and half struggles not to confess the love she feels for him, her emotional turmoil is expressed both in what she does allow herself to say and in her disjointed manner of saying it. Her style is richly allusive, its implications stopping just short of a direct avowal: the wine and sheaves define her sexual longing (Loofbourow, p. 138) and her trancelike repetitions suggest her distracted passion. She suppresses any expression of causal relationships, although they are obvious to a reader aware of her love for Esmond. She uses the correlative "and" when the subordinate "because" would be more exact; she speaks in brief, simply constructed sentences and offers only sketchy connections between them; she focuses intensely on a series of factual details, which stand in place of the feelings she refuses to express more directly. The effect is one of extreme fragmentation, but the verbal style suggests the very quality of her subjective experience, indicating that she has not yet come to terms with the emotional dislocations of a disintegrating marriage, an adulterous passion, and a sudden widowhood. "My lord was cold, and my Harry was likely to die; and my brain was in a fever; and we had no wine"—she is unable to order these details, unwilling to define precisely the connections between them.

Beatrix's speeches to Esmond, which also center around strongly conflicting feelings, are similarly marked by patterns of emphatic opposition. When she tells him that "a woman of my spirit . . . is to be won by gallantry, and not by sighs and rueful faces," yet also insists that "had you been a great man, you might have been good-humoured; but being nobody, sir, you are too great a man for me; and I'm afraid of you" (*Henry Esmond,* III, chap. 4), her recurrent paradoxes, accusing Esmond first of being ineffectual and then of being overbearing, suggest that she experiences her own longings and responses in contradictory terms. Typically, she frames her interpretations as extravagant absolutes. Esmond will "never fall into a passion; but . . . never forgive"; she has "no heart," but "would do anything" for "the man that could touch it" (*Henry Esmond,* III, chaps. 4, 7). Like most of Thackeray's characters, she is too ready to translate situations into incompatible alternatives or intolerable extremes. But Thackeray uses such intractable oppositions expressively as well as critically. His characters' highly mannered speeches testify that ambivalent passions and contradictory emotional drives are integral to his vision of the human experience.

In the more poignant atmosphere of **The Newcomes,** where the central characters find themselves emotionally marooned in a sea of social rapacity, similar stylizations of language may be found, but what is especially striking is a childlike simplicity of speech, most notable in Clive, the Colonel, and Rosey, which evokes a bewildered but radical innocence. Though it may be found elsewhere in Thackeray's fiction, the special prominence of the childlike language here exerts a decisive influence on the tone of the novel as a whole, suggesting how ill fitted the protagonists are to deal with the stern realities of socioeconomic calculation. Clive Newcome is a child who cannot come to terms with the "adult" cynicism of the world around him, and there is an aching tension between his simple, inadequate diction and the emotional desolation it articulates:

> Still! once means always in these things, father, doesn't it? Once means today and yesterday, and for ever and ever. . . . Do you know you never spoke twice in your life about my mother? You didn't care for her . . . your heart was with the other. So is mine. It's fatal; it runs in the family, father. . . . Did Madame de Florac play *you* false when she married her husband? It was her fate, and she underwent it. We all bow to it, we are in the track and the car passes over us.
>
> (*Newcomes,* II, chap. 30)

Although this passage illustrates Clive's fatalistic passivity and his victimization by self-pity, its gloomy resignation is an appropriate response to the society of **The Newcomes,** which refuses to acknowledge sincerity and demands suppression of tenderness. Clive's readiness to feel doomed in no way diminishes the reality of his ruin. Despite the sentimental pathos of his speech, the very ordinariness of the language plays against the uncompromising extremity of his grief ("once means always," "for ever and ever," "it's fatal") to suggest the impossibility of finding in words an adequate expression for emotional experience. Such thwarted emotionality is a continuing concern of this novel, but Thackeray's manipulations of language suggest that the frustration of feeling comes not simply from a hostile environment but also from the inability of his characters to bring their feelings to creative resolution, whether through failures of will and understanding, or because, as it sometimes seems in Thackeray, emotion ultimately eludes both our knowledge and our control.

In a novel so concerned with society's oppressiveness, Thackeray's device of having characters submerge their feelings in a mass of factual detail works especially well, for the emphasis on externality heightens the sense of limitation imposed by social roles and social situations. The courtship scenes between Clive and Ethel at the Hôtel de Florac derive much of their expressive power from the setting. Only the description of the statues in the garden, so much more eloquent than the conversation of the lovers, expresses the sense of ruin and decay Clive will not permit himself to speak:[10]

> In the centre of that avenue is a fountain, surmounted by a Triton so gray and moss-eaten, that though he holds his conch to his swelling lips, curling his tail in the arid basin, his instrument has had a sinecure for at least fifty years. . . . At the end of the lime-tree avenue is a broken-nosed damp Faun, with a marble pan-pipe, who pipes to the spirit ditties which I believe never had any tune. . . . There is Cupid, who has been at the point of kissing Psyche this half-century at least, though the delicious event has never come off through all those blazing summers and dreary winters; there is Venus and her Boy under the damp little dome of a cracked old temple.
>
> (*Newcomes,* II, chap. 9)

In their talk Clive and Ethel confine themselves to trivialities which express their real feelings only tangentially. Ethel's refusal to acknowledge that she is attracted to Clive depends on her conviction that she can do without love in arranging her marriage, but even Clive, who is more open in his love, underplays it, giving it up too readily, as if not fully aware of what it will cost him. Again, the childlike tone of his speech betrays his insufficient awareness of consequences and complexities:

> I love you so, that if I thought another had your heart, an honest man, a loyal gentleman . . . I think I could go back with a God bless you, and take to my pictures again, and work on in my own humble way. You seem like a queen to me, somehow; and I am but a poor, humble fellow, who might be happy, I think, if you were. In those balls, where I have seen you surrounded by those brilliant young men, noble and wealthy, admirers like me, I have often thought, "How could I aspire to such a creature, and ask her to forego a palace to share the crust of a poor painter?"
>
> (*Newcomes,* II, chap. 9)

He deflects the full force of passion into a storybook interpretation of their love, in which he appears the humble youngest son of an obscure family and Ethel the exalted princess of a fairytale;[11] and his expression of adoring veneration too readily substitutes a consideration of their respective social positions for a direct expression of feeling.

Ethel Newcome is even more preoccupied with rank and role than Clive is; she seems to feel that if one adopts the proper social form, it will guarantee the proper management of feeling. Her conversations with Clive are constructed out of exemplary but impersonal theories of good behavior: "I won't say a word about the—the regard which you express for me. I think you have it. Indeed, I do. But it were best not said, Clive; best for me, perhaps, not to own that I know it. In your speeches, my poor boy—and you will please not to make any more, or I never can see you or speak to you again, never—you forgot one part of a girl's duty: obedience to her parents" (*Newcomes,* II, chap. 9). The copybook correctness of these sentiments shows Ethel's immersion in social formulae; her thoughts are so entirely shaped by worldly precepts that she cannot begin to sound her own emotional depths. When she grows impatient with the role she has chosen in life, she talks of retiring to a convent, still clinging to external molds for shaping her thoughts and feelings.[12] Even when she imagines accepting Clive as a lover, it is by casting him in other roles—as an army officer or an artist already successful and wealthy—so that she will not have to relinquish her fantasies of affluence and power. She cannot acknowledge the impulses which draw her to Clive except in a way that distorts and diminishes what he really is.

Even though Clive is exasperated when Ethel defines their relationship in formal terms which deny her feelings, he too gives way to the apparent importance of external definition, as his feeling that she "ought" to have a high place in society shows. That their intimate conversation should be so pervaded with considerations of rank and form testifies to the terrible weight social demands place on private emotion in the world of *The Newcomes.* Although Clive and Ethel neither articulate nor understand the emotional ruin they are creating for themselves, the decaying, moss-grown statues provide an expressive context for their unacknowledged feelings, giving depth and poignancy to designedly inadequate communications. They speak in language so conventional, their few expressions of love are so indirect and subdued, that their emotions seem somehow beyond them, neither comprehended nor effectively realized.

What is striking in *The Newcomes,* indeed, is the way social expectations and social proprieties virtually replace the direct expression of feeling. Rosey can articulate her dissatisfaction with Clive as a husband only by objecting to his discourteous eagerness to go off and paint before breakfast. How or whether this affects her internally the reader is left to guess. In a letter to Laura, Ethel conveys the distress of a chance meeting with Clive simply by summarizing the details of the encounter. Madame de Florac warns Ethel against marriages of convenience by relating her own grief in a narrative dominated by social definitions of obligation:

> My poor father took the pride of his family into exile with him. Our poverty only made his pride the greater. Even before the emigration a contract had been passed between our family and the Count de Florac. I could not be wanting to the word given by my father. For how many long years have I kept it! But when I see a young girl who may be the victim—the subject of a marriage of convenience, as I was—my heart pities her. . . . There are some laws so cruel that nature revolts against them, and breaks them—or we die in keeping them. You smile—I have been nearly fifty years dying—*n'est-ce pas?*—and am here an old woman, complaining to a young girl.

> (*Newcomes,* II, chap. 9)

As social demands stifle the most vital emotions, a curious sense of detachment results, a detachment especially clear in the speeches of Madame de Florac. She calls attention to her immediate situation ("you smile," "an old woman, complaining to a young girl") as if she were merely watching herself on stage, setting the prosaic reality of ordinary moments and ordinary gestures against the years of anguish as one such moment succeeds another. Her calmly factual tone as she asserts she has been dying for fifty years creates the impression that her social self has become dissociated from the passionate one. And in the last chapters of *The Newcomes,* Thackeray's use of Pendennis as narrator comes to reinforce this sense of separation between private emotion and social reality, for though Pendennis maintains a sympathetically helpful presence throughout the adversities of Clive and the Colonel, he is powerless to relieve or even share in their anguish. As he himself puts it: "If Clive came to visit us, as he very rarely did, after an official question or two regarding the health of his wife and child, no farther mention was made of his family affairs. . . . I did not press the confidence which he was unwilling to offer, and thought best to respect his silence. I had a thousand affairs of my own; who has not in London? If you die to-morrow, your dearest friend will feel for you a hearty pang of sorrow, and go

to his business as usual" (*Newcomes,* II, chap. 37). Although Ethel relieves their financial plight, although Florac and his mother resolve that the Colonel "shall not want," no one can restore his broken spirit or revive Clive's youthful gaiety and confidence. Friends and narrator alike remain outsiders.

II

The distinctive quality of subjective experience as defined by Thackeray emerges clearly when he is compared with a writer who makes very different decisions about how to depict inner realities. George Eliot's novels contrast strongly with Thackeray's in their style of presenting subjective experience. When Thackeray's characters think, their thoughts almost never embody a sustained ratiocinative process. Whereas George Eliot's characters often follow prolonged and well-ordered lines of thought (even if we do not admire the conclusions they reach), Thackeray's characters shift quickly from one idea to another, the connective links being associative or emotional, rather than rational. Their moments of reflection are brief and fragmentary, and narrative passages designed to follow a character's thoughts usually do so through a proliferation of physical details and external actions which indicate the internal experience. A passage describing Arthur Pendennis's melancholy when he completes his undistinguished college career and comes home to a life without any apparent future catches Thackeray's characteristic flavor:

> Pen came back to Fairoaks, and to his books and to his idleness, and loneliness and despair. He commenced several tragedies, and wrote many copies of verses of a gloomy cast. He formed plans of reading and broke them. He thought about enlisting—about the Spanish legion—about a profession. He chafed against his captivity, and cursed the idleness which had caused it. Helen said he was breaking his heart, and was sad to see his prostration. As soon as they could afford it, he should go abroad—he should go to London—he should be freed from the dull society of two poor women. It *was* dull—very, certainly. The tender widow's habitual melancholy seemed to deepen into a sadder gloom; and Laura saw with alarm that the dear friend became every year more languid and weary, and that her pale cheek grew more wan.

> (*Pendennis,* I, chap. 21)

Pen's unfocused restlessness emerges in the rapid sequence of his pretentious activities and insubstantial daydreams. The emphasis is on his impatient feelings and fantasies, not on any serious attempt to think over his situation. When he thinks "about enlisting," the tell-tale construction of the gerund shows his avoidance of the more purposeful movement from subject to verb in a completely formed idea. Significantly, his escapist thoughts about the Spanish legion are more specific than his vague notion of finding "a profession." He curses his idleness instead of confronting it. The quick movement away from Pendennis to Helen and then to Laura, who registers Helen's sorrow through its outward signs, is also something that happens often in Thackeray. His narrative passages remind the reader that several perspectives exist and that many characters are likely to be involved in what one character sees as his own exclusive problem.

George Eliot's characters, though they are often as skillful as Thackeray's at egoistic blindness, are made more capable of analytical reflection. This is not to argue that their thinking is always more illuminating—Casaubon's reflections on his marriage may be articulate, but they do not yield valuable insights—but rather, that the mode of thought George Eliot presents differs from that found in Thackeray. Both authors create characters of limited understanding—the mental lives of Hetty Sorrel and Rosey Mackenzie seem equally impoverished. But on the other end of the scale, George Eliot creates characters whose intellectual command of their circumstances far excels anything found in Thackeray. Even George Eliot's more limited characters, moreover, enjoy a greater harmony between intention and impulse than is common in Thackeray. Hetty Sorrel seeks her destiny in a way that Rosey Mackenzie does not. Becky Sharp's fusion of will and desire, conscious and unconscious self, would seem to be perfect, yet Thackeray momentarily suggests quite another perspective. When the narrator comments that "her success excited, elated, and then bored her" (*Vanity Fair,* II, chap. 16), he invites us to see Becky's resourceful career as a compulsive quest, a restless drive for conquest that can never be satisfied.

George Eliot is more concerned than Thackeray is to trace the interaction between irrational impulse and deliberate thought: certainly Lydgate's decision to marry Rosamond cannot be called well considered. But George Eliot enables her readers to experience the process through which this decision comes. She is interested in the way the self sets noble promptings against baser ones, the way character emerges in—and indeed is partially formed by—its struggles with temptation. Bulstrode's gradual immersion in duplicity and crime is laid out as an orderly progression, with several turning points when he could have resisted but instead allowed himself to drift into opportunities for unscrupulous gain. Lydgate's gradual subjugation by Rosamond is explained as the victory of his sympathetic warmth and acquiescent passivity over his exasperated anger and resentment. Dorothea's decision to speak with Rosamond about Lydgate's difficulties results from the triumph of her habit of compassionate involvement over her momentary experience of jealous contempt. Although George Eliot's novels dramatize the complexity of the emotional forces influencing moments of significant choice and view with compassion those which are re-

solved ignobly or unwisely, they make it clear that the responsibility for the decision rests with the character who makes it and that other possibilities were open.

The characterization in Thackeray's novels, on the other hand, rarely allows the reader to experience directly the process by which characters arrive at decisions; they tend to be presented as faits accomplis. Pendennis's resolve to see no more of Fanny Bolton crystallizes suddenly around a memory stirred by the "sabbath evening, as the church bells were ringing"; and the reader learns fully of this abrupt and simple subjective process not at the moment of its occurrence, when Pen rushes away from Fanny in confusion, but afterwards, when he defends himself to Bows: "I thought of my own home, and of women angelically pure and good, who dwell there; and I was running hither, as I met you, that I might avoid the danger which besets me" (*Pendennis,* II, chap. 11). Esmond's decision to make no claim on the Castlewood property and title also comes instantaneously, in the irrevocable form of a deathbed pledge, and again there are only terse summaries of the internal struggle his generosity costs him: "He had had good cause for doubt and dismay; for mental anguish as well as resolution" (*Henry Esmond,* I, chap. 14). "Should he bring down shame and perplexity upon all those beings to whom he was attached by so many tender ties of affection and gratitude? . . . He had debated this matter in his conscience, whilst his poor lord was making his dying confession. On one side were ambition, temptation, justice even; but love, gratitude, and fidelity, pleaded on the other. And when the struggle was over in Harry's mind, a glow of righteous happiness filled it" (*Henry Esmond,* II, chap. 1). These neatly balanced abstractions are the most intimate view Esmond permits of one of his life's most significant commitments, yet other characters in Thackeray make decisions equally momentous with even less elaboration of the subjective processes behind them. When the wreckage of Barnes's marriage persuades Ethel Newcome to abandon her worldly aspirations, the reader is not invited to participate sympathetically as she weighs priorities or lives through emotional turmoil: the decision is made quickly, simply, and outside the novel.

A specific comparison of characters at moments of crucial decision sharply focuses the differences between the two authors. The style of the process by which Lydgate commits himself to maintaining a sympathetic rapport with Rosamond contrasts markedly with the style of Lady Castlewood's decision not to marry Esmond:

> He went out of the house, but as his blood cooled he felt that the chief result of the discussion was a deposit of dread within him at the idea of opening with his wife in future subjects which might again urge him to violent speech. It was as if a fracture in delicate crystal had begun, and he was afraid of any movement that might make it fatal. His marriage would be a mere

piece of bitter irony if they could not go on loving each other. He had long ago made up his mind to what he thought was her negative character—her want of sensibility, which showed itself in disregard both of his specific wishes and of his general aims. The first great disappointment had been borne: the tender devotedness and docile adoration of the ideal wife must be renounced, and life must be taken up on a lower stage of expectation, as it is by men who have lost their limbs. But the real wife had not only her claims, she had still a hold on his heart, and it was his intense desire that the hold should remain strong. In marriage, the certainty, "She will never love me much," is easier to bear than the fear, "I shall love her no more." Hence, after that outburst, his inward effort was entirely to excuse her, and to blame the hard circumstances which were partly his fault. He tried that evening, by petting her, to heal the wound he had made in the morning, and it was not in Rosamond's nature to be repellent or sulky; indeed, she welcomed the signs that her husband loved her and was under control. But this was something quite distinct from loving *him*.

(George Eliot, *Middlemarch*, chap. 64)

Although the language in this passage fully articulates the extent of Lydgate's suffering, it evolves an orderly response to his emotional collision with Rosamond. Lydgate first identifies and registers his most profound reaction to the scene, evaluating the probable consequences of any future clashes. He reviews his previous experience of disappointment, of which the disillusionment occasioned by this quarrel is a graver continuation. He acknowledges both the present state of his affection and the desirability of maintaining it, and he resolves on the mode of conduct to pursue. Lydgate's struggle with conflicting feelings is made very clear, but the reader experiences this troubled interlude as a process which can be intelligibly ordered and rationally explained. The very vocabulary supports this impression: "the chief result," "he had long ago made up his mind," "the ideal wife must be renounced," "certainty . . . is easier to bear than . . . fear," "hence . . . his inward effort."

Of course, the degree of conscious control in Lydgate's thinking is not exaggerated. He continues to blind himself to the full extent of Rosamond's deficiencies, and he refuses to understand that his marriage is already a piece of bitter irony. His perception of Rosamond's want of sensibility depends on her failure to adopt his concerns; the egocentric bias of his perceptions persists. There is also a touch of melodramatic self-pity in the simile involving lost limbs. But even with a character like Lydgate, whose understanding is flawed, George Eliot depicts a reflective mode of thinking in which chronological and causal relationships remain clear and in which rational judgment informs the process of drawing conclusions and formulating resolutions.

Rachel Esmond's agitated speech to Henry creates a quite different impression:

"Hush!" she said again, and raised her hand up to his lip. "I have been your nurse. You could not see me, Harry, when you were in the small-pox, and I came and sat by you. Ah! I prayed that I might die, but it would have been in sin, Henry. Oh, it is horrid to look back to that time. It is over now and past, and it has been forgiven me. When you need me again, I will come ever so far. When your heart is wounded, then come to me, my dear. Be silent! let me say all. You never loved me, dear Henry—no, you do not now, and I thank heaven for it. I used to watch you, and knew by a thousand signs that it was so. Do you remember how glad you were to go away to college? 'Twas I sent you. I told my papa that, and Mr. Atterbury too, when I spoke to him in London. And they both gave me absolution—both—and they are godly men, having authority to bind and to loose. And they forgave me, as my dear lord forgave me before he went to heaven."

(*Henry Esmond*, II, chap. 6)

Although Rachel, like Lydgate, is clearly struggling with conflicting feelings, hers are neither so directly nor so completely identified. She has two strong reasons for refusing Esmond—her fear that he doesn't love her and her wish to absolve herself of guilt for her past love by denying her present feeling. Her speeches to Esmond in the scene from which this passage is taken half identify these reasons, but in a fragmented way and never with complete explicitness. True to Thackeray's form, Rachel emphasizes roles ("I have been your nurse," "'Twas I sent you" to college, "they both gave me absolution") and facts (Harry's smallpox, his departure for college) which imply the complex emotions she will not articulate openly. Her curious digression to Harry's illness (why should being his nurse prevent her from marrying him?) cannot be understood unless the reader remembers her sudden jealousy when his infection reveals his attentions to Nancy Sievewright. The reader must also recall her speech to Esmond in prison: "Why did you not die when you had the small-pox—and I came myself and watched you, and you didn't know me in your delirium—and you called out for me, though I was there at your side?" (*Henry Esmond*, II, chap. 1), a speech which shows her treasuring, but not acknowledging, a sign that Henry does love her.

When Rachel asserts that she wanted to die, but "it would have been in sin," she is developing her earlier statement that "I would love you still—yes, there is no sin in such a love as mine now." These cryptic remarks hint at the erotic emphasis in her love but stop characteristically short of outright confession. And the suppression of rational connections in her speech further enhances the impression, so prevalent in Thackeray, of passion stifled and denied before it can develop. Whereas George Eliot's reconstruction of Lydgate's thoughts and feelings emphasizes the way one is joined to the next, Thackeray's presentation of Lady Castlewood deliberately severs such links. It is through the barest nuances of vocabulary and emphasis that Thackeray defines some of the most important currents in her feelings. Her statement that the "horrid time" is now "over . . . and past, and it has been forgiven me" discloses, but only indirectly, one of the central elements in her decision to refuse Esmond: her determination to extricate herself entirely from her complicated and painful feelings about her marriage and the man who tempted her adulterous love. Something "over and past" and clearly "horrid" is easier to come to terms with than something immediate, continuing, tempting as well as tormenting. Rachel prefers to be "forgiven" and to cling to a maternal definition of her love, but her emphatic, extravagant language measures the desperation in this effort.

Subtle linguistic details suggest the outlines of complex psychological processes throughout Rachel's speech. The extent of her wish to shape reality to her own emotional needs, for example, is suggested in her eagerness to "say all," meaning both everything that is on her mind and also everything that can ever be said about her relationship with Esmond, excluding any interpretations from his point of view. Her effort to take over all interpretations of his emotional state accounts for the absoluteness of her statement that "you never loved me" and that "a thousand signs" showed it. (In fact, she offers only one not very compelling piece of evidence, Esmond's eagerness for college.) The strenuousness of this attempt to manage her wayward passion for Esmond, to package and seal it forever as dignified maternal solicitude, shows in the ritualistic, indeed, formulaic quality of her final sentences where the repeated insistence on absolution and forgiveness—"they both gave me absolution—both," "having authority to bind and to loose," "they forgave me," "my dear lord forgave me"—suggests warding off evil with magical incantations. The true confusion of her feelings, however, emerges in her inability to settle on the precise arrangement she wishes for their relationship. First adopting the generous position that "when you need me again, I will come ever so far," she then shifts to a more gratifying arrangement in which Esmond seeks her out: "When your heart is wounded, then come to me, my dear."[13] This passage does not create the same impression of emotions nearly out of control that comes earlier in the reconciliation scene. Like Lydgate, Rachel has made a decision and she adheres to it tenaciously. But the passionate commentary which punctuates her factual summaries (wishing to die, thanking Heaven that Henry doesn't love her, craving absolution), the rush of brief, simply constructed sentences, the conspicuous omission of connections when connections are needed, suggest that the details of her speech mean more than she will say, perhaps more than she can say.[14]

* * *

George Eliot's way of depicting character, then, gives far more prominence to rational reflection and con-

scious control than Thackeray's. It is perhaps impossible to separate character altogether from the narrative voice which presents it; and George Eliot's narrative voice, which renders thoughts and actions so thoroughly intelligible, embodies the possibilities for understanding and sympathy towards which her best characters move. At the same time, its commitment to the endeavor for comprehensive insight supplies the reader with a hortatory example, summoning her or him to strive after similarly luminous interpretations. Indeed, in the more thoughtful of her characters and in her lucid narrative presence, George Eliot may overemphasize intelligibility and coherence, presenting an idealized version of human thought, a hopeful proclamation of its finest potentialities.

Thackeray, on the other hand, is more inclined to present the mind as it would function without the intervention of shapely rationality. His narrative perspective is more likely to immerse the reader in an abundance of emotional, physical, and factual details. He recreates the immediacies of subjective experience, the way circumstances, perceptions, feelings, fantasies jostle against each other in a single moment of awareness.

From time to time, of course, a narrative voice does step in with interpretations and analyses, perspectives that do not belong to a particular character. When little George leaves Amelia for his grandfather Osborne's house, Amelia attempts to convince herself that his egoistic prattle expresses genuine devotion, but the narrative comment makes clear her wish to be misled: "The poor mother was fain to content herself with these selfish demonstrations of attachment, and tried to convince herself how sincerely her son loved her" (*Vanity Fair,* II, chap. 15). Such remarks, however, tend to be fugitive; the commentary moves quickly to another perspective, another incident, another character, another feeling. Although, like George Eliot's narrative commentary, such passages hold out the possibility of interpretation, this kind of mental activity is far less available to Thackeray's characters. Understanding and insight are possible in the world of Thackeray's fiction, but they are unlikely to prevail. Thackeray does not provide his readers with models of sustained intellectual analysis; rather, he offers juxtapositions which, though they may stimulate reflection, do not embody it.

Thackeray's fiction is especially concerned with the wild and various forces of human irrationality: fantasies, illusions, longings, compulsions. Emotions as he depicts them have an obstreperous energy which has little to do with conscious notions of desirable behavior. Sometimes this is a matter of humor and delight. In *Pendennis* it is hilarious when decorously respectable characters erupt in fierce passion, as when Helen and Dr. Portman, confronting what they think is Pen's guilty involvement with the Fotheringay, tremble, turn pale, fling themselves, cry out, roar, growl, shriek, and gasp, all in the space of two pages (**Pendennis,** I, chap. 6). But by the time of **Henry Esmond** and **The Newcomes,** the discrepancy between social surface and passionate inner self is a matter for sorrowful regret. The tension between conscious will and unruly impulse is differently defined in different characters: Lord Castlewood's conscious self, for example, watches dismayed and helpless as irresistible compulsions lead to ruin (**Henry Esmond,** I, chaps. 12, 13, 14); in Lady Castlewood, the balance is reversed—consciously, she works to assert complete control over her deepest longings, denying and repressing them but driving herself to emotional exhaustion and nearly hysterical desperation. Beatrix Esmond shows both tendencies: her conscious self is at the mercy of a compulsive quest for triumph, for conquest of ever more splendid suitors and of the worldly wealth and power they represent, yet it is too successful in overruling another desperate desire, a longing for a lover who could somehow release in her a flood of passionate feeling (**Henry Esmond,** III, chap. 7). Yet whatever the difference in the pattern, the impression of unresolvable conflict is the same. Because the style of Thackeray's characterization conveys with such moving intensity these frustrated encounters between the self and passionate impulse, his most interesting fiction makes the process of moral judgment a complicated one. The determination to arrive at verdicts is shaken by the terrible sense of loss and destruction which permeates so much of his writing. Although he makes it very clear that his characters deceive, flatter, and indulge themselves, his novels so question the possibility of any reasonable accommodation between profound feeling and the controlling intelligence which attempts to shape it to social roles and requirements that critical judgment is supplanted by a more ambiguous mood of rueful contemplation.

Notes

1. F. R. Leavis, *The Great Tradition* (1948; rpt. ed., New York: New York University Press, 1967), p. 21.

2. See John Loofbourow, *Thackeray and the Form of Fiction* (Princeton: Princeton University Press, 1964); Juliet McMaster, *Thackeray: The Major Novels* (Manchester: University of Toronto Press, 1971); J. Hillis Miller, *The Form of Victorian Fiction* (Notre Dame, Ind.: University of Notre Dame Press, 1968); James H. Wheatley, *Patterns in Thackeray's Fiction* (Cambridge: M.I.T. Press, 1969).

3. [William C. Roscoe], "W. M. Thackeray, Artist and Moralist," *National Review,* 2 (January 1856), 178, 179.

4. [George Henry Lewes], *Leader,* 1 (21 December 1850), 929-930; reprinted in *Thackeray: The Critical Heritage,* edited by Geoffrey Tillotson and Donald Hawes (London: Routledge & Kegan Paul, 1968), p. 107.

5. See Bernard J. Paris's remarks on Thackeray's characterization in his article, "The Psychic Structure of *Vanity Fair,*" *Victorian Studies,* 10 (1967), 389-410.

6. Consider, for example, the willful deprivations of Amelia Sedley's widowhood or that of Rachel Esmond or Henry Esmond's renunciation of his fortune; all are motivated in part by considerations of self-esteem.

7. William Makepeace Thackeray, *Vanity Fair,* I, chap. 26, in *The Works of William Makepeace Thackeray* (London: Smith, Elder, & Co., 1869), 22 vols. All subsequent citations of Thackeray's novels will refer to this edition of his works.

8. Gordon N. Ray, in his biography of Thackeray, *Thackeray: The Uses of Adversity, 1811-1846* and *Thackeray: The Age of Wisdom, 1847-1863* (London: Oxford University Press, 1955 and 1958), discusses the profound influence of the Brookfield affair on Thackeray. The involvement with Jane Brookfield gave new vitality to Thackeray's emotional life; its ending seems to have left Thackeray feeling burnt-out, cut off from all that was most passionate in himself. This impression is borne out by Gordon Ray's edition of Thackeray's *Letters* (Cambridge: Harvard University Press, 1945-46), 4 vols.

9. Both Barbara Hardy, in her chapter "The Expressive Things," in *The Exposure of Luxury* ([London]: Peter Owen, 1972; Pittsburgh: University of Pittsburgh Press, n.d.), and Juliet McMaster, in her essay, "Thackeray's Things: Time's Local Habitation," in *The Victorian Experience: The Novelists,* edited by Richard A. Levine (Athens: Ohio University Press, 1976), pp. 49-86, note the importance of objects used expressively in Thackeray. Hardy particularly emphasizes the way Thackeray uses objects to show the idolatry of his characters, their vain fascination with impressive exteriors, while McMaster calls attention to the way objects serve to focus themes of time and memory, calling forth Proustian sets of associations. In this connection, McMaster also discusses the importance of Rachel's hand, noting that it is "the link of continuity in a life during which he has regarded her as goddess, guilty widow, mother, and wife" (p. 62).

10. I am indebted to Jean Sudrann's sensitive discussion of this passage in "'The Philosopher's Property': Thackeray and the Use of Time," *Victorian Studies,* 10 (1967), 359-388, where she notes that "the mythological figures of Triton and Faun, of Venus, Cupid and Psyche speak ironically of a

free joy of life and passion in the formal pattern-ing of the quaint old garden" (p. 382).

11. Juliet McMaster, in "Theme and Form in *The New-comes*," *Nineteenth-Century Fiction,* 23 (1968), 177-188, discusses Thackeray's use of fairytale motifs throughout *The Newcomes*.

12. James Wheatley offers an illuminating discussion of external forms and roles in Thackeray, in his chapter "*Vanity Fair*: Wisdom and Art." He finds that Thackeray's depiction of "mixed motivation" creates the impression of "an inner emotional self struggling for expression against external frustra-tions" (p. 80), but he finds less evidence of this pattern than I do in Thackeray's later fiction.

13. This shift is so slight that it seems inadvertent, but Thackeray quite commonly uses such small de-tails to convey significant meaning. Using a simi-lar shift in his description of Esmond and Rach-el's embrace at the close of this reconciliation scene—"and as a brother folds a sister to his heart; and as a mother cleaves to her son's breast—so for a few moments Esmond's beloved mistress came to him and blessed him,"—Thackeray em-phasizes the uncertainties of their relationship, for which neither set of family roles seems appropri-ate. The ambiguity of "mistress" further asserts the ambiguity of the relationship, for it may desig-nate both a lady of the manor, to whom a vassal owes fealty, and a woman who inspires erotic de-votion.

14. It may seem irrelevant to compare a narrative pas-sage from George Eliot with a dramatic speech from Thackeray, as the narrative passage will nec-essarily explain more than the dramatic one. The differences noted here, however, may be found, though not so markedly, in narrative passages from Thackeray and dramatic ones from George Eliot. When Dorothea speaks to Rosamond of unfaith-fulness in marriage, there is a sense of veiled emo-tion, for Dorothea is speaking indirectly both of her own alienation from Casaubon and her present unhappiness about Will; yet her sentences follow a coherent progression, indicating a capacity for analytic thought: "marriage drinks up all our power of giving and getting," "the marriage stays with us like a murder"—and a conscious acknowl-edgement of her own feelings; "the feeling may be very dear—it has taken hold of us unawares" (*Middlemarch*, chap. 81). Unlike Rachel, Dorothea is both willing and able to recognize her feelings: though she struggles to control them, she does not attempt to deny them. On the other hand, as we have seen, Thackeray's narrative reconstruction of Amelia's thoughts about her marriage shows just as clearly as Rachel's speeches a self unable to come to terms with its feelings.

Donald Hawes (essay date spring-summer 1981)

SOURCE: Hawes, Donald. "Thackeray and French Lit-erature in Perspective." *Studies in the Novel* 13, nos. 1-2 (spring-summer 1981): 5-20.

[*In the following essay, Hawes discusses the evolution of Thackeray's attitudes toward French literature over the course of his career.*]

Thackeray's criticism of French literature has been com-prehensively discussed by Lidmila Pantůčková,[1] follow-ing several considerations of the subject, notably George Saintsbury's comments in his Introduction to the sec-ond volume of the **Oxford Thackeray** and Robert S. Garnett's Appendixes to the **New Sketch Book** (1906). My aim is to put his opinions in perspective, showing how they relate to those held by some of his English contemporaries. We can then arrive, perhaps, at a better understanding of his inconsistencies and shifting view-points and of what is original and what is conventional in his attitudes. His criticism of French literature ex-tends over all his career, and is expressed formally and informally, in review articles, fiction, and letters. I shall concentrate on his journalistic work between 1833 and 1846, especially that in the *National Standard,* the **Paris Sketch Book,** the *Foreign Quarterly Review,* and *Fras-er's Magazine,* as reprinted in the **Oxford Thackeray.**

The dominating French literary figures of the 1830s and 1840s, at least in English eyes, were Hugo, Balzac, George Sand, Dumas, Sue, Soulié, and de Kock. Henry Lytton Bulwer observed in his *France, Social, Literary, Political* (1834) that "from the fall of Napoleon [French], philosophy and letters have been gradually as-suming an ardent spirit and a vivid colouring, analo-gous with the glory and the fever of that man's reign."[2] In the 1830s, and to a lesser extent in the 1840s, many English critics denigrated or opposed the work and ideas of these new and startling writers for a number of rea-sons, which included fear or disapproval of the 1830 Revolution, a neoclassical distaste for Romanticism, a partly Evangelical insistence on a strict moral code, and a feeling that novels were inferior works of literature.[3] Underlying these hostile opinions was the long-established distrust between the two nations, frequently evident in foreign affairs; there was talk of war in 1840 and 1844, for instance. "In the first place, and don't let us endeavour to disguise it, they hate us," Thackeray declared in **"Napoleon and his System,"** one of the es-says in his **Paris Sketch Book** (reprinted in **Oxford Thackeray,** Vol. II).

One of the most notorious attacks on French novels was Croker's in the *Quarterly Review* (April 1836), in which he considered books by de Kock, Hugo, Dumas, Balzac, Raymond, Masson, and George Sand. Like other con-temporary English observers, he relates the novels to political and social conditions, which he analyzes in an attempt to show the connection between crime in France and the July Revolution: "the MOUNTAIN which, in 1793, affrighted and desolated the world with its volcanic explosions, now pours from the same crater a less noisy but more spreading and destructive deluge of molten lava." As for the novels themselves, he singles out two distinctive features as deplorable: the exhibition of "the extreme laxity of female morals" and "the extreme grossness with which such instances are detailed." An article on "Modern French Romance" in the *Dublin Review* (November 1840), attributed to either John Steinmetz or Charles de Coux, reads almost like an absurdly hysterical parody of Croker's: "we defy Lucifer himself, if he could take up a pen, to outdo the French romancers of the present day" (specifically, George Sand, Hugo, Balzac, Soulié, and de Kock). Although the reviewer manages slightly to modify this generalization by finding, for example, "beauties" in *Notre Dame de Paris*, he ends up going far beyond Croker's statistics of crime, threatening to show on a future occasion "how in many cases the novelists of that unhappy country have led their readers to the scaffold." In the course of his survey in the *Edinburgh Review* (July 1843) of the nine volumes of *Les Français, peints par eux-mêmes* (1840-42), Abraham Hayward also notes "the eternal recurrence of matrimonial infidelity" in French light literature, and sees the lack of firm standards in French life and literature as due to revolution, since "where all are striving to be the equals of their superiors, or the superiors of their equals, the prevalent tone must be one of uneasy, dissatisfied, restless, pushing pretension."[4] Similarly, Henry Lytton Bulwer attributed the immorality and excesses in the drama of Hugo and Dumas to their need to satisfy the tastes of "an immense plebeian public" instead of a "polished or privileged class."[5] Another visitor to France, Mrs. Trollope, while admiring Parisian gaiety and elegance, thought that the "oil which feeds the lamp of revolutionary genius is foul, and such noxious vapours rise with the flame as must needs check its brightness." She took comfort in her opinion that France itself seemed "to be ashamed" of Hugo, whose dramas she found "disgusting." But she excepted George Sand from her criticisms: "there is so much of the divine spirit of real genius within her, that it seems as if she could not sink in the vortex that has engulfed her companions."[6] More ambiguously, Thackeray reported to readers of his *National Standard* on 29 June 1833 that he "was surprised and delighted with the great progress made by the Parisians since last year. Talk of the 'march of mind' in England, La jeune France completely distances us: all creeds, political, literary, and religious, have undergone equal revolutions and met with equal contempt." He then ironically and disapprovingly summarized Pétrus Borel's *Champavert* as a typical product of the movement (I, 32-35).

On the other hand, thoughtful and even enthusiastic defenders of French literature existed. Lady Morgan, in her *France in 1829-30* (1830), welcomed the opportune appearance of new French writing "to relieve the present age from the decrepitude and mediocrity which immediately preceded it" and praised "that fire which lives and glows in the pages" of de Vigny's *Cinq Mars*. It is doubtful, however, whether Thackeray would have taken her opinion seriously, since he believed that the information provided by her and Mrs. Trollope "not to be worth a sixpence" (II, 97). Mrs. Gore, another authoress mocked by him (in **"Punch's Prize Novelists"** and elsewhere), pleaded in her Preface to her edition of some of Charles de Bernard's stories—"badly translated," according to Thackeray (VI, 320)—for sympathetic understanding for "that philosophical satirist of a state of society unhinged by revolutions," indicating that "to judge the French people from deductions based upon the ideas and customs of England, often leads to most erroneous conclusions." Although in that Preface she described him as "one of the most popular, and decidedly the most original of modern French novelists," in her *Paris in 1841* (1842) she numbered him amongst those French writers who "constitute rather a via lactea of literary glory, than a constellation of stars of the first magnitude." Lady Blessington, in *The Idler in France* (1841), recommended Hugo's "powerfully written" *Les Derniers Jours d'un condamné*.[7] There were sympathetic reviewers in the *Westminster Review,* the *Athenaeum,* and the *Foreign Quarterly Review.* Andrew Bisset attempted, perhaps not very convincingly, to refute Croker in the *Westminster Review* (July 1836), on the grounds that works of fiction are exaggerated, "giving a most undue prominence and importance to follies and vices, as well as violent passions." In any case, the French had just emerged from a period of social violence, and their literature had broken free from eighteenth-century restraints.[8] G. H. Lewes, the most prominent of the favorable critics, strongly argued in the *Westminster Review* (October 1842) against the practice of anonymity, which gave an ignorant or prejudiced English critic the license to use unjust and hypocritical methods of attack. Criticism, he wrote, "always stabs in the name of public morals—it slanders on religious scruples. While lauding to the skies the corrupt literature of its own party, it 'shudders' at the thought of a 'French novel'; while deifying—, it curses George Sand."[9] He himself wrote in the *Foreign Quarterly Review* (July 1844) a searching appreciation of her and Balzac, "indisputably the greatest of their class, now living in France," emphasizing, however, that Balzac "should be strictly forbidden to young women."[10]

Ignorance was seen as a typical English fault, as Alexis de Tocqueville pointed out: "Admirable narrations are published in London, of what happens in the East and West Indies; the political and social condition of the antipodes is tolerably well known in England; but of the institutions of France the English have hardly even a superficial notion."[11] Nevertheless, information was available, not only in the periodicals and travellers' books I have mentioned but also in G. W. M. Reynolds's popular descriptive anthology, *The Modern Literature of France* (1839; second edition, 1841), and in Raymond de Véricour's *Modern French Literature* (1842). Furthermore, the popularity amongst the general reading public of the French novelists of the time was so great that if translations can be taken as a trustworthy guide Dumas, de Vigny, Hugo, Balzac, George Sand, and Sue "belong almost as much to English literature as to French."[12] Nor is it surprising, after all, that these authors found a market in England. The names of three of the friendly observers, Lady Morgan, Mrs. Gore, and Lady Blessington, are reminders that the two decades in England were marked by romanticism, sometimes of a debased kind, and that readers of the Annuals and of fashionable, historical, and Newgate novels were likely to enjoy much that came from the French novelists. Those read most widely were Dumas and Sue. The latter's *Les Mystères de Paris* "has been sold by tens of thousands in London in various shapes, in American editions, and illustrated English translations," Thackeray wrote on 16 July 1845 to Macvey Napier.[13] And on 13 March 1847 he drew in *Punch* two cab drivers, one of whom is asking the other, "I say, Jim, vich do you give the prufferance? Eugene Shue or Halexander Dumas?" (IX, 538). It has been calculated, too, that "fully one-half of the plays written in England between 1800 and 1850 must have been suggested by Parisian models."[14] At the risk of oversimplifying a complex pattern of response, we can say that on one side stood the common reader and playgoer (whose enjoyment of French writers has no equivalent today) and a few observers and critics. On the other were ranged quite formidable critics who were perturbed or enraged by what they thought to be works of viciousness and absurdity. The ambivalence apparent in Thackeray's criticism of French literature can perhaps be understood, if not justified, as a combination of these attitudes. As early as 1832, his opinions, recorded in his diary, seem to fluctuate as he reads modern French writers in Paris. On 16 August, he thinks that "the gentlemen of the Ecole Romantique have thrown away all these prejudices, but still seem no wise better or more poetical than their rigid predecessors." By 9 September, he has read "Notre Dame de Paris of W[h]. [he thinks] most highly as a work of genius, though it is not perhaps a fine novel."[15]

G. M. Young suggested that "a boy born in 1810 . . . entered manhood with the ground rocking under his feet as it had rocked in 1789." As we have seen, that description of his own feelings in the early 1830s would have seemed exaggerated to Thackeray, who often responded to the France of the July Monarchy with a certain amount of detached amusement and understanding rather than with fear, indignation, or hysteria. He could, it is true, join in the popular pastime of mocking Louis Philippe, but he could also generously sympathize with him as "the wisest, the greatest—the most miserable man in Europe" (III, 497). Young also noted the spread of Evangelicalism, saying, with some overemphasis, that "by the beginning of the nineteenth century virtue was advancing on a broad invincible front."[16] Thackeray was personally aware of this increasing emphasis on virtuous behavior in all walks of life, if only from his mother with her Evangelical leanings and from such Cambridge contemporaries as the future Archdeacon Allen (the prototype of Dobbin, according to Lady Ritchie's introduction to *Vanity Fair* in the Biographical Edition), who recorded in his diary earnest conversations and a Bible reading with him in February 1830.[17] Against these typical manifestations of Englishness, we must pose a knowledge and love of France that by the time he was twenty-one had made him an "old Paris hand," although as he argued in "On Some Fashionable French Novels," this was qualified by inevitable insularity: an English gentleman who has dwelt for some time in Paris has "seen an immense number of wax candles, cups of tea, glasses of orgeat, and French people, in best clothes, enjoying the same; but intimacy there is none; we see but the outsides of the people . . . with our English notions, and moral and physical constitution, it is quite impossible that we should become intimate with our brisk neighbours" (II, 94, 96).

Another essentially English factor that must be considered, although it has been discussed on innumerable occasions, is "gentlemanliness," that blend of assumptions that affects much criticism of French literature in the 1830s and 1840s. The period of Thackeray's life coincided with the period when a particular concept of the "English gentleman" was clarified. Simon Raven, a recent historian of the phenomenon, has explained that up to about 1840 outward conformity to the rules of decorum was sufficient, but that in the decades following Thomas Arnold's Rugby headmastership "responsibility, philanthropy, 'regularity in affairs'; faith, duty, sobriety; chastity and prudence; 'private persuasion and social persecution'" were "strictly accounted in any reckoning of the English gentleman."[18] Support for Raven's analysis can be found retrospectively in *Guesses at Truth* (1827), where the Hare brothers say that a gentleman "in the vulgar, superficial way of understanding the word, is the Devil's Christian" and that it is necessary "to throw aside these polisht and too current counterfeits for something valuable and sterling."[19] In his well-known definition of "gentleman" in the *Book of Snobs,* Thackeray seems to retain something of the pre-Arnoldian idea, since he makes clear that the gentleman should exercise the desirable qualities of honesty, generosity, and so on "in the most graceful outward manner" (IX, 270). It is significant that he finds de Bernard "more remarkable than any other French author, to our notion, for writing like a gentleman," with "ease, grace, and *ton,* in his style, which, if we judge aright, cannot be discovered in Balzac, or Soulié, or Dumas" (II, 109).

He openly defended the necessity for deception, "for it is good to pretend to the virtue of chastity even though we do not possess it; nay, the very restraint which the hypocrisy lays on a man is not unapt, in some instances, to profit him" (III, 385). That statement, which occurs in his *Times* review of Fielding's works (2 September 1840), had been anticipated by remarks he had made in the course of a criticism of novels by Count Horace de Viel-Castel: "If *mariages de convenance* take place here (as they will wherever avarice, and poverty, and desire, and yearning after riches are to be found), at least, thank God, such unions are not arranged upon a regular organised *system*; there is a fiction of attachment with us, and there is a consolation in the deceit ('the homage,' according to the old *mot* of Rochefoucauld, 'which vice pays to virtue'), for the very falsehood shows that the virtue exists somewhere" (II, 110-11). In his comments preceding his review of Reybaud's *Jérôme Paturot,* he expresses a gentlemanly distaste for the coarseness of Balzac, Dumas, and Soulié, sounding a little like so many English critics:

> These are hard words. But a hundred years hence (when, of course, the frequenters of the circulating library will be as eager to read the works of Soulié, Dumas, and the rest, as now), a hundred years hence, what a strange opinion the world will have of the French society of to-day! Did all married people, we may imagine they will ask, break a certain commandment?—They all do in the novels. Was French society composed of murderers, of forgers, of children without parents, of men consequently running the risk of marrying their grandmothers by mistake; of disguised princes, who lived in the friendship of amiable cutthroats and spotless prostitutes; who gave up the sceptre for the *savate,* and the stars and pigtails of the court for the chains and wooden shoes of the galleys? All these characters are quite common in French novels, and France in the nineteenth century was the politest country in the world. What must have the rest of the world have been?

(VI, 320)

I am not sure how seriously we should take these comments, for Thackeray affects in this genial essay, written in his later *Fraser's* manner, a dislike for unhappy endings and distressing scenes: he would, he says, pardon "the man who brought Cordelia to life" in a later version of *King Lear*; he has read "the *Nelly* part of the *Old Curiosity Shop*" only once, whereas he has "Dick Swiveller and the Marchioness by heart"; he prefers Sam Weller and Mr. Pickwick to Sikes's murder and "the Jew's nightmare" (VI, 322). And his remarks on men who run "the daily risk of marrying their grandmothers by mistake" reveal an amused aversion rather than horror, and ignore, in any case, popular conventions of secret parentage in the plots of English novels.

Nevertheless, even if he genuinely disapproved of such plots and characters in French fiction and could argue

in favor of hypocrisy, he admitted that he admired the comparative frankness allowed to such novelists as Sue, envying him as he envied Fielding:

> But here, and we shall not probably grudge it to him, a French satirist has a certain advantage which, with our modest public, an English novelist cannot possess. The former is allowed to speak more freely than the latter; and in consequence, perhaps the best parts of M. Sue's book [*Les Mystères de Paris*] are the most hideous, as where he describes the naked villainies of a certain monstrous notary who figures in the latter volumes. There can be no mistake about *him*: and the vigorous, terrible description of the man is wholesome, though bitter. There is a kind of approach to virtue in a good hearty negation of vice. It is best, no doubt, to contemplate only the good; and to be forced backwards, as it were, towards it, from a shrinking fright and abhorrence, occasioned by some dreadful exhibition of the opposite principle; but at least let us have no mistake between the one and the other, and not be led to a guilty sympathy for villainy, by having it depicted to us as exceedingly specious, agreeable, generous, and virtuous at heart.

(V, 471)

He had frequently argued—and had attempted to show in his first novel **Catherine**—that a forthright representation of evil was healthier and more truthful than the romantic depiction of crime and criminals in English Newgate novels—an argument commonly used by his fellow-Fraserians when assailing Bulwer but not used by reviewers of French novels.

Given such circumstances as the powerful criticisms of immorality in French literature expressed by influential critics, the pervasiveness of Evangelicalism, and the codification of gentlemanliness, Thackeray's "John Bullish" stance on occasions, particularly his concern with moral and ethical issues, is unremarkable. Commentators as various as Taine, Saintsbury, and Mario Praz have considered that his work was marred, in different ways and degrees, by his adherence to a moral code that could allow, in Saintsbury's words, "outside disturbers" to distract his powers of observation in literary matters.[20] In assessing his criticism of *Les Mystères de Paris,* Miss Pantůčková has recently said, for example, that "in comparison with Marx's generous, magnanimous and deeply human attitude to human individuals, even to those who are degraded and downtrodden into the mud of their society, Thackeray's moralistic point of view seems too narrow-minded."[21] It can be argued, however, that such a concern is a correct and salutary one. It is apposite to cite here a question put by a modern French critic, Jean Lozes, when discussing the naivety of Dobbin and Colonel Newcome: "mais à la fin, les vraies valeurs ne sont-elles pas préférables à une intelligence de combines menant à l'escroquerie physique et morale?"[22] But apart from any disapproval of "outside disturbers" and also indeed from any defense of them, what is remarkable is Thackeray's frequent independence of the typically English views of morality expressed by many of his contemporaries. Reynolds, it is true, in his Introduction to *The Modern Literature of France* approvingly noted that "the French author paints the truth in all its nudity" (p. xvii), but generally speaking it is difficult to find amongst reviewers such things as avowals of the social need for hypocrisy, admiration for Sue's candor in portraying villainy, or—as we shall see—a sense of delighted engagement with French literature. The *Athenaeum,* for one, could allow no justification of Sue's outspokenness. For its reviewer of *Les Mystères de Paris,* it was "a grave question" whether details of evil "are admissible in a work of Art." But, he continued, "we are sure that when employed to dress out a first invention so distorted and defective, the result of good will be miserably small, as compared with the bad amount of curiosity stirred, appetite sharpened, and feverish excitement maintained."[23] Thackeray thought that "curiosity," "appetite," and "feverish excitement" could be admirable qualities stimulated by a narrative and should therefore be given their full share of appreciative recognition.

In frankly acknowledging the entertainment Sue gave him, Thackeray aligned himself with popular opinion rather than with the critics. A current of enthusiasm runs through his comments on *Les Mystères de Paris*: "In spite of probability, and in spite of morality, and in spite of better judgement, here are six volumes that any novel-reader who begins must read through. Although one knows the author to be a quack, one cannot deny that he is a clever fellow; although the story is entirely absurd, yet it is extremely interesting; and although it may run on for half a dozen more volumes, it is probable we shall read every one of them" (V, 472). Similarly, he had argued previously, Charles de Bernard may offend the sense of English propriety, but "we follow him in his lively malicious account of [his characters'] manners, without risk of lighting upon any such horrors as Balzac or Dumas have provided for us" (II, 99); he is sparkling, gentlemanly, witty, and amusing. And he has no reservations about Reybaud's novel, because *Jérôme Paturot* is "a good, cheerful, clear, kind-hearted, merry, smart, bitter, sparkling romance" (VI, 323). Even his generally hostile reception of the books by Hugo and Dumas on the Rhine is qualified by appreciative comments. Hugo may be pretentious and dishonest. But "if the road and the scenery is tiresome, at any rate the traveller examining them is always amusing;—that strange, grotesque, violent, pompous, noble figure of a poet, with his braggart modesty, and wonderful simplicity of conceit, his kind heart yearning towards all small things and beauties of nature, small children, birds, flowers, &c., his rich, flowing, large eloquence, and his grim humour" (V, 376). And Dumas, whom he later admired unreservedly, "has both humour and eloquence, and in spite of his hectoring manner his heart is both

manly and kind" (V, 439). It may not be perverse to suggest that the comedy, zestful detail, and contemptuous rhetoric that he uses in his examination of George Sand's "philosophy" in *Spiridion* testify to a kind of enjoyment (e.g., II, 228, 237, 246-47).

This explicit delight in reading some French literature is unique amongst contemporary reviewers' attitudes. G. H. Lewes considered that a novelist could be regarded from three points of view: "as a Moralist, an Artist, and an Entertaining Writer." He admitted that "the first question with ordinary readers being: Is the work interesting? the first point the critic pronounces on, is naturally in answer to that question," but he "could wish it were otherwise." Conceding that "novels are read for amusement," he made it plain that "they should be criticised with other views." Having the novels of Balzac and George Sand particularly in mind, Lewes emphasized that the critic of fiction "is bound, before all things, closely to scrutinise and severely to condemn all departures from truth and morality, beside which the 'interest' [i.e., the entertainment value] of a work sinks into insignificance."[24] While Thackeray would have agreed with Lewes's priorities, he would surely have insisted that "interest" was more significant than Lewes allowed it to be. If we are inclined to dismiss Thackeray's insistence on this as superficial, we should remember first that he knew from his own experience how vital it was for a novelist to entertain his readers and secondly that his positive critical attitude in this respect could encourage others to find the practice of reading French literature pleasurable and rewarding.

With this independence of judgment almost always goes a liveliness of approach and expression, whether he is reviewing fiction or nonfiction. Compare the freshness and energy of Thackeray's review of Victor Hugo's *Le Rhin* with Francis Palgrave's calm and dull appraisal of the book in the *Quarterly Review* (March 1843). The keynote of the latter is struck by his preliminary statement that the work is "amongst the most innocuous productions of a very able but exaggerated and mischievous writer." Or with the two articles on *Le Rhin* in *Fraser's Magazine* (April and May 1843), consisting of summaries and a full discussion of the political issues raised by Hugo.[25] Thackeray enthusiastically condemns or mocks or praises it and is therefore likely to make the reader of his review want to read and argue about it. He even vivifies the journeyman work of retelling plots, that unenterprising but occasionally useful feature of many nineteenth-century reviews of fiction. Saintsbury found his "rehash" of *Jérôme Paturot* even better than the original (VI, xvi), and the same can be said for his summary of Soulié's *Le Bananier* (V, 483-99).

Such vivacious renderings of criticism and paraphrase, which direct our attention to Thackeray's own handling of language, make it unsurprising to find that with the exception of Lewes he seems to be alone amongst contemporary critics in attending to the prose style of the books under review. Although the validity of some of his assessments may be questioned, his qualifications for judging literary French were unexceptionable, since he had not only mastered the language and had read as widely in French literature as any of his fellow-reviewers but he had also translated or adapted French prose and poetry. The "philosophy" of *Spiridion* may, in his opinion, be typically French in its frantic freakishness, but George Sand's "style is a noble, and, as far as a foreigner can judge, a strange tongue, beautifully rich and pure . . . and for those who are not afraid of the matter of the novel, the manner will be found most delightful" (II, 232-33). Always alert to linguistic pomposity, he laughed at the "mixture of sublimity and absurdity, affectation and nature" he found in Hugo's *Etude sur Mirabeau* (I, 51), implying that this typified what he later called "the French propensity towards braggadocio" (III, 415). But in his review of Hugo's *Le Rhin,* he recognized one essential difference that exists between the English and French languages, pointing out "the literal translation of such fine words is always unfortunate in English, where words are used with somewhat more precision, and where such sounding phrases as *une magnifique nature, une noble poësie, une féconde histoire,* appear very bald indeed." He suggests, unjustly using the nature of English expression as his criterion, that "perhaps it would be a good precaution for imaginative writers to take in general, and whenever they have produced a sentence peculiarly dignified and sonorous, to try how it would look in another language, and whether the sense will still bear the transplantation." These reservations do not prevent him from appreciatively quoting in French Hugo's description of a storm ("it would be a shame, as we fancy, to alter a single word in it; so complete does it seem to be") and conveying its essence with brilliant concision: "It bursts into the narrative, and is over in a page, like the event it describes" (V, 370-71, 382). The reviewer in *Fraser's Magazine* contents himself with saying that "Victor Hugo's style, especially in prose, is vivid."[26]

Thackeray's criticism of French literature suffers by being concerned so much with the second-rate, which admittedly he often relished. We have no extensive reviews of the fiction of Stendhal, Balzac, and Hugo. He apparently rates de Bernard above these, and one of his favorite poets is Béranger. He was by no means alone in these preferences, which can be found amongst some of the friendly commentators already mentioned. But apart from personal predilections and the influence of contemporary fashion, one reason for his prolonged attention to the second-rate—a reason sometimes strangely forgotten—is that he usually reviewed what he was paid to review, always "glad to help [his] purse along."[27] Equally, he had occasionally to conform to the style or policy of a periodical. The constraints are no-

ticeable in some of his work for the *Foreign Quarterly Review.* One of his first articles for it, **"The Last Fifteen Years of the Bourbons,"** is un-Thackerayan in its solidity and solemnity, perhaps because it represented a bid for the editorship. In any case, John Forster, who became editor in early 1842, sought to give *"an English interest"* to the quarterly, as advertisements stated; he wanted his contributors to adopt an earnest, healthy, and manly tone. At the same time, the publicity claimed that a "popular character" would be introduced in its pages, and in this respect Thackeray was spontaneously obedient, as in his comments on Sue.[28]

Acknowledging his deficiencies and omissions, which owe much to social and cultural circumstances, we can see that what in general distinguishes Thackeray as a critic of French literature from his contemporaries is the fact that, unlike them, he was an English novelist. One of his premises, stated at the beginning of **"On Some French Fashionable Novels,"** was that the "sham story" appeared "a great deal more agreeable, life-like, and natural than the true one" and that "all who, from laziness as well as principle, are inclined to follow the easy and comfortable study of novels, may console themselves with the notion that they are studying matters quite as important as history, and that their favourite duodecimos are as instructive as the biggest quartos in the world" (II, 92). Such an assumption would have been unacceptable to many reviewers. For one thing, it was a direct contradiction of Carlyle's vehement and influential argument in "Biography": "let any one bethink him how impressive the smallest historical *fact* may become, as contrasted with the grandest *fictional event.*"[29] A practicing travel-writer as well, Thackeray valued firsthand, honest, and vivid responses to new scenes and experiences. As a creator and observer, engaged directly with solving problems of form and content, and having (in Saintsbury's words) "a curious impulsiveness and inconsistency which has something to do with the unequalled truth to nature and the wonderful fresh variety of his style and thought" (II, xvii-xviii), he was readier and freer than most English critics to appreciate the ways in which French writers drew their fictional personages, arranged their plots, reflected post-1830 France, embodied schemes of "philosophy," or reported events and scenes. As a hard-working author, pressed for money in the 1830s and early 1840s, he could also appreciate the commercial and mercenary aspects of their production of books. It is outside the scope of this article to assess what influence they may have had on his own writing, although this has often been noted and analyzed, sometimes with inconclusive results. Balzac, de Bernard, de Kock, Dumas, and Reybaud, for example, have been seen to have connections of various kinds and extents with his work.[30] The important fact that he was an imaginative writer is apparent in the style and atmosphere of his reviews. As some of my quotations have shown, his prose has a distinctive responsiveness and elegance, missing from the formal and lackluster prose of many of his fellow-critics. His way of writing leans toward the free-ranging, allusive approach of William Maginn, his friend and mentor in his early days as a journalist. But Maginn frequently bludgeons or wildly overpraises; he uses crude expressions, feeble jokes, and obscure references indiscriminately. Thackeray's more refined inventiveness and versatility of illustration amuses, illuminates, and emphasizes, as in his examination of the "prodigious" fecundity of French novelists, whom he compares to vendors of wines, religious relics, and souvenirs of Shakespeare and battle:

> And as the famous wine merchants at Frankfort who purchased the Johannisberg [sic] vintage of 1811, have been selling it ever since, by simply mixing a very little of the wine of that famous year with an immense quantity of more modern liquor; so do these great writers employ smaller scribes, whose works they amend and prepare for press. Soulié and Dumas can thus give the Soulié or Dumas flavour to any article of tolerable strength in itself; and so prepared, it is sent into the world with the Soulié or Dumas seal and signature, and eagerly bought and swallowed by the public as genuine. The retailers are quite aware of the mixture, of which indeed the authors make no secret; but if the public must have Johannisberg of 1811 and no other, of course the dealers will supply it, and hence the vast quantity of the article in the market. Have we not seen in the same way how, to meet the demands of devotion, the relicis of the saints have multiplied themselves; how Shakespeare's mulberry-tree has been cut down in whole forests, and planed and carved by regiments of turners and upholsterers; and how, in the plains of Waterloo, crosses, eagles, and grapeshot are still endlessly growing?

(V, 482)

Similarly, his unexpected but precise collocations of epithets are evidence of an acutely observant and essentially personal scrutiny of character or text. As evidence, consider the strings of adjectives he attaches to *Jérôme Paturot,* Hugo, and Janin, in passages quoted elsewhere in this article. Always present in his reviews is an air of effortless animation and zest, which can appear in a sentence like this, about Sue: "He is, then, as we fancy, a quack, certainly; but one of the cleverest quacks now quacking; and a great deal more amusing than many dullards of his trade, who have a perfect belief in themselves, and outrage art, sense, and style, out of their confidence that their stupid exaggerations are the result of a vast imagination and an undoubted genius" (V, 462). Or in this, from **"Madame Sand and the New Apocalypse"** in the *Paris Sketch Book*: "Monsieur de Balzac feels himself to be inspired; Victor Hugo is a god; Madame Sand is a god; that tawdry man of genius, Jules Janin, who writes theatrical reviews for the *Débats,* has divine intimations; and there is scarce a beggarly, beardless scribbler of poems and prose, but tells you, in his preface, of the sainteté of the *sacerdoce*

littéraire; or a dirty student, sucking tobacco and beer, and reeling home with a grisette from the chaumière, who is not convinced of the necessity of a new 'Messianism,' and will hiccup, to such as will listen, chapters of his own drunken Apocalypse" (II, 228). This liveliness, which springs partly from a vigorous choice of words, is also related to variation of sentence-structure, including a felicitous use of such colloquial elements as exclamations, questions and answers, confidences, asides, and conversational tags and phrases, as in this comment made in the course of his summary of the plot of *Jérôme Paturot*:

> May, one cannot help repeating, may all literary characters at the end of the first volume of their lives, find such an uncle! but alas! this is the only improbable part of the book. There is no such blessed resource for the penny-a-liner in distress. All he has to do is to write more lines, and get more pence, and wait for grim Death, who will carry him off in the midst of a penny, and lo! where is he? You read in the papers that yesterday, at his lodgings in Grub Street, "died Thomas Smith, Esq., the ingenious and delightful author, whose novels have amused us all so much. This eccentric and kind-hearted writer has left a wife and ten children, who, we understand, are totally unprovided for, but we are sure that the country will never allow them to want." Smith is only heard of once or twice again. A publisher discovers a novel left by that lamented and talented author; on which another publisher discovers another novel by the same hand: and "Smith's last work," and the "last work of Smith," serve the bibliopolists' turn for a week, are found entirely stupid by the public; and so Smith, and his genius, and his wants, and his works pass away out of this world for ever.

(VI, 330-31)

Sometimes, with an effect of memorable contrast, Thackeray writes the kind of brief, pithy sentence that I have already noted in connection with his praise of Hugo's description of a storm. As another instance, here is his summing-up of Soulié's productivity: "He publishes circulating libraries at once" (V, 482). Apart from its other features, therefore, his criticism can be clearly separated from that of his contemporaries simply because of its unique Thackerayan power of expression.

Despite his conventional belief that absurdities and moral dangers were characteristic of French literature, he continually contended that English readers had a great deal to gain from it. It was valuable, in his opinion, for its truthfulness about evil, narrative verve, fluency and euphony of language, and the opportunities it gave English people to make enlightening comparisons and contrasts between the two nations. Lewes, it must be admitted, was the superior critic in some respects, with his serious, probing explorations, based on consistent critical theories that led him to emphasize the importance of tradition, objectivity, and true proportion—in other words, aspects of an English classicism more balanced and informed than the dogmas of such conservative critics as Croker.[31] To Thackeray, on the other hand, can be applied most of the description he himself gave of Janin, whom he both abused and admired: "the man who writes a weekly *feuilleton* in the *Journal des Débats* with such indisputable brilliancy and wit, and such a happy mixture of effrontery, and honesty, and poetry, and impudence, and falsehood, and impertinence, and good feeling, that one can't fail to be charmed with the compound" (IV, 174). Seen in relation to what other English critics were saying about French literature, from Lewes's sympathy to the *Dublin Review*'s hostility, the prejudices and weaknesses in Thackeray's criticism can be understood (although not completely excused) and its positive qualities enhanced. It has much to offer: a wide range of interests and approaches that reflect both formal and popular opinion, an intimate concern with the actual business and process of writing novels and travelbooks, enthusiasm, and imagination.

Notes

1. Lidmila Pantůčková, "Thackeray as a Reader and Critic of French Literature," *Brno Studies in English,* 9, No. 166 (Brno: Universita J. E. Purkyně, 1970), 37-126.

2. Henry Lytton Bulwer, *France, Social, Literary, Political* (London: Bentley, 1834), II, 227.

3. For full discussions see Marcel Moraud, *Le Romantisme français en Angleterre de 1814 a 1848* (Paris: Librairie ancienne Honoré Champion, 1933), pp. 189-425, and D. O. Evans, "French Romanticism and British Reviewers," *French Quarterly,* 9 (Dec. 1927), 225-37.

4. *Quarterly Review,* 56 (Apr. 1836), 65-131; *Dublin Review,* 9 (Nov. 1840), 353-96; *Edinburgh Review,* 78 (July 1843), 114-56. For *Dublin Review* attribution, see *Wellesley Index to Victorian Periodicals,* ed. Walter E. Houghton, II (London: Routledge and Kegan Paul, 1972), 31.

5. Bulwer, *France* [*France, Social, Literary, Political*], II, 347.

6. Frances Trollope, *Paris and the Parisians in 1835* (London: Bentley, 1836), I, 64, 151, 153; II, 259.

7. Lady Morgan, *France in 1829-30* (London: Saunders and Otley, 1830), I, 272; II, 60; *The Lover and the Husband; the Woman of a Certain Age, &c.,* ed. Mrs. Gore (London: Bentley, 1841), pp. v, viii; Mrs. Gore, *Paris in 1841* (*Heath's Picturesque Annual for 1842,* Longman, 1842), p. 266; Countess of Blessington, *The Idler in France* (London: Colburn, 1841), II, 52.

8. *Westminster Review,* 25 (July 1836), 300-310.

9. Ibid., 38 (Oct. 1842), 466-86.

10. *Foreign Quarterly Review,* 33 (July 1844), 265-98.

11. *Westminster Review,* 25 (Apr. 1836), 138.

12. W. Roberts, "Dumas and Sue in English," *Nineteenth Century and After,* 92 (Nov. 1922), 760-66. Quotation from p. 760.

13. *Letters and Private Papers of William Makepeace Thackeray,* ed. Gordon N. Ray (London: Oxford Univ. Press, 1945-46), II, 202.

14. Allardyce Nicoll, *A History of English Drama 1660-1900,* IV (Cambridge: Cambridge Univ. Press, 1955), 79.

15. *Letters and Private Papers* [*Letters and Private Papers of William Make peace Thackeray*], I, 224, 228.

16. G. M. Young, *Portrait of an Age,* ed. G. Kitson Clark (London: Oxford Univ. Press, 1977), pp. 21, 24.

17. Gordon N. Ray, *Thackeray: The Uses of Adversity* (London: Oxford Univ. Press, 1955), p. 132.

18. Simon Raven, *The English Gentleman* (London: Blond, 1961), pp. 45-46, 51.

19. [Julius and Augustus Hare], *Guesses at Truth,* new ed. (London: Macmillan, 1871), p. 158.

20. George Saintsbury, *A History of Criticism* (Edinburgh and London: Blackwood, 1900-4), III, 501.

21. Pantůčková, "Thackeray as a Reader and Critic of French Literature," p. 73.

22. Jean Lozes, "Le Snob et le gentleman," *Caliban,* 8 (1971), 39-47. Quotation from p. 45.

23. *Athenaeum,* 27 Apr. 1844, p. 375.

24. *Foreign Quarterly Review,* 33 (July 1844), 291, 293.

25. *Quarterly Review,* 71 (Mar. 1843), 315-31; *Fraser's Magazine,* 27 (Apr. 1843), 411-26; 27 (May 1843), 584-96.

26. *Fraser's Magazine,* 27 (Apr. 1843), 415.

27. *Letters and Private Papers,* II, 64-65.

28. Ray, [*Thackeray:*] *Uses of Adversity,* p. 321; *Wellesley Index to Victorian Periodicals,* II, 134-35.

29. Thomas Carlyle, *English and Other Critical Essays* (London: Dent, Everyman's Library, 1915), p. 73.

30. See for example, George Saintsbury, *History of the French Novel* (London: Macmillan, 1917,

1919), II, 54n, 294; A. Carey Taylor, "Balzac et Thackeray," *Revue de littérature comparée,* 34 (1960), 354-69; Raymond Maitre, "Balzac, Thackeray, et Charles de Bernard," *Revue de littérature comparée,* 50 (1950), 278-93; Robert A. Colby, *Thackeray's Canvass of Humanity* (Columbus: Ohio State Univ. Press, 1979), chaps. 4, 5, 8, 9, and 10.

31. See Morris Greenhut, "George Henry Lewes and the Classical Tradition in English Criticism," *Review of English Studies,* 24 (Apr. 1948), 126-37.

Helene E. Roberts (essay date spring-summer 1981)

SOURCE: Roberts, Helene E. "'The Sentiment of Reality': Thackeray's Art Criticism." *Studies in the Novel* 13, nos. 1-2 (spring-summer 1981): 21-39.

[*In the following essay, Roberts evaluates Thackeray's career as an art critic.*]

During the twenty-two years between 1833 and 1854 William Makepeace Thackeray wrote thirty-four pieces on art for the periodicals and newspapers. The core of these writings can be found in his fourteen contributions on art to *Fraser's Magazine* in the eleven years between 1837 and 1847. These issues included reviews of the London art exhibitions of 1838, 1839, 1840, 1844, and 1845 and the Paris art exhibitions of 1839 and 1841.[1] In addition to these reviews in *Fraser's Magazine,* Thackeray reviewed art exhibitions for the *National Standard* in 1833, the *Times* in 1838, *Ainsworth's Magazine* in 1842, the *Pictorial Times* in 1843, and the *Morning Chronicle* in 1844 through 1846.[2] Thackeray also contributed six reviews of annuals and gift books, criticizing the illustrations at length, for the *Times* in 1838 and for *Fraser's Magazine* between 1837 and 1847. He again turned to the subject of book and periodical illustration in his article **"Caricature and Lithography in Paris"** published in the *Westminster Review* in 1839. This article was later included in his *Paris Sketch Book* as was his review **"On the French School of Painting"** from *Fraser's Magazine* of that same year. Thackeray also wrote a long adulatory essay on his friend and teacher, the illustrator George Cruikshank, for the *Westminster Review* of 1840; and, in 1854, he contributed his only piece on art in the 1850s, a review of *Pictures of Life and Character* in the *Quarterly Review* of his friend, the illustrator John Leech.[3] Four slight comic pieces published in *Punch* during 1843 complete the list of Thackeray's writings on art for the periodical and newspaper press.[4]

A few articles that were once attributed to Thackeray are no longer considered to be his. Others however may yet be discovered. Thackeray's writings on art not pub-lished in periodicals or newspapers include his lecture on Hogarth, part of his series on **English Humourists of the Eighteenth Century,** and the text for his friend Louis Marvy's engravings in *Sketches after English Landscape Painters.*[5] Material relevant to his attitudes about art may also be gleaned from his novels, short stories, literary criticisms, and letters. These thirty-four pieces on art from the periodicals and the supplementary writings form a substantial group and allow an assessment of Thackeray's taste in art, his aesthetic principles, and his contribution to Victorian art criticism.

Of all the English art critics of the first half of the nineteenth century Thackeray can be compared only with Hazlitt, Haydon, and Ruskin in combining a knowledge of the technical aspects of art, a grounding in the aesthetic theories of his day, and an unusual command of the English language. Alone among art critics he displayed a playful wit and an ebullient sense of fun.

His technical knowledge of art was gained during the years 1833 to 1841 during which time he seriously studied to become an artist. In July of 1833, although already involved in journalism and the proprietor of the *National Standard,* he wrote his mother, "I have been thinking very seriously of turning artist—I think I can draw better than do anything else & certainly like it better."[6] During the next few years he copied paintings in the Louvre, studied at the Life Academy and in the studios of Baron Gros and in the studios of landscape painters Edmond le Poittevin and Charles Lafond. In London he entered Henry Sass's academy, an establishment devoted primarily to preparing aspiring candidates to the Royal Academy schools. By 1835 he felt able to report to his mother: "I know I have got the stuff to make as good a painter as the very best of them."[7] Other days found him more discouraged about his progress, but it was his marriage in 1836 and the necessity of making a living that forced him to forsake art for the more immediately lucrative rewards of journalism. As late as 1841 he was still hoping to have the time to get back to painting.

His talent for sketching served him well during his journalistic career and he employed it frequently to illustrate his writings. Whether Thackeray's talents were sufficient to sustain a career in art is debatable, but these years of training gave him a sympathy for the problems faced by painters. When Thackeray reviewed Maclise's painting *Macbeth,* one senses not only the recollected frustrations, but also a judgment arising from personal experience. "The wonderful knowledge and firmness with which each individual figure and feature are placed down upon the canvass will be understood and admired by the public, but the artist still more, who knows the difficulty of these things, which seem so easy."[8] Thackeray's years as an art student gave him close friends among artists in both France and

England. Daniel Maclise became his close friend, and later, a fellow contributor to *Fraser's Magazine*. Thackeray also knew and corresponded with Frank Stone, George Cattermole, Henry Cole, and F. B. Lewis. Although he disapproved of the bohemian life of French art students, he was cognizant of French art, and, to a lesser extent, of German art as well. His experience, his personal contacts, and his wide reading in magazines and newspapers made him an exceedingly well-informed art critic.

Thackeray's taste in art reflected a Victorian sensibility, and that reason helps to explain why his art criticism has suffered neglect. His personal preferences can be shown by reference to his review of June, 1838 in *Fraser's Magazine*. In that review he lists the seven artists he would propose for academic titles and sketches himself in his critical persona of Michael Angelo Titmarsh crowning William Mulready as King of Painters. Below Mulready he lists Charles Lock Eastlake with the title of Archbishop followed by Duke William Etty. Next he places Charles and Edwin Landseer with the now forgotten Lord Charles preceding Edwin, dubbed Earl of Landseer. Placed in capital letters, though smaller in size than Mulready's name, is Prince Daniel Maclise. Baron Henry Briggs completes his list. None are names revered today.

Henry Perronet Briggs, although also a painter of historical and Shakespearean scenes, is praised by Thackeray for his portraits. "He is out and out," claims Thackeray, "the best portrait painter of the set."[9]

Throughout Thackeray's criticism he praised Daniel Maclise highly. "He has power of drawing such as never possessed by any other," Thackeray claimed in 1838; and again, a year later, he wrote that "this young man has the greatest power of hand that was ever had, perhaps by any painter in any time or country."[10] But Thackeray added that he wanted polish, thought, and cultivation. Thackeray was impressed with Maclise's clarity of detail: "every leaf in every tree is depicted," he boasted.[11] In 1840 he praised Maclise's "daguerreotypic eye."[12] Thackeray could also be critical of Maclise. In reviewing his *Macbeth* in 1840, he praised "the variety of attitude and light" and his "science, workmanship and feeling," and found the figures "grandly" and "nobly designed," but he was displeased with its overall effect. "It is a grim comedy," he concluded "rather than a tragedy."[13] Thackeray was pleased with Maclise's *Hamlet* of 1842, calling it "one of the most startling, wonderful pictures that the English school has ever produced." He noted the crowd that "always collect before it" wondering at "the prodigeous talent" of Maclise.[14]

Edwin Landseer gained Thackeray's respect for painting "the most dexterious pictures that ever were painted," but he added, "not great pictures." "He can paint all manner of birds and beasts as no body else can," Thackeray confided, but he is forced to admit, "to tell you a secret, I do not think he understands how to paint the great beast man, quite so well."[15] To Thackeray, man was the most important subject, and he praised Edwin's brother Charles more highly. Thackeray admired Charles's drawing, coloring, effect, and careful painting of details. "In this matter of costume," he wrote, "nobody can be more scrupulous than Mr. Charles Landseer."[16]

Thackeray levelled complaints of a different type against William Etty's paintings. He had great admiration for Etty's use of color and ability to paint flesh, comparing him on several occasions to Rubens and Titian, but he felt Etty offended propriety and that his paintings should be kept in the Academy and not be placed in public view. "A great curtain of fig leaves should be hung over every one of this artist's pictures," he suggested in 1839, "and the world should pass on, content to know that there are some glorious colors painted beneath."[17] Thackeray particularly found the *Sleeping Nymph* of 1838 objectionable. "Most richly painted, but," he complained, "tipsy looking, coarse and so naked as to be unfit for appearance among respectable people."[18] Thackeray's comparison of Etty with Rubens and Titian was not altogether a compliment, for he suggested that Titian and Rubens, with their "dashing worldly notions" had undermined the "beautiful system of faith" which had formerly sustained art. "Portraits of saints and martyrs, with eyes turned heavenward," he wrote, "now gave way to wicked likenesses of men of blood, or dangerous devilish sensuous portraits of tempting women."[19]

In contrast to Etty's pagan voluptuousness, Charles Lock Eastlake exemplified for Thackeray "purity and religious feeling."[20] If Thackeray praised Etty for painting with color "as luscious as Rubens, as rich almost as Titian," he praised Eastlake for keeping "the true faith" and eschewing the "temptations of Titian and his like."[21] Thackeray even ventured the opinion that Eastlake's paintings could hang with those of Raphael. In reviewing Eastlake's *Salutation of the Aged Friar* in 1840, he called it "as pure as a Sabbath-hymn sung by the voices of children."[22] The painting, he continued, has "hardly any subject at all" but "brings the spectator to a delightful peaceful state of mind and gives him matter to ponder upon long after."[23] Thackeray found faults in Eastlake's paintings: they are deficient in power, the coloring is inaccurate, the figures are repeated, "the drawing lacks vigour" and the flesh tints lack variety, but Thackeray excused all these faults because Eastlake's "chief requisites," grace and tender feelings, and his "undefinable arch-quality of sentiment," outweigh all these defects.[24] In reviewing Eastlake's works—the pattern is the same—Thackeray admitted their weaknesses, but expressed reverence for their purity and ability to touch him.

To Thackeray, Mulready was the King of Painters. He called his *Seven Ages* the "crowning picture of the exhibition" in 1838. He found faults in the drawing, but the "intention" he wrote, "is godlike." Each of the figures, he felt, had "a grace and soul of its own." Thackeray described each figure lovingly: "the portly justice, and old quarrelsome soldier, the lover leaning apart, and whispering sweet things in his pretty mistresses ear; the baby hanging on her gentle mother's bosom; the schoolboy, rosy and lazy; the old man, crabbed and stingy; and the old, old man of all, sans teeth, sans eyes, sans ears, sans everything." He praised the painting for its expressions. The figures are not copies of the stoney antique, or neoclassic caricatures. Evoking Shakespeare, Thackeray claimed they were like a "great poet would draw, who thinks profoundly and truly, and never forgets grace and beauty withal."[25]

Although Thackeray could criticize Mulready for using unnatural colors, he generally praised Mulready's drawing, expression, finish, composition, and color. Most of all it is Mulready's choice of "very simple, homely subjects" that pleased him.[26] Mulready, Thackeray declared, "manages to affect and delight one, as much as a painter can."[27] In reviewing *First Love* in 1840, Thackeray entered nostalgically into the mood of the painting, asking the viewers to remember the words lovers had whispered into their ears. He praised Mulready's "delicacy and tenderness," classing him with Eastlake as possessing "the poetry of picture-making above other English contemporary painters."[28] Two years later he again mentioned them as his favorites. "I always begin with the works of these gentlemen," he confessed in 1842, "and look at them oftenest and longest."[29]

Thackeray's list of preferences among the painters and his reviews of their work bring out three major concerns which were to characterize his art criticism: (1) the technical excellence of the painting, (2) the correspondence of the painting to the real world, and (3) its ability to evoke sentimental responses. The concerns are not solely those of Thackeray, but of other art critics as well. These concerns, in fact, are central to a description of the major changes in critical criteria which took place during the first half of the nineteenth century. Not only had the importance of technical rules diminished greatly during these fifty years, but the meaning of one of the critics' favorite criteria, that of "truth to nature" had shifted significantly. In the early part of the century nature appeared in her idealized perfect form, but by midcentury she had largely recaptured her stripes and even her warts. Furthermore, the basic goal of art had been changed. Where at the beginning of the century critics praised art for elevating the mind, by midcentury they preferred that it move the heart. Thackeray was not the sole initiator of these changes, but he was very much a part of them.

Standards of technical criticism changed least of all during the nineteenth century. If critics at midcentury questioned the infallibility of principles of academic instruction, they still judged artists according to the criteria of composition, design, coloring, and expression that had been formulated in the seventeenth century by Roger de Piles. The *Artist's Repository,* England's first art periodical (originally published from 1785 to 1795 and reissued several times in the nineteenth century) reproduced de Piles's "Balance of Painters" with its numerical rating of artists according to the four technical criteria.[30] Other periodicals discussed de Piles, but in an increasingly negative vein as the century progressed. In 1818 the *Annals of the Fine Arts,* for example, disparagingly referred to "the usual technical nonsense of de Piles and other theorists."[31] As the century neared its midpoint critics still used these same terms, checking off an artist's competence in the four categories of composition, design, coloring, and expression as well as in breadth, finish, handling, keeping, execution, and similar technical designations. But the critics' main concerns lay elsewhere and their use of technical criteria seemed like an obligatory concession to an artistic tradition rather than a vital or definitive rule for judgment.

Thackeray's brief training as an artist made him a competent judge of technical difficulties. There is hardly a painting that Thackeray reviews of which he does not judge the technical competence. He writes of Mulready's *Whistonian Controversy* for example: "in drawing so admirable, in expression so fine, in finish so exquisite, in composition so beautiful, in humour and beauty of expression so delightful, . . . and . . . the colouring brilliant, rich, astonishingly luminous, and intense."[32] Thackeray not only gave unusual attention and judgment in technical matters, he even occasionally analyzed the means artists used to gain their effects. He describes how Eastlake produced his flesh-tints "by the most careful stippling, with a brilliant composition of lake and burnt sienna, cooled off as they come to the edge with a little blue."[33] Although Thackeray pays serious attention to technical competence, he makes it abundantly clear that it is not these characteristics of the painting that decide its ultimate success. In review after review he praises the technical competence of the painter, but faults the painting on other counts, or conversely he points out many technical failures in the painting, but declares it a success. Thackeray gave due attention to the artistic technique of a painting, but it was not his ultimate judgment. More important was the age old criterion of "truth to nature," but it was a literal and commonplace nature rather than an ideal nature that Thackeray took as his model.

Reynolds's *Discourses* provided the touchstone for aesthetic theory at the turn of the century. One of Reynolds's basic principles was that it was the duty of artists to find the central and perfect form of nature, an "ideal beauty," as he described it in his third discourse, "superior to what is to be found in individual nature." One must go to nature for a model, but one must perfect what one finds there. "The mere copier of nature," he advised his students, "can never produce any great thing." All objects found in nature have their blemishes and defects. It is only through contemplation of natural forms that an artist can arrive at "an abstract idea of their forms more perfect than any one original."[34] The artist corrects nature, making her imperfect state into Ideal Beauty. Reviewers early in the century frequently invoked "truth to nature," but it was in Reynolds's ideal beauty that they found their pattern. "Nature, Nature," admonished Charles Taylor in the *Artist's Repository,* "but *liberally,* not literally attended to."[35] Critics at mid-century also invoked the criterion of "truth to nature"; they too desired a certain modification of reality and avoidance of an overly naturalistic rendering of the ugly and sordid aspects of reality, but they generously praised the accurately painted and highly finished details that allowed them to recognize familiar settings and make out the complex stories of genre paintings. They wished a readily recognizable nature, one that reminded them of a sentimental English childhood, not an arcadian landscape peopled with nymphs and shepherds.

This second criterion, that of truth to nature, was also important to Thackeray. The "beauty of nature is . . . neither more nor less than art" he wrote in *Fraser's Magazine* in 1838.[36] He warned artists not to substitute technical facility for the close observation of nature. "Look at Nature and Blush!" he demanded in 1839; "see how much nobler she is than your pettifogging art!—how much more beautiful Truth is than your miserable tricked-up lies."[37] Nature should not only be the inspiration for art, but the model. "Copy Nature," he recommended, "don't content yourself with the recollections of her—be not satisfied with pretty tricks of drawing and color."[38] He was quick to condemn artists, even those he favored, for deviating from a faithful rendition of nature. Even Mulready could be criticized for using "gaudy prismatic colours . . . wonderfully captivating to the eye . . . it is pleasant but wrong. We never saw it in nature."[39] His interpretation of nature was a literal one. He could not, for example, rise to encompass Turner's vision of the cosmic essence of nature and freely admitted his inability to understand Turner. In 1839 Thackeray condemned Turner's *Pluto and Proserpina* on the grounds that

> He has forsaken Nature, or attempted (like your French barbers) to embellish it. . . . Why will he not stick to copying her majestical countenance, instead of daubing it with some absurd antics and fard of her [*sic*] own! Fancy pea-green skies, crimson-lake trees, and orange and purple grass—fancy cataracts, rainbows, suns, moons, and thunderbolts—shake them well up with a quantity of gambouge, and you will have an idea of a fancy picture by Turner.[40]

Thackeray condemned falsity to nature in whatever form he found it. He condemned the coldness of classical art, the pretensions of neoclassic art, the pomposity of history painting, and the affectation of the gift book engravings, for all violated truth to nature. Unlike Reynolds, Thackeray did not feel that the ideal perfection of Greek art epitomized nature. "Why," he asked, "is yonder simpering Venus de Medicis to be our standard of beauty?"[41] Thackeray recounted the "manifold deadly errors" of Greek art. "It carried corporeal beauty to a pitch of painful perfection," he complained, "and defies the body and bones truly." There is no blood in the veins, no warmth in the marble bosom, and no fire in the dull eyes. Thackeray dismisses these classical sculptures as "monsters of beauty" lacking in human warmth and sentiment.[42]

French neoclassic copies from the antique pleased him even less. "The bloated, unnatural, stilted, spouting, sham sublime" he called them. "Borrowed from statuary" they had the same "misty, stony-green, dismal hue" and obligatory "white mantles, white urns, white columns, white statues." He complained of the "endless straight noses, long eyes, round chins, short upper lips, just as they are ruled down for you in the drawing books, as if the latter were the revelations of beauty issued by supreme authority."[43] Thackeray admitted that David had talent for painting portraits and common life, but he regretted that he had felt it necessary to attempt the heroic. He "failed signally," Thackeray proclaimed, "and what is worse carried the whole nation blundering after him."[44] Thackeray condemned the British romantic school of historic painting as well for being swaggering and theatrical with "sentiment so maudlin it makes you sick."[45] Poor Benjamin Robert Haydon bore the brunt of his displeasure, gaining good marks only for his earnest effort. To Thackeray history paintings were usually "pieces of canvas from 12 to 30 feet long, representing for the most part personages who never existed . . . performing actions that never occurred, and dressed in costumes they never could have worn."[46] Sir Walter Scott received a large portion of the blame for the interest in historical revivals which resulted in paintings with "no originality, no honesty of thought"; Thackeray condemned these "paltry archaeological quackeries which have no Faith, no Truth, no Life in them."[47]

Thackeray could not find the representation of the "great, beautiful, various, divine face of nature" in technical facility, grandiose landscapes, classical perfection, neoclassic sham, nor in heroic history paintings.[48] Neither could he find it in the artificiality and affectation of *Keepsake* prints. "There is not one of these beauties with her great eyes and slim waists that looks as if it has been painted from a human figure," he thundered. "It is but a slovenly, ricketty, wooden imitation of it, tricked out in some tawdry feathers and frippery, and no more like a real woman than the verses which accompany the plate are like real poetry."[49]

Where did Thackeray find real truth to nature? He found it in genre paintings by Maclise and Mulready. He found it in portraits and landscapes. He found it in the Düsseldorf and Dutch schools, and he found it in the French painter Meissonier. In praise of the French painter's *Chess Players,* Thackeray wrote that it was "a picture painted with a minuteness and accuracy of a daguerreotype."[50] Thackeray had used the same analogy of a daguerreotype to praise a painting by Maclise. He appreciated the clarity of details that photography afforded. In paintings he wanted the high finish that allowed details to be clearly seen, not, for example, the heavy impasto of the modern French landscape school. In praise of Meissonier's painting, he declared that "the chess men are no bigger than pin-heads" yet "every one of them [is] an accurate portrait."[51]

Above all, he wanted paintings to give him a sense of reality. In his criticism he frequently uses adjectives like "actual," "real," "precise," "exact," "faithful," "accurate," "correct," and nouns like "minuteness," "truth," "reality," "fidelity," and the French term *actualité.*" Thackeray's liking for the real and his sense of truth to nature were not satisfied merely by photographic realism. He also demanded a feeling of animation and movement in the figures, and he demanded subjects that reflected the variety of nature and of life around him. "Nature made every man with a nose and eyes of his own, she gave him a character of his own too," he declared; "a man, as a man, from a dustman up to Aeschylus, is God's work, and good to read, as all works are."[52]

Despite the lack of photographic realism in Daumier's work, Thackeray found this quality of variety and diversity of real life exemplified in his Robert Macaire series. Descendants will "have the advantage of knowing intimately and exactly, the manners of life and being of their grandsires," he wrote, and can call up their ghosts to "live, love, quarrel, swindle, suffer or struggle on blindly as of yore."[53] The immediacy, vividness, and reality of the depictions made them especially memorable. "The personages are real," Thackeray observed, "and the scenes remain imprinted on the brain as if we had absolutely been present at their acting."[54]

Thackeray's taste was not for bombast and elevated rhetoric, but for paintings of commonplace subjects with a human scale. "Earthy we are and of the earth; glimpses of the sublime are but rare to us," he wrote in 1839; "let us thankfully remain below, being merry and humble."[55] In 1843 he praised the young British artists for adopting "small subjects" and "simple and homely [*sic*] themes." He approved of their choice of "a simple

sentiment, an agreeable quiet incident, a tea-table tragedy or a bread and butter idyl," for their subjects, and added, "bread and butter can be digested by every man."[56]

It was not only as subjects of paintings that Thackeray welcomed the common man, but as viewers and even judges of art. In Paris he confessed that he "loved to go to the picture gallery" on Sunday to see the "thousand happy people of the working sort amusing themselves."[57] The people's taste, Thackeray thought, would improve and refine itself, at least if artists did not cater to the sensational, as did the annuals, and consciously encourage bad taste. "The pit," he declared, knows just as much about what is good art "as the boxes know."[58] Even if someone's taste is bad according to critical standards, he asks, does he not have a right to satisfy this taste? "Why should not the poor in spirit be provided for as well as the tremendous geniuses?" he demands. "The kind and beneficent Genius of Art has pleasures for all according to their degree."[59] Thackeray himself professed to a plebeian taste. "I think in my heart," he confessed in 1839, "I am fonder of pretty third-rate pictures than of your great thundering first-rates."[60]

Thackeray's art student days in Paris put him in touch with the art criticism of Theophile Thore and Gustave Planche, who discussed realism before there was even much of a French realist school of painters. The socialist Thore who wrote regularly in the periodicals from 1833 to 1868 espoused the cause of a popular art which would reflect the social life and human concerns of the people. Planche, whom Thackeray called an imposter and a quack, also wrote frequent art criticism from 1830 to 1857.[61] But, although he used the term *realisme* as early as 1833, he was hostile to both photographic verisimilitude and commonplace subject matter.

Thackeray praised the photographic clarity of details in painting and the popular appeal of contemporary subjects, but these were not in themselves enough. The ultimate test of reality coincided with the third critical criterion—does it touch the heart? Instead of demanding that a painting reflect only the appearance of real life, he seemed to require that it also evoke a similar emotional response in the viewer. "Skill and handling are great parts of the painter's trade," he declared, "but heart is the first."[62] The ability of a painting to touch the heart could validate its sincerity and its reality. "Look to have your *heart* touched by them," he advised, "the best paintings address themselves to the best feelings of it."[63] When a painting comes straight to the heart, he had written in 1837, "all criticism and calculation vanishes at once—for the artist has attained the great end, which is to strike far deeper than the sight."[64] Heart is a word Thackeray equates with sentiment which he also calls the "arch-quality" and the "first quality of a picture."[65] That the viewer's emotional response is a true guide to the worth of a painting is a statement with which few modern critics except I. A. Richards would agree. Yet it was a theory that forms the basis for Thackeray's judgment of art and for that of many early Victorian art critics. The theory assumed that emotional responses are based on the associations called into play by the painting, or indeed, by the natural scene that it depicts. It was a theory that had its roots in the eighteenth century.

Aesthetic writers on sentiment in the eighteenth century and romantic critics of the nineteenth century frequently failed to distinguish between a response to nature or to art. Paintings are seen as the substitute for the natural scene, both evoking similar associations and sentiments. Critics during the early part of the century, however, felt that the appropriate response should culminate in a moral elevation of mind. John Landseer, the father of Edwin and Charles, and the editor of the *Review of Publications of Art,* reviewed Turner's *Pope's Villa at Twickenham* in 1808. His review, though far above average in its mode of expression provides an example of the reading of moral sentiment into the meaning of a painting.

> Its author [Turner] developed the mysteries of the arcana of affinities between art and moral sentiment. The tranquil state of the human intellect, like that of a river, is the time when it is most susceptible of reflection. At such a time the mind, willingly enthralled by a certain feeling of melancholy pleasure, is instinctively led to compare the permanency of nature herself with the fluctuations of fashion and the vicissitudes of taste; and in the scene before us, the Thames flows on as it has ever flowed, with silent majesty, while the mutable and multifarious works which hands have erected on its banks, have mournfully succeeded each other.[66]

The "melancholy pleasure" and refined moral elevation produced by such paintings and the associations they evoked depended largely on a knowledge of romantic poetry, an experience of the subtle connotations of landscape gardening and a leisurely mode of existence. By midcentury most patrons of art lacked these amenities. Although they still looked for paintings to provide them with provocative associations, these associations were geared more to the sentiments provided by a bustling middle-class life, views from the kitchen window and poetry in the *Keepsake* and *Book of Beauty.* Painters and critics responded to this change in patronage with paintings and critical criteria reflecting a more mundane sentiment that emanated from the heart rather than the mind.

This sentimental response to paintings or to the natural scene might not come naturally; the viewer must be schooled in the appropriate trains of associations. This schooling was provided most vividly by Archibald Alison, but associationism was very much in the air during the early and middle part of the nineteenth century. Alison was discussed and referred to with familiarity in writings on art, and the word "associationism" was a frequently used one in art criticism. Alison emphasized the state of reverie into which the viewer would fall as he contemplated a painting. "We lost ourselves amid the number of images that pass before our minds," Alison wrote, "and we awaken at last from this play of fancy, as from the charm of a romantic dream."[67] Many of Thackeray's criticisms describe a similar experience. On seeing a painting of Rome he confessed that "reminiscences rushed back on a sudden with affecting volubility."[68] Maclise's *Olivia and Malvolio,* he acknowledged, "creates for the beholder a very pleasant melancholy train of thought as every good picture does in its kind."[69] When in the Louvre, Thackeray claimed that he could not pass Poussin's *Landscape with Diogenes* "without bearing away a certain pleasing dreamy feeling of awe and musing."[70] This process of evoking associations allowed for a very free response which might have little do with the artist's intentions. Thackeray was quick to point this out, describing each painting as having its "own private existence, independent of the progenitor." The same painting, he admitted, "inspires one man with joy that fills another with compassion."[71] Alison had met this objection by demanding that the painter carefully and consciously control the train of associations arising out of a painting by keeping to a single emotional mood and by reiterating that mood in all parts of that painting. Thackeray, too, expected the artist to control the associations evoked by the painting. The artist's choice of proper subject matter supported by the innuendoes suggested by the clearly demarcated details and facial expressions would lead the viewer to follow the charted train of associations and arrive at the desired sentimental response.

Thackeray admitted that topographical scenes and landscapes evoked many associations, but they did not appeal to him. "I do not care a fig for all the old town-halls in the world," he confessed, "though they be drawn ever so skillfully." To Thackeray the human situation was more provocative and capable of striking the heart. "The most sublime, beautiful, fearful sight in all nature," he wrote, "is surely the face of man, wonderful in its expressions of grief or joy, daring or endurance, thought, hope or pain."[72] His reaction to Turner's *Slavers Throwing Overboard the Dead and Dying* and to François Biard's *Slave Trade,* reviewed sequentially in 1840, makes clear his preference for the close observation of human expression. He calls Turner's painting a "most tremendous piece of colour that ever was seen; it sets the corner of the room on fire."[73] But, he asks, is it sublime or ridiculous? It does not move him as Biard's painting does. The *Slave Trade* depicts a group of blacks captured by an African chieftain who are being turned over to the slave traders. In particular Thackeray is moved by the face of a woman who is being branded by a trader. "I never saw anything so exquisitely pathetic as that face. God Bless you Monsieur Biard, for painting it!" he exclaimed. "It stirs the heart more than a hundred thousand tracts. It must convert every man who has seen it."[74] Turner has been judged the superior painter to the forgotten Biard, and Turner's painting is far more tumultuous, yet it is less moving to Thackeray. In Biard's painting he can see the posture of the bodies and the expression of the faces and empathize with the pain and grief.

Associationist criticism most frequently focused on landscape scenes or those scenes with poetic, literary, or moral themes, but Thackeray also described the associations of patriotic fervor, Christian love, and childhood memories. Of human situations wrought with emotional associations, childhood must rank very high. Certainly Victorian painters, and in particular Thomas Webster, played on this theme most successfully. Webster's *Leaving School* exhibited in 1842 released a poignant stream of associations in Thackeray.

> Oh, that first night at school; those bitter, bitter tears at night, as you lay awake in the silence, poor little lonely boy, yearning after love and home. Life has sorrows enough, God knows, but I swear, none like that! I was thinking about all this as I looked at Mr. Webster's picture, and behold it turned itself into an avenue of lime-trees, and a certain old stile that led to a stubble-field; and it was evening, about the 14th of September, and after dinner, (how that *last* glass of wine used to choke and burn in the throat!) and presently, a mile off, you heard, horribly distinct, the whirring of the well-known Defiance coach wheels. It was up in a moment—the trunk on the roof; and bah! from that day I can't bear to see mothers and children parting.[75]

Patriotism also had strong emotional associations for the Victorians. The *Fighting Temeraire*, one of the few paintings by Turner which gained Thackeray's unreserved approval moved him to a eulogy on the old champions of British battles. "We Cockneys feel our hearts leap up when we recall them to memory," he declared, "and every clerk on Thread-needle Street feels the strength of a Nelson, when he thinks of the mighty actions performed by him." Turner, Thackeray claims, "makes you see and think of a great deal more than the objects before you." Thackeray's associations on this occasion, as on many others, turn to music. The *Fighting Temeraire,* he declares, "when the art of translating colours into music or poetry shall be discovered, will be a magnificent national ode."[76]

Thackeray praised Biard, who moved his heart to moral sentiments; Webster, who led him to reminisce about the pathos of childhood; Turner, who lifted him to patriotic fervor; and Eastlake, who elevated him to the purity of religious feelings. That feeling he described as "a calm that comes not of feeling, but with the over-

flowing of it—a tender yearning sympathy and love of God's beautiful world and creatures.'"[77]

Thackeray compared the associations evoked by Eastlake's best paintings to something heavenly. On the other hand the wrong kind of subject matter and treatment could lead to evil and ugly associations. Some of the *Keepsake* prints, for example, rendered art "little better than a kind of prostitution." Thackeray was particularly harsh in condemning sensuality. He wondered if Etty's works should be shown in public and viewed the *Keepsake* prints as far from innocent. "Ladies in voluptuous attitudes and various stages of deshabille," he described them, contrived "to awaken dormant sensibilities of misses in their teens or tickle the worn out palates of elderly rakes and roués.'"[78]

Paintings with morbid associations also gained his disapproval. Of Delacroix, he asks, "How can you manage with a few paint-bladders and a dirty brush, and a careless hand, to dash down such savage histories as these, and fill people's minds with thoughts so dreadful?'"[79] Whenever he passes the section of Delacroix's paintings in the Louvre, he turns his head away and looks at the painting of a fat woman with a parrot on the opposite wall. The "convulsionary school," he calls Delacroix and his ilk, and accuses them, like Racine of dealing in "sparkling undertaker's wit.'"[80]

Thackeray liked paintings "full of gladness, vigour and sunshine," but he will not abide the overly sentimental either. He is particularly harsh on Richard Redgrave and the "fiddle-faddle," "namby-pamby" style of "milk-and-watery pathos.'"[81] Of Redgrave's *Governess,* Thackeray wrote, "This is, indeed, a love of lollypops with a vengeance, a regular babyhood of taste, about which a man with a manly stomach may be allowed to protest a little peevishly, and implore the public to give up such puling food." The incident is an everyday occurrence, not high tragedy. "If we are to cry for every governess who leaves home," he observed, "what a fund of pathos the *Times* advertisements would afford daily.'"[82]

Thackeray has often been dismissed as an art critic because, it is claimed, he is too literary. But given the context of Victorian criticism, this is an unfair accusation. Unlike many of his critical colleagues he did not weave little stories around the paintings he reviewed. He reported his responses, described the associations invoked by the paintings, and gave a substantial account of technical competence. One of his most humorous reviews, in fact, satirizes his colleagues' propensities to indulge in idle fancies and to write narratives to accompany the actions depicted in the paintings. In reviewing Etty's *Prodigal Son* in 1838, he adopts an inflated prose to describe in melodramatic terms the welcome home of the despairing prodigal. He creates brief biographies of the "dear, kind, stout, old mother" with her tears and prayers, "the poor young thing down in the village" who has pined for his return, the neighbor boy, gone to college and now deep in debt, and the old housekeeper and butler who kill the Guernsey calf. Thackeray even enumerates a mock menu including calf's head soup, boiled knuckle of veal, veal cutlets, calf's foot jelly, and eleven other delicacies provided by the fatted calf.[83]

Thackeray's sense of humor is evident in his art criticism. He usually frames the comments on paintings with humorous vignettes concerning the misadventures of Michael Angelo Titmarsh. Although he is more serious in the main body of the criticism, his satiric wit is not wholly restrained. His satire operates most frequently in artful choice of words and descriptive phrases, but occasionally, as in his criticism of the *Prodigal Son,* it flourishes in a more sustained parody. His humor was also evident in his criticism of Charles Landseer's *Return of the Dove to the Ark,* which Thackeray reviewed in 1844. He severely reprimanded Landseer for not treating the subject with the reverence and respect that it deserved. "The ark is vulgarized here and reduced to the proportions of a Calais steamer," he complains, "the animals like real animals, and the dove is only a girl's pet."[84] What would happen, he asks, if all poetic themes were treated so familiarly. His sense of humor leads him to imagine paintings of Hector shaving before going to face Achilles, or Priam in a nightcap, and Hecuba in curl papers asleep in their fourposter as Troy is being sacked. Thackeray felt Charles Landseer took too many liberties with his subject, trivializing a religious theme and seeking easy popularity by turning it into a genre painting. If Thackeray argued for more commonplace subjects that touched the heart, he did not wish to have subjects of a more elevated nature demeaned. He effectively demonstrated the point of his criticism through his witty examples.

Any judgment of Thackeray's art criticism must take into account the fact that he was writing as a journalist faced with deadlines and the necessity of appealing to a public. In most instances he is reviewing exhibitions and is limited to commenting on the paintings exhibited. He is guilty of inconsistencies and largely neglects landscape painting. He does not develop a system of aesthetics, leaving his readers to piece together one as best they can. But he can provide an insight into the Victorian sensibility that turned away from the heroic themes of academic painting to the commonplace sentiments of genre painting. Like most Victorians he is moved by the affective aspects of art.

He is remorseless in denouncing the sham, the pretentiousness, and the morbid and licentious themes of academic art to celebrate the manly, vigorous "sentiment of reality" to be found in the best of genre painting. The "sentiment of reality," Thackeray's own term which he used in writing of Dickens, exemplifies his own outlook and points to his unique contribution to Victorian art criticism.[85] Thackeray took the older criterion of truth to nature and shifted its import to realism. In practical terms this meant a greater commitment to photographic verisimilitude, and it included a much broader spectrum of subject matter and even justified a more popular judgment of taste. Ultimately in Thackeray's aesthetics the sentiment that a painting can invoke gauges its truth or reality. The sentiment is largely based on associations suggested by the subject matter. Thackeray most vividly describes these associations but strictly monitors their propriety. The artist must choose a proper subject and treat it in a manner that leads these trains of associations to culminate in the desired sentiment. It is in his sensibility to the quality of sentiment, in his tying of sentiment to reality, and in his pungency of expression that the main interest in his art criticism lies. Twentieth-century sensibilities are not compatible with this way of looking at painting, but if modern viewers are to understand Victorian art, they must be willing to try to let their associations flow and their hearts be moved. William Makepeace Thackeray's art criticism can provide an exemplary guide for this exercise.

Notes

1. Edward M. White, "Thackeray's Contributions to *Fraser's Magazine,*" in *Studies in Bibliography; Papers of the Bibliographic Society of the University of Virginia,* ed. Fredson Bowers, Vol. 19, 1966, pp. 67-84.

2. Issues of *Fraser's Magazine,* the *National Standard,* and *Ainsworth's Magazine* were examined at the Dartmouth College Library, Houghton Library, and the Harvard College Library. The review from the *Times* is reprinted in Harold Strong Gulliver, *Thackeray's Literary Apprenticeship* (Valdosta, 1934), pp. 112-13. Thackeray's contributions to the *Morning Chronicle* are reprinted in *Contributions to the Morning Chronicle,* ed. Gordon N. Ray (Urbana: Univ. of Illinois Press, 1955), pp. 27-30; 142-53. Thackeray's articles in the *Pictorial Times* are reprinted in *Stray Papers, Being Stories, Reviews, Verses and Sketches (1821-1847),* ed. Lewis Melville (London: Hutchinson, 1901). Many of Thackeray's art criticisms from *Fraser's Magazine* are reprinted in various editions of his *Works.*

3. Thackeray's essay on George Cruikshank has been reprinted in two separate editions: *An Essay on the Genius of George Cruikshank,* edited with a prefatory note on Thackeray as an artist and art critic by W. E. Church (London: George Redway, 1884) and *An Essay on the Genius of George Cruikshank* (London: Henry Hooper, 1840). The review of John Leech's book is in the *Quarterly Review,* Vol. 96, 1854-55.

4. Reprinted in "Contributions to *Punch,* Etc." in *Works,* Vol. 6 (Biographical Edition, New York, London: Harper and Brothers, 1898), and in various other editions of *Works.*

5. The essay on English humorists can be found in various editions of the *Works* (Louis Marvy, *Sketches after English Landscape Painters,* with short notices by W. M. Thackeray [London: David Bogue, n.d.]).

6. *The Letters and Private Papers of William Makepeace Thackeray,* ed. Gordon N. Ray (Cambridge: Harvard Univ. Press, 1945), I, Letter 74, p. 262.

7. Ibid., Letter No. 87, p. 291.

8. "A Pictorial Rhapsody; Concluded," *Fraser's Magazine,* Vol. 22, Jul. 1840, pp. 114-15.

9. "Strictures on Pictures," *Fraser's Magazine,* Vol. 17, June 1838, p. 759.

10. "A Second Lecture on the Fine Arts," *Fraser's Magazine,* Vol. 19, June 1839, p. 746.

11. "Letters on the Fine Arts; No. 3, The Royal Academy," *The Pictorial Times,* 13 May 1843, in *Stray Papers,* ed. Lewis Melville (London: Hutchinson, 1901), p. 216.

12. *Fraser's Magazine,* Vol. 22, July 1840, p. 113.

13. Ibid., p. 115.

14. "An Exhibition Gossip," *Ainsworth's Magazine,* Vol. 1, 1842, p. 321.

15. *Fraser's Magazine,* Vol. 17, June 1838, p. 761.

16. "A Pictorial Rhapsody," *Fraser's Magazine,* Vol. 21, June 1840, p. 729.

17. *Fraser's Magazine,* Vol. 19, June 1839, p. 745.

18. Ibid., Vol. 17, June 1838, p. 763.

19. Ibid., p. 761.

20. Ibid., p. 760.

21. Ibid., p. 761.

22. Ibid., Vol. 21, June 1840, p. 725.

23. Ibid.

24. Ibid.

25. Ibid., Vol. 17, June 1838, p. 760.

26. *Ainsworth's Magazine,* Vol. 1, 1842, p. 319.

27. Ibid., p. 320.

28. *Fraser's Magazine,* Vol. 21, June 1840, pp. 726-27.

29. *Ainsworth's Magazine,* Vol. 1, 1842, p. 320.

30. "A Dictionary of Principles and Terms of Art," *The Artist's Repository and Drawing Magazine,* Vol. 4, n.d., pp. 21-25.

31. *Annals of the Fine Arts,* Vol. 3, 1818, p. 88.

32. "May Gambols," *Fraser's Magazine,* Vol. 29, June 1844, p. 706.

33. *Fraser's Magazine,* Vol. 21, June 1840, p. 725.

34. Sir Joshua Reynolds, *Discourses on Art* (London: Collier-Macmillan, 1966), pp. 43, 46.

35. "Miscellanies," Part 1, *The Artist's Repository and Drawing Magazine,* Vol. 5, n.d., p. 109.

36. *Fraser's Magazine,* Vol. 17, June 1838, p. 759.

37. "Our Annual Execution," *Fraser's Magazine,* Vol. 19, Jan. 1839, p. 67.

38. Ibid.

39. *Fraser's Magazine,* Vol. 21, June 1840, p. 726.

40. Ibid., Vol. 19, June 1839, p. 744.

41. "On the French School of Painting," *Fraser's Magazine,* Vol. 20, Dec. 1839; citation quoted from reprinted version in *"Sketch Books," Works,* Vol. 5, pp. 44-45 (Biographical Edition, New York, London: Harper, 1898).

42. *Fraser's Magazine,* Vol. 21, June 1840, p. 724.

43. Ibid., Vol. 20, Dec. 1839, in *Works,* Vol. 5, pp. 45, 48.

44. Ibid., p. 52.

45. "Picture Gossip," *Fraser's Magazine,* Vol. 31, June 1845, p. 714.

46. "The Exhibition at Paris," *Times,* 5 April 1838, rpt. in Gulliver, p. 213.

47. *Fraser's Magazine,* Vol. 29, June 1844, p. 707.

48. Ibid., Vol. 24, July 1841, p. 200.

49. "A Word on the Annuals," *Fraser's Magazine,* Vol. 16, Dec. 1837, p. 761.

50. "On Men and Pictures," *Fraser's Magazine,* Vol. 24, July 1841, p. 200.

51. Ibid.

52. *Fraser's Magazine,* Vol. 20, Dec. 1839, in *Works,* Vol. 5, pp. 45, 48.

53. "Caricatures and Lithography in Paris," *Paris Sketch Book,* in *Works* (Biographical Edition, New York, London: Harper, 1898), Vol. 5, pp. 164-65.

54. Ibid.

55. *Fraser's Magazine,* Vol. 20, Dec. 1839, in *Works,* Vol. 5, p. 56.

56. "Letters on the Fine Arts; No. 3, The Royal Academy," *Pictorial Times,* 13 May 1843. Citation from reprinted version in *Stray Papers,* ed. Lewis Melville (London: Hutchinson, 1901), p. 213.

57. *Fraser's Magazine,* Vol. 24, July 1841, in *Works,* Vol. 23 (London: Smith & Elder, 1886), p. 181.

58. "Letters on the Fine Arts; No. 2, The Objections against Art Unions," *Pictorial Times,* I, 8 Apr. 1843. Citation from reprinted version in *Stray Papers,* ed. Lewis Melville (London: Hutchinson, 1901), p. 210.

59. Ibid., p. 211.

60. *Fraser's Magazine,* Vol. 20, Dec. 1839, in *Works,* Vol. 5, p. 56.

61. *Fraser's Magazine,* Vol. 17, June 1838, p. 759.

62. Ibid., Vol. 21, June 1840, p. 725.

63. Ibid.

64. Ibid., Vol. 19, June 1839, p. 745.

65. Ibid., Vol. 21, June 1840, p. 725.

66. *Review of Publications of Art,* Vol. 1, 1808, p. 158.

67. Archibald Alison, *Essays on the Nature and Principles of Taste,* 4th ed. (Edinburgh, 1815), Vol. 1, p. 6.

68. *Fraser's Magazine,* Vol. 31, June 1845, p. 713.

69. Ibid., Vol. 22, July 1840, p. 113.

70. *Fraser's Magazine,* Vol. 20, Dec. 1839, in *Works,* Vol. 5, p. 55.

71. *Fraser's Magazine,* Vol. 24, July 1841, p. 186.

72. Ibid., Vol. 22, July 1840, p. 115.

73. Ibid., Vol. 21, June 1840, p. 731.

74. Ibid.

75. *Ainsworth's Magazine,* Vol. 1, 1842, pp. 321-22.

76. *Fraser's Magazine,* Vol. 19, June 1839, p. 744.

77. Ibid., Vol. 21, June 1840, p. 724.

78. "A Word on the Annuals," *Fraser's Magazine,* Vol. 16, Dec. 1837, p. 758.

79. *Fraser's Magazine,* Vol. 24, July 1841, p. 200.

80. Ibid., Vol. 29, June 1844, p. 712.

81. Ibid., Vol. 24, July 1841, p. 188; Vol. 29, June 1844, pp. 703-4; Vol. 31, June 1845, p. 716.

82. Ibid., Vol. 31, June 1845, pp. 716-17.

83. Ibid., Vol. 17, June 1838, pp. 763-64.

84. Ibid., Vol. 29, June 1844, p. 703.

85. *Letters* [*The Letters and Private Papers of William Makepeace Thackeray*], Vol. 2, Letter No. 772, p. 772.

Juliet McMaster (essay date spring-summer 1981)

SOURCE: McMaster, Juliet. "Funeral Baked Meats: Thackeray's Last Novel." *Studies in the Novel* 13, nos. 1-2 (spring-summer 1981): 133-55.

[*In the following essay, McMaster characterizes themes of death and deterioration in Thackeray's novel* The Adventures of Philip. *In spite of the work's morbid subject matter, McMaster contends, the book is characterized by an underlying "lively" quality, largely because of the "chaotic energy and vitality" of its protagonist.*]

The wedding of Philip Firmin and Charlotte Baynes is a very dismal affair. Although the Pendennis children, the bridesmaids, are rigged out in new dresses and bonnets for the occasion, "everybody else looked so quiet and demure, that when we went into the church, three or four street urchins knocking about the gate, said, 'Look at 'em. They're going to be 'ung.' And so the words are spoken, and the indissoluble knot is tied. Amen. For better, for worse . . ." (p. 484).[1] The reader is teasingly required to choose his interpretation—the decisive words that are spoken could be either the marriage service or the urchins' pronouncement, and the indissoluble knot could refer as readily to the noose as to holy wedlock. It is no surprise to hear that the celebration afterwards is not very merry: "The marriage table did coldly furnish forth a funeral kind of dinner." The incident and narration are typical of *The Adventures of Philip,* Thackeray's last novel, in the alignment of love with death, and in the portrayal of a social ritual that is grimly accompanied by the rattle of the bones.

Philip is in many ways a tired novel, a book of the declining years, as Thackeray himself and many readers have admitted. It is characterized by a low-pressure narrative, a hero we cannot sympathize with, reactionary social attitudes,[2] lapses in inspiration. And yet it is also galvanized by an intense though intermittent energy, which erupts in the brawling violence of the protagonist, Philip, and in the irascibility and occasional panic of the narrator, Pendennis. At the literal level it is often languid, as we lounge in the Pendennis drawing room and listen to cozy snatches of domestic chat: fervid but obtuse morality from Laura, whimsical and half-hearted self-defense from Pen. But at the metaphoric level we have death, murder, violence, horror. The combination is not always successful. But it can be deeply disturbing, as the characters grope for life and health, and feel their capable strong hands touching some ghastly memento mori; and it can be humorous, too, Thackeray here having developed a taste for the macabre to match Dickens's. Thackeray's last completed novel, in fact, has much in common with Dickens's, *Our Mutual Friend,* in that both are almost obsessively concerned with death.

The social vision in **Philip** is one of the respectable arrangements of society as forming a thin crust over the abyss. Death has of course always had its prominent place in Thackeray's novels. His characters do their feverish social climbing in the context of mortality: Becky's sparkling smile collapses into the haggard grimace of guilt in her unguarded moments, Sedley and Osborne and all their successes and failures are mown down in the same chapter by time's fell hand, and Jos in Brussels performs his comic routine with his valet with the present fear of death upon him.[3] In **Philip** this vision is intensified, and our sense of the fragility of the respectable facade becomes keener, and the interest in the facade itself less, in proportion as what it fronts becomes insistent. Thackeray discovers endless ways of envisaging the tidy surface, the horror beneath.

The Twysdens, among the scores of social ménages that he creates in his work, are especially remarkable for the distance between the pretension and the reality. Becky and Rawdon in Curzon Street certainly put up a more glittering front, but then they do not really fool or seriously try to fool anyone, for everyone knows they are living on nothing a year and that the crash will come sooner or later. But the Twysdens keep up an agonized and desperate pretense—they starve themselves in private in order to throw lavish dinners, and gush about love and duty while clawing for the highest bidder in the marriage market. Their prestige is maintained at a ghastly expense, while they shudder under scanty coverlids or before niggard fires. The grave yawns under their paltry devices in economy: "My love, I have saved a halfpenny out of Mary's beer. Isn't it time to dress for the duchess's; and don't you think John might wear that livery of Thomas's who only had it a year, and died of the smallpox?" (p. 110). The next livery for John will be his shroud. The running head for this passage is "Thrift, thrift, Horatio." One would certainly expect funeral baked meats to be carefully preserved in that family. Indeed we see Mrs. Twysden prudently looking forward to the marriage tables as she leaves Philip alone with Agnes:

> Mamma, I say, has left the room at last, bowing with a perfect sweetness and calm grace and gravity; and she has slipped down the stairs . . . to the lower regions, and with perfect good breeding is torturing the butler

on his bottle-rack—is squeezing the housekeeper in her jam-closet—is watching the three cold cutlets, shuddering in the larder behind the wires. . . . And meanwhile our girl and boy are prattling in the drawing room.

(p. 113)

The billing and cooing go on over "the lower regions," a hell complete with appropriate tortures for the domestic Ixion.

In the person of Mrs. Baynes, another matron who stretches every nerve and sinew to maintain the family gentility, the strain is more apparent, and the demon visibly snarls behind the social simper: "She would pay us the most fulsome compliments with anger raging out of her eyes. . . . It was 'Oh, how kind you are to her, Mrs. Pendennis! How can I ever thank you and Mr. P., I am sure'; and she looked as if she could poison both of us, as she went away, curtsying and darting dreary parting smiles" (p. 245).

The smile that is a social mask to conceal sentiments anything but joyful is vividly envisaged in the description of Dr. Firmin, another character who conceals impending ruin behind a display of prosperity.

> By the way, that smile of Firmin's was a very queer contortion of the handsome features. As you came up to him, he would draw his lips over his teeth, causing his jaws to wrinkle (or dimple if you will) on either side. Meanwhile his eyes looked out from his face, quite melancholy and independent of the little transaction in which the mouth was engaged. Lips said, "I am a gentleman of fine manners and fascinating address, and I am supposed to be happy to see you. How do you do?" Dreary, sad, as into a great blank desert, looked the dark eyes.

(p. 24)

That is one of the many powerful passages in **Philip,** and the doctor's smile is another of the images of the thin veneer that is a front for desperation, like the footman's livery contaminated by small-pox, or the lovers' courtship conducted over the hell of the servants' hall. It is quite characteristic of the progress of the novel that the smile should presently be viewed as detachable. Madame de Smolensk, running a genteel boardinghouse on the brink of bankruptcy, always dresses elegantly for dinner among her boarders: "the worthy woman took that smile out of some cunning box on her scanty toilet-table—that smile which she wore all the evening along with the rest of her toilette, and took out of her mouth when she went to bed, and to think—to think how both ends were to be made to meet" (p. 277).

One of the successful comic sequences of the novel is that where General Baynes, wretchedly guilty at having agreed to break the match between Charlotte and Philip, becomes so hot-tempered in his own defense that when his old friend and then his brother-in-law point out his shabby conduct he feels obliged to challenge them, successively. As the retired military men, who for years have been relegated to domestic roles, square their stooped shoulders and talk of honor, recruiting seconds, and sending messages, according to the approved ritual, they are interrupted by the incursion of another ritual— the general's wife comes to see if they will join her table at whist. Another panicky smile must be summoned: "The bloodthirsty hypocrites instantly smoothed their ruffled brows and smiled on her with perfect courtesy" (p. 388). The stirring of murderous instincts in the genteel boardinghouse affords an occasion for a lot of well-managed comic business, as the boarders look on in shocked excitement, the wives join the row, and Philip, the young man at issue, dramatically bursts into the center of the action. The story at the literal level maintains the comedy and averts tragedy, for in the event "the fratricidal bullet" is not fired (p. 405); but the violence is done at the metaphorical and psychological level. While Baynes is fighting off the monitors who keep reiterating the unwanted promptings of his own conscience, the narrator moves into a macabre psychological allegory:

> Baynes will out-bawl that prating monitor, [an incommodious conscience] and thrust that inconvenient preacher out of sight, out of hearing, drive him with angry words from our gate. Ah! in vain we expel him; and bid John say, not at home! There he is when we wake, sitting at our bed-foot. We throw him overboard for daring to put an oar in our boat. Whose ghastly head is that looking up from the water and swimming alongside us, row we never so swiftly? Fire at him. Brain him with an oar, one of you, and pull on! Flash goes the pistol. Surely that oar has stove the old skull in? See! there comes the awful companion popping up out of water again, and crying, "Remember, remember, I am here, I am here!"

(p. 395)

This is the major sphere of action in *Philip*; the events of the story are jaded, unexciting, and often the narrator can hardly bother to narrate them. But the panic and hatred within, the irrational fantasies and suppressed desperation that find their strangled expression in gestures and images—this is the major stratum of interest, erupting recurrently into the cooler world of social accommodation.

The sense of impending explosion is strong at the outset of the novel, when Dr. Firmin's past sexual and financial sins rumble in the background and finally burst into light, to make his son possibly illegitimate and certainly penniless; no wonder Philip feels his home is mined, and claims, "I walk with a volcano under my feet, which may burst any day and annihilate me" (p. 141). The other main movements in the action similarly evoke the violent internal upheaval, the serene exterior. General Baynes benignly welcomes Philip as his daughter's suitor, because the marriage would usefully cancel his financial obligation to Philip; the narrator can see the implications of his benignity: Charlotte is to be "her father's ransom" (p. 256), and later the image of her as Iphigenia to her father's Agamemnon is developed. The cozy romantic arrangements are motivated by more than love. The Little Sister, too, adopts the seductive mannerisms of courtship in order to snare Tufton Hunt when she steals the forged bill from him. "'Law bless me, Mr. Hunt,' then says the artless creature, 'who ever would have thought of seeing *you,* I do declare!' And she makes a nice cheery little curtsy, and looks quite gay, pleased, and pretty; and so did Judith look gay, no doubt, and smile, and prattle before Holofernes" (p. 558).

The fascinating interplay between death and the niceties of social behavior at one point moves the narrator to speculate, "If a gentleman is sentenced to be hung, I wonder is it a matter of comfort to him or not to know beforehand the day of the operation?" (p. 158). Execution is a recurrent source of imagery. As nemesis encroaches, Dr. Firmin speculates on the form his "execution" is to take: "A day passes: no assassin darts at the doctor as he threads the dim opera-colonnade passage on his way to his club. A week goes by: no stiletto is plunged into his well-wadded breast as he steps from his carriage at some noble patient's door. Philip says he never knew his father more pleasant, easy, good-humoured, and affable than during this period" (p. 158-59). Agnes Twysden's marriage to Woolcomb is also an "execution" (p. 188). And Pendennis savors the neat justice of the fact that Dr. Guillotin himself was decapitated by his own efficient machine (p. 217).

Mental discomfort is recurrently envisaged as physical pain. A hostile review of Pendennis's latest publication is elaborated as a flogging (p. 217); Philip in his jealousy broods Othello-like on "daggers, ropes, and poisons, has it comes to this?" (p. 177); Charlotte's parents in trying to separate her from Philip "stab her to the heart" (p. 410), and "stretched Philip on an infernal rack of torture" (p. 412). And Charlotte in turn tortures her rival in the affections of her children, the Little Sister: "Tortures I know she was suffering. Charlotte had been stabbing her. Women will use the edge sometimes, and drive the steel in" (p. 546). Some of this metaphorical violence, of course, is fairly routine inflated language, familiar enough in romance, and even here satirized in the posturings of the absconded swindler Dr. Firmin, whose letters enlarge on the agonies of exile and the thorns of life on which he bleeds. And some of the hyperbole is deliberately deflated by the narrator's humorous tone, as when he finds himself quite by mistake beginning to feel sorry for Mrs. Baynes: "If I contemplate that wretched old Niobe much longer, I shall begin to pity her. Away softness! Take out thy arrows, the poisoned, the barbed, the rankling, and prod me the old creature well, god of the silver bow!" (p. 426). But often there is an almost hysteric intensity in the vision, that endues moments in *Philip* with the chilling power of Gothic. Mrs. Baynes, the "cruel, shrivelled, bilious, plain old woman" (p. 410), gathers something of the force of nightmare. "You should have seen that fiend and her livid smile, as she was drilling her gimlets into my heart," says Philip of his mother-in-law; "I can see her face now: her cruel yellow face, and her sharp teeth, and her grey eyes" (p. 364). And the coolly callous remark of Tufton Hunt, who proposes to blackmail the Doctor, has the fine Thackerayan power of understatement: "I prescribe bleeding" (p. 95).

His wife has become so terrible to General Baynes that at night he hides under the counterpane and "lies quite mum" for fear she should discover he is awake and proceed to "torture" him. Contemplating such violence and fear in apparently harmonious domestic relations, the narrator is moved to wonder why more husbands do not resort to the bolster, like Othello, and then comments on his comment, "Horrible cynicism! Yes—I know. These propositions served raw are savage, and shock your sensibility; cooked with a little piquant sauce, they are welcome at quite polite tables" (p. 409). The metaphor is an appropriate one for *Philip,* which within the bounds of a fiction palatable to the readership of the *Cornhill*[4] still has as its staple the raw propositions that, under the polite forms and energetically maintained surfaces, husbands and wives torment each other, parents victimize their children, and people lay traps and pounce on victims.

The culinary metaphor is one of many, for Thackeray develops the view of human relations as carnivorous, as a system of people devouring people. The image is not new in his work,[5] but here it occurs with such frequency as to be almost a theme in itself. Often the reference is jocular, as in the conversation about Pendennis and his mother in the opening pages:

> "My dear, if that child were hungry, you would chop off your head to make him broth," says the doctor, sipping his tea.
>
> "Potage à la bonne femme," says Mr. Pendennis. "Mother, we have it at the club. You would be done with milk, eggs, and a quantity of vegetables. You would be put to simmer for many hours in an earthen pan . . ."
>
> (p. 2)

It is not mere joking. Helen Pendennis, as we remember from the earlier novel, has as her family crest a pelican feeding her young with her blood, and maternal self-sacrifice is her métier. As Pen eats mother soup, Philip may dine off minced wife. "If [that dish which you liked] consisted of minced Charlotte . . . you know she would cheerfully chop herself up, and have herself

served with a little cream-sauce and sippets of toast" (p. 510). Another item on the cannibal menu is hashed author: Mugford the editor "likes always to have at least one man served up and hashed small in the *Pall Mall Gazette*" (p. 218). When Philip understands his good fortune in having escaped marriage with Agnes Twysden, he sees her as anthropophagous: "I might have been like that fellow in the *Arabian Nights,* who married Amina—the respectable woman, who dined upon grains of rice, but supped upon cold dead body" (p. 272). Dr. Firmin is a father who feeds off his own offspring.[6] His recurrent plunder, first of Philip's fortune and then of his income, is seen as a process of drawing blood. "My patriarch has tied me up, and had the knife in me repeatedly," says Philip. "He does not sacrifice me at one operation; but there will be a final one some day, and I shall bleed no more" (p. 555). Pendennis concurs that "that devouring dragon of a doctor had stomach enough for the blood of all of us" (p. 554). After he has cheated his son of his inheritance, the doctor spreads the rumor that it was the son who ruined his father. This second betrayal by which the father throws his son to the wolves is envisaged in elaborate detail:

> Have you never heard to what lengths some bankrupts will go? To appease the wolves who chase them in the winter forest, have you not read how some travellers will cast all their provisions out of the sledge? then, when all the provisions are gone, don't you know that they will fling out perhaps the sister, perhaps the mother, perhaps the baby, the little, dear, tender innocent? Don't you see him tumbling among the howling pack, and the wolves gnashing, gnawing, crashing, gobbling him up in the snow? Oh, horror—horror!
>
> (p. 378)

It is quite characteristic of Thackeray's habit of admitting in himself the sins he castigates in others that eventually he should see the writer as an ogre too. In that fascinatingly self-regarding passage in which he counts his words as he writes them, and calculates how much he will get paid for them, and how he can feed his family and servants on the proceeds, he eventually concludes, "Wife, children, guests, servants, charwoman, we are all actually making a meal off Philip Firmin's bones as it were" (p. 522).

In *Philip* Thackeray spreads wide what he says in more concentrated form in his *Roundabout Paper* on **"Ogres,"** which he wrote in the course of the novel's serial run. Here at the outset the author himself is an ogre, hungrily approaching a topic for his monthly essay: "I came to my meal with an ogre-like appetite and gusto. Fee, faw, fum! Wife, where is that tender little Princekin? Have you trussed him, and did you stuff him nicely, and have you taken care to baste him, and do him, not too brown, as I told you? Quick! I am hungry!" (XVII, 519-20). With similar gusto he expatiates on the social behavior and domestic habits of ogres, creating a gruesome personnel of Humguffins, and Raw-heads, and tossing off grisly jokes: "And if Lady Ogre-ham happens to die—I won't say to go the way of all flesh, that is too revolting . . ." (XVII, 523). His main thesis is that "there is no greater mistake than to suppose that ogres have ceased to exist. We all *know* ogres. Their caverns are round us, and about us." He explains:

> I mean, madam, that in the company assembled in your genteel drawing-room, who bow here and there and smirk in white neckcloths, you receive men who elbow through life successfully enough but are ogres in private: men wicked, false, rapacious, flattering; cruel hectors at home; smiling courtiers abroad; causing wives, children, servants, parents, to tremble before them, and smiling and bowing as they bid strangers welcome into their castles.
>
> (XVII, 522)

That is the vision of family and social relations in **Philip,** though there it is worked out in realistic terms as well as at the more violent metaphorical level. The really savage, pitiless people are those who should be your nearest and dearest.[7] It is within their own families that the ogres bare their sharpened fangs. Philip is robbed by his father, and betrayed by his cousin-fiancée. Charlotte is sacrificed and cheated by her mother. The two pathetic Misses Boldero are left in pawn by their mother, who skips without notice from Madame de Smolensk's boardinghouse, leaving her bills unpaid and her daughters dependent on the cheated landlady. The marriages too are ogrous. There is more than a hint that Dr. Firmin effectually did away with Philip's mother (who presumably went the way of all flesh); Mrs. Baynes terrorizes her husband, Woolcomb beats his wife. Mrs. Twysden, as we have seen, entertains guests who smirk in white neckcloths at the price of cheating and victimizing her servants. These are the people who are smiling courtiers abroad but ogres in private. "I say, there are men who have crunched the bones of victim after victim; in whose closets lie skeletons picked frightfully clean" (XVII, 522). Dr. Firmin, of course, has skeletons both figurative and literal on his premises, having a guilty past and an anatomical specimen, "a dilapidated skeleton in a corner," which has been used for medical studies.

The vision of intimate relations as a process of devouring modulates from the comic to the horrible. The two parents are the characters in whom Thackeray best realizes the potential of his cannibal theme for an intense balance between humor and horror. Dr. Firmin, with his flashing diamond ring and his patent subterfuges, is manifestly a posturing humbug, whose portrait is sold for a few shillings to his creditors amidst roars of laughter. But even when his poses and his humbug are taken into account, he remains a figure of powerfully sinister proportions. Mrs. Baynes is an absurd snob, and Philip and Pendennis gleefully expose her boardinghouse pre-

tensions. But she too is never finally put down, but, in being associated with Lady Macbeth and vampires, continues to inspire dread. As a farewell embrace to her daughter, we hear, she "put a lean, hungry face against Charlotte's lip" (p. 445). The grotesque vision of the ogre crunching bones has been pared down to the adjectives, "lean, hungry." But the image as vividly conveys greed and possessiveness unmitigated by gentleness or tolerance. There are ogres all round us.

Dr. Firmin is not only a devourer; in certain aspects he is Death incarnate.[8] It is around him that Thackeray clusters his imagery of death most insistently. His residence is on Old Parr Street—"It *is* a funereal street, Old Parr Street, certainly; the carriages which drive there ought to have feathers on the roof, and the butlers who open the doors should wear weepers" (p. 18). In this gloomy setting, as symbolically laden as Spenser's Cave of Despair, he makes his house a museum of mementos mori, which include his own portrait:

> Over the sideboard was the doctor, in a black velvet coat and a fur collar, his hand on a skull, like Hamlet. Skulls of oxen, horned, with wreaths, formed the cheerful ornaments of the cornice. On the side-table glittered a pair of cups, given by grateful patients, looking like receptacles rather for funereal ashes than for festive flowers or wine. Brice, the butler, wore the gravity and costume of an undertaker.
>
> (p. 16)

And his surgery, once a dissecting room for medical students, is equipped with a special side door for "having *the bodies* in and out" (p. 19). Not only does Dr. Firmin handle skulls and possess skeletons, he is himself a kind of death's-head, having "very white false teeth, which perhaps were a little too large for his mouth, and these grinned in the gas-light very fiercely. On his cheeks were black whiskers, . . . and his bald head glittered like a billiard-ball" (p. 7). In certain lights, we are reminded, his eye sockets are mere shadowy hollows under his brow (p. 197)—an effect that Walker attempted to capture in his illustration for Number 5. His medical vocation, which one would expect to make him a healing and life-giving figure, in fact does the opposite, as his function of counting his patients' heartbeats acts rather like Death's hourglass in a Danse Macabre. He "hangs on to the nobility by the pulse," we hear (p. 76), and he is thus depicted in the initial to the first chapter. In fact at the outset we hear how he neglects his son in his serious illness in order to minister to a "grand dook" (p. 3). When Tufton Hunt sees Firmin's carriage in the unfashionable district of Tottenham Court Road, where the doctor claims to have patients, he produces one of his worn-out Latin tags: "'Pallida mors aequo pede—hey, doctor? . . .' 'aequo pede,' sighs the doctor, casting up his fine eyes to the ceiling" (p. 124). There is the possibility for the double reading again. According to one we are dealing with the affected humbug with his pretentious display of school-boy Latin quotations; according to the other we can see him as pallid death himself, calling impartially on rich and poor. It is another of the features of the Danse Macabre that the agile skeleton comes in many guises, and his grinning teeth and bony shins may protrude from palmer's weeds or cardinal's robes. The doctor's appurtenances, his watch and his diamond ring and his scented handkerchief, and his habit of "smiling behind his teeth," affect one like the disguises of Holbein's Death.

But although in Dr. Firmin we find an almost allegorical personification of death, he is only the most obvious manifestation in a novel that deals in mortality at large. Pen and Philip meet at Grey Friars, now remembered as a multiple graveyard ("I think in the time of the Plague great numbers of people were buried there" [p. 9]), and establish their adult relationship over the loss of their mothers—"When Philip Firmin and I met again, there was crape on both our hats" (p. 21). We have many glimpses of the chilling or welcome summons of death. Again Thackeray hovers between the horrible and the facetious. Madame de Smolensk's clientèle, who are in all conscience a rather ghoulish gathering, are once imagined as being augmented by a group of Banquo-like revenants: "If twenty gibbering ghosts had come to the boarding-house dinner, madame would have gone on carving her dishes, and smiling and helping the live guests, the paying guests; leaving the dead guests to gibber away and help themselves" (p. 278). Considering the assembly literally present are by no means all paying guests, we find the figure is a little more than hypothetical.

In Lord Ringwood we are shown a worldly old reprobate who is haunted not so much by fear of his own death in the future as by the ghosts of his dead past, including his own dead self. He dare not stay in his own town mansion when he is in town (his irrational terror has a certain pathos, like that of General Baynes, hiding under the counterpane from his wife), because there he is haunted by the family portraits, "ghostly images of dead Ringwoods—his dead son, who had died in his boyhood; his dead brother attired in the uniform of his day; . . . Lord Ringwood's dead self, finally, as he appeared still a young man, when Lawrence painted him. . . . 'Ah! that's the fellow I least like to look at,' the old man would say, scowling at the picture" (p. 303). His death, when it occurs, is the occasion for the familiar display of pomp and ceremony. We get the *Times* obituary verbatim, with its solemnity about how "the Lord of many thousand acres, and, according to report, of immense wealth, was dead" (p. 320). Golden lads and girls all must (it seems), as chimney sweepers, come to dust. The initial for that chapter, a skull with a coronet, is a fit emblem for a large part of the novel. Indeed throughout the novel the chapter initials, which

Thackeray continued to execute himself after he had delegated the full-page illustrations to Walker,[9] provide a further set of variations on the theme of mortality.

The influence of Ringwood's death spreads to the Christmas pantomime, attended by the Pendennis family, and presently Pendennis is as gloomy as though he were at a burial (p. 322). As narrator Pendennis is our vehicle for the consciousness of mortality.[10] One memorable passage shows him as more than half in love with easeful death himself. He professes to be glad his youth is over, glad that the pains of life are nearer at their end than their beginning, glad he does not have to live through again the thousand ills that flesh is heir to:

> No. I do not want to go to school again. I do not want to hear Trotman's sermon over again. Take me out and finish me. Give me the cup of hemlock at once. Here's a health to you, my lads. . . . Ha! I feel the co-o-ld stealing, stealing upwards. Now it is in my ankles—no more gout in my foot: now my knees are numb. . . .
>
> What is this funeral chant, when the pipes should be playing gaily, as Love, and Youth, and Spring, and Joy are dancing under the windows?
>
> (p. 238)

It is a remarkable soliloquy, and representative again of the general tone and theme of *Philip,* which is half the time celebrating energy and vitality, and the other half giving way to the death wish; half the time studying the frantic struggle to maintain an appearance, the other half exposing beneath the fixed smile the grin of the death's-head. The narrative again becomes a funeral chant at the death of General Baynes, whose passing is the occasion for the narrator to picture again his own death, and this time the reader's too: "A drive to the cemetery, followed by a coach with four acquaintances dressed in decorous black, who separate and go to their homes or clubs, and wear your crape for a few days after—can most of us expect much more?" Writer, reader, pauper, hero, are all required to keep in mind "how lonely they are, and what a little dust will cover them" (p. 443).

* * *

Pendennis as the narrator is much more prominent in *Philip* than he was in the similar set-up in *The Newcomes,* where he was again the biographer of a younger friend from Grey Friars. In fact his increased prominence has been considered as one of the faults of the novel, since the unlimited license he takes to launch into a Roundabout-Paper-like digression inevitably takes its toll on the pace of the narrative. We have here a structure something like that of *Tristram Shandy,* where the narrator ostensibly intends to write the story of his Uncle Toby's amours, but is always writing about himself, whether he is progressing in or digressing from his other narrative. "But the story is not *de me*—it regards Philip," Pendennis is always obliged to remind himself (p. 553); "I feel that I am wandering from Philip's adventures to his biographer's," he apologizes again (p. 607). In fact, of course, the Pendennis digression, like the Shandean one, is "digressive, and it is progressive too—and at the same time,"[11] for Pen is as much Thackeray's (and his own) real subject as Philip.[12] This writer has long been aware that there is no such thing as an objective history, and so long as a history must be subjective, it is just as well that the reader should know something of whose subjectivity he is dealing with. Pendennis is explicit enough about the limitations of his point of view to make it clear that the Jamesian critics would have little to teach him: "People there are in our history who do not seem to me to have kindly hearts at all; and yet, perhaps, if a biography could be written from their point of view, some other novelist might show how Philip and *his* biographer were a pair of selfish worldlings unworthy of credit: how Uncle and Aunt Twysden were most exemplary people, and so forth" (p. 618). However, the narrator is ready to accept the responsibility for his subjective account: "This I say—*Ego*—as my friend's biographer," he announces boldly (p. 618). It is worth examining a little more the content of the subjectivity of the "friend's biographer."

Philip Firmin, clearly enough, is one of Thackeray's projections of himself. If Henry Esmond was a "handsome likeness," a rather delicate, formal, and self-satisfied self-portrait, Philip is the big, shouldering, boisterous, imprudent, undignified troublemaker part of Thackeray that John Carey has called the Prodigal.[13] The biographical parallels with Thackeray's own career are clear enough, and have been pointed out by Ray[14] and others. Philip is described at the outset as "A brave, handsome, blundering, downright young fellow, with broad shoulders, high spirits, and quite fresh blushes on his face, with very good talents (though he has been woefully idle, and requested to absent himself temporarily from his university), the possessor of a competent fortune and the heir of another" (p. 46): in all but the "handsome," he resembles Thackeray at the same age. Then, again like Thackeray, he loses the fortunes, dabbles in law, becomes a hack writer, falls in love with a childlike girl in the Paris of the reign of Louis Philippe and imprudently marries her, and proceeds to try to support a growing family on the inadequate earnings of his pen. Mrs. Baynes is Mrs. Shawe as Charlotte is Isabella. There are recognizable points of detail too. Philip, disappointed of the side dishes at Mugford's dinner when the celebrated Mr. Lyon sends word he is not coming (p. 221), is again Thackeray, who was deprived of ortolans when his hostess heard Dickens could not attend her dinner.[15] And Mrs. Baynes reneges on the payment of her daughter's income as did Mrs. Shawe.

It is equally clear that Pendennis is also Thackeray. He also has been through the storms of youth that he witnesses in Philip—the imprudent early marriage, the writing for a living; and, barring the ever-clinging Laura, his professional and domestic situation is clearly enough identified with his author's. The authorial "I" often refers to the historical author rather than the fictional one. The first part of the Little Sister's history, we hear, "I myself printed some twenty years ago" (p. 132)—in fact of course Thackeray had not yet invented Pendennis in 1840, when he published *A Shabby-Genteel Story.* In manner, too, he seems to have touched in details of the self-portrait. Ray describes, in the older Thackeray, the mixture between the rigid propriety of his bearing on formal occasions, and the great warmth and complete unreserve in convivial company and among children.[16] "His manner is cold," says Mrs. Mugford of Pendennis, "not to say 'aughty. He seems to be laughing at people sometimes. . . . But he is a true friend, Mrs. Brandon says he is. And when you know him, his heart is good" (p. 307). There are other details: Pendennis, like Thackeray, was given an embroidered waistcoat which was so flamboyant he scarcely dared wear it (p. 262); Pendennis, like Thackeray, agonizes over having made a fool of himself in delivering an after-dinner speech (p. 607).[17]

All of this has been often noticed and well enough documented—Thackeray evidently drew on elements of his own experience for both of his two main characters. But the special feature here, it seems to me, is that Pen is Thackeray the Older, looking at Philip, who is Thackeray the Younger. The self-consciousness here is so intense as to be something like Donne's "dialogue of one." Thackeray, braver than Lord Ringwood, is ready to look his "dead self" firmly in the eye, and come to terms with it—or at least to make the attempt.

It is beyond the scope of this paper to examine fully the implications of this narrative stance; but if we do see the novel as the late Thackeray's view of his early self, we have a means of accounting for some of the things in it that have bothered many readers. Pendennis's unfailing sympathy for his turbulent friend, whose failings he frequently acknowledges but never punishes,[18] is readily understandable. He is not the one to bring down poetic justice on himself, although he tries to live up to his claim that in his account he has nothing extenuated, nor set down aught in malice (p. 329).

Criticism of Thackeray has often focussed on the change in him that seems to have occurred at about the time of *Vanity Fair.* Gordon Ray sees the change as beneficial, as an access of sympathy and humanity that enlarged the scope of his work and enabled him to enter The Age of Wisdom.[19] Joseph Baker finds the change to be for the worse, *Philip* being a "recantation" of the admirable values embodied in *Vanity Fair*; and John Carey has recently argued for a Thackeray who, after the satiric triumphs of the early work, sold out to a flabby Victorian establishment.[20] Thackeray's own view of the matter, if that is indeed what we have in *Philip,* is certainly of interest.

Pendennis is obviously both envious and faintly ashamed of Philip. He knows himself to be more talented and intelligent, as well as more successful, but he cannot help admiring the unfailing ability of the young man to live straightforwards, unreflectingly encountering his life and unselfconsciously responding to it. Philip is outspoken, knowing what he thinks and likes and dislikes, and pronouncing his convictions with force if not subtlety: when he reviews a work, he declares it is "written by the greatest genius, or the greatest numskull that the world now exhibits" (p. 112). As for his judgments of people, "In the man whom he hates he can see no good; and in his friend no fault" (p. 639). In the face of these extremes, Pendennis is rather apologetic about his qualified judgments, his tact, and his prudently equivocal pronouncements. He acknowledges in advance some of Carey's accusations, and parodies his own tactful compositions. There *was* a time, he says, in his youth, when he had been called "a dangerous man":

> Now, I am ready to say that Nero was a monarch with many elegant accomplishments, and considerable natural amiability of disposition. I praise and admire success wherever I meet it. I make allowance for faults and shortcomings, especially in my superiors; and feel that, did we know all, we should judge them very differently. People don't believe me, perhaps, quite so much as formerly. But I don't offend: I trust I don't offend.
>
> (p. 58)

Such honest self-exposure, prompted by a scrutiny of the difference between the past and present selves, is a triumph of self-recognition. Pendennis's readiness to acknowledge the admixture of good even in villains—in another passage he defends Iago, Tartuffe, Macbeth, and Blifil, and suggests they have been much maligned (p. 307)—is the mark of the creator of characters like Becky, Major Pendennis, Beatrix, and Dr. Firmin. Philip would not be capable of creating such complex amalgams of good and evil. But he might have written *Catherine,* the book intended to show that the defense of criminals is immoral.[21]

Philip's independence of class is another characteristic that Pendennis cannot help admiring, being achingly dependent on it himself. "He is one of the half-dozen men I have seen in my life," records Pendennis, "upon whom rank made no impression" (p. 264). Philip, though he has a fine taste in wine, can drink beer cheerfully among Bohemian cronies when he has lost his money, and he can and does tell his great-uncle Lord Ringwood to go to hell (p. 310)—a gesture that sets Pendennis fairly trembling. On the other hand, though Philip is no snob, he is thoroughly arrogant. His independence is born of a habit of command that he retains even when he has not the money to maintain the status of an independent gentleman. He is no republican, as his patronage of the Little Sister and his resentment of Mugford's familiarities testify. The young Thackeray may have been an outspoken castigator of snobbery, but he too took his stand on being a gentleman. Pendennis's more reflective class-consciousness would at least have saved him from some of the unpleasantness that Philip causes—for instance in insulting the amiable Mrs. Ravenswing.

Philip, in this dialogue of one, makes some judgments on his biographer too: "'You call me reckless, and prodigal, and idle, and all sorts of names, because I live in a single room, do as little work as I can, and go about with holes in my boots: and you flatter yourself you are prudent, because you have a genteel house, a grave flunkey out of livery, . . . to wait when you give your half dozen dreary dinner parties. Wretched man! You are a slave: not a man'" (p. 271). Since Thackeray is the creator of both incarnations of himself, of both Philip's accusations and Pendennis's self-exposure, we can at least assume that he has grown in humility. Philip is not prone to self-analysis or self-accusation; it is Pendennis and Thackeray who can discover and contemplate the image of their present self as slavish.

Pendennis's faculty for self-examination does not make him any the happier. He is the writer of *Vanity Fair,* who aims at achieving an increase in consciousness, rather than an anaesthetizing entertainment: "This, dear friends and companions, is my amiable object—to walk with you through the Fair, to examine the shops and the shows there; and that we should all come home after the flare, and the noise, and the gaiety, and be perfectly miserable in private" (*Vanity Fair,* ch. 19). In *Philip,* as we have seen, it is not so much the external panorama we examine, the shops and the shows, as the internal prospect, the pain and the fury that is within and behind the show. Or rather, Philip watches the shops and the shows, Pendennis watches Philip, and Thackeray watches Pendennis watching Philip.[22] We have here something like a Thackerayan version of *The Heart of Darkness,* with Philip as the young idealist Kurtz, Pen as the Kurtz who has seen "the horror"—and, perhaps, Thackeray as the Marlow whose experience and wisdom encompass both.

It is Pendennis who, like Thackeray, has the haunting consciousness of mortality upon him; and perhaps that is partly why both seek out and admire the chaotic energy and vitality of Philip.[23] In a passage which Thackeray transcribed in a letter to the Baxters,[24] thus accentuating its personal ring, Pendennis writes, "indeed, it is rather absurd for elderly fingers to be still twanging Dan Cupid's toy bow and arrows. Yesterday is gone— yes, but very well remembered; and we think of it the more now we know that To-morrow is not going to bring us much" (p. 71). The portrait of the dead self is executed by the dying self.

But for all that, I would still say **Philip** is a very lively book, for a book about mortality.

Notes

1. For my text of *The Adventures of Philip* I use volume 16 of *The Oxford Thackeray,* ed. George Saintsbury, 17 vols. (London: Oxford Univ. Press, 1908).

2. See Joseph E. Baker, "Thackeray's Recantation," *PMLA,* 77 (1962), 586-94. Baker's suggestion that Thackeray "became a pillar of 'The Establishment' after having started as an 'Angry Young Man'" has found recent support in the general thesis of John Carey that after *Vanity Fair* Thackeray sold out to gentility (*Thackeray: Prodigal Genius* [London: Faber and Faber, 1977]).

3. In her powerful study of *Vanity Fair,* Dorothy Van Ghent singles out this episode as one to which we react "with an impulse of horrified laughter—the intuitive horror having no other outlet than in a sense of the absurd" (*The English Novel: Form and Function* [New York: Rinehart, 1953], p. 146). Similar effects are frequently achieved in *Philip.*

4. Thackeray as editor of the *Cornhill* was very cautious about possible offense to his readers, and rejected a story of Trollope's because it was about adultery. See *Letters and Private Papers of William Makepeace Thackeray,* ed. Gordon N. Ray (London: Oxford Univ. Press, 1945-46), IV, 206-8.

5. In his fine chapter on the suggestiveness of food and drink in Thackeray's fiction John Carey singles out the siren, the cannibal woman like Becky, as "a recurrent Thackeray nightmare" (p. 88).

6. I have discussed the father-son relation in *Philip* in *Thackeray: The Major Novels* (Toronto: Univ. of Toronto Press, 1971), pp. 216-19.

7. Joseph Baker and, more recently, Jack P. Rawlins, have been offended by the cozy cliquishness in *Philip,* according to which Pendennis adopts an attitude of My Hero Right or Wrong, and the gentlemen stick together. Baker sees this exclusiveness as a travesty of the parable of the Good Samaritan, which Thackeray invokes in his title, because it misses the point of the parable, which is that the traveller who has fallen among thieves is aided not by his own kind, but by an outsider, a

Samaritan. But Thackeray is concerned here less with class alignments than with familial ones. Both the thieves and the uncharitable Levites are generally of the traveller's own tribe—Dr. Firmin, the Twysdens and the Ringwoods; while those who aid him are those on whom he has no direct claim—the Pendennises, Madame de Smolensk, and Dr. Goodenough. See Baker, cited above, and Jack P. Rawlins, *Thackeray's Novels: A Fiction That Is True* (Berkeley: Univ. of California Press, 1974), p. 224.

8. I have touched on this aspect of Dr. Firmin in "Thackeray's Things: Time's Local Habitation," in *The Victorian Experience: The Novelists,* ed. Richard Levine (Athens: Ohio Univ. Press, 1976), pp. 59-60.

9. See John Harvey, *Victorian Novelists and Their Illustrators* (London: Sidgwick and Jackson, 1970), p. 102.

10. I am indebted to a fine paper by Ina Ferris, "Narrative Strategy in *The Adventures of Philip,*" delivered at the conference of the Association of Canadian University Teachers of English at London, Ontario, 25 May 1978.

11. *Tristram Shandy* [1759-69], I, ch. 22.

12. See Ferris.

13. Carey, *Thackeray: Prodigal Genius.*

14. Gordon N. Ray, *Thackeray: The Uses of Adversity (1811-46)* (London: Oxford Univ. Press, 1955), pp. 149, 183, 186, 219; *Thackeray: The Age of Wisdom* (1847-1863) (London: Oxford Univ. Press, 1958), pp. 387 ff.

15. See *Letters* [*Letters and Private Papers of William Makepeace Thackeray*], III, 455.

16. Ray, *Thackeray: The Age of Wisdom,* pp. 323-24.

17. See *Letters,* II, 540.

18. Rawlins discusses the lack of consequence between action and judgment in the plot of *Philip,* pp. 215 ff.

19. See "*Vanity Fair*: One Version of the Novelist's Responsibility," *Essays by Divers Hands,* 25 (1950), 87-99, as well as his two-volume biography.

20. Baker, "Thackeray's Recantation"; Carey, *Thackeray: Prodigal Genius,* especially pp. 9-33.

21. Compare Rawlins: "[Thackeray's] career essentially begins in a response to Bulwer-Lytton's glorification of murder in *Eugene Aram*; Thackeray's determination to cut through the glitter of style and expose the hard truth of moral absolutism

cuts too deeply, and he ends up [in *Philip*] writing a book sanctioning 'a glorious crime, a most righteous robbery'" (p. 225).

22. I might note here another stage in the interpretations of this novel. Baker saw it as a study of class cliquishness; Rawlins points out that "Thackeray's clique is much more exclusive," a small group of friends (pp. 224-25). The present reading further restricts the circle of essential interest—to the author's contemplation of himself. Thackeray acknowledged that "Writing novels is . . . thinking about one's self" (*Letters*, III, 645)—this is more than usually true of *Philip*.

23. It is interesting to note that whereas in mid-career Thackeray drew on recent experience for the most intense relationships in his novels (Ray has convincingly demonstrated the connection of Jane Brookfield with Rachel Esmond), later he excavated his earlier past. The pains and joys of his courtship of Isabella, and particularly the agony of the parent's attempt at match-breaking, are recalled in the relation of George Warrington and Theo in *The Virginians* as well as in that of Philip and Charlotte. Thackeray showed this process of the progressive recollection of the past in the dying delirium of Colonel Newcome, who briefly but consistently lives his life backwards into childhood (*The Newcomes*, ch. 80).

24. *Letters*, IV, 214.

Judith L. Fisher (essay date autumn 1982)

SOURCE: Fisher, Judith L. "The Aesthetic of the Mediocre: Thackeray and the Visual Arts." *Victorian Studies* 26, no. 1 (autumn 1982): 65-82.

[*In the following essay, Fisher illustrates connections between Thackeray's appreciation of the visual arts and his literary sensibility. Fisher concludes that Thackeray's "aesthetic of mediocrity" reflects a fundamental aversion to extreme emotion.*]

"What a marvellous power is this of the painter's! How [*sic*] each great man can excite us at his will. . . . How much instruction and happiness have we gained from these men, and how grateful should we be to them!"[1] So Thackeray summed up his love of art in 1840. He tried to pass on his enthusiasm to readers through his art criticism. Thackeray felt obliged to ensure that the middle-class patrons of art had a "gentlemanly" taste, even as he realized that his art world was primarily a marketplace: "You each do your duty in your calling, and according to your genius, but you want to be paid for what you do. . . . You will do

nothing dishonest in the pursuit of your trade; but will you not yield a little 'to the exigencies of the public service?'"[2] In art criticism as well as in fiction, as Gordon Ray has noted, Thackeray attained his position among his contemporaries "chiefly by redefining the gentlemanly ideal to fit a middle-class rather than an aristocratic context."[3] His consciousness of his bourgeois audience showed in his basic aesthetic position—in his rejection of the heroic sublime in favor of mediocre or beautiful art.

Mediocre art was genre, landscape, and narrative painting suitable for the family parlour and dining room. Thackeray praises the "pleasures of mediocrity" and admits that "I think in my heart I am fonder of pretty third-rate pictures than of your great thundering first-rates."[4] His "third-rates" generally told a story with a moral and aroused the sympathy of the viewer. As simplistic as this painting may sound, based on such art works, Thackeray evolved a social and visual aesthetic. His likes and dislikes in art were moral choices, not just visual preferences. Thackeray believed that "high" or sublime art, typified by classical sculpture and High Renaissance painting, tempted viewers to indulge in dangerous passions which would disrupt their social and domestic responsibilities. Art on the lowest end of the aesthetic scale—"namby-pamby" art as Thackeray called it—encouraged a falsely romanticized perception of life.[5]

I

Thackeray's artistic taste was nurtured in his childhood and confirmed in his youthful attempt to be a painter. The coldness and, in Thackeray's eyes, brutality of the English public school, Charterhouse, where the awkward, sensitive boy endured ragging and loneliness, contrasted sharply with the domestic warmth of Larkbeare in Devon where "King Billy" ruled over all, even the Queen Mother, Mrs. Carmichael-Smyth. Thus the family hearth represented love and security while the outside masculine world only threatened. It is important to note that Thackeray's early essays into drawing were caricatures done at Charterhouse and landscapes and domestic scenes from Larkbeare.

The positive morality associated with the home was strengthened during Thackeray's two tenures in Parisian *ateliers* (1833, 1834-35). The studios of Edmund Le Poittevin, Lafond, and Baron Antoine Jean Gros, where Thackeray worked, stressed the French tradition of grandiose history painting demanded by the École des Beaux Arts and Académie. As Thackeray spent his requisite hours copying plaster casts of antique statuary and imitating the "masters" at the Louvre, he gradually discovered that not only was his talent smaller than he had originally thought, but also that there was an inherent insincerity in a typical upper-middle-class Englishman trying to paint the fall of Troy or the Battle of Water-loo. (Years later when Thackeray was to describe the Battle of Waterloo in *Vanity Fair,* he would concentrate on the domestic viewpoint—the women left behind.)

Thackeray nevertheless delighted in the freedom and camaraderie of the studio, remembering the art students in after years as "the kindest folk alive" and reveling in their "innocent gaiety" and "jovial suppers."[6] But his own strict sense of propriety, fostered by his mother's evangelicalism, made Thackeray critical of what he considered to be the lax morals which accompanied the French art students' free behavior. During his second stay in Paris, Thackeray found the "merriment and hu-mour" of the artists to be undignified and even im-moral—and, more importantly, he connected their sup-posed moral degeneracy to the quality of their art work.

> The conduct of the model, a pretty little woman, the men & the master of the establishment was about as disgusting as possible—the girl wd not pose but in-stead sung songs & cut capers; the men from sixty to sixteen seemed to be in habits of perfect familiarity with the model; and Lafond himself a venerable man with a riband of honor maintained a complete superior-ity by the extreme bathos of his blackguard-ism. . . .—It is no wonder that the French are such poor painters with all this.
>
> (*Letters* [*The Letters and Private Papers of William Makepeace Thackeray*], I, 277)

To this sense of propriety, shared by his reading audi-ence, Thackeray added professional training as an artist and a naturally discerning eye. Between his Parisian *atelier* experiences, Thackeray studied in London with Henry Sass, a well-known English studio master who taught Daniel Maclise, Frank Stone, and W. P. Frith. Thackeray became and remained close friends with the rising generation of English painters—Maclise, Stone, George Cattermole—and was also instructed for a time by one of the reigning giants of illustration, George Cruikshank. His knowledge of the art world combined with his training and versatility with the pen to make Thackeray the most readable and knowledgeable (despite some of his suspect judgments) of the art crit-ics writing for popular journals. His aesthetic system is not as precise as Ruskin's, and his taste is not as "ex-quisite" as Pater's, but Thackeray's aesthetic choices are an invaluable guide to the growth of middle-class Victorian taste.

In advancing his peculiar aesthetic which, among other values, encouraged viewers to avoid Michelangelo and Poussin (at least to avoid extended exposure), Thack-eray was intensely aware of who his audience was. He was an early example of a Victorian art critic for a par-venu class extremely self-conscious about its respect-ability and uninitiated into the mysteries of art.[7] As Ri-chard Stein has observed, the presence of an untaught

audience merged with the writer's personal aesthetic to produce the phenomenon of a composite aesthetic such as that of Ruskin or Pater which focused on recreating the writer's emotional response to a work of art as a method of teaching the audience how to respond.[8]

Thackeray did not command the same respect among artists as did John Ruskin, W. M. Rossetti, or Walter Pater, for two reasons. Instead of serious aesthetic trea-tises, Thackeray wrote humorous satiric essays designed for the casual reader of popular magazines. His serious aesthetic preferences were usually masked by a comic persona, often Michael Angelo Titmarsh, and even state-ments of moral indignation were expressed in outbursts of comic hyperbole. Underneath his comic mask, none-theless, Thackeray shared Ruskin's view of the basic moral purpose of any work of art. Beauty itself was a moral quality, so good art was inherently didactic. But like Shakespeare's Touchstone or Feste, Thackeray hid his gravity behind a self-ironic harlequin mask, antici-pating the persona of *Vanity Fair.* Thus it was easy to lose sight of the hearty drink under the froth. Thackeray also reflected the mainstream of English middle-class taste. Many of his opinions are identical to those of art critics in other popular journals such as the *Athenaeum* and *Edinburgh Review.* Thackeray's personal favorites, Daniel Maclise, Charles Eastlake, William Henry Hunt, Edwin Landseer, and William Etty, were among the most popular (that is, financially successful) painters of their day. While he disdained some popular movements, such as the Nazarene and Neoclassic, most of the paint-ings he chose to admire and recommend to his audience were cabinet pieces. He found the French Romantics—Delacroix among them—too extreme; Turner he found incomprehensible; and he ignored the Pre-Raphaelites and the burgeoning French Realist school.[9] Thackeray was, however, aware of his inadequacies as when, in *Sketches After English Landscape Painters* (1850), he admitted that Turner was, perhaps, great, but one had to be of the initiate to understand this greatness (*Sketches After English Landscape Painters*). In fact, Thacker-ay's entire aesthetic is based on a recognition of one's inadequacies as much as on his recommendation of the positive values of mediocrity.

Although Thackeray was no Ruskin, he rose above the ordinary hack critic of his time who was sent "indiffer-ently to a police-office or a picture-gallery" (**PR ["A Pictorial Rhapsody"]**, I, 721). Thackeray's criticism and illustrations earned him a considerable reputation with the general public as a man of taste. Russell Stur-gis, for example, writing in 1880 on "Thackeray as a Draughtsman" for *Scribner's Monthly* praised Thack-eray for his genuine artistic ability. Sturgis's opinion was seconded by John Brown and Anthony Trollope who both felt Thackeray never realized his potential as an artist. Trollope wrote in his biography of Thackeray that "looking at the wit displayed in the drawings, I feel inclined to say that had he persisted he would have been a second Hogarth."[10]

Trollope's comparison of Thackeray with Hogarth was based on the elements of caricature in both artists' work. This tendency to pictorial caricature in Thackeray's illustrations appeared in his art criticism as verbal ridicule of artistic pretension. W. E. Church, evaluating the art criticism, noted Thackeray's impartiality and honesty: "In criticising some of his artist contemporaries, he was as nobly fearless as Hazlitt in what he wrote, and equally zealous with Ruskin to promote a taste for everything pure and simple, honest, grand, and beautiful in art. Sham art, gaudy or meretricious art he hated and detested, and derided; while much of the spurious and sickly sentimental art of his time he scorched with the fire of his sarcasm."[11]

Thackeray's impartial criticism distressed artist friends such as Stone and Maclise. Edward Fitzgerald said that Thackeray's "annual comments on the exhibitions were often a great trial to his friends and Frank Stone told him that Thackeray would get himself horse-whipped one day."[12] Thackeray's biting sense of the ridiculous did occasionally make his criticism painful, although not at the expense of its common sense. Like Church, John Brown also compared Thackeray's criticism to Ruskin's when he said it was not "easy to imagine better criticisms of art than those from Mr. Thackeray's hand." His criticism had its seat in reason, and it was more objective, cool, and critical than Ruskin's.[13]

Thackeray wrote forty-one reviews, essays, and blurbs on the arts from 1837 to 1863, most of them between 1837 and 1848. The nature of the writing varies from short satirical "squibs" in *Punch*, usually poking fun at the practices of the Royal Academy of Art, to straightforward reviews of exhibits in London and Paris, some of which develop into lengthy disquisitions on the state of the arts. A third kind of article was the specialized essay on particular artists or media, for instance the studies of John Leech, George Cruikshank, and **"Caricatures and Lithography in Paris."** While writing for the *Pictorial Times,* Thackeray entered into the Art Union controversy (a debate over the aesthetic propriety of raffling off paintings to the masses for a few shillings), his only excursion into the political side of the art world. For Louis Marvy, a French artist and friend who was forced to emigrate to England after the Revolution of 1848, Thackeray wrote text for **Sketches After English Landscape Painters** (1850). And finally he wrote satirical essays such as **"The Artists"** and **"The Painter's Bargain"** which drew heavily on his own artistic experience. Accompanying all this writing were Thackeray's drawings which adorned *Punch, Fraser's Magazine,* and his own novels.

II

Thackeray was primarily interested in contemporary English and French art. When he discussed classical, Renaissance, or neoclassical art, he compared the art of yesteryear with the art of 1840. Surprisingly classical and Renaissance art came off badly in Thackeray's estimation because he felt that their sublimity was too overwhelming for his audience. Classical art was too removed from a Victorian audience by its very perfection: "It carries corporeal beauty to a pitch of painful perfection, and deifies the body and bones truly; but, by dint of sheer beauty, it leaves humanity altogether inhuman—quite heartless and passionless." Classical statues were "monsters of beauty . . . out of the reach of human sympathy." The Thackeray who, as we shall see, valued sentiment above all else in a work of art, cannot sympathize with an art which, although truthful, seemed to imply that "human joy and sorrow, passion and love, were mean and contemptible in themselves" (**PR**, I, 724).

While classical art was unsuitable because it could not touch the human heart, Renaissance and Baroque paintings were inappropriate because they touched the heart—and libido—too deeply. Although Thackeray appreciated the power of Michelangelo and Poussin, he was extremely uncomfortable with their effect on him and could not recommend untrained eyes to see their work more than once. His response to Michelangelo's *Last Judgment,* for example, was a Burkean pain/pleasure reaction: "the spectator's sense amounts almost to pain." This "modern sublime," which Thackeray contrasted to the "Greek sublime," was too intense for a person with ordinary sensibilities. He could not imagine Michelangelo "with our small physical endowments and weaknesses, a man like ourselves" (**FS** [**"On the French School of Painting"**], 682). Michael Angelo Titmarsh (the self-mockery in the surname is evident) tries to disguise the overwhelming effect of a sublime artist like Nicholas Poussin by laughingly comparing his response to drunkenness: "And what is . . . Poussin . . . but romanée-galée,—heavy, sluggish,—the luscious odour almost sickens you; a sultry sort of drink; your limbs sink under it,—you feel as if you had been drinking hot blood" (**FS,** 688).

The extremes of passion represented in such paintings and the disastrous effect of the normal person's response to them evolved, finally, into the siren-figure in Thackeray's novels who entices, tempts, and inevitably brings the male to the brink of moral degradation. In *Pendennis,* the result of Pen's repressed sexual passion for Fanny Bolton, a figure corrupted by cheap romances, is a nearly fatal fever. Nine years earlier Thackeray made the same association between extreme emotional indulgence and illness, using paintings as the dangerous agents. "First-rate paintings," Thackeray claimed, referring to the works of Michelangelo and Poussin again, affect one like a bout of dissipation: "An ordinary man would be whirled away in a fever, or would hobble off this mortal stage in a premature gout-fit, if he too early or too often indulged in such tremendous drink" (**FS,** 688).

But as inhuman as the classical sublime and overwhelming as the "modern sublime" may be, Thackeray, nevertheless, recognized their artistic truth in the very strength of his own response. "Truth" tested by the power of one's response to the work of art was of paramount importance to Thackeray, for the emotional response was the agent for the moral effect of the painting. A false painting was one which expressed insincere emotion, thus arousing either no emotion or a false sympathy in the viewer which would lead either to no moral response, or, possibly, to an immoral response. It was this issue of artistic truth which led Thackeray to reject neoclassicism and other brands of nineteenth-century "high" art, including the traditional category of grandiose history painting. The problem with the contemporary historical mythological paintings of Benjamin West or David Scott was that artists could not possibly know anything of what they painted and simply obeyed some dictum from past "authorities." Thackeray thought that the neoclassic painting of David, romantic pieces by John Martin, and pseudohistorical works like Benjamin Robert Haydon's misled the viewer because they projected a false historical truth, one not grounded in the artist's experience.

Thackeray criticized neoclassical art in particular. The neoclassic failed because modern artists could only follow a formal tradition and were unable to share the vision of their predecessors. Tradition in art had become tyranny, according to Thackeray.[14] Original classical and Renaissance art works were beautiful, but copies of the works or the style were merely pieces of "Drury-Lane" trickery—and the greatest deception of this modern version of the traditional sublime was that people believed it to be the highest art only because they had been told it was so, not because they had had any personal experiences with the values expressed in the paintings. Thackeray's grounds for rejecting neoclassicism were similar to the objections of the French Realist Courbet, who dismissed the historical formula because "the art of painting can only consist of the representation of objects which are visible and tangible for the artist"; therefore the artists of one century are "basically incapable of reproducing the aspect of a past or future century."[15] Formula is indeed the word which characterizes Thackeray's view of this school of painting. In **"On the French School of Painting"** he goes so far as to outline the requirements for a proper neoclassical painting.[16]

The natural consequences of being bound by a tradition one did not understand was that painters resorted to the-atricality, to tricks of form, to achieve the desired effect. The resulting "theatrical heroic," as Thackeray called it in **"Picture Gossip,"** relied on exaggerated and unnatural color, form, and expression, which made the painting sensational instead of sublime. John Martin's *Deluge,* for instance, titillated viewers with its lurid red lighting and immense waves crashing down on tiny figures, but its unnecessary exaggeration conveyed no genuine sentiment or particular understanding of the moral significance of the Flood. To Thackeray "such monstrous theatrical effects are sadly painful," especially when condensed to a canvas of a size suitable for the middle-class parlour.[17] Also falling into the category of theatrical were the *Chevaliers de la Mort,* as Thackeray dubbed the French Romantic artists, who, he felt, had an obsession with death (**FS,** 682-683). In singling out for censure Delacroix's *Massacre at Scio, Medea Going to Murder her Children,* and Guerin's *Cain, After the Death of Abel,* Thackeray was letting his desire for morally edifying subject matter cloud his aesthetic judgment. But the two were one and the same; how could a painting be beautiful if the subject was grotesque? Why should murder, Thackeray asked, "be considered so eminently sublime and poetical?" Such painting may corrupt or mislead artists by making them think they are creating great art when they are simply being animalistic. When a young artist such as Paul Falconer Poole paints a violent picture like *Moors beleaguered in Valencia* in 1844, he may "fancy [he is] exhibiting 'power'; whereas nothing is so easy. Any man with mere instinct can succeed in the brutal in art."[18]

"Mere instinct" was one focal point of Thackeray's distrust of sublime art. Instinct could lead one to extremes of passion which Thackeray identified with the animal. In rejecting passion he was not only rejecting sensuality in the subjects of such paintings as Delacroix's *Massacre* where the violence is voluptuous, but also his own sensuousness as demonstrated in his reaction to Michelangelo. Violence, moreover, is not the only means of arousing extreme passion; much more subtle and effective is the appeal of female sexuality. As Thackeray recoiled from the sensuality of nude models and of his fictional sirens, so he drew back from sensuality in painting. His ambivalence toward William Etty's work illustrates this attitude. Although he could compare Etty's *Judgment of Paris* to Rubens's work and his *Andromeda* to Titian's, he still felt Etty was not for the "profanum vulgus"—another instance of Thackeray protecting the untrained eye (and in this instance, the untrained senses, too). For besides Etty's superb coloring, one must consider what his brush colored: "His figures *are* drawn, and a deuced deal *too much* drawn. A great, large curtain of fig-leaves should be hung over every one of this artist's pictures, and the world should pass on, content to know that there are some glorious colours painted beneath. His colour, indeed, is sublime: . . . but his taste! Not David nor Girodet ever offended propriety so—scarcely even Peter Paul himself" (**SL** [**"A Second Lecture on the Fine Arts"**], 745).

No Etty, Martin, Poussin, Michelangelo, or Praxiteles; painting should reinforce the conventional values, not disturb them. But Thackeray did not frown on all kinds of sublime art; he found a mediocre sublime suitable for public consumption in what he called "Christian art."[19] Not to be confused with Nazarene art (Catholic art in Thackeray's vocabulary) which Thackeray disliked for its pseudomedieval style, the Christian sublime had distinct limitations of subject and treatment. It was a "humbler sort of high art" which by its very humility "may be even more sublime than greatness."[20] Charles Eastlake and his religious works exemplified the Christian artist and painting for Thackeray. Eastlake's piety was expressed on canvas as "a tender, yearning sympathy and love for God's beautiful world and creatures," and created an art which leaves one "in that unspeakable, complacent, grateful condition, which . . . is the highest aim of the art" (**PR**, I, 724-725). If modern sublime art was religious in tone though not always in subject matter, it followed that the office of an artist like Eastlake was sacred: "The great artist who is the priest of nature is consecrated especially to this service of praise [of God]; and though it may have no direct relation to religious subjects, the view of a picture of the highest order does always . . . fill the mind with an inexpressible content and gratitude towards the Maker who has created such beautiful things for our use" (**PR**, I, 724).

This religious sublime substituted sentiment for the terror or awe inspired by the traditional sublime of Michelangelo. Sentiment Thackeray called the "secret of the sublime" and valued it more than technical skill. Thackeray, however, was quick to admit that he could not define sentiment, that it rested "with the individual entirely" (**PR**, I, 725), yet he was nevertheless confident in classifying much Victorian religious painting as "high" art.

III

Thackeray's humbler sublime was really much closer to beautiful or "low" art than to sublime art. In praising Eastlake he turned from negative criticism, rejecting sublimity, to positive criticism, approving mediocre art. As early as 1839 Thackeray noted an improvement in art which was actually a notice of the increase in genre and landscape paintings at the expense of historical art. He claimed that a "great stride has been taken in matters of art" with the rise of the younger Associates of the Royal Academy (**SL**, 743). The genre and literary subjects of Frank Stone, Daniel Maclise, and Charles Robert Leslie, as well as the older works of Sir David Wilkie, suited the Briton's commercial attitude toward art; the canvases were moderate sizes and the subjects

pleasant and undemanding. Thackeray's own preference for the ordinary, or "moderate-sized sublimity" (**EG** [**"Exhibition Gossip"**], 319), was satisfied by the new generation of artists who imitated nature and "painted from *the heart.*"[21] Instead of grand historical subjects, "tales from Hume and Gibbon," and sublime literary subjects such as Milton or Shakespeare's tragedies, these younger artists painted domestic scenes from *The Vicar of Wakefield* and Shakespeare's comedies. Thackeray's ideal of this mediocre painting included "a gentle sentiment, an agreeable, quiet incident, a tea-table tragedy, or a bread-and-butter idyl . . . [which] can be digested by every man" (**L** [**"Letters on the Fine Arts No. 3"**], 3, 136).

The main recommendation of these less pretentious paintings was their sentimental appeal, for while sentiment may have been the secret of the sublime, it was the substance of the mediocre. So important was sentiment that it overrode any fault in execution. In a work like Wilkie's *Grace Before Meat* or Eastlake's *Our Lord and the Little Children,* the expression was the standard by which the painting was to be judged, not the execution. Wilkie's work was "a little misty and feeble, perhaps, in drawing and substance," but "these pictures come straight to the heart, and then all criticism and calculation vanishes at once,—for the artist has attained his great end, which is, to strike far deeper than the sight; and we have no business to quarrel about defects in form and colour, which are but little parts of the great painter's skill" (**SL,** 745). Mediocre paintings were to be read; that is, they contained clues which, if properly interpreted, would reveal the painting's moral to the viewer. To be properly read, however, the subject must be familiar to the audience, thus the emphasis on popular literature and contemporary scenes. The entire emphasis on didacticism led art critics, Thackeray among them, to stress subject, not artistic values.

There was, accordingly, far less criticism of unnaturalness, bad drafting, and poor coloration in Thackeray's discussions of domestic or landscape painting than in his tirades against heroic art. When he was discussing an artist who particularly appealed to him, such as his old teacher George Cruikshank, he would even contradict his own insistence on imitating nature.[22] That Cruikshank's cows did not look like cows mattered "not the least" to Thackeray. After all, "can a man be supposed to imitate everything?" (**GC** [**"George Cruikshank"**], 29). He went so far as to claim in the same article about Cruikshank and a year later in a piece about the Louvre, that faulty execution could actually add to the effect of a painting. Of one of Cruikshank's engravings for *Oliver Twist,* Sykes's farewell to his dog, Thackeray commented, "the poor cur is not too well drawn, the landscape is stiff and formal; but in this case the faults, if faults they be, of execution rather add to than diminish the effect of the picture: it has a strange, wild, dreary, broken-hearted look" (**GC,** 57). Here the stiff-ness of execution gave the engraving a nightmarish quality, and Thackeray found a greater advantage yet in techniques which, while not stiff, were "unschooled." He said he could recognize "spiritual beauties" more easily in artists "whose powers of execution are mani-festly incomplete, than in artists whose hands are skil-ful and manner formed."[23] This assertion, however, glar-ingly contradicts Thackeray's approval of Wilkie, Eastlake, Maclise, Mulready, and Stone, all of whom specialized in the Victorian custom of "finishing" their paintings—hard-edged, niggling drawing covered by several coats of varnish.[24] Yet these painters who did finish were forgiven and admired because their pictures touched the heart.

Thackeray's tolerance for sentiment had its limitations; too much pathos combined with a lack of subtlety pro-duced "namby-pamby" paintings which were over-crowded with clues and sought only to stir extreme pity in the viewer. Such paintings were not didactic, but pa-thetic. Thackeray's favorite scapegoat in this school was Richard Redgrave, whom he always accused of mawkishness. His burlesque description of one version of Redgrave's *The Poor Teacher* (or *The Governess*) suffices to characterize this style.

> The Teacher's young pupils are at play in the garden, she sits sadly in the schoolroom, there she sits, poor dear!—the piano is open beside her, and (oh, harrow-ing thought!) "Home, sweet home!" is open in the music-book. She sits and thinks of that dear place, with a sheet of black-edged note-paper in her hand. They have brought her her tea and bread and butter on a tray. She has drunk the tea, *she has not tasted the bread and butter.* There is pathos for you! there is art! This is, in-deed, a love for lollypops with a vengeance, a regular babyhood of taste.
>
> (**PG** ["Picture Gossip"], 716)

Thackeray called Redgrave's painting "hysterical senti-mentality" and warned against the school whose growth in popularity was causing better painting to "melt away in a deluge of blubber" (**PG,** 717).

Thackeray's main objection to namby-pamby painting was its distortion of nature for the effect of sentiment—similar to his basic reason for rejecting grand historical painting. Adhering to nature, then, is a necessary crite-rion for any level of art. But exactly how did Thackeray define nature and the natural? He used the words to mean fidelity to physical detail, suitability to the audi-ence, and consistency within the art work. Thackeray would agree with Ruskin's assertion that a painter must paint within certain "optical laws,"[25] which at their sim-plest hold that a tree should be a recognizable species of tree, oak or elm, and should be colored as a tree. We find him complaining of William Mulready's color, for instance, as "pleasant, but wrong; we never saw it in

nature" (**PR,** I, 726). In Thackeray's conventional eyes, though, Turner was the most heinous offender against fidelity to natural detail. His pictures of the 1830s and 1840s either abandon or embellish nature; a characteris-tic "fancy picture" by Turner boasted "pea-green skies, crimson-lake trees, and orange and purple grass . . . cataracts, rainbows, suns, moons, and thunderbolts" (**SL,** 744). In contrast to Turner's "monstrosities" were realistic pictures like Maclise's *Gil Blas* which depicted "a poached egg, which one could swallow; a trout, that beats all the trout that was ever seen; a copper pan, scoured so clean that you might see your face in it; a green blind, through which the sun comes; and a wall, with the sun shining on it, that De Hooghe could not surpass" (**SL,** 746).

This contrast between Turner and Maclise typified Thackeray's demand for actuality in painting, or "actu-alité" as he called it (**SL,** 747). If an art work adhered to nature it would represent an immutable reality and, as we see in Maclise, one which was almost tangible. Demand for actuality—the impression that the subject existed as painted—was characteristic of English taste which preferred Dutch still life painters such as Hobbema and the Ruisdels. Thackeray picked on Turner again as the greatest offender against actuality. Even though Turner's *Rain, Steam and Speed* and *The Fight-ing Téméraire* won Thackeray's wholehearted approval for their realism, most of the later Turners disturbed Thackeray by their apparent ability to make something out of nothing.

Accidental discrepancies with nature caused by lack of skill Thackeray could excuse, but he found it hard to forgive the deliberate massacre of what one "really" saw. The very fact that a Turner appeared to be "actual" from a distance and was nothing but blobs of pigment when looked at closely only aggravated Thackeray's sense of betrayal because it was Thackeray's own senses that were being manipulated—he had no control over his own perception. Thackeray's attacks on Turner are pervaded by a sense of outrage at the artist's successful deceptions.

> As the traveller in the desert beholds at a distance pools of the most delightful water and shady palm trees for his camels to rest under, and urging on his footsore dromedary, finds at the desiderated spot that it is all bosh—no water, no date trees, no shade—only sand, rubbish, vanity, and vexation of spirit; so, as you look from afar off at Mr. TURNER'S pictures, you behold all sorts of wonderful and agreeable sights—Venice and the Adriatic flash out in the sunshine; ships loom through the haze at sea, or whales frisk and gambol there . . . but on coming up to the picture, behold it was all an illusion—a few washes of gamboge, putty, and vermillion are flicked over a canvass at hazard seemingly; it is only at a distance that they condescend to take a shape, but near at hand they are as intangible as Eurydice.[26]

This sounds like the Manager of the Performance in *Vanity Fair,* who "sits before the curtain on the boards and looks into the fair" as a "feeling of profound melancholy comes over him in his survey of the bustling place"; melancholy, because as an "experienced and disillusioned observer," Thackeray knew that what went on behind the curtain was "all bosh."

In order for a painting to be actual, however, it must, while faithfully copying nature, be appropriate in its choice and treatment of the subject. We can again refer to Turner as a negative example, but suitability, the second part of Thackeray's definition of the natural, goes beyond the technical and even beyond painting from one's experience to fulfilling the audience's expectations. To be natural, an artist must, like Eastlake or Wilkie, meet the expectations of his genre. Portraits should match their sitters; a politician should look like a politician, an actor like an actor. Malvolio must always be cross-gartered, the Vicar of Wakefield always kind and jovial. Thackeray particularly ridiculed the vulgarization of "great subjects." Charles Landseer's *Noah's Ark* was unnatural because it reduced the ark to "the proportions of a Calais steamer" (**MG** ["**May Gambols**"], 703). As Thackeray said, "it is best to do what you mean to do; better to kill a crow than to miss an eagle" (**MG,** 706).

A painting will not meet the expectations of its audience any more than it will be truthful unless it is consistent within itself. An artist should put nothing in a painting which does not add to the subject and should never overemphasize unimportant elements. Again Thackeray was close to Ruskin who explained realism, specifically Pre-Raphaelite realism, as trying "to conceive things as they are . . . giving every fact its own full power, and every incident and accessory its own true place" (*Art of England,* p. 33). Consistency, Thackeray said while discussing Cruikshank's "Jack's Carving the Name on the Beam" (from Ainsworth's *Jack Sheppard*) required not merely including the right elements but properly subordinating all parts of the picture to the main subject (**GC,** 55-56; **PR,** II, 116). This consistency can also be called propriety and is an adaptation of the eighteenth-century concept of decorum. The resulting idea of nature in art emphasized the permanent, visible, and conventional.

* * *

Thackeray's aesthetic of mediocrity reflected both his quest for reality and his withdrawal from difficult intangibles such as extreme emotion. Although this system was a most effective medium for teaching his public, Thackeray's responses were not merely public aesthetic reactions, but socio-moral reactions to demanding, often tragic art in a world where he found himself "growing more inclined to the pathetic daily" (**PG,** 717). Mediocre art was Thackeray's answer to his own problem: to find a style of art which was satisfying without being disturbing. While high art should be saved for "special occasions," mediocre art was for the pleasure of everyday use.[27] Mediocre art was not simply conservative formally; it actively reinforced one's domestic values. Thackeray recommends that Eastlake's *Our Lord and the Little Children* and *The Salutation of the Aged Friar* be lithographed and made available to people, for these pictures "are such placid, pious companions for a man's study, that the continual presence of them could not fail to purify his taste and his heart" (**PR,** I, 726).

Despite the pleasure mediocre art gave Thackeray, he was always aware of its limitations. It was not a weapon with which to improve the general human condition, but more a means of compromise with modern society whereby people were allowed a certain amount of success and domestic happiness if they gave up striving to be more than they were. Thackeray's novels follow this aesthetic pattern; the protagonists must give up not simply their own false pretenses, but almost any kind of vitality and meaningful social action. Mediocrity was to be enjoyed "in spite" of all things; Thackeray believed that the difficulties of the human situation would remain under any social order, and thus he "can only recommend you to enjoy honestly, to suffer bravely, and to wear a patient face"; we must "accept men and things as they are."[28]

Acceptance of the status quo necessitated two imperatives for Thackeray. Since one would find few heroes in life, one should realize that it is his or her lot to be ordinary, or "mediocre." Upon recognizing this "truth," one should then strive to know one's limitations and live as well as possible within them. Thackeray's belief that the mediocre was the common lot of most people was not without its compensations; after all, it was something to be a productive member of a group. In **"On Men and Pictures,"** Michael Angelo Titmarsh let out an exasperated cry at the folly of pursuing the impossible and emphasized that it was the common person, not the genius, who structured the world we live in:

> Why the deuce will men make light of the golden gift of mediocrity which for the most part they possess, and strive so absurdly at the sublime? What is it that makes a fortune in this world but energetic mediocrity? What is it that is so respected and prosperous as good, honest, emphatic, blundering dulness, bellowing commonplaces with its great healthy lungs, kicking and struggling with its big feet and fists, and bringing an awe-stricken public down on its knees before it?

> (**MP** ["**On Men and Pictures**"], 99)

Three things stand out in Thackeray's statement. First, his attitude toward mediocrity, a supposedly desirable state, is decidedly ambivalent. Although mediocrity is a "golden gift," it is also "blundering dullness." We have the same on-again, off-again attitude in his fiction, for as his protagonists achieve (sink into?) mediocrity, they are increasingly subject to Thackeray's jibes and made to seem almost ridiculously ineffectual—even though they are taking the "righteous path." Moreover, the mediocre is antiheroic as well as antigenius. Fortunes are made by "energetic mediocrity," not exceptional talent. As different from Carlyle as possible, Thackeray defined heroes as "persons with thews and sinews like your own, only they use them with somewhat more activity—with a voice like yours, only they shout a little louder—with the average portion of brains, in fact, but working them more" (**MP,** 99). Finally, Thackeray equated art with life by using the aesthetic term sublime as an emblem of social success. Thus, striving "so absurdly" at sublimity can be a social as well as an artistic phenomenon. Mediocrity, upon closer examination, appears less straightforward than Thackeray superficially presented it.

Significantly for himself and his fiction, Thackeray was careful to point out that the mediocre could be consciously chosen in art and in life. He felt that the artist and the viewing public should make a deliberate choice to adhere to their limitations. Mediocrity should not "fancy itself Genius";[29] it is mediocrity and should not masquerade as anything else. Knowing one's limitations applies to the medium, to the artist, and to the audience. Each artistic medium—oils, water color, sculpture—had its specific limits, and artists should not try to achieve greater effects than their media allowed (**PR,** II, 119). Then, too, artists who were not "gods, Miltons, Michelangelos, that can leave earth" should choose their subjects accordingly (**FS,** 685). For those who stuck to earth, such as Charles Eastlake and W. P. Frith, Thackeray had great praise. Even though he was not a master and lacked "power" in his work, Eastlake should be admired for "his skill in choosing such subjects as are best suited to his style of thinking, and least likely to shew his faults. In the pieces ordinarily painted by him, grace and tender feeling are the chief requisites; and I don't recollect a work of his in which he has aimed at other qualities" (**PR,** I, 726). Frith was even more down to earth; while an "ass will go and take the grand historic walk . . . Mr. Frith prefers the lowly path where there are plenty of flowers growing, and children prattling along the walks" (**PG,** 718). Thackeray saw in Frith a "thorough comprehension of his subject and his own abilities. And what a rare quality is this, to know what you can do!"

Thackeray elaborates his philosophy of the mediocre in his novels in which the protagonists follow a pattern of learning their own limitations through painful experience and come to accept a mediocre life as the one most suitable for them. In the case of Clive Newcome, for instance, it is the delusion of great artistic talent which Clive must finally see as a delusion. For Dobbin, it is the realization that Amelia, the great love of his life, was not worth the wait, and for Henry Esmond, perhaps the most deluded of them all, it is the stunning revelation that the glorious Beatrice has feet of clay. In each case the men settle for domestic tranquility—and know that they are settling for less.

Knowing one's own limitations is well enough; but one's audience, if one is an artist, must acknowledge theirs or they will not accept the art. The greater license allowed by the persona of Michael Angelo Titmarsh perhaps led Thackeray to overstate his genuine belief in the middle-of-the-road ethic. But to him as to Titmarsh, mediocrity was a blessing, and he thought that the public should find it so: "Let us thank Heaven, my dear sir, for according to us the power to taste and appreciate the pleasures of mediocrity. I have never heard that we were great geniuses. Earthy are we, and of the earth; glimpses of the sublime are but rare to us; leave we them to great geniuses, and to the donkeys; and if it nothing profits us, *aerias tentásse domos* along with them,—let us thankfully remain below, being merry and humble" (**FS,** 688).

There is an unspoken desire for safety in this ethic. If one remains earthbound, so to speak, with familiar objects and feelings, one risks nothing on the unknown. To venture into the sublime demands a release of who-knows-what kind of emotion, perhaps even a reorganization of one's perception of reality. The chances are that an untrained eye would be deceived or misled by sublimity or false sublimity—as so many of Thackeray's characters are. Thus he emphasized the visible content of the painting in his aesthetic as did many of his contemporaries. But the visual can mislead too; the final test must be the sincerity of one's emotional response to the visual. A didactic painting which could be "read" and inspired only cheerful associations and gentle emotions was undoubtedly safe. Safe, too, was the greater stimulation of the Victorian sublime. The standard of mediocrity, stemming from Thackeray's personal needs, was also an effective teaching device which as a visual aesthetic encouraged the "best kind of art," and as a moral philosophy in the novels allowed for feeling without passion.

Notes

1. William Makepeace Thackeray, "A Pictorial Rhapsody," *Fraser's,* 21 (1840), 732. Hereafter cited as PR, I in the text.

2. William Makepeace Thackeray, "Letters on the Fine Arts. No. 1: The Art Unions," *Pictorial Times,* 18 March 1843, p. 13. Hereafter cited as L, 1 in the text.

3. Gordon Ray, *The Uses of Adversity 1811-1846* (New York: McGraw-Hill, 1955), p. 13.

4. William Makepeace Thackeray, "On the French School of Painting," *Fraser's,* 20 (1839), 688. Hereafter cited as FS in the text.

5. Thackeray uses the term "namby-pamby" to describe a category of art works in "Picture Gossip," *Fraser's,* 31 (1845), 715. He probably acquired the term from reading Alexander Pope. "Picture Gossip" will hereafter be referred to as PG in the text. For a literary version of the artistic distinction between high and low art, see David Masson, "*Pendennis* and *Copperfield*: Thackeray and Dickens," *North British Review,* 15 (1851), 57-89.

6. William Makepeace Thackeray, *The Newcomes,* 2 vols. (London: Smith & Elder, 1911), I, 219. Similar sentiments appear in Thackeray's early diary. See *The Letters and Private Papers of William Makepeace Thackeray,* ed. Gordon Ray, 4 vols. (Cambridge, Massachusetts: Harvard University Press, 1945), I, 267.

7. For information about the quality of the Victorian art audience, see Frank Davis, *Victorian Patrons of Art* (London: Country Life, 1963); Peter Ferriday, "The Victorian Art Market," *Country Life,* 139 (1966), 1456-58, 1567-78; G. Robert Stange, "Art Criticism as a Prose Genre," in *The Art of Victorian Prose,* ed. George Levine and William Madden (New York: Oxford University Press, 1968); and John Steegman, *Victorian Taste* (Cambridge, Massachusetts: M.I.T. Press, 1971).

8. Richard Stein, *Ritual of Interpretation* (Cambridge, Massachusetts: Harvard University Press, 1975), p. 4.

9. See respectively, FS, 682-683; William Makepeace Thackeray, "A Second Lecture on the Fine Arts," *Fraser's,* 19 (1839), 744. Hereafter cited as SL in the text. Thackeray never mentions either the Pre-Raphaelites or the Realists in any of his criticism.

10. Anthony Trollope, *Thackeray* (London: Macmillan, 1879), pp. 30-31.

11. W. E. Church, *Thackeray as Artist and Art Critic* (privately printed [1890?]), pp. viii-ix.

12. Harold Gulliver, *Thackeray's Literary Apprenticeship* (Valdosta, Georgia: Southern Stationery and Printing Co., 1934), p. 87.

13. John Brown and Henry Lancaster, "Thackeray," *North British Review,* 40 (1864), 133.

14. See, for example, FS, 681: "It was the absurd maxim of our forefathers, that because these subjects had been the fashion twenty centuries ago, they must remain so in *saecula saeculorum*; because to these lofty heights giants had scaled, be-

hold the race of pigmies must get upon stilts and jump at them likewise!"

15. Linda Nochlin, *Realism* (New York: Penguin, 1973), p. 25.

16. The formula is as follows: "Borrowed from statuary in the first place, the colour of the paintings seems as much as possible to participate in it; they are mostly of a misty, stony, green, dismal hue, as if they had been painted in a world where no colour was. In every picture there are, of course, white mantles, white urns, white columns, white statues—those *obligés* accomplishments of the sublime. There are the endless straight noses, long eyes, round chins, short upper lips, just as they are ruled down for you in the drawing-books, as if the latter were the revelations of beauty, issued by supreme authority, from which there was no appeal? [*sic*]" (FS, 681).

17. William Makepeace Thackeray, "A Pictorial Rhapsody Concluded," *Fraser's,* 22 (1840), 117.

18. William Makepeace Thackeray, "May Gambols; or, Titmarsh in the Picture Galleries," *Fraser's,* 29 (1844), 712. Hereafter cited as MG in the text.

19. See William Makepeace Thackeray, "Strictures on Pictures," *Fraser's,* 17 (1838), 758-764 and PR, I, 724 where Thackeray praises the "Christian school."

20. William Makepeace Thackeray, "Exhibition Gossip," *Ainsworth's Magazine,* 1 (1842), 319. Hereafter cited as EG in the text.

21. William Makepeace Thackeray, "Letters on the Fine Arts. No. 3: The Royal Academy," *Pictorial Times,* 13 May 1843, p. 136. Hereafter cited as L, 3 in the text.

22. William Makepeace Thackeray, "George Cruikshank," *Westminster Review,* 34 (1840), 1-60. Hereafter cited as GC in the text.

23. William Makepeace Thackeray, "On Men and Pictures," *Fraser's,* 24 (1841), 104. Hereafter cited as MP in the text.

24. A term used by John Dodds in *Age of Paradox* (New York: Rinehart, 1952), p. 259.

25. John Ruskin, *Art of England* (New York: D. D. Merrill [188-]), p. 41.

26. William Makepeace Thackeray, "Exhibition of the Royal Academy," *Morning Chronicle,* 7 May 1846, in *Contributions to the Morning Chronicle,* ed. Gordon Ray (Urbana: University of Illinois Press, 1955), pp. 147-148.

27. "What a comfort it is, as I have often thought, that they [paintings] are not all masterpieces, and that

there is a good stock of mediocrity in this world, and that we only light upon genius now and then, at rare angel intervals, handed round like tokay at dessert, in a few houses, and in very small quantities only! Fancy how sick one would grow of it, if one had no other drink!" (MP, 101).

28. W. C. Roscoe, "Thackeray's Art and Morality," *National Review,* 2 (1856) in *Thackeray: The Critical Heritage,* ed. Geoffrey Tillotson and Donald Hawes (New York: Barnes & Noble, 1968), p. 278.

29. William Makepeace Thackeray, "Our Annual Execution," *Fraser's,* 19 (1839), 58.

Deborah A. Thomas (essay date summer 1985)

SOURCE: Thomas, Deborah A. "Bondage and Freedom in Thackeray's *Pendennis." Studies in the Novel* 17, no. 2 (summer 1985): 138-57.

[*In the following essay, Thomas examines the thematic tension between constraint and freedom in the novel.*]

I

". . . knowing how mean the best of us is, let us give a hand of charity to Arthur Pendennis, with all his faults and shortcomings, who does not claim to be a hero, but only a man and a brother."[1] With these words, Thackeray concludes *The History of Pendennis,* a novel that Victorian readers commonly admired and modern readers commonly ignore.[2] According to George Saintsbury, who viewed the book as "from first to last . . . prodigal of delights," at the time of creating *Pendennis* "Thackeray must have felt like Prometheus Unbound"—in the sense that the success of *Pendennis*'s predecessor, *Vanity Fair,* had finally brought Thackeray professional recognition and a feeling of his full artistic power (I, xiv-xv, xiii). Ironically, in light of Saintsbury's remark about Thackeray's newfound sense of creative freedom, the closing words of the novel echo a contemporary antislavery slogan. Furthermore, Thackeray's use of the slogan is significant. Although this particular motif in the novel has not been explicitly analyzed by critics, the tension between freedom and bondage—suggested by the motto—is a dominant idea in the novel as a whole.

The abolitionist slogan involved here is "Am I Not a Man and a Brother?" It originally appeared on a seal, produced in 1787 by the well-known potter Josiah Wedgwood, for the Society for the Abolition of the Slave Trade. Wedgewood also reproduced the design on seals and cameos that were distributed widely to promote the Society's cause. (These particular cameos have recently been described as "early examples of campaign buttons."[3] They became fashionable and were frequently used in jewelry for both men and women.) The Wedgewood design depicted a black man, in chains, with one knee bent to the ground and his bound hands upraised; the motto appeared around the upper border of the seal or cameo. At the time of the publication of *Pendennis* (1848-1850), the picture of the bound and kneeling black man, along with the associated motto, had been commonly used in antislavery material for over half a century and had become a familiar part of the early and mid-Victorian scene. For example, the illustration by "Phiz" (Hablot Knight Browne) entitled "The Discovery of Jingle in the Fleet," for Dickens's *Pickwick Papers* (1836-1837) contains a placard in the background that Michael Steig identifies as "the famous antislavery poster, 'Am I Not a Man and a Brother?,'" although the words are not legible in the Phiz engraving.[4] No allusion to this poster appears in Dickens's text; however, Phiz evidently felt that Victorian readers would recognize the design as a familiar emblem. Although Dickens did not refer to the slogan in this particular context, he echoed it frequently elsewhere. For instance, in Chapter 14 of *Bleak House* (1852-1853), Caddy Jellyby complains of her enforced drudgery as her mother's amanuensis: "Talk of Africa! I couldn't be worse off if I was a what's-his-name—man and a brother!" Although Mrs. Jellyby's eyes are so fixed on Borrioboola-Gha that she cannot perceive her daughter's misery, Caddy insists: "I won't be a slave all my life. . . ."[5]

Thackeray's own familiarity with this antislavery slogan before *Pendennis* is evident in his paper **"On Some Political Snobs,"** published in *Punch,* 4 July 1846, as part of *The Snobs of England* series. In this paper, Thackeray's persona protests about the outrageous costume of the typical footman:

> We can't be men and brothers as long as that poor devil is made to antic before us in his present fashion—as long as the unfortunate wretch is not allowed to see the insult passed upon him by that ridiculous splendour. This reform must be done. We have abolished negro slavery. John must now be *emancipated from plush.*[6]

The note by John Sutherland to the phrase "men and brothers," in his edition of *The Book of Snobs,* explains that "'Am I not a man and a brother?' was the abolitionists' motto, and a favourite catchphrase of Thackeray's."[7] In an article dealing with Thackeray's use of this slogan in some of his other writings, Sutherland remarks about this reference in *Pendennis* that the allusion "is wittily appropriate. As literary men . . . Arthur and Thackeray are slaves to the pen, and the writing man's emancipation from the indignity of the literary profession was one of Thackeray's lifelong campaigns."[8] Sutherland does not develop the implications of this allusion in the context of *Pendennis,* but these implications warrant more attention. Clearly Thackeray's use of the words "a man and a brother" at the end of *Pendennis* is an overt allusion to the popular antislavery slogan, just as his remark about the need of "a hand of charity" for Arthur Pendennis suggests the upraised hands of the kneeling slave in the abolitionist emblem. However, Thackeray's play of wit here is not confined simply to Arthur Pendennis's writing career (or to his own). This concluding evocation of the idea of slavery in particular and bondage in general is the culmination of a motif that runs throughout the previous portions of the book.

II

The most explicit—and explicitly pejorative—use of the idea of slavery in the novel is evident in the subplot. Within the overall subject of the development of Arthur Pendennis, as a young man and as a writer, is an intricate subplot dealing with the affairs of Sir Francis Clavering and his family, who impinge upon the life of young Pendennis—informally known as Pen—in connection with his possible marriage to Sir Francis's stepdaughter, Blanche Amory. Blanche is affected and hypocritical. In Saintsbury's words, she "is extremely nice—one would not, I think, marry her, except in polygamous and cloistral countries, but that is about all that can be said against her" (I, xix-xx). Her stepfather is a dissolute reprobate who married Blanche's mother for the latter's money and is now squandering her fortune. Her mother, Lady Clavering—nicknamed the Begum—is the good-natured and well-meaning daughter of a deceased wealthy English lawyer in Calcutta, whose fortune—according to the valet of Arthur Pendennis's uncle—was probably "wrung out of the pore starving blacks" (II, 781). The antecedents of the Begum's money and thus the Claverings' current wealth are definitely shady. However, the emphasis of the latter portion of the novel lies on the schemes of young Pendennis's uncle, Major Pendennis, to wring some of this money out of Sir Francis Clavering's clutches to benefit the Pendennis family instead.

On the fringe of the Clavering entourage is a mysterious, somewhat melodramatic individual who goes by the name of Colonel Altamont and possesses some kind of secret influence over Sir Francis Clavering. The hidden reason for this influence is that Altamont is actually Lady Clavering's first husband, John Amory, the father of Blanche Amory. (More precisely, he is assumed to be Lady Clavering's first husband until the end of the novel reveals that he was married before he met the woman who has become Lady Clavering.) John Amory is believed to have died—although the circumstances were hushed up—after being sentenced to a penal colony for forging his father-in-law's name. In fact, Amory escaped from Botany Bay, killing a man in the process. Now in England, he extorts money from Sir Francis by

threatening to reveal that the Clavering marriage is no marriage. Altamont's power over the wretched Sir Francis is a form of slavery. As Major Pendennis—a former officer in India and New South Wales who recognizes Amory and guesses the secret—thinks to himself, "Clavering . . . who would lose everything by Amory's appearance, would be a slave in the hands of a person who knew so fatal a secret" (II, 803). The Major's pragmatic conclusion is that Clavering should be a slave not in Altamont's hands but in the Major's own. With the power of this secret and without his nephew's knowledge, he blackmails Clavering into agreeing to give up his seat in Parliament in favor of young Arthur Pendennis, who is to marry Blanche and who will be further advanced by an exceptionally large dowry. Young Pen is thus to be enriched by a type of slave trade, a situation in which he somewhat naively acquiesces when, without knowing the reason for the Major's bargain with Clavering, Pen laughingly agrees with his friend Warrington's objection: "You're going to sell yourself, and Heaven help you!" (II, 802). As the narrator points out, this kind of traffic in human bodies is the way of the world: "And if every woman and man in this kingdom, who has sold her or himself for money or position, as Mr. Pendennis was about to do, would but purchase a copy of his memoirs, what tons of volumes Messrs. Bradbury and Evans would sell!" (II, 839). The despicable nature of slavery in this sense of human exploitation for money or self-advancement is even more obvious in yet another, smaller episode enclosed within this subplot.

While the Major is planning to profit from Clavering's secret, the Major's valet, Morgan, resolves to turn the secret to his own advantage. Like his longtime employer, whose pragmatism he mirrors, Morgan has a thoroughly selfish attitude, without the veneer of the Major's gentlemanly conduct and the slightly tempering effect provided by the Major's wider concern for the Pendennis name. Thus, when he overhears the conversation in which the Major confronts and masters Clavering, Morgan concludes to himself that everyone affected by the transaction would be willing to pay him to keep it quiet: "It may be a reg'lar enewity to me. Every one of 'em must susscribe" (II, 870).

From the Major's point of view, the valet is simply a convenient "animal" (II, 880). At the start of a sequence of events that leads to the dissolution of their master-servant relationship, the Major takes out his ill temper on Morgan at the end of a somewhat unsatisfactory holiday:

> In all his dealings with Morgan, his valet, he had been exceedingly sulky and discontented. He had sworn at him and abused him for many days past. He had scalded his mouth with bad soup at Swindon. He had left his umbrella in the railroad carriage: at which piece of forgetfulness, he was in such a rage, that he cursed

Morgan more freely than ever. Both the chimneys smoked furiously in his lodgings; and when he caused the windows to be flung open, he swore so acrimoniously, that Morgan was inclined to fling him out of window, too, through that opened casement.

(II, 874)

In reality, through various shady speculations, Morgan has gradually become more wealthy than his employer. The valet has acquired a great deal of money and has quietly purchased the house in which the Major has his lodging. However, the Major is too entrenched in the traditional distinction between servants and gentlemen to see Morgan's wealth, when it is brought to the Major's attention, as anything more than a surprising aberration. The employer continues to view the valet as simply a creature intended to serve his master's needs. Like an abused child who vents his unhappiness by abusing a lowlier person than himself, at the end of the passage quoted above, Morgan takes out his feelings on his unfortunate landlady, Mrs. Brixham:

> Whilst the Major was absent from his lodgings, Morgan had been seated in the landlady's parlour, drinking freely of hot brandy-and-water, and pouring out on Mrs. Brixham some of the abuse which he had received from his master upstairs. Mrs. Brixham was Morgan's slave. He was his landlady's landlord. He had bought the lease of the house which she rented; he had got her name and her son's to acceptances, and a bill of sale which made him master of the luckless widow's furniture. The young Brixham was a clerk in an insurance office, and Morgan could put him into what he called quod any day. Mrs. Brixham was a clergyman's widow, and Mr. Morgan, after performing his duties on the first floor, had a pleasure in making the old lady fetch him his boot-jack and his slippers. She was his slave.

(II, 874-77)

Mrs. Brixham's forced servitude here is underscored by Thackeray's illustration, entitled **"Mr. Morgan at His Ease,"** showing Mrs. Brixham kneeling before Morgan and undoing his boots. Not only does Morgan treat Mrs. Brixham as a slave, but he openly terms her housemaid "Slavey" (II, 885). The valet's unpleasant treatment of these women manifests the element of slavery inherent in his own treatment by the Major.

Ultimately, the relationship between Morgan and the Major becomes a power struggle, as each of these two self-seeking and self-protective individuals seeks to force the other to his knees. The term "knees" is not just a figure of speech, for the scene of Mrs. Brixham on her knees to Morgan is echoed in various guises through the subsequent sequence of events. When the Major returns home and summons Morgan, the latter grudgingly assumes the position into which he has just forced Mrs. Brixham and "knelt down to take his [the Major's] boots off with due subordination . . ." (II, 877). As this scene progresses, Morgan reaches the

point where he can no longer bear the Major's abuse. Morgan defies the Major. The Major discharges Morgan. Revealing his ownership of the house, Morgan states his defiance more emphatically: "I'll be your beast, and your brute, and your dog, no more, Major Pendennis 'Alf Pay" (II, 879). At this point, the reader's sympathies lie at least partly with Morgan, who has asserted himself against an old oppressor. Nonetheless, the subsequent elaboration about Morgan's exploitation of Mrs. Brixham—in contrast to the Major's more gentlemanly, although still self-protective conduct—makes clear that of these two worldlings, Morgan and the Major, Morgan is the more despicable.

After their confrontation, the former valet and the former master separate for the night, resolving to settle their accounts in the morning. Mrs. Brixham—in danger of financial ruin at the imminent departure of her lodger, the Major—then reveals to the Major her financial bondage to Morgan and the extent of the latter's lust for power. In Mrs. Brixham's words, "I—I must own to you, that I went down on my knees to him, sir; and he said, with a dreadful oath against you, that he would have you on your knees" (II, 882). As events ensue, however, the Major retains both his head and his footing. When Morgan demands payment for not revealing the Major's attempt at blackmail, the old officer pulls a pistol from his desk and threatens to shoot his former servant: "Kneel down and say your prayers, sir, for by the Lord you shall die" (II, 887). When Morgan, in terror, summons a policeman from the street, the Major calmly explains that the pistol is not loaded and accuses Morgan of theft, guessing—correctly—that Morgan must have appropriated items from the Major's wardrobe. To prevent a formal charge of theft and a public search of his trunks (containing not only minor items of the Major's property but more serious evidence of Morgan's other disreputable transactions), Morgan then reluctantly writes and signs a document, dictated by the Major, in which the ex-servant not only admits to robbing the Major and uttering "falsehoods regarding his and other honourable families" (II, 892) but also frees Mrs. Brixham of Morgan's financial claims on her. Thus the Major puts Morgan in a position in which he dares not try to damage the Major's reputation since the Major—by holding the valet's signed confession—is equally able to damage Morgan. The Major also incidentally frees himself from any pleas for charity by Mrs. Brixham, who had earlier begged him for financial help.

The episode of Morgan and Mrs. Brixham presents the idea of slavery in its most reprehensible and exploitive light. In this context, the Major's mistreatment of Morgan is not so bad as the latter's abuse of Mrs. Brixham since Morgan—as a hired servant—is potentially free to leave the Major's service and eventually does so. However, the Major's blackmail of Clavering is presented as a kind of inescapable bondage, and the Major's plans for his nephew involve permanent bondage as well. As Pen says painfully to his uncle, after Morgan in turn reveals the full dimensions of the Major's scheme to the young man who is to profit by it, "If you had told me this tale sooner . . . I should not have found myself tied to an engagement from which I can't, in honour, recede" (II, 908). The Major's initial response is one of self-congratulation: "No, begad, we've fixed you—and a man who's fixed to a seat in Parliament, and a pretty girl, with a couple of thousand a year, is fixed to no bad thing, let me tell you" (II, 908). Pen quickly makes clear, however, that he has no desire to profit from the Major's scheme once he understands its sordid roots. When Morgan attempts to sell the secret to him, assuming that Pen—like his uncle—is "trafficking with this wretched old Begum's misfortune; and would extort a seat in Parliament out of that miserable Clavering," Pen indignantly resolves to have nothing to do with the trade (II, 904). He also sees the consequences of his decision to withdraw from this kind of traffic as fitting punishment for his earlier worldly willingness to sell himself. As he declares to his uncle, "I am rightly punished by the event, and having sold myself for money and a seat in Parliament, by losing both" (II, 909).

To his uncle's dismay, Pen's decision is to renounce his seat in Parliament as well as Blanche's extra dowry and to reaffirm his commitment to marry Blanche with nothing except her original, modest dowry from her maternal grandfather's wealth. Only at this point, seeing the failure of his plans to improve the worldly standing of the Pendennises and echoing the words of another mistaken meddler in marital transactions, Cardinal Wolsey in *Henry VIII,* does the Major actually fall to his knees as he vainly begs Pen not to throw away his chance of worldly gain: "And—and Shakespere was right—and Cardinal Wolsey—begad—'and had I but served my God as I've served you'—yes, on my knees, by Jove, to my own nephew . . ." (II, 910). This image of kneeling, emphasized in Chapters 67, 68, and 70, may reflect the pose of the kneeling slave in the antislavery emblem. At any rate, the image is a sign of subordination, evoking the suggestion of slavery and indicating the ugliness inherent in the Major's scheme to have Pen "sell" himself for worldly advantage. The motif of slavery, in turn, links the novel's diverse secondary strands dealing with Altamont, Clavering, Morgan, Mrs. Brixham, and the Major's interactions with these characters. Traffic in human beings, Thackeray seems to be indicating, is one of the activities of the kind of world that is Vanity Fair. In Bunyan's words, in *Pilgrim's Progress,* "at this Fair are all such merchandise sold as houses, lands, trades, places, honors, preferments, titles, countries, kingdoms, lusts, pleasures, and delights of all sorts, as whores, bawds, wives, husbands, children, masters, servants,

lives, blood, bodies, souls, silver, gold, pearls, precious stones, and what not."[9] In this context, in *Pendennis,* Thackeray depicts the idea of slavery in a negative light.

III

Nonetheless, Thackeray's view of slavery—both in *Pendennis* and elsewhere—is complex. As Sutherland has pointed out, many of Thackeray's remarks about black men and women reflect an attitude that today we would call racist.[10] However, the institution of slavery also seems to have fascinated Thackeray. When he visited the United States in 1852-1853, a little more than two years after his completion of *Pendennis,* he wrote to his mother, "There was scarce any sensation of novelty until now when the slaves come on to the scene; and straightway the country assumes an aspect of the queerest interest. . . ."[11] Firsthand observation of Negroes in the American South convinced Thackeray of their inherent difference from whites:

> They are not my men & brethren, these strange people with retreating foreheads, with great obtruding lips & jaws: with capacities for thought, pleasure, endurance quite different to mine . . . they don't seem to me to be the same as white men, any more than asses are the same animals as horses; I don't mean this disrespectfully, but simply that there is such a difference of colour, habits, conformation of brains, that we must acknowledge it, & can't by any rhetorical phrase get it over; Sambo is not my man & my brother; the very aspect of his face is grotesque & inferior. I can't help seeing & owning this; at the same time of course denying any white man's right to hold this fellow-creature in bondage & make goods & chattels of him & his issue; but where the two races meet this weaker one must knock under; if it is to improve it must be on its own soil, away from the domineering whites. . . .[12]

Thackeray's argument here is subtle. On the one hand, he viewed blacks as not only different from but also as inferior to whites. On the other hand, he viewed slavery as inherently wrong and condemned its exploitative aspects. As he explained in an earlier letter from America to his mother, alluding to Harriet Beecher Stowe's currently popular, passionately antislavery *Uncle Tom's Cabin,* "I don't believe Blacky *is* my man & my brother, though God forbid I should own him or flog him, or part him from his wife & children. But the question is a much longer [one than] is set forth in Mrs. Stowe's philosophy. . . ."[13] Controversy as to the rights, wrongs, and relevance to Britons of the subject of slavery was a familiar aspect of the mid-Victorian world. During the months in which *Pendennis* was published (November 1848-December 1850), the *Times* of London printed a number of leading articles calling for an end to the current British blockade of part of the coast of Africa in an effort to stop the slave trade and commenting on the intensifying disagreement over slavery in the United

States.[14] In such articles, the *Times* attempted to treat the topic of slavery somewhat evenhandedly as a social evil but also as a problem with no simple or immediate solution.[15] More one-sidedly in *Fraser's Magazine,* December 1849, referring to the recent emancipation of blacks in the British West Indies, Carlyle declared that "Quashee, if he will not help in bringing out the spices, will get himself made a slave again (which state will be a little less ugly than his present one), and with beneficent whip, since other methods avail not, will be compelled to work"—a position which received a strong rebuttal from John Stuart Mill in the subsequent issue of *Fraser's.*[16] In the context of this current attention to "the Negro Question," it does not seem remarkable that the subject of slavery was in Thackeray's mind while working on *Pendennis.* Moreover, given the current awareness of the problematic nature of the topic as well as his own characteristic tendency to try to see both sides of every issue, it does not seem surprising that Thackeray's treatment of the idea of slavery in *Pendennis* is double-edged.

While Thackeray gives an obviously negative view of the subject of slavery in the subplot, in the main plot—dealing with the development of Arthur Pendennis from youth to maturity—he presents the concept of slavery in an ambiguously positive light. In the household in which the protagonist is raised, the most important individuals who care for him are his mother, Helen, and his informally adopted sister, Laura. Well-meaningly, but foolishly, these women have allowed Pen to treat them as slaves:

> What had made Pen at home such a dandy and such a despot? The women had spoiled him, as we like them and as they like to do. They had cloyed him with obedience, and surfeited him with sweet respect and submission, until he grew weary of the slaves who waited upon him, and their caresses and cajoleries excited him no more.
>
> (II, 677)

The narrator is quick to joke that his analysis of the reason for Pen's problem should not be construed as a manifesto for women's independence: "does any one dare to suppose that the writer would incite the women to revolt? Never, by the whiskers of the Prophet, again he says. He wears a beard, and he likes his women to be slaves. What man doesn't?" (II, 677-78). Nonetheless, Thackeray seems to be perceptively suggesting that, however much one may desire the submission of others, the consequences of satisfying this desire—when carried to an extreme—can adversely affect the despot. In Pen's case, the consequences in terms of his character of his early spoiling by "the slaves who waited upon him" form the central subject of this "History of Pendennis, His Fortunes and Misfortunes, His Friends and His Greatest Enemy," the full title of the book. As the narrator explains, part way through the novel,

> Pen's greatest enemy was himself: and as he had been pampering, and coaxing, and indulging that individual all his life, the rogue grew insolent, as all spoiled servants will be; and at the slightest attempt to coerce him, or make him do that which was unpleasant to him, became frantically rude and unruly.
>
> (II, 642)

The thrust of the novel is to show Pen's belated and reluctant development of self-discipline. His psyche must be taught to become a useful servant rather than a "spoiled" one. Thus, by the end of the novel, Pen has become "a man and a brother"—i.e., a slave—in the relatively positive sense that he has outgrown his self-centered dandyism and accepted his bondage to the responsibilities of adult life. The shift is not a simple one, however. Throughout the book, Thackeray maintains a tension between Pen's movement toward bondage and his impulse toward freedom.

Evidence of this conflict between bondage and freedom is apparent in two literary allusions near the beginning of the novel. In Chapter 2, referring obliquely to knowledge that would make a woman blush, acquired by boys in public schools, the narrator remarks, "I don't say that the boy is lost, or that the innocence has left him which he had from 'Heaven, which is our home,' but that the shades of the prison-house are closing very fast over him, and that we are helping as much as possible to corrupt him" (I, 20). The allusion is, of course, to Wordsworth's "Ode: Intimations of Immortality from Recollections of Early Childhood," describing the "growing Boy" whose heavenly recollections gradually "fade into the light of common day." Wordsworth's view of human development as a process of gradual accommodation to "the light of common day" parallels much of the course of *The History of Pendennis.* In Wordsworth's terms, the novel shows the "earnest pains" with which the growing child (Arthur Pendennis) "dost . . . provoke / The years to bring the inevitable yoke."

At the same time, while the allusion to Wordsworth's poem suggests the idea of the movement from freedom to bondage, the motto of the Pendennises suggests the urge to move from captivity to freedom. The motto, "Nec tenui penna," also first mentioned in Chapter 2, comes from the opening lines of Book II, Ode 20, of Horace's *Odes:* "Non usitata nec tenui ferar/penna" (freely translated "Mine are no weak or borrowed wings").[17] In the passage from which this quotation comes, the poet imagines himself being transformed into a bird:

> Mine are no weak or borrowed wings: they'll bear
> Me, bard made bird, through the compliant air,
> Earthbound no longer, leaving far behind
> The cities and the envy of mankind.
> Dearest Maecenas, I who was the child
> Of a poor family, I who have been styled

Your shadow, need not as a shadow lie
Penned by the Styx, nor die as others die.
Already the rough skin is forming on
My ankles; metamorphosis into swan
Moves up my body; downy plumage springs
On arms and elbows; shoulder-blades sprout wings.
And now I rise, singing, a portent more
Talked of than Icarus was, ready to soar
Over the roaring Bosphorus, the quicksands
Of Syrtes and the Hyperborean lands.
In Colchis and in Dacia, where they feign
Scorn of our Marsian troops, in ignorant Spain,
In farthest Thrace my verses shall be known:
Gauls shall drink Horace as they do the Rhone.[18]

The motto appears in Chapter 2 of *Pendennis* as part of "the Pendennis coat of arms, and crest, an eagle looking towards the sun" (I, 26), on Pen's father's memorial slab. However, the motto, in many ways, appropriately suggests the career of young Arthur Pendennis, who repeatedly struggles to soar out of his "mother's nest" (I, 183), and who ultimately achieves fame as a writer. Ironically, however, Pen eventually returns to his "home-nest" (I, 199) by returning to his childhood home and marrying his adopted sister Laura. Similarly, Horace's allusion to Icarus ironically suggests that Pen ultimately cannot escape what he early perceives as the "captivity" (I, 257) of home. Thus, while this echo of Horace superficially implies Pen's struggles toward freedom, like the echo of Wordsworth it also implies Pen's ultimate movement into bondage by the ordinary obligations of life. This progression into a form of slavery is apparent in Pen's attitude toward the three major aspects of his life on which the novel concentrates: his marriage, his work, and his mother.

As Pen's good friend Warrington declares in Chapter 53, evidently thinking of the misguided marriage that has blighted his own life, "We are the slaves of destiny. Our lots are shaped for us, and mine is ordained long ago" (II, 685). A major theme in the novel is the danger that Pen may be trapped by Warrington's kind of unfortunate marital commitment. The novel's comically striking first chapter focuses directly on this sort of marital mistake as young Pendennis (heir to the family's modest estate of Fairoaks) proudly announces his engagement to an actress almost a decade older than himself, and his uncle, Major Pendennis, prepares to rush to the scene of the potential disaster to prevent the marriage from taking place. The actress, Emily Costigan (professionally known as "Miss Fotheringay"), is ill-educated and unintelligent, but prudent. As the narrator comments about her three cautious letters to young Pen (letters actually written by someone else): "The young wiseacre had pledged away his all for this: signed his name to endless promissory notes, conferring his heart upon the bearer: bound himself for life, and got back twopence as an equivalent" (I, 106). By Chapter 17, as a beginning student at the University of Oxbridge, Pen recalls Miss Fotheringay with embarrassment: "To think

that he, Pendennis, had been enslaved by such a woman . . ." (I, 209). However, other characters in the book are not so lucky, and Pen subsequently has two more narrow escapes.

As Dickens demonstrates with the examples of Stephen Blackpool and Louisa Bounderby in *Hard Times* (1854), divorce was virtually unobtainable for ordinary men and women in the mid-Victorian period, and marriage "for better for worse" could lead to lifelong misery if "worse" or worst ensued. The example of Warrington shows the negative results of the kind of misalliance from which the Major rescued Pen. As Warrington remarks in Chapter 57 about Pen's aborted relationship with Emily Fotheringay, prior to describing his own secret marriage: "What would have been Arthur's lot now, had he been tied at nineteen to an illiterate woman older than himself, with no qualities in common between them . . ." (II, 732). Warington then reveals that as a younger man he made the mistake of actually contracting such a union—a revelation that he provides at the height of an argument between Pen and the latter's mother, in order to prevent Pen's "threatened . . . similar union" (II, 733) with Fanny Bolton, a flirtatious lower-class young woman whom Pen has resisted and his mother has maligned. Much earlier, Pen's mother had her own unhappy love affair. As the narrator explains near the beginning of the novel, Helen was unable to marry her cousin, Francis Bell, despite their mutual love, since Bell had impetuously engaged himself previously "—and his hand pledged to that bond in a thousand letters—to a coarse, ill-tempered, ill-favoured, ill-mannered, middle-aged woman" (l, 96). Unhappily but honorably, Francis Bell fulfilled his obligation of marriage, from which he was released by his wife's death only after Helen had become Mrs. Pendennis. Laura—whom Pen ultimately weds—is the child of Francis Bell's second marriage, informally adopted by Helen after both of Laura's parents die. The examples of George Warrington and Francis Bell function in the novel as cautionary tales. They reinforce the idea that Pen ought to marry a woman whom he genuinely loves and with whom he has, in Warrington's words, "qualities in common."

Because both mutual love and mutual qualities are lacking, it is evident that Major Pendennis's subsequent scheme to marry his nephew to Blanche Amory for worldly reasons is as inappropriate as Pen's adolescent, near-marriage with "the Fotheringay." Luckily, Pen escapes (by declining the money and the seat in Parliament, without which Blanche prefers a wealthier suitor). Other mismatches in the novel turn out badly, as revealed by the experiences of Lady Clavering (who marries two successive scoundrels, Amory and Clavering) and Mrs. Lightfoot (who marries a fellow servant many years her junior, uses her savings to establish him as an innkeeper, and endures his alcoholism in return). In the context of these actual and potential marital mistakes, Thackeray seems to be suggesting that Pen's decision to marry Laura is an intelligent exercise of free will. By the end of the book, Pen finally discovers his genuine love for Laura. She is not only his social equal but, as his semi-sister, of all the young women in the novel, she has most in common with him. Nonetheless, the conspicuous emphasis on the potentially galling nature of marital ties throughout the book suggests Thackeray's awareness that all marriage involves a loss of freedom and that the marriage of Laura and Pen will be no exception. (The comic discovery at the end of the novel of the disreputable John Armstrong/Amory/Altamont's multiple marriages serves as a parody of this notion of the normally restrictive nature of marital ties.) Indeed, unlike the conventional happily-ever-after ending of fairy tales, the narrator questions the future happiness of Pen and Laura—and does not fully allay the doubts he raises—in his final paragraph, concluding with his allusion to the antislavery motto. The implication is that Pen as a married person is "a man and a brother"—i.e., in some sense a slave (as Laura is as well).[19] However, Thackeray's use of the idea of bondage is not confined to the subject of Pen's marriage. Even more explicitly, he links the notion of slavery to the concept of Pen's work.

Like marriage, work in this book is perceived as a form of bondage which responsible adults inevitably accept. Initially, any kind of serious labor is something which young Pen is only too eager to avoid. Early in the novel, the reader sees Pen as a schoolboy—"in no ways remarkable either as a dunce or as a scholar" (I, 19). When his uncle arrives to take Pen home to his dying father's bedside, Pen is being lectured by the doctor at school for errors in construing Greek. After his father's death once Pen realizes his importance as the deceased man's only child and his new role as "chief . . . and lord" (I, 25) of his mother's household, his first decision is that he will never return to school: "In the midst of the general grief, and the corpse still lying above, he had leisure to conclude that he would have it *all* holidays for the future, that he wouldn't get up till he liked, or stand the bullying of the doctor any more . . ." (I, 25-26). After this "liberation from bondage" (I, 57), as the narrator later describes the leaving of school, Pen pursues his own course of study: "He had a natural taste for reading every possible kind of book which did not fall into his school-course. It was only when they forced his head into the waters of knowledge that he refused to drink" (I, 29). Pen's self-indulgent reading—reflecting his fondness for "novels, plays, and poetry" (I, 19)—is unwitting but excellent preparation for his eventual career as a writer. In the context of Pen's adolescence, however, it simply reflects the young protagonist's inclination to shirk more disciplined study.

Once at Oxbridge, Pen's distaste for serious work continues, although his reputation for ability among his fellow students is large: "'Ah, if Pendennis of Boniface would but try.' the men said, 'he might do anything'" (I, 222). According to the narrator. Pen's fame among the undergraduates is comparable to that held in "negro-gangs . . . [by] private black sovereigns . . . to whom they pay an occult obedience, besides that which they publicly profess for their owners and drivers" (I, 222). The problem for Pendennis at this point is that he has not learned to manage himself and is not willing to let wiser heads drive or lead him. His career at college is described in the title to Chapter 19 as a "Rake's Progress." His return to Fairoaks, after failing his degree examinations, is characterized in the title of Chapter 21 as the "Prodigal's Return." At Laura's urging, he goes back in a subdued mood to Oxbridge, where "He went into a second examination, and passed with perfect ease" (I, 257). Nevertheless, rather than making any effort to use his education and native talents at this point, Pen returns to mope at Fairoaks—an attitude that elicits Laura's proper Victorian scorn: "He wastes his life and energies away among us, tied to our apron-strings. He interests himself in nothing: he scarcely cares to go beyond the garden-gate. . . . Why is he not facing the world, and without a profession?" (I, 317). Laura continues her denunciation of Pen: "All men . . . must work. They must make themselves names and a place in the world" (I, 317). When Pen lackadaisically makes his first proposal of marriage to Laura—motivated by his mother's wishes rather than his own—Laura emphatically rejects him in words that link the obligations of marriage with the obligations of work:

> What do you offer in exchange to a woman for her love, honour, and obedience? If ever I say these words, dear Pen, I hope to say them in earnest, and by the blessing of God to keep my vow. But you—what tie binds you? You do not care about many things which we poor women hold sacred. . . . Go and work; go and mend, dear Arthur, for I see your faults, and dare speak of them now. . . .
>
> (I, 347-48)

Only after Pen is propelled to London by Laura and discovers his true vocation as a writer, does he finally accept this Victorian ethic of work.

Dedication to one's profession can be overdone, as demonstrated in Chapter 29 by the example of the "selfish" (I, 368) over-zealousness of the law student Mr. Paley. In contrast, what Laura has in mind is altruistically oriented, energetic but not obsessive work—eventually taking the form of writing "good books . . . such as might do people good to read" (II, 864). By Chapter 44, Pen has finally become enthusiastic about the value of earnest labor. He observes to his friend George Warrington: "Who ordered toil as the condition of life, ordered weariness, ordered sickness, ordered poverty, failure, success—to this man a foremost place, to the other a nameless struggle with the crowd—to that a shameful fall, or paralysed limb, or sudden accident—to each some work upon the ground he stands on, until he is laid beneath it" (II, 572).

In Pen's case (as his name suggests), the work which he has found to do is writing—prompted by Warrington's example and Pen's own need of money on which to live. Immediately, to Warrington's delight, Pen begins to rail at the publisher Mr. Bungay as a "slave-driver" (I, 415), but Pen eagerly enlists as a writer for Bungay's *Pall Mall Gazette*. Moreover, while still retaining too much integrity to write an unfavorable review of a good book, Pen is generally happy to accommodate his abilities to the needs of Bungay and whatever other publishers will accept his work. As the narrator explains,

> When you want to make money by Pegasus (as he must, perhaps, who has no other saleable property), farewell poetry and aerial flights: Pegasus only rises now like Mr. Green's balloon, at periods advertised beforehand, and when the spectators' money has been paid. Pegasus trots in harness, over the stony pavement, and pulls a cart or a cab behind him. Often Pegasus does his work with panting sides and trembling knees, and not seldom gets a cut of the whip from his driver.
>
> (I, 450)

In Warrington's words, Pen has become a "literary hack" (I, 449)—in the sense that his "Pegasus" has become a hired cab horse. The profession of authorship is presented here as a form of servitude, although it is a servitude that Pen readily accepts and the narrator condones. As the latter explains,

> Do not let us . . . be too prodigal of our pity upon Pegasus. . . . If he gets the whip, Pegasus very often deserves it, and I for one am quite ready to protest . . . against the doctrine which some poetical sympathizers are inclined to put forward, viz., that men of letters, and what is called genius, are to be exempt from the prose duties of this daily, bread-wanting, tax-paying life, and are not to be made to work and pay like their neighbours.
>
> (I, 450)

The idea of authorship as servitude is carried even further when Warrington suggests that he and Pen sell Pen's autobiographical novel *Walter Lorraine* to one of the rival publishers, Mr. Bacon and Mr. Bungay. The terms that Warrington uses to describe this transaction metaphorically suggest that they are selling *Walter Lorraine* into slavery:

> No, we won't burn him: we will carry him to the Egyptian, and sell him. We will exchange him away for money—yea, for silver and gold, and for beef and for liquors, and for tobacco and for raiment. This youth will fetch some price in the market: for he is a comely lad, though not over strong; but we will fatten him up, and give him the bath, and curl his hair, and we will sell him for a hundred piastres to Bacon or to Bungay.
>
> (II, 522-23)

In this sense, as Sutherland observes in the comment quoted earlier, the remark about Pen as "a man and a brother" at the end of the novel refers to the protagonist's profession of authorship. The narrator's concluding comment, however, is not an isolated witticism. Rather, it evolves not only from the novel's general concern with the motif of bondage but from the particular emphasis on writing as servitude and/or slavery earlier in the book. In the novel as a whole, the narrator's attitude toward this form of slavery seems largely one of toleration while still recognizing the often difficult nature of the writer's life. The slavery here, of course, is not seriously exploitative. Pen is selling his writing, rather than his own person as he almost did in the Blanche Amory episode. Furthermore, he reserves the right (as in the instance of the review) not to compromise his integrity. These differences are important reasons why slavery in this context seems acceptable, while in the Major's plans concerning his nephew and Blanche, slavery was a negative concept. At any rate, by the end of the novel, Pen has generally accepted his bondage to the world of work.

Moreover, by the end of the book, Pen is bound not only by his marital responsibilities and his work but by his inescapable awareness of his mother's values. Robert Bledsoe has argued provocatively that Pen ultimately discovers that he can achieve psychological security only by ceasing any effort to dissociate himself from his mother's wishes: "final freedom from the terrors of insecurity involves Pen's willing enslavement to the mindlessness of Helen's sentimentality."[20] In this reading of the novel, "Helen is the most important character,"[21] and "Pendennis does not grow up and away from his mother, as in a more conventional *Bildungsroman*. On the contrary, he grows up and back to her, rejecting the great world for Laura, whose arms are 'as tender as Helen's.'"[22] To some extent, this interpretation of the novel is perceptive, although Pen's ultimate return after Helen's death to the simple values of duty, home, and religion—and his choice of a wife in whom Helen has instilled these values—does not seem so abnormal when one considers that they were popularly approved and strongly emphasized values of the Victorian period.[23] In addition, Laura seems more than just "the agent of Helen's will" as Bledsoe perceives her.[24] By the time Laura finally accepts Pen, she has developed into an independent young woman whom Warrington admires, to whom Pynsent (an aristocratically connected public official) has proposed, and who Lady Rockminster (her patroness) thinks is too good for Pen. As Juliet McMaster emphasizes, "Pen does not marry her [Laura] until *he* wants to, and that is after his mother's death."[25] In the end, Pen remains the central character. By the conclusion of the novel, he is bound by other obligations than just his memory of his mother. Nonetheless, as Bledsoe has rightly pointed out, the pattern of the novel is circular rather than linear. Like the biblical prodigal son to whom he is frequently compared, Pen ultimately returns to "the home-nest" (I, 199) where he chafed as a boy. However, to some degree at least, at the end of the novel, there is evidence that Pen is "chafing" (I, 199) once again.

As a writer in London, Pen amply demonstrates his ability to see more than one side of a question. Pen declares to Warrington in Chapter 61, "The truth, friend! . . . where is the truth? Show it me. That is the question between us. I see it on both sides" (II, 801). In context, Warrington dismisses Pen's indifferent, relativist attitude as preparation for his worldly decision to marry Blanche. Nonetheless, even after Pen has returned to Helen's and Laura's simple values, he retains—or is plagued by—his ability to see the opposite side of every issue. He explains to Laura in Chapter 71 that he is still unable to rid himself of scepticism:

> But will come in spite of us. But is reflection. But is the sceptic's familiar, with whom he has made a compact; and if he forgets it, and indulges in happy daydreams, or building of air-castles, or listens to sweet music, let us say, or to the bells ringing to church, But taps at the door, and says, 'Master, I am here. You are my master; but I am yours. Go where you will you can't travel without me. I will whisper to you when you are on your knees at church. I will be at your marriage pillow. I will sit down at your table with your children. I will be behind your death-bed curtain.'
>
> (II, 916)

Even in the last paragraph of the novel, foreshadowing his future life, Pen is still described as subject to "fits of moodiness and solitude" (II, 977). As Robert A. Colby has pointed out, the ambivalence in Pen's character is evident in the two successive forms of Thackeray's cover illustration, showing the protagonist pulled between a mermaidlike woman and small satyr (or satyrs) on one side and an idealized Victorian woman and youthful cherub (or cherubs), with a church in the background, on the other.[26] Colby explains, "In the monthly parts, Pen looks in the direction of the good woman; by the time the story is published in book form Pen's eyes have shifted toward the sea nymph."[27] Thus, by the end of the novel, Thackeray seems to be quietly implying that the protagonist may not be entirely content with what Bledsoe has described as "Pen's willing enslavement" to Helen's world view. Like many other adults, both in the Victorian period and our own, he has returned to the values inculcated in his youth, but remains fitfully conscious of their limitations. This consciousness of his chains makes his constraint all the more evident.

In terms of Pen's development, his eventual bondage to his marriage, his work, and the values of his mother is presented as a positive form of slavery, although it is one that Pen does not accept with total docility and for which at the end, according to the narrator, he deserves the reader's "hand of charity." None of us, the narrator suggests, is perfect, and Pen—fettered as he is—is one of us. His chains are the intangible ones of marriage, work, and traditional values. He has eschewed the extortion, exploitation, and outright selling of human beings for tangible profit inherent in Major Pendennis's and Morgan's schemes. This emphasis on limitation and restraint in the main plot of the novel may explain why so many, less willingly inhibited, modern readers find this novel less appealing than our Victorian predecessors did. The emphasis on limitations certainly explains why Pen does not seduce Fanny Bolton, despite his obvious opportunity, a deliberately self-denying action that sometimes evokes incredulity among post-Victorian readers. Thackeray's point, however, is that Pendennis is never an entirely willing slave to the conventions he accepts. In a similar vein, in the preface, Thackeray explains that he will accept contemporary conventions of the novel and refrain from giving all the details about his protagonist's development as a young man. Nevertheless, he will strain against the restriction as best he can:

> Since the author of *Tom Jones* was buried, no writer of fiction among us has been permitted to depict to his utmost power a MAN. We must drape him, and give him a certain conventional simper. Society will not tolerate the Natural in our Art. Many ladies have remonstrated and subscribers left me because in the course of the story, I described a young man resisting and affected by temptation. My object was to say that he had the passions to feel, and the manliness and generosity to overcome them. You will not hear—it is best to know it—what moves in the real world, what passes in society, in the clubs, colleges, mess-rooms,—what is the life and talk of your sons. A little more frankness than is customary has been attempted in this story. . . .
>
> (I, xxxii-xxxiii)

The idea of bondage, and the impulse against bondage, is thus a dominant motif in the novel. At the end of the book, Arthur Pendennis is presented simply as a human being, limited in many senses as Thackeray is suggesting other human beings are also bound.

Notes

1. *The History of Pendennis: His Fortunes and Misfortunes, His Friends and His Greatest Enemy,* ed. George Saintsbury, 2 vols. (1908; rpt. London: Oxford Univ. Press, n.d.), II, 977. Citations from the novel, as well as to its editor's introduction, appear in the text.

2. Gordon N. Ray observes that *Pendennis* was "a book for which . . . [Thackeray's] contemporar-

ies felt particular affection as the epitome of his genial wisdom" (*Thackeray: The Age of Wisdom* [New York: McGraw-Hill, 1958], p. 108). Samuel C. Chew and Richard D. Altick remark that "*Pendennis . . .* has had its enthusiastic admirers but is little read today" (*A Literary History of England,* ed. Albert C. Baugh, 2nd ed. [New York: Appleton-Century-Crofts, 1967], p. 1358).

3. Anthony Burton, *Josiah Wedgwood: A Biography* (New York: Stein and Day, 1976), caption for illustration facing p. 176. For additional discussions of the Wedgwood emblem, see Burton, pp. 199-203; Eliza Meteyard, *The Life of Josiah Wedgwood* (London: Hurst and Blackett, 1866), II, 565-67; and Howard Temperly, *British Antislavery, 1833-1870* (Columbia: Univ., of South Carolina Press, 1972), p. 3.

4. Michael Steig, *Dickens and Phiz* (Bloomington: Indiana Univ. Press, 1978), p. 14. See Steig's illustration 22.

5. Charles Dickens, *Bleak House,* ed. George Ford and Sylvère Monod (New York: Norton, 1977), pp. 166-67.

6. William Makepeace Thackeray, *The Book of Snobs,* ed. John Sutherland (New York: St. Martin's, 1978), p. 72.

7. *The Book of Snobs,* p. 221, n. 1.

8. John Sutherland, "Thackeray as Victorian Racialist," *Essays in Criticism,* 20 (1970), 443.

9. John Bunyan, *The Pilgrim's Progress,* ed. Roger Sharrock (Harmondsworth: Penguin, 1965), p. 125. The episode involving Morgan and the Major which is analyzed in my text is also discussed by Barbara Hardy, although Hardy stresses the element of reversal in this series of events (*The Exposure of Luxury: Radical Themes in Thackeray* [Pittsburgh: Univ. of Pittsburgh Press, 1972], pp. 37-44).

10. Sutherland, "Thackeray as Victorian Racialist," pp. 441-45.

11. *The Letters and Private Papers of William Makepeace Thackeray,* ed. Gordon N. Ray (Cambridge: Harvard Univ. Press, 1946), III, 198-99, to Mrs. Carmichael-Smyth, 13 February 1853.

12. *Letters and Private Papers,* III, 199, to Mrs. Carmichael-Smyth, 13 February 1853.

13. *Letters and Private Papers,* III, 187, to Mrs. Carmichael-Smyth, 26 January 1853. Words in brackets appear in brackets in *Letters and Private Papers.*

14. For examples of articles about the blockade, see the *Times,* 13 January 1849, p. 4, cols. 4-5; 27 April 1849, p. 4, cols. 5-6; 24 May 1849, p. 4, cols. 5-6; 21 June 1849, p. 4, col. 6-p. 5, col. 1; 16 November 1849, p. 4, cols. 3-4; 22 July 1850, p. 4, cols. 3-4; 17 August 1850, p. 4, cols. 5-6. For examples of articles about slavery in the United States, see the *Times,* 11 January 1849, p. 4, col. 6-p. 5, col. 1; 24 January 1850, p. 4, cols. 2-3; 23 March 1850, p. 5, cols. 3-5; 30 August 1850, p. 4, cols. 3-4; 12 September 1850, p. 4, col. 6-p. 5, col. 1; 20 September 1850, p. 4, cols. 3-4; 25 October 1850, p. 4, cols. 2-3; 8 November 1850, p. 4, cols. 4-5; 19 November 1850, p. 4, cols. 1-3.

15. For examples of the *Times*'s effort at evenhandedness in its treatment of the topic of slavery, see the articles of 8 May 1849, p. 5, cols. 5-6 (in which the *Times* objects to accusations that the British press is cold or hostile to the antislavery cause) and 13 December 1850, p. 4, cols. 3-4 (in which the *Times* declares that "Except under the just provocation caused by the exuberant impudence of brother JONATHAN in his remarks on the country of his ancestors, no prudent Englishman would deny that there are two sides to the question of American slavery"—p. 4, col. 3).

16. [Thomas Carlyle], "Occasional Discourse on the Negro Question," *Fraser's Magazine,* 40 (1849), 675; [John Stuart Mill], "The Negro Question," *Fraser's Magazine,* 41 (1850), 25-31. Carlyle subsequently reprinted his essay as *Occasional Discourse on the Nigger Question* (1853). In 1865-1867, Carlyle and Mill were again emphatically at odds in the racially related Governor Eyre Case—a controversy involving a British governor of Jamaica who had harshly suppressed a Negro insurrection. For a discussion of this case, as well as the different positions taken by Carlyle, Mill, and their followers, see George H. Ford, "The Governor Eyre Case in England," *University of Toronto Quarterly,* 17 (1948), 219-33.

17. *The Odes of Horace,* trans. James Michie (New York: Orion Press, 1963), p. 157. A literal translation of "Nec tenui penna" is "and not upon a thin wing." Donald Hawes gives the translation of this motto as "'[Mine are] no weak wings'" (*The History of Pendennis,* ed. Donald Hawes, introd. J. I. M. Stewart (Harmondsworth: Penguin, 1972], p. 789, n.8. I am indebted for helpful discussions of this allusion to Professor Joseph P. McGowan, Chairman, Department of English; and Emeritus Professor John I. McEnerney, former Chairman, Department of Classical Studies, Villanova University.

18. *The Odes of Horace,* pp. 157, 159.

19. As Thackeray remarked later in a letter to his daughters, "You see what you do when you

marry.—what slaves you become—well? and what immense happiness you enjoy I daresay with the right man" *The Letters and Private Papers of William Makepeace Thackeray,* ed. Gordon N,. Ray (Cambridge: Harvard Univ. Press, 1946), IV, 28, to Anne and Harriet Thackeray, 8 March 1857.

20. Robert Bledsoe, "*Pendennis* and the Power of Sentimentality: A Study of Motherly Love," *PMLA,* 91 (1976), 871.

21. Bledsoe, p. 871.

22. Bledsoe, p. 882.

23. For example, see Walter E. Houghton, *The Victorian Frame of Mind, 1830-1870* (New Haven: Yale Univ. Press, 1957), pp. 94-99, 218-62, 341-48, as well as Alexander Welsh's discussions of "The Hearth" and "The Spirit of Love and Truth" in *The City of Dickens* (Oxford: Clarendon, 1971), pp. 141-79.

24. Bledsoe, p. 876.

25. Juliet McMaster, *Thackeray: The Major Novels* (Toronto: Univ. of Toronto Press, 1971), p. 202.

26. Robert A. Colby, *Thackeray's Canvass of Humanity: An Author and His Public* (Columbus: Ohio State Univ. Press, 1979), pp. 301-03.

27. Robert A. Colby, *Fiction with a Purpose: Major and Minor Nineteenth-Century Novels* (Bloomington: Indiana Univ. Press, 1967), p. 144.

Robert P. Fletcher (essay date spring 1991)

SOURCE: Fletcher, Robert P. "The Dandy and the Fogy: Thackeray and the Aesthetics/Ethics of the Literary Pragmatist." *ELH* 58, no. 2 (spring 1991): 383-404.

[*In the following essay, Fletcher highlights motifs of ephemerality, despair, and transcendence in Thackeray's fiction. Fletcher suggests that for Thackeray, literary expression was primarily a means of combating the fundamental "emptiness of existence."*]

I. INTRODUCTION

As he recounts Becky Sharp's rise to respectability, the narrator of *Vanity Fair* pauses, as he does frequently, to redescribe "our" relation to his fair heroine:

> It is all vanity to be sure: but who will not own to liking a little of it? I should like to know what well-constituted mind, merely because it is transitory, dislikes roast beef? That is a vanity; but may every man who reads this, have a wholesome portion of it through life, I beg: ay, though my readers were five hundred thousand. Sit down, gentlemen, and fall to, with a good

> hearty appetite; the fat, the lean, the gravy, the horse-radish as you like it—don't spare it. Another glass of wine, Jones, my boy—a little bit of the Sunday side. Yes, let us eat our fill of the vain thing, and be thankful therefor. And let us make the best of Becky's aristocratic pleasures likewise—for these too, like all other mortal delights, were but transitory.[1]

Thackeray creates in this passage a perspective that takes away as it gives a probationary sympathy to Becky's ambition, and to a possible reader's response to it. Our desire for the ephemeral products of existence is first validated; we shouldn't feel guilty for liking roast beef. Thackeray's feel for the transitory nature of experience here yields not an abstemious despair, but an unapologetic relish for our "vain things." "Well-constituted minds" give due attention to the here and now. Yet the chummy exhortation is undercut by his admission in the last sentence that both our and Becky's pleasures are "*but* transitory," as if—even though he admits the persuasive force of roast beef—he would posit something *less* transitory than temporal existence. Thus he has his roast beef and eats it too; he celebrates Becky's actions while qualifying (by temporalizing) their success. This wry sympathy is tame, however, compared to the irony in the advice that we should "make the best of Becky's aristocratic pleasures," for here the narrator counsels us to consume "Becky Sharp" as we do roast beef. The novel itself is offered as just one more of those vain things which are transitory, and by implication our desire for more than a transitory performance is a vanity in itself. The perspective has suddenly doubled, and we get caught in the middle, implicated by our enjoyment of Becky when we thought our voyeurism was harmless reading.

A couple of questions of interest for how we read Thackeray (and other literature) are involved in this short intrusion: how are the author's fascination with and valuing of temporal existence and his positing of something transcendent to it related? And of what good is a narrative so infused with irony? These questions of value (of experience and of literature) for a "well-constituted mind" hinge on Thackeray's concept of *vanity,* that word that pervades virtually all of his work. Depending on context, almost anything and everything presented in a Thackerayan novel is vain (or valueless): material products, words, beliefs, life, love. The last of these is sometimes raised into a transcendent value, but at the end of his (currently) most valued work, *Vanity Fair,* even it is qualified, its contingency made apparent in the ironic dampening of Dobbin's ardor for Amelia.

And yet, for a novelist troubled by the emptiness of existence, Thackeray writes books abounding in its materials: turtle soup and good claret, polished boots and shiny buttons, well-turned calves and bare arms fill his novels with the upper-middle class culture of his day. Vain can also mean conceited, or puffed up (certainly

Jos Sedley personifies this definition), and Thackeray is fascinated by those who are particularly full of themselves and of life. Philip Firmin, the hero of his last complete novel, is one of Thackeray's most potent swaggerers. If at his most serious, Thackeray despairs over the futility of human endeavor, he just as often celebrates the vitality of those who, like Becky Sharp, chase after "pleasures." Few novelists are more conscious than Thackeray of how both culture and literature are forever being reconstituted through redescriptions—the existing sign is found to be empty and is remade into something to be proud of, at least temporarily. And no Victorian novelist is more conscious of his own part in this process. His status as ironist and his foothold in the canon derive from his recognition of the paradox that is the subject of Barbara Herrnstein Smith's recent book: when we invest something with meaning and/or value, the contingency of that investment subjects it to eventual devaluation—whether it be the fashions we wear, the books we write and read, or the lives we live.[2]

If his consciousness of the fragility of value doesn't lead him to abandon the thrills of the fair, it does, however, occasionally open him to utopian yearnings for something not subject to change. Thackeray's sentiment today loses him more readers than his irony, but rather than coming from a soft head (a common accusation from unappreciative critics), it arises out of his intellectual realization of the impermanence of life, coupled with an appreciation of the distinctiveness of each life.[3] Richard Rorty reads a Philip Larkin poem as an expression of the human need to find something in life both idiosyncratic and universal—of the desire to be both poet and philosopher.[4] Thackeray communicates this same drive to create both the unique—whether as dandy or novelist—and the representative. His irony, which undercuts every performance (even his own), and his sentiment, which treasures the human urge to perform, are both elements of a temperament which I designate, after Rorty, as that belonging to the protopragmatist.[5] Thackeray values human effort to act or to know or to believe, while he questions the value of individual acts, knowledge, and beliefs. As a consequence of this pragmatic temperament, Thackerayan narratives are a blend of inquiry and provisional assertion, heuristic in their project to reassess the significance of human action. This disposition of mind lies behind the theme of vanity and influences Thackeray's concepts of fiction, narrative, and the ethical function of literature.

II. THACKERAY AS AN IRONIST

One of the easiest ways into Thackeray's literary pragmatism is through irony, doubtless a critical path itself tangled by numerous remappings. When seen as a literary tool, it can be appropriated by writers with radically different philosophies. William Empson's so-called single irony merely requires the use of an incongruity in one standpoint to bolster another that the writer finds more attractive. The attempt to provide an example of this use of irony, however, might be tricky, as we would quite easily find a point of dispute in whether the writer really endorses the point of view left intact. This problem of where irony stops once it starts brings us to Empson's double irony, labeled variously by others as Romantic irony, unstable irony, dialectic, or reflexivity.[6] Here, rather than one viewpoint being permanently adopted in place of an earlier or more conventional one, the writer retreats from each position, only conditionally accepting any view as a resting point. Every view is qualified, and every use of language is rhetorically marked as self-conscious.

In all such theories, irony includes a self-consciousness about one's own language. When the thoroughgoing ironist sees a particular use of language as not necessary but only possible, sees it is as subject to troping (through parody, for instance) as human life is itself to mutability, the ironist can bring an awareness of this shift in value to his or her own life. According to Rorty, the realization that contingency underwrites human culture allows the ironist to attempt his or her own self-creation through language. The ironist *redescribes* self and the world, and in so doing, creates a distinctive identity, the difference from all other "I's," the loss of which, Rorty claims, is what we fear when we contemplate death (*CIS* [*Contingency, Irony, and Solidarity*], 23). But the ironist also realizes the contingency of that proud act of invention, and knowing it subject to change, holds it tentatively, until another act of redescribing makes it obsolete. Rorty's irony, then, is more philosophy than technique, or rather, the technique and philosophy are often found together. This description fits Thackeray both as critic and practicing novelist; coincident with his brilliance as literary parodist and ironist is a pragmatism that reenacts the conflicting desires to be unique and universal, of the moment and lasting.

Drawn from his readings of Nietzsche, Heidegger, Wittgenstein, Freud, William James, Donald Davidson, and others, Rorty's description of the ironist is of one who conducts inquiry into previously held notions of reality, and of self and others, through redescription. How we are like and unlike others is the ironist's constant object of discovery and reassessment. This figure itself seems to be a good model for understanding Thackeray's fascination with his culture's morality and modes of existence. In *The Book of Snobs,* Thackeray embodies the paradox of the individual seeking distance from a language (in this case, that of snobbery) to a point less open to questioning, and in the end reproducing the same language:

> It is a great mistake to judge of Snobs lightly, and
> think they exist among the lower classes merely. An

immense percentage of Snobs, I believe, is to be found in every rank of this mortal life. You must not judge hastily or vulgarly of Snobs: to do so shows that you are yourself a Snob. I myself have been taken for one.

(Works [The Works of William Makepeace Thackeray], 6:305)

In fact, snobbery for Thackeray is related to irony in an important way. Both the ironist and the snob distance themselves from the language of the other; but snobs take their position (and its accompanying language) as superior to that of the other, as somehow stable or permanently valuable (or more "realistic"), while ironists see their alternative life or language as just one more contingency. We might say snobs are ironists unaware that they are being ironic about one very much like themselves. And the slyly placed point of dispute in the quotation above is just how aware Mr. Snob is.

Thackeray's willingness to explore and question "final vocabularies" (Rorty, *CIS*, 73)—those of his culture as well as his own—needs itself to be explored anew. I find evidence for this brand of philosophical irony (which pragmatists would argue enlists under its banner such diverse figures as Emerson and Nietzsche, Wordsworth and Derrida) in Thackeray's novels and journalism.[7] Rorty's statement that "since there is nothing beyond vocabularies which serves as a criterion of choice between them, criticism is a matter of looking on this picture and on that, not of comparing both pictures with the original" (*CIS*, 80) sounds like the basis for Thackeray's evaluative art criticism, in which he unabashedly favors one picture over another, not because it captures an ideal or a truth, but because the clothes on the figures suit him and his culture better.[8] On the other hand, in his travel books he provides a perspective on his own culture as well as the foreign one; the Fat Contributor is first an advocate for English ways but then the satirist of English tourists' habits—seemingly embodying, so to speak, Rorty's claim that "nothing can serve as a criticism of a person save another person, or of a culture save an alternative culture—for persons and cultures are, for us, incarnated vocabularies" (*CIS*, 80).[9] Thackeray embraces the relation between subjective voice speaking and the meaning found in the object, unlike—as Smith points out—critics in the early and mid-twentieth century (*CV [Contingencies of Value]*, 17-29). While the snob, the ironist, and the sentimentalist seem to usurp each other's position in Thackeray's mind, their vocabularies finally play against one another to remind him and us that they are each only a vocabulary.

Of course snobs and ironists live in Vanity Fair. Thackeray's concept of vanity has its place in a philosophical tradition stretching from the utilitarians to the pragmatism formulated by Charles Sanders Peirce at the end of the nineteenth century and developed in the twentieth

by William James, John Dewey, and now Rorty. Common to all are both the process by which old truths are overturned in favor of new ones and the attitude of inquiry engendered by that process. Thackeray's inquiries take the form of fictions interspersed with intrusive self-assessments which posit possible relations between the fiction and the reader's own language, thus ironically exposing the latter as one description. An examination of Thackeray's irony, therefore, leads us to his concept of fiction and his concern with its uses.

III. Exploring, Exposing, and Exploiting the Power of Fiction

Modern philosophers and literary theorists engage the problem of truth and fiction (as well as the related one of reality and literature) on a theoretical level. Thackeray, although not articulating their formulations, did anticipate in his narratives and criticism the concerns of those who ponder the connections between fiction and the world, and among fiction, our selves, and the values we define.

In *On the Margins of Discourse,* Smith divides language use into fictive discourse and natural discourse in order to get at the former's distinctive features.[10] Unlike speech-act theorist John Searle, who opposes "real world talk" to "parasitic discourse" by designating nonfictional uses of language as "natural," she does not imply that nonfictional uses of language are of more value.[11] Fictive discourse is no more artificial for Smith than other discourse; its ontological status is, if not the same, just as secure. But there *is* something distinctive about it. She cites children's ability at an early age to tell (and understand as fictions) imaginative stories, as well as Gregory Bateson's claim for the significance of the chimpanzee's ability to distinguish real aggression from fake aggression (or play).[12]

The way we respond to utterances (or texts) depends to a great extent on our classifications of them, based upon conventional markers. As Robert Newsom points out in his book *A Likely Story,* the deeply engrossed viewer of a scary movie has classified the experience of seeing a film as one of watching a fiction; this classification makes available a second frame of reference which forestalls the necessity of the viewer getting up and running out of the theater when the monster on the screen stalks as if towards the audience.[13] Yet, as Woody Allen's *The Purple Rose of Cairo* so whimsically shows, people nonetheless can and do blur the "margin" between fictive text and real discourse. Smith points to the effectiveness of modern advertising and the "sentimental" value of prefabricated greeting card verse to reveal how we sometimes use and interpret fictive utterances as "natural" (*OMD [On the Margins of Discourse]*, 55-60). The conventions which allow us to interpret something as fiction are exploited in other nonfictive contexts. We learn from our lifelong experience with language when the conventions that characterize fictive discourse apply and when they don't, but there is always the potential for confusion, purposeful or otherwise.

Thackeray as novelist and critic is fascinated by the problem of fiction, what constitutes it and how we use it. His parodies—both **"Novels by Eminent Hands"** and the many snippets in the novels, such as the beginning of the "Vauxhall" chapter of *Vanity Fair*—evidence his sensitivity to how we use language to form our understanding of experiences. As Bateson argues that different "maps" can be applied to the same "territory" and thereby constitute different kinds of knowledge, so Thackeray shows that different "plots" (which includes stylistic variation) can be applied to the same "story" and thereby yield different fictions.[14] He plays such stylized "language games" against one another, exaggerating the markers of Lever's or Disraeli's distinctive vocabularies, for instance, so as to eliminate the representational bond to reality each claims to possess. The conventions of such romances have for him the status of "prefabricated discourse," to use Smith's term; they are overused tools which—though they can stand out when exaggerated in parody—can still be effective when used well. Thackeray's strenuous attacks on the Newgate Novel proceed from an ambivalence about the ways in which Bulwer and others (Thackeray even classified Dickens among them) could adapt prefabricated forms of fiction (romance), complete with markers signaling they were meant to be interpreted *as* fiction, to subjects (crimes) commonly described in a rhetoric conventionally taken to be "natural discourse" and thereby blur the margins between the two. He objected to Bulwer and company, therefore, not only on account of the unnaturalness of describing criminals as heroes, but because he was acutely aware of the potential unnaturalness of all discourse. No vocabulary is more originally attached to reality than any other; each is merely a construct, a compelling fiction imposed by humans and competing with others quite as capable of describing a given reality if used well and read as natural. As Smith argues, there are no hard and fast rules for when and when not to read something as fiction, and we occasionally cross over from doing the one to the other without being aware of the switch (*OMD*, 41-75). In *Catherine,* his own attempt to expose the fictionality of Newgate fictions, Thackeray encountered the difficulty of employing a conventional discourse that is marked as fictional without finding it as persuasive as reality. He began with parody, but (like Fielding in *Joseph Andrews*) found it difficult to carry out the exercise to novel length without creating a coherent orchestration of language which he found convincing himself. Thackeray appropriated the narrative formula but found his heroine more than formulaic:

> Your letter with compliments has just come to hand; it is very ingenious in you to find such beauties in Catherine which was a mistake all through—it was not made disgusting enough that is the fact, and the triumph of it would have been to make readers so horribly horrified as to cause them to give up or rather throw up the book and all of it's [*sic*] kind, whereas you see the author had a sneaking kindness for his heroine, and did not like to make her utterly worthless.[15]

Two years later Thackeray returned to this topic of how fictional convention can become part of our natural discourse. Barry Lyndon, unlike Catherine and his own literary ancestor Fielding's Jonathan Wild, tells his own story. Despite his insistence on plain speaking, he frequently lapses into romance, sometimes unwittingly, sometimes quite consciously, as when he reflects on his challenge for his cousin's hand:

> "I'll have his blood, or he shall have mine; and this riband shall be found dyed in it. Yes! and if I kill him, I'll pin it on his breast, and then she may go take back her token." This I said because I was very much excited at the time, and because I had not read my novels and romantic plays for nothing.[16]

Although Barry can detect in retrospect the artificiality of his younger self's language, at other times he adopts a heroic idiom without being aware of its rhetorical nature, as, for instance, when he describes himself as a romantic gambler-gentleman:

> Is *this* not something like boldness? does *this* profession not require skill, and perseverance, and bravery? Four crowned heads looked on at the game, and an imperial princess, when I turned up the ace of hearts and made Paroli, burst into tears. No man on the European Continent held a higher position than Redmond Barry then; and when the Duke of Courland lost, he was pleased to say that we had won nobly: and so we had, and spent nobly what we won.
>
> (**BL** [*The Memoirs of Barry Lyndon*], 130)

We enjoy the braggadocio at this point; we simultaneously laugh at Barry and participate in this fictional (in a double sense—perhaps "fictive fictional"?) life. Only later, when he terrorizes Lady Lyndon into marrying him, are we made aware of the consequences that Barry's fictions about himself have for others, and of how our crediting those stories (as readers of *Barry Lyndon*) somehow implicates us in their effectiveness. When he enters Lady Lyndon's world as her suitor, Barry poses as the gothic villain—"Terror, be sure of that," he tells us, "is not a bad ingredient of love" (218)—and succeeds in instilling a fear and fascination in his object. Through Barry's tireless efforts, this initial contact becomes a "story of her ladyship's passionate attachment for me," and our PR wizard is not slow "in profiting by these rumours" (228). He continues his progress:

> Every one thought I was well with the widowed countess, though no one could show that I said so. But there is a way of proving a thing even while you contradict

it, and I used to laugh and joke so a propos that all men began to wish me joy of my great fortune, and look up to me as the affianced husband of the greatest heiress in the kingdom. The papers took up the matter.

(228)

Thackeray makes his scoundrel a master at manipulating the public voice of gossip, because the novelist understands how much of personal belief is made up of such culturally shared fictions. If Barry can convince the world of this "love story" he can persuade Lady Lyndon as well that "Fate works with agents, great and small; and by means over which they have no control the destinies of men and women are accomplished" (231). She does eventually succumb to Barry's artfully constructed "fate" and marries him. Throughout the novel, "fate," "luck," and "fortune" serve the failed Barry's own purposes as comforting fictions to explain away his imprisoned end. The novel is largely about belief in fictions: Barry's own, Lady Lyndon's, and most importantly the reader's belief in Barry Lyndon. Thackeray deliberately juggles the moments when we have to credit some of what Barry says with those when we know he is lying, and even adds in a third level of "editor" complete with interpretive tastes for "poetical justice [which] overtakes the daring and selfish hero" (234), all to show us the temptation we have when reading to forget the fictionality of the discourse, or of such things as "poetical justice." The novel itself succeeds in "proving a thing even while [it] contradict[s] it" by getting us to reflexively credit (as a fiction) a fictional liar's life.

Thackeray focuses so much of his attention on Barry Lyndon and other scoundrels because of their ability to manipulate the conventions governing discursive transactions in an amusing (albeit insidious) way. The dangerous liar is he who not only violates the "basic assumption of the linguistic marketplace" that referents are implied by a verbal or textual event and are to be inferred "in accord with the relevant rules and conventions" (Smith, *OMD*, 100), but keeps that event coherent and, above all, interesting as well. In other words he is the potential fiction writer. If Barry Lyndon fails at sustaining a coherent narrative (and from the first sentence of the novel Thackeray makes a point of providing plenty of room for interpretive inferences that contradict Barry's own), he succeeds in making his story interesting, in making himself an interesting character.

Thackeray and other writers who employ such unreliable narrators understand and exploit the rules of a language game which dictate that

a natural utterance [or text] constitutes, for the listener, not only an invitation and provocation, but ultimately an *obligation,* to respond to the speaker. When we "listen" to someone, as distinguished from merely noticing or overhearing what he says—in other words, when we

identify ourselves as his audience—we implicitly agree to make ourselves available to that speaker as the instrument of his interests. We agree not only to hear but to *heed* his promises, excuses, questions, and commands—and also, of course, his assertions. Most simply, but most significantly, we agree *to understand what he means,* that is, to infer the motives and circumstances that occasioned his utterance.

(Smith, *OMD*, 101-2)

When we "listen" to a narrative we agree, at least initially, to accept what the narrator presents to us as true, until we detect a violation of the good faith needed to play the game. Even then we have to credit some of what we are told—or stop playing the game with this speaker (or writer), or play our own game—as is often the case with the speaker-less (presence-less) text. What happens, Thackeray seems to be asking in **Barry Lyndon,** when we know the rules are being transgressed without being suspended (Barry claims to be an autobiographer not a fiction writer), and we find the discourse interesting nonetheless? Are we then believing a fiction to be true? Can we always, while we are enjoying ourselves with the story, keep the fictive and natural utterances clearly distinguished? And what are the consequences of such a play with the conventions of discourse? Thackeray's project is to educate his readers in their habits of reading and of belief. Probability and credulity are always at issue for Thackeray, not only in his criticism of others, but in his own novels as well. He seems—as a novelist—to be more interested in how we read and believe than in whether particular beliefs are true. His protopragmatism evidences itself in this preoccupation with how we know and its consequences for how we live.

IV. SKEPTICISM AND BELIEF; VANITY AND VALUE

The interest in fiction's sway with readers that I have been tracing in the last section is related to Thackeray's own struggles with skepticism and belief. His theological doubts instill an epistemological uncertainty, or vice versa. Taken together these conditions both make possible the fictions he writes and help determine his eventual difficulty with writing fiction at all.

Gordon Ray has documented Thackeray's recurring struggles with skepticism, first under the influence of Edward Fitzgerald, and later as he took in the intellectual currents of mid-century.[17] Ray cites extensively chapter 61 of **Pendennis,** "The Way of the World," wherein the dialectic between the skeptical, worldly Pen and the resolute, dutiful George Warrington does indeed reflect the author's own conflict between doubt and certainty. The cynical Pen argues that absolute faith in one's own voice breeds dogmatism and persecution; he cites historical examples to support his position. So far he is in the right. Even Warrington and the narrator

admire the young dandy's tolerance of human imper-
fection and rejection of cant. But Pen uses these realizations to justify an indifference to all human endeavor
and all morality, and this is where he trips up. Thackeray's will to believe is embodied in the fogy Warrington,
who insists that the struggle itself, "the protest" against
the impotence of skepticism, is all. To Pen's "sneering
acquiescence in the world as it is; or if you like so to
call it, . . . belief qualified with scorn in all things extant" (*Works,* 2:614-15) is opposed Warrington's sense
of duty. In this tension between belief and doubt is
Thackeray's peculiar appreciation of fiction born, for in
the incongruity of this desire to believe with an ironic
distance from forms of belief we find an important element in our understanding of fictive discourse, the
mind's simultaneous use of two frames of reference,
the ability to believe while not believing. Thackeray's
temperament, exemplified by this coincidence of skepticism and the will to believe, suits him to his chosen
task of uncovering vanity, that double-sided coin of
conceit and emptiness, which shows us how human culture can be both legal tender and counterfeit at the same
time.

If vanity allows Thackeray to express his skeptic side,
it also permits him to celebrate the attempt to believe,
the attempt to find value. To be self-consciously vain of
something is to be cognizant of overvaluing the item
even while enjoying it. In this sense of vanity Thackeray himself recognizes what Smith calls the "contingencies of value." Although we always want to believe
in things, people, ideas, and words, without qualification, we find our understanding of each depends upon
particular contexts and chance events, and must be kept
current through revision.

Belief, then, becomes for Thackeray an ideal that is
never fully realized. His temperament of mind favors
habits of inquiry once again akin to those of pragmatism. He had been tutored at Cambridge by William
Whewell, who lectured on connections between science
and morality and was writing his *History of the Induc-
tive Sciences* while Thackeray attended, and later in
life, as a moderate liberal, he admired science's and society's advances. I believe a healthy skepticism, which
Richard Poirier has deemed a prerequisite to "the deed
of writing," finds its expression in Thackeray's work in
the significant role that discovery and inquiry play in
his novels.[18] His chatty narrators may endorse particular
values (which we may or may not agree with as we
read him now), but they more importantly rehearse the
act of valuing, because Thackeray sees how we are capable of changing the nature of things we experience
(for ourselves) when we redescribe them:

> A word of kindness or acknowledgment, or a single
> glance of approbation, might have changed Esmond's
> opinion of the great man; and instead of a satire, which

his pen cannot help writing, who knows but that the
humble historian might have taken the other side of
panegyric? We have but to change the point of view,
and the greatest action looks mean; as we turn the
perspective-glass, and a giant appears a pigmy. You
may describe, but who can tell whether your sight is
clear or not, or your means of information accurate?

(*Works,* 7:222)

Because of this dialogic element in Thackeray's work, I
pair as analogous the concepts of skepticism and vanity,
and belief and value (sentimental or otherwise). When
we value something we often believe in it quite fer-
vently (as Thackeray shows in a pathetic character like
Old Osborne). Thackeray's skepticism is best described
by the term vanity because the latter hints at the vague
notion of something beyond the contingent which instills him with his sentimental melancholy. Perhaps this
frame of mind derives from his remarkable sense of the
contingency of things past. In a **"Roundabout"** essay
on a fragment by Charlotte Brontë, he speculates about
the text (and by implication about aesthetic texts in
general): "If the Has Been, why not the Might Have
Been?" (*Works,* 12:187). Not only might things have
been different, they "Might Have Been" represented
differently, and these two, Thackeray realizes—through
his inquiries into probability in narrative—can be very
nearly the same.

Once philosophers realize (as Thackeray does) that particular values are possibilities but not necessities, they
begin to downplay abstract moral law in favor of individual narratives—the moral function of which depends
on such a relativistic ethics. Rorty has described narrative's central role in exploring the value of particular
ethical paradigms—in fact, he calls the history of intellectual and moral progress "a history of increasingly
useful metaphors" (*CIS,* 9). This role is certainly the
one Thackeray saw good fictional narratives playing in
his own society. However, fictions which either attempt
to hide their fictionality or propose too easily a "transcendent" or "romantic" truth come under his severest
scrutiny. His own voice, on the other hand, is always
clearly that of an individual relating the events of his
experience: that is, always clearly in a rhetorical situation complete with all the hazards of argument and deception. Thackeray's narratives depend heavily on a
discernible scaffold of hypothesis and inference for
their persuasiveness, and their goal is discovery of new
ways of talking about reality, and new descriptions of it
that encompass older ones. The ironist specializes in redescribing reality in partially neologistic jargon (Rorty,
CIS, 78); Thackeray's attempts to redefine such things
as snobbery, worldly success, and the gentleman are
signs of his interest in using narrative as heuristic.[19] He
realizes there are no values which are not contingent
and no vocabularies which are final. Perhaps the most
interesting result, for his readers, of his doubts and de-

sire to believe is the effect his uncertainty has on the form of his novels. Uncertain of himself as well as others, Thackeray writes narrative which involves a great deal of speculation, playful and serious at once.

V. Thackerayan Narrative as Cognitive Play

Reading Thackeray's novels as representations of our need to reassess and revise cognitive activity and its accompanying moral judgements allows us to appreciate certain distinctive features of Thackeray's art, while not denying that many of his individual assessments and judgements are not ours. Thackeray can still make us aware of the "independent charms of epistemic activity" (Smith, *OMD*, 117). In life we are mainly concerned with cognitive ends which are rewarded by the everyday world. In art we are made aware of cognitive activities—how we know what we know—and Thackeray's narratives reward readers for taking their cues to examine how they use cultural and narrative conventions to form their worlds. On the other hand, Thackeray's unrevised racial views as, for instance, in the character of Woolcomb in *Philip,* are offensive to us (and undoubtedly have lost him many readers). His individual assessments stand up less well than his interest in assessing. But even in that novel, as Alexander Welsh has argued (Welsh, *Thackeray*), we can find valuable Thackeray's use of fiction for heuristic purposes.

I think it is worth pursuing the suggestion Welsh has made that Thackerayan narrative is distinctive for its predominantly speculative tenor. According to Rorty, narrative is one of the pragmatist's primary tools for helping us see and revise our intellectual habits (*CIS,* vxi). Fictional narrative helps us invent new vocabularies, since—as we have seen—its places of intersection with our present vocabulary help loosen the latter's hold on our knowledge of the world. Smith sees fictional narratives as examples of "cognitive play," places where we test out new descriptions of the world and of our place in it with relatively few consequences (when, that is, we can clearly keep distinguished the "margins"). These aesthetic toys and ethical tools allow us to grasp the "structural relations" (Smith, *OMD*, 117) of our world and modify them, and perhaps consequently modify the world outside us. In order to so work and allow us to learn, cognitive activity must be

> characterized by, among other things, a combination— either a balance or a particular ratio—of novelty and familiarity, repetition and variation, conformity and disparity, redundancy and information. Learning is most graciously invited by a situation that appears to some extent unknown but that promises knowability.
>
> (Smith, *OMD*, 118)

It is the testing of such patterns that Thackeray's novels rehearse. And so he blends the old vocabularies of his world with hypotheses about how they relate to one another.

One of Thackeray's most direct discussions of this stitching together of observation and inference occurs in an intrusion by Pendennis into his narrative of the Newcome family. According to this theory, the novelist "puts this and that together: from the footprint finds the foot; from the foot, the brute who trod upon it" (*Works,* 8:491). The entire passage compares the novelist's job to the paleontologist's, describing the former as one who, like Professor Agassiz, speculates from a "fragment of a bone" (*Works,* 8:491). The fragment, the historical evidence, in the novelist's case consists of language, the vocabularies and conventions of culture, both past and present. But much must be expanded upon, revised, and thus discovered. Thackeray's blends of commentary and action in his narratives work like the scientist's hypothesis and experiment. The narrator proposes something as happening, or as a past happening, or even as a possible happening, and then interprets it for us, proposing meanings for it and possibly even applying the meanings to his readers' lives. Smith writes of our "epistemic fixation" (*OMD*, 117), our hunger for information, knowledge, and interpretations for us in turn to interpret. Thackeray's narrators enact that processing. The delight is in watching this acute mind tracing the patterns and making us aware of our own tracings.

One of the most fruitful places to go exploring for this cognitive activity is Chapter 64 of *Vanity Fair*, aptly labeled "A Vagabond Chapter."[20] As that title suggests, it seems indeed wandering, nomadic, as it follows the fortunes of Becky, the novel's irrepressible vagabond, who strays ever more after Rawdon leaves her. We catch up with her in this chapter by following her retreat to the Continent and her subsequent ways of life. Filled with ambiguities and evasions about just what Becky does and does not do, how others do or do not act towards her, and why they might or might not have done so, it resists our desire to rest from interpretation. For every piece of evidence of Becky's guilt there is an extenuating circumstance, a sympathetic reading of the incident, or a complete displacement of responsibility. Becky is depicted as more acted upon than acting in her "*abattement* and degradation" (625). The snobbish Lady Slingstones who hound her are accompanied by such wolves as the lecherous Grinstone who "showed his teeth and laughed in her face with a familiarity that was not pleasant" (627). The point of view wanders in the chapter from a distanced perspective on "poor little Becky" (627) to "our little wanderer's" (632) own thoughts, endearingly presented, at George Osborne's grave, until we are indirectly given her genuine anxiety upon encountering Lord Steyne and being rejected. Throughout the chapter, Thackeray has manipulated us through vocabulary and point of view to keep us off balance as to just how much we are to sympathize with Becky.

The chapter starts off very clearly with the distinction between "the moral world" and "vice" (624), even though it teases us with the distinction between appearance and reality in the elaborate description of Becky as siren. The narrator obviously sets out to satirize the "truly-refined English or American female" who doesn't want vice represented. But in that complaint over censorship a comfortable dichotomy between appearance and reality, and moral and immoral, is itself set up for the purpose of knocking it down. Supposedly we have the decorous (unreal) world of novels and the (real) world of vice, personified by Becky, in her role of mermaid. But as we have seen, the rest of the chapter undermines—through its wavering point of view, conflicting scenes, and ambiguous images—that very category of vice. Even the central metaphor contributes to this collapsing of the dichotomy, though it seems to support the absolute morality of good and bad, woman and demon. The siren is supposedly half woman, half fish, and the mocking opening paragraph warns us against following the creatures into "their native element," where they "are about no good, . . . revelling and feasting on their wretched pickled victims" (625). But as we have seen, within two pages Becky is herself presented as victim, subject to the teeth of other predators. The metaphor of siren is retained, however, with very interesting results. As she is chased from place to place and made more and more lonely through this persecution, she is presented as "perched upon the French coast" (626); she shares "in sea-bathing" and takes walks "upon the jetty" (627), attracts temporary companions with "the sweetness of her singing" (629) and her "graces and fascinations" (630-31). Thackeray has exploited a different interpretation of the siren figure as one of banishment and loneliness to put in question his own earlier use of it. To discredit completely the alignment of his projected readers with good and the sirens with bad, he associates Becky with Mrs. Hook Eagles, "a woman without a blemish in her character" who makes Becky's acquaintance "at sea, where they were swimming together" (630). Thus the harpy and the siren become momentarily bosom companions (surely Thackeray is here drawing from the alternative tradition of depicting sirens as half bird, not fish), and the language not only of novels, but of morality is criticized.

The chapter, then, is truly vagabond, not only in its interest in Becky's leading an unsettled, irregular, or disreputable life, but in its own roving, straying, narration, its point of view seemingly not subject to control or restraint. At its beginning we are presented with a clear distinction between surface and depth, decorum and vice; after its explorations of those oppositions we are left with an opaque verbal and narrative surface, its depth (that is, the "truth" about Becky) imperceptible. The play of the narrative, which is dominated by speculative qualifiers like "perhaps" and "I don't think" and "very likely," comes up with no definite answers to the question of "her history [which] was after all a mystery" (629), but it does discover (and discredit) the conventions of a couple of language games. Throughout Thackeray's work we can find such play with possible meanings, possible responses, and the possible worlds which are implied by both.

There are several ramifications (for other narratives as well as Thackeray's) of this use of fiction for cognitive play, one of which is the improvisational form that such narratives employ. Part of Thackeray's genius is his ability to develop his characters and plots as his narrative discoveries change them. Thus, the narrator's attitude toward Amelia Sedley develops as she does, from admiration for a typical heroine (devoted and passive) to impatience with an obsessive and manipulative woman. He can also suddenly find some interesting qualities in Rawdon Crawley, after he (and we) had him pegged as a stupid bully. The figure of the dandy can signify independence (in Arthur Pendennis) or utter dependence on society (in the Major), depending on context. At the end of **The Newcomes,** like Scott at the end of *Old Mortality,* Thackeray even leaves the plot open—anticipating the "modern" phenomenon of "open" texts—by suggesting that the picture we might have of the hero and heroine married is only wishful thinking. He thus emphasizes both how readers participate in creating the novel by bringing their common vocabulary of novelistic conventions to the text and how his dissatisfaction with conventional forms (of literature and knowledge) gives him a certain daring independence with which to play the game. Finally, in **Henry Esmond,** according to Ray, Thackeray's most planned novel, his hero's melancholy sense of change and nostalgia for the past (represented by the faithful woman, Rachel Esmond) make one of the very subjects of the novel the extent to which chance and improvisation make up our (or at least, according to this passage, men's) experience:

> What is the meaning of fidelity in love, and whence the birth of it? 'Tis a state of mind that men fall into, and depending on the man rather than the woman. We love being in love, that's the truth on't. If we had not met Joan, we should have met Kate, and adored her. We know our mistresses are no better than many other women, nor no prettier, nor no wiser, nor no wittier. 'Tis not for these reasons we love a woman, or for any special quality or charm I know of; we might as well demand that a lady should be the tallest woman in the world, like the Shropshire giantess, as that she should be a paragon in any other character, before we began to love her.
>
> (**Works,** 7:272-73)

Another consequence of both Thackeray's role as ironist and his use of narrative for cognitive play is his understanding of the ethical import of fiction. Since he sees vocabularies not as pictures of the world but as tools for discovery (and for deception), and since he reenacts in his fiction the revisions we constantly make, he is sensitive to the social conflicts that occur when differing vocabularies (complete with their differing values) meet.

VI. THACKERAY'S AESTHETIC AND ETHICAL PRAGMATISM

To say that it is impossible not to be sometimes a snob is to acknowledge in a wonderfully provocative way how we *must* sometimes inscribe limits to irony even if we consider ourselves complete ironists. We must credit some uses of language at least some of the time. We have to interpret ourselves and others and texts, even if we realize at the same time the inevitable limitations of those readings; we cannot perpetually expect a better reading and still function in our social worlds. If the snob tries to play up his claims and the claims of those he values to truth, the ironist works against this exclusivity, to subvert it in favor of a general leveling, an understanding of the contingency of every vocabulary. Hence, as Rorty says, the ironist, who questions the necessary existence of a permanent moral order, has always seemed hostile to human solidarity (*CIS*, xv). This subversive enterprise is also the topic of Harold Bloom's "agonistic" theory of literature and Thackeray's declaration in **The English Humourists**: "Yesterday's preacher becomes the text for today's sermon" (**Works,** 7:424).[21] The recognition of his own snobbery, however, signifies Thackeray's awareness that the ironic process does not go on forever in any individual mind; the revolution (and semiosis) must come to a place of rest at least for a while. It is in this conflict between the status quo and the radical (past meanings and the interpretive impulse, in the analogous terms from hermeneutics) that literature exists for Thackeray. Along with the ironist's subversiveness Thackeray displays his distrust of revolutionary zeal. Despite the implications of Barbara Hardy's excellent book *The Exposure of Luxury: Radical Themes in Thackeray,* I find him more a pragmatist than a radical, at least philosophically.[22] Realizing the contingency of all vocabularies, he was both bemused and deeply troubled by the competitiveness of existence.

In the pair of dandies, Arthur and Major Pendennis, we see how a cultural entity could signify something valuable at one moment and vain the next. This seemingly cavalier method of using the figure to mean different things in different contexts, what we might call being the novelist-as-dandy, is another example of the ironist in Thackeray. He shows how circumstance helps determine meaning and value by adding one significant variable, age, to the club man, the Major, thereby changing his significance. This role of the novelist-as-dandy captures the bubble-bursting, mocking function of redescription. The young dandy stands as individual, independent of the social conventions of family and work, and, in the metaphors of Thackeray's universe, as the figure of self-creation. His waistcoats and gloves are signs from this *private* vocabulary, which is analogous to innumerable other such vocabularies we ourselves form. But occurring with regularity in Thackeray's discourse is the competing *public* vocabulary of George Warrington, or the fogy, or the preacher, whose earnestness quite frequently displaces the puppet-master's irony. Both these vocabularies, which occasion a doubleness itself an irony, are crucial for forming Thackeray's sense of psychic struggles in individual selves, in the literature they write and read, and in society. With such conflicting voices as part of his own make-up, Thackeray seems to appreciate how completely the self is formed by competing vocabularies. As his use of the dandy indicates, he admires the ability (while also being wary of it) of those who consciously re-create themselves (through recreation and play). The dandy has and exercises choice, though it is a choice limited by the contingencies that have formed his past.

The voice of the preacher, on the other hand, employs the vocabulary not of self-creation, but of self-transcendence. When he preaches vanity, the fogy is emphasizing the contingency of the self created, and expressing the hope (at times seemingly vain in itself) that there is something *not* subject to such contextual determination. As I pointed out at the beginning of this essay, Thackeray fails eventually to find anything immune to devaluation and realizes it. He finds that all of life cannot be held in a single language; its contradictions demand compromise. At times, this realization invigorates him, while at others it defeats him.

This awareness of struggle instills his theory and practice of fiction with a slant toward ethical inquiry that is the final product of his own inquiries. Since the snob uses language as a tool—or a weapon, really—to exclude others, the exposure of the snob comes about through an ironic perspective on *his* language. But of course the catch-22 is that to call someone a snob is to be a snob, to use that same language of exclusion against him. The result for Thackeray is that the examination of the languages of snobbery (of value) becomes a fixation, the only ethical role literature can play well. It cannot, according to Thackeray's practice of it, safeguard us from valueless enterprises and thoughts—to think that it can is to be a literary snob. The snob's comfort in judging others comes from his ability to hold that person off at a distance and thereby turn him into a thing for ridicule. The snob can voyeuristically enjoy the "meanness" of others, as Mr. Snob enjoys the Ponto family. Thackeray's play is to turn the language of snobbery—which reifies the other—*reflexively* back upon himself and us. To objectify someone, to suspend the rules of how to respond to, or "listen to" (in Smith's words), a person, is to be a snob. Thackeray forces his readers to examine their language and their actions, to see how like the other's they are. This inquiry into his society's (and our) ethical vocabularies is the main subject of the Thackerayan novel. To see how the old preacher is turned into text by the next one, how the father is revised by the son, is to see how we have arrived where we are, and where we will wind up when we in turn are redescribed. This sort of epistemic activity is Thackeray's only ethical value for narrative. But, like Patricia Meyer Spacks, Thackeray also asks whether we can ever have "narrative without ethics."²³ And like her, he concludes that reading and writing fictions "heightens ethical self-consciousness" (Spacks ["The Novel as Ethical Paradigm"], 185). For Thackeray, fictional narratives imitate not so much an outer reality, but the cognitive activity of human beings, the "*text*ure of ethical life" (Spacks, 186; emphasis added).

Smith describes the different language uses in society and literature (labelled as natural and fictive discourse) in terms of the metaphors of linguistic *marketplace* and linguistic *playground* (*OMD,* 119). In society language is a tool of exchange; we give and receive real or bogus information for immediate practical ends. Literature is the playground where we can try on vocabularies, see how they are different from our old ones, see if they fit us, with relatively few consequences (other than the knowledge of the nature of vocabularies gained in the process), because the rules governing reactions to linguistic acts are suspended in this "Fableland," to use Thackeray's name for it. The pair of metaphors encompasses both the competitive and playful sides of rhetorical practice, and the satisfactions of both. Thackeray's use of Bunyan's place of business, Vanity *Fair,* in its turn, entails both of Smith's terms. For a fair involves both the business of the *marketplace* and the games of the *playground,* just as Thackeray's theory and practice of fiction realizes both the hazards and satisfactions of existence in a world of competing descriptions.

Notes

1. *The Works of William Makepeace Thackeray,* The Biographical Edition, 13 vols. (New York and London: Harper & Brothers, 1899), 1:488. Further references to this edition will appear in the text.

2. Barbara Herrnstein Smith, *Contingencies of Value* (Cambridge, MA: Harvard Univ. Press, 1988). Further references will appear in the text, cited as *CV.*

3. For two examples of twentieth-century impatience with Thackeray's sentiment, see J. Y. T. Greig, *Thackeray: A Reconsideration* (London: Oxford Univ. Press, 1950) and John Carey, *Thackeray: Prodigal Genius* (London: Faber and Faber, 1977).

4. Richard Rorty, *Contingency, Irony, and Solidarity* (Cambridge: Cambridge Univ. Press, 1989), 23-26. Further references will appear in the text, cited as *CIS.*

5. Richard Rorty ("Freud and Moral Reflection," *Pragmatism's Freud,* ed. Joseph Smith and William Kerrigan [Baltimore: Johns Hopkins Univ. Press, 1986]) applies this epithet to David Hume, a man whom Thackeray was both fascinated and disturbed by. In his review of Burton's biography of Hume, Thackeray depicts the great skeptic as two people, one publicly dangerous, the other privately quite personable. See *Contributions to the Morning Chronicle,* ed. Gordon Ray (Urbana: Univ. of Illinois Press, 1955), 113-117. Rorty also indirectly claims Thackeray as a precursor of Neopragmatism because he contributed to our "acquisition of new vocabularies of moral reflection" by inventing "terms like . . . *a Becky Sharpe* [*sic*]" (11).

6. Though these terms are hardly interchangeable, they all capture Rorty's sense of irony as the realization that each vocabulary we adopt is a convention, a made thing, that isn't necessarily better or worse than any other possible vocabulary. I derive the terms from (respectively) William Empson, "Tom Jones," *Kenyon Review* 20 (Spring, 1958):218-19; Anne Mellor, *English Romantic Irony* (Cambridge, MA: Harvard Univ. Press, 1980); Wayne Booth, *A Rhetoric of Irony* (Chicago: Univ. of Chicago Press, 1974); Kenneth Burke, "Four Master Tropes," *A Grammar of Motives* (Berkeley: Univ. of California Press, 1962); Robert Siegle, *The Politics of Reflexivity: Narrative and the Constitutive Poetics of Culture* (Baltimore: Johns Hopkins Univ. Press, 1986).

7. Richard Poirier, *The Renewal of Literature: Emersonian Reflections* (New York: Random House, 1987), discusses Emerson and Wordsworth as pragmatists, while Rorty (note 4) credits Nietzsche for first doing philosophy from an ironic perspective, which has allowed for the thoroughgoing irony of Derrida. What all these figures have in common is the habit of talking of things not in "final" or metaphysical terms, but in figurative, that is rhetorically self-conscious, language.

8. Contrast, for instance, his praise for the caricaturist Daumier's topically dressed figures (*Works* [*The Works of William Makepeace Thackeray*], 5:142-66) with his scorn for David's idealizing neoclassical work (5:41-57), both in *The Paris Sketchbook.*

9. See *From Cornhill to Grand Cairo,* where in one paragraph on the Tomb of the Sepulchre, Thackeray expresses both scorn for English tourists' au-

dacity and admiration for the Anglican Church's simplicity compared to that of the Roman Catholic (*Works,* 5:694-95).

10. Barbara Herrnstein Smith, *On the Margins of Discourse* (Chicago: Univ. of Chicago Press, 1978). Further references will appear in the text, cited as *OMD.*

11. John R. Searle, *Speech Acts: An Essay in the Philosophy of Language* (1969; reprint Cambridge: Cambridge Univ. Press, 1980), 78.

12. Smith (note 10), 124-32, 210-11 n.7.

13. Robert Newsom, *A Likely Story* (New Brunswick: Rutgers Univ. Press, 1988), 118-125.

14. Gregory Bateson, "A Theory of Play and Fantasy," *Psychiatric Research Reports* 2 (1955): 39-51; reprinted in Robert E. Innis, ed., *Semiotics: An Introductory Anthology* (Bloomington: Indiana Univ. Press, 1985), 129-44.

15. *The Letters and Private Papers of William Makepeace Thackeray,* ed. Gordon Ray, 4 vols. (London: Oxford Univ. Press, 1945), 1:432-33.

16. William Makepeace Thackeray, *The Memoirs of Barry Lyndon, Esq.,* ed. Andrew Sanders (Oxford: Oxford Univ. Press, 1984), 40. Further references to this edition will appear in the text, cited as *BL.*

17. Gordon Ray, *Thackeray,* 2 vols. (New York: McGraw-Hill, 1955). See 1:131-32 and 2:121-23, 367-69.

18. Poirier (note 7), 3.

19. Alexander Welsh, Introduction to *Thackeray: A Collection of Critical Essays* (Englewood Cliffs, NJ: Prentice-Hall, 1968), 5; and "Theories of Science and Romance, 1870-1920," *Victorian Studies* [17] (1973): 146.

20. This chapter has received several critical treatments, two of which I am particularly indebted to: Nina Auerbach, *Woman and the Demon: The Life of a Victorian Myth* (Cambridge, MA: Harvard Univ. Press, 1982) 89 and passim; and John Loofbourow, *Thackeray and the Form of Fiction* (Princeton: Princeton Univ. Press, 1964), 60-66.

21. Harold Bloom, *Agon: Towards a Theory of Revisionism* (New York: Oxford Univ. Press, 1982).

22. Barbara Hardy, *The Exposure of Luxury: Radical Themes in Thackeray* (London: Peter Owen Ltd., 1972).

23. Patricia Meyer Spacks, "The Novel as Ethical Paradigm," *Novel: A Forum on Fiction* 21.2/3 (1988): 184.

Elizabeth Rosdeitcher (essay date fall 1996)

SOURCE: Rosdeitcher, Elizabeth. "Empires at Stake: Gambling and the Economic Unconscious in Thackeray." *Genre: Forms of Discourse and Culture* 29, no. 3 (fall 1996): 407-28.

[*In the following essay, Rosdeitcher assesses conflicts among ideas about capitalism, community, and culture in Thackeray's fiction.*]

In a scene at the end of *Vanity Fair,* Thackeray depicts a casino in the German town of Pumpernickel which for the week of carnival occupies the Town Hall. The scene offers an explicit allegory of an emerging tension between national identity and the marketplace. In place of the governing body which ordinarily conducts public affairs in the Town Hall, "one of the great German companies" sets up games of chance. This brief glimpse of an economic enterprise that serves as the vehicle for collective identity, and, as we will see, for national identity, reflects a notion of the economy that began in the eighteenth century. As Susan Buck-Morss proposes in a recent essay, "[I]t was not the political notion of nationalism but the economic notion of a collective based on the depersonalized exchange of goods upon which, historically, the liberal-democratic tradition rests"; and this new sense that "the exchange of goods . . . is capable of functioning as the fundament of collective life . . . can be traced to a particular historical site: Europe (specifically England and France) during the eighteenth-century Enlightenment" (439). The scene at Pumpernickel conveys the problematic nature of the alliance between nation-states and a transnational or global economy: While the town prohibits its own citizens from gambling in order to protect them, it admits into the casino "strangers, peasants, ladies . . . and any one who chose to win or lose money" (755), and thereby unsettles the borders of national identity by letting in those who usually inhabit its margins.[1]

This essay addresses Thackeray's representation of a notion of the economy, consistently figured as gambling, which both defines and threatens collective identities. I begin with a reading of *Barry Lyndon* (1844) which traces the historical development of an economic subject, one whose identity is predicated on the future rather than preordained by the past; and I close with a reading of *Vanity Fair* (1847-48) to suggest how the earlier notions of identity become appropriated within a more wide-ranging view of British society and a more complex—and more marketable—fictional form. In *Vanity Fair* gambling represents the mechanism by which the marketplace seduces us, and this dynamic is contained in the novel itself in the figure of Becky Sharp. The workings of this economy is finally complicitous with Thackeray's own fictional enterprise.

Eighteenth-century England and France, where Buck-Morss locates the origins of the new sense of the economy as the basis of collective life, has particular relevance to the British-French rivalry that is central to both *Barry Lyndon* and *Vanity Fair.* In *Barry Lyndon,* itself set in the eighteenth century, British-French antagonism is the pivotal rivalry of the Seven Years War in which *Barry Lyndon* becomes a soldier; and in *Vanity Fair* not only do we have the battle of Waterloo, but the novel's central character, Becky Sharp, with her French mother and English father, internalizes this opposition. Thackeray makes explicit the way in which notions of the economy underlie the process of national self-definition in these two newly emerging capitalist democracies, competing for colonial possessions and world markets. Their struggles in fact take the form of a gambling transaction.

Recent criticism of *Vanity Fair* universally acknowledges the place of economic concepts in Thackeray's most widely read novel. In a detailed analysis of women's duplicitous language in *Vanity Fair,* Lisa Jadwin notes that Thackeray locates the beginnings of Becky's linguistic skill in her poverty and her early dealings with creditors and tradesmen; Sandy Morey Norton, who finds in Thackeray's own uses of a double-voiced language an ambivalence toward imperialist projects, identifies Becky's desire with that of the capitalist: "It is never clear exactly what Becky wants, except that, like any true capitalist, she always wants more" (134). In a more explicit analysis of economic details, Andrew Miller considers the way economic form underpins a "dynamic of desire and disenchantment" in Thackeray that pervades the experience of his characters and the form of the novel; and Gary Dyer examines nineteenth-century attitudes toward women and commerce in a discussion of the rhetoric surrounding charity bazaars and "fancy fairs" in which women participated as Becky does at the end of *Vanity Fair.* Even Robert Fletcher's discussion of Thackeray's "literary pragmatism" which claims Thackeray as a precursor to a pragmatist philosophical tradition from Nietzsche to Rorty takes into account the way questions of economic value are put into play alongside considerations of linguistic value. Recognition of the significance of economic ideas in Thackeray is not limited to the most recent criticism. In *The Exposure of Luxury* Barbara Hardy contends that reading Thackeray is, in fact, like reading some of the major social and economic theorists: "To read him is to read a fictional form of Veblen's *Theory of the Leisure Class* or Marcel Mauss's *Essai sur le don,* or Galbraith's *The Affluent Society*" (20). Yet, while each of Thackeray's critics stress the economic, they fail to recognize the problematic way in which the economic simultaneously underlies and threatens the notion of an enlightened bourgeois subject and citizen.

Thackeray's preoccupation with the economic extended to his consideration of the writer's social status. In an 1846 essay on the death of Laman Blanchard, a fellow journalist just eight years his senior, for example, Thackeray objects to the terms on which an obituary evaluates Blanchard's career. The obituary unwittingly situates the author in a speculative marketplace where both chance and profitable investments determine his ultimate place in the hierarchy of literary evaluation. The language of the obituary implicitly conveys a notion of authorship modelled on gambling and financial speculation: Blanchard lacked "fortunate chances" and was unable to "invest" his talent in a way that would yield the "prizes . . . of weighty reputation or popular renown" (472) which would in turn increase his winnings. Thackeray critiques this assessment of Blanchard's career by envisioning the author as a different kind of economic subject. Instead of gauging the success of the writer on the ability to accumulate prizes, Thackeray proposes that success be measured by the work's usefulness to the public. Thackeray draws what he calls "an unpolite shoeblack comparison," equating the writer's work with labor that has such concrete and purposeful ends as the blacking of boots.

Thackeray's resistance to the evaluation of Blanchard's career as a series of speculations emerged out of his own deep familiarity with the attractions and the dangers of such a model. His own early experiences—his addiction to gambling, his work for a bill-discounting firm, the loss of his patrimony through his investment in the India Bank—gave him direct knowledge of the effects and pervasiveness of gambling and speculation. The widespread buying and selling of railway shares during the 1840s in which Thackeray also participated, and the financial panic that resulted in 1845, must have made the impact of the speculative marketplace again more acutely perceptible to him. Yet, if Thackeray resisted such a speculative model in evaluating the biography of his fellow writer, his own biographers have not. Peter Shillingsburg describes *Vanity Fair* as "the watershed of Thackeray's career as a businessman, transforming him from the investor/gambler, the writer waiting upon publishers with his goods, into the propertied tradesman who built himself a debt-free mansion at Palace Green, Kensington" (28). Thackeray's early career was a "high-risk speculative venture without guaranteed returns" (35)—the future was uncertain insofar as his work took on value only after it had been produced; after *Vanity Fair,* on the contrary, Thackeray engaged in a more secure economic venture in that his name and reputation guaranteed in advance the value of all his work. Making the speculative paradigm again explicit, the two volumes of Gordon Ray's biography hinge on the moment when *Vanity Fair* first wins Thackeray the "prizes" of reputation and popularity, following the series of setback and losses, of failed investments and reckless gambling, that make up the first volume. Ray concludes the first volume by noting that to Thackeray the "real professional service" of *Vanity Fair* "was in multiplying the value of all his future work. Henceforth he was paid not as a clever magazine writer, but as a great popular favorite" (428). Despite Thackeray's own efforts to evaluate writers' work according to other criteria, the speculative model itself outlived Thackeray, providing the terms for our own criticism and our assessment of his life.

Edmund Burke argued that the effect of the French Revolution and of the breakdown of the traditional social order generally would be to "metamorphose France from a great kingdom into one great playtable; to turn its inhabitants into a nation of gamesters; to make speculation as extensive as life; . . . [and] mix it with all its concerns" (189). Burke's complaint was that political equality would make money the sole determinant of social status and all individuals subject to the same haphazard fluctuations of the market.

Burkean rhetoric bores Barry Lyndon. At the height of his fortune, Barry wins a seat in Parliament where "during Mr. Burke's interminable speeches," he recalls, "I used always to go to sleep" (262); and yet, Barry, too, interprets his experiences as though they made up one unending game of chance. He unwittingly betrays the extent to which, as Burke puts it, "the spirit and symbols of gaming" have entered into "the minutest matters" of his existence and at the same time become "as extensive as life" (Burke [*Reflections on the Revolution in France*] 189). All events are either the result of good or bad luck; and the chapter headings such as "More Runs of Luck," "In Which the Luck Goes Against Barry," "Barry . . . Attains the Height of his Luck," and "In Which the Luck of Barry Lyndon Begins to Waver" reflect this structure as does Thackeray's initial title of the novel, **The Luck of Barry Lyndon**.[2] Gambling infuses both the lives and deaths of everyone who surrounds Barry. His father, who was "as brave a fellow as ever tossed a bumper or called a main," dies early in Barry's life "at the Chester races" (51). An uncle, whom Barry meets later in the novel, is a professional gamester who inducts Barry into his trade. When his friend Captain Fagan is shot and killed in the war, his last words to Barry are, "I should have left you a hundred guineas . . . but for a cursed run of ill-luck last night at faro" (120). It is no accident that the home of Barry's birth was later "used as a gambling-house" (257). He is literally born into a world defined through gambling.

Not only does gambling pervade all of Barry's adventures, it also structures both his character and the narrative itself. Barry Lyndon's life takes the shape of a series of gambling transactions. Walter Benjamin's observation that the gambler's experience is made up of a series of disconnected moments in which each *coup* is screened off from those which precede and follow describes the episodic form of Thackeray's narrative. Like the gambler who "gives short shrift to [a] weighty past" (Benjamin ["On Some Motifs in Baudelaire"] 177),

Barry Lyndon begins each episode with a new name and a made-up past that conceals his social origins. Further, that which Richard Proctor, a nineteenth-century theorist of gambling, defined as the "fatal confidence" characteristic of the gambler punctuates Barry's own discourse: "I had no doubts of the future," he maintains throughout, "I knew I was born to make a figure in the world" (162). Like the gambler, again, his thoughts are focussed on the future rather than the past. When he first leaves home to pursue his adventures, he confesses that "I rode away, thinking, . . . not so much of the kind mother left alone, and of the home behind me, as of to-morrow, and all the wonders it would bring" (96). Each episode reflects a new attempt to recast himself in the image of the gentleman, to realize in the future what he claims to have inherited in the past. The writing of the memoirs itself proves to be his final attempt to do so; it is his final act of speculation in which we, his future readers, participate. As Barry indicates early in his narrative, "My day is over . . . my race is run," and he writes only "for those who shall come after me" (63). Conceiving of his life as a race, the narrative itself becomes his last wager on its outcome, on the status he will achieve among his future readers. (He does not, however, win this bet; we see through his aristocratic pretensions repeatedly, particularly when he reports the accusations of others who call him a low-born adventurer, an impostor, and a scoundrel.)

Thackeray shows us that in contrast to Burke's vision of future France as a colossal gaming hall, Europe itself was *already* "one great playtable" before democratic ideals diminished the power of the nobility. When Barry attends the courts of Europe as a professional gamester, he describes a scene where "play was patronised and the professors of that science always welcome" (189), where "the dice-box rattled every where and all the world played" (191), or simply, where "every body was a gambler" (191). Throughout the novel, he encounters noblemen such as Monsieur de Galgenstein distinguished by his "propensity to gambling and extravagance" (135), Sir Charles Lyndon, "a constant frequenter" of the play-table characterized by "the spirit and gallantry with which he pursued his favorite pastime" (240), and Monsieur de Magny who "had been almost ruined at play, as his father had before him" and who "if he saw a dice-box, it was impossible to prevent him from handling it" (196).

The gambling of the traditional nobility, however, differs from the gambling of those like Barry Lyndon aspiring to its ranks. It reflects a distinction between individuals whose social identity was fixed by the past, by birth and lineage, and those whose identity was predicated on the future, whose status was subject, in other words, to chance, and open to speculation in all its meanings. As Thomas M. Kavanagh describes in his discussion of gambling in eighteenth-century France, gambling for the true nobleman was "an occasion . . . to demonstrate his independence from money as money" (38). It was unacceptable "to play with the primary intention of winning money; to cheat; or, when losing, to act in such a way as to reveal an inordinate attachment to money" (39). High-stakes gambling affirmed that one's position in society was grounded in one's ancestry, in particular, in the acts of valor one's ancestors performed on the battlefield: "To be noble was to have demonstrated—personally or vicariously through an ancestor—a willingness to risk one's life in battle beside one's king" (43). Gambling became a symbolic substitute, like the duel, through which members of the nobility reenact the formation of the class structure on the battlefields of medieval Europe (45). It had the additional advantage of conveying their detachment from money, and their sense of a "fixed, inherited" identity (47). Gambling is thus the activity through which members of the nobility enact their particular relationship to wealth and the social structure.

For those aspiring to the ranks of the nobility, and for the recently ennobled, gambling had a different social function. It both performed and represented the new social process whereby one could transform one's identity through money. In play at the gaming table was the hope of remaking oneself in the image of the nobility through one's future winnings; the identity one hoped to achieve in the future was one which was defined by its foundation in the past. The illusion could be sustained in the act of gambling itself, by gambling as if one was indifferent to loss or gain, as if, in other words, one already had aristocratic origins. Thus Barry Lyndon gambles like an aristocrat, displaying a daring and boldness, a "gay manner of losing" (191) and the willingness to "spen[d] nobly what we had won" (185). He also maintains of his life with his uncle as a gamester that "when we were not at cards, we would pass hours over Gwillim or d'Hozier, reading the genealogies and making ourselves acquainted with the relationships of our class" (181). Barry and his uncle simultaneously uphold the pretense of aristocratic identity even as they gamble to attain it. Although of his uncle he discovers that "all his show was on his back," this show consists of an elaborate coat of arms painted on his carriage denoting his (presumably) ancient heritage but which was simply part of his "stock in trade" as a gamester (170).

Within this new social and economic structure, pretense, disguise—in short, fiction—serves as a form of credit. Barry observes, for example, that, as a soldier in the Prussian army, he had "only artifice to attain [his] end" (162), and confesses that "the advantage of having a gentlemanlike appearance has saved me many a time by procuring me credit when my fortunes were at the lowest ebb" (148). Truth itself becomes a form of currency. Like money, its value depends on others' belief in its validity.[3] When Barry's stories are believed to be genuine, they gain him the credit through which he can make them true in the future; when they are proved false, they lose their value, and he loses his identity. Moreover, we will see in the depiction of the Seven Years War in which Barry participates, that nations as well as individuals are engaged in this new form of gambling, of seeking to authenticate a fictional identity.

Only a short catalogue of Barry's adventures can convey their serial, episodic nature that lends the novel the form of a series of gambling transactions; gambling is not only a common pastime and finally his trade, but a paradigm for each adventure insofar as fiction and disguise serve as currency putting at risk an identity which depends, like money, on other's belief in its validity. When Barry first leaves home, he leaves his past behind him as well in what he calls "his first day's entrance into the world" (97). He takes on a new name, a false family history, and pretending to be an English gentleman, enters a new social milieu. As it happens, all the members of his hosts' society, whose dinners are "seasoned . . . by a plentiful store of anecdotes" (103) and by gambling, employ similar forms of deceit; they are all impostors like Barry who use their false identities in order to obtain what they perceive to be his wealth and connections. As he soon recognizes,

> Here was a doctor, who never had a patient, cheek by jowl with an attorney, who never had a client; neither had a guinea—each had a good horse to ride in the park, and the best of clothes to their backs. A sporting clergyman without a living; several young wine-merchants, who consumed much more liquor than they had or sold; and men of similar character, formed the society at the house into which, by ill-luck, I was thrown.
>
> (106-107)

Through the use of deceit and pretense, the members of this society risk their status in order to improve it.

When Barry himself is found out, both his wealth and pretenses discredited, he finds himself in the company of men in the lowest ranks of society, those who "had taken refuge from poverty, or the law" (112) by joining the British army on its way to Germany. Again, Barry finds a way out of these circumstances through an elaborate use of disguise and fiction, exchanging the identity of a delirious officer with his own. Then, like another roll of the dice, he leaves his past behind him, setting off with his new identification papers and a full purse. With this new identity he claims once again that he was "once more . . . in my proper sphere, and determined never again to fall from the rank of a gentleman" (129).

His next attempt to "keep up the character of the English gentleman" with a group of Prussian officers again takes the form of a wager in which he risks the loss of his social position. His conversations in which he "talked to them about my English estates with a fluency that almost made me believe in the stories which I invented" (129) fittingly accompanies his gambling in which he "lost a few pieces to his excellency the first huntmaster of his highness" (129). When the inconsistencies in his stories are detected, however, "the game was up" (134), and his identity is once again diminished to the anonymity of a soldier without name or fortune, this time without even a nation, for he is forced into the service of the Prussian army. Here, however, he begins the game again, convincing a naive Prussian captain of his noble ancestry to attain a more noble position, one again involving deception—he becomes a spy. He finally lands in the service of a "gentleman" who is in fact his uncle, a professional gambler who leads the same transitory life as himself, and Barry becomes a counter-spy by joining forces with his uncle. Their experience as gamblers conforms to the repetitive pattern and has the same logic as the adventures which precede it. At each new court to which they travel, they assert their high birth, and when these assertions are invalidated, they become "beggars" and must "begin the world again" (188).

Throughout these adventures the identity of war and gambling illustrates their common function. Implicitly at work in the novel is Elaine Scarry's description of the function of war to substantiate as real an identity that is as yet only a fiction. Scarry labels war a contest comparing it to "duelling or, especially if the risks are incalculable, gambling" (85). More specifically, she proposes that war occurs "when the system of national self-belief is without any compelling source of substantiation. . . . That is, *it is when a country has become to its population a fiction that wars begin*" (131, emphasis in original). As if to confirm the parallel symbolic function of war and gambling, we find that gambling in ***Barry Lyndon*** is practiced at all levels of the military and social hierarchy, among the lowly soldiers as well as the statesmen and diplomats. Barry reports that in the English regiment "drinking and gambling were . . . our principal pastimes" (122), and in the Prussian regiment, "[t]hose who had anything to risk gambled" (147). When he becomes a professional gambler, he gambles with "the young men of the different embassies" (173). Among these men, he finds "a young *attaché* of the English embassy, my Lord Deuceace, afterwards Viscount Earl of Crabs in the English peerage" (170), Russian attachés, and Mr. Charles Fox, "then only my Lord Holland's dashing son, afterwards the greatest of European orators and statesmen" (170-71). The main struggles between England and France, in America over possession of colonial territories and in Europe for power within various principalities, become part of a contest to authenticate national self-definitions.

Through the figure of Barry's uncle, Thackeray further asserts the identity of war and gambling. While "the real end of Monsieur de Balibari was play," he arrives in Berlin where Barry is stationed on a "mission from the Austrian court:—it was to discover whether a certain quantity of alloyed ducats which had been traced to Berlin, were from the king's treasury" (170). At stake for both nations and gamblers is the value of their currency, the representation of wealth and status, that through war or gambling they seek to validate and their opponents hope to undo.

Thackeray vividly reveals the function of violence in the process of substantiating a fictional identity in a duel Barry fights to defend his claims to nobility. As Kavanagh explains with respect to the ancien regime in France, both gambling and duelling reenact the formation of the class structure on the battlefields of medieval Europe. And as Barry tells us, "my first affair of honour . . . was on the score of my nobility with young Sir Rumford Bumford of the English embassy. . . . I shot Sir Rumford Bumford in the leg, . . . and I promise you that none of the young gentlemen questioned the authenticity of my pedigree or laughed at my Irish crown again" (182). In the violence of the duel, by shooting Sir Rumford Bumford in the leg, Barry authenticates his false pedigree; his action epitomizes the violence of war as it works to authenticate the origins of a nation.

Thackeray thus charts the beginnings of a new social process whereby identities are projected into the future, rather than preordained by the past. But it retains the older social form as a disguise. In gambling older social systems persist within the newer one. Hence it both erases the past and sets up a false one in its place. Individuals enact a new relationship to money and the social structure while appearing to articulate an old one. In this sense it is significant that Barry joins an army going east, to the old feudal culture of Germany, rather than west, to the new world. The subjects of the speculative marketplace perpetually seek to remake themselves in the image of the nobility, seeing in their future winnings the means to transform themselves into an ideal image of "the perfect gentleman" or man of fashion, a subject of an older economic system and of the courtly or aristocratic culture of a feudal society. Fiction becomes complicitous with this project as part of the means by which this new identity is brought about.[4]

While Thackeray thus shares Burke's view of a world dominated by gambling and speculation, he attributes this to the way old values persist within a new economy: individuals continue to valorize the ideals of the aristocracy rather than recognize new ones. The essay in which Thackeray proposes that the shoeblack rather than the speculator should serve as an economic model for the writer illustrates his difference from Burke, his attempt to replace the old system with a new respect for that which was not the proper sphere for gentlemen.[5]

* * *

Insofar as **Barry Lyndon** distances the reader from its narrator's attempt to glorify his own deeds, to hold himself up as a hero, Thackeray diminishes the fetishistic power of his characters over the readers, deprives us of such pleasurable but illusory effects, and consequently interferes with the process of identification. We have no desire to imagine ourselves in Barry's place or to worship his qualities. **Vanity Fair** would appear to do the same. Thackeray characteristically distinguishes his novel from the kind of fiction that appeals to our desire for the satisfying illusions of romance or heroism.[6] By the close of the novel Thackeray appears to have demonstrated the vanity of all human wishes. Amelia confronts the truth about George, Dobbin sees through his idolatry of Amelia, and all such similar desires prove vain in both senses of the word: not only do they reflect our own egotism, but are futile as well, for they will never be satisfied. In this sobering manner Thackeray ostensibly deflates the value of all our investments, emotional or otherwise, and we humbly resign ourselves to profiting in knowledge what we have lost in pleasure. The apparent mastery we attain in the realization that all our wishes are vain coincides with Dobbin's final success in shutting Becky out of his household. Thackeray shelters the reader as Dobbin does his family, allaying the threat Becky poses either to corrupt the innocent or exploit them for her own gain. Our safety and stability, like that of Dobbin's family, rest on her exclusion.

The exclusion of Becky, however, is not so easily accomplished, and the order Thackeray restores at the end of the novel barely reflects the conditions that have prevailed throughout. Thackeray consistently interferes with the reader's capacity to condemn Becky once and for all, and this difficulty in making a final judgement of her consequently keeps us from reaching the state of rest and equilibrium, stability and order, seemingly achieved at the end. Robert Fletcher calls attention to Thackeray's refusal to give us the "epistemic fix" we are looking for: "For every piece of evidence of Becky's guilt there is an extenuating circumstance, a sympathetic reading of the incident, or a complete displacement of responsibility" (397). Thackeray dramatizes the reader's predicament in his famous defense of the propriety of his novel in which he portrays Becky as a siren whose "hideous tail" lies below the waterline where all improper activity takes place. "[I]t is a labor lost" to see what transpires below the surface, though we "look into it ever so curiously" (760). Try as we might to peer beyond the surface of this text and despite our knowledge of Becky's character, her guilt remains maddeningly hidden from view.

Thackeray refuses us the stability that depends on making Becky our opposite, allows us no such neat dichotomies, but rather continually muddies the water of our own self-reflection. We are never quite sure where we stand, what position to take with respect to Becky, and our own moral ground seems to crumble beneath our feet. The novel instills a condition of doubt and uncertainty in the reader which only ostensibly ends when Dobbin instates his paternal authority. This condition also constitutes games of chance. Thackeray produces within the reader that which gambling was said to effect in its players, its tendency to unleash, as Kavanagh explains, "not a single passion but . . . a monstrously self-perpetuating synthesis of antithetical passions—desire and fear, hope and disappointment, joy and regret, anger and hatred" (61). Gambling renders the self beyond rational self-control, upsetting all notions of an enlightened bourgeois subject and citizen. As Thackeray saw in his own 1829 gambling experiences in Paris, "the interest of the game . . . is so powerful that I could not tear myself away until I lost my last piece—I dreamed of it all night—and thought of nothing else for several days" (**Letters** [**The Letters and Private Papers of William Makepeace**] 90-91); and a few weeks later, his letters suggest that the lesson he derives from his gambling experience is the lesson of the unconscious: "it has taught me not to trust so much in myself as before my pride or ignorance would have led me to do; it has shown that I could not, (as few could) resist the temptation of gambling, and therefore it has taught me to keep away from it" (**Letters** 96).

Kavanagh proposes that the many conflicting emotions present in the gambler rendered him incapable of rational action. Likewise, the various responses Becky elicits in the narrator, characters, and readers alike, make it all the more difficult to dismiss her, and thereby to stabilize ourselves or recover the moral integrity of a Dobbin. Given this effect, we can speculate that the commercial success of the novel and its value as an investment in Thackeray's career is due in part to this particular role Becky plays within it. In contrast to **Barry Lyndon, Vanity Fair** does not defuse through distance and satire the fetishistic power of its characters. Becky's power is literally that of the commodity in the marketplace which succeeds when it incites the uncontrollable and contradictory passions of the gambler. Gambling, in other words, represents the mechanism by which commodities seduce us; and this mechanism is contained within the novel itself. That gambling, for example, preoccupies each of the main characters Becky seduces, suggests that the passion for both are one and the same: for Rawdon Crawley, gambling is the most prominent of a series of vices that make up his "infernal character"—"he's a gambler—he's a drunkard—he's a profligate in every way" (121); George Osborne is betting "frantically" (339) during his questionable dealings with Becky in Brussels; and Jos Sedley meets

Becky at the play-table in Pumpernickel before she leads him away and becomes his lover.

Like Barry, Becky's experience takes the form of the gambling transactions that become her central activity. Like Barry, who leaves home "thinking of tomorrow, and all the wonders it would bring," (96), Becky forms "visions of the future" (105) on meeting Jos, and when she first arrives at the Crawley mansion, "lay awake for a long, long time, thinking of the morrow, and of the new world into which she was going, and of her chances for success there" (84). When she is in exile from England, moreover, she travels, like Barry, from place to place, posing as a member of fashionable society, and subsequently being "found out" and "hav[ing] all her work to begin again" (765-66). As Thackeray describes in "A Vagabond Chapter," which recounts Becky's life on the continent—"from Boulogne to Dieppe, from Dieppe to Caen, from Caen to Tours," she tries each time "to be respectable, and alas! [is] always found out some day or other and pecked out of the cage by the real daws" (766). During these travels she inhabits a series of boarding houses where above all aspects of the life of fashion, "what she preferred was the *écartet* at night, and she played audaciously" (769). And like Barry Lyndon, the narrator insists on the degree to which Becky's "history was after all a mystery" (765). Repeatedly denying the past and starting anew, her experience assumes the logic of gambling.

In the shift from a male to a female gambler, however, the emphasis changes. In **Barry Lyndon** characters and nations were subjected to the process represented in gambling of substantiating a fictional identity. In **Vanity Fair** Becky embodies, in a way Barry did not, the economy itself, particularly as it threatens the identities of both individuals and nations. As a woman she is symbolically linked with the irrational desires on which the marketplace depends. While on one hand, individuals (seemingly) act voluntarily on their interests to shape the economy, the summation of individual intentions, as Adam Smith observed, has unforeseeable effects and an irrational logic of its own. As Susan Buck-Morss remarks, the "invisible hand" placed the economy "beyond the knowledge (and therefore the power) of the state," reflecting "something monstrous in the system that, sublimely out of control, threatens to escape every kind of constraining boundary" (Buck-Morss ["Envisioning Capital"] 452). Becky's threat to both characters and readers alike coincides with the threat posed by the marketplace and its particular commodities (the novel, itself, for example).

This dynamic is played out on a larger scale in the novel with direct reference to the way economic practices both construct and dissolve national identities. In the scene at Brussels which precedes the battle of Waterloo, Thackeray articulates the character of both Brit-

ish and Belgian nations in economic terms. We see a strange coalescence, for example, between soldiers on the battlefield and consumers in the marketplace: "[I]t may be said as a rule," the narrator reports, "that every Englishman in the Duke of Wellington's army paid his way. . . . The remembrance of such a fact surely becomes a nation of shopkeepers. It was a blessing for a commerce-loving country to be overrun by such an army of customers: and to have such creditable warriors to feed" (318). Both England ("a nation of shopkeepers") and Belgium ("a commerce-loving country") are primarily economic constructs, a body of citizens united by bonds of economic devotion. Moreover, the literal signification of the army as a military unit fades into metaphor, as the (literal) army becomes "an army of customers," and this suggestive phrase hints at the common predicament of the consumers/ soldiers who make up this army: consumers spend their money with the hopes of remaking themselves according to an idealized self-image, as soldiers seek the "chances of honour" in battle. In George Osborne, this notion of war as a form of gambling is most pronounced. As he goes to battle and ultimately to his death, George Osborne imagines himself as "one of the players" in a "great game": "What a fierce excitement of doubt, hope, and pleasure. What tremendous hazards of loss or gain! What were all the games of chance compared to this one?" (350). The pleasure of both forms of gambling lies in the fantasy they allow one to invoke.

In the detailed representation of "Vanity Fair" at Brussels, the limits of national identity are further explored as the analogy implicit in the phrase "an army of customers" continues to unfold. Nations mete out fate like games of chance when the soldiers and their wives are dealt "a great piece of good fortune" to be stationed in Brussels "where the Vanity Fair booths were laid out with the most tempting liveliness and splendour" (322). When Thackeray lists the amusements at Brussels, it does not seem arbitrary that he places gambling first, for as Benjamin suggests, gambling is representative of all other pleasures (198). Each pleasure appears to transmute itself magically into the next in a sentence that reflects this unfolding:

> Gambling was here in profusion, and dancing in plenty: feasting was there to fill with delight that great gourmand of a Jos: there was a theatre where a miraculous Catalani was delighting all hearers: beautiful rides, all enlivened with martial splendour; a rare old city, with strange costumes and wonderful architecture, to delight the eyes of little Amelia . . . and fill her with charming surprises.
>
> (322)

Gambling appears as the one pleasure out of which the others emerge because the money for which one gambles allows for the possibility of all other enjoyments, and as Thackeray notes, George Osborne was "flush of money" during this short interlude. But the function of the various forms of amusement reflect that of gambling in another sense as well. As Walter Benjamin observed, gambling constructs a history of isolated moments detached from both past and future, and serves as "a device for giving events the character of a shock, detaching them from the context of experience" (198). This "device" operates in the lives of Thackeray's "travellers": not only do the novelties "fill" Amelia with "charming surprises"—like the outcome of a wager, she can predict neither the content nor the effect of such novelties—but the travellers lose sight of the future that most probably awaits them, absorbed in "the business of life and living, and the pursuits of pleasure, especially, . . . as if no end were to be expected of them, and no enemy in front" (322). The British travellers live in a present much like that of the gambler, away from the habitual routines that make up their identities and their past, with an illusory sense of the future. As Kavanagh describes it, "[a]bsorbed in the impassioned present of the wager" and "los[ing] all sense of past and future," gamblers are figures "of solipsistic idiosyncrasy closed to everything beyond the immediate present" (61). Such a condition defies all notions of a rational or coherent subject, and precludes the possibility of collective identity as well—as the characters lose sight of their purpose, they loosen their ties to the nation in whose name they are presumably acting.

At home the financial losses suffered by Mr. Sedley signify in turn the impact of war on the economy. Rumors of Napoleon's advance create a financial panic and diminish the value of all his assets, precipitating Mr. Sedley's loss of his fortune, the breakdown of his identity and eventual death. When Thackeray begins to hint at the impending decline and fall of Mr. Sedley early in the novel, he suggests not only that war destabilizes the marketplace but that the paradigms of the marketplace also dominate both the war itself and the language used to represent it. "Mr. Sedley," he tells us, "conducted his mysterious operations in the City, a stirring place in those days when war was raging all over Europe and empires were being staked" (133). The "mysterious operations" that characterize Mr. Sedley's financial dealings seemingly possess a hidden agency of their own that dominates the representation of war itself, for while the marketplace, of course, responds to the rise and fall of empires, the workings of the stock exchange is registered in the war as well, lending it the form of a wager with "empires" for "stakes." The logic of gambling presides over war, as it does over nations more generally, conveying the extent to which economic processes both ground and undercut national identity.[7]

In fact, as in Burke's projections for France's future and *Barry Lyndon,* gambling enters into practically all aspects of life in this novel. Thackeray affirms Burke's

belief that speculation was entering into all matters of life and death, even organizing the very distinction between them. For John Sedley, for example, death is characterized simply by an absence of gambling: "[t]here came one morning and sunrise," the narrator exhorts, "when all the world got up and set about its various works and pleasures, with the exception of old John Sedley, who was not to fight with fortune, or to hope or scheme any more" (722); and in reflecting on Amelia's misfortune, he considers "how mysterious and often unaccountable it is—that lottery of life which gives to this man the purple and fine linen and sends to the other rags for garments and dogs for comfort" (678). Of course, it is not by chance that such metaphors occur: each instance harks back to the literal speculations on the market. Gambling represents a new sociosymbolic order pervading the political, economic, and social practices through which individual and collective identities of a nation take shape. It also reflects the precariousness of this order.

As in **Barry Lyndon** the war against France reflects the contest and rivalry between two competing capitalist nations each seeking to expand its boundaries, increase its colonial possessions, and enhance the value of its currency. They define themselves against one another, projecting onto each other the qualities they wish to reject in themselves, and above all seeking to invalidate the other's credibility. For example, in the scene at Pumpernickel at the end of **Vanity Fair** they do this by sending home dispatches to their governments denouncing the other's stories as false, and "cutting at each other with epigrams that were as sharp as razors" (752). As the narrator, suddenly participating in the war of slander, explains:

> For instance, on our side we would write, "The interests of Great Britain in this place and throughout the whole of Germany, are perilled by the continuance in office of the present French envoy; this man is of a character so infamous that he will stick at no falsehood, or hesitate at no crime, to attain his ends. . . ." On their side they would say, "M. de Tapeworm continues his system of stupid insular arrogance and vulgar falsehood against the greatest nation in the world."
>
> (752)

Each faction tries to diminish the value of the other's identity the way they try to devalue each other's currency or discredit the stories they tell about one another.

As I proposed at the beginning of this essay, Thackeray offers an allegory of the tension between a national identity and the marketplace in the gambling which takes place at the fair in the German town of Pumpernickel where the Town Hall has been temporarily turned into a casino:

> [T]here was a room for *trente-et-quarante* and roulette established, for the week of the festivities only, and by one of the great German companies from Ems or Aix-

la-Chappelle. The officers or inhabitants of the town were not allowed to play at these games, but strangers, peasants, ladies, were admitted, and any one who chose to win or lose money.

(755)

Such a scene resembles the democratic political and social order that Burke envisions and fears, ruled entirely by speculation. Ordinarily the place for a male governing body to conduct the public affairs of the town, the Town Hall is now controlled by economic forces, the "great German companies" who put into place a system in which chance and the irrational passions of the players govern the course of events (with the odds clearly stacked in favor of the German companies). That the German government prohibits its own "officers and inhabitants" from gambling, but admits anyone else as long as they have money, indicates the perceived threat that this economy posed to national identity. In fact, as Susan Buck-Morss explains, "[i]n Germany, where commercial interdependence was in advance of political unity, the tendency of the economy to escape national boundaries was a cause of complaint rather than affirmation" (fn. 454). Hence those usually at the borders of its identity and excluded from the public affairs of the Town Hall—"strangers, peasants, ladies"—are now being let in.

As we follow Amelia's son Georgy into the casino which he, too, has been forbidden to enter, the narrator focusses exclusively on the women as if their presence was most indicative of a break with the usual social decorum and the distinctions on which national identity rests: "Women were playing; they were masked, some of them; this license was allowed in these wild times of carnival" (755). The masks erase individual identities and signal the participation in a collective process centered on the exchange of money; and while the license of carnival lifts the prohibition against women gambling, whether for pleasure or profit, their masks also make the women more like the money with which they gamble, causing them to take on its non-descript quality as solely a means of exchange.[8] The indifference of the companies as to who is let in to the casino, as long as they have money, moreover, contributes to the production of what Georg Simmel describes as an "ominous analogy between money and prostitution" (377) whereby "we experience in the nature of money itself something of the essence of prostitution. The indifference as to its use, the lack of attachment to any individual because it is unrelated to any of them, the objectivity inherent in money as a mere means which excludes any emotional relationship" (376-77).

When Thackeray reintroduces Becky into the novel after her long absence, she appears at first anonymously at the roulette-table as "[a] woman with light hair, in a low dress by no means as fresh as it had been, and with a black mask on" (755). The heavily insinuating tone of the narrator's description of the dress that is both seductive and overused, the admonitory "by no means," itself bespeaks Simmel's "ominous analogy." Moreover, Becky's position in the casino is analogous to both gambling itself and the gamblers. Like the gambling that lures the players into enormous expenditure, Becky lures on Jos. But her gambling aligns her with the gamblers, too, for the same superstitions and false systems common to gamblers characterize her playing. As the narrator notes, she "only ventured money on the colours after the red or black had come up a certain number of times" (755), and tells Georgy to place her bet, which he does and wins, in accordance with the "power that arranges that . . . for beginners" (756). As a woman, Becky simultaneously possesses the coercive power of the market and is subject to this power as well.

Becky's seduction of Jos at the roulette-table parallels the gambling of both Jos and his courier, Mr. Kirsch. While Becky lures Jos away, for example, "Mr Kirsch, having lost all his money by this time, followed his master out into the moonlight, where the illuminations were winking out and the transparency over our mission was scarcely visible" (758). That "the transparency" of the mission which houses the British travellers was "scarcely visible" conveys the effect Becky has, which is also that of gambling, of dislocating the travellers, causing them to lose their bearing with respect to their nation. Most striking, however, the "illuminations" that "were winking out" refer ambiguously both to the stars and to Becky whose eyes "twinkled strangely" through the eyelets of her mask and make her "strange to look at" (755). Thackeray has previously insisted on this link when Becky, walking out at night with Rawdon, remarks, "'O those stars, those stars!'" while "turning her twinkling green eyes up towards them" (127). To align Becky with the stars is to align her with the fate or future which they seem to hold and with our wishes about that fate. It also identifies her with the speculative economy which like gambling depends on our hopes for the future, and whose "mysterious operations" nature was often thought to govern like the celestial bodies themselves.[9]

Her effect on the spectators in the casino—that "It was strange to look at her"—can perhaps be identified with the strangeness and fascination of one's own denied wishes and fears, on the split between moral and immoral on which the economy depends and with which it conspires. Becky embodies this very split: She is both like the society in which she moves, mimicking it perfectly, yet different; she has the form of a woman, but hides the "hideous tail" of a monster; like the narrator and his implied reader, she is English, but she is also French. Because she embodies a split on which the identity of her own culture depends, Dobbin and Thackeray's closing gesture is ultimately doomed to failure, even as it guarantees the success of the novel: to drive Becky out of the household or out of the nation, will ultimately prove to be as vain as all our wishes, for neither the household nor the nation would exist without her.

Notes

1. We can, of course, see in this predicament the origin of current tensions. Buck-Morss, for example, cites Labor Secretary Robert Reich who points out that "as borders become ever more meaningless in economic terms, those citizens best positioned to thrive in the world market are tempted to slip the bonds of national allegiance, and by so doing disengage themselves from their less favored fellows" (438). In *Specters of Marx,* Derrida also observes evidence of this dilemma:

   > How can one overlook . . . the economic war that is raging today both between [the United States and the European Community] and within the European Community? How can one minimize the conflicts of the GATT treaty and all that it represents, which the complex strategies of protectionism recall every day, not to mention the economic war with Japan and all the contradictions at work within the trade between the wealthy countries and the rest of the world, the phenomena of pauperization and the ferocity of "foreign debt," the effects of what the *Manifesto* called "the epidemic of overproduction" and "the state of momentary barbarism" [p. 13] it can induce in so-called civil societies?

   (63)

2. When it was first published serially in *Fraser's* in 1844, the novel's title was *The Luck of Barry Lyndon; A Romance of the Last Century.* In 1856 the novel was reissued with the title *The Memoirs of Barry Lyndon, Esquire.* Thackeray never approved the change in title, and as Martin Anisman suggests in the introduction to his edition of the novel, "The theme of the novel turns on the word 'luck' of the 1844 title" (17). My own perspective on the novel clearly reasserts the centrality of this concept.

3. This observation accords in various ways with what many critics have identified as the value of fiction in Thackeray's work more generally, of Thackeray's tendency to bring to the surface the fictionality of his texts. Alexander Welsh describes Thackeray's later fiction, *Pendennis* (1848-50), *The Newcomes* (1853-55), and *Philip* (1861-62), as an attempt "to communicate the nature of his experiments by performing them on the surface of the narrative." Hence his characters are not "concrete characters but genuine creations of narrative experiments." His purpose was not to "maintain[]

the illusion of reality" but "to conduct experiments, invent the scenes, pose the alternatives—to speculate, reconstruct and generalize" (5). Robert Fletcher develops these notions in his exploration of Thackeray as a literary pragmatist in whom a tension between skepticism and the will to believe "suits him to his chosen task of uncovering vanity, a double-sided coin of conceit and emptiness, which shows us how human culture can be both legal tender and counterfeit at the same time" (394).

4. We might compare the process of identity-formation in which *Barry Lyndon* is perpetually engaged—his effort to see himself and have others see him as an aristocratic English gentleman—to Lacan's representation of this process in the mirror-stage characterized by the subject's quest for an ideal, and of course, fictional, self-image. It is intriguing that when Lacan elaborates the process "which manufactures for the subject . . . the succession of phantasies that extends from a fragmented body image to a form of its totality" (4), he, too, resorts to images of a feudal society. "The formation of the I" he states, "is symbolized in dreams by a fortress or stadium—its inner arena and enclosure, surrounded by marshes and rubbish-tips, dividing it into two opposed fields of contest where the subject flounders in quest of the lofty, remote inner castle" (5).

5. "Shoeblacking" seems, in fact, to have special connotations in Thackeray as a code word for honest, unassuming labor. During his final days in prison Barry Lyndon serves a short stint "blacking boots for wealthier prisoners" until his mother saves him from the indignity of "those actions unworthy of a man and a gentleman" (386). In his earlier novel *The Ravenswing* (1843), Thackeray again dignifies this occupation through his portrait of the landlord of "The Bootjack Hotel," who "had, in the outset of life, performed the duties of boots in some inn even more frequented than his own, and, far from being ashamed of his origin, as many persons are in the days of their prosperity, had thus solemnly recorded it over the hospitable gates of his hotel" (239).

6. As George Levine elaborates in *The Realistic Imagination,* particularly with respect to Thackeray, such strategies make up the conventional repertoire of realist fiction.

7. The relationship between economy and empire implied in Thackeray's language is, of course, complex and overdetermined. Historians such as E. J. Hobsbawm and Perry Anderson offer detailed accounts of this relationship and the extent to which, as Anderson states, "massive investment

surplus and limited internal markets" fuelled imperial expansion (24).

8. In her analysis in "Women on the Market," Luce Irigaray provides a comparison of money to women on the basis of their common function as exchange value in a speculative economy. Thackeray's depiction of the masked women in the casino resonates in many ways with Irigaray's notion of the way women as general equivalents are "reduced to some common feature" such that "each looks exactly like every other," and "have the same phantom-like reality" (175).

9. Tatiana Holway charts the emergence throughout the nineteenth century of the belief that "scientific law," particularly that of astronomy, determined the economic cycles, which culminated in William Jevons's claim in the 1870s, "that the cause for speculative cycles 'can only be found in some great and widespread meteorological influence recurring at like periods'" (15).

Works Cited

Anderson, Perry. "Origins of the Present Crisis." *English Questions.* London: Verso, 1992.

Benjamin, Walter. "On Some Motifs in Baudelaire." *Illuminations.* Ed. Hannah Arendt. Trans. Harry Zohn. New York: Schocken Books, 1968.

Buck-Morss, Susan. "Envisioning Capital: Political Economy on Display." *Critical Inquiry* 21 (1995): 434-67.

Burke, Edmund. *Reflections on the Revolution in France.* New York: E. P. Dutton & Co., 1960.

Derrida, Jacques. *Specters of Marx: The State of Debt, the Work of Mourning, and the New International.* Trans. Peggy Kamuf. New York: Routledge, 1994.

Dyer, Gary. "The '*Vanity Fair*' of Nineteenth-Century England: Commerce, Women, and the East in the Ladies' Bazaar." *Nineteenth-Century Literature.* 46 (1991): 196-222.

Fletcher, Robert P. "The Dandy and the Fogy: Thackeray and the Aesthetics/Ethics of the Literary Pragmatist." *ELH* 58 (1991): 383-404.

Hardy, Barbara. *The Exposure of Luxury: Radical Themes in Thackeray.* London: Peter Owen, 1972.

Holway, Tatiana. "The Game of Speculation: Economics and Representation." *Dickens Quarterly* 9.3 (1992): 103-14.

Irigaray, Luce. "Women on the Market." *This Sex Which Is Not One.* Trans. Catherine Porter. Ithaca: Cornell UP, 1985.

Jadwin, Lisa. "The Seductiveness of Female Duplicity in *Vanity Fair*." *SEL* [*Studies in English Literature*] 32 (1992): 663-87.

Kavanagh, Thomas M. *Enlightenment and the Shadows of Chance: The Novel and the Culture of Gambling in Eighteenth-Century France.* Baltimore: The Johns Hopkins UP, 1993.

Lacan, Jacques. "The Mirror Stage." *Ecrits: A Selection.* New York: W. W. Norton & Company, 1977. 1-7.

Levine, George. *The Realistic Imagination: English Fiction from Frankenstein to Lady Chatterly.* Chicago: U of Chicago P, 1981.

Miller, Andrew. "*Vanity Fair* through Plate Glass." *PMLA* 105 (1990): 1042-54.

Norton, Sandy Morey. "The Ex-Collector of Boggley-Wollah: Colonialism in the Empire of *Vanity Fair*." *Narrative* 1 (1993): 124-37.

Ray, Gordon. *Thackeray: The Uses of Adversity, 1811-1846.* New York: The Mcgraw-Hill Book Company, Inc., 1955.

Scarry, Elaine. *The Body in Pain: The Making and Unmaking of the World.* New York: Oxford UP, 1985.

Shillingsburg, Peter L. *Pegasus in Harness: Victorian Publishing and W. M. Thackeray.* Charlottesville: UP of Virginia, 1992.

Simmel, Georg. *The Philosophy of Money.* Ed. David Frisby. Trans. Tom Bottomore and David Frisby. New York: Routledge, 1990.

Thackeray, William Makepeace. "A Brother of the Press on the History of a Literary Man, Laman Blanchard, and the Chances of the Literary Profession." *The Complete Works of Thackeray.* Vol. 25. New York: Harper & Brothers, 1914. 465-79.

———. *The Letters and Private Papers of William Makepeace Thackeray.* Vol. I: 1817-1840. Ed. Gordon N. Ray. London: Oxford UP, 1945.

———. *The Luck of Barry Lyndon.* Ed. Martin J. Anisman. New York: New York UP, 1970.

———. *Vanity Fair.* New York: New American Library, 1981.

Welsh, Alexander. *Introduction. Thackeray: A Collection of Critical Essays.* Ed. Alexander Welsh. Englewood Cliffs, NJ: Prentice Hall, Inc., 1968.

Brian McCuskey (essay date summer 1999)

SOURCE: McCuskey, Brian. "Fetishizing the Flunkey: Thackeray and the Uses of Deviance." *Novel: A Forum on Fiction* 32, no. 3 (summer 1999): 384-400.

[*In the following essay, McCuskey documents representations of male sexuality in Thackeray's novels. McCus-*

key posits that Thackeray's fetishization of male servants reflects his deep ambivalence toward Victorian social hierarchies.]

> The devotees of fetishes regard them as abnormalities, it is true, but only rarely as symptoms of illness; usually they are quite content with them or even extol the advantages they offer for erotic gratification.
>
> —Freud, "Fetishism" 198

I.

Midway through William Thackeray's **History of Pendennis** (1848-50), the narrator stops for a moment in the street to admire Lady Clavering's London mansion:

> One of the leaves of the hall door was opened, and John—one of the largest of his race—was leaning against the door pillar, with his ambrosial hair powdered, his legs crossed; beautiful, silk-stockinged; in his hand his cane, gold-headed, dolichoskion. Jeames was invisible, but near at hand, waiting in the hall, with the gentleman who does not wear livery, and ready to fling down the roll of haircloth over which her Ladyship was to step to her carriage. These things and men, the which to tell of demands time, are seen in the glance of a practised eye.
>
> (393)

Thackeray takes in the spectacle of servants who conspicuously display and consume their employer's wealth; all dressed up with no place to go, these footmen perform symbolic rather than domestic duties. "Their role was not in basic material production as such," John Gillis explains with reference to male servants in Victorian society, "but in the elaboration of the social and cultural symbols appropriate to the social status of their employers" (152). Ever watchful for a chance to satirize the pretensions of the leisure classes, Thackeray suspends his narrative to point out the utterly objectified servants whom Andrew Miller has described as "a logical extreme of a culture fashioned from commodities" (14). Thackeray's eye, "practised" in decoding the semiotics of urban life, calls attention to a scene that illustrates the excesses and idiosyncrasies of Vanity Fair.

The narrator moves on, but the passage is curious enough to tempt us to lag behind and wonder what other practices might be involved in looking so closely at servants. Even without the help of a suggestive epigraph, a post-Freudian reader sees immediately that the flunkey has been fetishized, his body fragmented into a collection of parts that are in turn eroticized by the narrator. The footman's hair is "ambrosial," inviting us to smell and even taste it; his legs are not only "beautiful, silk-stockinged" but also "crossed," inviting us to hear the whisper of silk on silk; and, of course, he holds a cane, tipped with gold, inviting us to visualize why else he might deserve the Homeric epithet *dolichoskion*—for

a spear "casting a long shadow." The description in fact serves as a neat inventory of the classic Freudian fetishes; we need only note the narrator's interest just prior to this passage—the shoe buckles which "John and Jeames, the footmen, wear, and which we know are large, and spread elegantly over the foot" (393)—to round out the list.

As the adjective "practised" also suggests, this scene is not an isolated instance in Thackeray's writing; he frequently takes the time to ogle male servants and savor fetishistic details. Elsewhere in **Pendennis** [*The History of Pendennis*], we notice "the tightest leather breeches" (306) and the "gloves as large as Doolan's" (364) worn by various flunkeys; in **Barry Lyndon** (1844), we meet the hero's "huge body-servant Fritz lolling behind with curling moustaches and long queue, his green livery barred with silver lace" (208); in **The Book of Snobs** (1848), we are told that "peach-coloured liveries laced with silver, and pea-green plush inexpressibles, render the De Mogyns' flunkeys the pride of the ring when they appear in Hyde Park" (42). Censuring lazy and conceited servants, Mrs. Beeton's *Book of Household Management* (1861) warned what would happen "when the lady of fashion chooses her footman without any other consideration than his height, shape, and *tournure* of his calf" (961). In Thackeray's fiction, however, it is not the lady but the gentleman of fashion who best appreciates "that delightful quivering swagger of the calves, which has always had a frantic fascination for us" (**Book of Snobs** 15), and who admires "gigantic footmen" with bodies "too big to be contained in Becky's little hall" (**Vanity Fair** 588).

Thackeray's obsession with the figures and accessories of male servants complicates recent critical discussions of his representation of male sexuality. Both Eve Kosofsky Sedgwick and Joseph Litvak have argued that Thackerayan gentlemen exempt themselves from the experience of sexual desire. Sedgwick suggests that Thackeray's bachelors, in "response to the strangulation of homosexual panic" that underwrites their patriarchal power, exhibit "a garrulous and visible refusal of anything that could be interpreted as genital sexuality, toward objects male or female" (192). Litvak, on the other hand, contends that Thackeray disavows sexual desire in order to claim a superior class sophistication predicated on a surfeit of experience: "Thackeray's desire not to desire is at the same time a desire to be, as well as a desire for, the kind of man whose apparent libidolessness only signifies the more decisively, and the more seductively, that he has had and done it all" (235). Neither of these descriptions, because they assume that homosexual desire must necessarily be masked, can accommodate a publicly fetishized flunkey. Thackeray's frantic (but not panicked) fascination with the servant's virile body and displaced phallus demonstrates both an investment in genital sexuality and an enthusiastic libido—as well as a certain contempt for the closet.

The purpose of this essay is to provide an alternative to the dominant model of reading Victorian fiction as an open secret for homosexuality and to discover in what ways the direct representation of sexual deviance might be useful for a bourgeois writer. The central question: Why would Thackeray so conspicuously consume footmen as the fetishized objects of a flamboyantly homosexual desire? Miller suggests that such moments of social and sexual ambivalence testify to the "wavering instability of all social categories, including those of gender and class, when seen through the heat of Thackerayan desire" for commodities (17). That is, the rise of capitalism tends to reduce all erotic impulses to a single material lust; commodity fetishism is the only desire experienced fully by the denizens of Vanity Fair. The narrator, however, seems to experience a distinctly sexual charge in fetishizing the flunkey, whose clothing and accessories signify mainly to the extent that they double for or point toward the displaced phallus. Nor have class and gender categories wavered and collapsed altogether; Thackeray's eye singles out only male servants and ignores that much more obvious target of the fetishist's gaze: the maid. As Emily Apter has shown, the figure of the maid—with her boots, stockings, and apron—recurs as the "quintessential fetish object" in nineteenth-century literature (190); it seems all the more peculiar, given her availability as a symbol, that Thackeray would deliberately overlook her.

To explain this anomaly, this essay traces what Freud calls the "symbolic connection of thought" (*Three Essays* [*Three Essays on the Theory of Sexuality*] 21) between Thackeray's fetishized flunkeys and various forms of Victorian castration anxiety—social as well as sexual. As we will see, Thackeray's satirical representation of the servant class allows him to analyze the interdependence of sexual and commodity fetishism, well before Freud and Marx provided these terms, and allows us to amplify the hermeneutic power of the twin theories by applying them jointly to the central ideological project of Thackeray's fiction: the definition and exaltation of the gentleman. Following the lead of most Victorian writers, whose emphasis on the famous "disinterestedness" of the gentleman entailed a corresponding negation of his sexuality, literary and cultural critics have stressed the way that the gentleman jettisons the burden of sexual desire in order to maintain social and ethical altitude. While still accounting for strategies of disavowal, this essay contends that Thackeray cannily exploits the power and pleasure of sexuality—and especially of deviant sexuality—in order to consolidate more thoroughly the gentleman's subjective power and cultural authority.

Thackeray's ambivalence about social norms has been well-documented, as he cynically critiques a culture in which he knows he remains invested, and there is no reason to think that his attitude toward sexual norms is any less conflicted or self-conscious. It is possible to read Thackeray's fetishizing of the flunkey ironically, as an inside joke for an audience in-the-know (*he* knows that *we* know that he *does* not because we *could* not *really* desire the flunkey), but we should be wary lest getting the joke means forgetting other possible readings, in which Thackeray's knowing heterosexism appears both less assumed and less assured. Noting Thackeray's recollection of being ordered to "Come & frig me" by another Charterhouse boy, Litvak points out that while Thackeray "was obviously not 'gay-identified'" as a writer, "the meaning of his not being gay-identified is anything *but* obvious" (223-24). We will therefore start with the obvious, allowing ourselves to get the joke, and proceed from there to other significations of the fetish that are, however deviant, "not known to the world at large and therefore not prohibited" (Freud, "Fetishism" 200).

II.

The inside joke, of course, is on the snob outside. Without an invitation to the very best dinners, the lower-middle-class snob sees little of high society apart from the liveried footmen who not only stand *for* the upper-class privilege he desires but also stand *between* him and those dinners. The narrator of **Vanity Fair** (1847-48) fancies that the "august portals" of fashionable London houses are "guarded by grooms of the chamber with flaming silver forks with which they prong all those who have not the right of the *entrée*" (583). Standing in the street, with nothing to look at but liveries, the snob suffers the pangs of a social ambition so intense that he cannot help but fetishize the flunkey who is (in Freudian terms) both a surrogate for the object of desire and a reminder of his alienation from it. The snob, in the throes of his frustrated commodity fetishism, fixates on each detail of the liveried footman and transforms boots, silk, cane, hair, and calves into sexualized objects that he can consume as a voyeur—a displaced and diminished version of the other, more satisfying forms of consumption denied to him. Thackeray's inside joke is that, at best, the snob is impotent; at worst, perverted. Employing Apter's terms, we might then describe Thackeray's representation of the flunkey as a form of "critical fetishism"; that is, "an aesthetic of fetishization that reflexively exposes the commodity as an impostor value" (12). The snob's material lust becomes so excessive, so grotesque, that we renounce his grubby values and take the higher ground already staked out by Thackeray, who critiques commodity culture from the socially elevated and ethically superior position of a gentleman, the insider who remains above it all.

The problem for Thackeray is that his joke backfires, causing repercussions that begin to erode that higher ground and to expose the gentleman himself as an "impostor value." To start with, the flunkey is as much a fetish object for his employers as he is for the snob. His livery both signifies and substitutes for wealth that in many cases does not actually exist; or rather, as those householders who live well on nothing a year in **Vanity Fair** can attest, it exists mainly as an effect of the servant's plush and powder. The flunkey finds himself fetishized by anxious employers who invest each part of his body and article of his livery with social significance, an attention to detail whose equivalence with sexual obsession underscores the fact that all aspects of the employer's identity—sexual as well as social—hinge upon the flunkey's display. We should note that Thackeray's descriptions do not much exaggerate this attention to detail; Victorian household manuals advised employers, for example, to hire footmen of "equal height to avoid the incongruity of appearance that men-servants of unequal height would present" (*Servants' Practical Guide* 160). The flunkey's appearance must be congruous in every detail with the wealth and status of his employers: the more ornamented and objectified their servants, the more manifest their possession of wealth, and the more secure their class position.

Employers also take the objectification of flunkeys to oppressive extremes because servants are the rudest reminders that, in Vanity Fair, possession is nine-tenths illusion. Commodities in Thackeray's fiction always tend to slip through the grasp of their owners and return to the free marketplace where they are picked up by other owners, who in turn experience not material gratification but psychological frustration when the commodities slip away again. This vicious cycle—what Miller calls an "interminable dynamic of desire and disenchantment" (25)—determines the career path of servants, whose loyalty lasts only as long as next quarter's wages. "It has often struck you, O thoughtful Dives! that this respect, and these glories, are for the main part transferred, with your fee simple, to your successor—that the servants will bow, and the tenants shout, for your son as for you; that the butler will fetch him the wine (improved by a little keeping) that's now in your cellar" (*Pendennis* 639). The ease with which servants find other situations interrupts the bourgeois fantasy of absolute ownership. When Mr. Sedley goes bankrupt, the collapse of the household does not overly trouble the servants, who "did not break their hearts at parting from their adored master and mistress" (**Vanity Fair** 216). Similarly, when the elder Pendennis dies, his servants transfer their allegiance to young Pen with an alacrity that would be as dismaying to the dead man as it is exhilarating to his heir: "All the servants there assembled in great silence . . . rose up at his entrance and bowed or curtseyed to [Pen]. They never used to do so last holidays, he felt at once and with indescribable pleasure" (**Pendennis** 55-56). Servants publicize a truth that bourgeois culture represses: ownership is not a power to be exercised but a position to be inhabited, often only briefly, within an economic system that does not register the life or death of any one individual.

It now makes sense why servants have an especially nasty habit of turning up at scenes of bankruptcy and death in Thackeray's fiction, appearing like vultures to circle their employers—whether dead, destitute, or disgraced—and snatch up the goods left behind before moving on themselves. Henry Esmond's valet, Lockwood, scavenges the field of battle where Henry lies wounded; John Osborne's butler buys up Mr. Sedley's wine for his master; Isidor the Belgian valet, attending upon Jos Sedley during Waterloo, fantasizes about inheriting that dandy's wardrobe; Fifine, Becky Sharp's maid, pockets the jewels that her shamed mistress has been forced to relinquish. Bruce Robbins has argued that the servant who appears during deathbed scenes in English fiction restores a "lost communal significance" to death and thus functions as "the authoritative image of the continuity of the generations" (120). Quite the reverse is true in Thackeray's fiction, however: the continuity guaranteed there by servants is the merciless continuity of capitalism, which is directly responsible for the loss of the communal significance that Robbins wishes to recover. The servant does not act as the herald of a "broader, more universal communion" in death (Robbins [*The Servant's Hand*] 121), but rather as the broker for a broader, more universal alienation.

Broad and universal enough, in fact, that both servant and master find themselves equally objectified under capitalism—the servant at the hands of his master, of course, but also the master at the hands of his servant. Through the ministrations of servants, the commodity form reaches from the public sphere into the private chamber and transforms the occupant who dresses there. When Thackeray introduces us to Major Pendennis at the opening of **Pendennis,** we barely get a glimpse of him through all the window-dressing. Instead, we are called upon to admire the work of his dexterous valet:

> One fine morning in the full London season, Major Arthur Pendennis came over from his lodgings, according to his custom, to breakfast at a certain Club in Pall Mall, of which he was a chief ornament. At a quarter past ten the Major invariably made his appearance in the best blacked boots in all London, with a checked morning cravat that never was rumpled until dinner time, a buff waistcoat which bore the crown of his sovereign on the buttons, and linen so spotless that Mr Brummell himself asked the name of his laundress. . . . Pendennis's coat, his white gloves, his whiskers, his very cane, were perfect of their kind as specimens of the costume of a military man *en retraite.* . . . His nose was of the Wellington pattern. His hands and wristbands were beautifully long and white. On the latter he wore handsome gold buttons

given to him by his Royal Highness the Duke of York, and on the others more than one elegant ring, the chief and largest of them being emblazoned with the famous arms of Pendennis.

(37)

The touch of the servant utterly commodifies the master's body, which fragments and eventually disappears—accessorized into oblivion. We see rings but not fingers, boots but not feet, cravat but not a neck. However, the master's body has not actually disintegrated; it has instead become indistinguishable from the commodities it proudly displays. In the description of the Major, the list of flashy accessories includes his whiskers; his features fit a certain reproducible "pattern," much like a set of china or cut of cloth; gloves and hands and wristbands fuse together into a uniform whiteness. Later in the novel, we learn that the Major's decaying body parts are promptly replaced by the valet with over-the-counter goods: the Major has "a little morocco box, which it must be confessed contained the Major's back teeth," and "Morgan, his man, made a mystery of mystery of his wigs: curling them in private places: introducing them privily to his master's room" (*Pendennis* 101). The commodification of the gentleman is complete once he becomes an "ornament" whose chief function is to circulate in society as the hollow signifier of his own wealth and status.

Victorian commodity culture therefore calls into question any essential difference between gentleman and servant; the flunkey—powdered, silk-stockinged, and bespangled—announces himself as a grotesque but recognizable double of his master. "My dear Flunkeys," as Thackeray says in *The Book of Snobs,* "are but the types of their masters in this world" (15). Male servants model not only liveries but also a cynical theory of subjectivity under capitalism: in Vanity Fair, you are what you wear. If Thackeray's characters, as John Carey has observed, tend to "regard their fellow men as a kind of mobile boutique" (76), they do so because there is little else to contemplate. Strip away the clothes and accessories of any man—servant, Snob, or master—and one finds only "underwaistcoats, more underwaistcoats, and then nothing" (Thackeray, *Four Georges* 108). This particular description targets the foppish and corrupt George IV, but Thackeray's representation of the objectified and emptied self prompts us to wonder more generally whether there is "nothing" to distinguish one man from another apart from commodities that refuse identification with any one man for very long.

Alexander Welsh has argued that "Thackeray and other English novelists were preoccupied with sorting gentlemen from non-gentlemen, whether on frivolous or moral grounds, because they were engaged in defining a social class" (115). Thackeray insists on a difference of innate character: gentlemen are distinguished from both working men below and aristocrats above by their exceptional virtue, integrity, and, above all else, indifference to materialism. Because gentlemanliness thus appears to be "a moral and not just a social category" (Gilmour [*The Idea of the Gentleman*] 3), the gentleman can stake his claim to cultural authority on an essential ethical superiority rather than an arbitrary economic advantage. *Vanity Fair* offers Thackeray's most famous definition of the gentleman: a man "whose aims are generous, whose truth is constant, and not only constant in its kind but elevated in its degree" (720). Thackeray therefore grants the gentleman a heightened subjective power—a self that is both more authentic and more fully developed than the selves of other men—that both precedes and legitimates his class power.

However, if commodity culture identifies and orders individuals only on the basis of clothing, not character, then the gentleman's authority has a much flimsier foundation: linen rather than moral fiber. Having aspired to the higher ground above servants and snobs, Thackeray finds himself back on the common ground of commodity culture, where the gentleman's claim to an exceptional moral standard elevated above the marketplace seems dubious—and even duplicitous. "Through the gentlemanly code," Ina Ferris contends, "writers like Thackeray attempted to bring virtue into commerce or, more precisely, to encourage the formation of virtues useful to a high-risk and volatile economy" (414). That is, Victorian literature manufactures the gentleman as a panacea for the moral maladies of industrial capitalism. In Ferris's terms, he is "a counter to the anonymous and volatile power of money" (407) who nonetheless collaborates with that power; his principles help to stabilize and accelerate the growth of a credit economy. Gentlemanliness, having been disrobed by servants, stands revealed as an impostor value, itself a grubby and guilty product of commodity culture.

III.

The disrobing of the gentleman leads Thackeray to an inevitable but unacceptable conclusion: anyone can "turn gentleman," as one servant says (*Pendennis* 703), as long as he has the right clothes and a hefty bankbook. The compulsively rehearsed subplot of the servant who rises into trade and even higher society approaches and avoids this conclusion over and over again. Under capitalism, Thackeray worries, the character of a gentleman does not signify, and so an enterprising servant like Jeames de la Pluche may ascend on a bubble of railway speculation into high society, despite the fact that his "conshns whispers to [him], 'Jeames, you'r hony a footman in disguise hafter all'" (*Diary* [*The Diary of C. Jeames de la Pluche, Esq.*] 144). Nonetheless, however many servants follow Jeames above stairs, Thackeray continues to insist that the gentleman's distinct and exceptional character does in fact exist, even if it cannot be apprehended directly as a material fact. As Clive Newcome confidently declares, "I can't tell you what it is, or how it is, . . . only one can't help seeing the difference. It isn't rank and that; only somehow there are some men gentlemen and some not" (*Newcomes* 68).

To help us see the difference, even if he cannot tell us what it is, Thackeray displaces the problem from the field of economic relations to the field of sexual relations, where the gentleman's character, viewed from a different angle, might show up more clearly. Another reiterated and parallel subplot then emerges: the servant as a sexual rival to the master. In the very early *Yellowplush Papers* [*The Yellowplush Correspondence*] (1837-38), the flunkey Yellowplush and his master Deuceace lust after the same women, and this pattern continues in the later stories: Pendennis and Mirobolant, a French cook, both pursue the coquettish Blanche Amory (whom Morgan the valet also ogles); Jeames de le Pluche vies with Captain Silvertop for the hand of Lady Angelina; Bedford, the butler in *Lovel the Widower* (1860), pays court to Bessy, the governess whom both Lovel and his friend Batchelor admire. In each of these cases, the narrative deflates the servant's presumption: Yellowplush's nods and winks are never reciprocated; Pen publicly humiliates Mirobolant; Angelina spurns the ex-footman in favor of the Captain; and Bessy firmly rejects the advances of Bedford. No matter how rich, educated, or dandified the servant becomes, women instinctively perceive and respond to the innate superiority of the gentleman; their sexual choices make visible and tangible a subjective difference whose existence otherwise remains very much in question.

This solution can only be provisional, however, because Thackeray's fiction also illustrates the ways in which the commodity form has already invaded and occupied the realm of sexuality, rendering the notion of female choice problematic. In *Vanity Fair,* as both Carey and Miller have demonstrated, sexual desire circulates and finds expression only through objects; the physical lust for bodies and the material lust for goods cannot readily be distinguished. Romance becomes a form of speculation; marriage, a long-term mutual fund; divorce, bankruptcy:

> Warm friendship and thorough esteem and confidence . . . are safe properties invested in the prudent marriage stock, multiplying and bearing an increasing value with every year. Many a young couple of spendthrifts get through their capital of passion in the first twelve months, and have no love left for the daily demands of after life. Oh me! for the day when the bank account is closed, and the cupboard is empty, and the firm of Damon and Phyllis insolvent!
>
> (Thackeray, *Newcomes,* 393)

As romantic and economic interests become conflated, women find themselves positioned between men as objects to be shared, exchanged, or fought over. Jeff

Nunokawa has argued that the Victorian novel expresses anxiety about the traffic in women "not because they are thus cast as property, but rather because such property is thus cast among the uncertainties of the marketplace" (7). At the moment the domestic angel becomes a commodity to be exchanged between father and fiancé, she also becomes caught up in the vicious economic cycle of possession, loss, and frustration that mesmerized Thackeray. Her sexual choice therefore cannot be trusted to last: choosing the gentleman over the servant may be more of a temporary dalliance than a permanent alliance. Furthermore, because not only the female body but also female desire itself has been commodified, her sexual choice necessarily involves economic motives: even if she does cling to the gentleman, it may have more to do with his clothes than with his character. There is always the possibility that a well-dressed servant will get the girl and cuckold the gentleman. When the appalled Major Pendennis wonders aloud if Blanche Amory may have "encouraged" the French cook's attentions, his valet replies with a sinister double negative: "Servants don't know them kind of things the least" (*Pendennis* 387).

Nunokawa contends that because the domestic angel is inevitably "discharged from her situation as safe estate and subject to the restless fate of capital," Victorian novels habitually refigure her within the realm of the ideal, far from the marketplace: "What can't be held *to* the heart for long can be held *in* it forever: property that can't be kept up in the external world is sustained instead in the figure of a woman whose dimensions are defined less by the material shapes of house or body than by a lover's fond thoughts or sorrowful memory" (13). In other words, the Victorian novel counters the commodification of women with its own strategies of dematerialization. Nunokawa's theory applies neatly to the work of Charles Dickens and George Eliot, but Thackeray's fiction refuses this solution. Instead, his novels constitute an ongoing struggle to dematerialize not the angel but the gentleman as a disembodied moral signifier, thereby rescuing him from the "restless fate of capital" while delivering her up to it. The angel finds herself utterly objectified within sexual relations governed by a strictly economic logic: "We young ladies in the world," Ethel Newcome says bitterly, "when we are exhibiting, ought to have little green tickets pinned on our backs, with 'Sold' written on them; it would prevent trouble and any future haggling, you know" (*Newcomes* 289). The gentleman, on the other hand, liberates himself from the material world by publicly disavowing sexual desire, thereby avoiding the humiliation by servants and the betrayal by women that, taken together, call his cultural authority into question. No wonder that the aptly named Mr. Batchelor of *Lovel the Widower* prefers his "comfortable, cool bachelor's bed" to the honeymoon suite (254): rejecting the pleasures of sex, the gentleman reclaims the privileges of class. The fact that women desire him underscores his gentlemanliness; the fact that he does not desire women keeps that gentlemanliness detached from the sexual and economic fields in which it would quickly deconstruct.

In renouncing sexual relations with women, however, the gentleman consolidates his social power only to jeopardize his masculinity in other ways. Ina Ferris notes that the gentleman's asceticism "tends to position him also outside energy, sexuality, and action" (421) and therefore feminizes him, prompting the gentleman to recuperate his masculinity by socializing with other men in taverns and clubs. However, she does not pursue the possibility that the gentleman's detached position might make him sexually suspect or, worse, that his preference for male company might heighten rather than deflect suspicion. There is a fine line between asceticism and impotence or, still worse, between asceticism and perversion; publicly disavowing desire may camouflage either private shortcomings or deviant preferences—thus making asceticism a virtue of necessity. Sedgwick argues that the nervous Thackerayan bachelor who sexually anaesthetizes himself from homosexual panic nonetheless feels "no urgency about proving that he actually could" fall in love with women; the "comfortably frigid campiness of Thackeray's bachelors gives way to something that sounds more inescapably like panic" only later in the century (194). As Litvak demonstrates, however, Thackeray even at mid-century does worry enough about identifying the gentleman's social sophistication with sexual deviance to fatten up and sacrifice Jos Sedley—who yokes effeminacy to appetite rather than asceticism—as a proto-homosexual scapegoat.

To head off a looming sex scandal before it can blacken the gentleman's character, Thackeray sacrifices the servant in precisely the same way: the fetishized flunkey assigns effeminacy to working-class rather than ruling-class masculinity, keeping the gentleman above suspicion and the servant under surveillance. Noting Thackeray's frequent protests against "this heaping of gold lace, gaudy colours, blooming plushes, on honest John Trot" (**"On a Chalk-Mark"** [**"On a Chalk-Mark on the Door"**] 137), Catherine Peters concludes that Thackeray objects to liveries because they dehumanize flunkeys: "The uniform was unfair to the man who had to dress up in gold lace and powder his hair, for it cut him off from ordinary human beings, conferring a false sense of importance on both employer and servant" (130). But Thackeray protests too much: his effusive descriptions of the flunkey call attention, again and again, to how quickly and easily working-class masculinity degenerates under pressure. "When you get to a glorified flunkey, in lace, plush, and aiguillettes, wearing a bouquet that nobody wears, a powdered head that nobody wears, a gilt cocked-hat only fit for a baboon," Thackeray observes, "I say the well-constituted man

can't help grinning at this foolish, monstrous, useless, shameful caricature of a man" (**"On Some Political Snobs"** 274). Thackeray champions his own "well-constituted" character even as the flunkey's collapses into caricature, monstrously feminized by trimmings, flowers, and a silly hat. Even worse, the flunkey compounds his humiliation by embracing the terms of service; later in the century, Edith Ellis (wife of Havelock) chastises the footman as an "overfed mannikin [*sic*]" who "does not seem to miss his manhood" (10). Far from defending flunkeys against public disgrace, Thackeray exaggerates their emasculation and prolongs their shame, serving them up to the public appetite for scandal that would otherwise threaten to consume gentlemen.

Thackeray's "frantic fascination" with male servants redoubles the insult: the flunkey's emasculation is so complete, his manhood so entirely missing, that he becomes a female object of desire, ogled sarcastically and derisively by gentlemen passersby. The performance of an apparently cross-class and homoerotic attraction to the servant allows the narrator to inflict an ultimately class-based and heterosexist injury on the servant. At the same time, the gentleman's campy performance helps him to disavow deviant sexuality and thus to defuse the scandal. William Cohen has argued that scandal, as a cultural phenomenon, constructs sexuality as both secret and unspeakable, thereby amplifying its own powers of discovery and disclosure: "The Victorian scandals most revealing about the imagination of sexual privacy are therefore those that concern the sexual activity construed as most insistently covert, sex between men" (5). But if homosexuality is by definition the most secret and unspeakable of desires, then the man who acts *out* that desire publicly is unlikely to be accused of acting *upon* it privately. The structure of scandal dictates that homosexual desire acknowledged so openly cannot be genuine; it must be a hoax, and to be a hoax, it follows that the hoaxer cannot himself be homosexual. As the organizers of fraternity drag shows know, the outrageous performance of sexual deviance redounds upon the sexual orthodoxy of the participants: there is nothing questionable about men putting on lipstick and dresses, as long as it is clearly a put-on.

Both the drag shows and Thackeray therefore invert and exploit what we now recognize as the logic of Freudian repression. If the truth of prohibited desire cannot be spoken directly, then prohibited desire spoken directly cannot be true; the gentleman who so freely confesses his fetish for the flunkey cannot *really* be a homosexual. Furthermore, because the gentleman's performed desire is doubly deviant (both homoerotic and fetishistic), it therefore seems so outrageous as to be impossible. Freud, in fact, would come to identify homosexuality and fetishism as two distinct and mutually exclusive responses to castration anxiety; he argues that the fetish is a defense mechanism that "saves the fetishist from being a homosexual" ("Fetishism" 200). In this way, flaunting that "frantic fascination" with the servant's clothes and accessories, the sexually anxious and ambivalent gentleman chooses to make a spectacle rather than a scandal of himself.

IV.

Given the sophistication of Thackeray's narrators, however, one wonders whether there might be a play within the play here: a double feint, in which the sexual deviant theatrically "outs" himself both to sustain his normative public identity and to satisfy his non-normative private desires more freely. Our suspicion heightens once we recognize that Thackeray's gentlemen—so fond of slumming—enact *social* deviance in precisely this way. The upper-class George Warrington, for example, drinks beer "like a coalheaver" to bring his social status into relief through its flagrant contravention: "And yet you couldn't but perceive that he was a gentleman" (*Pendennis* 312). However, the "great satisfaction" with which Warrington wipes his beard leaves no doubt that he also genuinely *enjoys* his beer, preferring it to more refined beverages (*Pendennis* 312). Extending this logic from social to sexual deviance, and prompted by our epigraph, we must ask of fetishized flunkeys what "advantages they offer for erotic gratification" that normative heterosexual relations cannot provide.

Fetish objects in and of themselves might appeal to gentlemen wracked by the sexual doubts and social anxieties described above. Andrew Miller has argued that fetish objects in Thackeray's fiction "simultaneously suggest the possibility of plenitude and of lack" (26) and therefore epitomize the experience of alienation in commodity culture, where you must desire what you cannot possess. But we should note that those fetish objects make other more productive and pleasurable experiences available as well: after all, as Freud points out, "the fetishist has no trouble in getting what other men have to woo and exert themselves to obtain" ("Fetishism" 200-201). In organizing his sexuality around objects rather than bodies, the gentleman-fetishist can indulge his erotic impulses without incurring any of the risks associated with female sexuality under capitalism. Furthermore, because he desires a class of objects (boots, stockings, lace) rather than a unique object, he need not fear losing his object of desire to other owners; fetish objects can substitute for each other as well as for the displaced phallus. Finally, and most importantly, because the gentleman-fetishist as Thackeray conceives him is essentially a voyeur, he consumes the object by looking at it rather than buying it—a form of possession that commodity culture cannot spoil, since market forces have no power to divert his line of sight. Fetishism is the one form of desire partially enabled rather than completely frustrated by commodity culture, which encourages the mass production and public display of precisely those objects that most incite the fetishist's imagination.

But why fetishize flunkeys and their accoutrements? Why not fetishize maids, safely positioning the gentleman within the field of heterosexual relations where he might deviate from the norm without defying it? We can begin to answer this question by identifying the way that the logic of Freudian repression might cooperate with the logic of commodity culture: better not to be able to speak the truth of desire, because any desire brought into the open will always and necessarily be thwarted. Thackeray again inverts and exploits this logic to provide another option for the wary gentleman apart from sexual anaesthesia or disavowal: the public organization of desire around objects that are in fact undesirable. If the logic of Victorian commodity culture dictates that desire must lead to alienation, then one must desire only those things whose alienation—rather than possession—heightens erotic pleasure or increases social advantage. Pendennis best exemplifies this rather perverse strategy, as he races through the novel instinctively pursuing either inappropriate or indecent objects of sexual desire and social ambition: an Irish actress, a porter's daughter, a career in hack journalism, a rotten pocket borough. As the lower-class women slip away from him, Pen experiences an immediate sense of relief more pleasurable than the anticipated sexual gratification; as his dubious career goals are thwarted, Pen enjoys the sense of a higher destiny being reserved for him. Furthermore, by conspicuously *not* desiring the objects associated with that higher destiny, such as his more-than-sister Laura and his family's country home, Pen improves his chances of eventually capitalizing on them: at the end of the novel, he marries the long-neglected Laura (whose new aristocratic connections make her even more attractive) and returns to his equally long-neglected home (whose land, with a new railway running through it, now yields a comfortable independence). In short, the artful Pen gets what he wants by not wanting what he gets; other men who wear their desire on their sleeve, like the crass Harry Foker, who pursues Blanche until she disgraces him, or the clumsy Jos, who wins Becky only to be murdered by her, or the sentimental Dobbin, who marries a spoiled Amelia, get only what they do not want.

In this way, Thackeray turns the logic of commodity culture against itself on behalf of the gentleman, who sustains his class power and gender identity not by disavowing desire (and thereby feminizing himself) but by desiring objects that should themselves be disavowed. The gentleman therefore demonstrates publicly the social and sexual energies that define him as masculine, but he does not expend those energies on objects whose certain alienation would put his cultural authority at risk, as women humiliate him sexually and servants surpass him financially. Instead, he directs them only toward objects that he has everything to gain by *losing,* not winning, and he waits for the more fitting and lucrative rewards that seem to accrue all the more naturally for the gentleman because he does not directly seek them. The logic of commodity culture dictates that the gentleman will never be called to account for indecent or inappropriate desires, since those desires by definition never stand a chance of being fulfilled.

This logic determines another way of explaining, *pace* Sedgwick, why homosocial relations in Thackeray's fiction so often verge on the homoerotic: male friendships are a good place for the gentleman to demonstrate his depth of feeling and therefore to intimate his sexual capacity precisely because he does not fear losing men as objects of desire, as must ultimately happen. Thus Pen lives in domestic bliss with Warrington, proving himself to be a compassionate and devoted partner, until that day when Laura becomes available and he must part from his friend: "Are you going to divorce me, Arthur," asks Warrington wryly, "and take unto yourself a wife?" (*Pendennis* 723). Thackeray's other "true" Victorian gentlemen engage in similarly ambiguous and expansive relations with male friends—Dobbin with George Osborne and Clive Newcome with J. J. Ridley—and in each case the homoerotic bond paves the way for and then gives way to a heterosexual marriage. The male friends separate, whether through death or discretion, and accept their necessary and proper alienation from one another: Dobbin mourns a discredited George; Warrington lives alone at a respectable distance from Pen; and J. J. Ridley drops out of *The Newcomes* (1853-55) so quickly that the narrator concludes with an apology for ignoring him.

Fetishizing the flunkey therefore provides the gentleman with an opportunity to enlarge his sexual capacity even further—signaling a reserve of libidinal energy to match his emotional depth. As he lingers over the body of the servant, investing each physical and sartorial detail with erotic potential, the narrator demonstrates that he and gentlemen like him are quite capable of experiencing ardor and even indulging lust. In displacing his presumably heterosexual desires onto an explicitly homoerotic object, however, he risks nothing in the affair. According to the logic of commodity culture, he will ultimately find himself alienated from such indecent objects, leaving his normative sexuality intact and unquestioned; furthermore, according to the logic of Freudian repression, he cannot be accused of harboring indecent desires if he can so guiltlessly and publicly express them. Returning to the front steps of Lady Clavering's mansion, we should note that just prior to the narrator's comments "keen-sighted Mr Pen" has been gazing up at "the virgin bedroom of Miss Blanche Amory" (*Pendennis* 392). As Pen draws near to the object of his affection, the narrator immediately routes his own and

Pen's attention away from the bedroom above and toward the flunkeys below, allowing the gentleman's sexual potency to manifest itself freely. Just after the narrator's interjection, his and Pen's attention swings back to the women, who now emerge from the house into view of "the enraptured observer of female beauty who happened to be passing at the time" (394). The "practised eye" that began by fetishizing the flunkey ends up "enraptured" by women instead; the gentleman's sexuality remains within conventional boundaries, but not before demonstrating its range and power.

This glimpse of an excessive and transgressive eroticism ultimately accentuates the gentleman's ethical distinction. Thackeray's gentlemen are far more famous for social than for sexual transgressions: their habitual slumming through the urban underworld constitutes a "sophisticated game of class" that "functions primarily as a sign of the gentleman's freedom rather than as social critique" (Ferris ["Thackeray and the Ideology of the Gentleman"] 426). The gentleman crosses class lines in order to demonstrate that his unique character exempts him from strict obedience to social etiquette and custom. But there is an overlooked and important parallel here: fetishizing the flunkey constitutes an equally sophisticated game of gender that signifies the gentleman's singularity in precisely the same way—by violating the heterosexual model of Victorian courtship and marriage. Thackeray plays these risky games for a very high stake: to secure for the gentleman an autonomous and expansive subjectivity. The most expedient way for the gentleman to demonstrate that the ethical values he represents are elemental—embodied and expressed from within—is to set them in opposition to social and sexual norms that are imposed from without. As John Kucich points out, "Postromantic ethics leads inevitably to the proud consciousness of having broken the rules that bind others to convention, and, as such, it actively resists aligning itself with official morality" (26). Taken together, the fleeting transgressions of the gentleman help to internalize and essentialize his ethical privilege, granting him a subjective freedom that in turn underwrites his cultural authority. The gentleman's social and sexual exceptionability translates directly into ethical exceptionality; rejecting the objects coveted by servants and snobs, the gentleman takes a lower road that turns out to be the higher ground.

Thackeray's fiction therefore counters mid-century arguments, most famously advanced by John Henry Newman, that the gentlemanly virtues of disinterestedness and self-control had degenerated into passivity and propriety. In *The Idea of a University* (1852), Newman very politely indicts the gentleman for his lack of initiative, his avoidance of controversy, and his affinity with mere comfort and convenience: "Hence it is that it is almost a definition of the gentleman to say he is one who never inflicts pain" (159). Newman probes the manners of the gentleman and finds nothing beneath the surface, no "clashing of opinion, or collision of feeling" (159) that, by testing the limits of the gentleman's disinterestedness and self-control, would verify his ethical position and his subjective power. The superficial respectability that dismayed Newman also troubled Thackeray, who worried that the figure of the gentleman, as appropriated and moralized by the rising middle class, might become utterly housebroken. Hence Thackeray's nostalgia for the age of duelling, when gentlemen *did* inflict pain, through the controlled discharge of violence that demonstrated both their strength of will and their depth of feeling. As a middle-class figure, however, the civilized Victorian gentleman is compelled to lay down the arms of his aristocratic precursors and to seek other means of proving his moral courage and plumbing his subjective depths.

Newman offers one solution, arguing that religious faith can restore both integrity and interiority to the gentleman: "The Church aims at regenerating the very depths of the heart" (154). For the deeply skeptical Thackeray, however, "all that chandlery and artificial flower-show" of Catholicism, all its "fine copes and embroideries," constitutes only more of the same superficiality and hypocrisy of which the gentleman stands accused (*Letters* [*The Letters and Private Papers of William Makepeace Thackeray*] 676). Leaving a lecture by Newman in 1850, Thackeray reportedly declared, "It is either Rome or Babylon, and for me it is Babylon" (Ray [*Thackeray*] 121). With precisely the same ironic twist in his fiction, Thackeray rejects orthodox religion and instead embraces deviant sexuality as a means of testing and authenticating the gentleman's subjective power. This is why Thackeray's gentleman do not renounce their homoerotic desires so dramatically and finally as Dickens's David Copperfield (watching Steerforth drown) or Eugene Wrayburn (battling Bradley Headstone): the gentlemen of Vanity Fair instead need to protect and preserve their deviance as the guarantor of their cultural authority. Their fetishized flunkeys do not merely constitute a curious side effect of Victorian commodity culture. Instead, just as the fetishized flunkey resides within the respectable bourgeois home, so too does sexual deviance reside at the center of bourgeois culture—in the depths of the heart of the gentleman.

Works Cited

Apter, Emily. *Feminizing the Fetish: Psychoanalysis and Narrative Obsession in Turn-of-the-Century France*. Ithaca: Cornell UP, 1991.

Beeton, Isabella. *The Book of Household Management*. London: S. O. Beeton, 1861.

Carey, John. *Thackeray: Prodigal Genius*. London: Faber and Faber, 1977.

Cohen, William. *Sex Scandal: The Private Parts of Victorian Fiction*. Durham: Duke UP, 1996.

Ellis, Edith. *Democracy in the Kitchen*. London, [1890].

Ferris, Ina. "Thackeray and the Ideology of the Gentleman." *The Columbia History of the British Novel*. Ed. John Richetti. New York: Columbia UP, 1994. 407-28.

Freud, Sigmund. "Fetishism." *Collected Papers*. Ed. James Strachey. Vol. 5. New York: Basic Books, 1959. 198-204.

———. *Three Essays on the Theory of Sexuality*. Ed. James Strachey. New York: Basic Books, 1962.

Gillis, John. "Servants, Sexual Relations, and the Risks of Illegitimacy in London, 1801-1900." *Feminist Studies* 5 (1979): 142-73.

Gilmour, Robin. *The Idea of the Gentleman in the Victorian Novel*. London: George Allen and Unwin, 1981.

Kucich, John. *The Power of Lies: Transgression in Victorian Fiction*. Ithaca: Cornell UP, 1994.

Litvak, Joseph. "Kiss Me, Stupid: Sophistication, Sexuality, and *Vanity Fair*." *Novel* 29.2 (1996): 223-42.

Miller, Andrew. *Novels Behind Glass: Commodity, Culture, and Victorian Narrative*. Cambridge: Cambridge UP, 1995.

Newman, John Henry. *The Idea of a University*. Ed. Martin J. Svaglic. Notre Dame: U of Notre Dame P, 1982.

Nunokawa, Jeff. *The Afterlife of Property: Domestic Security and the Victorian Novel*. Princeton: Princeton UP, 1994.

Peters, Catherine. *Thackeray's Universe: Shifting Worlds of Imagination and Reality*. London: Faber and Faber, 1987.

Ray, Gordon. *Thackeray: The Age of Wisdom, 1847-1863*. New York: McGraw-Hill, 1958.

Robbins, Bruce. *The Servant's Hand: English Fiction From Below*. New York: Columbia UP, 1986.

Sedgwick, Eve Kosofsky. *Epistemology of the Closet*. Berkeley: U of California P, 1990.

The Servants' Practical Guide. London: Frederick Warne, 1880.

Thackeray, William. *Barry Lyndon*. Harmondsworth: Penguin, 1975.

———. *The Book of Snobs. The Works of William Makepeace Thackeray*. Kensington Edition. Vol. 22. New York: Charles Scribner's Sons, 1904. 1-266.

———. *The Diary of C. Jeames de la Pluche, Esq. The Works of William Makepeace Thackeray*. Kensington

Edition. Vol. 23. New York: Charles Scribner's Sons, 1904. 129-203.

―――. *The Four Georges. The Works of William Makepeace Thackeray.* Kensington Edition. Vol. 26. New York: Charles Scribner's Sons, 1904. 1-145.

―――. *The History of Pendennis.* Harmondsworth: Penguin, 1986.

―――. *The Letters and Private Papers of William Makepeace Thackeray.* Ed. Gordon Ray. Vol. 2. Cambridge: Harvard UP, 1946.

―――. *Lovel the Widower. The Works of William Makepeace Thackeray.* Kensington Edition. Vol. 28. New York: Charles Scribner's Sons, 1904. 195-370.

―――. *The Newcomes.* Harmondsworth: Penguin, 1996.

―――. "On a Chalk-Mark on the Door." *The Roundabout Papers. The Works of William Makepeace Thackeray.* Kensington Edition. Vol. 27. New York: Charles Scribner's Sons, 1904. 125-140.

―――. "On Some Political Snobs." *The Works of William Makepeace Thackeray.* Kensington Edition. Vol. 22. New York: Charles Scribner's Sons, 1904. 273-77.

―――. *Vanity Fair.* Harmondsworth: Penguin, 1985.

Welsh, Alexander. "Introduction." *Thackeray: A Collection of Critical Essays.* Englewood Cliffs: Prentice-Hall, 1968. 1-14.

Edgar F. Harden (essay date 2000)

SOURCE: Harden, Edgar F. "*The History of Pendennis.*" In *Thackeray the Writer: From* Pendennis *to* Denis Duval, pp. 1-28. Basingstoke, England: Macmillan Press Ltd., 2000.

[*In the following essay, Harden explores Thackeray's association of theatricality with identity in the development of Pen's character.*]

During his career as a writer before the appearance of *Vanity Fair,* Thackeray had published 568 pieces as a contributor to newspapers and periodicals—works that included parodies, burlesques, extravaganzas, political reports, art criticism, book reviews, tales, comic verses, and installments of a full-length novel.[1] In addition he had published 7 works as separate imprints, most of them containing new material ranging from pictorial caricature and news reporting to travel books reflecting his experiences in Ireland and on a journey to the Near East. During the serial appearance of *Vanity Fair* on 19 occasions between January 1847 and July 1848, Thackeray also wrote and published 88 pieces for magazines and periodicals, besides drawing and publishing 106 comic illustrations. What was he to do after the appearance of the masterpiece that had established him as one of England's two leading novelists? Clearly, more of the same: continuing the incredibly energetic, bubbling flow of usually comic, occasionally more somber journalism, and of course beginning another ambitious serial novel.

In *Vanity Fair* Thackeray had for the first time in his imaginative life articulated a comprehensive system of forces defining a moral universe. Inevitably, therefore, all of his subsequent works unfolded within the force-field of this powerful articulation. Henceforth the words "Vanity Fair" openly defined the assumptions of the author in his fictions and non-fictions, and also identified the fundamental signpost that his readers needed in order for them to see and to understand the comical and absurd world that he and they shared—both the fictional world and the reality that it reflected.

He had also given quintessential definition to the Thackerayan narrator—an omnipresent, protean figure who mirrors the archetypal configurations of human society, and who reflects Thackeray's belief that one cannot see and understand the ambiguities of human existence from a single, stable point of view. Every utterance is the utterance of a moment, trapped in the flux of time and therefore limited. Consequently, his narrator manifests an intense historical awareness that constantly reveals itself in the precise, concrete details of an evoked visible world, as well as in his persistent consciousness of the flow of time, which ages both things and human experience, diminishing both and calling the value of both into question. Thackeray's satire, therefore, operates in creative interaction with this historical awareness. It is a satire that can be limited and local, but that also ranges beyond time and place, radically challenging a reader's most fundamental assumptions about human life. The brilliant wit and comedy of a Thackerayan narrative like *Vanity Fair* constantly entertain us, but the frequent shifting of narrative perspective also reminds us of the profound indeterminacy at the heart of it.

His next narrative, a serial, like all but one of its successors, **The History of Pendennis. His Fortunes and Misfortunes, His Friends and His Greatest Enemy** (November 1848-December 1850) is also a novel without a hero, and a novel firmly set in the Fair. **Pendennis,** however, is a case-study, so to speak, and like ensuing Thackerayan narratives reveals the same general types and the same recurring patterns of human conduct and lives rendered in *Vanity Fair,* but it also illustrates a certain human individuality. Whereas the emblematic illustration on the monthly wrappers of the serial parts of *Vanity Fair* had emphasized the role of the clown-narrator addressing his audience of fellow fools, the corresponding illustration on the wrappers of **Penden-**

nis pictured the title-figure making a choice between two female figures, one representing worldly temptation and the other the fulfillments of domesticity—an archetypal choice rendered in individual terms.

Pendennis is Thackeray's pre-eminent version of the great nineteenth-century theme of the young man from the provinces, impoverished, simple, and under-educated, but intelligent and full of high hopes, who comes to a disillusioning but also maturing understanding of himself and of his place in the world. In tracing Pen's progress, Thackeray typically drew upon his own experiences: boyhood memories of Larkbeare in Devon, youthful absurdity and victimization at Cambridge, naïve beginnings in bohemian Grub Street, and presumably silly posturings on the fringes of fashionable life in London.

As these statements suggest, however, the novel gives great emphasis not only to Pen but also to the various contexts of his existence. All of the characters are prominent inhabitants of the Fair, possess the inevitable limitations of their virtues, have to give up enticing possibilities, and—although they may seek to have their conduct governed by desirable values—can find only limited happiness. In typical Thackerayan fashion, Pen is quite flawed, a crucial aspect of Thackeray's presentation of him being the ironic relationship between Pen's hopes and enthusiasms and the narrator's more mature perspectives. At the same time, however, as Thackeray reveals that Laura's love is a partial renewal of Helen Pendennis's love for her son ("and arms as tender as Helen's once more enfold him"[2]), the novelist implies his awareness that he is dramatizing his own frustrated need for domestic affection.

Clearly the most prominent literality and metaphor defining the context of Pen's life is theatricality, which the novel renders with notable elaborateness and rich comedy. In *Pendennis,* theatricality epitomizes human isolation as well as intended deception—of oneself as well as of others—and can be seen as an analogue of *Vanity Fair*'s charade and puppet metaphors. In Thackeray all the world tends to be a stage and all men and women merely players, yet one can at times perceive one's "true" being and communicate it directly. Although other individuals tend to see one's behavior as performance, and although one's "true" being tends to dissipate and delude itself as well as others in a surrender to role-playing, it can also express itself even amid the theatrics.

Surrounding the histrionic title-figure we see various characters who illuminate for us and sometimes for him the extensiveness and complexity of theatrical behavior. In showing us a series of responses to such behavior, extending from a considerable number of actual playhouse visits to a variety of social gatherings and private conversations, the narrator focuses our attention especially upon the degree of a character's ability to distinguish between the human actor and the role. We see Pen's growth, for example, not only by the gradual change in his attitude towards the Fotheringay but also by the decline of his interest in Mrs. Leary and by the fact that in the latter instance he does not, as he had with the Fotheringay, confuse the performer with the role—unlike the still naïve Mr. Huxter.

From the very beginning of Pen's early infatuation during a performance of *The Stranger*—a play about a man imprisoned by a role that isolates him from himself as well as from others—the narrator emphasizes both the extent of Pen's confusion and the degree to which it separates him from the audience of which he is a part. The narrator gives us an elaborate sense of the play's sham, from its extraordinary dialogue, costumes, properties and style of acting, to the considerably disengaged behavior of the actors, and he frequently reminds us of the reactions of spectators other than Pen. To the initiated Foker, "The Stranger" is Bingley in tights and Hessians, and the woman opposite him is "the Fotheringay" (I, iv, 35), but in Pen's eyes she is "Mrs. Haller" (I, iv, 36), even when he sees her privately (I, v, 48). To us she begins "her business," but to the awestruck Pen "she's speaking." A further contrast is provided by her coach, Bows, who, even while about to be overcome by the pathos of a moment, is able to cry out "Bravo" in approval of his pupil's successful handling of her part. Whatever the limitations of Bows himself, this ability to respond sympathetically even while he knows he is observing a rehearsed mimetic act points to a larger ability possessed by the narrator, who can respond to what is genuine within the sham—to the "reality of love, children, and forgiveness of wrong" that is to be found "in the midst of the balderdash" (I, iv, 37).

The theatricality into which Pen's infatuation leads him becomes especially evident when he arranges to see *Hamlet* with his mother; by deciding that "the play should be the thing" (I, vi, 56) to test Helen, he implicitly acknowledges that his own life is a play, within which *Hamlet* will be staged. Like Hamlet, he is both actor and stage-manager, but because Helen has no knowledge of his intentions, she responds to the play-within-the-play as a stage-piece without a dramatic context and sees only a beautiful Ophelia (I, vi, 59). The next spectators who witness a performance of *Hamlet*—Dr. Portman and Major Pendennis—have that additional knowledge and therefore see more than a character in a play. The clergyman finds her not only "a very clever actress" but also a woman "endowed with very considerable personal attractions," while the Major ignores her abilities as a Shakespearean performer and comments on her physical attractiveness as an object of sexual desire: "Gad, . . . the young rascal has not made a bad choice." The Major's attention focuses on the larger human drama within which *Hamlet* is being played; more aware than Dr. Portman of the audience in the theatre and perfectly cognizant of an actress's ability to be alertly self-conscious, the Major sees her appeal for male admiration in the look she gives Sir Derby Oaks and he cynically thinks: "that's their way" (I, ix, 90). It is Dolphin who gives professional testimony to the Fotheringay's mastery of attitudinizing and her ability to learn the occasional "dodge" (I, xiv, 124).

Although Pen attends the Chatteris theatre night after night, he fails to see the mechanical quality of the dull girl's performance, and even when personal contact between them has ended and he has become a mere spectator, he does not become aware that he has always seen her as though across footlights. The memory of his passion and a persistent sense of his humiliation bring him to watch her in London, but by the next year "she was not the same, somehow." At last he seems to recognize "coarse and false" accents, "the same emphasis on the same words," and her "mechanical sobs and sighs" (I, xx, 190). His continuing association of her with misery, repudiation, and failure, however, makes understandable his following visit, after he has been plucked at Oxbridge.

When next he sees her—in a theatre audience, appropriately—she has changed her name and position; having become Lady Mirabel, she has permanently joined the audience and henceforth spends her energies perfecting her new, and now metaphorical role. By a striking complication, then, fantasy—the belief that an ignorant actress could be socially acceptable as a wife—having been exposed as illusion, suddenly becomes fact and yet retains its illusoriness; the fantasy becomes a reality that yet remains fantastic. London society has its private reservations (I, xxix, 282, 284), but publicly it allows the role to define the person and thereby encourages her to simulate the part she has chosen by marrying Sir Charles Mirabel, that most "theatrical man" (II, vi, 53).[3]

Her success in finding acceptance, moreover, not only implicates London society but also helps make her come to seem like a lady in her own right. The range of her accomplishments gradually increases, from patronizing new authors (II, vi, 60-1) to penning neat little notes (II, x, 100-1). Major Pendennis comes to term her "a most respectable woman, received everywhere—everywhere, mind" (II, vi, 53). She gives receptions and seems to Pen "as grave and collected as if she had been born a Duchess, and had never seen a trap-door in her life" (II, vi, 60). The main implications are clear: not only do people almost inevitably play roles, often deluding even themselves, but with money and a certain amount of study they find their great arena in society—where human beings are isolated from each other by the very roles that fit the overall performance.

The precocious Harry Foker serves as a perfect introduction to these two arenas, both in Chatteris and London. He also makes an appearance at the moment of Pen's re-emergence into London life and again that evening at the theatre (I, xxix, 281). In Chatteris he knows all the actors and in his own way unconsciously emulates them as well. Difficult to identify at first beneath his elaborate costume (I, iii, 29), Foker, like "one of our great light comedians," offers us "great pleasure and an abiding matter for thought" (I, iv, 34). Whether calling for "his mixture," ordering turtle, venison, and carefully chilled wine, dancing the hornpipe while "looking round for the sympathy of his groom, and the stable men" (I, iii, 30), or twirling "like Harlequin in the Pantomime" (I, xiii, 117), Foker is playing his role as man of the world with all the enthusiasm of youthful naïvety.

For all his simplicity, of course, he does have a certain shrewd acuteness of insight, especially into devious behavior: hence the irony of his partly duplicating Pen's early infatuation and of his failure to perceive the degree to which Miss Amory, an even more accomplished performer than the Fotheringay, is providing herself with "two strings to her bow" (I, x, 93). In terms of the general theatrical metaphor, Foker's illusion is epitomized for us when, after being smitten with Blanche, he feels he needs a new appearance, and in response to his command, *"Cherchy alors une paire de tongs,—et—curly moi un pew,"* the valet wonders "whether his master was in love or was going masquerading" (II, i, 8).[4] As the woodcut initial of the third last chapter reminds us, in seeking Blanche he plays Clown to Pen's Harlequin; yet, to his credit, Foker finally draws a just conclusion from the evidence presented to him about her.

Like Foker and especially Pen, Alcides Mirobolant shows how vanity and infatuation motivate theatrical behavior. A superlatively unconscious role-player, Mirobolant receives unusual attention from the novelist for a minor character because of his usefulness in parodying those who are self-deluded and, in the unconsciously ironic words of Morgan, those who "has as much pride and insolence as if they was real gentlemen" (I, xxxvii, 360). Like Pen in London, Mirobolant possesses an exalted sense of his own professional importance; in addition to his own library, pictures, and piano, he requires an array of assistants, his own maid, his own apartments, and all the deference due to a hypersensitive artist—a role that he plays even in private: "It was a grand sight to behold him in his dressing-gown composing a *menu*. He always sate down and played the piano for some time before that. If interrupted, he remonstrated pathetically with his little maid. Every great artist, he said, had need of solitude to perfectionate his works" (I, xxiii, 218). As a deluded lover, like the youthful Pen he uses loftily inflated language for the very earthbound object of his passion, and he conceives of himself in an overtly theatrical way: in re-plying to his confidante, who accuses him of being per-fidious, he says, "with a deep bass voice, and a tragic accent worthy of the Porte St. Martin and his favourite melo-dramas, 'Not perfidious, but fatal. Yes, I am a fa-tal man, Madame Fribsbi. To inspire hopeless passion is my destiny'" (I, xxiv, 234).

But it is as a mock-gentleman that he most clearly serves to parody the attitudinizing of young Pen. At the Baymouth ball, where his vanity conflicts directly with Pen's, Mirobolant's self-esteem clothes itself in a blue ribbon and a three-pointed star, but even then Arthur fails to see the implications: the idea "that such an indi-vidual should have any feeling of honour at all, did not much enter into the mind of this lofty young aristocrat, the apothecary's son" (I, xxvii, p. 262). As a Gascon, Mirobolant stands on the one side of Pen, while Costi-gan, Mirobolant's Irish counterpart, stands on the other; both represent parodic versions of the strut and swagger found in Pen.

Because Mirobolant has an exaggerated belief in the distinctions that set him apart, he insists that he is a *chef,* not a *cuisinier,* and that being a *Chevalier de Juil-let* he has a special duty to defend his honor—like that other mock-gentleman, Costigan, by means of a duel. Here too, his attitude shows itself akin to Pen's theatri-cal sense of his own dignity, both in his own formal challenge to a fellow schoolboy and in his response to Mirobolant's tapping him on the shoulder. The conflict between the two expresses itself in such approved melo-dramatic forms as the grinding of teeth, the jabbering of oaths, the stamping of feet, the challenge to a duel, and the high incidence of French, but like most melodra-matic threats in the book it is quickly deflated.

The connectedness of all this role-playing receives fur-ther extension in the depiction of another highly theatri-cal figure who believes himself to be a thorough man of the world: "General or Captain Costigan—for the latter was the rank which he preferred to assume" (I, v, 43). Costigan is a mock-gentleman and a mock-warrior—a veritable "Sir Lucius O'Trigger, which character he had performed with credit, both off and on the stage" (I, xii, 108). He resembles the infatuated Pen as an often un-conscious role-player, but where the boy is drunk on poetry and adolescent longings, the source of Costi-gan's illusions is a Celtic imagination excessively stimulated by alcohol.

Ending as a fixture of the singer's table at the Back Kitchen, this performer inevitably characterizes himself in theatrical terms, speaking often and sadly "of his re-semblance to King Lear in the plee—of his having a thankless choild, bedad" (II, iv, 36). When "this aged buffoon" (II, xvii, 163) finds himself in pawn for drink, however—at "the Roscius's Head, Harlequin Yard,

Drury Lane" (II, iv, 37), of course—he successfully ap-peals to that same child, but, inevitably, with an in-vented story. In fact, "the Captain was not only unac-customed to tell the truth,—he was unable even to think it—and fact and fiction reeled together in his muzzy, whiskified brain" (I, v, 45). Inevitably, then, his lan-guage is highly theatrical, for he cannot distinguish himself from his role. Appropriately making his initial appearance in the company of an actor, Costigan ha-bitually speaks with elaborate rhetoric; he exaggerates the language and "[suits] the action to the word" (I, xi, 102).

Inordinate in his sense of honor, and extravagant also in his sense of embarrassment, which he is capable of ex-pressing "in a voice of agony, and with eyes brimful of tears" (I, xii, 108), he unwittingly serves to parody Pen's own excessive pride and shame from the very be-ginning of the novel to the moment when the series of jokes by Warrington and others about Pen's "noble" family and his residence at Fairoaks "Castle" culmi-nates as the imagination of the "tipsy mountebank" (I, xiii, 115) actually bodies forth the marvellous structure and the impressive life lived there: "I've known um since choildhood, Mrs. Bolton; he's the proproietor of Fairoaks Castle, and many's the cooper of Clart I've dthrunk there with the first nobilitee of his neetive coun-tee" (II, viii, 83). As a dueller we cannot take him even as seriously as Sir Lucius, but since Costigan has a re-spect for people that is based chiefly upon their wealth or future prospects, we can perceive in him a comic representation of the values of the fashionable society to which he constantly alludes and which he uses to help bolster his role. He thereby reveals his similarity to Major Pendennis.

The Major, another old warrior of limited financial means and fictional ancestry, actually associates with the kind of people Costigan pretends to have known, but such association produces a false sense of personal importance not unlike Costigan's: as the narrator ironi-cally puts it, "The Major lived in such good company that he might be excused for feeling like an Earl" (I, vii, 70). At one point he even seems to feel like a Duke, for after greeting Wellington the Major begins "to imi-tate him unconsciously" (I, xxxvii, 363). In fact, we have a strong impression of his being an actor. Like his chest, "manfully wadded with cotton" (I, viii, 81), he is perfect on the outside but rickety within—both physi-cally and metaphorically. Hence the considerable em-phasis on his elaborate toilettes, which become more lengthy and complicated as he grows more feeble, and which become the basis for the narrator's elevating Ma-jor Pendennis to the mock-eminence of "hero" along-side Costigan (II, x, 100).

Like Sir Charles Mirabel, an inveterate "theatrical man" (II, vi, 53), "Colonel" Altamont, a notorious imposter, and those two aged youths, Blondel and Colchicum (II, vii, 72), Major Pendennis wears a wig—and that fact receives unusual attention in the novel, as does the elaborate and mysterious curling the wig receives. To a number of scoffers, it even defines him; he is "Wigsby" (I, xxix, 282, II, vi, 54, xxix, 294). Indeed, on one memorable occasion, later briefly re-evoked (I, xiv, 126), it is used to epitomize not only age but sham sentiment, as he tells a story of losing a young heiress: "We returned our letters, sent back our locks of hair (the Major here passed his fingers through his wig), we suffered—but we recovered" (I, vii, 71). Here, as often elsewhere, Major Pendennis is also an actor in the broadest sense: one whose wholehearted commitment to the values of Vanity Fair marks him as a participant in fundamental and extended illusion. We see this in the very ring he wears so prominently, "emblazoned with the famous arms of Pendennis" (I, i, 2). Like Bingley's it is a sham ring, and like the family motto as interpreted by the Major (II, xxxii, 318), it represents a dedication to worldly aspirations alone.

Though the linking of Major Pendennis and Costigan is established from the very beginning of the novel in Pen's letter to his uncle, no one would question that the Major is a far more conscious and adept poseur than Costigan; like most role-players, indeed, like Becky Sharp, however, he himself is partly taken in by the illusion he tries to sustain. With "a mournful earnestness and veracity," he urges young Pen to begin his genealogical studies but not to concentrate upon the pedigrees, for many are "very fabulous, and there are few families that can show such a clear descent as our own" (I, ix, 85; repeated II, xix, 185). So too, the Major believes that his conduct is "perfectly virtuous" as well as perfectly "respectable" (I, ix, 86).

One of the judgments that best epitomizes him appears in the delightful phrase, "He was perfectly affable" (I, i, 2). Such a desirable quality as affability, of course, can give great pleasure and amusement, even when it is the perfection of pose. If the performance is carried on at great length, however, we come to see the human strain and debilitation involved, as the Major's condition after his performance at the Gaunt House ball demonstrates. Like Pen, Blanche, Lady Clavering, and Lord Steyne, who introduces himself to her "at the request of the obsequious Major Pendennis" (II, vii, 69), the Major participates in many a "little play" (II, vii, 70) that goes to make up the entertainment of the evening. But since extended perfection is too much to ask of a human, to be "perfectly affable" for very long is to be inhumanly artificial.

Though the Major is capable of such consistency, we also see flaws from the very start of the performance, not only in his neglect of the humble rural petitioner in favor of the entreaties of more fashionable women but also in the "rage and wonder" (I, i, 3) that show themselves on his face and make Glowry feel for his lancet. Later in the novel, therefore, when we are told "it was curious how emotion seemed to olden him" (II, xiv, 137), the narrator is saying not simply that emotion ages the Major but also that emotion reveals his age; being a break in the pose, it discloses the aging process that has been taking place underneath, much as the sudden glimpse of Becky's haggard face opposite Rawdon asleep in his chair shows us how the unremitting effort to maintain her role has debilitated her.

Finally, the passage of time[5] not only reveals weakness and leads to artifice that is both more elaborate and more apparent, but it also changes the perspective in which the artifice is viewed. The Major's practised grin comes to be termed a smirk (II, vi, 54, xviii, 180, xx, 202) and thereby, like Smirke himself, more of a subject for caricature. His club, Bays's, even comes in the eyes of young men to take on the name of Dolphin's theatre: "It's a regular museum" (I, xxxvii, 362). Likewise, as men of the Major's time begin to die and he becomes more isolated, he thereby seems more theatrical and more clearly a subject for laughter. Hence it is appropriate that he at last retires from "the Pall Mall *pavé*," where "he has walked . . . long enough" (II, xxxi, 311), as a stage actor might at last retire from the boards. He never fully understands the play, however, even when he recalls so potentially illuminating an example as Sheridan's comedy—"We have him at a deadlock, like the fellow in the play—the Critic, hey?" (II, xxxii, 318)—for in **Pendennis** as in *The Critic,* contrivance is easily overcome by counter-contrivance, and the Major's elaborate plot, like Puff's, is negated by the recalcitrance of actors who alter their parts.

The Major never really understands the meaning of his part either, not even towards the end when he quotes Shakespeare's Wolsey and implicitly identifies himself with that role. Shakespeare's great worldling came at last to recognize that the cause of his defeat and misery lay in himself, that one cannot build on corruption; hence his injunction: "Be just and fear not." It is a mark of Pen's maturity that he understands this and renounces the corruption, but Major Pendennis does not. Hence his pitifully theatrical act of kneeling to Pen and his final comment: "'"and had I but served my God as I've served you"'—. . . I mightn't have been—Goodnight, sir, you needn't trouble yourself to call again.' . . . He looked very much oldened; it seemed as if the contest and defeat had quite broken him" (II, xxxii, 320).

Major Pendennis believes that his desires for his nephew, which he thinks of as unselfish, have only exposed him to defeat and misery. Implying, then, that unselfishness opens one to unhappiness, he inverts the meaning of Wolsey's speech and maintains his own worldly consistency, just as he does when he accepts

Pen's marriage to Laura because Lady Rockminster approves. Though we are told that he "became very serious in his last days," that seriousness seems to take the form solely of telling "his stories" to Laura or listening to her reading to him (II, xxxvii, 371). His stories could hardly be very edifying and one has reason for doubting whether he understands what she reads any more than he understood the folly of Wolsey or Cymbeline (II, xiv, 137-38).

The man whom Strong finally calls "Jack Alias" (II, xxxvii, 370) seems for a time to represent the triumph of theatricality. Whether his real name is "John Armstrong," like the famous outlaw, or whether that is as fictitious as "Ferdinand," "Amory," and "Altamont," it is as "Colonel Altamont, of the body-guard of his Highness the Nawaub of Lucknow" (I, xxvi, 256), that he is introduced and generally known in the novel. Appearing in a black wig (I, xxvii, 263) and in accompanying "whiskers, dyed evidently with the purple of Tyre" (I, xxvi, 256), beribboned like Mirobolant, bejewelled like the mountebank, Bloundell-Bloundell, with whom he associates on several occasions, and generally overdressed, Altamont is a blatant masquerader whose function is to emphasize the spuriousness of the relationships in the Clavering family and elsewhere, to serve as a standard for measuring other kinds of make-believe in the novel, and finally to demonstrate the basic folly of human plots and exploitative desires.

As a thoroughgoing performer, he endures repeated exposure, so deeply does he believe in his role or roles, as we can see when, in speaking of himself, he tells Strong that "a man of honour may take any name he chooses" (II, v, 46) or, at an equally comic moment, in excusing some deplorable behavior of his, he calmly says to Sir Francis Clavering: "I told you I was drunk, and that ought to be sufficient between gentleman and gentleman" (II, v, 49). Altamont not only has difficulty in distinguishing himself from his role, but he also, with the assistance of drink, confuses matters in the actual theatre as well, to the exasperation of Captain Strong: "I took him to the play the other night; and, by Jove, sir, he abused the actor who was doing the part of villain in the play, and swore at him so, that the people in the boxes wanted to turn him out. The after-piece was the 'Brigand,' where Wallack comes in wounded, you know, and dies. When he died, Altamont began to cry like a child, and said it was a d——d shame, and cried and swore so, that there was another row, and everybody laughing" (II, iv, 40).

Altamont, in short, is the epitome of disorder in the novel, for he is not only the chief threat but he is compulsive, even joyful in his unruliness, and his last cry is an exultant challenge to all comers: "Hurray, who's for it!" (II, xxxvii, 368). A true squire of Alsatia (II, iv, 33), he cannot be permanently assimilated by society, nor

does he really wish to be. A brigand, an outlaw, an ex-convict, guilty of forgery and manslaughter, he is even more fundamentally what Strong terms him at the end of the novel: "a madman" (II, xxxvii, 360). Full of "wild stories and adventures" (II, vi, 56), he represents a romantically alluring irrationality to simple novel-reading females like Miss Snell and Miss Fribsby; exploiting one after the other, like "a perfect Don Juan" (II, xxxvii, 369), he offers in return "to give anybody a lock of his hair" (II, xxxvii, 370).

Only Pen deliberately renounces the attempt to trade off of what Altamont seems to represent; consequently he is free to find stability in a good marriage. Altamont, of course, renounces nothing and, being the irrational force that he is, sweeps free of all attempts to capture him. All these plots fail and it is entirely fitting that Altamont should escape the careful Morgan because of a drunken innkeeper's sudden fears, and because of a most theatrical man's unexpected impulse of dashing down the gutterpipe that separates Altamont from his pursuers, being reminded of that "aisy sthratagem by remembering his dorling Emilie, when she acted the pawrt of Cora in the Plee—and by the bridge in Peza-wro, bedad" (II, xxxvii, 370). And with that phrase, we are carried back to the beginning of the novel and realize that all these plots reflect each other.

Though equally as much a masquerader as her father, Blanche Amory is of a rather different kind, despite certain similarities. For one thing, an important part of her alien tone comes from habits she has picked up in France. Called "the French girl" (I, xxvii, 258) by one character, she uses French not only to crown herself with a false name but especially to express her affectations, notably her sentimental ones. Her flippant and arch use of the Gallic tongue, however, reveals not only affectation but moral insensitivity—lightly calling Pen a *"monstre,"* for example, as a means of teasing him about supposedly having a sexual dalliance with Fanny (II, xx, 201).

Blanche's exposure to French literature, especially the romances of George Sand, causes her to play at being in love with literary heroes and to change capriciously from one to another; she indulges the same expectations and conducts herself in the same way when she transfers her attentions to actual human beings. It is little wonder, therefore, that she encourages Mirobolant (I, xxxvii, 360), flirts simultaneously with Foker and Pen, and at last, in a desperate search for legitimacy, marries an apparently bogus count with a superlatively grand name: de Montmorenci (the same family with which Becky Sharp claimed kinship) de Valentinois.

When she has no other audience she enjoys posing to herself, whether in a mirror or in her book of verse, the title of which serves the narrator as a metonym for her

(II, xxvii, 275). When she is not "the Muse," "*Mes Larmes*," or "the Lady of *Mes Larmes*," then she is often "the Sylphide," and like Marie Taglioni in the ballet of that name (I, xxxix, 377), she simulates an ethereal being whose association with earth-bound humanity proves impossible. As a *"femme incomprise"* (I, xxiii, 216), she cultivates sentiment and so, "by practice" (I, xxiv, 227), increases both her dissatisfaction and its expression. Irony becomes one form of utterance, especially irony directed against members of the Clavering family. At other times her annoyance takes the form of open quarrels with them, even before visitors like Laura and Major Pendennis.

Though at moments she feels a certain chagrin at having let her role slip, she always has another at hand. Most capable of responding to her circumstances by speaking dramatically and making "appropriate, though rather theatrical" gestures, she characteristically thinks of herself as "a heroine" (II, xxxvii, 366). When paying a patronizing and inquisitive visit to Fanny Bolton, for example, "Blanche felt a queen stepping down from her throne to visit a subject, and enjoyed all the bland consciousness of doing a good action" (II, xxvii, 274). Inevitably, Mrs. Bolton, a former member of the theatre, sees the play-acting and, worse, the prostitution of feeling.

Blanche wants "an establishment" (II, vi, 59) and wide social acceptance, but she also wants to continue her immature indulgence in "dreaming pretty dramas" (II, xxxiv, 329). Playing at being in love with Pen and genuinely attracted by Foker's wealth, her performance for each at the piano (captured also, for emphasis, by two illustrations) helps to epitomize her artful duplicity. Though she plays various characters, she also has certain stock gestures and devices that recur in her performances: "If ever this artless young creature met a young man, . . . she confided in him, so to speak—made play with her beautiful eyes—spoke in a tone of tender interest, and simple and touching appeal, and left him, to perform the same pretty little drama in behalf of his successor." If at first there are "very few audiences before whom Miss Blanche could perform" (I, xxvi, 246), she does for a time secure more attention, but her repetitions become apparent to Pen, as had the Fotheringay's.

When Pen asks her whether she wishes him "to come wooing in a Prince Prettyman's dress from the masquerade warehouse, and . . . feed my pretty princess with *bonbons*?" her answer is, of course, "*Mais j'adore les bonbons, moi*" (II, xxvi, 266). Indeed, it is Pen's ability as a play-actor that in part makes her equivocate between him and the wealthy Foker, for with the latter she has to carry much of the burden of the relationship. Hence also we understand part of the "strange feeling of exultation" that takes "possession of Blanche's mind"

(II, xxxvii, 365) when she loses Foker at last. It takes possession of her mind because, as several people in the novel point out, she has no heart; like Becky Sharp she can feel no kindness, warmth, sympathy, or love.

Without these capabilities, "life is nothing" (I, xxiv, 227) indeed, and Blanche unwittingly emphasizes the emptiness of her life for us by variously repeating, in effect, her cry: "*Il me faut des émotions*" (II, xxxv, 345). As one who from a very early age "had begun to gush" (I, xxiv, 227), she appropriately tells Pen, in her deceptive letter, "To you I bring the gushing poesy of my being" (II, xxxiv, 331); even at this point, however, he fails to realize how complete a sham she is, for "he saw more than existed in reality" (II, xxxv, 345). What really exists at the heart of this circle of sham emotions is precisely nothing; at the center of the roles, their motive and epitome, exists complete emptiness, for the self has been dissipated through a surrender to role-playing. With the Fotheringay we are amused by seeing the ironic discrepancy between her theatrical role and her dull, stolid, everyday self, but with Blanche Amory, the more we see into her the more we understand that behind the role is only a void.

The last form of theatricalism by which Pen is tested derives rather intimately from the actual theatre; it is represented by Fanny Bolton, whose mother was "in the profession once, and danced at the Wells." Fanny herself has attended a day-school run by two former actresses and she is "a theatrical pupil" of Bows's, like the Fotheringay. "She has a good voice and a pretty face and figure for the stage," and having heard "of her mother's theatrical glories, . . . longs to emulate [them]" (II, iv, 34-35). Like her mother, Fanny is a "theatrical person" (II, ix 96). Hence she responds readily to spectacle and freely participates in the illusions to which it gives rise.

Vauxhall is therefore a perfect place for her romance to begin. It offers singing, horse-riding, fireworks, dancing, and a general glitter that makes it seem to "blaze before her with a hundred million of lamps, with a splendour such as the finest fairy tale, the finest pantomime she had ever witnessed at the theatre, had never realised" (II, viii, 82). She is of course ready to make a hero of the young man who takes her through such a wealth of splendor as Vauxhall, and somewhat like Blanche and her Savoyard organ-grinder (I, xxiv, 228), she romanticizes Pen by imagining hardship as well as glory: "I'm sure he's a nobleman, and of ancient famly, and kep out of his estate." Thinking of Bulwer's *The Lady of Lyons*, she asks, "And if everybody admires Pauline . . . for being so true to a poor man—why should a gentleman be ashamed of loving a poor girl?" (II, xiii, 124). The other member of "this couple of fools" (II, xi, 108), as the narrator forthrightly terms them, her mother, encourages these fantasies with recollections of former actresses who married theatrical men of one kind or another: not only the Fotheringay, but Emily Budd, who danced Columbine in *Harlequin Hornpipe* (II, x, 98, xiii, 125).

Fanny, who, like young Pen (I, viii, 78), would "do on the stage" (II, xxxiv, 334), eventually has to accept Huxter as her harlequin, but the brief association with Pen helps the girl to supplement her powers of fantasy with cunning, notably when she coaxes information about him out of Costigan, "tripping about the room as she had seen the dancers do at the play" (II, xi, 107), flattering him, learning what she wants to know, and then abandoning him. Though she suffers "fever and agitation, and passion and despair" (II, xvii, 167), the "drama" (II, xxvi, 263) with Pen ends when she consoles herself like the heroine of Pen's poem, Ariadne. As he sees at last, the ultimate root of her theatricality lies in her "coquetry and irrepressible desire of captivating mankind" (II, xxxvi, 348).[6]

The object of much of this role-playing, cool or passionate, is of course also frequently theatrical in his behavior, but less so as he grows older. Pen's lack of a father, his spoiled domination of Helen and young Laura, his reading of Inchbald's *Theatre* (I, iii, 24), and supplementary literature, his lively imagination, adolescent longings, isolation, and inexperience all help to account for his youthful fantasies. He becomes a reciter of gloomy, romantic verses, a poet-playwright himself, and a person most ready to respond to the pathos and beauty of Ophelia and Mrs. Haller by seeing himself in the appropriate roles: "He was Hamlet jumping into Ophelia's grave: he was the Stranger taking Mrs. Haller to his arms, beautiful Mrs. Haller" (I, vii, 69). He puts on "his most princely air" (I, vi, 64) when addressing inferior mortals like Dr. Portman, while with the Major he strings up his nerves for "his tragic and heroical air," "armed *cap-à-pié* as it were, with lance couched and plumes displayed" (I, viii, 77). It is only appropriate that the conclusion of the affair should be parodied by Hobnell, who "flung himself into a theatrical attitude near a newly-made grave, and began repeating Hamlet's verses over Ophelia, with a hideous leer at Pen" (I, xv, 135).

After the end of this first major episode of his life, however, his extravagant theatricalism is essentially at an end. Though Pen momentarily looks down at Fanny, "splendidly protecting her, like Egmont at Clara in Goethe's play" (II, viii, 84-85), and sees himself as a potential Faust to her Margaret, he terms that vision "nonsense," and vows there will be none of that "business" (II, ix, 93) for him. Finally, when he asks Blanche, "will you be the . . . Lady of Lyons, and love the penniless Claude Melnotte?" (II, xxxiv, 329), he is acting a part more to amuse her than to satisfy himself.

Along with these romantic roles, Pen has, from the very beginning of the novel, tried to simulate "a man of the world." The family legends, his father's pretensions, and his own tacit pseudoaristocratic position as "head of the Pendennises" (I, i, 5), provide initial encouragement, as does the Fotheringay affair itself, for Pen becomes "famous" (I, xix, 176) at the university by making known his former passion for her, who is now a successful London actress: "his brow would darken, his eyes roll, his chest heave with emotion as he recalled that fatal period of his life, and described the woes and agonies which he had suffered" (I, xix, 175). Strutting, swaggering, entertaining bounteously, and indulging expensive tastes for clothing, jewelry, rare editions, prints, and gambling, while neglecting his studies (somewhat like his creator), Pen boyishly overplays his role—nowhere more so than in his admiring association with Bloundell-Bloundell, who is as flamboyantly fraudulent as Macheath (I, xx, 186), and whose stories Pen believes as implicitly as Fanny does Costigan's.

During the "Ball-Practising" (I, xxvii, 257), Pen seems at his most typical as a would-be man of the world when "performing *cavalier seul* . . . [and] drawling through that figure" (I, xxvii, 260), but, as before, his triumphs end, like Fitz-Boodle's: though he and Blanche whirl round "as light and brisk as a couple of opera-dancers," they bump into recalcitrant actuality. His "waltzing career" (I, xxvii, 261) having ended, he soon turns to law and then to a literary career (again like his creator). Here Warrington, the novel's primary counterforce to pretensions of theatricality, makes sure that Pen is taken down at the start, calling Pen's old poem about Ariadne "miserable weak rubbish" that is "mawkish and disgusting," and his Prize Poem both "pompous and feeble" (I, xxxii, 312). Pen therefore begins with humble hack-writing for bread and gradually moves up to the modest eminence of being a published novelist.

In his parallel social career, however, away from Warrington's superintendence, Pen's mimetic instincts seem more under the influence of personal vanity: "Pen was sarcastic and dandyfied when he had been in the company of great folks; he could not help imitating some of their airs and tones, and having a most lively imagination, mistook himself for a person of importance very easily." Living in prominent society, we are reminded, makes one an actor, as we see again when Pen tells Foker of the Major's efforts to secure Blanche for him, and when, by "flinging himself into an absurd theatrical attitude," he reveals not only "high spirits" (II, vii, 72) but also perhaps a mostly unconscious discomfort at what he sees and may sense of the Major's plotting.

Pen's next bit of theatricalism shows clear discomfort, however—this time at a lurking purpose in himself—as he tries to dispel "a gloomy and rather guilty silence" when he and Fanny happen to meet Bows in the porter's doorway by attempting "to describe, in a jocular manner, the transactions of the night previous, and . . . to give an imitation of Costigan vainly expostulating with the check-taker at Vauxhall. It was not a good imitation" (II, x, 97), and Bows understands why. Deciding that his "calling is not seduction" (II, xi, 110), Pen turns again to Blanche Amory and to his more public aspirations. Having played the part of the experienced old gentleman to Laura and Fanny, he now tries it on Warrington: "I am older than you, George, in spite of your grizzled whiskers, and have seen much more of the world than you have in your garret here, shut up with your books and your reveries and your ideas of one-and-twenty" (II, xxiii, 232). Though a severe judgment, it is clearly self-serving, causing Warrington to respond with a shrewd exposure of Pen's motive for proclaiming himself a worldly old Sadducee, one who takes things as they are: "This is the meaning of your scepticism, . . . my poor fellow. You're going to sell yourself" (II, xxiii, 238).

Pen in effect accepts a stock role imposed upon him; in the appropriately ironic words of Morgan, he is now "young Hopeful" (II, xxx, 303). Before the play is over, however, Pen clearly sees that he must not accept a ready-made role: "you must bear your own burthen, fashion your own faith, think your own thoughts, and pray your own prayer" (II, xxxv, 340). When he puts on his last "tragedy air" and tells Lady Rockminster that "a villain has transplanted me" (II, xxxvi, 347) in the affections of Blanche Amory, the pose reflects in part his mortified vanity, and consequently it distorts the truth about Foker in the use of the word "villain"; hence that theatrical and inappropriate term must be rejected. Even more, however, the exaggerated pose also represents a conscious self-parody that is a sign of health and insight, and that is rooted in a joyous new sense of his own identity that has arisen from Laura's agreement to marry him. His last role is decidedly self-effacing: together with Laura he serves the Huxters by arranging to soften the father, "bring in the young people, extort the paternal benediction, and finish the comedy" (II, xxxvi, 349). Finally, as the novel's last sentence tells us, he "does not claim to be a hero, but only a man and a brother" (I, xxxvii, 372).

That tempered claim is an emancipation, the ultimate mark of Pen's maturity, for it implies his awareness that when theatricalism is mere strutting and gesticulating—without humility and the recognition of kinship, which includes charity—it is an epitome of human isolation. In effect, he understands at last the meaning of that short and quietly resonant scene with Bows on Chatteris bridge, when two isolations meet in brief sympathy (I, xiv, 128). Warrington, of course, has long had a similar understanding, and therefore it is entirely fitting that at the end of the novel he not only affirms his kinship to Pen and Laura, his "brother and sister" as he

calls them, but that also, by "practising in the nursery here, in order to prepare for the part of Uncle George" (II, xxxvii, 370), he acknowledges the potentially positive value of theatricality. *The History of Pendennis* reminds us that we all inevitably play roles in the overarching comedy, but that we need to choose them with great care so as to dramatize genuine feelings of sympathy and love, and thereby to bring a temporary end to human isolation.

* * *

Like the narrator of *The Book of Snobs* and *Vanity Fair*,[7] his counterpart in *Pendennis* maintains a close relationship with the individual members of his audience, addressing them sometimes as males, sometimes as females, often as mature, and at least once as youthful. Continuing the practice established in those earlier works, he addresses the reader as "worthy" (I, xv, 129, xix, 170, II, xv, 144), "respected" (I, xiii, 115, II, iii, 27), "friendly" (I, xvi, 142), and even "beloved" (II, xiii, 119). We are called "brother and sister" (II, xxiii, 229) and "Brother wayfarer" (I, xviii, 165) because we are members of the human family sharing the experience of living in the Fair and attempting to make our way through it. As such we are collaborators who help bring his narrative into being and who authenticate it. Like him we know the implied answer to the question, "which of us knows his fate?" (I, iii, 32). Although our infatuations mock us all, young "Pen is a man who will console himself like the rest of us" (I, xv, 130). "We should all of us, I am sure, have liked to see the Major's grin, when the worthy old gentleman made his time-honoured joke" (I, xviii, 164). "What generous person is there that has not been so deceived" (I, xxv, 240) as Laura was in Blanche? In short, it is not simply his tale but "our tale" (II, xxxvii, 367).

At the same time, he invites us to participate more amusedly and at other times more profoundly in the comicality, absurdity, folly, and darkness of human life. Costigan's tattered hat, boots, and gloves suggest that "Poverty seems as if it were disposed, before it takes possession of a man entirely, to attack his extremities first" (I, v, 44). "When a gentleman is cudgelling his brain to find any rhyme for sorrow, besides borrow and to-morrow, his woes are nearer at an end than he thinks for" (I, xv, 131). "How lonely we are in the world; how selfish and secret, everybody! . . . you and I are but a pair of infinite isolations, with some fellow-islands a little more or less near to us" (I, xvi, 143).

If *performance* crucially defines our behavior as inhabitants of Vanity Fair—indeed, almost forty of the characters are literally actors, actresses, and dancers—so too does our reenactment of archetypal configurations articulated in literature, in history, and in mythological awareness. At times we see the mirroring by means of proverbial or proverb-like narrative statements. The experiences of Smirke literally tumbling head over heels off his horse in an impossible love-sick hope to see Helen and to move her emotions, and of Pen rushing off in a whirlwind to see with rapture the performance of a dull actress both prompt the comical observation "Thus love makes fools of all of us" (I, iv, 40). Nevertheless, even in response to fractured French, we must acknowledge that *"Etre soul au monde est bien ouneeyong"* (I, xvi, 144).

Old Lord Colchicum's sexual pursuit of a young female circus rider with the help of Tom Tufthunt leads to the sardonic remark: "When Don Juan scales the wall, there's never a want of a Leporello to hold the ladder" (II, viii, 83). Contradictory views of marriage remind the narrator of "the old allegory of the gold and silver shield, about which the two knights quarrelled, each [being] right according to the point from which he looks: so about marriage; the question whether it is foolish or good, wise or otherwise, depends upon the point of view from which you regard it" (I, vii, 67). The most fundamental Thackerayan articulation of the archetypal nature of our performances is of course his frequently quoted Horatian epitome: *Mutato nomine, de te fabula narratur* (With a change of name, the tale is told of you [II, xxxiv, 335]).

Pen's father taking his pedigree out of a trunk recalls to the narrator Sterne's officer calling for his sword (I, ii, 8). Helen, silently keeping within herself what her love has divined of her son's secret thoughts and feelings, prompts narrative recollection of Mary "keep[ing] these things in her heart" (I, iii, 29). More comically, men and women are like Titania seeing "good looks in donkey's ears, wit in their numskulls, and music in their bray" (II, xxvi, 264). "Was Titania the first who fell in love with an ass, or Pygmalion the only artist who has gone crazy about a stone?" (I, v, 52). Garbetts, the actor, unexpectedly meeting a lawyer who has got out a writ against him, "with a face as blank as Macbeth's when Banquo's ghost appears upon him, gasped some inarticulate words, and fled out of the room" (I, xiii, 117).

The Major is an unsatisfactory Mentor to Pen's Telemachus (II, vi, 53). The Major and Costigan reenact the prelude to the battle of Fontenoy (chapter vignette: I, xi, 97). Warrington is a Diogenes (I, xxxiii, 327, II, viii, 80). The love-sick Foker could "no more escape the common lot than Achilles, or Ajax, or Lord Nelson, or Adam our first father" (II, i, 1). Foker is like "the heir in Horace pouring forth the gathered wine of his father's vats; . . . human nature is pretty much the same in Regent Street as in the Via Sacra" (II, xxxiii, 324). Fanny is the Ariadne of Shepherd's Inn (II, xxvi, 263). Blanche is Foker's Armida (II, xxxvii, 362). Strong is down on his luck like "Marius at Miturnæ, Charles Ed-

ward in the Highlands, Napoleon before Elba" (II, xxiii, 226). The headmaster of Greyfriars School loses his momentary magnificence like Cinderella after the ball (I, ii, 18). And Smirke, like so many Thackerayan characters, has an unwanted Horatian companion riding behind him on his pony: black Care (I, xvi, 143).

Pen often sees himself in terms of prototypes. With absurd youthful pretentiousness he introduces himself as someone with an Odysseus-like breadth of experience, *qui mores hominum multorum videt et urbes* (who has seen the many cities and customs of men [I, i, 5]). By pompously quoting Thackeray's master, Horace, who is conveying Homer's characterization of Odysseus, Pen unwittingly identifies for readers one of Thackeray's basic assumptions: our culture transmits archetypal renderings of human experience that provide the basis for an understanding of our own experience (if we are capable of it). Given his slow growth into understanding, Pen youthfully creates romantic images of himself adopted from his reading: he is a fire-worshipper, he is Conrad, he is Selim—not from real experience, but from exotic, near-Eastern fantasies by Moore and Byron (I, iii, 25).

Gradually, however, he sees himself more in terms of actual historical experience and literary articulation. He seeks counterparts for his feelings in passages from Anacreon and Lucretius, and from late seventeenth and early eighteenth century poets like "Waller, Dryden, Prior" and similar poets of pre-Romantic elegance and sophistication. He sees his mother in terms of Andromache (I, iii, 27). He is Hamlet, the Stranger, the reader of Waller, Herrick, and Béranger. He vows like Montrose to make the Fotheringay "famous with his sword and glorious by his pen" (I, vii, 69). He sees himself as Egmont, as Leicester (II, viii, 85), and as Claude Melnotte (II, xxxiv, 329). He vows not to be Faust with Margaret (II, ix, 93).

More usually, of course, the *narrator* sees him in archetypal and of course often ironic terms. Pen is like the love-sick swain in Ovid (I, iii, 26). He rides out in quest of Dulcinea (I, iii, 28). With the laming of his horse he is as frantic with vexation as Richard at Bosworth (I, vi, 54). He listens to his uncle's tales with the avidity of Desdemona (I, ix, 85). He uses Smirke "as Corydon does the elm-tree, to cut out his mistress's name upon. He made him echo with the name of the beautiful Amaryllis" (I, xvi, 142). After the break-up of his relationship with the Fotheringay, Pen "sate sulking, Achilles-like in his tent, for the loss of his ravaged Briseis" (I, xvi, 146). At college, Pen is a "reckless young Amphitryon" (I, xx, 185) and a prodigal son (I, xxi, 194, xxii, 207). In notable contradistinction to Pen's pseudo near-Eastern Byronism, moreover, Thackeray finds a quintessential archetype of human experience in a figure from a masterpiece of the near-East, *The Ara-*

bian Nights' Entertainments, in order to articulate a reality fundamental to all the wanderers in Vanity Fair: Alnaschar (I, xxxii, 317), a naïve dreamer of impossible dreams who destroys them with his arrogant overreaching. The dreams are as fragile as glass, and the dreamer is a victim of his unwittingly self-destructive fantasies. So too, Thackeray would seem to be saying, are we all.

Notes

1. See Edgar F. Harden, *A Checklist of Contributions by William Makepeace Thackeray to Newspapers, Periodicals, Books, and Serial Parts Issues, 1828-1864* (Victoria, B.C.: English Literary Studies, 1996).

2. *"The History of Pendennis. His Fortunes and Misfortunes, His Friends and His Greatest Enemy." A Critical Edition,* ed. Peter L. Shillingsburg (New York and London: Garland, 1991), Vol. II, ch. xxxvi, p. 347. (References identify page numbers for those readers using the Garland edition, and volume and chapter numbers for other readers.) For permission to quote extensively from my article, "Theatricality in *Pendennis*" [Ariel 4 (1973)], I am indebted to the Editors of *Ariel.*

3. A number of other actresses, circus riders, and the like, including retired performers, appear in offstage capacities, from Miss Blenkinsop and her father (I, xxix, 281-83), Miss Rougemont, Mrs. Calverley, Mademoiselle Coralie, and Madame Brack (II, ii, 13-15), Mademoiselle Caracoline (II, viii, 84), and Fanny Bolton's teachers (II, viii, 84), to Princess Obstropski (II, xviii, 177-78), who, like Lady Mirabel, has married into society.

4. Here, as elsewhere in *Pendennis,* when French is employed it generally serves as the language of artifice, especially when used by Blanche. Foker and his "polyglot valet, . . . who was of no particular country, and spoke all languages indifferently ill" (II, i, 7), otherwise converse in English.

5. For a perceptive discussion of time in *Pendennis,* see Jean Sudrann, "'The Philosopher's Property': Thackeray and the Use of Time," *Victorian Studies,* 10 (1967): 359-88, especially 363-78.

6. Laura and Helen, though generally free from a tendency to behave theatrically, do succumb when agitated by wounded pride and jealousy, especially during the Fanny Bolton episode. Warrington is the character least prone to theatricalism—mainly because he is the least vulnerable to pride.

7. For more extended discussion of the narrator in *Vanity Fair,* see Edgar F. Harden, Vanity Fair. A Novel without a Hero. *A Reader's Companion* (New York: Twayne, 1995), pp. 71-94, and Harden, *Thackeray the Writer: From Journalism to* Vanity Fair (London: Macmillan, 1998), pp. 175-82.

Nicholas Dames (essay date June 2001)

SOURCE: Dames, Nicholas. "Brushes with Fame: Thackeray and the Work of Celebrity." *Nineteenth-Century Literature* 56, no. 1 (June 2001): 23-51.

[*In the following essay, Dames studies the intermingling of private and public life in Thackeray's fiction.*]

Little is known about the first voyage of William Makepeace Thackeray to England, at the age of five, from his birthplace in Calcutta, but what we do know of this trip involves the sighting of what we might now, with a debt to Thackeray himself, call a celebrity. On 8 March 1817 the Indiaman *Prince Regent* put in at St. Helena, and Lawrence Barlow, Thackeray's native servant, escorted his charge inland.[1] As Thackeray was later to remember it in his 1855 lectures on *The Four Georges:* "[Barlow] took me [on] a long walk over rocks and hills until we reached a garden, where we saw a man walking. 'That is he,' said [Barlow]; 'that is Bonaparte! He eats three sheep every day, and all the little children he can lay his hands on!'"[2] While Thackeray left out so much else of the voyage, which involved his departure from his mother and five months of difficult travel to an entirely unknown locale, this one incident—a casual encounter with fame—persisted in his memory. Three times Thackeray sent fictional characters on similar, if usually belated, pilgrimages: in *Pendennis* (1848) Colonel Altamont brags of having seen and been presented to Napoleon at St. Helena; and in *The Newcomes* (1853-55) both Clive Newcome and his father, Colonel Newcome, visit Napoleon's tomb on trips from India. Thackeray's biographers and critics have continued to mention the anecdote from his first voyage to England, and it has provided rich thematic material, particularly in relation to the deeply equivocal role of servants in his mature work.[3] One simple fact about this scene, however, has remained unnoticed: its survival as Thackeray's only recollection of this most pivotal voyage. What replaces or displaces memories more familial, possibly more traumatic, and certainly more personal, is a brush with fame—a brush so incidental as to have left nothing but Barlow's words and Bonaparte's image, yet so vivid as to have mnemonic priority.

This scene suggests to us a process of consciousness whereby our personal circumstances yield in importance to the sudden, and not-to-be-forgotten, collision with fame of an unprecedented and even monstrous sort. This process is so continual in Thackeray's fiction that we can adduce it as a general rule: fame has a cognitive and mnemonic appeal that overrules, and might even organize, merely individual facts. Put another way, the allure of a public world of fame extends its reach into and over a realm of memory and desire that is only putatively private. Even as the brushes with fame in Thackeray's fiction diminish toward a fame of an increasingly attenuated sort, from the deposed Emperor to minor and temporary London "notables," the process of attention to them remains in place, and the manner in which the publicity of these encounters so frequently overwhelms the quiet privacy of other moments is remarkably consistent. With only a slight anachronism, we might call these moments "celebrity sightings," and call their participants "celebrity seekers." In fact, what is increasingly at stake in the depiction of the famous in Thackeray's fiction is the gradual formation of a new category of public experience called *the celebrity,* unmoored from the political or aristocratic underpinnings of older forms of public notoriety and increasingly unlike earlier conceptualizations of fame. In the "celebrity," mid-Victorian culture found a social and perceptual category that could not only become more conceptually promiscuous—subsuming martial, literary, artistic, financial, governmental, and criminal fame into one form—but that could also root itself more deeply into the heretofore private consciousness of the public and, therefore, could reorient consciousness (particularly memory) toward a newly configured public realm.

Any study of celebrity in Victorian Britain must run along two axes: first, the institutions and practices that brought it into being; and second, the forms of consciousness that it produced.[4] More than other mid-Victorian social satirists and observers, Thackeray comes into play as a figure whose addiction to and disdain for the emergent category of the celebrity is so palpable and readable that he furnishes us with several clues to the social and institutional origins of celebrity, as well as to a history of its alterations to cognition and memory. Much recent work on Thackeray has spotlighted the complex interactions between a public realm driven by market dynamics and a private realm struggling to maintain its independence; Janice Carlisle's study of Thackeray's relations with his audience, along with Andrew H. Miller's influential account of commodified consciousness in *Vanity Fair* (1847-48), are two of the most compelling.[5] Indeed, how nineteenth-century authors may have been "spotlighted" themselves by increasingly sophisticated systems of publicity is a topic of growing interest, as authors whose public profiles may have seemed shadowy or obscure, from Henry James to Elizabeth Barrett Browning, are discussed through the public-sphere theories of Jürgen Habermas, Pierre Bourdieu, and Richard Sennett.[6] Thackeray, more than most writers working within this public sphere, opens up for us the space where these relations between consciousness and publicity become

most visible and most vexed: the celebrity. With the glimpse of Napoleon in his garden we enter a world in which what Leo Braudy has called the eighteenth century's "international European fame culture" metamorphoses into a culture of celebrity in which the grand figures of the past (Rousseau, Bonaparte, Byron) mix with a considerably more varied, and more constantly changing, group of figures.[7] Suddenly the ceremonial, dramatic, and historically pivotal acts of the famous turn into the reciprocally ratifying, random encounter between celebrity and observer, each briefly entering the other's orbit and reanimating a deadened private world. Through an analysis of the collisions with celebrity in Thackeray's mid-career fiction, we might in fact encounter our own attitude toward celebrities in the age of its formation.

* * *

Many, if not most, of Thackeray's characters are animated or enlivened by life with the famous—they are celebrity seekers of more or less proficiency. Arthur Pendennis, for one, spends the days of his London youth breakfasting "with a Peer, a Bishop, a parliamentary orator, two blue ladies of fashion, a popular preacher, the author of the last new novel, and the very latest lion imported from Egypt or from America," refreshing himself for his journalistic labor with a social set deliberately composed of the indiscriminately well known.[8] Pen's casual acquaintances are no different, ranging from the Upper Temple law student Lowton, who introduces himself to Pen by pointing out "the notabilities in the Hall" (I, 295), to the pathetic Captain Sumph, "an ex-beau still about town, and related in some indistinct manner to Literature and the Peerage" (I, 338), whose dinner conversations consist primarily of anecdotes relating to his friendship with Byron and his time spent at Missolonghi. Charles Honeyman, the fashionable preacher of *The Newcomes,* is notable for nothing other than his proficiency at spotting the sort of minor celebrity known only to cognoscenti, while the best possible field for these activities is provided by Maria Newcome (Clive Newcome's aunt), whose parties are dedicated to in-the-know fame. Even Thackeray's characters situated outside the nineteenth century evince a similar passion: in *The History of Henry Esmond* (1852), besides the lengthier portraits of Marlborough, Steele, and Addison, there are smaller vignettes of encounters with Swift, Pope, Congreve, and others. Compared to equally sprawling social fictions by Dickens, Trollope, and George Eliot, Thackeray's world positively swarms with notables, major and minor, emergent and fading, as well as with the less famous who are nonetheless adept at noticing these figures at parties, in crowds, or on the street.

But are these figures "celebrities"? Or to ask a more precise question, when did the "figure" of celebrity emerge and take shape, and what other figural systems for classifying public fame competed with it? Some opening postulates are called for here. First, the word "celebrity" in its current meaning—a person of public fame—does not appear until the late 1840s, and Thackeray is among its first users.[9] In this usage Thackeray is performing one of the analytic, and one might even say journalistic, tasks for which his intellect seemed most suited: discovering a new social category that had previously been invisible, and attaching to it a name whose immediate insertion into common use quickly elevates it from neologism to shorthand communication. "Snob," of course, is the most notable of these successes, and "bohemia" is similarly a Thackerayan term whose use has become so necessary that its coiner is almost entirely obscured.[10] Even if "celebrity" is not precisely a Thackerayan coinage, it is nonetheless a term whose use Thackeray latched onto early in its history, and one that he found particularly congenial.

The second postulate is that the word "celebrity" in its early phase—the 1850s and 1860s—coexisted with a series of roughly similar terms whose usage overlapped. Although we can distinguish the nuances of "celebrity" from these cognate terms, we can also, in the process, establish the contours of this newer figure of fame in a fairly detailed manner. In getting to celebrity, that is, we need to take a detour through what celebrity is *not*.

The first "figure" of fame common to mid-Victorian discourse is the "notability" or the "notable," the figure of *popularity*. We might initially catch some of the sense of these terms by noticing that while none of Thackeray's major characters are celebrities, quite a few of them are notables, and many of them manage to achieve popularity. This popularity and notability, however, always resides within a circumscribed sphere—and that is precisely the important connotation of the "notable": notability and the public fame it offers remain limited to a particular circle, and since each circle has its own small set of notabilities, to be a "notable" is to subject oneself to a deeply relativistic sense of fame. To be popular, in other words, is always to be popular to some defined group. Pendennis achieves "popularity" within the confines of Oxbridge, a public fame so specific that Thackeray can define its limits with some precision:

> Monsieur Pen at Oxbridge had his school, his faithful band of friends, and his rivals. When the young men heard at the haberdashers' shops that Mr. Pendennis, of Boniface, had just ordered a crimson satin cravat, you would see a couple of dozen crimson satin cravats in Main Street in the course of the week—and Simon, the Jeweller, was known to sell no less than two gross of Pendennis pins, from a pattern which the young gentleman had selected in his shop.
>
> . . . Among the young ones Pen became famous and popular: not that he did much, but there was a general determination that he could do a great deal if he chose.
>
> (I, 177, 179)

This is a precious enough fame, although Thackeray is at pains to note that the Oxbridge hierarchy would be entirely ignorant of it and that outside of the university its currency proves untransferable. Always in the wake of the notable is the ironic, and ironizing, awareness that every circle has its own. In 1863 the Scottish divine Patrick C. Beaton writes in *Fraser's Magazine*: "All courts have their notables. . . . All cities have their notables. London has its Lord Mayor, whom our French neighbours still persist in believing to be next in influence and authority to the Queen, and its court of aldermen, all of whom, doubtless, are notable men in their way. The literary, the scientific, the artistic, the religious, the fashionable world, all have their notables, not to mention many others of a nondescript character."[11] Thackeray himself wrote for *Fraser's* in the 1830s, and the journal had much to do with the formation of a Victorian celebrity discourse. But Beaton, contrary to any notion of celebrity, emphasizes the benumbing and belittling sense that all "notables" find their identical image in the smallest of their brethren. Thackeray echoes this idea in *Pendennis*: "A man may be famous in the Honour-lists and entirely unknown to the undergraduates: who elect kings and chieftains of their own, whom they admire and obey, as negro-gangs have private black sovereigns in their own body, to whom they pay an occult obedience, besides that which they publicly profess for their owners and drivers" (I, 179).

More august than notability, but no less problematic, is the fame of the "lion." "Common *Lionism*," Carlyle's well-known phrase uttered in the context of a description of the fate of Robert Burns, remains the term's touchstone; always with the lion, the quasi-celebrity, comes the question of lionizing—of how the ordinary is transformed into the known, as well as the savage and all-too-visible effects of that transformative process. Carlyle's description in *On Heroes, Hero-Worship, and the Heroic in History* (1841) of Burns's persecution by "Lion-hunters" contains one of the earliest usages of "celebrity," a term that for Carlyle will, like candlelight, "shew *what* man, not in the least make him a better or other man."[12] Carlyle's passage is the originary source within mid-Victorian conversations on fame for the figure of the lion as the distorted, inflated, comically and frighteningly toothsome image of public notoriety.[13]

Thackeray was certainly familiar with this Carlylean usage: in **"The Lion Huntress of Belgravia,"** one of his 1850 contributions to *Punch,* he presents the diary of a female hostess and devotée of fame: "They call me the Lion Huntress. I own that I love the society of the distinguished and the great. A mere cultivator of frivolous fashion, a mere toady of the great, I despise; but genius, but poetry, but talent, but scientific reputation, but humour, but eccentricity above all, I adore."[14] She adds: "Indeed what is there in life worth living for but the enjoyment of the society of men of talent and celebrity?" (p. 325). The incoherent categorical mixtures of celebrity are here, but one remains aware in Thackeray's sketch that the hostess is not merely entertaining the famous but also creating them; not merely hunting lions but also making them. And if lionizing is a potentially fatal process, as Carlyle contended had been the case with Burns, then the lion itself is dangerous: as Thackeray's Belgravian hostess says, "it gives one a sort of thrill" to have in one's home a lion "who has hanged twenty-five Polish Colonels, like Count Knoutoff; or shot a couple of hundred Carlist officers before breakfast, like General Garbanzos, than whom I never met a more mild, accomplished, and elegant man" (p. 331). For Victorian commentators the indiscriminacy of lionizing, combined with the sudden glare of attention that the "lion" figured, produced an image of the terrors of the transformative processes of publicity, a fear that this sort of fame was not tameable.

Neither the notable nor the lion is quite a celebrity; sharing a certain overlapping territory but contributing quite different nuances, these terms teach us largely what preexisted celebrity in the decades of its emergence. A look at one of the initial entrances into English of the "celebrity" is illuminating. In *The Newcomes* Charles Honeyman, interpreting for Colonel Newcome a room of Maria Newcome's invited celebrities, says:

> Let me whisper to you that your kinswoman is rather a searcher after what we call here *notabilities*. . . . That is Mr. Huff, the political economist, talking with Mr. Macduff, the member for Glenlivat. That is the Coroner for Middlesex conversing with the great surgeon Sir Cutler Sharp, and that pretty little laughing girl talking with them is no other than the celebrated Miss Pinnifer, whose novel of Ralph the Resurrectionist created such a sensation after it was abused in the Trimestrial Review. It was a little bold certainly—I just looked at it at my club—after hours devoted to parish duty a clergyman is sometimes allowed, you know, *desipere in loco*—there are descriptions in it certainly startling—ideas about marriage not exactly orthodox—but the poor child wrote the book actually in the nursery, and all England was ringing with it before Dr. Pinnifer, her father, knew who was the author. That is the Doctor asleep in the corner by Miss Rudge, the American authoress, who I daresay is explaining to him the difference between the two Governments. My dear Mrs. Newcome, I am giving my brother-in-law a little sketch of some of the celebrities who are crowding your salon to-night. What a delightful evening you have given us![15]

Alongside all these "notabilities" we find "a young barrister, already becoming celebrated as a contributor to some of our principal reviews," as well as "Professor Quartz and Baron Hammerstein, celebrated geologists from Germany," and an unnamed cavalry officer who is a "literary man of celebrity, and by profession an attorney" (I, 74). And although Honeyman self-consciously terms these men "notabilities," the newer word "celebrity" begins to dominate the passage, in one of the first uses of the word in English as a substantive noun. Honeyman's knowingness here is clearly satirized, and yet it just as clearly marks him out for the kind of narratorial snobophobia that, as Joseph Litvak has argued of Thackeray, masks an equivalent homophobia.[16] But while Honeyman is so obviously a celebrity-seeker of the most parasitical sort, that is no reason why his knowledge—the knowingness about the various *demimondes* of London that he flaunts so readily—is invalid: the idea that a fashionable preacher should be so well informed about such medical, political, and literary celebrities argues well enough for their status *as* celebrities, no longer confined to the narrow circles of influence and regard that distinguish, and in turn extinguish, the merely "notable."

Further, there is no danger to, or from, these "lions," save the merely feline dangers of a certain catty gossip passed from guest to guest—no threatened demise at the hands of lion-hunters, no fear that these lions pose any ethical or even criminal questions. Unlike Napoleon, these lions do not threaten to eat sheep—and thus "lion," with its connotations of distortion and danger, is the incorrect term. Mrs. Newcome does not so much lionize these figures—that is, create their fame—as participate in their aura as celebrities, as figures meant to be observed, brushed up against, talked about, and above all *recognized*.

Celebrity is a term that is absolute (in contrast to the relativism of popularity) and expressive of a certain passiveness (as opposed to the active quality of "lionizing"). Someone who is a celebrity to one person or group is, within a mass culture, a celebrity to all, and even if the mark of celebrity has been lowered from Napoleon to teenage authors of scandalous novels, that is no reason why the celebrity of the latter cannot eventually equal the celebrity of the former—a principle that Thackeray divined and that has been amply borne out in our own time. Once one becomes a celebrity, from whatever field, then one's membership in that field is less relevant than one's status *as celebrity*, no longer a "notable among the undergraduates" but a notability proper, a celebrity above all else. The very erratic and catholic mixture of guests at Mrs. Newcome's home is a vision of a culture of celebrity in which institutional boundaries mean little except for the overarching institution—the daily and periodical press—that licenses them all and from which, presumably, Honeyman has gathered much of his insider's information. Those who most misunderstand celebrity in Thackeray's fiction, such as Major Pendennis, do so not from a failure to read the newspaper (itself inconceivable in Thackeray's world) but from a failure to read it well and thoroughly—a failure that usually involves concentrating solely on the aristocratic world and its movements. Mrs. Newcome, for one, is past that particular boundary: "Dr. Windus is a man of science and his name is of European celebrity!" she responds to her husband when he complains of her dull guests; "Any intellectual person would prefer such company to the titled nobodies into whose family your brother has married" (*The Newcomes,* I, 152).

In an analogous manner, what had been the active process of lionizing—lion-hunters descending upon Carlyle's great or the nation's talentless in an indiscriminate pack, looking to transform—can only be understood in Thackeray's writing as an entirely mysterious process of celebrity-construction, and only articulated in passive phrases. Thus the force of the original locution of celebrity—"celebrated as"—makes us ask: celebrated by whom? Honeyman's syntax ("A young barrister already becoming celebrated") precludes an answer: the process has already started, and wherever it takes place, it does not take place *here,* exactly, but always somewhere else, always with reference to a phantasmatic other who has initiated the distinction that we only recognize.[17] The knowingness that defines Honeyman, and that, in another temperament, might expose these "celebrities" as frauds, is yet powerless to explain how the mysteries of celebrity have originated.

The theoretical term that does much of the work of "celebrity," although in a less awestruck fashion, is *charisma,* as first articulated by Max Weber and later developed by Pierre Bourdieu. "Charm and charisma," Bourdieu writes, "in fact designate the power, which certain people have, to impose their own self-image as the objective and collective image of their body and being; to persuade others, as in love or faith, to abdicate their generic power of objectification and delegate it to the person who should be its object, who thereby becomes an absolute subject, without an exterior (being his own Other), fully justified in existing, legitimated."[18] In opposition to the lion-hunter's objectifying, which denies the true greatness (or true poverty) of the hunted by the process of a violent adulatory caricature, charisma is the celebrity's defense against being objectified, a seigneurial right to objectify the other as Observer, as Fan. And as Weber perceived, the sign of charisma is a freely given "recognition" on the part of the observer, one that legitimates the charismatic leader but also, paradoxically and yet necessarily, legitimates the recognizer.[19] The social history of the nineteenth century is remarkably full of vivid instances of charismatic authority, particularly in the arts, from which the relevant instances of the performances of Rachel, or of Paganini, might be adduced.[20] If we need to make any readjustment to Weberian charisma in order to match it to mid-Victorian "celebrity," however, it is to remove from Weber's term any sense of its necessary linkage to talent, efficacy, or lastingness. As Leo Braudy puts it in

The Frenzy of Renown, the early nineteenth century learned how "success could easily be confused with visibility, celebrity with fame"; but the recognition of the ephemerality, or delusiveness, of celebrity was never an effective critique against its power (p. 425). Concerning Mr. Wagg, one of a host of writers populating *Pendennis,* Pen may laugh at what is called "Mr. Wagg's celebrity" and say that "he is a dunce, and that any body could write his books" (I, 253), but this assertion hardly injures Wagg's status, which might feed equally well on denunciations as on praise. As a variety of fame, celebrity was from the start both inured to the criticisms that might see through its hollowness and resistant to the ephemerality that often defined its essence.

* * *

Joshua Reynolds's famous painting *Garrick between Tragedy and Comedy* (1762) formed the basis for Thackeray's ironically allusive cover drawings for *Pendennis*'s serial and book publications—a more or less leering Pen tugged at by a nude blonde siren on one side and a maternal brunette on the other. Thus, the painting has always offered an excellent imagistic basis from which to discuss Thackeray's continual ambivalences, his characteristic inability to decide between what might seem like oppositional alternatives.[21] Similarly, the characteristic of Thackeray's writing that appears most marked in his relations to Victorian celebrity is the fierce quality with which he upholds strongly different attitudes toward it. At once resenting the floodlit, falsely intimate publicity it brings and yet seeking to penetrate any barriers of privacy that might screen out the light, Thackeray offers us as well a paradigmatic example of the dual, even dialectical, relations that Victorian mass-culture increasingly held toward the celebrities it began to produce. The first of the two oscillating relations that Thackeray illuminates for us involves privacy and publicity; the second involves distortion, monstrosity, and caricature. For the sake of taxonomical convenience I will term the first relation the "dynamic of publicity" and the second the "dynamic of monstrosity"; as we will see, however, both of these processes are instances of a larger fact about Victorian celebrity-formation: it involved a continual shuttling between mutually antithetical concepts.[22]

The "dynamic of publicity" is the gesture of both protesting against the invasions of privacy to which the celebrity is subjected and yet performing those very invasions in the service of puncturing the aura of the given celebrity, thereby demonstrating a knowingness that might discern true celebrity from both false, mindless fandom and from accurate estimations of worth. It is not entirely surprising, of course, that the same public that so eagerly consumes information on the private life of the famous might also inveigh most heavily against the methods used to gather that information. What is perhaps more striking is that, rather than an aberration, the dynamic of publicity might be an essential characteristic of a mass public's response to celebrity.

Indeed, the most well-known facts about Thackeray's own dealings with publicity bear out this idea. One example is the famous "Garrick Club Affair" of 1858, in which Thackeray went to extremes to punish Edmund Yates, the writer of a particularly vicious and personal critique of Thackeray in *Town Talk,* for Yates's invasion of the *cordon sanitaire* of the gentleman's club. And an earlier example is Thackeray's impulsive resignation from *Punch* in 1851 over the publication of a starkly critical cartoon depicting Napoleon III as "A Beggar on Horseback," complete with bloody sword, liquor flask, and dead bodies.[23] In both of these instances Thackeray expended personal and career capital to defend a certain sanctity and dignity of public life from invasions of an increasingly aggressive press. Many of his sketches were written to the same effect, particularly when the target was the gentleman's club and its inhabitants. In **"Strange to Say, on Club Paper"** (1863), from the **Roundabout Papers,** Thackeray complains at length about an obituary of Field-Marshal Lord Clyde, published in the *Observer,* in which the writer notices that a codicil from Clyde's will, signed at Chatham, has been written on the paper of the Athenæum Club—with the obvious implication that the rich and respected Clyde was in the habit of stealing paper from his club and carrying it with him to the country. The all-seeing eye of the press has seized upon a detail, Thackeray wants us to notice, and has used that ambiguous detail of private habits to impugn a public figure, subtly and without overt claims.

The true explanation for the codicil, Thackeray argues, is that Clyde's lawyer wrote it at the Athenæum and sent it to Chatham for Clyde's signature. Yet in Thackeray's view the falseness of the implied accusation is only a symptom of the real problem, which for him amounts to a systemic reportorial invasion of the smallest facts of private existence. Imagining himself as a latter-day Jeremiah sent to alert his fellow club-members, Thackeray envisions stationing himself as an outdoor "Pall Mall preacher" to deliver his public lecture on the evils of the press. But he chooses a curious location for this fantasy: "I would have taken post under the statue of Fame, say, where she stands distributing wreaths to the three Crimean Guardsman."[24] In other words, Thackeray is not only defending privacy but fame itself, which is under attack from the deflations of the press; a more ancient concept of fame, depending on martial valor (Clyde's courage, the sacrifice of Crimean soldiers) must be protected from the depredations of mass publicity.

However much the Clyde incident may have obtained in Thackeray's thinking about real-life public figures,

within his fiction Thackeray presents the private failings of a variety of public figures (many of them military), subjecting them to a critique that has often enraged his readers. The Marlborough of **Henry Esmond [The History of Henry Esmond]** is duplicitous and endlessly greedy for power; when Thackeray has Addison say that "we must paint our great Duke . . . not as a man, which no doubt he is, with weaknesses like the rest of us, but as a hero," Esmond responds with a severe argument against this sort of distorted panegyric in favor of a more intimate picture of Marlborough's flaws.[25] So constant is this process in Thackeray's historical fiction that it forms the centerpiece of Georg Lukács's seminal attack on Thackeray's "distortion of history, its degradation to the level of the trivial and the private."[26] Steele is a genial drunk, Addison a phlegmatic courtier, Swift a choleric panderer to power—traits that obtain not only within **Henry Esmond** but also within Thackeray's lectures on **The Four Georges** and **The English Humourists** (1851), where we are invited to ask of a public figure, as Thackeray asks of Swift, "Would we have liked to live with him?"[27]

Beyond these facts we have the early Thackeray of *Fraser's Magazine,* the journal that under the proprietorship of William Maginn was perhaps most notable among Victorian periodicals for propagating a journalism dependent upon a mock-respectful attitude toward cultural nobilities, one that poked sophisticated fun at the figures whose exposure in the journal made it alluring. In 1836 Maginn—usually noted as the model for Captain Shandon in **Pendennis,** who runs the very Fraserian *Pall Mall Gazette*—originated a series of pictorial and verbal portraits of the newly notable entitled "The Gallery of Literary Characters," which included sketches of Sir John Soane and Michael Faraday, among others. The tone of the sketches is instructive, combining an "insider's knowledge" of the figure with an elaborately mock-panegyric style that is subtle enough to be read as simple praise: it is a deflation couched as a celebration, one in which the celebration invites the readers and the deflation allows them access to a knowingness that at once acknowledges and ridicules the power of the minor celebrity in question.[28] Of course, Thackeray himself was well acquainted with the journalistic machinery so often used to invade the sacrosanct privacy of public figures, and he was as adept at making those invasions as he was at protesting them. Thackeray's story **"Ravenswing,"** which was published in *Fraser's* in 1843, is nothing less than an acute and detailed depiction of the creation of an operatic celebrity through a skilled manipulation of advance publicity. The story's narrator, very much in tune with the tone that *Fraser's* maintained, takes pleasure in describing the creation of what now goes under the name of "buzz," one that all but drowns out the sound of the eponymous character's admittedly mediocre singing.

The game of knowingness that *Fraser's* made so attractive, and that is such a strong part of Thackeray's depiction of celebrity, remains central to an understanding of the second dynamic in play in Victorian celebrity-formation. The "dynamic of monstrosity" may be summarized as the dual gesture of enlarging the image of the celebrity in question, combined with the pleasure of puncturing this enlarged image. Inflation and deflation, in a continual combination, comprise the game of celebrity in Thackeray's fiction, where the great are routinely built up out of the small in order to be forcibly returned back to the small. Much of the work of celebrity in Thackeray's writings might be called the work of "debunking," such as this moment from *The Newcomes* when Pendennis, George Warrington, the Reverend Honeyman, and Clive Newcome sit around a dinner table astonishing the older Colonel Newcome with their in-the-know deflations of the famous:

> He heard opinions that amazed and bewildered him. He heard that Byron was no great poet, though a very clever man. He heard that there had been a wicked persecution against Mr. Pope's memory and fame, and that it was time to reinstate him: that his favourite, Dr. Johnson, talked admirably, but did not write English: that young Keats was a genius to be estimated in future days with young Raphael: and that a young gentleman of Cambridge who had lately published two volumes of verses, might take rank with the greatest poets of all.
>
> (I, 195)

The shocked Colonel responds that the young men "will be sneering at Shakespeare next"—a comment that does not prevent them from progressing to pictorial art, where they debunk Haydon and canonize Turner.

This scene is not only (or not merely) a representative picture of changing tastes in the mid-1830s: it is more crucially a moment where an entirely new attitude toward fame begins to reveal itself, one in which debunking and deifying go hand in hand and in which the very unusual quality of one's judgment, a sort of novelty for novelty's sake, becomes prized. It is, in short, the discourse of fame-as-celebrity, where a more or less fixed canon of the famous is replaced by the quick, capricious, and always-subject-to-revision judgments of a "knowing class"—here composed of two journalists, an artist, and a clergyman—that engages itself in the pleasures of smart praise and even smarter critique. We might be reminded here of Thackeray's own brush with extreme literary fame: his brief meeting with Goethe during a youthful stay in Weimar in 1831. In an 1855 letter to G. H. Lewes, Thackeray records both his awe at the great man and a gleefully satirical comment about him: "I recollect I was at first astonished, and then somewhat relieved, when I found he spoke French with not a good accent."[29] This is also a world in which all publicity is good publicity; in *The Newcomes* Fred Bayham relates how, in an effort to help out Charles Honeyman and attract crowds to his sermons, he writes savage reviews of these sermons in the *Pall Mall Gazette*: "I wrote an article of controversial biography in the *P.M.G.* [*Pall Mall Gazette*], set the business going in the daily press; and the thing was done, Sir" (II, 55). This is the incipient world of the "star"—and it is no accident that one of the first usages of this word in its current range of meaning is in *Pendennis,* where Warrington puffs Pen's book to the publisher Bacon by proclaiming, "I tell you he's a star; he'll make a name, sir. He's a new man, sir" (I, 317).

But why is it a dynamic of "monstrosity"? Why term the inflation and deflation of the celebrity as "monstrous"? To answer this question, it is instructive to return to Thackeray's childhood sighting of Napoleon, the savage sheep-eater of his servant's imagination, as well as to his anger at the caricature of Napoleon III in *Punch*: in both cases we have an enlargement and distortion of the image (usually the body-image) of the public figure that creates something disturbing and uncategorizable—a monster.[30] It is well established that Thackeray found himself literally and figuratively enlarged in the years of what Gordon N. Ray calls his "rise to celebrity" ([Thackeray:] *Age of Wisdom,* p. 35), and that this enlargement left him open to a variety of puncturing critiques, such as Yates's article in *Town Talk*. In Thackeray's work the celebrity has a linkage to something powerful and unsettling at once, something that calls for immediate deflation; thus the frequent combination in Thackeray's prose of locutions of "celebrity" and locutions of infamy, such as his introduction in the 1862 sketch **"Dessein's"** of "the notorious, nay, celebrated Mr. Laurence Sterne."[31] The dual gesture here is at every moment canceling itself out: to call Sterne a celebrity, to "celebrate" him, involves a concomitant gesture of pointing to his unsavory "notoriety," which hardly invalidates—indeed might even enhance—his celebrity status. To praise is not necessarily to avoid puncturing, and to puncture is not necessarily to impair the quality or intensity of celebrity.

Thus, the dynamics of celebrity in Thackeray's writing, whereby the celebrity is at once exalted and punctured, and whereby the machinery of publicity that creates celebrities is at once targeted as an ill and exploited as a tool, are systematically conflicted. These are social attitudes and processes, as is evident from the sorts of *milieux* in which they are situated in Thackeray's work: at dinner tables, before Pall Mall clubs, in open and even litigious contestation with enemies, and in public acts such as resignations, reviews, and profiles. But however much one ties the processes and shapes of celebrity to public institutions such as the periodical press or public moments such as dinner conversations and published evaluations, there remains a stratum of analysis left untouched—the very structuring of consciousness that a sphere of celebrity might create. To this end, it is necessary to return to one particular genre of Thackerayan celebrity, one whose very frequency testifies to its hold upon mental, and particularly mnemonic, habits: the casual brush with fame.

* * *

On Clive Newcome's first trip to Paris, his host, the Vicomte de Florac, directs his attention not to architectural features but to Parisian celebrities: "He pointed out to us no end of famous people at the opera—a few of the Fauxbourg St. Germain, and ever so many of the present people:—M. Thiers, and Count Molé, and Georges Sand, and Victor Hugo, and Jules Janin—I forget half their names" (*The Newcomes,* I, 204). These are "present people" indeed, who put the feudalized notables of St. Germain into the shade and who make Clive feel more than ever "present" himself, both in the sense of up-to-date and, crucially, *in place,* in a recognizable and defined space that is legitimated by the celebrities who inhabit it. Politicians, writers, and critics define this sphere, which not coincidentally gathers in a theater, where—if the first form of modern celebrity comes from the stage and its "stars," such as the tragedian Rachel—the glare of celebrity has switched from the footlights to the audience itself. Thackeray's major characters continually orient themselves, and understand the significance of their new locales, through casual sightings of the famous. Arthur Pendennis, upon first arriving in London, meets with a reporter for the *Star,* who shows him a minor celebrity: "As they passed by Brompton, this gentleman pointed out to Pen Mr. Hurtle, the reviewer, walking with his umbrella. Pen craned over the coach to have a long look at the great Hurtle. . . . Pen thought it was quite an honour to have seen the great Mr. Hurtle, whose works he admired" (I, 280). However satirical the portrait of Pen's celebrity-hunting is—however minor a celebrity this Hurtle might be—Pen's reaction is so thoroughly consistent with the reactions of other Thackeray characters meeting with more august fame (such as Clive meeting Victor Hugo, or Esmond meeting Swift and Congreve) that it deserves a closer look. What we have here, in fact, is a small example of a structure of consciousness that for Thackeray is often routed through the fame of celebrity: a fantasized intimacy that colors these scenes, a memory that organizes itself through encounters with fame, and finally a mass consciousness whose sameness is guaranteed by the mass fame that any of us might, for a time, glimpse.

The false, or phantasmatic, intimacy of celebrity is revealed in the effect of that key detail of Mr. Hurtle's appearance, his umbrella. In itself absolutely innocuous, this slight addition to the encounter, the one detail of Hurtle's appearance caught by Pen, not only humanizes "the great Hurtle" but also provides the central fantasy of all of Thackeray's presentations of the famous: they might *always* be caught in the act of humanizing themselves, whether through the sort of foibles that Lukács deplored or through the irrelevant, but suddenly totemic, detail that makes the celebrity seem closer to us. Even the famous, we learn with relief, try to avoid getting wet. This is not solely a gesture of deflation—catching the great in the act of being ordinary—but also an act of imaginative identification, whereby the great are revealed as fantasized intimates without losing their aura of fame; to learn that Hurtle carries an umbrella, or that Steele drinks to excess, is not to rob them of their celebrity but merely to add to it a leering, and yearning, knowledge that even the celebrity can act like us. This is of course often a moment for Thackeray to parody the pretend intimates of the famous: in *Pendennis* Captain Shandon of the *Pall Mall Gazette,* even while in debtor's prison, "spoke of the characters of the day, and great personages of the fashion, with easy familiarity and jocular allusions, as if it was his habit to live amongst them. He told anecdotes of their private life, and of conversations he had, and entertainments at which he had been present, and at which such and such a thing had occurred. Pen was amused to hear the shabby prisoner in a tattered dressing-gown talking glibly about the great of the land" (I, 324). But this ridiculous affectation of pretending to intimacy with celebrities is by no means restricted to Shandon; in fact, it constitutes a general response to the famous: the establishment of a "familiarity" that is as pathetically phantasmatic as it is common.[32]

Yet the consciousness of celebrity depicted by Thackeray does not stop with a "fan" yearning for intimacy with his chosen object, for a casual encounter with the famous organizes a series of facts about biography, memory, and witnessing—in short, it gives shape to a life. Here is Pendennis and his uncle bumping into one of the early nineteenth century's pinnacles of fame, the Duke of Wellington:

> Master Pen was not displeased to accompany his illustrious relative, who pointed out a dozen great men in their brief transit through St. James's Street, and got bows from a Duke at a crossing, a Bishop (on a cob), and a Cabinet Minister with an umbrella. The Duke gave the elder Pendennis a finger of a pipe-clayed glove to shake, which the Major embraced with great veneration; and all Pen's blood tingled, as he found himself in actual communication, as it were, with this famous man, (for Pen had possession of the Major's left arm, whilst that gentleman's other wing was engaged with his Grace's right,) and he wished all Grey Friars' School, all Oxbridge University, all Paternoster Row and the Temple, and Laura and his mother at Fairoaks, could be standing on each side of the street, to see the meeting between him and his uncle, and the most famous duke in Christendom.
>
> (I, 363)

Almost literally electric, the celebrity's energy is conducted from the proffered finger, through the Major's right arm, to the left arm that Pen's holds; here Pen's fantasy is of a collective witnessing of the event, a collectivity that in fact summarizes his own life at that moment, from school to university to occupation and back to "home."[33] As much as the event encapsulates an embodied fantasy of intimacy—and we should note as well the Cabinet Minster's umbrella, a recurrent trope of Thackeray's—it also helps to bring all of Pen's life into focus, condensed by the meeting with a celebrity.

The brush with fame in Thackeray's writings provides a node of memory onto which other, more merely biographical, facts can hang and around which they can cohere. As surely as the moment before death is supposed to permit one's life to flash before one's eyes, the glare of the celebrity's light puts one's own life into relief. Continually in Thackeray's sketches and longer fictions his narrators and characters recall pivotal moments of private biography through their coalescence with public facts about the famous. For Thackeray himself those facts were often organized around the famous of his youth, including George IV; for instance, in **"De Juventute"** (1860), from the ***Roundabout Papers,*** Thackeray affirms that simply by staring at a coin with George IV's image on it, a person can "conjure back his life there"; and in **"On a Peal of Bells"** (1862) he recalls a day from youth because it was the day his sovereign was crowned.[34]

This phenomenon is an early account of what psychological theorists and neuroscientists today term "flashbulb memories": strongly vivid recollections of private facts insofar as those facts combine with a moment of public trauma; the sort of memory licensed, and in fact culturally validated, by the question "where were you when you heard that President Kennedy was shot?"[35] Where were you, Thackeray asks, when you heard that George IV was crowned? Increasingly in Thackeray's work the private facts of memory are only accessible by reference to what some public figure, caught in a flashbulb of fame, was doing at the time, or how that public figure, the nascent celebrity, intersected with one's own life.

The lengthy, and often-cited, sketch **"On Some Carp at Sans Souci"** (1863) is especially relevant here. In this sketch Thackeray imagines an encounter with a ninety-year-old inmate of a workhouse, who cannot herself recall any salient biographical facts; indeed she need not, because Thackeray can remember them for her—with reference, of course, to the famous that Grandmother Goody Two-shoes has encountered:

> My good old creature, you can't of course remember, but that little gentleman for whom your mother was laundress in the Temple was the ingenious Mr. Goldsmith, author of a *History of England,* the *Vicar of Wakefield,* and many diverting pieces. . . . That gentle-

man who well-nigh smothered you by sitting down on you as you lay in a chair asleep was the learned Mr. S. Johnson, whose history of *Rasselas* you have never read, my poor soul. . . . That tipsy Scotch gentleman who used to come to the chambers sometimes, and at whom everybody laughed, wrote a more amusing book than any of the scholars, your Mr. Burke and your Mr. Johnson, and your Doctor Goldsmith. Your father often took him home in a chair to his lodgings; and has done as much for Parson Sterne in Bond Street, the famous wit. . . . With the help of a "Wade's Chronology," I can make out ever so queer a history for you, my poor old body, and a pedigree as authentic as many in the peerage-books.[36]

The biography that Thackeray sketches here is fantastic, but that is no argument against its plausibility. Thackeray's underlying claim is that our distinctiveness—that is, what makes us stand out, even among classes distant from celebrity—relies upon the very real chance that we have met, seen, touched, or known a famous individual. The paradox, of course, is that this very uniqueness also makes our memories identical to everyone else's—the consequence of a mass memory based on public figures. Thackeray invents a plausible, if unverifiable, biography for old Goody based on a chronology of public events, which only reduces her uniqueness by the very extent to which it provides us with any detail at all. The memory that is organized through brushes with fame is, as Thackeray shows us, a memory that is all the more a property of a mass public, and therefore all the more susceptible to being shaped by mass publicity.

For those who have noted and despaired at this condition of modern memory—its strange reliance upon the managed character of modern public celebrity—the hoped-for revenge is usually that the celebrity will have a shorter than usual shelf life. Theodor Adorno comments: "Just as voluntary memory and utter oblivion always belonged together, organized fame and remembrance lead ineluctably to nothingness, the foretaste of which is perceptible in the hectic doings of all celebrities. . . . The inhuman indifference and contempt instantaneously visited on the fallen idols of the culture industry reveals the truth about their fame, though without granting those disdainful of it any better hopes of posterity."[37] To the extent, that is, that celebrities reach within our memories and consciousnesses, they forfeit the ability to pass into a memory that might represent real *history*; their imminent obsolescence, Adorno claims, prevents their passage into anything more lasting than a temporary place in the annals of publicity. This is not a revenge that is wreaked upon the celebrity in Thackeray's world, however, where in fact history and celebrity come to coincide almost completely. Adorno's unusually compensatory thesis, whereby the celebrity is barred from historical remembrance as a consequence of his or her all-too-vivid presence in modern industrialized life, does not apply to Thackeray, for whom no sort of history is finally more effective and more memorable than a history *of* celebrities. In this way the work of celebrity, altering social and even cognitive forms, extends even further—into what we might even call a historiography.

* * *

One important aspect of Thackeray's celebrities as a group is that they are at once so obviously "real," insofar as they are often factual historical figures (Wellington, Hugo, Steele), and yet so unreal in what Thackeray excludes from them. Nowhere in Thackeray's writings, for instance, do we find what we might expect of Victorian culture—the female star, such as Rachel, whose life on the stage is matched by an ineradicable personal allure. We do have **Pendennis**'s Emily Fotheringay, but her brief career is undermined for the reader by the aromas of alcohol and poverty wafting from the dressing room. Since Thackeray's celebrities are exclusively, almost "unrealistically," male—far from the stage or entertainment, and yet so pervasively based on actual historical personages—it remains difficult to say how "real" they are. Perhaps, however, this question is finally less pertinent than the question of how celebrity as a rhetorical and cultural *figure* becomes a sign for reality itself in Thackeray's writing—how it becomes, finally, one of his more useful "reality effects."

Roland Barthes's well-known analysis of historical characters within fiction is pertinent here: when seen closely they are "absurdly improbable," but when seen peripherally, out of the corner of the narratorial eye, "they are superlative effects of the real."[38] If we alter the sense of Barthes's distinction somewhat, then the consequences for Thackeray become clear. By enlarging the category of the "historical character" to the "celebrity" (from Napoleon, that is, to a category where Wellington and Hurtle can coexist), and by changing the emphasis from the historical character seen on the periphery to the "brush with fame" (the fortuitous and random encounter with the charismatic figure), we see a prime example of a reality-effect not simply experienced by Thackeray's readers but by Thackeray's characters as well. If the celebrity has become a "superlative effect of the real," then perhaps it is because celebrities have now become, for a novel-reading public, superlative guarantors of reality. In Thackeray's putatively realist fictions, in other words, an important category of realist technique depends upon some newly shared cultural assumptions: the celebrity, whether inside or outside of fiction, is a perfect reality-effect; and we in fact borrow our sense of reality from the celebrity—when we meet one, we have reality conferred upon us. In these assumptions Thackeray is an exemplary instance of how the celebrity not only grew in Victorian culture but also grew into one of the culture's primary indexes of what

"reality" might be—the reality that the reflected glare of celebrity casts upon us.

In practice, then, our sense of Thackeray's "realism" should be redirected from the everyday and quotidian to the spectacular—but nonetheless possible, within the everyday—world of the intersection between publicity and privacy. Barthes's familiar accounts of what constitutes a reality-effect—famously, and paradigmatically, a barometer hanging on a wall, from Flaubert's *Trois Contes*—should in Thackeray be represented instead by very unusual encounters with celebrities: it is no longer the weather but, in a sense, the cultural figures who tell us which way the wind is blowing.[39] Politically this is a world of personalization, or even—to use a term of Mary Poovey's—vivification: the birthplace of a privatized, biographical, even trivialized version of historical process in which, in the words of Habermas, "the accidental fate of the so-called man in the street or that of systematically managed stars attain publicity, while publicly relevant developments and decisions are garbed in private dress and through personalization distorted to the point of unrecognizability."[40] But this personalization, which brings an end to Habermas's "critical public sphere" of the eighteenth century is only possible if the "star"—the celebrity—becomes a sign for reality, not simply an escape from it. When he meets Wellington, Pendennis's entire world is suddenly floodlit by a sense of its heightened reality, and thus any one of Thackeray's characters requires access to figures of publicity in order to feel "real." The question of how real Thackeray's celebrities might be can only be answered as follows: they themselves are the ultimate form that reality takes within Thackeray's writings; they are more real than any objects, details, or private facts. In other words, the work that celebrities perform is preeminently the work of guaranteeing the reality of the world around us.

Notes

1. See Gordon N. Ray, *Thackeray: The Uses of Adversity, 1811-1846* (New York: McGraw-Hill, 1955), pp. 65-66, for the few details of the voyage that have emerged subsequent to Thackeray's death.

2. Thackeray, *The Four Georges,* in *The Works of William Makepeace Thackeray, Kensington Edition,* 32 vols. (New York: Charles Scribner's Sons, 1904), XXVI, 70. Hereafter referred to as *Works.*

3. Bruce Robbins's reading of the anecdote is particularly compelling, as it concentrates on how Barlow's "imagination enjoys and amplifies the insatiable appetite and the evil intentions with regard to his own situation" (*The Servant's Hand: English Fiction from Below* [New York: Columbia Univ. Press, 1986], p. 106).

4. Michael Warner has offered a similar, useful warning about reducing any analysis of a modern "pub-

lic" to its institutions or specific manifestations: "the publicity of the public sphere never reduces to information, discussion, will formation, or any of the other scenarios by which the public sphere represents itself. The mediating rhetorical dimension of a public context must be built into each individual's relation to it, as a meaningful reference point against which something could be grasped as information, discussion, will formation" ("The Mass Public and the Mass Subject," in *The Phantom Public Sphere,* ed. Bruce Robbins [Minneapolis: Univ. of Minnesota Press, 1993], p. 236).

5. See Carlisle, *The Sense of an Audience: Dickens, Thackeray, and George Eliot at Mid-Century* (Athens: Univ. of Georgia Press, 1981); and Miller, *Novels behind Glass: Commodity Culture and Victorian Narrative* (Cambridge: Cambridge Univ. Press, 1995), pp. 14-49.

6. Two important recent examples include Richard Salmon, *Henry James and the Culture of Publicity* (Cambridge: Cambridge Univ. Press, 1997); and Linda M. Shires, "The Author as Spectacle and Commodity: Elizabeth Barrett Browning and Thomas Hardy," in *Victorian Literature and the Victorian Visual Imagination,* ed. Carol T. Christ and John O. Jordan (Berkeley and Los Angeles: Univ. of California Press, 1995), pp. 198-212.

7. See Braudy, *The Frenzy of Renown: Fame and Its History* (New York: Oxford Univ. Press, 1986), p. 371.

8. Thackeray, *The History of Pendennis,* ed. Peter L. Shillingsburg, 2 vols. in 1 (New York: Garland, 1991), I, 356. Further references are to this edition and appear in the text.

9. The *OED* [*Oxford English Dictionary*] lists 1849 as the first appearance of "celebrity" in its current guise, although the first attribution is not to Thackeray; he frequently used the word, however, in serial numbers of *Pendennis* that appear prior to the summer of 1849. There are a number of suggestive studies of celebrity *avant la lettre,* particularly in the Romantic period: see Susan Wolfson, "'The Mouth of Fame': Gender, Transgression, and Romantic Celebrity," in *Essays on Transgressive Readings: Reading Over the Lines,* ed. Georgia Johnston (Lewiston, N.Y.: Edwin Mellen, 1997), pp. 3-34; and Ghislane McDayter, "Conjuring Byron: Byromania, Literary Commodification and the Birth of Celebrity," in *Byromania: Portraits of the Artist in Nineteenth- and Twentieth-Century Culture,* ed. Frances Wilson (New York: St. Martin's Press, 1999), pp. 43-62. For an acute reading of Romantic celebrity memoirs written by women, see Catherine B. Burroughs, *Closet Stages: Joanna Baillie and the Theater Theory of*

British Romantic Women Writers (Philadelphia: Univ. of Pennsylvania Press, 1997).

10. For what is still the essential discussion of Thackeray's invention of "bohemia," see Eve Kosofsky Sedgwick, *Epistemology of the Closet* (Berkeley and Los Angeles: Univ. of California Press, 1990), pp. 193-95.

11. [Patrick C. Beaton], "A Chapter on Notables," *Fraser's Magazine,* 67 (1863), 479.

12. *On Heroes, Hero-Worship, and the Heroic in History,* ed. Michael K. Goldberg, Joel J. Brattin, and Mark Engel (Berkeley and Los Angeles: Univ. of California Press, 1993), p. 166.

13. For the links between Thackerayan narrative and Carlyle's "heroes," see Ian Ousby, "Carlyle, Thackeray, and Victorian Heroism," *The Yearbook of English Studies,* 12 (1982), 152-68.

14. Thackeray, "The Lion Huntress of Belgravia," in *Works,* XXXI, 324.

15. Thackeray, *The Newcomes: Memoirs of a Most Respectable Family,* ed. Peter L. Shillingsburg, 2 vols. in 1 (Ann Arbor: Univ. of Michigan Press, 1996), I, 75.

16. See *Strange Gourmets: Sophistication, Theory, and the Novel* (Durham, N.C.: Duke Univ. Press, 1997), p. 56.

17. Michael Warner has termed this process "the moment of special imaginary reference" ("Mass Public" ["The Mass Public and the Mass Subject"], p. 236).

18. Pierre Bourdieu, *Distinction: A Social Critique of the Judgement of Taste,* trans. Richard Nice (Cambridge, Mass.: Harvard Univ. Press, 1984), p. 208.

19. "It is recognition on the part of those subject to authority which is decisive for the validity of charisma. This is freely given and guaranteed by what is held to be a 'sign' or proof, originally always a miracle, and consists in devotion to the corresponding revelation, hero worship, or absolute trust in the leader" (Max Weber, *The Theory of Social and Economic Organization,* ed. Talcott Parsons, trans. A. M. Henderson and Talcott Parsons [New York: Free Press, 1947], p. 359).

20. For Rachel, see Rachel M. Brownstein, *Tragic Muse: Rachel of the Comédie-Française* (New York: Alfred A. Knopf, 1993); for Paganini, see Richard Sennett, *The Fall of Public Man* (New York: W. W. Norton, 1977), pp. 200-203; and for an examination of the symphony conductor as an image for a certain, scientized version of charis-

matic power, see Alison Winter, *Mesmerized: Powers of Mind in Victorian Britain* (Chicago: Univ. of Chicago Press, 1998), pp. 310-12.

21. Martin Meisel has provided a compelling reading of Reynolds's painting as an allegory for Thackeray's ambivalence toward his position as both artist and marketable performer: "For Thackeray, the honor of the artist and the honor of the public performer are two faces of one situation—his own. One face, however, like Reynolds' Tragedy, speaks from the vantage of superiority. It enjoins a respect for the integrity and honesty of the work, and a qualitative standard quite apart from fashion and the market. The other face acts from the disadvantage of dependence. It requires a success that entails cajoling an audience subject to fashion and providing the market, though the performer cannot afford to seem willing to go to any lengths for popularity" (*Realizations: Narrative, Pictorial, and Theatrical Arts in Nineteenth-Century England* [Princeton: Princeton Univ. Press, 1983], p. 347). Meisel's reading of Thackeray's dual relationship to his craft bears a strong relation to my reading of Thackeray's deeply ambivalent relation to his sudden celebrity as well as his culture's sudden embrace of "celebrity." For complementary readings of Thackeray's habitual ambivalences, see Miller's analysis of a "dynamic of desire and disenchantment" (*Novels behind Glass*, p. 22); and for a reading of Thackeray's syntactical, and conceptual, collapse of antithetical concepts, see Elaine Scarry, "Enemy and Father: Comic Equilibrium in Number Fourteen of *Vanity Fair*," *Journal of Narrative Technique*, 10 (1980), 145-55.

22. This "dynamic shuttling" might not be solely a property of Victorian celebrity discourse; Michael Warner has analyzed the modern "double movement of identification and alienation" characteristic of contemporary response to public icons ("Mass Public," p. 252). Of additional interest is Jacqueline Rose's recent account of celebrity, in which the paradoxes it encapsulates are read as examples of perversion or even sadism (see "The Cult of Celebrity," *New Formations*, no. 36 [1999], 9-20).

23. Both Peter L. Shillingsburg and Gordon N. Ray provide detailed accounts of the resignation and how Thackeray handled his indignation over the caricatures; see Shillingsburg, *Pegasus in Harness: Victorian Publishing and W. M. Thackeray* (Charlottesville: Univ. Press of Virginia, 1992), pp. 80-84; and Ray, *Thackeray: The Age of Wisdom, 1847-1863* (New York: McGraw-Hill, 1958), p. 172.

24. Thackeray, "'Strange to Say, on Club Paper,'" in *Works*, XXVII, 413-14.

25. Thackeray, *The History of Henry Esmond*, ed. Edgar F. Harden (New York: Garland, 1989), p. 212.

26. See *The Historical Novel*, trans. Hannah and Stanley Mitchell (London: Merlin Press, 1962), p. 204.

27. Thackeray, *The English Humourists of the Eighteenth Century*, in *Works*, XXVI, 153.

28. *Fraser's* was not the only journal, of course, beginning a discourse of celebrity. One other relevant example was *Bentley's Miscellany*, which under the proprietorship of W. H. Ainsworth issued a study of "American Notabilities" in November 1861—including Lincoln, Jefferson Davis, and George McClellan—and the more ironical "Parisian Notabilities" in October 1864, in which figures from Napoleon III to the *feuilletoniste* Vicomte Ponson du Terrail were simultaneously "celebrated" and derided (see "American Notabilities: Lincoln—Jeff Davis—Stephens—Fremont—Beauregard—M'Clellan—Banks," *Bentley's Miscellany*, 50 [1861], 456-64; and "Parisian Notabilities," *Bentley's Miscellany*, 56 [1864], 343-55). The procedure of these journals is best summarized by Flaubert, whose definition of "celebrity" ran as follows: "S'inquiéter du moindre détail de leur vie intime afin de pouvoir les dénigrer [Look into the smallest details of their private lives so that you can disparage them]" (Flaubert, *Le Dictionnaire des idées reçues; et, Le Catalogue des idées chic*, ed. Anne Herschberg Pierrot [Paris: Librairie Générale Française, 1997], p. 57; my translation).

29. Thackeray, letter to G. H. Lewes, 28 April 1855, in *The Letters and Private Papers of William Makepeace Thackeray*, ed. Gordon N. Ray, 4 vols. (Cambridge, Mass.: Harvard Univ. Press, 1945-46), III, 444. The letter is also printed separately as "Goethe in His Old Age," in *Works*, XXX, 452-56.

30. Bourdieu's analysis of the manner in which caricature—one of Thackeray's talents—relates to the enlargement of the image of the charismatic figure is useful here: "It would seem that the logic whereby the 'great' are perceived as physically greater than they are applies very generally, and that authority of whatever sort contains a power of seduction which it would be naive to reduce to the effect of self-interested servility. That is why political contestation has always made use of caricature, a distortion of the bodily image intended to break the charm and hold up to ridicule one of the principles of the effect of authority imposition" (*Distinction*, p. 208).

31. Thackeray, "Dessein's," in *Works,* XXVII, 348.

32. It is interesting to note, when thinking of the fantasized familiarity with the great that Thackeray's characters so often possess, that Thackeray's own prose style was critiqued by Trollope—otherwise Thackeray's greatest admirer—for what Trollope called its "affected familiarity": "He indulges too frequently in little confidences with individual readers, in which pretended allusions to himself are frequent" (Anthony Trollope, *Thackeray* [London: Macmillan, 1879], p. 201).

33. I owe the term "collective witnessing" to Michael Warner, who discusses it in relation to one of the salient facts of modern mass consumption, in which "our desires have become recognizable through their display in the media; and in the moment of wanting them, we imagine a collective consumer witnessing our wants and choices. The public discourse of the mass media has increasingly come to rely on the intimacy of this collective witnessing in its rhetorics of publicity, iconic and consumerist alike" ("Mass Public," p. 242).

34. See Thackeray, "De Juventute," and "On a Peal of Bells," in *Works,* XXVII, 80, 322.

35. See Daniel L. Schacter, *Searching for Memory: The Brain, the Mind, and the Past* (New York: Basic Books, 1996), pp. 195-201, for a lucid summary of recent research into what constitutes "flashbulb memories," a summary that in fact employs the "when Kennedy was shot" example as central. If there is anything missing from this account, as from research on the topic in general, it is a more theoretical consideration of what in modern mass culture might be so effective at tying personal recollection to public, and in fact celebritized (thus the "flashbulb"), events.

36. Thackeray, "On Some Carp at Sans Souci," in *Works,* XXVII, 362-63.

37. *Minima Moralia: Reflections from Damaged Life,* trans. E. F. N. Jephcott (London: Verso, 1978), pp. 100-101.

38. Barthes, *S/Z,* trans. Richard Miller (New York: Hill and Wang, 1974), p. 102.

39. See Roland Barthes, "The Reality Effect," in his *The Rustle of Language,* trans. Richard Howard (London: Blackwell, 1986), pp. 141-48.

40. Jürgen Habermas, *The Structural Transformation of the Public Sphere: An Inquiry into a Category of Bourgeois Society,* trans. Thomas Burger (Cambridge, Mass.: MIT Press, 1989), pp. 171-72. For an account of what Poovey calls "vivification," see her *Making a Social Body: British Cultural Formation, 1830-1864* (Chicago: Univ. of Chicago Press, 1995), p. 9.

Edward T. Barnaby (essay date fall 2001)

SOURCE: Barnaby, Edward T. "Thackeray as Metahistorian, or the Realist *Via Media.*" *CLIO: A Journal of Literature, History, and the Philosophy of History* 31, no. 1 (fall 2001): 33-55.

[*In the following essay, Barnaby considers a central ideological tension in Thackeray's historical fiction, one embodied in a struggle between subjective and objective narrative styles.*]

The writings of Thackeray provide a particularly rich starting point for an inquiry into the relationship between the novel and what Guy Debord calls the "society of the spectacle" wrought by capitalist ideology.[1] Debord describes a process of reification in modern consumer culture through which the individual is transformed into a politically immobilized spectator who contemplates society rather than attempting to act within it. This reification also takes place on the level of time and history in that capitalist culture is predicated on a shift from what Debord identifies as the cyclical time of agrarian society to the "irreversible" linear time of industrial progress. The issue on which Marxist critics have been unable to reach a consensus, however, is whether the novel participates in the process of reifying society within the logic of capitalism or liberates its readers from ideological blindness by making this capitalist transformation visible to them. The answer to this question lies partly in what Hayden White identifies as the meta-historical perspective of the novel that makes visible the ideological perspectives through which history is narrated.[2] We find Thackeray positioning the historical novel between two divergent approaches to historiographical practice in his day, namely, the subjectivity of Carlyle's Germanism and the objectivity of a more scientist French model. In identifying and parodying these extremes in historical representation, Thackeray creates a generic vacuum that his works fill with the ironic perspective of literary realism. Providing even further depth to this appraisal of Thackeray's historical consciousness is the fact that he was somewhat of a frustrated historian himself, producing a discrete body of works about, and delivering lectures on, particularly historical subjects. Examining the function of ideology in these more explicitly historical forms of representation will clarify the novel's particular relationship to ideology, as well as the novel's tendency to overlap the territory of the historian.

Thackeray's satire of historiography in **The Second Funeral of Napoleon** as little more than "works of fiction" full of heroes "whom it can do one no earthly good to remember" emerges largely in response to the imported German philosophy of Thomas Carlyle, particularly Carlyle's treatise *On Heroes, Hero-Worship and the Heroic in History.*[3] The occasion of Thackeray's epistolary report from France is the exhumation of the emperor's exiled corpse and its subsequent transfer to the temple in Paris that had been constructed in Napoleon's honor. The ceremonial pomp and reverence that accompanied this political gesture serves for Thackeray as visible testimony to both the shallow spectacle that is public history and the fallibility of cultural memory. Thackeray wonders whether the fashionable esteem for Greek and Roman culture would persist if, instead of what one reads in a history text, one was "to know really what those monsters were" (361). Applying this argument to the historical figures of his own culture, Thackeray observes that "many of our English worthies are no better. You are not in a situation to know the real characters of any one of them. They appear before you in their public capacities, but the individuals you know not" (360).

This distinction between a public and private persona does not exist for Carlyle. He understands the mission of historiography to be the composition of an inspiring narrative about "Great Men" whose ideas and actions influenced the course of human events and formed the cultural horizons "of whatsoever the general mass of men contrived to do or attain" (239). Carlyle explains that "all things that we see standing accomplished in the world," namely the visual spectacle of the past, exist as the "outer material result, the practical realization and embodiment, of Thoughts that dwelt in the Great Men" (239). In one sense, this idea parallels the Marxist concept of superstructures that spring from the invisible undercurrents of historical process. At the same time, it relies upon a romantic notion of the role of the individual in history that, as Lukács argues in *The Historical Novel,* lends itself to fascist reconstructions of the past.[4]

Perhaps more important to Carlyle than the Great Men themselves, however, is the viability of the narrative that perpetuates their memory. With the ironic historical consciousness characteristic of German philosophy in the nineteenth century, Carlyle identifies the true hero of history as the poet who can best mediate past ages and the present. Historiography tells its readers more about the character of the author than about the figures of the past. According to Carlyle, "how a man, of some wide thing that he has witnessed, will construct a narrative, what kind of picture and delineation he will give of it,—is the best measure you could get of what intellect is in the man" (336). The true historian confronts the subjectivity of true insight. The poet-historian cannot evade crucial decisions by hiding behind a wall of uninterpreted facts or by attempting to conceal his or her presence in the text as a narrator—including decisions regarding "which circumstance is vital and shall stand prominent; which unessential, fit to be suppressed; where is the true beginning, the true sequence and ending" (Carlyle [*On Heroes, Hero-Worship and the Heroic in History*], 336). As with the eye of a portrait painter, for example, the poet-historian must distort the total, objective image of history in order to allow what is most significant to become visible to the observer.

It is a poetic historiography that most thoroughly recaptures what Carlyle regards as the purest form of historical record, that of oral tradition. He uses the image of "an enormous camera-obscura magnifier" to describe the process by which "Tradition" cultivates the memory of great individuals in the collective cultural consciousness. Like the expanded images produced by the camera-obscura, mythical traditions distort the stature of historical figures beyond realistic dimensions, yet both representations are still grounded in an essential reality. In spite of transcending the boundaries of the science of historical inquiry toward a more phenomenological appreciation of history, myth, and historical poesis, one remains able "to discern, far in the uttermost distance, some gleam as of a small real light shining in the centre of that enormous camera-obscura image; to discern that the centre of it all was not a madness and nothing, but a sanity and something" (Carlyle, 262). Carlyle distinguishes between the artificial amassing of historical data in print culture versus the more organic process of oral culture through which the essence of history is preserved, insofar as "a thing grows in the human Memory, in the human Imagination, when love, worship and all that lies in the human Heart, is there to encourage it" (262). Tradition operates according to the natural passage of time into historical consciousness. Carlyle explains that it is not with the scientific apparatus of "date or document" but through the appearance "here and there [of] some dumb monumental cairn" and the aesthetic selectivity of tradition that "any great man would grow mythic" (262).

It is against these myth-fostering dynamics of tradition that Carlyle contrasts the reductive logic of modern historical consciousness. He disparages the mania of modern historians for causality and their rigid adherence to the dictates of scientific method in accounting for the sphere of human action, which is not in itself consistently rational. Carlyle takes great issue, for example, with the modern notion of environmental determinism in which individuals are regarded as products of their time. It is absurd to Carlyle to regard "the time" as having sovereignty over the human will, as if the time were alive and the individual not, and as if "the time called him forth, the Time did everything, he nothing" (250). Equally offensive to Carlyle are mechanistic theories of the universe that reduce the experience of history to that of "wheel-and-pinion 'motives,' self-interests, checks, balances; . . . the clank of spinning-jennies, and parliamentary majorities" (399). He prefers instead the image of Idgrasil, the tree of life from Norse mythology, on whose leaves is inscribed "a biography, every fibre there an act or word" and whose boughs are "Histories of Nations" (257). Budding and withering represent "events, things suffered, things done, catastrophes." The winds that shake the tree are "the breath of Human Passion," and the sound of its rustling is "the noise of Human Existence." While mythical in origin, this organic image of historical process places no boundaries on the further development of culture, unlike the excessive romanticism of the nineteenth-century historical perspective that tended to confer a latter-day sense of futility and belatedness upon the present.

Certain critics regard *On Heroes and Hero-Worship* as one of Carlyle's more philosophically eccentric works, arguing that it exhibits a certain oversimplification not found elsewhere in his writing that is perhaps due in part to the structural constraints of its lecture format.[5] However, the lectures share the basic sentiments of Carlyle's essays "On History" and "On History Again." Here he makes similar observations regarding the roots of history in oral texts; the problem of representing the simultaneous nature of historical reality as a narrative succession; the need for the poetic vision of an *artist* to reconstruct history as opposed to the mechanical preoccupations of an *artisan*; and the need for historical *compression* lest memory become too overwhelmed with material detail to grasp more holistic insights.[6] The intense irony of Carlyle's historical consciousness and his equally ironic awareness of the instability of all media of historical representation leads him to a highly subjective stance in which history practically deconstructs itself as he writes it. Described as a "visionary historian" and his work as a "marriage of history, vision, and art," Carlyle is argued to have held historically factual "that which is recognized by the whole man rising up in a creative oneness of self, to an intuition, in an essentially fictive moment, of the eternal realities."[7] Others have concluded that it is in autobiography and epic that Carlyle sought true historical insight.[8]

In terms of Thackeray's response to Carlyle, however, it is only fitting that Thackeray would seize upon the more extreme of Carlyle's manifestos as being the easier to satirize. Thackeray rejects Carlyle's notion that a pageant of "Great Men" is the only fully accessible and meaningful form of history. He deliberately avoids dealing with the "larger-than-life" figures of typical historical interest that already have been distorted by the camera-obscura of hero worship. Instead he attempts to make visible the historical experience of fictional individuals living within a historical society and age. In response to Carlyle's image of the uncultured valet who "does not know a hero when he sees him" and is naively awed by the spectacle of royalty, Thackeray advances the disinterested perspective of the *valet-de-chambre* and his pragmatic rejection of the very concept of heroism as a model for historical narratives to emulate. Thackeray writes, "we are with the mob in the crowd, not with the great folks in the procession. We are not the Historic Muse, but her ladyship's attendant,

tale-bearer—valet-de-chambre—for whom no man is a hero.'"[9] He seeks to penetrate to a level of history untainted by hero-worship, one that exists beyond the inflated public identities revered by the "Humbug-worshippers" who prefer a sanitized history "written on fig leaves."[10] What Carlyle regards as poetic insight into historical process Thackeray regards as deceit and a blurring of the boundary between history and fiction to the point of unintelligibility. Perusing samples of contemporary historiography, Thackeray wonders "whether I should . . . endeavor . . . to imitate the remarkable character about whom I was reading, or whether I should fling aside the book and the hero of it, as things altogether base, unworthy, laughable, and get a novel" (359).

While one aspect of Thackeray's satire is clearly directed toward the influence of German philosophy on the historiographic practices of his time, an opposite trend in historicism emerging simultaneously in the French academy also elicits a response from the novelist. It is in this sense that Thackeray's satire draws upon the traditional tactic of identifying a *via media* between two extremes, in this case positing the realism of the novel as a corrective to the subjectivity of German historiography and the pretensions to objectivity of the French school. Phillipe Carrard's study *Poetics of the New History* identifies the literary structures that inform the writing of French historiography, many of which are satirized by Thackeray in **Vanity Fair** and **Henry Esmond**.[11] Thackeray uses narrative in a way that foregrounds convention instead of concealing it, in contrast to the prevailing wisdom of manuals of historiographic method, such as the *Introduction to the Study of History* by Langlois. Carrard observes that Langlois counsels against "authorial intrusion" and regards strict adherence to the chronological presentation of events and the logic of causality as providing the most "natural" appearance to the historical representation of events while minimizing the amount of "dramatic deformation" (7). Carrard explains that such tactics, combined with the use of deliberately "plain" and non-metaphorical language, represent an attempt to purify historical discourse of the author's "enunciation" by removing all "focalization" from the narrative in order to conceal the historian's act of mediation (19, 105). Carrard also notes that Chartier has critiqued this brand of historiography for generating an erroneous faith in the possibility of representing history from an entirely objective stance (9).

Thackeray exhibits an awareness of this power of a properly construed historical narrative in his review of "Gisquet's Memoirs," in which he notes that the lack of novelty of the piece and its inferior literary style did not prevent its success "because the facts *thus brought together* cannot fail to make an impression."[12] Thackeray's narrators in **Vanity Fair** and **Henry Esmond**, however, are designed not only to demonstrate the various ways in which a given set of historical facts can be "brought together," but also to demonstrate the not-so-scientific manner in which those facts are obtained and selected. Sometimes they even need to be told twice and from various perspectives, in defiance of historiographic principles of objectivity and linearity, as the narrator of *Vanity Fair* confesses in chapter 25: "our history is destined in this Chapter to go backwards and forwards in a very irresolute manner seemingly, and having conducted our story to to-morrow presently, we shall immediately again have occasion to step back to yesterday, so that the whole of the tale may get a hearing" (246).

While Thackeray's use of plot has been effectively analyzed in light of his preoccupation with time as an antagonistic agent of decay, the plots of *Vanity Fair* and *Henry Esmond* might also be seen as performing a specifically satirical function with regard to what White calls the "emplotment" of historical narrative. The observation that Thackeray comments ironically on the artificial structure of narrative by prolonging his plots until the resolution begins to unravel is certainly relevant to a discussion of his critique of historical representation.[13] However, Thackeray also depicts the process of constructing a narrative of events as a series of choices that are available to an author, whether of a novel or a history. Each subsequent choice further diminishes the objectivity of the narrative and renders absurd the scientific model of historiography, according to which two accounts of the same event should theoretically be interchangeable.

Thackeray portrays Henry Esmond as subscribing to this fallacy at several points in the *History* [*The History of Henry Esmond*]. Regarding the court case that ensued upon Lord Castlewood's death, Henry writes: "'tis needless to narrate here, as the reports of the lawyers already have chronicled them, the particulars or issue of that trial" (170). One who has read Browning's *The Ring and the Book* knows better. Not until General Webb is wrongly maligned in the reportage of the battle of Wynendael does Henry learn that it is never "needless" to recount a narrative, even if one does so only to make its flaws visible and introduce a corrective. The task of describing Henry's first experience of battle is similarly displaced onto alternate narrators. Henry explains that the campaign "may be dismissed very briefly here" because "a score of books have been written concerning it" (200). However, this replacement of a significant moment of Henry's personal history with a mere cross-reference to general accounts of Marlborough's career produces quite an ironic gap in narration between the public and private spheres.

The opening lines of chapter thirty in *Vanity Fair,* in which the narrator dismisses any "claim to rank among the military novelists," do not share the same spirit of deference to existing narratives that one finds in *Henry Esmond.* They do speak, however, to Thackeray's systematic multiplication of narrative perspectives throughout the novel so as to foreground the variety of stories that remain untold due to the choices made by a given narrator. In this case, the narrator chooses to "go no farther with the [regiment] than to the city gate" and not to rewrite what "all of us have read" about the battle of Waterloo or rehearse a tale that is in "every Englishman's mouth." The decision to allow the story of Waterloo to remain untold within his narrative is conspicuous, considering that the narrator himself observes that "you and I . . . are never tired of hearing and recounting the history of that famous action" (293, 326).

Nowhere, however, does the narrator more clearly catalog his narrative options for the benefit of the reader than in chapter six of *Vanity Fair,* in which he retells the plot of the first five chapters from within a variety of generic conventions. Instead of endowing his story with the sense of authority that asserts how things were, Thackeray's narrator informs the reader that he has been forced to choose his narrative from among several alternatives, namely the genteel, the romantic, and the facetious. As his alternate readings of the plot demonstrate, the choice of narrative affects not only setting, characterization, and diction but also the reader's impression of the event. White identifies in *Metahistory* a similar variety of possible emplotments for historical writing in the form of tragic, comic, epic, and satiric structures. Just as each of these forms has its own ideological implications when used to construct a historical account, the genres Thackeray identifies illustrate the way in which any representation of narrative events can be packaged for different social strata and filtered through various lenses of conservatism, sentimentality, or irony.

It is Thackeray's stated attempt to "preserve our middle course modestly amidst those scenes and personages with which we are most familiar" that identifies as satiric his motive for offering these extreme examples of "how this story *might* have been written, if the author had but a mind" (52). In the tradition of Dryden's invocation of the *via media* in *Religio Laici* and Swift's positioning of a sedate Martin Luther between papal megalomania and the rage of Calvin in *A Tale of a Tub,* Thackeray's satire operates by identifying certain generic conventions as literary extremes and then positing his own style as normative and, relatively speaking, realistic. This necessitates a strategic use of irony on Thackeray's part, for irony, as White explains, not only presupposes a realistic perspective in its antagonism toward more figurative formulations of reality, but also appears "intrinsically" realistic and objective because of its self-critical perspective (37-38).

Another ironic moment in *Vanity Fair* that allows Thackeray to position realism as an objective norm comes when the narrator pauses to indulge "those who like to lay down the History-book, and to speculate upon what *might* have happened in the world, but for the fatal occurrence of what actually did take place" (277). He argues that, if Napoleon had waited until the Congress of Vienna pitted the nations of Europe against one another, his bid to regain control of France might have gone uncontested. The narrator abruptly concludes this hypothetical game, however, and turns once again to the realm of historical reality by asking "but what would have become of our story and all our friends, then?" For a moment he has successfully transferred the plot and characters of *Vanity Fair* into the sphere of the historical real by inserting an ironic distance between the fictional story and his temporary suspension of historical fact.

Such transparency of emplotment is also visible in *Henry Esmond.* The anxiety Henry suffers on the night of the Pretender's return to English soil begins as a crisis of personal resolve and ends in a crisis of narration: "He wished the deed undone, for which he had laboured so. He was not the first that has regretted his own act, or brought about his own undoing. Undoing? Should he write that word in his late years? No, on his knees before Heaven, rather be thankful for what then he deemed his misfortune, and which hath caused the whole subsequent happiness of his life" (416). Henry resists a fatalistic or tragic construction of the events, preferring instead to conclude his history with the comic reversal of a *deus ex machina* and a favorable resolution of the conflict. In one sense, this scene illustrates the way in which Henry manipulates the events of his life in order to make them conform to dramatic structures that allow him to construct a meaningful past. At the same time, Henry's self-willed shift from tragedy to comedy demonstrates that neither of these narrative alternatives is prioritized in terms of its realism. It is the protagonist's ironic break from the predestined outcomes of plot that positions the real outside of the jurisdiction of plot (and, by implication, positions Henry Esmond within the realm of the real). This concept of realism as the transcendence of plot also appears in Thackeray's article about the memoirs of "Le Duc de Normandie," in which he advances the anti-Aristotelian notion "that the very *improbability* of the narrative argues for its veracity" and thus implies that the domain of reality and history must be distinguished from the domain of dramatic emplotment.[14]

Thackeray parallels Henry's desire to depart from the plot of the novel with Henry's willingness to rewrite the lineage of his family, which is essentially the "plot" of society in the form of a narrative of succession. The revelation that Henry had previously sacrificed his title for the sake of Lady Esmond's orphaned children comes after the Duke of Hamilton, Beatrix's betrothed, refuses to allow her to accept Henry's wedding gift or any gift

"from gentlemen that bear a name they have no right to" (367). During the ensuing discussion, both Lady Castlewood and Lady Esmond defend Henry's honor as a "kinsman and benefactor" whose actions, which include saving Lady Esmond's son from being killed by Lord Mohun, merit any honorary title he is given. Ironically, after the unfavorable reference to Mohun, the Duke attempts to evade his own common lineage with Mohun, stressing that they are "connected . . . by marriage—though neither by blood nor friendship." This scene depicts a variety of attempts to deny or transcend the social "plot" that controls the inheritance of aristocratic names and titles.

Perhaps, then, it is an overstatement for a sensitive reader of Thackeray to claim that the issue of lineage "is Thackeray's way of posing, and resolving, the problem of history," especially in light of the above discussion of his use of narrative to satirize historiography.[15] The process by which lineage is constructed and deconstructed, however, is certainly foregrounded in *Henry Esmond* in such a way that it becomes an ironic mirror in which the historical enterprise is made visible as a similarly subjective process of construction. Thackeray's strategy of using the conventions of a private history to expose the subjectivity of public history becomes transparent in the closing pages of the novel. Lowering the curtain on his autobiographical performance, so to speak, Henry writes, "with the sound of King George's trumpets, all the vain hopes of the weak and foolish young pretender were blown away; and with that music, too, I may say, the drama of my own life was ended" (461-62). All is revealed to be pageantry as a fanfare accompanies the denouement and order is simultaneously restored in both the private and public spheres. The artificial conventions of the well-made play that Henry uses to shape the events of his life into a history are linked by Thackeray to the arbitrary temporal boundaries of the reigns of monarchs that typically inform the structure of history on the public level.

What is one to make of the fact that, even after the drama of his life has supposedly ended, Henry moves to America and founds the estate that becomes the subject of another novel, *The Virginians*? Some critics, as discussed above, have regarded this as part of Thackeray's tactic of prolonging the plot to illustrate the destabilizing effect of time on even the most poetic resolution of conflict. However, it also points to the inherent fictionality and untruthfulness of any historical representation that pretends to objective realism yet contains a denouement, especially, as in this case, when the events of public and private are so conveniently made to coincide. Thackeray's satire thus anticipates the current skepticism in the academy toward periodization as a form of history riddled with ideological metanarratives. Regarding the practice of historians to date the onset of the Victorian period five years before the accession of Queen Victoria in order to include the Reform Bill of 1832, Elliot Gilbert writes, "nothing could more clearly reveal the extent to which history, for all its aspirations to objective, scientific truth, in fact approaches to the condition of imaginative literature."[16]

It is this issue that Thackeray addresses during his *Lectures on the English Humourists* when he satirizes history for its pretensions to objective truth by observing that, unlike the novelist who makes no claims to truth, the historian has political motives for engaging in false representation. After berating the Muse of History for condescending to her "lighter sisters" while being herself a fabricator of speeches, a panegyrical flatterer, and a mouthpiece for the Dons, Thackeray turns to the subject of autobiography.

> You offer me an autobiography; I doubt all autobiographies I ever read except those, perhaps, of Mr. Robinson Crusoe, Mariner, and writers of his class. These have no object in setting themselves right with the public or their own consciences; these have no motive for concealment or half truths; these call for no more confidence than I can cheerfully give, and do not force me to tax my credulity or to fortify it by evidence. I take up a volume of Dr. Smollett, or a volume of the "Spectator," and say the fiction carries a greater amount of truth in solution than the volume which purports to be all true.[17]

Thackeray contrasts the novelist's honesty in openly displaying his narrative techniques with the historiographer's suspicious repression of the act of literary production, as if historiography were an unmediated representation of the past that has no narrator. In addition, then, to pointing out the fictional quality of the narratives that determine the structure of history, Thackeray also directs his satire against the ideal of the objective historian by dramatizing the partisan and irrational ways in which people interpret and construe the events of their time. It is no coincidence that such a project also resembles an attack on the rationalist concept of the public sphere, since undermining the concept of a single, objective account of history involves exposing it as little more than the allegedly official record of a fictional "nation" told from the perspective of the dominant class under the authority of an equally fictional concept of universal reason.

A clear example of Thackeray's satire of objectivity and reason in public matters is Henry Esmond's admission that, in hindsight, he would have sided with Addison's politics and been a Whig instead of a Tory. Once again expressing a desire to rewrite the plot by hypothesizing about what he would do "were my time to come over again," Henry points to the arbitrary and private motivations behind an individual's views on society, arguing that "'tis men rather than principles that com-

monly bind them. A kindness or a slight puts a man under one flag or the other, and he marches with it to the end of the campaign" (372). Not only are political associations dictated by the emotions but the consistent nature of one's views is the result of blind momentum and not steadfast rational principle. Following a passage in which Churchill is harangued by Webb, Henry addresses future readers of his memoirs in order to instruct them not to "judge of the great duke by what a contemporary has written of him. No man . . . ever deserved better the very greatest praise and the strongest censure. If the present writer joins with the latter faction, very likely a private pique of his own may be the cause of his ill-feeling" (243). This suggests with great irony that the writing of history requires the exclusion of eyewitness testimony because of its inherent biases. There is also Thackeray's footnote to the effect that this aside was "written on a leaf inserted into the MS. book, and dated 1744, probably after he had heard of the duchess's death," which suggests that Henry's historiographical method is contaminated by a eulogizing impulse instead of remaining faithful to his immediate impressions (the very impressions he has, of course, already conceded to be emotionally biased). One might ask what materials are left to the historian that can legitimately be regarded as either factual or objective.

In analyzing Thackeray's oblique treatment of Waterloo in *Vanity Fair,* John Schad suggests that this decision on the part of the novelist to remain below deck during the battle was in itself politically motivated. Schad argues that the 1819 massacre at Peterloo was strongly linked in the popular consciousness of the time with Waterloo and, in the mind of historian David Thomson, "did much to offset the Tory credit for Waterloo."[18] After outlining various reasons Thackeray would have been sensitive to this issue while writing *Vanity Fair,* Schad asks whether the novel's "ostentatious avoidance of the battle [is] in some sense an unwitting reflection, or even parody of this more general departure from the straight line of Tory history" (26). It is possible to appreciate the irony that Schad suggests here without posing a definitive answer to his question. Perhaps, however, a more stable example of exposing the political unconscious of historiography is Thackeray's analysis in *Vanity Fair* of Napoleon's failed return from exile. The narrator questions the claim of the "historians on our side" who report that "the armies of the allied powers were all providentially on a war-footing" and were thus prepared to resist Napoleon's surprise return (277). The narrator offers the alternative explanation that the countries were actually armed in order to defend the controversial stakes they all had claimed while redrawing the map of Europe at the Congress of Vienna.

In identifying the "historians on our side" as he does, Thackeray drives a partisan divide through the center of the concept of objective and rational historical inquiry.

British historians regard the preparedness of their nation to repel Napoleon as providentially inspired not only in order to condemn Napoleon's imperialism with the authority of divine justice but also to conceal the fact that Britain already had raised an army to assert its own imperialistic ambitions in Europe. Henry Esmond explicitly criticizes historiographers for rationalizing the violent impulses of society by representing only the aspects of war that glorify the British: "Why does the stately Muse of History, that delights in describing the valour of heroes and the grandeur of conquest, leave out these scenes, so brutal mean, and degrading, that yet form by far the greater part of the drama of war?" (235). The narrator of **Vanity Fair** similarly accuses historians of perpetuating a cycle of violence between England and France, as the incessant rehearsal of the events by those who "are never tired of hearing and recounting the history of that famous action" produces a "remembrance" that "rankles still" in the minds of the French. The narrator sees "no end to the so-called glory and shame, and to the alternations of successful and unsuccessful murder, in which two high-spirited nations might engage," presumably urged on by partisan accounts of the battle as *glorious* or *shameful* instead of a broader recognition on both sides of the Channel that they are merely "carrying out bravely the Devil's code of honour" (326).

To shift momentarily from the historian to the poet, consider Henry's complaint to Addison after reading Addison's poem *The Campaign:* "You hew out of your polished verses a stately image of smiling victory. . . . You great poets should show it as it is—ugly and horrible, not beautiful and serene. Oh, sir, had you made the campaign, believe me, you never would have sung it so" (255). At first glance, Henry's comments appear to define realism as the opposite of poetic idealization, a form of showing-it-as-it-is that implies that reality is inherently ugly and horrible, whereas poetic representation is inherently beautiful and serene. However, Addison's response to Henry that "'tis a panegyric I mean to write, and not a satire" suggests instead the existence of two generic extremes with no alternative that could be considered a middle ground. Once again Thackeray's skill as a satirist becomes apparent when one observes that Henry's criticism of Addison for idealizing warfare is the same criticism that he voices against historians in general. Not only has history been satirized to resemble the distorting medium of idealized poetry, but satire itself has been located at the opposite extreme as dwelling excessively upon the vulgar. This creates a generic vacuum that Thackeray's novel itself, because it identifies and reconciles both extremes, must fill.

As discussed above with regard to his presentation of alternative narratives in chapter six of **Vanity Fair,** Thackeray uses this ironic construction of a spectrum ranging from panegyric to satire in order to position the

realism of **Henry Esmond** as the middle course. Engaging in a strategy that could be used to describe the function of the realist novel in general, Thackeray presents a multiplicity of narrative perspectives in order to expose the partisan perspective of the single narrative advanced in the guise of totality by the historian and, in Addison's case, the poet. It is in this sense that Thackeray exemplifies Lukács's argument that the historical novel exposes fascist attempts to advance a partisan view of history as an objective and totalitarian one. Certainly **Vanity Fair,** as "A Novel Without a Hero," and even **The History of Henry Esmond,** as an ironic rethinking of the genre of the memoir, portray the concept of the hero "artistically from a social-historical standpoint and not merely an individual-biographical standpoint" (Lukács [*The Historical Novel*], 341). At the same time, Thackeray's attack on an aristocratic-centered historiography and his attempt to position ironic realism as the normative middle course of literary representation could be regarded as participating in what Fredric Jameson describes as the realist novel's "systematic undermining and demystification, the secular 'decoding,' of those preexisting inherited traditional or sacred narrative paradigms which are its initial givens . . . whereby populations are effectively reprogrammed for life and work in the new world of market capitalism."[19] Is it possible, then, that even White's metahistorical perspective cannot entirely find liberation from ideology?

It appears that Thackeray adopts the metahistorical perspective to a point that is sufficient to dissolve any veneer of objectivity remaining within the historical text, yet not enough to undermine the realist claims of his own novels. Jameson observes that, regardless of their mission to destabilize previous paradigms of representation, at some point "realistic novelists are forced by their own narrative and aesthetic vested interests into a repudiation of revolutionary change" in favor of the "evocation of the solidity of their object of representation" (193). It is thus Carlyle, characterized by what Cumming describes as his continual raising and frustration of generic expectations and his literary techniques that "complicate the presentation of fact," who emerges as the true metahistorian here.[20] Carlyle is willing to allow his corrosive irony to consume the very platform on which he stands by alienating the very medium of language and the narrative through which he must convey history. Thackeray uses such metahistorical irony only to undermine the claims of other literary representations of history and make room for the particular historical voice of his novels, ultimately resorting to the "containment strategies" that Jameson identifies as the ideological underpinnings of realism.

Perhaps it is in this spirit of a capitalist reprogramming of the reader that Thackeray chooses an economic metaphor to describe the reduction of history to mere gossip when Henry observes that "my lady's woman carries her mistress's private history to the servants' scandal-market, and exchanges it against the secrets of other abigails" (135). Is there an extent to which Thackeray himself participates in a process of stripping history of its ideological power and converting it into a form of intellectual currency destined for capitalist consumption? While one could argue that his satires of history in *Vanity Fair* and *Henry Esmond* accomplish this on a philosophical level, Thackeray's *The Four Georges* and *Lectures on the English Humourists* represent his literal exploitation of the growing market for historiography in Victorian society. Both sets of lectures, which Gilbert characterizes as "based in part on the overflow of his research for *Esmond*," recycle historical data for economic gain (255). As Macaulay notes in his journal after attending Thackeray's lecture on Steele, "the truth is that Thackeray knows little of those times, & his audience generally less." It is clear from the remainder of Macaulay's comments that he values Thackeray's lectures primarily as entertainment for the spectator and as a source of income for the speaker: "Poor fellow—He is full of humour and imagination, & I only wish that these lectures may answer both in the way of fame & money. He told me as I was going that the scheme had almost set him up—& I told him, & from my heart that I wished he had made ten times as much."[21]

The way in which Thackeray markets his knowledge of history to promote *The Four Georges* suggests an alignment between the lecture tour and the dynamics of the spectacle identified by Debord. Thackeray's introduction to the first lecture makes clear that the value of the presentation lies purely in its ability to entertain, "to amuse for a few hours with talk about the old society," and not to offer "grave historical treatises" (2). As if justifying to potential clients the particular service that he will provide, Thackeray explains his intent to capitalize on "the result of many a day's and night's pleasant reading [i.e., research for his novels] to try and while away a few winter evenings for my hearers" (2). The content of the lectures, however, participates in the spirit of his novels by critiquing traditional historiography for its myopic perspective regarding class representation, its idealization of public figures and its preoccupation with the political and military spheres. It is "not about battles, about politics, about statesmen and measures of state" that Thackeray wishes to speak, "but to sketch the manners and life of the old world" (2). In effect, Thackeray wishes to resurrect the experience of society as it was lived and not simply to catalog people and events that have arbitrarily risen to celebrity. Similar to the narrator's conscious decision not to treat the Battle of Waterloo directly in *Vanity Fair* is Thackeray's desire to write the history of "every-day figures and inhabitants—not so much with heroes fighting immense battles and inspiring repulsed battalions to engage; or statesmen locked up in darkling cabinets and meditating ponderous laws or dire conspiracies—as with people occupied with their every-day work or pleasure" (16). He speaks of a wish to "people the old world" as if with fictional characters, thus allowing the historical conditions themselves to take the foreground instead of magnifying a particular historical figure or dramatizing a particular event.

It is in this sense that Thackeray's historiography transcends the level of a spectacle for mass consumption and participates actively, like the novel, in making visible the gaps in historical representation that are otherwise overlooked within the narrow horizons constructed by ideology. For example, he incorporates the testimony of travel literature of the early eighteenth century into his historical narrative, thus expanding the scope of the historical landscape beyond the walls of the court. "Shut out by woods from the beggared country" and "away from the noise and brawling of the citizens and buyers," accounts of courtly life fail to include the conditions of the peasantry and exclude this alternative perspective on life under monarchical rule (7). Thackeray points both the historian and his audience "out of your palace-windows beyond the trim-cut forest vistas" to where "misery is lying outside" and there are "half-burned cottages and trembling peasants gathering piteous harvests" (7). Thackeray severely questions the moral example set by an aristocracy that allows such conditions to persist, in spite of the fact that it is this social class that the history books idealize and elevate as candidates for hero-worship. It is with this spirit that Thackeray concludes his lectures, prompted especially by his disgust with George IV, when he departs from the monarchical title characters to discuss those he regards as true gentlemen deserving of the eye of history, namely, Walter Scott, Robert Southey, and Cuthbert Collingwood.

It is revealing that Thackeray's preferred point of access to the history of the period was popular magazines such as the *Spectator* and *Tatler*, precisely because they are "full of delightful glimpses of the town life of those days" (31). In spite of his desire to remain on the level of manners and popular culture, however, Thackeray's subject in *The Four Georges* clearly demands that he probe public records as well. With regard to George IV, Thackeray tries "reading him in scores of volumes, hunting him through old magazines and newspapers, having him here at a ball, there at a public dinner, there at races and so forth," only to find that of this great historical figure there is "nothing but a coat and a wig and a mask smiling below it—nothing but a great simulacrum" (102).

This enterprise leads to Thackeray's great frustration with the lack of substance behind the public persona of "George IV," which is essentially constructed out of official documents that the king signed but did not himself write. Unwilling to afford any semblance of a private dimension to this political facade, Thackeray muses that even the king's private letters were spelled by someone else. Thackeray's tireless attempt to tunnel beneath the mute monoliths of the historical landscape is evidenced in this passage in which he is apparently more interested in the obscure life of the clerk whose words were placed in the mouth of the king than in the king himself: "He put a great George P. or George R. at the bottom of the page and fancied he had written the paper: some bookseller's clerk, some poor author, some man did the work" (102). Practically abandoning the task of historiography altogether by the end of the lecture, Thackeray withdraws from the futility of trying to "get at the character" of his subject and questions, "will men of the future have nothing better to do than to unswathe and interpret that royal old mummy?" (103).

The tension between Thackeray's participation in the society of the spectacle and his simultaneous unmasking of that spectacle is most clearly seen in his discussion during the lectures of "the triumph of the monarchical principle" in which "feudalism was beaten down" (12). Thackeray not only makes visible the shift from one mode of politico-economic power to another but also anticipates Louis Althusser's argument that aesthetic culture is merely an apparatus of the state.[22] Thackeray explains that "it was the rule to be dazzled by princes, and people's eyes winked quite honestly at that royal radiance" (14). He describes the elaborate pageants and ceremonies that made use of classical allegory to position the monarch as practically divine, evidently with such effectiveness that "the proudest and most ancient gentry of the land" not only consented to his rule, but also competed to perform "menial service for him" (12). Thackeray identifies the royal procession to the Crystal Palace as a striking visual image of the clash between the feudal and industrial modes of production. He revels in the irony of one group of spectators, awed by the performance of the monarchy, subscribing to its mythos and patronizing its rituals, making its way toward the Great Exhibition to join another group of spectators engrossed in the alternative performance of modern industrial capitalism (12-13). He boils the authority of the monarchy down to its ability to convince the populace to tip its hat to an inherently meaningless symbol, as in the story of William Tell, who refused to salute Gesler's hat when it was raised upon a pole in the town square.

Having cornered his audience into feeling scorn for any society so duped by spectacle into complicity, however, Thackeray observes, "I make no comment upon the spectators' behavior; all I say is, that Gesler's cap is still up in the market-place of Europe, and not a few folks are still kneeling to it" (13). That the spectacle of monarchy has merely been replaced by the spectacle of the free market is the metahistorical perspective that

emerges from Thackeray's lectures on *The Four Georges.* It thus appears that his initial claim for the sheer entertainment value of his lectures derives in reality from an episode of Socratic modesty. However, Thackeray's apparent ambivalence toward the behavior of the spectators, recommending that they view "these old-world ceremonies . . . as you will, according to your mood; and with scorn or with respect, or with anger and sorrow as your temper leads you," suggests the indulgence of what Nietzsche refers to as "suprahistorical" cynicism on the part of the narrator. This mode of presenting insight to the public while ambivalent to the nature of its response or perhaps even skeptical that a response will be made is symptomatic of a society paralyzed by spectacle. Toward the end of the lectures, Thackeray struggles once again with his ambivalence regarding the fundamental purpose of historiography, whether it be moral or aesthetic, perhaps providing grounds for judgment or merely images for contemplation. Leaving no room for the definition of a middle ground, he asks, "Shall we regard it as preachers and moralists, and cry Woe, against the open vice and selfishness and corruption; or look at it as we do at the king in the pantomime, with his pantomime wife and pantomime courtiers, whose big heads he knocks together, whom he pokes with his pantomime sceptre, whom he orders to prison under the guard of his pantomime beef-eaters, as he sits down to dine on his pantomime pudding?" (127). For Thackeray the lecturer, historical inquiry is both "as serious as a sermon, and as absurd and outrageous as Punch's puppet-show" (127). As historiographer, he appears uncomfortable in either role. As novelist, he seems to accommodate both.

Irrespective of his ambiguous relationship to the ideology of the spectacle, it is clear that Thackeray's satire creates a vacuum between extremes in the practice of historiography that the realistic novel as he writes it is ripe to fill. The nature of Thackeray's metahistorical commentary in the lectures on the *Four Georges* and *The Second Funeral of Napoleon* demonstrates his desire to shift historiography in the direction of the novel. Jane Millgate seems to have misconstrued the dynamics of his satire in regarding Thackeray's use of the "devices of the historian" in the form of "prefaces, footnotes, and the whole edited memoirs format" as a means of both exposing "the bias of the first-person narrator" and locating "points at which modifications [to the novel] might be needed, and something of the form they should take" (53). Her observation that the effect of such paratextual devices "to shift the fiction quite perceptibly in the direction of history" (53) was achieved "perhaps in ways not fully appreciated by Thackeray himself" (53) is an understatement indeed, especially since it appears that Thackeray was engaged, on the contrary, in a systematic satire of historiography that portrayed it as little more than disguised fiction. As Laurence Lerner suggests regarding Henry Esmond's suspect abilities as a historian, "we are invited to treat Esmond's decorous storytelling as he treats Addison's poem," not to look for ways to conceal its subjectivity.[23] In arguing that the scholarly apparatus of historiography is "being exploited by the novelist in the interests of a license in the handling both of event and interpretation such as no historian could permit himself" (53), Millgate fails to recognize in Thackeray's novels the implication that certain historians of his time permit themselves to manipulate the interpretation of historical events toward ideological ends, while others conceal this act within a scientistic method.

Notes

1. Guy Debord, *The Society of the Spectacle,* trans. Donald Nicholson-Smith (1967; reprint, New York: Zone, 1995).

2. Hayden White, *Metahistory: The Historical Imagination in Nineteenth-Century Europe* (Baltimore: Johns Hopkins UP, 1973).

3. William Makepeace Thackeray, *The Second Funeral of Napoleon* (1841; reprint, Boston: Dana Estes, n.d.), 359; Thomas Carlyle, *On Heroes, Hero-Worship and the Heroic in History* (1841; reprint, New York: Dutton, 1967).

4. Georg Lukács, *The Historical Novel,* trans. Hannah and Stanley Mitchell (1937; reprint, Lincoln: U of Nebraska P, 1983).

5. Albert J. LaValley, *Carlyle and the Idea of the Modern: Studies in Carlyle's Prophetic Literature and Its Relation to Blake, Nietzsche, Marx and Others* (New Haven: Yale UP, 1968), 138.

6. Carlyle, "On History" (1830), 56, 59, 61; "On History Again" (1833), 109; in *A Carlyle Reader: Selections from the Writings of Thomas Carlyle,* ed. G. B. Tennyson (New York: Cambridge UP, 1984).

7. John P. Farrell, "Transcendental Despair: *The French Revolution,*" 109 and Brian John, "The Fictive World: *Past and Present,*" 77, 87 in *Modern Critical Views: Thomas Carlyle,* ed. Harold Bloom (New York: Chelsea, 1986).

8. A. Dwight Culler, "Mill, Carlyle, and the Spirit of the Age," *Modern Critical Views: Thomas Carlyle,* 132.

9. Thackeray, *The Four Georges,* (1861; reprint, Boston: Dana Estes, n.d.), 29.

10. Thackeray, *The Second Funeral of Napoleon,* 361-62.

11. Philippe Carrard, *Poetics of the New History: French Historical Discourse from Braudel to Chartier* (Baltimore: Johns Hopkins UP, 1992);

Thackeray, *Vanity Fair, a Novel Without a Hero,* ed. Peter Shillingsburg (1847; reprint, New York: W. W. Norton, 1994); Thackeray, *The History of Henry Esmond, Esq.,* ed. Donald Hawes (1852; reprint, Oxford: Oxford UP, 1991).

12. Quoted in Geoffrey C. Stokes, "Thackeray as Historian: Two Newly Identified Contributions to *Fraser's Magazine,*" *Nineteenth-Century Fiction* 22 (1967): 283, emphasis added.

13. See J. M. Rignall, "Thackeray's *Henry Esmond* and the Struggle against the Power of Time," *The Nineteenth-Century British Novel,* ed. Jeremy Hawthorn (London: Edward Arnold, 1986), 81-94.

14. Quoted in Stokes, "Thackeray as Historian," 287, emphasis added.

15. Karen Chase, "The Kindness of Consanguinity: Family History in *Henry Esmond,*" *Modern Language Studies* 16 (1986): 214.

16. Elliot L. Gilbert, "'To Awake from History': Carlyle, Thackeray, and *A Tale of Two Cities,*" *Dickens Studies Annual* 12 (1983): 252.

17. Thackeray, *The English Humourists of the Eighteenth Century,* ed. Ernest Rhys (1853; reprint, London: J. M. Dent & Sons, 1924), 89-90.

18. Quoted in John Schad, "Reading the Long Way Round: Thackeray's *Vanity Fair,*" *Yearbook of English Studies* 26 (1996): 26.

19. Fredric Jameson, *The Political Unconscious: Narrative as a Socially Symbolic Act* (Ithaca: Cornell UP, 1981), 152.

20. Mark Cumming, *A Disemprisoned Epic: Form and Vision in Carlyle's French Revolution* (Philadelphia: U of Pennsylvania P, 1988), 51, 57.

21. Quoted in Jane Millgate, "History *versus* Fiction: Thackeray's Response to Macaulay," *Costerus: Essays in English and American Language and Literature* 2 (1974): 48.

22. See Louis Althusser, "Ideology and Ideological State Apparatuses," *Lenin and Philosophy, and Other Essays,* trans. Ben Brewster (London: New Left, 1971).

23. Laurence Lerner, "The Unsaid in *Henry Esmond,*" *Essays in Criticism* 45 (1995): 157.

David Kurnick (essay date winter 2006)

SOURCE: Kurnick, David. "Empty Houses: Thackeray's Theater of Interiority." *Victorian Studies* 48, no. 2 (winter 2006): 257-67.

[*In the following essay, Kurnick exposes Thackeray's "moral ambivalence" toward the theater, focusing on his novel* Lovel the Widower. *Kurnick contends that the undercurrent of emotional loss in the work stems from the author's nostalgia for a "lost possibility of performance."*]

The nineteenth century has long been justifiably regarded as the golden age of the realist novel, the period when long narrative fiction achieved undisputed cultural respectability and intellectual seriousness. But some of the most innovative recent critical work in Victorian studies has addressed the struggles and uncertainties attendant on the novel's quest for cultural hegemony. I'm thinking in particular of books like Emily Allen's *Theater Figures: The Production of the Nineteenth-Century British Novel* and J. Jeffrey Franklin's *Serious Play: The Cultural Form of the Nineteenth-Century Realist Novel.* Despite the differing emphases and arguments of these works, they share an acute awareness of the theater's central role in nineteenth-century English culture. Allen and Franklin both argue that the novel consolidated its cultural centrality by means of a strenuous competition with its theatrical other.

Allen demonstrates, for example, that novelists conjured the image of theater to create distinctions between *novels*: the figure of theater drew off energies of embodiment, femininity, and mass entertainment that the serious novel needed to render abject in order to establish itself as a private, disembodied, respectable artistic object. Franklin's account similarly emphasizes a model of generic competition, whereby novelists like William Makepeace Thackeray and George Eliot discipline theatrical characters in order to supplant what Franklin calls "the subject of performance" with "the subject of reading" (126). Allen and Franklin are both drawing on and contributing to the important work of historians who have traced the transformations in dramatic culture over the course of the nineteenth century. A series of changes in theater architecture, playwriting, acting styles, and urban planning affected English theatergoing in profound ways that have been summed up as effecting a gradual "novelization" of the theater. The disappearance of the last big urban fairgrounds, the shortening of theatrical bills of fare to make evening entertainment coincide with the suburban commuter trains, the introduction of family-oriented matinees, the evaporation of the stage apron and thus the curtailing of interaction between actor and audience, the eventual triumph of the proscenium arch so that stage action receded and took on the air of a parallel reality, the increased emphasis on realism in stage design and on decorum and passivity in audiences, the developing interest in psychological realism in characterization: together, these developments transformed a theatrical and public culture to reflect the new prominence of the private, domestically oriented, psychologically absorbed form of the realist novel.[1]

The critics I've mentioned have understandably argued that the major realist novelists are quite happy about, if not themselves complicit in, this disciplining of theatrical culture. As I've indicated, these critics assume that antagonism sets the terms for the relations among artistic forms: the decline of the theater coincides with the novel's victory. This model makes intuitive sense—and as I've suggested, it has brought a new dynamism to the study of the novel's evolution. But I would like to question the notion that the models of "contest" (Franklin [*Serious Play*] 87) and "competition" (Allen [*Theater Figures*] 17) provide the only, or best, lens through which to comprehend the relations between genres. It seems important, for example, to recall that some of the writers most closely associated with the novel's cultural prestige, among them George Eliot, Henry James, and, later, James Joyce, attempted to write for the stage. Strangely—but not, I want to suggest, entirely coincidentally—these are also among the novelists we most associate with the refinement of techniques for representing consciousness. That these authors are frequently described as apostles of inwardness, and that they could be vocal about their distaste for the actual theater, should not blind us to the fact that at crucial moments in their novelistic careers, the theater seemed to hold a promise—occasionally financial, but also aesthetic and ethical—that the novel did not. The strange theatrical interludes in these exemplary novelistic careers, I'd suggest, should at the very least prompt us to reconsider the model of generic competition.

I'll focus on a revealing stretch in the career of Thackeray—a writer whose volubly expressed contempt for "sham" and pretense might make him seem the most antitheatrical of Victorian novelists. To be sure (as generations of critics have shown) it is possible to demonstrate that Thackeray's hatred of theatricality coexists with a powerful attraction to it. This is a valuable insight, but it is not my point here. In fact, I want to suggest that focusing on Thackeray's moral ambivalence about an abstraction called "theatricality" may obscure his attachment to a very real theatrical culture. The coordinates of this attachment are more ethical than moral—more concerned, that is, with the social spaces the theater creates and the forms of life it fosters than with the necessity of judging the fact of performance according to a rubric of right-or-wrong. I'll be examining Thackeray's 1854 play entitled **The Wolves and the Lamb** alongside his 1860 short novel, **Lovel the Widower,** a narrative he derived from that play after repeated efforts to have it staged were frustrated. In tracing the unexpected mutations the story undergoes in its retreat from the theater, I'll also suggest that this late novel's most innovative formal and tonal features derive from its melancholic relation to a lost possibility of performance.

The novelistic voice Thackeray creates in *Lovel* [*Lovel the Widower*], I'll argue, conveys a palpable nostalgia for a dwindling mid-Victorian theatrical world that, as we have seen, was ceding symbolic centrality to an increasingly valorized private and domestic sphere. I hope that this analysis of how Thackeray's theatrical desire shapes his fiction indicates that we need a more capacious model of generic interaction than one that understands literary forms as engaged in a kind of Darwinian struggle for survival.[2] I want to remind us that writers don't always know what's good for "their" genre, or even which genre is "theirs." And even if we can be sure that the novel was in competition with the theater, we should recall that competitors view one another with longing and desire as well as with enmity, and that victors often ambivalently memorialize the values of their defeated rivals. Far from triumphing in the eclipse of the theater, some of the period's most interesting novelists registered their own ascendancy ruefully. Further, this sense of loss actually produced some of the literary techniques that we now regard as most characteristically novelistic: I'll conclude by suggesting that the stream of consciousness that is among the novel's best-known techniques for representing psychic experience in fact takes its form from the novel's frustrated theatrical desire.

Thackeray wrote *The Wolves and the Lamb* in 1854, at the height of his fame. He intended the play for the Olympic Theatre in the West End, but the manager there rejected it after a hasty reading, as did the manager of the Haymarket to whom Thackeray next submitted it. In fact its only performance occurred at a housewarming party Thackeray threw when he and his daughters moved into their large house at Palace Green, Kensington, in 1862. The playbills Thackeray had printed up for the party claimed that this was a performance by the "W. M. T. House Theatricals": the pun's reference to an "empty house" alludes first of all to the fact that the furnishings hadn't yet arrived at Palace Green on the occasion of this performance; secondly, it reminds the spectators of the play's inability to command the attention of a real theatrical "house"; thirdly, and most interestingly, by metaphorically hollowing out the space of domestic felicity, it sounds a strangely melancholic note on the occasion of a housewarming.[3]

This somewhat sour pun is all the more striking when we consider the blandly orthodox domesticity celebrated in the play itself. *The Wolves and the Lamb* is a routine domestic comedy of the type that was increasingly finding favor in mid-century London.[4] And perhaps one reason for the failure of Thackeray's play to gain a place on the stage is the unconvincing eagerness with which it mimics the ascendant hominess of the West End theater. The play's headnote indicates that the stage represents "*two drawing-rooms opening into one another*" (373). In offering his hypothetical viewers this image of the domestic receding into itself, it is as if Thackeray wants to recall us to the derivation of "drawing room" from the word "withdraw," while at the same time doubling and intensifying the scene's domesticity.

This visual frame offers an apt introduction to the plot of the play, which pays similarly insistent homage to the space of the home. The lamb of its title is the widower Milliken, a "*wealthy City Merchant*" (372) who falls in love with his children's governess Julia Prior. When it's revealed that Miss Prior's previous employment was dancing in an "Oriental ballet," Milliken's respectable in-laws are of course horrified (412). But by far the most surprising thing about the revelation of Julia's theatrical past is how anodyne it proves—how easily contained in the space of the home. In notable contrast to Thackeray's other theatrically marked heroines like *Vanity Fair*'s Becky Sharpe, *Pendennis*'s Blanche Amory, or *Henry Esmond*'s Beatrix—all of whom prove unable to change their performative stripes, and accordingly provoke their creator's denunciation—Julia proves fully assimilable in the Milliken family. The marriage comes off in the end, and Julia shows herself more than willing to repress her theatrical past in exchange for a position in the Milliken home. It is as if, in the context of a theatrical culture busy making itself over in the image of the home, Thackeray can barely work up his customary fervor over the theatrical; he seems only able to rehearse, mechanically, the domestic ideology the form demands of him.

The only bump in these proceedings is provided by a strangely peripheral character with the suggestive name of Captain Touchit. An old friend of the hero who is simply visiting the house as the action transpires, this character remains entirely marginal to the unfolding of the play's action, with little real place in any summary of its plot. Thackeray signals Touchit's externality most clearly by positioning him as the only character who recognizes the incongruity of the play's relative lack of interest in the question of theater. Touchit does this by insisting on verbally reminding the other characters of the theatrical medium in which they exist. Stumbling onto the play's climactic scene, for example, he exclaims, "What is this comedy going on, ladies and gentlemen? The ladies on their elderly knees—Miss Prior with her hair down her back. Is it tragedy or comedy?—is it a rehearsal for a charade, or are we acting for Horace's birthday?" (437). The outburst hints at some of the multifariousness of the theatrical culture *The Wolves and the Lamb* otherwise ignores. If the play as a whole seems happily to participate in the domestication of the theater described by Allen and Franklin, it is only Captain Touchit who even seems to register that that eclipse is underway.

A connection to theatrical spaces outside the home in fact turns out to be precisely what most characterizes Touchit. A former tenant in the boarding house kept by the Prior family, Touchit is the only character with a living experience of Julia Prior's theatrical past. He is, moreover, much more eager than she to discuss it, to bring those alternate theatrical spaces briefly to verbal life on this stage. In his only tête-à-tête with Julia, and over her protests, he reminisces about one of their fellow-lodgers: "What a heap of play-tickets, diorama-tickets, concert-tickets he used to give you!" (401-02). But Julia quickly cuts short this drift into the past and into theatrical spaces distinct from the withdrawn drawing room in which they find themselves.

Touchit seems more firmly linked to theatrical culture than the actress Julia Prior, but there are indications at the end of the play that he may be discarded not on grounds of impropriety but of sheer irrelevance: "And you will come down and see us often, Touchit, won't you?" Milliken asks vaguely in the play's penultimate line, but the question goes unanswered by Touchit, who, a few lines earlier, has indicated his intention not to "interrupt this felicity" and to dine instead at his club (445). This non-exchange makes evident the increased demarcation between inside and outside, home and world—between the spectacle of domesticity and the pleasures of the theater—that is characteristic both of the refortified Milliken home and of the paradoxically withdrawn theatrical space it occupies. Touchit is a container for the memory of these external spaces the play ignores, and his silence mirrors the play's confusion about what to do with this extra-domestic character. Touchit's exile from the conclusion of *The Wolves and the Lamb* suggests that a stage committed to mirroring the enclosure of the home can afford no space for the articulation of that theatrical memory.

Paradoxically enough, it is only in the novel that this character, an embodied repository of the theatrical past, will find his voice. *The Wolves and the Lamb* forces us to imagine Touchit's interior response to the play's final question; but the 1860 novel *Lovel the Widower,* which Thackeray adapted out of his failed play, opens with and is sustained by a torrent of Touchit's language. The emotional focus and innovative force of *Lovel the Widower* derive from the way it finds a narrative form for the experience of dramatic failure. Retreating from the scene of his theatrical frustration, Thackeray discovers a lush narrative expanse, a subtly contoured, acoustically rich space of interior consciousness. The story has remained essentially the same, but Thackeray has transformed its meaning by giving power of narration to the most peripheral character. The 1860 novel creates its flamboyant interior monologue out of that liminal space between theatrical past and domestic present inhabited by Captain Touchit.

"Who shall be the hero of this tale?" the novel opens. "Not I who write it" (197). The phrase signals a clear dissent from the famous Dickensian opening that is its most immediate point of reference: unlike David Copperfield, who coyly wonders *whether* he will turn out to be the hero of the life-story that bears his name, this narrator flatly refuses to move center stage. "I am but the Chorus of the Play," he clarifies—and takes off on a fifteen-page bravura rant in which we tour an echo chamber reverberating with past and present arguments, blandishments, resentments. No one else speaks, but we are nonetheless awash in voices:

> I am but the Chorus of the Play. I make remarks on the conduct of the characters: I narrate their simple story. There is love and marriage in it: there is grief and disappointment: the scene is in the parlour, and the region beneath the parlour. No: it may be the parlour and the kitchen, in this instance, are on the same level. . . . I don't think there's a villain in the whole performance. There is . . . an old haunter of Bath and Cheltenham boarding-houses (about which how can I know anything, never having been in a boarding-house at Bath or Cheltenham in my life?). . . .
>
> The principal personage you may very likely think to be no better than a muff. But is many a respectable man of our acquaintance much better? . . . Yes, perhaps even this one is read and written by—Well? *Quid rides*? Do you mean that I am painting a portrait which hangs before me every morning in the looking glass when I am shaving? *Après*? Do you suppose that I suppose that I have not infirmities like my neighbors? . . .
>
> I wish with all my heart I was about to narrate a story with a good mother-in-law for a character; but then you know, my dear madam, all good women in novels are insipid. This woman certainly was not. . . . Aha! my good lady Baker! I was a *mauvais sujet*, was I?—I was leading Fred [Lovel] into smoking, drinking, and low bachelor habits, was I? I, his old friend, who have borrowed money from him any time these twenty years, was not fit company for you and your precious daughter? Indeed! . . .
>
> Before entering upon the present narrative, may I take leave to inform a candid public that, though it is all true, there is not a word of truth in it; that though Lovel is alive and prosperous, and you very likely have met him, yet I defy you to point him out; that his wife (for he is Lovel the Widower no more) is not the lady you imagine her to be.

(197-202)

Are you talking to me? we may well ask. Where are we? *When* are we? Are you telling a story, conducting a quarrel, rehearsing a grudge, announcing a performance—speaking to a public, to Lady Baker, to yourself? How many of us are there in here? Certainly some of these sentences take up the tone of the stentorian moralist so despised by Thackeray's modernist critics, just as some could be characterized as the "confiding garrulities" beloved of his nineteenth-century readers (Rideing [*Thackeray's London*] 5). But Touchit's narration displays a new mobility and restlessness that have led Geoffrey Tillotson to describe *Lovel* as anticipating the development of the "stream of consciousness" (27). This metaphor may be too placid, however, to account for a speech act that seems so fitful, so devious and panicked. In the opening pages of *Lovel,* we have entered a narrative space where the referential trajectory of language seems prone to odd inflections, where the scope of the audience and the status of the utterance are undergoing constant and seemingly unstoppable warpings: curse shades into entreaty, narration into quarrelsome conversation, reminiscence into hallucination.

Can we trace some of the contours of the shadow theater mapped out by this torrent of language? We are both "upstairs" and "downstairs" (in the "parlour" and the "kitchen"); we are at once in the middle-class home (in the seat of "love and marriage") and out of it (our speaker suspiciously disavows familiarity with "cheap boarding-houses"); we are at once at the threshold of Lovel's story ("before entering upon the present narrative") and after it ("he is Lovel the Widower no more"); we are on the stage but peripheral to its action. So multifarious, so nearly ubiquitous is this narrative voice, that it might seem the voice of casually authoritative omniscience—if it weren't for the fact that it is so drenched in tones of spleen, loss, resentment, and sheer embodied breathlessness. It is as if this speaker were suffering in his person the exhausting effects of every narrative swerve, every spatial and temporal translation.

As I have indicated, the characterological location of this ubiquity that seems to have no place to rest is *The Wolves and the Lamb*'s Captain Touchit. But he appears here under a name that offers an embarrassingly bald explanation for his placelessness and for his quasi-paranoid narrative style: "I shall call myself Mr. Batchelor, if you please" (216). Meanwhile, his friend Milliken has been rechristened with a name, "Lovel," that rounds out the domestic sphere's logic of affective exclusivity. If, as our narrator assures us, "there is love and marriage in it," Frederick *Lovel* is clearly where it's at—and Mr. Batchelor is just as clearly out of it. The love/Lovel pun offered in the first lines of the story constitutes an almost crass joke against those who find themselves unaccommodated by the domestic present: it's not merely that the bachelor is excluded from the domestic hearth but that this hearth has now explicitly become the space of "love." The obviousness of this effect is clearly part of Thackeray's intent and an important element of the story's pathos. It is difficult, after all, to ignore the social abjection and sheer tactile need embodied in a Batchelor whose "real" name is Touchit.[5] Batchelor's bitterness in these opening pages suggests that the wellsprings of Thackerayan narration lie in a resentment about the equation between domesticity and affective plenitude.[6]

As I began by noting, the genre that has been understood as best accommodating the increasing prominence of the private sphere is the novel. But Batchelor's eminently novelistic voice is given its affective contours by his obsession with the memory of theater. His social need, that is, is a symptom of the disappearance of a "stage" that could accommodate him. If Tillotson is correct that Batchelor's voice is an early example of the modernist stream of consciousness, *Lovel the Widower*'s theatrical background indicates that this technique for the exploration of interiority derives not from a push toward psychological realism but from the vacuum created by the loss of a commonly accessible public culture. The stream of consciousness, in other words, would owe less to the representational demands of a generic "subject" than to the specific social melancholia of the *mauvais sujet* who is exiled from the domestic enclosure and who stubbornly holds onto a theatrical space fading into oblivion. Batchelor's narration, I am suggesting, is a panicked report from an evaporating culture of theatricality.

Batchelor's interior monologue is thus not a sign of his accommodation of the new novelistic order but a symptom of his alienation from it. The "subject of performance" is indeed rendered obsolete in *Lovel the Widower,* but this supercession is not only mourned by the novel, but mourned *as* one of its most well-known formal innovations. Far from being a triumphant alternative to the theatrical, novelistic interiority emerges as a container for an unaccommodated theatricality. George Levine has argued for Thackeray's status as the novelist most representative of mid-Victorian realist conventions and most aware of their ethical limitations.[7] If we accept this description, *Lovel the Widower* makes movingly explicit the extent to which those conventions—especially the premium placed on privacy and psychology—derive from a soured appetite for publicity. I think that Thackeray's attachment to that public world might prompt us to reconsider the antagonistic rubrics underlying the critical approaches with which I began. Do novelists really behave like good rational actors, playing to win in contests with generic opponents? Might not novelists, like everyone else, become perversely attached to their own losing ventures? Might not their very successes radiate the same ideological ambivalence as do their failures? I've argued that Thackeray's Mr. Batchelor does not gleefully herald the invention of novelistic interiority as much as he grumblingly *makes do* with it. I want to close by suggesting that the extraordinary sensitivity of Thackeray's narration to the contours of domestic, psychological, and theatrical space should alert us to the persistence of a public desire even in a form, like the psychological novel, apparently most given over to the public's erasure.

Notes

1. Franklin and Allen both discuss these changes, which are explored as well in Baer, Booth, Davis and Emeljanow, Hadley, Innes, and Wiles.

2. Moretti offers the strongest case for a Darwinian generic history. As I hope this paper will suggest, Moretti's application of the law of the jungle to the evolution of genre may underestimate the elements of nostalgia, ambivalence, and attachment to failure that can motivate human subjects and cultural production.

3. On this play's composition and the housewarming production, see Ray, 2: 234, 391.

4. See in particular Booth as well as Davis and Emeljanow.

5. There is a striking resonance between Thackeray's Touchit and Henry James's Ralph Touchett from *Portrait of a Lady* (1881), both in name and in their position as observing bachelors. McMaster invokes James's string of bachelor/observers in describing *Lovel* [*Lovel the Widower*] (4). But she seems unaware of Batchelor's original identity as Touchit, and so does not point out the connection between one of James's better-known bachelors and Thackeray's frustrated theatrical ambition. The connection seems to me suggestive for a queer genealogy of Jamesian spectatorship: the question that the alluring Ralph frequently provokes in readers—namely, in what context *could* he perform?—has a very specific antecedent in Thackeray's failed play.

6. In her incisive comments on *Lovel the Widower,* Sedgwick reads the novel as demonstrating the bachelor's "basic strategy" of "a preference of atomized male individualism to the nuclear family (and a corresponding demonization of women, especially mothers)" (192). My focus is on the abject back-story to the bachelor-narrator's "strategy" and "preference[s]," which I would thus read in more defensive, less voluntaristic, terms. I want to suggest that his "male individualism" and his misogyny are both informed by an exclusion from the family that is increasingly seen in the period as the mother's natural cultural location. Because Mr. Batchelor's character derives from a palpable envy, its coordinates are perhaps less aptly described as elements of a "perference" than as a manifestation of *amor fati*—making a virtue of necessity.

7. For Levine's discussion of Thackeray's realism, see 131-80.

Works Cited

Allen, Emily. *Theater Figures: The Production of the Nineteenth-Century British Novel.* Columbus: Ohio State UP, 2003.

Baer, Marc. *Theatre and Disorder in Late Georgian London.* Oxford: Oxford UP, 1992.

Booth, Michael. *Theatre in the Victorian Age.* Cambridge: Cambridge UP, 1991.

Davis, Jim, and Victor Emeljanow. *Reflecting the Audience: London Theatregoing, 1840-1880.* Iowa City: U of Iowa P, 2001.

Franklin, J. Jeffrey. *Serious Play: The Cultural Form of the Nineteenth-Century Realist Novel.* Philadelphia: U of Pennsylvania P, 1999.

Hadley, Elaine. *Melodramatic Tactics: Theatricalized Dissent in the English Marketplace, 1800-1885.* Stanford: Stanford UP, 1995.

Innes, Christopher. *A Sourcebook on Naturalist Theatre.* London: Routledge, 2000.

Levine, George. *The Realistic Imagination: English Fiction from Frankenstein to Lady Chatterley.* Chicago: U of Chicago P, 1981.

McMaster, Juliet. *Thackeray: The Major Novels.* Toronto: U of Toronto P, 1971.

Moretti, Franco. *Graphs, Maps, Trees: Abstract Models for a Literary History.* London: Verso, 2005.

Ray, Gordon. *Thackeray.* 2 vols. New York: McGraw-Hill, 1955-58.

Rideing, William H. *Thackeray's London: A Description of His Haunts and the Scenes of His Novels.* London: J. W. Jarvis and Son, 1885.

Sedgwick, Eve Kosofsky. *Epistemology of the Closet.* Berkeley: U of California P, 1990.

Thackeray, William Makepeace. *Lovel the Widower.* 1860. *The Works of William Makepeace Thackeray.* Vol. 28. New York: Charles Scribner's Sons, 1903-04. 195-370.

———. *The Wolves and the Lamb.* 1854. *The Works of William Makepeace Thackeray.* Vol. 28. New York: Charles Scribner's Sons, 1903-04. 371-445.

Tillotson, Geoffrey. *Thackeray the Novelist.* Cambridge: Cambridge UP, 1954.

Wiles, David. *A Short History of Western Performance Space.* Cambridge: Cambridge UP, 2003.

Vanessa Warne (essay date summer 2006)

SOURCE: Warne, Vanessa. "Thackeray Among the Annuals: Morality, Cultural Authority and the Literary Annual Genre." *Victorian Periodicals Review* 39, no. 2 (summer 2006): 158-78.

[*In the following essay, Warne analyzes the relationship between bourgeois literary culture and social ambition in Thackeray's fiction.*]

Published in monthly numbers between October 1848 and December 1850, William Makepeace Thackeray's *The History of Pendennis* depicts the publishing culture of the preceding era. Set in mid-1820s London, the novel's often unflattering portrayal of literary men offended several of Thackeray's contemporaries, notable among them James Forster and John Douglas Cook.[1] Thackeray defended himself and his novel in a January 1850 letter to the *Morning Chronicle*. In it, he explains, "I hope that a comic writer, because he describes an author as improvident, and another as a parasite, may not only be guiltless of a desire to vilify his profession, but may really have its honour at heart."[2] As recent criticism on the novel has noted, in addition to being improvident and parasitical, authors in *Pendennis* are portrayed—perhaps most damningly of all—as paid labourers.[3] Employed by profit-oriented publishers and obliged to write for a paying public, Thackeray's men of letters are involved in fundamentally commercial endeavours and are obliged to "work and pay like their neighbours."[4]

Arthur Pendennis is no exception. Short on money, he takes advantage of a rivalry between two publishers, Bacon and Bungay. Former partners, these men compete in various genres: "no sooner does one bring out a book of travels, or poems, a magazine or periodical, quarterly, or monthly, or weekly, or annual, but the rival is in the field with something similar."[5] Pendennis becomes a regular contributor to Bungay's weekly, the *Pall Mall Gazette,* and eventually manoeuvres Bacon and Bungay into a bidding war over his first novel. He begins his career more modestly, however, by making pseudonymous contributions to a literary annual published by Bacon. Typical of the genre, the *Spring Annual* is:

> a beautiful gilt volume . . . edited by Lady Violet Lebas, and numbering amongst its contributors not only the most eminent, but the most fashionable poets of our time. . . . The book was daintily illustrated with pictures of reigning beauties, or other prints of a tender and voluptuous character; and, as these plates were prepared long beforehand, requiring much time in engraving, it was the eminent poets who had to write for the plates, and not the painters who illustrated the poems.[6]

Pendennis writes **"The Church Porch,"** a poem for an engraving, and also contributes a ballad written at an earlier date. Initially elated by Bacon's decision to accept and pay for these pieces, the young writer discovers a downside to publishing-house rivalries when the *Spring Annual* is reviewed in the *Pall Mall Gazette*. Unaware of Pendennis's involvement with the annual, Bungay's reviewer "cruelly mauled"[7] the book, showing "no more mercy than a bull would have on a parterre."[8] More than simply a lesson for an unseasoned author, this episode allows Thackeray to characterize literary annuals as objects of both critical disdain and commercial exchange: having "cut up the volume to his heart's content," the reviewer "sold it to a bookstall, and purchased a pint of brandy with the proceeds."[9]

Thackeray's depiction of the *Spring Annual* is drawn from personal experience. Like Pendennis, Thackeray contributed to literary annuals, publishing three poems and two short stories in *The Keepsake* and *Fisher's Drawing-Room Scrapbook*.[10] However, unlike his fictional hero, Thackeray began contributing to annuals well into his career, starting with **"The Anglers"** in 1847. The poem, like the vast majority of annual poetry, was written to accompany an engraving; other contributions, such as **"Lucy's Birthday,"** appeared in annuals but were not composed for them. Thackeray also wrote three reviews of literary annuals for *Fraser's Magazine* and the *Times,* specifically **"A Word on the Annuals"** (*Fraser's Magazine,* December 1837), **"The Annuals"** (*The Times,* 2 November 1838) and **"Our Annual Execution"** (*Fraser's Magazine,* January 1839), together with several reviews that make passing reference to annuals, notably **"A Second Lecture on the Fine Arts, By Michael Angelo Titmarsh, Esquire"** (*Fraser's Magazine,* June 1839), **"About a Christmas Book"** (*Fraser's Magazine,* December 1845) and **"A Grumble about the Christmas Books"** (*Fraser's Magazine,* January 1847).[11] These reviews consistently characterize annuals as aesthetic and moral failures and attempt to put an end to their popularity and commercial success. Merciless critic turned contributor, Thackeray expresses perspectives on the literary annual genre that are both complex and revealing.[12] This essay examines Thackeray's objections to annuals and demonstrates the ways in which these objections were informed both by a perceived rivalry between literary annuals and periodicals and by a related desire to control the cultural appetites of middle-class consumers.

MIDDLE-CLASS AMBITION AND THE NOVELS

An important feature of early Victorian print culture, the typical annual is an elaborately bound book pairing poetry and prose with engravings of portraits and landscapes. Published in November and December, annuals were designed for gift giving and were particularly popular with middle-class women, a group to whom they were marketed heavily. Rudolph Ackermann published the first English annual, the *Forget Me Not,* in 1823. In 1826, nine different annuals were in circulation; by 1830, the number had risen to 43. Despite its early success, however, the genre was relatively short lived: by 1850, only 11 titles remained and by 1860 the publication of literary annuals had virtually ended.[13]

What almost all critics and commentators who look back on the rise and decline of annuals have in common is an awareness of the genre's association with aristocratic culture and of the appeal that this association held for middle-class readers. Featuring portraits of lords and ladies, as well as poems by them, many annuals celebrated aristocrats, their lifestyles and their values. Writing in 1855, Richard Madden reflected on the genre's popularity:

> These luxuries of literature were got up especially for the entertainment of ladies and gentlemen of fashionable circles, but not exclusively for the elite of English society. The tastes of belles and beaux of the boudoir of all grades aspiring to distinctions were to be catered for.[14]

Striking a similar note, Edward Bulwer-Lytton attributed the popularity of annuals to middle-class interest in aristocratic culture:

> In proportion as the aristocracy had become social, and fashion allowed the members of the more mediocre classes a hope to outstep the boundaries of fortune, and be quasi-aristocrats themselves, people eagerly sought for representations of the manners which they aspired to imitate, and the circles to which is was not impossible to belong.[15]

Twentieth-century critics have made similar links between annuals and the middle-class ambition to become "quasi-aristocrats." For instance, Glennis Stephenson associates annuals with "cultural emulation,"[16] while Daniel Riess observes that "the gift books appealed to the bourgeois desire for possessions displaying their owners' refined taste and sophistication."[17]

Thackeray's novels contain numerous portraits of annual readers and their bourgeois desires. As Rowland McMaster, Peter Shillingsburg and others have shown, references to newspapers and magazines are standard, if not definitive, aspects of Thackeray's novel writing.[18] The same can be said of references to annuals. Appearing in the decade following his literary annual reviews, his novels reveal that annuals remained a preoccupation with Thackeray even after the popularity of the genre had begun to decline. In *Pendennis,* Thackeray creates the *Spring Annual,* a fictional title which allows him to depict both a contributor to annuals and a ruthless reviewer of them. References to annuals in *Vanity Fair* and *The Newcomes* are more scarce but manage nonetheless to comment on the motivations of annual-reading audiences.

In *Vanity Fair,* Thackeray makes a brief but revealing reference to annuals. Owned by Becky Sharpe and eventually stolen by her similarly ambitious and avaricious French maid, a collection of gilt-edged annuals make an appearance at a climactic point in the narrative. When Rawdon discovers Becky entertaining Lord Steyne, Mademoiselle Fifine decides to leave and to take Becky's books with her:

> The game, in her opinion, was over in that little domestic establishment. Fifine went off in a cab, as we have known more exalted persons of her nation to do under similar circumstances: but, more provident or lucky than these, she secured not only her own property, but some of her mistress's (if indeed that lady could be said to have any property at all)—and not only carried off the trinkets before alluded to, and some favorite dresses on which she had long kept her eye, but four richly gilt Louis Quatorze candlesticks, six gilt Albums, Keepsakes and Books of Beauty, a gold enamelled snuff-box which had once belonged to Madame du Barri, and the sweetest little inkstand and mother-of-pearl blotting-book, which Becky used when she composed her charming little pink notes, had vanished from the premises in Curzon Street together with Mademoiselle Fifine, and all the silver laid on the table for the little *festin* which Rawdon interrupted.[19]

Material expressions of Becky's appetite for wealth and social status, the items Fifine steals are showy and decorative. Like the "enamelled" snuffbox and "gilt" candlesticks, the "six gilt Albums, Keepsakes and Books of Beauty" are identified by association as conspicuous luxury items, superficially attractive but lacking in genuine value. By grouping the books with a snuff-box "which had once belonged to Madame du Barri," Thackeray also links annuals with Becky's social ambition and aristocratic aspirations. Of course, in light of Rawdon and Becky's strained finances, it is highly likely that these books, like Becky's jewels, are ill-gotten gifts from Lord Steyne. It is also worth noting that their new owner is not unlike their former one: Fifine shares Becky's taste for showy but insubstantial luxury goods and has a less than spotless character. Although a very small part of the novel, the episode adds depth to Thackeray's portrayal of an earlier era and connects annuals with both social climbing and sexual impropriety.

Like *Vanity Fair, The Newcomes* also aligns annuals with socially ambitious and acquisitive women. When Rosey Mackenzie visits the Newcomes, she talks with Ethel Newcome about an assortment of annuals. Rosey, who examines the "'Books of Beauty,' 'Flowers of Loveliness,' and so forth," "thought the prints very sweet and pretty; she thought the poetry very pretty and sweet."[20] Thackeray, who had reviewed the same titles for *Fraser's Magazine* in 1837, uses the scene to reveal Rosey's vapidity. When asked to choose between two poems, Rosey fails to express a preference: "Which did she like best, Mr Niminy's 'Lines to a Bunch of Violets,' or Miss Piminy's 'Stanzas to a Wreath of Roses'? Miss Mackenzie was quite puzzled to say which of these masterpieces she preferred; she found them alike so pretty."[21] In addition to being an obvious satire on the aesthetics of annuals, this exchange offers insight into the social function of these books. Viewing annuals, Rosey is provided with an opportunity to demonstrate her conversational skills, cultural knowledge and aesthetic judgment. When she asks her mother to choose for her, Mrs. Mackenzie, also known as "The Cam-paigner," decides to recoup the opportunity on which her daughter fails to capitalize: "'How, my darling love, can I pretend to know?' mamma says. 'I have been a soldier's wife, battling about the world. I have not had your advantages. I had no drawing-masters, nor music-master, as you have. You, dearest child, must instruct me in these things.'"[22] Mrs. Mackenzie's statement sig-nals a shift in her family's cultural status and portrays her daughter as someone with a cultural education wor-thy of the *nouveau riches* Newcomes. When she suc-ceeds in marrying Rosey to Clive, Mrs. Mackenzie translates cultural capital into an elevation in economic status. Although brief, this drawing-room exchange of-fers insight into the extent to which the reading of an-nuals was a social activity, an activity which played a role in the formation, clarification, and performance of social arrangements informed and structured by cultural forms of power. Moreover, by depicting middle-class women like Rosey as ignorant and indiscriminate con-sumers of annuals, Thackeray justifies his own detailed and sustained criticism of annuals as a necessary peda-gogical intervention. Last but not least, Thackeray's representation of annuals in **The Newcomes** associates the possession and consumption of these books with forms of class ambition embodied by Mrs. Mackenzie and figured as morally suspect.

PUBLISHING PRACTICES AND STEEL PLATES

While some annual readers were, like Becky Sharpe, motivated by a fascination with the aristocracy and by a desire for self-display, others purchased annuals to sat-isfy appetites for visual art. It is, in fact, difficult to overestimate the role of annuals in the cultural lives of early Victorian middle-class art lovers. John Seed has argued that "in all sorts of ways, art was a constituent of middle-class private life by the middle of the nine-teenth century—as a topic of conversation, a passion for accumulation, an object of fantasy, a speculative in-vestment, a cultural marker."[23] However, as Francis Haskell notes, the material possession of original works of art remained the domain of the upper classes: "[t]he opportunity to see original pictures . . . was relatively limited, and the overwhelming mass of the population— even that part of the population specifically concerned with art—had to be content with reproductions and the written word."[24] The publishers of literary annuals re-sponded to these circumstances, offering audiences an opportunity to view reproductions of privately owned and otherwise inaccessible works of art. They also pro-vided the middle class with an affordable, but nonethe-less refined, means of owning, collecting and displaying art. Implicitly encouraging the adoption of the aesthetic values of the aristocracy, annuals allowed the middle classes to develop and accumulate a kind of cultural wealth that, though it could not alter their lack of eco-nomic power, could perhaps compensate them for it.

Middle-class art lovers also invested in *catalogues rai-sonnés* and in periodicals. The success of books such as William Hazlitt's *Sketches of the Principal Picture Gal-leries in England* (1824) and the advent of specialized art periodicals, among them the *Art-Journal* (1838-1912) and *Arnold's Magazine of the Fine Arts* (1831-1834), demonstrate the growth in interest in art and art criticism, as does the inclusion of reviews of art exhibi-tions in non-specialist periodicals such as the *Examiner,* the *Times,* and *The National Standard* (a weekly literary magazine which Thackeray owned and edited from May 1833 to February 1834).[25] Thackeray, who reviewed art exhibitions for the *Morning Chronicle, Fraser's Maga-zine* and the *Pictorial Times,* played an important role in the development of art journalism and in the democ-ratization of so-called high art.[26] Not unlike his essays on art, prominent among them **"Strictures for Pic-tures"** and **"On Men and Pictures,"** Thackeray's re-views of literary annuals are a form of art criticism, a point made elsewhere by Judith Fisher and Helene Rob-erts. Writing about reproductions, Thackeray not only brought together two of the most important sources of art for the middle classes, the written word and the en-graving, but also advised middle-class readers about the consumption and evaluation of a form of art which they could and did collect.

In reviews of annuals, Thackeray pays particular atten-tion to methods of reproduction, commenting at length on the annuals' reliance on steel-plate engraving and on the impact of this technology on middle-class taste. In an 1838 *Times* review, Thackeray argues that annuals have increased the availability of the works of estab-lished and legitimate artists but have also made avail-able "the worst drawings of the worst daubers."[27] He goes so far as to blame annuals and their indiscriminate use of steel plates for ruining the already poor taste of the English public:

> We can (thanks to the wondrous perfection of steel engraving) issue out thousands of beautiful pictures where only tens could be printed before; it is as easy to multiply Reynoldses or Wilkies as to take off a thou-sand of the worst drawings of the worst daubers, and the consequence is, that with all these facilities the public has acquired such a taste for art as is far worse than regular barbarism.[28]

Thackeray's comments are a timely engagement with the nature of art in an age of mechanical reproduction. Advancements in steel-plate engraving had enabled the large-scale production of high-quality, affordable prints and had consequently changed the early Victorian art world.[29] These advancements played a particularly key role in the development and proliferation of the literary annual. The reproduction of privately owned paintings and the widespread circulation of engravings to middle-class consumers are, in fact, definitive features of the genre. Pairing paternalistic comments about public taste with criticism of engraving technology, Thackeray's response to the sale and circulation of affordable prints was not an unusual one. As Francis Klingender has shown, "The process was often regarded with contempt, perhaps because of the very fact that it enabled reproductions of pictures and works of art to be circulated cheaply to rich and poor alike."[30] Thackeray, responding both to what is circulated and to whom, sympathizes with the public's desire for pictures but expresses concerns about standards of taste and cultural guidance.

Thackeray also laments the negative influence of this technology on artists and engravers working for the literary annual industry. In an 1839 review, tellingly titled **"Our Annual Execution,"** Thackeray describes portraits contained in the *Tableaux of the Affections* as:

> bad figures, badly painted and drawn, standing in the midst of bad landscapes; the whole engraved in that mean, weak, conventional manner which engravers have nowadays—in which there is no force, breadth, texture, nor feeling of drawing; but only the paltry smoothness and effect which are the result of purely mechanical skill, and which a hundred workhouse-boys or tailor's apprentices would learn equally well—better than a man of genius would do.[31]

Thackeray's discussion of the "purely mechanical skill" of the engraver is noteworthy. Aligned with "workhouse-boys or tailor's apprentices" and with the machinery that reproduces their work, the once-artistic engravers are, in Thackeray's opinion, tainted by new technology. Artists fare no better. As Thackeray explains, "It seems to us that a painter who remains long at this work must ruin his eye, his hand, and his taste."[32] In addition to these degradations, the originality and honesty of artists are lessened by exposure to this technology. In a discussion of *Finden's Tableaux* for 1839, Thackeray notes that "'The Minstrel of Provence' is very curiously like a head by an English painter, Mr. F. Stone, and one might, by carrying the inquiry further, detect still further plagiarisms, were they worth the pains of detection."[33]

In the same review, Thackeray connects artistic plagiarism with steel plates and with the reuse of these plates by publishers. Because steel plates are highly durable, publishers could, and did, recycle them and use the same engraving in different publications. According to Thackeray, this practice encouraged plagiarism. Adding ephemerality and similitude to his growing list of aesthetic objections to annual art, he explains:

> painters may indulge in copying foreign artists without fear of detection or censure; for the prints of ancient annuals, numbered with the dead (so complete is the forgetfulness of the public, and so fleeting the reputation of these works of art), appear years afterwards, resuscitated, in works with a different binding and title, and have, with many, all the air of novelty.[34]

In an earlier review in which Thackeray comments on the reuse of plates, he targets John Fisher, the publisher of several annuals, including *Fisher's Drawing-Room Scrapbook*:

> The unwary public, who purchase Mr. Fisher's publications, will be astonished, if they knew but the secret, with the number of repetitions, and the ingenuity with which one plate is made to figure, now in the *Scrap-Book,* now in the *Views of Syria,* and now in the *Christian Keepsake.* Heaven knows how many more periodicals are issued from the same establishment, and how many different titles are given to each individual print![35]

The exposure of Mr. Fisher's practices identifies annuals as a poor investment for art lovers: their artistic content has been seen before in other books or, in the case of plagiarized images, in paintings. Portraying the recycling of prints as "secret" and embarrassing, Thackeray derides the cultural legitimacy of annuals and links annuals with both compromised aesthetics and compromised ethics. This reaction to the reuse of plates can perhaps be understood as one manifestation of widespread cultural interest in the originality of works of art. Responding to the early nineteenth century's culture of mass reproduction, Thackeray assigns engraved images what both Walter Benjamin and John Berger describe as the "aura" of originality, a characteristic possessed by paintings but not possessed by copies of them.[36] Lamenting the reprinting of prints, Thackeray shifts the cultural fetishization of originality away from the painting or sketch, tying it instead to the original printing run of an engraving.

It is also worth noting that Thackeray's exclamation "Heaven knows how many more periodicals are issued from the same establishment, and how many different titles are given to each individual print!"[37] identifies annuals with unrestrained activity and suggests that the publishing practices of this industry are not only deceptive but promiscuous.[38] Ten years later, in 1847, Thackeray complains again about Fisher and the recycling of steel plates. In **"A Grumble About the Christmas Books,"** he notes:

> Old critical hands, in taking up Mr. Fisher's book, recognize old friends with new titles among the prints— old pictures with wonderful subjects marvelously gathered together from all quarters. Pictorially, The Drawing-room Scrap-book is a sea-pie, made up of scraps that have been served at many tables before.[39]

The fact that Thackeray published his poem **"The Anglers"** in the very same issue of the *Drawing-Room Scrapbook* did not prevent him from linking these books with promiscuity. Portraying annuals as indiscriminate, unrestricted, and composed, like sea-pies, of diverse things, he repeatedly identifies the genre as a poor investment and a poor influence on taste. A precursor to Thackeray's depiction of an annual that gets traded in for brandy in **Pendennis,** the book-as-pie metaphor undercuts the high-class aura of the genre. Deflating the association of annuals with the aristocracy, marking them instead as emblematic of frugal middle-class domesticity, this image discourages purchasers motivated primarily by class interest and ambition and may, perhaps, have tempered even the most ardent appetite for art.

ART AND INDECENCY

Thackeray, who devoted a significant portion of his reviews to issues of reproduction, to the printing, reprinting, and copying of images, reserved his most virulent comments for the subject matter of annual art. Paying particular attention to the visual representation of women, his reviews protest the idealization of female bodies in annuals and, in doing so, anticipate late twentieth-century responses to these books.[40] In a representative passage appearing in *Fraser's,* he lamented the unnatural character of women's portraits in *The Keepsake*:

> There is not one of these beauties, with her great eyes, and slim waist, that looks as if it had been painted from a human figure. It is but a slovenly, ricketty, wooden imitation of it, tricked out in some tawdry feathers and frippery, and no more like a real woman than the verses which accompany the plate are like real poetry.[41]

Not unlike publishers who try to pass off old plates as new ones, these artists counterfeit women, misrepresenting artificial ones as real. In his *Times* review, Thackeray proposes that portraits like these were "drawn with the mind, as it were, and not with the eye, and are, in consequence, merely conventional women, with those long eyelashes and tapering boneless fingers, which women luckily do not possess."[42] In a particularly poetic passage from *Fraser's,* he describes idealized female bodies as monstrous:

> Oh Medora, Yuleika, Juana, Juanita, Juanette, and Company!—oh ye of the taper fingers and six-inch eyes! shut those great fringes of eyelashes, close those silly coral slits of mouths. Avaunt, ye spider-waisted monsters! who have flesh, but no bones, silly bodies, but no souls. Oh ye, O young artists! who were made for better things than to paint such senseless gimcracks, and make fribble furniture for tawdry drawing-room tables, look at Nature and blush![43]

More than monstrous, these women demonstrate the link between idealization and sexualization: Thackeray's unmistakably vaginal image of "coral slits of mouths" and his suggestive descriptions of bodies without souls characterize annual art not only as unnatural but also as erotic, if not pornographic.

Interspersed between comments on plagiarism and secret reprintings, Thackeray's discussion of the representation of women reveals a preoccupation with the mo-

rality or, more accurately, the immorality of literary annuals. Connected by a strong moral component, his arguments about the corrupt artistic and publishing practices of the genre and his discussion of its portrayal of women both combine ethics with aesthetics. Judith Fisher identifies a preference for mediocrity as a defining characteristic of Thackeray's art criticism, and Helene Roberts argues that the ability to move audiences was what Thackeray valued most. When it comes to literary annuals, however, morality is the criterion for assessment which Thackeray privileges and prefers. Morality is, for instance, central to his discussion of Letitia Elizabeth Landon's *Flowers of Loveliness* (1838). Thackeray comments on a number of engravings from this volume but he focuses on K. Meadows's "The Pansies." Describing the image, he calls one of the female figures portrayed by Meadows:

> the fat, indecency in "The Pansies" whose shoulders are exposed as shoulders never ought to be, and drawn as shoulders never were. Another fat creature, in equal dishabille, embraces Fatima, No. 1; a third, archly smiling, dances away, holding in her hand a flower—there is no bone or muscle in that coarse bare bosom, those unnatural naked arms, and fat dumpy fingers. The idea of the picture is coarse, mean, and sensual—the execution of it no better.[44]

Readers of this review who had already purchased *The Flowers of Loveliness* may have been surprised by how much the female figures Meadows portrays differ from Thackeray's hyperbolic characterization of them as fat, arch, and undressed. As the highlighting of "exposed" shoulders, "dishabille," a "coarse bare bosom" and "naked arms" makes clear, the image's moral failings are Thackeray's focus; he makes only passing mention of its "execution." In a similar attack on two paintings by Alfred Edward Chalon reproduced in *The Book of Beauty* for 1838, Thackeray explains, "the former is a caricature of a woman, and the other—it is difficult to speak of the other—such a piece of voluptuous loveliness is dangerous to look at or describe."[45]

When Thackeray comments on the morality of annual art, he makes a distinction between art and the kinds of erotic images he labels "caricatures" or "pieces of voluptuous loveliness." Recent scholarship on aesthetics and pornography can shed light on the nature and operation of this distinction. Allison Pease has argued that the representation of sexual acts is not a prerequisite of pornography; pornography is instead about the elicitation of sexual desire.[46] Audience reaction is thus key to the classification of an image or text as obscene or indecent. Chastising artists for arousing audiences (not to mention reviewers), Thackeray appears to be working with similar ideas about the distinction between art and erotic images. He asks,

> Who sets them to this wretched work?—to paint these eternal fancy portraits, of ladies in voluptuous attitudes

and various stages of dishabille, to awaken the dormant sensibilities of misses in their teens, or tickle the worn-out palates of elderly rakes and roués?[47]

Awakening "dormant sensibilities," "tickling" more experienced "palates," the engravings contained in the annuals are sexually stimulating and thus "dangerous to look at" for men and women alike. Thackeray's characterization of the indecency of annuals is also shaped by the class status of viewers. Attending to the socially and historically contingent nature of definitions of pornography, Lisa Sigel observes that:

> in the nineteenth century, the application of labels such as pornography, obscenity and indecency hinged upon access. It was presumed that certain people could look at representations with limited emotional, social and legal consequences while others could not. Objects became indecent through the act of viewing or reading.[48]

Sigel goes on to note that "High art that could be viewed in museums by the bourgeois became pornographic when reproduced and sold on the streets to the poor."[49] In the case of literary annuals, the images under scrutiny are produced by reputable printers and sold in stores to middle-class consumers. Despite these differences, the readers Thackeray describes in his reviews fail to view images with appropriately limited emotions:

> "How sweet!" says miss, examining some voluptuous Inez, or some loving Haidee, and sighing for an opportunity to imitate her. "How rich!" says the gloating old bachelor, who has his bed-room hung round with them, or the dandy young shopman, who can afford to purchase two or three of the most undressed; and the one dreams of opera-girls and French milliners, and the other, of the "splendid women" that he has seen in Mr. Yate's last new piece at the Adelphi.[50]

In this passage, Thackeray portrays annuals and the prints they contain as debased, middle-class mockeries of the upper-class art gallery. He makes a similar equation when he follows a description of the contents of *The Keepsake* with the sarcastic remark: "this is the *catalogue raisonné* of the Keepsake gallery for the present year."[51] Significantly, Thackeray ties the middle-class art collection to sexual rather than cultural forms of pleasure. Motivated by a desire for women, not art, the old bachelor decorates his bedroom with images from the annuals, while the shopman, in more pressed circumstances, chooses to purchase only "the most undressed."[52] Heightening the already significant eroticism of the passage, Thackeray has the men dream about sexually available women, one about opera singers, the other about actresses. The young female viewer has a different but no less worrisome response. Inspired by the sexual appeal of other women, she responds by desiring an opportunity to be desired. Sighing, gloating, and dreaming, the middle-class art consumers Thackeray imagines are moved by the images contained in annuals but are not moved in acceptable ways.

Here and elsewhere, Thackeray conflates, or, at the very least, contaminates, an interest in art with an interest in sex, transforming the middle-class consumer who desires art into someone is search of sexual titillation rather than cultural edification. A supplement to his more strictly aesthetic critique, commentary on the immorality of annuals makes his opposition to the genre two-pronged. Linking annuals, art criticism, and sex, Thackeray attempts to shape and control both the morality and the art education of middle-class readers and, in doing so, demonstrates the proximity of culture and morality that characterized the early Victorian era. Commenting on the changing relationship between economic capital and cultural authority in the late 1700s and early 1800s, Leonore Davidoff and Catherine Hall argue that "Middle-class farmers, manufacturers, merchants and professionals in this period, critical of many aspects of aristocratic privilege and power, sought to translate their increasing economic weight into a moral and cultural authority."[53] Blurring sexual and cultural appetites, Thackeray uses his reviews of annuals to undermine the moral and cultural credibility of a genre, a genre which specialized in representing the aristocracy to the middle class. Not unlike images of sea-pies, the eroticisation of annuals was a deterrent intended to discourage middle-class consumers and to reform, if not put an end to, a genre.

Thackeray's opposition to annuals was expressed in moral and aesthetic terms, but was it founded in moral and aesthetic concerns? The virulence of his attacks suggests that the sentiments he expresses were sincere, but was the disgust he articulated his primary motivation or did it instead mask a different set of concerns, concerns which were not articulated in his reviews but are made manifest by his decision to contribute to a genre he claimed to detest? In what follows I propose that Thackeray's opposition to the annual genre was a manifestation of the competitive character of the early Victorian literary marketplace and, as such, had more to do with the rivalry for readers than with either morality or aesthetics.

ANNUALS VERSUS PERIODICALS

Thackeray's negative assessment of annuals anticipates and reflects a larger cultural shift in the values and self-conceptions of the middle class. By the middle decades of the Victorian period, annuals, closely identified with the early Victorian middle class's desire to view and own art, had become, for a new generation of readers, an unpleasant reminder of a period marked by dependence on the upper class for cultural knowledge and direction. Although the popularity of literary annuals was short-lived, links between the annuals, cultural appetite and class status make the dismissal of this genre as a passing fancy problematic. Reflecting connections between status and taste, cultural knowledge and power, art and morality, Thackeray's commentary on annuals offers insight into numerous facets of nineteenth-century print culture, not least among them the complex and fluid relationship between middle-class consumers, the book publishing industry, and the Victorian periodical press.

Although demonstrated by his novels, the nature of this relationship is most readily apparent in his reviews. In the 1839 review for *Fraser's Magazine,* Thackeray commented on his role as a critic of the literary annual genre. He writes, "unless we cry out, it is not improbable that the public will begin to fancy . . . that the verses which [annuals] contain are real poetry, and the pictures real painting: and thus painters, poets and public will be spoiled alike."[54] In the same review, Thackeray takes credit for reforming annuals when he notes, "Thank Heaven, the *nudities* have gone out of fashion!—the public has to thank *us* for that."[55] Here and elsewhere, Thackeray portrays himself as a defender of taste and morality, tries to influence the practices of artists and publishers, and attempts to educate reading audiences about art, morality and connections between the two. He also attempts to educate readers about the differences between annuals and magazines. While magazines and newspapers are distinguished from annuals by obvious physical differences, by different prices, and by less frequent periodic publication, art is something they have in common. Annuals contain engravings, periodicals contain articles, but both offer the middle classes access to art and seek to educate these same classes about art. Thackeray, an art critic and annual reviewer writing for numerous magazines and newspapers, was in a unique position to recognize this fact. When he directs the middle-class gaze away from immodestly bare shoulders and from affordable reproductions of aristocratically-owned art, Thackeray also directs readers away from literary annuals towards periodicals. Using periodical reviews to police the annual genre, he reveals his perception of annuals as rivals to newspapers and magazines, portrays the press as a reliable and effective source of art criticism, and identifies newspapers and magazines as morally and culturally trustworthy alternatives to annuals.

Thackeray's esteem for the periodical press and the periodical reviewer is given particularly memorable expression in an 1839 article for *Fraser's Magazine.* In it, Thackeray digresses from a discussion of the Spring art exhibitions to comment on the impact of annuals on painters:

> Woe to the painter who falls into the hand of Mr. Charles Heath! (I speak, of course, not of Mr. Heath personally, but in a Pickwickian sense—of Mr. Heath the Annual-monger). He ruins the young artist, sucks his brains out, emasculates his genius so as to make it fit company for the purchasers of Annuals! Take, for instance, that unfortunate young man, Mr. Corbould,

> who gave great promise two years since, painted a pretty picture last year, and now—he has been in the hands of the Annual-mongers, and has left well-nigh all his vigour behind him. . . . Away, Mr. Corbould! away while it is yet time, out of the hands of these sickly, heartless Annual-sirens! And ten years hence, when you have painted a good, vigorous, healthy picture, bestow the tear of gratitude upon Titmarsh, who tore you from the lap of your crimson-silk-and-gilt-edged Armida.[56]

Using the characteristically hyperbolic voice of his alter ego Michael Angelo Titmarsh, Thackeray humorously transforms art criticism into romance narrative. The literary annual genre is a siren, the critic a chivalrous hero, while the artist is an emasculated victim, having left "all his vigour behind him" and opted for the luxurious lap of the feminized and demonized annuals. Uniting many of Thackeray's bugbears—sexual desire, the deplorability of public taste, and the commercialization of art—this romance anticipates a happy ending for Mr. Corbould but fails to foresee, let alone explain, the reversal that would occur "ten years hence" when Thackeray, the critic, was himself seduced by "sickly, heartless Annual-sirens."[57] As noted above, Thackeray's contributions to annuals began in the same year as the publication of his final literary annual review and coincided with the publication of *Vanity Fair* (1847-1848), *The History of Pendennis* (1848-1850), and *The Newcomes* (1853-1855). How are we to understand a change of heart that followed a decade of negative periodical reviews? Moreover, how are we to reconcile his decision to contribute to annuals with the continued criticism of annuals in his novels?

Commenting on these developments, Donald Hawes has argued that Thackeray was swayed by female friends and contributed to annuals for personal rather than professional reasons. According to Hawes, his decision to contribute to annuals was "doubtless due to his friendship with Lady Blessington in the last two or three years of her life and with her two nieces (one of whom, Eileen Power, succeeded her as editress of the *Keepsake* in 1850)."[58] However, Thackeray's correspondence with the Countess of Blessington complicates Hawes's reading of events by demonstrating the inextricability of the personal and the professional. When, for instance, Thackeray wrote to Blessington in September 1848, he sent her a story that he described in his opening line as "a little sketch wh. I hope will be suitable for the pages of the Keepsake."[59] After some chatter about a recent trip to Brighton, Thackeray gets down to business:

> But now the real and important part of this note— *There will be a place vacant in the Post Office soon* that of Assistant Secretary at present held by Mr. James Campbell. What a place for a man of letters! I think if Lord Clanricarde would give it to me I would satisfy my employers, and that my profession would be pleased

by hearing of the appointment on one of us. I wonder might I write to him, or is there any kind person who would advocate my cause?[60]

The contribution to the *Keepsake* may have been prompted by friendship, but it is difficult to overlook the fact that it arrives with a request for Blessington to aid Thackeray in securing a desirable government position and that its discussion is a preamble to the "real and important part of this note." Thackeray's subscription offers additional evidence of the inextricability of the personal and the professional: pairing affection with obligation, he signs the letter, "Always dear Lady Blessington your very much obliged W M Thackeray."[61]

This exchange suggests that Thackeray's contributions to annuals did not result from a change of heart about the genre but from a desire for financial security.[62] Written in the weeks preceding his portrayal of Pendennis's pecuniary dealings with a fictional annual editor, this letter offers evidence of the practical, and perhaps even tactical, nature of Thackeray's relations with the annual genre. Whereas Hawes sought an explanation for the inconsistencies in Thackeray's dealings with annuals in his relationships with literary women, Kathryn Ledbetter and Terence Hoagwood have focused on the professional concerns that shaped Thackeray's relationships with annuals and the women who edited them. Describing the "agenda" of his reviews as one that "opposes the appearance of women in the literary profession,"[63] they argue that "regular reviews of annuals in the periodicals suggests that literary annuals were too popular to ignore. Since men such as Thackeray could not ignore the annuals, they often satirized them, degrading the genre as silly and, of course, female."[64] They also propose that Thackeray's opposition to annuals was linked to professional rivalries: "as a member of the new group of middle-class writers filling the pages of literary periodicals, Thackeray and other reviewers were fighting in a competitive war for readers."[65]

Both his correspondence and his decision to contribute to annuals support the claim that the incongruous aboutface that characterizes Thackeray's relationship to the annuals can be attributed to the fight for readers and, more narrowly, to financial motivations. His opposition to the style and sensuality of annuals may have been genuine; when viewed in relation to his decision to contribute to annuals, it seems more likely, however, that the artistic quality and the eroticism of annual art provided Thackeray with useful fodder for, as well as a justification of, his attack on annuals, an attack which served the larger goal of directing middle-class consumers away from annuals and towards newspapers and magazines. His objections to the immorality and indecency of annuals were undeniably virulent but, even if genuine, they were easily forgotten. Thackeray's willingness to write both for and against the annuals indicates that what lay behind his efforts to control the cultural appetites of his readers, ostensibly his concern for middle-class morality and taste, was in reality the competition over readers that existed between authors and between the genres with which they were allied.

A manifestation of the widespread trade in culture which he both commented on and participated in, the evolution of Thackeray's relationship to annuals is consistent with the fundamentally commercial character of the literary culture of the early Victorian period. When paid to write reviews, Thackeray did so; when his rising reputation made him a desirable contributor to annuals, he made the most of a new field of opportunity. If the annual happened to be edited by an influential and well-connected friend, so much the better. His negative reviews of annuals did not prevent editors of these books from accepting his work, nor did his appearance in annuals prevent him from portraying the genre negatively in his novels. Pragmatic and adaptable, Thackeray is like other successful literary players of his day, moving between genres, taking work where they could get it, and, in doing so, managing not only to influence the cultural and moral development of the middle class but also to "work and pay like their neighbours."[66]

Notes

1. For a more detailed discussion of Forster's and Cook's responses to *Pendennis,* see Mark Cronin, "Henry Gowan, William Makepeace Thackeray, and 'The Dignity of Literature Controversy,'" *Dickens Quarterly* 16 (1999): 104-115.

2. William Makepeace Thackeray, *The Letters of William Makepeace Thackeray,* ed. Gordon Ray (Cambridge, MA: Harvard University Press, 1945), 2: 635.

3. For recent criticism on *Pendennis,* see Richard Pearson's chapter "Mediahood and Manhood in *Pendennis*" *W. M. Thackeray and the Mediated Text: Writing for Periodicals in the Mid-Nineteenth Century* (Burlington, VT: Ashgate, 2000); Peter Shillingsburg, *Pegasus in Harness: Victorian Publishing and W. M. Thackeray* (Charlottesville: University Press of Virginia, 1992); and Mark Cronin, "The Rake, The Writer, and The Stranger: Textual Relations between *Pendennis* and *David Copperfield,*" *Dickens Studies Annual* 24 (1996): 215-240.

4. William Makepeace Thackeray, *The History of Pendennis* (New York: Scribner's, 1917), 408.

5. Ibid., 366.

6. Ibid., 359-60.

7. Ibid., 406.

8. Ibid.

9. Ibid., 407.

10. In *An Index to the Annuals 1820-1850: The Authors* (Worcester: Andrew Boyle, 1967), Andrew Boyle lists four contributions by Thackeray to *The Keepsake*: the short stories "An Interesting Event" (1849) and "Voltigeur" (1851), and the poems "The Pen and the Album" (1853) and "Lucy's Birthday" (1854). He further notes the contribution of one poem, "The Anglers," to *Fisher's Drawing Room Scrapbook* in 1847.

11. For more information on the attribution of these articles to Thackeray, see Donald Hawes, "Thackeray and the Annuals," *Ariel* 7 (1976): 3-31.

12. Briefly combining reviewing with contributing, Thackeray's final article on annuals discusses the *Scrapbook* for 1847, the annual in which "The Anglers" appears. Despite this fact, Thackeray's review is a negative one.

13. These statistics were compiled by A. Bose and appear on page 38 of "The Verse of the English 'Annuals,'" *Review of English Studies* 4 (1953): 38-51. For information on the start and end dates of individual annuals, see Bose's source: Frederick Faxon's *Literary Annuals and Gift-books: A Bibliography* (Pinner: Private Libraries, 1973).

14. Richard Robert Madden, ed., *The Literary Life and Correspondence of the Countess of Blessington,* (New York: Harper, 1855), 2:227.

15. Edward Bulwer-Lytton, *England and the English,* (London: R. Bentley, 1834), 1:2.

16. Glennis Stephenson, *Letitia Landon: The Woman Behind L. E. L* (New York: Manchester University Press, 1995), 135.

17. Riess, Daniel, "Letitia Landon and the Dawn of English Post-Romanticism," *SEL [Studies in English Literature]* 36 (1996): 819.

18. See Rowland McMaster, *Thackeray's Cultural Frame of Reference* (Montreal: McGill-Queen's University Press, 1991) and Shillingsburg, *Pegasus in Harness.*

19. William Makepeace Thackeray, *Vanity Fair,* ed. Peter Shillingsburg (New York: Garland, 1989), 490.

20. William Makepeace Thackeray, *The Newcomes,* ed. David Pascoe (London: Penguin, 1996), 248.

21. Ibid.

22. Ibid.

23. John Seed, "'Commerce and the Liberal Arts': The Political Economy of Art in Manchester, 1775-1860," in *The Culture of Capital: Art, Power and the Nineteenth-Century Middle Class,* ed. Janet Wolff and John Seed (Manchester: Manchester University Press, 1988), 65.

24. Francis Haskell, *Rediscoveries on Art: Taste, Fashion and Collecting in England and France* (Oxford: Phaidon, 1976), 166.

25. For general information on art criticism in Victorian periodicals, see Helene E. Roberts, "Art Reviewing in Early Nineteenth-Century Art Periodicals," *Victorian Periodicals Review* 19 (1973): 9-20. For information on Thackeray's involvement with the *National Standard,* see Pearson. For analysis of Thackeray's art criticism, see Helene E. Roberts, "'The Sentiment of Reality': Thackeray's Art Criticism," *Studies in the Novel* 13 (1981): 21-39; Edgar F. Harden, *Thackeray the Writer: From Journalism to Vanity Fair* (New York: St. Martin's, 1998); Judith L. Fisher, "The Aesthetics of the Mediocre: Thackeray and the Visual Arts," *Victorian Studies* 26 (1982): 65-82; and Hawes. In his article, Hawes concurs with Thackeray about the failings of annuals, explaining that Thackeray is "virtually alone in his just and witty dispensation of praise and blame" (23). Hawes also refers to annuals as "trash and trivia" (24) and explains that "it would be pleasing to claim that Thackeray helped to destroy the popularity of the Annuals" (27). Unfortunately, this perspective prevents Hawes from commenting critically on the cultural significance of this genre and also limits his analysis of Thackeray's reviews.

26. For information on the democratization of art, see Linda Dowling, *The Vulgarization of Art: The Victorians and Aesthetic Democracy* (Charlottesville: University Press of Virginia, 1996).

27. William Makepeace Thackeray, "The Annuals" *The Times,* 2 November 1838, 5.

28. Ibid.

29. For general information on steel-plate engraving, see David Alexander, *Painters and Engravers: The Reproductive Print* (New Haven: Yale University Press, 1980). For a detailed discussion of the relationship between steel-plate engraving and the annual industry, see Kathryn Ledbetter, "'The Copper and Steel Manufactory' of Charles Heath," *Victorian Review* 28 (2002): 21-30.

30. Francis Klingender, *Art and the Industrial Revolution* (London: Evelyn, Adams and Mackay, 1968), 67.

31. William Makepeace Thackeray, "Our Annual Execution," *Fraser's Magazine,* January 1839, 59.

32. Thackeray, "The Annuals," 5.

33. Ibid.

34. Ibid.

35. William Makepeace Thackeray, "A Word on the Annuals," *Fraser's Magazine,* December 1837, 762.

36. See Walter Benjamin, *Illuminations,* trans. Harry Zohn (New York: Harcourt, 1968) and John Berger, *Ways of Seeing* (London: Penguin, 1972).

37. Ibid.

38. It is worth noting that Thackeray uses the word "periodicals" in reference to literary annuals in this passage, something he also does in a passage from *Pendennis* quoted above. Annuals do not possess the traits of ephemerality and affordability normally associated with the output of the periodical press. Thackeray's use of the term reminds us that what annuals, magazines, and newspapers have in common is the periodic nature of their publication.

39. William Makepeace Thackeray, "A Grumble about the Christmas Books," *Fraser's Magazine,* January 1847, 123.

40. A number of twentieth-century critics have commented on the gender politics of annuals. For example, Peter Manning, in "Wordsworth in the *Keepsake, 1829,*" in *Literature in the Market Place: Nineteenth-Century British Publishing and Reading Practices,* ed. John Jordan and Robert Patten (Cambridge: Cambridge University Press, 1995), characterizes "the essence of the annual" as "the construction of a single image of the feminine under the guise of variety and discrimination" (63). Glennis Stephenson strikes a similar note when she suggests that "the annuals played a central role in the construction and consolidation of a female domestic ideal" (144).

41. Thackeray, "A Word on the Annuals," 761.

42. Thackeray, "The Annuals," 5.

43. Thackeray, "Our Annual Execution," 67.

44. Thackeray, "A Word on the Annuals," 761.

45. Ibid., 763.

46. Alison Pease, *Modernism, Mass Culture, and the Aesthetics of Obscenity* (Cambridge: Cambridge University Press, 2000).

47. Ibid., 758.

48. Lisa Sigel, *Governing Pleasures: Pornography and Social Change in England, 1815-1914* (New Brunswick, NJ: Rutgers University Press, 2002), 4.

49. Ibid., 157.

50. Thackeray, "A Word on the Annuals," 758.

51. Thackeray, "Our Annual Execution," 61.

52. When he describes annual art displayed on walls, Thackeray is referring to the practice of selling prints from annuals separately, as off-prints that could be displayed without damaging the books. These prints could not, apparently, be similarly excused from damaging the morality of consumers.

53. Leonore Davidoff and Catherine Hall, *Family Fortunes: Men and Women in the English Middle Class 1780-1850* (London: Hutchinson, 1987), 30.

54. Thackeray, "Our Annual Execution," 58.

55. Ibid., 67.

56. William Makepeace Thackeray, "A Second Lecture on the Fine Arts, by Michael Angelo Titmarsh, Esq.," *Fraser's Magazine,* June 1839, 748-49.

57. For a different treatment of this passage, see Harden (Chapter Two).

58. Hawes, 29. I am indebted to Kathryn Ledbetter for pointing out that Hawes's identification of the editor of the 1850 *Keepsake* as Eileen Power is belied by the volume's Preface, which is signed with the initials "M.A.P.," identifying the editor as Marguerite Power.

59. Thackeray, *Letters* [*The Letters of William Makepeace Thackeray*], 2: 426.

60. Ibid.

61. Ibid.

62. In subsequent letters to Blessington, Thackeray described himself as "anxious to get employment" (2: 427) and continued to discuss the Post Office position. Thackeray's efforts to secure the position were unsuccessful.

63. Terence Hoagwood and Kathryn Ledbetter, "*Coloured Shadows*": *Contexts in Publishing, Printing, and Reading Nineteenth-Century British Women Writers* (New York: Palgrave, 2005), 80.

64. Ibid., 81.

65. Ibid.

66. Thackeray, *Pendennis* [*The History of Pendennis*], 408.

Sarah Rose Cole (essay date September 2006)

SOURCE: Cole, Sarah Rose. "The Aristocrat in the Mirror: Male Vanity and Bourgeois Desire in William Makepeace Thackeray's *Vanity Fair.*" *Nineteenth-Century Literature* 61, no. 2 (September 2006): 137-70.

[*In the following essay, Cole examines themes of masculinity and social mobility in the novel.*]

"It may be consoling to the middle classes," William Makepeace Thackeray ironically proclaims in his review of William Jesse's *Life of George Brummell* (1844), "to think that the great Brummell, the conqueror of all the aristocratic dandies of his day, nay, the model of dandyhood for all time, was one of them, of the lower order. . . . Let men who aspire to the genteel, then, never be discouraged."[1] In taking the apparently dissident figure of the dandy Brummell as a symbol of "men who aspire to the genteel," Thackeray confronts his middle-class readers with the uncomfortable notion that Brummell's outrageous artifice is only a more successful version of their own performance of gentility. The upstart Brummell, whose triumph depends on his relationship to "the aristocratic dandies," is at once a unique person—the "model of dandyhood for all time"—and an embodiment of a common middle-class fantasy of aristocratic distinction. Although Ellen Moers, in her classic history *The Dandy,* opposes the "anti-bourgeois virtues" of the dandy to "the heavy earnestness of the Victorian pose,"[2] Thackeray makes the paradoxical suggestion that Beau Brummell is really a typical Victorian bourgeois.

In his 1844 essay on Brummell, as in his later full-length satires **The Book of Snobs** (1846-47) and **Vanity Fair** (1847-48), Thackeray mischievously suggests that the Victorian bourgeoisie was driven not by utilitarian calculation or domestic ideology, but by the desire for aristocratic status—a desire that turns ordinary middle-class men into lesser versions of Beau Brummell. Not only are Thackeray's middle-class male characters obsessed with aristocratic concepts of gentility, but they are also, like the dandy Brummell, flagrantly vain. From **Vanity Fair**'s George Osborne and Jos Sedley to the eponymous hero of **Pendennis,** by way of the jewelry-obsessed Bob Browns and Mr. Specs who populate his journalistic sketches, Thackeray continually depicts middle-class men who are mesmerized by their own physical appearance. The result is a composite picture that bears little resemblance to Victorian ideals, or to later stereotypes, of Victorian middle-class manhood. Rather than striving for professional success, moral earnestness, or marital bliss, Thackeray's bourgeois men are generally in pursuit of an admiring gaze—often a male gaze—that will validate their own fantasies of a Brummell-like physical perfection and social ascent. Why does Thackeray mark his bourgeois social-climbers with a vanity that seems to work against conventions of middle-class masculinity? In pursuit of this question, I make two moves in this essay: first, I explore recent historiographical models that cast new light on Thackeray's vision of nineteenth-century class relations, and then I investigate how and why Thackeray figures the bourgeois desire for gentility as a set of homoerotic and autoerotic desires for the male body. Focusing on **Vanity Fair** and on a constellation of journalistic sketches, I argue that Thackeray continually invokes the figure of the mirror-gazing man—an image fraught with implicit gender reversal—in order to shock his readers into acknowledging the artificial and performative nature of their own class personae.

For Thackeray male vanity signals the process of fantasy and fakery that he calls "Snobbism." It is well known that Thackeray coined the word "snob" (or, at least, he changed "snob" from an obscure slang term to a word on the tip of every Victorian tongue).[3] Thackeray's concept of "Snobbism," however, needs to be carefully distinguished from the modern sense of the word. For Thackeray and his Victorian readers snobbery was not the arrogance of a secure elite, but rather the showy gentility of an insecure bourgeoisie that wanted to get into the aristocracy. "Snobbishness," as Walter Bagehot defines it in an 1864 essay on Thackeray's works, is "the habit of 'pretending to be higher in the social scale than you really are.'"[4] Because of such imitative and performative practices, the snob—in the world of Thackeray's novels and sketches—is always likely to be staring into the mirror, in the hope of seeing an aristocrat.

* * *

As a writer whose particular province is the social border-zone where snobbery flourishes, Thackeray requires us to take a stance on one of the most central, and most perplexing, questions of nineteenth-century British history: the relations between the bourgeoisie and the aristocracy. Pointing to "the extent and prevalence of Lord-olatry" in England, Thackeray insists that "it is impossible, in our condition of society, not to be sometimes a Snob" (**Book of Snobs,** pp. 14, 15). Recent developments in historical scholarship allow us to see this sweeping assertion as a polemical response to a social system in which the bourgeoisie and the aristocracy were indeed inseparably linked. Moving beyond the long-standing debate that sought to determine whether the hegemonic class of nineteenth-century Britain was the bourgeoisie or the aristocracy, historians have increasingly focused on the myriad ways in which the landed and commercial elites interacted and cooperated. Whether in Amanda Vickery's study of women's experience in provincial "genteel" society or in P. J. Cain and A. G. Hopkins's account of landed magnates and City merchant-bankers fusing in a "gentlemanly capitalism" that powered the British empire, we find a new picture of collaboration, rather than competition, between the middle classes and the owners of landed estates.[5] Vickery, who explicitly seeks to counter Leonore Davidoff and Catherine Hall's account of a rising bourgeoisie distinguished by its "separate spheres" ideology, rewrites the history of the early nineteenth century by focusing on the "enmeshed relationship" between "minor gentry, professional and mercantile families" in provincial society (*Gentleman's Daughter,*

p. 17).[6] Complementing Vickery's study of local ties, Cain and Hopkins focus instead on the national and imperial level, where a vigorously capitalist aristocracy joined forces with "the merchant princes and bankers of the City" to create an imperial economic system in which "profitable enterprise" was "compatible with gentility" (*British Imperialism,* pp. 46, 49).

In taking "gentility" as a key to cross-class relations, these recent scholarly works bear some resemblance to Thackeray's own critique of his social-climbing contemporaries. Yet Thackeray's interpretation of gentility—as an aristocratic value that turns the middle classes into abject snobs—is closer to the older historical model of bourgeois "gentrification" put forward from the 1960s through the 1980s by historians such as Perry Anderson, Martin Wiener, and Lawrence Stone and Jeanne C. Fawtier Stone.[7] Representing the most important counternarrative to the modern historical orthodoxy of the rise of the bourgeoisie, the "gentrification" model proposed that the British aristocracy maintained its traditional hegemony by "psychologically coopting those below them into the status hierarchy of gentility" (Stone and Stone, *An Open Elite,* pp. 411, 410), thus preventing the middle class from seizing the social and political power promised by industrial capitalism. In contrast to this narrative of aristocratic domination, however, more recent historians such as Vickery, Cain, and Hopkins confirm Penelope J. Corfield's conclusion that the concept of gentility served above all to "blur divisions among England's élite, divisions that might otherwise have been more rigid: between titled and untitled society; between business and land; between professionals and non-professionals; between town and country; and between the upper class and bourgeoisie."[8]

If the ruling class of nineteenth-century Britain was actually a fusion of landed, commercial, and professional elites, then why did Thackeray—like so many other Victorian writers and modern historians—believe so firmly in the existence of a distinct "middle class" that must either conquer the aristocracy or be conquered? This conundrum can be helpfully rephrased by adopting the key questions that Dror Wahrman poses in *Imagining the Middle Class*: "how, why, and when did the British come to *believe* that they lived in a society centred around a 'middle class'?" (p. 1). Wahrman's answer is that political debates leading up to the 1832 Reform Bill created "the particular historical narrative which depicts the 'middle class' as triumphantly rising on the crest of the tide of social transformation, a narrative which since then has become so familiar" (*Imagining the Middle Class,* p. 17). As Wahrman points out, given the gradual pace of industrialization and "the existence of large and vibrant 'middling' social groups already by the *early* eighteenth century," "there was

nothing inevitable" about the sudden emergence of the "middle class" into social consciousness between around 1820 and 1832 (*Imagining the Middle Class,* pp. 3, 8).

Drawing on Wahrman's insight that the triumph of the middle class was a concept *invented* in the early nineteenth century, rather than a social development that occurred in that era, I would suggest that this narrative of middle-class triumph soon generated its counternarratives of middle-class failure—just as the modern historical orthodoxy of Victorian bourgeois hegemony generated its counternarrative of aristocratic hegemony. Faced with the blurred boundaries between the commercial and the landed classes, an important minority of self-identified "middle-class" writers concluded that the middle class was selling out to the aristocracy. The sophisticated and ironic Thackeray, here, appears surprisingly in the company of the radical industrialist Richard Cobden, who complained in 1863 that "manufacturers and merchants as a rule seem only to desire riches that they may be enabled to prostrate themselves at the feet of feudalism."[9] Closer to Thackeray's distinctive set of concerns is the *Fraser's Magazine* serial "The Age of Veneer" (1850), where the anonymous writer declares: "Society in this country is imitative. . . . Each grade or class strives to hook itself on to its superior; is proud, not of its own self-created virtues, position, or other speciality, but of its resemblance to the nearest aristocratic model within the range of its ken."[10] Though "The Age of Veneer" is best known as the probable inspiration for Charles Dickens's upstart speculator Mr. Veneering in *Our Mutual Friend* (1864-65), the concept of an "imitative" society seems more Thackerayan than Dickensian, using matters of style to capture the paradox of a commercial society clinging to an "aristocratic model."[11]

In the social world of Thackeray's writings, the desire for traditional aristocratic rank reacts in unpredictable ways with the more fluid, commodity-oriented desires typical of capitalist culture. Recent scholarship on *Vanity Fair* has focused mainly on the second type of social desire, especially on the fantasies and fetishes of commodity culture. According to Andrew Miller, "More than any other Victorian novel, Thackeray's book [*Vanity Fair*] imagines the fetishistic reduction of the material environment to commodities, to a world simultaneously brilliant and tedious," one in which characters experience a "dynamic of desire and disenchantment" in their intense relationship to material goods.[12] Joseph Litvak, seeking an alternative to Miller's "way of pathologizing the erotics of the marketplace," argues that Thackeray and his characters do not merely submit to commodity culture, but rather strategically use material objects in pursuit of their desire for "sophistication."[13] Miller's and Litvak's readings have been crucial in showing how Thackeray eroticizes social and economic processes. But by shifting attention to the relation between aristocratic and capitalist culture, we can see something new about social desire in Thackeray's writing: the way in which aristocratic status, one of the most desirable possessions of all, is *not* for sale in *Vanity Fair.*

For Thackeray aristocratic status is not merely a privileged relation to consumption, a position of leisure and sophistication that could potentially be reached by anyone wealthy or savvy enough. Even if, as Thackeray claims in **The Book of Snobs,** only a few generations are needed for a family to rise from the upper middle class into the peerage, this pace is still glacial compared to the instant satisfactions (or lack of satisfactions) offered by consumer culture: "when the City Snob's money has been washed during a generation or so; has been washed into estates, and woods, and castles and town-mansions; it is allowed to pass current as real aristocratic coin" (**Book of Snobs,** p. 37). Rather than placing his hopes in movable goods, the successful bourgeois aspirant to aristocratic rank must buy a landed estate and wait for his son to come out "a full-blown aristocrat" with a gentleman's education (**Book of Snobs,** p. 37). Only in exceptional cases—and then only temporarily—can a real-life George Brummell or a fictional Becky Sharp use their genius for glamour to remake themselves into the equals, or even masters, of their aristocratic models. And after Brummell and Becky each fall into disgrace and flee to the Continent, their one-time patrons, the Prince Regent and Lord Steyne, remain unscathed: socially scandalous, physically repulsive, and utterly secure in their inherited rank.

* * *

In *Vanity Fair* the "great Brummell" appears only in the other characters' fantasies. The middle-class male snobs whom we actually meet are instead comic figures of failed dandyism: the handsome but naive George Osborne, whose vanity prevents him from noticing the contempt of his aristocratic gambling buddies, and the fat, ridiculously overdressed Jos Sedley, who imagines that "he and Brummell were the leading bucks of the day."[14] In the long-standing critical debate over Thackeray's attitudes toward dandyism, little has been made of the fact that his vainest characters are usually middle-class professionals rather than members of an idle aristocracy. Although the concept of the dandy as a middle-class artist who takes on an "aristocratic pose" has long been familiar to scholars of late-Victorian aestheticism, studies of Thackeray and early-Victorian dandyism have tended to focus on the *opposition* between the dandy and the middle-class artist.[15] Beginning with Ellen Moers's and Robin Gilmour's complementary studies of "the dandy" and "the gentleman," scholars have treated Thackeray as an ambivalent defender of Victorian bourgeois values against an aristocratic Regency dandyism

that he secretly admired.[16] Moers's work, in particular, has been lastingly influential in classifying Thackeray as a middle-class "anti-dandiacal" writer, alongside his *Fraser's Magazine* colleagues William Maginn and Thomas Carlyle.[17]

Yet Thackeray's treatment of dandyism differs from that of Maginn and Carlyle in important but usually overlooked ways. Writing in 1830, during the period that Dror Wahrman describes as crucial to the invention of the rising middle class, Maginn does indeed oppose middle-class values to the "vanity" of aristocratic dandies: after criticizing dandies as "vain young foplings" who consider it "a mark of superior breeding . . . to express contempt of the middle classes of society," Maginn then sets the record straight with a long paean to the superior "genius" and "self-denial" of the middle classes.[18] Carlyle, whose references to Maginn's essay in *Sartor Resartus* (1833-34) are well known, continues Maginn's attack on the dandy-aristocrat by inventing the character of "Lord Herringbone," a nobleman whose single-minded vanity reveals the solipsism of an aristocracy that lives as a parasite on the productive classes of society.[19] Unlike these *Fraser's* writings, however, Thackeray's novels and sketches do not use the scandalous image of the mirror-gazing man to criticize a decadent aristocracy or show up the contrasting virtues of the middle class. Instead, Thackeray's target is his own class of middle-class "gentlemen" and their parasitic imitation of the aristocracy.

Among Thackeray's many treatments of male vanity, *Vanity Fair* solicits particular attention, both because it remains Thackeray's best-known work and because of the provocation of the novel's title. What kind of "vanity" does *Vanity Fair* thematize? Is it the traditional moral concern—the emptiness of worldly ambitions—as it was in the "Vanity Fair" chapter of John Bunyan's *Pilgrim's Progress* (1678)? Or is it the everyday modern concern: the question of just how much time someone spends looking in the mirror? The answer to both questions, of course, is "yes." In a novel that moves unpredictably between didacticism and gossip, it is scarcely surprising to find an interplay between the two meanings of "vanity," as Thackeray alternates between delivering sermons on the "vain, wicked, foolish" world (*Vanity Fair,* p. 71) and telling comic stories about the toilettes of second-rate Regency dandies. Here, as so often, Thackeray seems to stand on a crossroads, where *Pilgrim's Progress* meets the celebrity magazine *Vanity Fair,* and where the religious anathema against worldliness turns suddenly into a sophisticated world-weariness. In the novel's conclusion, the narrator directly quotes Ecclesiastes: "Ah! *Vanitas Vanitatum!* Which of us is happy in this world? Which of us has his desire? or, having it, is satisfied?" (*Vanity Fair,* p.

624) But elsewhere, the narrator's commentary on vanity turns from moral preaching to blasé social observation about men who love to look in the mirror:

> We have talked of Joseph Sedley being as vain as a girl—Heaven help us! the girls have only to turn the tables and say of one of their own sex, "She is as vain as a man," and they will have perfect reason. The bearded creatures are quite as eager for praise, quite as finikin over their toilettes, quite as proud of their personal advantages, quite as conscious of their powers of fascination as any coquette in the world.
>
> (*Vanity Fair,* p. 19)

Despite the obvious differences between Thackeray's biblical conclusion and his catty commentary on mirror-gazing men, both passages make a similar claim about the universality of one kind of vanity or another. According to the narrator of *Vanity Fair,* we all suffer the vanity of frustrated or misplaced desire; and all of us, men as well as women, have the vanity of coquettes. But the narrator's claims about universal vanity are undercut, in important and surprising ways, by *Vanity Fair*'s own cast of characters: among the major characters, it is only men who exhibit vanity of the mirror-gazing kind. While the timid Jos and the swashbuckling soldier George are equally addicted to the stereotypically female vice of mirror gazing, the novel's two heroines are both remarkable for their lack of physical vanity. The ambitious Becky Sharp, who cares for her own appearance only as a weapon of social conquest, typically looks in the mirror only to "take a rapid survey of matters in the glass" on the way to a social or sexual seduction (*Vanity Fair,* p. 431). Becky's foil, the self-effacing Amelia Sedley, is similarly uninterested in the mirror, though for different reasons: she transfers her own "pride and vanity" onto her "image of George" as a heroic lover (pp. 229, 228). Although in the quotation above the narrator urges women to "turn the tables" by reversing the stock phrase "vain as a girl," *Vanity Fair* leaves no need for such a female intervention. Thackeray depicts a world in which *no* "coquette in the world" is in fact so vain as a man.

The most obvious provocation offered by male vanity is the transgression of gender boundaries; the very act of coupling the words "male" and "vanity" implies a gender reversal, "turn[ing] the tables" on the stereotype of female vanity. Yet, although Thackeray's comedy often relies on gender reversal, his early writings up through *Vanity Fair* are most preoccupied with a different kind of transgression: the crossing of social class boundaries. In making male vanity central to the comedy of *Vanity Fair,* Thackeray uses the affective shock created by gender transgression in order to dramatize the less immediately provocative problem of class transgression. How could middle-class readers be persuaded that their imitation of the aristocracy negated their own true nature? I would suggest that Thackeray mixed a class

transgression with a gender transgression in order to create the toxic compound of *bourgeois male vanity*: a condition that renders the middle-class snob doubly unnatural. When a middle-class man becomes addicted to mirror gazing, he adopts a vice that is usually attributed to women or to male aristocrats—in other words, to those who are expected to be idle and decorative. At one stroke (or rather, with one loving look in the mirror), the vain bourgeois man crosses the lines of both class and gender.

By linking male vanity to bourgeois social-climbing, Thackeray adapts and reverses a traditional set of representations that associate male vanity with an effeminate aristocracy. Such representations—promoted equally by the post-Regency vogue for dandy fiction and by anti-dandiacal reactions such as those of Carlyle and Maginn—perpetuated a cultural construct that had little to do with actual nineteenth-century aristocratic practices. According to historians such as Linda Colley and Paul Langford, the British aristocracy had already transformed itself into a "service elite" in the late eighteenth century, thus devaluing elegant leisure in favor of a patrician brand of "manliness" based on patriotic duty.[20] Similarly, Michèle Cohen traces the decline of the Restoration ideals of gentlemanly polish and conversational charm, which became associated with "effeminacy" and "foppery"; during the course of the eighteenth century, upper-class men began to identify instead with a mode of blunt taciturnity that was supposed to be peculiarly English, "sincere and manly."[21] Yet the literary image of the idle and decorative aristocrat persisted because, as Eve Kosofsky Sedgwick suggests, it was a powerful ideological construction. Discerning a "feminization of the aristocracy as a whole" in British literature of the eighteenth and nineteenth centuries, Sedgwick finds that "the abstract image of the entire [aristocratic] class . . . came to be seen as ethereal, decorative, and otiose in relation to the vigorous and productive values of the middle class."[22]

Within this general feminization of the aristocracy, I would suggest, male vanity forms a particularly important crux. We might think here of Jane Austen's *Persuasion* (1818), where the contrast between classes is signaled by men's attitudes toward their complexions: the spendthrift Sir Walter Elliot, defined by his "vanity of person and of situation," fusses with face creams, while the rising middle-class naval officers, Admiral Croft and Captain Wentworth, carelessly expose their complexions to sun and wind.[23] Despite intervening changes in actual aristocratic gender modes, such nineteenth-century representations scarcely differ from William Hogarth's classic satire *Marriage A-la-mode* (1743-45), where we see the penniless Lord Squanderfield turning his back disdainfully on his wealthy bourgeois bride in order to gaze at the real object of his narcissistic desire—his own aristocratic figure, which has, ironically, just been sold to the highest bidder.

When Thackeray lectured on Hogarth in *The English Humourists* (published 1853), he singled out *Marriage à-la-mode* for particular praise, but his own satirical use of male vanity reverses the class stereotypes that Hogarth employed.[24] In *Vanity Fair* it is the bourgeois George Osborne and Jos Sedley who become feminized by their uncontrollable vanity, while the hypermasculine aristocrat Rawdon Crawley symbolically sacrifices his own fashionable ornaments to his all-consuming passion for Becky. Rawdon's future moral regeneration is signaled when he offers to sell his "pins, and rings, and watch and chain, and things" for Becky's support, in a bonfire of vanity that frees him to ride off to Waterloo "with a kit as modest as that of a serjeant, and with something like a prayer on his lips for the woman he was leaving" (*Vanity Fair,* p. 260). Rawdon's incongruously business-like inventory—"my driving cloak, lined with sable fur, £50" (p. 260)—transforms the trappings of a Regency rake into the vehicle for the kind of marital commitment and responsibility that, ironically, is lacking in the bourgeois match of George and Amelia. When Thackeray prefigures George's later marital neglect of Amelia through an early incident involving a diamond shirt pin, he signals that George's primary flaw as a husband will not be his philandering (which remains more talk than action), but rather an addictive vanity that works against conventional gender roles. Borrowing money from one of his many male admirers, William Dobbin, George sets out to buy a present for Amelia but instead finds himself "attracted by a handsome shirt-pin in a jeweller's window which he could not resist" (*Vanity Fair,* p. 107). Having placed himself, rather than his fiancée, in the position of decorative object, George ends up giving Amelia no gift other than the chance to observe his own augmented beauty: "He beamed on her from the drawing room door—magnificent—with ambrosial whiskers—like a god . . . and she thought his diamond shirt pin (which she had not known him to wear before,) the prettiest ornament ever seen" (*Vanity Fair,* p. 108).

Not only is the middle-class George implicitly feminized by the vanity that the upper-class Rawdon easily discards, but his combination of vanity and snobbery also puts George in a position of feminine subordination to Rawdon himself. Determined to make his appearance among "gentlemen, and men of the world and fashion" (*Vanity Fair,* p. 177), George allows his middle-class cash to be drained away by Rawdon's suspiciously infallible gambling skills. Drawing on the traditional verbal overlap between gambling and sexual seduction (both kinds of temptation, in nineteenth-century novels, usually result in ruin), Thackeray writes: "Rawdon was making a victim of [George] as he had

done of many before, and as soon as he had used him would fling him off with scorn" (*Vanity Fair,* p. 252). Thus, far from triumphing over an obsolete aristocracy, Thackeray's representative bourgeois snob ends up, like a naive woman, being seduced and abandoned by a male aristocrat.

Thackeray's reversal of the literary stereotypes for male aristocrats and bourgeoisie becomes even more flagrant in his next novel, *Pendennis* (1848-50), where the feminized bourgeois and the masculinized aristocrat take center stage as a Victorian Odd Couple, living together in the Temple. When we first meet the bohemian aristocrat Warrington, he is dressed in a "ragged old shooting jacket" and "drinking beer like a coal-heaver" while teasing his middle-class friend Arthur Pendennis for being a "dandy" and for drinking tea like a woman.[25] Within the terms of the middle-class ideological construction described by Sedgwick, then, Thackeray's first two major novels depict a world turned upside-down. Instead of seeing a "vigorous" middle class supersede a "decorative" aristocracy, we watch effete bourgeois dandies kowtowing to manly aristocrats. In Thackeray's novels, this reversal of bourgeois ideals serves to call into question the effects of the bourgeois pursuit of gentility. But in his sketches and essays, Thackeray sometimes approaches the problem from the other direction, by presenting bourgeois and aristocratic men as he thinks they *should* be. This more prescriptive stance (though one liberally laced with irony) is most visible in his serialized conduct book, **"Mr. Brown's Letters to a Young Man About Town"** (1849). In this essay series, which appeared in *Punch* during the serial run of *Pendennis,* Thackeray implies that effeminacy and male vanity are appropriate for idle aristocrats, while middle-class men who are vain must be condemned as snobs.

In **"Mr. Brown's Letters"** Thackeray takes on a persona aptly described by Robert A. Colby as a "Victorian middle-class Lord Chesterfield," a worldly-wise Londoner writing letters of advice to his lawyer nephew, Bob (*Thackeray's Canvass of Humanity,* p. 277). Addressing not only the shadowy "Bob" but also the presumably middle-class and male reader, Thackeray's conduct book aims to produce an urbane, elegant, but unpretentious and unsnobbish bourgeois style of living, one that will not be dependent on imitation of aristocratic habits. In one of the few scholarly discussions of this work, Colby points out that old Mr. Brown "serves as a corrective" to Major Pendennis: during the simultaneous serial publications of *Pendennis* and **"Mr. Brown's Letters"**, while Major Pendennis was teaching his nephew Arthur to be a social-climbing dandy, Mr. Brown was cautioning his own nephew Bob against "tuft-hunting" and ostentatious dress (*Thackeray's Canvass of Humanity,* p. 306, n. 5). What has not yet been discussed, however, is that **"Mr. Brown's Letters"** actively works to restore the typical bourgeois and aristocratic male gender roles that Thackeray's own novels call into question.

Male vanity is Thackeray's entry point into this project, as the series begins with a letter in which Mr. Brown teaches Bob to stop dressing like a mock-aristocrat: Bob must shave off his fashionable little beard and give up his "sham turquoise buttons," which he wears because he "cannot afford to buy real stones."[26] Though promising to exemplify his teachings "in your [i.e., Bob's] own person" (**"Mr. Brown's Letters,"** p. 115), Mr. Brown in fact pays much more attention to the contrasting "person" of a genuine aristocratic dandy, Lord Hugo, who functions as the feminized object of a masculine bourgeois gaze. Declaring that he has Lord Hugo "perfectly before [his] mind's eye," Mr. Brown commands young Bob to "look at every article" of Lord Hugo's clothing, and emphasizes: "see how absurd it is of you to attempt to imitate him" (p. 115). Conjuring up a scene in which Lord Hugo displays himself in his "private box at the Lyceum," Mr. Brown directs Bob's gaze across the imaginary theater in order to scrutinize every item of Lord Hugo's dress, from his hands "gloved as tightly and delicately as a lady's" to the jewels that "meander down his pink shirt-front" (p. 115). Mr. Brown not only emphasizes the feminine cut and color of the aristocrat's clothes, but he also specifically links this effete elegance to Lord Hugo's idleness. As far as Mr. Brown is concerned, Lord Hugo is nothing but a static spectacle, a well-framed image: "He sits in a splendid side box, or he simpers out of the windows at WHITE's [Club], or you see him grinning out of a cab by the Serpentine—a lovely and costly picture, surrounded by a costly frame" (p. 115). In contrast, middle-class gentlemen like Bob Brown should go to parks and theaters in order to see rather than to be seen. "You and I, my good BOB," says Mr. Brown, "if we want to see a play, do not disdain an order from our friend the Newspaper Editor, or to take a seat in the pit" (p. 115). By writing a theater review, or by sitting inconspicuously below the audience's line of sight, the Browns of this world can not only save money, but also properly position themselves to analyze the show—whether the show is onstage or up in Lord Hugo's private box.

In **"Mr. Brown's Letters to a Young Man About Town"** Thackeray both objectifies the male body and sets strict limits to that process of objectification: in the prescriptive world of Mr. Brown, the aristocratic man solicits the gaze and the bourgeois man does the gazing. The danger, however, is that the bourgeois man will gaze in a covetous and imitative way, like Bob Brown, rather than with the proper sense of difference. The solution—a rhetorical strategy that manages to negotiate between bourgeois pride and class envy, visual pleasure and ironic distance, aristocratic artifice and bourgeois naturalness—is a humorous flight around the idea that class divisions are *natural*. Aristocratic men become a wholly different species, and the bourgeois intellectual gains a scientist's authority in the process of admiring them:

> There is nothing disagreeable to me in the notion of a dandy any more than there is in the idea of a peacock, or a cameleopard, or a prodigious gaudy tulip, or an astonishingly bright brocade. There are all sorts of animals, plants, and stuffs in Nature, from peacocks to tom-tits, and from cloth of gold to corduroy, whereof the variety is assuredly intended by Nature, and certainly adds to the zest of life. Therefore I do not say that LORD HUGO is a useless being, or bestow the least contempt upon him. Nay, it is right gratifying and natural that he should be, and be as he is—handsome and graceful, splendid and perfumed, beautiful—whiskered and empty-headed, a sumptuous dandy and man of fashion.

(**"Mr. Brown's Letters,"** p. 115)

When Mr. Brown describes male vanity as a "natural" trait only for aristocratic peacocks, he implicitly condemns middle-class male vanity as unnatural. Yet Thackeray's advice manual is far from being a straightforward celebration of bourgeois naturalness and manliness. In defending Lord Hugo's dandyism, Mr. Brown also seems to defend his own right to enjoy ogling other men: it is not only the vain aristocrat himself, but also Mr. Brown who finds Lord Hugo's "beautiful" appearance "right gratifying." Throughout his first letter Mr. Brown objectifies and aestheticizes Lord Hugo, in a process that can best be explained by adapting Brian McCuskey's concept of Thackeray's "uses of deviance."[27] Although McCuskey focuses on Thackeray's descriptions of male servants (thus of men socially below, rather than above, the middle-class gentleman), his analysis allows us to see Thackeray's objectification of the male figure as a strategic move, an apparent sexual "deviance" that actually strengthens the social authority of the middle-class narrator. According to McCuskey, Thackeray fetishizes the dressed-up bodies of fancy footmen in order to assign "effeminacy to working-class rather than ruling-class masculinity, keeping the gentleman above suspicion and the servant under surveillance" ("Fetishizing the Flunkey," p. 393). By turning a male servant into "a female object of desire," McCuskey argues, Thackeray's narrators "inflict an ultimately class-based and heterosexist injury on the servant" (p. 393). The same process, I would suggest, occurs when Thackeray's Mr. Brown uses a homoerotic gaze to subordinate Lord Hugo, a man who otherwise stands above him in social rank (and even sits above him in the theater). Although McCuskey's simplified category of "ruling-class masculinity" ignores the tensions between bourgeoisie and aristocrats, I would like to build on his central argument: that Thackeray invokes same-sex desire in an open and purposeful way in order to manage class anxieties. While the major queer readings of Thackeray by Eve Kosofsky Sedgwick and Joseph Litvak treat homosexual desire as something that, in Mc-Cuskey's words, "must necessarily be masked" ("Fetishizing the Flunkey," p. 385), I see Thackeray deliberately invoking, rather than anxiously suppressing, both homoeroticism and homosexual panic in order to dramatize the bourgeois obsession with the aristocracy.[28]

When Thackeray employs the homoerotic gaze as a strategy to place the bourgeois man in a position of power over both servants and aristocrats, he usually does so on behalf of his own narratorial "I." Whether the narrator is named "Mr. Brown" or "William Makepeace Thackeray," it is he who fits McCuskey's description of the "gentleman" who makes a sophisticated use out of apparent deviance. When it comes to the majority of actual middle-class male *characters* in Thackeray's novels and sketches, however, the textual "uses of deviance" turn out to be quite different. The bourgeois snobs who populate Thackeray's fictional world are abjected, rather than empowered, by the homoeroticism and gender reversal that Thackeray associates with cross-class male desire. In *Vanity Fair* and *The Book of Snobs,* middle-class men do just what Bob Brown is being trained not to do: they gaze at aristocrats with a hopeless longing that leads to foolish attempts at visual imitation. Thus, Thackeray's vainest middle-class men, such as *Vanity Fair*'s George and Jos, are also the ones most likely to humiliate themselves by their visual fixation on male aristocrats. When in "the presence of a lord," Jos can "look at nothing else," while the more enterprising George would (as Rawdon scornfully puts it) "go to the deuce to be seen with a Lord" (*Vanity Fair,* pp. 560, 122). These two types of obsession with the male figure—the narcissistic and the homosocial—are repeatedly connected, and equally castigated, in Thackeray's attacks on the "snob." As Joseph Litvak has argued, Thackeray's "snobophobia" often shades into homophobia, since the snob's desire to *be like* an aristocrat threatens to become a desire *for* the aristocrat (*Strange Gourmets,* pp. 56-57). Rather than pointing to a larger, submerged homophobia as the real motive of Thackeray's "snobophobia," however, it is more helpful to see Thackeray attacking snobs for having the *wrong kind* of desire for male aristocrats.[29] Instead of feminizing and objectifying aristocrats, as Mr. Brown does, snobs objectify themselves while granting power to the aristocrats whom they adore and imitate.

In *The Book of Snobs* Thackeray presents the whole relationship between the British middle classes and the nobility as a process that moves inevitably from aristocrat-worship to self-objectification, or (to put it more simply) from snobbery to vanity. In the chapter "The Influence of the Aristocracy on Snobs," Thackeray imagines the Peerage as the fetish-object of Britain's social religion:

> How can we help Snobbishness, with such a prodigious national institution erected for its worship? . . . What man can withstand this prodigious temptation? Inspired by what is called a noble emulation, some people grasp at honours and win them; others, too weak or mean, blindly admire and grovel before those who have gained them.
>
> (***Book of Snobs,*** p. 15)

In some ways, Thackeray's attack on the Peerage is typical of the early, politically radical incarnation of *Punch* magazine. During the 1840s, when *The Snobs of England* (Thackeray's original title for the work) was serialized in *Punch,* the magazine's writers used comedy to expose the "injustice" and "abuse of power and privilege . . . perpetrated by members of what we should now call 'the Establishment': the great landowners, aristocrats, prelates, capitalists, MPs and magistrates."[30] Yet, unlike *Punch*'s leading writer Douglas Jerrold, who focused on the sufferings of the poor and the inhumanity of the powerful, Thackeray concentrated—as he would throughout his literary career—on the ways in which the "Establishment" psychologically corrupts the middle class. Addressing readers who may falsely imagine themselves as "calm moralists" immune to snobbery, Thackeray asks: "of these calm moralists, is there one I wonder whose heart would not throb with pleasure if he could be seen walking arm-in-arm with a couple of Dukes down Pall Mall?" (***Book of Snobs,*** p. 15) No longer calling upon a generalized "we," which presumably embraces a readership of both sexes, Thackeray here moves from his overall picture of the British class system to an individual scenario that is specifically male and homosocial. Rather than addressing female snobs who might, perhaps, fantasize about being seen dancing with a duke at a public ball, Thackeray instead addresses male snobs whose vanity is linked to the "throb" of "pleasure" that comes from an (imagined) association with male aristocrats. Even in this relatively impersonal and disembodied scenario, Thackeray gestures toward the comic focus on male vanity that will become so central to *Vanity Fair.*

In the characterizations of George and Jos, Thackeray develops the message that is implied in *The Book of Snobs*: that the middle-class male snob is unmanned, both by his feminine vanity and by his submissive adoration of male aristocrats. Such a process of unmanning is most immediately apparent in Jos, whose own father dismisses him contemptuously as "vain selfish lazy and effeminate" (*Vanity Fair,* p. 46). But, since readers are equally likely to dismiss Jos in the same terms, he could scarcely be accepted as an object lesson for "men who aspire to the genteel." That, I propose, is why Thackeray doubles the role of the vain bourgeois snob, using Jos for broad comedy and George for more topical satire. By setting up a range of parallels between the flagrantly effeminate Jos and the athletic soldier George—both sons of City merchants, both engaged in imperial service, both vain and snobbish, both ambiguously involved in flirtations with Becky Sharp—Thackeray points to the more subtle feminization and abjection of snobs who appear to fit masculine norms, as George does. As Joseph Litvak observes about **The Book of Snobs,** Thackeray swings "between universalizing and minoritizing paradigms," sometimes treating the entire population of Britain as snobs and sometimes using homophobic imagery to imply that snobs are a perverse, unnatural minority (*Strange Gourmets,* p. 58).[31]

In **Vanity Fair,** I would suggest, Thackeray uses the resources of fiction to mediate between these "universalizing and minoritizing" images of the snob. In a novel about soldiers and their wives, the "stout civilian" Jos stands out as a socially deviant snob, while the *normalcy* of snobbery among the British bourgeoisie is embodied by George, "the champion of his school and his regiment" (**Vanity Fair,** pp. 265, 264). Thus, when Litvak focuses his reading of **Vanity Fair** on Jos, whom he presents as the "protogay scapegoat" for Thackeray's "*snobophobia*" (*Strange Gourmets,* pp. 17, 56), Thackeray's universalizing paradigm of snobbery is lost. Instead, we can use the insights of queer reading and gender studies in order to take seriously Thackeray's claim that "it is impossible, in our condition of society, not to be sometimes a Snob." If we want to understand how Thackeray attacks the norms of British gentility by depicting the majority of middle-class men as subtly unmanned by their snobbery, then we should look more closely at scenes of male vanity involving that paragon of military glamour, Captain George Osborne.

* * *

In **Vanity Fair**'s earliest description of a mirror-gazing George, there is, crucially, someone else looking into his mirror: Becky Sharp. Looking "towards the glass," George "caught Miss Sharp's eye fixed keenly upon him, on which he blushed a little, and Rebecca thought in her heart, '*Ah, mon beau Monsieur,* I think I have *your* gage'—the little artful minx!" (**Vanity Fair,** p. 40). Caught in the act of mirror gazing, George blushes, as the hyperfeminine Amelia has just done. (Earlier in the same scene, when Amelia demurely remains silent at the dinner table, Thackeray tells us that "Miss Amelia only made a smile and a blush" [p. 40]—a coy locution that emphasizes the connection between blushing and being a young "miss.") Despite Thackeray's blasé assurance that men are "quite as proud of their personal advantages . . . as any coquette in the world" (**Vanity Fair,** p. 19), a residual thrill of gender transgression clings to the scene of male vanity. This electric charge of transgression arises from the collision of George and Becky: the man who has eyes only for his own beauty, and the woman with the penetrating gaze, who takes the "gage" of her male object.

The reversal of gender roles becomes even clearer when we realize that in this scene Becky (as well as George)

is looking in the mirror for the first time in the novel. Typically, Becky immediately looks beyond her own reflection in order to "fix" another character's weaknesses, which she will eventually turn to her advantage. George, in contrast, will be continually defined by his failures to see, his inability to look beyond his own inflated self-image in order to understand social realities. Over and over again we find Thackeray ironizing George's point of view with a similar formulation. Becky's romantic involvement with Rawdon is "invisible" to George, who (with unconscious irony) tries to impress Rawdon by warning him against Becky "with a knowing look" (**Vanity Fair,** p. 126). Later, having transferred his snobbish desires to the newly fashionable Mrs. Rawdon Crawley, George becomes "lost in pompous admiration of his own irresistible powers of pleasing," and he does not "perceive" that Becky is flirting with him only in order to arouse the jealousy of General Tufto (**Vanity Fair,** p. 250). After George is disinherited by his father, he greets his father's lawyers with a "swaggering martial air" in order to show his superior gentility, and thus does not "see the sneer of contempt" that dismisses him as a pauper (p. 230).

When Thackeray begins chapter 13 of **Vanity Fair** with an illustration of George looking in the mirror, the most obvious message is that vanity makes George as blind to Amelia's attractions as he is to the nuances of social power. "I fear the gentleman to whom Miss Amelia's letters were addressed was rather an obdurate critic" (**Vanity Fair,** p. 104), Thackeray writes, pointedly starting the sentence in the middle of the mirror in order to suggest whose face George prefers to Amelia's. The cartoon blatantly illustrates George's self-absorption: the word "I" (the first word of the new chapter) is written across the picture. But where is the self that absorbs him? On closer scrutiny, we find that the "I" is written on the mirror itself, where the capital letter seems to be the focal point of George's gaze. In other words, George looks desirously toward an imagined "I," which exists in the mirror—and which, of course, turns out to be the narrator's own "I," in a sentence that makes George an object of speculation.

This cartoon, in fact, allegorizes George's vanity rather than merely illustrating it. A dependent narcissist rather than a self-sufficient egoist, George is in love with an "I" that appears only in the mirror and that is ultimately constructed by the gaze of others. In order to understand this interplay between vanity and insecurity, we might recall how George is willing to "go to the deuce to be seen with a Lord." The elusiveness of George's "I" in the mirror cartoon, I would suggest, points to his struggle to be become a "man of fashion" in the fullest sense: not just a fashionably dressed man, but one accepted in aristocratic circles. According to the *Oxford English Dictionary,* a man or woman "of fashion" is someone who "moves in upper-class society, and conforms to its rules with regard to dress, expenditure, and habits." When George longs for approval from "men of the world and fashion," he wants to be recognized not only as an urban sophisticate, but also as someone qualified to take his place among aristocrats. Thus, his apparently happy self-objectification—his concentration on his own remarkable good looks—takes on an anxious, even desperate quality when he solicits the gaze that is supposed to certify his class status.

While George's narcissistic gaze will always be stopped short (literally or figuratively) by the mirror, the sharp gaze of Becky Sharp will later be extended by magnifying devices: a real, though comic, telescope when she spies on Miss Briggs at Brighton; a cartoon spyglass when, in the capital illustration to chapter 64, Becky appears in the costume of Napoleon, gazing across the sea from her place of exile. This cartoon image recalls an earlier scene in which Becky looks out across the Channel, from Brighton, and tells George that she can almost see the other side: "her bright green eyes streamed out, and shot into the night as if they *could* see through it" (*Vanity Fair,* p. 213). The capital illustration of Becky's spyglass pairs off with the capital illustration of George's mirror, in a parallel reversal of the gendered gaze. From his first entrance into *Vanity Fair,* George is caught up in the pervasive pattern of transgendering that allows Becky to figure as the female Napoleon.

The fact that George and Becky appear as paired examples of gender reversal is no coincidence, since these two characters are the most determined social climbers in *Vanity Fair.* In both cases, Thackeray marks the crossing of class borders as unnatural by connecting snobbery (in the Victorian sense of the word) to the more obvious unnaturalness of gender reversal. The penetrating social mastery of the female Napoleon finds its necessary inverse in the effeminate ineffectuality of George's social ambitions.

This presentation of snobbery as gender reversal is all the more effective for its relative subtlety: to casual social observers (including most of the novel's other characters), both George and Becky *look* like model and conventional examples of their respective sexes. Unlike the openly effeminate Jos Sedley, the athletic George is seen as a "hero" by the other middle-class characters: "wherever he went, women and men had admired and envied him" (*Vanity Fair,* p. 264). Unlike Becky's sometime patroness, the stout, domineering spinster Miss Crawley, Becky is a "pretty little wife" who "look[s] the image of youthful innocence and girlish happiness" (pp. 212, 211). Thus, rather than being overtly signaled through physical cross-gendering, George's effeminacy and Becky's masculinity appear only in minute behavioral signals that link gender reversal to inappropriate social ambitions.

Thackeray's double presentation of George—making him at once an example of conventional, heterosexual masculinity and an example of effeminate, homoerotic snobbery—reaches its greatest intensity in the chapters that surround the capital illustration of George looking in the mirror. In the context of the surrounding text, the visual image of George's vanity suggests not just self-infatuation but a perversion of the male gaze away from its proper direction: the body of Amelia. At the end of the previous chapter it is the narrator himself who certifies Amelia's desirability, as he changes from an omniscient storyteller to a specifically male subject whose penetratingly heterosexual gaze contrasts with George's mirror gazing. Teasingly invoking, rather than describing, Amelia's virginal bedroom, the narrator presents himself as an excited voyeur: "I . . . can steal in and out of her chamber like Iachimo,—like Iachimo? No—that's a bad part—I will only act Moonshine and peep harmless into the bed where faith and beauty and innocence lie dreaming" (*Vanity Fair,* p. 103). By casting himself first as the bedroom-invading villain of *Cymbeline* and then as a Peeping Tom, the narrator parades a comically exaggerated sense of sexual guilt.

Like the domestic hauntings analyzed by Sharon Marcus in her discussion of London ghost stories, Thackeray's invasion of Amelia's bedroom registers the anxieties provoked by realist fiction's necessary invasion of privacy.[32] Although the narrator's appearance as a Peeping Tom is a self-ironizing gesture, it nonetheless points to the "contradiction" that Marcus sees between "domestic ideology," which "advocated a privacy that required concealing the home from view," and "realism, which paradoxically attempted to put private life on display *as private*" (*Apartment Stories,* p. 127). Thackeray's performance of sexual guilt, however, also serves a more immediate strategic purpose: by presenting Amelia's body as the irresistibly compelling object of his own masculine gaze, the narrator makes George's indifference to Amelia look like a failure of natural heterosexual desire.

In the pages of the novel that follow, Thackeray repeatedly dramatizes George's failure to desire Amelia, while leaving the meanings of this failure surprisingly ambiguous. In George's own account, he is bored by Amelia only because her lifelong loyalty makes no appeal to his masculine taste for conquest, a taste that he likens to gambling: "She's faultless, I know she is. But you see there's no fun in winning a thing unless you play for it" (*Vanity Fair,* p. 106). But Thackeray undermines George's conventionally masculine self-explanation by implying that George's desires are not actually directed toward women who require seduction, but toward male figures: his own image and the upper-class dandies whom he snobbishly pursues. George's eagerness to make a social "engagement" with Rawdon's gambling circle stands in contrast to his apathy toward his marital engagement—explicitly so, when he assures Rawdon that he is "not on duty" to Amelia (p. 123). But, while the all-male world of gambling proves more alluring to George than do Amelia's domestic attractions, the homosocial relations of gambling actually serve to feminize rather than masculinize George. Thackeray takes the apparently conventional metaphor of gambling as sexual conquest and turns it against George, when he reveals that gambling, for George, is usually a losing proposition—and, specifically, a proposition of losing to aristocratic men, who "get what money they like out of him," as Rawdon succinctly puts it (*Vanity Fair,* p. 122). Although George is such an "obdurate critic" of Amelia (p. 104), he turns out to be all too easy when it comes to the "young men of the first fashion" (p. 123) whom he meets by gambling with Rawdon.

One of George's aristocratic exploiters, twice named in *Vanity Fair* but never actually seen (pp. 111, 122), is the Honorable Mr. Deuceace, a name that serves as a hint about the erotic charge of cross-class gambling. When Thackeray revised his first successful serial, *The Yellowplush Correspondence* (1838) for book publication in *Comic Tales and Sketches* (1841) he gave the adventures of Deuceace (as narrated by the valet Yellowplush) a new collective title: **"The Amours of Mr. Deuceace."**[33] Ambiguously referring to Deuceace's gambling exploits as well as his pursuit of rich women, the title of **"Amours"** suits a work that—even more openly than *Vanity Fair*—presents the relationship between aristocratic gamblers and their feminized bourgeois victims in humorously homoerotic terms. When Deuceace, the impoverished son of an earl, sends an invitation to the rich bourgeois Dawkins, the recipient practically swoons with snobbish excitement, as the servant Yellowplush records in his own idiosyncratic spelling: "I saw young Dawkins blush with delite as he red the note; he . . . roat in a hand quite trembling with pleasyer" (**"Amours of Mr. Deuceace,"** p. 58). In the meantime, Deuceace competes with another upper-class gambler who is also "after" Dawkins; each refuses to "give him up" to the other (**"Amours of Mr. Deuceace,"** pp. 60-61).

It seems, then, to be an axiom of Thackeray's works that middle-class men are incapable of winning at cards against aristocratic men. Given the blatant improbability of such a social law, we might well ask what larger satirical point Thackeray seeks to convey in his stylized picture of "green" middle-class men (*Vanity Fair,* p. 122) and card-sharping toffs. The answer lies in Thackeray's need to come up with a concrete sign of the imbalance in cultural power between aristocrats and their middle-class idolaters. Given the British bourgeoisie's adeptness at imitating "the nearest aristocratic model within the range of its ken" ("Age of Veneer," p. 240), a snob such as George is unlikely to be caught out in overt social gaffes. Thus, even while Rawdon plots to

"have him" (in several senses of the word) at a card game, he acknowledges that George's looks and manners are indistinguishable from those of upper-class men: "You wouldn't see any difference" is Rawdon's answer to Miss Crawley's anxious question of whether George is "presentable" (*Vanity Fair,* p. 122). The "difference" that cannot be seen, however, becomes visible in scenarios of gambling, where the middle-class man unconsciously begs to be cheated by the aristocrats he admires. Thus, it is gambling that marks the minute yet all-important difference between aristocratic "men of fashion" and bourgeois dandies who are merely *fashionable.*

Within the sphere of Britain's ruling classes, this invisible difference between aristocrats and upper bourgeoisie marks the divide between male "bodies that matter" and those that do not.[34] In representations of aristocratic vanity, the aristocrat's pride in his appearance is linked to the fact that his body is both literally and symbolically important. Like Hogarth's Lord Squanderfield, the aristocrat is the physical carrier of the family "blood" (which he can sell only by selling *himself* in a cross-class marriage); like Thackeray's Lord Hugo, he symbolically represents the idleness of his class by showing off his impractically labor-intensive elegance. In contrast, George Osborne's handsome appearance is emptied of such social significance; his body demonstrates neither genteel idleness nor noble blood. Yet George is not only able to pass (however temporarily) as an aristocrat, but he also fulfills nineteenth-century ideals of aristocratic male beauty more than does any other character in *Vanity Fair.* In making this representational choice, Thackeray eschews the more obvious comic potential of the bourgeois would-be dandy, such as naive Bob Brown, with his fake turquoise buttons, or fat Jos Sedley, who *"would* have his clothes made too tight" (*Vanity Fair,* p. 19). Thackeray even, improbably, shows George returning from army service in the West Indies with his "pale interesting" complexion intact (p. 40), looking like an upper-class Guardsman who has never served outside of England, while Jos and Dobbin are left with "yellow" faces from tropical diseases (pp. 16, 40). By granting George an eerie immunity to the physical traces of imperial service, Thackeray allows him to match the Byronic pattern—pale, dark-haired, and graceful, with "an air at once swaggering and melancholy, languid and fierce" (*Vanity Fair,* p. 180)—that would continue to mark the aristocratic seducer in Victorian novels both high and low (from Dickens's *David Copperfield* [1849-50] and Anthony Trollope's *The Way We Live Now* [1874-75] to Ellen Wood's best-selling melodrama *East Lynne* [1861]). This is the same physical type that, in Thackeray's comic sketches, helps to sum up aristocratic stock-characters such as the Honorable Deuceace in *The Yellowplush Correspondence* and

Lord Hugo in **"Mr. Brown's Letters to a Young Man About Town."** Why, then, does the "cockney-dandy" George Osborne get to look like this (*Vanity Fair,* p. 618)?

In George's deceptively aristocratic figure, Thackeray embodies the desires and delusions that fuel bourgeois snobbery. George, with his flagrant vanity, fetishizes his own body because it seems to certify that he belongs by right among the "young men of the first fashion." But George's figure also becomes the vehicle for the vicarious vanity of his even more snobbish father, whose main hope in life is to see "the name of Osborne ennobled in the person of his son" (*Vanity Fair,* p. 179). Although his ambitions for George sometimes take a concrete and feasible form (for example, that George should marry Rhoda Swartz and use her fabulous wealth to buy his way into Parliament), Mr. Osborne also dwells obsessively on his son's good looks:

> What pride he had in his boy! He was the handsomest child ever seen. Everybody said he was like a nobleman's son. A royal princess had remarked him, and kissed him, and asked his name in Kew Gardens. What city-man could show such another? . . . he remembered George . . . on the day when he was presented to the Prince Regent at the levee, when all Saint James's couldn't produce a finer young fellow.
>
> (*Vanity Fair,* p. 203)

In this passage of free indirect discourse, Mr. Osborne's language suggests that George is more valuable as an object of display—a prize possession to "show" or "produce"—than as a son whose own actions might someday ennoble the family. This further linkage between snobbery and gender reversal—the fact that Mr. Osborne objectifies his handsome son rather than his plain daughters—should scarcely be surprising, in light of the Thackerayan strategies that I have been analyzing. What I would like to emphasize, however, is the element of irrational fantasy involved in the Osbornes' family dynamics: like George himself, Mr. Osborne seems to believe that the family is *already* ennobled in George's "person," simply because of how that "person" looks.

In *Vanity Fair* Thackeray suggests that middle-class Britons not only desire to become aristocratic, but they also live in the fixed illusion that they are *already* aristocratic, that their own pursuit of fashion and gentility places them within the charmed circle of the social elite. By portraying middle-class illusions as key agents of aristocratic power, Thackeray dramatizes a process strikingly close to the Gramscian concept of hegemony: the dominance of a ruling class that, in Terry Eagleton's words, establishes "leadership in social life by diffusing [its] own 'world view' throughout the fabric of society as a whole, thus equating [its] own interests with the interests of society at large."[35]

Whether the aristocracy actually succeeded in imposing its "world view" on the rest of nineteenth-century British society remains a matter of historical debate; but Thackeray was not the only contemporary observer to take the fusion of the British aristocracy and bourgeoisie as a sign that the middle classes had willingly surrendered. Alexis de Tocqueville, seeking to understand the overthrow of the French nobility by comparison with the tenacity of the British landed elite, concluded that the British social system kept the bourgeoisie tame by nourishing their fantasies of social ascent:

> The reason why the English middle class, far from being actively hostile to the aristocracy, inclined to fraternize with it was not so much that the aristocracy kept open house as that its barriers were ill defined; not so much that entrance into it was easy as that you never knew when you had got there. The result was that everyone who hovered on its outskirts nursed the agreeable illusion that he belonged to it and joined forces with it in the hope of acquiring prestige or some practical advantage under its aegis.[36]

Thackeray's novels and sketches, more than any other Victorian oeuvre, focus on dramatizing precisely these processes: the hopes, stratagems, and illusions of those hovering about the "ill defined" barriers of the British aristocracy, hoping to get in. Above all, Thackeray takes aim at the "agreeable illusion" of bourgeois participation in aristocratic gentility, an illusion that he seeks to uncover and destroy in his readers as well as in his characters. In his treatment of bourgeois male vanity, Thackeray not only portrays snobbery as a perverting and feminizing force, but he also captures the vertiginous experience of a class system that seems to him at once rigid and open. Never knowing when they "had got there," Thackeray's bourgeois social climbers stand in the anteroom of aristocratic power, practicing their genteel airs before the mirror while they wait to be invited inside.

Notes

1. William Makepeace Thackeray, rev. of *The Life of George Brummell, Esq.,* by William Jesse (May 1844), rpt. in Thackeray, *Contributions to the "Morning Chronicle,"* ed. Gordon N. Ray (Urbana: Univ. of Illinois Press, 1955), p. 32. In using a mock-inspirational tone to address social climbers, Thackeray in his Brummell essay prefigures the *Vanity Fair* chapter "How to Live Well on Nothing a Year," where Becky Sharp's "pursuit of fashion under difficulties" parodies George Lillie Craik's popular self-help story *The Pursuit of Learning under Difficulties* (1830) (see Robert A. Colby, *Thackeray's Canvass of Humanity: An Author and His Public* [Columbus: Ohio State Univ. Press, 1979], pp. 246, 270).

2. See Moers, *The Dandy: Brummell to Beerbohm* (New York: Viking Press, 1960), p. 14.

3. See John Sutherland, "Appendix: The Etymology of Snob," in William Makepeace Thackeray, *The Book of Snobs,* ed. Sutherland (St. Lucia: Univ. of Queensland Press, 1978), pp. 235-37 (further references to *The Book of Snobs* are to this edition and appear in the text). See also the entry for "Snob" in the *Oxford English Dictionary.*

4. [Walter Bagehot], "Sterne and Thackeray," *National Review,* 18 (April 1864); rpt. in *Thackeray: The Critical Heritage,* ed. Geoffrey Tillotson and Donald Hawes (London: Routledge, 1966), p. 354.

5. See Vickery, *The Gentleman's Daughter: Women's Lives in Georgian England* (New Haven: Yale Univ. Press, 1998), p. 1; and Cain and Hopkins, *British Imperialism, 1688-2000,* 2d ed. (London: Pearson Education, 2002), p. 3. Other major recent histories have, at the very least, downplayed the concept of a power struggle between unitary bourgeois and aristocratic classes. For example, in the New Oxford History of Britain, K. Theodore Hoppen emphasizes the diversity of attitudes and identities within the Victorian middle classes: "Entrepreneurs and professional men, shopkeepers and clerks, were not all stamped out of identical moulds. They were not all thirsting for revenge upon the aristocracy and the agricultural interest" (Hoppen, *The Mid-Victorian Generation, 1846-1886* [Oxford: Clarendon Press, 1998], p. 32).

6. See Leonore Davidoff and Catherine Hall, *Family Fortunes: Men and Women of the English Middle Class, 1780-1850* (Chicago: Univ. of Chicago Press, 1987). For Vickery's rejection of the "separate spheres" model, see *The Gentleman's Daughter,* pp. 1-11; for her more explicit critique of Davidoff and Hall, see Amanda Vickery, "Golden Age to Separate Spheres? A Review of the Categories and Chronology of English Women's History," *Historical Journal,* 36 (1993), 383-414.

7. See Perry Anderson, "Origins of the Present Crisis" (1964) and "The Figures of Descent" (1987), rpt. in Anderson, *English Questions* (London and New York: Verso, 1992), pp. 15-47 and 121-92; Wiener, *English Culture and the Decline of the Industrial Spirit, 1850-1980* (Cambridge: Cambridge Univ. Press, 1981); Stone and Stone, *An Open Elite? England, 1540-1880* (Oxford: Clarendon Press, 1984). In taking the term "gentrification" to sum up this historical model, I am following the usage of Dror Wahrman (see Wahrman, *Imagining the Middle Class: The Political Representation of Class in Britain, c. 1780-1840* [Cambridge: Cambridge Univ. Press, 1995], p. 5).

8. Corfield, "The Rivals: Landed and Other Gentlemen," in *Land and Society in Britain, 1700-1914: Essays in Honour of F. M. L. Thompson,* ed. Neg-

ley Harte and Roland Quinault (Manchester: Manchester Univ. Press, 1996), p. 23.

9. Richard Cobden, quoted in Anderson, "The Figures of Descent," p. 126.

10. [Anon.], "The Age of Veneer," *Fraser's Magazine,* 42 (1850), 240.

11. On the Dickens connection, see Owen Knowles, "Veneering and the Age of Veneer: A Source and Background for *Our Mutual Friend,*" *The Dickensian,* 81 (1985), 88-96.

12. Miller, *Novels behind Glass: Commodity Culture and Victorian Narrative* (Cambridge: Cambridge Univ. Press, 1995), pp. 9, 22.

13. Litvak, *Strange Gourmets: Sophistication, Theory, and the Novel* (Durham, N.C.: Duke Univ. Press, 1997), p. 160, n. 23.

14. William Makepeace Thackeray, *Vanity Fair: A Novel without a Hero,* ed. Peter L. Shillingsburg (New York: Garland Publishing, 1989), p. 18. Further references are to this edition and appear in the text.

15. See Regenia Gagnier, *Idylls of the Marketplace: Oscar Wilde and the Victorian Public* (Stanford: Stanford Univ. Press, 1986), p. 57. Other important discussions of the ambiguous class-identity of the Wildean dandy include Alan Sinfield, *The Wilde Century: Effeminacy, Oscar Wilde and the Queer Moment* (New York: Columbia Univ. Press, 1994), pp. 69-75; and Joseph Bristow, *Effeminate England: Homoerotic Writing after 1885* (New York: Columbia Univ. Press, 1995), pp. 29-42.

16. See Moers, *The Dandy*; and Gilmour, *The Idea of the Gentleman in the Victorian Novel* (London: George Allen and Unwin, 1981). More recently, Claire Nicolay has revised but not discarded this view of Thackeray (see Nicolay, "Delightful Coxcombs to Industrious Men: Fashionable Politics in *Cecil* and *Pendennis,*" *Victorian Literature and Culture,* 30 [2002], 289-304).

17. Moers's pairing of Thackeray and Carlyle as "anti-dandiacals" (see *The Dandy,* pp. 169-92) is adopted, for example, by Gagnier (see *Idylls of the Marketplace,* pp. 70, 76).

18. [Maginn], "Mr. Edward Lytton Bulwer's Novels; and Remarks on Novel-Writing," *Fraser's Magazine,* 1 (1830), 314-15.

19. See Thomas Carlyle, *Sartor Resartus: The Life and Opinions of Herr Teufelsdröckh in Three Books,* ed. Rodger L. Tarr (Berkeley and Los Angeles: Univ. of California Press, 2000), p. 201.

20. See Colley, *Britons: Forging the Nation, 1707-1837* (New Haven: Yale Univ. Press, 1992), pp.

192-93; and Langford, *Public Life and the Prop-ertied Englishman, 1689-1798: The Ford Lectures, Delivered in the University of Oxford, 1990* (Oxford: Clarendon Press, 1991), pp. 569-81.

21. See Cohen, *Fashioning Masculinity: National Identity and Language in the Eighteenth Century* (London and New York: Routledge, 1996), pp. 9, 3.

22. Eve Kosofsky Sedgwick, *Between Men: English Literature and Male Homosocial Desire* (New York: Columbia Univ. Press, 1985), p. 93.

23. Jane Austen, *Persuasion,* in *"Northanger Abbey" and "Persuasion,"* ed. R. W. Chapman, vol. 5 of *The Works of Jane Austen,* 5 vols. (New York: Oxford Univ. Press, 1969), p. 4.

24. After introducing *Marriage A-la-mode* as "the most important and highly wrought of the Hogarth comedies," Thackeray focuses on describing Plate I; among other details, he notes that "my lord is admiring himself in the glass." See William Make-peace Thackeray, *The English Humourists of the Eighteenth Century: A Series of Lectures* (New York: Harper and Brothers, 1853), pp. 190-91.

25. William Makepeace Thackeray, *The History of Pendennis,* ed. Peter L. Shillingsburg, 2 vols. in 1 (New York: Garland Publishing, 1991), I, 286-88. Because critics generally discuss Warrington as an embodiment of Thackeray's anti-dandiacal ideal of the gentleman, they have ignored the odd fact that Warrington's social background is aristocratic rather than bourgeois. It is significant that War-rington's rank is exactly the same as that of the Regency buck Rawdon Crawley, also the younger son of a baronet. Later, in *The Virginians* (1857-59), Thackeray would further emphasize War-rington's aristocratic lineage by revealing him as a direct descendant of Henry Esmond (the true heir of the Viscountcy of Castlewood).

26. William Makepeace Thackeray, "Mr. Brown's Let-ters to a Young Man About Town," *Punch,* 16 (1849), 115.

27. See McCuskey, "Fetishizing the Flunkey: Thack-eray and the Uses of Deviance," *Novel,* 32 (1999), 384-400.

28. The works I refer to here are Litvak, *Strange Gourmets*; and Eve Kosofsky Sedgwick, *Episte-mology of the Closet* (Berkeley and Los Angeles: Univ. of California Press, 1990).

29. Litvak suggests that Thackeray's *"snobophobia"* is a mask for his *"homophobia"* (*Strange Gour-mets,* p. 56); this is the main point of divergence between Litvak's reading and my own, since I see social-class anxieties as more than just a mask for sexual anxieties.

30. Michael Slater, *Douglas Jerrold, 1803-1857* (London: Duckworth, 2002), p. 121.

31. The terms "minoritizing" and "universalizing," here, are adapted from Sedgwick, *Epistemology of the Closet* (see Sedgwick's "Introduction: Axiom-atic," pp. 1-63).

32. See Marcus, *Apartment Stories: City and Home in Nineteenth-Century Paris and London* (Berkeley and Los Angeles: Univ. of California Press, 1999), pp. 116-27.

33. William Makepeace Thackeray, "The Amours of Mr. Deuceace," in his *Comic Tales and Sketches,* Vol. I (London: Hugh Cunningham, 1841). In Thackeray's original *Fraser's Magazine* serial (1838), the first Deuceace story was simply titled "Dimond Cut Dimond" (see "Dimond Cut Di-mond," in *The Yellowplush Correspondence,* rpt. in William Makepeace Thackeray, *"Flore et Zephyr"; "The Yellowplush Correspondence"; "The Tremendous Adventures of Major Gahagan,"* ed. Peter L. Shillingsburg [New York: Garland Publishing, 1991], pp. 27-39). But in *Comic Tales and Sketches,* edited by Thackeray himself under his pen name Michael Angelo Titmarsh, "Dimond Cut Dimond" becomes the first section of "The Amours of Mr. Deuceace," and this title was sub-sequently retained in Victorian editions of *The Yellowplush Papers* [*The Yellowplush Correspon-dence*].

34. Here I take liberties with Judith Butler's memo-rable phrase, since I am concerned with represen-tations of social class, and not with Butler's theo-retical model (see Butler, *Bodies That Matter: On the Discursive Limits of "Sex"* [New York and London: Routledge, 1993]).

35. Eagleton, *Ideology: An Introduction* (London and New York: Verso, 1991), p. 116. See also Antonio Gramsci, *Selections from the Prison Notebooks of Antonio Gramsci,* ed. Quintin Hoare and Geoffrey Nowell Smith (London: International Publishers, 1971).

36. Alexis de Tocqueville, *The Old Régime and the French Revolution,* trans. Stuart Gilbert (Garden City, N.Y.: Doubleday and Doubleday, 1955), pp. 88-89.

FURTHER READING

Bibliographies

Flamm, Dudley. *Thackeray's Critics: An Annotated Bib-liography of British and American Criticism, 1831-1901.* Chapel Hill: University of North Carolina Press, 1966, 184 p.

Provides a detailed survey of Thackeray criticism from the nineteenth century.

Goldfarb, Sheldon. *William Makepeace Thackeray: An Annotated Bibliography, 1976-1987.* New York: Garland, 1989, 175 p.

Includes annotated listings for more than four hundred critical studies devoted to Thackeray's work.

Biographies

Peters, Catherine. *Thackeray's Universe: Shifting Worlds of Imagination and Reality.* London: Faber and Faber, 1987, 292 p.

Analyzes the various tensions between art and life that helped shape Thackeray's identity as a writer.

Taylor, D. J. *Thackeray,* London: Chatto & Windus, 1999, 494 p.

Explores the diverse complexities and contradictions that defined Thackeray's personality.

Criticism

Brewer, Kenneth L., Jr. "Colonial Discourse and William Makepeace Thackeray's *Irish Sketch Book.*" *Papers on Language and Literature* 29, no. 3 (July 1993): 259-83.

Discusses the interplay of "high" and "low" culture in Thackeray's writings about Ireland.

Ferris, Ina. "The Breakdown of Thackeray's Narrator: *Lovel the Widower.*" *Nineteenth-Century Fiction* 32, no. 1 (June 1977): 36-53.

Explores elements of narrative experimentation in the novel.

Fisher, Judith Law. "Siren and Artist: Contradiction in Thackeray's Aesthetic Ideal." *Nineteenth-Century Fiction* 39, no. 4 (March 1985): 392-419.

Documents the friction among issues of desire, morality, and artistic expression in Thackeray's work.

Fletcher, Robert P. "'The Foolishest of Existing Mortals': Thackeray, 'Gurlyle,' and the Character(s) of Fiction." *CLIO: A Journal of Literature, History, and the Philosophy of History* 24, no. 2 (winter 1995): 113-25.

Examines the relationship between historical knowledge and fictional representation in the writings of Thackeray and Carlyle.

Law, Joe K. "Thackeray and the Uses of Opera." *Review of English Studies: A Quarterly Journal of English Literature and the English Language* 39, no. 156 (November 1988): 502-12.

Highlights Thackeray's use of operatic elements in his fiction.

Loomis, Chauncey C., Jr. "Thackeray and the Plight of the Victorian Satirist." *English Studies: A Journal of English Letters and Philology* 49, no. 1 (February 1968): 1-19.

Appraises Thackeray's satirical writings in relation to prevailing Victorian attitudes toward the genre.

McAuliffe, John. "Taking the Sting out of the Traveller's Tale: Thackeray's *Irish Sketchbook.*" *Irish Studies Review* 9, no. 1 (April 2001): 25-40.

Considers the role of the unreliable narrator in Thackeray's writings on Ireland.

Melville, Lewis. "Thackeray's Originals." In *Some Aspects of Thackeray,* pp. 140-79. London: Stephen Swift and Co. Ltd, 1911.

Examines some of the real-life models for Thackeray's fictional characters.

Merrill, Katharine. "Characterization in the Beginning of Thackeray's *Pendennis.*" *PMLA: Publications of the Modern Language Association of America* 15, no. 2 (1900): 233-52.

Addresses questions of characterization and structure in the novel's early chapters.

Ousby, Ian. "Carlyle, Thackeray, and Victorian Heroism." *Yearbook of English Studies* 12 (1982): 152-68.

Treats certain "shared assumptions and shared concerns" in the two authors' conceptions of heroism.

Palmieri, Frank. "Cruikshank, Thackeray, and the Victorian Eclipse of Satire." *SEL: Studies in English Literature, 1500-1900* 44, no. 4 (October 2004): 753-77.

Investigates Thackeray's early comic writings within the framework of Victorian satire from the 1830s and 1840s.

Ray, Gordon N. "Thackeray's 'Book of Snobs.'" *Nineteenth-Century Fiction* 10, no. 1 (June 1955): 22-33.

Interprets Thackeray's essays in the context of class conflict in Victorian England.

Saintsbury, George. *A Consideration of Thackeray.* London: Oxford University Press, 1931, 273 p.

Offers a detailed survey of Thackeray's body of work.

Simons, Gary. "Thackeray's Contributions to the *Times.*" *Victorian Periodicals Review* 40, no. 4 (January 2007): 332-54.

Appraises the literary merit of Thackeray's early critical writings.

Sinha, Susanta Kumar. "Authorial Voice in Thackeray: A Reconsideration." *English Studies: A Journal of English Language and Literature* 64, no. 3 (June 1983): 233-46.

Considers the question of authorial presence in Thackeray's fiction, identifying a moral purpose underlying Thackeray's narrative commentaries.

Sutherland, John. "The Genesis of Thackeray's *Denis Duval*." *Review of English Studies: A Quarterly Journal of English Literature and the English Language* 37, no. 146 (May 1986): 226-33.

Describes some of the source materials for Thackeray's final, unfinished novel.

Thomas, Deborah A. "Thackeray, Capital Punishment, and the Demise of Jos Sedley." *Victorian Literature and Culture* 33, no. 1 (2005): 1-20.

Considers the ambiguity surrounding Joseph Sedley's mysterious death in the novel *Vanity Fair* against the backdrop of Victorian attitudes toward capital punishment.

Tillotson, Geoffrey, and Donald Hawes. *Thackeray: The Critical Heritage.* London: Routledge & Kegan Paul, 1968, 392 p.

Presents a range of contemporary critical reactions to Thackeray's major and minor works.

Tobias, Richard Clark. "American Criticism of Thackeray 1848-1855." *Nineteenth-Century Fiction* 8, no. 1 (June 1953): 53-65.

Examines the emergence of Thackeray's critical reputation in the United States.

Wheatley, James H. *Patterns in Thackeray's Fiction.* Cambridge: The M.I.T. Press, 1969, 157 p.

Explores the evolution of Thackeray's narrative strategies and thematic concerns throughout his body of work.

Additional coverage of Thackeray's life and career is contained in the following sources published by Gale: *British Writers,* **Vol. 5;** *British Writers: The Classics,* **Vol. 2;** *Concise Dictionary of British Literary Biography, 1832-1890; Dictionary of Literary Biography,* **Vols. 21, 55, 159, 163;** *DISCovering Authors; DISCovering Authors: British Edition; DISCovering Authors: Canadian Edition; DISCovering Authors Modules: Most-studied Authors* **and** *Novelists; DISCovering Authors 3.0; Literature Resource Center; Nineteenth-Century Literature Criticism,* **Vols. 5, 14, 22, 43, 169;** *Novels for Students,* **Vol. 13;** *Reference Guide to English Literature,* **Ed. 2;** *Something About the Author,* **Vol. 23;** *Twayne's English Authors; World Literature and Its Times,* **Vol. 3; and** *World Literature Criticism,* **Vol. 6.**

How to Use This Index

The main references

Calvino, Italo
  1923-1985 .... CLC 5, 8, 11, 22, 33, 39,
                                   73; SSC 3, 48

---

list all author entries in the following Gale Literary Criticism series:

AAL = *Asian American Literature*
BG = *The Beat Generation: A Gale Critical Companion*
BLC = *Black Literature Criticism*
BLCS = *Black Literature Criticism Supplement*
CLC = *Contemporary Literary Criticism*
CLR = *Children's Literature Review*
CMLC = *Classical and Medieval Literature Criticism*
DC = *Drama Criticism*
FL = *Feminism in Literature: A Gale Critical Companion*
GL = *Gothic Literature: A Gale Critical Companion*
HLC = *Hispanic Literature Criticism*
HLCS = *Hispanic Literature Criticism Supplement*
HR = *Harlem Renaissance: A Gale Critical Companion*
LC = *Literature Criticism from 1400 to 1800*
NCLC = *Nineteenth-Century Literature Criticism*
NNAL = *Native North American Literature*
PC = *Poetry Criticism*
SSC = *Short Story Criticism*
TCLC = *Twentieth-Century Literary Criticism*
WLC = *World Literature Criticism, 1500 to the Present*
WLCS = *World Literature Criticism Supplement*

The cross-references

See also CA 85-88, 116; CANR 23, 61;
DAM NOV; DLB 196; EW 13; MTCW 1, 2;
RGSF 2; RGWL 2; SFW 4; SSFS 12

---

list all author entries in the following Gale biographical and literary sources:

AAYA = *Authors & Artists for Young Adults*
AFAW = *African American Writers*
AFW = *African Writers*
AITN = *Authors in the News*
AMW = *American Writers*
AMWR = *American Writers Retrospective Supplement*
AMWS = *American Writers Supplement*
ANW = *American Nature Writers*
AW = *Ancient Writers*
BEST = *Bestsellers*
BPFB = *Beacham's Encyclopedia of Popular Fiction: Biography and Resources*
BRW = *British Writers*
BRWS = *British Writers Supplement*
BW = *Black Writers*
BYA = *Beacham's Guide to Literature for Young Adults*
CA = *Contemporary Authors*
CAAS = *Contemporary Authors Autobiography Series*
CABS = *Contemporary Authors Bibliographical Series*
CAD = *Contemporary American Dramatists*
CANR = *Contemporary Authors New Revision Series*
CAP = *Contemporary Authors Permanent Series*
CBD = *Contemporary British Dramatists*
CCA = *Contemporary Canadian Authors*
CD = *Contemporary Dramatists*
CDALB = *Concise Dictionary of American Literary Biography*

CDALBS = *Concise Dictionary of American Literary Biography Supplement*
CDBLB = *Concise Dictionary of British Literary Biography*
CMW = *St. James Guide to Crime & Mystery Writers*
CN = *Contemporary Novelists*
CP = *Contemporary Poets*
CPW = *Contemporary Popular Writers*
CSW = *Contemporary Southern Writers*
CWD = *Contemporary Women Dramatists*
CWP = *Contemporary Women Poets*
CWRI = *St. James Guide to Children's Writers*
CWW = *Contemporary World Writers*
DA = *DISCovering Authors*
DA3 = *DISCovering Authors 3.0*
DAB = *DISCovering Authors: British Edition*
DAC = *DISCovering Authors: Canadian Edition*
DAM = *DISCovering Authors: Modules*
   DRAM: *Dramatists Module;* **MST:** *Most-studied Authors Module;*
   MULT: *Multicultural Authors Module;* **NOV:** *Novelists Module;*
   POET: *Poets Module;* **POP:** *Popular Fiction and Genre Authors Module*
DFS = *Drama for Students*
DLB = *Dictionary of Literary Biography*
DLBD = *Dictionary of Literary Biography Documentary Series*
DLBY = *Dictionary of Literary Biography Yearbook*
DNFS = *Literature of Developing Nations for Students*
EFS = *Epics for Students*
EW = *European Writers*
EWL = *Encyclopedia of World Literature in the 20th Century*
EXPN = *Exploring Novels*
EXPP = *Exploring Poetry*
EXPS = *Exploring Short Stories*
FANT = *St. James Guide to Fantasy Writers*
FW = *Feminist Writers*
GFL = *Guide to French Literature,* Beginnings to 1789, 1798 to the Present
GLL = *Gay and Lesbian Literature*
HGG = *St. James Guide to Horror, Ghost & Gothic Writers*
HW = *Hispanic Writers*
IDFW = *International Dictionary of Films and Filmmakers: Writers and Production Artists*
IDTP = *International Dictionary of Theatre: Playwrights*
LAIT = *Literature and Its Times*
LAW = *Latin American Writers*
JRDA = *Junior DISCovering Authors*
MAICYA = *Major Authors and Illustrators for Children and Young Adults*
MAICYAS = *Major Authors and Illustrators for Children and Young Adults Supplement*
MAWW = *Modern American Women Writers*
MJW = *Modern Japanese Writers*
MTCW = *Major 20th-Century Writers*
NCFS = *Nonfiction Classics for Students*
NFS = *Novels for Students*
PAB = *Poets: American and British*
PFS = *Poetry for Students*
RGAL = *Reference Guide to American Literature*
RGEL = *Reference Guide to English Literature*
RGSF = *Reference Guide to Short Fiction*
RGWL = *Reference Guide to World Literature*
RHW = *Twentieth-Century Romance and Historical Writers*
SAAS = *Something about the Author Autobiography Series*
SATA = *Something about the Author*
SFW = *St. James Guide to Science Fiction Writers*
SSFS = *Short Stories for Students*
TCWW = *Twentieth-Century Western Writers*
WLIT = *World Literature and Its Times*
WP = *World Poets*
YABC = *Yesterday's Authors of Books for Children*
YAW = *St. James Guide to Young Adult Writers*

Literary Criticism Series
Cumulative Author Index

Beattie, Ann 1947- ..... **CLC 8, 13, 18, 40, 63, 146; SSC 11**
　See also AMWS 5; BEST 90:2; BPFB 1; CA 81-84; CANR 53, 73, 128; CN 4, 5, 6, 7; CPW; DA3; DAM NOV, POP; DLB 218, 278; DLBY 1982; EWL 3; MAL 5; MTCW 1, 2; MTFW 2005; RGAL 4; RGSF 2; SSFS 9; TUS

Beattie, James 1735-1803 .... **NCLC 25**
　See also DLB 109

Beauchamp, Kathleen Mansfield 1888-1923 . **SSC 9, 23, 38, 81; TCLC 2, 8, 39, 164; WLC 4**
　See also BPFB 2; BRW 7; CA 104; 134; DA; DA3; DAB; DAC; DAM MST; DLB 162; EWL 3; EXPS; FW; GLL 1; MTCW 2; RGEL 2; RGSF 2; SSFS 2, 8, 10, 11; TEA; WWE 1

Beaumarchais, Pierre-Augustin Caron de 1732-1799 .... **DC 4; LC 61**
　See also DAM DRAM; DFS 14, 16; DLB 313; EW 4; GFL Beginnings to 1789; RGWL 2, 3

Beaumont, Francis 1584(?)-1616 .. **DC 6; LC 33**
　See also BRW 2; CDBLB Before 1660; DLB 58; TEA

Beauvoir, Simone de 1908-1986 .... **CLC 1, 2, 4, 8, 14, 31, 44, 50, 71, 124; SSC 35; WLC 1**
　See also BPFB 1; CA 9-12R; 118; CANR 28, 61; DA; DA3; DAB; DAC; DAM MST, NOV; DLB 72; DLBY 1986; EW 12; EWL 3; FL 1:5; FW; GFL 1789 to the Present; LMFS 2; MTCW 1, 2; MTFW 2005; RGSF 2; RGWL 2, 3; TWA

Beauvoir, Simone Lucie Ernestine Marie Bertrand de
　See Beauvoir, Simone de

Becker, Carl (Lotus) 1873-1945 ..... **TCLC 63**
　See also CA 157; DLB 17

Becker, Jurek 1937-1997 .... **CLC 7, 19**
　See also CA 85-88; 157; CANR 60, 117; CWW 2; DLB 75, 299; EWL 3; RGHL

Becker, Walter 1950- .... **CLC 26**

Becket, Thomas a 1118(?)-1170 .... **CMLC 83**

Beckett, Samuel 1906-1989 ... **CLC 1, 2, 3, 4, 6, 9, 10, 11, 14, 18, 29, 57, 59, 83; DC 22; SSC 16, 74; TCLC 145; WLC 1**
　See also BRWC 2; BRWR 1; BRWS 1; CA 5-8R; 130; CANR 33, 61; CBD; CDBLB 1945-1960; CN 1, 2, 3, 4; CP 1, 2, 3, 4; DA; DA3; DAB; DAC; DAM DRAM, MST, NOV; DFS 2, 7, 18; DLB 13, 15, 233, 319, 321, 329; DLBY 1990; EWL 3; GFL 1789 to the Present; LATS 1:2; LMFS 2; MTCW 1, 2; MTFW 2005; RGSF 2; RGWL 2, 3; SSFS 15; TEA; WLIT 4

Beckford, William 1760-1844 .... **NCLC 16, 214**
　See also BRW 3; DLB 39, 213; GL 2; HGG; LMFS 1; SUFW

Beckham, Barry (Earl) 1944- .... **BLC 1:1**
　See also BW 1; CA 29-32R; CANR 26, 62; CN 1, 2, 3, 4, 5, 6; DAM MULT; DLB 33

Beckman, Gunnel 1910- .... **CLC 26**
　See also CA 33-36R; CANR 15, 114; CLR 25; MAICYA 1, 2; SAAS 9; SATA 6

Becque, Henri 1837-1899 .... **DC 21; NCLC 3**
　See also DLB 192; GFL 1789 to the Present

Becquer, Gustavo Adolfo 1836-1870 .... **HLCS 1; NCLC 106**
　See also DAM MULT

Beddoes, Thomas Lovell 1803-1849 .. **DC 15; NCLC 3, 154**
　See also BRWS 11; DLB 96

Bede c. 673-735 .... **CMLC 20**
　See also DLB 146; TEA

Bedford, Denton R. 1907-(?) .... **NNAL**

Bedford, Donald F.
　See Fearing, Kenneth (Flexner)

Beecher, Catharine Esther 1800-1878 .... **NCLC 30**
　See also DLB 1, 243

Beecher, John 1904-1980 .... **CLC 6**
　See also AITN 1; CA 5-8R; 105; CANR 8; CP 1, 2, 3

Beer, Johann 1655-1700 .... **LC 5**
　See also DLB 168

Beer, Patricia 1924- .... **CLC 58**
　See also BRWS 14; CA 61-64; 183; CANR 13, 46; CP 1, 2, 3, 4, 5, 6; CWP; DLB 40; FW

Beerbohm, Max
　See Beerbohm, (Henry) Max(imilian)

Beerbohm, (Henry) Max(imilian) 1872-1956 .... **TCLC 1, 24**
　See also BRWS 2; CA 104; 154; CANR 79; DLB 34, 100; FANT; MTCW 2

Beer-Hofmann, Richard 1866-1945 .... **TCLC 60**
　See also CA 160; DLB 81

Beg, Shemus
　See Stephens, James

Begiebing, Robert J(ohn) 1946- .... **CLC 70**
　See also CA 122; CANR 40, 88

Begley, Louis 1933- .... **CLC 197**
　See also CA 140; CANR 98, 176; DLB 299; RGHL; TCLE 1:1

Behan, Brendan (Francis) 1923-1964 .... **CLC 1, 8, 11, 15, 79**
　See also BRWS 2; CA 73-76; CANR 33, 121; CBD; CDBLB 1945-1960; DAM DRAM; DFS 7; DLB 13, 233; EWL 3; MTCW 1, 2

Behn, Aphra 1640(?)-1689 .. **DC 4; LC 1, 30, 42, 135; PC 13, 88; WLC 1**
　See also BRWS 3; DA; DA3; DAB; DAC; DAM DRAM, MST, NOV, POET; DFS 16, 24; DLB 39, 80, 131; FW; TEA; WLIT 3

Behrman, S(amuel) N(athaniel) 1893-1973 .... **CLC 40**
　See also CA 13-16; 45-48; CAD; CAP 1; DLB 7, 44; IDFW 3; MAL 5; RGAL 4

Bekederemo, J. P. Clark
　See Clark Bekederemo, J.P.

Belasco, David 1853-1931 .... **TCLC 3**
　See also CA 104; 168; DLB 7; MAL 5; RGAL 4

Belcheva, Elisaveta Lyubomirova 1893-1991 .... **CLC 10**
　See also CA 178; CDWLB 4; DLB 147; EWL 3

Beldone, Phil "Cheech"
　See Ellison, Harlan

Beleno
　See Azuela, Mariano

Belinski, Vissarion Grigoryevich 1811-1848 .... **NCLC 5**
　See also DLB 198

Belitt, Ben 1911- .... **CLC 22**
　See also CA 13-16R; CAAS 4; CANR 7, 77; CP 1, 2, 3, 4, 5, 6; DLB 5

Belknap, Jeremy 1744-1798 .... **LC 115**
　See also DLB 30, 37

Bell, Gertrude (Margaret Lowthian) 1868-1926 .... **TCLC 67**
　See also CA 167; CANR 110; DLB 174

Bell, J. Freeman
　See Zangwill, Israel

Bell, James Madison 1826-1902 ..... **BLC 1:1; TCLC 43**
　See also BW 1; CA 122; 124; DAM MULT; DLB 50

Bell, Madison Smartt 1957- ..... **CLC 41, 102, 223**
　See also AMWS 10; BPFB 1; CA 111, 183; CAAE 183; CANR 28, 54, 73, 134, 176; CN 5, 6, 7; CSW; DLB 218, 278; MTCW 2; MTFW 2005

Bell, Marvin (Hartley) 1937- ...... **CLC 8, 31; PC 79**
　See also CA 21-24R; CAAS 14; CANR 59, 102; CP 1, 2, 3, 4, 5, 6, 7; DAM POET; DLB 5; MAL 5; MTCW 1; PFS 25

Bell, W. L. D.
　See Mencken, H(enry) L(ouis)

Bellamy, Atwood C.
　See Mencken, H(enry) L(ouis)

Bellamy, Edward 1850-1898 ..... **NCLC 4, 86, 147**
　See also DLB 12; NFS 15; RGAL 4; SFW 4

Belli, Gioconda 1948- .... **HLCS 1**
　See also CA 152; CANR 143; CWW 2; DLB 290; EWL 3; RGWL 3

Bellin, Edward J.
　See Kuttner, Henry

Bello, Andres 1781-1865 .... **NCLC 131**
　See also LAW

Belloc, (Joseph) Hilaire (Pierre Sebastien Rene Swanton) 1870-1953 .... **PC 24; TCLC 7, 18**
　See also CA 106; 152; CLR 102; CWRI 5; DAM POET; DLB 19, 100, 141, 174; EWL 3; MTCW 2; MTFW 2005; SATA 112; WCH; YABC 1

Belloc, Joseph Peter Rene Hilaire
　See Belloc, (Joseph) Hilaire (Pierre Sebastien Rene Swanton)

Belloc, Joseph Pierre Hilaire
　See Belloc, (Joseph) Hilaire (Pierre Sebastien Rene Swanton)

Belloc, M. A.
　See Lowndes, Marie Adelaide (Belloc)

Belloc-Lowndes, Mrs.
　See Lowndes, Marie Adelaide (Belloc)

Bellow, Saul 1915-2005 ...... **CLC 1, 2, 3, 6, 8, 10, 13, 15, 25, 33, 34, 63, 79, 190, 200; SSC 14, 101; WLC 1**
　See also AITN 2; AMW; AMWC 2; AMWR 2; BEST 89:3; BPFB 1; CA 5-8R; 238; CABS 1; CANR 29, 53, 95, 132; CDALB 1941-1968; CN 1, 2, 3, 4, 5, 6, 7; DA; DA3; DAB; DAC; DAM MST, NOV, POP; DLB 2, 28, 299, 329; DLBD 3; DLBY 1982; EWL 3; MAL 5; MTCW 1, 2; MTFW 2005; NFS 4, 14, 26; RGAL 4; RGSF 2; SSFS 12, 22; TUS

Belser, Reimond Karel Maria de 1929- .... **CLC 14**
　See also CA 152

Bely, Andrey
　See Bugayev, Boris Nikolayevich

Belyi, Andrei
　See Bugayev, Boris Nikolayevich

Bembo, Pietro 1470-1547 .... **LC 79**
　See also RGWL 2, 3

Benary, Margot
　See Benary-Isbert, Margot

Benary-Isbert, Margot 1889-1979 .... **CLC 12**
　See also CA 5-8R; 89-92; CANR 4, 72; CLR 12; MAICYA 1, 2; SATA 2; SATA-Obit 21

Benavente (y Martinez), Jacinto 1866-1954 .... **DC 26; HLCS 1; TCLC 3**
　See also CA 106; 131; CANR 81; DAM DRAM, MULT; DLB 329; EWL 3; GLL 2; HW 1, 2; MTCW 1, 2

Blake, William 1757-1827 . **NCLC 13, 37, 57, 127, 173, 190, 201; PC 12, 63; WLC 1**
See also AAYA 47; BRW 3; BRWR 1; CD-BLB 1789-1832; CLR 52; DA; DA3; DAB; DAC; DAM MST, POET; DLB 93, 163; EXPP; LATS 1:1; LMFS 1; MAICYA 1, 2; PAB; PFS 2, 12, 24; SATA 30; TEA; WCH; WLIT 3; WP

Blanchot, Maurice 1907-2003 .... **CLC 135**
See also CA 117; 144; 213; CANR 138; DLB 72, 296; EWL 3

Blasco Ibanez, Vicente 1867-1928 . **TCLC 12**
See also BPFB 1; CA 110; 131; CANR 81; DA3; DAM NOV; DLB 322; EW 8; EWL 3; HW 1, 2; MTCW 1

Blatty, William Peter 1928- .... **CLC 2**
See also CA 5-8R; CANR 9, 124; DAM POP; HGG

Bleeck, Oliver
See Thomas, Ross (Elmore)

Bleecker, Ann Eliza 1752-1783 .... **LC 161**
See also DLB 200

Blessing, Lee (Knowlton) 1949- .... **CLC 54**
See also CA 236; CAD; CD 5, 6; DFS 23, 26

Blight, Rose
See Greer, Germaine

Blind, Mathilde 1841-1896 .... **NCLC 202**
See also DLB 199

Blish, James (Benjamin) 1921-1975 . **CLC 14**
See also BPFB 1; CA 1-4R; 57-60; CANR 3; CN 2; DLB 8; MTCW 1; SATA 66; SCFW 1, 2; SFW 4

Bliss, Frederick
See Card, Orson Scott

Bliss, Gillian
See Paton Walsh, Jill

Bliss, Reginald
See Wells, H(erbert) G(eorge)

Blixen, Karen (Christentze Dinesen)
1885-1962 ... **CLC 10, 29, 95; SSC 7, 75**
See also CA 25-28; CANR 22, 50; CAP 2; DA3; DLB 214; EW 10; EWL 3; EXPS; FW; GL 2; HGG; LAIT 3; LMFS 1; MTCW 1; NCFS 2; NFS 9; RGSF 2; RGWL 2, 3; SATA 44; SSFS 3, 6, 13; WLIT 2

Bloch, Robert (Albert) 1917-1994 .... **CLC 33**
See also AAYA 29; CA 5-8R, 179; 146; CAAE 179; CAAS 20; CANR 5, 78; DA3; DLB 44; HGG; INT CANR-5; MTCW 2; SATA 12; SATA-Obit 82; SFW 4; SUFW 1, 2

Blok, Alexander (Alexandrovich)
1880-1921 .... **PC 21; TCLC 5**
See also CA 104; 183; DLB 295; EW 9; EWL 3; LMFS 2; RGWL 2, 3

Blom, Jan
See Breytenbach, Breyten

Bloom, Harold 1930- .... **CLC 24, 103, 221**
See also CA 13-16R; CANR 39, 75, 92, 133, 181; DLB 67; EWL 3; MTCW 2; MTFW 2005; RGAL 4

Bloomfield, Aurelius
See Bourne, Randolph S(illiman)

Bloomfield, Robert 1766-1823 ..... **NCLC 145**
See also DLB 93

Blount, Roy, Jr. 1941- .... **CLC 38**
See also CA 53-56; CANR 10, 28, 61, 125, 176; CSW; INT CANR-28; MTCW 1, 2; MTFW 2005

Blount, Roy Alton
See Blount, Roy, Jr.

Blowsnake, Sam 1875-(?) .... **NNAL**

Bloy, Leon 1846-1917 .... **TCLC 22**
See also CA 121; 183; DLB 123; GFL 1789 to the Present

Blue Cloud, Peter (Aroniawenrate)
1933- .... **NNAL**
See also CA 117; CANR 40; DAM MULT; DLB 342

Bluggage, Oranthy
See Alcott, Louisa May

Blume, Judy 1938- .... **CLC 12, 30**
See also AAYA 3, 26; BYA 1, 8, 12; CA 29-32R; CANR 13, 37, 66, 124, 186; CLR 2, 15, 69; CPW; DA3; DAM NOV, POP; DLB 52; JRDA; MAICYA 1, 2; MAICYAS 1; MTCW 1, 2; MTFW 2005; NFS 24; SATA 2, 31, 79, 142, 195; WYA; YAW

Blume, Judy Sussman
See Blume, Judy

Blunden, Edmund (Charles)
1896-1974 .... **CLC 2, 56; PC 66**
See also BRW 6; BRWS 11; CA 17-18; 45-48; CANR 54; CAP 2; CP 1, 2; DLB 20, 100, 155; MTCW 1; PAB

Bly, Robert (Elwood) 1926- .... **CLC 1, 2, 5, 10, 15, 38, 128; PC 39**
See also AMWS 4; CA 5-8R; CANR 41, 73, 125; CP 1, 2, 3, 4, 5, 6, 7; DA3; DAM POET; DLB 5, 342; EWL 3; MAL 5; MTCW 1, 2; MTFW 2005; PFS 6, 17; RGAL 4

Boas, Franz 1858-1942 .... **TCLC 56**
See also CA 115; 181

Bobette
See Simenon, Georges (Jacques Christian)

Boccaccio, Giovanni 1313-1375 ... **CMLC 13, 57; SSC 10, 87**
See also EW 2; RGSF 2; RGWL 2, 3; TWA; WLIT 7

Bochco, Steven 1943- .... **CLC 35**
See also AAYA 11, 71; CA 124; 138

Bode, Sigmund
See O'Doherty, Brian

Bodel, Jean 1167(?)-1210 .... **CMLC 28**

Bodenheim, Maxwell 1892-1954 .... **TCLC 44**
See also CA 110; 187; DLB 9, 45; MAL 5; RGAL 4

Bodenheimer, Maxwell
See Bodenheim, Maxwell

Bodker, Cecil 1927-
See Bodker, Cecil

Bodker, Cecil 1927- .... **CLC 21**
See also CA 73-76; CANR 13, 44, 111; CLR 23; MAICYA 1, 2; SATA 14, 133

Boell, Heinrich (Theodor)
1917-1985 ..... **CLC 2, 3, 6, 9, 11, 15, 27, 32, 72; SSC 23; TCLC 185; WLC 1**
See also BPFB 1; CA 21-24R; 116; CANR 24; CDWLB 2; DA; DA3; DAB; DAC; DAM MST, NOV; DLB 69, 329; DLBY 1985; EW 13; EWL 3; MTCW 1, 2; MTFW 2005; RGHL; RGSF 2; RGWL 2, 3; SSFS 20; TWA

Boerne, Alfred
See Doeblin, Alfred

Boethius c. 480-c. 524 .... **CMLC 15**
See also DLB 115; RGWL 2, 3; WLIT 8

Boff, Leonardo (Genezio Darci)
1938- .... **CLC 70; HLC 1**
See also CA 150; DAM MULT; HW 2

Bogan, Louise 1897-1970 .... **CLC 4, 39, 46, 93; PC 12**
See also AMWS 3; CA 73-76; 25-28R; CANR 33, 82; CP 1; DAM POET; DLB 45, 169; EWL 3; MAL 5; MBL; MTCW 1, 2; PFS 21; RGAL 4

Bogarde, Dirk
See Van Den Bogarde, Derek Jules Gaspard Ulric Niven

Bogat, Shatan
See Kacew, Romain

Bogomolny, Robert L(ee) 1938- .... **SSC 41; TCLC 11**
See Tsushima, Shuji
See also CA 121, 164; DLB 182; EWL 3; MJW; RGSF 2; RGWL 2, 3; TWA

Bogosian, Eric 1953- .... **CLC 45, 141**
See also CA 138; CAD; CANR 102, 148; CD 5, 6; DLB 341

Bograd, Larry 1953- .... **CLC 35**
See also CA 93-96; CANR 57; SAAS 21; SATA 33, 89; WYA

Boiardo, Matteo Maria 1441-1494 .... **LC 6**

Boileau-Despreaux, Nicolas
1636-1711 .... **LC 3, 164**
See also DLB 268; EW 3; GFL Beginnings to 1789; RGWL 2, 3

Boissard, Maurice
See Leautaud, Paul

Bojer, Johan 1872-1959 .... **TCLC 64**
See also CA 189; EWL 3

Bok, Edward W(illiam)
1863-1930 .... **TCLC 101**
See also CA 217; DLB 91; DLBD 16

Boker, George Henry 1823-1890 . **NCLC 125**
See also RGAL 4

Boland, Eavan 1944- ... **CLC 40, 67, 113; PC 58**
See also BRWS 5; CA 143, 207; CAAE 207; CANR 61, 180; CP 1, 6, 7; CWP; DAM POET; DLB 40; FW; MTCW 2; MTFW 2005; PFS 12, 22

Boland, Eavan Aisling
See Boland, Eavan

Boll, Heinrich (Theodor)
See Boell, Heinrich (Theodor)

Bolt, Lee
See Faust, Frederick (Schiller)

Bolt, Robert (Oxton) 1924-1995 ...... **CLC 14; TCLC 175**
See also CA 17-20R; 147; CANR 35, 67; CBD; DAM DRAM; DFS 2; DLB 13, 233; EWL 3; LAIT 1; MTCW 1

Bombal, Maria Luisa 1910-1980 .... **HLCS 1; SSC 37**
See also CA 127; CANR 72; EWL 3; HW 1; LAW; RGSF 2

Bombet, Louis-Alexandre-Cesar
See Stendhal

Bomkauf
See Kaufman, Bob (Garnell)

Bonaventura .... **NCLC 35**
See also DLB 90

Bonaventure 1217(?)-1274 .... **CMLC 79**
See also DLB 115; LMFS 1

Bond, Edward 1934- .... **CLC 4, 6, 13, 23**
See also AAYA 50; BRWS 1; CA 25-28R; CANR 38, 67, 106; CBD; CD 5, 6; DAM DRAM; DFS 3, 8; DLB 13, 310; EWL 3; MTCW 1

Bonham, Frank 1914-1989 .... **CLC 12**
See also AAYA 1, 70; BYA 1, 3; CA 9-12R; CANR 4, 36; JRDA; MAICYA 1, 2; SAAS 3; SATA 1, 49; SATA-Obit 62; TCWW 1, 2; YAW

Bonnefoy, Yves 1923- . **CLC 9, 15, 58; PC 58**
See also CA 85-88; CANR 33, 75, 97, 136; CWW 2; DAM MST, POET; DLB 258; EWL 3; GFL 1789 to the Present; MTCW 1, 2; MTFW 2005

Bonner, Marita
See Occomy, Marita (Odette) Bonner

Bonnin, Gertrude 1876-1938 .... **NNAL**
See also CA 150; DAM MULT; DLB 175

Bontemps, Arna(ud Wendell)
1902-1973 ..... **BLC 1:1; CLC 1, 18; HR 1:2**
See also BW 1; CA 1-4R; 41-44R; CANR 4, 35; CLR 6; CP 1; CWRI 5; DA3; DAM MULT, NOV, POET; DLB 48, 51; JRDA; MAICYA 1, 2; MAL 5; MTCW 1, 2; SATA 2, 44; SATA-Obit 24; WCH; WP

Boot, William
See Stoppard, Tom

Booth, Irwin
See Hoch, Edward D.

Booth, Martin 1944-2004 .... **CLC 13**
See also CA 93-96, 188; 223; CAAE 188; CAAS 2; CANR 92; CP 1, 2, 3, 4

Booth, Philip 1925-2007 .... **CLC 23**
See also CA 5-8R; 262; CANR 5, 88; CP 1, 2, 3, 4, 5, 6, 7; DLBY 1982

Booth, Philip Edmund
See Booth, Philip

Booth, Wayne C. 1921-2005 .... **CLC 24**
See also CA 1-4R; 244; CAAS 5; CANR 3, 43, 117; DLB 67

Booth, Wayne Clayson
See Booth, Wayne C.

Borchert, Wolfgang 1921-1947 .... **TCLC 5**
See also CA 104; 188; DLB 69, 124; EWL 3

Borel, Petrus 1809-1859 .... **NCLC 41**
See also DLB 119; GFL 1789 to the Present

Borges, Jorge Luis 1899-1986 ... **CLC 1, 2, 3, 4, 6, 8, 9, 10, 13, 19, 44, 48, 83; HLC 1; PC 22, 32; SSC 4, 41, 100; TCLC 109; WLC 1**
See also AAYA 26; BPFB 1; CA 21-24R; CANR 19, 33, 75, 105, 133; CDWLB 3; DA; DA3; DAB; DAC; DAM MST, MULT; DLB 113, 283; DLBY 1986; DNFS 1, 2; EWL 3; HW 1, 2; LAW; LMFS 2; MSW; MTCW 1, 2; MTFW 2005; PFS 27; RGHL; RGSF 2; RGWL 2, 3; SFW 4; SSFS 17; TWA; WLIT 1

Borne, Ludwig 1786-1837 .... **NCLC 193**
See also DLB 90

Borowski, Tadeusz 1922-1951 .... **SSC 48; TCLC 9**
See also CA 106; 154; CDWLB 4; DLB 215; EWL 3; RGHL; RGSF 2; RGWL 3; SSFS 13

Borrow, George (Henry)
1803-1881 .... **NCLC 9**
See also BRWS 12; DLB 21, 55, 166

Bosch (Gavino), Juan 1909-2001 ..... **HLCS 1**
See also CA 151; 204; DAM MST, MULT; DLB 145; HW 1, 2

Bosman, Herman Charles
1905-1951 .... **TCLC 49**
See also CA 160; DLB 225; RGSF 2

Bosschere, Jean de 1878(?)-1953 ... **TCLC 19**
See also CA 115; 186

Boswell, James 1740-1795 ... **LC 4, 50; WLC 1**
See also BRW 3; CDBLB 1660-1789; DA; DAB; DAC; DAM MST; DLB 104, 142; TEA; WLIT 3

Boto, Eza
See Biyidi, Alexandre

Bottomley, Gordon 1874-1948 ..... **TCLC 107**
See also CA 120; 192; DLB 10

Bottoms, David 1949- .... **CLC 53**
See also CA 105; CANR 22; CSW; DLB 120; DLBY 1983

Boucicault, Dion 1820-1890 .... **NCLC 41**
See also DLB 344

Boucolon, Maryse
See Conde, Maryse

Bourcicault, Dion
See Boucicault, Dion

Bourdieu, Pierre 1930-2002 .... **CLC 198**
See also CA 130; 204

Bourget, Paul (Charles Joseph)
1852-1935 .... **TCLC 12**
See also CA 107; 196; DLB 123; GFL 1789 to the Present

Bourjaily, Vance (Nye) 1922- .... **CLC 8, 62**
See also CA 1-4R; CAAS 1; CANR 2, 72; CN 1, 2, 3, 4, 5, 6, 7; DLB 2, 143; MAL 5

Bourne, Randolph S(illiman)
1886-1918 .... **TCLC 16**
See also AMW; CA 117; 155; DLB 63; MAL 5

Boursiquot, Dionysius
See Boucicault, Dion

Bova, Ben 1932- .... **CLC 45**
See also AAYA 16; CA 5-8R; CAAS 18; CANR 11, 56, 94, 111, 157; CLR 3, 96; DLBY 1981; INT CANR-11; MAICYA 1, 2; MTCW 1; SATA 6, 68, 133; SFW 4

Bova, Benjamin William
See Bova, Ben

Bowen, Elizabeth (Dorothea Cole)
1899-1973 . **CLC 1, 3, 6, 11, 15, 22, 118; SSC 3, 28, 66; TCLC 148**
See also BRWS 2; CA 17-18; 41-44R; CANR 35, 105; CAP 2; CDBLB 1945-1960; CN 1; DA3; DAM NOV; DLB 15, 162; EWL 3; EXPS; FW; HGG; MTCW 1, 2; MTFW 2005; NFS 13; RGSF 2; SSFS 5, 22; SUFW 1; TEA; WLIT 4

Bowering, George 1935- .... **CLC 15, 47**
See also CA 21-24R; CAAS 16; CANR 10; CN 7; CP 1, 2, 3, 4, 5, 6, 7; DLB 53

Bowering, Marilyn R(uthe) 1949- .... **CLC 32**
See also CA 101; CANR 49; CP 4, 5, 6, 7; CWP; DLB 334

Bowers, Edgar 1924-2000 .... **CLC 9**
See also CA 5-8R; 188; CANR 24; CP 1, 2, 3, 4, 5, 6, 7; CSW; DLB 5

Bowers, Mrs. J. Milton 1842-1914
See Bierce, Ambrose (Gwinett)

Bowie, David
See Jones, David Robert

Bowles, Jane (Sydney) 1917-1973 ..... **CLC 3, 68**
See also CA 19-20; 41-44R; CAP 2; CN 1; EWL 3; MAL 5

Bowles, Jane Auer
See Bowles, Jane (Sydney)

Bowles, Paul 1910-1999 ..... **CLC 1, 2, 19, 53; SSC 3, 98; TCLC 209**
See also AMWS 4; CA 1-4R; 186; CAAS 1; CANR 1, 19, 50, 75; CN 1, 2, 3, 4, 5, 6; DA3; DLB 5, 6, 218; EWL 3; MAL 5; MTCW 1, 2; MTFW 2005; RGAL 4; SSFS 17

Bowles, William Lisle 1762-1850 . **NCLC 103**
See also DLB 93

Box, Edgar
See Vidal, Gore

Boyd, James 1888-1944 .... **TCLC 115**
See also CA 186; DLB 9; DLBD 16; RGAL 4; RHW

Boyd, Nancy
See Millay, Edna St. Vincent

Boyd, Thomas (Alexander)
1898-1935 .... **TCLC 111**
See also CA 111; 183; DLB 9; DLBD 16, 316

Boyd, William 1952- .... **CLC 28, 53, 70**
See also CA 114; 120; CANR 51, 71, 131, 174; CN 4, 5, 6, 7; DLB 231

Boyesen, Hjalmar Hjorth
1848-1895 .... **NCLC 135**
See also DLB 12, 71; DLBD 13; RGAL 4

Boyle, Kay 1902-1992 .... **CLC 1, 5, 19, 58, 121; SSC 5, 102**
See also CA 13-16R; 140; CAAS 1; CANR 29, 61, 110; CN 1, 2, 3, 4, 5; CP 1, 2, 3, 4, 5; DLB 4, 9, 48, 86; EWL 3; MAL 5; MTCW 1, 2; MTFW 2005; RGAL 4; RGSF 2; SSFS 10, 13, 14

Boyle, Mark
See Kienzle, William X.

Boyle, Patrick 1905-1982 .... **CLC 19**
See also CA 127

Boyle, T. C.
See Boyle, T. Coraghessan

Boyle, T. Coraghessan 1948- ..... **CLC 36, 55, 90; SSC 16**
See also AAYA 47; AMWS 8; BEST 90:4; BPFB 1; CA 120; CANR 44, 76, 89, 132; CN 6, 7; CPW; DA3; DAM POP; DLB 218, 278; DLBY 1986; EWL 3; MAL 5; MTCW 2; MTFW 2005; SSFS 13, 19

Boz
See Dickens, Charles (John Huffam)

Brackenridge, Hugh Henry
1748-1816 .... **NCLC 7**
See also DLB 11, 37; RGAL 4

Bradbury, Edward P.
See Moorcock, Michael

Bradbury, Malcolm (Stanley)
1932-2000 .... **CLC 32, 61**
See also CA 1-4R; CANR 1, 33, 91, 98, 137; CN 1, 2, 3, 4, 5, 6, 7; CP 1; DA3; DAM NOV; DLB 14, 207; EWL 3; MTCW 1, 2; MTFW 2005

Bradbury, Ray 1920- ... **CLC 1, 3, 10, 15, 42, 98, 235; SSC 29, 53; WLC 1**
See also AAYA 15; AITN 1, 2; AMWS 4; BPFB 1; BYA 4, 5, 11; CA 1-4R; CANR 2, 30, 75, 125, 186; CDALB 1968-1988; CN 1, 2, 3, 4, 5, 6, 7; CPW; DA; DA3; DAB; DAC; DAM MST, NOV, POP; DLB 2, 8; EXPN; EXPS; HGG; LAIT 3, 5; LATS 1:2; LMFS 2; MAL 5; MTCW 1, 2; MTFW 2005; NFS 1, 22, 29; RGAL 4; RGSF 2; SATA 11, 64, 123; SCFW 1, 2; SFW 4; SSFS 1, 20; SUFW 1, 2; TUS; YAW

Bradbury, Ray Douglas
See Bradbury, Ray

Braddon, Mary Elizabeth
1837-1915 .... **TCLC 111**
See also BRWS 8; CA 108; 179; CMW 4; DLB 18, 70, 156; HGG

Bradfield, Scott 1955- .... **SSC 65**
See also CA 147; CANR 90; HGG; SUFW 2

Bradfield, Scott Michael
See Bradfield, Scott

Bradford, Gamaliel 1863-1932 .... **TCLC 36**
See also CA 160; DLB 17

Bradford, William 1590-1657 .... **LC 64**
See also DLB 24, 30; RGAL 4

Bradley, David, Jr. 1950- ...... **BLC 1:1; CLC 23, 118**
See also BW 1, 3; CA 104; CANR 26, 81; CN 4, 5, 6, 7; DAM MULT; DLB 33

Bradley, David Henry, Jr.
See Bradley, David, Jr.

Bradley, John Ed 1958- .... **CLC 55**
See also CA 139; CANR 99; CN 6, 7; CSW

Bradley, John Edmund, Jr.
See Bradley, John Ed

Bradley, Marion Zimmer
1930-1999 .... **CLC 30**
See also AAYA 40; BPFB 1; CA 57-60; 185; CAAS 10; CANR 7, 31, 51, 75, 107; CPW; DA3; DAM POP; DLB 8; FANT; FW; GLL 1; MTCW 1, 2; MTFW 2005; SATA 90, 139; SATA-Obit 116; SFW 4; SUFW 2; YAW

Bradshaw, John 1933- .... **CLC 70**
See also CA 138; CANR 61

Bradstreet, Anne 1612(?)-1672 .... **LC 4, 30, 130; PC 10**
See also AMWS 1; CDALB 1640-1865; DA; DA3; DAC; DAM MST, POET; DLB 24; EXPP; FW; PFS 6; RGAL 4; TUS; WP

Brady, Joan 1939- .... **CLC 86**
See also CA 141

Bragg, Melvyn 1939- .... **CLC 10**
See also BEST 89:3; CA 57-60; CANR 10,
48, 89, 158; CN 1, 2, 3, 4, 5, 6, 7; DLB
14, 271; RHW

Brahe, Tycho 1546-1601 .... **LC 45**
See also DLB 300

Braine, John (Gerard) 1922-1986 . **CLC 1, 3,
41**
See also CA 1-4R; 120; CANR 1, 33; CD-
BLB 1945-1960; CN 1, 2, 3, 4; DLB 15;
DLBY 1986; EWL 3; MTCW 1

Braithwaite, William Stanley (Beaumont)
1878-1962 ...... **BLC 1:1; HR 1:2; PC 52**
See also BW 1; CA 125; DAM MULT; DLB
50, 54; MAL 5

Bramah, Ernest 1868-1942 .... **TCLC 72**
See also CA 156; CMW 4; DLB 70; FANT

Brammer, Billy Lee
See Brammer, William

Brammer, William 1929-1978 .... **CLC 31**
See also CA 235; 77-80

Brancati, Vitaliano 1907-1954 .... **TCLC 12**
See also CA 109; DLB 264; EWL 3

Brancato, Robin F(idler) 1936- .... **CLC 35**
See also AAYA 9, 68; BYA 6; CA 69-72;
CANR 11, 45; CLR 32; JRDA; MAICYA
2; MAICYAS 1; SAAS 9; SATA 97;
WYA; YAW

Brand, Dionne 1953- .... **CLC 192**
See also BW 2; CA 143; CANR 143; CWP;
DLB 334

Brand, Max
See Faust, Frederick (Schiller)

Brand, Millen 1906-1980 .... **CLC 7**
See also CA 21-24R; 97-100; CANR 72

Branden, Barbara 1929- .... **CLC 44**
See also CA 148

Brandes, Georg (Morris Cohen)
1842-1927 .... **TCLC 10**
See also CA 105; 189; DLB 300

Brandys, Kazimierz 1916-2000 .... **CLC 62**
See also CA 239; EWL 3

Branley, Franklyn M(ansfield)
1915-2002 .... **CLC 21**
See also CA 33-36R; 207; CANR 14, 39;
CLR 13; MAICYA 1, 2; SAAS 16; SATA
4, 68, 136

Brant, Beth (E.) 1941- .... **NNAL**
See also CA 144; FW

Brant, Sebastian 1457-1521 .... **LC 112**
See also DLB 179; RGWL 2, 3

Brathwaite, Edward Kamau
1930- ..... **BLC 2:1; BLCS; CLC 11; PC
56**
See also BRWS 12; BW 2, 3; CA 25-28R;
CANR 11, 26, 47, 107; CDWLB 3; CP 1,
2, 3, 4, 5, 6, 7; DAM POET; DLB 125;
EWL 3

Brathwaite, Kamau
See Brathwaite, Edward Kamau

Brautigan, Richard (Gary)
1935-1984 .... **CLC 1, 3, 5, 9, 12, 34, 42;
PC 94; TCLC 133**
See also BPFB 1; CA 53-56; 113; CANR
34; CN 1, 2, 3; CP 1, 2, 3, 4; DA3; DAM
NOV; DLB 2, 5, 206; DLBY 1980, 1984;
FANT; MAL 5; MTCW 1; RGAL 4;
SATA 56

Brave Bird, Mary
See Crow Dog, Mary

Braverman, Kate 1950- .... **CLC 67**
See also CA 89-92; CANR 141; DLB 335

Brecht, (Eugen) Bertolt (Friedrich)
1898-1956 ..... **DC 3; TCLC 1, 6, 13, 35,
169; WLC 1**
See also CA 104; 133; CANR 62; CDWLB
2; DA; DA3; DAB; DAC; DAM DRAM,
MST; DFS 4, 5, 9; DLB 56, 124; EW 11;
EWL 3; IDTP; MTCW 1, 2; MTFW 2005;
RGHL; RGWL 2, 3; TWA

Brecht, Eugen Berthold Friedrich
See Brecht, (Eugen) Bertolt (Friedrich)

Bremer, Fredrika 1801-1865 .... **NCLC 11**
See also DLB 254

Brennan, Christopher John
1870-1932 .... **TCLC 17**
See also CA 117; 188; DLB 230; EWL 3

Brennan, Maeve 1917-1993 ... **CLC 5; TCLC
124**
See also CA 81-84; CANR 72, 100

Brenner, Jozef 1887-1919 .... **TCLC 13**
See also CA 111; 240

Brent, Linda
See Jacobs, Harriet A(nn)

Brentano, Clemens (Maria)
1778-1842 .... **NCLC 1, 191; SSC 115**
See also DLB 90; RGWL 2, 3

Brent of Bin Bin
See Franklin, (Stella Maria Sarah) Miles
(Lampe)

Brenton, Howard 1942- .... **CLC 31**
See also CA 69-72; CANR 33, 67; CBD;
CD 5, 6; DLB 13; MTCW 1

Breslin, James
See Breslin, Jimmy

Breslin, Jimmy 1930- .... **CLC 4, 43**
See also CA 73-76; CANR 31, 75, 139, 187;
DAM NOV; DLB 185; MTCW 2; MTFW
2005

Bresson, Robert 1901(?)-1999 .... **CLC 16**
See also CA 110; 187; CANR 49

Breton, Andre 1896-1966 .. **CLC 2, 9, 15, 54;
PC 15**
See also CA 19-20; 25-28R; CANR 40, 60;
CAP 2; DLB 65, 258; EW 11; EWL 3;
GFL 1789 to the Present; LMFS 2;
MTCW 1, 2; MTFW 2005; RGWL 2, 3;
TWA; WP

Breton, Nicholas c. 1554-c. 1626 .... **LC 133**
See also DLB 136

Breytenbach, Breyten 1939(?)- .. **CLC 23, 37,
126**
See also CA 113; 129; CANR 61, 122;
CWW 2; DAM POET; DLB 225; EWL 3

Bridgers, Sue Ellen 1942- .... **CLC 26**
See also AAYA 8, 49; BYA 7, 8; CA 65-68;
CANR 11, 36; CLR 18; DLB 52; JRDA;
MAICYA 1, 2; SAAS 1; SATA 22, 90;
SATA-Essay 109; WYA; YAW

Bridges, Robert (Seymour)
1844-1930 .... **PC 28; TCLC 1**
See also BRW 6; CA 104; 152; CDBLB
1890-1914; DAM POET; DLB 19, 98

Bridie, James
See Mavor, Osborne Henry

Brin, David 1950- .... **CLC 34**
See also AAYA 21; CA 102; CANR 24, 70,
125, 127; INT CANR-24; SATA 65;
SCFW 2; SFW 4

Brink, Andre 1935- .... **CLC 18, 36, 106**
See also AFW; BRWS 6; CA 104; CANR
39, 62, 109, 133, 182; CN 4, 5, 6, 7; DLB
225; EWL 3; INT CA-103; LATS 1:2;
MTCW 1, 2; MTFW 2005; WLIT 2

Brinsmead, H. F.
See Brinsmead, H(esba) F(ay)

Brinsmead, H. F(ay)
See Brinsmead, H(esba) F(ay)

Brinsmead, H(esba) F(ay) 1922- ...... **CLC 21**
See also CA 21-24R; CANR 10; CLR 47;
CWRI 5; MAICYA 1, 2; SAAS 5; SATA
18, 78

Brittain, Vera (Mary) 1893(?)-1970 . **CLC 23**
See also BRWS 10; CA 13-16; 25-28R;
CANR 58; CAP 1; DLB 191; FW; MTCW
1, 2

Broch, Hermann 1886-1951 ... **TCLC 20, 204**
See also CA 117; 211; CDWLB 2; DLB 85,
124; EW 10; EWL 3; RGWL 2, 3

Brock, Rose
See Hansen, Joseph

Brod, Max 1884-1968 .... **TCLC 115**
See also CA 5-8R; 25-28R; CANR 7; DLB
81; EWL 3

Brodkey, Harold (Roy) 1930-1996 .. **CLC 56;
TCLC 123**
See also CA 111; 151; CANR 71; CN 4, 5,
6; DLB 130

Brodsky, Iosif Alexandrovich 1940-1996
See Brodsky, Joseph
See also AAYA 71; AITN 1; AMWS 8; CA
41-44R; 151; CANR 37, 106; CWW 2;
DA3; DAM POET; DLB 285, 329; EWL
3; MTCW 1, 2; MTFW 2005; RGWL 2, 3

Brodsky, Joseph . **CLC 4, 6, 13, 36, 100; PC
9; TCLC 219**
See Brodsky, Iosif Alexandrovich

Brodsky, Michael 1948- .... **CLC 19**
See also CA 102; CANR 18, 41, 58, 147;
DLB 244

Brodsky, Michael Mark
See Brodsky, Michael

Brodzki, Bella .... **CLC 65**

Brome, Richard 1590(?)-1652 .... **LC 61**
See also BRWS 10; DLB 58

Bromell, Henry 1947- .... **CLC 5**
See also CA 53-56; CANR 9, 115, 116

Bromfield, Louis (Brucker)
1896-1956 .... **TCLC 11**
See also CA 107; 155; DLB 4, 9, 86; RGAL
4; RHW

Broner, E(sther) M(asserman)
1930- .... **CLC 19**
See also CA 17-20R; CANR 8, 25, 72; CN
4, 5, 6; DLB 28

Bronk, William (M.) 1918-1999 .... **CLC 10**
See also CA 89-92; 177; CANR 23; CP 3,
4, 5, 6, 7; DLB 165

Bronstein, Lev Davidovich
See Trotsky, Leon

Bronte, Anne
See Bronte, Anne

Bronte, Anne 1820-1849 ..... **NCLC 4, 71, 102**
See also BRW 5; BRWR 1; DA3; DLB 21,
199, 340; NFS 26; TEA

Bronte, (Patrick) Branwell
1817-1848 .... **NCLC 109**
See also DLB 340

Bronte, Charlotte
See Bronte, Charlotte

Bronte, Charlotte 1816-1855 .... **NCLC 3, 8,
33, 58, 105, 155; WLC 1**
See also AAYA 17; BRW 5; BRWC 2;
BRWR 1; BYA 2; CDBLB 1832-1890;
DA; DA3; DAB; DAC; DAM MST, NOV;
DLB 21, 159, 199, 340; EXPN; FL 1:2;
GL 2; LAIT 2; NFS 4; TEA; WLIT 4

Bronte, Emily
See Bronte, Emily (Jane)

Bronte, Emily (Jane) 1818-1848 ... **NCLC 16,
35, 165; PC 8; WLC 1**
See also AAYA 17; BPFB 1; BRW 5;
BRWC 1; BRWR 1; BYA 3; CDBLB
1832-1890; DA; DA3; DAB; DAC; DAM
MST, NOV, POET; DLB 21, 32, 199, 340;
EXPN; FL 1:2; GL 2; LAIT 1; TEA;
WLIT 3

Buchanan, George 1506-1582 .... **LC 4**
See also DLB 132
Buchanan, Robert 1841-1901 .... **TCLC 107**
See also CA 179; DLB 18, 35
Buchheim, Lothar-Guenther
1918-2007 .... **CLC 6**
See also CA 85-88; 257
Buchner, (Karl) Georg
1813-1837 .... **NCLC 26, 146**
See also CDWLB 2; DLB 133; EW 6;
RGSF 2; RGWL 2, 3; TWA
Buchwald, Art 1925-2007 .... **CLC 33**
See also AITN 1; CA 5-8R; 256; CANR 21,
67, 107; MTCW 1, 2; SATA 10
Buchwald, Arthur
See Buchwald, Art
Buck, Pearl S(ydenstricker)
1892-1973 .... **CLC 7, 11, 18, 127**
See also AAYA 42; AITN 1; AMWS 2;
BPFB 1; CA 1-4R; 41-44R; CANR 1, 34;
CDALBS; CN 1; DA; DA3; DAB; DAC;
DAM MST, NOV; DLB 9, 102, 329; EWL
3; LAIT 3; MAL 5; MTCW 1, 2; MTFW
2005; NFS 25; RGAL 4; RHW; SATA 1,
25; TUS
Buckler, Ernest 1908-1984 .... **CLC 13**
See also CA 11-12; 114; CAP 1; CCA 1;
CN 1, 2, 3; DAC; DAM MST; DLB 68;
SATA 47
Buckley, Christopher 1952- .... **CLC 165**
See also CA 139; CANR 119, 180
Buckley, Christopher Taylor
See Buckley, Christopher
Buckley, Vincent (Thomas)
1925-1988 .... **CLC 57**
See also CA 101; CP 1, 2, 3, 4; DLB 289
Buckley, William F., Jr. 1925-2008 ... **CLC 7,
18, 37**
See also AITN 1; BPFB 1; CA 1-4R; 269;
CANR 1, 24, 53, 93, 133, 185; CMW 4;
CPW; DA3; DAM POP; DLB 137; DLBY
1980; INT CANR-24; MTCW 1, 2;
MTFW 2005; TUS
Buckley, William Frank
See Buckley, William F., Jr.
Buckley, William Frank, Jr.
See Buckley, William F., Jr.
Buechner, Frederick 1926- ..... **CLC 2, 4, 6, 9**
See also AMWS 12; BPFB 1; CA 13-16R;
CANR 11, 39, 64, 114, 138; CN 1, 2, 3,
4, 5, 6, 7; DAM NOV; DLBY 1980; INT
CANR-11; MAL 5; MTCW 1, 2; MTFW
2005; TCLE 1:1
Buell, John (Edward) 1927- .... **CLC 10**
See also CA 1-4R; CANR 71; DLB 53
Buero Vallejo, Antonio 1916-2000 ... **CLC 15,
46, 139, 226; DC 18**
See also CA 106; 189; CANR 24, 49, 75;
CWW 2; DFS 11; EWL 3; HW 1; MTCW
1, 2
Bufalino, Gesualdo 1920-1996 .... **CLC 74**
See also CA 209; CWW 2; DLB 196
Bugayev, Boris Nikolayevich
1880-1934 .... **PC 11; TCLC 7**
See also CA 104; 165; DLB 295; EW 9;
EWL 3; MTCW 2; MTFW 2005; RGWL
2, 3
Bukowski, Charles 1920-1994 ... **CLC 2, 5, 9,
41, 82, 108; PC 18; SSC 45**
See also CA 17-20R; 144; CANR 40, 62,
105, 180; CN 4, 5; CP 1, 2, 3, 4, 5; CPW;
DA3; DAM NOV, POET; DLB 5, 130,
169; EWL 3; MAL 5; MTCW 1, 2;
MTFW 2005; PFS 28
Bulgakov, Mikhail 1891-1940 .... **SSC 18;
TCLC 2, 16, 159**
See also AAYA 74; BPFB 1; CA 105; 152;
DAM DRAM, NOV; DLB 272; EWL 3;
MTCW 2; MTFW 2005; NFS 8; RGSF 2;
RGWL 2, 3; SFW 4; TWA

Bulgakov, Mikhail Afanasevich
See Bulgakov, Mikhail
Bulgya, Alexander Alexandrovich
1901-1956 .... **TCLC 53**
See also CA 117; 181; DLB 272; EWL 3
Bullins, Ed 1935- ...... **BLC 1:1; CLC 1, 5, 7;
DC 6**
See also BW 2, 3; CA 49-52; CAAS 16;
CAD; CANR 24, 46, 73, 134; CD 5, 6;
DAM DRAM, MULT; DLB 7, 38, 249;
EWL 3; MAL 5; MTCW 1, 2; MTFW
2005; RGAL 4
Bulosan, Carlos 1911-1956 .... **AAL**
See also CA 216; DLB 312; RGAL 4
**Bulwer-Lytton, Edward (George Earle
Lytton)** 1803-1873 .... **NCLC 1, 45**
See also DLB 21; RGEL 2; SFW 4; SUFW
1; TEA
Bunin, Ivan
See Bunin, Ivan Alexeyevich
Bunin, Ivan Alekseevich
See Bunin, Ivan Alexeyevich
Bunin, Ivan Alexeyevich 1870-1953 ... **SSC 5;
TCLC 6**
See also CA 104; DLB 317, 329; EWL 3;
RGSF 2; RGWL 2, 3; TWA
Bunting, Basil 1900-1985 ...... **CLC 10, 39, 47**
See also BRWS 7; CA 53-56; 115; CANR
7; CP 1, 2, 3, 4; DAM POET; DLB 20;
EWL 3; RGEL 2
Bunuel, Luis 1900-1983 ... **CLC 16, 80; HLC
1**
See also CA 101; 110; CANR 32, 77; DAM
MULT; HW 1
Bunyan, John 1628-1688 .. **LC 4, 69; WLC 1**
See also BRW 2; BYA 5; CDBLB 1660-
1789; CLR 124; DA; DAB; DAC; DAM
MST; DLB 39; RGEL 2; TEA; WCH;
WLIT 3
Buravsky, Alexandr .... **CLC 59**
Burchill, Julie 1959- .... **CLC 238**
See also CA 135; CANR 115, 116
Burckhardt, Jacob (Christoph)
1818-1897 .... **NCLC 49**
See also EW 6
Burford, Eleanor
See Hibbert, Eleanor Alice Burford
Burgess, Anthony 1917-1993 . **CLC 1, 2, 4, 5,
8, 10, 13, 15, 22, 40, 62, 81, 94**
See also AAYA 25; AITN 1; BRWS 1; CA
1-4R; 143; CANR 2, 46; CDBLB 1960 to
Present; CN 1, 2, 3, 4, 5; DA3; DAB;
DAC; DAM NOV; DLB 14, 194, 261;
DLBY 1998; EWL 3; MTCW 1, 2; MTFW
2005; NFS 15; RGEL 2; RHW; SFW 4;
TEA; YAW
Buridan, John c. 1295-c. 1358 ...... **CMLC 97**
Burke, Edmund 1729(?)-1797 .... **LC 7, 36,
146; WLC 1**
See also BRW 3; DA; DA3; DAB; DAC;
DAM MST; DLB 104, 252, 336; RGEL
2; TEA
Burke, Kenneth (Duva) 1897-1993 ... **CLC 2,
24**
See also AMW; CA 5-8R; 143; CANR 39,
74, 136; CN 1, 2; CP 1, 2, 3, 4, 5; DLB
45, 63; EWL 3; MAL 5; MTCW 1, 2;
MTFW 2005; RGAL 4
Burke, Leda
See Garnett, David
Burke, Ralph
See Silverberg, Robert
Burke, Thomas 1886-1945 .... **TCLC 63**
See also CA 113; 155; CMW 4; DLB 197
Burney, Fanny 1752-1840 .... **NCLC 12, 54,
107**
See also BRWS 3; DLB 39; FL 1:2; NFS
16; RGEL 2; TEA

Burney, Frances
See Burney, Fanny
Burns, Robert 1759-1796 ... **LC 3, 29, 40; PC
6; WLC 1**
See also AAYA 51; BRW 3; CDBLB 1789-
1832; DA; DA3; DAB; DAC; DAM MST,
POET; DLB 109; EXPP; PAB; RGEL 2;
TEA; WP
Burns, Tex
See L'Amour, Louis
Burnshaw, Stanley 1906-2005 ..... **CLC 3, 13,
44**
See also CA 9-12R; 243; CP 1, 2, 3, 4, 5, 6,
7; DLB 48; DLBY 1997
Burr, Anne 1937- .... **CLC 6**
See also CA 25-28R
Burroughs, Edgar Rice 1875-1950 . **TCLC 2,
32**
See also AAYA 11; BPFB 1; BYA 4, 9; CA
104; 132; CANR 131; DA3; DAM NOV;
DLB 8; FANT; MTCW 1, 2; MTFW
2005; RGAL 4; SATA 41; SCFW 1, 2;
SFW 4; TCWW 1, 2; TUS; YAW
Burroughs, William S. 1914-1997 . **CLC 1, 2,
5, 15, 22, 42, 75, 109; TCLC 121; WLC
1**
See also AAYA 60; AITN 2; AMWS 3; BG
1:2; BPFB 1; CA 9-12R; 160; CANR 20,
52, 104; CN 1, 2, 3, 4, 5, 6; CPW; DA;
DA3; DAB; DAC; DAM MST, NOV,
POP; DLB 2, 8, 16, 152, 237; DLBY
1981, 1997; EWL 3; GLL 1; HGG; LMFS
2; MAL 5; MTCW 1, 2; MTFW 2005;
RGAL 4; SFW 4
Burroughs, William Seward
See Burroughs, William S.
Burton, Sir Richard F(rancis)
1821-1890 .... **NCLC 42**
See also DLB 55, 166, 184; SSFS 21
Burton, Robert 1577-1640 .... **LC 74**
See also DLB 151; RGEL 2
Buruma, Ian 1951- .... **CLC 163**
See also CA 128; CANR 65, 141
Busch, Frederick 1941-2006 .. **CLC 7, 10, 18,
47, 166**
See also CA 33-36R; 248; CAAS 1; CANR
45, 73, 92, 157; CN 1, 2, 3, 4, 5, 6, 7;
DLB 6, 218
Busch, Frederick Matthew
See Busch, Frederick
Bush, Barney (Furman) 1946- .... **NNAL**
See also CA 145
Bush, Ronald 1946- .... **CLC 34**
See also CA 136
Busia, Abena, P. A. 1953- .... **BLC 2:1**
Bustos, F(rancisco)
See Borges, Jorge Luis
Bustos Domecq, H(onorio)
See Bioy Casares, Adolfo; Borges, Jorge
Luis
Butler, Octavia E. 1947-2006 .... **BLC 2:1;
BLCS; CLC 38, 121, 230, 240**
See also AAYA 18, 48; AFAW 2; AMWS
13; BPFB 1; BW 2, 3; CA 73-76; 248;
CANR 12, 24, 38, 73, 145, 240; CLR 65;
CN 7; CPW; DA3; DAM MULT, POP;
DLB 33; LATS 1:2; MTCW 1, 2; MTFW
2005; NFS 8, 21; SATA 84; SCFW 2;
SFW 4; SSFS 6; TCLE 1:1; YAW
Butler, Octavia Estelle
See Butler, Octavia E.
Butler, Robert Olen, (Jr.) 1945- ...... **CLC 81,
162; SSC 117**
See also AMWS 12; BPFB 1; CA 112;
CANR 66, 138; CN 7; CSW; DAM POP;
DLB 173, 335; INT CA-112; MAL 5;
MTCW 2; MTFW 2005; SSFS 11, 22
Butler, Samuel 1612-1680 . **LC 16, 43; PC 94**
See also DLB 101, 126; RGEL 2

Butler, Samuel 1835-1902 .... **TCLC 1, 33;**
WLC 1
See also BRWS 2; CA 143; CDBLB 1890-
1914; DA; DA3; DAB; DAC; DAM MST,
NOV; DLB 18, 57, 174; RGEL 2; SFW 4;
TEA

Butler, Walter C.
See Faust, Frederick (Schiller)

Butor, Michel (Marie Francois)
1926- .... **CLC 1, 3, 8, 11, 15, 161**
See also CA 9-12R; CANR 33, 66; CWW
2; DLB 83; EW 13; EWL 3; GFL 1789 to
the Present; MTCW 1, 2; MTFW 2005

Butts, Mary 1890(?)-1937 ... **SSC 124; TCLC**
77
See also CA 148; DLB 240

Buxton, Ralph
See Silverstein, Alvin; Silverstein, Virginia
B(arbara Opshelor)

Buzo, Alex
See Buzo, Alexander (John)

Buzo, Alexander (John) 1944- .... **CLC 61**
See also CA 97-100; CANR 17, 39, 69; CD
5, 6; DLB 289

Buzzati, Dino 1906-1972 .... **CLC 36**
See also CA 160; 33-36R; DLB 177; RGWL
2, 3; SFW 4

Byars, Betsy 1928- .... **CLC 35**
See also AAYA 19; BYA 3; CA 33-36R,
183; CAAE 183; CANR 18, 36, 57, 102,
148; CLR 1, 16, 72; DLB 52; INT CANR-
18; JRDA; MAICYA 1, 2; MAICYAS 1;
MTCW 1; SAAS 1; SATA 4, 46, 80, 163;
SATA-Essay 108; WYA; YAW

Byars, Betsy Cromer
See Byars, Betsy

Byatt, Antonia Susan Drabble
See Byatt, A.S.

Byatt, A.S. 1936- .... **CLC 19, 65, 136, 223;**
SSC 91
See also BPFB 1; BRWC 2; BRWS 4; CA
13-16R; CANR 13, 33, 50, 75, 96, 133;
CN 1, 2, 3, 4, 5, 6; DA3; DAM NOV,
POP; DLB 14, 194, 319, 326; EWL 3;
MTCW 1, 2; MTFW 2005; RGSF 2;
RHW; SSFS 26; TEA

Byrd, William II 1674-1744 .... **LC 112**
See also DLB 24, 140; RGAL 4

Byrne, David 1952- .... **CLC 26**
See also CA 127

Byrne, John Keyes 1926-2009 .... **CLC 19**
See also CA 102; CANR 78, 140; CBD;
CD 5, 6; DFS 13, 24; DLB 13; INT CA-
102

Byron, George Gordon (Noel)
1788-1824 ..... **DC 24; NCLC 2, 12, 109,**
149; PC 16, 95; WLC 1
See also AAYA 64; BRW 4; BRWC 2; CD-
BLB 1789-1832; DA; DA3; DAB; DAC;
DAM MST, POET; DLB 96, 110; EXPP;
LMFS 1; PAB; PFS 1, 14, 29; RGEL 2;
TEA; WLIT 3; WP

Byron, Robert 1905-1941 .... **TCLC 67**
See also CA 160; DLB 195

C. 3. 3.
See Wilde, Oscar

Caballero, Fernan 1796-1877 .... **NCLC 10**

Cabell, Branch
See Cabell, James Branch

Cabell, James Branch 1879-1958 .... **TCLC 6**
See also CA 105; 152; DLB 9, 78; FANT;
MAL 5; MTCW 2; RGAL 4; SUFW 1

Cabeza de Vaca, Alvar Nunez
1490-1557(?) .... **LC 61**

Cable, George Washington
1844-1925 .... **SSC 4; TCLC 4**
See also CA 104; 155; DLB 12, 74; DLBD
13; RGAL 4; TUS

Cabral de Melo Neto, Joao
1920-1999 .... **CLC 76**
See also CA 151; CWW 2; DAM MULT;
DLB 307; EWL 3; LAW; LAWS 1

Cabrera Infante, G. 1929-2005 ... **CLC 5, 25,**
45, 120; HLC 1; SSC 39
See also CA 85-88; 236; CANR 29, 65, 110;
CDWLB 3; CWW 2; DA3; DAM MULT;
DLB 113; EWL 3; HW 1, 2; LAW; LAWS
1; MTCW 1, 2; MTFW 2005; RGSF 2;
WLIT 1

Cabrera Infante, Guillermo
See Cabrera Infante, G.

Cade, Toni
See Bambara, Toni Cade

Cadmus and Harmonia
See Buchan, John

Caedmon fl. 658-680 .... **CMLC 7**
See also DLB 146

Caeiro, Alberto
See Pessoa, Fernando

Caesar, Julius
See Julius Caesar

Cage, John (Milton), (Jr.)
1912-1992 .... **CLC 41; PC 58**
See also CA 13-16R; 169; CANR 9, 78;
DLB 193; INT CANR-9; TCLE 1:1

Cahan, Abraham 1860-1951 .... **TCLC 71**
See also CA 108; 154; DLB 9, 25, 28; MAL
5; RGAL 4

Cain, Christopher
See Fleming, Thomas

Cain, G.
See Cabrera Infante, G.

Cain, Guillermo
See Cabrera Infante, G.

Cain, James M(allahan) 1892-1977 .. **CLC 3,**
11, 28
See also AITN 1; BPFB 1; CA 17-20R; 73-
76; CANR 8, 34, 61; CMW 4; CN 1, 2;
DLB 226; EWL 3; MAL 5; MSW; MTCW
1; RGAL 4

Caine, Hall 1853-1931 .... **TCLC 97**
See also RHW

Caine, Mark
See Raphael, Frederic (Michael)

Calasso, Roberto 1941- .... **CLC 81**
See also CA 143; CANR 89

Calderon de la Barca, Pedro
1600-1681 . **DC 3; HLCS 1; LC 23, 136**
See also DFS 23; EW 2; RGWL 2, 3; TWA

Caldwell, Erskine 1903-1987 ... **CLC 1, 8, 14,**
50, 60; SSC 19; TCLC 117
See also AITN 1; AMW; BPFB 1; CA 1-4R;
121; CAAS 1; CANR 2, 33; CN 1, 2, 3,
4; DA3; DAM NOV; DLB 9, 86; EWL 3;
MAL 5; MTCW 1, 2; MTFW 2005;
RGAL 4; RGSF 2; TUS

Caldwell, (Janet Miriam) Taylor (Holland)
1900-1985 .... **CLC 2, 28, 39**
See also BPFB 1; CA 5-8R; 116; CANR 5;
DA3; DAM NOV, POP; DLBD 17;
MTCW 2; RHW

Calhoun, John Caldwell
1782-1850 .... **NCLC 15**
See also DLB 3, 248

Calisher, Hortense 1911-2009 .... **CLC 2, 4, 8,**
38, 134; SSC 15
See also CA 1-4R; CANR 1, 22, 117; CN
1, 2, 3, 4, 5, 6, 7; DA3; DAM NOV; DLB
2, 218; INT CANR-22; MAL 5; MTCW
1, 2; MTFW 2005; RGAL 4; RGSF 2

Callaghan, Morley Edward
1903-1990 ..... **CLC 3, 14, 41, 65; TCLC**
145
See also CA 9-12R; 132; CANR 33, 73;
CN 1, 2, 3, 4; DAC; DAM MST; DLB
68; EWL 3; MTCW 1, 2; MTFW 2005;
RGEL 2; RGSF 2; SSFS 19

Callimachus c. 305B.C.-c.
240B.C. .... **CMLC 18**
See also AW 1; DLB 176; RGWL 2, 3

Calvin, Jean
See Calvin, John

Calvin, John 1509-1564 .... **LC 37**
See also DLB 327; GFL Beginnings to 1789

Calvino, Italo 1923-1985 .... **CLC 5, 8, 11, 22,**
33, 39, 73; SSC 3, 48; TCLC 183
See also AAYA 58; CA 85-88; 116; CANR
23, 61, 132; DAM NOV; DLB 196; EW
13; EWL 3; MTCW 1, 2; MTFW 2005;
RGHL; RGSF 2; RGWL 2, 3; SFW 4;
SSFS 12; WLIT 7

Camara Laye
See Laye, Camara

Cambridge, A Gentleman of the University
of
See Crowley, Edward Alexander

Camden, William 1551-1623 .... **LC 77**
See also DLB 172

Cameron, Carey 1952- .... **CLC 59**
See also CA 135

Cameron, Peter 1959- .... **CLC 44**
See also AMWS 12; CA 125; CANR 50,
117, 188; DLB 234; GLL 2

Camoens, Luis Vaz de 1524(?)-1580
See Camoes, Luis de

Camoes, Luis de 1524(?)-1580 . **HLCS 1; LC**
62; PC 31
See also DLB 287; EW 2; RGWL 2, 3

Camp, Madeleine L'Engle
See L'Engle, Madeleine

Campana, Dino 1885-1932 .... **TCLC 20**
See also CA 117; 246; DLB 114; EWL 3

Campanella, Tommaso 1568-1639 .... **LC 32**
See also RGWL 2, 3

Campbell, Bebe Moore 1950-2006 . **BLC 2:1;**
CLC 246
See also AAYA 26; BW 2, 3; CA 139; 254;
CANR 81, 134; DLB 227; MTCW 2;
MTFW 2005

Campbell, John Ramsey
See Campbell, Ramsey

Campbell, John W(ood, Jr.)
1910-1971 .... **CLC 32**
See also CA 21-22; 29-32R; CANR 34;
CAP 2; DLB 8; MTCW 1; SCFW 1, 2;
SFW 4

Campbell, Joseph 1904-1987 .... **CLC 69;**
TCLC 140
See also AAYA 3, 66; BEST 89:2; CA 1-4R;
124; CANR 3, 28, 61, 107; DA3; MTCW
1, 2

Campbell, Maria 1940- .... **CLC 85; NNAL**
See also CA 102; CANR 54; CCA 1; DAC

Campbell, Ramsey 1946- ... **CLC 42; SSC 19**
See also AAYA 51; CA 57-60, 228; CAAE
228; CANR 7, 102, 171; DLB 261; HGG;
INT CANR-7; SUFW 1, 2

Campbell, (Ignatius) Roy (Dunnachie)
1901-1957 .... **TCLC 5**
See also AFW; CA 104; 155; DLB 20, 225;
EWL 3; MTCW 2; RGEL 2

Campbell, Thomas 1777-1844 .... **NCLC 19**
See also DLB 93, 144; RGEL 2

Campbell, Wilfred
See Campbell, William

Campbell, William 1858(?)-1918 ..... **TCLC 9**
See also CA 106; DLB 92

Campbell, William Edward March
1893-1954 .... **TCLC 96**
See also CA 108; 216; DLB 9, 86, 316;
MAL 5

Campion, Jane 1954- .... **CLC 95, 229**
See also AAYA 33; CA 138; CANR 87

Campion, Thomas 1567-1620 . **LC 78; PC 87**
See also CDBLB Before 1660; DAM POET;
DLB 58, 172; RGEL 2

Child, Mrs.
See Child, Lydia Maria
Child, Philip 1898-1978 .... **CLC 19, 68**
See also CA 13-14; CAP 1; CP 1; DLB 68;
RHW; SATA 47
Childers, (Robert) Erskine
1870-1922 .... **TCLC 65**
See also CA 113; 153; DLB 70
Childress, Alice 1920-1994 .... **BLC 1:1; CLC
12, 15, 86, 96; DC 4; TCLC 116**
See also AAYA 8; BW 2, 3; BYA 2; CA 45-
48; 146; CAD; CANR 3, 27, 50, 74; CLR
14; CWD; DA3; DAM DRAM, MULT,
NOV; DFS 2, 8, 14, 26; DLB 7, 38, 249;
JRDA; LAIT 5; MAICYA 1, 2; MAIC-
YAS 1; MAL 5; MTCW 1, 2; MTFW
2005; RGAL 4; SATA 7, 48, 81; TUS;
WYA; YAW
Chin, Frank (Chew, Jr.) 1940- .... **AAL; CLC
135; DC 7**
See also CA 33-36R; CAD; CANR 71; CD
5, 6; DAM MULT; DLB 206, 312; LAIT
5; RGAL 4
Chin, Marilyn (Mei Ling) 1955- .... **PC 40**
See also CA 129; CANR 70, 113; CWP;
DLB 312; PFS 28
Chislett, (Margaret) Anne 1943- ...... **CLC 34**
See also CA 151
Chitty, Thomas Willes 1926- .... **CLC 6, 11**
See also CA 5-8R; CN 1, 2, 3, 4, 5, 6; EWL
3
Chivers, Thomas Holley
1809-1858 .... **NCLC 49**
See also DLB 3, 248; RGAL 4
Chlamyda, Jehudil
See Peshkov, Alexei Maximovich
Ch'o, Chou
See Shu-Jen, Chou
Choi, Susan 1969- .... **CLC 119**
See also CA 223; CANR 188
Chomette, Rene Lucien 1898-1981 .. **CLC 20**
See also CA 103
Chomsky, Avram Noam
See Chomsky, Noam
Chomsky, Noam 1928- .... **CLC 132**
See also CA 17-20R; CANR 28, 62, 110,
132, 179; DA3; DLB 246; MTCW 1, 2;
MTFW 2005
Chona, Maria 1845(?)-1936 .... **NNAL**
See also CA 144
Chopin, Kate
See Chopin, Katherine
Chopin, Katherine 1851-1904 .... **SSC 8, 68,
110; TCLC 127; WLCS**
See also AAYA 33; AMWR 2; BYA 11, 15;
CA 104; 122; CDALB 1865-1917; DA3;
DAB; DAC; DAM MST, NOV; DLB 12,
78; EXPN; EXPS; FL 1:3; FW; LAIT 3;
MAL 5; MBL; NFS 3; RGAL 4; RGSF 2;
SSFS 2, 13, 17, 26; TUS
Chretien de Troyes c. 12th cent. - . **CMLC 10**
See also DLB 208; EW 1; RGWL 2, 3;
TWA
Christie
See Ichikawa, Kon
Christie, Agatha (Mary Clarissa)
1890-1976 .. **CLC 1, 6, 8, 12, 39, 48, 110**
See also AAYA 9; AITN 1, 2; BPFB 1;
BRWS 2; CA 17-20R; 61-64; CANR 10,
37, 108; CBD; CDBLB 1914-1945; CMW
4; CN 1, 2; CPW; CWD; DA3; DAB;
DAC; DAM NOV; DFS 2; DLB 13, 77,
245; MSW; MTCW 1, 2; MTFW 2005;
NFS 8; RGEL 2; RHW; SATA 36; TEA;
YAW
Christie, Ann Philippa
See Pearce, Philippa
Christie, Philippa
See Pearce, Philippa

Christine de Pisan
See Christine de Pizan
Christine de Pizan 1365(?)-1431(?) ...... **LC 9,
130; PC 68**
See also DLB 208; FL 1:1; FW; RGWL 2,
3
Chuang-Tzu c. 369B.C.-c.
286B.C. .... **CMLC 57**
Chubb, Elmer
See Masters, Edgar Lee
Chulkov, Mikhail Dmitrievich
1743-1792 .... **LC 2**
See also DLB 150
Churchill, Caryl 1938- .... **CLC 31, 55, 157;
DC 5**
See also BRWS 4; CA 102; CANR 22, 46,
108; CBD; CD 5, 6; CWD; DFS 25; DLB
13, 310; EWL 3; FW; MTCW 1; RGEL 2
Churchill, Charles 1731-1764 .... **LC 3**
See also DLB 109; RGEL 2
Churchill, Chick
See Churchill, Caryl
Churchill, Sir Winston (Leonard Spencer)
1874-1965 .... **TCLC 113**
See also BRW 6; CA 97-100; CDBLB
1890-1914; DA3; DLB 100, 329; DLBD
16; LAIT 4; MTCW 1, 2
Chute, Carolyn 1947- .... **CLC 39**
See also CA 123; CANR 135; CN 7
Ciardi, John (Anthony) 1916-1986 . **CLC 10,
40, 44, 129; PC 69**
See also CA 5-8R; 118; CAAS 2; CANR 5,
33; CLR 19; CP 1, 2, 3, 4; CWRI 5; DAM
POET; DLB 5; DLBY 1986; INT
CANR-5; MAICYA 1, 2; MAL 5; MTCW
1, 2; MTFW 2005; RGAL 4; SAAS 26;
SATA 1, 65; SATA-Obit 46
Cibber, Colley 1671-1757 .... **LC 66**
See also DLB 84; RGEL 2
Cicero, Marcus Tullius
106B.C.-43B.C. .... **CMLC 3, 81**
See also AW 1; CDWLB 1; DLB 211;
RGWL 2, 3; WLIT 8
Cimino, Michael 1943- .... **CLC 16**
See also CA 105
Cioran, E(mil) M. 1911-1995 .... **CLC 64**
See also CA 25-28R; 149; CANR 91; DLB
220; EWL 3
Circus, Anthony
See Hoch, Edward D.
Cisneros, Sandra 1954- .... **CLC 69, 118, 193;
HLC 1; PC 52; SSC 32, 72**
See also AAYA 9, 53; AMWS 7; CA 131;
CANR 64, 118; CLR 123; CN 7; CWP;
DA3; DAM MULT; DLB 122, 152; EWL
3; EXPN; FL 1:5; FW; HW 1, 2; LAIT 5;
LATS 1:2; LLW; MAICYA 2; MAL 5;
MTCW 2; MTFW 2005; NFS 2; PFS 19;
RGAL 4; RGSF 2; SSFS 3, 13, 27; WLIT
1; YAW
Cixous, Helene 1937- .... **CLC 92, 253**
See also CA 126; CANR 55, 123; CWW 2;
DLB 83, 242; EWL 3; FL 1:5; FW; GLL
2; MTCW 1, 2; MTFW 2005; TWA
Clair, Rene
See Chomette, Rene Lucien
Clampitt, Amy 1920-1994 .... **CLC 32; PC 19**
See also AMWS 9; CA 110; 146; CANR
29, 79; CP 4, 5; DLB 105; MAL 5; PFS
27
Clancy, Thomas L., Jr. 1947- ... **CLC 45, 112**
See also AAYA 9, 51; BEST 89:1, 90:1;
BPFB 1; BYA 10, 11; CA 125; 131;
CANR 62, 105, 132; CMW 4; CPW;
DA3; DAM NOV, POP; DLB 227; INT
CA-131; MTCW 1, 2; MTFW 2005
Clancy, Tom
See Clancy, Thomas L., Jr.

Clare, John 1793-1864 .. **NCLC 9, 86; PC 23**
See also BRWS 11; DAB; DAM POET;
DLB 55, 96; RGEL 2
Clarin
See Alas (y Urena), Leopoldo (Enrique
Garcia)
Clark, Al C.
See Goines, Donald
Clark, Brian (Robert)
See Clark, (Robert) Brian
Clark, (Robert) Brian 1932- .... **CLC 29**
See also CA 41-44R; CANR 67; CBD; CD
5, 6
Clark, Curt
See Westlake, Donald E.
Clark, Eleanor 1913-1996 .... **CLC 5, 19**
See also CA 9-12R; 151; CANR 41; CN 1,
2, 3, 4, 5, 6; DLB 6
Clark, J. P.
See Clark Bekederemo, J.P.
Clark, John Pepper
See Clark Bekederemo, J.P.
See also AFW; CD 5; CP 1, 2, 3, 4, 5, 6, 7;
RGEL 2
Clark, Kenneth (Mackenzie)
1903-1983 .... **TCLC 147**
See also CA 93-96; 109; CANR 36; MTCW
1, 2; MTFW 2005
Clark, M. R.
See Clark, Mavis Thorpe
Clark, Mavis Thorpe 1909-1999 ...... **CLC 12**
See also CA 57-60; CANR 8, 37, 107; CLR
30; CWRI 5; MAICYA 1, 2; SAAS 5;
SATA 8, 74
Clark, Walter Van Tilburg
1909-1971 .... **CLC 28**
See also CA 9-12R; 33-36R; CANR 63,
113; CN 1; DLB 9, 206; LAIT 2; MAL 5;
RGAL 4; SATA 8; TCWW 1, 2
Clark Bekederemo, J.P. 1935- .... **BLC 1:1;
CLC 38; DC 5**
See Clark, John Pepper
See also AAYA 79; BW 1; CA 65-68;
CANR 16, 72; CD 6; CDWLB 3; DAM
DRAM, MULT; DFS 13; DLB 117; EWL
3; MTCW 2; MTFW 2005
Clarke, Arthur
See Clarke, Arthur C.
Clarke, Arthur C. 1917-2008 .. **CLC 1, 4, 13,
18, 35, 136; SSC 3**
See also AAYA 4, 33; BPFB 1; BYA 13;
CA 1-4R; 270; CANR 2, 28, 55, 74, 130;
CLR 119; CN 1, 2, 3, 4, 5, 6, 7; CPW;
DA3; DAM POP; DLB 261; JRDA; LAIT
5; MAICYA 1, 2; MTCW 1, 2; MTFW
2005; SATA 13, 70, 115; SATA-Obit 191;
SCFW 1, 2; SFW 4; SSFS 4, 18; TCLE
1:1; YAW
Clarke, Arthur Charles
See Clarke, Arthur C.
Clarke, Austin 1896-1974 .... **CLC 6, 9**
See also CA 29-32; 49-52; CAP 2; CP 1, 2;
DAM POET; DLB 10, 20; EWL 3; RGEL
2
Clarke, Austin C. 1934- .... **BLC 1:1; CLC 8,
53; SSC 45, 116**
See also BW 1; CA 25-28R; CAAS 16;
CANR 14, 32, 68, 140; CN 1, 2, 3, 4, 5,
6, 7; DAC; DAM MULT; DLB 53, 125;
DNFS 2; MTCW 2; MTFW 2005; RGSF
2
Clarke, Gillian 1937- .... **CLC 61**
See also CA 106; CP 3, 4, 5, 6, 7; CWP;
DLB 40
Clarke, Marcus (Andrew Hislop)
1846-1881 .... **NCLC 19; SSC 94**
See also DLB 230; RGEL 2; RGSF 2
Clarke, Shirley 1925-1997 .... **CLC 16**
See also CA 189

Colum, Padraic 1881-1972 .... **CLC 28**
    See also BYA 4; CA 73-76; 33-36R; CANR
    35; CLR 36; CP 1; CWRI 5; DLB 19;
    MAICYA 1, 2; MTCW 1; RGEL 2; SATA
    15; WCH

Colvin, James
    See Moorcock, Michael

Colwin, Laurie (E.) 1944-1992 .... **CLC 5, 13,**
    23, 84
    See also CA 89-92; 139; CANR 20, 46;
    DLB 218; DLBY 1980; MTCW 1

Comfort, Alex(ander) 1920-2000 .... **CLC 7**
    See also CA 1-4R; 190; CANR 1, 45; CN
    1, 2, 3, 4; CP 1, 2, 3, 4, 5, 6, 7; DAM
    POP; MTCW 2

Comfort, Montgomery
    See Campbell, Ramsey

Compton-Burnett, I(vy)
    1892(?)-1969 .... **CLC 1, 3, 10, 15, 34;**
    TCLC 180
    See also BRW 7; CA 1-4R; 25-28R; CANR
    4; DAM NOV; DLB 36; EWL 3; MTCW
    1, 2; RGEL 2

Comstock, Anthony 1844-1915 ...... **TCLC 13**
    See also CA 110; 169

Comte, Auguste 1798-1857 .... **NCLC 54**

Conan Doyle, Arthur
    See Doyle, Sir Arthur Conan

Conde (Abellán), Carmen
    1901-1996 .... **HLCS 1**
    See also CA 177; CWW 2; DLB 108; EWL
    3; HW 2

Conde, Maryse 1937- .... **BLC 2:1; BLCS;**
    CLC 52, 92, 247
    See also BW 2, 3; CA 110; 190; CAAE 190;
    CANR 30, 53, 76, 171; CWW 2; DAM
    MULT; EWL 3; MTCW 2; MTFW 2005

Condillac, Etienne Bonnot de
    1714-1780 .... **LC 26**
    See also DLB 313

Condon, Richard 1915-1996 ...... **CLC 4, 6, 8,**
    10, 45, 100
    See also BEST 90:3; BPFB 1; CA 1-4R;
    151; CAAS 1; CANR 2, 23, 164; CMW
    4; CN 1, 2, 3, 4, 5, 6; DAM NOV; INT
    CANR-23; MAL 5; MTCW 1, 2

Condon, Richard Thomas
    See Condon, Richard

Condorcet
    See Condorcet, marquis de Marie-Jean-
    Antoine-Nicolas Caritat

Condorcet, marquis de
    Marie-Jean-Antoine-Nicolas Caritat
    1743-1794 .... **LC 104**
    See also DLB 313; GFL Beginnings to 1789

Confucius 551B.C.-479B.C. .... **CMLC 19, 65;**
    WLCS
    See also DA; DA3; DAB; DAC; DAM
    MST

Congreve, William 1670-1729 ... **DC 2; LC 5,**
    21; WLC 2
    See also BRW 2; CDBLB 1660-1789; DA;
    DAB; DAC; DAM DRAM, MST, POET;
    DFS 15; DLB 39, 84; RGEL 2; WLIT 3

Conley, Robert J. 1940- .... **NNAL**
    See also CA 41-44R; CANR 15, 34, 45, 96,
    186; DAM MULT; TCWW 2

Connell, Evan S., Jr. 1924- .... **CLC 4, 6, 45**
    See also AAYA 7; AMWS 14; CA 1-4R;
    CAAS 2; CANR 2, 39, 76, 97, 140; CN
    1, 2, 3, 4, 5, 6; DAM NOV; DLB 2, 335;
    DLBY 1981; MAL 5; MTCW 1, 2;
    MTFW 2005

Connelly, Marc(us Cook) 1890-1980 . **CLC 7**
    See also CA 85-88; 102; CAD; CANR 30;
    DFS 12; DLB 7; DLBY 1980; MAL 5;
    RGAL 4; SATA-Obit 25

Connolly, Paul
    See Wicker, Tom

Connor, Ralph
    See Gordon, Charles William

Conrad, Joseph 1857-1924 ..... **SSC 9, 67, 69,**
    71; TCLC 1, 6, 13, 25, 43, 57; WLC 2
    See also AAYA 26; BPFB 1; BRW 6;
    BRWC 1; BRWR 2; BYA 2; CA 104; 131;
    CANR 60; CDBLB 1890-1914; DA; DA3;
    DAB; DAC; DAM MST, NOV; DLB 10,
    34, 98, 156; EWL 3; EXPN; EXPS; LAIT
    2; LATS 1:1; LMFS 1; MTCW 1, 2;
    MTFW 2005; NFS 2, 16; RGEL 2; RGSF
    2; SATA 27; SSFS 1, 12; TEA; WLIT 4

Conrad, Robert Arnold
    See Hart, Moss

Conroy, Pat 1945- .... **CLC 30, 74**
    See also AAYA 8, 52; AITN 1; BPFB 1;
    CA 85-88; CANR 24, 53, 129; CN 7;
    CPW; CSW; DA3; DAM NOV, POP;
    DLB 6; LAIT 5; MAL 5; MTCW 1, 2;
    MTFW 2005

Constant (de Rebecque), (Henri) Benjamin
    1767-1830 .... **NCLC 6, 182**
    See also DLB 119; EW 4; GFL 1789 to the
    Present

Conway, Jill K. 1934- .... **CLC 152**
    See also CA 130; CANR 94

Conway, Jill Kathryn Ker
    See Conway, Jill K.

Conybeare, Charles Augustus
    See Eliot, T(homas) S(tearns)

Cook, Michael 1933-1994 .... **CLC 58**
    See also CA 93-96; CANR 68; DLB 53

Cook, Robin 1940- .... **CLC 14**
    See also AAYA 32; BEST 90:2; BPFB 1;
    CA 108; 111; CANR 41, 90, 109, 181;
    CPW; DA3; DAM POP; HGG; INT CA-
    111

Cook, Roy
    See Silverberg, Robert

Cooke, Elizabeth 1948- .... **CLC 55**
    See also CA 129

Cooke, John Esten 1830-1886 .... **NCLC 5**
    See also DLB 3, 248; RGAL 4

Cooke, John Estes
    See Baum, L(yman) Frank

Cooke, M. E.
    See Creasey, John

Cooke, Margaret
    See Creasey, John

Cooke, Rose Terry 1827-1892 ...... **NCLC 110**
    See also DLB 12, 74

Cook-Lynn, Elizabeth 1930- .... **CLC 93;**
    NNAL
    See also CA 133; DAM MULT; DLB 175

Cooney, Ray .... **CLC 62**
    See also CBD

Cooper, Anthony Ashley 1671-1713 .. **LC 107**
    See also DLB 101, 336

Cooper, Dennis 1953- .... **CLC 203**
    See also CA 133; CANR 72, 86; GLL 1;
    HGG

Cooper, Douglas 1960- .... **CLC 86**

Cooper, Henry St. John
    See Creasey, John

Cooper, J. California (?)- .... **CLC 56**
    See also AAYA 12; BW 1; CA 125; CANR
    55; DAM MULT; DLB 212

Cooper, James Fenimore
    1789-1851 .... **NCLC 1, 27, 54, 203**
    See also AAYA 22; AMW; BPFB 1;
    CDALB 1640-1865; CLR 105; DA3;
    DLB 3, 183, 250, 254; LAIT 1; NFS 25;
    RGAL 4; SATA 19; TUS; WCH

Cooper, Susan Fenimore
    1813-1894 .... **NCLC 129**
    See also ANW; DLB 239, 254

Coover, Robert 1932- .. **CLC 3, 7, 15, 32, 46,**
    87, 161; SSC 15, 101
    See also AMWS 5; BPFB 1; CA 45-48;
    CANR 3, 37, 58, 115; CN 1, 2, 3, 4, 5, 6,
    7; DAM NOV; DLB 2, 227; DLBY 1981;
    EWL 3; MAL 5; MTCW 1, 2; MTFW
    2005; RGAL 4; RGSF 2

Copeland, Stewart (Armstrong)
    1952- .... **CLC 26**

Copernicus, Nicolaus 1473-1543 .... **LC 45**

Coppard, A(lfred) E(dgar)
    1878-1957 .... **SSC 21; TCLC 5**
    See also BRWS 8; CA 114; 167; DLB 162;
    EWL 3; HGG; RGEL 2; RGSF 2; SUFW
    1; YABC 1

Coppee, Francois 1842-1908 .... **TCLC 25**
    See also CA 170; DLB 217

Coppola, Francis Ford 1939- ... **CLC 16, 126**
    See also AAYA 39; CA 77-80; CANR 40,
    78; DLB 44

Copway, George 1818-1869 .... **NNAL**
    See also DAM MULT; DLB 175, 183

Corbiere, Tristan 1845-1875 .... **NCLC 43**
    See also DLB 217; GFL 1789 to the Present

Corcoran, Barbara (Asenath)
    1911- .... **CLC 17**
    See also AAYA 14; CA 21-24R; 191; CAAE
    191; CAAS 2; CANR 11, 28, 48; CLR
    50; JRDA; MAICYA 2; MAIC-
    YAS 1; RHW; SAAS 20; SATA 3, 77;
    SATA-Essay 125

Cordelier, Maurice
    See Giraudoux, Jean(-Hippolyte)

Cordier, Gilbert
    See Scherer, Jean-Marie Maurice

Corelli, Marie
    See Mackay, Mary

Corinna c. 225B.C.-c. 305B.C. ...... **CMLC 72**

Corman, Cid 1924-2004 .... **CLC 9**
    See also CA 85-88; 225; CAAS 2; CANR
    44; CP 1, 2, 3, 4, 5, 6, 7; DAM POET;
    DLB 5, 193

Corman, Sidney
    See Corman, Cid

Cormier, Robert 1925-2000 .... **CLC 12, 30**
    See also AAYA 3, 19; BYA 1, 2, 6, 8, 9;
    CA 1-4R; CANR 5, 23, 76, 93; CDALB
    1968-1988; CLR 12, 55; DA; DAB; DAC;
    DAM MST, NOV; DLB 52; EXPN; INT
    CANR-23; JRDA; LAIT 5; MAICYA 1,
    2; MTCW 1, 2; MTFW 2005; NFS 2, 18;
    SATA 10, 45, 83; SATA-Obit 122; WYA;
    YAW

Corn, Alfred (DeWitt III) 1943- .... **CLC 33**
    See also CA 179; CAAE 179; CAAS 25;
    CANR 44; CP 3, 4, 5, 6, 7; CSW; DLB
    120, 282; DLBY 1980

Corneille, Pierre 1606-1684 .. **DC 21; LC 28,**
    135
    See also DAB; DAM MST; DFS 21; DLB
    268; EW 3; GFL Beginnings to 1789;
    RGWL 2, 3; TWA

Cornwell, David
    See le Carre, John

Cornwell, David John Moore
    See le Carre, John

Cornwell, Patricia 1956- .... **CLC 155**
    See also AAYA 16, 56; BPFB 1; CA 134;
    CANR 53, 131; CMW 4; CPW; CSW;
    DAM POP; DLB 306; MSW; MTCW 2;
    MTFW 2005

Cornwell, Patricia Daniels
    See Cornwell, Patricia

Cornwell, Smith
    See Smith, David (Jeddie)

Corso, Gregory 1930-2001 .... **CLC 1, 11; PC 33**
See also AMWS 12; BG 1:2; CA 5-8R; 193; CANR 41, 76, 132; CP 1, 2, 3, 4, 5, 6, 7; DA3; DLB 5, 16, 237; LMFS 2; MAL 5; MTCW 1, 2; MTFW 2005; WP

Cortazar, Julio 1914-1984 ... **CLC 2, 3, 5, 10, 13, 15, 33, 34, 92; HLC 1; SSC 7, 76**
See also BPFB 1; CA 21-24R; CANR 12, 32, 81; CDWLB 3; DA3; DAM MULT, NOV; DLB 113; EWL 3; EXPS; HW 1, 2; LAW; MTCW 1, 2; MTFW 2005; RGSF 2; RGWL 2, 3; SSFS 3, 20; TWA; WLIT 1

Cortes, Hernan 1485-1547 .... **LC 31**

Cortez, Jayne 1936- .... **BLC 2:1**
See also BW 2, 3; CA 73-76; CANR 13, 31, 68, 126; CWP; DLB 41; EWL 3

Corvinus, Jakob
See Raabe, Wilhelm (Karl)

Corwin, Cecil
See Kornbluth, C(yril) M.

Cosic, Dobrica 1921- .... **CLC 14**
See also CA 122; 138; CDWLB 4; CWW 2; DLB 181; EWL 3

Costain, Thomas B(ertram) 1885-1965 .... **CLC 30**
See also BYA 3; CA 5-8R; 25-28R; DLB 9; RHW

Costantini, Humberto 1924(?)-1987 . **CLC 49**
See also CA 131; 122; EWL 3; HW 1

Costello, Elvis 1954- .... **CLC 21**
See also CA 204

Costenoble, Philostene
See Ghelderode, Michel de

Cotes, Cecil V.
See Duncan, Sara Jeannette

Cotter, Joseph Seamon Sr. 1861-1949 .... **BLC 1:1; TCLC 28**
See also BW 1; CA 124; DAM MULT; DLB 50

Couch, Arthur Thomas Quiller
See Quiller-Couch, Sir Arthur (Thomas)

Coulton, James
See Hansen, Joseph

Couperus, Louis (Marie Anne) 1863-1923 .... **TCLC 15**
See also CA 115; EWL 3; RGWL 2, 3

Coupland, Douglas 1961- .... **CLC 85, 133**
See also AAYA 34; CA 142; CANR 57, 90, 130, 172; CCA 1; CN 7; CPW; DAC; DAM POP; DLB 334

Coupland, Douglas Campbell
See Coupland, Douglas

Court, Wesli
See Turco, Lewis

Courtenay, Bryce 1933- .... **CLC 59**
See also CA 138; CPW

Courtney, Robert
See Ellison, Harlan

Cousteau, Jacques-Yves 1910-1997 .. **CLC 30**
See also CA 65-68; 159; CANR 15, 67; MTCW 1; SATA 38, 98

Coventry, Francis 1725-1754 .... **LC 46**
See also DLB 39

Coverdale, Miles c. 1487-1569 .... **LC 77**
See also DLB 167

Cowan, Peter (Walkinshaw) 1914-2002 .... **SSC 28**
See also CA 21-24R; CANR 9, 25, 50, 83; CN 1, 2, 3, 4, 5, 6, 7; DLB 260; RGSF 2

Coward, Noel (Peirce) 1899-1973 . **CLC 1, 9, 29, 51**
See also AITN 1; BRWS 2; CA 17-18; 41-44R; CANR 35, 132; CAP 2; CBD; CD-BLB 1914-1945; DA3; DAM DRAM; DFS 3, 6; DLB 10, 245; EWL 3; IDFW 3, 4; MTCW 1, 2; MTFW 2005; RGEL 2; TEA

Cowley, Abraham 1618-1667 .. **LC 43; PC 90**
See also BRW 2; DLB 131, 151; PAB; RGEL 2

Cowley, Malcolm 1898-1989 .... **CLC 39**
See also AMWS 2; CA 5-8R; 128; CANR 3, 55; CP 1, 2, 3, 4; DLB 4, 48; DLBY 1981, 1989; EWL 3; MAL 5; MTCW 1, 2; MTFW 2005

Cowper, William 1731-1800 ..... **NCLC 8, 94; PC 40**
See also BRW 3; DA3; DAM POET; DLB 104, 109; RGEL 2

Cox, William Trevor
See Trevor, William

Coyne, P. J.
See Masters, Hilary

Coyne, P.J.
See Masters, Hilary

Cozzens, James Gould 1903-1978 . **CLC 1, 4, 11, 92**
See also AMW; BPFB 1; CA 9-12R; 81-84; CANR 19; CDALB 1941-1968; CN 1, 2; DLB 9, 294; DLBD 2; DLBY 1984, 1997; EWL 3; MAL 5; MTCW 1, 2; MTFW 2005; RGAL 4

Crabbe, George 1754-1832 ... **NCLC 26, 121; PC 97**
See also BRW 3; DLB 93; RGEL 2

Crace, Jim 1946- .... **CLC 157; SSC 61**
See also BRWS 14; CA 128; 135; CANR 55, 70, 123, 180; CN 5, 6, 7; DLB 231; INT CA-135

Craddock, Charles Egbert
See Murfree, Mary Noailles

Craig, A. A.
See Anderson, Poul

Craik, Mrs.
See Craik, Dinah Maria (Mulock)

Craik, Dinah Maria (Mulock) 1826-1887 .... **NCLC 38**
See also DLB 35, 163; MAICYA 1, 2; RGEL 2; SATA 34

Cram, Ralph Adams 1863-1942 ..... **TCLC 45**
See also CA 160

Cranch, Christopher Pearse 1813-1892 .... **NCLC 115**
See also DLB 1, 42, 243

Crane, (Harold) Hart 1899-1932 .... **PC 3; TCLC 2, 5, 80; WLC 2**
See also AMW; AMWR 2; CA 104; 127; CDALB 1917-1929; DA; DA3; DAB; DAC; DAM MST, POET; DLB 4, 48; EWL 3; MAL 5; MTCW 1, 2; MTFW 2005; RGAL 4; TUS

Crane, R(onald) S(almon) 1886-1967 .... **CLC 27**
See also CA 85-88; DLB 63

Crane, Stephen (Townley) 1871-1900 .... **PC 80; SSC 7, 56, 70; TCLC 11, 17, 32, 216; WLC 2**
See also AAYA 21; AMW; AMWC 1; BPFB 1; BYA 3; CA 109; 140; CANR 84; CDALB 1865-1917; CLR 132; DA; DA3; DAB; DAC; DAM MST, NOV, POET; DLB 12, 54, 78; EXPN; EXPS; LAIT 2; LMFS 2; MAL 5; NFS 4, 20; PFS 9; RGAL 4; RGSF 2; SSFS 4; TUS; WYA; YABC 2

Cranmer, Thomas 1489-1556 .... **LC 95**
See also DLB 132, 213

Cranshaw, Stanley
See Fisher, Dorothy (Frances) Canfield

Crase, Douglas 1944- .... **CLC 58**
See also CA 106

Crashaw, Richard 1612(?)-1649 .. **LC 24; PC 84**
See also BRW 2; DLB 126; PAB; RGEL 2

Cratinus c. 519B.C.-c. 422B.C. ..... **CMLC 54**
See also LMFS 1

Craven, Margaret 1901-1980 .... **CLC 17**
See also BYA 2; CA 103; CCA 1; DAC; LAIT 5

Crawford, F(rancis) Marion 1854-1909 .... **TCLC 10**
See also CA 107; 168; DLB 71; HGG; RGAL 4; SUFW 1

Crawford, Isabella Valancy 1850-1887 .... **NCLC 12, 127**
See also DLB 92; RGEL 2

Crayon, Geoffrey
See Irving, Washington

Creasey, John 1908-1973 .... **CLC 11**
See also CA 5-8R; 41-44R; CANR 8, 59; CMW 4; DLB 77; MTCW 1

Crebillon, Claude Prosper Jolyot de (fils) 1707-1777 .... **LC 1, 28**
See also DLB 313; GFL Beginnings to 1789

Credo
See Creasey, John

Credo, Alvaro J. de
See Prado (Calvo), Pedro

Creeley, Robert 1926-2005 .... **CLC 1, 2, 4, 8, 11, 15, 36, 78, 266; PC 73**
See also AMWS 4; CA 1-4R; 237; CAAS 10; CANR 23, 43, 89, 137; CP 1, 2, 3, 4, 5, 6, 7; DA3; DAM POET; DLB 5, 16, 169; DLBD 17; EWL 3; MAL 5; MTCW 1, 2; MTFW 2005; PFS 21; RGAL 4; WP

Creeley, Robert White
See Creeley, Robert

Crenne, Helisenne de 1510-1560 .... **LC 113**
See also DLB 327

Crevecoeur, Hector St. John de
See Crevecoeur, Michel Guillaume Jean de

Crevecoeur, Michel Guillaume Jean de 1735-1813 .... **NCLC 105**
See also AMWS 1; ANW; DLB 37

Crevel, Rene 1900-1935 .... **TCLC 112**
See also GLL 2

Crews, Harry 1935- .... **CLC 6, 23, 49**
See also AITN 1; AMWS 11; BPFB 1; CA 25-28R; CANR 20, 57; CN 3, 4, 5, 6, 7; CSW; DA3; DLB 6, 143, 185; MTCW 1, 2; MTFW 2005; RGAL 4

Crichton, John Michael
See Crichton, Michael

Crichton, Michael 1942-2008 .. **CLC 2, 6, 54, 90, 242**
See also AAYA 10, 49; AITN 2; BPFB 1; CA 25-28R; 279; CANR 13, 40, 54, 76, 127, 179; CMW 4; CN 2, 3, 6, 7; CPW; DA3; DAM NOV, POP; DLB 292; DLBY 1981; INT CANR-13; JRDA; MTCW 1, 2; MTFW 2005; SATA 9, 88; SATA-Obit 199; SFW 4; YAW

Crispin, Edmund
See Montgomery, (Robert) Bruce

Cristina of Sweden 1626-1689 .... **LC 124**

Cristofer, Michael 1945(?)- .... **CLC 28**
See also CA 110; 152; CAD; CANR 150; CD 5, 6; DAM DRAM; DFS 15; DLB 7

Cristofer, Michael Ivan
See Cristofer, Michael

Criton
See Alain

Croce, Benedetto 1866-1952 .... **TCLC 37**
See also CA 120; 155; EW 8; EWL 3; WLIT 7

Crockett, David 1786-1836 .... **NCLC 8**
See also DLB 3, 11, 183, 248

Crockett, Davy
See Crockett, David

Crofts, Freeman Wills 1879-1957 .. **TCLC 55**
See also CA 115; 195; CMW 4; DLB 77; MSW

Croker, John Wilson 1780-1857 .... **NCLC 10**
See also DLB 110

Crommelynck, Fernand 1885-1970 .. **CLC 75**
  See also CA 189; 89-92; EWL 3
Cromwell, Oliver 1599-1658 .... **LC 43**
Cronenberg, David 1943- .... **CLC 143**
  See also CA 138; CCA 1
Cronin, A(rchibald) J(oseph)
  1896-1981 .... **CLC 32**
  See also BPFB 1; CA 1-4R; 102; CANR 5;
  CN 2; DLB 191; SATA 47; SATA-Obit 25
Cross, Amanda
  See Heilbrun, Carolyn G(old)
Crothers, Rachel 1878-1958 .... **TCLC 19**
  See also CA 113; 194; CAD; CWD; DLB
  7, 266; RGAL 4
Croves, Hal
  See Traven, B.
Crow Dog, Mary (?)- .... **CLC 93; NNAL**
  See also CA 154
Crowfield, Christopher
  See Stowe, Harriet (Elizabeth) Beecher
Crowley, Aleister
  See Crowley, Edward Alexander
Crowley, Edward Alexander
  1875-1947 .... **TCLC 7**
  See also CA 104; GLL 1; HGG
Crowley, John 1942- .... **CLC 57**
  See also AAYA 57; BPFB 1; CA 61-64;
  CANR 43, 98, 138, 177; DLBY 1982;
  FANT; MTFW 2005; SATA 65, 140; SFW
  4; SUFW 2
Crowne, John 1641-1712 .... **LC 104**
  See also DLB 80; RGEL 2
Crud
  See Crumb, R.
Crumarums
  See Crumb, R.
Crumb, R. 1943- .... **CLC 17**
  See also CA 106; CANR 107, 150
Crumb, Robert
  See Crumb, R.
Crumbum
  See Crumb, R.
Crumski
  See Crumb, R.
Crum the Bum
  See Crumb, R.
Crunk
  See Crumb, R.
Crustt
  See Crumb, R.
Crutchfield, Les
  See Trumbo, Dalton
Cruz, Victor Hernandez 1949- ... **HLC 1; PC
  37**
  See also BW 2; CA 65-68, 271; CAAE 271;
  CAAS 17; CANR 14, 32, 74, 132; CP 1,
  2, 3, 4, 5, 6, 7; DAM MULT, POET; DLB
  41; DNFS 1; EXPP; HW 1, 2; LLW;
  MTCW 2; MTFW 2005; PFS 16; WP
Cryer, Gretchen (Kiger) 1935- .... **CLC 21**
  See also CA 114; 123
Csath, Geza
  See Brenner, Jozef
Cudlip, David R(ockwell) 1933- .... **CLC 34**
  See also CA 177
Cullen, Countee 1903-1946 ..... **BLC 1:1; HR
  1:2; PC 20; TCLC 4, 37, 220; WLCS**
  See also AAYA 78; AFAW 2; AMWS 4; BW
  1; CA 108; 124; CDALB 1917-1929; DA;
  DA3; DAC; DAM MST, MULT, POET;
  DLB 4, 48, 51; EWL 3; EXPP; LMFS 2;
  MAL 5; MTCW 1, 2; MTFW 2005; PFS
  3; RGAL 4; SATA 18; WP
Culleton, Beatrice 1949- .... **NNAL**
  See also CA 120; CANR 83; DAC
Culver, Timothy J.
  See Westlake, Donald E.

Culver, Timothy J.
  See Westlake, Donald E.
Cum, R.
  See Crumb, R.
Cumberland, Richard
  1732-1811 .... **NCLC 167**
  See also DLB 89; RGEL 2
Cummings, Bruce F(rederick)
  1889-1919 .... **TCLC 24**
  See also CA 123
Cummings, E(dward) E(stlin)
  1894-1962 .. **CLC 1, 3, 8, 12, 15, 68; PC
  5; TCLC 137; WLC 2**
  See also AAYA 41; AMW; CA 73-76;
  CANR 31; CDALB 1929-1941; DA;
  DA3; DAB; DAC; DAM MST, POET;
  DLB 4, 48; EWL 3; EXPP; MAL 5;
  MTCW 1, 2; MTFW 2005; PAB; PFS 1,
  3, 12, 13, 19, 30; RGAL 4; TUS; WP
Cummins, Maria Susanna
  1827-1866 .... **NCLC 139**
  See also DLB 42; YABC 1
Cunha, Euclides (Rodrigues Pimenta) da
  1866-1909 .... **TCLC 24**
  See also CA 123; 219; DLB 307; LAW;
  WLIT 1
Cunningham, E. V.
  See Fast, Howard
Cunningham, J. Morgan
  See Westlake, Donald E.
Cunningham, J(ames) V(incent)
  1911-1985 .... **CLC 3, 31; PC 92**
  See also CA 1-4R; 115; CANR 1, 72; CP 1,
  2, 3, 4; DLB 5
Cunningham, Julia (Woolfolk)
  1916- .... **CLC 12**
  See also CA 9-12R; CANR 4, 19, 36; CWRI
  5; JRDA; MAICYA 1, 2; SAAS 2; SATA
  1, 26, 132
Cunningham, Michael 1952- .... **CLC 34, 243**
  See also AMWS 15; CA 136; CANR 96,
  160; CN 7; DLB 292; GLL 2; MTFW
  2005; NFS 23
Cunninghame Graham, R. B.
  See Cunninghame Graham, Robert
  (Gallnigad) Bontine
Cunninghame Graham, Robert (Gallnigad)
  Bontine 1852-1936 .... **TCLC 19**
  See also CA 119; 184; DLB 98, 135, 174;
  RGEL 2; RGSF 2
Curnow, (Thomas) Allen (Monro)
  1911-2001 .... **PC 48**
  See also CA 69-72; 202; CANR 48, 99; CP
  1, 2, 3, 4, 5, 6, 7; EWL 3; RGEL 2
Currie, Ellen 19(?)- .... **CLC 44**
Curtin, Philip
  See Lowndes, Marie Adelaide (Belloc)
Curtin, Phillip
  See Lowndes, Marie Adelaide (Belloc)
Curtis, Price
  See Ellison, Harlan
Cusanus, Nicolaus 1401-1464
  See Nicholas of Cusa
Cutrate, Joe
  See Spiegelman, Art
Cynewulf c. 770- .... **CMLC 23**
  See also DLB 146; RGEL 2
Cyrano de Bergerac, Savinien de
  1619-1655 .... **LC 65**
  See also DLB 268; GFL Beginnings to
  1789; RGWL 2, 3
Cyril of Alexandria c. 375-c. 430 . **CMLC 59**
Czaczkes, Shmuel Yosef Halevi
  See Agnon, S.Y.
Dabrowska, Maria (Szumska)
  1889-1965 .... **CLC 15**
  See also CA 106; CDWLB 4; DLB 215;
  EWL 3

Dabydeen, David 1955- .... **CLC 34**
  See also BW 1; CA 125; CANR 56, 92; CN
  6, 7; CP 5, 6, 7; DLB 347
Dacey, Philip 1939- .... **CLC 51**
  See also CA 37-40R, 231; CAAE 231;
  CAAS 17; CANR 14, 32, 64; CP 4, 5, 6,
  7; DLB 105
Dacre, Charlotte c. 1772-1825(?) . **NCLC 151**
Dafydd ap Gwilym c. 1320-c. 1380 ..... **PC 56**
Dagerman, Stig (Halvard)
  1923-1954 .... **TCLC 17**
  See also CA 117; 155; DLB 259; EWL 3
D'Aguiar, Fred 1960- ..... **BLC 2:1; CLC 145**
  See also CA 148; CANR 83, 101; CN 7;
  CP 5, 6, 7; DLB 157; EWL 3
Dahl, Roald 1916-1990 ...... **CLC 1, 6, 18, 79;
  TCLC 173**
  See also AAYA 15; BPFB 1; BRWS 4; BYA
  5; CA 1-4R; 133; CANR 6, 32, 37, 62;
  CLR 1, 7, 41, 111; CN 1, 2, 3, 4; CPW;
  DA3; DAB; DAC; DAM MST, NOV,
  POP; DLB 139, 255; HGG; JRDA; MAI-
  CYA 1, 2; MTCW 1, 2; MTFW 2005;
  RGSF 2; SATA 1, 26, 73; SATA-Obit 65;
  SSFS 4; TEA; YAW
Dahlberg, Edward 1900-1977 . **CLC 1, 7, 14;
  TCLC 208**
  See also CA 9-12R; 69-72; CANR 31, 62;
  CN 1, 2; DLB 48; MAL 5; MTCW 1;
  RGAL 4
Daitch, Susan 1954- .... **CLC 103**
  See also CA 161
Dale, Colin
  See Lawrence, T(homas) E(dward)
Dale, George E.
  See Asimov, Isaac
d'Alembert, Jean Le Rond
  1717-1783 .... **LC 126**
Dalton, Roque 1935-1975(?) ..... **HLCS 1; PC
  36**
  See also CA 176; DLB 283; HW 2
Daly, Elizabeth 1878-1967 .... **CLC 52**
  See also CA 23-24; 25-28R; CANR 60;
  CAP 2; CMW 4
Daly, Mary 1928- .... **CLC 173**
  See also CA 25-28R; CANR 30, 62, 166;
  FW; GLL 1; MTCW 1
Daly, Maureen 1921-2006 .... **CLC 17**
  See also AAYA 5; 58; BYA 6; CA 253;
  CANR 37, 83, 108; CLR 96; JRDA; MAI-
  CYA 1, 2; SAAS 1; SATA 2, 129; SATA-
  Obit 176; WYA; YAW
Damas, Leon-Gontran 1912-1978 ... **CLC 84;
  TCLC 204**
  See also BW 1; CA 125; 73-76; EWL 3
Dana, Richard Henry Sr.
  1787-1879 .... **NCLC 53**
Dangarembga, Tsitsi 1959- .... **BLC 2:1**
  See also BW 3; CA 163; NFS 28; WLIT 2
Daniel, Samuel 1562(?)-1619 .... **LC 24**
  See also DLB 62; RGEL 2
Daniels, Brett
  See Adler, Renata
Dannay, Frederic 1905-1982 .... **CLC 3, 11**
  See also BPFB 3; CA 1-4R; 107; CANR 1,
  39; CMW 4; DAM POP; DLB 137; MSW;
  MTCW 1; RGAL 4
D'Annunzio, Gabriele 1863-1938 ... **TCLC 6,
  40, 215**
  See also CA 104; 155; EW 8; EWL 3;
  RGWL 2, 3; TWA; WLIT 7
Danois, N. le
  See Gourmont, Remy(-Marie-Charles) de
Dante 1265-1321 .... **CMLC 3, 18, 39, 70; PC
  21; WLCS**
  See also DA; DA3; DAB; DAC; DAM
  MST, POET; EFS 1; EW 1; LAIT 1;
  RGWL 2, 3; TWA; WLIT 7; WP

Deighton, Leonard Cyril 1929- ..... **CLC 4, 7, 22, 46**
See also AAYA 57, 6; BEST 89:2; BPFB 1; CA 9-12R; CANR 19, 33, 68; CDBLB 1960- Present; CMW 4; CN 1, 2, 3, 4, 5, 6, 7; CPW; DA3; DAM NOV, POP; DLB 87; MTCW 1, 2; MTFW 2005

Dekker, Thomas 1572(?)-1632 ..... **DC 12; LC 22, 159**
See also CDBLB Before 1660; DAM DRAM; DLB 62, 172; LMFS 1; RGEL 2

de Laclos, Pierre Ambroise Franois
See Laclos, Pierre-Ambroise Francois

Delacroix, (Ferdinand-Victor-)Eugene 1798-1863 .... **NCLC 133**
See also EW 5

Delafield, E. M.
See Dashwood, Edmee Elizabeth Monica de la Pasture

de la Mare, Walter (John) 1873-1956 ..... **PC 77; SSC 14; TCLC 4, 53; WLC 2**
See also CA 163; CDBLB 1914-1945; CLR 23; CWRI 5; DA3; DAB; DAC; DAM MST, POET; DLB 19, 153, 162, 255, 284; EWL 3; EXPP; HGG; MAICYA 1, 2; MTCW 2; MTFW 2005; RGEL 2; RGSF 2; SATA 16; SUFW 1; TEA; WCH

de Lamartine, Alphonse (Marie Louis Prat)
See Lamartine, Alphonse (Marie Louis Prat) de

Delaney, Franey
See O'Hara, John (Henry)

Delaney, Shelagh 1939- .... **CLC 29**
See also CA 17-20R; CANR 30, 67; CBD; CD 5, 6; CDBLB 1960 to Present; CWD; DAM DRAM; DFS 7; DLB 13; MTCW 1

Delany, Martin Robison 1812-1885 .... **NCLC 93**
See also DLB 50; RGAL 4

Delany, Mary (Granville Pendarves) 1700-1788 .... **LC 12**

Delany, Samuel R., Jr. 1942- .... **BLC 1:1; CLC 8, 14, 38, 141**
See also AAYA 24; AFAW 2; BPFB 1; BW 2, 3; CA 81-84; CANR 27, 43, 116, 172; CN 2, 3, 4, 5, 6, 7; DAM MULT; DLB 8, 33; FANT; MAL 5; MTCW 1, 2; RGAL 4; SATA 92; SCFW 1, 2; SFW 4; SUFW 2

Delany, Samuel Ray
See Delany, Samuel R., Jr.

de la Parra, (Ana) Teresa (Sonojo) 1890(?)-1936 .... **HLCS 2; TCLC 185**
See also CA 178; HW 2; LAW

Delaporte, Theophile
See Green, Julien (Hartridge)

De La Ramee, Marie Louise 1839-1908 .... **TCLC 43**
See also CA 204; DLB 18, 156; RGEL 2; SATA 20

de la Roche, Mazo 1879-1961 .... **CLC 14**
See also CA 85-88; CANR 30; DLB 68; RGEL 2; RHW; SATA 64

De La Salle, Innocent
See Hartmann, Sadakichi

de Laureamont, Comte
See Lautreamont

Delbanco, Nicholas 1942- ..... **CLC 6, 13, 167**
See also CA 17-20R, 189; CAAE 189; CAAS 2; CANR 29, 55, 116, 150; CN 7; DLB 6, 234

Delbanco, Nicholas Franklin
See Delbanco, Nicholas

del Castillo, Michel 1933- .... **CLC 38**
See also CA 109; CANR 77

Deledda, Grazia (Cosima) 1875(?)-1936 .... **TCLC 23**
See also CA 123; 205; DLB 264, 329; EWL 3; RGWL 2, 3; WLIT 7

Deleuze, Gilles 1925-1995 .... **TCLC 116**
See also DLB 296

Delgado, Abelardo (Lalo) B(arrientos) 1930-2004 .... **HLC 1**
See also CA 131; 230; CAAS 15; CANR 90; DAM MST, MULT; DLB 82; HW 1, 2

Delibes, Miguel
See Delibes Setien, Miguel

Delibes Setien, Miguel 1920- .... **CLC 8, 18**
See also CA 45-48; CANR 1, 32; CWW 2; DLB 322; EWL 3; HW 1; MTCW 1

DeLillo, Don 1936- ..... **CLC 8, 10, 13, 27, 39, 54, 76, 143, 210, 213**
See also AMWC 2; AMWS 6; BEST 89:1; BPFB 1; CA 81-84; CANR 21, 76, 92, 133, 173; CN 3, 4, 5, 6, 7; CPW; DA3; DAM NOV, POP; DLB 6, 173; EWL 3; MAL 5; MTCW 1, 2; MTFW 2005; NFS 28; RGAL 4; TUS

de Lisser, H. G.
See De Lisser, H(erbert) G(eorge)

De Lisser, H(erbert) G(eorge) 1878-1944 .... **TCLC 12**
See also BW 2; CA 109; 152; DLB 117

Deloire, Pierre
See Peguy, Charles (Pierre)

Deloney, Thomas 1543(?)-1600 .... **LC 41; PC 79**
See also DLB 167; RGEL 2

Deloria, Ella (Cara) 1889-1971(?) ..... **NNAL**
See also CA 152; DAM MULT; DLB 175

Deloria, Vine, Jr. 1933-2005 .... **CLC 21, 122; NNAL**
See also CA 53-56; 245; CANR 5, 20, 48, 98; DAM MULT; DLB 175; MTCW 1; SATA 21; SATA-Obit 171

Deloria, Vine Victor, Jr.
See Deloria, Vine, Jr.

del Valle-Inclan, Ramon (Maria)
See Valle-Inclan, Ramon (Maria) del

Del Vecchio, John M(ichael) 1947- .. **CLC 29**
See also CA 110; DLBD 9

de Man, Paul (Adolph Michel) 1919-1983 .... **CLC 55**
See also CA 128; 111; CANR 61; DLB 67; MTCW 1, 2

de Mandiargues, Andre Pieyre
See Pieyre de Mandiargues, Andre

DeMarinis, Rick 1934- .... **CLC 54**
See also CA 57-60, 184; CAAE 184; CAAS 24; CANR 9, 25, 50, 160; DLB 218; TCWW 2

de Maupassant, (Henri Rene Albert) Guy
See Maupassant, (Henri Rene Albert) Guy de

Dembry, R. Emmet
See Murfree, Mary Noailles

Demby, William 1922- ...... **BLC 1:1; CLC 53**
See also BW 1, 3; CA 81-84; CANR 81; DAM MULT; DLB 33

de Menton, Francisco
See Chin, Frank (Chew, Jr.)

Demetrius of Phalerum c. 307B.C.- .... **CMLC 34**

Demijohn, Thom
See Disch, Thomas M.

De Mille, James 1833-1880 .... **NCLC 123**
See also DLB 99, 251

Democritus c. 460B.C.-c. 370B.C. . **CMLC 47**

de Montaigne, Michel (Eyquem)
See Montaigne, Michel (Eyquem) de

de Montherlant, Henry (Milon)
See Montherlant, Henry (Milon) de

Demosthenes 384B.C.-322B.C. ...... **CMLC 13**
See also AW 1; DLB 176; RGWL 2, 3; WLIT 8

de Musset, (Louis Charles) Alfred
See Musset, Alfred de

de Natale, Francine
See Malzberg, Barry N(athaniel)

de Navarre, Marguerite 1492-1549 .... **LC 61, 167; SSC 85**
See also DLB 327; GFL Beginnings to 1789; RGWL 2, 3

Denby, Edwin (Orr) 1903-1983 .... **CLC 48**
See also CA 138; 110; CP 1

de Nerval, Gerard
See Nerval, Gerard de

Denham, John 1615-1669 .... **LC 73**
See also DLB 58, 126; RGEL 2

Denis, Julio
See Cortazar, Julio

Denmark, Harrison
See Zelazny, Roger

Dennis, John 1658-1734 .... **LC 11, 154**
See also DLB 101; RGEL 2

Dennis, Nigel (Forbes) 1912-1989 ...... **CLC 8**
See also CA 25-28R; 129; CN 1, 2, 3, 4; DLB 13, 15, 233; EWL 3; MTCW 1

Dent, Lester 1904-1959 .... **TCLC 72**
See also CA 112; 161; CMW 4; DLB 306; SFW 4

Dentinger, Stephen
See Hoch, Edward D.

De Palma, Brian 1940- .... **CLC 20, 247**
See also CA 109

De Palma, Brian Russell
See De Palma, Brian

de Pizan, Christine
See Christine de Pizan

De Quincey, Thomas 1785-1859 ..... **NCLC 4, 87, 198**
See also BRW 4; CDBLB 1789-1832; DLB 110, 144; RGEL 2

De Ray, Jill
See Moore, Alan

Deren, Eleanora 1908(?)-1961 .. **CLC 16, 102**
See also CA 192; 111

Deren, Maya
See Deren, Eleanora

Derleth, August (William) 1909-1971 .... **CLC 31**
See also BPFB 1; BYA 9, 10; CA 1-4R; 29-32R; CANR 4; CMW 4; CN 1; DLB 9; DLBD 17; HGG; SATA 5; SUFW 1

Der Nister 1884-1950 .... **TCLC 56**
See also DLB 333; EWL 3

de Routisie, Albert
See Aragon, Louis

Derrida, Jacques 1930-2004 ...... **CLC 24, 87, 225**
See also CA 124; 127; 232; CANR 76, 98, 133; DLB 242; EWL 3; LMFS 2; MTCW 2; TWA

Derry Down Derry
See Lear, Edward

Dersonnes, Jacques
See Simenon, Georges (Jacques Christian)

Der Stricker c. 1190-c. 1250 .... **CMLC 75**
See also DLB 138

Desai, Anita 1937- . **CLC 19, 37, 97, 175, 271**
See also BRWS 5; CA 81-84; CANR 33, 53, 95, 133; CN 1, 2, 3, 4, 5, 6, 7; CWRI 5; DA3; DAB; DAM NOV; DLB 271, 323; DNFS 2; EWL 3; FW; MTCW 1, 2; MTFW 2005; SATA 63, 126

Desai, Kiran 1971- .... **CLC 119**
See also BYA 16; CA 171; CANR 127; NFS 28

de Saint-Luc, Jean
See Glassco, John

EWL 3; LAIT 3; MAL 5; MTCW 1, 2; MTFW 2005; NFS 6; RGAL 4; RGHL; RHW; SSFS 27; TCLE 1:1; TCWW 1, 2; TUS

Dodgson, Charles Lutwidge
See Carroll, Lewis

Dodsley, Robert 1703-1764 .... **LC 97**
See also DLB 95; RGEL 2

Dodson, Owen (Vincent)
1914-1983 .... **BLC 1:1; CLC 79**
See also BW 1; CA 65-68; 110; CANR 24; DAM MULT; DLB 76

Doeblin, Alfred 1878-1957 .... **TCLC 13**
See also CA 110; 141; CDWLB 2; DLB 66; EWL 3; RGWL 2, 3

Doerr, Harriet 1910-2002 .... **CLC 34**
See also CA 117; 122; 213; CANR 47; INT CA-122; LATS 1:2

Domecq, H(onorio) Bustos
See Bioy Casares, Adolfo; Borges, Jorge Luis

Domini, Rey
See Lorde, Audre

Dominic, R. B.
See Hennissart, Martha

Dominique
See Proust, (Valentin-Louis-George-Eugene) Marcel

Don, A
See Stephen, Sir Leslie

Donaldson, Stephen R. 1947- ... **CLC 46, 138**
See also AAYA 36; BPFB 1; CA 89-92; CANR 13, 55, 99; CPW; DAM POP; FANT; INT CANR-13; SATA 121; SFW 4; SUFW 1, 2

Donleavy, J(ames) P(atrick) 1926- .... **CLC 1, 4, 6, 10, 45**
See also AITN 2; BPFB 1; CA 9-12R; CANR 24, 49, 62, 80, 124; CBD; CD 5, 6; CN 1, 2, 3, 4, 5, 6, 7; DLB 6, 173; INT CANR-24; MAL 5; MTCW 1, 2; MTFW 2005; RGAL 4

Donnadieu, Marguerite
See Duras, Marguerite

Donne, John 1572-1631 ... **LC 10, 24, 91; PC 1, 43; WLC 2**
See also AAYA 67; BRW 1; BRWC 1; BRWR 2; CDBLB Before 1660; DA; DAB; DAC; DAM MST, POET; DLB 121, 151; EXPP; PAB; PFS 2, 11; RGEL 3; TEA; WLIT 3; WP

Donnell, David 1939(?)- .... **CLC 34**
See also CA 197

Donoghue, Denis 1928- .... **CLC 209**
See also CA 17-20R; CANR 16, 102

Donoghue, Emma 1969- .... **CLC 239**
See also CA 155; CANR 103, 152; DLB 267; GLL 2; SATA 101

Donoghue, P.S.
See Hunt, E. Howard

Donoso (Yanez), Jose 1924-1996 ... **CLC 4, 8, 11, 32, 99; HLC 1; SSC 34; TCLC 133**
See also CA 81-84; 155; CANR 32, 73; CD-WLB 3; CWW 2; DAM MULT; DLB 113; EWL 3; HW 1, 2; LAW; LAWS 1; MTCW 1, 2; MTFW 2005; RGSF 2; WLIT 1

Donovan, John 1928-1992 .... **CLC 35**
See also AAYA 20; CA 97-100; 137; CLR 3; MAICYA 1, 2; SATA 72; SATA-Brief 29; YAW

Don Roberto
See Cunninghame Graham, Robert (Gallnigad) Bontine

Doolittle, Hilda 1886-1961 . **CLC 3, 8, 14, 31, 34, 73; PC 5; WLC 3**
See also AAYA 66; AMWS 1; CA 97-100; CANR 35, 131; DA; DAC; DAM MST, POET; DLB 4, 45; EWL 3; FL 1:5; FW; GLL 1; LMFS 2; MAL 5; MBL; MTCW 1, 2; MTFW 2005; PFS 6, 28; RGAL 4

Doppo
See Kunikida Doppo

Doppo, Kunikida
See Kunikida Doppo

Dorfman, Ariel 1942- .... **CLC 48, 77, 189; HLC 1**
See also CA 124; 130; CANR 67, 70, 135; CWW 2; DAM MULT; DFS 4; EWL 3; HW 1, 2; INT CA-130; WLIT 1

Dorn, Edward (Merton)
1929-1999 .... **CLC 10, 18**
See also CA 93-96; 187; CANR 42, 79; CP 1, 2, 3, 4, 5, 6, 7; DLB 5; INT CA-93-96; WP

Dor-Ner, Zvi .... **CLC 70**

Dorris, Michael 1945-1997 .... **CLC 109; NNAL**
See also AAYA 20; BEST 90:1; BYA 12; CA 102; 157; CANR 19, 46, 75; CLR 58; DA3; DAM MULT, NOV; DLB 175; LAIT 5; MTCW 2; MTFW 2005; NFS 3; RGAL 4; SATA 75; SATA-Obit 94; TCWW 2; YAW

Dorris, Michael A.
See Dorris, Michael

Dorsan, Luc
See Simenon, Georges (Jacques Christian)

Dorsange, Jean
See Simenon, Georges (Jacques Christian)

Dorset
See Sackville, Thomas

Dos Passos, John (Roderigo)
1896-1970 ... **CLC 1, 4, 8, 11, 15, 25, 34, 82; WLC 2**
See also AMW; BPFB 1; CA 1-4R; 29-32R; CANR 3; CDALB 1929-1941; DA; DA3; DAB; DAC; DAM MST, NOV; DLB 4, 9, 274, 316; DLBD 1, 15; DLBY 1996; EWL 3; MAL 5; MTCW 1, 2; MTFW 2005; NFS 14; RGAL 4; TUS

Dossage, Jean
See Simenon, Georges (Jacques Christian)

Dostoevsky, Fedor Mikhailovich
1821-1881 .. **NCLC 2, 7, 21, 33, 43, 119, 167, 202; SSC 2, 33, 44; WLC 2**
See also AAYA 40; DA; DA3; DAB; DAC; DAM MST, NOV; DLB 238; EW 7; EXPN; LATS 1:1; LMFS 1, 2; NFS 28; RGSF 2; RGWL 2, 3; SSFS 8; TWA

Dostoevsky, Fyodor
See Dostoevsky, Fedor Mikhailovich

Doty, Mark 1953(?)- .... **CLC 176; PC 53**
See also AMWS 11; CA 161, 183; CAAE 183; CANR 110, 173; CP 7; PFS 28

Doty, Mark A.
See Doty, Mark

Doty, Mark Alan
See Doty, Mark

Doty, M.R.
See Doty, Mark

Doughty, Charles M(ontagu)
1843-1926 .... **TCLC 27**
See also CA 115; 178; DLB 19, 57, 174

Douglas, Ellen 1921- .... **CLC 73**
See also CA 115; CANR 41, 83; CN 5, 6, 7; CSW; DLB 292

Douglas, Gavin 1475(?)-1522 .... **LC 20**
See also DLB 132; RGEL 2

Douglas, George
See Brown, George Douglas

Douglas, Keith (Castellain)
1920-1944 .... **TCLC 40**
See also BRW 7; CA 160; DLB 27; EWL 3; PAB; RGEL 2

Douglas, Leonard
See Bradbury, Ray

Douglas, Michael
See Crichton, Michael

Douglas, Michael
See Crichton, Michael

Douglas, (George) Norman
1868-1952 .... **TCLC 68**
See also BRW 6; CA 119; 157; DLB 34, 195; RGEL 2

Douglas, William
See Brown, George Douglas

Douglass, Frederick 1817(?)-1895 .. **BLC 1:1; NCLC 7, 55, 141; WLC 2**
See also AAYA 48; AFAW 1, 2; AMWC 1; AMWS 3; CDALB 1640-1865; DA; DA3; DAC; DAM MST, MULT; DLB 1, 43, 50, 79, 243; FW; LAIT 2; NCFS 2; RGAL 4; SATA 29

Dourado, (Waldomiro Freitas) Autran
1926- .... **CLC 23, 60**
See also CA 25-28R, 179; CANR 34, 81; DLB 145, 307; HW 2

Dourado, Waldomiro Freitas Autran
See Dourado, (Waldomiro Freitas) Autran

Dove, Rita 1952- . **BLC 2:1; BLCS; CLC 50, 81; PC 6**
See also AAYA 46; AMWS 4; BW 2; CA 109; CAAS 19; CANR 27, 42, 68, 76, 97, 132; CDALBS; CP 5, 6, 7; CSW; CWP; DA3; DAM MULT, POET; DLB 120; EWL 3; EXPP; MAL 5; MTCW 2; MTFW 2005; PFS 1, 15; RGAL 4

Dove, Rita Frances
See Dove, Rita

Doveglion
See Villa, Jose Garcia

Dowell, Coleman 1925-1985 .... **CLC 60**
See also CA 25-28R; 117; CANR 10; DLB 130; GLL 2

Downing, Major Jack
See Smith, Seba

Dowson, Ernest (Christopher)
1867-1900 .... **TCLC 4**
See also CA 105; 150; DLB 19, 135; RGEL 2

Doyle, A. Conan
See Doyle, Sir Arthur Conan

Doyle, Sir Arthur Conan
1859-1930 ..... **SSC 12, 83, 95; TCLC 7; WLC 2**
See also AAYA 14; BPFB 1; BRWS 2; BYA 4, 5, 11; CA 104; 122; CANR 131; CD-BLB 1890-1914; CLR 106; CMW 4; DA; DA3; DAB; DAC; DAM MST, NOV; DLB 18, 70, 156, 178; EXPS; HGG; LAIT 2; MSW; MTCW 1, 2; MTFW 2005; NFS 28; RGEL 2; RGSF 2; RHW; SATA 24; SCFW 1, 2; SFW 4; SSFS 2; TEA; WCH; WLIT 4; WYA; YAW

Doyle, Conan
See Doyle, Sir Arthur Conan

Doyle, John
See Graves, Robert

Doyle, Roddy 1958- .... **CLC 81, 178**
See also AAYA 14; BRWS 5; CA 143; CANR 73, 128, 168; CN 6, 7; DA3; DLB 194, 326; MTCW 2; MTFW 2005

Doyle, Sir A. Conan
See Doyle, Sir Arthur Conan

Dr. A
See Asimov, Isaac; Silverstein, Alvin; Silverstein, Virginia B(arbara Opshelor)

Drabble, Margaret 1939- ...... **CLC 2, 3, 5, 8, 10, 22, 53, 129**
See also BRWS 4; CA 13-16R; CANR 18, 35, 63, 112, 131, 174; CDBLB 1960 to Present; CN 1, 2, 3, 4, 5, 6, 7; CPW; DA3; DAB; DAC; DAM MST, NOV, POP; DLB 14, 155, 231; EWL 3; FW; MTCW 1, 2; MTFW 2005; RGEL 2; SATA 48; TEA

Drakulic, Slavenka 1949- .... **CLC 173**
See also CA 144; CANR 92

Feuchtwanger, Lion 1884-1958 .... **TCLC 3**
    See also CA 104; 187; DLB 66; EWL 3;
    RGHL

Feuerbach, Ludwig 1804-1872 ..... **NCLC 139**
    See also DLB 133

Feuillet, Octave 1821-1890 .... **NCLC 45**
    See also DLB 192

Feydeau, Georges (Leon Jules Marie)
    1862-1921 .... **TCLC 22**
    See also CA 113; 152; CANR 84; DAM
    DRAM; DLB 192; EWL 3; GFL 1789 to
    the Present; RGWL 2, 3

Fichte, Johann Gottlieb
    1762-1814 .... **NCLC 62**
    See also DLB 90

Ficino, Marsilio 1433-1499 .... **LC 12, 152**
    See also LMFS 1

Fiedeler, Hans
    See Doeblin, Alfred

Fiedler, Leslie A(aron) 1917-2003 ..... **CLC 4,
    13, 24**
    See also AMWS 13; CA 9-12R; 212; CANR
    7, 63; CN 1, 2, 3, 4, 5, 6; DLB 28, 67;
    EWL 3; MAL 5; MTCW 1, 2; RGAL 4;
    TUS

Field, Andrew 1938- .... **CLC 44**
    See also CA 97-100; CANR 25

Field, Eugene 1850-1895 .... **NCLC 3**
    See also DLB 23, 42, 140; DLBD 13; MAI-
    CYA 1, 2; RGAL 4; SATA 16

Field, Gans T.
    See Wellman, Manly Wade

Field, Michael 1915-1971 .... **TCLC 43**
    See also CA 29-32R

Fielding, Helen 1958- .... **CLC 146, 217**
    See also AAYA 65; CA 172; CANR 127;
    DLB 231; MTFW 2005

Fielding, Henry 1707-1754 .... **LC 1, 46, 85,
    151, 154; WLC 2**
    See also BRW 3; BRWR 1; CDBLB 1660-
    1789; DA; DA3; DAB; DAC; DAM
    DRAM, MST, NOV; DLB 39, 84, 101;
    NFS 18; RGEL 2; TEA; WLIT 3

Fielding, Sarah 1710-1768 .... **LC 1, 44**
    See also DLB 39; RGEL 2; TEA

Fields, W. C. 1880-1946 .... **TCLC 80**
    See also DLB 44

Fierstein, Harvey (Forbes) 1954- ..... **CLC 33**
    See also CA 123; 129; CAD; CD 5, 6;
    CPW; DA3; DAM DRAM, POP; DFS 6;
    DLB 266; GLL; MAL 5

Figes, Eva 1932- .... **CLC 31**
    See also CA 53-56; CANR 4, 44, 83; CN 2,
    3, 4, 5, 6, 7; DLB 14, 271; FW; RGHL

Filippo, Eduardo de
    See de Filippo, Eduardo

Finch, Anne 1661-1720 ..... **LC 3, 137; PC 21**
    See also BRWS 9; DLB 95; PFS 30

Finch, Robert (Duer Claydon)
    1900-1995 .... **CLC 18**
    See also CA 57-60; CANR 9, 24, 49; CP 1,
    2, 3, 4, 5, 6; DLB 88

Findley, Timothy (Irving Frederick)
    1930-2002 .... **CLC 27, 102**
    See also CA 25-28R; 206; CANR 12, 42,
    69, 109; CCA 1; CN 4, 5, 6, 7; DAC;
    DAM MST; DLB 53; FANT; RHW

Fink, William
    See Mencken, H(enry) L(ouis)

Firbank, Louis 1942- .... **CLC 21**
    See also CA 117

Firbank, (Arthur Annesley) Ronald
    1886-1926 .... **TCLC 1**
    See also BRWS 2; CA 104; 177; DLB 36;
    EWL 3; RGEL 2

Firdaosi
    See Ferdowsi, Abu'l Qasem

Firdausi
    See Ferdowsi, Abu'l Qasem

Firdavsi, Abulqosimi
    See Ferdowsi, Abu'l Qasem

Firdavsii, Abulqosim
    See Ferdowsi, Abu'l Qasem

Firdawsi, Abu al-Qasim
    See Ferdowsi, Abu'l Qasem

Firdosi
    See Ferdowsi, Abu'l Qasem

Firdousi
    See Ferdowsi, Abu'l Qasem

Firdousi, Abu'l-Qasim
    See Ferdowsi, Abu'l Qasem

Firdovsi, A.
    See Ferdowsi, Abu'l Qasem

Firdovsi, Abulgasim
    See Ferdowsi, Abu'l Qasem

Firdusi
    See Ferdowsi, Abu'l Qasem

Fish, Stanley
    See Fish, Stanley Eugene

Fish, Stanley E.
    See Fish, Stanley Eugene

Fish, Stanley Eugene 1938- .... **CLC 142**
    See also CA 112; 132; CANR 90; DLB 67

Fisher, Dorothy (Frances) Canfield
    1879-1958 .... **TCLC 87**
    See also CA 114; 136; CANR 80; CLR 71;
    CWRI 5; DLB 9, 102, 284; MAICYA 1,
    2; MAL 5; YABC 1

Fisher, M(ary) F(rances) K(ennedy)
    1908-1992 .... **CLC 76, 87**
    See also AMWS 17; CA 77-80; 138; CANR
    44; MTCW 2

Fisher, Roy 1930- .... **CLC 25**
    See also CA 81-84; CAAS 10; CANR 16;
    CP 1, 2, 3, 4, 5, 6, 7; DLB 40

Fisher, Rudolph 1897-1934 ...... **BLC 1:2; HR
    1:2; SSC 25; TCLC 11**
    See also BW 1, 3; CA 107; 124; CANR 80;
    DAM MULT; DLB 51, 102

Fisher, Vardis (Alvero) 1895-1968 .... **CLC 7;
    TCLC 140**
    See also CA 5-8R; 25-28R; CANR 68; DLB
    9, 206; MAL 5; RGAL 4; TCWW 1, 2

Fiske, Tarleton
    See Bloch, Robert (Albert)

Fitch, Clarke
    See Sinclair, Upton

Fitch, John IV
    See Cormier, Robert

Fitzgerald, Captain Hugh
    See Baum, L(yman) Frank

FitzGerald, Edward 1809-1883 ...... **NCLC 9,
    153; PC 79**
    See also BRW 4; DLB 32; RGEL 2

Fitzgerald, F(rancis) Scott (Key)
    1896-1940 ... **SSC 6, 31, 75; TCLC 1, 6,
    14, 28, 55, 157; WLC 2**
    See also AAYA 24; AITN 1; AMW; AMWC
    2; AMWR 1; BPFB 1; CA 110; 123;
    CDALB 1917-1929; DA; DA3; DAB;
    DAC; DAM MST, NOV; DLB 4, 9, 86,
    219, 273; DLBD 1, 15, 16; DLBY 1981,
    1996; EWL 3; EXPN; EXPS; LAIT 3;
    MAL 5; MTCW 1, 2; MTFW 2005; NFS
    2, 19, 20; RGAL 4; RGSF 2; SSFS 4, 15,
    21, 25; TUS

Fitzgerald, Penelope 1916-2000 . **CLC 19, 51,
    61, 143**
    See also BRWS 5; CA 85-88; 190; CAAS
    10; CANR 56, 86, 131; CN 3, 4, 5, 6, 7;
    DLB 14, 194, 326; EWL 3; MTCW 2;
    MTFW 2005

Fitzgerald, Robert (Stuart)
    1910-1985 .... **CLC 39**
    See also CA 1-4R; 114; CANR 1; CP 1, 2,
    3, 4; DLBY 1980; MAL 5

FitzGerald, Robert D(avid)
    1902-1987 .... **CLC 19**
    See also CA 17-20R; CP 1, 2, 3, 4; DLB
    260; RGEL 2

Fitzgerald, Zelda (Sayre)
    1900-1948 .... **TCLC 52**
    See also AMWS 9; CA 117; 126; DLBY
    1984

Flanagan, Thomas (James Bonner)
    1923-2002 .... **CLC 25, 52**
    See also CA 108; 206; CANR 55; CN 3, 4,
    5, 6, 7; DLBY 1980; INT CA-108; MTCW
    1; RHW; TCLE 1:1

Flaubert, Gustave 1821-1880 .... **NCLC 2, 10,
    19, 62, 66, 135, 179, 185; SSC 11, 60;
    WLC 2**
    See also DA; DA3; DAB; DAC; DAM
    MST, NOV; DLB 119, 301; EW 7; EXPS;
    GFL 1789 to the Present; LAIT 2; LMFS
    1; NFS 14; RGSF 2; RGWL 2, 3; SSFS
    6; TWA

Flavius Josephus
    See Josephus, Flavius

Flecker, Herman Elroy
    See Flecker, (Herman) James Elroy

Flecker, (Herman) James Elroy
    1884-1915 .... **TCLC 43**
    See also CA 109; 150; DLB 10, 19; RGEL
    2

Fleming, Ian 1908-1964 ... **CLC 3, 30; TCLC
    193**
    See also AAYA 26; BPFB 1; BRWS 14; CA
    5-8R; CANR 59; CDBLB 1945-1960;
    CMW 4; CPW; DA3; DAM POP; DLB
    87, 201; MSW; MTCW 1, 2; MTFW
    2005; RGEL 2; SATA 9; TEA; YAW

Fleming, Ian Lancaster
    See Fleming, Ian

Fleming, Thomas 1927- .... **CLC 37**
    See also CA 5-8R; CANR 10, 102, 155;
    INT CANR-10; SATA 8

Fleming, Thomas James
    See Fleming, Thomas

Fletcher, John 1579-1625 . **DC 6; LC 33, 151**
    See also BRW 2; CDBLB Before 1660;
    DLB 58; RGEL 2; TEA

Fletcher, John Gould 1886-1950 .... **TCLC 35**
    See also CA 107; 167; DLB 4, 45; LMFS
    2; MAL 5; RGAL 4

Fleur, Paul
    See Pohl, Frederik

Flieg, Helmut
    See Heym, Stefan

Flooglebuckle, Al
    See Spiegelman, Art

Flying Officer X
    See Bates, H(erbert) E(rnest)

Fo, Dario 1926- .... **CLC 32, 109, 227; DC 10**
    See also CA 116; 128; CANR 68, 114, 134,
    164; CWW 2; DA3; DAM DRAM; DFS
    23; DLB 330; DLBY 1997; EWL 3;
    MTCW 1, 2; MTFW 2005; WLIT 7

Foden, Giles 1967- .... **CLC 231**
    See also CA 240; DLB 267; NFS 15

Fogarty, Jonathan Titulescu Esq.
    See Farrell, James T(homas)

Follett, Ken 1949- .... **CLC 18**
    See also AAYA 6, 50; BEST 89:4; BPFB 1;
    CA 81-84; CANR 13, 33, 54, 102, 156;
    CMW 4; CPW; DA3; DAM NOV, POP;
    DLB 87; DLBY 1981; INT CANR-33;
    MTCW 1

Follett, Kenneth Martin
    See Follett, Ken

Fondane, Benjamin 1898-1944 ..... **TCLC 159**

Fontane, Theodor 1819-1898 . **NCLC 26, 163**
    See also CDWLB 2; DLB 129; EW 6;
    RGWL 2, 3; TWA

Fonte, Moderata 1555-1592 .... **LC 118**

Fontenelle, Bernard Le Bovier de
1657-1757 .... **LC 140**
See also DLB 268, 313; GFL Beginnings to
1789

Fontenot, Chester .... **CLC 65**

Fonvizin, Denis Ivanovich
1744(?)-1792 .... **LC 81**
See also DLB 150; RGWL 2, 3

Foote, Horton 1916-2009 .... **CLC 51, 91**
See also CA 73-76; CAD; CANR 34, 51,
110; CD 5, 6; CSW; DA3; DAM DRAM;
DFS 20; DLB 26, 266; EWL 3; INT
CANR-34; MTFW 2005

Foote, Mary Hallock 1847-1938 .. **TCLC 108**
See also DLB 186, 188, 202, 221; TCWW
2

Foote, Samuel 1721-1777 .... **LC 106**
See also DLB 89; RGEL 2

Foote, Shelby 1916-2005 .... **CLC 75, 224**
See also AAYA 40; CA 5-8R; 240; CANR
3, 45, 74, 131; CN 1, 2, 3, 4, 5, 6, 7;
CPW; CSW; DA3; DAM NOV, POP;
DLB 2, 17; MAL 5; MTCW 2; MTFW
2005; RHW

Forbes, Cosmo
See Lewton, Val

Forbes, Esther 1891-1967 .... **CLC 12**
See also AAYA 17; BYA 2; CA 13-14; 25-
28R; CAP 1; CLR 27; DLB 22; JRDA;
MAICYA 1, 2; RHW; SATA 2, 100; YAW

Forche, Carolyn 1950- .. **CLC 25, 83, 86; PC
10**
See also CA 109; 117; CANR 50, 74, 138;
CP 4, 5, 6, 7; CWP; DA3; DAM POET;
DLB 5, 193; INT CA-117; MAL 5;
MTCW 2; MTFW 2005; PFS 18; RGAL
4

Forche, Carolyn Louise
See Forche, Carolyn

Ford, Elbur
See Hibbert, Eleanor Alice Burford

Ford, Ford Madox 1873-1939 ... **TCLC 1, 15,
39, 57, 172**
See also BRW 6; CA 104; 132; CANR 74;
CDBLB 1914-1945; DA3; DAM NOV;
DLB 34, 98, 162; EWL 3; MTCW 1, 2;
NFS 28; RGEL 2; RHW; TEA

Ford, Henry 1863-1947 .... **TCLC 73**
See also CA 115; 148

Ford, Jack
See Ford, John

Ford, John 1586-1639 .... **DC 8; LC 68, 153**
See also BRW 2; CDBLB Before 1660;
DA3; DAM DRAM; DFS 7; DLB 58;
IDTP; RGEL 2

Ford, John 1895-1973 .... **CLC 16**
See also AAYA 75; CA 187; 45-48

Ford, Richard 1944- .... **CLC 46, 99, 205**
See also AMWS 5; CA 69-72; CANR 11,
47, 86, 128, 164; CN 5, 6, 7; CSW; DLB
227; EWL 3; MAL 5; MTCW 2; MTFW
2005; NFS 25; RGAL 4; RGSF 2

Ford, Webster
See Masters, Edgar Lee

Foreman, Richard 1937- .... **CLC 50**
See also CA 65-68; CAD; CANR 32, 63,
143; CD 5, 6

Forester, C(ecil) S(cott) 1899-1966 . **CLC 35;
TCLC 152**
See also CA 73-76; 25-28R; CANR 83;
DLB 191; RGEL 2; RHW; SATA 13

Forez
See Mauriac, Francois (Charles)

Forman, James
See Forman, James D.

Forman, James D. 1932- .... **CLC 21**
See also AAYA 17; CA 9-12R; CANR 4,
19, 42; JRDA; MAICYA 1, 2; SATA 8,
70; YAW

Forman, James Douglas
See Forman, James D.

Forman, Milos 1932- .... **CLC 164**
See also AAYA 63; CA 109

Fornes, Maria Irene 1930- .... **CLC 39, 61,
187; DC 10; HLCS 1**
See also CA 25-28R; CAD; CANR 28, 81;
CD 5, 6; CWD; DFS 25; DLB 7, 341; HW
1, 2; INT CANR-28; LLW; MAL 5;
MTCW 1; RGAL 4

Forrest, Leon (Richard)
1937-1997 .... **BLCS; CLC 4**
See also AFAW 2; BW 2; CA 89-92; 162;
CAAS 7; CANR 25, 52, 87; CN 4, 5, 6;
DLB 33

Forster, E(dward) M(organ)
1879-1970 ...... **CLC 1, 2, 3, 4, 9, 10, 13,
15, 22, 45, 77; SSC 27, 96; TCLC 125;
WLC 2**
See also AAYA 2, 37; BRW 6; BRWR 2;
BYA 12; CA 13-14; 25-28R; CANR 45;
CAP 1; CDBLB 1914-1945; DA; DA3;
DAB; DAC; DAM MST, NOV; DLB 34,
98, 162, 178, 195; DLBD 10; EWL 3;
EXPN; LAIT 3; LMFS 1; MTCW 1, 2;
MTFW 2005; NCFS 1; NFS 3, 10, 11;
RGEL 2; RGSF 2; SATA 57; SUFW 1;
TEA; WLIT 4

Forster, John 1812-1876 .... **NCLC 11**
See also DLB 144, 184

Forster, Margaret 1938- .... **CLC 149**
See also CA 133; CANR 62, 115, 175; CN
4, 5, 6, 7; DLB 155, 271

Forsyth, Frederick 1938- .... **CLC 2, 5, 36**
See also BEST 89:4; CA 85-88; CANR 38,
62, 115, 137, 183; CMW 4; CN 3, 4, 5, 6,
7; CPW; DAM NOV, POP; DLB 87;
MTCW 1, 2; MTFW 2005

Fort, Paul
See Stockton, Francis Richard

Forten, Charlotte
See Grimke, Charlotte L(ottie) Forten

Forten, Charlotte L. 1837-1914
See Grimke, Charlotte L(ottie) Forten

Fortinbras
See Grieg, (Johan) Nordahl (Brun)

Foscolo, Ugo 1778-1827 .... **NCLC 8, 97**
See also EW 5; WLIT 7

Fosse, Bob 1927-1987 .... **CLC 20**
See also CA 110; 123

Fosse, Robert L.
See Fosse, Bob

Foster, Hannah Webster
1758-1840 .... **NCLC 99**
See also DLB 37, 200; RGAL 4

Foster, Stephen Collins
1826-1864 .... **NCLC 26**
See also RGAL 4

Foucault, Michel 1926-1984 . **CLC 31, 34, 69**
See also CA 105; 113; CANR 34; DLB 242;
EW 13; EWL 3; GFL 1789 to the Present;
GLL 1; LMFS 2; MTCW 1, 2; TWA

Fouque, Friedrich (Heinrich Karl) de la
Motte 1777-1843 .... **NCLC 2**
See also DLB 90; RGWL 2, 3; SUFW 1

Fourier, Charles 1772-1837 .... **NCLC 51**

Fournier, Henri-Alban 1886-1914 ... **TCLC 6**
See also CA 104; 179; DLB 65; EWL 3;
GFL 1789 to the Present; RGWL 2, 3

Fournier, Pierre 1916-1997 .... **CLC 11**
See also CA 89-92; CANR 16, 40; EWL 3;
RGHL

Fowles, John 1926-2005 .... **CLC 1, 2, 3, 4, 6,
9, 10, 15, 33, 87; SSC 33**
See also BPFB 1; BRWS 1; CA 5-8R; 245;
CANR 25, 71, 103; CDBLB 1960 to
Present; CN 1, 2, 3, 4, 5, 6, 7; DA3; DAB;
DAC; DAM MST; DLB 14, 139, 207;

EWL 3; HGG; MTCW 1, 2; MTFW 2005;
NFS 21; RGEL 2; RHW; SATA 22; SATA-
Obit 171; TEA; WLIT 4

Fowles, John Robert
See Fowles, John

Fox, Paula 1923- .... **CLC 2, 8, 121**
See also AAYA 3, 37; BYA 3, 8; CA 73-76;
CANR 20, 36, 62, 105; CLR 1, 44, 96;
DLB 52; JRDA; MAICYA 1, 2; MTCW
1; NFS 12; SATA 17, 60, 120, 167; WYA;
YAW

Fox, William Price (Jr.) 1926- .... **CLC 22**
See also CA 17-20R; CAAS 19; CANR 11,
142; CSW; DLB 2; DLBY 1981

Foxe, John 1517(?)-1587 .... **LC 14, 166**
See also DLB 132

Frame, Janet 1924-2004 ...... **CLC 2, 3, 6, 22,
66, 96, 237; SSC 29**
See also CA 1-4R; 224; CANR 2, 36, 76,
135; CN 1, 2, 3, 4, 5, 6, 7; CP 2, 3, 4;
CWP; EWL 3; MTCW 1,2; RGEL 2;
RGSF 2; SATA 119; TWA

France, Anatole
See Thibault, Jacques Anatole Francois

Francis, Claude .... **CLC 50**
See also CA 192

Francis, Dick 1920- .... **CLC 2, 22, 42, 102**
See also AAYA 5, 21; BEST 89:3; BPFB 1;
CA 5-8R; CANR 9, 42, 68, 100, 141, 179;
CDBLB 1960 to Present; CMW 4; CN 2,
3, 4, 5, 6; DA3; DAM POP; DLB 87; INT
CANR-9; MSW; MTCW 1, 2; MTFW
2005

Francis, Paula Marie
See Allen, Paula Gunn

Francis, Richard Stanley
See Francis, Dick

Francis, Robert (Churchill)
1901-1987 .... **CLC 15; PC 34**
See also AMWS 9; CA 1-4R; 123; CANR
1; CP 1, 2, 3, 4; EXPP; PFS 12; TCLE
1:1

Francis, Lord Jeffrey
See Jeffrey, Francis

Frank, Anne(lies Marie)
1929-1945 .... **TCLC 17; WLC 2**
See also AAYA 12; BYA 1; CA 113; 133;
CANR 68; CLR 101; DA; DA3; DAB;
DAC; DAM MST; LAIT 4; MAICYA 2;
MAICYAS 1; MTCW 1, 2; MTFW 2005;
NCFS 2; RGHL; SATA 87; SATA-Brief
42; WYA; YAW

Frank, Bruno 1887-1945 .... **TCLC 81**
See also CA 189; DLB 118; EWL 3

Frank, Elizabeth 1945- .... **CLC 39**
See also CA 121; 126; CANR 78, 150; INT
CA-126

Frankl, Viktor E(mil) 1905-1997 ...... **CLC 93**
See also CA 65-68; 161; RGHL

Franklin, Benjamin
See Hasek, Jaroslav (Matej Frantisek)

Franklin, Benjamin 1706-1790 .. **LC 25, 134;
WLCS**
See also AMW; CDALB 1640-1865; DA;
DA3; DAB; DAC; DAM MST; DLB 24,
43, 73, 183; LAIT 1; RGAL 4; TUS

Franklin, Madeleine
See L'Engle, Madeleine

Franklin, Madeleine L'Engle
See L'Engle, Madeleine

Franklin, Madeleine L'Engle Camp
See L'Engle, Madeleine

Franklin, (Stella Maria Sarah) Miles
(Lampe) 1879-1954 .... **TCLC 7**
See also CA 104; 164; DLB 230; FW;
MTCW 2; RGEL 2; TWA

Franzen, Jonathan 1959- .... **CLC 202**
See also AAYA 65; CA 129; CANR 105,
166

Fraser, Antonia 1932- .... **CLC 32, 107**
  See also AAYA 57; CA 85-88; CANR 44,
  65, 119, 164; CMW; DLB 276; MTCW 1,
  2; MTFW 2005; SATA-Brief 32

Fraser, George MacDonald
  1925-2008 .... **CLC 7**
  See also AAYA 48; CA 45-48, 180; 268;
  CAAE 180; CANR 2, 48, 74; MTCW 2;
  RHW

Fraser, Sylvia 1935- .... **CLC 64**
  See also CA 45-48; CANR 1, 16, 60; CCA
  1

Frater Perdurabo
  See Crowley, Edward Alexander

Frayn, Michael 1933- .... **CLC 3, 7, 31, 47,**
  176; DC 27
  See also AAYA 69; BRWC 2; BRWS 7; CA
  5-8R; CANR 30, 69, 114, 133, 166; CBD;
  CD 5, 6; CN 1, 2, 3, 4, 5, 6, 7; DAM
  DRAM, NOV; DFS 22; DLB 13, 14, 194,
  245; FANT; MTCW 1, 2; MTFW 2005;
  SFW 4

Fraze, Candida (Merrill) 1945- .... **CLC 50**
  See also CA 126

Frazer, Andrew
  See Marlowe, Stephen

Frazer, J(ames) G(eorge)
  1854-1941 .... **TCLC 32**
  See also BRWS 3; CA 118; NCFS 5

Frazer, Robert Caine
  See Creasey, John

Frazer, Sir James George
  See Frazer, J(ames) G(eorge)

Frazier, Charles 1950- .... **CLC 109, 224**
  See also AAYA 34; CA 161; CANR 126,
  170; CSW; DLB 292; MTFW 2005; NFS
  25

Frazier, Charles R.
  See Frazier, Charles

Frazier, Charles Robinson
  See Frazier, Charles

Frazier, Ian 1951- .... **CLC 46**
  See also CA 130; CANR 54, 93

Frederic, Harold 1856-1898 ... **NCLC 10, 175**
  See also AMW; DLB 12, 23; DLBD 13;
  MAL 5; NFS 22; RGAL 4

Frederick, John
  See Faust, Frederick (Schiller)

Frederick the Great 1712-1786 .... **LC 14**

Fredro, Aleksander 1793-1876 .... **NCLC 8**

Freeling, Nicolas 1927-2003 .... **CLC 38**
  See also CA 49-52; 218; CAAS 12; CANR
  1, 17, 50, 84; CMW 4; CN 1, 2, 3, 4, 5,
  6; DLB 87

Freeman, Douglas Southall
  1886-1953 .... **TCLC 11**
  See also CA 109; 195; DLB 17; DLBD 17

Freeman, Judith 1946- .... **CLC 55**
  See also CA 148; CANR 120, 179; DLB
  256

Freeman, Mary E(leanor) Wilkins
  1852-1930 .... **SSC 1, 47, 113; TCLC 9**
  See also CA 106; 177; DLB 12, 78, 221;
  EXPS; FW; HGG; MBL; RGAL 4; RGSF
  2; SSFS 4, 8, 26; SUFW 1; TUS

Freeman, R(ichard) Austin
  1862-1943 .... **TCLC 21**
  See also CA 113; CANR 84; CMW 4; DLB
  70

French, Albert 1943- .... **CLC 86**
  See also BW 3; CA 167

French, Antonia
  See Kureishi, Hanif

French, Marilyn 1929- .. **CLC 10, 18, 60, 177**
  See also BPFB 1; CA 69-72; CANR 3, 31,
  134, 163; CN 5, 6, 7; CPW; DAM DRAM,
  NOV, POP; FL 1:5; FW; INT CANR-31;
  MTCW 1, 2; MTFW 2005

French, Paul
  See Asimov, Isaac

Freneau, Philip Morin 1752-1832 .. **NCLC 1,**
  111
  See also AMWS 2; DLB 37, 43; RGAL 4

Freud, Sigmund 1856-1939 .... **TCLC 52**
  See also CA 115; 133; CANR 69; DLB 296;
  EW 8; EWL 3; LATS 1:1; MTCW 1, 2;
  MTFW 2005; NCFS 3; TWA

Freytag, Gustav 1816-1895 .... **NCLC 109**
  See also DLB 129

Friedan, Betty 1921-2006 .... **CLC 74**
  See also CA 65-68; 248; CANR 18, 45, 74;
  DLB 246; FW; MTCW 1, 2; MTFW
  2005; NCFS 5

Friedan, Betty Naomi
  See Friedan, Betty

Friedlander, Saul 1932- .... **CLC 90**
  See also CA 117; 130; CANR 72; RGHL

Friedman, B(ernard) H(arper)
  1926- .... **CLC 7**
  See also CA 1-4R; CANR 3, 48

Friedman, Bruce Jay 1930- ...... **CLC 3, 5, 56**
  See also CA 9-12R; CAD; CANR 25, 52,
  101; CD 5, 6; CN 1, 2, 3, 4, 5, 6, 7; DLB
  2, 28, 244; INT CANR-25; MAL 5; SSFS
  18

Friel, Brian 1929- .. **CLC 5, 42, 59, 115, 253;**
  DC 8; SSC 76
  See also BRWS 5; CA 21-24R; CANR 33,
  69, 131; CBD; CD 5, 6; DFS 11; DLB
  13, 319; EWL 3; MTCW 1; RGEL 2; TEA

Friis-Baastad, Babbis Ellinor
  1921-1970 .... **CLC 12**
  See also CA 17-20R; 134; SATA 7

Frisch, Max 1911-1991 ...... **CLC 3, 9, 14, 18,**
  32, 44; TCLC 121
  See also CA 85-88; 134; CANR 32, 74; CD-
  WLB 2; DAM DRAM, NOV; DFS 25;
  DLB 69, 124; EW 13; EWL 3; MTCW 1,
  2; MTFW 2005; RGHL; RGWL 2, 3

Fromentin, Eugene (Samuel Auguste)
  1820-1876 .... **NCLC 10, 125**
  See also DLB 123; GFL 1789 to the Present

Frost, Frederick
  See Faust, Frederick (Schiller)

Frost, Robert 1874-1963 . **CLC 1, 3, 4, 9, 10,**
  13, 15, 26, 34, 44; PC 1, 39, 71; WLC 2
  See also AAYA 21; AMW; AMWR 1; CA
  89-92; CANR 33; CDALB 1917-1929;
  CLR 67; DA; DA3; DAB; DAC; DAM
  MST, POET; DLB 54, 284, 342; DLBD
  7; EWL 3; EXPP; MAL 5; MTCW 1, 2;
  MTFW 2005; PAB; PFS 1, 2, 3, 4, 5, 6,
  7, 10, 13; RGAL 4; SATA 14; TUS; WP;
  WYA

Frost, Robert Lee
  See Frost, Robert

Froude, James Anthony
  1818-1894 .... **NCLC 43**
  See also DLB 18, 57, 144

Froy, Herald
  See Waterhouse, Keith (Spencer)

Fry, Christopher 1907-2005 ... **CLC 2, 10, 14**
  See also BRWS 3; CA 17-20R; 240; CAAS
  23; CANR 9, 30, 74, 132; CBD; CD 5, 6;
  CP 1, 2, 3, 4, 5, 6, 7; DAM DRAM; DLB
  13; EWL 3; MTCW 1, 2; MTFW 2005;
  RGEL 2; SATA 66; TEA

Frye, (Herman) Northrop
  1912-1991 .... **CLC 24, 70; TCLC 165**
  See also CA 5-8R; 133; CANR 8, 37; DLB
  67, 68, 246; EWL 3; MTCW 1, 2; MTFW
  2005; RGAL 4; TWA

Fuchs, Daniel 1909-1993 .... **CLC 8, 22**
  See also CA 81-84; 142; CAAS 5; CANR
  40; CN 1, 2, 3, 4, 5; DLB 9, 26, 28;
  DLBY 1993; MAL 5

Fuchs, Daniel 1934- .... **CLC 34**
  See also CA 37-40R; CANR 14, 48

Fuentes, Carlos 1928- .. **CLC 3, 8, 10, 13, 22,**
  41, 60, 113; HLC 1; SSC 24; WLC 2
  See also AAYA 4, 45; AITN 2; BPFB 1;
  CA 69-72; CANR 10, 32, 68, 104, 138;
  CDWLB 3; CWW 2; DA; DA3; DAB;
  DAC; DAM MST, MULT, NOV; DLB
  113; DNFS 2; EWL 3; HW 1, 2; LAIT 3;
  LATS 1:2; LAW; LAWS 1; LMFS 2;
  MTCW 1, 2; MTFW 2005; NFS 8; RGSF
  2; RGWL 2, 3; TWA; WLIT 1

Fuentes, Gregorio Lopez y
  See Lopez y Fuentes, Gregorio

Fuertes, Gloria 1918-1998 .... **PC 27**
  See also CA 178, 180; DLB 108; HW 2;
  SATA 115

Fugard, (Harold) Athol 1932- . **CLC 5, 9, 14,**
  25, 40, 80, 211; DC 3
  See also AAYA 17; AFW; CA 85-88; CANR
  32, 54, 118; CD 5, 6; DAM DRAM; DFS
  3, 6, 10, 24; DLB 225; DNFS 1, 2; EWL
  3; LATS 1:2; MTCW 1; MTFW 2005;
  RGEL 2; WLIT 2

Fugard, Sheila 1932- .... **CLC 48**
  See also CA 125

Fujiwara no Teika 1162-1241 .... **CMLC 73**
  See also DLB 203

Fukuyama, Francis 1952- .... **CLC 131**
  See also CA 140; CANR 72, 125, 170

Fuller, Charles (H.), (Jr.) 1939- ..... **BLC 1:2;**
  CLC 25; DC 1
  See also BW 2; CA 108; 112; CAD; CANR
  87; CD 5, 6; DAM DRAM, MULT; DFS
  8; DLB 38, 266; EWL 3; INT CA-112;
  MAL 5; MTCW 1

Fuller, Henry Blake 1857-1929 .... **TCLC 103**
  See also CA 108; 177; DLB 12; RGAL 4

Fuller, John (Leopold) 1937- .... **CLC 62**
  See also CA 21-24R; CANR 9, 44; CP 1, 2,
  3, 4, 5, 6, 7; DLB 40

Fuller, Margaret
  See Ossoli, Sarah Margaret (Fuller)

Fuller, Roy (Broadbent) 1912-1991 ... **CLC 4,**
  28
  See also BRWS 7; CA 5-8R; 135; CAAS
  10; CANR 53, 83; CN 1, 2, 3, 4, 5; CP 1,
  2, 3, 4, 5; CWRI 5; DLB 15, 20; EWL 3;
  RGEL 2; SATA 87

Fuller, Sarah Margaret
  See Ossoli, Sarah Margaret (Fuller)

Fuller, Thomas 1608-1661 .... **LC 111**
  See also DLB 151

Fulton, Alice 1952- .... **CLC 52**
  See also CA 116; CANR 57, 88; CP 5, 6, 7;
  CWP; DLB 193; PFS 25

Furey, Michael
  See Ward, Arthur Henry Sarsfield

Furphy, Joseph 1843-1912 .... **TCLC 25**
  See also CA 163; DLB 230; EWL 3; RGEL
  2

Furst, Alan 1941- .... **CLC 255**
  See also CA 69-72; CANR 12, 34, 59, 102,
  159; DLBY 01

Fuson, Robert H(enderson) 1927- .... **CLC 70**
  See also CA 89-92; CANR 103

Fussell, Paul 1924- .... **CLC 74**
  See also BEST 90:1; CA 17-20R; CANR 8,
  21, 35, 69, 135; INT CANR-21; MTCW
  1, 2; MTFW 2005

Futabatei, Shimei 1864-1909 .... **TCLC 44**
  See also CA 162; DLB 180; EWL 3; MJW

Futabatei Shimei
  See Futabatei, Shimei

Futrelle, Jacques 1875-1912 .... **TCLC 19**
  See also CA 113; 155; CMW 4

GAB
  See Russell, George William

Garth, Will
See Hamilton, Edmond; Kuttner, Henry
Garvey, Marcus (Moziah, Jr.)
1887-1940 ..... **BLC 1:2; HR 1:2; TCLC 41**
See also BW 1; CA 120; 124; CANR 79; DAM MULT; DLB 345
Gary, Romain
See Kacew, Romain
Gascar, Pierre
See Fournier, Pierre
Gascoigne, George 1539-1577 .... **LC 108**
See also DLB 136; RGEL 2
Gascoyne, David (Emery)
1916-2001 .... **CLC 45**
See also CA 65-68; 200; CANR 10, 28, 54; CP 1, 2, 3, 4, 5, 6, 7; DLB 20; MTCW 1; RGEL 2
Gaskell, Elizabeth Cleghorn
1810-1865 .... **NCLC 5, 70, 97, 137, 214; SSC 25, 97**
See also BRW 5; CDBLB 1832-1890; DAB; DAM MST; DLB 21, 144, 159; RGEL 2; RGSF 2; TEA
Gass, William H. 1924- . **CLC 1, 2, 8, 11, 15, 39, 132; SSC 12**
See also AMWS 6; CA 17-20R; CANR 30, 71, 100; CN 1, 2, 3, 4, 5, 6, 7; DLB 2, 227; EWL 3; MAL 5; MTCW 1, 2; MTFW 2005; RGAL 4
Gassendi, Pierre 1592-1655 .... **LC 54**
See also GFL Beginnings to 1789
Gasset, Jose Ortega y
See Ortega y Gasset, Jose
Gates, Henry Louis, Jr. 1950- ... **BLCS; CLC 65**
See also BW 2, 3; CA 109; CANR 25, 53, 75, 125; CSW; DA3; DAM MULT; DLB 67; EWL 3; MAL 5; MTCW 2; MTFW 2005; RGAL 4
Gatos, Stephanie
See Katz, Steve
Gautier, Theophile 1811-1872 .. **NCLC 1, 59; PC 18; SSC 20**
See also DAM POET; DLB 119; EW 6; GFL 1789 to the Present; RGWL 2, 3; SUFW; TWA
Gautreaux, Tim 1947- .... **CLC 270**
See also CA 187; CSW; DLB 292
Gay, John 1685-1732 .... **LC 49**
See also BRW 3; DAM DRAM; DLB 84, 95; RGEL 2; WLIT 3
Gay, Oliver
See Gogarty, Oliver St. John
Gay, Peter 1923- .... **CLC 158**
See also CA 13-16R; CANR 18, 41, 77, 147; INT CANR-18; RGHL
Gay, Peter Jack
See Gay, Peter
Gaye, Marvin (Pentz, Jr.)
1939-1984 .... **CLC 26**
See also CA 195; 112
Gebler, Carlo 1954- .... **CLC 39**
See also CA 119; 133; CANR 96, 186; DLB 271
Gebler, Carlo Ernest
See Gebler, Carlo
Gee, Maggie 1948- .... **CLC 57**
See also CA 130; CANR 125; CN 4, 5, 6, 7; DLB 207; MTFW 2005
Gee, Maurice 1931- .... **CLC 29**
See also AAYA 42; CA 97-100; CANR 67, 123; CLR 56; CN 2, 3, 4, 5, 6, 7; CWRI 5; EWL 3; MAICYA 2; RGSF 2; SATA 46, 101
Gee, Maurice Gough
See Gee, Maurice
Geiogamah, Hanay 1945- .... **NNAL**
See also CA 153; DAM MULT; DLB 175

Gelbart, Larry
See Gelbart, Larry (Simon)
Gelbart, Larry (Simon) 1928- .... **CLC 21, 61**
See also CA 73-76; CAD; CANR 45, 94; CD 5, 6
Gelber, Jack 1932-2003 ...... **CLC 1, 6, 14, 79**
See also CA 1-4R; 216; CAD; CANR 2; DLB 7, 228; MAL 5
Gellhorn, Martha (Ellis)
1908-1998 .... **CLC 14, 60**
See also CA 77-80; 164; CANR 44; CN 1, 2, 3, 4, 5, 6 7; DLBY 1982, 1998
Genet, Jean 1910-1986 .. **CLC 1, 2, 5, 10, 14, 44, 46; DC 25; TCLC 128**
See also CA 13-16R; CANR 18; DA3; DAM DRAM; DFS 10; DLB 72, 321; DLBY 1986; EW 13; EWL 3; GFL 1789 to the Present; GLL 1; LMFS 2; MTCW 1, 2; MTFW 2005; RGWL 2, 3; TWA
Genlis, Stephanie-Felicite Ducrest
1746-1830 .... **NCLC 166**
See also DLB 313
Gent, Peter 1942- .... **CLC 29**
See also AITN 1; CA 89-92; DLBY 1982
Gentile, Giovanni 1875-1944 .... **TCLC 96**
See also CA 119
Geoffrey of Monmouth c.
1100-1155 .... **CMLC 44**
See also DLB 146; TEA
George, Jean
See George, Jean Craighead
George, Jean Craighead 1919- .... **CLC 35**
See also AAYA 8, 69; BYA 2, 4; CA 5-8R; CANR 25; CLR 1, 80, 136; DLB 52; JRDA; MAICYA 1, 2; SATA 2, 68, 124, 170; WYA; YAW
George, Stefan (Anton) 1868-1933 . **TCLC 2, 14**
See also CA 104; 193; EW 8; EWL 3
Georges, Georges Martin
See Simenon, Georges (Jacques Christian)
Gerald of Wales c. 1146-c. 1223 ... **CMLC 60**
Gerhardi, William Alexander
See Gerhardie, William Alexander
Gerhardie, William Alexander
1895-1977 .... **CLC 5**
See also CA 25-28R; 73-76; CANR 18; CN 1, 2; DLB 36; RGEL 2
Gerome
See Thibault, Jacques Anatole Francois
Gerson, Jean 1363-1429 .... **LC 77**
See also DLB 208
Gersonides 1288-1344 .... **CMLC 49**
See also DLB 115
Gerstler, Amy 1956- .... **CLC 70**
See also CA 146; CANR 99
Gertler, T. .... **CLC 34**
See also CA 116; 121
Gertrude of Helfta c. 1256-c.
1301 .... **CMLC 105**
Gertsen, Aleksandr Ivanovich
See Herzen, Aleksandr Ivanovich
Ghalib
See Ghalib, Asadullah Khan
Ghalib, Asadullah Khan
1797-1869 .... **NCLC 39, 78**
See also DAM POET; RGWL 2, 3
Ghelderode, Michel de 1898-1962 ..... **CLC 6, 11; DC 15; TCLC 187**
See also CA 85-88; CANR 40, 77; DAM DRAM; DLB 321; EW 11; EWL 3; TWA
Ghiselin, Brewster 1903-2001 .... **CLC 23**
See also CA 13-16R; CAAS 10; CANR 13; CP 1, 2, 3, 4, 5, 6, 7
Ghose, Aurabinda 1872-1950 .... **TCLC 63**
See also CA 163; EWL 3
Ghose, Aurobindo
See Ghose, Aurabinda

Ghose, Zulfikar 1935- .... **CLC 42, 200**
See also CA 65-68; CANR 67; CN 1, 2, 3, 4, 5, 6, 7; CP 1, 2, 3, 4, 5, 6, 7; DLB 323; EWL 3
Ghosh, Amitav 1956- .... **CLC 44, 153**
See also CA 147; CANR 80, 158; CN 6, 7; DLB 323; WWE 1
Giacosa, Giuseppe 1847-1906 .... **TCLC 7**
See also CA 104
Gibb, Lee
See Waterhouse, Keith (Spencer)
Gibbon, Edward 1737-1794 .... **LC 97**
See also BRW 3; DLB 104, 336; RGEL 2
Gibbon, Lewis Grassic
See Mitchell, James Leslie
Gibbons, Kaye 1960- .... **CLC 50, 88, 145**
See also AAYA 34; AMWS 10; CA 151; CANR 75, 127; CN 7; CSW; DA3; DAM POP; DLB 292; MTCW 2; MTFW 2005; NFS 3; RGAL 4; SATA 117
Gibran, Kahlil 1883-1931 ..... **PC 9; TCLC 1, 9, 205**
See also CA 104; 150; DA3; DAM POET, POP; DLB 346; EWL 3; MTCW 2; WLIT 6
Gibran, Khalil
See Gibran, Kahlil
Gibson, Mel 1956- .... **CLC 215**
Gibson, William 1914-2008 .... **CLC 23**
See also CA 9-12R; 279; CAD; CANR 9, 42, 75, 125; CD 5, 6; DA; DAB; DAC; DAM DRAM, MST; DFS 2; DLB 7; LAIT 2; MAL 5; MTCW 2; MTFW 2005; SATA 66; SATA-Obit 199; YAW
Gibson, William 1948- .... **CLC 39, 63, 186, 192; SSC 52**
See also AAYA 12, 59; AMWS 16; BPFB 2; CA 126; 133; CANR 52, 90, 106, 172; CN 6, 7; CPW; DA3; DAM POP; DLB 251; MTCW 2; MTFW 2005; SCFW 2; SFW 4; SSFS 26
Gibson, William Ford
See Gibson, William
Gide, Andre (Paul Guillaume)
1869-1951 ...... **SSC 13; TCLC 5, 12, 36, 177; WLC 3**
See also CA 104; 124; DA; DA3; DAB; DAC; DAM MST, NOV; DLB 65, 321, 330; EW 8; EWL 3; GFL 1789 to the Present; MTCW 1, 2; MTFW 2005; NFS 21; RGSF 2; RGWL 2, 3; TWA
Gifford, Barry 1946- .... **CLC 34**
See also CA 65-68; CANR 9, 30, 40, 90, 180
Gifford, Barry Colby
See Gifford, Barry
Gilbert, Frank
See De Voto, Bernard (Augustine)
Gilbert, W(illiam) S(chwenck)
1836-1911 .... **TCLC 3**
See also CA 104; 173; DAM DRAM, POET; DLB 344; RGEL 2; SATA 36
Gilbert of Poitiers c. 1085-1154 .... **CMLC 85**
Gilbreth, Frank B(unker), Jr.
1911-2001 .... **CLC 17**
See also CA 9-12R; SATA 2
Gilchrist, Ellen (Louise) 1935- .. **CLC 34, 48, 143, 264; SSC 14, 63**
See also BPFB 2; CA 113; 116; CANR 41, 61, 104; CN 4, 5, 6, 7; CPW; CSW; DAM POP; DLB 130; EWL 3; EXPS; MTCW 1, 2; MTFW 2005; RGAL 4; RGSF 2; SSFS 9
Gildas fl. 6th cent. - .... **CMLC 99**
Giles, Molly 1942- .... **CLC 39**
See also CA 126; CANR 98
Gill, Eric
See Gill, (Arthur) Eric (Rowton Peter Joseph)

Author Index

Handke, Peter 1942- .... **CLC 5, 8, 10, 15, 38, 134; DC 17**
See also CA 77-80; CANR 33, 75, 104, 133, 180; CWW 2; DAM DRAM, NOV; DLB 85, 124; EWL 3; MTCW 1, 2; MTFW 2005; TWA

Handler, Chelsea 1976(?)- .... **CLC 269**
See also CA 243

Handy, W(illiam) C(hristopher)
1873-1958 .... **TCLC 97**
See also BW 3; CA 121; 167

Hanley, James 1901-1985 ..... **CLC 3, 5, 8, 13**
See also CA 73-76; 117; CANR 36; CBD; CN 1, 2, 3; DLB 191; EWL 3; MTCW 1; RGEL 2

Hannah, Barry 1942- .. **CLC 23, 38, 90, 270; SSC 94**
See also BPFB 2; CA 108; 110; CANR 43, 68, 113; CN 4, 5, 6, 7; CSW; DLB 6, 234; INT CA-110; MTCW 1; RGSF 2

Hannon, Ezra
See Hunter, Evan

Hanrahan, Barbara 1939-1991 .... **TCLC 219**
See also CA 121; 127; CN 4, 5; DLB 289

Hansberry, Lorraine (Vivian)
1930-1965 ... **BLC 1:2, 2:2; CLC 17, 62; DC 2; TCLC 192**
See also AAYA 25; AFAW 1, 2; AMWS 4; BW 1, 3; CA 109; 25-28R; CABS 3; CAD; CANR 58; CDALB 1941-1968; CWD; DA; DA3; DAB; DAC; DAM DRAM, MST, MULT; DFS 2; DLB 7, 38; EWL 3; FL 1:6; FW; LAIT 4; MAL 5; MTCW 1, 2; MTFW 2005; RGAL 4; TUS

Hansen, Joseph 1923-2004 .... **CLC 38**
See also BPFB 2; CA 29-32R; 233; CAAS 17; CANR 16, 44, 66, 125; CMW 4; DLB 226; GLL 1; INT CANR-16

Hansen, Karen V. 1955- .... **CLC 65**
See also CA 149; CANR 102

Hansen, Martin A(lfred)
1909-1955 .... **TCLC 32**
See also CA 167; DLB 214; EWL 3

Hanson, Kenneth O(stlin) 1922- .... **CLC 13**
See also CA 53-56; CANR 7; CP 1, 2, 3, 4, 5

Hardwick, Elizabeth 1916-2007 .... **CLC 13**
See also AMWS 3; CA 5-8R; 267; CANR 3, 32, 70, 100, 139; CN 4, 5, 6; CSW; DA3; DAM NOV; DLB 6; MBL; MTCW 1, 2; MTFW 2005; TCLE 1:1

Hardwick, Elizabeth Bruce
See Hardwick, Elizabeth

Hardwick, Elizabeth Bruce
See Hardwick, Elizabeth

Hardy, Thomas 1840-1928 . **PC 8, 92; SSC 2, 60, 113; TCLC 4, 10, 18, 32, 48, 53, 72, 143, 153; WLC 3**
See also AAYA 69; BRW 6; BRWC 1, 2; BRWR 1; CA 104; 123; CDBLB 1890-1914; DA; DA3; DAB; DAC; DAM MST, NOV, POET; DLB 18, 19, 135, 284; EWL 3; EXPN; EXPP; LAIT 2; MTCW 1, 2; MTFW 2005; NFS 3, 11, 15, 19; PFS 3, 4, 18; RGEL 2; RGSF 2; TEA; WLIT 4

Hare, David 1947- . **CLC 29, 58, 136; DC 26**
See also BRWS 4; CA 97-100; CANR 39, 91; CBD; CD 5, 6; DFS 4, 7, 16; DLB 13, 310; MTCW 1; TEA

Harewood, John
See Van Druten, John (William)

Harford, Henry
See Hudson, W(illiam) H(enry)

Hargrave, Leonie
See Disch, Thomas M.

Hariri, Al- al-Qasim ibn 'Ali Abu Muhammad al-Basri
See al-Hariri, al-Qasim ibn 'Ali Abu Muhammad al-Basri

Harjo, Joy 1951- ..... **CLC 83; NNAL; PC 27**
See also AMWS 12; CA 114; CANR 35, 67, 91, 129; CP 6, 7; CWP; DAM MULT; DLB 120, 175, 342; EWL 3; MTCW 2; MTFW 2005; PFS 15; RGAL 4

Harlan, Louis R(udolph) 1922- .... **CLC 34**
See also CA 21-24R; CANR 25, 55, 80

Harling, Robert 1951(?)- .... **CLC 53**
See also CA 147

Harmon, William (Ruth) 1938- .... **CLC 38**
See also CA 33-36R; CANR 14, 32, 35; SATA 65

Harper, F. E. W.
See Harper, Frances Ellen Watkins

Harper, Frances E. W.
See Harper, Frances Ellen Watkins

Harper, Frances E. Watkins
See Harper, Frances Ellen Watkins

Harper, Frances Ellen
See Harper, Frances Ellen Watkins

Harper, Frances Ellen Watkins
1825-1911 . **BLC 1:2; PC 21; TCLC 14, 217**
See also AFAW 1, 2; BW 1, 3; CA 111; 125; CANR 79; DAM MULT, POET; DLB 50, 221; MBL; RGAL 4

Harper, Michael S(teven) 1938- ..... **BLC 2:2; CLC 7, 22**
See also AFAW 2; BW 1; CA 33-36R, 224; CAAE 224; CANR 24, 108; CP 2, 3, 4, 5, 6, 7; DLB 41; RGAL 4; TCLE 1:1

Harper, Mrs. F. E. W.
See Harper, Frances Ellen Watkins

Harpur, Charles 1813-1868 .... **NCLC 114**
See also DLB 230; RGEL 2

Harris, Christie
See Harris, Christie (Lucy) Irwin

Harris, Christie (Lucy) Irwin
1907-2002 .... **CLC 12**
See also CA 5-8R; CANR 6, 83; CLR 47; DLB 88; JRDA; MAICYA 1, 2; SAAS 10; SATA 6, 74; SATA-Essay 116

Harris, Frank 1856-1931 .... **TCLC 24**
See also CA 109; 150; CANR 80; DLB 156, 197; RGEL 2

Harris, George Washington
1814-1869 .... **NCLC 23, 165**
See also DLB 3, 11, 248; RGAL 4

Harris, Joel Chandler 1848-1908 ..... **SSC 19, 103; TCLC 2**
See also CA 104; 137; CANR 80; CLR 49, 128; DLB 11, 23, 42, 78, 91; LAIT 2; MAICYA 1, 2; RGSF 2; SATA 100; WCH; YABC 1

Harris, John (Wyndham Parkes Lucas) Beynon 1903-1969 .... **CLC 19**
See also BRWS 13; CA 102; 89-92; CANR 84; DLB 255; SATA 118; SCFW 1, 2; SFW 4

Harris, MacDonald
See Heiney, Donald (William)

Harris, Mark 1922-2007 .... **CLC 19**
See also CA 5-8R; 260; CAAS 3; CANR 2, 55, 83; CN 1, 2, 3, 4, 5, 6, 7; DLB 2; DLBY 1980

Harris, Norman .... **CLC 65**

Harris, (Theodore) Wilson 1921- ... **BLC 2:2; CLC 25, 159**
See also BRWS 5; BW 2, 3; CA 65-68; CAAS 16; CANR 11, 27, 69, 114; CD-WLB 3; CN 1, 2, 3, 4, 5, 6, 7; CP 1, 2, 3, 4, 5, 6, 7; DLB 117; EWL 3; MTCW 1; RGEL 2

Harrison, Barbara Grizzuti
1934-2002 .... **CLC 144**
See also CA 77-80; 205; CANR 15, 48; INT CANR-15

Harrison, Elizabeth (Allen) Cavanna
1909-2001 .... **CLC 12**
See also CA 9-12R; 200; CANR 6, 27, 85, 104, 121; JRDA; MAICYA 1; SAAS 4; SATA 1, 30; YAW

Harrison, Harry 1925- .... **CLC 42**
See also CA 1-4R; CANR 5, 21, 84; DLB 8; SATA 4; SCFW 2; SFW 4

Harrison, Harry Max
See Harrison, Harry

Harrison, James
See Harrison, Jim

Harrison, James Thomas
See Harrison, Jim

Harrison, Jim 1937- .... **CLC 6, 14, 33, 66, 143; SSC 19**
See also AMWS 8; CA 13-16R; CANR 8, 51, 79, 142; CN 5, 6; CP 1, 2, 3, 4, 5, 6; DLBY 1982; INT CANR-8; RGAL 4; TCWW 2; TUS

Harrison, Kathryn 1961- .... **CLC 70, 151**
See also CA 144; CANR 68, 122

Harrison, Tony 1937- .... **CLC 43, 129**
See also BRWS 5; CA 65-68; CANR 44, 98; CBD; CD 5, 6; CP 2, 3, 4, 5, 6, 7; DLB 40, 245; MTCW 1; RGEL 2

Harriss, Will(ard Irvin) 1922- .... **CLC 34**
See also CA 111

Hart, Ellis
See Ellison, Harlan

Hart, Josephine 1942(?)- .... **CLC 70**
See also CA 138; CANR 70, 149; CPW; DAM POP

Hart, Moss 1904-1961 .... **CLC 66**
See also CA 109; 89-92; CANR 84; DAM DRAM; DFS 1; DLB 7, 266; RGAL 4

Harte, (Francis) Bret(t)
1836(?)-1902 ... **SSC 8, 59; TCLC 1, 25; WLC 3**
See also AMWS 2; CA 104; 140; CANR 80; CDALB 1865-1917; DA; DA3; DAC; DAM MST; DLB 12, 64, 74, 79, 186; EXPS; LAIT 2; RGAL 4; RGSF 2; SATA 26; SSFS 3; TUS

Hartley, L(eslie) P(oles) 1895-1972 ... **CLC 2, 22**
See also BRWS 7; CA 45-48; 37-40R; CANR 33; CN 1; DLB 15, 139; EWL 3; HGG; MTCW 1, 2; MTFW 2005; RGEL 2; RGSF 2; SUFW 1

Hartman, Geoffrey H. 1929- .... **CLC 27**
See also CA 117; 125; CANR 79; DLB 67

Hartmann, Sadakichi 1869-1944 ... **TCLC 73**
See also CA 157; DLB 54

Hartmann von Aue c. 1170-c.
1210 .... **CMLC 15**
See also CDWLB 2; DLB 138; RGWL 2, 3

Hartog, Jan de
See de Hartog, Jan

Haruf, Kent 1943- .... **CLC 34**
See also AAYA 44; CA 149; CANR 91, 131

Harvey, Caroline
See Trollope, Joanna

Harvey, Gabriel 1550(?)-1631 .... **LC 88**
See also DLB 167, 213, 281

Harvey, Jack
See Rankin, Ian

Harwood, Ronald 1934- .... **CLC 32**
See also CA 1-4R; CANR 4, 55, 150; CBD; CD 5, 6; DAM DRAM, MST; DLB 13

Hasegawa Tatsunosuke
See Futabatei, Shimei

Hasek, Jaroslav (Matej Frantisek)
1883-1923 .... **SSC 69; TCLC 4**
See also CA 104; 129; CDWLB 4; DLB 215; EW 9; EWL 3; MTCW 1, 2; RGSF 2; RGWL 2, 3

Hunter, Mollie 1922- .... **CLC 21**
See also AAYA 13, 71; BYA 6; CANR 37,
78; CLR 25; DLB 161; JRDA; MAICYA
1, 2; SAAS 7; SATA 2, 54, 106, 139;
SATA-Essay 139; WYA; YAW

Hunter, Robert (?)-1734 .... **LC 7**

Hurston, Zora Neale 1891-1960 ..... **BLC 1:2;**
CLC 7, 30, 61; DC 12; HR 1:2; SSC 4,
80; TCLC 121, 131; WLCS
See also AAYA 15, 71; AFAW 1, 2; AMWS
6; BW 1, 3; BYA 12; CA 85-88; CANR
61; CDALBS; DA; DA3; DAC; DAM
MST, MULT, NOV; DFS 6; DLB 51, 86;
EWL 3; EXPN; EXPS; FL 1:6; FW; LAIT
3; LATS 1:1; LMFS 2; MAL 5; MBL;
MTCW 1, 2; MTFW 2005; NFS 3; RGAL
4; RGSF 2; SSFS 1, 6, 11, 19, 21; TUS;
YAW

Husserl, E. G.
See Husserl, Edmund (Gustav Albrecht)

Husserl, Edmund (Gustav Albrecht)
1859-1938 .... **TCLC 100**
See also CA 116; 133; DLB 296

Huston, John (Marcellus)
1906-1987 .... **CLC 20**
See also CA 73-76; 123; CANR 34; DLB
26

Hustvedt, Siri 1955- .... **CLC 76**
See also CA 137; CANR 149

Hutcheson, Francis 1694-1746 .... **LC 157**
See also DLB 252

Hutchinson, Lucy 1620-1675 .... **LC 149**

Hutten, Ulrich von 1488-1523 .... **LC 16**
See also DLB 179

Huxley, Aldous (Leonard)
1894-1963 .... **CLC 1, 3, 4, 5, 8, 11, 18,**
35, 79; SSC 39; WLC 3
See also AAYA 11; BPFB 2; BRW 7; CA
85-88; CANR 44, 99; CDBLB 1914-1945;
DA; DA3; DAB; DAC; DAM MST, NOV;
DLB 36, 100, 162, 195, 255; EWL 3;
EXPN; LAIT 5; LMFS 2; MTCW 1, 2;
MTFW 2005; NFS 6; RGEL 2; SATA 63;
SCFW 1, 2; SFW 4; TEA; YAW

Huxley, T(homas) H(enry)
1825-1895 .... **NCLC 67**
See also DLB 57; TEA

Huygens, Constantijn 1596-1687 .... **LC 114**
See also RGWL 2, 3

Huysmans, Joris-Karl 1848-1907 ... **TCLC 7,**
69, 212
See also CA 104; 165; DLB 123; EW 7;
GFL 1789 to the Present; LMFS 2; RGWL
2, 3

Hwang, David Henry 1957- .... **CLC 55, 196;**
DC 4, 23
See also CA 127; 132; CAD; CANR 76,
124; CD 5, 6; DA3; DAM DRAM; DFS
11, 18; DLB 212, 228, 312; INT CA-132;
MAL 5; MTCW 2; MTFW 2005; RGAL
4

Hyatt, Daniel
See James, Daniel (Lewis)

Hyde, Anthony 1946- .... **CLC 42**
See also CA 136; CCA 1

Hyde, Margaret O. 1917- .... **CLC 21**
See also CA 1-4R; CANR 1, 36, 137, 181;
CLR 23; JRDA; MAICYA 1, 2; SAAS 8;
SATA 1, 42, 76, 139

Hyde, Margaret Oldroyd
See Hyde, Margaret O.

Hynes, James 1956(?)- .... **CLC 65**
See also CA 164; CANR 105

Hypatia c. 370-415 .... **CMLC 35**

Ian, Janis 1951- .... **CLC 21**
See also CA 105; 187

Ibanez, Vicente Blasco
See Blasco Ibanez, Vicente

Ibarbourou, Juana de
1895(?)-1979 .... **HLCS 2**
See also DLB 290; HW 1; LAW

Ibarguengoitia, Jorge 1928-1983 ..... **CLC 37;**
TCLC 148
See also CA 124; 113; EWL 3; HW 1

Ibn Arabi 1165-1240 .... **CMLC 105**

Ibn Battuta, Abu Abdalla
1304-1368(?) .... **CMLC 57**
See also WLIT 2

Ibn Hazm 994-1064 .... **CMLC 64**

Ibn Zaydun 1003-1070 .... **CMLC 89**

Ibsen, Henrik (Johan) 1828-1906 .. **DC 2, 30;**
TCLC 2, 8, 16, 37, 52; WLC 3
See also AAYA 46; CA 104; 141; DA; DA3;
DAB; DAC; DAM DRAM, MST; DFS 1,
6, 8, 10, 11, 15, 16, 25; EW 7; LAIT 2;
LATS 1:1; MTFW 2005; RGWL 2, 3

Ibuse, Masuji 1898-1993 .... **CLC 22**
See also CA 127; 141; CWW 2; DLB 180;
EWL 3; MJW; RGWL 3

Ibuse Masuji
See Ibuse, Masuji

Ichikawa, Kon 1915-2008 .... **CLC 20**
See also CA 121; 269

Ichiyo, Higuchi 1872-1896 .... **NCLC 49**
See also MJW

Idle, Eric 1943- .... **CLC 21**
See also CA 116; CANR 35, 91, 148

Idris, Yusuf 1927-1991 .... **SSC 74**
See also AFW; DLB 346; EWL 3; RGSF 2,
3; RGWL 3; WLIT 2

Ignatieff, Michael 1947- .... **CLC 236**
See also CA 144; CANR 88, 156; CN 6, 7;
DLB 267

Ignatieff, Michael Grant
See Ignatieff, Michael

Ignatow, David 1914-1997 .... **CLC 4, 7, 14,**
40; PC 34
See also CA 9-12R; 162; CAAS 3; CANR
31, 57, 96; CP 1, 2, 3, 4, 5, 6; DLB 5;
EWL 3; MAL 5

Ignotus
See Strachey, (Giles) Lytton

Ihimaera, Witi (Tame) 1944- .... **CLC 46**
See also CA 77-80; CANR 130; CN 2, 3, 4,
5, 6, 7; RGSF 2; SATA 148

Il'f, Il'ia
See Fainzilberg, Ilya Arnoldovich

Ilf, Ilya
See Fainzilberg, Ilya Arnoldovich

Illyes, Gyula 1902-1983 .... **PC 16**
See also CA 114; 109; CDWLB 4; DLB
215; EWL 3; RGWL 2, 3

Imalayen, Fatima-Zohra
See Djebar, Assia

Immermann, Karl (Lebrecht)
1796-1840 .... **NCLC 4, 49**
See also DLB 133

Ince, Thomas H. 1882-1924 .... **TCLC 89**
See also IDFW 3, 4

Inchbald, Elizabeth 1753-1821 ...... **NCLC 62**
See also DLB 39, 89; RGEL 2

Inclan, Ramon (Maria) del Valle
See Valle-Inclan, Ramon (Maria) del

Incogniteau, Jean-Louis
See Kerouac, Jack

Infante, G(uillermo) Cabrera
See Cabrera Infante, G.

Ingalls, Rachel 1940- .... **CLC 42**
See also CA 123; 127; CANR 154

Ingalls, Rachel Holmes
See Ingalls, Rachel

Ingamells, Reginald Charles
See Ingamells, Rex

Ingamells, Rex 1913-1955 .... **TCLC 35**
See also CA 167; DLB 260

Inge, William (Motter) 1913-1973 ..... **CLC 1,**
8, 19
See also CA 9-12R; CAD; CDALB 1941-
1968; DA3; DAM DRAM; DFS 1, 3, 5,
8; DLB 7, 249; EWL 3; MAL 5; MTCW
1, 2; MTFW 2005; RGAL 4; TUS

Ingelow, Jean 1820-1897 .... **NCLC 39, 107**
See also DLB 35, 163; FANT; SATA 33

Ingram, Willis J.
See Harris, Mark

Innaurato, Albert (F.) 1948(?)- ... **CLC 21, 60**
See also CA 115; 122; CAD; CANR 78;
CD 5, 6; INT CA-122

Innes, Michael
See Stewart, J(ohn) I(nnes) M(ackintosh)

Innis, Harold Adams 1894-1952 .... **TCLC 77**
See also CA 181; DLB 88

Insluis, Alanus de
See Alain de Lille

Iola
See Wells-Barnett, Ida B(ell)

Ionesco, Eugene 1912-1994 ... **CLC 1, 4, 6, 9,**
11, 15, 41, 86; DC 12; WLC 3
See also CA 9-12R; 144; CANR 55, 132;
CWW 2; DA; DA3; DAB; DAC; DAM
DRAM, MST; DFS 4, 9, 25; DLB 321;
EW 13; EWL 3; GFL 1789 to the Present;
LMFS 2; MTCW 1, 2; MTFW 2005;
RGWL 2, 3; SATA 7; SATA-Obit 79;
TWA

Iqbal, Muhammad 1877-1938 .... **TCLC 28**
See also CA 215; EWL 3

Ireland, Patrick
See O'Doherty, Brian

Irenaeus St. 130- .... **CMLC 42**

Irigaray, Luce 1930- .... **CLC 164**
See also CA 154; CANR 121; FW

Irish, William
See Hopley-Woolrich, Cornell George

Irland, David
See Green, Julien (Hartridge)

Iron, Ralph
See Schreiner, Olive (Emilie Albertina)

Irving, John 1942- . **CLC 13, 23, 38, 112, 175**
See also AAYA 8, 62; AMWS 6; BEST
89:3; BPFB 2; CA 25-28R; CANR 28, 73,
112, 133; CN 3, 4, 5, 6, 7; CPW; DA3;
DAM NOV, POP; DLB 6, 278; DLBY
1982; EWL 3; MAL 5; MTCW 1, 2;
MTFW 2005; NFS 12, 14; RGAL 4; TUS

Irving, John Winslow
See Irving, John

Irving, Washington 1783-1859 . **NCLC 2, 19,**
95; SSC 2, 37, 104; WLC 3
See also AAYA 56; AMW; CDALB 1640-
1865; CLR 97; DA; DA3; DAB; DAC;
DAM MST; DLB 3, 11, 30, 59, 73, 74,
183, 186, 250, 254; EXPS; GL 2; LAIT
1; RGAL 4; RGSF 2; SSFS 1, 8, 16;
SUFW 1; TUS; WCH; YABC 2

Irwin, P. K.
See Page, P(atricia) K(athleen)

Isaacs, Jorge Ricardo 1837-1895 ... **NCLC 70**
See also LAW

Isaacs, Susan 1943- .... **CLC 32**
See also BEST 89:1; BPFB 2; CA 89-92;
CANR 20, 41, 65, 112, 134, 165; CPW;
DA3; DAM POP; INT CANR-20; MTCW
1, 2; MTFW 2005

Isherwood, Christopher 1904-1986 ... **CLC 1,**
9, 11, 14, 44; SSC 56
See also AMWS 14; BRW 7; CA 13-16R;
117; CANR 35, 97, 133; CN 1, 2, 3; DA3;
DAM DRAM, NOV; DLB 15, 195; DLBY
1986; EWL 3; IDTP; MTCW 1, 2; MTFW
2005; RGAL 4; RGEL 2; TUS; WLIT 4

Ishiguro, Kazuo 1954- . **CLC 27, 56, 59, 110, 219**
See also AAYA 58; BEST 90:2; BPFB 2; BRWS 4; CA 120; CANR 49, 95, 133; CN 5, 6, 7; DA3; DAM NOV; DLB 194, 326; EWL 3; MTCW 1, 2; MTFW 2005; NFS 13; WLIT 4; WWE 1
Ishikawa, Hakuhin
See Ishikawa, Takuboku
Ishikawa, Takuboku 1886(?)-1912 ..... **PC 10; TCLC 15**
See Ishikawa Takuboku
See also CA 113; 153; DAM POET
Isidore of Seville c. 560-636 .... **CMLC 101**
Iskander, Fazil (Abdulovich) 1929- .. **CLC 47**
See also CA 102; DLB 302; EWL 3
Iskander, Fazil' Abdulevich
See Iskander, Fazil (Abdulovich)
Isler, Alan (David) 1934- .... **CLC 91**
See also CA 156; CANR 105
Ivan IV 1530-1584 .... **LC 17**
Ivanov, V.I.
See Ivanov, Vyacheslav
Ivanov, Vyacheslav 1866-1949 .... **TCLC 33**
See also CA 122; EWL 3
Ivanov, Vyacheslav Ivanovich
See Ivanov, Vyacheslav
Ivask, Ivar Vidrik 1927-1992 .... **CLC 14**
See also CA 37-40R; 139; CANR 24
Ives, Morgan
See Bradley, Marion Zimmer
Izumi Shikibu c. 973-c. 1034 .... **CMLC 33**
J. R. S.
See Gogarty, Oliver St. John
Jabran, Kahlil
See Gibran, Kahlil
Jabran, Khalil
See Gibran, Kahlil
Jaccottet, Philippe 1925- .... **PC 98**
See also CA 116; 129; CWW 2; GFL 1789 to the Present
Jackson, Daniel
See Wingrove, David
Jackson, Helen Hunt 1830-1885 .... **NCLC 90**
See also DLB 42, 47, 186, 189; RGAL 4
Jackson, Jesse 1908-1983 .... **CLC 12**
See also BW 1; CA 25-28R; 109; CANR 27; CLR 28; CWRI 5; MAICYA 1, 2; SATA 2, 29; SATA-Obit 48
Jackson, Laura (Riding) 1901-1991 .. **CLC 3, 7; PC 44**
See also CA 65-68; 135; CANR 28, 89; CP 1, 2, 3, 4, 5; DLB 48; RGAL 4
Jackson, Sam
See Trumbo, Dalton
Jackson, Sara
See Wingrove, David
Jackson, Shirley 1919-1965 . **CLC 11, 60, 87; SSC 9, 39; TCLC 187; WLC 3**
See also AAYA 9; AMWS 9; BPFB 2; CA 1-4R; 25-28R; CANR 4, 52; CDALB 1941-1968; DA; DA3; DAC; DAM MST; DLB 6, 234; EXPS; HGG; LAIT 4; MAL 5; MTCW 2; MTFW 2005; RGAL 4; RGSF 2; SATA 2; SSFS 1, 27; SUFW 1, 2
Jacob, (Cyprien-)Max 1876-1944 .... **TCLC 6**
See also CA 104; 193; DLB 258; EWL 3; GFL 1789 to the Present; GLL 2; RGWL 2, 3
Jacobs, Harriet A(nn) 1813(?)-1897 .... **NCLC 67, 162**
See also AFAW 1, 2; DLB 239; FL 1:3; FW; LAIT 2; RGAL 4
Jacobs, Jim 1942- .... **CLC 12**
See also CA 97-100; INT CA-97-100

Jacobs, W(illiam) W(ymark) 1863-1943 .... **SSC 73; TCLC 22**
See also CA 121; 167; DLB 135; EXPS; HGG; RGEL 2; RGSF 2; SSFS 2; SUFW 1
Jacobsen, Jens Peter 1847-1885 .... **NCLC 34**
Jacobsen, Josephine (Winder) 1908-2003 .... **CLC 48, 102; PC 62**
See also CA 33-36R; 218; CAAS 18; CANR 23, 48; CCA 1; CP 2, 3, 4, 5, 6, 7; DLB 244; PFS 23; TCLE 1:1
Jacobson, Dan 1929- .... **CLC 4, 14; SSC 91**
See also AFW; CA 1-4R; CANR 2, 25, 66, 170; CN 1, 2, 3, 4, 5, 6, 7; DLB 14, 207, 225, 319; EWL 3; MTCW 1; RGSF 2
Jacopone da Todi 1236-1306 .... **CMLC 95**
Jacqueline
See Carpentier (y Valmont), Alejo
Jacques de Vitry c. 1160-1240 ...... **CMLC 63**
See also DLB 208
Jagger, Michael Philip
See Jagger, Mick
Jagger, Mick 1943- .... **CLC 17**
See also CA 239
Jahiz, al- c. 780-c. 869 .... **CMLC 25**
See also DLB 311
Jakes, John 1932- .... **CLC 29**
See also AAYA 32; BEST 89:4; BPFB 2; CA 57-60, 214; CAAE 214; CANR 10, 43, 66, 111, 142, 171; CPW; CSW; DA3; DAM NOV, POP; DLB 278; DLBY 1983; FANT; INT CANR-10; MTCW 1, 2; MTFW 2005; RHW; SATA 62; SFW 4; TCWW 1, 2
Jakes, John William
See Jakes, John
James I 1394-1437 .... **LC 20**
See also RGEL 2
James, Alice 1848-1892 .... **NCLC 206**
See also DLB 221
James, Andrew
See Kirkup, James
James, C(yril) L(ionel) R(obert) 1901-1989 .... **BLCS; CLC 33**
See also BW 2; CA 117; 125; 128; CANR 62; CN 1, 2, 3, 4; DLB 125; MTCW 1
James, Daniel (Lewis) 1911-1988 .... **CLC 33**
See also CA 174; 125; DLB 122
James, Dynely
See Mayne, William (James Carter)
James, Henry Sr. 1811-1882 .... **NCLC 53**
James, Henry 1843-1916 .... **SSC 8, 32, 47, 108; TCLC 2, 11, 24, 40, 47, 64, 171; WLC 3**
See also AMW; AMWC 1; AMWR 1; BPFB 2; BRW 6; CA 104; 132; CDALB 1865-1917; DA; DA3; DAB; DAC; DAM MST, NOV; DLB 12, 71, 74, 189; DLBD 13; EWL 3; EXPS; GL 2; HGG; LAIT 2; MAL 5; MTCW 1, 2; MTFW 2005; NFS 12, 16, 19; RGAL 4; RGEL 2; RGSF 2; SSFS 9; SUFW 1; TUS
James, M. R.
See James, Montague (Rhodes)
James, Mary
See Meaker, Marijane
James, Montague (Rhodes) 1862-1936 .... **SSC 16, 93; TCLC 6**
See also CA 104; 203; DLB 156, 201; HGG; RGEL 2; RGSF 2; SUFW 1
James, P. D.
See White, Phyllis Dorothy James
James, Philip
See Moorcock, Michael
James, Samuel
See Stephens, James
James, Seumas
See Stephens, James

James, Stephen
See Stephens, James
James, T.F.
See Fleming, Thomas
James, William 1842-1910 .... **TCLC 15, 32**
See also AMW; CA 109; 193; DLB 270, 284; MAL 5; NCFS 5; RGAL 4
Jameson, Anna 1794-1860 .... **NCLC 43**
See also DLB 99, 166
Jameson, Fredric 1934- .... **CLC 142**
See also CA 196; CANR 169; DLB 67; LMFS 2
Jameson, Fredric R.
See Jameson, Fredric
James VI of Scotland 1566-1625 .... **LC 109**
See also DLB 151, 172
Jami, Nur al-Din 'Abd al-Rahman 1414-1492 .... **LC 9**
Jammes, Francis 1868-1938 .... **TCLC 75**
See also CA 198; EWL 3; GFL 1789 to the Present
Jandl, Ernst 1925-2000 .... **CLC 34**
See also CA 200; EWL 3
Janowitz, Tama 1957- .... **CLC 43, 145**
See also CA 106; CANR 52, 89, 129; CN 5, 6, 7; CPW; DAM POP; DLB 292; MTFW 2005
Jansson, Tove (Marika) 1914-2001 ... **SSC 96**
See also CA 17-20R; 196; CANR 38, 118; CLR 2; 125; CWW 2; DLB 257; EWL 3; MAICYA 1, 2; RGSF 2; SATA 3, 41
Japrisot, Sebastien 1931-
See Rossi, Jean-Baptiste
Jarrell, Randall 1914-1965 .... **CLC 1, 2, 6, 9, 13, 49; PC 41; TCLC 177**
See also AMW; BYA 5; CA 5-8R; 25-28R; CABS 2; CANR 6, 34; CDALB 1941-1968; CLR 6, 111; CWRI 5; DAM POET; DLB 48, 52; EWL 3; EXPP; MAICYA 1, 2; MAL 5; MTCW 1, 2; PAB; PFS 2; RGAL 4; SATA 7
Jarry, Alfred 1873-1907 .... **SSC 20; TCLC 2, 14, 147**
See also CA 104; 153; DA3; DAM DRAM; DFS 8; DLB 192, 258; EW 9; EWL 3; GFL 1789 to the Present; RGWL 2, 3; TWA
Jarvis, E.K.
See Ellison, Harlan; Silverberg, Robert
Jawien, Andrzej
See John Paul II, Pope
Jaynes, Roderick
See Coen, Ethan
Jeake, Samuel, Jr.
See Aiken, Conrad (Potter)
Jean-Louis
See Kerouac, Jack
Jean Paul 1763-1825 .... **NCLC 7**
Jefferies, (John) Richard 1848-1887 .... **NCLC 47**
See also DLB 98, 141; RGEL 2; SATA 16; SFW 4
Jeffers, John Robinson
See Jeffers, Robinson
Jeffers, Robinson 1887-1962 .... **CLC 2, 3, 11, 15, 54; PC 17; WLC 3**
See also AMWS 2; CA 85-88; CANR 35; CDALB 1917-1929; DA; DAC; DAM MST, POET; DLB 45, 212, 342; EWL 3; MAL 5; MTCW 1, 2; MTFW 2005; PAB; PFS 3, 4; RGAL 4
Jefferson, Janet
See Mencken, H(enry) L(ouis)
Jefferson, Thomas 1743-1826 . **NCLC 11, 103**
See also AAYA 54; ANW; CDALB 1640-1865; DA3; DLB 31, 183; LAIT 1; RGAL 4
Jeffrey, Francis 1773-1850 .... **NCLC 33**
See also DLB 107

Leger, Alexis
   See Leger, (Marie-Rene Auguste) Alexis
   Saint-Leger

**Leger, (Marie-Rene Auguste) Alexis
   Saint-Leger** 1887-1975 .. **CLC 4, 11, 46;
   PC 23**
   See also CA 13-16R; 61-64; CANR 43;
   DAM POET; DLB 258, 331; EW 10;
   EWL 3; GFL 1789 to the Present; MTCW
   1; RGWL 2, 3

Leger, Saintleger
   See Leger, (Marie-Rene Auguste) Alexis
   Saint-Leger

Le Guin, Ursula K. 1929- ...... **CLC 8, 13, 22,
   45, 71, 136; SSC 12, 69**
   See also AAYA 9, 27; AITN 1; BPFB 2;
   BYA 5, 8, 11, 14; CA 21-24R; CANR 9,
   32, 52, 74, 132; CDALB 1968-1988; CLR
   3, 28, 91; CN 2, 3, 4, 5, 6, 7; CPW; DA3;
   DAB; DAC; DAM MST, POP; DLB 8,
   52, 256, 275; EXPS; FANT; FW; INT
   CANR-32; JRDA; LAIT 5; MAICYA 1,
   2; MAL 5; MTCW 1, 2; MTFW 2005;
   NFS 6, 9; SATA 4, 52, 99, 149, 194;
   SCFW 1, 2; SFW 4; SSFS 2; SUFW 1, 2;
   WYA; YAW

Lehmann, Rosamond (Nina)
   1901-1990 .... **CLC 5**
   See also CA 77-80; 131; CANR 8, 73; CN
   1, 2, 3, 4; DLB 15; MTCW 2; RGEL 2;
   RHW

Leiber, Fritz (Reuter, Jr.)
   1910-1992 .... **CLC 25**
   See also AAYA 65; BPFB 2; CA 45-48; 139;
   CANR 2, 40, 86; CN 2, 3, 4, 5; DLB 8;
   FANT; HGG; MTCW 1, 2; MTFW 2005;
   SATA 45; SATA-Obit 73; SCFW 1, 2;
   SFW 4; SUFW 1, 2

Leibniz, Gottfried Wilhelm von
   1646-1716 .... **LC 35**
   See also DLB 168

Leino, Eino
   See Lonnbohm, Armas Eino Leopold

Leiris, Michel (Julien) 1901-1990 ..... **CLC 61**
   See also CA 119; 128; 132; EWL 3; GFL
   1789 to the Present

Leithauser, Brad 1953- .... **CLC 27**
   See also CA 107; CANR 27, 81, 171; CP 5,
   6, 7; DLB 120, 282

le Jars de Gournay, Marie
   See de Gournay, Marie le Jars

Lelchuk, Alan 1938- .... **CLC 5**
   See also CA 45-48; CAAS 20; CANR 1,
   70, 152; CN 3, 4, 5, 6, 7

Lem, Stanislaw 1921-2006 ..... **CLC 8, 15, 40,
   149**
   See also AAYA 75; CA 105; 249; CAAS 1;
   CANR 32; CWW 2; MTCW 1; SCFW 1,
   2; SFW 4

Lemann, Nancy (Elise) 1956- .... **CLC 39**
   See also CA 118; 136; CANR 121

Lemonnier, (Antoine Louis) Camille
   1844-1913 .... **TCLC 22**
   See also CA 121

Lenau, Nikolaus 1802-1850 .... **NCLC 16**

L'Engle, Madeleine 1918-2007 .... **CLC 12**
   See also AAYA 28; AITN 2; BPFB 2; BYA
   2, 4, 5, 7; CA 1-4R; 264; CANR 3, 21,
   39, 66, 107; CLR 1, 14, 57; CPW; CWRI
   5; DA3; DAM POP; DLB 52; JRDA;
   MAICYA 1, 2; MTCW 1, 2; MTFW 2005;
   SAAS 15; SATA 1, 27, 75, 128; SATA-
   Obit 186; SFW 4; WYA; YAW

L'Engle, Madeleine Camp Franklin
   See L'Engle, Madeleine

Lengyel, Jozsef 1896-1975 .... **CLC 7**
   See also CA 85-88; 57-60; CANR 71;
   RGSF 2

Lenin 1870-1924 .... **TCLC 67**
   See also CA 121; 168

Lenin, N.
   See Lenin

Lenin, Nikolai
   See Lenin

Lenin, V. I.
   See Lenin

Lenin, Vladimir I.
   See Lenin

Lenin, Vladimir Ilyich
   See Lenin

Lennon, John (Ono) 1940-1980 .. **CLC 12, 35**
   See also CA 102; SATA 114

Lennox, Charlotte Ramsay
   1729(?)-1804 .... **NCLC 23, 134**
   See also DLB 39; RGEL 2

Lentricchia, Frank, Jr.
   See Lentricchia, Frank

Lentricchia, Frank 1940- .... **CLC 34**
   See also CA 25-28R; CANR 19, 106, 148;
   DLB 246

Lenz, Gunter .... **CLC 65**

Lenz, Jakob Michael Reinhold
   1751-1792 .... **LC 100**
   See also DLB 94; RGWL 2, 3

Lenz, Siegfried 1926- .... **CLC 27; SSC 33**
   See also CA 89-92; CANR 80, 149; CWW
   2; DLB 75; EWL 3; RGSF 2; RGWL 2, 3

Leon, David
   See Jacob, (Cyprien-)Max

Leonard, Dutch
   See Leonard, Elmore

Leonard, Elmore 1925- .... **CLC 28, 34, 71,
   120, 222**
   See also AAYA 22, 59; AITN 1; BEST 89:1,
   90:4; BPFB 2; CA 81-84; CANR 12, 28,
   53, 76, 96, 133, 176; CMW 4; CN 5, 6, 7;
   CPW; DA3; DAM POP; DLB 173, 226;
   INT CANR-28; MSW; MTCW 1, 2;
   MTFW 2005; RGAL 4; SATA 163;
   TCWW 1, 2

Leonard, Elmore John, Jr.
   See Leonard, Elmore

Leonard, Hugh
   See Byrne, John Keyes

Leonov, Leonid (Maximovich)
   1899-1994 .... **CLC 92**
   See also CA 129; CANR 76; DAM NOV;
   DLB 272; EWL 3; MTCW 1, 2; MTFW
   2005

Leonov, Leonid Maksimovich
   See Leonov, Leonid (Maximovich)

Leopardi, (Conte) Giacomo
   1798-1837 .... **NCLC 22, 129; PC 37**
   See also EW 5; RGWL 2, 3; WLIT 7; WP

Le Reveler
   See Artaud, Antonin (Marie Joseph)

Lerman, Eleanor 1952- .... **CLC 9**
   See also CA 85-88; CANR 69, 124, 184

Lerman, Rhoda 1936- .... **CLC 56**
   See also CA 49-52; CANR 70

Lermontov, Mikhail Iur'evich
   See Lermontov, Mikhail Yuryevich

Lermontov, Mikhail Yuryevich
   1814-1841 .... **NCLC 5, 47, 126; PC 18**
   See also DLB 205; EW 6; RGWL 2, 3;
   TWA

Leroux, Gaston 1868-1927 .... **TCLC 25**
   See also CA 108; 136; CANR 69; CMW 4;
   MTFW 2005; NFS 20; SATA 65

Lesage, Alain-Rene 1668-1747 .... **LC 2, 28**
   See also DLB 313; EW 3; GFL Beginnings
   to 1789; RGWL 2, 3

Leskov, N(ikolai) S(emenovich) 1831-1895
   See Leskov, Nikolai (Semyonovich)

Leskov, Nikolai (Semyonovich)
   1831-1895 ... **NCLC 25, 174; SSC 34, 96**
   See also DLB 238

Leskov, Nikolai Semenovich
   See Leskov, Nikolai (Semyonovich)

Lesser, Milton
   See Marlowe, Stephen

Lessing, Doris 1919- .. **CLC 1, 2, 3, 6, 10, 15,
   22, 40, 94, 170, 254; SSC 6, 61; WLCS**
   See also AAYA 57; AFW; BRWS 1; CA
   9-12R; CAAS 14; CANR 33, 54, 76, 122,
   179; CBD; CD 5, 6; CDBLB 1960 to
   Present; CN 1, 2, 3, 4, 5, 6, 7; CWD; DA;
   DA3; DAB; DAC; DAM MST, NOV;
   DFS 20; DLB 15, 139; DLBY 1985; EWL
   3; EXPS; FL 1:6; FW; LAIT 4; MTCW 1,
   2; MTFW 2005; NFS 27; RGEL 2; RGSF
   2; SFW 4; SSFS 1, 12, 20, 26; TEA;
   WLIT 2, 4

Lessing, Doris May
   See Lessing, Doris

Lessing, Gotthold Ephraim
   1729-1781 .... **DC 26; LC 8, 124, 162**
   See also CDWLB 2; DLB 97; EW 4; RGWL
   2, 3

Lester, Julius 1939- .... **BLC 2:2**
   See also AAYA 12, 51; BW 2; BYA 3, 9,
   11, 12; CA 17-20R; CANR 8, 23, 43, 129,
   174; CLR 2, 41, 143; JRDA; MAICYA 1,
   2; MAICYAS 1; MTFW 2005; SATA 12,
   74, 112, 157; YAW

Lester, Richard 1932- .... **CLC 20**

Levenson, Jay .... **CLC 70**

Lever, Charles (James)
   1806-1872 .... **NCLC 23**
   See also DLB 21; RGEL 2

Leverson, Ada Esther
   1862(?)-1933(?) .... **TCLC 18**
   See also CA 117; 202; DLB 153; RGEL 2

Levertov, Denise 1923-1997 .. **CLC 1, 2, 3, 5,
   8, 15, 28, 66; PC 11**
   See also AMWS 3; CA 1-4R, 178; 163;
   CAAE 178; CAAS 19; CANR 3, 29, 50,
   108; CDALBS; CP 1, 2, 3, 4, 5, 6; CWP;
   DAM POET; DLB 5, 165, 342; EWL 3;
   EXPP; FW; INT CANR-29; MAL 5;
   MTCW 1, 2; PAB; PFS 7, 17; RGAL 4;
   RGHL; TUS; WP

Levi, Carlo 1902-1975 .... **TCLC 125**
   See also CA 65-68; 53-56; CANR 10; EWL
   3; RGWL 2, 3

Levi, Jonathan .... **CLC 76**
   See also CA 197

Levi, Peter (Chad Tigar)
   1931-2000 .... **CLC 41**
   See also CA 5-8R; 187; CANR 34, 80; CP
   1, 2, 3, 4, 5, 6, 7; DLB 40

Levi, Primo 1919-1987 ...... **CLC 37, 50; SSC
   12, 122; TCLC 109**
   See also CA 13-16R; 122; CANR 12, 33,
   61, 70, 132, 171; DLB 177, 299; EWL 3;
   MTCW 1, 2; MTFW 2005; RGHL;
   RGWL 2, 3; WLIT 7

Levin, Ira 1929-2007 .... **CLC 3, 6**
   See also CA 21-24R; 266; CANR 17, 44,
   74, 139; CMW 4; CN 1, 2, 3, 4, 5, 6, 7;
   CPW; DA3; DAM POP; HGG; MTCW 1,
   2; MTFW 2005; SATA 66; SATA-Obit
   187; SFW 4

Levin, Ira Marvin
   See Levin, Ira

Levin, Ira Marvin
   See Levin, Ira

Levin, Meyer 1905-1981 .... **CLC 7**
   See also AITN 1; CA 9-12R; 104; CANR
   15; CN 1, 2, 3; DAM POP; DLB 9, 28;
   DLBY 1981; MAL 5; RGHL; SATA 21;
   SATA-Obit 27

Levine, Albert Norman
   See Levine, Norman

Lively, Penelope 1933- .... **CLC 32, 50**
See also BPFB 2; CA 41-44R; CANR 29,
67, 79, 131, 172; CLR 7; CN 5, 6, 7;
CWRI 5; DAM NOV; DLB 14, 161, 207,
326; FANT; JRDA; MAICYA 1, 2;
MTCW 1, 2; MTFW 2005; SATA 7, 60,
101, 164; TEA
Lively, Penelope Margaret
See Lively, Penelope
Livesay, Dorothy (Kathleen)
1909-1996 .... **CLC 4, 15, 79**
See also AITN 2; CA 25-28R; CAAS 8;
CANR 36, 67; CP 1, 2, 3, 4, 5; DAC;
DAM MST, POET; DLB 68; FW; MTCW
1; RGEL 2; TWA
Livius Andronicus c. 284B.C.-c.
204B.C. .... **CMLC 102**
Livy c. 59B.C.-c. 12 .... **CMLC 11**
See also AW 2; CDWLB 1; DLB 211;
RGWL 2, 3; WLIT 8
Li Yaotang
See Jin, Ba
Lizardi, Jose Joaquin Fernandez de
1776-1827 .... **NCLC 30**
See also LAW
Llewellyn, Richard
See Llewellyn Lloyd, Richard Dafydd Viv-
ian
Llewellyn Lloyd, Richard Dafydd Vivian
1906-1983 .... **CLC 7, 80**
See also CA 53-56; 111; CANR 7, 71; DLB
15; SATA 11; SATA-Obit 37
Llosa, Jorge Mario Pedro Vargas
See Vargas Llosa, Mario
Llosa, Mario Vargas
See Vargas Llosa, Mario
Lloyd, Manda
See Mander, (Mary) Jane
Lloyd Webber, Andrew 1948- .... **CLC 21**
See also AAYA 1, 38; CA 116; 149; DAM
DRAM; DFS 7; SATA 56
Llull, Ramon c. 1235-c. 1316 .... **CMLC 12**
Lobb, Ebenezer
See Upward, Allen
Locke, Alain (Le Roy)
1886-1954 .... **BLCS; HR 1:3; TCLC 43**
See also AMWS 14; BW 1, 3; CA 106; 124;
CANR 79; DLB 51; LMFS 2; MAL 5;
RGAL 4
Locke, John 1632-1704 .... **LC 7, 35, 135**
See also DLB 31, 101, 213, 252; RGEL 2;
WLIT 3
Locke-Elliott, Sumner
See Elliott, Sumner Locke
Lockhart, John Gibson 1794-1854 .. **NCLC 6**
See also DLB 110, 116, 144
Lockridge, Ross (Franklin), Jr.
1914-1948 .... **TCLC 111**
See also CA 108; 145; CANR 79; DLB 143;
DLBY 1980; MAL 5; RGAL 4; RHW
Lockwood, Robert
See Johnson, Robert
Lodge, David 1935- .... **CLC 36, 141**
See also BEST 90:1; BRWS 4; CA 17-20R;
CANR 19, 53, 92, 139; CN 1, 2, 3, 4, 5,
6, 7; CPW; DAM POP; DLB 14, 194;
EWL 3; INT CANR-19; MTCW 1, 2;
MTFW 2005
Lodge, Thomas 1558-1625 .... **LC 41**
See also DLB 172; RGEL 2
Loewinsohn, Ron(ald William)
1937- .... **CLC 52**
See also CA 25-28R; CANR 71; CP 1, 2, 3,
4
Logan, Jake
See Smith, Martin Cruz
Logan, John (Burton) 1923-1987 .... **CLC 5**
See also CA 77-80; 124; CANR 45; CP 1,
2, 3, 4; DLB 5

Lo-Johansson, (Karl) Ivar
1901-1990 .... **TCLC 216**
See also CA 102; 131; CANR 20, 79, 137;
DLB 259; EWL 3; RGWL 2, 3
Lo Kuan-chung 1330(?)-1400(?) .... **LC 12**
Lomax, Pearl
See Cleage, Pearl
Lomax, Pearl Cleage
See Cleage, Pearl
Lombard, Nap
See Johnson, Pamela Hansford
Lombard, Peter 1100(?)-1160(?) ... **CMLC 72**
Lombino, Salvatore
See Hunter, Evan
London, Jack 1876-1916
See London, John Griffith
London, John Griffith 1876-1916 .... **SSC 4,
49; TCLC 9, 15, 39; WLC 4**
See also AAYA 13, 75; AITN 2; AMW;
BPFB 2; BYA 4, 13; CA 110; 119; CANR
73; CDALB 1865-1917; CLR 108; DA;
DA3; DAB; DAC; DAM MST, NOV;
DLB 8, 12, 78, 212; EWL 3; EXPS;
JRDA; LAIT 3; MAICYA 1, 2; MAL 5;
MTCW 1, 2; MTFW 2005; NFS 8, 19;
RGAL 4; RGSF 2; SATA 18; SFW 4;
SSFS 7; TCWW 1, 2; TUS; WYA; YAW
Long, Emmett
See Leonard, Elmore
Longbaugh, Harry
See Goldman, William
Longfellow, Henry Wadsworth
1807-1882 .... **NCLC 2, 45, 101, 103; PC
30; WLCS**
See also AMW; AMWR 2; CDALB 1640-
1865; CLR 99; DA; DA3; DAB; DAC;
DAM MST, POET; DLB 1, 59, 235;
EXPP; PAB; PFS 2, 7, 17; RGAL 4;
SATA 19; TUS; WP
Longinus c. 1st cent. - .... **CMLC 27**
See also AW 2; DLB 176
Longley, Michael 1939- .... **CLC 29**
See also BRWS 8; CA 102; CP 1, 2, 3, 4, 5,
6, 7; DLB 40
Longstreet, Augustus Baldwin
1790-1870 .... **NCLC 159**
See also DLB 3, 11, 74, 248; RGAL 4
Longus fl. c. 2nd cent. - .... **CMLC 7**
Longway, A. Hugh
See Lang, Andrew
Lonnbohm, Armas Eino Leopold
See Lonnbohm, Armas Eino Leopold
Lonnbohm, Armas Eino Leopold
1878-1926 .... **TCLC 24**
See also CA 123; EWL 3
Lonnrot, Elias 1802-1884 .... **NCLC 53**
See also EFS 1
Lonsdale, Roger .... **CLC 65**
Lopate, Phillip 1943- .... **CLC 29**
See also CA 97-100; CANR 88, 157; DLBY
1980; INT CA-97-100
Lopez, Barry (Holstun) 1945- .... **CLC 70**
See also AAYA 9, 63; ANW; CA 65-68;
CANR 7, 23, 47, 68, 92; DLB 256, 275,
335; INT CANR-7, CANR-23; MTCW 1;
RGAL 4; SATA 67
Lopez de Mendoza, Inigo
See Santillana, Inigo Lopez de Mendoza,
Marques de
Lopez Portillo (y Pacheco), Jose
1920-2004 .... **CLC 46**
See also CA 129; 224; HW 1
Lopez y Fuentes, Gregorio
1897(?)-1966 .... **CLC 32**
See also CA 131; EWL 3; HW 1
Lorca, Federico Garcia
See Garcia Lorca, Federico
Lord, Audre
See Lorde, Audre

Lord, Bette Bao 1938- .... **AAL; CLC 23**
See also BEST 90:3; BPFB 2; CA 107;
CANR 41, 79; INT CA-107; SATA 58
Lord Auch
See Bataille, Georges
Lord Brooke
See Greville, Fulke
Lord Byron
See Byron, George Gordon (Noel)
Lord Dunsany
See Dunsany, Edward John Moreton Drax
Plunkett
Lorde, Audre 1934-1992 .... **BLC 1:2, 2:2;
CLC 18, 71; PC 12; TCLC 173**
See also AFAW 1, 2; BW 1, 3; CA 25-28R;
142; CANR 16, 26, 46, 82; CP 2, 3, 4, 5;
DA3; DAM MULT, POET; DLB 41; EWL
3; FW; GLL 1; MAL 5; MTCW 1, 2;
MTFW 2005; PFS 16; RGAL 4
Lorde, Audre Geraldine
See Lorde, Audre
Lord Houghton
See Milnes, Richard Monckton
Lord Jeffrey
See Jeffrey, Francis
Loreaux, Nichol .... **CLC 65**
Lorenzini, Carlo 1826-1890 .... **NCLC 54**
See also CLR 5, 120; MAICYA 1, 2; SATA
29, 100; WCH; WLIT 7
Lorenzo, Heberto Padilla
See Padilla (Lorenzo), Heberto
Loris
See Hofmannsthal, Hugo von
Loti, Pierre
See Viaud, (Louis Marie) Julien
Lottie
See Grimke, Charlotte L(ottie) Forten
Lou, Henri
See Andreas-Salome, Lou
Louie, David Wong 1954- .... **CLC 70**
See also CA 139; CANR 120
Louis, Adrian C. .... **NNAL**
See also CA 223
Louis, Father M.
See Merton, Thomas (James)
Louise, Heidi
See Erdrich, Louise
Lovecraft, H. P. 1890-1937 .... **SSC 3, 52;
TCLC 4, 22**
See also AAYA 14; BPFB 2; CA 104; 133;
CANR 106; DA3; DAM POP; HGG;
MTCW 1, 2; MTFW 2005; RGAL 4;
SCFW 1, 2; SFW 4; SUFW
Lovecraft, Howard Phillips
See Lovecraft, H. P.
Lovelace, Earl 1935- .... **CLC 51**
See also BW 2; CA 77-80; CANR 41, 72,
114; CD 5, 6; CDWLB 3; CN 1, 2, 3, 4,
5, 6, 7; DLB 125; EWL 3; MTCW 1
Lovelace, Richard 1618-1658 ..... **LC 24, 158;
PC 69**
See also BRW 2; DLB 131; EXPP; PAB;
RGEL 2
Low, Penelope Margaret
See Lively, Penelope
Lowe, Pardee 1904- .... **AAL**
Lowell, Amy 1874-1925 ... **PC 13; TCLC 1, 8**
See also AAYA 57; AMW; CA 104; 151;
DAM POET; DLB 54, 140; EWL 3;
EXPP; LMFS 2; MAL 5; MBL; MTCW
2; MTFW 2005; PFS 30; RGAL 4; TUS
Lowell, James Russell 1819-1891 ... **NCLC 2,
90**
See also AMWS 1; CDALB 1640-1865;
DLB 1, 11, 64, 79, 189, 235; RGAL 4

Machiavelli, Niccolo 1469-1527 ... **DC 16; LC 8, 36, 140; WLCS**
See also AAYA 58; DA; DAB; DAC; DAM MST; EW 2; LAIT 1; LMFS 1; NFS 9; RGWL 2, 3; TWA; WLIT 7

MacInnes, Colin 1914-1976 .... **CLC 4, 23**
See also CA 69-72; 65-68; CANR 21; CN 1, 2; DLB 14; MTCW 1, 2; RGEL 2; RHW

MacInnes, Helen (Clark)
1907-1985 .... **CLC 27, 39**
See also BPFB 2; CA 1-4R; 117; CANR 1, 28, 58; CMW 4; CN 1, 2; CPW; DAM POP; DLB 87; MSW; MTCW 1, 2; MTFW 2005; SATA 22; SATA-Obit 44

Mackay, Mary 1855-1924 .... **TCLC 51**
See also CA 118; 177; DLB 34, 156; FANT; RGEL 2; RHW; SUFW 1

Mackay, Shena 1944- .... **CLC 195**
See also CA 104; CANR 88, 139; DLB 231, 319; MTFW 2005

Mackenzie, Compton (Edward Montague)
1883-1972 .... **CLC 18; TCLC 116**
See also CA 21-22; 37-40R; CAP 2; CN 1; DLB 34, 100; RGEL 2

Mackenzie, Henry 1745-1831 .... **NCLC 41**
See also DLB 39; RGEL 2

Mackey, Nathaniel 1947- .... **BLC 2:3; PC 49**
See also CA 153; CANR 114; CP 6, 7; DLB 169

Mackey, Nathaniel Ernest
See Mackey, Nathaniel

MacKinnon, Catharine A. 1946- .... **CLC 181**
See also CA 128; 132; CANR 73, 140, 189; FW; MTCW 2; MTFW 2005

Mackintosh, Elizabeth
1896(?)-1952 .... **TCLC 14**
See also CA 110; CMW 4; DLB 10, 77; MSW

Macklin, Charles 1699-1797 .... **LC 132**
See also DLB 89; RGEL 2

MacLaren, James
See Grieve, C(hristopher) M(urray)

MacLaverty, Bernard 1942- ..... **CLC 31, 243**
See also CA 116; 118; CANR 43, 88, 168; CN 5, 6, 7; DLB 267; INT CA-118; RGSF 2

MacLean, Alistair (Stuart)
1922(?)-1987 .... **CLC 3, 13, 50, 63**
See also CA 57-60; 121; CANR 28, 61; CMW 4; CP 2, 3, 4, 5, 6, 7; CPW; DAM POP; DLB 276; MTCW 1; SATA 23; SATA-Obit 50; TCWW 2

Maclean, Norman (Fitzroy)
1902-1990 .... **CLC 78; SSC 13**
See also AMWS 14; CA 102; 132; CANR 49; CPW; DAM POP; DLB 206; TCWW 2

MacLeish, Archibald 1892-1982 ... **CLC 3, 8, 14, 68; PC 47**
See also AMW; CA 9-12R; 106; CAD; CANR 33, 63; CDALBS; CP 1, 2; DAM POET; DFS 15; DLB 4, 7, 45; DLBY 1982; EWL 3; EXPP; MAL 5; MTCW 1, 2; MTFW 2005; PAB; PFS 5; RGAL 4; TUS

MacLennan, (John) Hugh
1907-1990 .... **CLC 2, 14, 92**
See also CA 5-8R; 142; CANR 33; CN 1, 2, 3, 4; DAC; DAM MST; DLB 68; EWL 3; MTCW 1, 2; MTFW 2005; RGEL 2; TWA

MacLeod, Alistair 1936- .. **CLC 56, 165; SSC 90**
See also CA 123; CCA 1; DAC; DAM MST; DLB 60; MTCW 2; MTFW 2005; RGSF 2; TCLE 1:2

Macleod, Fiona
See Sharp, William

MacNeice, (Frederick) Louis
1907-1963 .... **CLC 1, 4, 10, 53; PC 61**
See also BRW 7; CA 85-88; CANR 61; DAB; DAM POET; DLB 10, 20; EWL 3; MTCW 1, 2; MTFW 2005; RGEL 2

MacNeill, Dand
See Fraser, George MacDonald

Macpherson, James 1736-1796 .... **CMLC 28; LC 29; PC 97**
See also BRWS 8; DLB 109, 336; RGEL 2

Macpherson, (Jean) Jay 1931- .... **CLC 14**
See also CA 5-8R; CANR 90; CP 1, 2, 3, 4, 6, 7; CWP; DLB 53

Macrobius fl. 430- .... **CMLC 48**

MacShane, Frank 1927-1999 .... **CLC 39**
See also CA 9-12R; 186; CANR 3, 33; DLB 111

Macumber, Mari
See Sandoz, Mari(e Susette)

Madach, Imre 1823-1864 .... **NCLC 19**

Madden, (Jerry) David 1933- .... **CLC 5, 15**
See also CA 1-4R; CAAS 3; CANR 4, 45; CN 3, 4, 5, 6, 7; CSW; DLB 6; MTCW 1

Maddern, Al(an)
See Ellison, Harlan

Madhubuti, Haki R. 1942- .... **BLC 1:2; CLC 2; PC 5**
See also BW 2, 3; CA 73-76; CANR 24, 51, 73, 139; CP 2, 3, 4, 5, 6, 7; CSW; DAM MULT, POET; DLB 5, 41; DLBD 8; EWL 3; MAL 5; MTCW 2; MTFW 2005; RGAL 4

Madison, James 1751-1836 .... **NCLC 126**
See also DLB 37

Maepenn, Hugh
See Kuttner, Henry

Maepenn, K. H.
See Kuttner, Henry

Maeterlinck, Maurice 1862-1949 .... **DC 32; TCLC 3**
See also CA 104; 136; CANR 80; DAM DRAM; DLB 192, 331; EW 8; EWL 3; GFL 1789 to the Present; LMFS 2; RGWL 2, 3; SATA 66; TWA

Maginn, William 1794-1842 .... **NCLC 8**
See also DLB 110, 159

Mahapatra, Jayanta 1928- .... **CLC 33**
See also CA 73-76; CAAS 9; CANR 15, 33, 66, 87; CP 4, 5, 6, 7; DAM MULT; DLB 323

Mahfouz, Nagib
See Mahfouz, Naguib

Mahfouz, Naguib 1911(?)-2006 . **CLC 52, 55, 153; SSC 66**
See also AAYA 49; AFW; BEST 89:2; CA 128; 253; CANR 55, 101; DA3; DAM NOV; DLB 346; DLBY 1988; MTCW 1, 2; MTFW 2005; RGSF 2; RGWL 2, 3; SSFS 9; WLIT 2

Mahfouz, Naguib Abdel Aziz Al-Sabilgi
See Mahfouz, Naguib

Mahfouz, Najib
See Mahfouz, Naguib

Mahfuz, Najib
See Mahfouz, Naguib

Mahon, Derek 1941- .... **CLC 27; PC 60**
See also BRWS 6; CA 113; 128; CANR 88; CP 1, 2, 3, 4, 5, 6, 7; DLB 40; EWL 3

Maiakovskii, Vladimir
See Mayakovski, Vladimir (Vladimirovich)

Mailer, Norman 1923-2007 ... **CLC 1, 2, 3, 4, 5, 8, 11, 14, 28, 39, 74, 111, 234**
See also AAYA 31; AITN 2; AMW; AMWC 2; AMWR 2; BPFB 2; CA 9-12R; 266; CABS 1; CANR 28, 74, 77, 130; CDALB 1968-1988; CN 1, 2, 3, 4, 5, 6, 7; CPW; DA; DA3; DAB; DAC; DAM MST, NOV, POP; DLB 2, 16, 28, 185, 278; DLBD 3; DLBY 1980, 1983; EWL 3; MAL 5; MTCW 1, 2; MTFW 2005; NFS 10; RGAL 4; TUS

Mailer, Norman Kingsley
See Mailer, Norman

Maillet, Antonine 1929- .... **CLC 54, 118**
See also CA 115; 120; CANR 46, 74, 77, 134; CCA 1; CWW 2; DAC; DLB 60; INT CA-120; MTCW 2; MTFW 2005

Maimonides, Moses 1135-1204 ..... **CMLC 76**
See also DLB 115

Mais, Roger 1905-1955 .... **TCLC 8**
See also BW 1, 3; CA 105; 124; CANR 82; CDWLB 3; DLB 125; EWL 3; MTCW 1; RGEL 2

Maistre, Joseph 1753-1821 .... **NCLC 37**
See also GFL 1789 to the Present

Maitland, Frederic William
1850-1906 .... **TCLC 65**

Maitland, Sara (Louise) 1950- .... **CLC 49**
See also BRWS 11; CA 69-72; CANR 13, 59; DLB 271; FW

Major, Clarence 1936- ...... **BLC 1:2; CLC 3, 19, 48**
See also AFAW 2; BW 2, 3; CA 21-24R; CAAS 6; CANR 13, 25, 53, 82; CN 3, 4, 5, 6, 7; CP 2, 3, 4, 5, 6, 7; CSW; DAM MULT; DLB 33; EWL 3; MAL 5; MSW

Major, Kevin (Gerald) 1949- .... **CLC 26**
See also AAYA 16; CA 97-100; CANR 21, 38, 112; CLR 11; DAC; DLB 60; INT CANR-21; JRDA; MAICYA 1, 2; MAICYAS 1; SATA 32, 82, 134; WYA; YAW

Maki, James
See Ozu, Yasujiro

Makin, Bathsua 1600-1675(?) .... **LC 137**

Makine, Andrei 1957-
See Makine, Andrei

Makine, Andrei 1957- .... **CLC 198**
See also CA 176; CANR 103, 162; MTFW 2005

Malabaila, Damiano
See Levi, Primo

Malamud, Bernard 1914-1986 .. **CLC 1, 2, 3, 5, 8, 9, 11, 18, 27, 44, 78, 85; SSC 15; TCLC 129, 184; WLC 4**
See also AAYA 16; AMWS 1; BPFB 2; BYA 15; CA 5-8R; 118; CABS 1; CANR 28, 62, 114; CDALB 1941-1968; CN 1, 2, 3, 4; CPW; DA; DA3; DAB; DAC; DAM MST, NOV, POP; DLB 2, 28, 152; DLBY 1980, 1986; EWL 3; EXPS; LAIT 4; LATS 1:1; MAL 5; MTCW 1, 2; MTFW 2005; NFS 27; RGAL 4; RGHL; RGSF 2; SSFS 8, 13, 16; TUS

Malan, Herman
See Bosman, Herman Charles; Bosman, Herman Charles

Malaparte, Curzio 1898-1957 .... **TCLC 52**
See also DLB 264

Malcolm, Dan
See Silverberg, Robert

Malcolm, Janet 1934- .... **CLC 201**
See also CA 123; CANR 89; NCFS 1

Malcolm X
See Little, Malcolm

Malebranche, Nicolas 1638-1715 .... **LC 133**
See also GFL Beginnings to 1789

Malherbe, Francois de 1555-1628 .... **LC 5**
See also DLB 327; GFL Beginnings to 1789

Mallarme, Stephane 1842-1898 ...... **NCLC 4, 41, 210; PC 4**
See also DAM POET; DLB 217; EW 7; GFL 1789 to the Present; LMFS 2; RGWL 2, 3; TWA

Mallet-Joris, Francoise 1930- .... **CLC 11**
See also CA 65-68; CANR 17; CWW 2; DLB 83; EWL 3; GFL 1789 to the Present

McGahern, John 1934-2006 .... **CLC 5, 9, 48, 156; SSC 17**
See also CA 17-20R; 249; CANR 29, 68, 113; CN 1, 2, 3, 4, 5, 6, 7; DLB 14, 231, 319; MTCW 1

McGinley, Patrick (Anthony) 1937- . **CLC 41**
See also CA 120; 127; CANR 56; INT CA-127

McGinley, Phyllis 1905-1978 .... **CLC 14**
See also CA 9-12R; 77-80; CANR 19; CP 1, 2; CWRI 5; DLB 11, 48; MAL 5; PFS 9, 13; SATA 2, 44; SATA-Obit 24

McGinniss, Joe 1942- .... **CLC 32**
See also AITN 2; BEST 89:2; CA 25-28R; CANR 26, 70, 152; CPW; DLB 185; INT CANR-26

McGivern, Maureen Daly
See Daly, Maureen

McGivern, Maureen Patricia Daly
See Daly, Maureen

McGrath, Patrick 1950- .... **CLC 55**
See also CA 136; CANR 65, 148; CN 5, 6, 7; DLB 231; HGG; SUFW 2

McGrath, Thomas (Matthew) 1916-1990 .... **CLC 28, 59**
See also AMWS 10; CA 9-12R; 132; CANR 6, 33, 95; CP 1, 2, 3, 4, 5; DAM POET; MAL 5; MTCW 1; SATA 41; SATA-Obit 66

McGuane, Thomas 1939- .. **CLC 3, 7, 18, 45, 127**
See also AITN 2; BPFB 2; CA 49-52; CANR 5, 24, 49, 94, 164; CN 2, 3, 4, 5, 6, 7; DLB 2, 212; DLBY 1980; EWL 3; INT CANR-24; MAL 5; MTCW 1; MTFW 2005; TCWW 1, 2

McGuane, Thomas Francis III
See McGuane, Thomas

McGuckian, Medbh 1950- .... **CLC 48, 174; PC 27**
See also BRWS 5; CA 143; CP 4, 5, 6, 7; CWP; DAM POET; DLB 40

McHale, Tom 1942(?)-1982 .... **CLC 3, 5**
See also AITN 1; CA 77-80; 106; CN 1, 2, 3

McHugh, Heather 1948- .... **PC 61**
See also CA 69-72; CANR 11, 28, 55, 92; CP 4, 5, 6, 7; CWP; PFS 24

McIlvanney, William 1936- .... **CLC 42**
See also CA 25-28R; CANR 61; CMW 4; DLB 14, 207

McIlwraith, Maureen Mollie Hunter
See Hunter, Mollie

McInerney, Jay 1955- .... **CLC 34, 112**
See also AAYA 18; BPFB 2; CA 116; 123; CANR 45, 68, 116, 176; CN 5, 6, 7; CPW; DA3; DAM POP; DLB 292; INT CA-123; MAL 5; MTCW 2; MTFW 2005

McIntyre, Vonda N. 1948- .... **CLC 18**
See also CA 81-84; CANR 17, 34, 69; MTCW 1; SFW 4; YAW

McIntyre, Vonda Neel
See McIntyre, Vonda N.

McKay, Claude
See McKay, Festus Claudius

McKay, Festus Claudius 1889-1948 ...... **BLC 1:3; HR 1:3; PC 2; TCLC 7, 41; WLC 4**
See also AFAW 1, 2; AMWS 10; BW 1, 3; CA 104; 124; CANR 73; DA; DAB; DAC; DAM MST, MULT, NOV, POET; DLB 4, 45, 51, 117; EWL 3; EXPP; GLL 2; LAIT 3; LMFS 2; MAL 5; MTCW 1, 2; MTFW 2005; PAB; PFS 4; RGAL 4; TUS; WP

McKuen, Rod 1933- .... **CLC 1, 3**
See also AITN 1; CA 41-44R; CANR 40; CP 1

McLoughlin, R. B.
See Mencken, H(enry) L(ouis)

McLuhan, (Herbert) Marshall 1911-1980 .... **CLC 37, 83**
See also CA 9-12R; 102; CANR 12, 34, 61; DLB 88; INT CANR-12; MTCW 1, 2; MTFW 2005

McMahon, Pat
See Hoch, Edward D.

McManus, Declan Patrick Aloysius
See Costello, Elvis

McMillan, Terry 1951- .. **BLCS; CLC 50, 61, 112**
See also AAYA 21; AMWS 13; BPFB 2; BW 2, 3; CA 140; CANR 60, 104, 131; CN 7; CPW; DA3; DAM MULT, NOV, POP; MAL 5; MTCW 2; MTFW 2005; RGAL 4; YAW

McMurtry, Larry 1936- .... **CLC 2, 3, 7, 11, 27, 44, 127, 250**
See also AAYA 15; AITN 2; AMWS 5; BEST 89:2; BPFB 2; CA 5-8R; CANR 19, 43, 64, 103, 170; CDALB 1968-1988; CN 2, 3, 4, 5, 6, 7; CPW; CSW; DA3; DAM NOV, POP; DLB 2, 143, 256; DLBY 1980, 1987; EWL 3; MAL 5; MTCW 1, 2; MTFW 2005; RGAL 4; TCWW 1, 2

McMurtry, Larry Jeff
See McMurtry, Larry

McNally, Terrence 1939- ... **CLC 4, 7, 41, 91, 252; DC 27**
See also AAYA 62; AMWS 13; CA 45-48; CAD; CANR 2, 56, 116; CD 5, 6; DA3; DAM DRAM; DFS 16, 19; DLB 7, 249; EWL 3; GLL 1; MTCW 2; MTFW 2005

McNally, Thomas Michael
See McNally, T.M.

McNally, T.M. 1961- .... **CLC 82**
See also CA 246

McNamer, Deirdre 1950- .... **CLC 70**
See also CA 188; CANR 163

McNeal, Tom .... **CLC 119**
See also CA 252; CANR 185; SATA 194

McNeile, Herman Cyril 1888-1937 .... **TCLC 44**
See also CA 184; CMW 4; DLB 77

McNickle, (William) D'Arcy 1904-1977 .... **CLC 89; NNAL**
See also CA 9-12R; 85-88; CANR 5, 45; DAM MULT; DLB 175, 212; RGAL 4; SATA-Obit 22; TCWW 1, 2

McPhee, John 1931- .... **CLC 36**
See also AAYA 61; AMWS 3; ANW; BEST 90:1; CA 65-68; CANR 20, 46, 64, 69, 121, 165; CPW; DLB 185, 275; MTCW 1, 2; MTFW 2005; TUS

McPhee, John Angus
See McPhee, John

McPherson, James Alan, Jr.
See McPherson, James Alan

McPherson, James Alan 1943- . **BLCS; CLC 19, 77; SSC 95**
See also BW 1, 3; CA 25-28R, 273; CAAE 273; CAAS 17; CANR 24, 74, 140; CN 3, 4, 5, 6; CSW; DLB 38, 244; EWL 3; MTCW 1, 2; MTFW 2005; RGAL 4; RGSF 2; SSFS 23

McPherson, William (Alexander) 1933- .... **CLC 34**
See also CA 69-72; CANR 28; INT CANR-28

McTaggart, J. McT. Ellis
See McTaggart, John McTaggart Ellis

McTaggart, John McTaggart Ellis 1866-1925 .... **TCLC 105**
See also CA 120; DLB 262

Mda, Zakes 1948- .... **BLC 2:3; CLC 262**
See also CA 205; CANR 151, 185; CD 5, 6; DLB 225

Mda, Zanemvula
See Mda, Zakes

Mda, Zanemvula Kizito Gatyeni
See Mda, Zakes

Mead, George Herbert 1863-1931 . **TCLC 89**
See also CA 212; DLB 270

Mead, Margaret 1901-1978 .... **CLC 37**
See also AITN 1; CA 1-4R; 81-84; CANR 4; DA3; FW; MTCW 1, 2; SATA-Obit 20

Meaker, M. J.
See Meaker, Marijane

Meaker, Marijane 1927- .... **CLC 12, 35**
See also AAYA 2, 23; BYA 1, 7, 8; CA 107; CANR 37, 63, 145, 180; CLR 29; GLL 2; INT CA-107; JRDA; MAICYA 1, 2; MAICYAS 1; MTCW 1; SAAS 1; SATA 20, 61, 99, 160; SATA-Essay 111; WYA; YAW

Meaker, Marijane Agnes
See Meaker, Marijane

Mechthild von Magdeburg c. 1207-c. 1282 .... **CMLC 91**
See also DLB 138

Medoff, Mark (Howard) 1940- .... **CLC 6, 23**
See also AITN 1; CA 53-56; CAD; CANR 5; CD 5, 6; DAM DRAM; DFS 4; DLB 7; INT CANR-5

Medvedev, P. N.
See Bakhtin, Mikhail Mikhailovich

Meged, Aharon
See Megged, Aharon

Meged, Aron
See Megged, Aharon

Megged, Aharon 1920- .... **CLC 9**
See also CA 49-52; CAAS 13; CANR 1, 140; EWL 3; RGHL

Mehta, Deepa 1950- .... **CLC 208**

Mehta, Gita 1943- .... **CLC 179**
See also CA 225; CN 7; DNFS 2

Mehta, Ved 1934- .... **CLC 37**
See also CA 1-4R, 212; CAAE 212; CANR 2, 23, 69; DLB 323; MTCW 1; MTFW 2005

Melanchthon, Philipp 1497-1560 .... **LC 90**
See also DLB 179

Melanter
See Blackmore, R(ichard) D(oddridge)

Meleager c. 140B.C.-c. 70B.C. ...... **CMLC 53**

Melies, Georges 1861-1938 .... **TCLC 81**

Melikow, Loris
See Hofmannsthal, Hugo von

Melmoth, Sebastian
See Wilde, Oscar

Melo Neto, Joao Cabral de
See Cabral de Melo Neto, Joao

Meltzer, Milton 1915- .... **CLC 26**
See also AAYA 8, 45; BYA 2, 6; CA 13-16R; CANR 38, 92, 107; CLR 13; DLB 61; JRDA; MAICYA 1, 2; SAAS 1; SATA 1, 50, 80, 128; SATA-Essay 124; WYA; YAW

Melville, Herman 1819-1891 ..... **NCLC 3, 12, 29, 45, 49, 91, 93, 123, 157, 181, 193; PC 82; SSC 1, 17, 46, 95; WLC 4**
See also AAYA 25; AMW; AMWR 1; CDALB 1640-1865; DA; DAB; DAC; DAM MST, NOV; DLB 3, 74, 250, 254; EXPN; EXPS; GL 3; LAIT 1, 2; NFS 7, 9; RGAL 4; RGSF 2; SATA 59; SSFS 3; TUS

Members, Mark
See Powell, Anthony

Membreno, Alejandro .... **CLC 59**

Menand, Louis 1952- .... **CLC 208**
See also CA 200

Montgomery, (Robert) Bruce
1921(?)-1978 .... **CLC 22**
See also CA 179; 104; CMW 4; DLB 87;
MSW

Montgomery, L(ucy) M(aud)
1874-1942 .... **TCLC 51, 140**
See also AAYA 12; BYA 1; CA 108; 137;
CLR 8, 91; DA3; DAC; DAM MST; DLB
92; DLBD 14; JRDA; MAICYA 1, 2;
MTCW 2; MTFW 2005; RGEL 2; SATA
100; TWA; WCH; WYA; YABC 1

Montgomery, Marion, Jr. 1925- .... **CLC 7**
See also AITN 1; CA 1-4R; CANR 3, 48,
162; CSW; DLB 6

Montgomery, Marion H. 1925-
See Montgomery, Marion, Jr.

Montgomery, Max
See Davenport, Guy (Mattison, Jr.)

Montherlant, Henry (Milon) de
1896-1972 .... **CLC 8, 19**
See also CA 85-88; 37-40R; DAM DRAM;
DLB 72, 321; EW 11; EWL 3; GFL 1789
to the Present; MTCW 1

Monty Python
See Chapman, Graham; Cleese, John
(Marwood); Gilliam, Terry; Idle, Eric;
Jones, Terence Graham Parry; Palin,
Michael

Moodie, Susanna (Strickland)
1803-1885 .... **NCLC 14, 113**
See also DLB 99

Moody, Hiram
See Moody, Rick

Moody, Hiram F. III
See Moody, Rick

Moody, Minerva
See Alcott, Louisa May

Moody, Rick 1961- .... **CLC 147**
See also CA 138; CANR 64, 112, 179;
MTFW 2005

Moody, William Vaughan
1869-1910 .... **TCLC 105**
See also CA 110; 178; DLB 7, 54; MAL 5;
RGAL 4

Mooney, Edward 1951- .... **CLC 25**
See also CA 130

Mooney, Ted
See Mooney, Edward

Moorcock, Michael 1939- ...... **CLC 5, 27, 58, 236**
See also AAYA 26; CA 45-48; CAAS 5;
CANR 2, 17, 38, 64, 122; CN 5, 6, 7;
DLB 14, 231, 261, 319; FANT; MTCW 1,
2; MTFW 2005; SATA 93, 166; SCFW 1,
2; SFW 4; SUFW 1, 2

Moorcock, Michael John
See Moorcock, Michael

Moorcock, Michael John
See Moorcock, Michael

Moore, Al
See Moore, Alan

Moore, Alan 1953- .... **CLC 230**
See also AAYA 51; CA 204; CANR 138,
184; DLB 261; MTFW 2005; SFW 4

Moore, Brian 1921-1999 ... **CLC 1, 3, 5, 7, 8, 19, 32, 90**
See also BRWS 9; CA 1-4R; 174; CANR 1,
25, 42, 63; CCA 1; CN 1, 2, 3, 4, 5, 6;
DAB; DAC; DAM MST; DLB 251; EWL
3; FANT; MTCW 1, 2; MTFW 2005;
RGEL 2

Moore, Edward
See Muir, Edwin

Moore, G. E. 1873-1958 .... **TCLC 89**
See also DLB 262

Moore, George Augustus
1852-1933 .... **SSC 19; TCLC 7**
See also BRW 6; CA 104; 177; DLB 10,
18, 57, 135; EWL 3; RGEL 2; RGSF 2

Moore, Lorrie
See Moore, Marie Lorena

Moore, Marianne (Craig)
1887-1972 .... **CLC 1, 2, 4, 8, 10, 13, 19, 47; PC 4, 49; WLCS**
See also AMW; CA 1-4R; 33-36R; CANR
3, 61; CDALB 1929-1941; CP 1; DA;
DA3; DAB; DAC; DAM MST, POET;
DLB 45; DLBD 7; EWL 3; EXPP; FL 1:6;
MAL 5; MBL; MTCW 1, 2; MTFW 2005;
PAB; PFS 14, 17; RGAL 4; SATA 20;
TUS; WP

Moore, Marie Lorena 1957- ...... **CLC 39, 45, 68, 165**
See also AMWS 10; CA 116; CANR 39,
83, 139; CN 5, 6, 7; DLB 234; MTFW
2005; SSFS 19

Moore, Michael 1954- .... **CLC 218**
See also AAYA 53; CA 166; CANR 150

Moore, Thomas 1779-1852 .... **NCLC 6, 110**
See also DLB 96, 144; RGEL 2

Moorhouse, Frank 1938- .... **SSC 40**
See also CA 118; CANR 92; CN 3, 4, 5, 6,
7; DLB 289; RGSF 2

Mora, Pat 1942- .... **HLC 2**
See also AMWS 13; CA 129; CANR 57,
81, 112, 171; CLR 58; DAM MULT; DLB
209; HW 1, 2; LLW; MAICYA 2; MTFW
2005; SATA 92, 134, 186

Moraga, Cherrie 1952- ... **CLC 126, 250; DC 22**
See also CA 131; CANR 66, 154; DAM
MULT; DLB 82, 249; FW; GLL 1; HW 1,
2; LLW

Moran, J.L.
See Whitaker, Rod

Morand, Paul 1888-1976 .... **CLC 41; SSC 22**
See also CA 184; 69-72; DLB 65; EWL 3

Morante, Elsa 1918-1985 .... **CLC 8, 47**
See also CA 85-88; 117; CANR 35; DLB
177; EWL 3; MTCW 1, 2; MTFW 2005;
RGHL; RGWL 2, 3; WLIT 7

Moravia, Alberto
See Pincherle, Alberto

Morck, Paul
See Rolvaag, O.E.

More, Hannah 1745-1833 ...... **NCLC 27, 141**
See also DLB 107, 109, 116, 158; RGEL 2

More, Henry 1614-1687 .... **LC 9**
See also DLB 126, 252

More, Sir Thomas 1478(?)-1535 ... **LC 10, 32, 140**
See also BRWC 1; BRWS 7; DLB 136, 281;
LMFS 1; NFS 29; RGEL 2; TEA

Moreas, Jean
See Papadiamantopoulos, Johannes

Moreton, Andrew Esq.
See Defoe, Daniel

Moreton, Lee
See Boucicault, Dion

Morgan, Berry 1919-2002 .... **CLC 6**
See also CA 49-52; 208; DLB 6

Morgan, Claire
See Highsmith, Patricia

Morgan, Edwin 1920- .... **CLC 31**
See also BRWS 9; CA 5-8R; CANR 3, 43,
90; CP 1, 2, 3, 4, 5, 6, 7; DLB 27

Morgan, Edwin George
See Morgan, Edwin

Morgan, (George) Frederick
1922-2004 .... **CLC 23**
See also CA 17-20R; 224; CANR 21, 144;
CP 2, 3, 4, 5, 6, 7

Morgan, Harriet
See Mencken, H(enry) L(ouis)

Morgan, Jane
See Cooper, James Fenimore

Morgan, Janet 1945- .... **CLC 39**
See also CA 65-68

Morgan, Lady 1776(?)-1859 .... **NCLC 29**
See also DLB 116, 158; RGEL 2

Morgan, Robin (Evonne) 1941- .... **CLC 2**
See also CA 69-72; CANR 29, 68; FW;
GLL 2; MTCW 1; SATA 80

Morgan, Scott
See Kuttner, Henry

Morgan, Seth 1949(?)-1990 .... **CLC 65**
See also CA 185; 132

Morgenstern, Christian (Otto Josef
Wolfgang) 1871-1914 .... **TCLC 8**
See also CA 105; 191; EWL 3

Morgenstern, S.
See Goldman, William

Mori, Rintaro
See Mori Ogai

Mori, Toshio 1910-1980 ... **AAL; SSC 83, 123**
See also CA 116; 244; DLB 312; RGSF 2

Moricz, Zsigmond 1879-1942 .... **TCLC 33**
See also CA 165; DLB 215; EWL 3

Morike, Eduard (Friedrich)
1804-1875 .... **NCLC 10, 201**
See also DLB 133; RGWL 2, 3

Morin, Jean-Paul
See Whitaker, Rod

Mori Ogai 1862-1922 .... **TCLC 14**
See also CA 110; 164; DLB 180; EWL 3;
MJW; RGWL 3; TWA

Moritz, Karl Philipp 1756-1793 .... **LC 2, 162**
See also DLB 94

Morland, Peter Henry
See Faust, Frederick (Schiller)

Morley, Christopher (Darlington)
1890-1957 .... **TCLC 87**
See also CA 112; 213; DLB 9; MAL 5;
RGAL 4

Morren, Theophil
See Hofmannsthal, Hugo von

Morris, Bill 1952- .... **CLC 76**
See also CA 225

Morris, Julian
See West, Morris L(anglo)

Morris, Steveland Judkins (?)-
See Wonder, Stevie

Morris, William 1834-1896 . **NCLC 4; PC 55**
See also BRW 5; CDBLB 1832-1890; DLB
18, 35, 57, 156, 178, 184; FANT; RGEL
2; SFW 4; SUFW

Morris, Wright (Marion) 1910-1998 . **CLC 1, 3, 7, 18, 37; TCLC 107**
See also AMW; CA 9-12R; 167; CANR 21,
81; CN 1, 2, 3, 4, 5, 6; DLB 2, 206, 218;
DLBY 1981; EWL 3; MAL 5; MTCW 1,
2; MTFW 2005; RGAL 4; TCWW 1, 2

Morrison, Arthur 1863-1945 .... **SSC 40; TCLC 72**
See also CA 120; 157; CMW 4; DLB 70,
135, 197; RGEL 2

Morrison, Chloe Anthony Wofford
See Morrison, Toni

Morrison, James Douglas
1943-1971 .... **CLC 17**
See also CA 73-76; CANR 40

Morrison, Jim
See Morrison, James Douglas

Morrison, John Gordon 1904-1998 ... **SSC 93**
See also CA 103; CANR 92; DLB 260

Morrison, Toni 1931- . **BLC 1:3, 2:3; CLC 4, 10, 22, 55, 81, 87, 173, 194; WLC 4**
See also AAYA 1, 22, 61; AFAW 1, 2;
AMWC 1; AMWS 3; BPFB 2; BW 2, 3;
CA 29-32R; CANR 27, 42, 67, 113, 124;
CDALB 1968-1988; CLR 99; CN 3, 4, 5,
6, 7; CPW; DA; DA3; DAB; DAC; DAM
MST, MULT, NOV, POP; DLB 6, 33, 143,
331; DLBY 1981; EWL 3; EXPN; FL 1:6;
FW; GL 3; LAIT 2, 4; LATS 1:2; LMFS

2; MAL 5; MBL; MTCW 1, 2; MTFW
2005; NFS 1, 6, 8, 14; RGAL 4; RHW;
SATA 57, 144; SSFS 5; TCLE 1:2; TUS;
YAW

Morrison, Van 1945- .... **CLC 21**
See also CA 116; 168

Morrissy, Mary 1957- .... **CLC 99**
See also CA 205; DLB 267

Mortimer, John 1923-2009 .... **CLC 28, 43**
See also CA 13-16R; CANR 21, 69, 109,
172; CBD; CD 5, 6; CDBLB 1960 to
Present; CMW 4; CN 5, 6, 7; CPW; DA3;
DAM DRAM, POP; DLB 13, 245, 271;
INT CANR-21; MSW; MTCW 1, 2;
MTFW 2005; RGEL 2

Mortimer, John Clifford
See Mortimer, John

Mortimer, Penelope (Ruth)
1918-1999 .... **CLC 5**
See also CA 57-60; 187; CANR 45, 88; CN
1, 2, 3, 4, 5, 6

Mortimer, Sir John
See Mortimer, John

Morton, Anthony
See Creasey, John

Morton, Thomas 1579(?)-1647(?) .... **LC 72**
See also DLB 24; RGEL 2

Mosca, Gaetano 1858-1941 .... **TCLC 75**

Moses, Daniel David 1952- .... **NNAL**
See also CA 186; CANR 160; DLB 334

Mosher, Howard Frank 1943- .... **CLC 62**
See also CA 139; CANR 65, 115, 181

Mosley, Nicholas 1923- .... **CLC 43, 70**
See also CA 69-72; CANR 41, 60, 108, 158;
CN 1, 2, 3, 4, 5, 6, 7; DLB 14, 207

Mosley, Walter 1952- .... **BLCS; CLC 97, 184**
See also AAYA 57; AMWS 13; BPFB 2;
BW 2; CA 142; CANR 57, 92, 136, 172;
CMW 4; CN 7; CPW; DA3; DAM MULT,
POP; DLB 306; MSW; MTCW 2; MTFW
2005

Moss, Howard 1922-1987 . **CLC 7, 14, 45, 50**
See also CA 1-4R; 123; CANR 1, 44; CP 1,
2, 3, 4; DAM POET; DLB 5

Mossgiel, Rab
See Burns, Robert

Motion, Andrew 1952- .... **CLC 47**
See also BRWS 7; CA 146; CANR 90, 142;
CP 4, 5, 6, 7; DLB 40; MTFW 2005

Motion, Andrew Peter
See Motion, Andrew

Motley, Willard (Francis)
1909-1965 .... **CLC 18**
See also AMWS 17; BW 1; CA 117; 106;
CANR 88; DLB 76, 143

Motoori, Norinaga 1730-1801 .... **NCLC 45**

Mott, Michael (Charles Alston)
1930- .... **CLC 15, 34**
See also CA 5-8R; CAAS 7; CANR 7, 29

Mountain Wolf Woman 1884-1960 . **CLC 92;
NNAL**
See also CA 144; CANR 90

Moure, Erin 1955- .... **CLC 88**
See also CA 113; CP 5, 6, 7; CWP; DLB
60

Mourning Dove 1885(?)-1936 .... **NNAL**
See also CA 144; CANR 90; DAM MULT;
DLB 175, 221

Mowat, Farley 1921- .... **CLC 26**
See also AAYA 1, 50; BYA 2; CA 1-4R;
CANR 4, 24, 42, 68, 108; CLR 20; CPW;
DAC; DAM MST; DLB 68; INT CANR-
24; JRDA; MAICYA 1, 2; MTCW 1, 2;
MTFW 2005; SATA 3, 55; YAW

Mowat, Farley McGill
See Mowat, Farley

Mowatt, Anna Cora 1819-1870 ..... **NCLC 74**
See also RGAL 4

Mo Yan
See Moye, Guan

Moye, Guan 1956(?)- .... **CLC 257**
See also CA 201; EWL 3; RGWL 3

Mo Yen
See Moye, Guan

Moyers, Bill 1934- .... **CLC 74**
See also AITN 2; CA 61-64; CANR 31, 52,
148

Mphahlele, Es'kia 1919-2008 .... **BLC 1:3;
CLC 25, 133**
See also AFW; BW 2, 3; CA 81-84; 278;
CANR 26, 76; CDWLB 3; CN 4, 5, 6;
DA3; DAM MULT; DLB 125, 225; EWL
3; MTCW 2; MTFW 2005; RGSF 2;
SATA 119; SATA-Obit 198; SSFS 11

Mphahlele, Ezekiel
See Mphahlele, Es'kia

Mphahlele, Zeke
See Mphahlele, Es'kia

Mqhayi, S(amuel) E(dward) K(rune Loliwe)
1875-1945 .... **BLC 1:3; TCLC 25**
See also CA 153; CANR 87; DAM MULT

Mrozek, Slawomir 1930- .... **CLC 3, 13**
See also CA 13-16R; CAAS 10; CANR 29;
CDWLB 4; CWW 2; DLB 232; EWL 3;
MTCW 1

Mrs. Belloc-Lowndes
See Lowndes, Marie Adelaide (Belloc)

Mrs. Fairstar
See Horne, Richard Henry Hengist

M'Taggart, John M'Taggart Ellis
See McTaggart, John McTaggart Ellis

Mtwa, Percy (?)- .... **CLC 47**
See also CD 6

Mueller, Lisel 1924- .... **CLC 13, 51; PC 33**
See also CA 93-96; CP 6, 7; DLB 105; PFS
9, 13

Muggeridge, Malcolm (Thomas)
1903-1990 .... **TCLC 120**
See also AITN 1; CA 101; CANR 33, 63;
MTCW 1, 2

Muhammad 570-632 .... **WLCS**
See also DA; DAB; DAC; DAM MST;
DLB 311

Muir, Edwin 1887-1959 . **PC 49; TCLC 2, 87**
See also BRWS 6; CA 104; 193; DLB 20,
100, 191; EWL 3; RGEL 2

Muir, John 1838-1914 .... **TCLC 28**
See also AMWS 9; ANW; CA 165; DLB
186, 275

Mujica Lainez, Manuel 1910-1984 ... **CLC 31**
See also CA 81-84; 112; CANR 32; EWL
3; HW 1

Mukherjee, Bharati 1940- ..... **AAL; CLC 53,
115, 235; SSC 38**
See also AAYA 46; BEST 89:2; CA 107,
232; CAAE 232; CANR 45, 72, 128; CN
5, 6, 7; DAM NOV; DLB 60, 218, 323;
DNFS 1, 2; EWL 3; FW; MAL 5; MTCW
1, 2; MTFW 2005; RGAL 4; RGSF 2;
SSFS 7, 24; TUS; WWE 1

Muldoon, Paul 1951- .... **CLC 32, 72, 166**
See also BRWS 4; CA 113; 129; CANR 52,
91, 176; CP 2, 3, 4, 5, 6, 7; DAM POET;
DLB 40; INT CA-129; PFS 7, 22; TCLE
1:2

Mulisch, Harry (Kurt Victor)
1927- .... **CLC 42, 270**
See also CA 9-12R; CANR 6, 26, 56, 110;
CWW 2; DLB 299; EWL 3

Mull, Martin 1943- .... **CLC 17**
See also CA 105

Muller, Wilhelm .... **NCLC 73**

Mulock, Dinah Maria
See Craik, Dinah Maria (Mulock)

Multatuli 1820-1881 .... **NCLC 165**
See also RGWL 2, 3

Munday, Anthony 1560-1633 .... **LC 87**
See also DLB 62, 172; RGEL 2

Munford, Robert 1737(?)-1783 .... **LC 5**
See also DLB 31

Mungo, Raymond 1946- .... **CLC 72**
See also CA 49-52; CANR 2

Munro, Alice 1931- .... **CLC 6, 10, 19, 50, 95,
222; SSC 3, 95; WLCS**
See also AITN 2; BPFB 2; CA 33-36R;
CANR 33, 53, 75, 114, 177; CCA 1; CN
1, 2, 3, 4, 5, 6, 7; DA3; DAC; DAM MST,
NOV; DLB 53; EWL 3; MTCW 1, 2;
MTFW 2005; NFS 27; RGEL 2; RGSF 2;
SATA 29; SSFS 5, 13, 19; TCLE 1:2;
WWE 1

Munro, H(ector) H(ugh) 1870-1916 . **SSC 12,
115; TCLC 3; WLC 5**
See also AAYA 56; BRWS 6; BYA 11; CA
104; 130; CANR 104; CDBLB 1890-
1914; DA; DA3; DAB; DAC; DAM MST,
NOV; DLB 34, 162; EXPS; LAIT 2;
MTCW 1, 2; MTFW 2005; RGEL 2;
SSFS 1, 15; SUFW

Munro, Hector H.
See Munro, H(ector) H(ugh)

Murakami, Haruki 1949- .... **CLC 150, 274**
See also CA 165; CANR 102, 146; CWW
2; DLB 182; EWL 3; MJW; RGWL 3;
SFW 4; SSFS 23

Murakami Haruki
See Murakami, Haruki

Murasaki, Lady
See Murasaki Shikibu

Murasaki Shikibu 978(?)-1026(?) .. **CMLC 1,
79**
See also EFS 2; LATS 1:1; RGWL 2, 3

Murdoch, Iris 1919-1999 .. **CLC 1, 2, 3, 4, 6,
8, 11, 15, 22, 31, 51; TCLC 171**
See also BRWS 1; CA 13-16R; 179; CANR
8, 43, 68, 103, 142; CBD; CDBLB 1960
to Present; CN 1, 2, 3, 4, 5, 6; CWD;
DA3; DAB; DAC; DAM MST, NOV;
DLB 14, 194, 233, 326; EWL 3; INT
CANR-8; MTCW 1, 2; MTFW 2005; NFS
18; RGEL 2; TCLE 1:2; TEA; WLIT 4

Murfree, Mary Noailles 1850-1922 .. **SSC 22;
TCLC 135**
See also CA 122; 176; DLB 12, 74; RGAL
4

Murglie
See Murnau, F.W.

Murnau, Friedrich Wilhelm
See Murnau, F.W.

Murnau, F.W. 1888-1931 .... **TCLC 53**
See also CA 112

Murphy, Richard 1927- .... **CLC 41**
See also BRWS 5; CA 29-32R; CP 1, 2, 3,
4, 5, 6, 7; DLB 40; EWL 3

Murphy, Sylvia 1937- .... **CLC 34**
See also CA 121

Murphy, Thomas (Bernard) 1935- ... **CLC 51**
See also CA 101; DLB 310

Murphy, Tom
See Murphy, Thomas (Bernard)

Murray, Albert 1916- .... **BLC 2:3; CLC 73**
See also BW 2; CA 49-52; CANR 26, 52,
78, 160; CN 7; CSW; DLB 38; MTFW
2005

Murray, Albert L.
See Murray, Albert

Murray, James Augustus Henry
1837-1915 .... **TCLC 117**

Murray, Judith Sargent
1751-1820 .... **NCLC 63**
See also DLB 37, 200

Murray, Les(lie Allan) 1938- .... **CLC 40**
See also BRWS 7; CA 21-24R; CANR 11, 27, 56, 103; CP 1, 2, 3, 4, 5, 6, 7; DAM POET; DLB 289; DLBY 2001; EWL 3; RGEL 2

Murry, J. Middleton
See Murry, John Middleton

Murry, John Middleton
1889-1957 .... **TCLC 16**
See also CA 118; 217; DLB 149

Musgrave, Susan 1951- .... **CLC 13, 54**
See also CA 69-72; CANR 45, 84, 181; CCA 1; CP 2, 3, 4, 5, 6, 7; CWP

Musil, Robert (Edler von)
1880-1942 ... **SSC 18; TCLC 12, 68, 213**
See also CA 109; CANR 55, 84; CDWLB 2; DLB 81, 124; EW 9; EWL 3; MTCW 2; RGSF 2; RGWL 2, 3

Muske, Carol
See Muske-Dukes, Carol

Muske, Carol Anne
See Muske-Dukes, Carol

Muske-Dukes, Carol 1945- .... **CLC 90**
See also CA 65-68, 203; CAAE 203; CANR 32, 70, 181; CWP; PFS 24

Muske-Dukes, Carol Ann
See Muske-Dukes, Carol

Muske-Dukes, Carol Anne
See Muske-Dukes, Carol

Musset, Alfred de 1810-1857 . **DC 27; NCLC 7, 150**
See also DLB 192, 217; EW 6; GFL 1789 to the Present; RGWL 2, 3; TWA

Musset, Louis Charles Alfred de
See Musset, Alfred de

Mussolini, Benito (Amilcare Andrea)
1883-1945 .... **TCLC 96**
See also CA 116

Mutanabbi, Al-
See al-Mutanabbi, Ahmad ibn al-Husayn Abu al-Tayyib al-Jufi al-Kindi

My Brother's Brother
See Chekhov, Anton (Pavlovich)

Myers, L(eopold) H(amilton)
1881-1944 .... **TCLC 59**
See also CA 157; DLB 15; EWL 3; RGEL 2

Myers, Walter Dean 1937- ...... **BLC 1:3, 2:3; CLC 35**
See also AAYA 4, 23; BW 2; BYA 6, 8, 11; CA 33-36R; CANR 20, 42, 67, 108, 184; CLR 4, 16, 35, 110; DAM MULT, NOV; DLB 33; INT CANR-20; JRDA; LAIT 5; MAICYA 1, 2; MAICYAS 1; MTCW 2; MTFW 2005; SAAS 2; SATA 41, 71, 109, 157, 193; SATA-Brief 27; WYA; YAW

Myers, Walter M.
See Myers, Walter Dean

Myles, Symon
See Follett, Ken

Nabokov, Vladimir (Vladimirovich)
1899-1977 .... **CLC 1, 2, 3, 6, 8, 11, 15, 23, 44, 46, 64; SSC 11, 86; TCLC 108, 189; WLC 4**
See also AAYA 45; AMW; AMWC 1; AMWR 1; BPFB 2; CA 5-8R; 69-72; CANR 20, 102; CDALB 1941-1968; CN 1, 2; CP 2; DA; DA3; DAB; DAC; DAM MST, NOV; DLB 2, 244, 278, 317; DLBD 3; DLBY 1980, 1991; EWL 3; EXPS; LATS 1:2; MAL 5; MTCW 1, 2; MTFW 2005; NCFS 4; NFS 9; RGAL 4; RGSF 2; SSFS 6, 15; TUS

Naevius c. 265B.C.-201B.C. .... **CMLC 37**
See also DLB 211

Nagai, Kafu 1879-1959 .... **TCLC 51**
See also CA 117; 276; DLB 180; EWL 3; MJW

Nagai, Sokichi
See Nagai, Kafu

Nagai Kafu
See Nagai, Kafu

na gCopaleen, Myles
See O Nuallain, Brian

na Gopaleen, Myles
See O Nuallain, Brian

Nagy, Laszlo 1925-1978 .... **CLC 7**
See also CA 129; 112

Naidu, Sarojini 1879-1949 .... **TCLC 80**
See also EWL 3; RGEL 2

Naipaul, Shiva 1945-1985 .... **CLC 32, 39; TCLC 153**
See also CA 110; 112; 116; CANR 33; CN 2, 3; DA3; DAM NOV; DLB 157; DLBY 1985; EWL 3; MTCW 1, 2; MTFW 2005

Naipaul, Shivadhar Srinivasa
See Naipaul, Shiva

Naipaul, V.S. 1932- .. **CLC 4, 7, 9, 13, 18, 37, 105, 199; SSC 38, 121**
See also BPFB 2; BRWS 1; CA 1-4R; CANR 1, 33, 51, 91, 126; CDBLB 1960 to Present; CDWLB 3; CN 1, 2, 3, 4, 5, 6, 7; DA3; DAB; DAC; DAM MST, NOV; DLB 125, 204, 207, 326, 331; DLBY 1985, 2001; EWL 3; LATS 1:2; MTCW 1, 2; MTFW 2005; RGEL 2; RGSF 2; TWA; WLIT 4; WWE 1

Nakos, Lilika 1903(?)-1989 .... **CLC 29**

Napoleon
See Yamamoto, Hisaye

Narayan, R.K. 1906-2001 ...... **CLC 7, 28, 47, 121, 211; SSC 25**
See also BPFB 2; CA 81-84; 196; CANR 33, 61, 112; CN 1, 2, 3, 4, 5, 6, 7; DA3; DAM NOV; DLB 323; DNFS 1; EWL 3; MTCW 1, 2; MTFW 2005; RGEL 2; RGSF 2; SATA 62; SSFS 5; WWE 1

Nash, Frediric Ogden
See Nash, Ogden

Nash, Ogden 1902-1971 ...... **CLC 23; PC 21; TCLC 109**
See also CA 13-14; 29-32R; CANR 34, 61, 185; CAP 1; CP 1; DAM POET; DLB 11; MAICYA 1, 2; MAL 5; MTCW 1, 2; RGAL 4; SATA 2, 46; WP

Nashe, Thomas 1567-1601(?) . **LC 41, 89; PC 82**
See also DLB 167; RGEL 2

Nathan, Daniel
See Dannay, Frederic

Nathan, George Jean 1882-1958 .... **TCLC 18**
See also CA 114; 169; DLB 137; MAL 5

Natsume, Kinnosuke
See Natsume, Soseki

Natsume, Soseki 1867-1916 .... **TCLC 2, 10**
See also CA 104; 195; DLB 180; EWL 3; MJW; RGWL 2, 3; TWA

Natsume Soseki
See Natsume, Soseki

Natti, (Mary) Lee 1919- .... **CLC 17**
See also CA 5-8R; CANR 2; CWRI 5; SAAS 3; SATA 1, 67

Navarre, Marguerite de
See de Navarre, Marguerite

Naylor, Gloria 1950- . **BLC 1:3; CLC 28, 52, 156, 261; WLCS**
See also AAYA 6, 39; AFAW 1, 2; AMWS 8; BW 2, 3; CA 107; CANR 27, 51, 74, 130; CN 4, 5, 6, 7; CPW; DA; DA3; DAC; DAM MST, MULT, NOV, POP; DLB 173; EWL 3; FW; MAL 5; MTCW 1, 2; MTFW 2005; NFS 4, 7; RGAL 4; TCLE 1:2; TUS

Neal, John 1793-1876 .... **NCLC 161**
See also DLB 1, 59, 243; FW; RGAL 4

Neff, Debra .... **CLC 59**

Neihardt, John Gneisenau
1881-1973 .... **CLC 32**
See also CA 13-14; CANR 65; CAP 1; DLB 9, 54, 256; LAIT 2; TCWW 1, 2

Nekrasov, Nikolai Alekseevich
1821-1878 .... **NCLC 11**
See also DLB 277

Nelligan, Emile 1879-1941 .... **TCLC 14**
See also CA 114; 204; DLB 92; EWL 3

Nelson, Alice Ruth Moore Dunbar
1875-1935 .... **HR 1:2**
See also BW 1, 3; CA 122; 124; CANR 82; DLB 50; FW; MTCW 1

Nelson, Willie 1933- .... **CLC 17**
See also CA 107; CANR 114, 178

Nemerov, Howard 1920-1991 .... **CLC 2, 6, 9, 36; PC 24; TCLC 124**
See also AMW; CA 1-4R; 134; CABS 2; CANR 1, 27, 53; CN 1, 2, 3; CP 1, 2, 3, 4, 5; DAM POET; DLB 5, 6; DLBY 1983; EWL 3; INT CANR-27; MAL 5; MTCW 1, 2; MTFW 2005; PFS 10, 14; RGAL 4

Nepos, Cornelius c. 99B.C.-c. 24B.C. .... **CMLC 89**
See also DLB 211

Neruda, Pablo 1904-1973 .. **CLC 1, 2, 5, 7, 9, 28, 62; HLC 2; PC 4, 64; WLC 4**
See also CA 19-20; 45-48; CANR 131; CAP 2; DA; DA3; DAB; DAC; DAM MST, MULT, POET; DLB 283, 331; DNFS 2; EWL 3; HW 1; LAW; MTCW 1, 2; MTFW 2005; PFS 11, 28; RGWL 2, 3; TWA; WLIT 1; WP

Nerval, Gerard de 1808-1855 ... **NCLC 1, 67; PC 13; SSC 18**
See also DLB 217; EW 6; GFL 1789 to the Present; RGSF 2; RGWL 2, 3

Nervo, (Jose) Amado (Ruiz de)
1870-1919 .... **HLCS 2; TCLC 11**
See also CA 109; 131; DLB 290; EWL 3; HW 1; LAW

Nesbit, Malcolm
See Chester, Alfred

Nessi, Pio Baroja y
See Baroja, Pio

Nestroy, Johann 1801-1862 .... **NCLC 42**
See also DLB 133; RGWL 2, 3

Netterville, Luke
See O'Grady, Standish (James)

Neufeld, John (Arthur) 1938- .... **CLC 17**
See also AAYA 11; CA 25-28R; CANR 11, 37, 56; CLR 52; MAICYA 1, 2; SAAS 3; SATA 6, 81, 131; SATA-Essay 131; YAW

Neumann, Alfred 1895-1952 .... **TCLC 100**
See also CA 183; DLB 56

Neumann, Ferenc
See Molnar, Ferenc

Neville, Emily Cheney 1919- .... **CLC 12**
See also BYA 2; CA 5-8R; CANR 3, 37, 85; JRDA; MAICYA 1, 2; SAAS 2; SATA 1; YAW

Newbound, Bernard Slade 1930- .... **CLC 11, 46**
See also CA 81-84; CAAS 9; CANR 49; CCA 1; CD 5, 6; DAM DRAM; DLB 53

Newby, P(ercy) H(oward)
1918-1997 .... **CLC 2, 13**
See also CA 5-8R; 161; CANR 32, 67; CN 1, 2, 3, 4, 5, 6; DAM NOV; DLB 15, 326; MTCW 1; RGEL 2

Newcastle
See Cavendish, Margaret Lucas

Newlove, Donald 1928- .... **CLC 6**
See also CA 29-32R; CANR 25

Newlove, John (Herbert) 1938- .... **CLC 14**
See also CA 21-24R; CANR 9, 25; CP 1, 2, 3, 4, 5, 6, 7

Nye, Robert 1939- .... **CLC 13, 42**
   See also BRWS 10; CA 33-36R; CANR 29,
   67, 107; CN 1, 2, 3, 4, 5, 6, 7; CP 1, 2, 3,
   4, 5, 6, 7; CWRI 5; DAM NOV; DLB 14,
   271; FANT; HGG; MTCW 1; RHW;
   SATA 6
Nyro, Laura 1947-1997 .... **CLC 17**
   See also CA 194
Oates, Joyce Carol 1938- .. **CLC 1, 2, 3, 6, 9,
   11, 15, 19, 33, 52, 108, 134, 228; SSC 6,
   70, 121; WLC 4**
   See also AAYA 15, 52; AITN 1; AMWS 2;
   BEST 89:2; BPFB 2; BYA 11; CA 5-8R;
   CANR 25, 45, 74, 113, 129, 165; CDALB
   1968-1988; CN 1, 2, 3, 4, 5, 6, 7; CP 5,
   6, 7; CPW; CWP; DA; DA3; DAB; DAC;
   DAM MST, NOV, POP; DLB 2, 5, 130;
   DLBY 1981; EWL 3; EXPS; FL 1:6; FW;
   GL 3; HGG; INT CANR-25; LAIT 4;
   MAL 5; MBL; MTCW 1, 2; MTFW 2005;
   NFS 8, 24; RGAL 4; RGSF 2; SATA 159;
   SSFS 1, 8, 17; SUFW 2; TUS
O'Brian, E.G.
   See Clarke, Arthur C.
O'Brian, Patrick 1914-2000 .... **CLC 152**
   See also AAYA 55; BRWS 12; CA 144; 187;
   CANR 74; CPW; MTCW 2; MTFW 2005;
   RHW
O'Brien, Darcy 1939-1998 .... **CLC 11**
   See also CA 21-24R; 167; CANR 8, 59
O'Brien, Edna 1932- ..... **CLC 3, 5, 8, 13, 36,
   65, 116, 237; SSC 10, 77**
   See also BRWS 5; CA 1-4R; CANR 6, 41,
   65, 102, 169; CDBLB 1960 to Present;
   CN 1, 2, 3, 4, 5, 6, 7; DA3; DAM NOV;
   DLB 14, 231, 319; EWL 3; FW; MTCW
   1, 2; MTFW 2005; RGSF 2; WLIT 4
O'Brien, E.G.
   See Clarke, Arthur C.
O'Brien, Fitz-James 1828-1862 ..... **NCLC 21**
   See also DLB 74; RGAL 4; SUFW
O'Brien, Flann
   See O Nuallain, Brian
O'Brien, Richard 1942- .... **CLC 17**
   See also CA 124
O'Brien, Tim 1946- .... **CLC 7, 19, 40, 103,
   211; SSC 74, 123**
   See also AAYA 16; AMWS 5; CA 85-88;
   CANR 40, 58, 133; CDALBS; CN 5, 6,
   7; CPW; DA3; DAM POP; DLB 152;
   DLBD 9; DLBY 1980; LATS 1:2; MAL
   5; MTCW 2; MTFW 2005; RGAL 4;
   SSFS 5, 15; TCLE 1:2
Obstfelder, Sigbjoern 1866-1900 .... **TCLC 23**
   See also CA 123
O'Casey, Brenda
   See Haycraft, Anna
O'Casey, Sean 1880-1964 .... **CLC 1, 5, 9, 11,
   15, 88; DC 12; WLCS**
   See also BRW 7; CA 89-92; CANR 62;
   CBD; CDBLB 1914-1945; DA3; DAB;
   DAC; DAM DRAM, MST; DFS 19; DLB
   10; EWL 3; MTCW 1, 2; MTFW 2005;
   RGEL 2; TEA; WLIT 4
O'Cathasaigh, Sean
   See O'Casey, Sean
Occom, Samson 1723-1792 .... **LC 60; NNAL**
   See also DLB 175
Occomy, Marita (Odette) Bonner
   1899(?)-1971 ..... **HR 1:2; PC 72; TCLC
   179**
   See also BW 2; CA 142; DFS 13; DLB 51,
   228
Ochs, Phil(ip David) 1940-1976 .... **CLC 17**
   See also CA 185; 65-68
O'Connor, Edwin (Greene)
   1918-1968 .... **CLC 14**
   See also CA 93-96; 25-28R; MAL 5

O'Connor, (Mary) Flannery
   1925-1964 .... **CLC 1, 2, 3, 6, 10, 13, 15,
   21, 66, 104; SSC 1, 23, 61, 82, 111;
   TCLC 132; WLC 4**
   See also AAYA 7; AMW; AMWR 2; BPFB
   3; BYA 16; CA 1-4R; CANR 3, 41;
   CDALB 1941-1968; DA; DA3; DAB;
   DAC; DAM MST, NOV; DLB 2, 152;
   DLBD 12; DLBY 1980; EWL 3; EXPS;
   LAIT 5; MAL 5; MBL; MTCW 1, 2;
   MTFW 2005; NFS 3, 21; RGAL 4; RGSF
   2; SSFS 2, 7, 10, 19; TUS
O'Connor, Frank 1903-1966
   See O'Donovan, Michael Francis
O'Dell, Scott 1898-1989 .... **CLC 30**
   See also AAYA 3, 44; BPFB 3; BYA 1, 2,
   3, 5; CA 61-64; 129; CANR 12, 30, 112;
   CLR 1, 16, 126; DLB 52; JRDA; MAI-
   CYA 1, 2; SATA 12, 60, 134; WYA; YAW
Odets, Clifford 1906-1963 ..... **CLC 2, 28, 98;
   DC 6**
   See also AMWS 2; CA 85-88; CAD; CANR
   62; DAM DRAM; DFS 3, 17, 20; DLB 7,
   26, 341; EWL 3; MAL 5; MTCW 1, 2;
   MTFW 2005; RGAL 4; TUS
O'Doherty, Brian 1928- .... **CLC 76**
   See also CA 105; CANR 108
O'Donnell, K. M.
   See Malzberg, Barry N(athaniel)
O'Donnell, Lawrence
   See Kuttner, Henry
O'Donovan, Michael Francis
   1903-1966 .... **CLC 14, 23; SSC 5, 109**
   See also BRWS 14; CA 93-96; CANR 84;
   DLB 162; EWL 3; RGSF 2; SSFS 5
Oe, Kenzaburo 1935- .. **CLC 10, 36, 86, 187;
   SSC 20**
   See also CA 97-100; CANR 36, 50, 74, 126;
   CWW 2; DA3; DAM NOV; DLB 182,
   331; DLBY 1994; EWL 3; LATS 1:2;
   MJW; MTCW 1, 2; MTFW 2005; RGSF
   2; RGWL 2, 3
Oe Kenzaburo
   See Oe, Kenzaburo
O'Faolain, Julia 1932- .... **CLC 6, 19, 47, 108**
   See also CA 81-84; CAAS 2; CANR 12,
   61; CN 2, 3, 4, 5, 6, 7; DLB 14, 231, 319;
   FW; MTCW 1; RHW
O'Faolain, Sean 1900-1991 ...... **CLC 1, 7, 14,
   32, 70; SSC 13; TCLC 143**
   See also CA 61-64; 134; CANR 12, 66; CN
   1, 2, 3, 4; DLB 15, 162; MTCW 1, 2;
   MTFW 2005; RGEL 2; RGSF 2
O'Flaherty, Liam 1896-1984 .... **CLC 5, 34;
   SSC 6, 116**
   See also CA 101; 113; CANR 35; CN 1, 2,
   3; DLB 36, 162; DLBY 1984; MTCW 1,
   2; MTFW 2005; RGEL 2; RGSF 2; SSFS
   5, 20
Ogai
   See Mori Ogai
Ogilvy, Gavin
   See Barrie, J(ames) M(atthew)
O'Grady, Standish (James)
   1846-1928 .... **TCLC 5**
   See also CA 104; 157
O'Grady, Timothy 1951- .... **CLC 59**
   See also CA 138
O'Hara, Frank 1926-1966 .... **CLC 2, 5, 13,
   78; PC 45**
   See also CA 9-12R; 25-28R; CANR 33;
   DA3; DAM POET; DLB 5, 16, 193; EWL
   3; MAL 5; MTCW 1, 2; MTFW 2005;
   PFS 8, 12; RGAL 4; WP
O'Hara, John (Henry) 1905-1970 . **CLC 1, 2,
   3, 6, 11, 42; SSC 15**
   See also AMW; BPFB 3; CA 5-8R; 25-28R;
   CANR 31, 60; CDALB 1929-1941; DAM
   NOV; DLB 9, 86, 324; DLBD 2; EWL 3;
   MAL 5; MTCW 1, 2; MTFW 2005; NFS
   11; RGAL 4; RGSF 2

O'Hehir, Diana 1929- .... **CLC 41**
   See also CA 245; CANR 177
O'Hehir, Diana F.
   See O'Hehir, Diana
Ohiyesa
   See Eastman, Charles A(lexander)
Okada, John 1923-1971 .... **AAL**
   See also BYA 14; CA 212; DLB 312; NFS
   25
Okigbo, Christopher 1930-1967 ..... **BLC 1:3;
   CLC 25, 84; PC 7; TCLC 171**
   See also AFW; BW 1, 3; CA 77-80; CANR
   74; CDWLB 3; DAM MULT, POET; DLB
   125; EWL 3; MTCW 1, 2; MTFW 2005;
   RGEL 2
Okigbo, Christopher Ifenayichukwu
   See Okigbo, Christopher
Okri, Ben 1959- .... **BLC 2:3; CLC 87, 223**
   See also AFW; BRWS 5; BW 2, 3; CA 130;
   138; CANR 65, 128; CN 5, 6, 7; DLB
   157, 231, 319, 326; EWL 3; INT CA-138;
   MTCW 2; MTFW 2005; RGSF 2; SSFS
   20; WLIT 2; WWE 1
Old Boy
   See Hughes, Thomas
Olds, Sharon 1942- .. **CLC 32, 39, 85; PC 22**
   See also AMWS 10; CA 101; CANR 18,
   41, 66, 98, 135; CP 5, 6, 7; CPW; CWP;
   DAM POET; DLB 120; MAL 5; MTCW
   2; MTFW 2005; PFS 17
Oldstyle, Jonathan
   See Irving, Washington
Olesha, Iurii
   See Olesha, Yuri (Karlovich)
Olesha, Iurii Karlovich
   See Olesha, Yuri (Karlovich)
Olesha, Yuri (Karlovich) 1899-1960 . **CLC 8;
   SSC 69; TCLC 136**
   See also CA 85-88; DLB 272; EW 11; EWL
   3; RGWL 2, 3
Olesha, Yury Karlovich
   See Olesha, Yuri (Karlovich)
Oliphant, Mrs.
   See Oliphant, Margaret (Oliphant Wilson)
Oliphant, Laurence 1829(?)-1888 .. **NCLC 47**
   See also DLB 18, 166
Oliphant, Margaret (Oliphant Wilson)
   1828-1897 .... **NCLC 11, 61; SSC 25**
   See also BRWS 10; DLB 18, 159, 190;
   HGG; RGEL 2; RGSF 2; SUFW
Oliver, Mary 1935- ... **CLC 19, 34, 98; PC 75**
   See also AMWS 7; CA 21-24R; CANR 9,
   43, 84, 92, 138; CP 4, 5, 6, 7; CWP; DLB
   5, 193, 342; EWL 3; MTFW 2005; PFS
   15
Olivier, Laurence (Kerr) 1907-1989 . **CLC 20**
   See also CA 111; 150; 129
O.L.S.
   See Russell, George William
Olsen, Tillie 1912-2007 .... **CLC 4, 13, 114;
   SSC 11, 103**
   See also AAYA 51; AMWS 13; BYA 11;
   CA 1-4R; 256; CANR 1, 43, 74, 132;
   CDALBS; CN 2, 3, 4, 5, 6, 7; DA; DA3;
   DAB; DAC; DAM MST; DLB 28, 206;
   DLBY 1980; EWL 3; EXPS; FW; MAL
   5; MTCW 1, 2; MTFW 2005; RGAL 4;
   RGSF 2; SSFS 1; TCLE 1:2; TCWW 2;
   TUS
Olson, Charles (John) 1910-1970 .. **CLC 1, 2,
   5, 6, 9, 11, 29; PC 19**
   See also AMWS 2; CA 13-16; 25-28R;
   CABS 2; CANR 35, 61; CAP 1; CP 1;
   DAM POET; DLB 5, 16, 193; EWL 3;
   MAL 5; MTCW 1, 2; RGAL 4; WP
Olson, Merle Theodore
   See Olson, Toby

Olson, Toby 1937- .... **CLC 28**
See also CA 65-68; CAAS 11; CANR 9, 31, 84, 175; CP 3, 4, 5, 6, 7
Olyesha, Yuri
See Olesha, Yuri (Karlovich)
Olympiodorus of Thebes c. 375-c. 430 .... **CMLC 59**
Omar Khayyam
See Khayyam, Omar
Ondaatje, Michael 1943- ..... **CLC 14, 29, 51, 76, 180, 258; PC 28**
See also AAYA 66; CA 77-80; CANR 42, 74, 109, 133, 172; CN 5, 6, 7; CP 1, 2, 3, 4, 5, 6, 7; DA3; DAB; DAC; DAM MST; DLB 60, 323, 326; EWL 3; LATS 1:2; LMFS 2; MTCW 2; MTFW 2005; NFS 23; PFS 8, 19; TCLE 1:2; TWA; WWE 1
Ondaatje, Philip Michael
See Ondaatje, Michael
Oneal, Elizabeth 1934- .... **CLC 30**
See also AAYA 5, 41; BYA 13; CA 106; CANR 28, 84; CLR 13; JRDA; MAICYA 1, 2; SATA 30, 82; WYA; YAW
Oneal, Zibby
See Oneal, Elizabeth
O'Neill, Eugene (Gladstone) 1888-1953 ... **DC 20; TCLC 1, 6, 27, 49; WLC 4**
See also AAYA 54; AITN 1; AMW; AMWC 1; CA 110; 132; CAD; CANR 131; CDALB 1929-1941; DA; DA3; DAB; DAC; DAM DRAM, MST; DFS 2, 4, 5, 6, 9, 11, 12, 16, 20, 26; DLB 7, 331; EWL 3; LAIT 3; LMFS 2; MAL 5; MTCW 1, 2; MTFW 2005; RGAL 4; TUS
Onetti, Juan Carlos 1909-1994 ... **CLC 7, 10; HLCS 2; SSC 23; TCLC 131**
See also CA 85-88; 145; CANR 32, 63; CDWLB 3; CWW 2; DAM MULT, NOV; DLB 113; EWL 3; HW 1, 2; LAW; MTCW 1, 2; MTFW 2005; RGSF 2
O'Nolan, Brian
See O Nuallain, Brian
O Nuallain, Brian 1911-1966 .... **CLC 1, 4, 5, 7, 10, 47**
See also BRWS 2; CA 21-22; 25-28R; CAP 2; DLB 231; EWL 3; FANT; RGEL 2; TEA
Ophuls, Max
See Ophuls, Max
Ophuls, Max 1902-1957 .... **TCLC 79**
See also CA 113
Opie, Amelia 1769-1853 .... **NCLC 65**
See also DLB 116, 159; RGEL 2
Oppen, George 1908-1984 ..... **CLC 7, 13, 34; PC 35; TCLC 107**
See also CA 13-16R; 113; CANR 8, 82; CP 1, 2, 3; DLB 5, 165
Oppenheim, E(dward) Phillips 1866-1946 .... **TCLC 45**
See also CA 111; 202; CMW 4; DLB 70
Oppenheimer, Max
See Ophuls, Max
Opuls, Max
See Ophuls, Max
Orage, A(lfred) R(ichard) 1873-1934 .... **TCLC 157**
See also CA 122
Origen c. 185-c. 254 .... **CMLC 19**
Orlovitz, Gil 1918-1973 .... **CLC 22**
See also CA 77-80; 45-48; CN 1; CP 1, 2; DLB 2, 5
Orosius c. 385-c. 420 .... **CMLC 100**
O'Rourke, Patrick Jake
See O'Rourke, P.J.
O'Rourke, P.J. 1947- .... **CLC 209**
See also CA 77-80; CANR 13, 41, 67, 111, 155; CPW; DAM POP; DLB 185

Orris
See Ingelow, Jean
Ortega y Gasset, Jose 1883-1955 ...... **HLC 2; TCLC 9**
See also CA 106; 130; DAM MULT; EW 9; EWL 3; HW 1, 2; MTCW 1, 2; MTFW 2005
Ortese, Anna Maria 1914-1998 .... **CLC 89**
See also DLB 177; EWL 3
Ortiz, Simon
See Ortiz, Simon J.
Ortiz, Simon J. 1941- . **CLC 45, 208; NNAL; PC 17**
See also AMWS 4; CA 134; CANR 69, 118, 164; CP 3, 4, 5, 6, 7; DAM MULT, POET; DLB 120, 175, 256, 342; EXPP; MAL 5; PFS 4, 16; RGAL 4; SSFS 22; TCWW 2
Ortiz, Simon Joseph
See Ortiz, Simon J.
Orton, Joe
See Orton, John Kingsley
Orton, John Kingsley 1933-1967 .... **CLC 4, 13, 43; DC 3; TCLC 157**
See also BRWS 5; CA 85-88; CANR 35, 66; CBD; CDBLB 1960 to Present; DAM DRAM; DFS 3, 6; DLB 13, 310; GLL 1; MTCW 1, 2; MTFW 2005; RGEL 2; TEA; WLIT 4
Orwell, George
See Blair, Eric (Arthur)
Osborne, David
See Silverberg, Robert
Osborne, Dorothy 1627-1695 .... **LC 141**
Osborne, George
See Silverberg, Robert
Osborne, John 1929-1994 .... **CLC 1, 2, 5, 11, 45; TCLC 153; WLC 4**
See also BRWS 1; CA 13-16R; 147; CANR 21, 56; CBD; CDBLB 1945-1960; DA; DAB; DAC; DAM DRAM, MST; DFS 4, 19, 24; DLB 13; EWL 3; MTCW 1, 2; MTFW 2005; RGEL 2
Osborne, Lawrence 1958- .... **CLC 50**
See also CA 189; CANR 152
Osbourne, Lloyd 1868-1947 .... **TCLC 93**
Osceola
See Blixen, Karen (Christentze Dinesen)
Osgood, Frances Sargent 1811-1850 .... **NCLC 141**
See also DLB 250
Oshima, Nagisa 1932- .... **CLC 20**
See also CA 116; 121; CANR 78
Oskison, John Milton 1874-1947 .... **NNAL; TCLC 35**
See also CA 144; CANR 84; DAM MULT; DLB 175
Ossoli, Sarah Margaret (Fuller) 1810-1850 .... **NCLC 5, 50, 211**
See also AMWS 2; CDALB 1640-1865; DLB 1, 59, 73, 183, 223, 239; FW; LMFS 1; SATA 25
Ostriker, Alicia 1937- .... **CLC 132**
See also CA 25-28R; CAAS 24; CANR 10, 30, 62, 99, 167; CWP; DLB 120; EXPP; PFS 19, 26
Ostriker, Alicia Suskin
See Ostriker, Alicia
Ostrovsky, Aleksandr Nikolaevich
See Ostrovsky, Alexander
Ostrovsky, Alexander 1823-1886 .. **NCLC 30, 57**
See also DLB 277
Osundare, Niyi 1947- .... **BLC 2:3**
See also AFW; BW 3; CA 176; CDWLB 3; CP 7; DLB 157
Otero, Blas de 1916-1979 .... **CLC 11**
See also CA 89-92; DLB 134; EWL 3
O'Trigger, Sir Lucius
See Horne, Richard Henry Hengist

Otto, Rudolf 1869-1937 .... **TCLC 85**
Otto, Whitney 1955- .... **CLC 70**
See also CA 140; CANR 120
Otway, Thomas 1652-1685 ... **DC 24; LC 106**
See also DAM DRAM; DLB 80; RGEL 2
Ouida
See De La Ramee, Marie Louise
Ouologuem, Yambo 1940- .... **CLC 146**
See also CA 111; 176
Ousmane, Sembene 1923-2007 .... **BLC 1:3, 2:3; CLC 66**
See also AFW; BW 1, 3; CA 117; 125; 261; CANR 81; CWW 2; EWL 3; MTCW 1; WLIT 2
Ovid 43B.C.-17 .... **CMLC 7, 108; PC 2**
See also AW 2; CDWLB 1; DA3; DAM POET; DLB 211; PFS 22; RGWL 2, 3; WLIT 8; WP
Owen, Hugh
See Faust, Frederick (Schiller)
Owen, Wilfred (Edward Salter) 1893-1918 ... **PC 19; TCLC 5, 27; WLC 4**
See also BRW 6; CA 104; 141; CDBLB 1914-1945; DA; DAB; DAC; DAM MST, POET; DLB 20; EWL 3; EXPP; MTCW 2; MTFW 2005; PFS 10; RGEL 2; WLIT 4
Owens, Louis (Dean) 1948-2002 .... **NNAL**
See also CA 137, 179; 207; CAAE 179; CAAS 24; CANR 71
Owens, Rochelle 1936- .... **CLC 8**
See also CA 17-20R; CAAS 2; CAD; CANR 39; CD 5, 6; CP 1, 2, 3, 4, 5, 6, 7; CWD; CWP
Oz, Amos 1939- ...... **CLC 5, 8, 11, 27, 33, 54; SSC 66**
See also CA 53-56; CANR 27, 47, 65, 113, 138, 175; CWW 2; DAM NOV; EWL 3; MTCW 1, 2; MTFW 2005; RGHL; RGSF 2; RGWL 3; WLIT 6
Ozick, Cynthia 1928- . **CLC 3, 7, 28, 62, 155, 262; SSC 15, 60, 123**
See also AMWS 5; BEST 90:1; CA 17-20R; CANR 23, 58, 116, 160, 187; CN 3, 4, 5, 6, 7; CPW; DA3; DAM NOV, POP; DLB 28, 152, 299; DLBY 1982; EWL 3; EXPS; INT CANR-23; MAL 5; MTCW 1, 2; MTFW 2005; RGAL 4; RGHL; RGSF 2; SSFS 3, 12, 22
Ozu, Yasujiro 1903-1963 .... **CLC 16**
See also CA 112
Pabst, G. W. 1885-1967 .... **TCLC 127**
Pacheco, C.
See Pessoa, Fernando
Pacheco, Jose Emilio 1939- .... **HLC 2**
See also CA 111; 131; CANR 65; CWW 2; DAM MULT; DLB 290; EWL 3; HW 1, 2; RGSF 2
Pa Chin
See Jin, Ba
Pack, Robert 1929- .... **CLC 13**
See also CA 1-4R; CANR 3, 44, 82; CP 1, 2, 3, 4, 5, 6, 7; DLB 5; SATA 118
Packer, Vin
See Meaker, Marijane
Padgett, Lewis
See Kuttner, Henry
Padilla (Lorenzo), Heberto 1932-2000 .... **CLC 38**
See also AITN 1; CA 123; 131; 189; CWW 2; EWL 3; HW 1
Paerdurabo, Frater
See Crowley, Edward Alexander
Page, James Patrick 1944- .... **CLC 12**
See also CA 204
Page, Jimmy 1944-
See Page, James Patrick

Page, Louise 1955- .... **CLC 40**
    See also CA 140; CANR 76; CBD; CD 5,
    6; CWD; DLB 233
Page, P(atricia) K(athleen) 1916- ...... **CLC 7,
    18; PC 12**
    See also CA 53-56; CANR 4, 22, 65; CCA
    1; CP 1, 2, 3, 4, 5, 6, 7; DAC; DAM MST;
    DLB 68; MTCW 1; RGEL 2
Page, Stanton
    See Fuller, Henry Blake
Page, Thomas Nelson 1853-1922 .... **SSC 23**
    See also CA 118; 177; DLB 12, 78; DLBD
    13; RGAL 4
Pagels, Elaine
    See Pagels, Elaine Hiesey
Pagels, Elaine Hiesey 1943- .... **CLC 104**
    See also CA 45-48; CANR 2, 24, 51, 151;
    FW; NCFS 4
Paget, Violet 1856-1935 .. **SSC 33, 98; TCLC
    5**
    See also CA 104; 166; DLB 57, 153, 156,
    174, 178; GLL 1; HGG; SUFW 1
Paget-Lowe, Henry
    See Lovecraft, H. P.
Paglia, Camille 1947- .... **CLC 68**
    See also CA 140; CANR 72, 139; CPW;
    FW; GLL 2; MTCW 2; MTFW 2005
Pagnol, Marcel (Paul)
    1895-1974 .... **TCLC 208**
    See also CA 128; 49-52; DLB 321; EWL 3;
    GFL 1789 to the Present; MTCW 1;
    RGWL 2, 3
Paige, Richard
    See Koontz, Dean R.
Paine, Thomas 1737-1809 .... **NCLC 62**
    See also AMWS 1; CDALB 1640-1865;
    DLB 31, 43, 73, 158; LAIT 1; RGAL 4;
    RGEL 2; TUS
Pakenham, Antonia
    See Fraser, Antonia
Palamas, Costis
    See Palamas, Kostes
Palamas, Kostes 1859-1943 .... **TCLC 5**
    See also CA 105; 190; EWL 3; RGWL 2, 3
Palamas, Kostis
    See Palamas, Kostes
Palazzeschi, Aldo 1885-1974 .... **CLC 11**
    See also CA 89-92; 53-56; DLB 114, 264;
    EWL 3
Pales Matos, Luis 1898-1959 .... **HLCS 2**
    See Pales Matos, Luis
    See also DLB 290; HW 1; LAW
Paley, Grace 1922-2007 ... **CLC 4, 6, 37, 140,
    272; SSC 8**
    See also AMWS 6; CA 25-28R; 263; CANR
    13, 46, 74, 118; CN 2, 3, 4, 5, 6, 7; CPW;
    DA3; DAM POP; DLB 28, 218; EWL 3;
    EXPS; FW; INT CANR-13; MAL 5;
    MBL; MTCW 1, 2; MTFW 2005; RGAL
    4; RGSF 2; SSFS 3, 20, 27
Paley, Grace Goodside
    See Paley, Grace
Palin, Michael 1943- .... **CLC 21**
    See also CA 107; CANR 35, 109, 179;
    SATA 67
Palin, Michael Edward
    See Palin, Michael
Palliser, Charles 1947- .... **CLC 65**
    See also CA 136; CANR 76; CN 5, 6, 7
Palma, Ricardo 1833-1919 .... **TCLC 29**
    See also CA 168; LAW
Pamuk, Orhan 1952- .... **CLC 185**
    See also CA 142; CANR 75, 127, 172;
    CWW 2; NFS 27; WLIT 6
Pancake, Breece Dexter 1952-1979 . **CLC 29;
    SSC 61**
    See also CA 123; 109; DLB 130
Pancake, Breece D'J
    See Pancake, Breece Dexter

Panchenko, Nikolai .... **CLC 59**
Pankhurst, Emmeline (Goulden)
    1858-1928 .... **TCLC 100**
    See also CA 116; FW
Panko, Rudy
    See Gogol, Nikolai (Vasilyevich)
Papadiamantis, Alexandros
    1851-1911 .... **TCLC 29**
    See also CA 168; EWL 3
Papadiamantopoulos, Johannes
    1856-1910 .... **TCLC 18**
    See also CA 117; 242; GFL 1789 to the
    Present
Papadiamantopoulos, Yannis
    See Papadiamantopoulos, Johannes
Papini, Giovanni 1881-1956 .... **TCLC 22**
    See also CA 121; 180; DLB 264
Paracelsus 1493-1541 .... **LC 14**
    See also DLB 179
Parasol, Peter
    See Stevens, Wallace
Pardo Bazan, Emilia 1851-1921 .... **SSC 30;
    TCLC 189**
    See also EWL 3; FW; RGSF 2; RGWL 2, 3
Paredes, Americo 1915-1999 .... **PC 83**
    See also CA 37-40R; 179; DLB 209; EXPP;
    HW 1
Pareto, Vilfredo 1848-1923 .... **TCLC 69**
    See also CA 175
Paretsky, Sara 1947- .... **CLC 135**
    See also AAYA 30; BEST 90:3; CA 125;
    129; CANR 59, 95, 184; CMW 4; CPW;
    DA3; DAM POP; DLB 306; INT CA-129;
    MSW; RGAL 4
Paretsky, Sara N.
    See Paretsky, Sara
Parfenie, Maria
    See Codrescu, Andrei
Parini, Jay (Lee) 1948- .... **CLC 54, 133**
    See also CA 97-100, 229; CAAE 229;
    CAAS 16; CANR 32, 87
Park, Jordan
    See Kornbluth, C(yril) M.; Pohl, Frederik
Park, Robert E(zra) 1864-1944 ..... **TCLC 73**
    See also CA 122; 165
Parker, Bert
    See Ellison, Harlan
Parker, Dorothy (Rothschild)
    1893-1967 . **CLC 15, 68; PC 28; SSC 2,
    101; TCLC 143**
    See also AMWS 9; CA 19-20; 25-28R; CAP
    2; DA3; DAM POET; DLB 11, 45, 86;
    EXPP; FW; MAL 5; MBL; MTCW 1, 2;
    MTFW 2005; PFS 18; RGAL 4; RGSF 2;
    TUS
Parker, Robert B. 1932- .... **CLC 27**
    See also AAYA 28; BEST 89:4; BPFB 3;
    CA 49-52; CANR 1, 26, 52, 89, 128, 165;
    CMW 4; CPW; DAM NOV, POP; DLB
    306; INT CANR-26; MSW; MTCW 1;
    MTFW 2005
Parker, Robert Brown
    See Parker, Robert B.
Parker, Theodore 1810-1860 .... **NCLC 186**
    See also DLB 1, 235
Parkes, Lucas
    See Harris, John (Wyndham Parkes Lucas)
    Beynon
Parkin, Frank 1940- .... **CLC 43**
    See also CA 147
Parkman, Francis, Jr. 1823-1893 .. **NCLC 12**
    See also AMWS 2; DLB 1, 30, 183, 186,
    235; RGAL 4
Parks, Gordon 1912-2006 . **BLC 1:3; CLC 1,
    16**
    See also AAYA 36; AITN 2; BW 2, 3; CA
    41-44R; 249; CANR 26, 66, 145; DA3;
    DAM MULT; DLB 33; MTCW 2; MTFW
    2005; SATA 8, 108; SATA-Obit 175

Parks, Suzan-Lori 1964(?)- ..... **BLC 2:3; DC
    23**
    See also AAYA 55; CA 201; CAD; CD 5,
    6; CWD; DFS 22; DLB 341; RGAL 4
Parks, Tim(othy Harold) 1954- ...... **CLC 147**
    See also CA 126; 131; CANR 77, 144; CN
    7; DLB 231; INT CA-131
Parmenides c. 515B.C.-c.
    450B.C. .... **CMLC 22**
    See also DLB 176
Parnell, Thomas 1679-1718 .... **LC 3**
    See also DLB 95; RGEL 2
Parr, Catherine c. 1513(?)-1548 .... **LC 86**
    See also DLB 136
Parra, Nicanor 1914- ... **CLC 2, 102; HLC 2;
    PC 39**
    See also CA 85-88; CANR 32; CWW 2;
    DAM MULT; DLB 283; EWL 3; HW 1;
    LAW; MTCW 1
Parra Sanojo, Ana Teresa de la 1890-1936
    See de la Parra, (Ana) Teresa (Sonojo)
Parrish, Mary Frances
    See Fisher, M(ary) F(rances) K(ennedy)
Parshchikov, Aleksei 1954- .... **CLC 59**
    See also DLB 285
Parshchikov, Aleksei Maksimovich
    See Parshchikov, Aleksei
Parson, Professor
    See Coleridge, Samuel Taylor
Parson Lot
    See Kingsley, Charles
Parton, Sara Payson Willis
    1811-1872 .... **NCLC 86**
    See also DLB 43, 74, 239
Partridge, Anthony
    See Oppenheim, E(dward) Phillips
Pascal, Blaise 1623-1662 .... **LC 35**
    See also DLB 268; EW 3; GFL Beginnings
    to 1789; RGWL 2, 3; TWA
Pascoli, Giovanni 1855-1912 .... **TCLC 45**
    See also CA 170; EW 7; EWL 3
Pasolini, Pier Paolo 1922-1975 .. **CLC 20, 37,
    106; PC 17**
    See also CA 93-96; 61-64; CANR 63; DLB
    128, 177; EWL 3; MTCW 1; RGWL 2, 3
Pasquini
    See Silone, Ignazio
Pastan, Linda (Olenik) 1932- .... **CLC 27**
    See also CA 61-64; CANR 18, 40, 61, 113;
    CP 3, 4, 5, 6, 7; CSW; CWP; DAM
    POET; DLB 5; PFS 8, 25
Pasternak, Boris 1890-1960 ... **CLC 7, 10, 18,
    63; PC 6; SSC 31; TCLC 188; WLC 4**
    See also BPFB 3; CA 127; 116; DA; DA3;
    DAB; DAC; DAM MST, NOV, POET;
    DLB 302, 331; EW 10; MTCW 1, 2;
    MTFW 2005; NFS 26; RGSF 2; RGWL
    2, 3; TWA; WP
Patchen, Kenneth 1911-1972 .... **CLC 1, 2, 18**
    See also BG 1:3; CA 1-4R; 33-36R; CANR
    3, 35; CN 1; CP 1; DAM POET; DLB 16,
    48; EWL 3; MAL 5; MTCW 1; RGAL 4
Patchett, Ann 1963- .... **CLC 244**
    See also AAYA 69; AMWS 12; CA 139;
    CANR 64, 110, 167; MTFW 2005
Pater, Walter (Horatio) 1839-1894 . **NCLC 7,
    90, 159**
    See also BRW 5; CDBLB 1832-1890; DLB
    57, 156; RGEL 2; TEA
Paterson, A(ndrew) B(arton)
    1864-1941 .... **TCLC 32**
    See also CA 155; DLB 230; RGEL 2; SATA
    97
Paterson, Banjo
    See Paterson, A(ndrew) B(arton)

Paterson, Katherine 1932- .... **CLC 12, 30**
See also AAYA 1, 31; BYA 1, 2, 7; CA 21-24R; CANR 28, 59, 111, 173; CLR 7, 50, 127; CWRI 5; DLB 52; JRDA; LAIT 4; MAICYA 1, 2; MAICYAS 1; MTCW 1; SATA 13, 53, 92, 133; WYA; YAW

Paterson, Katherine Womeldorf
See Paterson, Katherine

Patmore, Coventry Kersey Dighton
1823-1896 .... **NCLC 9; PC 59**
See also DLB 35, 98; RGEL 2; TEA

Paton, Alan 1903-1988 ..... **CLC 4, 10, 25, 55, 106; TCLC 165; WLC 4**
See also AAYA 26; AFW; BPFB 3; BRWS 2; BYA 1; CA 13-16; 125; CANR 22; CAP 1; CN 1, 2, 3, 4; DA; DA3; DAB; DAC; DAM MST, NOV; DLB 225; DLBD 17; EWL 3; EXPN; LAIT 4; MTCW 1, 2; MTFW 2005; NFS 3, 12; RGEL 2; SATA 11; SATA-Obit 56; TWA; WLIT 2; WWE 1

Paton Walsh, Gillian
See Paton Walsh, Jill

Paton Walsh, Jill 1937- .... **CLC 35**
See also AAYA 11, 47; BYA 1, 8; CA 262; CAAE 262; CANR 38, 83, 158; CLR 2, 6, 128; DLB 161; JRDA; MAICYA 1, 2; SAAS 3; SATA 4, 72, 109, 190; SATA-Essay 190; WYA; YAW

Patsauq, Markoosie 1942- .... **NNAL**
See also CA 101; CLR 23; CWRI 5; DAM MULT

Patterson, (Horace) Orlando (Lloyd)
1940- .... **BLCS**
See also BW 1; CA 65-68; CANR 27, 84; CN 1, 2, 3, 4, 5, 6

Patton, George S(mith), Jr.
1885-1945 .... **TCLC 79**
See also CA 189

Paulding, James Kirke 1778-1860 ... **NCLC 2**
See also DLB 3, 59, 74, 250; RGAL 4

Paulin, Thomas Neilson
See Paulin, Tom

Paulin, Tom 1949- .... **CLC 37, 177**
See also CA 123; 128; CANR 98; CP 3, 4, 5, 6, 7; DLB 40

Pausanias c. 1st cent. - .... **CMLC 36**

Paustovsky, Konstantin (Georgievich)
1892-1968 .... **CLC 40**
See also CA 93-96; 25-28R; DLB 272; EWL 3

Pavese, Cesare 1908-1950 .... **PC 13; SSC 19; TCLC 3**
See also CA 104; 169; DLB 128, 177; EW 12; EWL 3; PFS 20; RGSF 2; RGWL 2, 3; TWA; WLIT 7

Pavic, Milorad 1929- .... **CLC 60**
See also CA 136; CDWLB 4; CWW 2; DLB 181; EWL 3; RGWL 3

Pavlov, Ivan Petrovich 1849-1936 . **TCLC 91**
See also CA 118; 180

Pavlova, Karolina Karlovna
1807-1893 .... **NCLC 138**
See also DLB 205

Payne, Alan
See Jakes, John

Payne, Rachel Ann
See Jakes, John

Paz, Gil
See Lugones, Leopoldo

Paz, Octavio 1914-1998 . **CLC 3, 4, 6, 10, 19, 51, 65, 119; HLC 2; PC 1, 48; TCLC 211; WLC 4**
See also AAYA 50; CA 73-76; 165; CANR 32, 65, 104; CWW 2; DA; DA3; DAB; DAC; DAM MST, MULT, POET; DLB 290, 331; DLBY 1990, 1998; DNFS 1;

EWL 3; HW 1, 2; LAW; LAWS 1; MTCW 1, 2; MTFW 2005; PFS 18, 30; RGWL 2, 3; SSFS 13; TWA; WLIT 1

p'Bitek, Okot 1931-1982 . **BLC 1:3; CLC 96; TCLC 149**
See also AFW; BW 2, 3; CA 124; 107; CANR 82; CP 1, 2, 3; DAM MULT; DLB 125; EWL 3; MTCW 1, 2; MTFW 2005; RGEL 2; WLIT 2

Peabody, Elizabeth Palmer
1804-1894 .... **NCLC 169**
See also DLB 1, 223

Peacham, Henry 1578-1644(?) .... **LC 119**
See also DLB 151

Peacock, Molly 1947- .... **CLC 60**
See also CA 103, 262; CAAE 262; CAAS 21; CANR 52, 84; CP 5, 6, 7; CWP; DLB 120, 282

Peacock, Thomas Love
1785-1866 .... **NCLC 22; PC 87**
See also BRW 4; DLB 96, 116; RGEL 2; RGSF 2

Peake, Mervyn 1911-1968 .... **CLC 7, 54**
See also CA 5-8R; 25-28R; CANR 3; DLB 15, 160, 255; FANT; MTCW 1; RGEL 2; SATA 23; SFW 4

Pearce, Ann Philippa
See Pearce, Philippa

Pearce, Philippa 1920-2006 .... **CLC 21**
See also BYA 5; CA 5-8R; 255; CANR 4, 109; CLR 9; CWRI 5; DLB 161; FANT; MAICYA 1; SATA 1, 67, 129; SATA-Obit 179

Pearl, Eric
See Elman, Richard (Martin)

Pearson, Jean Mary
See Gardam, Jane

Pearson, Thomas Reid
See Pearson, T.R.

Pearson, T.R. 1956- .... **CLC 39**
See also CA 120; 130; CANR 97, 147, 185; CSW; INT CA-130

Peck, Dale 1967- .... **CLC 81**
See also CA 146; CANR 72, 127, 180; GLL 2

Peck, John (Frederick) 1941- .... **CLC 3**
See also CA 49-52; CANR 3, 100; CP 4, 5, 6, 7

Peck, Richard 1934- .... **CLC 21**
See also AAYA 1, 24; BYA 1, 6, 8, 11; CA 85-88; CANR 19, 38, 129, 178; CLR 15, 142; INT CANR-19; JRDA; MAICYA 1, 2; SAAS 2; SATA 18, 55, 97, 110, 158, 190; SATA-Essay 110; WYA; YAW

Peck, Richard Wayne
See Peck, Richard

Peck, Robert Newton 1928- .... **CLC 17**
See also AAYA 3, 43; BYA 1, 6; CA 81-84; 182; CAAE 182; CANR 31, 63, 127; CLR 45; DA; DAC; DAM MST; JRDA; LAIT 3; MAICYA 1, 2; NFS 29; SAAS 1; SATA 21, 62, 111, 156; SATA-Essay 108; WYA; YAW

Peckinpah, David Samuel
See Peckinpah, Sam

Peckinpah, Sam 1925-1984 .... **CLC 20**
See also CA 109; 114; CANR 82

Pedersen, Knut 1859-1952 .. **TCLC 2, 14, 49, 151, 203**
See also AAYA 79; CA 104; 119; CANR 63; DLB 297, 330; EW 8; EWL 8; MTCW 1, 2; RGWL 2, 3

Peele, George 1556-1596 .... **DC 27; LC 115**
See also BRW 1; DLB 62, 167; RGEL 2

Peeslake, Gaffer
See Durrell, Lawrence (George)

Peguy, Charles (Pierre)
1873-1914 .... **TCLC 10**
See also CA 107; 193; DLB 258; EWL 3; GFL 1789 to the Present

Peirce, Charles Sanders
1839-1914 .... **TCLC 81**
See also CA 194; DLB 270

Pelagius c. 350-c. 418 .... **CMLC 112**

Pelecanos, George P. 1957- .... **CLC 236**
See also CA 138; CANR 122, 165; DLB 306

Pelevin, Victor 1962- .... **CLC 238**
See also CA 154; CANR 88, 159; DLB 285

Pelevin, Viktor Olegovich
See Pelevin, Victor

Pellicer, Carlos 1897(?)-1977 .... **HLCS 2**
See also CA 153; 69-72; DLB 290; EWL 3; HW 1

Pena, Ramon del Valle y
See Valle-Inclan, Ramon (Maria) del

Pendennis, Arthur Esquir
See Thackeray, William Makepeace

Penn, Arthur
See Matthews, (James) Brander

Penn, William 1644-1718 .... **LC 25**
See also DLB 24

PEPECE
See Prado (Calvo), Pedro

Pepys, Samuel 1633-1703 ... **LC 11, 58; WLC 4**
See also BRW 2; CDBLB 1660-1789; DA; DA3; DAB; DAC; DAM MST; DLB 101, 213; NCFS 4; RGEL 2; TEA; WLIT 3

Percy, Thomas 1729-1811 .... **NCLC 95**
See also DLB 104

Percy, Walker 1916-1990 .... **CLC 2, 3, 6, 8, 14, 18, 47, 65**
See also AMWS 3; BPFB 3; CA 1-4R; 131; CANR 1, 23, 64; CN 1, 2, 3, 4; CPW; CSW; DA3; DAM NOV, POP; DLB 2; DLBY 1980, 1990; EWL 3; MAL 5; MTCW 1, 2; MTFW 2005; RGAL 4; TUS

Percy, William Alexander
1885-1942 .... **TCLC 84**
See also CA 163; MTCW 2

Perdurabo, Frater
See Crowley, Edward Alexander

Perec, Georges 1936-1982 .... **CLC 56, 116**
See also CA 141; DLB 83, 299; EWL 3; GFL 1789 to the Present; RGHL; RGWL 3

Pereda (y Sanchez de Porrua), Jose Maria de 1833-1906 .... **TCLC 16**
See also CA 117

Pereda y Porrua, Jose Maria de
See Pereda (y Sanchez de Porrua), Jose Maria de

Peregoy, George Weems
See Mencken, H(enry) L(ouis)

Perelman, S(idney) J(oseph)
1904-1979 .. **CLC 3, 5, 9, 15, 23, 44, 49; SSC 32**
See also AAYA 79; AITN 1, 2; BPFB 3; CA 73-76; 89-92; CANR 18; DAM DRAM; DLB 11, 44; MTCW 1, 2; MTFW 2005; RGAL 4

Peret, Benjamin 1899-1959 .... **PC 33; TCLC 20**
See also CA 117; 186; GFL 1789 to the Present

Peretz, Isaac Leib
See Peretz, Isaac Loeb

Peretz, Isaac Loeb 1851(?)-1915 ...... **SSC 26; TCLC 16**
See also CA 109; 201; DLB 333

Peretz, Yitzkhok Leibush
See Peretz, Isaac Loeb

Portillo (y Pacheco), Jose Lopez
See Lopez Portillo (y Pacheco), Jose
Portillo Trambley, Estela
1927-1998 .... HLC 2; TCLC 163
See also CA 77-80; CANR 32; DAM
MULT; DLB 209; HW 1; RGAL 4
Posey, Alexander (Lawrence)
1873-1908 .... NNAL
See also CA 144; CANR 80; DAM MULT;
DLB 175
Posse, Abel .... CLC 70, 273
See also CA 252
Post, Melville Davisson
1869-1930 .... TCLC 39
See also CA 110; 202; CMW 4
Postman, Neil 1931(?)-2003 .... CLC 244
See also CA 102; 221
Potok, Chaim 1929-2002 ... CLC 2, 7, 14, 26,
112
See also AAYA 15, 50; AITN 1, 2; BPFB 3;
BYA 1; CA 17-20R; 208; CANR 19, 35,
64, 98; CLR 92; CN 4, 5, 6; DA3; DAM
NOV; DLB 28, 152; EXPN; INT CANR-
19; LAIT 4; MTCW 1, 2; MTFW 2005;
NFS 4; RGHL; SATA 33, 106; SATA-Obit
134; TUS; YAW
Potok, Herbert Harold -2002
See Potok, Chaim
Potok, Herman Harold
See Potok, Chaim
Potter, Dennis (Christopher George)
1935-1994 .... CLC 58, 86, 123
See also BRWS 10; CA 107; 145; CANR
33, 61; CBD; DLB 233; MTCW 1
Pound, Ezra (Weston Loomis)
1885-1972 .. CLC 1, 2, 3, 4, 5, 7, 10, 13,
18, 34, 48, 50, 112; PC 4, 95; WLC 5
See also AAYA 47; AMW; AMWR 1; CA
5-8R; 37-40R; CANR 40; CDALB 1917-
1929; CP 1; DA; DA3; DAB; DAC; DAM
MST, POET; DLB 4, 45, 63; DLBD 15;
EFS 2; EWL 3; EXPP; LMFS 2; MAL 5;
MTCW 1, 2; MTFW 2005; PAB; PFS 2,
8, 16; RGAL 4; TUS; WP
Povod, Reinaldo 1959-1994 .... CLC 44
See also CA 136; 146; CANR 83
Powell, Adam Clayton, Jr.
1908-1972 .... BLC 1:3; CLC 89
See also BW 1, 3; CA 102; 33-36R; CANR
86; DAM MULT; DLB 345
Powell, Anthony 1905-2000 ... CLC 1, 3, 7, 9,
10, 31
See also BRW 7; CA 1-4R; 189; CANR 1,
32, 62, 107; CDBLB 1945-1960; CN 1, 2,
3, 4, 5, 6; DLB 15; EWL 3; MTCW 1, 2;
MTFW 2005; RGEL 2; TEA
Powell, Dawn 1896(?)-1965 .... CLC 66
See also CA 5-8R; CANR 121; DLBY 1997
Powell, Padgett 1952- .... CLC 34
See also CA 126; CANR 63, 101; CSW;
DLB 234; DLBY 01; SSFS 25
Power, Susan 1961- .... CLC 91
See also BYA 14; CA 160; CANR 135; NFS
11
Powers, J(ames) F(arl) 1917-1999 ..... CLC 1,
4, 8, 57; SSC 4
See also CA 1-4R; 181; CANR 2, 61; CN
1, 2, 3, 4, 5, 6; DLB 130; MTCW 1;
RGAL 4; RGSF 2
Powers, John R. 1945- .... CLC 66
See also CA 69-72
Powers, John
See Powers, John R.
Powers, Richard 1957- .... CLC 93
See also AMWS 9; BPFB 3; CA 148;
CANR 80, 180; CN 6, 7; MTFW 2005;
TCLE 1:2
Powers, Richard S.
See Powers, Richard

Pownall, David 1938- .... CLC 10
See also CA 89-92, 180; CAAS 18; CANR
49, 101; CBD; CD 5, 6; CN 4, 5, 6, 7;
DLB 14
Powys, John Cowper 1872-1963 ... CLC 7, 9,
15, 46, 125
See also CA 85-88; CANR 106; DLB 15,
255; EWL 3; FANT; MTCW 1, 2; MTFW
2005; RGEL 2; SUFW
Powys, T(heodore) F(rancis)
1875-1953 .... TCLC 9
See also BRWS 8; CA 106; 189; DLB 36,
162; EWL 3; FANT; RGEL 2; SUFW
Pozzo, Modesta
See Fonte, Moderata
Prado (Calvo), Pedro 1886-1952 ... TCLC 75
See also CA 131; DLB 283; HW 1; LAW
Prager, Emily 1952- .... CLC 56
See also CA 204
Pratchett, Terence David John
See Pratchett, Terry
Pratchett, Terry 1948- .... CLC 197
See also AAYA 19, 54; BPFB 3; CA 143;
CANR 87, 126, 170; CLR 64; CN 6, 7;
CPW; CWRI 5; FANT; MTFW 2005;
SATA 82, 139, 185; SFW 4; SUFW 2
Pratolini, Vasco 1913-1991 .... TCLC 124
See also CA 211; DLB 177; EWL 3; RGWL
2, 3
Pratt, E(dwin) J(ohn) 1883(?)-1964 . CLC 19
See also CA 141; 93-96; CANR 77; DAC;
DAM POET; DLB 92; EWL 3; RGEL 2;
TWA
Premacanda
See Srivastava, Dhanpat Rai
Premchand
See Srivastava, Dhanpat Rai
Premchand, Munshi
See Srivastava, Dhanpat Rai
Prem Chand, Munshi
See Srivastava, Dhanpat Rai
Prescott, William Hickling
1796-1859 .... NCLC 163
See also DLB 1, 30, 59, 235
Preseren, France 1800-1849 .... NCLC 127
See also CDWLB 4; DLB 147
Preussler, Otfried 1923- .... CLC 17
See also CA 77-80; SATA 24
Prevert, Jacques (Henri Marie)
1900-1977 .... CLC 15
See also CA 77-80; 69-72; CANR 29, 61;
DLB 258; EWL 3; GFL 1789 to the
Present; IDFW 3, 4; MTCW 1; RGWL 2,
3; SATA-Obit 30
Prevost, (Antoine Francois)
1697-1763 .... LC 1
See also DLB 314; EW 4; GFL Beginnings
to 1789; RGWL 2, 3
Price, Edward Reynolds
See Price, Reynolds
Price, Reynolds 1933- .. CLC 3, 6, 13, 43, 50,
63, 212; SSC 22
See also AMWS 6; CA 1-4R; CANR 1, 37,
57, 87, 128, 177; CN 1, 2, 3, 4, 5, 6, 7;
CSW; DAM NOV; DLB 2, 218, 278;
EWL 3; INT CANR-37; MAL 5; MTFW
2005; NFS 18
Price, Richard 1949- .... CLC 6, 12
See also CA 49-52; CANR 3, 147; CN 7;
DLBY 1981
Prichard, Katharine Susannah
1883-1969 .... CLC 46
See also CA 11-12; CANR 33; CAP 1; DLB
260; MTCW 1; RGEL 2; RGSF 2; SATA
66

Priestley, J(ohn) B(oynton)
1894-1984 .... CLC 2, 5, 9, 34
See also BRW 7; CA 9-12R; 113; CANR
33; CDBLB 1914-1945; CN 1, 2, 3; DA3;
DAM DRAM, NOV; DLB 10, 34, 77,
100, 139; DLBY 1984; EWL 3; MTCW
1, 2; MTFW 2005; RGEL 2; SFW 4
Prince 1958- .... CLC 35
See also CA 213
Prince, F(rank) T(empleton)
1912-2003 .... CLC 22
See also CA 101; 219; CANR 43, 79; CP 1,
2, 3, 4, 5, 6, 7; DLB 20
Prince Kropotkin
See Kropotkin, Peter (Aleksieevich)
Prior, Matthew 1664-1721 .... LC 4
See also DLB 95; RGEL 2
Prishvin, Mikhail 1873-1954 .... TCLC 75
See also DLB 272; EWL 3 !**
Prishvin, Mikhail Mikhailovich
See Prishvin, Mikhail
Pritchard, William H(arrison)
1932- .... CLC 34
See also CA 65-68; CANR 23, 95; DLB
111
Pritchett, V(ictor) S(awdon)
1900-1997 ... CLC 5, 13, 15, 41; SSC 14
See also BPFB 3; BRWS 3; CA 61-64; 157;
CANR 31, 63; CN 1, 2, 3, 4, 5, 6; DA3;
DAM NOV; DLB 15, 139; EWL 3;
MTCW 1, 2; MTFW 2005; RGEL 2;
RGSF 2; TEA
Private 19022
See Manning, Frederic
Probst, Mark 1925- .... CLC 59
See also CA 130
Procaccino, Michael
See Cristofer, Michael
Proclus c. 412-c. 485 .... CMLC 81
Prokosch, Frederic 1908-1989 ...... CLC 4, 48
See also CA 73-76; 128; CANR 82; CN 1,
2, 3, 4; CP 1, 2, 3, 4; DLB 48; MTCW 2
Propertius, Sextus c. 50B.C.-c.
16B.C. .... CMLC 32
See also AW 2; CDWLB 1; DLB 211;
RGWL 2, 3; WLIT 8
Prophet, The
See Dreiser, Theodore
Prose, Francine 1947- .... CLC 45, 231
See also AMWS 16; CA 109; 112; CANR
46, 95, 132, 175; DLB 234; MTFW 2005;
SATA 101, 149, 198
Protagoras c. 490B.C.-420B.C. ...... CMLC 85
See also DLB 176
Proudhon
See Cunha, Euclides (Rodrigues Pimenta)
da
Proulx, Annie
See Proulx, E. Annie
Proulx, E. Annie 1935- ...... CLC 81, 158, 250
See also AMWS 7; BPFB 3; CA 145;
CANR 65, 110; CN 6, 7; CPW 1; DA3;
DAM POP; DLB 335; MAL 5; MTCW 2;
MTFW 2005; SSFS 18, 23
Proulx, Edna Annie
See Proulx, E. Annie
Proust, (Valentin-Louis-George-Eugene)
Marcel 1871-1922 ..... SSC 75; TCLC 7,
13, 33, 220; WLC 5
See also AAYA 58; BPFB 3; CA 104; 120;
CANR 110; DA; DA3; DAB; DAC; DAM
MST, NOV; DLB 65; EW 8; EWL 3; GFL
1789 to the Present; MTCW 1, 2; MTFW
2005; RGWL 2, 3; TWA
Prowler, Harley
See Masters, Edgar Lee
Prudentius, Aurelius Clemens 348-c.
405 .... CMLC 78
See also EW 1; RGWL 2, 3

Prudhomme, Rene Francois Armand
1839-1907
See Sully Prudhomme, Rene-Francois-Armand

Prus, Boleslaw 1845-1912 .... **TCLC 48**
See also RGWL 2, 3

Prynne, William 1600-1669 .... **LC 148**

Prynne, Xavier
See Hardwick, Elizabeth

Pryor, Aaron Richard
See Pryor, Richard

Pryor, Richard 1940-2005 .... **CLC 26**
See also CA 122; 152; 246

Pryor, Richard Franklin Lenox Thomas
See Pryor, Richard

Przybyszewski, Stanislaw
1868-1927 .... **TCLC 36**
See also CA 160; DLB 66; EWL 3

Pseudo-Dionysius the Areopagite fl. c. 5th
cent. - .... **CMLC 89**
See also DLB 115

Pteleon
See Grieve, C(hristopher) M(urray)

Puckett, Lute
See Masters, Edgar Lee

Puig, Manuel 1932-1990 .... **CLC 3, 5, 10, 28, 65, 133; HLC 2**
See also BPFB 3; CA 45-48; CANR 2, 32, 63; CDWLB 3; DA3; DAM MULT; DLB 113; DNFS 1; EWL 3; GLL 1; HW 1, 2; LAW; MTCW 1, 2; MTFW 2005; RGWL 2, 3; TWA; WLIT 1

Pulitzer, Joseph 1847-1911 .... **TCLC 76**
See also CA 114; DLB 23

Pullman, Philip 1946- .... **CLC 245**
See also AAYA 15, 41; BRWS 13; BYA 8, 13; CA 127; CANR 50, 77, 105, 134; CLR 20, 62, 84; JRDA; MAICYA 1, 2; MAICYAS 1; MTFW 2005; SAAS 17; SATA 65, 103, 150, 198; SUFW 2; WYAS 1; YAW

Purchas, Samuel 1577(?)-1626 .... **LC 70**
See also DLB 151

Purdy, A(lfred) W(ellington)
1918-2000 .... **CLC 3, 6, 14, 50**
See also CA 81-84; 189; CAAS 17; CANR 42, 66; CP 1, 2, 3, 4, 5, 6, 7; DAC; DAM MST, POET; DLB 88; PFS 5; RGEL 2

Purdy, James 1923-2009 .... **CLC 2, 4, 10, 28, 52**
See also AMWS 7; CA 33-36R; CAAS 1; CANR 19, 51, 132; CN 1, 2, 3, 4, 5, 6, 7; DLB 2, 218; EWL 3; INT CANR-19; MAL 5; MTCW 1; RGAL 4

Purdy, James Amos
See Purdy, James

Pure, Simon
See Swinnerton, Frank Arthur

Pushkin, Aleksandr Sergeevich
See Pushkin, Alexander (Sergeyevich)

Pushkin, Alexander (Sergeyevich)
1799-1837 .... **NCLC 3, 27, 83; PC 10; SSC 27, 55, 99; WLC 5**
See also DA; DA3; DAB; DAC; DAM DRAM, MST, POET; DLB 205; EW 5; EXPS; PFS 28; RGSF 2; RGWL 2, 3; SATA 61; SSFS 9; TWA

P'u Sung-ling 1640-1715 .... **LC 49; SSC 31**

Putnam, Arthur Lee
See Alger, Horatio, Jr.

Puttenham, George 1529(?)-1590 ...... **LC 116**
See also DLB 281

Puzo, Mario 1920-1999 .... **CLC 1, 2, 6, 36, 107**
See also BPFB 3; CA 65-68; 185; CANR 4, 42, 65, 99, 131; CN 1, 2, 3, 4, 5, 6; CPW; DA3; DAM NOV, POP; DLB 6; MTCW 1, 2; MTFW 2005; NFS 16; RGAL 4

Pygge, Edward
See Barnes, Julian

Pyle, Ernest Taylor 1900-1945 .... **TCLC 75**
See also CA 115; 160; DLB 29; MTCW 2

Pyle, Ernie
See Pyle, Ernest Taylor

Pyle, Howard 1853-1911 .... **TCLC 81**
See also AAYA 57; BYA 2, 4; CA 109; 137; CLR 22, 117; DLB 42, 188; DLBD 13; LAIT 1; MAICYA 1, 2; SATA 16, 100; WCH; YAW

Pym, Barbara (Mary Crampton)
1913-1980 .... **CLC 13, 19, 37, 111**
See also BPFB 3; BRWS 2; CA 13-14; 97-100; CANR 13, 34; CAP 1; DLB 14, 207; DLBY 1987; EWL 3; MTCW 1, 2; MTFW 2005; RGEL 2; TEA

Pynchon, Thomas 1937- .. **CLC 2, 3, 6, 9, 11, 18, 33, 62, 72, 123, 192, 213; SSC 14, 84; WLC 5**
See also AMWS 2; BEST 90:2; BPFB 3; CA 17-20R; CANR 22, 46, 73, 142; CN 1, 2, 3, 4, 5, 6, 7; CPW 1; DA; DA3; DAB; DAC; DAM MST, NOV, POP; DLB 2, 173; EWL 3; MAL 5; MTCW 1, 2; MTFW 2005; NFS 23; RGAL 4; SFW 4; TCLE 1:2; TUS

Pythagoras c. 582B.C.-c. 507B.C. . **CMLC 22**
See also DLB 176

Q
See Quiller-Couch, Sir Arthur (Thomas)

Qian, Chongzhu
See Ch'ien, Chung-shu

Qian, Sima 145B.C.-c. 89B.C. .... **CMLC 72**

Qian Zhongshu
See Ch'ien, Chung-shu

Qroll
See Dagerman, Stig (Halvard)

Quarles, Francis 1592-1644 .... **LC 117**
See also DLB 126; RGEL 2

Quarrington, Paul 1953- .... **CLC 65**
See also CA 129; CANR 62, 95

Quarrington, Paul Lewis
See Quarrington, Paul

Quasimodo, Salvatore 1901-1968 .... **CLC 10; PC 47**
See also CA 13-16; 25-28R; CAP 1; DLB 114, 332; EW 12; EWL 3; MTCW 1; RGWL 2, 3

Quatermass, Martin
See Carpenter, John (Howard)

Quay, Stephen 1947- .... **CLC 95**
See also CA 189

Quay, Timothy 1947- .... **CLC 95**
See also CA 189

Queen, Ellery
See Dannay, Frederic; Hoch, Edward D.; Lee, Manfred B.; Marlowe, Stephen; Sturgeon, Theodore (Hamilton); Vance, Jack

Queneau, Raymond 1903-1976 ..... **CLC 2, 5, 10, 42**
See also CA 77-80; 69-72; CANR 32; DLB 72, 258; EW 12; EWL 3; GFL 1789 to the Present; MTCW 1, 2; RGWL 2, 3

Quevedo, Francisco de 1580-1645 ...... **LC 23, 160**

Quiller-Couch, Sir Arthur (Thomas)
1863-1944 .... **TCLC 53**
See also CA 118; 166; DLB 135, 153, 190; HGG; RGEL 2; SUFW 1

Quin, Ann 1936-1973 .... **CLC 6**
See also CA 9-12R; 45-48; CANR 148; CN 1; DLB 14, 231

Quin, Ann Marie
See Quin, Ann

Quincey, Thomas de
See De Quincey, Thomas

Quindlen, Anna 1953- .... **CLC 191**
See also AAYA 35; AMWS 17; CA 138; CANR 73, 126; DA3; DLB 292; MTCW 2; MTFW 2005

Quinn, Martin
See Smith, Martin Cruz

Quinn, Peter 1947- .... **CLC 91**
See also CA 197; CANR 147

Quinn, Peter A.
See Quinn, Peter

Quinn, Simon
See Smith, Martin Cruz

Quintana, Leroy V. 1944- ...... **HLC 2; PC 36**
See also CA 131; CANR 65, 139; DAM MULT; DLB 82; HW 1, 2

Quintilian c. 40-c. 100 .... **CMLC 77**
See also AW 2; DLB 211; RGWL 2, 3

Quiroga, Horacio (Sylvestre)
1878-1937 ... **HLC 2; SSC 89; TCLC 20**
See also CA 117; 131; DAM MULT; EWL 3; HW 1; LAW; MTCW 1; RGSF 2; WLIT 1

Quoirez, Francoise 1935-2004 ... **CLC 3, 6, 9, 17, 36**
See also CA 49-52; 231; CANR 6, 39, 73; CWW 2; DLB 83; EWL 3; GFL 1789 to the Present; MTCW 1, 2; MTFW 2005; TWA

Raabe, Wilhelm (Karl) 1831-1910 . **TCLC 45**
See also CA 167; DLB 129

Rabe, David (William) 1940- .. **CLC 4, 8, 33, 200; DC 16**
See also CA 85-88; CABS 3; CAD; CANR 59, 129; CD 5, 6; DAM DRAM; DFS 3, 8, 13; DLB 7, 228; EWL 3; MAL 5

Rabelais, Francois 1494-1553 .... **LC 5, 60; WLC 5**
See also DA; DAB; DAC; DAM MST; DLB 327; EW 2; GFL Beginnings to 1789; LMFS 1; RGWL 2, 3; TWA

Rabi'a al-'Adawiyya c. 717-c.
801 .... **CMLC 83**
See also DLB 311

Rabinovitch, Sholem 1859-1916 .... **SSC 33; TCLC 1, 35**
See also CA 104; DLB 333; TWA

Rabinovitsh, Sholem Yankev
See Rabinovitch, Sholem

Rabinowitz, Sholem Yakov
See Rabinovitch, Sholem

Rabinowitz, Solomon
See Rabinovitch, Sholem

Rabinyan, Dorit 1972- .... **CLC 119**
See also CA 170; CANR 147

Rachilde
See Vallette, Marguerite Eymery; Vallette, Marguerite Eymery

Racine, Jean 1639-1699 .. **DC 32; LC 28, 113**
See also DA3; DAB; DAM MST; DLB 268; EW 3; GFL Beginnings to 1789; LMFS 1; RGWL 2, 3; TWA

Radcliffe, Ann (Ward) 1764-1823 ... **NCLC 6, 55, 106**
See also DLB 39, 178; GL 3; HGG; LMFS 1; RGEL 2; SUFW; WLIT 3

Radclyffe-Hall, Marguerite
See Hall, Radclyffe

Radiguet, Raymond 1903-1923 ...... **TCLC 29**
See also CA 162; DLB 65; EWL 3; GFL 1789 to the Present; RGWL 2, 3

Radishchev, Aleksandr Nikolaevich
1749-1802 .... **NCLC 190**
See also DLB 150

Radishchev, Alexander
See Radishchev, Aleksandr Nikolaevich

Radnoti, Miklos 1909-1944 .... **TCLC 16**
See also CA 118; 212; CDWLB 4; DLB 215; EWL 3; RGHL; RGWL 2, 3

Remington, Frederic S(ackrider)
1861-1909 .... **TCLC 89**
See also CA 108; 169; DLB 12, 186, 188;
SATA 41; TCWW 2
Remizov, A.
See Remizov, Aleksei (Mikhailovich)
Remizov, A. M.
See Remizov, Aleksei (Mikhailovich)
Remizov, Aleksei (Mikhailovich)
1877-1957 .... **TCLC 27**
See also CA 125; 133; DLB 295; EWL 3
Remizov, Alexey Mikhaylovich
See Remizov, Aleksei (Mikhailovich)
Renan, Joseph Ernest 1823-1892 . **NCLC 26, 145**
See also GFL 1789 to the Present
Renard, Jules(-Pierre) 1864-1910 .. **TCLC 17**
See also CA 117; 202; GFL 1789 to the
Present
Renart, Jean fl. 13th cent. - .... **CMLC 83**
Renault, Mary
See Challans, Mary
Rendell, Ruth 1930- .... **CLC 28, 48, 50**
See also BEST 90:4; BPFB 3; BRWS 9;
CA 109; CANR 32, 52, 74, 127, 162; CN
5, 6, 7; CPW; DAM POP; DLB 87, 276;
INT CANR-32; MSW; MTCW 1, 2;
MTFW 2005
Rendell, Ruth Barbara
See Rendell, Ruth
Renoir, Jean 1894-1979 .... **CLC 20**
See also CA 129; 85-88
Rensie, Willis
See Eisner, Will
Resnais, Alain 1922- .... **CLC 16**
Revard, Carter 1931- .... **NNAL**
See also CA 144; CANR 81, 153; PFS 5
Reverdy, Pierre 1889-1960 .... **CLC 53**
See also CA 97-100; 89-92; DLB 258; EWL
3; GFL 1789 to the Present
Reverend Mandju
See Su, Chien
Rexroth, Kenneth 1905-1982 .... **CLC 1, 2, 6, 11, 22, 49, 112; PC 20, 95**
See also BG 1:3; CA 5-8R; 107; CANR 14,
34, 63; CDALB 1941-1968; CP 1, 2, 3;
DAM POET; DLB 16, 48, 165, 212;
DLBY 1982; EWL 3; INT CANR-14;
MAL 5; MTCW 1, 2; MTFW 2005;
RGAL 4
Reyes, Alfonso 1889-1959 .... **HLCS 2; TCLC 33**
See also CA 131; EWL 3; HW 1; LAW
Reyes y Basoalto, Ricardo Eliecer Neftali
See Neruda, Pablo
Reymont, Wladyslaw (Stanislaw)
1868(?)-1925 .... **TCLC 5**
See also CA 104; DLB 332; EWL 3
Reynolds, John Hamilton
1794-1852 .... **NCLC 146**
See also DLB 96
Reynolds, Jonathan 1942- .... **CLC 6, 38**
See also CA 65-68; CANR 28, 176
Reynolds, Joshua 1723-1792 .... **LC 15**
See also DLB 104
Reynolds, Michael S(hane)
1937-2000 .... **CLC 44**
See also CA 65-68; 189; CANR 9, 89, 97
Reza, Yasmina 1959- .... **DC 34**
See also AAYA 69; CA 171; CANR 145;
DFS 19; DLB 321
Reznikoff, Charles 1894-1976 .... **CLC 9**
See also AMWS 14; CA 33-36; 61-64; CAP
2; CP 1, 2; DLB 28, 45; RGHL; WP
Rezzori, Gregor von
See Rezzori d'Arezzo, Gregor von
Rezzori d'Arezzo, Gregor von
1914-1998 .... **CLC 25**
See also CA 122; 136; 167

Rhine, Richard
See Silverstein, Alvin; Silverstein, Virginia
B(arbara Opshelor)
Rhodes, Eugene Manlove
1869-1934 .... **TCLC 53**
See also CA 198; DLB 256; TCWW 1, 2
R'hoone, Lord
See Balzac, Honore de
Rhys, Jean 1890-1979 .... **CLC 2, 4, 6, 14, 19, 51, 124; SSC 21, 76**
See also BRWS 2; CA 25-28R; 85-88;
CANR 35, 62; CDBLB 1945-1960; CD-
WLB 3; CN 1, 2; DA3; DAM NOV; DLB
36, 117, 162; DNFS 2; EWL 3; LATS 1:1;
MTCW 1, 2; MTFW 2005; NFS 19;
RGEL 2; RHW; TEA; WWE 1
Ribeiro, Darcy 1922-1997 .... **CLC 34**
See also CA 33-36R; 156; EWL 3
Ribeiro, Joao Ubaldo (Osorio Pimentel)
1941- .... **CLC 10, 67**
See also CA 81-84; CWW 2; EWL 3
Ribman, Ronald (Burt) 1932- .... **CLC 7**
See also CA 21-24R; CAD; CANR 46, 80;
CD 5, 6
Ricci, Nino 1959- .... **CLC 70**
See also CA 137; CANR 130; CCA 1
Ricci, Nino Pio
See Ricci, Nino
Rice, Anne 1941- .... **CLC 41, 128**
See also AAYA 9, 53; AMWS 7; BEST
89:2; BPFB 3; CA 65-68; CANR 12, 36,
53, 74, 100, 133; CN 6, 7; CPW; CSW;
DA3; DAM POP; DLB 292; GL 3; GLL
2; HGG; MTCW 2; MTFW 2005; SUFW
2; YAW
Rice, Elmer (Leopold) 1892-1967 ...... **CLC 7, 49**
See also CA 21-22; 25-28R; CAP 2; DAM
DRAM; DFS 12; DLB 4, 7; EWL 3;
IDTP; MAL 5; MTCW 1, 2; RGAL 4
Rice, Tim(othy Miles Bindon)
1944- .... **CLC 21**
See also CA 103; CANR 46; DFS 7
Rich, Adrienne 1929- ..... **CLC 3, 6, 7, 11, 18, 36, 73, 76, 125; PC 5**
See also AAYA 69; AMWR 2; AMWS 1;
CA 9-12R; CANR 20, 53, 74, 128;
CDALBS; CP 1, 2, 3, 4, 5, 6, 7; CSW;
CWP; DA3; DAM POET; DLB 5, 67;
EWL 3; EXPP; FL 1:6; FW; MAL 5;
MBL; MTCW 1, 2; MTFW 2005; PAB;
PFS 15, 29; RGAL 4; RGHL; WP
Rich, Barbara
See Graves, Robert
Rich, Robert
See Trumbo, Dalton
Richard, Keith
See Richards, Keith
Richards, David Adams 1950- .... **CLC 59**
See also CA 93-96; CANR 60, 110, 156;
CN 7; DAC; DLB 53; TCLE 1:2
Richards, I(vor) A(rmstrong)
1893-1979 .... **CLC 14, 24**
See also BRWS 2; CA 41-44R; 89-92;
CANR 34, 74; CP 1, 2; DLB 27; EWL 3;
MTCW 2; RGEL 2
Richards, Keith 1943- .... **CLC 17**
See also CA 107; CANR 77
Richardson, Anne
See Roiphe, Anne
Richardson, Dorothy Miller
1873-1957 .... **TCLC 3, 203**
See also BRWS 13; CA 104; 192; DLB 36;
EWL 3; FW; RGEL 2
**Richardson (Robertson), Ethel Florence
Lindesay** 1870-1946 .... **TCLC 4**
See also CA 105; 190; DLB 197, 230; EWL
3; RGEL 2; RGSF 2; RHW

Richardson, Henrietta
See Richardson (Robertson), Ethel Florence
Lindesay
Richardson, Henry Handel
See Richardson (Robertson), Ethel Florence
Lindesay
Richardson, John 1796-1852 .... **NCLC 55**
See also CCA 1; DAC; DLB 99
Richardson, Samuel 1689-1761 ...... **LC 1, 44, 138; WLC 5**
See also BRW 3; CDBLB 1660-1789; DA;
DAB; DAC; DAM MST, NOV; DLB 39;
RGEL 2; TEA; WLIT 3
Richardson, Willis 1889-1977 .... **HR 1:3**
See also BW 1; CA 124; DLB 51; SATA 60
Richler, Mordecai 1931-2001 .... **CLC 3, 5, 9, 13, 18, 46, 70, 185, 271**
See also AITN 1; CA 65-68; 201; CANR
31, 62, 111; CCA 1; CLR 17; CN 1, 2, 3,
4, 5, 7; DAC; DAM MST, NOV;
DLB 53; EWL 3; MAICYA 1, 2; MTCW
1, 2; MTFW 2005; RGEL 2; RGHL;
SATA 44, 98; SATA-Brief 27; TWA
Richter, Conrad (Michael)
1890-1968 .... **CLC 30**
See also AAYA 21; AMWS 18; BYA 2; CA
5-8R; 25-28R; CANR 23; DLB 9, 212;
LAIT 1; MAL 5; MTCW 1, 2; MTFW
2005; RGAL 4; SATA 3; TCWW 1, 2;
TUS; YAW
Ricostranza, Tom
See Ellis, Trey
Riddell, Charlotte 1832-1906 .... **TCLC 40**
See also CA 165; DLB 156; HGG; SUFW
Riddell, Mrs. J. H.
See Riddell, Charlotte
Ridge, John Rollin 1827-1867 ...... **NCLC 82; NNAL**
See also CA 144; DAM MULT; DLB 175
Ridgeway, Jason
See Marlowe, Stephen
Ridgway, Keith 1965- .... **CLC 119**
See also CA 172; CANR 144
Riding, Laura
See Jackson, Laura (Riding)
Riefenstahl, Berta Helene Amalia
1902-2003 .... **CLC 16, 190**
See also CA 108; 220
Riefenstahl, Leni
See Riefenstahl, Berta Helene Amalia
Riffe, Ernest
See Bergman, Ingmar
Riffe, Ernest Ingmar
See Bergman, Ingmar
Riggs, (Rolla) Lynn
1899-1954 .... **NNAL; TCLC 56**
See also CA 144; DAM MULT; DLB 175
Riis, Jacob A(ugust) 1849-1914 ..... **TCLC 80**
See also CA 113; 168; DLB 23
Rikki
See Ducornet, Erica
Riley, James Whitcomb 1849-1916 .... **PC 48; TCLC 51**
See also CA 118; 137; DAM POET; MAI-
CYA 1, 2; RGAL 4; SATA 17
Riley, Tex
See Creasey, John
Rilke, Rainer Maria 1875-1926 .... **PC 2; TCLC 1, 6, 19, 195**
See also CA 104; 132; CANR 62, 99; CD-
WLB 2; DA3; DAM POET; DLB 81; EW
9; EWL 3; MTCW 1, 2; MTFW 2005;
PFS 19, 27; RGWL 2, 3; TWA; WP
Rimbaud, (Jean Nicolas) Arthur
1854-1891 ... **NCLC 4, 35, 82; PC 3, 57; WLC 5**
See also DA; DA3; DAB; DAC; DAM
MST, POET; DLB 217; EW 7; GFL 1789
to the Present; LMFS 2; PFS 28; RGWL
2, 3; TWA; WP

EWL 3; EXPN; LAIT 4; MAICYA 1, 2;
MAL 5; MTCW 1, 2; MTFW 2005; NFS
1; RGAL 4; RGSF 2; SATA 67; SSFS 17;
TUS; WYA; YAW

Salisbury, John
See Caute, (John) David

Sallust c. 86B.C.-35B.C. .... **CMLC 68**
See also AW 2; CDWLB 1; DLB 211;
RGWL 2, 3

Salter, James 1925- .... **CLC 7, 52, 59, 275;
SSC 58**
See also AMWS 9; CA 73-76; CANR 107,
160; DLB 130; SSFS 25

Saltus, Edgar (Everton) 1855-1921 . **TCLC 8**
See also CA 105; DLB 202; RGAL 4

Saltykov, Mikhail Evgrafovich
1826-1889 .... **NCLC 16**
See also DLB 238.

Saltykov-Shchedrin, N.
See Saltykov, Mikhail Evgrafovich

Samarakis, Andonis
See Samarakis, Antonis

Samarakis, Antonis 1919-2003 .... **CLC 5**
See also CA 25-28R; 224; CAAS 16; CANR
36; EWL 3

Samigli, E.
See Schmitz, Aron Hector

Sanchez, Florencio 1875-1910 .... **TCLC 37**
See also CA 153; DLB 305; EWL 3; HW 1;
LAW

Sanchez, Luis Rafael 1936- .... **CLC 23**
See also CA 128; DLB 305; EWL 3; HW 1;
WLIT 1

Sanchez, Sonia 1934- . **BLC 1:3, 2:3; CLC 5,
116, 215; PC 9**
See also BW 2, 3; CA 33-36R; CANR 24,
49, 74, 115; CLR 18; CP 2, 3, 4, 5, 6, 7;
CSW; CWP; DA3; DAM MULT; DLB 41;
DLBD 8; EWL 3; MAICYA 1, 2; MAL 5;
MTCW 1, 2; MTFW 2005; PFS 26; SATA
22, 136; WP

Sancho, Ignatius 1729-1780 .... **LC 84**

Sand, George 1804-1876 .... **DC 29; NCLC 2,
42, 57, 174; WLC 5**
See also DA; DA3; DAB; DAC; DAM
MST, NOV; DLB 119, 192; EW 6; FL 1:3;
FW; GFL 1789 to the Present; RGWL 2,
3; TWA

Sandburg, Carl (August) 1878-1967 . **CLC 1,
4, 10, 15, 35; PC 2, 41; WLC 5**
See also AAYA 24; AMW; BYA 1, 3; CA
5-8R; 25-28R; CANR 35; CDALB 1865-
1917; CLR 67; DA; DA3; DAB; DAC;
DAM MST, POET; DLB 17, 54, 284;
EWL 3; EXPP; LAIT 2; MAICYA 1, 2;
MAL 5; MTCW 1, 2; MTFW 2005; PAB;
PFS 3, 6, 12; RGAL 4; SATA 8; TUS;
WCH; WP; WYA

Sandburg, Charles
See Sandburg, Carl (August)

Sandburg, Charles A.
See Sandburg, Carl (August)

Sanders, (James) Ed(ward) 1939- .... **CLC 53**
See also BG 1:3; CA 13-16R; CAAS 21;
CANR 13, 44, 78; CP 1, 2, 3, 4, 5, 6, 7;
DAM POET; DLB 16, 244

Sanders, Edward
See Sanders, (James) Ed(ward)

Sanders, Lawrence 1920-1998 .... **CLC 41**
See also BEST 89:4; BPFB 3; CA 81-84;
165; CANR 33, 62; CMW 4; CPW; DA3;
DAM POP; MTCW 1

Sanders, Noah
See Blount, Roy, Jr.

Sanders, Winston P.
See Anderson, Poul

Sandoz, Mari(e Susette) 1900-1966 .. **CLC 28**
See also CA 1-4R; 25-28R; CANR 17, 64;
DLB 9, 212; LAIT 2; MTCW 1, 2; SATA
5; TCWW 1, 2

Sandys, George 1578-1644 .... **LC 80**
See also DLB 24, 121

Saner, Reg(inald Anthony) 1931- .... **CLC 9**
See also CA 65-68; CP 3, 4, 5, 6, 7

Sankara 788-820 .... **CMLC 32**

Sannazaro, Jacopo 1456(?)-1530 .... **LC 8**
See also RGWL 2, 3; WLIT 7

Sansom, William 1912-1976 . **CLC 2, 6; SSC
21**
See also CA 5-8R; 65-68; CANR 42; CN 1,
2; DAM NOV; DLB 139; EWL 3; MTCW
1; RGEL 2; RGSF 2

Santayana, George 1863-1952 .... **TCLC 40**
See also AMW; CA 115; 194; DLB 54, 71,
246, 270; DLBD 13; EWL 3; MAL 5;
RGAL 4; TUS

Santiago, Danny
See James, Daniel (Lewis)

**Santillana, Inigo Lopez de Mendoza,
Marques de** 1398-1458 .... **LC 111**
See also DLB 286

Santmyer, Helen Hooven
1895-1986 .... **CLC 33; TCLC 133**
See also CA 1-4R; 118; CANR 15, 33;
DLBY 1984; MTCW 1; RHW

Santoka, Taneda 1882-1940 .... **TCLC 72**

Santos, Bienvenido N(uqui)
1911-1996 ... **AAL; CLC 22; TCLC 156**
See also CA 101; 151; CANR 19, 46; CP 1;
DAM MULT; DLB 312, 348; EWL;
RGAL 4; SSFS 19

Santos, Miguel
See Mihura, Miguel

Sapir, Edward 1884-1939 .... **TCLC 108**
See also CA 211; DLB 92

Sapper
See McNeile, Herman Cyril

Sapphire 1950- .... **CLC 99**
See also CA 262

Sapphire, Brenda
See Sapphire

Sappho fl. 6th cent. B.C.- ... **CMLC 3, 67; PC
5**
See also CDWLB 1; DA3; DAM POET;
DLB 176; FL 1:1; PFS 20; RGWL 2, 3;
WLIT 8; WP

Saramago, Jose 1922- .... **CLC 119, 275;
HLCS 1**
See also CA 153; CANR 96, 164; CWW 2;
DLB 287, 332; EWL 3; LATS 1:2; NFS
27; SSFS 23

Sarduy, Severo 1937-1993 .... **CLC 6, 97;
HLCS 2; TCLC 167**
See also CA 89-92; 142; CANR 58, 81;
CWW 2; DLB 113; EWL 3; HW 1, 2;
LAW

Sargeson, Frank 1903-1982 ..... **CLC 31; SSC
99**
See also CA 25-28R; 106; CANR 38, 79;
CN 1, 2, 3; EWL 3; GLL 2; RGEL 2;
RGSF 2; SSFS 20

Sarmiento, Domingo Faustino
1811-1888 .... **HLCS 2; NCLC 123**
See also LAW; WLIT 1

Sarmiento, Felix Ruben Garcia
See Dario, Ruben

Saro-Wiwa, Ken(ule Beeson)
1941-1995 .... **CLC 114; TCLC 200**
See also BW 2; CA 142; 150; CANR 60;
DLB 157

Saroyan, William 1908-1981 ... **CLC 1, 8, 10,
29, 34, 56; DC 28; SSC 21; TCLC 137;
WLC 5**
See also AAYA 66; CA 5-8R; 103; CAD;
CANR 30; CDALBS; CN 1, 2; DA; DA3;
DAB; DAC; DAM DRAM, MST, NOV;

DFS 17; DLB 7, 9, 86; DLBY 1981; EWL
3; LAIT 4; MAL 5; MTCW 1, 2; MTFW
2005; RGAL 4; RGSF 2; SATA 23; SATA-
Obit 24; SSFS 14; TUS

Sarraute, Nathalie 1900-1999 .... **CLC 1, 2, 4,
8, 10, 31, 80; TCLC 145**
See also BPFB 3; CA 9-12R; 187; CANR
23, 66, 134; CWW 2; DLB 83, 321; EW
12; EWL 3; GFL 1789 to the Present;
MTCW 1, 2; MTFW 2005; RGWL 2, 3

Sarton, May 1912-1995 ... **CLC 4, 14, 49, 91;
PC 39; TCLC 120**
See also AMWS 8; CA 1-4R; 149; CANR
1, 34, 55, 116; CN 1, 2, 3, 4, 5, 6; CP 1,
2, 3, 4, 5, 6; DAM POET; DLB 48; DLBY
1981; EWL 3; FW; INT CANR-34; MAL
5; MTCW 1, 2; MTFW 2005; RGAL 4;
SATA 36; SATA-Obit 86; TUS

Sartre, Jean-Paul 1905-1980 . **CLC 1, 4, 7, 9,
13, 18, 24, 44, 50, 52; DC 3; SSC 32;
WLC 5**
See also AAYA 62; CA 9-12R; 97-100;
CANR 21; DA; DA3; DAB; DAC; DAM
DRAM, MST, NOV; DFS 5, 26; DLB 72,
296, 321, 332; EW 12; EWL 3; GFL 1789
to the Present; LMFS 2; MTCW 1, 2;
MTFW 2005; NFS 21; RGHL; RGSF 2;
RGWL 2, 3; SSFS 9; TWA

Sassoon, Siegfried (Lorraine)
1886-1967 .... **CLC 36, 130; PC 12**
See also BRW 6; CA 104; 25-28R; CANR
36; DAB; DAM MST, NOV, POET; DLB
20, 191; DLBD 18; EWL 3; MTCW 1, 2;
MTFW 2005; PAB; PFS 28; RGEL 2;
TEA

Satterfield, Charles
See Pohl, Frederik

Satyremont
See Peret, Benjamin

Saul, John III
See Saul, John

Saul, John 1942- .... **CLC 46**
See also AAYA 10, 62; BEST 90:4; CA 81-
84; CANR 16, 40, 81, 176; CPW; DAM
NOV, POP; HGG; SATA 98

Saul, John W.
See Saul, John

Saul, John W. III
See Saul, John

Saul, John Woodruff III
See Saul, John

Saunders, Caleb
See Heinlein, Robert A.

Saura (Atares), Carlos 1932-1998 .... **CLC 20**
See also CA 114; 131; CANR 79; HW 1

Sauser, Frederic Louis
See Sauser-Hall, Frederic

Sauser-Hall, Frederic 1887-1961 ..... **CLC 18,
106**
See also CA 102; 93-96; CANR 36, 62;
DLB 258; EWL 3; GFL 1789 to the
Present; MTCW 1; WP

Saussure, Ferdinand de
1857-1913 .... **TCLC 49**
See also DLB 242

Savage, Catharine
See Brosman, Catharine Savage

Savage, Richard 1697(?)-1743 .... **LC 96**
See also DLB 95; RGEL 2

Savage, Thomas 1915-2003 .... **CLC 40**
See also CA 126; 132; 218; CAAS 15; CN
6, 7; INT CA-132; SATA-Obit 147;
TCWW 2

Savan, Glenn 1953-2003 .... **CLC 50**
See also CA 225

Savonarola, Girolamo 1452-1498 ...... **LC 152**
See also LMFS 1

Sax, Robert
See Johnson, Robert

Saxo Grammaticus c. 1150-c.
1222 .... **CMLC 58**
Saxton, Robert
See Johnson, Robert
Sayers, Dorothy L(eigh) 1893-1957 . **SSC 71;**
TCLC 2, 15
See also BPFB 3; BRWS 3; CA 104; 119;
CANR 60; CDBLB 1914-1945; CMW 4;
DAM POP; DLB 10, 36, 77, 100; MSW;
MTCW 1, 2; MTFW 2005; RGEL 2;
SSFS 12; TEA
Sayers, Valerie 1952- .... **CLC 50, 122**
See also CA 134; CANR 61; CSW
Sayles, John (Thomas) 1950- .... **CLC 7, 10,**
14, 198
See also CA 57-60; CANR 41, 84; DLB 44
Scamander, Newt
See Rowling, J.K.
Scammell, Michael 1935- .... **CLC 34**
See also CA 156
Scannel, John Vernon
See Scannell, Vernon
Scannell, Vernon 1922-2007 .... **CLC 49**
See also CA 5-8R; 266; CANR 8, 24, 57,
143; CN 1, 2; CP 1, 2, 3, 4, 5, 6, 7; CWRI
5; DLB 27; SATA 59; SATA-Obit 188
Scarlett, Susan
See Streatfeild, Noel
Scarron 1847-1910
See Mikszath, Kalman
Scarron, Paul 1610-1660 .... **LC 116**
See also GFL Beginnings to 1789; RGWL
2, 3
Schaeffer, Susan Fromberg 1941- ..... **CLC 6,**
11, 22
See also CA 49-52; CANR 18, 65, 160; CN
4, 5, 6, 7; DLB 28, 299; MTCW 1, 2;
MTFW 2005; SATA 22
Schama, Simon 1945- .... **CLC 150**
See also BEST 89:4; CA 105; CANR 39,
91, 168
Schama, Simon Michael
See Schama, Simon
Schary, Jill
See Robinson, Jill
Schell, Jonathan 1943- .... **CLC 35**
See also CA 73-76; CANR 12, 117, 187
Schelling, Friedrich Wilhelm Joseph von
1775-1854 .... **NCLC 30**
See also DLB 90
Scherer, Jean-Marie Maurice
1920- .... **CLC 16**
See also CA 110
Schevill, James (Erwin) 1920- .... **CLC 7**
See also CA 5-8R; CAAS 12; CAD; CD 5,
6; CP 1, 2, 3, 4, 5
Schiller, Friedrich von 1759-1805 ...... **DC 12;**
NCLC 39, 69, 166
See also CDWLB 2; DAM DRAM; DLB
94; EW 5; RGWL 2, 3; TWA
Schisgal, Murray (Joseph) 1926- .... **CLC 6**
See also CA 21-24R; CAD; CANR 48, 86;
CD 5, 6; MAL 5
Schlee, Ann 1934- .... **CLC 35**
See also CA 101; CANR 29, 88; SATA 44;
SATA-Brief 36
Schlegel, August Wilhelm von
1767-1845 .... **NCLC 15, 142**
See also DLB 94; RGWL 2, 3
Schlegel, Friedrich 1772-1829 .... **NCLC 45**
See also DLB 90; EW 5; RGWL 2, 3; TWA
Schlegel, Johann Elias (von)
1719(?)-1749 .... **LC 5**
Schleiermacher, Friedrich
1768-1834 .... **NCLC 107**
See also DLB 90

Schlesinger, Arthur M., Jr.
1917-2007 .... **CLC 84**
See Schlesinger, Arthur Meier
See also AITN 1; CA 1-4R; 257; CANR 1,
28, 58, 105, 187; DLB 17; INT CANR-
28; MTCW 1, 2; SATA 61; SATA-Obit
181
Schlink, Bernhard 1944- .... **CLC 174**
See also CA 163; CANR 116, 175; RGHL
Schmidt, Arno (Otto) 1914-1979 ...... **CLC 56**
See also CA 128; 109; DLB 69; EWL 3
Schmitz, Aron Hector 1861-1928 ..... **SSC 25;**
TCLC 2, 35
See also CA 104; 122; DLB 264; EW 8;
EWL 3; MTCW 1; RGWL 2, 3; WLIT 7
Schnackenberg, Gjertrud 1953- ...... **CLC 40;**
PC 45
See also AMWS 15; CA 116; CANR 100;
CP 5, 6, 7; CWP; DLB 120, 282; PFS 13,
25
Schnackenberg, Gjertrud Cecelia
See Schnackenberg, Gjertrud
Schneider, Leonard Alfred
1925-1966 .... **CLC 21**
See also CA 89-92
Schnitzler, Arthur 1862-1931 ..... **DC 17; SSC**
15, 61; TCLC 4
See also CA 104; CDWLB 2; DLB 81, 118;
EW 8; EWL 3; RGSF 2; RGWL 2, 3
Schoenberg, Arnold Franz Walter
1874-1951 .... **TCLC 75**
See also CA 109; 188
Schonberg, Arnold
See Schoenberg, Arnold Franz Walter
Schopenhauer, Arthur 1788-1860 . **NCLC 51,**
157
See also DLB 90; EW 5
Schor, Sandra (M.) 1932(?)-1990 ..... **CLC 65**
See also CA 132
Schorer, Mark 1908-1977 .... **CLC 9**
See also CA 5-8R; 73-76; CANR 7; CN 1,
2; DLB 103
Schrader, Paul (Joseph) 1946- . **CLC 26, 212**
See also CA 37-40R; CANR 41; DLB 44
Schreber, Daniel 1842-1911 .... **TCLC 123**
Schreiner, Olive (Emilie Albertina)
1855-1920 .... **TCLC 9**
See also AFW; BRWS 2; CA 105; 154;
DLB 18, 156, 190, 225; EWL 3; FW;
RGEL 2; TWA; WLIT 2; WWE 1
Schulberg, Budd 1914- .... **CLC 7, 48**
See also AMWS 18; BPFB 3; CA 25-28R;
CANR 19, 87, 178; CN 1, 2, 3, 4, 5, 6, 7;
DLB 6, 26, 28; DLBY 1981, 2001; MAL
5
Schulberg, Budd Wilson
See Schulberg, Budd
Schulman, Arnold
See Trumbo, Dalton
Schulz, Bruno 1892-1942 .. **SSC 13; TCLC 5,**
51
See also CA 115; 123; CANR 86; CDWLB
4; DLB 215; EWL 3; MTCW 2; MTFW
2005; RGSF 2; RGWL 2, 3
Schulz, Charles M. 1922-2000 .... **CLC 12**
See also AAYA 39; CA 9-12R; 187; CANR
6, 132; INT CANR-6; MTFW 2005;
SATA 10; SATA-Obit 118
Schulz, Charles Monroe
See Schulz, Charles M.
Schumacher, E(rnst) F(riedrich)
1911-1977 .... **CLC 80**
See also CA 81-84; 73-76; CANR 34, 85
Schumann, Robert 1810-1856 ...... **NCLC 143**
Schuyler, George Samuel 1895-1977 . **HR 1:3**
See also BW 2; CA 81-84; 73-76; CANR
42; DLB 29, 51

Schuyler, James Marcus 1923-1991 .. **CLC 5,**
23; PC 88
See also CA 101; 134; CP 1, 2, 3, 4, 5;
DAM POET; DLB 5, 169; EWL 3; INT
CA-101; MAL 5; WP
Schwartz, Delmore (David)
1913-1966 . **CLC 2, 4, 10, 45, 87; PC 8;**
SSC 105
See also AMWS 2; CA 17-18; 25-28R;
CANR 35; CAP 2; DLB 28, 48; EWL 3;
MAL 5; MTCW 1, 2; MTFW 2005; PAB;
RGAL 4; TUS
Schwartz, Ernst
See Ozu, Yasujiro
Schwartz, John Burnham 1965- .... **CLC 59**
See also CA 132; CANR 116, 188
Schwartz, Lynne Sharon 1939- .... **CLC 31**
See also CA 103; CANR 44, 89, 160; DLB
218; MTCW 2; MTFW 2005
Schwartz, Muriel A.
See Eliot, T(homas) S(tearns)
Schwarz-Bart, Andre 1928-2006 .... **CLC 2, 4**
See also CA 89-92; 253; CANR 109; DLB
299; RGHL
Schwarz-Bart, Simone 1938- . **BLCS; CLC 7**
See also BW 2; CA 97-100; CANR 117;
EWL 3
Schwerner, Armand 1927-1999 .... **PC 42**
See also CA 9-12R; 179; CANR 50, 85; CP
2, 3, 4, 5, 6; DLB 165
Schwitters, Kurt (Hermann Edward Karl
Julius) 1887-1948 .... **TCLC 95**
See also CA 158
Schwob, Marcel (Mayer Andre)
1867-1905 .... **TCLC 20**
See also CA 117; 168; DLB 123; GFL 1789
to the Present
Sciascia, Leonardo 1921-1989 .. **CLC 8, 9, 41**
See also CA 85-88; 130; CANR 35; DLB
177; EWL 3; MTCW 1; RGWL 2, 3
Scoppettone, Sandra 1936- .... **CLC 26**
See also AAYA 11, 65; BYA 8; CA 5-8R;
CANR 41, 73, 157; GLL 1; MAICYA 2;
MAICYAS 1; SATA 9, 92; WYA; YAW
Scorsese, Martin 1942- .... **CLC 20, 89, 207**
See also AAYA 38; CA 110; 114; CANR
46, 85
Scotland, Jay
See Jakes, John
Scott, Duncan Campbell
1862-1947 .... **TCLC 6**
See also CA 104; 153; DAC; DLB 92;
RGEL 2
Scott, Evelyn 1893-1963 .... **CLC 43**
See also CA 104; 112; CANR 64; DLB 9,
48; RHW
Scott, F(rancis) R(eginald)
1899-1985 .... **CLC 22**
See also CA 101; 114; CANR 87; CP 1, 2,
3, 4; DLB 88; INT CA-101; RGEL 2
Scott, Frank
See Scott, F(rancis) R(eginald)
Scott, Joan .... **CLC 65**
Scott, Joanna 1960- .... **CLC 50**
See also AMWS 17; CA 126; CANR 53,
92, 168
Scott, Joanna Jeanne
See Scott, Joanna
Scott, Paul (Mark) 1920-1978 ...... **CLC 9, 60**
See also BRWS 1; CA 81-84; 77-80; CANR
33; CN 1, 2; DLB 14, 207, 326; EWL 3;
MTCW 1; RGEL 2; RHW; WWE 1
Scott, Ridley 1937- .... **CLC 183**
See also AAYA 13, 43
Scott, Sarah 1723-1795 .... **LC 44**
See also DLB 39

DLB 6, 28, 52, 278, 332, 333; DLBY
1991; EWL 3; EXPS; HGG; JRDA; LAIT
3; MAICYA 1, 2; MAL 5; MTCW 1, 2;
MTFW 2005; RGAL 4; RGHL; RGSF 2;
SATA 3, 27; SATA-Obit 68; SSFS 2, 12,
16, 27; TUS; TWA

Singer, Israel Joshua 1893-1944 .... **TCLC 33**
See also CA 169; DLB 333; EWL 3

Singh, Khushwant 1915- .... **CLC 11**
See also CA 9-12R; CAAS 9; CANR 6, 84;
CN 1, 2, 3, 4, 5, 6, 7; DLB 323; EWL 3;
RGEL 2

Singleton, Ann
See Benedict, Ruth

Singleton, John 1968(?)- .... **CLC 156**
See also AAYA 50; BW 2, 3; CA 138;
CANR 67, 82; DAM MULT

Siniavskii, Andrei
See Sinyavsky, Andrei (Donatevich)

Sinibaldi, Fosco
See Kacew, Romain

Sinjohn, John
See Galsworthy, John

Sinyavsky, Andrei (Donatevich)
1925-1997 .... **CLC 8**
See also CA 85-88; 159; CWW 2; EWL 3;
RGSF 2

Sinyavsky, Andrey Donatovich
See Sinyavsky, Andrei (Donatevich)

Sirin, V.
See Nabokov, Vladimir (Vladimirovich)

Sissman, L(ouis) E(dward)
1928-1976 .... **CLC 9, 18**
See also CA 21-24R; 65-68; CANR 13; CP
2; DLB 5

Sisson, C(harles) H(ubert)
1914-2003 .... **CLC 8**
See also BRWS 11; CA 1-4R; 220; CAAS
3; CANR 3, 48, 84; CP 1, 2, 3, 4, 5, 6, 7;
DLB 27

Sitting Bull 1831(?)-1890 .... **NNAL**
See also DA3; DAM MULT

Sitwell, Dame Edith 1887-1964 ..... **CLC 2, 9,
67; PC 3**
See also BRW 7; CA 9-12R; CANR 35;
CDBLB 1945-1960; DAM POET; DLB
20; EWL 3; MTCW 1, 2; MTFW 2005;
RGEL 2; TEA

Siwaarmill, H. P.
See Sharp, William

Sjoewall, Maj 1935- .... **CLC 7**
See also BPFB 3; CA 65-68; CANR 73;
CMW 4; MSW

Sjowall, Maj
See Sjoewall, Maj

Skelton, John 1460(?)-1529 ..... **LC 71; PC 25**
See also BRW 1; DLB 136; RGEL 2

Skelton, Robin 1925-1997 .... **CLC 13**
See also AITN 2; CA 5-8R; 160; CAAS 5;
CANR 28, 89; CCA 1; CP 1, 2, 3, 4, 5, 6;
DLB 27, 53

Skolimowski, Jerzy 1938- .... **CLC 20**
See also CA 128

Skram, Amalie (Bertha)
1847-1905 .... **TCLC 25**
See also CA 165

Skvorecky, Josef 1924- . **CLC 15, 39, 69, 152**
See also CA 61-64; CAAS 1; CANR 10,
34, 63, 108; CDWLB 4; CWW 2; DA3;
DAC; DAM NOV; DLB 232; EWL 3;
MTCW 1, 2; MTFW 2005

Slade, Bernard 1930-
See Newbound, Bernard Slade

Slaughter, Carolyn 1946- .... **CLC 56**
See also CA 85-88; CANR 85, 169; CN 5,
6, 7

Slaughter, Frank G(ill) 1908-2001 ... **CLC 29**
See also AITN 2; CA 5-8R; 197; CANR 5,
85; INT CANR-5; RHW

Slavitt, David R. 1935- .... **CLC 5, 14**
See also CA 21-24R; CAAS 3; CANR 41,
83, 166; CN 1, 2; CP 1, 2, 3, 4, 5, 6, 7;
DLB 5, 6

Slavitt, David Rytman
See Slavitt, David R.

Slesinger, Tess 1905-1945 .... **TCLC 10**
See also CA 107; 199; DLB 102

Slessor, Kenneth 1901-1971 .... **CLC 14**
See also CA 102; 89-92; DLB 260; RGEL
2

Slowacki, Juliusz 1809-1849 .... **NCLC 15**
See also RGWL 3

Smart, Christopher 1722-1771 .... **LC 3, 134;
PC 13**
See also DAM POET; DLB 109; RGEL 2

Smart, Elizabeth 1913-1986 .... **CLC 54**
See also CA 81-84; 118; CN 4; DLB 88

Smiley, Jane 1949- ...... **CLC 53, 76, 144, 236**
See also AAYA 66; AMWS 6; BPFB 3; CA
104; CANR 30, 50, 74, 96, 158; CN 6, 7;
CPW 1; DA3; DAM POP; DLB 227, 234;
EWL 3; INT CANR-30; MAL 5; MTFW
2005; SSFS 19

Smiley, Jane Graves
See Smiley, Jane

Smith, A(rthur) J(ames) M(arshall)
1902-1980 .... **CLC 15**
See also CA 1-4R; 102; CANR 4; CP 1, 2,
3; DAC; DLB 88; RGEL 2

Smith, Adam 1723(?)-1790 .... **LC 36**
See also DLB 104, 252, 336; RGEL 2

Smith, Alexander 1829-1867 .... **NCLC 59**
See also DLB 32, 55

Smith, Alexander McCall 1948- ..... **CLC 268**
See also CA 215; CANR 154; SATA 73,
179

Smith, Anna Deavere 1950- ...... **CLC 86, 241**
See also CA 133; CANR 103; CD 5, 6; DFS
2, 22; DLB 341

Smith, Betty (Wehner) 1904-1972 .... **CLC 19**
See also AAYA 72; BPFB 3; BYA 3; CA
5-8R; 33-36R; DLBY 1982; LAIT 3;
RGAL 4; SATA 6

Smith, Charlotte (Turner)
1749-1806 .... **NCLC 23, 115**
See also DLB 39, 109; RGEL 2; TEA

Smith, Clark Ashton 1893-1961 .... **CLC 43**
See also AAYA 76; CA 143; CANR 81;
FANT; HGG; MTCW 2; SCFW 1, 2; SFW
4; SUFW

Smith, Dave
See Smith, David (Jeddie)

Smith, David (Jeddie) 1942- .... **CLC 22, 42**
See also CA 49-52; CAAS 7; CANR 1, 59,
120; CP 3, 4, 5, 6, 7; CSW; DAM POET;
DLB 5

Smith, Iain Crichton 1928-1998 .... **CLC 64**
See also BRWS 9; CA 21-24R; 171; CN 1,
2, 3, 4, 5, 6; CP 1, 2, 3, 4, 5, 6; DLB 40,
139, 319; RGSF 2

Smith, John 1580(?)-1631 .... **LC 9**
See also DLB 24, 30; TUS

Smith, Johnston
See Crane, Stephen (Townley)

Smith, Joseph, Jr. 1805-1844 .... **NCLC 53**

Smith, Kevin 1970- .... **CLC 223**
See also AAYA 37; CA 166; CANR 131

Smith, Lee 1944- .... **CLC 25, 73, 258**
See also CA 114; 119; CANR 46, 118, 173;
CN 7; CSW; DLB 143; DLBY 1983;
EWL 3; INT CA-119; RGAL 4

Smith, Martin
See Smith, Martin Cruz

Smith, Martin Cruz 1942- .. **CLC 25; NNAL**
See Smith, Martin Cruz
See also BEST 89:4; BPFB 3; CA 85-88;
CANR 6, 23, 43, 65, 119, 184; CMW 4;
CPW; DAM MULT, POP; HGG; INT
CANR-23; MTCW 2; MTFW 2005;
RGAL 4

Smith, Patti 1946- .... **CLC 12**
See also CA 93-96; CANR 63, 168

Smith, Pauline (Urmson)
1882-1959 .... **TCLC 25**
See also DLB 225; EWL 3

Smith, R. Alexander McCall
See Smith, Alexander McCall

Smith, Rosamond
See Oates, Joyce Carol

Smith, Seba 1792-1868 .... **NCLC 187**
See also DLB 1, 11, 243

Smith, Sheila Kaye
See Kaye-Smith, Sheila

Smith, Stevie 1902-1971 .... **CLC 3, 8, 25, 44;
PC 12**
See also BRWS 2; CA 17-18; 29-32R;
CANR 35; CAP 2; CP 1; DAM POET;
DLB 20; EWL 3; MTCW 1, 2; PAB; PFS
3; RGEL 2; TEA

Smith, Wilbur 1933- .... **CLC 33**
See also CA 13-16R; CANR 7, 46, 66, 134,
180; CPW; MTCW 1, 2; MTFW 2005

Smith, Wilbur Addison
See Smith, Wilbur

Smith, William Jay 1918- .... **CLC 6**
See also AMWS 13; CA 5-8R; CANR 44,
106; CP 1, 2, 3, 4, 5, 6, 7; CSW; CWRI
5; DLB 5; MAICYA 1, 2; SAAS 22;
SATA 2, 68, 154; SATA-Essay 154; TCLE
1:2

Smith, Woodrow Wilson
See Kuttner, Henry

Smith, Zadie 1975- .... **CLC 158**
See also AAYA 50; CA 193; DLB 347;
MTFW 2005

Smolenskin, Peretz 1842-1885 .... **NCLC 30**

Smollett, Tobias (George) 1721-1771 ... **LC 2,
46**
See also BRW 3; CDBLB 1660-1789; DLB
39, 104; RGEL 2; TEA

Snodgrass, Quentin Curtius
See Twain, Mark

Snodgrass, Thomas Jefferson
See Twain, Mark

Snodgrass, W. D. 1926-2009 .... **CLC 2, 6, 10,
18, 68; PC 74**
See also AMWS 6; CA 1-4R; CANR 6, 36,
65, 85, 185; CP 1, 2, 3, 4, 5, 6, 7; DAM
POET; DLB 5; MAL 5; MTCW 1, 2;
MTFW 2005; PFS 29; RGAL 4; TCLE
1:2

Snodgrass, William De Witt
See Snodgrass, W. D.

Snorri Sturluson 1179-1241 .... **CMLC 56**
See also RGWL 2, 3

Snow, C(harles) P(ercy) 1905-1980 ... **CLC 1,
4, 6, 9, 13, 19**
See also BRW 7; CA 5-8R; 101; CANR 28;
CDBLB 1945-1960; CN 1, 2; DAM NOV;
DLB 15, 77; DLBD 17; EWL 3; MTCW
1, 2; MTFW 2005; RGEL 2; TEA

Snow, Frances Compton
See Adams, Henry (Brooks)

Snyder, Gary 1930- . **CLC 1, 2, 5, 9, 32, 120;
PC 21**
See also AAYA 72; AMWS 8; ANW; BG
1:3; CA 17-20R; CANR 30, 60, 125; CP
1, 2, 3, 4, 5, 6, 7; DA3; DAM POET; DLB
5, 16, 165, 212, 237, 275, 342; EWL 3;
MAL 5; MTCW 2; MTFW 2005; PFS 9,
19; RGAL 4; WP

Stuart, Don A.
See Campbell, John W(ood, Jr.)

Stuart, Ian
See MacLean, Alistair (Stuart)

Stuart, Jesse (Hilton) 1906-1984 ... **CLC 1, 8, 11, 14, 34; SSC 31**
See also CA 5-8R; 112; CANR 31; CN 1, 2, 3; DLB 9, 48, 102; DLBY 1984; SATA 2; SATA-Obit 36

Stubblefield, Sally
See Trumbo, Dalton

Sturgeon, Theodore (Hamilton)
1918-1985 .... **CLC 22, 39**
See also AAYA 51; BPFB 3; BYA 9, 10; CA 81-84; 116; CANR 32, 103; DLB 8; DLBY 1985; HGG; MTCW 1, 2; MTFW 2005; SCFW; SFW 4; SUFW

Sturges, Preston 1898-1959 .... **TCLC 48**
See also CA 114; 149; DLB 26

Styron, William 1925-2006 .. **CLC 1, 3, 5, 11, 15, 60, 232, 244; SSC 25**
See also AMW; AMWC 2; BEST 90:4; BPFB 3; CA 5-8R; 255; CANR 6, 33, 74, 126; CDALB 1968-1988; CN 1, 2, 3, 4, 5, 6, 7; CPW; CSW; DA3; DAM NOV, POP; DLB 2, 143, 299; DLBY 1980; EWL 3; INT CANR-6; LAIT 2; MAL 5; MTCW 1, 2; MTFW 2005; NCFS 1; NFS 22; RGAL 4; RGHL; RHW; TUS

Styron, William Clark
See Styron, William

Su, Chien 1884-1918 .... **TCLC 24**
See also CA 123; EWL 3

Suarez Lynch, B.
See Bioy Casares, Adolfo; Borges, Jorge Luis

Suassuna, Ariano Vilar 1927- .... **HLCS 1**
See also CA 178; DLB 307; HW 2; LAW

Suckert, Kurt Erich
See Malaparte, Curzio

Suckling, Sir John 1609-1642 . **LC 75; PC 30**
See also BRW 2; DAM POET; DLB 58, 126; EXPP; PAB; RGEL 2

Suckow, Ruth 1892-1960 .... **SSC 18**
See also CA 193; 113; DLB 9, 102; RGAL 4; TCWW 2

Sudermann, Hermann 1857-1928 .. **TCLC 15**
See also CA 107; 201; DLB 118

Sue, Eugene 1804-1857 .... **NCLC 1**
See also DLB 119

Sueskind, Patrick 1949- .... **CLC 182**
See Suskind, Patrick
See also BPFB 3; CA 145; CWW 2

Suetonius c. 70-c. 130 .... **CMLC 60**
See also AW 2; DLB 211; RGWL 2, 3; WLIT 8

Su Hsuan-ying
See Su, Chien

Su Hsuean-ying
See Su, Chien

Sukenick, Ronald 1932-2004 ..... **CLC 3, 4, 6, 48**
See also CA 25-28R; 209; 229; CAAE 209; CAAS 8; CANR 32, 89; CN 3, 4, 5, 6, 7; DLB 173; DLBY 1981

Suknaski, Andrew 1942- .... **CLC 19**
See also CA 101; CP 3, 4, 5, 6, 7; DLB 53

Sullivan, Vernon
See Vian, Boris

Sully Prudhomme, Rene-Francois-Armand
1839-1907 .... **TCLC 31**
See also CA 170; DLB 332; GFL 1789 to the Present

Su Man-shu
See Su, Chien

Sumarokov, Aleksandr Petrovich
1717-1777 .... **LC 104**
See also DLB 150

Summerforest, Ivy B.
See Kirkup, James

Summers, Andrew James
See Summers, Andy

Summers, Andy 1942- .... **CLC 26**
See also CA 255

Summers, Hollis (Spurgeon, Jr.)
1916- .... **CLC 10**
See also CA 5-8R; CANR 3; CN 1, 2, 3; CP 1, 2, 3, 4; DLB 6; TCLE 1:2

Summers, (Alphonsus Joseph-Mary Augustus) Montague
1880-1948 .... **TCLC 16**
See also CA 118; 163

Sumner, Gordon Matthew
See Sting

Sun Tzu c. 400B.C.-c. 320B.C. ...... **CMLC 56**

Surdas c. 1478-c. 1583 .... **LC 163**
See also RGWL 2, 3

Surrey, Henry Howard 1517-1574 ... **LC 121; PC 59**
See also BRW 1; RGEL 2

Surtees, Robert Smith 1805-1864 .. **NCLC 14**
See also DLB 21; RGEL 2

Susann, Jacqueline 1921-1974 .... **CLC 3**
See also AITN 1; BPFB 3; CA 65-68; 53-56; MTCW 1, 2

Su Shi
See Su Shih

Su Shih 1036-1101 .... **CMLC 15**
See also RGWL 2, 3

Suskind, Patrick .... **CLC 182**
See Sueskind, Patrick
See also BPFB 3; CA 145; CWW 2

Suso, Heinrich c. 1295-1366 .... **CMLC 87**

Sutcliff, Rosemary 1920-1992 .... **CLC 26**
See also AAYA 10; BYA 1, 4; CA 5-8R; 139; CANR 37; CLR 1, 37, 138; CPW; DAB; DAC; DAM MST, POP; JRDA; LATS 1:1; MAICYA 1, 2; MAICYAS 1; RHW; SATA 6, 44, 78; SATA-Obit 73; WYA; YAW

Sutherland, Efua (Theodora Morgue)
1924-1996 .... **BLC 2:3**
See also AFW; BW 1; CA 105; CWD; DLB 117; EWL 3; IDTP; SATA 25

Sutro, Alfred 1863-1933 .... **TCLC 6**
See also CA 105; 185; DLB 10; RGEL 2

Sutton, Henry
See Slavitt, David R.

Su Yuan-ying
See Su, Chien

Su Yuean-ying
See Su, Chien

Suzuki, D. T.
See Suzuki, Daisetz Teitaro

Suzuki, Daisetz T.
See Suzuki, Daisetz Teitaro

Suzuki, Daisetz Teitaro
1870-1966 .... **TCLC 109**
See also CA 121; 111; MTCW 1, 2; MTFW 2005

Suzuki, Teitaro
See Suzuki, Daisetz Teitaro

Svareff, Count Vladimir
See Crowley, Edward Alexander

Svevo, Italo
See Schmitz, Aron Hector

Swados, Elizabeth 1951- .... **CLC 12**
See also CA 97-100; CANR 49, 163; INT CA-97-100

Swados, Elizabeth A.
See Swados, Elizabeth

Swados, Harvey 1920-1972 .... **CLC 5**
See also CA 5-8R; 37-40R; CANR 6; CN 1; DLB 2, 335; MAL 5

Swados, Liz
See Swados, Elizabeth

Swan, Gladys 1934- .... **CLC 69**
See also CA 101; CANR 17, 39; TCLE 1:2

Swanson, Logan
See Matheson, Richard

Swarthout, Glendon (Fred)
1918-1992 .... **CLC 35**
See also AAYA 55; CA 1-4R; 139; CANR 1, 47; CN 1, 2, 3, 4, 5; LAIT 5; NFS 29; SATA 26; TCWW 1, 2; YAW

Swedenborg, Emanuel 1688-1772 ..... **LC 105**

Sweet, Sarah C.
See Jewett, (Theodora) Sarah Orne

Swenson, May 1919-1989 ...... **CLC 4, 14, 61, 106; PC 14**
See also AMWS 4; CA 5-8R; 130; CANR 36, 61, 131; CP 1, 2, 3, 4; DA; DAB; DAC; DAM MST, POET; DLB 5; EXPP; GLL 2; MAL 5; MTCW 1, 2; MTFW 2005; PFS 16, 30; SATA 15; WP

Swift, Augustus
See Lovecraft, H. P.

Swift, Graham 1949- .... **CLC 41, 88, 233**
See also BRWC 2; BRWS 5; CA 117; 122; CANR 46, 71, 128, 181; CN 4, 5, 6, 7; DLB 194, 326; MTCW 2; MTFW 2005; NFS 18; RGSF 2

Swift, Jonathan 1667-1745 ..... **LC 1, 42, 101; PC 9; WLC 6**
See also AAYA 41; BRW 3; BRWC 1; BRWR 1; BYA 5, 14; CDBLB 1660-1789; CLR 53; DA; DA3; DAB; DAC; DAM MST, NOV, POET; DLB 39, 95, 101; EXPN; LAIT 1; NFS 6; PFS 27; RGEL 2; SATA 19; TEA; WCH; WLIT 3

Swinburne, Algernon Charles
1837-1909 ... **PC 24; TCLC 8, 36; WLC 6**
See also BRW 5; CA 105; 140; CDBLB 1832-1890; DA; DA3; DAB; DAC; DAM MST, POET; DLB 35, 57; PAB; RGEL 2; TEA

Swinfen, Ann .... **CLC 34**
See also CA 202

Swinnerton, Frank (Arthur)
1884-1982 .... **CLC 31**
See also CA 202; 108; CN 1, 2, 3; DLB 34

Swinnerton, Frank Arthur
1884-1982 .... **CLC 31**
See also CA 108; DLB 34

Swithen, John
See King, Stephen

Sylvia
See Ashton-Warner, Sylvia (Constance)

Symmes, Robert Edward
See Duncan, Robert

Symonds, John Addington
1840-1893 .... **NCLC 34**
See also BRWS 14; DLB 57, 144

Symons, Arthur 1865-1945 .... **TCLC 11**
See also BRWS 14; CA 107; 189; DLB 19, 57, 149; RGEL 2

Symons, Julian (Gustave)
1912-1994 .... **CLC 2, 14, 32**
See also CA 49-52; 147; CAAS 3; CANR 3, 33, 59; CMW 4; CN 1, 2, 3, 4, 5; CP 1, 3, 4; DLB 87, 155; DLBY 1992; MSW; MTCW 1

Synge, (Edmund) J(ohn) M(illington)
1871-1909 .... **DC 2; TCLC 6, 37**
See also BRW 6; BRWR 1; CA 104; 141; CDBLB 1890-1914; DAM DRAM; DFS 18; DLB 10, 19; EWL 3; RGEL 2; TEA; WLIT 4

Syruc, J.
See Milosz, Czeslaw

Szirtes, George 1948- .... **CLC 46; PC 51**
See also CA 109; CANR 27, 61, 117; CP 4, 5, 6, 7

Szymborska, Wislawa 1923- ... **CLC 99, 190; PC 44**
See also AAYA 76; CA 154; CANR 91, 133, 181; CDWLB 4; CWP; CWW 2; DA3; DLB 232, 332; DLBY 1996; EWL 3; MTCW 2; MTFW 2005; PFS 15, 27; RGHL; RGWL 3

T. O., Nik
See Annensky, Innokenty (Fyodorovich)

Tabori, George 1914-2007 .... **CLC 19**
See also CA 49-52; 262; CANR 4, 69; CBD; CD 5, 6; DLB 245; RGHL

Tacitus c. 55-c. 117 .... **CMLC 56**
See also AW 2; CDWLB 1; DLB 211; RGWL 2, 3; WLIT 8

Tadjo, Veronique 1955- .... **BLC 2:3**
See also EWL 3

Tagore, Rabindranath 1861-1941 .... **PC 8; SSC 48; TCLC 3, 53**
See also CA 104; 120; DA3; DAM DRAM, POET; DFS 26; DLB 323, 332; EWL 3; MTCW 1, 2; MTFW 2005; PFS 18; RGEL 2; RGSF 2; RGWL 2, 3; TWA

Taine, Hippolyte Adolphe 1828-1893 .... **NCLC 15**
See also EW 7; GFL 1789 to the Present

Talayesva, Don C. 1890-(?) .... **NNAL**

Talese, Gay 1932- .... **CLC 37, 232**
See also AITN 1; AMWS 17; CA 1-4R; CANR 9, 58, 137, 177; DLB 185; INT CANR-9; MTCW 1, 2; MTFW 2005

Tallent, Elizabeth 1954- .... **CLC 45**
See also CA 117; CANR 72; DLB 130

Tallmountain, Mary 1918-1997 .... **NNAL**
See also CA 146; 161; DLB 193

Tally, Ted 1952- .... **CLC 42**
See also CA 120; 124; CAD; CANR 125; CD 5, 6; INT CA-124

Talvik, Heiti 1904-1947 .... **TCLC 87**
See also EWL 3

Tamayo y Baus, Manuel 1829-1898 .... **NCLC 1**

Tammsaare, A(nton) H(ansen) 1878-1940 .... **TCLC 27**
See also CA 164; CDWLB 4; DLB 220; EWL 3

Tam'si, Tchicaya U
See Tchicaya, Gerald Felix

Tan, Amy 1952- ..... **AAL; CLC 59, 120, 151, 257**
See also AAYA 9, 48; AMWS 10; BEST 89:3; BPFB 3; CA 136; CANR 54, 105, 132; CDALBS; CN 6, 7; CPW 1; DA3; DAM MULT, NOV, POP; DLB 173, 312; EXPN; FL 1:6; FW; LAIT 3, 5; MAL 5; MTCW 2; MTFW 2005; NFS 1, 13, 16; RGAL 4; SATA 75; SSFS 9; YAW

Tandem, Carl Felix
See Spitteler, Carl

Tandem, Felix
See Spitteler, Carl

Tania B.
See Blixen, Karen (Christentze Dinesen)

Tanizaki, Jun'ichiro 1886-1965 ... **CLC 8, 14, 28; SSC 21**
See also CA 93-96; 25-28R; DLB 180; EWL 3; MJW; MTCW 2; MTFW 2005; RGSF 2; RGWL 2

Tanizaki Jun'ichiro
See Tanizaki, Jun'ichiro

Tannen, Deborah 1945- .... **CLC 206**
See also CA 118; CANR 95

Tannen, Deborah Frances
See Tannen, Deborah

Tanner, William
See Amis, Kingsley

Tante, Dilly
See Kunitz, Stanley

Tao Lao
See Storni, Alfonsina

Tapahonso, Luci 1953- .... **NNAL; PC 65**
See also CA 145; CANR 72, 127; DLB 175

Tarantino, Quentin (Jerome) 1963- .... **CLC 125, 230**
See also AAYA 58; CA 171; CANR 125

Tarassoff, Lev
See Troyat, Henri

Tarbell, Ida M(inerva) 1857-1944 . **TCLC 40**
See also CA 122; 181; DLB 47

Tarchetti, Ugo 1839(?)-1869 .... **SSC 119**

Tardieu d'Esclavelles, Louise-Florence-Petronille
See Epinay, Louise d'

Tarkington, (Newton) Booth 1869-1946 .... **TCLC 9**
See also BPFB 3; BYA 3; CA 110; 143; CWRI 5; DLB 9, 102; MAL 5; MTCW 2; RGAL 4; SATA 17

Tarkovskii, Andrei Arsen'evich
See Tarkovsky, Andrei (Arsenyevich)

Tarkovsky, Andrei (Arsenyevich) 1932-1986 .... **CLC 75**
See also CA 127

Tartt, Donna 1964(?)- .... **CLC 76**
See also AAYA 56; CA 142; CANR 135; MTFW 2005

Tasso, Torquato 1544-1595 .... **LC 5, 94**
See also EFS 2; EW 2; RGWL 2, 3; WLIT 7

Tate, (John Orley) Allen 1899-1979 .. **CLC 2, 4, 6, 9, 11, 14, 24; PC 50**
See also AMW; CA 5-8R; 85-88; CANR 32, 108; CN 1, 2; CP 1, 2; DLB 4, 45, 63; DLBD 17; EWL 3; MAL 5; MTCW 1, 2; MTFW 2005; RGAL 4; RHW

Tate, Ellalice
See Hibbert, Eleanor Alice Burford

Tate, James (Vincent) 1943- ..... **CLC 2, 6, 25**
See also CA 21-24R; CANR 29, 57, 114; CP 1, 2, 3, 4, 5, 6, 7; DLB 5, 169; EWL 3; PFS 10, 15; RGAL 4; WP

Tate, Nahum 1652(?)-1715 .... **LC 109**
See also DLB 80; RGEL 2

Tauler, Johannes c. 1300-1361 ...... **CMLC 37**
See also DLB 179; LMFS 1

Tavel, Ronald 1936-2009 .... **CLC 6**
See also CA 21-24R; CAD; CANR 33; CD 5, 6

Taviani, Paolo 1931- .... **CLC 70**
See also CA 153

Taylor, Bayard 1825-1878 .... **NCLC 89**
See also DLB 3, 189, 250, 254; RGAL 4

Taylor, C(ecil) P(hilip) 1929-1981 .... **CLC 27**
See also CA 25-28R; 105; CANR 47; CBD

Taylor, Edward 1642(?)-1729 ..... **LC 11, 163; PC 63**
See also AMW; DA; DAB; DAC; DAM MST, POET; DLB 24; EXPP; RGAL 4; TUS

Taylor, Eleanor Ross 1920- .... **CLC 5**
See also CA 81-84; CANR 70

Taylor, Elizabeth 1912-1975 .... **CLC 2, 4, 29; SSC 100**
See also CA 13-16R; CANR 9, 70; CN 1, 2; DLB 139; MTCW 1; RGEL 2; SATA 13

Taylor, Frederick Winslow 1856-1915 .... **TCLC 76**
See also CA 188

Taylor, Henry 1942- .... **CLC 44**
See also CA 33-36R; CAAS 7; CANR 31, 178; CP 6, 7; DLB 5; PFS 10

Taylor, Henry Splawn
See Taylor, Henry

Taylor, Kamala 1924-2004 .... **CLC 8, 38**
See also BYA 13; CA 77-80; 227; CN 1, 2, 3, 4, 5, 6, 7; DLB 323; EWL 3; MTFW 2005; NFS 13

Taylor, Mildred D. 1943- .... **CLC 21**
See also AAYA 10, 47; BW 1; BYA 3, 8; CA 85-88; CANR 25, 115, 136; CLR 9, 59, 90; CSW; DLB 52; JRDA; LAIT 3; MAICYA 1, 2; MTFW 2005; SAAS 5; SATA 135; WYA; YAW

Taylor, Peter (Hillsman) 1917-1994 .. **CLC 1, 4, 18, 37, 44, 50, 71; SSC 10, 84**
See also AMWS 5; BPFB 3; CA 13-16R; 147; CANR 9, 50; CN 1, 2, 3, 4, 5; CSW; DLB 218, 278; DLBY 1981, 1994; EWL 3; EXPS; INT CANR-9; MAL 5; MTCW 1, 2; MTFW 2005; RGSF 2; SSFS 9; TUS

Taylor, Robert Lewis 1912-1998 .... **CLC 14**
See also CA 1-4R; 170; CANR 3, 64; CN 1, 2; SATA 10; TCWW 1, 2

Tchekhov, Anton
See Chekhov, Anton (Pavlovich)

Tchicaya, Gerald Felix 1931-1988 .. **CLC 101**
See also CA 129; 125; CANR 81; EWL 3

Tchicaya U Tam'si
See Tchicaya, Gerald Felix

Teasdale, Sara 1884-1933 .... **PC 31; TCLC 4**
See also CA 104; 163; DLB 45; GLL 1; PFS 14; RGAL 4; SATA 32; TUS

Tecumseh 1768-1813 .... **NNAL**
See also DAM MULT

Tegner, Esaias 1782-1846 .... **NCLC 2**

Teilhard de Chardin, (Marie Joseph) Pierre 1881-1955 .... **TCLC 9**
See also CA 105; 210; GFL 1789 to the Present

Temple, Ann
See Mortimer, Penelope (Ruth)

Tennant, Emma 1937- .... **CLC 13, 52**
See also BRWS 9; CA 65-68; CAAS 9; CANR 10, 38, 59, 88, 177; CN 3, 4, 5, 6, 7; DLB 14; EWL 3; SFW 4

Tenneshaw, S.M.
See Silverberg, Robert

Tenney, Tabitha Gilman 1762-1837 .... **NCLC 122**
See also DLB 37, 200

Tennyson, Alfred 1809-1892 ... **NCLC 30, 65, 115, 202; PC 6; WLC 6**
See also AAYA 50; BRW 4; CDBLB 1832-1890; DA; DA3; DAB; DAC; DAM MST, POET; DLB 32; EXPP; PAB; PFS 1, 2, 4, 11, 15, 19; RGEL 2; TEA; WLIT 4; WP

Teran, Lisa St. Aubin de
See St. Aubin de Teran, Lisa

Terence c. 184B.C.-c. 159B.C. ...... **CMLC 14; DC 7**
See also AW 1; CDWLB 1; DLB 211; RGWL 2, 3; TWA; WLIT 8

Teresa de Jesus, St. 1515-1582 .... **LC 18, 149**

Teresa of Avila, St.
See Teresa de Jesus, St.

Terkel, Louis
See Terkel, Studs

Terkel, Studs 1912-2008 .... **CLC 38**
See also AAYA 32; AITN 1; CA 57-60; 278; CANR 18, 45, 67, 132; DA3; MTCW 1, 2; MTFW 2005; TUS

Terkel, Studs Louis
See Terkel, Studs

Terry, C. V.
See Slaughter, Frank G(ill)

Terry, Megan 1932- .... **CLC 19; DC 13**
See also CA 77-80; CABS 3; CAD; CANR 43; CD 5, 6; CWD; DFS 18; DLB 7, 249; GLL 2

Tertullian c. 155-c. 245 .... **CMLC 29**

Tertz, Abram
See Sinyavsky, Andrei (Donatevich)

Wambaugh, Joseph Aloysius
See Wambaugh, Joseph, Jr.

Wang Wei 699(?)-761(?) . **CMLC 100; PC 18**
See also TWA

Warburton, William 1698-1779 .... **LC 97**
See also DLB 104

Ward, Arthur Henry Sarsfield
1883-1959 .... **TCLC 28**
See also CA 108; 173; CMW 4; DLB 70;
HGG; MSW; SUFW

Ward, Douglas Turner 1930- .... **CLC 19**
See also BW 1; CA 81-84; CAD; CANR
27; CD 5, 6; DLB 7, 38

Ward, E. D.
See Lucas, E(dward) V(errall)

Ward, Mrs. Humphry 1851-1920
See Ward, Mary Augusta
See also RGEL 2

Ward, Mary Augusta 1851-1920 ... **TCLC 55**
See Ward, Mrs. Humphry
See also DLB 18

Ward, Nathaniel 1578(?)-1652 .... **LC 114**
See also DLB 24

Ward, Peter
See Faust, Frederick (Schiller)

Warhol, Andy 1928(?)-1987 .... **CLC 20**
See also AAYA 12; BEST 89:4; CA 89-92;
121; CANR 34

Warner, Francis (Robert Le Plastrier)
1937- .... **CLC 14**
See also CA 53-56; CANR 11; CP 1, 2, 3, 4

Warner, Marina 1946- .... **CLC 59, 231**
See also CA 65-68; CANR 21, 55, 118; CN
5, 6, 7; DLB 194; MTFW 2005

Warner, Rex (Ernest) 1905-1986 ...... **CLC 45**
See also CA 89-92; 119; CN 1, 2, 3, 4; CP
1, 2, 3, 4; DLB 15; RGEL 2; RHW

Warner, Susan (Bogert)
1819-1885 .... **NCLC 31, 146**
See also AMWS 18; DLB 3, 42, 239, 250,
254

Warner, Sylvia (Constance) Ashton
See Ashton-Warner, Sylvia (Constance)

Warner, Sylvia Townsend
1893-1978 .. **CLC 7, 19; SSC 23; TCLC
131**
See also BRWS 7; CA 61-64; 77-80; CANR
16, 60, 104; CN 1, 2; DLB 34, 139; EWL
3; FANT; FW; MTCW 1, 2; RGEL 2;
RGSF 2; RHW

Warren, Mercy Otis 1728-1814 ..... **NCLC 13**
See also DLB 31, 200; RGAL 4; TUS

Warren, Robert Penn 1905-1989 .. **CLC 1, 4,
6, 8, 10, 13, 18, 39, 53, 59; PC 37; SSC
4, 58; WLC 6**
See also AITN 1; AMW; AMWC 2; BPFB
3; BYA 1; CA 13-16R; 129; CANR 10,
47; CDALB 1968-1988; CN 1, 2, 3, 4;
CP 1, 2, 3, 4; DA; DA3; DAB; DAC;
DAM MST, NOV, POET; DLB 2, 48, 152,
320; DLBY 1980, 1989; EWL 3; INT
CANR-10; MAL 5; MTCW 1, 2; MTFW
2005; NFS 13; RGAL 4; RGSF 2; RHW;
SATA 46; SATA-Obit 63; SSFS 8; TUS

Warrigal, Jack
See Furphy, Joseph

Warshofsky, Isaac
See Singer, Isaac Bashevis

Warton, Joseph 1722-1800 ... **LC 128; NCLC
118**
See also DLB 104, 109; RGEL 2

Warton, Thomas 1728-1790 .... **LC 15, 82**
See also DAM POET; DLB 104, 109, 336;
RGEL 2

Waruk, Kona
See Harris, (Theodore) Wilson

Warung, Price
See Astley, William

Warwick, Jarvis
See Garner, Hugh

Washington, Alex
See Harris, Mark

Washington, Booker T(aliaferro)
1856-1915 .... **BLC 1:3; TCLC 10**
See also BW 1; CA 114; 125; DA3; DAM
MULT; DLB 345; LAIT 2; RGAL 4;
SATA 28

Washington, George 1732-1799 .... **LC 25**
See also DLB 31

Wassermann, (Karl) Jakob
1873-1934 .... **TCLC 6**
See also CA 104; 163; DLB 66; EWL 3

Wasserstein, Wendy 1950-2006 . **CLC 32, 59,
90, 183; DC 4**
See also AAYA 73; AMWS 15; CA 121;
129; 247; CABS 3; CAD; CANR 53, 75,
128; CD 5, 6; CWD; DA3; DAM DRAM;
DFS 5, 17; DLB 228; EWL 3; FW; INT
CA-129; MAL 5; MTCW 2; MTFW 2005;
SATA 94; SATA-Obit 174

Waterhouse, Keith (Spencer) 1929- . **CLC 47**
See also BRWS 13; CA 5-8R; CANR 38,
67, 109; CBD; CD 5; CN 1, 2, 3, 4, 5, 6,
7; DLB 13, 15; MTCW 1, 2; MTFW 2005

Waters, Frank (Joseph) 1902-1995 .. **CLC 88**
See also CA 5-8R; 149; CAAS 13; CANR
3, 18, 63, 121; DLB 212; DLBY 1986;
RGAL 4; TCWW 1, 2

Waters, Mary C. .... **CLC 70**

Waters, Roger 1944- .... **CLC 35**

Watkins, Frances Ellen
See Harper, Frances Ellen Watkins

Watkins, Gerrold
See Malzberg, Barry N(athaniel)

Watkins, Gloria Jean
See hooks, bell

Watkins, Paul 1964- .... **CLC 55**
See also CA 132; CANR 62, 98

Watkins, Vernon Phillips
1906-1967 .... **CLC 43**
See also CA 9-10; 25-28R; CAP 1; DLB
20; EWL 3; RGEL 2

Watson, Irving S.
See Mencken, H(enry) L(ouis)

Watson, John H.
See Farmer, Philip Jose

Watson, Richard F.
See Silverberg, Robert

Watts, Ephraim
See Horne, Richard Henry Hengist

Watts, Isaac 1674-1748 .... **LC 98**
See also DLB 95; RGEL 2; SATA 52

Waugh, Auberon (Alexander)
1939-2001 .... **CLC 7**
See also CA 45-48; 192; CANR 6, 22, 92;
CN 1, 2, 3; DLB 14, 194

Waugh, Evelyn 1903-1966 ... **CLC 1, 3, 8, 13,
19, 27, 44, 107; SSC 41; WLC 6**
See also AAYA 78; BPFB 3; BRW 7; CA
85-88; 25-28R; CANR 22; CDBLB 1914-
1945; DA; DA3; DAB; DAC; DAM MST,
NOV, POP; DLB 15, 162, 195; EWL 3;
MTCW 1, 2; MTFW 2005; NFS 13, 17;
RGEL 2; RGSF 2; TEA; WLIT 4

Waugh, Evelyn Arthur St. John
See Waugh, Evelyn

Waugh, Harriet 1944- .... **CLC 6**
See also CA 85-88; CANR 22

Ways, C.R.
See Blount, Roy, Jr.

Waystaff, Simon
See Swift, Jonathan

Webb, Beatrice (Martha Potter)
1858-1943 .... **TCLC 22**
See also CA 117; 162; DLB 190; FW

Webb, Charles 1939- .... **CLC 7**
See also CA 25-28R; CANR 114, 188

Webb, Charles Richard
See Webb, Charles

Webb, Frank J. .... **NCLC 143**
See also DLB 50

Webb, James, Jr.
See Webb, James

Webb, James 1946- .... **CLC 22**
See also CA 81-84; CANR 156

Webb, James H.
See Webb, James

Webb, James Henry
See Webb, James

Webb, Mary Gladys (Meredith)
1881-1927 .... **TCLC 24**
See also CA 182; 123; DLB 34; FW; RGEL
2

Webb, Mrs. Sidney
See Webb, Beatrice (Martha Potter)

Webb, Phyllis 1927- .... **CLC 18**
See also CA 104; CANR 23; CCA 1; CP 1,
2, 3, 4, 5, 6, 7; CWP; DLB 53

Webb, Sidney (James) 1859-1947 .. **TCLC 22**
See also CA 117; 163; DLB 190

Webber, Andrew Lloyd
See Lloyd Webber, Andrew

Weber, Lenora Mattingly
1895-1971 .... **CLC 12**
See also CA 19-20; 29-32R; CAP 1; SATA
2; SATA-Obit 26

Weber, Max 1864-1920 .... **TCLC 69**
See also CA 109; 189; DLB 296

Webster, John 1580(?)-1634(?) ...... **DC 2; LC
33, 84, 124; WLC 6**
See also BRW 2; CDBLB Before 1660; DA;
DAB; DAC; DAM DRAM, MST; DFS
17, 19; DLB 58; IDTP; RGEL 2; WLIT 3

Webster, Noah 1758-1843 .... **NCLC 30**
See also DLB 1, 37, 42, 43, 73, 243

Wedekind, Benjamin Franklin
See Wedekind, Frank

Wedekind, Frank 1864-1918 .... **TCLC 7**
See also CA 104; 153; CANR 121, 122;
CDWLB 2; DAM DRAM; DLB 118; EW
8; EWL 3; LMFS 2; RGWL 2, 3

Wehr, Demaris .... **CLC 65**

Weidman, Jerome 1913-1998 .... **CLC 7**
See also AITN 2; CA 1-4R; 171; CAD;
CANR 1; CD 1, 2, 3, 4, 5; DLB 28

Weil, Simone (Adolphine)
1909-1943 .... **TCLC 23**
See also CA 117; 159; EW 12; EWL 3; FW;
GFL 1789 to the Present; MTCW 2

Weininger, Otto 1880-1903 .... **TCLC 84**

Weinstein, Nathan
See West, Nathanael

Weinstein, Nathan von Wallenstein
See West, Nathanael

Weir, Peter (Lindsay) 1944- .... **CLC 20**
See also CA 113; 123

Weiss, Peter (Ulrich) 1916-1982 .. **CLC 3, 15,
51; TCLC 152**
See also CA 45-48; 106; CANR 3; DAM
DRAM; DFS 3; DLB 69, 124; EWL 3;
RGHL; RGWL 2, 3

Weiss, Theodore (Russell)
1916-2003 .... **CLC 3, 8, 14**
See also CA 9-12R; 189; 216; CAAE 189;
CAAS 2; CANR 46, 94; CP 1, 2, 3, 4, 5,
6, 7; DLB 5; TCLE 1:2

Welch, (Maurice) Denton
1915-1948 .... **TCLC 22**
See also BRWS 8, 9; CA 121; 148; RGEL
2

Welch, James (Phillip) 1940-2003 ..... **CLC 6,
14, 52, 249; NNAL; PC 62**
See also CA 85-88; 219; CANR 42, 66, 107;
CN 5, 6, 7; CP 2, 3, 4, 5, 6, 7; CPW;
DAM MULT, POP; DLB 175, 256; LATS
1:1; NFS 23; RGAL 4; TCWW 1, 2

Weldon, Fay 1931- . **CLC 6, 9, 11, 19, 36, 59, 122**
See also BRWS 4; CA 21-24R; CANR 16, 46, 63, 97, 137; CDBLB 1960 to Present; CN 3, 4, 5, 6, 7; CPW; DAM POP; DLB 14, 194, 319; EWL 3; FW; HGG; INT CANR-16; MTCW 1, 2; MTFW 2005; RGEL 2; RGSF 2

Wellek, Rene 1903-1995 .... **CLC 28**
See also CA 5-8R; 150; CAAS 7; CANR 8; DLB 63; EWL 3; INT CANR-8

Weller, Michael 1942- .... **CLC 10, 53**
See also CA 85-88; CAD; CD 5, 6

Weller, Paul 1958- .... **CLC 26**

Wellershoff, Dieter 1925- .... **CLC 46**
See also CA 89-92; CANR 16, 37

Welles, (George) Orson 1915-1985 .. **CLC 20, 80**
See also AAYA 40; CA 93-96; 117

Wellman, John McDowell 1945- ...... **CLC 65**
See also CA 166; CAD; CD 5, 6; RGAL 4

Wellman, Mac
See Wellman, John McDowell; Wellman, John McDowell

Wellman, Manly Wade 1903-1986 ... **CLC 49**
See also CA 1-4R; 118; CANR 6, 16, 44; FANT; SATA 6; SATA-Obit 47; SFW 4; SUFW

Wells, Carolyn 1869(?)-1942 .... **TCLC 35**
See also CA 113; 185; CMW 4; DLB 11

Wells, H(erbert) G(eorge) 1866-1946 . **SSC 6, 70; TCLC 6, 12, 19, 133; WLC 6**
See also AAYA 18; BPFB 3; BRW 6; CA 110; 121; CDBLB 1914-1945; CLR 64, 133; DA; DA3; DAB; DAC; DAM MST, NOV; DLB 34, 70, 156, 178; EWL 3; EXPS; HGG; LAIT 3; LMFS 2; MTCW 1, 2; MTFW 2005; NFS 17, 20; RGEL 2; RGSF 2; SATA 20; SCFW 1, 2; SFW 4; SSFS 3; SUFW; TEA; WCH; WLIT 4; YAW

Wells, Rosemary 1943- .... **CLC 12**
See also AAYA 13; BYA 7, 8; CA 85-88; CANR 48, 120, 179; CLR 16, 69; CWRI 5; MAICYA 1, 2; SAAS 1; SATA 18, 69, 114, 156; YAW

Wells-Barnett, Ida B(ell) 1862-1931 .... **TCLC 125**
See also CA 182; DLB 23, 221

Welsh, Irvine 1958- .... **CLC 144**
See also CA 173; CANR 146; CN 7; DLB 271

Welty, Eudora 1909-2001 .... **CLC 1, 2, 5, 14, 22, 33, 105, 220; SSC 1, 27, 51, 111; WLC 6**
See also AAYA 48; AMW; AMWR 1; BPFB 3; CA 9-12R; 199; CABS 1; CANR 32, 65, 128; CDALB 1941-1968; CN 1, 2, 3, 4, 5, 6, 7; CSW; DA; DA3; DAB; DAC; DAM MST, NOV; DFS 26; DLB 2, 102, 143; DLBD 12; DLBY 1987, 2001; EWL 3; EXPS; HGG; LAIT 3; MAL 5; MBL; MTCW 1, 2; MTFW 2005; NFS 13, 15; RGAL 4; RGSF 2; RHW; SSFS 2, 10, 26; TUS

Welty, Eudora Alice
See Welty, Eudora

Wen I-to 1899-1946 .... **TCLC 28**
See also EWL 3

Wentworth, Robert
See Hamilton, Edmond

Werewere Liking 1950- .... **BLC 2:2**
See also EWL 3

Werfel, Franz (Viktor) 1890-1945 ... **TCLC 8**
See also CA 104; 161; DLB 81, 124; EWL 3; RGWL 2, 3

Wergeland, Henrik Arnold 1808-1845 .... **NCLC 5**

Werner, Friedrich Ludwig Zacharias 1768-1823 .... **NCLC 189**
See also DLB 94

Werner, Zacharias
See Werner, Friedrich Ludwig Zacharias

Wersba, Barbara 1932- .... **CLC 30**
See also AAYA 2, 30; BYA 6, 12, 13; CA 29-32R, 182; CAAE 182; CANR 16, 38; CLR 3, 78; DLB 52; JRDA; MAICYA 1, 2; SAAS 2; SATA 1, 58; SATA-Essay 103; WYA; YAW

Wertmueller, Lina 1928- .... **CLC 16**
See also CA 97-100; CANR 39, 78

Wescott, Glenway 1901-1987 .. **CLC 13; SSC 35**
See also CA 13-16R; 121; CANR 23, 70; CN 1, 2, 3, 4; DLB 4, 9, 102; MAL 5; RGAL 4

Wesker, Arnold 1932- .... **CLC 3, 5, 42**
See also CA 1-4R; CAAS 7; CANR 1, 33; CBD; CD 5, 6; CDBLB 1960 to Present; DAB; DAM DRAM; DLB 13, 310, 319; EWL 3; MTCW 1; RGEL 2; TEA

Wesley, Charles 1707-1788 .... **LC 128**
See also DLB 95; RGEL 2

Wesley, John 1703-1791 .... **LC 88**
See also DLB 104

Wesley, Richard (Errol) 1945- .... **CLC 7**
See also BW 1; CA 57-60; CAD; CANR 27; CD 5, 6; DLB 38

Wessel, Johan Herman 1742-1785 .... **LC 7**
See also DLB 300

West, Anthony (Panther) 1914-1987 .... **CLC 50**
See also CA 45-48; 124; CANR 3, 19; CN 1, 2, 3, 4; DLB 15

West, C. P.
See Wodehouse, P(elham) G(renville)

West, Cornel 1953- .... **BLCS; CLC 134**
See also CA 144; CANR 91, 159; DLB 246

West, Cornel Ronald
See West, Cornel

West, Delno C(loyde), Jr. 1936- .... **CLC 70**
See also CA 57-60

West, Dorothy 1907-1998 ...... **HR 1:3; TCLC 108**
See also AMWS 18; BW 2; CA 143; 169; DLB 76

West, Edwin
See Westlake, Donald E.

West, (Mary) Jessamyn 1902-1984 ... **CLC 7, 17**
See also CA 9-12R; 112; CANR 27; CN 1, 2, 3; DLB 6; DLBY 1984; MTCW 1, 2; RGAL 4; RHW; SATA-Obit 37; TCWW 2; TUS; YAW

West, Morris L(anglo) 1916-1999 ..... **CLC 6, 33**
See also BPFB 3; CA 5-8R; 187; CANR 24, 49, 64; CN 1, 2, 3, 4, 5, 6; CPW; DLB 289; MTCW 1, 2; MTFW 2005

West, Nathanael 1903-1940 ...... **SSC 16, 116; TCLC 1, 14, 44**
See also AAYA 77; AMW; AMWR 2; BPFB 3; CA 104; 125; CDALB 1929-1941; DA3; DLB 4, 9, 28; EWL 3; MAL 5; MTCW 1, 2; MTFW 2005; NFS 16; RGAL 4; TUS

West, Owen
See Koontz, Dean R.

West, Paul 1930- .... **CLC 7, 14, 96, 226**
See also CA 13-16R; CAAS 7; CANR 22, 53, 76, 89, 136; CN 1, 2, 3, 4, 5, 6, 7; DLB 14; INT CANR-22; MTCW 2; MTFW 2005

West, Rebecca 1892-1983 ... **CLC 7, 9, 31, 50**
See also BPFB 3; BRWS 3; CA 5-8R; 109; CANR 19; CN 1, 2, 3; DLB 36; DLBY 1983; EWL 3; FW; MTCW 1, 2; MTFW 2005; NCFS 4; RGEL 2; TEA

Westall, Robert (Atkinson) 1929-1993 .... **CLC 17**
See also AAYA 12; BYA 2, 6, 7, 8, 9, 15; CA 69-72; 141; CANR 18, 68; CLR 13; FANT; JRDA; MAICYA 1, 2; MAICYAS 1; SAAS 2; SATA 23, 69; SATA-Obit 75; WYA; YAW

Westermarck, Edward 1862-1939 . **TCLC 87**

Westlake, Donald E. 1933-2008 ... **CLC 7, 33**
See also BPFB 3; CA 17-20R; 280; CAAS 13; CANR 16, 44, 65, 94, 137; CMW 4; CPW; DAM POP; INT CANR-16; MSW; MTCW 2; MTFW 2005

Westlake, Donald E. Edmund
See Westlake, Donald E.

Westlake, Donald Edwin
See Westlake, Donald E.

Westlake, Donald Edwin Edmund
See Westlake, Donald E.

Westmacott, Mary
See Christie, Agatha (Mary Clarissa)

Weston, Allen
See Norton, Andre

Wetcheek, J. L.
See Feuchtwanger, Lion

Wetering, Janwillem van de
See van de Wetering, Janwillem

Wetherald, Agnes Ethelwyn 1857-1940 .... **TCLC 81**
See also CA 202; DLB 99

Wetherell, Elizabeth
See Warner, Susan (Bogert)

Whale, James 1889-1957 .... **TCLC 63**
See also AAYA 75

Whalen, Philip (Glenn) 1923-2002 .... **CLC 6, 29**
See also BG 1:3; CA 9-12R; 209; CANR 5, 39; CP 1, 2, 3, 4, 5, 6, 7; DLB 16; WP

Wharton, Edith (Newbold Jones) 1862-1937 . **SSC 6, 84, 120; TCLC 3, 9, 27, 53, 129, 149; WLC 6**
See also AAYA 25; AMW; AMWC 2; AMWR 1; BPFB 3; CA 104; 132; CDALB 1865-1917; CLR 136; DA; DA3; DAB; DAC; DAM MST, NOV; DLB 4, 9, 12, 78, 189; DLBD 13; EWL 3; EXPS; FL 1:6; GL 3; HGG; LAIT 2, 3; LATS 1:1; MAL 5; MBL; MTCW 1, 2; MTFW 2005; NFS 5, 11, 15, 20; RGAL 4; RGSF 2; RHW; SSFS 6, 7; SUFW; TUS

Wharton, James
See Mencken, H(enry) L(ouis)

Wharton, William 1925-2008 ..... **CLC 18, 37**
See also CA 93-96; 278; CN 4, 5, 6, 7; DLBY 1980; INT CA-93-96

Wheatley (Peters), Phillis 1753(?)-1784 .... **BLC 1:3; LC 3, 50; PC 3; WLC 6**
See also AFAW 1, 2; CDALB 1640-1865; DA; DA3; DAC; DAM MST, MULT, POET; DLB 31, 50; EXPP; FL 1:1; PFS 13, 29; RGAL 4

Wheelock, John Hall 1886-1978 .... **CLC 14**
See also CA 13-16R; 77-80; CANR 14; CP 1, 2; DLB 45; MAL 5

Whim-Wham
See Curnow, (Thomas) Allen (Monro)

Whisp, Kennilworthy
See Rowling, J.K.

Whitaker, Rod 1931-2005 .... **CLC 29**
See also CA 29-32R; 246; CANR 45, 153; CMW 4

Whitaker, Rodney
See Whitaker, Rod

Whitaker, Rodney William
See Whitaker, Rod

White, Babington
See Braddon, Mary Elizabeth

White, E. B. 1899-1985 .... **CLC 10, 34, 39**
See also AAYA 62; AITN 2; AMWS 1; CA 13-16R; 116; CANR 16, 37; CDALBS; CLR 1, 21, 107; CPW; DA3; DAM POP; DLB 11, 22; EWL 3; FANT; MAICYA 1, 2; MAL 5; MTCW 1, 2; MTFW 2005; NCFS 5; RGAL 4; SATA 2, 29, 100; SATA-Obit 44; TUS

White, Edmund 1940- .... **CLC 27, 110**
See also AAYA 7; CA 45-48; CANR 3, 19, 36, 62, 107, 133, 172; CN 5, 6, 7; DA3; DAM POP; DLB 227; MTCW 1, 2; MTFW 2005

White, Edmund Valentine III
See White, Edmund

White, Elwyn Brooks
See White, E. B.

White, Hayden V. 1928- .... **CLC 148**
See also CA 128; CANR 135; DLB 246

White, Patrick (Victor Martindale)
1912-1990 ...... **CLC 3, 4, 5, 7, 9, 18, 65, 69; SSC 39; TCLC 176**
See also BRWS 1; CA 81-84; 132; CANR 43; CN 1, 2, 3, 4; DLB 260, 332; EWL 3; MTCW 1; RGEL 2; RGSF 2; RHW; TWA; WWE 1

White, Phyllis Dorothy James
1920- .... **CLC 18, 46, 122, 226**
See also BEST 90:2; BPFB 2; BRWS 4; CA 21-24R; CANR 17, 43, 65, 112; CD-BLB 1960 to Present; CMW 4; CN 4, 5, 6; CPW; DA3; DAM POP; DLB 87, 276; DLBD 17; MSW; MTCW 1, 2; MTFW 2005; TEA

White, T(erence) H(anbury)
1906-1964 .... **CLC 30**
See also AAYA 22; BPFB 3; BYA 4, 5; CA 73-76; CANR 37; CLR 139; DLB 160; FANT; JRDA; LAIT 1; MAICYA 1, 2; RGEL 2; SATA 12; SUFW 1; YAW

White, Terence de Vere 1912-1994 ... **CLC 49**
See also CA 49-52; 145; CANR 3

White, Walter
See White, Walter F(rancis)

White, Walter F(rancis)
1893-1955 ..... **BLC 1:3; HR 1:3; TCLC 15**
See also BW 1; CA 115; 124; DAM MULT; DLB 51

White, William Hale 1831-1913 ..... **TCLC 25**
See also CA 121; 189; DLB 18; RGEL 2

Whitehead, Alfred North
1861-1947 .... **TCLC 97**
See also CA 117; 165; DLB 100, 262

Whitehead, Colson 1969- ...... **BLC 2:3; CLC 232**
See also CA 202; CANR 162

Whitehead, E(dward) A(nthony)
1933- .... **CLC 5**
See also CA 65-68; CANR 58, 118; CBD; CD 5, 6; DLB 310

Whitehead, Ted
See Whitehead, E(dward) A(nthony)

Whiteman, Roberta J. Hill 1947- ...... **NNAL**
See also CA 146

Whitemore, Hugh (John) 1936- .... **CLC 37**
See also CA 132; CANR 77; CBD; CD 5, 6; INT CA-132

Whitman, Sarah Helen (Power)
1803-1878 .... **NCLC 19**
See also DLB 1, 243

Whitman, Walt(er) 1819-1892 .. **NCLC 4, 31, 81, 205; PC 3, 91; WLC 6**
See also AAYA 42; AMW; AMWR 1; CDALB 1640-1865; DA; DA3; DAB; DAC; DAM MST, POET; DLB 3, 64, 224, 250; EXPP; LAIT 2; LMFS 1; PAB; PFS 2, 3, 13, 22; RGAL 4; SATA 20; TUS; WP; WYAS 1

Whitney, Isabella fl. 1565-fl. 1575 ..... **LC 130**
See also DLB 136

Whitney, Phyllis A. 1903-2008 .... **CLC 42**
See also AAYA 36; AITN 2; BEST 90:3; CA 1-4R; 269; CANR 3, 25, 38, 60; CLR 59; CMW 4; CPW; DA3; DAM POP; JRDA; MAICYA 1, 2; MTCW 2; RHW; SATA 1, 30; SATA-Obit 189; YAW

Whitney, Phyllis Ayame
See Whitney, Phyllis A.

Whitney, Phyllis Ayame
See Whitney, Phyllis A.

Whittemore, (Edward) Reed, Jr.
1919- .... **CLC 4**
See also CA 9-12R, 219; CAAE 219; CAAS 8; CANR 4, 119; CP 1, 2, 3, 4, 5, 6, 7; DLB 5; MAL 5

Whittier, John Greenleaf
1807-1892 .... **NCLC 8, 59; PC 93**
See also AMWS 1; DLB 1, 243; RGAL 4

Whittlebot, Hernia
See Coward, Noel (Peirce)

Wicker, Thomas Grey
See Wicker, Tom

Wicker, Tom 1926- .... **CLC 7**
See also CA 65-68; CANR 21, 46, 141, 179

Wicomb, Zoe 1948- .... **BLC 2:3**
See also CA 127; CANR 106, 167; DLB 225

Wideman, John Edgar 1941- .. **BLC 1:3, 2:3; CLC 5, 34, 36, 67, 122; SSC 62**
See also AFAW 1, 2; AMWS 10; BPFB 4; BW 2, 3; CA 85-88; CANR 14, 42, 67, 109, 140, 187; CN 4, 5, 6, 7; DAM MULT; DLB 33, 143; MAL 5; MTCW 2; MTFW 2005; RGAL 4; RGSF 2; SSFS 6, 12, 24; TCLE 1:2

Wiebe, Rudy 1934- . **CLC 6, 11, 14, 138, 263**
See also CA 37-40R; CANR 42, 67, 123; CN 1, 2, 3, 4, 5, 6, 7; DAC; DAM MST; DLB 60; RHW; SATA 156

Wiebe, Rudy Henry
See Wiebe, Rudy

Wieland, Christoph Martin
1733-1813 .... **NCLC 17, 177**
See also DLB 97; EW 4; LMFS 1; RGWL 2, 3

Wiene, Robert 1881-1938 .... **TCLC 56**

Wieners, John 1934- .... **CLC 7**
See also BG 1:3; CA 13-16R; CP 1, 2, 3, 4, 5, 6, 7; DLB 16; WP

Wiesel, Elie 1928- ...... **CLC 3, 5, 11, 37, 165; WLCS**
See also AAYA 7, 54; AITN 1; CA 5-8R; CAAS 4; CANR 8, 40, 65, 125; CDALBS; CWW 2; DA; DA3; DAB; DAC; DAM MST, NOV; DLB 83, 299; DLBY 1987; EWL 3; INT CANR-8; LAIT 4; MTCW 1, 2; MTFW 2005; NCFS 4; NFS 4; RGHL; RGWL 3; SATA 56; YAW

Wiesel, Eliezer
See Wiesel, Elie

Wiggins, Marianne 1947- .... **CLC 57**
See also AAYA 70; BEST 89:3; CA 130; CANR 60, 139, 180; CN 7; DLB 335

Wigglesworth, Michael 1631-1705 .... **LC 106**
See also DLB 24; RGAL 4

Wiggs, Susan .... **CLC 70**
See also CA 201; CANR 173

Wight, James Alfred 1916-1995 .... **CLC 12**
See also AAYA 1, 54; BPFB 2; CA 77-80; 148; CANR 40; CLR 80; CPW; DAM POP; LAIT 3; MAICYA 2; MAICYAS 1; MTCW 2; SATA 86, 135; SATA-Brief 44; TEA; YAW

Wilbur, Richard 1921- .. **CLC 3, 6, 9, 14, 53, 110; PC 51**
See also AAYA 72; AMWS 3; CA 1-4R; CABS 2; CANR 2, 29, 76, 93, 139; CDALBS; CP 1, 2, 3, 4, 5, 6, 7; DA; DAB; DAC; DAM MST, POET; DLB 5, 169; EWL 3; EXPP; INT CANR-29; MAL 5; MTCW 1, 2; MTFW 2005; PAB; PFS 11, 12, 16, 29; RGAL 4; SATA 9, 108; WP

Wilbur, Richard Purdy
See Wilbur, Richard

Wild, Peter 1940- .... **CLC 14**
See also CA 37-40R; CP 1, 2, 3, 4, 5, 6, 7; DLB 5

Wilde, Oscar 1854(?)-1900 ... **DC 17; SSC 11, 77; TCLC 1, 8, 23, 41, 175; WLC 6**
See also AAYA 49; BRW 5; BRWC 1, 2; BRWR 2; BYA 15; CA 104; 119; CANR 112; CDBLB 1890-1914; CLR 114; DA; DA3; DAB; DAC; DAM DRAM, MST, NOV; DFS 4, 8, 9, 21; DLB 10, 19, 34, 57, 141, 156, 190, 344; EXPS; FANT; GL 3; LATS 1:1; NFS 20; RGEL 2; RGSF 2; SATA 24; SSFS 7; SUFW; TEA; WCH; WLIT 4

Wilde, Oscar Fingal O'Flahertie Willis
See Wilde, Oscar

Wilder, Billy
See Wilder, Samuel

Wilder, Samuel 1906-2002 .... **CLC 20**
See also AAYA 66; CA 89-92; 205; DLB 26

Wilder, Stephen
See Marlowe, Stephen

Wilder, Thornton (Niven)
1897-1975 .. **CLC 1, 5, 6, 10, 15, 35, 82; DC 1, 24; WLC 6**
See also AAYA 29; AITN 2; AMW; CA 13-16R; 61-64; CAD; CANR 40, 132; CDALBS; CN 1, 2; DA; DA3; DAB; DAC; DAM DRAM, MST, NOV; DFS 1, 4, 16; DLB 4, 7, 9, 228; DLBY 1997; EWL 3; LAIT 3; MAL 5; MTCW 1, 2; MTFW 2005; NFS 24; RGAL 4; RHW; WYAS 1

Wilding, Michael 1942- ...... **CLC 73; SSC 50**
See also CA 104; CANR 24, 49, 106; CN 4, 5, 6, 7; DLB 325; RGSF 2

Wiley, Richard 1944- .... **CLC 44**
See also CA 121; 129; CANR 71

Wilhelm, Kate
See Wilhelm, Katie

Wilhelm, Katie 1928- .... **CLC 7**
See also AAYA 20; BYA 16; CA 37-40R; CAAS 5; CANR 17, 36, 60, 94; DLB 8; INT CANR-17; MTCW 1; SCFW 2; SFW 4

Wilhelm, Katie Gertrude
See Wilhelm, Katie

Wilkins, Mary
See Freeman, Mary E(leanor) Wilkins

Willard, Nancy 1936- .... **CLC 7, 37**
See also BYA 5; CA 89-92; CANR 10, 39, 68, 107, 152, 186; CLR 5; CP 2, 3, 4, 5; CWP; CWRI 5; DLB 5, 52; FANT; MAICYA 1, 2; MTCW 1; SATA 37, 71, 127, 191; SATA-Brief 30; SUFW 2; TCLE 1:2

William of Malmesbury c. 1090B.C.-c. 1140B.C. .... **CMLC 57**

William of Moerbeke c. 1215-c. 1286 .... **CMLC 91**

William of Ockham 1290-1349 ..... **CMLC 32**

Wister, Owen 1860-1938 ..... **SSC 100; TCLC 21**
See also BPFB 3; CA 108; 162; DLB 9, 78, 186; RGAL 4; SATA 62; TCWW 1, 2

Wither, George 1588-1667 .... **LC 96**
See also DLB 121; RGEL 2

Witkacy
See Witkiewicz, Stanislaw Ignacy

Witkiewicz, Stanislaw Ignacy
1885-1939 .... **TCLC 8**
See also CA 105; 162; CDWLB 4; DLB 215; EW 10; EWL 3; RGWL 2, 3; SFW 4

Wittgenstein, Ludwig (Josef Johann)
1889-1951 .... **TCLC 59**
See also CA 113; 164; DLB 262; MTCW 2

Wittig, Monique 1935-2003 .... **CLC 22**
See also CA 116; 135; 212; CANR 143; CWW 2; DLB 83; EWL 3; FW; GLL 1

Wittlin, Jozef 1896-1976 .... **CLC 25**
See also CA 49-52; 65-68; CANR 3; EWL 3

Wodehouse, P(elham) G(renville)
1881-1975 .. **CLC 1, 2, 5, 10, 22; SSC 2, 115; TCLC 108**
See also AAYA 65; AITN 2; BRWS 3; CA 45-48; 57-60; CANR 3, 33; CDBLB 1914-1945; CN 1, 2; CPW 1; DA3; DAB; DAC; DAM NOV; DLB 34, 162; EWL 3; MTCW 1, 2; MTFW 2005; RGEL 2; RGSF 2; SATA 22; SSFS 10

Woiwode, L.
See Woiwode, Larry (Alfred)

Woiwode, Larry (Alfred) 1941- ... **CLC 6, 10**
See also CA 73-76; CANR 16, 94; CN 3, 4, 5, 6, 7; DLB 6; INT CANR-16

Wojciechowska, Maia (Teresa)
1927-2002 .... **CLC 26**
See also AAYA 8, 46; BYA 3; CA 9-12R; 183; 209; CAAE 183; CANR 4, 41; CLR 1; JRDA; MAICYA 1, 2; SAAS 1; SATA 1, 28, 83; SATA-Essay 104; SATA-Obit 134; YAW

Wojtyla, Karol (Jozef)
See John Paul II, Pope

Wojtyla, Karol (Josef)
See John Paul II, Pope

Wolf, Christa 1929- ...... **CLC 14, 29, 58, 150, 261**
See also CA 85-88; CANR 45, 123; CDWLB 2; CWW 2; DLB 75; EWL 3; FW; MTCW 1; RGWL 2, 3; SSFS 14

Wolf, Naomi 1962- .... **CLC 157**
See also CA 141; CANR 110; FW; MTFW 2005

Wolfe, Gene 1931- .... **CLC 25**
See also AAYA 35; CA 57-60; CAAS 9; CANR 6, 32, 60, 152; CPW; DAM POP; DLB 8; FANT; MTCW 2; MTFW 2005; SATA 118, 165; SCFW 2; SFW 4; SUFW 2

Wolfe, Gene Rodman
See Wolfe, Gene

Wolfe, George C. 1954- .... **BLCS; CLC 49**
See also CA 149; CAD; CD 5, 6

Wolfe, Thomas (Clayton)
1900-1938 .... **SSC 33, 113; TCLC 4, 13, 29, 61; WLC 6**
See also AMW; BPFB 3; CA 104; 132; CANR 102; CDALB 1929-1941; DA; DA3; DAB; DAC; DAM MST, NOV; DLB 9, 102, 229; DLBY 1985, 1997; EWL 3; MAL 5; MTCW 1, 2; NFS 18; RGAL 4; SSFS 18; TUS

Wolfe, Thomas Kennerly, Jr. 1931- .. **CLC 1, 2, 9, 15, 35, 51, 147**
See also AAYA 8, 67; AITN 2; AMWS 3; BEST 89:1; BPFB 3; CA 13-16R; CANR 9, 33, 70, 104; CN 5, 6, 7; CPW; CSW;

DA3; DAM POP; DLB 152, 185 185; EWL 3; INT CANR-9; LAIT 5; MTCW 1, 2; MTFW 2005; RGAL 4; TUS

Wolfe, Tom
See Wolfe, Thomas Kennerly, Jr.

Wolff, Geoffrey 1937- .... **CLC 41**
See also CA 29-32R; CANR 29, 43, 78, 154

Wolff, Geoffrey Ansell
See Wolff, Geoffrey

Wolff, Sonia
See Levitin, Sonia

Wolff, Tobias 1945- .... **CLC 39, 64, 172; SSC 63**
See also AAYA 16; AMWS 7; BEST 90:2; BYA 12; CA 114; 117; CAAS 22; CANR 54, 76, 96; CN 5, 6, 7; CSW; DA3; DLB 130; EWL 3; INT CA-117; MTCW 2; MTFW 2005; RGAL 4; RGSF 2; SSFS 4, 11

Wolitzer, Hilma 1930- .... **CLC 17**
See also CA 65-68; CANR 18, 40, 172; INT CANR-18; SATA 31; YAW

Wollstonecraft, Mary 1759-1797 .... **LC 5, 50, 90, 147**
See also BRWS 3; CDBLB 1789-1832; DLB 39, 104, 158, 252; FL 1:1; FW; LAIT 1; RGEL 2; TEA; WLIT 3

Wonder, Stevie 1950- .... **CLC 12**
See also CA 111

Wong, Jade Snow 1922-2006 .... **CLC 17**
See also CA 109; 249; CANR 91; SATA 112; SATA-Obit 175

Wood, Ellen Price
See Wood, Mrs. Henry

Wood, Mrs. Henry 1814-1887 ...... **NCLC 178**
See also CMW 4; DLB 18; SUFW

Wood, James 1965- .... **CLC 238**
See also CA 235

Woodberry, George Edward
1855-1930 .... **TCLC 73**
See also CA 165; DLB 71, 103

Woodcott, Keith
See Brunner, John (Kilian Houston)

Woodruff, Robert W.
See Mencken, H(enry) L(ouis)

Woodward, Bob 1943- .... **CLC 240**
See also CA 69-72; CANR 31, 67, 107, 176; MTCW 1

Woodward, Robert Upshur
See Woodward, Bob

Woolf, (Adeline) Virginia 1882-1941 .. **SSC 7, 79; TCLC 1, 5, 20, 43, 56, 101, 123, 128; WLC 6**
See also AAYA 44; BPFB 3; BRW 7; BRWC 2; BRWR 1; CA 104; 130; CANR 64, 132; CDBLB 1914-1945; DA; DA3; DAB; DAC; DAM MST, NOV; DLB 36, 100, 162; DLBD 10; EWL 3; EXPS; FL 1:6; FW; LAIT 3; LATS 1:1; LMFS 2; MTCW 1, 2; MTFW 2005; NCFS 2; NFS 8, 12, 28; RGEL 2; RGSF 2; SSFS 4, 12; TEA; WLIT 4

Woollcott, Alexander (Humphreys)
1887-1943 .... **TCLC 5**
See also CA 105; 161; DLB 29

Woolman, John 1720-1772 .... **LC 155**
See also DLB 31

Woolrich, Cornell
See Hopley-Woolrich, Cornell George

Woolson, Constance Fenimore
1840-1894 .... **NCLC 82; SSC 90**
See also DLB 12, 74, 189, 221; RGAL 4

Wordsworth, Dorothy 1771-1855 . **NCLC 25, 138**
See also DLB 107

Wordsworth, William 1770-1850 .. **NCLC 12, 38, 111, 166, 206; PC 4, 67; WLC 6**
See also AAYA 70; BRW 4; BRWC 1; CD-BLB 1789-1832; DA; DA3; DAB; DAC; DAM MST, POET; DLB 93, 107; EXPP; LATS 1:1; LMFS 1; PAB; PFS 2; RGEL 2; TEA; WLIT 3; WP

Wotton, Sir Henry 1568-1639 .... **LC 68**
See also DLB 121; RGEL 2

Wouk, Herman 1915- .... **CLC 1, 9, 38**
See also BPFB 2, 3; CA 5-8R; CANR 6, 33, 67, 146; CDALBS; CN 1, 2, 3, 4, 5, 6; CPW; DA3; DAM NOV, POP; DLBY 1982; INT CANR-6; LAIT 4; MAL 5; MTCW 1, 2; MTFW 2005; NFS 7; TUS

Wright, Charles 1932-2008 ... **BLC 1:3; CLC 49**
See also BW 1; CA 9-12R; 278; CANR 26; CN 1, 2, 3, 4, 5, 6, 7; DAM MULT, POET; DLB 33

Wright, Charles 1935- ... **CLC 6, 13, 28, 119, 146**
See also AMWS 5; CA 29-32R; CAAS 7; CANR 23, 36, 62, 88, 135, 180; CP 3, 4, 5, 6, 7; DLB 165; DLBY 1982; EWL 3; MTCW 1, 2; MTFW 2005; PFS 10

Wright, Charles Penzel, Jr.
See Wright, Charles

Wright, Charles Stevenson
See Wright, Charles

Wright, Frances 1795-1852 .... **NCLC 74**
See also DLB 73

Wright, Frank Lloyd 1867-1959 .... **TCLC 95**
See also AAYA 33; CA 174

Wright, Harold Bell 1872-1944 .... **TCLC 183**
See also BPFB 3; CA 110; DLB 9; TCWW 2

Wright, Jack R.
See Harris, Mark

Wright, James (Arlington)
1927-1980 .... **CLC 3, 5, 10, 28; PC 36**
See also AITN 2; AMWS 3; CA 49-52; 97-100; CANR 4, 34, 64; CDALBS; CP 1, 2; DAM POET; DLB 5, 169, 342; EWL 3; EXPP; MAL 5; MTCW 1, 2; MTFW 2005; PFS 7, 8; RGAL 4; TUS; WP

Wright, Judith 1915-2000 ... **CLC 11, 53; PC 14**
See also CA 13-16R; 188; CANR 31, 76, 93; CP 1, 2, 3, 4, 5, 6, 7; CWP; DLB 260; EWL 3; MTCW 1, 2; MTFW 2005; PFS 8; RGEL 2; SATA 14; SATA-Obit 121

Wright, L(aurali) R. 1939- .... **CLC 44**
See also CA 138; CMW 4

Wright, Richard 1908-1960 .. **BLC 1:3; CLC 1, 3, 4, 9, 14, 21, 48, 74; SSC 2, 109; TCLC 136, 180; WLC 6**
See also AAYA 5, 42; AFAW 1, 2; AMW; BPFB 3; BW 1; BYA 2; CA 108; CANR 64; CDALB 1929-1941; DA; DA3; DAB; DAC; DAM MST, MULT, NOV; DLB 76, 102; DLBD 2; EWL 3; EXPN; LAIT 3, 4; MAL 5; MTCW 1, 2; MTFW 2005; NCFS 1; NFS 1, 7; RGAL 4; RGSF 2; SSFS 3, 9, 15, 20; TUS; YAW

Wright, Richard B. 1937- .... **CLC 6**
See also CA 85-88; CANR 120; DLB 53

Wright, Richard Bruce
See Wright, Richard B.

Wright, Richard Nathaniel
See Wright, Richard

Wright, Rick 1945- .... **CLC 35**

Wright, Rowland
See Wells, Carolyn

Wright, Stephen 1946- .... **CLC 33**
See also CA 237

Wright, Willard Huntington
1888-1939 .... **TCLC 23**
See also CA 115; 189; CMW 4; DLB 306;
DLBD 16; MSW

Wright, William 1930- .... **CLC 44**
See also CA 53-56; CANR 7, 23, 154

Wroth, Lady Mary 1587-1653(?) .... **LC 30,
139; PC 38**
See also DLB 121

Wu Ch'eng-en 1500(?)-1582(?) .... **LC 7**

Wu Ching-tzu 1701-1754 .... **LC 2**

Wulfstan c. 10th cent. -1023 .... **CMLC 59**

Wurlitzer, Rudolph 1938(?)- ... **CLC 2, 4, 15**
See also CA 85-88; CN 4, 5, 6, 7; DLB 173

Wyatt, Sir Thomas c. 1503-1542 . **LC 70; PC
27**
See also BRW 1; DLB 132; EXPP; PFS 25;
RGEL 2; TEA

Wycherley, William 1640-1716 .... **LC 8, 21,
102, 136**
See also BRW 2; CDBLB 1660-1789; DAM
DRAM; DLB 80; RGEL 2

Wyclif, John c. 1330-1384 .... **CMLC 70**
See also DLB 146

Wylie, Elinor (Morton Hoyt)
1885-1928 .... **PC 23; TCLC 8**
See also AMWS 1; CA 105; 162; DLB 9,
45; EXPP; MAL 5; RGAL 4

Wylie, Philip (Gordon) 1902-1971 ... **CLC 43**
See also CA 21-22; 33-36R; CAP 2; CN 1;
DLB 9; SFW 4

Wyndham, John
See Harris, John (Wyndham Parkes Lucas)
Beynon

Wyss, Johann David Von
1743-1818 .... **NCLC 10**
See also CLR 92; JRDA; MAICYA 1, 2;
SATA 29; SATA-Brief 27

Xenophon c. 430B.C.-c. 354B.C. ... **CMLC 17**
See also AW 1; DLB 176; RGWL 2, 3;
WLIT 8

Xingjian, Gao 1940- .... **CLC 167**
See also CA 193; DFS 21; DLB 330;
MTFW 2005; RGWL 3

Yakamochi 718-785 .... **CMLC 45; PC 48**

Yakumo Koizumi
See Hearn, (Patricio) Lafcadio (Tessima
Carlos)

Yamada, Mitsuye (May) 1923- .... **PC 44**
See also CA 77-80

Yamamoto, Hisaye 1921- .... **AAL; SSC 34**
See also CA 214; DAM MULT; DLB 312;
LAIT 4; SSFS 14

Yamauchi, Wakako 1924- .... **AAL**
See also CA 214; DLB 312

Yan, Mo
See Moye, Guan

Yanez, Jose Donoso
See Donoso (Yanez), Jose

Yanovsky, Basile S.
See Yanovsky, V(assily) S(emenovich)

Yanovsky, V(assily) S(emenovich)
1906-1989 .... **CLC 2, 18**
See also CA 97-100; 129

Yates, Richard 1926-1992 .... **CLC 7, 8, 23**
See also AMWS 11; CA 5-8R; 139; CANR
10, 43; CN 1, 2, 3, 4, 5; DLB 2, 234;
DLBY 1981, 1992; INT CANR-10; SSFS
24

Yau, John 1950- .... **PC 61**
See also CA 154; CANR 89; CP 4, 5, 6, 7;
DLB 234, 312; PFS 26

Yearsley, Ann 1753-1806 .... **NCLC 174**
See also DLB 109

Yeats, W. B.
See Yeats, William Butler

Yeats, William Butler 1865-1939 . **DC 33; PC
20, 51; TCLC 1, 11, 18, 31, 93, 116;
WLC 6**
See also AAYA 48; BRW 6; BRWR 1; CA
104; 127; CANR 45; CDBLB 1890-1914;
DA; DA3; DAB; DAM DRAM,
MST, POET; DLB 10, 19, 98, 156, 332;
EWL 3; EXPP; MTCW 1, 2; MTFW
2005; NCFS 3; PAB; PFS 1, 2, 5, 7, 13,
15; RGEL 2; TEA; WLIT 4; WP

Yehoshua, A.B. 1936- .... **CLC 13, 31, 243**
See also CA 33-36R; CANR 43, 90, 145;
CWW 2; EWL 3; RGHL; RGSF 2; RGWL
3; WLIT 6

Yehoshua, Abraham B.
See Yehoshua, A.B.

Yellow Bird
See Ridge, John Rollin

Yep, Laurence 1948- .... **CLC 35**
See also AAYA 5, 31; BYA 7; CA 49-52;
CANR 1, 46, 92, 161; CLR 3, 17, 54, 132;
DLB 52, 312; FANT; JRDA; MAICYA 1,
2; MAICYAS 1; SATA 7, 69, 123, 176;
WYA; YAW

Yep, Laurence Michael
See Yep, Laurence

Yerby, Frank G(arvin) 1916-1991 . **BLC 1:3;
CLC 1, 7, 22**
See also BPFB 3; BW 1, 3; CA 9-12R; 136;
CANR 16, 52; CN 1, 2, 3, 4, 5; DAM
MULT; DLB 76; INT CANR-16; MTCW
1; RGAL 4; RHW

Yesenin, Sergei Aleksandrovich
See Esenin, Sergei

Yevtushenko, Yevgeny (Alexandrovich)
1933- ...... **CLC 1, 3, 13, 26, 51, 126; PC
40**
See also CA 81-84; CANR 33, 54; CWW
2; DAM POET; EWL 3; MTCW 1; PFS
29; RGHL; RGWL 2, 3

Yezierska, Anzia 1885(?)-1970 .... **CLC 46;
TCLC 205**
See also CA 126; 89-92; DLB 28, 221; FW;
MTCW 1; NFS 29; RGAL 4; SSFS 15

Yglesias, Helen 1915-2008 .... **CLC 7, 22**
See also CA 37-40R; 272; CAAS 20; CANR
15, 65, 95; CN 4, 5, 6, 7; INT CANR-15;
MTCW 1

Y.O.
See Russell, George William

Yokomitsu, Riichi 1898-1947 .... **TCLC 47**
See also CA 170; EWL 3

Yolen, Jane 1939- .... **CLC 256**
See also AAYA 4, 22; BPFB 3; BYA 9, 10,
11, 14, 16; CA 13-16R; CANR 11, 29, 56,
91, 126, 185; CLR 4, 44; CWRI 5; DLB
52; FANT; INT CANR-29; JRDA; MAI-
CYA 1, 2; MTFW 2005; SAAS 1; SATA
4, 40, 75, 112, 158, 194; SATA-Essay 111;
SFW 4; SUFW 2; WYA; YAW

Yonge, Charlotte (Mary)
1823-1901 .... **TCLC 48**
See also CA 109; 163; DLB 18, 163; RGEL
2; SATA 17; WCH

York, Jeremy
See Creasey, John

York, Simon
See Heinlein, Robert A.

Yorke, Henry Vincent 1905-1974 ...... **CLC 2,
13, 97**
See also BRWS 2; CA 85-88, 175; 49-52;
DLB 15; EWL 3; RGEL 2

Yosano, Akiko 1878-1942 ... **PC 11; TCLC 59**
See also CA 161; EWL 3; RGWL 3

Yoshimoto, Banana
See Yoshimoto, Mahoko

Yoshimoto, Mahoko 1964- .... **CLC 84**
See also AAYA 50; CA 144; CANR 98, 160;
NFS 7; SSFS 16

Young, Al(bert James) 1939- .... **BLC 1:3;
CLC 19**
See also BW 2, 3; CA 29-32R; CANR 26,
65, 109; CN 2, 3, 4, 5, 6, 7; CP 1, 2, 3, 4,
5, 6, 7; DAM MULT; DLB 33

Young, Andrew (John) 1885-1971 ...... **CLC 5**
See also CA 5-8R; CANR 7, 29; CP 1;
RGEL 2

Young, Collier
See Bloch, Robert (Albert)

Young, Edward 1683-1765 .... **LC 3, 40**
See also DLB 95; RGEL 2

Young, Marguerite (Vivian)
1909-1995 .... **CLC 82**
See also CA 13-16; 150; CAP 1; CN 1, 2,
3, 4, 5, 6

Young, Neil 1945- .... **CLC 17**
See also CA 110; CCA 1

Young Bear, Ray A. 1950- ... **CLC 94; NNAL**
See also CA 146; DAM MULT; DLB 175;
MAL 5

Yourcenar, Marguerite 1903-1987 ... **CLC 19,
38, 50, 87; TCLC 193**
See also BPFB 3; CA 69-72; CANR 23, 60,
93; DAM NOV; DLB 72; DLBY 1988;
EW 12; EWL 3; GFL 1789 to the Present;
GLL 1; MTCW 1, 2; MTFW 2005;
RGWL 2, 3

Yuan, Chu 340(?)B.C.-278(?)B.C. . **CMLC 36**

Yu Dafu 1896-1945 .... **SSC 122**
See also DLB 328; RGSF 2

Yurick, Sol 1925- .... **CLC 6**
See also CA 13-16R; CANR 25; CN 1, 2,
3, 4, 5, 6, 7; MAL 5

Zabolotsky, Nikolai Alekseevich
1903-1958 .... **TCLC 52**
See also CA 116; 164; EWL 3

Zabolotsky, Nikolay Alekseevich
See Zabolotsky, Nikolai Alekseevich

Zagajewski, Adam 1945- .... **PC 27**
See also CA 186; DLB 232; EWL 3; PFS
25

Zakaria, Fareed 1964- .... **CLC 269**
See also CA 171; CANR 151, 188

Zalygin, Sergei -2000 .... **CLC 59**

Zalygin, Sergei (Pavlovich)
1913-2000 .... **CLC 59**
See also DLB 302

Zamiatin, Evgenii
See Zamyatin, Evgeny Ivanovich

Zamiatin, Evgenii Ivanovich
See Zamyatin, Evgeny Ivanovich

Zamiatin, Yevgenii
See Zamyatin, Evgeny Ivanovich

Zamora, Bernice (B. Ortiz) 1938- .. **CLC 89;
HLC 2**
See also CA 151; CANR 80; DAM MULT;
DLB 82; HW 1, 2

Zamyatin, Evgeny Ivanovich
1884-1937 .... **SSC 89; TCLC 8, 37**
See also CA 105; 166; DLB 272; EW 10;
EWL 3; RGSF 2; RGWL 2, 3; SFW 4

Zamyatin, Yevgeny Ivanovich
See Zamyatin, Evgeny Ivanovich

Zangwill, Israel 1864-1926 ... **SSC 44; TCLC
16**
See also CA 109; 167; CMW 4; DLB 10,
135, 197; RGEL 2

Zanzotto, Andrea 1921- .... **PC 65**
See also CA 208; CWW 2; DLB 128; EWL
3

Zappa, Francis Vincent, Jr. 1940-1993
See Zappa, Frank
See also CA 108; 143; CANR 57

Zappa, Frank .... **CLC 17**
See Zappa, Francis Vincent, Jr.

Zaturenska, Marya 1902-1982 ..... **CLC 6, 11**
See also CA 13-16R; 105; CANR 22; CP 1,
2, 3

Literary Criticism Series
Cumulative Topic Index

This index lists all topic entries in Gale's *Children's Literature Review* (CLR), *Classical and Medieval Literature Criticism* (CMLC), *Contemporary Literary Criticism* (CLC), *Drama Criticism* (DC), *Literature Criticism from 1400 to 1800* (LC), *Nineteenth-Century Literature Criticism* (NCLC), *Short Story Criticism* (SSC), and *Twentieth-Century Literary Criticism* (TCLC). The index also lists topic entries in the Gale Critical Companion Collection, which includes the following publications: *The Beat Generation* (BG), *Feminism in Literature* (FL), *Gothic Literature* (GL), and *Harlem Renaissance* (HR).

Women Playwrights, Nineteenth-Century
NCLC 200: 225-334
    European authors, 227-65
    North American authors, 265-334

Women Writers, Seventeenth-Century LC 30:
2-58
    overview, 2-15
    women and education, 15-9
    women and autobiography, 19-31
    women's diaries, 31-9
    early feminists, 39-58

Women's Autobiography, Nineteenth Century NCLC 76: 285-368
    overviews and general studies, 287-300
    autobiographies concerned with religious
        and political issues, 300-15
    autobiographies by women of color, 315-38
    autobiographies by women pioneers,
        338-51
    autobiographies by women of letters,
        351-68

Women's Diaries, Nineteenth-Century NCLC
48: 308-54
    overview, 308-13
    diary as history, 314-25
    sociology of diaries, 325-34
    diaries as psychological scholarship, 334-43
    diary as autobiography, 343-8
    diary as literature, 348-53

Women's Periodicals LC 134: 292-382
    English women's periodicals: overviews,
        293-307

French women's periodicals: overviews,
    307-19
early imitators of Addison and Steele,
    320-42
The Female Spectator, 342-70
Journal des dames, 370-80

World War I Literature TCLC 34: 392-486
    overview, 393-403
    English, 403-27
    German, 427-50
    American, 450-66
    French, 466-74
    and modern history, 474-82

World War I Short Fiction SSC 71: 187-347
    overviews and general studies, 187-206
    female short fiction writers of World War I,
        206-36
    Central Powers
        Czechoslovakian writers of short fiction,
        236-44
        German writers of short fiction, 244-61
    Entente/Allied Alliance
        Australian writers of short fiction, 261-73
        English writers of short fiction, 273-305
        French writers of short fiction, 305-11
    Associated Power: American writers of
        short fiction, 311-46

Writers of the Lost Generation TCLC 178:
196-369
    overviews 197-225
    major figures 225-98
    women of the Lost Generation 298-341
    expatriate writers and Paris 341-68

**Writings on Syphilis in the Early Modern
Period** LC 144: 245-350
    overview 247-56
    William Clowes' *Short and Profitable Treatise* 256-57
    Fracastoro's *Syphilis* 257-89
    Medieval and Renaissance Literary Representations of Syphilis 289-333
    Eighteenth-Century Literary Representations of Syphilis 333-48

Yellow Journalism NCLC 36: 383-456
    overviews and general studies, 384-96
    major figures, 396-413

Yiddish Literature TCLC 130: 229-364
    overviews and general studies, 230-54
    major authors, 254-305
    Yiddish literature in America, 305-34
    Yiddish and Judaism, 334-64

Young Adult Literature, Contemporary CLC
234: 267-341
    general overviews, representative authors,
        and reviews, 270-83
    feminism and young adult literature for
        young women, 283-305
    interviews with YA authors, 305-14
    using YA fiction in the classroom, 314-26
    religious issues, sexual orientation, and alternative communities in YA lit, 326-41

Young Playwrights Festival
    1988 CLC 55: 376-81
    1989 CLC 59: 398-403
    1990 CLC 65: 444-8

NCLC Cumulative Nationality Index

AMERICAN

Adams, John **106**
Adams, John Quincy **175**
Alcott, Amos Bronson **1, 167**
Alcott, Louisa May **6, 58, 83**
Alger, Horatio Jr. **8, 83**
Allston, Washington **2**
Apess, William **73**
Audubon, John James **47**
Barlow, Joel **23**
Bartram, William **145**
Beecher, Catharine Esther **30**
Bellamy, Edward **4, 86, 147**
Bird, Robert Montgomery **1, 197**
Boker, George Henry **125**
Boyesen, Hjalmar Hjorth **135**
Brackenridge, Hugh Henry **7**
Brentano, Clemens (Maria) **1, 191**
Brown, Charles Brockden **22, 74, 122**
Brown, William Wells **2, 89**
Brownson, Orestes Augustus **50**
Bryant, William Cullen **6, 46**
Calhoun, John Caldwell **15**
Channing, William Ellery **17**
Child, Francis James **173**
Child, Lydia Maria **6, 73**
Chivers, Thomas Holley **49**
Cooke, John Esten **5**
Cooke, Rose Terry **110**
Cooper, James Fenimore **1, 27, 54, 203**
Cooper, Susan Fenimore **129**
Cranch, Christopher Pearse **115**
Crèvecoeur, Michel Guillaume Jean de **105**
Crockett, David **8**
Cummins, Maria Susanna **139**
Dana, Richard Henry Sr. **53**
Delany, Martin Robinson **93**
Dickinson, Emily (Elizabeth) **21, 77, 171**
Douglass, Frederick **7, 55, 141**
Dunlap, William **2**
Dwight, Timothy **13**
Emerson, Mary Moody **66**
Emerson, Ralph Waldo **1, 38, 98**
Field, Eugene **3**
Foster, Hannah Webster **99**
Foster, Stephen Collins **26**
Fuller, Margaret **5, 50, 211**
Frederic, Harold **10, 175**
Freneau, Philip Morin **1, 111**
Garrison, William Lloyd **149**
Hale, Sarah Josepha (Buell) **75**
Halleck, Fitz-Greene **47**
Hamilton, Alexander **49**
Hammon, Jupiter **5**
Harris, George Washington **23, 165**
Hawthorne, Nathaniel **2, 10, 17, 23, 39, 79, 95, 158, 171, 191**
Hawthorne, Sophia Peabody **150**
Hayne, Paul Hamilton **94**
Holmes, Oliver Wendell **14, 81**
Hooper, Johnson Jones **177**
Horton, George Moses **87**

Irving, Washington **2, 19, 95**
Jackson, Helen Hunt **90**
Jacobs, Harriet A(nn) **67, 162**
James, Alice **206**
James, Henry Sr. **53**
Jefferson, Thomas **11, 103**
Kennedy, John Pendleton **2**
Kirkland, Caroline M. **85**
Lanier, Sidney **6, 118**
Larcom, Lucy **179**
Lazarus, Emma **8, 109**
Lincoln, Abraham **18, 201**
Lippard, George **198**
Longfellow, Henry Wadsworth **2, 45, 101, 103**
Longstreet, Augustus Baldwin **159**
Lowell, James Russell **2, 90**
Madison, James **126**
Melville, Herman **3, 12, 29, 45, 49, 91, 93, 123, 157, 181, 193**
Mowatt, Anna Cora **74**
Murray, Judith Sargent **63**
Neal, John **161**
Osgood, Frances Sargent **141**
Parker, Theodore **186**
Parkman, Francis Jr. **12**
Parton, Sara Payson Willis **86**
Paulding, James Kirke **2**
Peabody, Elizabeth Palmer **169**
Pinkney, Edward **31**
Poe, Edgar Allan **1, 16, 55, 78, 94, 97, 117, 211**
Prescott, William Hickling **163**
Rowson, Susanna Haswell **5, 69, 182**
Sedgwick, Catharine Maria **19, 98**
Shaw, Henry Wheeler **15**
Sigourney, Lydia Howard (Huntley) **21, 87**
Simms, William Gilmore **3**
Smith, Joseph Jr. **53**
Smith, Seba **187**
Solomon, Northup **105**
Southworth, Emma Dorothy Eliza Nevitte **26**
Stowe, Harriet (Elizabeth) Beecher **3, 50, 133, 195**
Taylor, Bayard **89**
Tenney, Tabitha Gilman **122**
Thoreau, Henry David **7, 21, 61, 138, 207**
Thorpe, Thomas Bangs **183**
Timrod, Henry **25**
Trumbull, John **30**
Truth, Sojourner **94**
Tyler, Royall **3**
Very, Jones **9**
Warner, Susan (Bogert) **31, 146**
Warren, Mercy Otis **13**
Webster, Noah **30**
Webb, Frank J. **143**
Whitman, Sarah Helen (Power) **19**
Whitman, Walt(er) **4, 31, 81, 205**
Whittier, John Greenleaf **8, 59**
Willis, Nathaniel Parker **194**
Wilson, Harriet E. Adams **78**

Winnemucca, Sarah **79**
Winthrop, Theodore **210**

ARGENTINIAN

Echeverria, (Jose) Esteban (Antonino) **18**
Hernández, José **17**
Sarmiento, Domingo Faustino **123**

AUSTRALIAN

Adams, Francis **33**
Clarke, Marcus (Andrew Hislop) **19**
Gordon, Adam Lindsay **21**
Harpur, Charles **114**
Kendall, Henry **12**

AUSTRIAN

Grillparzer, Franz **1, 102**
Lenau, Nikolaus **16**
Nestroy, Johann **42**
Raimund, Ferdinand Jakob **69**
Sacher-Masoch, Leopold von **31**
Stifter, Adalbert **41, 198**

BRAZILIAN

Alencar, Jose de **157**
Alves, Antônio de Castro **205**

CANADIAN

Crawford, Isabella Valancy **12, 127**
De Mille, James **123**
Haliburton, Thomas Chandler **15, 149**
Lampman, Archibald **25, 194**
Moodie, Susanna (Strickland) **14, 113**
Richardson, John **55**
Traill, Catharine Parr **31**

CHINESE

Li Ju-chen **137**

COLOMBIAN

Isaacs, Jorge Ricardo **70**
Silva, José Asunción **114**

CUBAN

Avellaneda, Gertrudis Gómez de **111**
Casal, Julián del **131**
Heredia, José Maráa **209**
Manzano, Juan Francisco **155**
Martí (y Pérez), José (Julian) **63**
Villaverde, Cirilo **121**

CZECH

Macha, Karel Hynek **46**

DANISH

Andersen, Hans Christian **7, 79, 214**
Grundtvig, Nicolai Frederik Severin **1, 158**
Jacobsen, Jens Peter **34**
Kierkegaard, Søren **34, 78, 125**

NCLC-213 Title Index